WEDGWOOD

The New Illustrated Dictionary

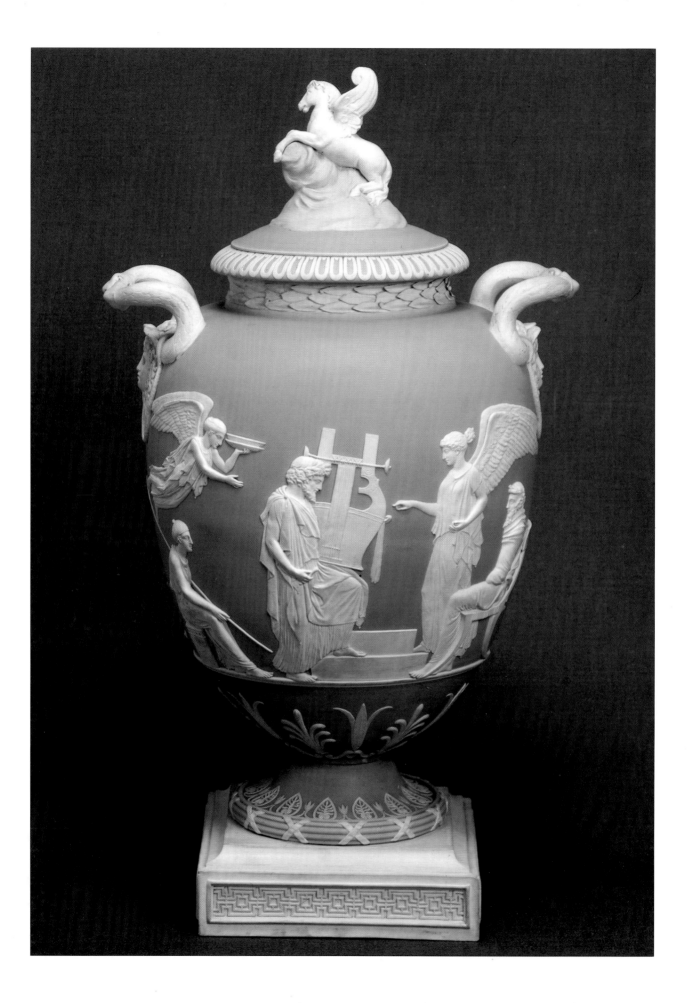

WEDGWOOD

The New Illustrated Dictionary

Robin Reilly

Antique Collectors' Club

First published 1995
© 1995 Robin Reilly
World copyright reserved

Reprinted 1996

ISBN 1 85149 209 7

The right of Robin Reilly to be identified as author of this work
has been asserted by him in accordance with
the Copyright, Designs and Patents Act 1988

British Library Cataloguing-in-Publication Data
A catalogue record for this book is available from the British Library

Frontispiece: *Apotheosis of Homer.* Greenish-buff jasper dip 'Pegasus' vase, with solid
pale blue clouds beneath the feet of the Pegasus figure and eggs at the centre of the snake
handles, on a solid white jasper plinth. Height 18in. c.1786.   *Nottingham Castle Museum*

Endpapers: The Wedgwood family in the grounds of Etruria Hall. Oil on panel,
47¾in. x 72½in., by George Stubbs, 1780. Right to left: Josiah Wedgwood, his wife Sarah,
and their children John, Josiah II, Susannah, Catherine, Thomas, Sarah and Mary Anne.
See Colour Plate 104.   *Wedgwood Museum*

Printed in England
by the Antique Collectors' Club Ltd., Woodbridge, Suffolk IP12 1DS
on Consort Royal Satin paper supplied by the Donside Mills, Aberdeen, Scotland

The Antique Collectors' Club

The Antique Collectors' Club was formed in 1966 and now has a five figure membership spread throughout the world. It publishes the only independently run monthly antiques magazine, *Antique Collecting*, which caters for those collectors who are interested in widening their knowledge of antiques, both by greater awareness of quality and by discussion of the factors which influence the price that is likely to be asked. The Antique Collectors' Club pioneered the provision of information on prices for collectors and the magazine still leads in the provision of detailed articles on a variety of subjects.

It was in response to the enormous demand for information on 'what to pay' that the price guide series was introduced in 1968 with the first edition of *The Price Guide to Antique Furniture* (completely revised 1978 and 1989), a book which broke new ground by illustrating the more common types of antique furniture, the sort that collectors could buy in shops and at auctions rather than the rare museum pieces which had previously been used (and still to a large extent are used) to make up the limited amount of illustrations in books published by commercial publishers. Many other price guides have followed, all copiously illustrated, and greatly appreciated by collectors for the valuable information they contain, quite apart from prices. The Antique Collectors' Club also publishes other books on antiques (including horology and art), garden history and architecture, and a full book list is available.

Club membership, open to all collectors, costs little. Members receive free of charge *Antique Collecting*, the Club's magazine (published ten times a year), which contains well-illustrated articles dealing with the practical aspects of collecting not normally dealt with by magazines. Prices, features of value, investment potential, fakes and forgeries are all given prominence in the magazine.

Among other facilities available to members are private buying and selling facilities, the longest list of 'For Sales' of any antiques magazine, an annual ceramics conference and the opportunity to meet other collectors at their local antique collectors' clubs. There are over eighty in Britain and more than a dozen overseas. Members may also buy the Club's publications at special pre-publication prices.

As its motto implies, the Club is an organisation designed to help collectors get the most out of their hobby: it is informal and friendly and gives enormous enjoyment to all concerned.

For Collectors —By Collectors —About Collecting

ANTIQUE COLLECTORS' CLUB
5 Church Street, Woodbridge, Suffolk IP12 1DS, UK
Tel: 01394 385501 Fax: 01394 384434
—————————— or ——————————
Market Street Industrial Park, Wappingers' Falls, NY 12590, USA
Tel: 914 297 0003 Fax: 914 297 0068

For
D. E. W.

Books by the same Author

Contents

Colour Plates

Introduction

The first edition of *The Dictionary of Wedgwood,* planned over a period of several years with George Savage, was originally intended to act as an extended index or glossary to a much larger work which would chart the entire history of the Wedgwood firm and of the family who controlled its destiny until 1967. In the event, for practical reasons, the *Dictionary* was written first and published in 1980. Two years later, George Savage died, before he was able to start work on the history, which was finally published in two volumes in 1989.

In the years between the publication of the two books, and during the succeeding years, I carried out further intensive research among the Wedgwood archives and benefited from the research of others. This confirmed some earlier attributions while contradicting others and made it clear that the first edition of the *Dictionary* required some amendment and might also be substantially enlarged. In particular, I wished to include the important discoveries that I had made about the production of eighteenth-century jasper and the Wedgwood copies of the Portland vase and some crucial new evidence about the formerly misunderstood white terracotta body. There was room, too, and an evident need for, more information about 19th- and 20th-century wares which could be met by my own recent research assisted by the pioneer work of Maureen Batkin published in 1982. It is my hope that this revised and more comprehensive edition may more nearly satisfy the needs of collectors of Wedgwood of all periods from the founding of the firm to the end of its existence as an independent public company in 1986.

As always, I owe a great debt of gratitude to the many museums, auction houses and collectors who have allowed me to plunder their collections and archives for illustrations and information. They are acknowledged in the text and captions to the illustrations of this book, but I must pay special tribute to the personal generosity of some great collectors: Dwight and Lucille Beeson, Misch and Nettie Buten and David Buten, Byron and Elaine Born, Eugene D. Buchanan, Herb and Sylvia Jacobs, Stuart and Carita Kadison, Sam and Sara Laver and Dave and Charlotte Zeitlin. They were among those discerning Americans whose passion for Wedgwood wares (at a time when they were but little appreciated in this country) ensured that some of the finest collections of modern times found a permanent home in the United States.

In recent years some of these collections have changed hands or have been dispersed: notably, the Buten Museum, removed to New York; the Beeson Collection, now entirely transferred to the Birmingham Museum of Art, Alabama, as a permanent monument to the generosity of Dwight and Lucille Beeson; the Born collection, dispersed after the deaths of both Byron and Elaine; and the Jacobs collection, sold by Christie's, New York, in 1993.

No work of this type could be undertaken without the wholehearted co-operation of the Trustees of the Wedgwood Museum, to whom I am indebted for the freedom to examine and, where required, to reproduce, manuscript material from the great accumulation deposited at Keele University. The captions bear witness to the generosity of the Wedgwood (now Waterford Wedgwood) Company in providing illustrations, without which this book would have been impossibly costly to produce. I have once more to record my gratitude to Gaye Blake-Roberts FMA, Curator of the Wedgwood Museum, and her assistants, Lynn Miller and Sharon Gater, whose own valuable research has been shared freely with me and whose cheerful and warm welcome at Barlaston has made my many visits there both rewarding and a pleasure.

My greatest debt, however, is to the late George Savage, who not only taught me much of what I know about ceramic history in the wider sense, and about connoisseurship, but was also responsible for the original concept of a dictionary devoted to the history and products of a single company. Without his vast knowledge of ceramics and his experience of organising such a project (evident in his *Dictionary of Antiques, Dictionary of 19th-Century Antiques* and, with Harold Newman, *The Illustrated Dictionary of Ceramics),* the first edition of this book would have been a nightmare to write and a far more seriously flawed publication than it was. My decision almost entirely to rewrite it is no reflection on the quality of our work together but rather an indication of the quantity and depth of research done during the past fifteen years.

R.R.
Somerset 1995

A Note on the captions to the Illustrations

Unless otherwise stated, all objects illustrated are of Wedgwood manufacture and are marked with the impressed or printed marks appropriate to their dates of production (see Appendix II).

Some explanation is required to clarify the method and conventions used in dating the objects described or illustrated. The word *'circa'* (abbreviated to 'c.') is used to indicate an approximate date extending five years on either side of the date given (e.g. 'c.1785' means that the piece was made between 1780 and 1790). Where two dates are given ('c.1780-90') the earlier is the first date at which the piece could have been made. Where the qualifying 'c.' does not appear, there is reason to believe that the date or dates given are precise.

A

Absolon, William (1751-1815)

An independent decorator working in Yarmouth from about 1790 on wares bought from a variety of sources, including Leeds* and Turner*, and Queen's ware* from Wedgwood's Etruria factory. His painting was naïve, and largely directed to the souvenir trade, the subjects varying from birds, botanical flowers and crude landscapes, to monograms, shields and trophies. A fruit centre at Norwich Castle Museum, marked WEDGWOOD impressed and 'Absolon Yarm' enamelled in red, is painted with a primitive representation of Britannia with naval trophies holding a portrait inscribed 'NELSON'. Absolon purchased 'white Biske', cane* ware and black basaltes* from Wedgwood between 1800 and 15 November 1810, when he complained of overcharging and closed his account. His signature is found also on Chinese porcelain and glass.

ACANTHUS. White stoneware teapot dipped in deep-blue jasper and ornamented with acanthus leaf and bell flower reliefs. c.1840.
Temple Newsam House, Leeds

Abundantia

Allegorical figure associated with peace, justice and good government, from which flowed ample supplies of food, the basic requirement of human well-being. She is found especially in Italian art with her principal attribute, the cornucopia*, and may, like Ceres* her classical prototype, hold a sheaf of corn in her hand and be accompanied by several children.
Wedgwood subject:
Abundantia, medallion 4in. x 3¼in., no.151 in 1777 Catalogue*

Acanthus

A plant, mainly of southern Europe, known also as bear's breech. The leaf has been used as a decorative motif for more than two thousand years, appearing on much Attic-Ionic architecture and ornament. Either stylised or naturalistically rendered, it is used for ceramic decoration or ornament in both painted and moulded forms. It occurs also in profile, known as an acanthus scroll. It was common in classical art and was frequently used by Wedgwood to decorate objects in the neo-classical* style.

Accum & Garden

See: Pyrophorous Vase

ABSOLON, William. Interior of Queen's ware fruit centre painted with primitive naval trophies and portrait of Nelson. c.1806.
Norwich Castle Museum

Achilles

The hero of Homer's *Iliad*. The son of Peleus, King of the Myrmidones, and the Nereid*, Thetis, he was educated by Phoenix in eloquence and the arts of war, and by Chiron, the centaur*, in the healing arts. According to legend, Thetis sought to make him immortal by dipping him in the river Styx but failed to immerse the heel by which she held him, which remained vulnerable to human assault. Later, to preserve him from the Trojan war, she sent him to live among the daughters of Lycomedes, King of Scyros. There, dressed as a woman, Achilles was discovered by Ulysses, but not before he had taken advantage of his disguise to impregnate Deidamia, daughter of Lycomedes, who bore him a son, Pyrrhus. Offered the choice between a short but heroic life and a long and inglorious one, Achilles chose the former and set out for the war, where he was, at first, in the forefront of the battle. After a quarrel with Agamemnon, however, he retired to sulk in his tent. His friend, Patroclus, nevertheless persuaded him to allow his men, horses and armour to be used. When Patroclus was slain, Achilles, stricken with grief and remorse, rejoined the battle. Wearing new armour, he killed numerous Trojans, including King Priam's son, Hector*, whose body he tied to his chariot and dragged round the walls of the city before yielding it to Priam, who came in person to beg for it. Achilles fell in the battle before Troy was taken, slain, it was said, by an arrow shot by Paris*, which struck him in the heel.

Achilles, and the legends associated with him, are subjects of many Wedgwood cameos*, medallions* and tablets*. These include an important series of large reliefs (on tablets about 6½in. x 18in.) depicting scenes from the life of Achilles, modelled by Pacetti* in 1788 and adapted from the Luna marble disc or puteal (c.800-400 BC) now in the Capitoline Museum, Rome. The series comprises five groups, used singly or in sequence according to the size and shape of the ground:

1. *Birth and Dipping of Achilles* (sometimes divided as two groups)
2. *Thetis delivering Achilles to Centaur and Achilles on the back of Centaur hunting the Lion* (also used as two groups)
3. *Achilles in Scyros among the Daughters of Lycomedes*

ACHILLES. Pen and wash drawing *Achilles on the back of Centaur hunting the Lion,* probably by Pacetti, c.1789. *Wedgwood Museum*

ACHILLES. Olive-green jasper dip tablet, 6⅛in. x 18in., *The Birth and Dipping of Achilles.* c.1910-18.

Dwight & Lucille Beeson Collection, Birmingham Museum, Alabama

4. *Achilles and Hector in combat before the walls of Troy*
5. *Achilles dragging the body of Hector around the walls of Troy*
A sixth scene by Pacetti, *Priam kneeling before Achilles begging the Body of his son Hector,* was modelled in 1788 from the so-called sarcophagus of Alexander Severus and Julia Mammaea, also in the Capitoline Museum.

A second version of *Achilles in Scyros,* taken from the same source as *Priam kneeling before Achilles,* is also attributed to Pacetti. This is frequently mis-described as *Sacrifice of Iphigenia.*

An earlier large version of *Priam begging the body of Hector from Achilles* (11½in. x 14in. or 13in. x 17½in., no.211, 1779 Catalogue) is unattributed. A third version of *Achilles in Scyros,* known also as *The Discovery of Achilles,* 9in. x 17in., was modelled by De Vaere*, 1789-90, probably working from an engraving in Winckelmann's *Antichi Inediti,* 1767 (Vol.I, fig.87). A second, smaller, version of *Achilles dragging the body of Hector around the walls of Troy* (the subject reversed and a figure of Achilles that dwarfs the horses) was probably copied from a cast by Tassie* from a gem by Pichler*.

Centaur teaching Achilles the Lyre, one of the Herculaneum* roundels (diameter 11½in.) intended for 'the Decoration of Large Halls and Stair Cases', dates from 1770-71, and Wedgwood's immediate source was a set of bas-relief copies in the possession of the Marquess of Lansdowne.

Acid-Etched Gold (Acid Gold)
A form of decoration, introduced in Britain by Minton in 1763, by which patterns are etched into the surface of the ware by the use of hydrofluoric acid. An acid-resistant transfer-print is applied to the glazed surface of the ware and rubbed firmly to produce perfect adhesion of the print before the paper is removed. The rest of the piece, back and front, is then 'stopped out' by coating it with acid-resistant material before immersing it in hydrofluoric acid. The acid 'bites' away the exposed parts of the glaze, etching the required pattern. The etched pattern is then given a first coat of 22-carat liquid gold, which is fired into the glaze. A second coating of gold is applied and the object fired again. The gold pattern is then burnished to produce a polished relief design against a matt gold ground. Patterns produced by this method are normally narrow border designs and are among the most costly to manufacture. The technique has been used also for the decoration of vases. The Wedgwood range of bone china tableware still includes a number of designs of this type.
See also: Gilding

Acorn
See: Finial

Adam Plaque
See: Zinkeisen, Anna

Adam, Robert (1728-92)
Architect and designer in the neo-classical* style. In 1752, Adam travelled to Italy and thence to Dalmatia, where his drawings of Diocletian's palace helped to form his early style as a designer. When, in 1762, he returned to Britain, he was appointed architect to the King. Robert Adam's work, and that of his brother James (1732-94), with whom he was in partnership in London, did much to promote neo-classicism in England. Their eldest brother, John, remained in Scotland, while a fourth, William, managed the family business set up in 1764. In 1773, the brothers Robert and James began to publish their chief designs in a series of engravings collected under the general title of *Works in Architecture.* These designs strongly influenced such manufacturers as Wedgwood and Boulton*, and there is evidence that the colours chosen by Wedgwood for his jasper* grounds were closely related to those used by Adam in interior decoration.

In 1771, Wedgwood referred in a letter to 'Mr Adams' *(sic),* who was employing modellers in Rome to make bas-reliefs*, a practice that Wedgwood followed seventeen years later. Despite its fashionable following, the Adam style*, as it has come to be known, was by no means universally admired. Among its sternest critics were Horace Walpole and Sir William Chambers*.
See: Adelphi; Chimneypieces

Adam Style
The English version of the neo-classical* style, introduced soon after 1760 by Robert and James Adam. It replaced the earlier rococo* style in the decorative arts and tended to supersede the Palladian style in architecture. Adam's repertory of ornament is classical and in many ways similar to the current French version of neo-classicism, although it was plainer and less luxurious. Festoons*, swags, medallions* and urns* were commonly employed for ornamental purposes. In contrast with the asymmetry of the preceding rococo style, there is a return to strict symmetry. The Adam style had very little effect on the porcelain of the period but the products of Wedgwood, especially Queen's ware*, basaltes* and jasper*, were strongly influenced by it. The prevailing Adam colour-schemes were repeated in the colouring of Wedgwood's jasper, and, although Robert Adam was not personally enthusiastic about them, jasper tablets* and medallions were used in a few Adam houses.
See: Chimneypieces

Adams, William (1746-1805)
John Adams, a saltglazed stoneware manufacturer of the Brick House*, Burslem, and at a second pottery at Cobridge, died in 1757, leaving as his heir, William, a minor aged nine. Josiah Wedgwood rented the Brick House from him in 1763.

Often erroneously described as a pupil of Wedgwood's, Adams was in business at Burslem from 1769 and opened a factory at Greengates, Tunstall, in 1779. Adams manufactured creamware* and basaltes* and began production of his own jasper* in the 1780s, including pale and dark blue, pale and dark green, lilac, pink and plum-colour. The quality of his jasper is close to that of Wedgwood but the colours are generally stronger and the blue more violet in shade. Some of these wares were mounted in Sheffield. Adams also made cane* ware with reliefs in cane, white, blue or olive-green.

ADAMS, William. Pair of solid bright-blue jasper ewers, height 10¾in., ornamented with figures of Muses. c.1795.   *Geoffrey Godden*

Some of his relief subjects are apparently identical to Wedgwood's and were either obtained from the same sources or direct copies. The principal marks were ADAMS & CO or ADAMS, impressed. The old story, repeated among descendants of the family, that Wedgwood stole the formula for jasper from their ancestor is without foundation. The firm continued in production at Tunstall and Stoke until 1966, when the business was acquired by Wedgwood and it became part of the enlarged Wedgwood Group*.

ADAMS, William. Garniture of three bright-blue jasper vases, height 11½in. and 9½in. c.1800.   *Christie's, New York*

Adelphi, The

A Greek word meaning 'brothers', and the name given by Robert Adam* and his brothers to the development in the neighbourhood of Charing Cross, between the Strand and the Thames. Much of this development was demolished in 1936 to make way for new building. The Adelphi Terrace, which no longer exists, has housed many notable figures, including Robert and James Adam, David Garrick and Bernard Shaw. The Royal Society of Arts* occupies a

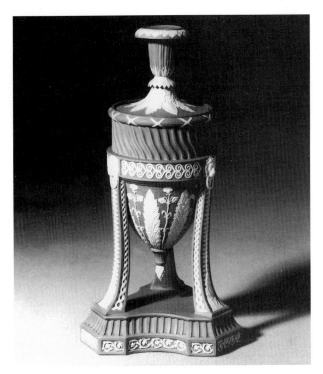

ADAMS, William. Solid pale-blue and white jasper tripod candlestick-vase, height 12in., with reversible lid, almost identical in shape to Wedgwood's. c.1790.   *Temple Newsam House, Leeds*

building in John Adam Street, the exterior of which is almost unaltered. Better architects than civil engineers or business managers, the Adam brothers ran into what their nephew William described as 'the underground stream of loss and expenditure', which gradually bore them towards bankruptcy. They escaped ruin only by disposing of all their assets, excepting only the Adelphi estate, by lottery. The success of this curious expedient enabled them to buy back much of their property and to complete the Adelphi scheme.

For Wedgwood's connection with the Adelphi, see: Showrooms

Adonis

A beautiful youth, beloved of Aphrodite, who died of wounds inflicted by a boar. The goddess was griefstricken by his death, and the gods allowed him to return from the underworld for six months of each year, which he spent with Aphrodite. His death and resurrection were celebrated at the Spring festivals and, according to legend, the anemone sprang from his blood.

Wedgwood subjects:

Adonis, medallion no.47 in 1773 Catalogue*
Death of Adonis, plaque 5½in. x 6in., no.186 in 1777 Catalogue*
(Venus (Aphrodite) and Adonis,* supplied by Hoskins & Grant* in 1775 but uncatalogued and possibly not produced)

Advertising

Josiah Wedgwood publicised his wares primarily by his use of impressed [trade] marks*, by publishing illustrated catalogues* and by cultivating patronage. His attitude to newspaper advertising was ambivalent. He told Bentley* in 1771: 'I would much rather not advertise at all if you think the sales are in such a way as to do without it'. His reluctance stemmed less from a lack of regard for the efficacy of the medium than from a dislike of the popular pastime of 'puffing' – the business of promoting goods, services or individuals in newspaper articles purporting to offer objective comment. He was especially wary of a critic self-styled as 'Anti-puffado' who had already criticised Wedgwood indirectly by attacking one of his agents. Wedgwood nevertheless acknowledged the necessity for advertising, which he used as early as 1769 to publicise his showrooms* in London, and from 1771 he advertised his wares freely in the newspapers, making the most of his royal appointments and patronage, the convenience and superiority of his showrooms and the generosity of his terms of business. Two years

Colour Plate 1. AGATE WARE. Two surface agate vases, one with reversible lid and candleholder, with traces of gilding on white terracotta stoneware plinths. Height 18in. and 14½in. c.1783.

Wedgwood Museum

Colour Plate 2. ALLEN, Thomas. Queen's ware wall plaque painted by Thomas Allen with a portrait of Falstaff against an elaborate raised-gold ground. Diameter 15in. Signed and dated 1881.
Wedgwood Museum

ADVERTISING. Three-colour (yellow and black dip) jasper octagonal advertising cameo, 1⅝in. x 1⅝in., ornamented with a caduceus and clasped hands of friendship between two cornucopiae. The moulded inscription reads: JOSIAH WEDGWOOD & SONS ETRURIA ENGLAND. c.1900.

Christie's, London

ADVERTISING. Trade advertisement for *Summer Sky,* Wedgwood's first two-colour earthenware tableware produced by fusing the lavender coloured body with plain Queen's ware.

Wedgwood Museum

later he even prepared to advertise his trade marks.

Although newspaper and magazine advertising was continued in the nineteenth century, it was directed principally at the trade and appeared mainly in trade publications. It was not until 1955 that Wedgwood set up its own Public Relations and Advertising department with offices in London. The first director, Alan Eden-Green, devised and put into operation a rational and consistent national advertising policy which played a full part in the rise of Wedgwood's fame in the second half of the twentieth century.

Aeneas

The son of Anchises and Aphrodite, Aeneas is one of the two great Trojan heroes, the other being Hector. Aeneas survived the fall of Troy because he was under the protection of Aphrodite and Poseidon (Neptune*). A favourite subject with artists is Aeneas bearing his father, Anchises, on his back from the flames of Troy. Aeneas took with him the Palladium* and, crossing into Europe, he eventually found his way to Latium, where he settled, becoming the ancestral hero of the Romans. Virgil's *Aeneid* is concerned with the wanderings of Aeneas before he reached Latium. He was driven by a storm on to the coast of North Africa, where he found

Dido, who fell in love with him. In Italy Aeneas founded the city of Lavinium, named after Lavinia (daughter of Latinus, King of the Aborigines) whom he married. After the death of Latinus, Aeneas became King of the Aborigines and the surviving Trojans and finally fell in battle against the Etruscans. His body was not found and it was assumed that he had been translated into Heaven.

Wedgwood subject:

Aeneas bearing Anchises from the flames of Troy, cameo, attributed to John Bacon, c.1769.

AESCULAPIUS. *(Left)* Early trial jasper medallion, 4½in. x 3½in., *Sacrifice to Aesculapius,* showing blistering and fire-cracks. c.1775.

Wedgwood Museum.

(Right) Wedgwood & Bentley jasper medallion, *Aesculapius,* height 3¼in.

Dwight & Lucille Beeson Collection, Birmingham Museum, Alabama

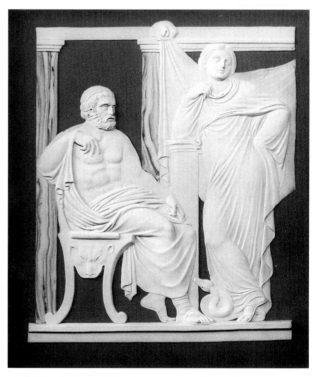

AESCULAPIUS. Solid blue jasper plaque, 9½in. x 8¼in., *Aesculapius and Hygeia,* by Camillo Pacetti. c.1790.

Dwight & Lucille Beeson Collection, Birmingham Museum, Alabama

Aerograph

An apparatus invented in 1890 for applying coloured grounds and glazes to the surface of pottery and porcelain, utilising compressed air to produce a fine spray. Extensively used by Wedgwood, especially in the 1950s for the production of bone china tea and coffee sets (e.g. *April* colours).

Aesculapius

The Greek God of medicine, although Homer refers to him only as a 'blameless physician' (rare enough in any period to be considered godlike). The son of Apollo*, Aesculapius was believed to cure the sick and restore the dead to life. Fearing that men might thus become immortal, Zeus slew him with a thunderbolt and placed him among the stars. Serpents, symbols of regeneration, were sacred to Aesculapius, and the cock was sacrificed to him. He is usually represented with a staff and serpent. Wedgwood referred to Dr Erasmus Darwin* as his 'favourite Aesculapius'.

Wedgwood subjects:

Aesculapius, cameo (probably via a cameo by Tassie*) after a Renaissance gem by Valerio Vicentino. This cameo figure usually appears alone, but it is occasionally found with the accompanying figure of Hygeia* as it appears in the original gem

Aesculapius and Hygeia, tablet 8¼in. x 6⅞in., also 9½in. x 8¼in., modelled by Pacetti*, 1788, from a marble relief now in the Capitoline Museum

Sacrifice to Aesculapius, medallion 4in. x 3⅜in., no.28 in 1773 Catalogue*

Aesop's Fables

A series of creamware* Royal shape (see: Tableware Shapes) dessert plates transfer-printed* in iron-red with subjects from *Aesop's Fables,* produced c.1765. Each square print has a rococo* border suspended from a tied ribbon by husk festoons* enamelled in bright green to match the enamelled edge. The rims of the plates are decorated with red transfer-printed sprays of flowers. Eleven such Fable plates are in the Victoria & Albert Museum, London (Schreiber Collection), and four in the British Museum. All the engraved scenes are copied or adapted from either Francis Barlow's* illustrations to *Aesop's Fables, with his Life,* (1687) or from Samuel Croxall's edition of 1722 and most of them are known on tiles introduced by Sadler* & Green c.1765. The discovery of a previously unrecorded letter (sold by Phillips,

AESOP'S FABLES. Queen's ware Royal shape dessert plate transfer-printed in red with 'Hunted Beaver' and a border of six flower sprays. The square centre, adapted from an engraving for tiles, is suspended from a ribbon bow and husk festoons enamelled in bright green. c.1771-5. *British Museum*

London 13 June 1991) from Wedgwood to Erasmus Darwin* describing almost identical designs for a set of 'small table plates', which Wedgwood proposed in July 1765 to send to the Queen for the Prince of Wales and Duke of York, makes this the most likely approximate date also for the plates in the two London museum collections. A twelfth plate in the Schreiber Collection is similarly decorated but for the central print of 'The Return of the Prodigal Son', also a subject known on Sadler & Green tiles.

Interpretations of *Aesop's Fables* were painted on Wedgwood earthenware by Emile Lessore*, almost precisely a century later, in 1866.

Aesthetic Movement

Movement starting in the late 1860s which developed from the Arts and Crafts Movement* of William Morris and his associates, with which it was to some extent at variance. It took for its guiding principle 'Art for Art's sake', adapted by Victor Cousin from Whistler, which was widely quoted. It gave place, about 1890, to Art Nouveau*. The Aesthetic Movement was popularised in America by Oscar Wilde during his lecture tours and lampooned by W.S. Gilbert in *Patience*. In British design, the Aesthetic Movement is irretrievably associated with the contemporary fashion for Japanese goods, and some of the most popular decorative motifs, such as the sunflower* and the peacock, were common to both.

See: Art Pottery; Japonisme

Agate Ware

Pottery made in imitation of polished agate, either by wedging coloured clays in the body (solid agate), by blending coloured slips* on the surface or by the application of metallic oxides. The colours blended together are brown, red, yellow and white (more rarely blue and green). Examples are known from ancient Rome, but notably from the T'ang dynasty of eighth-century China. Agate wares thrown on the potter's wheel show a spiral swirl on the outside, caused by the circular motion of the wheel, and a smeared effect on interior surfaces resulting from the pressure of the thrower's wet hand. This technique appears to have been used in Staffordshire as early as c.1730-40, prior to the introduction of moulds. Solid (moulded) agate may be easily distinguished from surface agate: the former shows a clear break in the veining where the two halves of the moulded piece have been joined (generally under the handles) and the colour and veining are visible in the interior of the vessel; surface agate shows matching striations over

AESTHETIC MOVEMENT. Majolica (Argenta) dessert plate in the form of a sunflower head on a wicker dish, decorated with brown and yellow glazes. The sunflower was a favourite motif of the Aesthetic Movement. *Wedgwood Museum*

AGATE. *(Left to right)* Early turned solid agate mugs of mingled reddish-brown and black clays (the smaller with a vein of white) of the type probably made by Wedgwood at the Ivy House. Unmarked. c.1755-60. *Wedgwood Museum.*
Wedgwood & Bentley solid agate lidded vase, height 6¾in., of wedged reddish-brown, black and cream-coloured clays. c.1774. *Christie's, London.*
19th-century solid agate candlesticks, height 6¼in., showing declining technique. c.1840. *Nottingham Castle.*
Black and white powder box from the range of Norman Wilson Unique Ware. A fine example of 20th-century agate technique in black and white. *Wedgwood Museum*

the whole body and the interior is uncoloured. Wedgwood wrote in his *Experiment Book** early in 1759: 'I had already made an imitation of Agate; which was esteemed beautiful & a considerable improvement; but people were surfeited with wares of these variegated colors'. He nevertheless continued to make surface agate and added other colours in imitation of semi-precious stones, including porphyry* and lapis lazuli*.

See: Colour Plate 1
See also: Crystalline; Marbling; Terracotta; Variegated Ware

AGRICULTURAL DEVICES. Part of a tea service, printed and enamelled in brown. c.1812. *Wedgwood Museum*

Agricultural Devices Pattern
Known also as 'Agricultural Implements', this design, printed and enamelled in brown was introduced on Queen's ware c.1810 and is widely regarded as one of the most distinguished patterns of the early nineteenth century. A service of this pattern was ordered by the Marchioness of Blandford in September 1813.

Agrippina (d. AD33)
Wife of Germanicus*, by whom she bore nine children, including a son who became the Emperor Caligula. She shared many of her husband's campaigns but, after his death in AD17, her popularity caused the Emperor Tiberius to banish her. One of her daughters, also Agrippina, married Nero.
Wedgwood subject:
Agrippina ('Agrepina'), bust 16½in., supplied by Hoskins & Grant, 1774

Ainslie, Sir Robert (1730?-1812)
Diplomat and numismatist, knighted in 1776. He was ambassador

to Constantinople, 1776-92, and in that capacity provided Wedgwood with models of tablewares (and probably also of hookahs*) to copy for the Turkish market. Other British envoys abroad who assisted Wedgwood & Bentley in this manner included Sir William Hamilton*, Lord Cathcart*, Sir Robert Liston* and Sir Robert Murray Keith*.

Alders, Thomas (fl. mid-18th century)
Manufacturer of buttons and knife handles in agate* and tortoise-shell* earthenware, black wares, 'scratch blue' and saltglazed stoneware*, whose factory was at Cliff Bank, Stoke-on-Trent. From 1752 to 1754 he was in partnership with John Harrison* and Josiah Wedgwood.

Ale Jug
See: Cambridge Ale Jug

Alexander the Great (356-323 BC)
Son of Philip II of Macedonia and Olympias. Educated by Aristotle*, he succeeded to the throne at the age of twenty. After putting down an insurrection in his own country, he led his forces into Greece, where he at once displayed military genius. Turning on the Persians, he defeated Darius at Issus. By 331 he had conquered Asia and two years later he entered India, where he was again uniformly successful in battle. In 326, however, his troops, exhausted and homesick, forced him to return to Macedonia. He died three years later. He founded the city of Alexandria at the beginning of 331.
Wedgwood subjects:
(Alexander, bust supplied by Hoskins & Grant*, 1779, but not catalogued and probably not made)
Alexander the Great, portrait medallion 2in. x 1½in., 1773
Alexander, 2 larger portrait medallions, 1777
Masque of Alexander, bas-relief modelled by Webber*, 1786

Algardi, Alessandro
See: Morpheus

All Draughtsmen's Assistant or Drawing Made Easy
Book by R. Sayer* and J. Bennett, published in 1771, compiled as a source of inspiration for decorators, fan painters etc., drawings from which are identifiable transfer-printed on pottery and porcelain. A river scene after Vernet from this source appears on Wedgwood Queen's ware*.

Allen, G. (fl.1820-50)
Engraver, in 1845, of the *Eastern Flowers* pattern, a Queen's ware tableware design in the *famille rose** style. No other pattern has been traced to Allen but the success of *Eastern Flowers,* which was reintroduced in 1952, makes it probable that he was responsible for others of a similar type.

ALLEN, Thomas. Circular wall plaque, diameter 15in., painted with a portrait of Jessica from 'The Merchant of Venice' against a richly patterned raised-gold ground. The plaque is one of a series portraying Shakespearian characters. Signed and dated 1881.
Wedgwood Museum

ALLEN, Thomas. *L'Allegro*, one of Thomas Allen's decorously draped semi-nude female figures, popular in the late-Victorian period, painted underglaze on a Queen's ware rectangular plaque, 20⅛in. x 14⅛in. Signed and dated 1891. *Wedgwood Museum*

Allen & Hordley (fl.1830-40)

Engravers responsible for the engraving in 1830 of a country house in a landscape, printed underglaze in blue with a rose border on Wedgwood Pearl* ware, as well as a similarly printed landscape pattern of 1832.

Allen, Thomas (1831-1915)

Painter, designer and first professional art director at the Etruria* factory. After training at the Stoke-on-Trent School of Design, Allen continued his studies in London before joining Minton's*, where he rapidly gained a reputation for fine painting. A vase painted by him in the Sèvres* manner was shown by Minton at the Great Exhibition of 1851, about a year before he was awarded a national scholarship to the newly-established South Kensington School of Design, where he remained until he returned to Minton in 1854. He was employed there until 1875/6 when, frustrated by low wages and the domination of the art department by Léon Arnoux and M.L. Solon, he transferred to Wedgwood, becoming in turn supervisor of the Fine Art Studio, chief designer and, in 1880, art director. He designed a number of successful tableware patterns for Wedgwood but his most admired work continued to be figure subjects for vases, including the decorously posed and chastely draped semi-nudes popular among Victorian art-lovers. His technique was undeniably superb, and he is widely regarded as the leading Staffordshire figure-painter of the 19th century. A pair of large vases painted by Allen with nymphs and *amorini* was shown in the Paris Exposition of 1878, where Wedgwood won a gold medal.

Allen's handpainted work for Wedgwood (unlike his work for Minton) was usually signed: 'Tho Allen', or with his monogram, and often dated. In addition to vases, he painted some excellent earthenware chargers or plaques with portraits of characters from Shakespeare on gold grounds (1881) and his *Columbia* pattern is still in production after more than a century of almost continuous popularity. He retired in 1904.

The following is a brief summary of Allen's most recognisable work:

Vases, ranging in height from about 15in. to more than 30in., richly decorated with figure subjects (often of a somewhat sentimental character) in reserves on coloured grounds

Plaques, 15in. in diameter, portraying characters from Shakespeare on a gold ground, signed and dated 1881 (also painted by other contemporary artists). See: Shakespeare Subjects

Rectangular or circular earthenware plaques painted with figure subjects in landscapes

Tableware patterns: *Ivanhoe, Banquet, Columbia, Swallow, Greek Musicians* (after paintings by Albert Moore)

A number of patterns for tiles printed in a single colour, or print and enamel, many of them adapted from his tableware patterns (e.g. *Ivanhoe, Banquet, Greek Musicians*)

See: Colour Plate 2

Alpine Pink

The name given to a bone china* coloured body* introduced by Norman Wilson* in 1936 and reintroduced for a short period in 1955. It was made in traditional shapes, shell dessert shapes (including Nautilus*) and Coupe/Savoy (see: Tableware Shapes).

Unsuccessful trials of stained bone china were made by Wedgwood in 1878, but further attempts made between 1882 and 1886 resulted in the production of shades of celadon, blue, yellow, pink and lilac. Examples of these are extremely rare and it is likely that they were made in very small quantities. Pink-stained bone china was used later by Harry Barnard* for some teaware shapes decorated with modelled slip*, c.1898-1902.

Althaea

Wife of Oeneus, King of Calydon, and mother of a great many children, including Meleager* and Deianeira. After the Calydonian Boar Hunt, Althaea hanged herself for having caused the death of Meleager.

Wedgwood subject:

Althaea, Mother of Meleager, Burning the Firebrand, medallion 3½in. x 2½in., no.50 in 1773 Catalogue*

Alumina

Aluminium oxide, a refractory white powder with a melting point of about 2,200°C., which is used in a variety of ways where it is desired to prevent two surfaces from sticking to each other: for example, the support of figures during firing.

American Bicentennial Editions

To celebrate the American Bicentennial in 1976, Wedgwood issued limited editions* of the following specially designed pieces:

Pair of plates, fluted blue and white jasper with inner border of thirteen applied stars: one plate with a centre ornament of the American eagle surrounded by applied jasper seals of the thirteen original colonies; the other ornamented with portrait medallions* of the thirteen signatories of the Declaration of Independence (Edition 5,000).

Five-colour Trophy Plate*, centre ornament portrait medallion of George Washington surrounded by rams' heads and floral swags, classical bas-reliefs and a formal applied border in pale-blue, white, cane, lilac and green jasper (Edition 300).

Three-colour goblet, height 5in., in pale-blue, white and green jasper, ornamented with portrait medallions of George Washington and Thomas Jefferson, floral swags, laurel border and three-colour diced* pattern. (Edition 200).

Two-handled mug, black and white jasper with gold design featuring the American eagle, designed by Richard Guyatt*. (Edition 500).

Queen's ware mug, the American eagle and flag within borders of thirteen stars and fifty stars, designed by Richard Guyatt. (Edition 5,000).

American Independence Series

A series of six pale-blue and white jasper plates with centre applied ornament depicting scenes from American history with moulded inscriptions and outer applied borders of thirteen stars. The scenes represented are: Boston Tea Party; Paul Revere's Ride; Battle of Concord; George Washington crossing the Delaware; Victory at Yorktown; and The Declaration Signed.

AMERICAN INDEPENDENCE SERIES. Cornwallis surrendering to the American forces at Yorktown, 1781. Jasper plate issued to commemorate the bicentennial in 1976. The stars represent the thirteen original colonies. *Wedgwood Museum*

America's Heritage Series

Six blue and white jasper plates, diameter 8in., with centre applied bas-relief ornament, moulded inscription, applied inner border of thirteen stars and outer moulded border of fifty smaller stars. Introduced in a 'limited' *(sic)* edition* of 15,000 sets. The centre bas-relief scenes are: The West by Land; The West by Sea; The Heartland by Rail; the Heartland by River; The World by Road; and The World by Air.

Andrieu, Bertrand

See: Bastille Medallions

ANDROMACHE. Plaster block mould of a bas-relief by John Bacon senior. *Wedgwood Museum*

Andromache

Wife of Hector*. On the capture of Troy, her son Scamandrius was hurled from the walls of the city. She fell to the share of Neoptolemus, son of Achilles*. Later she lived with Hector's brother, Helenus.
Wedgwood subject:
Andromache, circular medallion 8½in., no.197 in 1779 Catalogue*, modelled by John Bacon senior*, 1777

Andromeda

The daughter of Cepheus, King of Ethiopia. Her mother Cassiopaea boasted that her daughter was more beautiful than the Nereids*, which so angered Poseidon (Neptune*) that he sent a sea monster to ravage the country. The oracle of Ammon promised that the people should be saved if Andromeda were sacrificed to the monster. She was chained to a rock, where Perseus* found her. He slew the monster and made her his wife. She had, however, been promised to her uncle, Phineus, who attacked Perseus at the wedding. Perseus turned him to stone by confronting him with the Medusa's* head. After Andromeda's death the gods placed her among the stars.
Wedgwood subjects:
Andromeda, medallion 4¾in. x 4in., no.23 in 1773 Catalogue*
Marriage of Perseus and Andromeda, oval plaque 6in. x 9in., no.5 in 1773 Catalogue*

Angelini, Giuseppe (1742-1811)

Sculptor and modeller, who came to England from Rome about 1770 and joined the Royal Academy Schools in 1772. He was employed for a time by the sculptor Joseph Nollekens but in 1777 was in financial straits and was granted assistance by the Academy. By 1787 he was back in Rome, modelling for Wedgwood and working with Flaxman*, De Vaere*, Pacetti*, Dalmazzoni* and Webber.*
Angelini modelled the following bas-reliefs for Wedgwood in 1789. It is not, however, certain that all were reproduced:
Apollo and the Muse Erato
Apotheosis of a Young Prince
The Fable of Meleager (sometimes confused with *Death of a Roman Warrior** but it is a much larger composition using, in part, the same source)
The Nine Muses, adapted from the Sarcophagus of the Muses, then in the Capitoline Museum and now in the Louvre
Pluto carrying off Proserpine (known also as the *Rape of Persephone* and *The Procession of Persephone into the Underworld*), 9in. x 26¼in. Possibly finished by De Vaere
Reclining Figures (sometimes described as *Banquet* or *Roman Banquet*) from 'the top of the urn of the Muses', 3¼in. x 17¾in.
Several Geniuses Representing the Pleasures of the Elysian Fields
Two Fauns, Two Bacchantes & A Silenus (probably separate figures but none certainly identified)
Angelini was responsible for a further six models, none of which is titled or described in the relevant correspondence. They remain unidentified.

ANGELINI, Giuseppe. Dark-blue jasper dip tablet, 3¼in. x 17¼in., *Reclining Figures* (also 'Roman Banquet'), modelled in 1789. c.1790.
Sotheby's, London

Animal Figures

Wedgwood's early catalogues contain descriptions of a number of animal figures produced in black basaltes*. These include Egyptian Lions, Egyptian and Greek Sphinxes*, Griffins*, a large Elephant, and a Pug Dog. The Griffins and two pairs of Sphinxes were provided with 'nozzles to hold candles'. The Elephant, 14½in. x 16½in., must have been a formidable beast but was not a commercial success and none is known to have survived. Wedgwood wrote in May 1770: 'I fear we made a Bull [in a china shop] when we first made an Elephant' and promised to make no more until the present model was sold. The Pug was intended as a portrait of Hogarth's dog Trump*.

Although most of these figures were reproduced during the 19th century, no new animal figures appear to have been commissioned until 1913, when Ernest W. Light* modelled a number of birds and animals for Wedgwood. Another important series of animal figures was modelled by John Skeaping* in 1927 and single figures were reproduced from models by Alan Best* c.1935 and Arnold Machin* in the 1940s.

The existence of a black basaltes-type figure of a horse, bearing a WEDGWOOD mark, was first made public in 1985. This is undoubtedly from the same source (or copied from) the Leeds* creamware model and the mark appears to be spurious. No such figure is listed in the Wedgwood Catalogues, and, in the opinion of this author, the figure is a modern fake.
See: Candlesticks; Egyptian Taste

ANIMAL FIGURES. Four basalt animal figures by Ernest Light, all with glass eyes inset. Elephant (with white biscuit tusks) height 5in. c.1918.
Formerly Buten Museum

Annular Shape
See: Murray, Keith; Tableware Shapes

Anthemion
A stylised form of honeysuckle commonly employed as part of neo-classical decoration in the last quarter of the 18th century. It appears in two principal forms on both Wedgwood tablewares and ornamental wares: the anthemion border; and a border of alternating palmettes* and honeysuckle flowers.

Antimony
See: Glazes

Antinous
An extraordinarily handsome youth, born at Claudiopolis in Bithynia, he became the favourite of the Emperor Hadrian, accompanying him on all his journeys. He was drowned in the Nile in AD122.
Wedgwood subjects:
Antinous, bust 22in., supplied by Hoskins & Grant, 1774
Antinous, figure 12in., c.1859

Antique
Correctly, appertaining to ancient Greece and Rome. The word was used in this sense throughout the 18th century and well into the 19th, and it is so employed in this *Dictionary*. The use of 'antique' to describe something as old as a century or so is comparatively new. What are known as 'antique shops' were previously 'curiosity shops' and sold 'curios'. Shops dealing in genuine antiques – classical pottery, statuary and the like – were always rarities.

Antiquities of Herculaneum
Le Antichità di Ercolano Esposte, an account in nine volumes of the discoveries at Herculaneum, was published in Naples in 1771. *Antiquities of Herculaneum*, a translation by J. Martin and T. Lettice, edited by O.A. Bayard, began to appear in 1773. Wedgwood was a subscriber to the first volume, which appears to have been the only one published. Boulton* owned five volumes of the Italian original in 1771.

Antoninus Pius (AD86-161)
Roman Emperor, AD128-61. Before his death he adopted Marcus Aurelius*, as he himself had been adopted by Hadrian.
Wedgwood subject:
Antoninus Pius, bust 22in., supplied by Hoskins & Grant, 1774

ANTHEMION. Anthemion ornament used in different versions on the lid, body and plinth of a green jasper dip vase, height 8⅜in., c.1795.
Dwight & Lucille Beeson Collection, Birmingham Museum, Alabama

ANTONY, Mark. Solid blue and white jasper portrait medallion, oval height 3¼in.. of Mark Antony, the modelling attributed to Hackwood, 1775.

Dwight & Lucille Beeson Collection, Birmingham Museum, Alabama

Antony, Mark (83?-30 BC)

Marcus Antonius, Roman triumvir, orator and soldier. In Gaul, he joined the party of Julius Caesar, whose patronage he subsequently enjoyed. He took part in the campaigns in Greece, Palestine and Egypt, aided Caesar in Gaul and commanded the left wing of his army at Pharsalus in 48. Mark Antony was consul with Caesar in 44 and, after Caesar's death in that year, was made triumvir. He later quarrelled with Octavius and was defeated in battle near Modena. He fled to Egypt, where he allied himself with Cleopatra*. Defeated again by Octavius at Actium and deserted by his army, he committed suicide.
Wedgwood subjects:

Mark Antony, bust 10-11½in., catalogued in 1777: probably supplied by Hoskins & Grant, 1775

Mark Antony, portrait medallion, 1773 Catalogue (Class V): refinished, or possibly remodelled, by Hackwood* in 1775

APHRODITE. Basalt table centre, height 12¼in., the figure of *Aphrodite* on a rock pierced as a flower holder, standing in a shallow bowl with everted rim. c.1910. The figure was available also singly with the rock unpierced.   *Wedgwood Museum*

Aphrodite

Greek goddess of love; the daughter of Zeus and Dione, but, according to later poets, she sprang from the foam of the sea. The wife of Hephaestos (Vulcan*) and mistress of Ares (Mars*), she is often depicted with her son Eros (Cupid*). Best known among her lovers is Adonis*. A Queen's ware figure of Aphrodite, height 12¾in., was modelled by Arnold Machin* c.1942.

APOLLO. *(Left)* Wedgwood & Bentley jasper medallion, 3⅞in. x 3⅛in., *Apollo Musagetes*, probably the model supplied by John Flaxman senior in 1775.   *Wedgwood Museum*
(Right) Wedgwood & Bentley jasper medallion, 3⅞in. x 3⅛in., *Apollo Musagetes,* The ground of the medallion is impressed with a large letter 'B', probably indicating a trial or reference piece. *Wedgwood Museum*

Apollo

The son of Zeus and Leto, twin brother of Diana*, and one of the principal deities of the Greeks, Apollo was the god of prophecy, with numerous oracles. In this guise he is known as the Pythian Apollo. As the god of music he is connected with the Muses* and called Apollo Musagetes (leader of the Muses). He came to be identified with Helios, and thus became god of the sun, often being depicted as driving the chariot of the sun across the heavens. He was also the god of rewards and punishments, and of towns and colonies. The Romans became acquainted with him by way of the Greeks, probably during the third century BC.
Wedgwood subjects:

Apollo, figure 11in., supplied by J. Flaxman senior* in 1775

Apollo Belvedere. Cast supplied by Flaxman*, January 1789

Apollo [Musagetes] (nearly full-face, his lyre on a tree stump beside him), medallion. See next entry

Apollo [Musagetes] (in profile, his lyre on tree stump beside him), medallion. Either this or the previous medallion is that listed as no.44, 4in. x 3in., in the 1773 Catalogue*. The other is almost certainly the figure bought, with four figures of Muses, from J. Flaxman senior in March 1775 for half a guinea. Both are from the Wedgwood & Bentley period

Apollo and Marsyas) three octagonal medallions, each 3in. x 6in.
Apollo and Daphne) supplied as casts by Mrs Landré* for 7/6d
Apollo and Python) in 1769

Apollo instructing the Youthful Bacchus (known also as *Apollo and the Three Graces,* tablet 6½in. x 15in., probably modelled in Rome c.1790. Uncatalogued

Apollo and Nine Muses, tablet, 6⅛in. x 15¾in. (also in separate pieces 8in. x 5½in. or 3½in. x 2½in.) attributed to John Flaxman junior, c.1778-80

In addition, the figure of Apollo appears on several small cameos and also in a scene, *Apollo chasing Daphne* (source: D'Hancarville* Vol.I, Pl.84), painted on an 'Etruscan' vase*

*Apollo Vase**

APOLLO. Green jasper dip tablet, 6½in. x 15¾in., *Apollo instructing the Youthful Bacchus.* c.1880.   *Christie's, New York*

APOLLO VASE. Solid blue and white jasper vase, height 9½in., designed by John Goodwin in 1930 to celebrate the bicentenary of Josiah Wedgwood's birth. *Wedgwood Museum*

Apollo Vase

Pale-blue jasper dip* lidded vase, 9½in. high, designed by John Goodwin* in 1930 to celebrate the bicentenary of Josiah Wedgwood's birth. The lid is surmounted by the figure of Apollo* and the vase bears the Latin inscription in bas-relief: 'CC POSTNATUM CONDITOREM ANNO VIGET ARS ETRURIAE REDINTEGRATA' (freely translated as: 'Two hundred years after the birth of the founder, the thriving art of Etruria is renewed'). The vase was made in a limited edition of fifty, each being numbered.

Apothecary Jars

Queen's ware syrup and pill jars for apothecaries and druggists were among the range of chemical wares* made by Wedgwood during the 1780s. Storage jars in three sizes, described as 'Apothecary Jars' and decorated with geometric patterns, were designed by

Peter Wall* and Robert Minkin* for the Design '63* exhibition at the London Showrooms* in February 1963.

Apotheosis

Deification, canonisation of a saint, or the exaltation of a person, ideal or principle; also loosely used to convey the meaning of resurrection or ascension to glory. A fairly familiar subject in classical art, it was used by Wedgwood for a number of important bas-reliefs* for tablets*, at least two of which were successfully adapted for the ornamenting of vases. The most notable are *Apotheosis of Homer** and *Apotheosis of Virgil** by Flaxman*. Also recorded are *Apotheosis of a Young Prince* by Angelini* and *Apotheosis of Faustina,* wife of Marcus Aurelius* by Pacetti*.

Apotheosis of Homer

Known also as *A Victorious Citharist* and *The Crowning of a Citharist* (Wedgwood himself referred to it as 'Homer & Hesiod'), this design was copied faithfully in relief by Flaxman* from the red-figure* decoration on a calyx krater* bought by the British Museum from Sir William Hamilton* in 1772 and illustrated by d'Hancarville* (Vol.III, Pl.31). Wedgwood refers to this relief model in a letter to Bentley* dated 19 August 1778. Bentley interpreted the scene as 'some honour paid to the genius of Homer*', and Hamilton confirmed this, establishing the name by which it is now known. This accorded admirably with the veneration of 18th-century scholars and travellers for Homer as the supreme genius of the ancient world. Some eight years later, this bas-relief was chosen by Wedgwood as the principal ornament for his most important jasper vase to date, first produced in February 1786. In May of that year he presented a copy of it to the British Museum. Wedgwood considered it one of the finest vases he ever made and the bas-relief is widely regarded as the most important commission executed by Flaxman for Wedgwood. A superb example of the vase, in greenish-buff jasper dip* with the Pegasus* finial in white on solid pale-blue clouds, is in the Nottingham Castle Museum. A second example in this rare colour is in a private collection in the U.S.A. and a third was destroyed in the bombing of Hull during World War II.
See: Frontispiece

Apotheosis of Virgil

A large bas-relief subject designed and modelled by Flaxman, c.1785, as a companion piece to *Apotheosis of Homer**. It was used

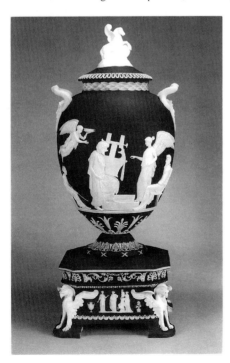

APOTHEOSIS OF HOMER. Black jasper dip *Apotheosis of Homer* vase on octagonal pedestal, height 24½in. c.1875-85.
Christie's, New York

APOTHEOSIS OF VIRGIL. Flaxman's bas-relief used as ornament for a fine black and white jasper dip vase, height (including 6½in. pedestal) 23¾in., 1795-1820.
Dwight & Lucille Beeson Collection, Birmingham Museum, Alabama

APOTHEOSIS OF VIRGIL. Large circular jasper plaque, diameter 12½in., presented to Henry Brownsword on the occasion of his retirement in 1903. *Wedgwood Museum*

as ornament both for jasper tablets and for vases, but it was probably designed specifically in order to provide a companion to the Homeric vase.

Apple shapes
See: Fruit and Vegetable Shapes

Applied Reliefs
See: Ornamenting

Apprenticeship
The system of apprenticeship, by which young men were bound to serve an employer for a stated number of years to learn a craft, declined steadily in England from the end of the seventeenth century. By 1740, formal apprenticeship in the potteries had become a comparatively rare undertaking, and a high proportion of those who were indentured became master potters. Throwing (see: Processes of Manufacture) was the most highly rated of all the potter's skills and only those who were expected to be master-craftsmen served such such an apprenticeship. Josiah Wedgwood was apprenticed to his brother, Thomas, of the Churchyard Works, for five years from 11 November 1744, 'to learn…the said Art of Throwing and Handleing'.

Apricot Brandy Bottle
Apricot brandy bottles, variously decorated, were made in several bodies, including Queen's ware* and jasper*, for Humphrey Taylor & Co in 1913.

APRICOT BRANDY BOTTLE. Solid green and white jasper liqueur bottle made for Humphrey Taylor & Co. Height 6¾in. c.1913.
Wedgwood Museum

April Colours
See: Aerograph

Arabesque
The term, from the Italian *arabeschi*, cannot be precisely defined. An arabesque consists of interlaced lines, bands and strapwork, sometimes largely abstract, sometimes floral and foliate. Originally adapted by Islamic craftsmen from Roman sources, it is related to the grotesques* with which it is sometimes confused. The principal difference is that arabesques arising from Islamic sources lack representations of living creatures, although these have sometimes been added by Christian designers. The term 'Moresque', often used for arabesques of the 19th century, is properly applied to those with sources in Spain or Sicily, both of which were at one time under Saracen domination.
See also: Hispano-Moresque Designs

Arbury Hall
See: Newdigate, Sir Roger

Architectural Details
From the existence of a few extremely rare examples, it appears that Wedgwood experimented with the production of small terracotta* architectural details moulded in relief. These may have been intended to be set in above the jambs of chimneypieces*, but there is no evidence that they were ever produced in quantity and it seems probable that the idea was soon abandoned.

ARGENTA. Lobster salad bowl with EPNS rim, the body printed and enamelled with a pattern of seaweed, the claw feet enamelled in scarlet. Diameter 10in. 1883. *Author's collection*

Ares
See: Mars

Argand lamp
A type of oil lamp invented c.1782 by a Swiss, Aimé Argand, and made in England by Boulton*. The wick is fed from a central reservoir, and air is supplied to the flame by a glass tube. It has the usual glass chimney. From about 1810 the wick was adjustable. Wedgwood was associated with the Birmingham manufacturer J. Hinks & Son in making lamps of this type in the 1870s.

Argenta
A form of Majolica* with pale-coloured grounds, introduced c.1879. It made possible the use of more delicate colourings and decoration and also responded to the fashion for *Japonisme**.

Argonaut
See: Shell Shapes

Argyll
A gravy-warmer, or 'gravy cup', said to have been invented by the third Duke of Argyll, c.1750, and first made in silver. Somewhat similar in shape to a covered coffee pot, it has a handle, usually at a

ARGYLL. Pearl ware gravy cup or 'Argyll'. height 6in., with Mared pattern painted in underglaze blue .c.1785. *Formerly Buten Museum*

right angle to the spout, and a central tube or separate compartment (often formed by a 'double wall') to contain hot water. It was made by both Wedgwood and Leeds, among others, in creamware*.

Ariadne

The daughter of Minos and Pasiphaë of Crete. She fell in love with Theseus and gave him the reel of thread with which he found his way out of the labyrinth of the Minotaur. Theseus promised to marry Ariadne, and she fled with him from Crete, but he deserted her and she was found by Dionysus (see: Bacchus), who made her his wife.

Wedgwood subjects:

Ariadne, miniature bust, height 4-4½in., on waisted socle, 1779

Ariadne, plaque (head), 8in. x 6in., supplied by John Flaxman senior in 1775. No.113 in 1777 Catalogue*

Ariadne, medallion (head), 2¾in. x 1¾in., no.120 in 1777 Catalogue*. A reduced version of the above medallion

Ariadne Reclining, figure length 10in., copied from a marble in the Vatican Museum. Catalogued in 1787

Triumph of Ariadne 'With choral figures'. tablet 10½in. x 14¼in., no.170 in 1777 Catalogue. From an antique marble or cast owned by Sir Roger Newdigate*

Triumph of Bacchus and Ariadne, tablet 9½in. x 23in. or 10¾in. x 26in., no.212 in 1779 Catalogue*

Aristophanes (c.444-380 BC)

Celebrated Greek poet and dramatist, believed to have been born in Athens. He is known particularly for satirical comedies, of which eleven have survived, directed against a variety of abuses of his time.

Wedgwood subject:

Aristophanes, miniature bust 4-4½in., 1779.

ARISTOPHANES. Wedgwood & Bentley miniature bust, height 4in., in white jasper on a black basaltes socle. c.1779. *Christie's, London*

ARIADNE. A copy in miniature, in the Carrara body, of a marble in the Vatican Museum, made also in black basaltes from about 1781. Height 9in. c.1870. *Wedgwood Museum*

Aristotle (384-322 BC)

Philosopher, born at Stagira in Macedonia. After the death of Alexander the Great in 322, Aristotle, regarded as a friend of Macedonia, thought it prudent to leave Athens, and he escaped to Chalcis in Euboea, where he died. A bust of Aristotle, 7-8in. high, was reproduced in black basaltes* by 1774.

Armorial Ware

Ware decorated with the coat of arms or crest of the owner. The fashion derived from armorial engraving on silver, and enamelled Chinese export porcelain commissioned from Europe. Wedgwood

ARMORIAL WARE. Queen's ware plate bat-printed in black and decorated in polychrome enamels with the arms of Honeywood and Courtenay. c.1778-90. *Wedgwood Museum*

ARMORIAL WARE. Queen's ware dessert dish, lined in blue and gold and painted with the Prince of Wales's feathers, from a service made for the Duke of Clarence in 1818. *City Museum & Art Gallery, Stoke-on-Trent*

was at first reluctant to accept orders of this nature, explaining to Bentley* in 1766: 'Crests are very bad things for us to meddle with...Plain ware, if it should not happen to be firsts [perfect], you will take off my hands as seconds [sell as substandard], which, if Crested, would be as useless as most other Crests and Crest wearers are'. By 1776, however, he was obliged to admit that 'The painting of Arms is now become serious business, and I must either lose or gain a great deal of business by it. However I must at all events come into it'. The earliest recorded Wedgwood service with armorial decoration was commissioned by Lady Warburton and was invoiced by Sadler*, who printed it on Queen's ware*, in March 1769. As the Crest Order Books* preserved in the Wedgwood Museum* testify, armorial ware became an essential, though always doubtfully profitable, part of Wedgwood's Queen's ware business and was later to be a small but prestigious part of Wedgwood's bone china* production. Recent research has revealed that some of Wedgwood's earliest armorial ware was bat-printed* and enamelled, not transfer-printed* as had been assumed. Modern coats of arms are reproduced in colour by lithography* or silk-screen* printing.

Armstrong, Samuel (fl.1769-74)
Painter at the Chelsea Decorating Studio*, who enamelled borders on the Frog* service.

Army Type Ware
Heavily potted earthenware crockery made under government contract for the use of the armed services during World War II. It was decorated with a black strip for the navy, a printed green cipher for the army and a plain pale blue band or badge for the Royal Air Force. Orders for this ware formed a substantial part of the new Barlaston* factory's production, providing nearly one-third of total home sales and more than 8 per cent of world sales in December 1941.

Art Deco
The name adopted to describe the decorative style that superseded Art Nouveau*. Art Deco sprang from several diverse sources, including Cubism, Expressionism and Fauvism, the work of the Deutscher Werkbund, designs for the Ballets Russes and an awakening interest in African & Central American Indian art. The Exposition Internationale des Arts Décoratifs et Industriels Modernes in Paris in 1925 included ceramics, glass, furniture and bookbinding as well as graphics and interior design, and the official catalogue illustrated more than 1,000 examples. By the early-1930s, the style had developed beyond such romantic forms as floral garlands, tassels and spirals to more geometrical designs. As its influence spread through Europe to America, it absorbed national characteristics and broadened its stylistic vocabulary to

ART DECO. *Pink Vandyke* border pattern handpainted over matt white glaze on Paris shape. 1934. *Photograph: Wedgwood*

ART DECO. Teaware handpainted with platinum lines and green leaves, with green enamel handles and knops. c.1937.
Author's collection

ART NOUVEAU. Old photograph of a selection of Lindsay Ware, produced in enamelled Queen's ware, c.1901. *Photograph: Wedgwood*

embrace Egyptian and Aztec architectural forms as well as those suggested by modern machinery. It was the first international decorative style to make wide use of the newly-developed plastics. Wedgwood is not generally associated with Art Deco design, but nevertheless could not ignore a movement of such popularity and produced a number of hand-painted Queen's ware* and bone china* patterns which are recognisably of the period.
See: Taplin, Millicent

Art Nouveau
An English style in the decorative arts which grew out of the Arts and Crafts Movement* and *japonisme** in the 1880s and achieved its greatest popularity on the Continent, where it is known variously as *Style Modern, Style Anglais, Jugendstil* and *Stile Liberty* (after the stylish London store which most enthusiastically promoted it). The qualities which distinguished it from other design movements were rejection of convention, simplicity and abstraction of nature. As Mario Amaya wrote: 'The major objective became a search for style that could institute a sense of design compatible with its age in all the applied arts' *(Art Nouveau*, 1966). Some of its most distinguished exponents, such as Walter Crane*, Charles Voysey and C.R. Ashbee, were leaders also of the Arts and Crafts Movement*, but their most innovative designs, realised in clean purity of line, belong to England's 'Modern Style'. Art Nouveau ornament was mostly floral, characterised by flowing, undulating lines, the 'swinging curves' which later inspired such great architects and designers as Arne Jacobsen, Georg Jensen, Frank Lloyd Wright and Mies Van de Rohe. It played a small part in the production of most pottery and porcelain factories but tended rather to inspire the work of studio potters. Cecil Wedgwood* wrote to W.R. Lethaby, then principal of the Central School of Art, in 1902: 'We are not at all wedded to "New Art", in fact personally speaking I think a great deal of it is very poor...not one out of a hundred of the purchasing Public has really good taste. As long as a thing is "new" it may be as ugly as sin'. This view was clearly at variance with that of his cousin and fellow director, Kennard Wedgwood*, who expressed a wish for 'a line of Vases entirely on New Art Lines' and commissioned Courtney Lindsay* to design them. Although England and Scotland produced some of the most famous names in Art Nouveau

design, the style never achieved widespread recognition or popularity in Britain. Since the revival of interest during the 1960s, however, much of what was best in the Art Nouveau style has been embraced as an important contribution to the grammar of architecture and design. The most obvious examples of Wedgwood design in this style are found in Lindsay's work, but there are other designs, notably in the Queen's ware Pattern Books* of the period, that demonstrate a nod in the direction of contemporary high fashion. Strong residual echoes of the style are noticeable also in many of the designs of Daisy Makeig-Jones*.

Art Pottery
Decorative pottery in the style of the Aesthetic Movement* and the Arts and Crafts Movement*, current from the late 1870s. Art pottery might be factory made or studio pottery and it was more profusely decorated than pottery intended for mere utility. For the most part 'art' wares were made by smaller factories, but Godfrey Wedgwood* showed considerable interest in them, and artists employed at Etruria* as well as commissioned freelance designers produced wares in this style. The term 'art' was widely used and applied to furniture, metalwork and glass.
See: Japonisme; Magnolia Ware; Majolica

Artemis (Artemisia)
Greek goddess, the daughter of Zeus and Leto, and sister of Apollo*. In Greece she was sometimes identified with Selene, but she is best known elsewhere, and principally identified in Wedgwood wares, by her Roman name, Diana*.
Wedgwood subject:
Artemisia, medallion 4in. x 5in., no.144 in 1777 Catalogue*

Artichoke
One of several vegetable and fruit forms used by Wedgwood, notably as a shape for custard cups* and for knops* and handles.

Arts and Crafts Movement
A movement which originated in England and exerted so powerful an influence on international taste, fashion and design that it persisted through the turn of the 19th century to become a permanent

ASTLE, Thomas. Thirty black basaltes cabinet medals of the Kings of England, from heads supplied by Astle. Ovals 2-2½in. high. c.1785.
Christie's, London

part of the industrial design heritage. The central belief of its founding fathers, first among whom was William Morris, was that a nation's art reflects its moral health. Its precepts were 'fitness for purpose' and 'honesty of production', and its aims, social and political, were to bring about a revival of simplicity and craftsmanship and to return art to the people. Although Morris's dream was a medieval fantasy, in part it was realised: he presided over a remarkable revival in handicrafts of all kinds. But craftsmen require employment, and neither craftsmanship nor fine materials come cheap. Demand was confined to the rich, and renewed interest quickly developed into a vogue which could be satisfied only by the very machines that Morris had hoped to discredit. Handicraft was simulated; 'art' products became the fashion; craftsmanship was degraded into quaintness. Nevertheless, Morris gave his name to a style that has outlived many more transient fashions and, at a time when the machine was threatening to become the master, and mass-production the permanent successor to craftsmanship, he gave expression to a need for genuineness of materials and work and for a quality of life already fast disappearing. The influence of the Arts and Crafts Movement on the pottery industry, and more especially on British studio potters, was considerable. One of its leading exponents, Walter Crane*, was commissioned to decorate vases for Wedgwood; undecorated wares, including tiles, were supplied to William De Morgan* and the Passenger* brothers to paint; the technique of inlaying* was revived for Thomas Mellor* and Charles Toft* to employ; and designers and painters at Etruria were put to work on 'Art Pottery'*. These were all expressions of the Wedgwoods' commitment to handcraft, a policy most evident in their long association with Emile Lessore*, which began a year before the founding of Morris's design firm and well in advance of the movement that inspired the widespread production of 'Art Pottery'. That commitment was reinforced early in the 20th century by the employment of Alfred and Louise Powell*.

Asparagus Pan
A footed dish, open at one end and rising to a tapered prow at the other, intended for the service of asparagus. It appears as design no.20 in the first Queen's Ware Catalogue, 1774.

Asparagus Tray (Server)
A flat receptacle, open at both ends, with low vertical sides, wider at one end than at the other, and about 3in. long. Sometimes erroneously described as knife rests, these were used to hold small bunches of asparagus spears arranged around a large dish.

Astle, Thomas (1735-1803)
Antiquary and palaeographer; elected Fellow of the Royal Society, 1766. His (Stowe) collection of manuscripts is now in the British Library, London. He supplied Wedgwood with portraits (probably from medals and engravings) for the series of thirty-six Kings of England, listed as Class IX, Section I in the 1773 Catalogue*. These were sold only in sets, with or without wooden cabinets.

Athene
Pallas Athene, goddess of wisdom.
See: Minerva

Atlas (Atlantes)
One of the Titans*, brother of Prometheus*. He and his brothers made war on Zeus, but they were defeated and Atlas was condemned to bear the Heavens on his shoulders. Atlantes are male statues used in place of columns in the support of buildings and occur in classical ornamental designs as supporters. Male versions of caryatids*, Atlantes appear as supporters on the so-called Michelangelo* vase.
Wedgwood subject:
Atlas supporting the world, cameo after an engraved gem by Giovanni Antonio de' Rossi

Attributes
By tradition, mythological figures were provided with a variety of attributes which served to identify them, and these are briefly discussed here as an aid to identification. These attributes come originally from Greek sources and have descended through the generations with certain modifications.

In general, the face was oval. Angularity was regarded as ugly, so the forehead was rounded. The style of the hair helps to identify the personage depicted: Jupiter* (Zeus) has curling hair and beard, with two locks over his forehead brushed upwards in a form somewhat resembling rams' horns; Neptune's* hair has often the appearance of being saturated with water; Pluto* has long, straight hair; Apollo* has long hair, tied on the top of the head and hanging down the back; Venus* and Diana* have hair either knotted at the nape of the neck or tied on top; Hercules* has hair best described as woolly.

The eyes were large and, in the case of virgin goddesses and vestals, modestly lowered. The eyebrows were fairly prominent. The mouth had a full lower lip above a rounded chin. The lips of divine beings were sometimes open, but in mortals they were closed. Teeth were shown only in the heads of satyrs, Sileni and fauns*. The pectoral muscles of men were large and prominent, especially in the figures of Hercules, and the belly was flat. The breasts of women tended to be small, almost virginal, and pointed, and the belly soft and rounded. The hands and feet were always carefully carved or modelled.

While these remarks apply principally to ancient sculpture, most later sculpture in the classical or neo-classical styles conformed to these principles closely, since it was directly inspired by surviving Greek and Roman sculpture and vase-painting. Individual attributes, such as Jupiter's thunderbolt, which accompany later representations of mythological figures, are described under the appropriate headings.

Often allied to figures of this kind are the allegorical subjects popular throughout the 18th century and to be found among Wedgwood figures and reliefs. Objects allegorical of the gods, which may even stand by themselves without an accompanying figure, are the laurel of Apollo (often in the form of a wreath), the vine and thyrsus* of Bacchus*, the eagle and thunderbolt of Jupiter, the crescent moon of Diana*, the lion-skin and club of Hercules and the caduceus* of Mercury*.

There are also figures symbolising such concepts as the Continents, the Elements*, the Seasons* and others. Everyone of education in the 18th century was expected to be able to recognise classical attributes and to interpret such symbolism.
See also: Horae; Trophies

Auckland, William Eden, 1st Baron (1744-1814)
English statesman, diplomat and 'man of business'; third son of Sir Robert Eden of West Auckland, Durham. A convinced Whig, who deserted the Opposition to serve the government under the Younger Pitt, Eden was one of Wedgwood's most influential patrons. He was minister plenipotentiary to France in 1786 and negotiated the Commercial Treaty. Wedgwood wrote him a long letter at that time on the subject of duties as they affected trade with France. Eden was created Baron Auckland in 1789. A year later, while serving as ambassador extraordinary at the Hague, he entertained Josiah II* and Tom Byerley* and arranged for them to show a copy of the Portland* vase to the Prince and Princess of Orange. Auckland wrote Wedgwood a letter of enthusiastic praise not only for the vase but also for the behaviour of the younger Josiah, but hinted that he was not convinced by Wedgwood's explanation of the relief figures.

Portrait medallions* of Lord and Lady Auckland were modelled about 1789 by Eley George Mountstephen* and reproduced in jasper* in 1790. Mountstephen's original pink wax model of Auckland's portrait was shown in the exhibition at the National Portrait Gallery, London, in 1973.

Auction Sale, December 1781
After the death of Thomas Bentley* in 1780, it became necessary to wind up the affairs of the Wedgwood & Bentley partnership for the production of ornamental* wares. The principal asset was the stock and the decision was taken to dispose of this by auction, over a period of eleven days with a break only for Sunday, at the auction rooms of Christie* & Ansell in Pall Mall, where the Royal Academy exhibitions had previously been held. The catalogue explicitly states that the sale was being held at the wish of the widowed Mrs Bentley, but there was, in fact, no alternative method of rapidly realising her share of the business at prices better than cost of manufacturing. The stock was sold in 1,200 lots, some of them of twenty-four or more pieces, and realised a total of £2,182.6.6. The catalogue of the sale is preserved in the archives of Messrs Christie, Manson & Woods in King Street, London, and the prices marked are a useful guide to the market at the time. Recent research into the details of the catalogue has revealed some important information about the Wedgwood & Bentley partnership.

Audubon Birds
See: Palliser, Herbert

Auerbach
Russian faïence factory, founded in the village of Domkino (Korchova district of the Tver province) in 1809 by Friedrich Christian Brinner. From 1810 the factory was owned by Andrei Auerbach and rapidly achieved distinction, becoming the leading pottery in Russia. Much of the cream-coloured earthenware, particularly the services with simple handpainted borders of vines or foliage, closely resembles Wedgwood's and appears to be in conscious imitation. The factory was sold in 1870 to the monopolist of the Russian ceramics industry, M.S. Kuznetsov.

Augustus Caesar (63 BC- AD14)
First Roman Emperor, adopted by his uncle, Julius Caesar*. His name was originally Octavian, and Augustus was a title conferred on him by the senate and the people in 27 BC. He was succeeded by Tiberius.
Wedgwood subjects:
Augustus, portrait medallion 3in. x 2½in., catalogued in 1777 (Class V, Illustrious Romans).
Augustus, bust about 22in., supplied by Hoskins & Grant*, 1774.

Auro Basalt
A range of black basalt* vases decorated with gilded and bronzed raised slip* introduced c.1885 in an attempt to imitate Japanese bronze styles. The gilded decoration was floral or leafage and was often cut off abruptly at the neck or foot of the vase (as if the design might be continued inside the neck or under the base), a feature of much oriental design.
See: Japonisme

Aurora
The Greek Eos, goddess of the Dawn. At the end of the night she rose from the bed of her husband, Tithonus, and in a chariot drawn

AUCKLAND, William Eden, 1st Baron. Jasper portrait medallion, modelled by Eley George Mountstephen. c.1789.
Brooklyn Museum: Emily Winthrop Miles Collection

by swift horses she ascended from Oceanus to the heavens to announce the coming of the Sun.
Wedgwood subjects:
Aurora, black transfer-print from an engraving, printed and enamelled in colours by William Greatbatch* on creamcolour teapots, some of which are attributed to Wedgwood, c.1777
Aurora, goddess of the Dawn, cameo, modelled by William Hackwood* from a cast supplied by Hoskins & Grant*, 1779

Austin, Arnold (fl.1904-47)
Like his father, James A. Austin, chief modeller at Etruria*, and later at the Barlaston* factory. He modelled a bust of Josiah Wedgwood taken from the monument at Stoke-on-Trent parish church.

Austin, Roy (1918-78)
The third generation of his family to be Wedgwood's chief modeller, Roy Austin was appointed in 1967, succeeding Eric Owen*. He attended Newcastle School of Art and Stoke-on-Trent College of Art until 1939, when he joined the Air Sea Rescue Corps, in which he served until the end of World War II. In 1950 he was appointed a visiting master to Stoke-on-Trent College of Art and was later a visiting lecturer at the Royal College of Art (School of Ceramics) and Central School of Art and Design in London.

Australia
See: Sydney Cove Medallion

Aventurine Glaze
See: Glazes

Ayoree Clay
Wedgwood's alternative name for Cherokee* clay.

AURO BASALT. Vase, height 6¼in., decorated with bronzed and gilded raised paste oak-leaf design. c.1885. *Wedgwood Museum*

B

Baby Feeder
Small spouted pot, similar in shape to a teapot or coffeepot, with a long, curved nipple spout. Baby feeders were made by Wedgwood in Queen's ware* and Pearl* ware throughout the 19th century.
See: Bubby Pot

Bacchae or Bacchantes (Maenads)
Female companions of Bacchus, represented as crowned with vine leaves and clothed in skins or swirling drapery. Often they are depicted beating tambourines. They were priestesses who, with the aid of wine, became frenzied during the Dionysiac festivals.
See: Bacchus

Bacchus
The Roman name associated with Dionysus, the son of Zeus and Semele. He wandered through Egypt, Syria and much of Asia teaching mankind the cultivation of the vine and the arts of civilisation. Usually portrayed as a naked youth, but occasionally as aged (when he is often confused with Silenus*), Bacchus was the god of wine. He wears a crown of vine leaves and grapes and holds a thyrsus*. The celebration of Bacchic festivals were especially frenzied and lascivious. Women taking part in them were known as Bacchantes, and Bacchus was accompanied also by fauns*, satyrs* and centaurs* who pursued the women. Small boys, the dolphin*, panther and ass were all associated with Bacchus, as were the vine, laurel and ivy. His triumphal car is drawn by goats, leopards or tigers. A large number of Wedgwood bas-reliefs* portray Bacchus and his attendants and the list has been complicated by alternative names for them, some of which were used in the Catalogues* and others added by later writers. The following have been certainly identified:

Bacchus, figure 11in., after the Michelangelo* marble, now in the Museo Nazionale, Florence, first catalogued 1773
Bacchus, figure 10¾in., after the Jacopo Sansovino marble, now in the Museo Nazionale, Florence, first catalogued 1774, supplied by Hoskins & Grant*, 1773
Bacchus, miniature bust 4-4½in., probably supplied by Hoskins & Grant, 1779
Bacchus and Panther, plaque 'rectangular and oval' 6in. x 11in., no.16 in 1773 Catalogue
Bacchus with an Urn and Grapes, medallion 3¼in. x 1¾in., no.229 in 1779 Catalogue (new models in 1776). After the bas-relief on the monument of Lysicrates at Athens, and probably copied

BABY FEEDER. Pearl ware baby feeder or 'bubby pot' decorated with Hibiscus pattern, printed underglaze in blue. Height 5½in. c.1815.
Formerly Buten Museum

BACCHUS. Black basaltes vase painted in encaustic colours with figures representing 'Bacchus Barbu' (Indian Bacchus), copied from d'Hancarville Vol.I, Plate 59. Unmarked. Wedgwood & Bentley, c.1775.
Wedgwood Museum

BACCHUS. Jasper tablet, *Education of Bacchus,* 7in. x 22⅞in. c.1920.
Dwight & Lucille Beeson Collection, Birmingham Museum, Alabama

BACCHUS. White terracotta biscuit 'Herculaneum Picture', *A Bacchanalian Figure* (known also as 'Herculaneum Dancer'), the ground and frame painted with matt dark red encaustic colour. Unmarked. Wedgwood & Bentley, c.1773.   *Merseyside Museums*

BACCHUS. Deep-blue jasper dip oval plaque *Birth of Bacchus*, modelled by William Hackwood in 1776 as a companion piece to his *Triumph of Bacchus*. The subject was first produced in this form because the composition of eleven figures could not be made in one piece. Oval length 11⅝in. c.1785.   *Nottingham Castle Museum*

from an engraving by Stuart* and Revett *(Die Althümer zu Athen)*; Robert Adam* reproduced the entire frieze at Stowe in 1771

Birth of Bacchus, plaque 6 in x 5in., no.1 in 1773 Catalogue*

Birth of Bacchus, plaque 5½in. x 7½in., modelled by Hackwood* 'from the antique' (after a marble vase by the Athenian sculptor Salpion*, now in the Naples Museum, and adapted from an engraving by Montfaucon*), 1776. No.118 in 1777 Catalogue

Birth of Bacchus, tablet 11in. x 23in., 'from Michelangelo's seal' (the original carnelian gem in the cabinet of the King of France reputedly once belonged to Michelangelo), modelled by Hackwood*. No.206 in 1773 Catalogue

Education of Bacchus, tablet 6¾in. x 11¼in. or 7in. x 22⅞in., probably copied in Rome, c.1790, from a sarcophagus in the

Capitoline Museum

Head of Bacchus, plaque 8in. x 6in., supplied by Flaxman senior*, 1775. No.112 in 1777 Catalogue. A smaller version of this head, 2¾in. x 1¾in., appears as no.121 in the same catalogue

Indian Bacchus, plaque 4in. x 5in., no.146 in 1777 Catalogue

Sacrifice to Bacchus, tablet 8¼in. x 14in. or 9½in. x 22in., modelled by Hackwood*, 1776. No.200 in 1779 Catalogue

Silenus with Infant Bacchus (known also as *Faun with Infant Bacchus* or *Borghese Faun)*, figure 18in., c.1790. The original statue, of which Wedgwood's is an inaccurate copy, is in the Louvre

Triumph of Bacchus, tablet 6½in. x 14in. or 7½in. x 10in., modelled by Hackwood, 1776. No.201 in 1777 Catalogue

Triumph of Bacchus and Ariadne, tablet 9½in. x 23in. or 10¾in. x 26in., no.212 in 1779 Catalogue

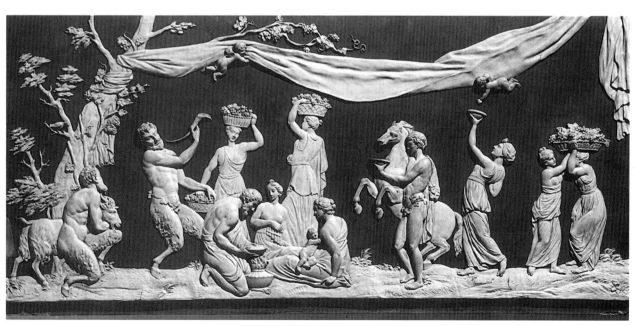

BACCHUS. Wedgwood & Bentley pale blue jasper tablet, *Birth of Bacchus,* 9⅜in. x 20½in. c.1779.   *Manchester Museum*

BACCHUS. Pale blue and white jasper plaque, *Bacchus and Panther*, 7in. x 9in. c.1785-90.
Dwight & Lucille Beeson Collection, Birmingham Museum, Alabama

BACCHUS. Drabware jug moulded with 'Bacchanalian boys' and branches of fruiting vine. Height 10in. c.1886.   *Wedgwood Museum*

A Bacchanalian Figure } 2 circular plaques 11½in. diameter, nos
A Bacchanalian Figure } 64-5 in 1773 Catalogue. 2 of 14 'Figures from paintings in the ruins of Herculaneum' taken from copies owned by Lord Lansdowne*

A Bacchanalian Piece, tablet 8in. x 10½in., after a bas-relief*, in the Newdigate* collection. No.174 in 1777 Catalogue

Bacchanalian Boys, 2 plaques 3½in. x 5in., probably after Duquesnoy*, nos 35-6 in 1777 Catalogue

Bacchanalian Boys at Play, plaque 6in. x 8in., 1773. Probably after Duquesnoy and obtained from Mrs Landré* in 1769. No.13 in 1773 Catalogue

Bacchanalian Sacrifice, 'long square tablet' 9in. x 21in., after bas-relief by Clodion*. No.71 in 1773 Catalogue

Bacchanalian Tablet, tablet 5½in. x 26in., from designs by Beauclerk*. No.244 in 1787 Catalogue. Made up from Group of Three Boys, Group of Two Boys and Four Boys Single (nos 241-3 in the same catalogue)

Bacchanalian Triumph, 'rectangular and oval' plaque 4in. x 6in., 1773. Probably obtained from Mrs Landré, 1769. No.12 in 1773 Catalogue

Bacchanalian Triumph, 'long square tablet' 9in. x 21in., after a bas-relief by Clodion. No.70 in 1773 Catalogue

Boys and Goat, Bacchanalians, tablet 7in. x 11½in. or 9in. x 12¾in., no.213 in 1779 Catalogue

Triumph of Bacchanalian Boys, small medallion 1½in. x 2in., no.190 in 1777 Catalogue

A Bacchante and Children, plaque 6in. x 8in., no. 37 in 1773 Catalogue

Two Bacchantes, separate figures for medallions by Angelini*, 1789

Bacon, John Senior RA (1740-99)

English sculptor, born in Southwark, London. Bacon is believed to have been apprenticed, at the age of fourteen, at a porcelain factory in Bow Churchyard, East London, and one or two porcelain models of exceptional quality have been attributed to him. He certainly worked, at some time, for Nicholas Crisp(e), a jeweller and potter at Lambeth. About 1769 he went to work for Coade* at Lambeth, at the same time studying at the Royal Academy Schools. A receipt dated 28 July 1769 shows that he was paid £9.15s for modelling work for Wedgwood. In the same year he won the first Gold Medal for sculpture ever awarded by the Royal Academy, and nine years later he received the Gold Medal of the Royal Society of Arts* for statues of Mars* and Venus*. His work for Wedgwood includes *Andromache** and *A Conquered Province* (nos. 197-8 in 1779 Catalogue) and probably the two large bas-reliefs *Night and Day* (nos. 77-80 in 1773 catalogue).

Baddeley, Edward Gerrard (fl.1834-89)

Engraver of Hanley; worked for Wedgwood at Etruria, 1852-77.

Baddeley, John (c.1720-71)

Potter of Shelton, Staffordshire, from whom, in 1762, Wedgwood bought pineapple* ware. Four years later he settled part of his bill with Baddeley by supplying him with cauliflower* block moulds (see: Moulds) to the substantial value of 12 guineas, later purchasing from him six dozen cauliflower cups and saucers. The explanation for these transactions appears to lie in Wedgwood's understanding of the waning popularity of rococo* vegetable and fruit shapes of which he was then clearing his warehouse. Wedgwood's high regard for Baddeley's ware was emphasised when he wrote in 1771 of 'Mr Baddeley who makes the best ware perhaps of any of the Potter's here' – next, of course, to his own.

Baddeley, William (fl.1795-1822)

Potter of Eastwood, Hanley, who used the impressed mark 'EASTWOOD', often on the lower front edge of his wares (not the base), from 1802-22. He has been accused of deliberately impressing the first four letters faintly in order to pass off his wares, which included creamwares*, Egyptian Black* and cane*, as Wedgwood. No substantive evidence has been found to support this charge.

Bagot, Sir William (1728-98)

Sixth baronet and 1st Baron Bagot of Blithfield, Staffordshire; M.P. for Staffordshire, 1754-80. An enthusiastic patron of Wedgwood's, Sir William insisted that his architect, James Wyatt, insert three jasper tablets* into his chimneypiece*, choosing for the purpose Flaxman's* *Apotheosis of Homer** and *Dancing Hours**. Wedgwood visited Blithfield to inspect the chimneypiece in July 1779.

BACON, John Senior. Plaster block mould, *A Conquered Province*, from a model by John Bacon.   *Wedgwood Museum*

Colour Plate 3. BAKEWELL, James. Shell-edge shape Queen's ware dessert dish decorated by James Bakewell with sprays of flowers in David Rhodes's rose-purple enamel ('calx cassii'). 8¼in. x 12¾in. Unmarked except for monogram 'JB' in enamel on base. c.1769.

Francis Rickerby Collection

Colour Plate 4. BAKEWELL, James. Queen's ware feather-edge shape plate enamelled, probably by James Bakewell, with sprays of flowers in black and yellow. Unmarked. c.1769. *Merseyside Museums*

Colour Plate 5. BARLASTON HALL. Queen's ware wall plaque (pierced for hanging) painted in purple lustre by Alfred Powell with a view of Barlaston Hall. Signed on reverse with monogram and inscribed 'Alfred Powell at Barlaston May 1942'. Diameter 23in.

Wedgwood Museum

Colour Plate 6. BARTON, Glenys. 'Sky Plateau II', a sculptured design in bone china by Glenys Barton, produced in a limited edition of four in 1977. Diameter 10in.   *Wedgwood Museum*

Colour Plate 7. BASKETS. Queen's ware pierced fruit basket and stand enamelled in rose-purple with sprays of flowers in the manner of James Bakewell. Diameter (basket) 7in. Unmarked, c.1770. The basket is shape no. 1 in the First Queen's Ware Catalogue, 1774.
L.A. Compton Collection

Colour Plate 8. BEAUCLERK, Lady Diana. Grey-blue jasper tablet with pale-blue wash on the upper surface only, ornamented with single figures and groups of boys after designs by Lady Diana Beauclerk. 6in. x 22½in. c.1787-90.
Nottingham Castle Museum

Colour Plate 9. BENTLEY, Thomas. Portrait of Thomas Bentley, Josiah Wedgwood's partner in the manufacture of Ornamental wares, 1768-80. After a portrait by J.F. Rigaud, RA (formerly attributed to Joseph Wright of Derby). Oil on canvas, 35¼in. x 27¾in. *Wedgwood Museum*

Colour Plate 10. BONE CHINA. First period bone china teapot and sugar box (oblong shape) with French tea cup and coffee cup, decorated with 'Rose colour ivy leaves on a pale blue ground'. Teapot height 6¼in. c.1818. *Formerly Buten Museum*

Colour Plate 11. BOUGH POT. Two-handled candlestick vase – bough-pot with candleholder, the body moulded to simulate bamboo, painted with a broad blue band and green leaves in encaustic colours. Height 8in. c.1785. *Wedgwood Museum*

Colour Plate 12. BOURNE, Edward. Pale-blue jasper dip portrait medallion of Edward Bourne in a laurel and fluted black jasper frame, modelled by William Hackwood in 1778. 6½in. x 5½in. Unmarked. c.1779. *Wedgwood Museum*

Colour Plate 13. BULB POT. Green dip jasper and solid blue jasper square pedestal bulb pots, each fitted with a loose grid, pierced for flowers, and a cup for a single bulb. Similar pedestals were used also for flower holders and as tall bases for vases. Height 7in. c.1790.
Wedgwood Museum

Colour Plate 14. CAMEO. Pair of white terracotta stoneware double-sided (back-to-back) octagonal cameos ornamented with figures of Aesculapius and Polymnia within decorative borders, painted in encaustic colours of reddish-brown, black and blue, ⅞in. x ⅞in. Unmarked. c.1773. Such terracotta cameos were supplied to Boulton in 1773 for mounting under 'crystals' (watch glasses).
Author's collection.

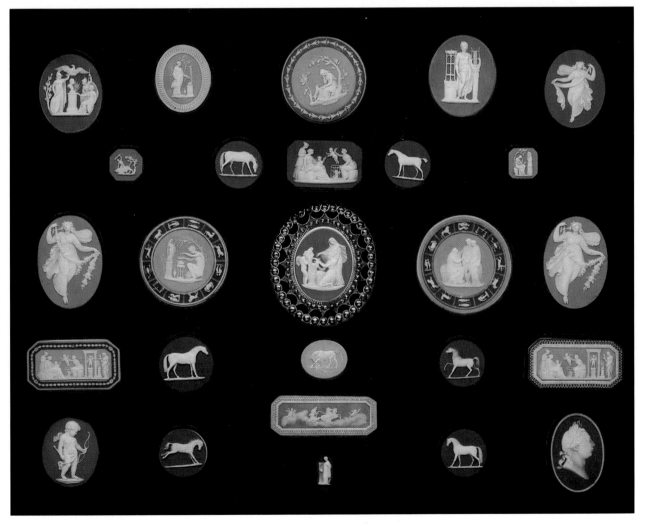

Colour Plate 15. CAMEO. Frame of three-colour, blue and lilac jasper cameos, the subjects including a portrait of George III, six Burch horses and a 'German cameo'. c.1785-90.
Wedgwood Museum

Colour Plate 16. CANDLE-STICKS. Pair of blue and white jasper candlesticks in the form of tree trunks entwined with vines and ivy, with white jasper figures of Cupids, representing *Autumn* and *Winter*. Height 10¾in. c.1785-90.

Nottingham Castle Museum

Colour Plate 17. CANE WARE. Cane footed cream bowl, cover and stand moulded to simulate bamboo and decorated with blue and white encaustic colours. Height 5¼in. c.1785-90.

City Museum & Art Gallery, Stoke-on-Trent

Colour Plate 18. CANE WARE. Cane bulb pot, the lid furnished with two cups for bulbs, moulded to simulate bamboo and decorated with green and black encaustic colours. Height 8½in. c.1785.

Wedgwood Museum

Colour Plate 20. CAULIFLOWER WARE. Creamware teapot and plate or stand, moulded in cauliflower pattern and decorated with transparent green and ivory-yellow glazes. Teapot height 4⅛in. Unmarked. Staffordshire (perhaps Wedgwood) or Yorkshire, c.1770.

L.A. Compton Collection

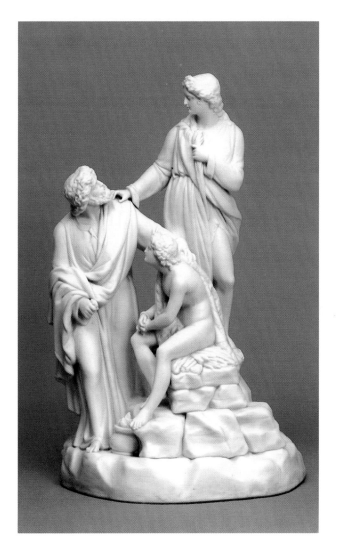

Colour Plate 21. CHAMBER WARE. Toilet set of the Celadon coloured body with platinum bands, comprising water jug, bowl, chamber pot, covered soap dish (with interior loose drainer) and toothbrush holder. Jug height 11¼in. c.1935. *Author's collection*

Colour Plate 19. CARRARA. *The Sacrifice* (Abraham sacrificing Isaac), modelled by William Beattie, and reproduced in the Carrara body, c.1857. Height 24in. *Formerly Buten Museum*

Colour Plate 22. CHESSMEN. Lilac and white and blue and white jasper dip chess set designed by John Flaxman junior in 1783-4. c.1785-95.
City Museum and Art Gallery, Stoke-on-Trent (contemporary chess and backgammon box, *Author's collection*)

Colour Plate 24. COMMEMORATIVE WARE. Wedgwood's first jasper Christmas Plate, diameter 8in., 1969, and the first Christmas Mug, height 4½in., 1971. The relief ornaments are, respectively, views of Windsor Castle and Piccadilly Circus 1971. *Wedgwood Museum*

Colour Plate 23. CHINOISERIE. *Pot-pourri* jar with pierced lid decorated with *Chinese Flowers* in enamel colours. Height 13½in. c.1820. *Wedgwood Museum*

Colour Plate 25. CONCHOLOGY. Queen's ware dessert service, the shapes based on the Nautilus and Pecten (scallop) shells, enamelled in blue and brown. Nautilus centre height 9in. c.1790-5.
Wedgwood Museum

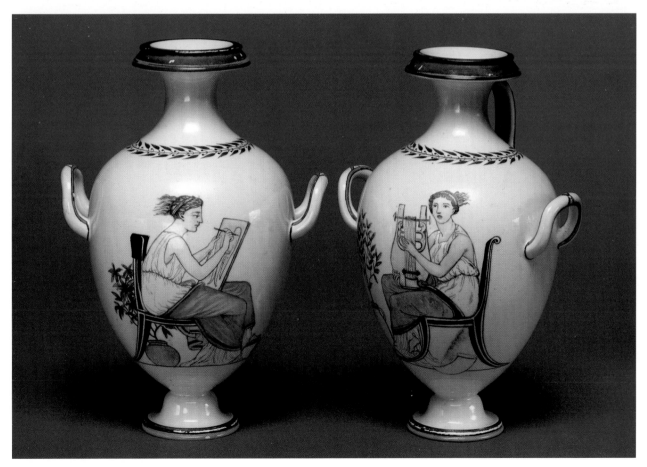

Colour Plate 26. CRANE, Walter. Pair of Queen's ware vases painted in enamel colours with figures representing 'Painting' and 'Music' after designs finished by Walter Crane in 1867. 1888.
Wedgwood Museum

Colour Plate 29. DAIRY WARE. Rosso antico settling pans ornamented with 'Egyptian' reliefs in black, the interiors washed with glazed black slip, made for Lady Anson's dairy at Shugborough in 1807. Octagonal pan 17¾in. x 22½in. x 3⅞in.   *National Trust, Shugborough*

Colour Plate 27. CUT-STEEL MOUNTS. Blue and white jasper cameos of the *Bourbonnais Shepherd* and *Poor Maria*, after designs by Lady Templetown, mounted in cut steel as shoe buckles, the latter with beads also of glass and jasper. The mounts are probably by Boulton & Fothergill. c.1785.   *Wedgwood Museum*

Colour Plate 28. CUTTS, John. First period bone china tea service with coffee cups of pattern no. 689 'Full Landscape' painted by John Cutts. c.1816.
Wedgwood Museum

Colour Plate 30. DANCING HOURS, THE. One of a pair of Wedgwood & Bentley solid grey-blue jasper tablets, the grounds washed with a darker blue and ornamented with white jasper figures of *The Dancing Hours* attributed to John Flaxman junior. 5⅜in. x 18in. c.1778.   *Wedgwood Museum*

Colour Plate 31. DE MORGAN, William. Queen's ware dish decorated with reduction-fired crimson lustre by Charles Passenger at William De Morgan's Fulham Pottery. Diameter 9¼in. c.1885.   *Mr & Mrs David Zeitlin Collection*

Colour Plate 32. DICED PATTERN. Tobacco jar of diced black jasper dip with ornaments of yellow quatrefoils and white olive foliage. Height 8in. c.1880-1900.   *Wedgwood Museum*

Colour Plate 33. DIP. Pale-green jasper dip tea bowl and saucer, the rim and interior lapidary-polished. Both bowl and saucer are as translucent as porcelain. c.1785.
Nottingham Castle Museum

Colour Plate 34. DOLPHIN. Pair of blue jasper dip dolphin tripod pastille burners with finely pierced lids. Height 5¼in. c.1800. *Wedgwood Museum*

Colour Plate 35. DRESSER, Christopher. Pearl ware cylindrical vase etched with a design by Christopher Dresser, groundlaid in ivory, enamelled in blue and gilded. Height 10½in. Signed. The design was registered in 1867. *Wedgwood Museum*

Colour Plate 36. EGYPTIAN COLLECTION. Gilded basalt plaque, 'Lord of the Diadems'. 8¾in. x 8in. 1976. *Wedgwood Museum*

Colour Plate 37. ENCAUSTIC PAINTING. Superb volute krater vase with mask handles, painted in encaustic colours with 'Offerings at a Shrine' copied from d'Hancarville's engravings of an Apulian krater purchased by the British Museum from the Hamilton collection in 1772. Height 33in. Unmarked. c.1790-5.

Mr & Mrs David Zeitlin Collection

Colour Plate 38. ENCAUSTIC PAINTING. Cane *déjeuner* set, or *solitaire,* moulded to simulate bamboo and decorated in encaustic colours. Oval tray 9¼in. 11in. c.1790.
Wedgwood Museum

39. ENGINE TURNED DECORATION. Two lilac jasper dip coffee cups and saucers, one with engine-turned diced pattern and applied green quatrefoils, the other with engine-turned fluting to the saucer and lower part of the cup. Height 2½in. c.1785-95. *Nottingham Castle Museum*

Colour Plate 40. EXOTIC BIRDS. Fine Pearl ware jug enamelled with 'exotic' birds and *(verso) Deutsche Blumen,* with a band of 'Brown Laurel' pattern at the neck. Height 8⅝in. c.1780.
Author's collection

Bail Handle

An overarching ceramic handle found on teapots and kettles. In the case of teapots, it replaces the handle on the side opposite to the spout. Wedgwood's bail handles were fixed but some factories made them to swivel downwards to one side. The bail handle first appears on some 17th century Chinese porcelain spouted wine pots exported to Europe for use as teapots. Wedgwood employed this type of handle principally for black basaltes* teapots and kettles, and more rarely for Queen's ware*, cane* and rosso antico*. The bail handle is also found on some 19th-century bone china* teapots.

Bailey, J.A. (1907-78)

Painter at Etruria* under the direction of John Goodwin*, 1928-30. He painted a series of game-bird centres on bone china with powder colour* borders.

Bain Marie

A French term for a covered basin, heated, or kept warm, by hot water. Part of a food warmer* or nursery* lamp. Made by Wedgwood in Queen's ware*.

Baker, Professor Robert William (1909-92)

Potter, designer and teacher, and first professor of ceramics at the Royal College of Art. 'Bobby' Baker trained at the Royal College of Art, London (1927-31), winning a painting scholarship to Italy, where he travelled widely and studied Renaissance art. He was employed first at Wimbledon School of Art, where he became especially interested in pottery, building his own kiln. Baker was convinced of the need for technical mastery, historical understanding and practical application in all design. This led him towards industrial pottery design rather than the studio work of the great craft potters and attracted the attention of government circles concerned with the needs of industry. After three years super-intending art instruction at Stoke-on-Trent, Baker was recommended by Josiah Wedgwood V*, then chairman both of the Wedgwood firm and of the board of governors of the Royal College of Art, for the newly created chair of ceramics, under the direction of the new rector of the College, Robin Darwin (like Josiah V, a direct descendant of the first Josiah Wedgwood). Baker remained professor there until 1959, rapidly acquiring an international reputation for the quality of his students, among them Peter Wall* and Robert Minkin*. Bobby Baker's long friendship with Josiah V and with Victor Skellern* was largely responsible for Wedgwood's success in attracting outstanding young designers to Barlaston* in the 1950s and 1960s.

Bakewell, James (fl.1750-77)

Painter at Burslem and at Wedgwood's Chelsea Decorating Studio* in London. He joined Wedgwood in the summer of 1768, employed to draw shapes of vases for reference purposes. At the end of 1769 he completed the decoration of a dessert service in black and yellow enamels, and six months later Wedgwood

BAIL HANDLE. Black basaltes rum kettles with bail handles: (left) Wedgwood & Bentley, c.1776, with sibyl knop, height 7¾in.; (right) with spaniel knop, c.1785.
Dwight & Lucille Beeson Collection, Birmingham Museum, Alabama

reported to Bentley*: 'Bakewell has set his mind on being a *good enamel Painter* and really improves very much in flowers and in Coppying figures'. Josiah sent him to London, where he evidently got into trouble and Wedgwood was soon complaining that he was overpaid. Bakewell stayed, nevertheless, at least until the end of 1777, when he was severely reprimanded by Bentley for some new misdemeanour. Apart from the 'Frog'* service, for which he is thought to have painted landscapes, Bakewell's work is known only by some attractive dessert wares, painted in a free style with naturalistic sprays of flowers in a deep pink, or black and yellow, which are attributed to him. This attribution is supported by the monogram JB, which appears on the base of some of the pieces, but it is certain that he was not the only painter using this style, which was that used for the dessert ware made to accompany the Empress Catherine's* Husk* service.

See: Colour Plates 3 and 4

See also: Cooper, Joseph; Dimcock, Thomas; Green, Thomas

Ball, Arthur (1896-1915)

Painter at Etruria* for about four years under the direction of John Goodwin. He was killed in World War I.

Ball Clay

Dark-coloured clay, which fires to a paler colour, quarried in Devon and Dorset but also found elsewhere in the world. It is used in earthenware and stoneware to lend plasticity to the body.

Bamboo Ware

Wares such as teapots, bulb pots, vases, etc., shaped or moulded in imitation of short lengths of cut bamboo. The use of bamboo forms

BAKEWELL, James. Queen's ware radish dish painted in rose-purple enamel with a single flower and Husk border in the manner associated with James Bakewell, c.1770. *Wedgwood Museum*

BAMBOO. Cane teaware in moulded bamboo shapes decorated with blue enamel and ornamented with scenes of *Bacchanalian Boys* after Duquesnoy. c.1790. *Christie's, London*

for this purpose was undoubtedly suggested by small Chinese porcelain wine pots and vases similarly moulded, which were popular in the early years of the 18th century. Wedgwood first made objects of this form from about 1780 in cane* ware and black basaltes*. Flower holders were made also in jasper*, c.1790. Bamboo-shaped objects were often decorated with encaustic* or glossy enamels and they included cane ware flower holders (groups of up to nine graduated bamboo canes on a simulated earth base), bough pots, bulb pots, dessert wares, tea wares and vases.

Bamboo shapes in primrose jasper decorated with terracotta jasper leaves, a colour scheme echoing the cane and rosso antico* of the early 19th century, were produced in 1977.

Bank House
House built for Thomas Bentley* on the Etruria* estate, 1767-8, but never occupied by him. It became the home of Josiah and Sarah Wedgwood* and their children until their own house, Etruria Hall* was completed, and, thereafter, it was occupied by Josiah's sister Catherine Willet and her family.

Banks, Sir Joseph (1743-1820)
English naturalist and friend of Josiah Wedgwood's. Educated at Harrow, Eton and Christ Church, Oxford, he accompanied Captain James Cook to the southern hemisphere in 1768 and was instrumental in introducing the sugar-cane and the bread-fruit tree to the West Indies. He was elected Fellow of the Royal Society and was president from 1778 until his death. Created a baronet in 1781, he received the Order of the Bath in 1795, becoming a Privy Councillor in 1797. Banks was a guest at meetings of the Lunar Society* and Josiah consulted him about several scientific problems, including his invention of a thermoscope to measure the heat of his ovens (see: Pyrometer). In 1789 Sir Joseph sent Wedgwood samples of white clay from New South Wales, shipped to him by the first governor, Captain Arthur Phillip, who wished to know if it was suitable for the production of porcelain*; and it was at Sir Joseph's house in Soho Square, on 1 May 1790, that Wedgwood showed his first perfect copy of the Portland vase*. A portrait of Sir Joseph was modelled by Flaxman* in 1775 and reproduced in jasper*, and a large portrait (long axis 10⅞in.) was adapted from it in 1779. A third portrait, a companion to one of Lady Banks, was not issued before 1781.
See: Sydney Cove Medallion

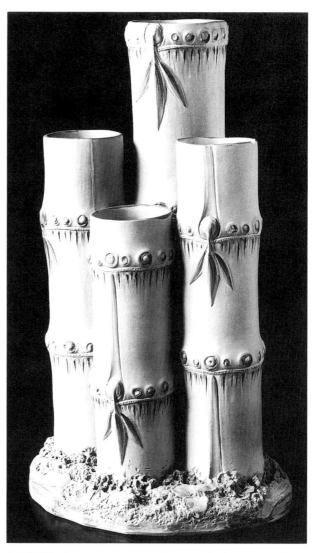

BAMBOO. Encaustic-painted cane flower-holder in the form of four bamboo canes embedded in a mound with scattered flowers. Height 10⅛in. c.1790. Such pieces were made in groups of up to nine canes.
Wedgwood Museum

Banks, Thomas, RA (1735-1805)
English sculptor, studied in the studio of Peter Scheemakers* and was later employed by William Kent. He received a premium from the Royal Society of Arts* in 1763 and a Gold medal from the Royal Academy seven years later for a bas-relief of *The Rape of Proserpine*. From 1772 to 1779 he was in Rome, and he spent nearly two years, between 1781 and 1783, at St Petersburg, executing commissions for the Empress Catherine II* and members of her court. In a letter to Sir William Hamilton* (16 June 1787), Wedgwood refers to 'Mr Banks, a very able statuary in London, whom you must have known in Italy, and another artist in town, [who] have promised to employ all the time they can spare for me'. No evidence has been found to associate Banks with any Wedgwood model, but he was at that period engaged in carving chimneypieces* for Beckford's Fonthill and Warren Hastings's Daylesford. It is possible, therefore, that Banks designed and carved marble chimneypieces specifically to accommodate Wedgwood tablets*.

Barberini Vase
See: Portland Vase

Barber's Bowl
Wide-rimmed, deep, oval or circular dish manufactured with a segment of the rim cut away so that the bowl could be fitted comfortably beneath the chin of the person being shaved. Commonly

BANKS, Sir Joseph. Lilac jasper dip portrait medallion, modelled by John Flaxman junior in 1775. Oval height 3½in. c.1785.
Wedgwood Museum

BANKS, Sir Joseph. Wedgwood & Bentley large-size blue and white jasper 'classicised' portrait medallion. Oval height 10¾in. 1779.
British Museum

made in European tin-glazed* earthenware and known also in Continental, Chinese and Japanese porcelain, barber's bowls were made in creamware by English manufacturers in the last quarter of the 18th century. Wedgwood's Queen's ware* examples are furnished with a pierced well for soap opposite the cut segment.

BARBER'S BOWL. Queen's ware oval barber's bowl. Width 9⅛in., height 2⅛in. c.1810.
Merseyside Museum

Barium Sulphate

Otherwise known as 'Cawk' or, in Josiah Wedgwood's code, as 'no.74' or 'radix jasperini'. An essential ingredient of the original jasper* body, of which it formed more than fifty per cent. The secret of Wedgwood's use of barium sulphate was closely guarded, and supplies of it were delivered to Etruria by roundabout routes to disguise its nature and destination. As Josiah told Bentley* in January 1775: 'I dare not have it the *nearest way,* nor *undisguis'd'*. Wedgwood's difficulty in differentiating chemically between barium carbonate, or witherite (Wheatstone, known to Josiah as 'Spath fusible', no.19 in his code) and barium sulphate (barytes, or heavy spar) was responsible for much of the frustration and delay that occurred in the invention of jasper.

Barlaston

The 382-acre estate, near the village of Barlaston, Staffordshire, bought by Wedgwood in 1936 as the site of the new factory. The foundation stone was laid on 10 September 1938. Architects for the factory were Keith Murray* and his partner Charles White. Louis de Soissons, already distinguished as architect of Welwyn Garden City, was responsible for the garden village of 100 houses for employees, with provision for future expansion to a total of 1,400 houses and shops. Financial backing was obtained from Friends' Provident Ltd and this was augmented by a bank loan. The earthenware factory was transferred from Etruria* in 1940 and the bone china* factory

BARLASTON. View of the main entrance, showroom and executive offices of the Barlaston factory, 1975. *Photograph: Wedgwood*

BARLASTON. Brown-Boveri electrically fired contra-flow tunnel ovens at the Barlaston factory, c.1955. Each oven was 272ft. in length. *Photograph: Wedgwood*

was completed in 1949, when the production of jasper*, discontinued in 1941 for the duration of the war, was resumed.

The new factory was the most advanced pottery in Britain. Firing was by Brown Boveri electric contra-flow tunnel ovens, the first to be used in this country, and all mechanical processes were powered by electricity. Since the original purchase and building programme, the estate has been increased to five hundred acres and the factory, planned for 700 workers with a possible extension to accommodate 1,000, has been expanded to employ more than

2,000. But an ambitious expansion plan, estimated to cost £9½ million, was halted in 1980 by high interest rates and a decline in the home market which made it necessary to lay off nearly twenty per cent of the enlarged work-force.

A purpose-built design studio was opened in the factory grounds in 1968, signalling the Company's continuing commitment to excellence of design. In the following year, a visitors' centre was completed, with a large demonstration area, where they may see many of the most interesting manufacturing processes, a lecture

BARLASTON. Aerial view of the extended Barlaston factory in 1975. The circular building on the right is the Design Studio opened by Lord Snowdon in 1968. *Photograph: Wedgwood*

theatre and cinema, and a new Wedgwood Museum*. Since the 1980s, the number of visitors to the factory has risen to more than 200,000 a year.

Production at the Barlaston factory has benefited from the continuous application of advanced technology – including the use of electronically controlled firing systems, lasers to monitor firing, spray drying and isostatic pressing – to traditional crafts, a crucial factor in combating rising costs without loss of quality.

Barlaston Hall

A fine 18th-century Palladian house, designed by Sir Robert Taylor in 1756, set on a small hill, a part of the estate bought by Wedgwood in 1936. The Hall, taken for a short period in 1904 by Josiah IV* (later 1st Baron Wedgwood of Barlaston) is described by his niece, Dame Veronica Wedgwood* (*The Last of the Radicals*, 1951): 'a beautiful house. A graceful double staircase of faded brick sweeps up to a broad terrace, on to which open the long windows of a great saloon…Inside, the doors have carved pediments, broken with baskets of fruit and cornucopias and touched with faded colours. The staircase, running up round a wide square well and surmounted by a little cloister-like gallery of panelled arches on slender double columns, is cantilevered out from the wall and runs up three floors without supports'. Probably wisely, Josiah IV decided that it was unsafe for his five active children and he moved his family to a house he built at nearby Moddershall.

By 1961 the house had fallen into disrepair caused by neglect and mining subsidence and the costs of restoration were estimated at £100,000. At this time a scheme was proposed to turn the house into a museum building with accommodation for caretakers, offices for curatorial staff, a lecture hall, and rooms for visiting notables. This was rejected by Wedgwood's directors as too costly. By the 1970s after a further decade of neglect, when ceilings had collapsed and most of the the lead had been stripped from the roof, restoration was estimated at £500,000. The Chairman, Sir Arthur Bryan*, having refused a contribution of £100,000 towards these costs offered by the Historic Building Council, then applied for permission to demolish the house. A public inquiry was held and consent refused. In 1981, Michael Heseltine, as Environment Minister, ordered repairs to be undertaken. A statement then issued by his department alleged that attempts to preserve the Hall, dating from 1955, had failed 'largely due to lack of interest and cooperation from Josiah Wedgwood Ltd', a view strongly challenged by Wedgwood's directors.

After a prolonged and public dispute, the Hall was finally sold by Wedgwood to Save Britain's Heritage for £1. Restoration to the fabric was put in hand and completed, at a cost of £400,000, in 1992, when the house was sold for £300,000 on condition that restoration of the interior – including plasterwork, woodwork and the staircase – should be completed by the new owners.

Barlaston Hall was the subject of a painting in purple lustre (see: Lustre Decoration) by Alfred Powell* on a circular Queen's ware plaque, 23in. diameter, in 1942.
See: Colour Plate 5

Barlaston Mug

Mug designed in 1940 to mark the opening of the new factory. The designs were the work of Eric Ravilious*, who drew the lithograph* himself. This was the first, and largely experimental, commercial application of lithography to Wedgwood Queen's ware*.

Barlaston Shape

A full range of tableware shapes designed in 1953 by Norman Wilson* and modelled by Eric Owen* to supersede the plain coloured bodies* in traditional shapes (see: Tableware Shapes), the popularity of which was beginning to decline. Two-colour clay* patterns, produced by combining the techniques of inlaying and slip*-decorating, included the following colours with cream colour: *Summer Sky* (lavender*), *Barlaston Green* (celadon*), *Havana* (chocolate-brown), *Harvest Moon* (cane-colour) and *Moonlight* (grey). Among the most successful lithographed patterns with enamelled borders were *Covent Garden*, *Ruby Mayfield*, *Penshurst* and *Woodbury*.

Barlow, Francis (1626-1704)

Painter and engraver, often described as the first English painter of sporting subjects whose name is known. His drawings for *Hunting, Hawking and Fishing* were engraved by Wenceslaus Hollar in 1671. His best known work is his 110 illustrations to the 1687 edition of *Aesop's Fables*, a number of which were copied for the decoration of some early Wedgwood creamware* dessert plates.

Barnard, Harry (1862-1933)

Artist, author, potter, designer and modeller; born in Canonbury, London. Barnard left school at fifteen to work in the modelling shop of the family business of silversmiths in St Martin's-le-Grand, but shortly afterwards enrolled at the Royal School (now Royal College) of Art to study drawing and modelling. He later attended evening classes at the Kennington Road City and Guilds School. During this period he was already employed by Doulton, whom he had joined in 1880. At the Doulton Lambeth studios he worked under Mark Marshall, making ornamental vases, commemorative jugs ornamented with portrait medallions*, and unique exhibition pieces in collaboration with Marshall, Hannah Barlow, Eliza Simmance and others. By the age of twenty-two he had become under-manager of the studios, which then employed 325 women and forty-five men and boys. During his fifteen years' service he invented or perfected many processes in production and decoration.

In 1895 he resigned and joined James Mackintyre of Cobridge, where he introduced a new form of decoration, a form of *pâte-sur-pâte*, which he called 'gesso'. Two years later he joined Wedgwood at Etruria*, where he applied his decorating techniques to bone china*, jasper*, majolica* and tiles*, becoming manager of the tile department in 1899.

In 1902 Barnard moved to London in the key sales position of London Manager, returning to Etruria in 1919. He was given the special task of expanding the Museum*, then in the charge of John Cook, but in the same year he was requested by Frank Wedgwood to produce a new edition of the Portland vase*, the trials for which occupied him for four years (as did Josiah I's for the issue of 1790),

BARLASTON. Queen's ware mugs, the turned shape by Keith Murray, the printed designs by Victor Skellern; *(left)* a presentation mug to commemorate the opening of the Barlaston factory; *(right)* commemorating the first biscuit and glost firing through electrically fired ovens at Barlaston. 1940. *Wedgwood Museum*

BARNARD, Harry. Modelled slip and gilded bone china broth set and oval bowl designed by Harry Barnard, 1898-1902.
Photograph: Wedgwood

BARNARD, Harry.
Typical pierced and
modelled-slip decoration on
a Queen's ware vase with
dark-blue ground. Artist's
signature incised. c.1900.
*Mr & Mrs David Zeitlin
Collection*

and he made his first good vase in 1923. During the following twelve
months he made thirteen vases, of which only seven were good, but
by the end of 1930 (the bicentenary year of Josiah's birth) he had
produced 195, of which only thirteen were rejected. Most of these
were mounted on a mirrored stand and sold for 20 guineas. Others
were set on a special stand, designed by Barnard, incorporating jasper
replicas of the four panels of the original sarcophagus in miniature.

In 1927 Barnard made the largest piece of Wedgwood ware ever
produced, a basalt* panel 53in. square and 5in. thick for Beeshy's*
English China Store at Ridgway, Ontario. The relief shows a
Georgian potter at work on the kick-wheel, with the words:
'Within the Potter's House...surrounded by the Shapes of Clay'
(Omar Khayyam) on the panel above. Barnard solved the problem
of firing such a large panel without warping by cutting it into forty-
two irregular shapes, like the pieces of a stained glass window, and
jointing them together in a previously-prepared screen when they
came out of the oven.

Four years later Harry Barnard fell victim to the retrenchment
made necessary at Wedgwood after years of trade depression. He
was in his seventieth year, and a less active man might have
expected to retire somewhat earlier. He accepted, with reluctance, a
cut of seventy-five per cent in his salary, but continued to lecture
on Wedgwood all round the country, and to make unique pieces of
his own design which were fired at Etruria. He died in January
1933 at Newcastle-under-Lyme.

Harry Barnard's work for Wedgwood, of which no full record
survives, included extensive repairs to the bust of Sir Walter
Raleigh (see: Hoskins & Grant), a bust of George Bernard Shaw
(1931), fifty-four portrait medallions and six busts for the Cameograph Company*, 195 Portland vases, the Beeshy basalt panel and
some original pieces of Queen's ware and jasper (particularly the
now rare crimson jasper) using trailed slip and sgraffito* techniques. In 1924 he published *Chats on Wedgwood Ware*, an
admirable short study of the subject.

Barnsley, Grace (1896-1975)
English pottery decorator. The daughter of Sidney Barnsley, she
was educated at Bedales (where she was a contemporary of Josiah
Wedgwood V's) and attended Birmingham Municipal Art School.
With her husband Oscar Davies, she opened the Roeginga Pottery
at Rainham, Kent, where she decorated matt glaze* pottery with
enamel colours. During the 1920s and 1930s she decorated individual pieces and some tablewares in Queen's ware* and bone
china* for Wedgwood, though she was never formally employed at
Etruria*. Her designs were mostly floral and the style closely
resembles that of her friend Louise Powell*.
See: Duopour

Barrett, George the Elder RA (1728-84)
A proficient landscape painter, born in Dublin, who was a founder-
member of the Royal Academy and succeeded, in spite of earning
2,000 guineas a year, in becoming bankrupt. He is regarded as one
of the founders of the British school of watercolour painters. His

two sons and a daughter earned their living as artists, the most
celebrated being George junior (1767-1842). Wedgwood obtained
landscapes from George Barrett senior, which were copied for the
'Frog'* service, but no evidence has been found to support
previous statements that Barret was employed at the Chelsea
Decorating Studio*.

Barrett (or Barratt), Joseph (fl.1760-75)
A painter who worked on the 'Frog'* service at the Chelsea
Decorating Studio*.

Bartoli, Pietro Santi (c.1635-1700)
Italian painter and engraver, known also as Il Perugino, who
studied under Poussin. Many of his engravings of antique and
Renaissance sculpture and monuments were published, with text
by the antiquary Giovanni Pietro Bellori (1636?-1700), in
*Admiranda Romanorum Antiquitatum Vestigia, Pitture Antiche
delle Grotte di Roma* and *Veterum Sepulcra*, the later editions of
which must surely have been familiar to Josiah Wedgwood,
although they do not appear to have been in his library.

Bartolozzi, Francesco (1727-1816)
Italian engraver who arrived in England in 1764. He made many
engravings after Angelica Kauffmann* and Giovanni Cipriani*. He
popularised the stipple engraving: one in which the picture is made
up of many small dots variably spaced rather than lines, with an
effect somewhat resembling an ordinary half-tone block. The
stipple technique was first employed for the decoration of pottery
and porcelain in the second half of the 18th century when it was
transferred by the process of bat printing*. Wedgwood's copies or
adaptations of engravings by Bartolozzi include:
*The Children of Flora (Spring)), The Marriage of Cupid and
Psyche, The Four Seasons, Summer, Winter, Group of Three
Boys* (after the watercolour by Lady Diana Beauclerk*) and a
mythological scene, after Cipriani, painted in encaustic colours
on a tablet *(British Museum)*
See also: Armorial Ware

BARTOLOZZI, Page from an earthenware pattern book illustrating
the *Bartolozzi* centre with *Adelphi* border, printed in green on a fawn
border with scarlet enamelling. c.1905.   *Wedgwood Museum*

Barton, Glenys (b.1944)
Born in the Potteries, Glenys Barton gained a place in the Ceramics
School of the Royal College of Art and then became a lecturer in
ceramics at the Camberwell College of Art. She was the British
prize winner at the International Ceramics Exhibition, 1972. In
1976 Glenys Barton was invited to become 'artist in residence' at
Barlaston*, an opportunity which gave her the use of facilities at
the factory to develop her designs for ceramic sculpture. Subsequently, on 14 June 1977, some thirty pieces of her work were

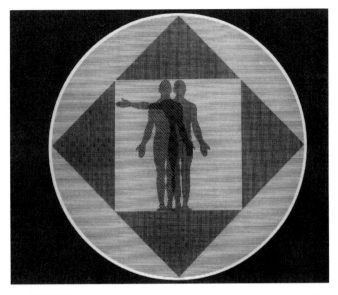

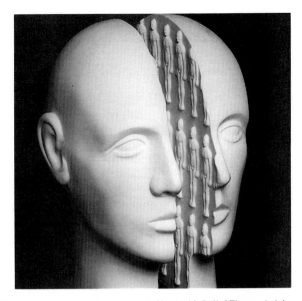

BARTON, Glenys. Two of twenty-six designs made in bone china in 1976-7: 'Man Diagram I', diameter 11in., and 'Head with Relief Figures, height 6½in.
Wedgwood Museum

shown by the Craft Advisory Committee at their Waterloo Place Gallery, London, in an exhibition titled *Man and Space: Glenys Barton at Wedgwood.* These were in bone china* and mainly featured the male nude figure, the torso or the head, in geometric and architectural settings. An illustrated catalogue was published, with an appreciation by Edward Lucie-Smith and a discussion of Glenys Barton's work in an historical context by John Mallet, Keeper of the Department of Ceramics, Victoria & Albert Museum. The majority of the pieces were produced in editions limited to four, with some of the less complex designs available in editions of from ten to fifty. Considerable difficulty was experienced in reproducing her sculptural pieces, the editions of which were oversubscribed, and they have thus become even rarer than the limits on their editions indicate.
See: Colour Plate 6

Basalt
A very hard, black, natural stone, used by the Egyptians and others for sculpture, and mainly worked with abrasive substances such as emery (carborundum). Basalt is also the modern name used for Wedgwood's black stoneware, formerly called black basaltes* because of its resemblance in appearance and hardness to the natural stone.

Basaltes, Bronzed and Gilt
Basaltes vases, urns and figures with the relief ornament, or the body of the figure, decorated with bronze and gold were made in small quantities for a short period from about 1875. This form of

hybrid decoration was evidently inspired by the fashion for Japanese bronzes.
See: Bronze and Gold; Bronzed Basaltes; Japonisme

Baskets
Baskets, used for fruit as part of a dessert service, were among Wedgwood's earliest shapes. 'Baskets & Stands' were supplied to Wedgwood by William Greatbatch* in 1760 at three shillings and sixpence each, and 'Chelsea Baskets & Stands' from the same source were nine shillings a dozen in 1763 (the difference in price

BASKETS. Plate 13, drawn by William Blake for the '1817' Catalogue, illustrating eight various basket shapes made by Wedgwood.
Photograph: Wedgwood

BASALTES, BRONZED and GILT. Octagonal black basaltes teacup and saucer ornamented with gilded and bronze classical figures and musical trophies, a style inspired by the vogue for Japanese bronzes. c.1875.
Christie's, New York

BASKETS. Queen's ware 'Footed Canoe Basket', illustrated as shape no.858 in the '1817' Catalogue.   *Wedgwood Museum*

BASKET WORK. Basketwork-moulded cane ware flower basket with pierced lid, height 3½in. c.1813.   *Wedgwood Museum*

being mainly in the intricacy of the shapes and the quality of decoration). Wedgwood made quite elaborate pierced Queen's ware* baskets for both of the handpainted services delivered to Catherine II* in 1770 and 1774, and similar baskets were available also undecorated or transfer-printed by Sadler* & Green. A 'Twig' basket*, made by interlacing strips of clay in the manner of basket weaving, is shown as design no.28 in the first (1774) Queen's ware Catalogue*. Later in the century, decorative and practical baskets were made in terracotta*, cane* ware and jasper*, and in the 19th century they were made also in white stoneware*, drab* ware and bone china*. No less than ten different shapes of baskets for fruit or eggs, appear in Plate 13 of the '1817' Catalogue, drawn by William Blake*. Queen's ware baskets of an early shape were among the reproductions of 18th-century shapes and patterns made for James Powell & Sons* about 1910.

See: Colour Plate 7
See also: Violet Basket

BASKET-TRELLIS-AND-FRUIT SHAPE. Creamware large teapot or punch pot, height 7in., moulded in relief, the lead glaze touched in with colour. c.1765. This pattern, often attributed to Wedgwood, was made by Greatbatch and others.   *Sotheby's, London*

Basket-trellis-and-fruit shape
The modern name used to describe the moulded shape of some unmarked creamware teapots, jugs, sugar bowls and tea canisters made by William Greatbatch* and supplied to Wedgwood, c.1762.

Basket Work
A popular moulded relief used frequently during the second half of the 18th century and intermittently thereafter for tablewares. It was especially useful as decoration for wide-rimmed plates and dishes. Wedgwood probably made at least one basket work pattern in salt-

glazed stoneware* and in tortoiseshell* and other coloured glazes* but these types of body and decoration had been discarded by him before he began regularly to mark his ware so identification is uncertain. He was supplied with basket work shapes, especially the basket-trellis-and-fruit* shape, by Greatbatch*, probably as early as 1762. In addition to tableware shapes in Queen's ware*, basket work moulding was used for the decoration of the 'dry bodies'*, the cane* ware body being most obviously suitable, and for the smear-glazed (see: Glazes) white stoneware* ('porcelain') body made c.1810-35. See: Tableware Shapes, *Osier*

Bas-relief
Term normally used in sculpture for ornament in low relief (raised only slightly above the level of the surface) as distinct from high relief *(alto relievo)* in which as much as half or two-thirds of the relief may project from the surface. Most jasper* ornament is in bas-relief, although there are a few examples which qualify for the description of *alto relievo* or high relief.

Bas-relief Ware
The name given to a white vitreous stoneware* body with jasper dip* and bas-relief ornament. This combination of bodies was introduced in 1817 as a substitute for jasper, which was discontinued in all forms except for slip and applied ornaments until 1845. Bas-relief ware continued in production for cameos and some vases, and for teawares and other objects that might be put to some practical use, until 1941. The white stoneware, known in the

BAS-RELIEF WARE. White stoneware mug dipped in olive-green jasper and ornamented with 'Sacrifice' figures. The interior is glazed over a white jasper slip. c.1910.   *Author's collection*

early years of its production as 'white porcelain', was one of the many bodies finally discarded when the move to Barlaston* was completed. It is easily identified, being a coarser and greyer body than that of the white jasper reliefs.

Bastille Medallions
The storming of the Bastille on 14 July 1789 was announced in London by the *Morning Post* in terms of glowing approval. Charles James Fox* hailed it as 'the greatest event...that ever happened in the world'. Josiah Wedgwood, Joseph Priestley* and William Blake* were among those radicals who shared this sympathy for the Revolution. Josiah wrote to Erasmus Darwin*: 'I know you will rejoice with me in the glorious revolution which has taken place in France. The politicians tell me that as a manufacturer I shall be ruined if France has her liberty, but I am willing to take my chance'. Later, with many others, he was to modify his enthusiasm, but meanwhile he was not slow to take advantage of powerful Whig support for the revolutionaries. He issued a number of 'French' medallions in jasper*, the most important of which were the two commemorating the storming and fall of the Bastille. Measuring 2⅞in. in diameter, the medallions bear the inscriptions: LE TRIOMPHE DE LA VALEUR FRANCOISE and LE DESPOTISME ABATTU above bas-relief scenes illustrating the event. Both are dated 1789. Although apparently copied from medals, these subjects are not after the celebrated medals by Bertrand Andrieu. Wedgwood's medallions were in production within fifteen weeks of the first announcement in London and they are especially notable for the method of their production, which employs (apparently for the first time) a mixture of jasper slip*, press moulding* and sprigging* to achieve a particular delicacy of lettering and shading.

Another pair of circular medallions, precise copies of the medals by Andrieu, appears only in black basaltes. Although marked, their attribution to Wedgwood has been challenged.
See: French Revolution

Bat
1. A thin disc of clay used in making plates on the jolley*
2. A slab of soft glue or gelatine employed in certain kinds of transfer-printing (see: Bat-printing)
3. A thin slab of fireclay* used in placing ware in the kiln
See: Processes of Manufacture

Bat Printing
In the latter half of the 18th century, 'bats' of soft animal glue or gelatine were used instead of paper for taking impressions from stipple engravings (see: Bartolozzi*). The impression was taken from the engraved plate on to the bat *in oil*, the surface of which was then dusted with powdered ceramic colour. As late as 1973, it was authoritatively stated that no bat-printing was done at Etruria*, and until 1981 no bat-printed Wedgwood had been identified of an earlier date than c.1810. Research carried out by David Drakard and Paul

BAT PRINTING. Detail of a purple bat-printed landscape on a drabware jug, illustrating the stippled effect of this type of engraving and printing. Height 4¼in. c.1827. *Mr & Mrs Samuel Laver Collection*

BASTILLE MEDALLIONS. Pair of layered blue and white jasper medallions: *Le Despotisme Abattu* and *Le Triomphe de la Valeur Françoise.* Diameter 2⅞in. 1789. *Nottingham Castle Museum*

Holdway, however, satisfactorily proved that much of Wedgwood's armorial* ware was decorated in this manner and it is now clear that bat-printing was used on Queen's ware* from about 1768.

In modern times an automatic transfer-printing machine is used. This takes an imprint from an inked copper plate on to an appropriately shaped gelatine pad, which is then lowered on to the article to print the design.
See: Transfer Printing

BAT PRINTING. Pearl ware beaker and jug, bat-printed with hare-coursing and fox-hunting scenes in puce and decorated with blue enamel lines. Jug height 5in. c.1810.
City Museum & Art Gallery, Stoke-on-Trent

Batavian Ware
See: Rockingham

Bateman, Josiah (fl.1800-42)
Salesman and traveller, first employed by Wedgwood in 1807. Tom Byerley*, asking that Bateman be appointed his assistant in London, described him as 'respectable' and 'a good man to depend upon', and praised his knowledge of the business. This early recommendation was amply justified by Bateman's faithful and intelligent service to Wedgwood during the following thirty-five years. From 1809, he travelled all over England and Scotland, selling Wedgwood's wares, suggesting new types of ware for production and reporting on the success or decline in popularity of others, collecting debts, assessing customers' honesty and credit, listening to gossip about competitors and, perhaps above all, insisting on satisfactory service to his customers. After Byerley's death in 1810, Bateman assumed the position of senior salesman, and he became one of Josiah II's* most trusted employees, whose knowledge and experience of the provincial market was probably unrivalled. His opinion and advice were often sought by Josiah II, with whom his relationship came closer to friendship than that of any of his contemporaries.

The orders sent to London and Etruria by Bateman between

BATEMAN, Samuel. Rectangular plaque painted in impasto technique, 20in. x 14⅛in. Signed and dated 1886. *Sotheby's, London*

1829 and 1842 have survived almost intact in two separate collections now reunited in the Wedgwood archives. Since the Oven Books*, and much other material relevant to that period, have not been preserved, Bateman's orders provide an exceptionally valuable record of the bodies, shapes and designs in production. In 1832 Bateman was reported as suffering from lumbago, and his health gradually declined until six years later he suffered a stroke. He continued to travel, but less far and less regularly. His last recorded journey was to Sussex in 1842.
See also: Gill, Charles

Bateman, S. (fl.1880-90)
Artist, whose signature appears on Wedgwood earthenware plaques and vases painted in an *impasto* technique in coloured slip*. Two plaques, 20in. x 14⅛in. and 12¼in. x 8⅛in., one showing fishing smacks on the Mersey and the other a scene of cows in a country stream, are dated 1886 and 1887, respectively. Nothing appears to be known of Bateman and no record of his work has been found in the Wedgwood archives. There is no evidence that he was ever employed at Etruria* and it is possible that he worked on Wedgwood 'blanks' in his own studio, though the presence of his monogram incised in the clay before firing does not support this.

Bath
See: Showrooms

Batteries, Electric
The '1880' Shape Book* (figs 2041 and 2032) illustrates cylindrical pots for electric batteries and a round porous cell. These were made for the construction of Leclanché cells, a type of electric battery in which the positive pole was a zinc rod and the negative pole a carbon rod placed inside a porous cell filled with manganese oxide and carbon, the whole being immersed in the pot, which was filled with sal ammoniac solution. This produced an electric current by chemical reaction when the circuit was closed between the positive and negative poles. Although the voltage was small, the current relatively weak, and the cell soon exhausted, it recovered fairly quickly, and it was therefore employed in the home in the 1880s for that novelty of the period, the electric bell, for which Wedgwood also made bell-pushes. Leclanché cells were usually made of glass, and the employment of pottery for the purpose was unusual.

In the same Shape Book, fig. 2040 is a Voltaic trough, a vessel of rectangular section employed for another type of cell which nevertheless worked on the same basic principle – the production of electricity by bringing together two dissimilar metals immersed in a suitable liquid. Its operation was similar to that of the Leclanché cell. The making of voltaic troughs was suggested to Josiah II* by Sir Humphry Davy* in 1808.

Bawden , Edward, CBE, RA, RDI (1903-89)
Artist, book-illustrator and designer, born at Braintree, Essex, in 1903. He studied at the Cambridge Art School and the Royal College of Art, London, where he later became Assistant Professor, School of Design. His friendship with Eric Ravilious*, a contemporary at the RCA, took him to Etruria* on a visit about 1936 but he did not receive his first commission from Wedgwood until ten years later. Soon after the outbreak of war in 1939, Bawden was appointed an official war artist, and he travelled extensively, and often uncomfortably, in various theatres of war, including France, the Mediterranean and the Middle East. In 1943, he spent five days in an open boat after the ship on which he was returning to England was torpedoed. In 1946 Sir Colin Anderson, Chairman of the New Zealand Shipping Line, commissioned Bawden to design ware to be made by Wedgwood for his ships and this was produced in 1948. Four years later, he designed *Heartsease* pattern for use on bone china* for the Orient Shipping Line. Bawden's work made use of a wide variety of artistic techniques – watercolour, engraving, calligraphy, lino-cut and line drawing – on as wide a variety of materials, including fabrics, metalwork, pottery and porcelain. He illustrated seventy books with wit and sensitivity and exhibited more than 200 works at the Royal Academy, of which he was elected a member in 1956.

BAWDEN, Edward. *Heartsease* pattern on bone china, designed by Bawden for the Orient Shipping line in 1952. *Wedgwood Museum*

Baxter, Alexander
See: Husk Service; 'Frog' Service

Beaded Edge
See: Tableware Shapes

Beads
See: Jasper; Ramshaw, Wendy

BEANE'S PATENT TEA INFUSER. Urn-shaped tea infuser with metal lining and spigot, the Queen's ware body, foot and lid printed in red.   *Formerly Buten Museum*

BEATTIE, WILLIAM. Carrara group, 'The Interpretation' (Joseph before Pharaoh) after a model by Beattie. Height 20½in. 1859.   *Photograph: Wedgwood*

Beane's Patent Tea Infuser

A Queen's ware urn-shaped vessel on a turned, tall pedestal foot, with a domed cover and a pewter spigot. Inside, a pewter container holds tea leaves at varying levels according to the number of cups of tea required, from two to six. The impressed mark is accompanied by a printed inscription: WEDGWOOD BEANES PATENT TEA INFUSER. The date code* on the example known is illegible. Made about 1880.

Beardmore, Hope (fl.1920-30)

Painter at Etruria. She worked closely with James Hodgkiss* and Arthur Dale Holland* on the decoration of bone china* ornamental pieces in the powder blue* and lustre* ranges introduced between 1910 and 1914. The ornamental ware pattern book contains several drawings of her painted designs, including landscapes and groups of sheep for use with powder blue grounds.

Beattie, William (fl.1829-67)

Sculptor and modeller in the neo-classical* style, who exhibited at the Royal Academy from 1829 to 1864 and at the Great Exhibition in 1851, where he displayed a large silver vase with a statuette of the Prince Consort. He was employed as a modeller by a number of Staffordshire potters, including Wedgwood, Minton*, Copeland (see: Spode) and Adams*. Parian* figures signed by him and inscribed 'AU of G' on the base were made for the Art Union of Glasgow. He was at Etruria* from 1856 to 1864, and his work for Wedgwood includes the following Carrara* figures and groups, several of which were made also in Majolica*:

America, figure, 14¾in.
Christ Healing the Blind Man, group, 21in.
Finding of Moses, group, 19½in.
Greek Flute Player, figure, 14in.
Interpretation, group, 20in., model after Benjamin Spence, 1867.
Isaak and Rebekah, group, 21½in.
Sacrifice. Abraham offering up his son, Isaac, group, 24in.
Scotland, figure, 13in.

BEATTIE, WILLIAM. Majolica group, 'Isaak and Rebekah', first produced in the Carrara body, decorated in transparent coloured glazes. Height 20in. c.1870.   *Henry Spencer & Sons, Retford*

BEAUCLERK, Lady Diana. Coloured stipple engraving by Bartolozzi after a watercolour drawing by Lady Diana Beauclerk. This group was copied by Wedgwood as *Group of Three Boys* and widely used, alone and with other figures after Beauclerk, for tablets and medallions and as ornament for teawares and other pieces. *Photograph: Wedgwood*

BEAUCLERK, Lady Diana. White stoneware ('porcelain') Club jug, height 6½in., with bright blue slip neck ornamented with fruiting vine and groups of boys after designs by Beauclerk. c.1820.
Wedgwood Museum

Beau, Alfred (fl.1870-80)

Painter and potter, whose work for Wedgwood has not been identified. He is thought to have worked as an 'outside' decorator for 'art wares', probably for only a short period. His name appears in correspondence with Godfrey Wedgwood* in 1880 in which it is mentioned that some ware decorated by him still remains in stock.

Beauclerk, Lady Diana (1734-1808)

Gifted amateur artist, who supplied drawings to Bartolozzi* for engraving and to Wedgwood for reproduction as bas-reliefs*. The daughter of the 3rd Duke of Marlborough, she married Lord Bolingbroke in 1757 and, when this union was dissolved, the witty but insanitary Topham Beauclerk. Horace Walpole was her devoted friend, praising her designs and collecting Wedgwood jasper* ornamented with bas-reliefs modelled from them. Her work is sometimes confused with that of Emma Crewe* and Lady Templetown*. All three designed in the sentimental manner that was part of the late neo-classical* style in the last quarter of the 18th century. 'Lady Di' supplied designs to Wedgwood from 1785 to 1789, the first of them being sent to Josiah by Charles James

Fox*. Three medallions and one tablet ornamented with her designs (all 'repaired' by Hackwood*) are listed in the 1787 Catalogue*:

Group of Three Boys, 5½in. x 4½in., no.241
Group of Two Boys, 5½in. x 4½in., no.242
Four Boys Single, 4½in. x 3¾in. 'and sizes down to 3 x 2¼', no.243
Bacchanalian Tablet, 26in. x 5½in., made up of 'the six preceding articles [figures], under arbours with panthers skins in festoons &c' (the grouping was varied), no.244

It is possible that others of her designs were added after 1787-8, the date of the last ornamental ware catalogues. There is evidence also of Wedgwood plates and flower vases decorated with 'cameos of brown and white and blue festoons' from designs by Lady Diana dated 1777 and once in the collection of Horace Walpole, but none has so far been traced.
See: Colour Plate 8

Bedford Vase

The name given to a black basaltes* vase made late in 1768 or early in 1769 and ornamented with a medallion in low relief. It was

BEAUCLERK, Lady Diana. Green jasper dip tablet of ten figures composed from groups and a single figure designed by Lady Diana Beauclerk. 6½in. x 24in. c.1795.
Dwight & Lucille Beeson Collection, Birmingham Museum, Alabama

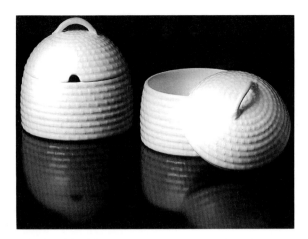

BEEHIVE SHAPE. Queen's ware beehive-shape honey pots decorated with Dysart glaze (see: Glazes). c.1955. *Wedgwood Museum*

one of the first vases to be ornamented in this manner. The shape cannot now be identified with certainty, although it is likely that it is the Vase No.1 shape with the added ornament of a single medallion on the front. Wedgwood wrote in February 1769: 'we have about a dozen of them ordered...Mr Cox* has been running about to several Noblemen this evening and says I must order 1000. He says the Medallion alone would sell it'. Wedgwood had established a useful connection with the Duke and Duchess of Bedford in 1765, when he had been permitted to copy 'patterns' (probably shapes) from a 'set of French [Sèvres*] China' at Woburn, and the Bedford vase was evidently named as a compliment to this influential patron. See: Vases, Ornamental; Woburn Abbey

Bedson, William (fl.1773-77)

Modeller at Etruria*. He is recorded in 1775 as the modeller of a set of heads of the French Kings from medals in the collection of Lord Bessborough. Josiah was not enthusiastic about them: 'they will serve to make a flourish in our next edition of the Catalogue but I fear they will be of little farther use'. Two years later, Bedson was sent to Arbury Hall, the seat of Sir Roger Newdigate*, to take plaster moulds from 'upwards of 30' bas-reliefs in his collection. With the arrival at Etruria of the Arbury moulds, Hackwood* and Bedson had as much modelling and repairing* 'absolutely upon the stocks as would last them two years'.

Beehive Shape

A shape imitating bound reeds or straw, first illustrated in the form of a honey pot in the '1817' Queen's ware* Catalogue*. The shape, which was used also for teaware and coffeeware, was introduced c.1800 (orders for beehive shape in blue or lilac jasper* were received in London in 1801). The shape was produced in cane* ware, jasper and black basaltes*, and from 1818 in the white stoneware* body often used with smear glaze (see: Glazes). A green glaze beehive-shape crocus pot and stand were produced c.1815. Honey pots in this shape have been produced in cane ware, Queen's ware with a yellow glaze*, green glaze or Dysart glaze and in the coloured bodies*.

Beer-Pump Handle

Jasper handles for public house beer pumps were made around 1900 and ornamented with a variety of decorative subjects. See: Spirit Barrel

Beeshy's English Store, Ridgway, Ontario

In 1927 this firm constructed an Old English front to their store and commissioned Wedgwood to supply a decorative panel to be installed above the entrance. The basalt* plaque supplied, measuring about 53in. square and weighing 800 lbs, is the largest object of its kind ever produced. Modelled by Harry Barnard*, it depicts a potter at work using the old kick-wheel, and a quotation, in relief, from *Omar Khayyam*.

Beeson Collection, Dwight and Lucille

One of the finest collections of Wedgwood wares ever privately assembled, the Dwight and Lucille Beeson Collection of more than

1,000 objects, including some 450 of the Wedgwood & Bentley period, was presented by the Beesons to the Birmingham Museum of Art, Alabama, over a period of several years, starting in 1976. The collection is especially notable for its two first edition Portland vases* – the 'Darwin' copy (no.12) and one of the rare slate blue versions – and the *Britannia Triumphant* group. It contains also two pieces of the 'Frog'* service, one enamelled in colour, and (purchased in 1990) a large Wedgwood & Bentley Queen's ware covered vase probably intended for decoration by George Stubbs*. Another acquisition of the greatest importance, purchased in 1992, was the Elizabeth Chellis library of books, letters and catalogues relating to 18th-century life and to English pottery and porcelain in general, and to Wedgwood in particular. A fully illustrated catalogue of the collection, compiled by Elizabeth Bryding Adams, was published in 1992.

Belanger, François-Joseph (1744-1818)

French neo-classical* architect and landscape gardener. Belanger studied at the Paris Academy of Architecture and enjoyed the encouragement of the Comte de Caylus*. His first work of importance was a pavilion for the Comte de Lauraguais*, the Hôtel de Brancas, in 1769. He travelled to England, where he made some designs for the Earl of Shelburne (later 1st Marquis of Lansdowne*) and in 1770 became Dessinateur au Cabinet to the Comte de Provence (later Louis XVIII) and in 1777 Premier Architect to the Comte d'Artois (later Charles X). Whether he ever visited Etruria* is uncertain but it is not improbable. Writing to Sir William Hamilton* in 1787, Wedgwood refers to: 'Mr Belanger, a celebrated architect in Paris, who has sent me some excellent reliefs in wax, and employs some of the best artists for me there. He very kindly makes a point of recommending my medallions and employs them in his own works. He is now fitting up a superb room for the Comte d'Artois in which he introduces many of these ornaments'. See: Porcelain

Bell, John, (1812-95)

Sculptor and modeller, born in Suffolk. He attended the Royal Academy schools in 1829, winning a Silver Medal from the Royal Society of Arts* four years later. His statue of 'The Archer', exhibited at the Royal Academy and subsequently sent to Westminster Hall, was widely admired but his varied designs for the exhibition of British Manufacture and Decorative Art in 1848 were less appreciated. His monument to the Brigade of Guards in London was frequently mocked and described by one critic as looking its 'best in a fog'. He was employed for several years by J.M. Blashfield, who had purchased all Coade's* models and moulds in 1836. Among Bell's best known work is an extraordinary 'deer-hound hall table' created in 1845 for the Coalbrookdale ironworks in Shropshire and a model of 'Una and the Lion', the latter reproduced in miniature by Minton*. Both Minton and Copeland (see: Spode) made a number of his models in Parian*, and two, the

BEESHY'S ENGLISH STORE. The largest Wedgwood basalt panel ever made, designed and modelled by Harry Barnard in 1927 for Beeshy's shop in Ridgeway, Ontario. *Photograph: Wedgwood*

BELL PULL. Oviform jasper bell pulls, the left-hand example twice-dipped and engine-turned to produce an intaglio pattern in blue. Height 2¾in. c.1785-95   *Wedgwood Museum*

Dolphin Salt and Bonfire spill vase, were reproduced by Wedgwood: the first in Pearl* ware and Majolica* (and possibly also Carrara*, though unrecorded); the second in Carrara.
See: Summerly's Art Manufactures

Bell Pull
Bell pulls were attached to one end of sashes or cords which hung down from the wall, the other end being connected by long wires to bells in the servants' quarters. Bell pulls were made by the porcelain factories, especially Worcester*, and in jasper* by Wedgwood, but they are comparatively rare. Wedgwood's were ovoid in shape, about 2¾in. in height and pierced to allow the cord to pass through. The same mould was used to produce a scent bottle, which was hollowed out a little and sealed at one end, and bell pulls were occasionally mounted in silver or Sheffield plate (see: Mounts, Metal) to create miniature vases or ewers. Jasper bell pulls were made by Wedgwood from c.1785 and early examples seem invariably to be jasper dip*, often with engine-turned patterns as well as ornament. Later, mid-19th century, examples were usually of solid jasper with ornament.

Bell, Vanessa (1879-1961)
Painter and designer. Daughter of Sir Leslie Stephen and elder sister of Virginia Woolf. Vanessa studied at the Royal Academy Schools. In 1907, she married the art critic, Clive Bell. With fellow members of the Bloomsbury Group, Duncan Grant* and Roger Fry, she helped to found the Omega Workshops (1913). Both she and Duncan Grant painted individual services on Wedgwood 'blanks', a teaset of hers being preserved by the National Trust, Monks House.

BELL, Vanessa. Pearl ware part teaset enamelled in blue, yellow and dark pink by Vanessa Bell, c.1932.   *National Trust, Monk's House*

Bell Works, Burslem
See: Brick House

Bellerophon
Son of the King of Corinth, Bellerophon was given the task of slaying the Chimaera* by the King of Lydia, who sought his destruction. Bellerophon succeeded, with the aid of his horse, Pegasus*, and eventually married the King's daughter, thus becoming heir to the throne. However, he incurred the wrath of the gods by attempting to ride to Heaven on Pegasus, and ended both blind and lame.
Wedgwood subject:
Bellerophon watering Pegasus below Parnassus, cameo, produced in several sizes, modelled by Hackwood* from an engraving after Sostratos or from a Tassie* gem of the same subject, 1773

Bellows, Charles
See: Portland Vase

Bent, James (c.1740-1812) and William (1742-1820)
James Bent and his younger brother William, apothecaries of Newcastle-under-Lyme, attended Josiah Wedgwood and his family for all complaints and accidents requiring medical attention, although Erasmus Darwin* was invariably called in as consultant if there was danger to life. James Bent was considered sufficiently accomplished as a surgeon to amputate Josiah Wedgwood's leg in 1768. The brothers Bent were also largely responsible for setting up and attendance on the private health scheme established by Wedgwood for the workers at Etruria*, on which Wedgwood spent about £100 a year. James Bent appears to have charged five shillings for house visits and one shilling for bleeding.

BENTLEY, A.H. ('Bert'). Queen's ware *Pomona* shape jardinière designed by Paul Follot. Height 8½in. The apples and leaves were applied by Bentley who recorded this piece as requiring twelve hours' work. c.1921.   *British Museum*

Bentley, A.H. ('Bert', 1878-1937)
Modeller and ornamenter. A craftsman of exceptional skill, Bentley worked at Etruria*, especially on jasper*, including – with Harry Barnard* – the 1923-30 edition of the Portland* vase, crimson jasper, and many reproductions of earlier portrait medallions*. Portrait medallions, usually with wreath borders and slotted for hanging, bearing the initials 'BB' and an elongated 'O' impressed, are from the Barnard and Bentley series of portraits begun in 1920 and catalogued by Barnard in 1922. Many of these do not bear the 'MADE IN ENGLAND' impressed mark expected on wares of this period and they are therefore often mistaken for 18th-century medallions. Portraits of Inigo Jones mispelled 'Indigo' are Bentley's work.

Bentley, Thomas (1730-80)
Josiah Wedgwood's partner in the production of ornamental wares, 1768-1780, and his closest friend. Bentley was born in the village of Scropton, some twelve miles south-west of Derby, the son of a well-to-do country gentleman, and educated at the Presbyterian

Academy at Findern, where he was given a conventional grounding in the classics. After seven years indentured to a wholesale merchant in Manchester, acquiring a sound training in accountancy, he travelled on the Continent, gaining some fluency in both French and Italian. In 1754 he married Hannah Oates, who died in childbirth five years later. By the time he met Wedgwood, in the spring of 1762, a chance encounter which both owed to Josiah's being confined to his bed for some days in Liverpool, he had been in business for several years as a general merchant with premises in King Street, Liverpool. At thirty-two, Bentley was already a figure of considerable importance in Liverpool. In 1757 he had taken a leading part, as one of the trustees, in the founding of Warrington Academy, for many years the centre of intellectual activity in Liverpool and the home of liberal nonconformism. In 1761 Joseph Priestley* became Tutor of Languages and Polite Literature at the Academy, and it was probably through Bentley that Wedgwood made his acquaintance.

Introduced by the surgeon and scholar, Dr Matthew Turner*, Wedgwood and Bentley quickly became firm friends and, when Wedgwood returned to Burslem, there began between the two men a regular correspondence which grew to huge proportions and ended only with Bentley's death. In 1764 Bentley entered into partnership with Samuel Boardman* at the Manchester Stocking Warehouse, Liverpool, and from that date he built up a solid and expanding trade in Wedgwood wares, selling them on commission to wholesale and retail customers both at home and abroad. By June 1766 Wedgwood was referring to him as a 'Pot mercht' and Bentley & Boardman were acting as Wedgwood's agent for his incoming shipments of clay through the port of Liverpool while Wedgwood, in turn, acted as their agent for pottery which he could not supply from his own factory. They were already trading partners in all but name and in November 1767 Wedgwood and Bentley signed an informal resolution to enter into partnership as manufacturers of ornamental wares 'Viz Vases, Figures, Flower-pots, Toylet Furniture, & such other Articles as they shall from Time to Time agree upon'. Wedgwood put up the entire capital, Bentley's share being borrowed from him at interest. The partnership books were opened on 14 November 1768 and the partnership of Wedgwood and Bentley was officially celebrated on 13 June 1769 when Wedgwood threw six black basaltes 'First Day's Vases'* to mark the opening of their new factory called Etruria*.

While he had been conducting negotiations with Bentley, Wedgwood had purchased the Ridgehouse Estate and had begun to build there a factory for the manufacture of ornamental ware. It was at first intended that Bentley should live in a house to be built for him on the estate but it was soon understood that he would be far more valuable to the partnership in London. By August 1769 he had already taken up residence in London to look after the new showrooms* in Newport Street and supervise the work given to David Rhodes* and the rest of the painters employed in the Chelsea Decorating Studio*.

For more than eleven years Bentley acted as Wedgwood's London Manager, a position that remained for two centuries the key managerial appointment in the Wedgwood organisation. In this

BENTLEY, Thomas. Black jasper dip portrait medallion, modelled by Joachim Smith in 1773-4. Oval height 5in. c.1781.
Manchester City Art Gallery

capacity he exerted considerable influence on Wedgwood's production, especially of ornamental wares, in which he had a financial interest, but also of 'useful' wares, which fell outside the partnership. Bentley's education, taste, social accomplishments and wide circle of friends were invaluable to Wedgwood in the acquisition of powerful patrons and the creation of a style that was at once distinctive and fashionable. No less important was his contribution as an experienced and inventive entrepreneur. Sadly, he did not live to see the introduction of vases in jasper*, which owed so much to his guidance.

Bentley married for the second time in 1772. After his death eight years later, it became necessary to wind up the partnership and allot to his widow (formerly Mary Stamford of Derby) her share. The entire stock was sold by auction at Christie* & Ansell in 1781.

Four portrait medallions* of Bentley were produced in jasper. The first, modelled by Joachim Smith* in 1773, shows him in court dress and is a companion to one of Josiah Wedgwood by the same artist. The other three are in the classical style (in Josiah's words, 'Al antique') and are attributed to Hackwood*, c.1778-80.

The memorial tablet to Bentley, placed by Wedgwood in Chiswick church, was principally the work of James 'Athenian' Stuart*. Part of the inscription reads:

Blessed with an elevated and comprehensive understanding
Informed in a variety of science
He possessed
A warm and brilliant imagination
A pure and elegant taste.

As friend, partner, confidant and guide, Bentley was irreplaceable. In the years following his death, Wedgwood had no one in whom he could confide with the same openness that had characterised his correspondence with Bentley, and no one who would offer him such honest counsel.

See: Colour Plate 9

Bentley & Boardman
See: Bentley, Thomas; Boardman, Samuel

Berlin Match Striker
See: Match Holders, Match Pots

Best, Alan (b.1910)
American sculptor, modeller and zoologist, born in Chicago. Probably through the friendship of Kennard Wedgwood*, Best was introduced to the Wedgwoods in England, becoming a visiting modeller at Etruria* in 1934. During the following year, he modelled six figures for reproduction in Queen's ware*. None was made in large quantities and all are now rare. During World War II Best served in the Merchant Navy. Later he lived in Canada, concentrating on zoological work.
Wedgwood figures:

Boxer
Rugby Player } Produced with Moonstone or Champagne
Sprinter } Matt Glaze
Weight Thrower

Mandarin Duck, produced in Dysart Glaze* or Celadon coloured body*
Panther, produced in plain cream colour or black glaze

BEST, Alan. Queen' ware figure, *The Weight Thrower*, height 9in. c.1935.
Dr & Mrs Jerome Mones Collection

Bevan, Silvanus (1691-1765)

The son of Silvanus and Jane Bevan of Swansea, Silvanus practised as an apothecary in London, founding the firm later to be known as Allen & Hanbury. His first marriage, in 1715, to Elizabeth, daughter of the celebrated master clockmaker, Daniel Quare, was attended by a number of eminent contemporaries, including Sarah, Duchess of Marlborough and William Penn. Elizabeth died in childbirth, and Silvanus married Martha Heathcote of Calthorpe. He was elected Fellow of the Royal Society in 1724. In the following year he took as his apprentice William Cookworthy*, later founder of the Plymouth porcelain factory.

Bevan was a competent ivory carver and several of his relief portraits were sent to Josiah Wedgwood by Samuel More* in 1778. Bevan's style, crude but lively, is easily recognisable and the following Wedgwood reproductions of his portraits have been identified: Sir Edward Hulse, Richard Mead, Sir Hans Sloane, Henry Pemberton and John Woodward (all physicians); William Penn; and two double portraits, of Silvanus and his second wife, and of his brother Timothy and his wife, Hannah. These last two portraits were evidently produced for the Bevan family, and, writing of them to Bentley* in October 1779, Wedgwood agreed to make copies in biscuit*, as requested, but added: 'there is so little difference in the expence to us…& so evident a great difference in the value, & consequently in the complim[en]t that I should prefer jasper* to give away'.

Bewick, Thomas (1753-1828)

The greatest of English wood engravers of the 18th century, Bewick was born a few miles from Newcastle-on-Tyne. He was apprenticed to the engraver Ralph Beilby, with whom, after a brief visit to London in 1776, he entered into partnership, never again leaving the Tyneside district. Among his most celebrated publications are *Select Fables*, 1784, *History of Quadrupeds*, 1790, and *History of British Birds*, 1797-1804. Less famous, perhaps, but

miniature masterpieces of observation, humour and technical skill, are his landscape vignettes, which he often used as tailpieces in his books. Some of these were used by Wedgwood as decoration on Queen's ware* table services, c.1775-80, and the 'Bewick' pattern was reintroduced, printed in black and red, or in green, on Queen's shape in the 1950s. There is no evidence to support the statement that Bewick (like his friend, Robert Pollard*) polished seals for Wedgwood.

Biancini, Angelo (b.1911)

Italian sculptor, educated at the Accademia di Santa Luca; Professor and Artistic Director, Instituto d'Arte, Faenza; regular exhibitor at Venice Biennali and Rome Quadriennali, 1934-58. In 1962, Professor Biancini visited Barlaston, at the invitation of Wedgwood's Managing Director, Maitland Wright, and modelled three busts – Star Wedgwood (Cecily Stella*, Maitland Wright's wife), Alan Wedgwood (son of Clement Tom Wedgwood*) and *Bella Carlyn* – and a double candlestick, for reproduction in a terracotta* body and black basaltes*. The quantities were very limited and these pieces are now rarely seen.

Bidet

Small, shallow bath on a narrow stand for female use, introduced into France in the latter part of the 18th century. Arthur Young, in his *Travels in France*, wrote that it was rare in England in 1790, and it remained so during the 19th century, when the word was regarded as extremely indelicate. Nevertheless, bidets were made by Wedgwood from about the middle of the century, although they are not illustrated, with other Chamber Ware*, in the '1880' Catalogue*

Billington, John (fl.1775-89)

Modeller at Etruria, 1789.

Bin Labels

Tablets of Queen's ware* or Pearl Ware*, made in rectangular, circular or triangular shapes to be suspended by string through a pierced hole from a wine bin. They were painted or stencilled with the name of the contents – Port, Sherry, Hock, Claret, Brandy etc – or were left blank with an unglazed surface for writing on. Such labels were made by many Staffordshire potters in the 19th century.
See: Wine Labels

Bird's Nest
See: Wall Brackets

Birks, Joseph and Simon (fl.1867-75)

Modellers, perhaps brothers, at Etruria*. c.1867-75.

BISCUIT. Garniture consisting of an ovoid lidded vase, height 10in., and two flower pots painted with groups of *putti* and borders of garlands and trophies. c.1820.   *Wedgwood Museum*

Biscuit

French term for unglazed earthenware or porcelain* which has (despite the name) been fired only once. The use of unglazed porcelain for modelling figures and groups was first introduced at Sèvres* by the art director J-J. Bachelier early in the 1750s, and by 1770 the practice had been adopted at Derby*. The fashion was revived in the 1840s with the introduction of Parian* ware (Wedgwood: Carrara*) which was at first produced unglazed. Other decorative wares, such as vases, are sometimes left in the biscuit state. Wedgwood's white terracotta* body was often left in biscuit, though the interiors of terracotta flowerpots* were usually glazed, and all the dry bodies*, including black basaltes* and jasper* are biscuit stonewares*.

Black

Colour produced by mixing cobalt* oxide, iron oxide and manganese* oxide. It formed the basis of black glazes, such as the so-called 'Jackfield'* glaze, and, mixed with the body, of such wares as black basaltes*. Manganese oxide alone yields a brown-black, and much early 'black' ware may be seen, under magnification and in strong light, to be an extremely dark brown colour.
See: Egyptian Black; Car

Black Basaltes (modern: Basalt)

The name given by Josiah Wedgwood to his black stoneware body, introduced in 1768. Black pottery, made from reddish-brown clay which burned black in firing, had been known in England since the Iron Age, and during the Roman occupation fine pots of this type were decorated with contrasting slip*, incised patterns or stamped ornament. Black-stained clay was used in Staffordshire from about 1750 to make a hard black earthenware, but there seems to be no evidence to support Simeon Shaw's* assertion that 'Egyptian black'* ware was in common production by 1754, when Wedgwood joined in partnership with Whieldon*. On the other hand, Shaw's statement that the clay for this body was stained by the use of 'car'*, an iron oxide suspended in the water drained from the local coal mines, is likely to be true since this material, when dried, formed a high proportion of Wedgwood's original black basaltes body.

Wedgwood claimed to have invented the black basaltes body as well as its name, and his basaltes or 'black porcelaine', as he often called it, was very different from any earlier black body made in Staffordshire. It owed its richer colour to the addition of manganese and its fine texture and extreme hardness to the use of sifted ball clay* and the high temperature at which it was fired.

First trials of Wedgwood's black basaltes may have been carried out in July 1766*. Certainly by September of the following year he had, as he told Bentley, something new and exciting at an advanced stage, and in August 1768 he sent Bentley 'first fruits' in the shape of '2 Etruscan bronze vases'. Prices were to be from eighteen shillings a pair for the largest size 'with the Satyrs head [handles]' to seven shillings and sixpence. He admitted these to be unusually high prices for pottery but explained that losses in firing

BLACK BASALTES. Fine, simple Wedgwood & Bentley vase with winged female figure handles and applied drapery swags. Height 9in. c.1775.
Kadison Collection

were so heavy that he had 'not one in 6 good' from the oven. Next month Wedgwood confirmed this early name for the new body and mentioned an 'Etruscan' teapot to be sent to Deborah Chetwynd*, but later it was decided that the name should be confined to those pieces decorated with encaustic* painting in the manner of ancient red-figure vases. The patent for the encaustic colours was taken out in 1769, at the same time as Wedgwood patented a method of bronzing the body (see: Bronzed Basaltes). From 1773, the plain black was known as 'basaltes', a name that, in its modern, shortened version of 'basalt', is now generally applied to all bodies of this type, whether Wedgwood's or from another manufacturer.

The shapes of Wedgwood's vases were drawn from a wide variety of sources. He had already accumulated a useful store of designs for his earlier variegated* vases and these were put to use for the new body. In addition, he copied shapes from vases seen in London shops or in the private collections of his patrons, from illustrations of Sir William Hamilton's* great collection, from books of engraved designs by Jacques de Stella*, Joseph Marie Vien*, Edmé Bouchardon* and others, and from illustrations to the works of the Comte de Caylus* and Bernard de Montfaucon*. The debt to Hamilton is scarcely calculable, for the illustrations of his collection provided Wedgwood with both shapes and painted decoration to copy, and later the inspiration for some of his most important bas-relief ornament.

BLACK BASALTES. Three Wedgwood & Bentley vases with engine-turned necks, two with sibyl finials and ornament of cameos and swags. The vases *left* and *right* illustrate Wedgwood's use of different handles and plinths on the same basic shape. Heights 11¼in.-15⅛in. c.1775.
Christie's, New York

Tea Set. Low. Round, Fluted Shape

Tea Set. Low, Oval. Fluted Shape

Tea Set, Honeysuckle

Tea Set, Etruria Shape

Tea Set, Arabesque

Tea Set. Octagon Shape

Coffee Set Antique Shape, Fluted

Tea Set. Silver Shape

BLACK BASALTES. Two pages from a Wedgwood catalogue, c.1914, showing teaware shapes, most of which (*Round* and *Oval Fluted, Honeysuckle, Etruria, Arabesque, Octagon, Antique, Silver* and *Parapet*) were in production by the first quarter of the 19th century.

Photograph: Wedgwood

Sugar Box

Teapot

Cream,
St. Louis Shape

Sugar Box

Teapot

Cream,
146 Shape

Tea & Saucer, Bute Shape

Coffee Set, Phillips, Fluted

Tea and Saucer, Brewster Shape

Sugar Box

Teapot

Cream,
Brewster Shape

Tea & Saucer, Fluted Shape

Sugar Box

Teapot

Jug. Phillips,
Fluted Shape

Jug, Parapet,
Fluted Shape

Square Clock. with Movement

Cream,
Round Fluted. Parapet Shape

Jug. Upright Shape

Bowl. Brewster Shape

Bowl, Bute Shape

Coffee Pot, York Shape

BLACK BASALTES. Three 18th-century black basaltes vases by Wedgwood's competitors: *(left and centre)* vases by Palmer, height 11in. and 9in., c.1776-7; *(right)* vase by Adams, height 9¼in., c.1790.

Christie's, London

Ornament for the vases and for 'useful' wares* was at first by incising patterns on the engine-turning* lathe, bas-reliefs* moulded in one with the vase being introduced by the end of 1769. By the autumn of that year Josiah was copying and enlarging small gems* for applied (sprigged) cameo ornaments, and these were soon combined with applied wreaths and swags. Not until 1776 was Wedgwood satisfied that he could use the technique of sprigging* for groups of figures or for the more intricate ornaments. Handles, finials* and ornaments were interchangeable, so that the variety of vases that could be made was almost infinite. By the summer of 1769, Wedgwood, the first English potter to make ornamental vases* a significant part of his factory's production, had created a 'Vase madness', a *universal passion* that he was having some difficulty in satisfying. The demand was so great that John Coward*, the woodcarver, was pressed into service to 'docter' or 'tinker' imperfect vases to make them fit for sale, adding wood covers or feet to those which lacked them. It is not to be supposed, however, that all those vases which now appear with such 'tinkered' additions are the work of Coward: most are later vases, repaired at a much later date.

The strong resemblance that black basaltes bears to bronze makes it an ideal medium for the reproduction of bronze figures* and medals* and for large library busts*. Figures were first mentioned in a letter from Wedgwood to Bentley dated 19 November 1769 in which he made clear his lack of enthusiasm for them, partly because he believed that skilled craftsmen would be better employed in making vases, for which there was so great a demand, and partly because the best figure makers tended also to be the most enthusiastic drinkers. 'If', he wrote, 'there was any such thing as getting one *sober* figure maker to bring up some Boys I shod like to ingage in that branch'. He asked Bentley to make inquiries

BLACK BASALTES. 'Capitoline Lion': one of a pair of figures copied from lions at either side of the staircase leading to the Capitol in Rome. Length 8¾in. Unmarked. Wedgwood & Bentley period, c.1768.

Author's collection

at the Bow* factory. He was, however, already engaged in making figures for candlesticks*, copying figures of a sphinx* and a triton*, lent to him by Sir William Chambers*. By 1773, when they were listed in the first Wedgwood & Bentley Catalogue*, at least eight models of Greek and Egyptian sphinxes were in production, with other models of *Neptune*; Triton*; Polyphemus*; Morpheus*; Infant Hercules* with the Serpent; Ganymede*;* two figures of *Bacchus** after Sansovino and Michelangelo*; *Egyptian Lions; Five Boys* after Fiammingo (Duquesnoy*); and an *Elephant.* Later 18th-century additions included a model of Hogarth's dog 'Trump'*, and statuettes of Voltaire* and Rousseau*. Altogether more than sixty figures were made during Josiah's lifetime. Surprisingly few black basaltes figures have been added in the 19th and 20th centuries, notably those after models by Clodion*, Edward Keys*, Nicolas Guinet, Thomas Woolner*, Carrier de Belleuse*, Ernest W. Light* and, most recently, Donald Brindley*. Although the total number of figures made in black basaltes is not negligible, the manufacture of figures in any ceramic body has never been a commercially significant part of Wedgwood's production.

Library busts*, on the other hand, were important to Wedgwood's reputation and prestige. No well-ordered town or country house was without a library, and the architecture, interior decoration and furniture design of the period provided numerous settings for busts of classical authors or modern heroes. Wedgwood obtained plaster moulds of suitable busts from Hoskins & Oliver* (later Hoskins & Grant*) as early as 1770 but little progress was made in reproducing them until 1773, when large busts of Horace* and Cicero* and a small bust of George II* were listed in the Catalogue. This modest beginning evidently excited favourable comment for the list was rapidly enlarged until, by 1787, there were ninety busts listed in the catalogues and probably as many as twelve others unlisted. Some twenty-five more were added in the 19th century, notably those by E.W. Wyon*, and many of the 18th-century busts were reproduced, but the fashion for the bust as a decorative object declined with the virtual extinction of the private library.

Among the earliest objects made in black basaltes were seals*, gems* – cameos* and intaglios*, copied from antique stones – and 'Cabinet medals'*, some double-sided, moulded from bronze originals. Seals were in production by 1769 and gems by the autumn of 1771. The first Wedgwood & Bentley Catalogue, published in 1773, lists large quantities of gems, as well as medals, small portrait medallions* and the first medallions* and plaques*. All ornament at this period was moulded in one piece with the ground. Later, for the largest tablets* and all pieces of exceptional quality, the relief was applied and sharpened before firing by the process known as undercutting*.

So versatile and strong was the black basaltes body that it was possible to use it for almost anything that the public would buy. Teawares and coffeewares were made in several shapes; inkpots* were made from 1775 in an increasing profusion of designs; picture frames* were produced to adorn portrait medallions, plaques and Herculaneum Pictures*; baptismal fonts* were created for parish churches; and Josiah even persuaded himself, in 1771, to make an enormous bowl to surmount the 'Demosthenes Lanthorn' (a copy of the Choragic Monument of Lysicrates) built in the grounds of Thomas Anson's seat at Shugborough, in Staffordshire.

Wedgwood's own description, in the 1779 Catalogue, of the basaltes body is instructive: 'a fine Black Porcelaine, having nearly the same properties as the Basaltes [the natural basalt stone], resisting the Attacks of Acid; being a Touchstone to Copper, Silver and Gold; admitting of a good Polish; and capable of bearing to be made red hot in a furnace frequently without Damage'. Black basaltes touchstones, for the use of goldsmiths in testing the nature and quality of silver and gold in conjunction with acids, were marketed by Wedgwood in the 18th and 19th centuries.

Black basaltes continued to be popular and fashionable throughout the 18th century. By the time of his death, Josiah Wedgwood had brought the body to such a degree of perfection that any development was likely to be confined to variations of shape or alteration in the types of decoration.

'Black silverd ware', the suggestion of Tom Wedgwood* (Josiah's third son), appeared in 1793 and was still in production in small quantities twenty years later. Encaustic-painted basaltes enjoyed a revival in the early 19th century, and 'Black Chinese

BLACK BASALTES. Rare desk set of black basaltes ornamented with rosso antico figures of boys at play below a meander border. Taperstick height 2¼in.

Dwight & Lucille Beeson Collection, Birmingham Museum, Alabama

Flowers' – basaltes painted with flowers and foliage in the famille rose* style – was introduced c.1810. From about 1815, this style was adapted also to the painting of flowers and leaves in an English manner. The 'Chinese Flowers' style of this period, also painted on cane* and rosso antico*, is often described erroneously as 'Capri'* ware.

By 1815, there were twenty or more teapot shapes in production in basaltes, including 'arabesque'*, 'cane fluted' [bamboo*] and 'beehive'* and some shapes were available with spouts protected by Sheffield plate or silver sleeves. Large pastille burners* and pyrophorous vases* made their first appearance in basaltes in the first quarter of the century, and a small quantity of commemorative* coronation ware was produced in 1821.

For nearly forty years, from about 1830, the demand for black basaltes all but dried up. It was revived by the fashion for Japanese bronzes initiated by the London International Exhibition of 1862. This stimulated demand for European bronzes and for Wedgwood's black basaltes. During the next fifteen years or so, Wedgwood marketed not only plain and ornamented black basaltes but also gilded pieces, 'bronze' and gold busts, and some vases, figures, and even teawares ornamented with bronze reliefs and gilding. Twelve modern busts were commissioned from the sculptor E.W. Wyon* and many earlier models of all types were reproduced. In about 1885, in response to the demand for Art Pottery* and the continuing interest in Japonisme*, Cecil Wedgwood* introduced 'Auro Basalt'*.

From the 1880s the name was abbreviated to 'basalt'. Between 1900 and 1939 many of the 18th-century busts, figures and vases were reproduced and new figures were commissioned, notably a series of small statuettes of *Charles I, Oliver Cromwell, The Lady of the Lake, Olivia, Roderick Dhu* and the *Vicar of Wakefield,* c.1910, and about twenty-two animals and birds modelled by Ernest W. Light*. John Skeaping's* animal figures and several of Arnold Machin's* figures and busts, all more familiar in Queen's ware and matt glazes*, were also produced in the modern basalt body. A few of Keith Murray's* shapes were produced in basalt shortly before World War II and in 1963 Robert Minkin's* coffee-set was the most important of a number of shapes, some designed to make use of engine-turned decoration introduced in the Design '63* Exhibition. In the early 1970s, Donald Brindley* was commissioned to model busts of Queen Elizabeth II, Dwight D.Eisenhower, Abraham Lincoln , George Washington and John F. Kennedy for limited editions* of 2,000, and standing figures of *Hercules*, Leda and the Swan, Mercury**, and *Terpsichore.*

Of his black basaltes, Josiah Wedgwood wrote: 'The Black is sterling and will last for ever'. The bold and imaginative use of basalt in the 'Lunar' set on '225 Shape' (see: Tableware Shapes) was a successful attempt in 1984 to demonstrate that the body is not yet obsolete for use in ceramic tableware.
See: Basaltes, Bronzed and Gilt; Bronze and Gold; Cost Accounting; Silvered Basaltes; Vases, Ornamental

Blake, John Bradby (1745-73)

English naturalist, educated at Westminster School, who became a supercargo for the Honourable East India Company. In 1766, Blake went to Canton, where he obtained seeds and plants for propagation and also specimens of Chinese kaolin (white china clay) and fusible feldspathic rock *(pai-tun tzu,* or petuntse*) for Wedgwood's early trials of porcelain* manufacture. Blake's early death at the age of twenty-eight seems to have put an end to these first experiments with Chinese materials. His portrait medallion, modelled by Joachim Smith*, was listed in the 1779 Catalogue*. It

BLAKE, John Bradby. Pale-blue jasper dip portrait medallion modelled by Joachim Smith, c.1776. Oval height 1¾in. c.1785.
Wedgwood Museum

was incorrectly identified by Eliza Meteyard* as a portrait of Lord Gower (see: Stafford).

Blake, William (1757-1827)

Painter, engraver and poet. Apprenticed to James Basire in 1771, Blake studied at the Royal Academy Schools and exhibited at the Academy for the first time in 1780. During his lifetime he enjoyed little success as an artist, his work being incomprehensible to his contemporaries. What Thomas Hardy later described as 'the disproportioning of realities' was then little appreciated. Blake has since been recognised as one of the truly creative artists of his period and perhaps the greatest visionary artist of the British school. He supported himself mainly by book illustration. It has been assumed that he was introduced to Wedgwood by their mutual friend, Flaxman*, but it is also possible that the introduction was made by Erasmus Darwin*, who had met Blake as early as 1791. In 1815 Josiah II* commissioned from Blake the first eighteen plates to illustrate a new tableware catalogue. Although three copies of this '1817' Catalogue* are in the Wedgwood archives, there is no decisive evidence that it was ever published.

Blake is said to have painted the ceiling of Etruria Hall*, but the evidence is inconclusive and no trace of any such work has survived.

Blancmange Mould

A deep *intaglio* mould made in a wide variety of shapes and used to make the opaque jelly called blancmange.
See: Jelly Mould

BLANCMANGE MOULD. Two pages from Charles Gill's notebook, c.1810, showing drawings of some of the Queen's ware blancmange moulds then in production. *Wedgwood Museum*

BOEHM, Sir Joseph Edgar. Celadon jasper bust of William Ewart Gladstone by Sir Joseph Boehm, commissioned by Frederick Rathbone in 1879. Height 11¼in. c.1880. *British Museum*

Bleeding

When, during firing, the ground colour of jasper* runs into, and stains, the white relief, it is said to have 'bled'. This difficulty in production was largely responsible for Wedgwood's decision to mould his jasper reliefs separately and apply them by hand. The problem was encountered again in the 20th century in the production of crimson jasper. This colour was finally withdrawn because no method could be found to eliminate bleeding, and production losses were thus unacceptably high.

Block Mould

See: Mould

Blue John

A fluorspar with dark purple veinings, otherwise known as Derbyshire Spar, which Boulton* used for making vases mounted in ormolu*. Wedgwood experimented with its use when he was conducting his long series of experiments for jasper*. For secrecy, he referred to it as 'radix amethyst'. Blue John is found only at Treak Cliff, near Castleton, Derbyshire, and deposits are now almost exhausted.

Boardman, Samuel (fl.1764-95)

Partner with Thomas Bentley* from 1764 in the firm of Bentley & Boardman, at the Manchester Stocking Warehouse, King Street, Liverpool. The firm rapidly built up a considerable business with Wedgwood, especially for export. By the time Bentley joined in partnership with Wedgwood, the value of this was running at more than £20,000 a year. In addition, Bentley & Boardman acted as agents for much of Wedgwood's raw materials arriving by sea from the West country and acted as a useful 'filter' for the delivery of materials the precise nature of which Josiah wanted to be kept secret. Boardman was on good terms with Tom Byerley*, who chose to write to him the only detailed account of Josiah's death in 1795 which has survived.

Boden & Smith

'Toy'* makers and seal setters of 8 Temple Street, Birmingham, who ordered substantial quantities of Wedgwood's black basaltes seals* in 1773. Towards the end of that year Wedgwood wrote to Bentley* to complain that Boden & Smith had bought seals made by Voyez*.

Body

Term used to denote the composite material from which earthenware, stoneware* or porcelain* (fired or unfired) is made. Porcelain body is more specifically known as 'paste'.

Boehm, Sir Joseph Edgar (1834-90)

Sculptor, born in Vienna. He exhibited at the Royal Academy from 1862, rapidly becoming well known as a portrait sculptor. Elected R.A. in 1880, he was lecturer on sculpture at the Academy and Sculptor in Ordinary to Queen Victoria. He was appointed baronet in 1889. In 1880, Boehm's portrait bust of W.E. Gladstone* was reproduced in black basaltes* and in 'Celadon' jasper*, a colour specially prepared for it, to the order of the dealer and Wedgwood specialist, Frederick Rathbone.

Bone China

A form of porcelain* composed of china clay, feldspathic rock and flint with about fifty per cent of calcined animal bone (bone ash). It is fired at a lower temperature than the feldspathic porcelain made in Europe or the Orient, but is a purer white in colour, lighter in weight and less brittle. It also allows for the use of a wider palette of colours in decoration. The introduction of bone china is credited to Josiah Spode II* about 1799, although bone ash had been employed in the manufacture of artificial (soft-paste*) porcelain since 1748, when it was noted as an important ingredient in the Bow* porcelain patent. Other factories who used bone ash in their paste included Lowestoft, Chelsea* from about 1758, Derby* in 1770, and James Neale* in about 1785. What distinguished Spode's use of bone ash was that he used as much as double the quantity previously employed by any other factory and created a product that was finally understood to be superior, in essential manufacturing respects, to any other form of porcelain made in Britain or the rest of Europe.

In 1806, in recognition of the high quality of his bone china, Spode was appointed 'Potter and English Porcelain Manufacturer' to the Prince of Wales (later George IV). Wedgwood's entry into this new field of production was slow and nervous, and it was Josiah Bateman* who was most active in trying to persuade John Wedgwood* and his brother Josiah II* to catch up with their competitors. By August 1810, John had been persuaded of the need to make bone china at Etruria* and at last, in October 1811, Josiah II wrote: 'I am making China but cannot promise for time. I shall make teaware only at first'. The first Wedgwood bone china body contained little more than twenty-five per cent of bone ash, a proportion far lower than Spode's and scarcely qualifying the body to be described as bone china. The first delivery to London was made in June 1812.

From the start, Wedgwood had problems with design. John had advised that the patterns must be 'very splendid...form & good body & workmanship are very subsidiary to gilding and gaudy colours'. This advice that was both unwelcome to Josiah II and hard for him to accept and he never succeeded in producing patterns that were sufficiently rich and ornamental to capture a substantial part of the market. Wedgwood's patterns were generally elegant, sometimes beautiful and almost invariably restrained. Their quality was not questioned, but they were expensive and they were not in the height of fashion. The principal painters employed in the short period of manufacture were John Cutts*, whose landscapes were never popular, and Aaron Steele*, whose accurate paintings of birds have survived on dessert sets and some small violet baskets*. Patterns listed as 'Shirwin's Flowers' and 'Shirwin's rich border of flowers' may be the work of John Sherwin*, a flower painter employed at the Spode factory in 1806.

The first period of manufacture of bone china at Etruria was brought to an end about 1822, although orders for replacements were accepted as late as 1831. No evidence has been found to suggest that Wedgwood produced bone china dinnerware at this period except for a crested service made especially for the Sneyd* family. The regular range was limited to tewares and dessert services, the latter including some small covered cream bowls and stands, with the occasional production of such small ornamental pieces as candlesticks*, violet baskets, spill vases*, pyrophorous vases* and D-shaped bulb pots*. Some White ware* dinnerware was produced in patterns to match bone china teawares. All Wedgwood bone china of the first period, made between 1812 and 1831, is scarce, and the ornamental pieces are especially rare.

Wedgwood's first period bone china was marked WEDGWOOD in underglaze blue or onglaze red, purple, black or gold, sometimes with the pattern number in script onglaze. The onglaze marks appear to have been lightly fired for they have suffered excessively from wear.

BONE CHINA. First period bone china teaset decorated with pattern no.565, 'Chinese figures on a yellow ground', first produced in 1812.
Christie's, London

BONE CHINA. First period bone china tea service of pattern no.30, 'Vine leaf embossed, gold tendrils, gold edge, solid handles'. c.1815.
Formerly Buten Museum

No bone china was made at Etruria between 1831 and 1865, when some trials of a china body were made for the possible use of Emile Lessore*. More experiments were made in 1866 and again in 1870, and in some of these a quantity of feldspar was used. Production of bone china was reintroduced at Etruria in 1878 with a body containing nearly forty-seven per cent bone ash. After discussions with Minton's*, whose Patent Ovens were installed at Etruria, the old China Works there, adapted in the 1830s for the production of earthenware, were modernised. The stated intention was to 'produce articles of the highest quality for the requirements of the best markets, our chief object being to secure excellence'.

After 1878, when bone china was made in the full range of teaware and dinnerware shapes, the majority of bone china patterns were designed especially for the body. The influence of Japanese design (see: Japonisme) was strong and there was an equally strong leaning towards heavy floral decoration on tablewares, generally confined to borders and rims. Shell dessert ware shapes (see: Conchology), popular early in the century with lustre* decoration, were reproduced in bone china with gold-printed designs of shells and aquatic leaves and grasses, and a series of thirty-six small ornaments was made from shell shapes on stands in the form of coral branches.

In 1882 and 1886 small quantities of stained bone china were produced in shades of celadon, blue, yellow, pink and lilac. Vellum porcelain, raised gilding and 'jewelled' china (an effect produced by raised enamelling in imitation of pearls, turquoise, coral and jade) were all examples of efforts to compete with more successful rivals, especially Worcester* and Minton. There was great variety but little sign of an implicit style.

The beginning of the 20th century was a period of great difficulty for Wedgwood, but Edwardian taste was far more in line with the Wedgwood tradition of design than that of the Victorians. John Goodwin* presided over a return to conventional designs, safely grounded (as was much furniture design of the period) in adaptations of late 18th-century styles. Powder colours*, starting with powder blue, were introduced in 1910 and came to be of considerable importance to Wedgwood, both for rich tableware designs, such as the range of *Whitehall* patterns*, and for new ornamental wares. Daisy Makeig-Jones's* Fairyland Lustre* designs made a uniquely unconventional and imaginative contrast to this respectable and rather staid approach to design, the gaiety and richness of the decoration appealing especially to a people enduring the cares and restrictions of war and its aftermath. The continuing demand for more traditional craftsmanship was satisfied largely by the work of Alfred and Louise Powell* and their school of paintresses, and by James Hodgkiss*, Arthur Dale Holland* and Joseph Palin Thorley*.

During this period Wedgwood took its place among the leading manufacturers of bone china and progress was made towards the creation of a recognisable Wedgwood style in bone china tableware design. Victor Skellern's* lasting contribution was the establishment of such a style without allowing it to become static or stifled by tradition. He was a determined advocate of the introduction of lithograph* decoration on bone china, and an equally enthusiastic champion of silk-screen* printing.

After World War II, the market for fine bone china was identified as primarily in North America and secondly in the most prosperous section of the British population. These markets expanded rapidly but remained conservative. To such buyers, a Wedgwood bone china service was often a single, lifetime purchase, an heirloom to be preserved, and its form and decoration must be both respectably traditional and lastingly prestigious. Such a market does not encourage adventurous design. Wedgwood's few departures from the security of recognisable tradition – of which the '225' Shape (see: Tableware Shapes) introduced in 1984 is an outstanding example – have been made in defiance of the market, and few have reaped great commercial rewards.

Unlike Minton, Worcester, Copeland (Spode), Derby or Coalport, Wedgwood has produced little purely ornamental china in the 20th century. Lavishly decorated and gilded vases never fitted comfortably with Wedgwood's style, nor have bone china figures been a part of regular production. Some rather insipid figures, mostly of her young friends, were modelled by Kathleen Goodwin*, c.1923, and a small number of 'Audubon Birds' was modelled by Herbert Palliser*, c.1940, both series enamelled by Holland, but neither appears to have been especially popular. It was not until after the acquisition of the Coalport factory in 1967 that bone china figures were seriously considered to become part of Wedgwood's regular production.

The strength, whiteness and translucency of bone china have caused it to be widely considered to be the best porcelain for tableware ever invented and this opinion is amply validated by the determination of the Americans and the Japanese to break the British monopoly on its manufacture. It is not claimed to be the most beautiful of porcelains: Chinese porcelain, before it bowed to Western taste, and some of the fragile and costly European soft-paste porcelains, such as Sèvres or Swansea, might compete for that claim; but it is the porcelain which most nearly satisfies the combined requirements of beauty, utility and ease of manufacture.
See: Colour Plate 10

Book-Ends
Book-ends were made by Wedgwood in the 1930s, notably in matt glazes* from designs by Doris Lindner*, Keith Murray* and Erling B. Olsen*.

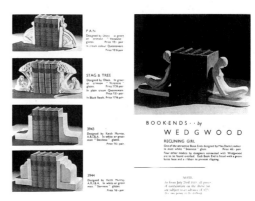

BOOK ENDS. Advertising leaflet illustrating book ends designed by Ehrling Olsen, Keith Murray and Doris Lindner, available in matt or Veronese glazes. 1935.
Wedgwood Museum

BORGHESE VASE. Imposing blue and white jasper vase, adapted from the antique marble formerly in the possession of the Borghese family in Rome. Height (vase) 18¾in., (pedestal) 12½in.
Lady Lever Art Gallery, Port Sunlight

Boot, Ralph (fl.1769-73)
Originally employed as a modeller at Burslem, Boot worked on figures* of 'Sphynxes, Lyons and Tritons'. Although Wedgwood considered that he modelled 'sad figures', it was still believed that he would become a 'useful hand'. Boot was transferred temporarily to work under Daniel Greatbatch* to help to meet the demand during the 'vase madness' of 1769-70 and remained at Etruria* where he continued to work on figures, which included triton and sphinx candlesticks* and finials* for vases.

Borghese Family
Celebrated Italian family, which originated in Siena in the 13th century, one member of which settled in Rome in the 16th century. His son became Pope Paul V, greatly increasing the family's influence and fortunes. In 1803, Prince Camillo Borghese married Napoleon's sister Pauline, whose semi-nude statue by Canova* is widely known. The family owned the Borghese Palace, one of the finest buildings in Rome, and the Villa Borghese, a summer residence outside the Porta del Popolo. The Villa's remarkable art collection was sold by Prince Borghese to Napoleon in 1806, but some of the works were returned to the Villa after Waterloo while others were placed in the Louvre. Both the Villa and the Palace are now the property of the State.
See also: Borghese Vase; Dancing Hours

Borghese Vase
Antique marble vase, now thought to be of Athenian workmanship, discovered in the sixteenth century and recorded in the Villa Borghese in 1645. Widely regarded as one of the finest marble vases in existence, it has been frequently copied in marble and bronze, in silver by Paul Storr (1808), and in Coade* stone, often as a companion to the Medici Vase. It was illustrated by Perrier*, whose book of engravings of statues and vases was in Wedgwood's library, and copied in Wedgwood's jasper, c.1785-90. The ten bas-relief figures from the Borghese Vase were copied by De Vaere* in Rome in 1788 and were reproduced as the ornament for a tablet*. At least one of the figures from the composition was also used separately. A dark red wax model of the vase, tentatively attributed to De Vaere, is in the Nottingham Castle Museum collection.
See: Borghese Family

Botanical Flowers
Term used in pottery and porcelain for floral decoration consisting of more or less exactly delineated flowers and foliage, generally copied from contemporary illustrations, and often named on the reverse of plates and dishes. In England the style was introduced at the Chelsea* factory in the 1750s with the so-called 'Hans Sloane' flowers, and it can be traced to Meissen*, where illustrated treatises on horticulture were used as a source of inspiration for porcelain decoration in the 1730s and 1740s.

The flower sprays of the Husk* service and some of those painted in rose-purple (calx cassii*) or yellow and black attributed to Bakewell* might be considered 'botanical', but their accuracy could be challenged as insufficiently precise. Unmarked creamware dessert services painted in this style, often with a chocolate-brown edge and belonging to the period 1790-1810 are frequently attributed to Wedgwood but the first authentic Wedgwood designs of this type are the underglaze-blue* printed patterns, *Hibiscus* (1806-7), *Peony* (1807) and *Water Lily* (1808). Wedgwood's *Botanical Flowers* pattern was produced in 1808-9 in two versions – printed and enamelled in colours and printed underglaze in blue. A few years later a third version was printed onglaze in red. Sources used for these patterns included issues of the *Botanist's Repository* and the *Botanical Magazine*. Botanical Flowers appear again, handpainted in naturalistic colours on bone china of the first period, c.1814, and with printed and enamelled decoration, c.1816. Wedgwood's introduction of this style of decoration was undoubtedly influenced by John Wedgwood's* deep interest in horticulture. He was one of the founders of the Royal Horticultural Society.
See: Underglaze Blue Printing

BOTANICAL FLOWERS. Two scalloped bone china dessert plates printed in black and enamelled in naturalistic colours with pattern no. 681 'Botanical Flowers with gold diamond border, gold edge'. c.1816.
Christie's, New York

Bouchardon, Edmé (1698-1762)
French sculptor, apprenticed to Coustou. He studied at the French Academy in Rome between 1723 and 1732 before returning to Paris, where he received royal patronage and achieved some fame. Etchings by Gabriel Huquier (1695-1772) of vases designed by

BOUCHARDON, Edmé. Etching by Gabriel Huquier after Bouchardon for his *Second Livre de Vases.*
Photograph: Wedgwood

BOUCHARDON, Edmé. Green jasper dip 'tendril' vase adapted from the design by Bouchardon. Height 6½in. c.1790.
Merseyside Museums

Bouchardon were published in Paris and issued in pirated editions by François Vivares (and possibly also others) in 1771. Wedgwood & Bentley adapted at least two of Bouchardon's designs for production in black basaltes* – the 'Merman' and the 'Tendril' vases – the latter being reproduced also in jasper* and, in the 19th century, in Majolica*. By 1788 Wedgwood owned a set of plasters of the Muses* by Bouchardon, though he thought them probably poor copies of the sculptor's work. They have not been identified with certainty in jasper.

Boucher, François (1703-70)
French painter and Court favourite of Madame de Pompadour, known especially for his pastoral and genre pieces. A scene of three women and a dog in a pastoral setting, after Boucher's *L'Amours Pastorales,* was copied by Wedgwood as transfer-printed* decoration for teapots and tea canisters, c.1771-80. In the 19th century, several of Boucher's paintings, including *Les Douceurs d'été* and *Rape of Europa* were copied by Lessore* as subjects for his painting on Wedgwood plaques. The source of the 'Boucher' candelabrum, the base of which was used also for a single candlestick and a fruit centre in Majolica*, is presumed to be a design by Boucher but it has not been identified.

BOUCHER, François. Majolica 'Boucher' fruit centre, height 8½in., decorated in transparent coloured glazes. 1869.   *Sotheby's. London*

Bough Pot
A bowl or vase fitted with a removable pierced cover, the holes regularly spaced and large enough to accommodate cut branches of blossom from flowering shrubs or small trees. After a visit to Etruria* in 1772 by a Mr and Mrs Southwell, 'both adept in these matters', Wedgwood noted their advice concerning the 'Essential properties of Bow pots' in his Commonplace Book*: 'To stand firm, but not look heavy. To hold a good quantity of flowers, unless they are small ones for a choice flower or two out of the

BOUCHER, François. Large Queen's ware plaque painted by Emile Lessore with 'Rape of Europa' after Boucher. Signed. Exhibited at the International Exhibition, 1862.   *Mr & Mrs Samuel Laver Collection*

BOUGH POT. White terracotta bough-pot – candlestick with pierced lid, fluted body and applied drapery swags, decorated with black slip underglaze.   *Mr & Mrs Samuel Laver Collection*

BOUGH POT. Combined bough pot and pastille burner in Pearl ware decorated in enamel colours and gold. The pierced cover is for flower arrangement; the solid inner plate for scented pastilles to lie on. Width 13½in. c.1820.
Christie's, New York

hothouse; – therefore they should be kept as wide as the beauty of their shape will admit of in the neck & top – but so as Not to turn out at the top, for that spreads the flowers disagreeably. To be of a different earth, colour, or composition, from the common earthenware in use at the time being, and To come at a moderate price'. Their uses were specified as 'some large for hearths, under slabs [marble-top console tables]...others less, and of the vase forms, for chimney pieces, and some very cheap for windows in common houses'. Wedgwood made bough pots in all of his ceramic bodies, especially the white terracotta*, black basaltes* and other dry bodies*, and very large quantities of them were sold in the 1781 auction of the Wedgwood & Bentley partnership stock.
See: Colour Plate 11
See also: Bulb Pots

Boulton, Matthew (1730-1809)
There were few manufacturers of decorative metalwork on a large scale in 18th-century England, and chief among them was Matthew Boulton. Born in Birmingham, Boulton inherited his father's toy-making business in 1759, the year in which Josiah Wedgwood had started his first factory at the Ivy House*. 'Toys'* in the metal trade were differently defined from those in the Potteries, comprising a wide variety of products, both useful and decorative, in polished iron, steel, brass, copper and silver, and ranging from tools and instruments used by such craftsmen as carpenters and millwrights to fashionable buttons and buckles and ornate candlesticks. Boulton's factory was concerned with the production of ornamental and decorative objects. By 1766, when he moved to his second, newly-built factory at Soho, Birmingham, he claimed to employ 500-600 people. His turnover doubled to £30,000 in the first twelve months at the new factory, which almost immediately came to be regarded as 'one of the wonders of the industrial world' and attracted a throng of visitors. For twenty years he was in partnership with John Fothergill, but by the time that Fothergill died in 1782 Boulton had lost much of his interest in the ornamental metal trade and was increasingly employed in the engine trade and his partnership in that business with James Watt*, which dated from 1775.

In 1765, Boulton was a leading figure in Birmingham business, and his Soho Works, which consisted of more than sixty workshops for a great variety of specialised processes, was already famous. Wedgwood determined to be taken round the Soho factory before the plans for his own Etruria* factory were too far advanced. After his first visit, in May 1766, he described Boulton as 'the first – or most complete manufacturer in England, in metal. He is very ingenious, Philosophical & Agreeable'. The two men found much in common and, although rivals in some branches of their manufacturing, became firm friends. With others of Wedgwood's friends, both Boulton and Watt were members of the Lunar Society*.

It was at Boulton's factory that Wedgwood first saw the improved engine-turning* lathe*, operated by a rosette*, and on another of his visits he examined the Argand lamp*. While Wedgwood was negotiating his partnership with Bentley* for the

manufacture of ornamental ware, Boulton was striving to 'supplant the French in the gilt business', making ormolu clock cases and vases in the French style. He discussed with Wedgwood the possibility of mounting variegated* wares and black basaltes* vases in ormolu but Bentley's reaction to the proposal was not favourable and nothing came of it. Boulton considered starting his own pottery to make what he wanted and Wedgwood wrote to Bentley (September 1769): 'It doubles my courage to have the first Manufacturer in England to encounter with...I like the Man, I like his spirit. – He will not be a mere snivelling copyist like the antagonists I have hitherto had'. Boulton decided against such direct competition and the two men went 'curio hunting' together in London, searching for vases to adapt or imitate.

Meanwhile, he bought Wedgwood's white terracotta* cameos*, painting the grounds in watercolour and setting them under glass in the lids of small boxes, but it was with the invention of jasper* that the trade between the two firms blossomed. Boulton made many small decorative objects such as shoe buckles, brooches, buttons and chatelaines* in both silver and cut-steel and these were greatly enhanced by the addition of jasper cameos.

Like Wedgwood, Boulton was an enthusiastic and successful exporter of his ornamental goods, and like Wedgwood, he enlisted the services of British ambassadors abroad, including Lord Cathcart*. One of Boulton's best markets was Russia and it was estimated by Wedgwood that the greater part of Boulton's production went abroad. At home, Boulton and Wedgwood supplied many of the same great houses and benefited from many of the same patrons. Both also borrowed models from Sir William Chambers*; both were supplied with models by the Flaxmans*; both seriously considered taking houses in the Adelphi* for their London showrooms, and both decided against doing so. Any comparison of Wedgwood and Boulton reveals more similarities: in background and education, in intelligence and energy, in inventiveness and ambition. Even the deficiencies in their managerial skills were similar. But there was one decisive difference between them: when those deficiencies were revealed, Wedgwood found solutions to them and his business continued to prosper; Boulton failed to identify the problem until it was too late to save his business. Before the end of the century, he was obliged to admit defeat and end all production of decorative metalwork. Thereafter he concentrated his remaining energies on the exploitation of the steam engine that he had helped Watt to develop. It was to provide motive power for many 18th-century factories, including Etruria.

Bouquetière
Flower pot, generally of circular or oval form, with a pierced cover to hold the stems of flowers or small branches of flowering shrubs. It was made in many forms during the 18th and early 19th centuries in Wedgwood's dry bodies*, although the term seems not to have been used contemporarily by Wedgwood.
See: Bough Pot

BOUQUETIERE. White terracotta biscuit bouquetière with pierced lid, decorated with matt black slip, the interior glazed. Height 8¼in. c.1785.
Dwight & Lucille Beeson Collection, Birmingham Museum, Alabama

BOURDALOU. Pearl ware slipper or bourdalou, printed in underglaze blue with a *capriccio* landscape. Length 10½in. c.1830.
Wedgwood Museum

Bourdalou

A small oval chamber pot for female use, made c.1710 to 1890 by leading Continental porcelain factories, in China for export, in England at Bow* and Derby*, in creamware* by Leeds* and Spode*, among others, and in Queen's ware* and Pearl* ware by Wedgwood. Bourdalous are supposed to derive their name from that of a preacher at the Court of Louis XIV, whose sermons were inconveniently long. Wedgwood referred to them as 'coach pots', which name indicates another use for them. The name current in the 19th century was 'crinoline slipper'. A bourdalou is illustrated as shape no.58 in Plate 12 of the '1790' Queen's Ware Catalogue*.

Bourn, James (fl.c.1760-80)

Turner at Wedgwood's Burslem factory, transferred to Etruria* in November 1769. Bourn was especially skilled in turning vases, particularly those of basaltes*, which caused difficulties to some turners because of the dark colour of the body. In 1774 Bourn is recorded as turning patterns for others to copy.
See: Engine-turning

Bourne, Edward (fl.1764-78)

Known as 'Old Bourne', he was a bricklayer from Chesterton, probably employed in maintaining the kilns and buildings at Etruria*. He was responsible for giving Wedgwood information about the Elers* brothers and their methods. Bourne was the subject of one of Hackwood's* finest portrait medallions*, signed on the truncation. In November 1778, Wedgwood wrote of it to Bentley*: 'Old Bournes is the man himself with every wrinkle crink & cranny in the whole visage'. The portrait exists with the

BOURNE, Edward. Pale-blue jasper dip portrait medallion in a laurel wreath and fluted black jasper frame, modelled by Hackwood in 1778. Oval height 6½in.
Wedgwood Museum

bricklayer's trowel in different positions on the field. Two moulds survive: one, inscribed 'Mr Byrne [sic] Bricklayer', is signed 'Wm Hackwood 1779'; the other (later) is marked 'Mr Bourne Bricklayer by Hackwood 1779'.
See: Colour Plate 12

Bourne, Semei (Simeon. fl.1805-15)

Engraver of Shelton, who produced engravings for Wedgwood c.1805-15. He is recorded as the supplier of at least one engraving for the *Water Lily** pattern in November 1806, and of engravings for a *Japan* pattern in November and December 1808.

Bourne, W. (fl.1770s)

Painter at the Chelsea Decorating Studio from 1770.

Bow Porcelain Factory

Factory in Bow, East London (properly Stratford-le-Bow) producing soft-paste porcelain, mainly between about 1750 and 1760. The history of the factory is lacunary, but two patents registered in 1744 and 1748 both refer to Cherokee clay* under the Indian name of *unaker*, although it is not known whether the clay was eventually used. The factory was the first to employ bone ash (see: Bone China) in the manufacture of porcelain and also the first to use transfer-printing* in the decoration. Robert Hancock*, the engraver, probably learnt the art of transfer-printing from John Brooks at Battersea before he worked at Bow. The process appears to have been abandoned when Hancock left for the Worcester* Porcelain Factory in 1756. Mr Tebo*, the repairer and modeller, first made his appearance at Bow. About 1760 the factory suffered serious financial reverses. It continued under John Crowther until the spring of 1776, when the stock and plant are thought to have been sold to William Duesbury*. Wedgwood was in possession of the Bow recipe for porcelain and noted it in his Commonplace Book* on 13 February 1759, commenting later that it was 'one of the worst processes for China making'. Catherine Willcox*, one of the most skilled painters at the Chelsea Decorating Studio*, was a daughter of Thomas Frye, one of the founders of the Bow factory.

Boydell, John (1719-1804)

Prominent publisher and engraver, studied at St Martin's Lane Academy and painted a series of watercolour topographical views along the Thames which he subsequently engraved. He set up as a printseller in 1751 and rapidly achieved success, He became Sheriff of London in 1785 and Lord Mayor in 1790. Boydell is frequently quoted as having been employed on the 'Frog'* service. There is no evidence for this statement but it is certain that he supplied Wedgwood with prints, and possibly also watercolour views, to be copied by artists employed at the Chelsea Decorating Studio*. The engraver John Pye*, who worked for Sadler* & Green, engraved landscapes for Boydell.

Boyle, John (d.1845)

Son of Zachariah Boyle (Z. Boyle & Son, Stoke-on-Trent); manufacturer of earthenware on his own account from 1826; partner with Herbert Minton*, 1836-41, in the firm of Minton & Boyle. Following a disagreement with Minton, Boyle formed a business with his brothers. In 1843 he joined Francis Wedgwood* at Etruria* as an equal partner, buying his half-share in instalments of

BRAINSTONE VASE. Black basaltes 'Brainstone' vase, shape no.140, the lidded bowl with swans'-heads supported on the wings of seated sphinxes. Height 13⅞in. This imposing piece was in production by April 1777 and was reproduced intermittently until 1938.

Formerly Buten Museum

£5,000 up to a maximum total of £20,000. Less than a year later the factory and the entire estate were put up for sale and it is probable that the reason for this sudden reversal of policy was the decline of Boyle's health. He died in 1845, just five months after the factory was withdrawn from sale, having failed to find a buyer at auction. Boyle's share was valued at £15,280, a sum for which Francis Wedgwood became responsible to the executors of Boyle's estate.
See: Brown, Robert

Brackets
See: Wall Brackets

Brainstone Vase
Name given to a large lidded bowl, height about 14in., moulded with a vermicular pattern and with swans'-head handles, supported by two seated winged sphinxes* on a deep, rectangular plinth moulded

BRAMMER, Leonard G. Dramatic view of the Etruria mill and mill-bank areas, c.1950. One of a series of drawings commissioned from Brammer shortly after the move of the factory to Barlaston.
Wedgwood Museum

with a Greek key fret*. Height about 14in. This vase, shape no.140, was certainly in production by 1777 and continued to be produced intermittently until 1938. Some of the later reproductions are either unmarked or lack the impressed 'ENGLAND' or 'MADE IN ENGLAND' marks that would identify them as modern.

Bramah, Joseph (1748-1814)
Inventor and cabinet-maker; patented Bramah locks and the Bramah hydraulic press, 1795. Joseph Bramah supplied Wedgwood with drawings and designs for chamber wares* and sanitary ('closet') ware*. In 1804 he wrote to Tom Byerley* suggesting that Wedgwood should manufacture 'artificial Teeth of such of your composition as is best suited for that purpose, and which would undoubtedly become an object of the very first Importance to human happiness'. He wrote 'feelingly, because from Sundry Accidents I have for some time lost all my Teeth in the Upper Jaw'. Nothing came of this proposal.
See: Dentures

Brammer, Leonard Griffith, RE (1906-1994)
English painter and engraver, born in Burslem. He studied at the Burslem School of Art from 1923 to 1926 under Gordon Forsyth and at the Royal College of Art, London, from 1926 to 1931. Brammer exhibited at the Royal Academy from 1930 and was elected RE 1956. He worked mainly in the Potteries and in 1950, shortly after the completion of the move to Barlaston*, he was commissioned by Wedgwood to draw and engrave a series of views of the Etruria* factory. These are now preserved in the Wedgwood Museum*.

Brandoin, Michel-Vincent (1735-1807)
A Swiss *émigré* painter working in England. Brandoin designed the Gessner* Monument in Zürich which shows the Muses* of Poetry and Painting mourning over a portrait of the poet. This was copied on a jasper* medallion to which Josiah refers in a letter dated 23 January 1790. Brandoin's original painting of the 'Pretty Mantua Maker' was copied, via an engraving by Charles Grignion*, for the transfer-printed decoration of Queen's ware*, c.1772.

BRANDOIN, Michel-Vincent. Queen's ware teapot transfer-printed in black with 'An Opera Girl of Paris in the Character of Flora' *(verso)* and 'The Pretty Mantua Maker' from engravings by Grignion after paintings by Brandoin. Height 8½in. Potter's marks only incised. Wedgwood, c.1772.
Norwich Castle Museum

Brewster Teapot
A circular or oval teapot with vertical sides and a narrow gallery surrounding the opening into which the lid is recessed. Made by Wedgwood in the 1780s in jasper* and subsequently in other bodies. The shape was inspired by contemporary silver.

Brick House ('Bell Works'), Burslem (1763-72)
Wedgwood moved to the Brick House Works, which became known locally as the Bell Works from his use of a bell instead of the traditional horn to summon his men to work, by the beginning of 1763. This second potworks, rented from the Adams* family, was much larger than the Ivy House* and the move coincided with two important developments closely affecting Wedgwood's business: regular production at William Greatbatch's* factory and

BRICK HOUSE. The Brick House ('Bell') Works. Reproduced from the line engraving published in Meteyard's *The Life of Josiah Wedgwood,* 1865, after an original drawing from memory by Aaron Wedgwood of Burslem.
Wedgwood Museum

Wedgwood's own manufacture of creamware for transfer-printing* in Liverpool. The first gave him a source of supply for goods which he no longer wished to make himself (for example: saltglazed* stoneware); the second almost guaranteed a substantial increase in business for creamware. It was probably during this period at the Brick House that Wedgwood produced most, if not all, of his cauliflower* and other rococo* 'greengrocery' wares. It was certainly at this factory that he produced the teaset which earned him, in 1766, permission from Queen Charlotte* to style himself 'Potter to Her Majesty', and the Husk* service for the Empress Catherine II*.

In November 1769 Wedgwood informed Bentley that he had received notice to quit the Brick House because his landlord William Adams wanted the premises for himself. However, Wedgwood did not move the 'Useful' works from the Brick House to Etruria* until the summer or autumn of 1772. A drawing from memory by Aaron Wedgwood, c.1864, shows the Brick House Works as extensive, with five ovens and substantial buildings for workshops and warehouses.

Bridgeman, Montague
See: Weaver-Bridgeman

Bridgewater, Francis Egerton, 3rd Duke of (1736-1803)
Francis Egerton, Duke of Bridgewater, devoted himself to the development of coal mines at Worsley (Lancashire) and, starting in 1759, he constructed, with the help of James Brindley*, a canal from Worsley to Manchester to facilitate the transport of coal from his mines. This was subsequently extended, once more with Brindley's involvement, to Liverpool. The Duke was again a prime mover in the scheme for the 'Grand Trunk' canal to connect the port of Hull, the Potteries and Liverpool and he has since come to be known as the founder of British inland navigation. Bridgewater became acquainted with Josiah Wedgwood through their mutual interest in canals and, as early as 1765, he gave Wedgwood an order for 'the completest Table service of Cream colour' that he could make. Like his brother-in-law Lord Gower (see: Stafford) he was among Wedgwood's most friendly patrons, advising him in 1767 against applying for a patent for the exclusive use of Cherokee clay* and confiding to him his plans for the improvement of transport and communications by the use of inland waterways.

The portrait medallion* for many years illustrated as of the Duke of Bridgewater (the mould at the factory is inscribed 'D.of Bridgewater 2nd April 1797') was correctly identified in 1965 by Vivian Scheidemantel as a portrait of Frederick William Charles I, King of Württemberg.

Brindley, Donald (fl.1960-85)
Sculptor, modeller and ceramic designer. Studied at the Royal College of Art before joining Coalport*, where he became chief designer. For Wedgwood he has modelled portrait medallions* of Queen Elizabeth II, the Duke of Edinburgh, and Earl Mountbatten; black basaltes* busts of Presidents Eisenhower (1970), Lincoln, Washington and Kennedy (1971), produced in limited editions of 2,000; and figures of *Hercules** and *Mercury** (basalt) and *Terpsichore* and *Leda and the Swan** (jasper*).

Brindley, James (1716-72)
Engineer who, in 1742, was a repairer of old machinery, including windmills and water-wheels used to crush flint for the Potteries at Leek (Staffordshire). Illiterate and unable to draw, he nevertheless introduced important improvements to the design of contemporary machines. He designed the canal for the Duke of Bridgewater* to run from the Worsley coal field to Manchester, subsequently

BRIDGEWATER, 3rd Duke of. Wax portrait, 2¾in. x 2½in., by Peter Rouw, signed and dated 1803. *National Portrait Gallery, London*

BRINDLEY, James. Engineer and designer of the Bridgewater and Trent & Mersey (Grand Trunk) canals. From an engraving.

Photograph: Wedgwood

extended it to Liverpool, and designed and started the construction of the Trent and Mersey canal, though he did not live to see it completed. When he died in September 1772, Josiah wrote of him: 'What the Public has lost can only be conceiv'd by those who best knew his Character & Talents – Talents for which this Age & Country are indebted for works that will... shew to future Ages how much good may be done by one single Genius, when happily employd upon works beneficial to Mankind...Millions yet unborn will revere & bless his memory'.

A jasper portrait medallion* of Brindley was probably adapted from a painting by Francis Parsons exhibited at the Society of Artists in 1771. No example of this medallion is known to exist, and the mould has been lost.

See: Canal, Trent and Mersey

Britannia Triumphant

Perhaps Wedgwood's most important group, it was modelled in solid blue and white jasper* c.1800 to celebrate British naval victories in the war against France. The tall pale-blue jasper cylindrical pedestal, incised to simulate stonework, is formed by the coiled clay method (rarely used at Etruria*, where throwing and turning or casting were the preferred methods) and ornamented with laurel-framed portrait medallions of Admirals Nelson and Duncan, Howe and St Vincent. These are set in pairs and divided by arched niches, probably intended for small statuettes which were either never modelled or are now lost. The pedestal is surmounted by a blue plinth bearing a splendid white jasper figure of *Britannia*, seated and holding in her left hand a portrait medallion* of George III* after the medal by Burch*. Her raised right hand, now empty, originally held a trident. By her side is a rather playful figure of a lion, and her right foot rests upon a fallen figure carrying a torch, evidently representing France. A shield ornamented with the British flag, a canon and an overturned cornucopia* compete the composition. The whole stands 32in. high.

Britannia (and the accompanying figures in the group) have in the past been firmly attributed to Henry Webber* on the basis of some similarity between the *Britannia* figure and that of the *Minerva** candlestick, also assigned to Webber. The latter attribution is now considered unsound, calling into question the identification of Webber as the modeller of the Britannia group. The most likely modeller of this sculptural piece is Flaxman*, but

no conclusive evidence has been found to sustain a firm attribution. All the portrait medallions on the pedestal are the recorded work of John De Vaere*, 1798, and the portrait of George III is after the Academy prize medal entry by Edward Burch, 1785, reissued to celebrate the restoration of the King's health in 1789. Original plaster moulds for the cylindrical pedestal are dated 26 April 1800. These separate fragments of evidence place the most likely date of the whole composition as 1798-1800, though it is unlikely to have been produced before the summer of 1800.

Ackermann's engraving, after a watercolour by T.H. Shepherd, of the Wedgwood & Byerley showrooms, published in 1809, clearly shows the Britannia group displayed inside a form of temple* which was designed in 1801 by William Theed*.

The 'Britannia Triumphant' group was acquired for the Dwight and Lucille Beeson* collection, Birmingham Museum of Art, Alabama, in 1991. Two jasper pedestals are in the Wedgwood Museum*, Barlaston.

BRITANNIA TRIUMPHANT. Solid pale blue and white jasper group on tall cylindrical pedestal. Height 32in. c.1802.

Dwight & Lucille Beeson Collection, Birmingham Museum, Alabama (group); Wedgwood Museum (pedestal)

Broadwood, John (1732-1812)

Maker of pianofortes. Until 1769 he was in partnership with Burckhardt Tschudi, a Swiss maker of harpsichords, who retired in his favour. Broadwood patented a 'new constructed pianoforte' in 1783. He achieved an international reputation and the cases of instruments made by him were sometimes inset with jasper cameos* and medallions*. Several examples have survived, most notably that designed by Thomas Sheraton for Manuel de Godoy in 1796, now preserved at the Heritage Foundation, Deerfield, Massachusetts.

Brock, Veda (fl.1960s)

Resident designer for Wedgwood, New York, 1964-7. She designed the best-selling 'Bridal' pattern *Belle Fleur* as well as *Westbury, Mimosa, Medina* and *Gold Damask*, all for bone china production.

Brockman, Richard (b.1930)

Studied at the Wimbledon College of Art, 1948-52 and the Royal College of Art, 1952-55. He joined Royal Tuscan, becoming Art Director in 1963 and in 1968 moved to Wedgwood as Art Director. designing the *Croft* range of oven – tableware in 1974. In 1980 he moved to California as Art Director of the Franciscan factory, acquired by Wedgwood in March 1979. He left the Company when Franciscan was sold in 1986.

Bronze and Gold

Brown stoneware* body decorated with richly gilt relief ornament introduced in 1875 for the production of ornamental vases. Quantities were small and the period of production short, probably because of difficulties in production, which included 'scumming'* and blistering.
See: Black Basaltes; Bronzed and Gilt; Bronzed Basaltes.

Bronzed Basaltes (Bronze Etruscan)

Often described by Josiah Wedgwood as 'bronz'd ware'. Black basaltes* vases and candlesticks* were bronzed by covering them with a small quantity of lightly fired metallic gold. About 1769 Boulton* was able to treat vases to make them resemble antique bronze. Wedgwood probably bought the information from Boulton and in 1769 took out a patent for 'the purpose of ornamenting earthen and porcelain ware with an Encaustic Gold Bronze, together with a peculiar Species of Encaustic Painting'*. The bronzing powder was prepared by dissolving pure gold in aqua regia (a mixture of hydrochloric and nitric acids), precipitating it in a minutely divided form by adding bronze filings. This powdered gold was then applied to the surface with a little flux*, using oil of turpentine as a medium. For an antique effect the gold powder was mixed with lamp black and caused to adhere with 'Dr Turner's* brown Varnish' and a light firing. Both processes were at best semi-permanent and only vestigial traces remain on surviving pieces treated by either. There is some natural confusion between 'Bronze Etruscan', the name used for bronzed basaltes, and 'Etruscan Bronze', which Josiah sometimes used to describe vases in the plain black basaltes body. Soon after the invention of the bronzing method in 1769, the plain black came to be known simply as 'Etruscan', and after 1773 as 'basaltes'.

Brookes, William (fl.1805-39)

Independent engraver of Hanley, who supplied Wedgwood with engravings for *Blue Bamboo* and *Blue Basket* patterns in 1805, the *Ferrara** pattern, 1832, and probably *Corinth*, 1811. He was responsible also for engraving certain items of *Blue Palisade*. Brookes is credited by Simeon Shaw* with being the originator of the idea of using a standard border for all plates in a service but differentiating between sizes by altering the centre decoration.
See: Underglaze Blue Printing

Brooklyn Bridge

A commemorative* plate decorated with a blue-printed view of Brooklyn Bridge to celebrate the tercentenary of Long Island (1636-1936). The central picture of the bridge is taken from a lithograph by John Pennell; the border vignettes illustrate important Long Island views.

Brown, Lancelot ('Capability'. 1715-1803)

Architect of country houses and landscape gardener in the Romantic or picturesque style. Born at Harle-Kirk, Northumberland, he laid out the grounds at Kew and Blenheim. He gained his sobriquet from the habit, when being shown a new site, of saying that it had 'capabilities'. Brown was appointed High Sheriff of Huntingdon in 1770.

Wedgwood first met Brown in London in May 1767 and referred to him in a letter to Bentley* as: 'the famous Brown [who] may be of much service to me'. In September 1774 he records a visit to Etruria* by Lord Gower (see: Stafford), the Duke of Bedford and 'the great Mr Brown. The latter, paid me many compliments, said he would make room for our Heads, speaking of himself as an Architect...He seems very much disposed to serve us'. Five years later, Brown renewed his offers of help and advice. Wedgwood showed him some of his jasper* tablets*, but both Brown and Lord Gower objected to the blue ground, unless it could be made into the colour of Lapis Lazuli*. 'I shew'd them', Wedgwood wrote sadly, 'a sea green & some other colors to which Mr Brown said they were pretty colors & he should not object to them for the ground of a room, but they did not come up to his ideas for the ground of a tablet, nor would any other color unless it was a copy of some natural, & valuable stone'. Brown advised Wedgwood to make tablets in white, to imitate statuary marble. As a result of this advice, Wedgwood considered the production of fired relief figures with flat backs (see: Half Figures) so that architects could fix them to grounds of their own choosing.

Brown, Robert (fl.1845-59)

Little is known of Robert Brown, who became a partner in the Wedgwood firm in 1846. On the death of his business partner John Boyle*, Francis Wedgwood* found himself in some financial difficulty, owing Boyle's estate more than £15,000. Sixteen months later, Robert Brown, one of the executors, took up the debt in return for a two-fifths share in the Wedgwood firm for four years and a half-share thereafter. The designation of the firm was, however, to continue as Josiah Wedgwood & Sons.

This new partnership was a success. Brown was both rich and competent. Llewellyn Jewitt, who may have known him, wrote of him as 'a man of enlarged understanding, of great experience, and of wonderful business talents. He realised a handsome fortune entirely by his own industry and exertions, and was possessed of a refined taste'. It is significant that during the period of his partnership Wedgwood's Carrara* was introduced and jasper* reappeared after an absence of fifteen years. In the illustrated catalogue of the Great Exhibition of 1851 it was remarked that the factory of 'Messrs Wedgwood & Brown' had shown 'its quota of beautiful works...some of the best articles originally designed or executed by its famous founder', and it was noted with approval that 'this eminent house [was] again prepared to assert its position among the principal art manufacturers of the present day'.

When Robert Brown died in May 1859, Francis Wedgwood's affairs had improved sufficiently to allow him to buy back Brown's share.

Brown China

See: Brown Stoneware; Glazes, *Rockingham*

BROWN STONEWARE. Brown stoneware ('porcelain') goblet-shape vase ornamented in white with 'Chinese Ornaments', the interior glazed. Height 9in. c.1810. *Wedgwood Museum*

Brown Stoneware

A hard chocolate-brown stoneware body known also as 'Stone Brown' and 'Brown Porcelain' introduced c.1807 and made with

BROWNSWORD, Henry. Queen's ware dish, printed in brown and enamelled in shaded blue with yellow highlights. Diameter 9¼in. Signed. 1867. *Mr & Mrs David Zeitlin Collection*

white relief ornaments, including *Chinese Flowers*. Several recipes were tried, using varying quantities of local red clays with 'Stoke brown' clay, black shavings and Cornwall stone, but the colour does not seem to have been popular and quantities were small. The Stone Brown body was reintroduced in 1875 for the production of ornamented gilt vases (see: Bronze and Gold) and, more occasionally, for enamelled decoration.

Brownsword, Henry (fl.1849-1903)

Modeller and painter at Etruria* for fifty-four years. He decorated Queen's ware* pieces, including ornamental dishes and Quiver vases* in a style easily mistaken for that of Emile Lessore*, whom he visited frequently, on Wedgwood's behalf, in Marlotte. With Lessore's son, Alfred, he was entrusted with the negotiations which resulted in Wedgwood's purchase in 1872 of the Rubelles patent, recipes and moulds for 'Tremblay' ware. A self-portrait in blue and white jasper* is in the Wedgwood Museum*.
See: Email Ombrant

Brownsword, John (fl.1812-25)

Decorator of bone china* of the first period, 1812-31.

Bryan, Sir Arthur (b.1923)

Chairman (1967-86) and Managing Director (1963-86) of Josiah Wedgwood & Sons. Born in Stoke-on-Trent and educated at Longton High School, Arthur Bryan served in aircrew with the RAFVR during World War II. In 1947 he joined Wedgwood, spending the following two years in the production and administration departments at Barlaston* before joining the sales department. In 1950 he became the traveller for the south of England and assistant London Manager, and three years later he succeeded Felton Wreford as London Manager. In 1955 he was appointed General Manager of the Wedgwood Rooms*, a pioneering retail organisation started two years earlier. In 1959 he became General Sales Manager and in the following year moved to New York as President of Josiah Wedgwood & Sons Inc. of America, in succession to Hensleigh Wedgwood*. His period as president was notable for a substantial increase in exports to the United States and, on the retirement of F. Maitland Wright and Norman Wilson* in 1963, Bryan was appointed Managing Director of the parent company. He was the first sole chief executive of Wedgwood to be chosen from outside the family.

When Josiah V* retired in 1967, Bryan succeeded him as Chairman. Earlier in the year the Company's shares were introduced for the first time to the London Stock Exchange.

During the first three months of 1966 Wedgwood had embarked on a policy of expansion, acquiring the businesses of William Adams*, Royal Tuscan (later Wedgwood Hotelware) and Susie Cooper*, and forming the Wedgwood Group*. The Group's size was soon more than quadrupled by the acquisitions of Coalport,

BRYAN, Sir Arthur. Managing Director of Wedgwood, 1963-86, and Chairman, 1967-86. Bryan masterminded a huge expansion of Wedgwood and the subsequent sale of the company to Waterford. *Photograph: Wedgwood*

Johnson Bros, J & G. Meakin, Midwinter, Crown Staffordshire and Mason's Ironstone, as well as by the considerable expansion of the Wedgwood factory at Barlaston. Diversification was attempted by the addition of King's Lynn Glass (later Wedgwood Glass), Galway Crystal, Merseyside Jewellers (makers of jewellery mountings) and Precision Studios (specialist producers of ceramic decorative materials). The Group formed a retail division through the rapid expansion of the Wedgwood Rooms and the purchase of important London china and glass shops in the West End: Gered of Piccadilly and Regent Street, and Goldsmiths and Silversmiths at Oxford Circus.

During the first fifteen years of Bryan's tenure of office as chief executive, Wedgwood grew from a family firm employing 2,400 people to a group of companies with more than 10,000 employees in the United Kingdom. By 1977 the Group's twenty factories accounted for twenty per cent of the British ceramic industry's output and twenty-five per cent of its exports. Nor was expansion confined to the acquisition of other companies: plans were put in hand to complete by the end of 1980 a £9½ million development programme to increase production capacity by about twenty-six per cent. In 1963 the firm's total sales amounted to little over £2 million; by 1986 they had grown to £152 million and profits had increased from £200,000 to £20 million. Arthur Bryan was knighted for services to export in 1976.

The policy of massive and rapid expansion appeared to be an unqualified success, but it had not been achieved without casualties. Increased borrowings and a reversal in trade conditions, which Sir Arthur attributed to 'exploitation by dumping from low labour cost, but not more highly skilled or efficient countries overseas' and 'an overvalued pound', called a halt to the grand £9½ million development programme and made it necessary to lay off nearly twenty per cent of the work-force in 1981-2. Moreover, the huge expansion in sales had been achieved largely as the result of major take-overs (Johnson Bros, for example was already one of the world's largest earthenware manufacturers before the firm was taken over by Wedgwood) exaggerated by spiralling inflation.

Some acquisitions failed to mature under Wedgwood's direction: the Franciscan Pottery in Glendale, California, bought in 1979 to provide a manufacturing base in the USA, was closed in 1984; Galway Crystal was sold after less than six years in the Wedgwood Group; and other companies, sometimes bought for controversial reasons, did not prove to be sympathetic bedfellows. There was also some criticism that the 'dash for growth' had done little for the quality of production or design.

The new Group was, however, resilient, and its more evident successes attracted the attention of predators. After fighting off a hostile bid from London International Group, a bid of £253 million from Waterford Glass, negotiated personally by Sir Arthur, was accepted in 1986. The two companies were consolidated as Waterford Wedgwood with Bryan as first President, from 1987 until his retirement in the following year, and Patrick Hayes, Waterford's chief executive, as Chairman. For a discussion of the consequences of this take-over, see: Wedgwood in the Twentieth Century.

Bubby Pot
A patent baby feeder* invented c.1777 by Dr Hugh Smith and known as 'Smith's Bubby Pot'. It was made by Wedgwood in plain and transfer-printed* Queen's ware*.

Bucknell, Leonard Holcombe (fl.1920-35)
Architect and designer, in partnership with his wife, Ruth Ellis*. As freelance designers, perhaps introduced by Sir Charles Holmes*, they produced for Wedgwood a number of designs for tableware patterns in 1931-2, including *Somerset*, *Cascade* and *Trellis*

Buddha
A rare figure in basalt* with painted glass eyes, height 5½in., produced c.1913. Glass eyes are also a feature of Ernest Light's* figures.

Bulb Pot
A pot or vase, known also as a root pot, often with a semi-circular front ('D-shape'), the removable lid pierced with holes for cut flowers or for planting bulbs. Bulb or root pots were a popular product of the Etruria* factory and a curious bulb holder was made in the form of a hedgehog (see: Hedgehog Crocus Pot). The lids of some large 18th-century bulb pots were fitted with small cups to hold hyacinth bulbs. At the porcelain factories, root pots were termed bough pots*, a term used also by Wedgwood for vases with lids pierced for flowers. They should not be confused with cassolettes*, pastille burners* or pot-pourri vases*, all of which have pierced covers of different types.
See: Colour Plate 13

BULB POT. Pair of white terracotta D-shape 'bulbous root pots' with moulded spiral flute pattern between bands of beads, and pierced grids, decorated with salmon-pink slip and glazed. c.1785-90.
Christie's, New York

Burch, Edward, RA (1730-1814)
Originally a waterman, who was accepted into the Royal Academy Schools in 1769 and elected a member only two years later. He achieved a considerable reputation as a gem engraver and modeller in wax, exhibiting at the Academy from 1771 to 1808 and at the Society of Artists, showing engraved gems*, models in wax and sulphurs*. He supplied Wedgwood with models between 1788 and 1790.
The following subjects are recorded in the Ledgers for 1788-9:

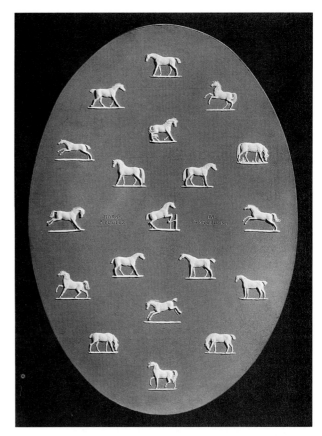

BURCH, Edward. Nineteen bas-relief studies of horses modelled by Burch in 1788-9, reproduced on a single tablet by Bert Bentley, c.1920.
Wedgwood Museum

BURCH, Edward. Blue jasper dip cameo portrait of George III modelled by Burch and issued to celebrate the King's temporary return to sanity in 1789. Oval height 1½in.
Wedgwood Museum

George III, portrait medallion* after the Academy Prize Medal entry, 1785
Queen Charlotte, portrait medallion
Dog, a large bas-relief (unidentified)
Dogs, 18 bas-relief models of dogs (unidentified)
Horses, 18 (possibly 19) bas-relief models of single horses, including *Cleopatra* and *Dungannon*. Several are after drawings by Stubbs
Signs of the Zodiac, a set

Burnishing
See: Processes of Manufacture

BUSTS. Wedgwood & Bentley black basaltes bust of Joseph Addison, height 14½in.

Dwight & Lucille Beeson Collection, Birmingham Museum, Alabama

Burdett, Peter Pever (c.1740-93)

Engraver, painter and cartographer of Old Hall Street, Liverpool. In 1771 Burdett wrote to Bentley*, claiming to have discovered a method of engraving to reproduce 'designs in imitation of Crayons & Brown Ink drawings'. This was apparently a technique for transferring aquatint to pottery, which Wedgwood described as 'the full effect of painting in one color', and it came with a recommendation from Sadler*, for whom Burdett may briefly have worked. Josiah was sufficiently interested to supply ware for trials, but a dispute sprang up between Sadler and Burdett about ownership of the invention, for which Burdett required a premium. Wedgwood therefore began experiments on his own, while continuing to negotiate with Burdett, who, as a sign of good faith, showed Wedgwood a faster method of lining (edging) plates and dishes. Impressed by this, Wedgwood invited Burdett to London to work at the Chelsea Decorating Studio* under Bentley's* direction. Burdett was soon dissatisfied with his treatment there and wrote a series of acrimonious letters which resulted in his leaving. He was paid only for some paintings of dead game, later copied for Wedgwood by Ralph Unwin*. Josiah wrote to Bentley in 1774: Your Burdetts...& all such flighty unsolid Genius's are very dangerous people to have any sort of connection with – They are absolutely mad themselves, & yet, in their own conceit, are too wise to be guided by anybody else'. Although trials of his new technique were made, nothing of Burdett's work has been certainly identified.

Burton, William (1863-1941)

Ceramic chemist and author, born in Manchester, the son of a grocer. After a short period as a schoolmaster, Burton obtained a scholarship to the Royal School of Mines. He joined Wedgwood as a chemist in 1887, remaining for five years and making some important experiments with lustre* decoration. He also noted in a

memorandum of c.1890 a method of covering earthenware with a form of silver-plating, using a solution of platinum in *aqua regia*. Some rare examples of this decoration exist on Wedgwood Queen's ware*, testifying to its use, at least experimentally, at Etruria*. While he was with Wedgwood he taught at the Wedgwood Institute, Burslem, and delivered two series of lectures at the Hanley Museum (now the City Museum & Art Gallery, Stoke-on-Trent).

In 1892 he was invited to become manager of the Pilkington Tile & Pottery Co., whose factory he planned without the aid of an architect. It was largely due to his research and experiments that Pilkington's Lancastrian Pottery was able to produce a superb range of ornamental lustre, decorated by such celebrated artists as Gordon Forsyth and Walter Crane*. The Royal Society of Arts* presented Burton with silver medals for his papers on the 'Pallette of the Potter' (1896) and 'Recent Advances in Pottery Decoration' (1901), and he was awarded an honorary MA degree by Manchester University in 1908. He retired from Pilkington's in 1915. He wrote a number of books on the history and manufacture of pottery, including *Josiah Wedgwood and his Pottery* published in 1922.

Busts

The Romans are credited with making the sculpted bust a statement about a particular human being, rather than about human beings in general as in the case of Greek sculpture. The popularity of portrait busts in late 18th-century England was characteristic not only of neo-classical* taste and the growing interest in Roman portraiture but also of a people that had come to a new appreciation of the importance of the individual and his family heritage and to revere history and the antique. Moreover, the town or country house library was the mark of the owner's culture and education, and the library bust was part of its essential furnishing. The architecture and furniture design of the period, with numerous broken pediments and shell or 'fan' recesses made allowance for the display of portrait busts. According to taste, these might be of classical

BUSTS. Plate 36 from Hepplewhite's Cabinet Maker and Upholsterer's Guide, 1794, displaying a library bust on a bureau bookcase.

Photograph: Wedgwood

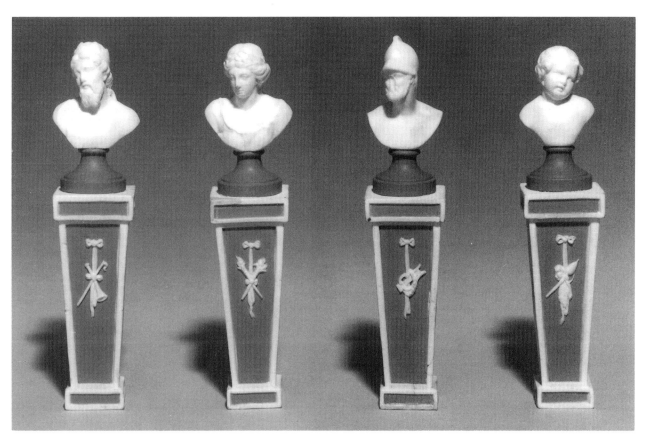

BUSTS. Four extremely rare miniature white jasper busts – Jupiter, Venus, Mars and Cupid – on solid blue jasper socles, mounted on blue jasper dip tapering pedestals. Mars and Cupid unmarked. Height 5¾in. c.1787. Five other examples of such busts are in the Royal Collection at Windsor Castle.
British Museum

authors or modern poets, statesmen or orators, actors or dramatists, divines or military heroes. Because of its strength and close resemblance to polished bronze, as well as the comparatively low cost of producing quantities of replicas in the body, black basaltes* was the ideal material for the production of busts of all sizes from the largest and most imposing at 25in. high for tall bookcases to miniatures of 4in. to mingle with candlesticks and small bronze figures on the chimneypiece*. Wedgwood also made a few busts in the *rosso antico** and white terracotta* bodies, and a small number of miniatures in white jasper* on blue or black socles.

Although Wedgwood bought plaster moulds of large busts of Cicero* and Horace* from Hoskins & Oliver* in May 1770, there is no clear evidence of his interest in making busts until February 1771, when he suggested to Bentley* that busts obtained from the Royal Academy would be 'less hackney'd & better in General' than any bought from the plaster figure and mould-makers. But sculptors were not much in evidence in the early years of the Academy and Wedgwood was resigned to continuing with the plaster shops. By buying moulds from Oliver, from which he would make reproductions in a more attractive and more durable form than anything in plaster, Wedgwood would be taking a large part of Oliver's business and might, in the foreseeable future, make plaster moulds unsaleable and reduce the business of the figure makers to mould-making. He therefore suggested that Bentley should buy all the original moulds of busts made for Wedgwood & Bentley at up to a guinea each to give Oliver a fair profit. Wedgwood could then make his own block mould* and working moulds as he required them.

Production was delayed for some three years, probably because Oliver's moulds were 'horrid dear' and there was difficulty in obtaining suitable moulds from elsewhere. The first (1773) Catalogue* listed only three: Cicero and Horace, and a small bust of George II* after an ivory by Rysbrack*. In February 1774 busts of Shakespeare (see: Shakespeare Subjects*), Plato*, Homer* and Aristotle* were bought from John Cheere* for half a guinea each, and heads of Zingara* and a Vestal* were obtained from the sculptor Richard Parker*. Bentley returned to Hoskins & Grant (Benjamin Grant having succeeded Oliver who had either retired or died in 1774) and bought a total of fifty-six busts from them in 1774 and 1775. All were 'Plaster Casts Prepar'd to Mould from' – the equivalent of block moulds, from which Wedgwood would take his own (intaglio) working moulds. There is clear evidence that at this date Wedgwood was taking his moulds in clay (baked fireclay would last longer than plaster) and that all his busts were press-moulded* rather than slip-cast*. Wedgwood & Bentley had created

BUSTS. Queen's ware bust of Ernest Bevin (1881-1951) modelled by Arnold Machin, 1953. Height 11in. *Wedgwood Museum*

a rich market for black basaltes busts and they were preparing to take best advantage of it.

By the end of 1774 Wedgwood had set on two men, one 'a new hand' (the young William Hackwood*) to work on busts alone and was asking Bentley for 'Maiden ones – I mean [busts] from Gentns collections which have not yet found their way into the Plaister shops'. He was now confident that he could furnish Bentley in London with 'a collection of the *finest Heads* in this World'. The choice of subjects was no doubt dependent to a large extent on what was immediately available from the plaster-makers' yards. At first the busts were almost exclusively of classical subjects: of the earliest lists, only those of George II, Shakespeare, Inigo Jones and 'Palladio' (an invented portrait, accepted as authentic as late as 1970) were not. The second collection supplied by Hoskins & Grant included a wealth of British writers, Sir Isaac Newton and three great figures in the history of medicine – Hippocrates*, Galen and William Harvey – probably suggested by Erasmus Darwin*. Later additions were Voltaire*, Rousseau*, Montesquieu and David Garrick, and in 1778 busts of five great Dutchmen were ordered by the Egbert de Vrij Temminck*, Burgomaster of Amsterdam. The 1787 Ornamental Ware Catalogue, the last English edition published in Josiah's lifetime, listed ninety busts of eighty-two subjects. Few were added between 1787 and Josiah's death in 1795, the most important being a superb bust of Mercury* attributed to Flaxman*. Although busts exist with the marks of other factories, notably Turner*, Enoch Wood* and Wood & Caldwell, no other 18th-century factory produced black basaltes busts in such quantity or on such a scale as Etruria.

The fashion for library busts declined in the 19th century but there was some revival of interest in them in the second half of the century, when many of the early models were reissued, usually on socles of a different form from those used in the 18th century. Fifteen of the modern busts listed were modelled by the sculptor Edward William Wyon* and these were produced in the new Carrara* body as well as basaltes. A few busts were produced in bronzed basaltes* and also in the brown stoneware body.

Some busts continued to be made up to the beginning of World War II, with a few additions, such as Barnard's* bust of George Bernard Shaw and a fine portrait of Salvation Army General Bramwell Booth, but no large busts have been made since the move to Barlaston*. Small black basaltes busts (most of them modelled by Arnold Machin*) of Queen Elizabeth II and the Duke of Edinburgh, the Prince of Wales, Sir Winston Churchill, Franklin D. Roosevelt and John F. Kennedy have been produced, and busts of a similar size of Queen Elizabeth, the Queen Mother, Margaret Thatcher (then Prime Minister) and Field-Marshal Montgomery were issued in a modern form of Carrara in 1983.

Buten Museum of Wedgwood
Founded in 1957 by Harry M. Buten and his wife Nettie, this remarkable collection of some 10,000 pieces of all periods formed the only museum (excepting only the Wedgwood Museum* at Barlaston) dedicated entirely to the products and history of the Wedgwood firm. It was especially strong in examples from the Victorian period, long neglected and generally despised by collectors. Museum publications included several books by Harry Buten and his son, David, who succeeded him as Director (see: Bibliography) and reprints of standard, but long out of print, works on Wedgwood. The Buten Museum collection, formerly in Merion, Pennsylvania, was sold in the 1980s and removed, almost intact, to become part of the Nassau County Division of Museums at Port Washington.

Buttons
Ornate buttons, often more decorative than practical, were made in large quantities in the 18th century in a great variety of materials, including gold, silver, copper, brass, cut-steel*, pinchbeck*, French *passementerie,* porcelain*, glass, ivory and bone. They were worn more by men than women and were regularly made in sets, varying in number from five to thirty-five or even more, according to the splendour of the garment. Wedgwood's jasper* cameos* were especially well suited to this purpose and his connections with the Birmingham toy-makers, notably Boulton*, provided a ready source of mounts in gold, silver and cut-steel. Even before the invention of jasper, Boulton was taking quantities of Wedgwood's white terracotta* cameos and painting the grounds in watercolour before mounting them under convex glass.

Lapel buttons, ornamented with a miniature representation of the

BUTTONS. Jasper dip cameos of Hercules, and Apollo standing between an altar and a column supporting his lyre, mounted in silver as buttons, diameter 1¼in. c.1785.   *Wedgwood Museum*

Portland vase* in relief on various coloured jasper grounds, have been made since the 1950s. They were originally to be worn by Wedgwood's staff at trade shows but have since been supplied to members attending annual Wedgwood International Seminars.

Byerley, Josiah (fl.1790-1820)
Eldest son of Wedgwood's nephew, Tom Byerley*. Josiah was employed at Etruria from about 1800, but his work was sternly criticised by John Wedgwood* in a letter to Josiah II* in February 1804: 'Jos Byerley might have been of use but the absurd manner in which he has been brought up has rendered him totally inefficient for he knows nothing of the manufactory & sleeps his time over the correspondence solely...he is of no use but to fall into passions & get laughed at'. Shortly after this, Josiah was set up by his father as a potter in a small way at Fenton, making earthenware. After Tom Byerley's death in September 1810, Josiah, whose pottery had failed, applied to take over his late father's job as London Manager (see: Showrooms) and was re-employed at once. His experience of the firm and knowledge of its products was considered useful and the Wedgwoods wished to relieve the straits of Tom Byerley's family, who were in debt to the firm.

The younger Byerley seems to have shown unexpected energy in his new job, encouraging Josiah II to produce bone china*, stone china* and pyrophorous vases*, and making sensible suggestions about new products, especially the bone china patterns. There was, however, some doubt about his morals, and Josiah II felt obliged to ask Bateman* for confidential advice: 'I find', he wrote in December 1812, 'Mr Byerley's expences are greater than they ought to be, & I have been told that he keeps a mistress, & that you know it'. Bateman heatedly denied any knowledge of this sort but his reply showed no great enthusiasm for Byerley and it is no surprise to learn that the latter left the firm in 1814. He was succeeded in London by John Howorth*, described by Tom Byerley in 1802 as 'a man decidedly honest from principle'.

Byerley, Thomas (1747-1810)
Only son of Josiah's elder sister Margaret and a Commissioner of Excise, who died in 1763. Tom Byerley had early ambitions to be a writer or an actor, but lacked the necessary application for success in either career. Nor were his ambitions approved by his mother or

his uncle. Josiah Wedgwood employed him as a clerk at Burslem and later he worked with Bentley* in London. In 1768 he was helped by Josiah to emigrate to America, where, after some abortive ventures in other directions (one of which appears to have landed him in gaol, probably for debt), he settled in New York as a schoolmaster. In 1775, on the outbreak of the War of Independence, he prudently returned to England and Josiah again gave him a job as a clerk at Etruria*. His knowledge of French enabled him to translate and compose Josiah's correspondence with French customers, and he became a useful salesman and debt collector. When Josiah decided to have his children tutored at home, Byerley helped to instruct them, and it was Byerley who was trusted to fetch Josiah's favourite child, his daughter Susannah (later Darwin*), from the Bentleys'* house in London after she had been seriously ill in 1778. It was Byerley, too, who made the first serious attempt, on the same journey, as a travelling salesman for Wedgwood. By the age of thirty-three, Tom Byerley had become his uncle's most trusted and senior manager and he was a natural choice to take over as Manager of the London Showrooms* when Bentley died in 1780. He married Frances Bruckfield of Derby and fathered a numerous family, eight of whom were still living at home in 1803.

In 1787 Byerley visited Paris, and two years later he accompanied Josiah II* on an extended tour of the Continent where they displayed, for the first time outside England, a copy of the Portland vase*. Their travels took them to Holland, where they stayed with Lord Auckland* at the Hague, Germany, Switzerland and France.

In 1790 the partnership of Wedgwood, Sons and Byerley was established (see: Proprietors of Wedgwood) and Josiah I began gradually to withdraw from the business. After Josiah's death in January 1795, the young Wedgwoods, preferring the country to the Potteries, also withdrew from active management, leaving Byerley in control both of the factory and of the London showrooms, but without final authority over either. He has been unjustly blamed for the decline in Wedgwood's fortunes at this period. In spite of the magnitude of his task, the neglect of his partners and unfavourable trade conditions in Europe, sales continued to be satisfactory, orders exceeded production capacity and profits were better than average. The decline was due partly to a deterioration in standards

BYERLEY, Thomas. Blue jasper dip portrait medallion modelled by William Theed, 1810. Oval height 4in. *Wedgwood Museum*

of quality and mostly to the reckless extravagance of all the partners. In 1806 Josiah II returned to Staffordshire to manage the factory, while Byerley resumed his direction of affairs in London. His last years were beset by domestic worries, especially by perpetual financial difficulties, and he died in September 1810 after a short illness. His son Josiah* wrote: 'his fortitude remained to the last & his patience & resignation were quite exemplary'. His portrait medallion* was modelled by William Theed* in 1810.

Byres, James (1734-1817)

Scottish architect, turned antiquarian and dealer, living in Rome from c.1756. His first major purchase was a 'Picture of the Assumption by Poussin' (now in the National Gallery of Art, Washington) for Lord Exeter; his most important transaction the acquisition and illegal export of Poussin's *Seven Sacraments,* sold to the Duke of Rutland. In 1780 he bought the Barberini (later Portland*) vase from Donna Cornelia Barberini-Colonna and, after commissioning sixty plaster casts from James Tassie* from a mould by Giovanni Pichler*, sold it on to Sir William Hamilton* for £1,000. Ten years later, Byres retired to Scotland, where he died at the age of eighty-three. His portrait medallion*, from a model by James Tassie, was issued in 1779.

BYRES, James. Jasper portrait medallion modelled by James Tassie in 1779.   *Scottish National Portrait Gallery*

C

Cabaret à Deux
A set comprising two cups and saucers, cream jug, sugar box or dish, and either a teapot or a chocolate pot on a tray. It was probably the largest group of jasper teaware* made during the 18th century. The interiors of cups were often lapidary* polished, but it is clear that these sets were intended for 'cabinets' rather than for use. Similar sets were made in Wedgwood's cane ware* and later in other bodies, notably black basaltes* and bone china*.
See: Cabinet Pieces; Déjeuner Set; Trays

Cabinet Medals
See: Medals

Cabinet Pieces
Term applied to apparently 'useful' wares intended solely for ornament, and particularly to jasper* teaware and coffeeware (the hollow ware* having unglazed interiors) made in the 18th century. Such pieces were finely ornamented and often engine-turned*, with lapidary* polished rims (and sometimes also interiors). 'Cabinet' jasper of this type was made until the last quarter of the 19th century and some of these late pieces were of excellent quality, though the jasper body is more granular than that of the first period. A small quantity of jasper teaware of cabinet quality in both solid jasper and engine-turned* jasper dip* was made in 1955.

Cadbury Bournvita Set
Set comprising four beakers with saucers (which doubled as lids to keep the drink warm) a sugar basin and a lidded jug, made in cane-coloured coloured body*, *Honey Buff*, in 1934. The beakers were originally made for the firm of Cadbury in 1933, as an advertising exercise, to be supplied in exchange for coupons collected by customers. More than one million beakers were sold in two years, creating work for 200 workers at Etruria* at a time when sales were depressed. The flow-line belt system, introduced by Norman Wilson*, was used for the first time at Etruria* for the mass-production of these beakers.

CABINET PIECES. Extremely fine translucent white jasper chocolate pot ornamented with green and lilac ivy festoons, laurel and rosette borders in green, and two cameos in blue and white. c.1790.
Lady Lever Art Gallery, Port Sunlight

CADBURY BOURNVITA SET. *Honey Buff* coloured body lidded jug and beaker and saucer, the saucer designed to double as a lid to keep the drink hot. 1933. *Author's collection*

CABINET PIECES. Solid pale-blue and white jasper teaware ornamented with groups after Lady Templetown's designs. Two of the pieces have feet inlaid with bands of white jasper. c.1785-90.
Christie's, New York

Caddy (Shell) Spoon

Caddy spoons and caddy shells, the first with a shell-shaped bowl and conventional spoon handle, the second in the shape of a scallop shell, were made in the jasper*, cane*, rosso antico* and drab* dry bodies*, c.1815-28, and have been reproduced in jasper in the 20th century.

Cadell, Thomas (1742-1802)

London publisher in partnership with Andrew Millar in the Strand, London, from whom Wedgwood obtained a number of important books, including Hamilton's* *Antiquities*. His provision of prints for the Frog* service and the misprinting of his name as 'Cedell' have led to the misapprehension that he was a painter employed at the Chelsea Decorating Studio*

Cades, Giuseppe (1750-99)

Often identified as a modeller employed by Flaxman* and Webber* in Rome, Cades was a sculptor and gem* engraver, whose signed gem, *The Sale of Erotes*, a subject copied in cameo* by Wedgwood, was inspired by a mural painting in the Naples Museum. The subject was well known and popular during the second half of the 18th century and Wedgwood may have obtained a glass paste gem from Tassie* to use as his model. Cades was partly responsible for 18th-century decoration in the Borghese Palace, Rome.
See also: Borghese Family

Caduceus

The herald's wand or staff, carried by Hermes (Mercury*) in his role as messenger of the gods. In addition he wears a winged helmet and has wings on his heels. The caduceus is sometimes used by itself as an ornament, when it commonly stands in place of the figure of Hermes.

Caesar, Gaius Julius (106-44 BC)

Dictator and general. Agreed with Pompey and Crassus to divide the State between them. In 49, Caesar disobeyed the Senate's order to disband his army and marched on Rome. He defeated Pompey at Pharsalia in 48 and placed Cleopatra* and her brother Ptolemy on the throne of Egypt. Returning in triumph to Rome, Caesar refused the royal crown offered to him by Mark Antony*. He was assassinated on 15 March 44 BC.
Wedgwood subjects:
Portrait medallion, 1777
Bust supplied by Hoskins & Grant*, 1779.

Calcining

The process of heating a substance like flint* or ox bones (see: Bone China*) until it can be reduced to powder.

Calendar Plate

Queen's ware Calendar plates were introduced by Wedgwood in 1971. The first of the series was decorated with the Signs of the Zodiac*.

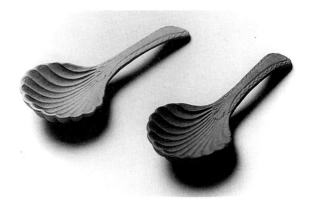

CADDY SHELL SPOONS. Drab 'porcelain' and rosso antico caddy spoons, length 3½in. Such spoons were made in all the dry bodies. c.1820. *Wedgwood Museum*

Calendar Tiles

Queen's ware rectangular tiles with a calendar on one side and on the other a printed decoration, usually a monochrome illustration of a subject from Boston, Massachusetts. Single tiles could be used as calendars or for wall decoration, since they were pierced for hanging, and they could also be employed as teapot stands. The mark is 'WEDGWOOD COPYRIGHT JONES, McDUFFEE & STRATTON'* with the year and name of the subject illustrated. Calendar tiles were produced from 1879 to 1929 but they are surprisingly scarce.

CALENDAR TILES. Calendar tiles for 1901 and 1907 printed with views of the Bunker Hill Monument and Harvard Stadium.
Sotheby's, London

Calx Casii

Purple of Cassius*. Wedgwood's name for a pinkish-purple enamel colour mixed by David Rhodes*. It was used for the *Husk* service in 1770 and also for the shell-edge shape dessert wares painted with botanical flowers* by James Bakewell* and others in the early 1770s.

CALENDAR PLATE. Calendar Plate for 1971, the year of its introduction. Each month is represented by the appropriate sign of the Zodiac. *Wedgwood Museum*

CAMBRIDGE ALE JUG. Set of three jugs, the largest height 6¼in., with a fourth jug enamelled with the crest of Trinity Hall, Cambridge. c.1895 and 1876.
Author's collection

Cambridge Ale Jugs

Jugs of squat shape, made in red body*, c.1850-90, for Woollard & Hattersley of Cambridge, who supplied them, enamelled with the appropriate college arms, to many of the university colleges.

CAMEO. Nine jasper dip cameos of various subjects and shapes, including a double portrait of George III and Queen Charlotte, a head of Christ and navette-shaped cameos of *Hebe* and a *Marine Venus*. Height 1⅛in.-2¾in. c.1785-95.
Christie's, London

Cameo

A term originally applied to gems* carved in low relief during the Greek and Roman period, and later extended to small objects, similarly carved, especially those of natural laminated material providing a background of contrasting colour to the relief (i.e. shell cameos). The word *cameo* means decoration in relief, irrespective of size, but by general usage it has become more or less confined to small objects of this kind, the larger being described as medallions*, plaques* or tablets*.

Antique gems* were avidly collected during the 18th century, and Wedgwood was able, on a number of occasions, to make use of existing collections as sources of designs for his replicas in cameo or intaglio*. Impressions of intaglios were taken in a mixture of sulphur and wax, and cameos could be cast in the normal way. Many such casts were made by James Tassie* for reproduction in his glass paste, and Wedgwood bought moulds from him. Wedgwood also employed gem engravers, among whom the most celebrated was probably Edward Burch, RA*.

In his 1779 Catalogue* of Ornamental Wares, Wedgwood refers to his cameos as fit for rings, buttons, lockets, bracelets, inlaying into fine cabinets, writing tables, bookcases etc. His sources, as he freely acknowledges, were the nobility and gentry (e.g. the Duke of Marlborough and Sir Watkin Williams Wynn*) in possession either of original gems or of fine impressions of gems in foreign collections. The cameos were first produced in black basaltes* or white terracotta* biscuit* ('waxen biscuit') with grounds enamelled in contrasting colours, and, from 1775, in stained jasper*. The jasper cameos were said to be like those of natural stone, and to admit of the same polish. Subjects listed in Wedgwood's catalogues included Egyptian mythology; Greek and Roman mythology; philosophers; the Trojan war; Roman history; illustrious men; and an appendix of recent additions. Some might better be described as small portrait medallions*.

At this time Wedgwood & Bentley advertised their willingness to make likenesses of their patrons, families and friends in the form of jasper cameos in sizes suitable for rings, lockets, seals or bracelets, from waxes or engraved stones, either in cameo or intaglio. The wax model for a portrait suitable for a ring, seal, or bracelet cost three guineas. For the jasper copies ('black and Blue onyx') either cameo or intaglio, the sum of 5 shillings was charged in lots of no less than ten. Cameos for rings were the same price, and those for bracelets 7s 6d. These too were sold in lots of ten or more. Portrait medallions were a great deal more costly.

Nearly all cameos were of jasper or white terracotta* biscuit. The latter were usually either plain or with enamelled grounds, but on some rare examples part of the relief has been coloured to give a three-colour effect. Double cameos – two cameos fused back-to-back and thus ornamented on both sides – were also made in terracotta and jasper. These are unmarked, as are the early terracotta biscuit examples. Jasper cameos were made in both the solid body and in jasper dip*, and many had bevelled and lapidary* polished edges. They might be mounted in cut-steel, silver, pinchbeck* or gold by such firms as Boulton* & Fothergill and Boden* & Smith. Subjects specially designed for Wedgwood included the cameos of horses by Burch* after Stubbs*. Examples exist of cameos with yellow, brown, green, black, blue and lilac grounds, but only the blue are commonly found and the experimental yellow is extremely rare. Also rare are early cameos of more than two colours, although small quantities were made in the 19th century, and again in 1959, and rather larger quantities have been produced since that date specifically for sale mounted as jewellery*.

Objects ornamented with Wedgwood cameos included *chatelaines**, combs, clock pendulums, clock cases*, watch cases, watch keys, snuff boxes, patch boxes, *étuis*, work boxes, writing desks, toothpick cases, metal vases and urns, metal lamps, coach panels, buckles, bracelets, lockets, buttons, rings, brooches, sword hilts*, opera glasses (monocular and binocular), scent bottles*, and *papier mâché** articles made by Henry Clay* of Birmingham and others. Cameos have been used also to ornament Wedgwood vases in Queen's ware, white terracotta, all the dry bodies* and bone china* and some rare three- and four-colour jasper cabinet pieces*.
See: Colour Plates 14 and 15

Cameograph Company, London

A company specialising in the production of bas-reliefs* and sculpture multiplied by the process of machine carving. Harry

CAMPANA. Black basaltes pastille burner and bough pot of Campana shape, enamelled in the *famille-rose* style. c.1820. Diameter 8in. *Sotheby's, London*

Barnard*, who modelled fifty-four medallions and six busts for the Cameograph Company, described the process as 'wonderful…and quite satisfactory for a foundation, but in translating it into such a material as our Jasper it required more work upon it which was entrusted to me'. The portrait medallions* reproduced in jasper have a curiously flat appearance in comparison with those cast from moulds. They include portraits of Edward VIII as Prince of Wales, George V, Queen Mary (Queen consort to George V), George VI as Duke of York, and Elizabeth, Duchess of York (later Queen consort to George VI), all c.1925.

Camera Obscura

Optical apparatus consisting of a box with an open side, over which a black curtain is hung. Fitted into the box at the top is a convex lens (mounted on bellows to allow focusing) above which is an adjustable angled mirror. The object to be copied is reflected in the mirror, and the image passes through the lens to form a picture on the white paper placed on the viewing table at the base of the box. The image appears the right way up but reversed. With his head under the curtain, any copier may trace over the outline of an image, but it required a professional draughtsman's technique to produce anything resembling a work of art. The invention of the camera obscura is often attributed to Giovanni Battista della Porta in 1569, but the principle was well known and employed many years earlier. It was used by the artists employed by Wedgwood to obtain 'real views' for the 'Frog'* service and by Thomas Daniel*. Thomas Wedgwood*, Josiah's youngest son, is believed to have been the first to make use of the camera obscura in photographic experiments.

Campana

A vase shape derived from the Greek krater*. It is of inverted bell shape with side handles well down on the shoulders. Originally made in ancient times, it was popular towards the end of the 18th century and during the Empire (Regency) period. The porcelain factories used it primarily as a vehicle for fine painting, and Wedgwood employed the shape extensively for basaltes* and jasper*. The vase 43, which is a campana shape, is still made in jasper.

Canal, Trent and Mersey

The state of communications between London and Liverpool was a considerable obstacle to the expansion of the pottery industry in Staffordshire. Roads were hardly better than cart tracks, impassable in winter, and the pack horse was widely used to transport both raw materials and the finished product. Josiah Wedgwood, already connected with a scheme to construct turnpike (toll) roads as early as 1760, supported a plan in 1765 to connect the rivers Trent and Mersey by canal, a proposal that would have the effect of linking the Potteries with Liverpool and Hull. Eventually, with all its branches, it linked the Potteries with the rest of England.

The success of the Duke of Bridgewater's* Worsley canal encouraged interested parties in Staffordshire to examine the prospects of a plan to link the Trent with the Mersey. Such a waterway would carry Lord Gower's (see: Stafford) coal and the products of the Potteries direct to the ports of Liverpool on the west coast and Hull on the east as well as providing access at greatly reduced costs for materials brought by the coastal trade from the West Country. Intensive lobbying by Wedgwood and his supporters, with influential help from Bridgewater and Gower, overcame obstinate opposition to the scheme, and in April 1766, Wedgwood, Bentley* and James Brindley* were among those who gave evidence before a committee of the House of Commons. The bill for the Trent and Mersey Canal received royal assent on 14 May. The 101 subscribers who formed the Company of Proprietors included Bridgewater, Gower, Thomas Whieldon*, Matthew Boulton*, and William Willet* and John Wedgwood of Smallwood (two of Josiah's brothers-in-law). The executive committee consisted of only seven members, including Brindley as Surveyor-General, all but one of whom were salaried. The exception was the Treasurer, Josiah Wedgwood, appointed, as he ruefully explained to Bentley, 'at £000 Per ann.' For this privilege, and for handling some £5,000 of the proprietors' money at any one time, he was obliged to offer personal security of £10,000. As an acknowledgement of his tireless work and the successful outcome of the campaign, he was invited to cut the first sod of the canal on 26 July 1766.

The Grand Trunk Canal, as it came to be known, was not completed until 1777, when it extended to ninety-three miles with seventy-five locks. The total cost was £200,000. The price of coal in Manchester was halved, the Duke of Bridgewater's profits from his coal mines rose in forty years from £406 in to £48,000, and the freight costs for raw materials and finished goods to and from the Potteries were reduced from 10d to 1½d per ton per mile.

A week before the cutting of the canal began, Wedgwood opened negotiations to buy the Ridgehouse Estate (see: Etruria), which lay directly in the path of the canal. His purchase of this site in 1767 gave his new factory exceptional advantages over any other in the area.

Canarsac, Lafon de (1821-1905)

Paris manufacturer of porcelain* who, in 1854, invented a technique of using photographs for ceramic decoration. He was awarded a medal for his exhibit at the London International Exhibition of 1862. The Victoria & Albert Museum, London, has a cup and saucer acquired at that time. Photographic printing was introduced experimentally at Etruria* in 1876.
See: Photolithography

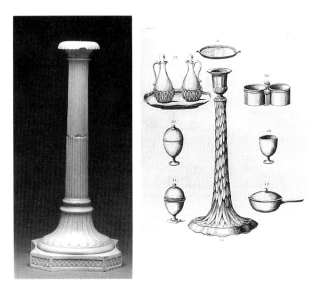

CANDLESTICKS AND CANDELABRA. Cream-colour fluted column candlestick with everted rim on a shaped octagonal base. Height 12in. Unmarked. c.1767. *Wedgwood Museum*

CANDLESTICKS AND CANDELABRA. Plate 7 from the '1790' Queen's ware Catalogue illustrating a tall table candlestick, shape no. 35. *Wedgwood Museum*

Candlesticks and Candelabra

Among the earliest objects made by Wedgwood, candlesticks exist in a wide variety of shapes and in almost every ceramic body produced by the firm since 1760. Early examples of green glaze*, tortoise-shell* and variegated* candlesticks have survived. Although many of the shapes are elegant enough to be considered purely ornamental, all

CANDLESTICKS AND CANDELABRA. Extremely rare Wedgwood & Bentley vase with two-branch candelabra fitted to the lid. Height 17½in. c.1778.
Dwight & Lucille Beeson Collection, Birmingham Museum, Alabama

appear to have been intended for use. In general, candlestick shapes followed closely the contemporary designs for silver, and a knowledge of English and Continental silver may often be of use in dating them. Candelabra – multi-branched candlesticks with nozzles for two or more candles – were made in the 18th century in both black basaltes* and jasper*, and in the 19th century in Majolica*.

Among the forms produced by Wedgwood are the following :

Chamber candlesticks (chambersticks). Short-stemmed candle-sticks provided with loop carrying handles and usually with cone-shaped snuffers, designed to light the owner to bed

Boucher. Three-branch candelabrum. The seated figure of a naked boy supporting on his shoulder a bowl which holds rustic branches. Made in Majolica*, c.1875

*Diana**. Two-branch candelabrum. A companion to *Minerva**

Dolphin*

Figure. e.g. *Ceres** and *Cybele**

Griffin*

Minerva. Two-branch candelabrum. Companion to *Diana*

Oak and Vine. Models by W.Beattie*. From c.1859 in Carrara*

Pillar. Simple tall pillar shapes, made from the 18th century in most bodies, often in turned jasper dip*

Reading. Turned, flared bell-shape. In most bodies, including bone china* of the first period

Rustic. Figures of boys representing Autumn and Winter attributed to Hackwood*

Satyr. Young satyrs holding vases or (after Clodion*) branches. From c. 1875 in Majolica and Carrara*

Sphinx*. Candleholders sprout somewhat oddly from the head of the figures of both the seated and the crouching sphinx in basaltes, rosso antico and basaltes, and jasper

Triton*

Vase-candlestick*

See: Colour Plate 16

CANDLESTICKS AND CANDELABRA. Queen's ware Pearl-glazed table candlestick moulded in an overlapping leaf pattern outlined in underglaze blue (Shape no.14 in 1774 Catalogue and no.35 in '1790' Catalogue). Height 12in. c.1778. *Author's collection*

CANDLESTICKS AND CANDELABRA. Pair of fine and very rare three-colour jasper two-branch candelabra, superbly modelled as figures of *Diana* and *Minerva* in white jasper on pale-blue bases with deep-blue palm-branch candleholders. Height 13¾in. c.1789.

Christie's, London

CANDLESTICKS AND CANDELABRA. Pair of pale-blue jasper dip figure candlesticks, probably representing *Juno* and *Ceres*. Height 10⅞in. c.1810. These figures, on variously modelled bases, appear to have been made as early as the end of 1780.

Temple Newsam House, Leeds

Cane Ware

A vitreous* biscuit* or dry body*, made largely from local marls, first catalogued by Wedgwood in 1787, when he described it as 'BAMBOO, or cane-coloured *bisqué* porcelain' of the same nature as his white terracotta* biscuit. By 1787 cane had been in production at Etruria* for at least ten years but no precise date can be given for its introduction. Trial pieces were made in 1771, when it was described as 'Fawn', but the first tablets* 'miscarried in firing' and Josiah scrapped the composition. Further experiments led next year to the production of sample quantities of 'Fawn flowerpots with white hoops', but no evidence has been found of orders for them. In 1776 some bamboo teapots were produced but Josiah was still not satisfied with the colour. By 1778 he was making cheap teapots in the new 'cane' body as well as flower pots. Probably there were other 'useful' shapes made in this body during the Wedgwood & Bentley period but no record of any has been found.

On 26 September 1779 Wedgwood informed Bentley* that he had made figures of Voltaire* and Rousseau* in cane. Only one example of the Voltaire figure in the cane body has been found. It is now in the British Museum and may be unique. The companion cane ware figure of Rousseau has remained unrecorded since 1779. Cane portrait medallions* of this period are extremely rare and the few surviving examples may be trial pieces.

Wedgwood remained dissatisfied with the cane body and further experiments with four different mixtures were carried out by the sixteen-year-old Josiah II* in 1783. None of these found favour with Wedgwood, but by the summer of 1786 the new body was established and 'Tea and Coffee Equipages' were being offered in bamboo shapes with enamelled patterns. By the time the 1787 Catalogue* was published the range had been extended to services for tea, coffee and chocolate, déjeuner sets* and cabinet pieces*, either plain or 'enriched with Grecian and Etruscan ornaments'.

The pigments used for the decoration of cane ware were usually the 'encaustic'* colours, a mixture of clay and enamels patented in 1769, though some later decoration includes conventional ceramic colours. Finely painted bamboo-shape tea and coffee wares with unglazed interiors were probably cabinet pieces, but equally fine bough pots*, bulb pots*, cassolettes* and vases* appear to have

CANE WARE. Small Wedgwood & Bentley cane 'bamboo' teapot. Height 3½in. c.1779.

Mr & Mrs Samuel Laver Collection

CANE WARE. Rare Wedgwood & Bentley cane portrait medallions: (*left* Samuel More; *right* William Shakespeare, modelled by Hackwood. Height (without frames) 3¼in. c.1779.

Christie's, New York

CANE WARE. Sugar box and teapot, the box with basket moulding. c.1788. *Wedgwood Museum*

been intended for use. A simpler and cheaper type of cane ware, with moulded relief ornament, was used for tea and coffee wares, jugs and mugs, the last sometimes strengthened by the addition of silver-plated rims. The interiors of some jugs and mugs were coated with a Pearl* slip*. All the forms of decoration and ornament used on black basaltes* – moulding, sprigged* ornament, engine-

CANE WARE. Amphora painted in encaustic colours, the obverse with two figures sacrificing at an altar, the reverse with a formal palmette design. Height 8⅜in. c.1790.
Dwight & Lucille Beeson Collection, Birmingham Museum, Alabama

CANE WARE. Bough pot in the form of a kylix flanked by a pair of canopic jars fitted as inkwells, with red ornaments and gilding in the 'Egyptian' taste. Height 5¼in. c.1810.
Mr & Mrs David Zeitlin Collection

CANE WARE. Three pieces, including a rare triangular tray and an unusually large helmet jug (height 10¼in.), decorated with encaustic painting. c.1790. *Photograph: Paine Art Centre*

turning*, encaustic* painting – were applied also to cane, but both the range of pieces and the quantities were small in comparison.

Among the most original and practical of cane ware pieces were the various forms of pie dishes* simulating pastry, which first appeared in 1786 and were made in good quantities throughout the 19th century. Large pot-pourri* vases painted with a *fêng huang* (phoenix) and Oriental flowers were made from c.1820.

Production of cane ware continued throughout the 19th century, achieving its greatest popularity between 1810 and 1840, when an improved composition with fresh shapes and ornament was introduced. During this period it was generally referred to as 'Cane porcelain'. Sprigged ornaments were added in white, red, blue, green, black, brown or grey stonewares, and the body was frequently finished with smear-glaze (see: Glazes). The most important developments in the decoration of early 19th-century cane were the introduction of 'beehive'*, 'basket-work'*.and 'arabesque'* embossed shapes for teawares and the varied use of contrasting bas-relief ornament. Cane wine coolers* were in production by 1811, and 'Leafage'* dessert plates and jugs are recorded at the same date. Some elaborate and curious 'beehive' benches appeared in 1800 and Pyrophorous vases* in assorted shapes were produced regularly from 1813. Among the rarest of cane ware pieces are the chessmen*, from Flaxman's* models, issued c.1820-30. Production of this attractive and versatile body was not finally discontinued until 1940.

See: Colour Plates 17 and 18
See also: Game Pie Dishes

CANE WARE. Octagonal shape teaware ornamented with fruiting vine in red body. c.1820. *Wedgwood Museum*

Canister
See: Tea Canister

Canopic Jars
A set of four jars in which the ancient Egyptians preserved the viscera of the deceased, usually for inhumation with the mummy. They were made at the Egyptian city of Canopus. Jars similar in style were employed for funerary purposes by the Etruscans as cinerary urns. The term 'Canopus vase' was used by Wedgwood for a human-headed vase in the Ptolemaic style after an illustration in Bernard de Montfaucon's* *L'Antiquité Expliquée,* Paris, 1719 (Plate CXXXII), which was in Josiah Wedgwood's library. Wedgwood & Bentley made two shapes: the first in one piece with a graceful waisted foot (which is not a feature of the Egyptian canopus); the second in two pieces, the upper part forming a lid, and the shape of the jar terminating abruptly at the foot, which is closer to the original. Both were decorated with encaustic* painting, and the second was made also in plain basaltes*, sometimes bolted to a square plinth.
See: Egyptian Taste

Canova, Antonio (1757-1852)
Influential neo-classical* sculptor, living in Rome from 1781. He went to Vienna in 1797 during Napoleon's invasion of Italy, but accepted the Emperor's invitation to Paris in 1802 and carved portraits of Napoleon and some of the Bonaparte family. In 1816 he was ennobled by the Pope for his part in ensuring the return to Italy of art treasures looted by the French armies. Wedgwood made 33in. models of Canova's statuettes of the boxers *Creugantes* and *Damoxenes,* though no examples have been found, and also reproduced Canova's bust of the Medici Venus* in Carrara*, c.1859.

CANOVA, Antonio. Black basaltes bust of *Venus* after the marble by Canova. Height 9½in. c.1820-30. *Formerly Buten Museum*

Capri Ware
The name given to the painted *Chinese Flowers* decoration in the famille rose style reproduced on black basaltes*, *rosso antico* and the red body* from c.1860. The quality of painting is generally much inferior to that of similarly decorated wares produced fifty years earlier and the pieces are usually finished with a reddish-brown enamel line.

CAPRI WARE. Inkstand in the form of a Roman lamp with taper-holder on a fixed base, decorated in the *famille-rose* style with orange-red enamel lines. Length 7in. c.1860. The more granular body, thinner enamelling and heavy lines distinguish this from the earlier, but similar, *Chinese Flowers* decoration. *Kadison Collection*

CANOPIC JARS. Canopic jar made in two pieces, the upper part forming a lid, painted in encaustic orange-red. Height 9½in. Unmarked. Wedgwood & Bentley period, c.1773. *Christie's, London*

Car
A waste product of coal mining, used in Staffordshire for colouring clays employed in the manufacture of pottery.
See: Black Basaltes; Egyptian Black

Carocchi, Fabbri & Co. (Gubbio, Italy)
Makers of reproductions of Italian *maiolica* established about 1857. According to Marryat *(Pottery and Porcelain),* a young man named Luigi 'Parocci' (certainly Carocchi), who was a pupil of the chemist, Professor Angelo Fabbri, rediscovered the method of producing the lustre* of Maestro Giorgio Andreoli (fl.1498-1553), not only the ruby colour but also other 'more rare tints'. On 13 April 1857, twenty plates thus decorated were taken for genuine early ware by those who saw them. It was this secret process that Pietro Gaj* offered to sell to Wedgwood in 1862.
See: Gubbio Lustre, Lustre Decoration

Carrara
Wedgwood's name for Parian*, introduced at Etruria* c.1848, and named after the celebrated white statuary marble from the quarries at Carrara in Northern Italy. The name did not become widely

CARRARA. Portrait medallions of 'Vespatian' and Augustus in moulded frames. Like many of the early black basaltes portraits (but not jasper), these are moulded in one piece with the ground and frame. Oval height 6in. Possibly trials, c.1849. *Wedgwood Museum*

CARRARA. Bust of George Stephenson by E.W. Wyon. Height 15in. Inscribed. c.1858. *Sotheby's, London*

CARRARA. *Charity*, by Carrier de Belleuse. Height 15in. This group was exhibited at the 1851 Great Exhibition. *Photograph: Wedgwood*

accepted and the term 'Parian' is more commonly used to describe the wares of all factories. After about 1870, even Laurence Wedgwood* resumed the use of 'Parian' in his notebooks. Thirty models were listed in Wedgwood's 1849 Price List and this figure was increased to more than one hundred, of which about a quarter were busts*, in the following twenty years. The variety of pieces was considerable: figures*, groups and busts, many of them reproduced from earlier models, were augmented by 'Miscellaneous Articles', which included honey-pots, spill-cases, candlesticks* and chessmen*. At least fifteen busts and several figures were obtained from Edward William Wyon*, one of the leading sculptors of the time, and others were modelled by Albert Carrier de Belleuse*. Thomas Woolner* and William Beattie*. Of the Etruria factory modellers who contributed new subjects for the Carrara body, only the work of Edward Keys* has so far been identified.

Other manufacturers, notably Minton*, made objects in a tinted Parian body and there is evidence that Wedgwood made stained Carrara chessmen in 1849. Wedgwood's bust of Gladstone*, examples of which are in the British Museum and the Manchester Museum, have been described as green-tinted Parian but are now known to be a rare Celadon* jasper* created specially for this work. A few coloured pieces were made in the third quarter of the 19th century and Carrara was used for coloured and gilded vases (see: Victoria Ware*) and a small quantity of a form of *pâte-sur-pâte*.

A particular curiosity is the Carrara reproduction of the Portland vase*. This was produced in plain white or with the ground painted in mazarine blue or black and glazed, c.1843

The following Wedgwood models have been recorded in Carrara. Their sources and dates of first production are shown, where these are known:

FIGURES

America, height 14½in.
*Apollo** (Belvedere), height 11in. (from a cast supplied by Flaxman*, 1789)
*Antinous** (Belvedere), height 11in.
*Ariadne**, 8in. x 9½in. 1849 Price List. Exhibited 1851
Autumn, height 15in. (after Clodion*)
Bacchante, height 15in. (after Clodion)
*Bacchus**, height 11in. (after Michelangelo*)
Broken Heart, height 12in. (E.Shenton* 1855)
Charity, 15in. x 18in. (Carrier de Belleuse*). 1862 Exhibition
Christ on the Mount, height 15in. Exhibited 1851

Cleopatra*, height 9½in. 1849 Price List
Crouching Venus, height 13in. Exhibited 1851
*Cupid**, height 7½ in. (after Falconet*). 1849 Price List
Cupid, height 24in. Exhibited 1851
Cupid with Bow, height 9in. 1849 Price List
*Diana**, 8⅞in. x 9½in. (after Flaxman). 1849 Price List. Exhibited 1851
Dream of Sorrow (ordered by Howell & James) 1866
England, height 13in. (W. Beattie*)
Eros and Euphrosyne, height 22in. (T. Woolner*)
Faith, height 18in. (Carrier de Belleuse), c.1859
*Faun**, height 15in. (after Clodion)
Faun with Flute (Faun with Pipes: Louvre), height 17in. 1849 Price List
Faun and Goat (Faun with Kid: Prado), height 23½ in.
Faun with Infant Bacchus, height 18in.
Forget-me-not, height 9in. (E. Keys). 1849 Price List
Grape Gatherer (male figure), height 10 in.
Grape Gatherer (female figure), height 10 in.
Greek Flute Player, height 14in. (W.Beattie)
Grief
Hiawatha, height 20in. (E.J. Kuntze*, 1863)
Hope, 9½in. x 9½in. (E.W. Wyon)
Hope, height 18in. (Carrier de Belleuse). c.1862
Infant Bacchus, height 13in. 1849 Price List.
Infant Hercules with the Serpent, 20in. x 17in. Exhibited 1851
Innocence, height 12in. 1849 Price List
Ireland, height 13in. (W. Beattie)
Madonna, height 13in. 1849 Price List. Exhibited 1851
Madonna on pedestal, height 15in. Exhibited 1851
May Day, height 10in. (E. Keys)
*Mercury**, height 11in. Exhibited 1851
Mercury, height 17in. (after Pigalle*). 1849 Price List. Exhibited 1851
Milton, height 17½in. (after Rysbrack*: moulds bought from T. & R. Boote)
Morpheus, 18in. x 24in. (after Algardi). Exhibited 1851
Nubian Water Carrier, height 9½in. (E.W. Wyon)
Nymph at the Fount, 10½ in. x 11½in. 1849 Price List
Poor Maria (from Sterne's* *Sentimental Journey*, height 12½in. (E. Keys). Exhibited 1851
*Psyche**, height 7½in. (after Falconet)
Reading Girl (Ordered by Howell & James) 1866
Satyr candlestick, height 14½in. (after Clodion)

Scotland, height 13in. (W. Beattie)
Shakespeare, height 17½in. (after Scheemakers*: mould bought from T. & R. Boote)
*Sleeping Boy**, on pedestal (after Fiammingo. See: Duquesnoy)
Spring, 10in.
Strawberry Girl, height 15in. (E. Shenton 1858)
Summer, height 10in.
The Marketer, height 6in.
*Triton** candlesticks (pair), height 11in. 1849 Price List
Venus Victrix, height 9½in.
*Venus**, height 18in. (after Pigalle). Exhibited 1851
Venus and Cupid, height 27in. Exhibited 1851
Wanderer (female figure), height 18in. (E. Shenton 1859)
Water Nymph, height 9in. (E. Keys). 1849 Price List
Winter, height 10in.

GROUPS
Abraham and Isaac (see: *The Sacrifice)*
Boy and Goat, height 8in.
Christ Healing the Blind, height 21in.
Cupid and Psyche, height 7½in. (the two figures after Falconet, listed above, on one plinth)
Cupid and Psyche, 22½in. x 12½in. (after N. Guinet*)
Finding of Moses, height 19½in. (W. Beattie)
Isaak and Rebekah, 21½in. x 18in. (W. Beattie)
Joseph before Pharaoh (see: *The Interpretation)*
May Day, height 10in. (E. Keys)
Oberon, 21in. x 13in. (E.W. Wyon)
The Interpretation, 20in. x 16in. (W. Beattie)
The Sacrifice, height 24in. (W. Beattie)
The Surprise, height 13in. (E. Keys)
Titania, 21in. x 13in. (E.W. Wyon 1853).
Venus and Cupid, height 15in. (Giovanni Meli*)
Venus and Cupid, 21in. x 12in. Exhibited 1851

BUSTS
John Bunyan, 14in. (E.W. Wyon). 1859 Price List
Robert Burns, 14in. (E.W. Wyon). 1859 Price List
Lord Byron, 14in. (E.W. Wyon). 1859 Price List.
Sir Colin Campbell, 16in. (E.W. Wyon). 1859 Price List
Jesus Christ, 8in. (after Michelangelo). 1849 Price List
Richard Cobden, 1865
Sir Robert Cranston (John S. Rhind*, 1905)
Princess Elizabeth Alexandra Mary (later Queen Elizabeth II), 16½in. (K.S. de Strobl*, 1937)
W.E.Gladstone*, 11¼in. (J.E. Boehm* 1879)
Sir Henry Havelock, 15in. (E.W. Wyon). 1859 Price List
Havelock (small size)
Thomas Henry Huxley, 12in. (R. Monti*, 1865)
Abraham Lincoln, 1867 Price List
John Locke, 8in. (after D. Le Marchand*). 1849 Price List
John Milton, 14¼in. (E.W. Wyon). 1859 Price List
George Moore, 15in. (E.W. Wyon). 1859 Price List
Sir Isaac Newton, 9in. (after Le Marchand). 1849 Price List
Lord Palmerston, 9½in. (E.W. Wyon). 1849 Price List
Palmerston, large size (E.W. Wyon 1866)
Pope Pius IX, 10in. 1849 Price List
Sir Walter Raleigh, 4in. 1849 Price List
Sir Walter Scott, 15in. (E.W. Wyon). 1859 Price List
William Shakespeare, 14in. (Flaxman). 1859 Price List
William Shakespeare, 11½in. (F.M. Miller* 1864)
George Stephenson, 15in. (E.W. Wyon 1858)
Robert Stephenson, 15in. (E.W. Wyon 1858)
Susanna. 1849 Price List
Alfred, Lord Tennyson, 18½in. 1892
Venus, 14in. (after Canova)
George Washington. 19½in. (Sir Francis Chantrey). 1849 Price List
James Watt*, 15in. (E.W. Wyon). 1859 Price List
Arthur Wellesley, Duke of Wellington, 15½in. (E.W. Wyon). 1859 Price List
John Wesley, 9in. 1849 Price List
Marquis of Zetland (T. Earle* 1868)
A reproduction of the Michelangelo tondo from the Royal Academy, and small busts of Queen Elizabeth, the Queen Mother, Field-Marshal Viscount Montgomery of Alamein and Mrs Margaret Thatcher were produced after the brief reintroduction of the Parian body in 1981.

CARRIER DE BELLEUSE. White stoneware oval basin ('Lamp tray'), dipped in lilac jasper with solid white jasper lion-mask handles, mounted on a Carrara base catalogued in 1859 as 'Supporting Group' by Carrier de Belleuse. Height 17½in. c.1866.   *Christie's, London*

PORTRAIT MEDALLIONS*
Augustus
Vespatian [*sic*]
Although these two portraits are the only ones so far traced, and they may have been trial pieces, it is likely that others exist.

MISCELLANEOUS MODELS
Butter Cooler, Sunflower shape
Candlesticks, Oak and Vine, height 10in. (W. Beattie)
Chess Pieces (Flaxman)
Honey Pot, Beehive Shape, height 4in.
Honey Pot, Beehive shape, 3in. x 3½in.
Match Box (long square)
Portland Vase, height 10in.
Spill Case, 'Bonfire', height 4½in. (J. Bell* 1848)
Spill Case, 'Muses', height 4in.
Spill Case, 'Muses', height 5in.
Supporting Group (Carrier de Belleuse 1859)
Table centre (Carrier de Belleuse 1861)
Vase 43 Shape (no cover), height 6in.
See: Colour Plate 19

Carrier de Belleuse, Albert Ernest (1824-87)
French sculptor and modeller for porcelain* who studied with the Ecole des Beaux Arts, Paris, in 1840. He established a large studio for sculpture and ornamental work, where one of his assistants was Auguste Rodin. Carrier reproduced statuary in large and small sizes, and made many pastiches for decorative purposes, usually signed 'Carrier'. He worked for a number of English factories, including Minton*, Copeland (Spode*), Brownfields and Wedgwood. His figures of *Faith*, *Hope* and *Charity* were reproduced by Wedgwood in Carrara* for the Great Exhibition of 1851. He also modelled for Wedgwood an imposing table centre and a 'Supporting Group'.

Carter, Benjamin (fl.1910-20)
Painter at Etruria* under the direction of John Goodwin*

Cartlidge, Susan
Paintress at Etruria* under the direction of John Goodwin*. Some of her work shown at the Paris Exposition Universelle of 1925.

Caryatid
Figure of a woman used in architecture in place of a column to support an entablature. Caryatids are the female form of Atlantes (see: Atlas). They occur in classical ornamental design, and Wedgwood used them to provide supports for a small number of fine basaltes* tripod vases of the Wedgwood & Bentley period.
See also: Michelangelo Lamp

CASTER. Embossed Queen's ware sugar caster, height 8¼in. c.1860.
Mr & Mrs Samuel Laver Collection

Cassandra

Daughter of Hecuba and Priam*, King of Troy, and desired by Apollo*. He was ready to confer on her the gift of prophecy if she would yield to him, but when she received the prophetic power she was no longer willing to fulfil her promise. In revenge, Apollo decreed that her prophecies should not be believed. After the fall of Troy, which she had foretold with irritating perseverance, Cassandra became part of the share of Agamemnon, who took her to Mycenae. There she was murdered by Clytemnestra and subsequently deified. Wedgwood subject:
Cassandra, medallion 7¼in. x 4½in., 'A fine figure in high relief from the king of France's cabinet', no.33 in 1779 Catalogue*.This model is often attributed, without evidence, to John Bacon*. In the 1788 Catalogue, it is listed as *Cassandra grasping the Palladium.*

Cassolette

A covered vase to contain perfumed substances for scenting a room. It has holes pierced in the shoulders, and usually in the cover also. Some mounted vases had a pierced metal band added between the mouth and the cover, thus changing them into cassolettes or pot-pourri* vases. Boulton called vases of this kind 'essence pots' or 'essence vases'. They were made also by Wedgwood in white terracotta*, variegated wares* and the dry bodies*, although Wedgwood's, being ceramic, were more likely to be pot-pourri vases, the essential difference between the two being that the cassolette contained dry ingredients while those for the pot-pourri vase were more often liquid.

Caster

A container for sugar, pepper or salt, generally with a high domed top or cover which is pierced to allow the contents to be sprinkled over food. Wedgwood made casters in Queen's ware* from about 1774 and later in Pearl* ware.
See: Cruet Set

Casting

The process of using a mould or moulds to duplicate an existing model by pouring in a liquid which later sets and hardens. The moulds are usually of fired clay or plaster of Paris. Plaster moulds are commonly used for slip-casting* because they readily absorb a good deal of moisture from semi-liquid clay. Fire-clay moulds are more commonly employed for press-moulding*, although plaster moulds may be used for this purpose.

Every cast begins with an original model from which a mould is taken. This may be modelled specifically for the purpose in clay or wax, or it may already exist in marble, bronze or wood. Since about 1745, moulds have been made from plaster of Paris, a fine powder which, when mixed with water, forms a plastic substance varying in consistency from dough to thin cream, according to the amount of water added. In this state it will take on the shape of anything with which it is brought into contact, and, after an interval which varies from five to thirty minutes according to the type of plaster being used, it becomes rigid. At the same time a certain amount of heat is generated and there is a slight increase in size.

To take moulding an ordinary portrait bust as an example, the workman must first decide how many pieces will be necessary, depending on the complexity of the model. A portrait of a clean-shaven, bald man requires fewer pieces than that of a woman with an elaborate coiffure, and a portrait of a bearded man may cause distinct difficulties since the pieces of the finished mould must draw away cleanly from the model without damaging the surface or themselves being damaged. There are several ways of overcoming these difficulties, either by modifying the model and trimming the cast afterwards or by multiplying the number of pieces in the mould. As each piece of the mould is finished, the edge is notched so that it fits accurately into the next piece, and when all the pieces have been made they are put together and a stronger outer case cast over them. Each piece, as it is made, is oiled to prevent it from adhering to the next.

The next step is to remove both the outer case and the inner notched pieces from the model and to fit them all together again with a hollow interior. They are now ready for use to cast either a block mould (patrix), from which working moulds (matrices) of the same kind may be cast, or to cast the objects themselves in slip. A hollow plaster block mould can be made by pouring in liquid plaster, swilling it around, and then pouring it off, repeating the process until the cast is of the required thickness or the plaster is beginning to set. For a slip cast, the slip is poured into the mould and left until a layer of sufficiently firm clay has adhered to the walls of the mould, after which the surplus is poured off and the remaining layer of clay left to harden and shrink away from the walls of the mould. The operations of making moulds and taking casts in plaster are highly skilled; the making of slip casts is less so.

Moulds intended for use in press-moulding are, of course, open, not closed. A bust is usually divided into the front (in one or more pieces) and a comparatively shallow back, and a ceramic body somewhat stiffer than slip is pressed into the mould by hand. After being extracted, the two halves of the object are luted together, using slip as an adhesive, and the mould seams and blemishes are removed by hand (a process known as fettling*).

Moulds for figures are made by dissecting the original model into parts, which are moulded and cast separately. The parts are then joined together ready for firing. Elsewhere (e.g. Hoskins & Grant*) notes will be found of certain busts bought ready-made which were later worked on by various modellers, notably Hackwood*. These, no doubt, were some of the tasks they performed. At first Hoskins (and others, such as Mrs Landré* and Richard Parker*) supplied Wedgwood with moulds in plaster, but later Wedgwood preferred to buy plaster models from which he could make his own moulds. Plaster-cast makers, such as Hoskins, often obtained permission to take casts from objects in private collections, and Josiah Wedgwood also acknowledges similar permissions in his catalogues.
See: Newdigate, Sir Roger; Processes of Manufacture; Repairers

Castleford

Pottery, founded by David Dunderdale at Castleford (near Leeds), c.1790-1821, making good quality creamware* and Pearlware* and fine white and black stonewares, mainly teapots and jugs moulded with low relief ornament in a manner inspired by Wedgwood's black basaltes*, white terracotta* and jasper*. Some of the creamware designs and shapes appear to be almost direct copies of Wedgwood's. 'Castleford type' jugs, particularly those with hunt scenes, were made by Wedgwood in the early 19th century, and also by other potters, notably Spode* and John Turner*.
The *Castleford Pottery Pattern Book* was published in 1796.

Catalogues

Josiah Wedgwood wrote to Bentley* on 13 September 1772 to suggest that they should produce a 'Printed Catalogue of the things we have'. The reference was to cameos* and medallions* and the proposed catalogue was probably intended primarily as an aid to customers and employees in identifying the subjects of their Wedgwood gems*. Next year saw the publication of the first Wedgwood & Bentley catalogue of ornamental wares. It was evidently useful and popular for it was reprinted with a few additions (the most important of which was the introduction of the 'fine white terracotta'*) in 1774, reprinted in French in the same year and reissued with six additional pages and a woodcut illustration of an inkstand in 1775. Larger, revised editions were published in 1777, 1779, 1787 and 1788. Further translations were published in French, Dutch and German in 1779 and again in French in 1787. These catalogues have become invaluable guides to the Wedgwood & Bentley ornamental wares and often provide the only reliable evidence of the earliest dates of production of individual pieces. The last Ornamental Ware Catalogue was divided under twenty headings ('Classes') with subsections (see: Ornamental Ware), the bodies employed being described in six categories. The catalogue contained two illustrations in colour of jasper* pieces and a diagrammatic woodcut illustration of Wedgwood's 'improved' inkstand (see: Ink Pot, Ink Standish).

In November 1773 Wedgwood was considering a Queen's ware* catalogue printed in French to send to agents and merchants abroad with samples of nine patterns. This catalogue, he decided, would 'not be complete without some copper plates of the principal vessels which will give a much better idea of them than the names only'. Next month, he wrote: 'I find the Catalogue of Usefull Ware will be a much more extensive thing than I expected'.

The first Queen's ware catalogue, printed by Joseph Cooper* of Drury Lane and illustrated with nine plates (showing thirty-five numbered articles) engraved by John Pye* was sent out in 1774, grandiosely entitled *A Catalogue of the different articles of Queen's Ware, which may be had either plain, gilt or embellished with Enamel Paintings, manufactured by Josiah Wedgwood, Potter to her Majesty*. The second 'Useful ware' catalogue (usually referred to as the '1790' Catalogue) was prepared for publication with thirteen engraved plates (showing eighty numbered shapes) and texts in English and French about 1793 but the surviving copies are uncorrected and so incomplete as to suggest that it was never published. A third Queen's ware catalogue, generally called the '1817' Catalogue, was issued in three versions between c.1817 and 1849 but no certain evidence has been found to show that it was ever formally published and it may have been used only at Etruria (and perhaps at the York Street showrooms* until their closure in 1828) for reference. The various editions of the Catalogue contained between thirty-nine and forty-six engraved plates, illustrating up to 386 engraved plates. The first eighteen plates were commissioned by Josiah II* from William Blake* in 1815; Plates 19 and 20 were engraved about 1816 by John Taylor Wedgwood*. The engravers of the rest remain unidentified and it is evident that five unnumbered plates were added at a later date, probably c.1835.

The '1880' Illustrated Catalogue of Shapes (published between 1878 and 1880) contains forty-four plates illustrating 319 shapes, many of the drawings being repetitions of those in the '1817' Catalogue. It was republished by the Wedgwood Society*, London, in 1971. The last Wedgwood illustrated catalogue, *Catalogue of Bodies, Glazes, and Shapes current for 1940-50*, was published in 1940. It contained 218 illustrated pages covering all types of ware then in production.

Second only in importance to the Ornamental ware and Queen's ware catalogues issued by Wedgwood is the auction sale catalogue of 1781, the *Catalogue of Cameos, Intaglios, Bas Reliefs, Medallions...joint property of Mr Wedgwood and Mrs Bentley which are to be sold by Auction by Messrs Christie & Ansell, 1781*. This is not illustrated but it contains descriptions of 1,200 lots, some containing twenty-four or more pieces, and there can be little doubt that the descriptions and the brief explanatory introduction were prepared with the assistance of Josiah Wedgwood himself or of Tom Byerley*. This catalogue, which received inadequate attention before 1989, conclusively resolves many questions about the division between 'ornamental' and 'useful' wares and the production of the Wedgwood & Bentley partnership.

Published catalogues of public and private collections and of important exhibitions of Wedgwood wares are listed under the appropriate heading in the Bibliography.

CATHERINE II (THE GREAT). Wedgwood & Bentley blue and white jasper portrait medallion after a medal by T. Ivanov, 1762. First produced by Wedgwood & Bentley, August 1779. Oval height 4⅝in.
Brooklyn Museum, Emily Winthrop Miles Collection

Cathcart, Charles, 9th Baron (1721-76)

Lieutenant-General and Ambassador to St Petersburg 1768-71; married, 1753, Jane Hamilton, sister of Sir William Hamilton*. In March 1768 Wedgwood informed Bentley* that he had 'spent several hours with Ld Cathcart our Embassador to Russia' and added, 'We are to do great things for each other'. Cathcart made an immediate start by lending Wedgwood prints from Hamilton's *Antiquités,* not then available in England. By September next year four Queen's ware* services were being assembled for the Russian consul in London and another, presumably for official use, for the Cathcarts. Later, 'some vases as patterns' were sent out to Lady Cathcart, evidently for her to display in the British Embassy as samples of Wedgwood's work from which orders might be forthcoming. It was no doubt through the influence of the Cathcarts that the first order from the Empress Catherine* – for the *Husk* service – was obtained in 1770 and this proved to be the foundation of a useful trade which owed at least as much to Jane Cathcart as to her husband. Wedgwood corresponded frequently with her and she was as unsparing in her efforts on his behalf as she was with severe, but constructive, criticism of the ware and, more especially, of poor packing and delays in delivery.

Jane Cathcart died in St Petersburg in 1771 and shortly afterwards Lord Cathcart gave up his post as Ambassador and returned to England. By then, however, the name of Wedgwood was established at Catherine's Court as the manufacturer of fine ornamental vases and the finest earthenware tablewares, and it was little more than eighteen months after Lady Cathcart's death that Wedgwood & Bentley received the order for the Frog* service. Russia was also one of Boulton's* best markets and, like Wedgwood, he owed much of his success there to the Cathcarts.

Catherine II (The Great) (1729-96)

Empress of Russia, born at Stettin, the daughter of the Prince of Anhalt-Zerbst; married Peter, heir to the Russian throne, in 1745. Her husband reigned as Peter III for only a few months before he was murdered, and their son, who became Paul I, also was assassinated. Catherine, a clever and ambitious woman, too often frustrated her own plans by promoting one or other of her many lovers to high office. She made extensive purchases of French decorative art, patronising the *ébéniste* David Roentgen and the Sèvres* porcelain factory. She bought Sir Robert Walpole's collection of paintings and ordered Queen's ware* services (the *Husk* and the Frog* services) from Wedgwood. The Scottish architect Charles Cameron designed three suites of apartments for Catherine's palace

CAULIFLOWER WARE. A group of cauliflower wares, decorated in bright green and pale ivory-yellow glazes, of the type made by Wedgwood and other Staffordshire and Yorkshire potters. Unmarked. Jug height 4½in. c.1765-70.

Dwight & Lucille Beeson Collection, Birmingham Museum, Alabama

at Tsarskoë Selo (St Petersburg), which were decorated with Wedgwood jasper* plaques in some of the rooms, including the Empress's bedroom. Unfortunately, the palace was destroyed during the siege of Leningrad.

Wedgwood, his judgement no doubt coloured by commercial considerations, described Catherine as 'a Woman of sense – fine taste & Spirit'. A small portrait medallion* in black basaltes* is listed in the 1773 Catalogue. By 1777, two jasper portraits were available, both after medals by T. Ivanov. A fourth portrait, of Catherine as *Minerva*, was modelled by Maria Feodorowna* in 1782. A black basaltes tablet, impressed on the reverse with the inscription 'CATHERINE II REWARDING ART AND PRO-TECTING COMMERCE', attributed to Flaxman*, c.1785, again shows the Empress flatteringly as *Minerva*.

CAULIFLOWER WARE. Page from a catalogue illustrating modern cauliflower wares in production at Etruria, c.1925-30. Note the stronger and clumsier shape of the handle, replacing the 18th-century scroll handle. *Photograph: Wedgwood*

Catherine Shape
See: Tableware Shapes

Caudle Set
Caudle in the 18th century was a warm, sweet drink, made from eggs, sugar, spices and bread or oatmeal, mixed with ale or wine, for the sick and their visitors. Caudle was served in covered cups, generally with two handles, with a conforming saucer. According to Simeon Shaw*, Wedgwood 'had the honour to present unto her Majesty Queen Charlotte*, a Candle Sett [*sic*], made of the best cream colour, and painted in the best style of the day by Thomas Daniel* and Daniel Steele*'. There appears to be no documentary evidence of this presentation, but the word 'Candle' is evidently a misprint for 'caudle', an error corrected later in Ward's *History of Stoke-on-Trent*. If this unsolicited gift was ever made, a distinct possibility in view of Wedgwood's methods of business, the most likely date for it would be between 1763 and 1765. The suggestion that Wedgwood's gift was of a 'candle' set (although no such set is recorded in the pottery or porcelain of any factory) and that the error of description is Ward's, is contradicted by the evidence of similar misprints of 'candle' for 'caudle' (notably in J.E. Nightingale, *Contributions Towards the History of Early English Porcelain*, 1881).

Cauliflower Ware
Cream-coloured ware modelled and coloured naturally in imitation of the cauliflower – usually a teapot, coffeepot, tea bowl, sugar box, cream jug or tureen and stand. The lower part was modelled to resemble the leaves and covered with green glaze*; the flower head was cream or yellow. Ware of this kind was made by Josiah Wedgwood from c.1759 and is a good example of Wedgwood in the rococo* style. Similar cauliflower ware was made by many other potters in Staffordshire, Yorkshire and Derbyshire in the 1760s.
See: Colour Plate 20
See also: Fruit and Vegetable Shapes

Cawk (Cauk)
Local term for a mineral, principally barium sulphate*, found in Derbyshire. Also known as barytes or heavy spar. It is an essential ingredient of jasper*.

Caylus, Ann-Claude-Phillippe de Tubières, Comte de (1692-1765)
A collector of antiquities who wrote an important work on classical and Egyptian art, *Receuil d'antiquités égyptiennes, étrusques,*

CELTIC ORNAMENTS. Queen's ware bread-and-butter plate and bone china 'York' cup and 'Empire' bowl decorated with various patterns of the *Celtic Ornaments* series designed by Daisy Makeig-Jones. c.1914-20.   *Formerly Buten Museum*

CENTAUR. Green and white jasper 'Herculaneum Picture', *Centaur*, in a cavetted frame of the same material moulded with the ground. Diameter 15⅞in. c.1790.
Dwight & Lucille Beeson Collection, Birmingham Museum, Alabama

grecques, romaines et gauloises, published in seven volumes between 1752 and 1767. With Winckelmann* and Sir William Hamilton*, the comte de Caylus may be regarded as one of the architects of the neo-classical* style. Wedgwood possessed the *Receuil,* and quotes it from time to time in his letters to Bentley*. In that book, Caylus, relying on the description by Pliny the Elder in *Historia Naturalis,* published a description of the early technique of encaustic* painting, the effect of which (but not the method) was imitated by Wedgwood.

CC
Wedgwood factory and trade abbreviation for Cream-colour, used especially in the descriptions of embossed Queen's ware* (e.g. CC on Lavender) and for the two-colour clay CC and Celadon slipware created for Keith Murray's* designs in the 1930s.

Ceiling Rose
A jasper ceiling rose with a central hole to be used in conjunction with a light fixture was made by Wedgwood at the end of the 19th century. An example, formerly in the Buten Museum*, is dated 1896.

Celadon
A glaze of varying shades of green covering Chinese stonewares of the Sung dynasty (960-1280) and later. A modified green, similar in shade was employed by the Chinese as a porcelain ground colour in the 18th century. The word is probably a corruption of Saladin (Salah-ed-din), the Saracen Sultan of Egypt in the 12th century, who was especially fond of ware decorated with this glaze. Wedgwood applied the term Celadon to a sea-green stained earthenware introduced c.1858. The existence of a pale-green stoneware body, in production about 1810, has led to the erroneous belief that the Celadon body was first introduced around this date. The term Celadon was used also to describe the pale green jasper* created specifically for a large bust of Gladstone* in 1879.
See: Coloured Bodies

Celtic Ornaments
Designs by Daisy Makeig-Jones* adapted from ornamental motifs in the 6th-century *Book of Kells* of which Wedgwood procured an expensive reproduction in 1916. Two patterns, which she named *St Chad's* and *Lindisfarne* (produced in two versions), were designed for Queen's ware tableware, but the *Celtic Ornaments* were principally for bone china* teaware and coffeeware and a few bone china ornamental pieces. Mother-of-pearl lustre* glazes were often applied over the ornamental wares, sometimes over coloured grounds. Bone china patterns, most of which occur in several versions, include *Tyrone, Celt, Armagh, St Chad's* and *Gothic Circles.*
See also: Fairyland Lustre; Ordinary Lustres

Centaur
Mythical being that was half-horse and half-man. Centaurs lived in a region of Mount Pelion and were said to be the offspring of Ixion and a cloud. Their conflict with the Lapiths is sometimes depicted in art. No doubt the legend grew from the contacts of settled peoples with nomadic tribes who were rarely out of the saddle. Chiron was a centaur famous for his wisdom. Jason, Peleus and Achilles* were among his pupils, and Hercules* was his friend. Centaurs, one female, figure in three of the 'Herculaneum Pictures'* made in 1770 in white terracotta* and black basaltes* from plaster models in the collection of the Marquis of Lansdowne*. These are circular plaques, diameter 11½in., listed as nos 57-9 in the 1773 Catalogue*.

Centrepiece
See Grand Plat Ménage

Ceracchi, Joseph (Giuseppe) (1751-1802)
Italian sculptor who came to England in 1773 and was employed by Robert Adam*. He exhibited several marble busts at the Royal Academy between 1776 and 1779 and carved the figures of 'Temperance' and 'Fortitude' for the Strand facade of Somerset House. Ceracchi moved to Philadelphia in 1791 and modelled busts of eminent Americans, including Benjamin Franklin, George Washington and Thomas Jefferson. Returning to Europe in 1795, he moved to Paris, where he became involved in a plot to assassinate Napoleon. He was guillotined in 1801. Ceracchi modelled in plaster a portrait of Dr Joseph Priestley* reproduced in Wedgwood's jasper* and black basaltes*. It was remodelled, probably by Hackwood*, for the series of large-size portrait medallions* in 1779.

Ceres
The Roman name for Demeter, goddess of agriculture and the fruits of the earth. The sister of Zeus (Jupiter*) and mother of Persephone (see: Proserpine*), Demeter is usually represented wearing a garland of corn and holding in her hands ears of corn, a torch or a basket. The Romans celebrated a festival in her honour, and her cult was of considerable political importance.
Wedgwood subjects:
Ceres, figure, 'A young female figure in the character of Ceres, sitting' (no dimensions given). Possibly the figure invoiced by T. Parker* in 1769. No.5 in 1773 Catalogue*
Ceres, figure 17in., no.35 in 1787 Catalogue. This is almost cer-

CERES. Solid blue and white jasper candlestick in the form of a figure of *Ceres* holding a torch, the moulded flames forming the candleholder. Height 12½in. c.1790. *Wedgwood Museum*

tainly the figure invoiced as 'Chrispagnia' (see: Crisphagnia) by Hoskins & Grant* in May 1779

Ceres, candlestick, height 12½in. (companion to a similar candlestick figure of *Cybele),* c.1786. Josiah Wedgwood commented on this figure in March 1786: 'Ceres being represented in most antiques with a lighted torch in her hand...was what gave the idea of a flame for the nozzle of the Candlestick she bears'.

Ceres, candlestick, height 11in. (companion to a similar candlestick figure of *Pomona),* c. 1780

Ceres, medallion 4in. x 3 in., no.48 in 1773 Catalogue

Ceres, circular medallion (head in profile), diameter 7¾in. Probably the head listed as no.115 *Summer* in the 1777 Catalogue (rectangular or oval 10in. x 8in.) and invoiced by Flaxman as one of a set of four 'Bass Releivos of the Seasons' in 1775

Ceres and Tryptolemus, medallions 7in. x 5½in. and 20in. x 14½in., after an antique gem, known also as *Venus and Cupid,* but catalogued simply as *Night,* nos 77 and 79 in the 1773 Catalogue

Sacrifice to Ceres or *Offering to Ceres,* tablet (see: Flora).

See also: Zingara

Chamber of Manufacturers
See: General Chamber of Manufacturers

Chamber Ware
Another name for toilet wares, which included chamber pots, washing bowls and water jugs, soap dishes*, toothbrush boxes* or holders and slop pails. Although there is little evidence of such objects being made during the lifetime of Josiah Wedgwood I, and they were never a large part of Wedgwood's total business, they were made in a great variety of decoration and several ceramic bodies throughout the 19th century. In addition to Queen's ware* and Pearl* ware, often richly decorated, the coloured bodies* were much used for 'Chamber services', and the use of White Ware* for this purpose is proof of its durability. A typical Chamber service of 1838 consisted of ewer and basin, soap and toothbrush trays, sponge tray, 'mouth bason' and ewer, 'footpail' and jug. Orders from London for such sets decorated with variegated lustre* were fairly common from about 1814, but the order received in November 1815 for 'gold Lustre Chamber pots' with matching shaving basins to be repeated in silver lustre appears to be unique. During

CHAMBER WARE. Pearl ware handbasin and soap box with 'Marble' decoration in the style first produced in White ware c.1845. Basin diameter 14½in. 1861. *Wedgwood Museum*

the 19th century, chamber services were often made in patterns matching the decoration of contemporary Wedgwood closet ware*.

A useful aid to the dating of chamber pots is their size. During the 18th century they were small because they were kept in a special cupboard in the sideboard, ready for the use of after dinner drinkers. Chamber pots of a larger size for bedroom use seem to have been an early 19th-century addition to the toilet ewer and basin because such objects are not illustrated *en suite* in the earliest shape books. The upper part of the house was, until then, served by what the English euphemistically call a 'commode' (properly the name for a decorative chest of drawers for the drawing-room). Wedgwood made pans for these in standard sizes in undecorated earthenware.

Wedgwood's manufacture of chamber pots towards the end of the 18th century is immortalised in a note to *The Rolliad (Probationary Odes VI),* published in 1795 as a political attack on William Pitt the Younger: 'I am told, that a scoundrel of a potter, one Mr Wedgewood [*sic*] is making 20,000 vile utensils, with a figure of Mr Pitt in the bottom; round the head is to be a motto,

We will spit
On Mr *Pitt*

and *other such* d-md rhymes, suited to the uses of the different vessels'. There is no record of any such chamber pots produced by

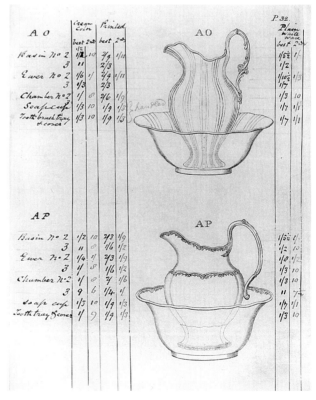

CHAMBER WARE. Plate 31 of the '1817' Catalogue, probably dating from about 1825, showing matching toilet sets from Wedgwood's Queen's ware chamber ware. *Wedgwood Museum*

CHAMBER WARE. Glazed cane earthenware chamber-pot decorated with *Liverpool Birds* pattern transfer-printed in black. Height 5⅝in. c.1860. *Author's collection*

Wedgwood, although political pots of this type were made by other Staffordshire potters.
See: Colour Plate 21

Chambers, Sir William (1726-96)
Born in Stockholm of an English father, William Chambers became a supercargo for the Swedish East India Company and travelled to China, where he studied oriental art, architecture and customs at first hand. Later he visited Italy and became one of the last of the Palladians in a neo-classical* world. In 1757 he published *Designs of Chinese Buildings, Furniture, Dresses, Machines, and Utensils...from the originals drawn in China by Mr Chambers.* Although the latter claim is now known to have been false, his illustrations were influential, as was his *Treatise on Civil Architecture,* published two years later. His most important work of architecture was Somerset House; his most extraordinary, the Pagoda in Kew Gardens. A view of the Kew Pagoda and Footbridge was among the 'Landskips' chosen to decorate the Frog* service in 1773.

Sir William, who was appointed architect to George III, was a figure of some influence and considerable pomposity, who thought little of the work of the brothers Adam* and, while admiring Wedgwood's black basaltes* figures and vases, remained generally unimpressed by jasper*, which he considered too close to Adam's 'filigree'. He nevertheless assisted Wedgwood by lending him models (triton* and probably the 'Capitoline' lions), advising him on the 'real difference between *Urns & Vases'*, and recommending Henry Webber* to him. A portrait medallion* of Sir William Chambers, modelled by Charles Peart* was produced in jasper in 1787.

CHAMBERS, Sir William. Solid blue and white jasper portrait medallion, modelled by Charles Peart. Oval height 3¾in. *Scottish National Portrait Gallery*

Champagne
A pale cane-coloured body introduced in 1930.
See: Coloured Bodies

Champagne Glaze
Deep cane-coloured lead glaze introduced in 1930.
See: Skeaping, John

CHARLOTTE, QUEEN. Creamware teapot with scroll handle transfer-printed with a portrait of Queen Charlotte after an engraving by F.G. Aliamet. Height 5in. c.1761-2. *Mrs R.D. Chellis Collection*

Champion, Richard (1743-91)
Porcelain manufacturer of Bristol who used Cornish feldspathic rock (growan stone) and china clay (kaolin*) to make hard-paste* porcelain*. The enterprise was started by William Cookworthy of Plymouth in 1768 and transferred to Bristol in 1772 with Champion as manager. Cookworthy patented the formula in 1768, obtaining a monopoly of the use of Cornish materials, which hampered the development in Staffordshire of both creamware* and porcelain. In 1773 Champion bought the factory and the patent and next year applied for an extension of the latter for another fifteen years. This was strenuously opposed by the Staffordshire potters, led by Wedgwood, who petitioned the House of Lords. Champion accepted a compromise solution, agreeing to amend his specification to the use of Cornish clay and stone in the manufacture of porcelain only. By 1781 Champion was bankrupt and turned to Wedgwood for assistance. No longer interested in the manufacture of porcelain, Wedgwood helped him to sell his patent to a company of eight Staffordshire potters (later the New Hall* Company of Shelton). Champion procured an appointment as Deputy-Paymaster to the Forces and in 1784 he emigrated to South Carolina, where he died.

Charlotte Mourning at the Tomb of Werther
A late 18th-century subject derived from Goethe's sentimental romance, *The Sorrows of Young Werther*. It depicts a young woman, Charlotte, standing by, or kneeling before, a column surmounted by an urn containing the ashes of her lover, who committed suicide for her sake. The subject was used by Wedgwood for a jasper bas-relief designed by Lady Templetown* in 1787 and modelled by Hackwood* in 1790.

Charlotte, Queen (1744-1818)
Consort of George III, to whom she bore fifteen children, Charlotte Sophia was the daughter of the Duke of Mecklenburg-Strelitz. She

CHARLOTTE, QUEEN. Blue jasper dip portrait medallion from a model by Isaac Gosset. Oval height 3½in. c.1785. *Wedgwood Museum*

CHATELAINE. Cut-steel chatelaine set with two oval blue and white jasper cameos, the pendant watch case set with a miniature on ivory and a jasper cameo of *Apollo*. c.1790.
Wedgwood Museum

took a keen interest in pottery and porcelain and ordered an important service from the Chelsea Porcelain Factory* in 1763. Josiah Wedgwood is said to have presented her with an enamelled creamware caudle* set about 1764 and in 1765 she ordered from Wedgwood 'a complete sett of tea things, with a gold ground & raised flowers upon it in green'. This was a full tea and coffee service for twelve, to include matching candlesticks*, melons* and fruit baskets*. The production of this service, and in particular the gilding*, caused Wedgwood considerable anxiety, but it was safely completed and delivered before the end of the year. The Queen was sufficiently pleased with it to order a creamware dinnerset and to permit Wedgwood to style himself 'Potter to Her Majesty'. Shortly thereafter he named his creamware 'Queen's ware'*, and the Queen's shape (see: Tableware Shapes*) also was named after her. None of the teaset appears to have survived.

Queen Charlotte's portrait appears in three engraved versions on Wedgwood creamware teapots and no less than seven portrait medallions*.
See: Chetwynd, Deborah; Gosset, Isaac; Hackwood, William

Chatelain, Jean Baptiste Claude (1710-71)
Draughtsman and engraver, born in Paris. He served as an officer in the French army before settling in London. Views by his hand, probably supplied by John Boydell*, were used in the decoration of the Frog* service, but Chatelain was never employed by Wedgwood either at Etruria* or at the Chelsea Decorating Studio*. Chatelain died two years before the 'Frog' service was painted.

Chatelaine
Ornamental clasp, worn at a woman's waist, with a chain from which were suspended keys, watch, *étui,* etc. Wedgwood's jasper cameos* were used to ornament silver, Sheffield plate and cut-steel* chatelaines towards the end of the 18th century.

Cheere, John (1709-87)
Younger brother of the celebrated sculptor, Sir Henry Cheere. John Cheere took over John Nost's yard near Green Park, London, together with Nost's stock of moulds for lead figures in 1737. He enjoyed a considerable reputation as a purveyor of statuary in lead and plaster and kept a large stock for the inspection of his customers. A contemporary (1772) description of Cheere's yard compares it to 'a country fair or market, made up of spruce squires, hay makers with rakes in their hands, shepherds and shepherdesses, bagpipers and pipers and fiddlers'. These garden ornaments would have been painted, in the fashion of the day, in naturalistic colours. Of more interest to Wedgwood were Cheere's portrait busts* adapted from the antique or from the work of such eminent sculptors as Coysevox, Roubiliac*, Rysbrack* and Scheemakers*. He supplied Wedgwood with busts of Plato*, Homer* and Aristotle* in 1774, and one of Shakespeare*, on which Hackwood* worked in the following year. Cheere appears to have invented his own method of 'bronzing' his statues and busts, which are nearly black with a subtle polish. In several reference books relating to Wedgwood wares his name is erroneously given as John Cheese.

CHEESE DISH. Basketwork Stilton cheese dish cover, height 9½in., diameter 8in., on a circular footed stand. Cover unmarked. A sketch of this cover appears with Bateman's order of 22 August 1825 for 'Cane basket work 1 nice Stilton cheese dish cover about 8½" diameter'.
Author's collection

Cheese Dishes
Flat dishes with shaped covers for storing and serving cheese, or dishes with sloping rectangular covers for wedges of cheese, do not appear in any of the Wedgwood Queen's ware* catalogues between 1774 and 1880. However, an order from Josiah Bateman* in August 1825 includes 'Cane basket work 1 nice Stilton cheese dish cover about 8½" diameter', and it is evident that tall cylindrical covers of this type were made. The '1880' Catalogue illustrates a barrel-shape Stilton cheese stand and a covered dish for toasted cheese and such dishes were made also in Majolica*. Wedge-shaped cheese dishes were made from the latter part of the 19th century until 1940 in decorated Queen's ware* and the coloured bodies*.

Cheese Hard
See: Leather Hard

Cheese Mould
See: Curd Mould

Chelsea Decorating Studio (1769-74)
Within a month of Bentley's* arrival in London towards the end of 1769, he rented a house in Cheyne Row, Chelsea, which he equipped as a decorating studio, complete with muffle kiln*. He moved David Rhodes* and his painters from the Newport Street showrooms* to this new accommodation and both he and Wedgwood set about recruiting suitable painters, able not only to decorate Queen's ware* services but also to paint the more sophisticated figures and groups on the black 'Etruscan'* vases. Ralph and Catherine Willcox* joined the Chelsea Decorating Studio in December and James Bakewell* followed them from Burslem next May, but Wedgwood was aware of the need to train painters to produce the quality of work that he required. As he wrote to Bentley in May 1770: 'You observe very justly that few hands can be got to paint flowers in the style we want them…*We must make them.* There is no other way.' The need for fine quality was emphasised by the order for the *Husk** service for Catherine* the Great in April 1770, and reinforced by her second order, for the enormous and demanding Frog* service, three years later. Rhodes was instructed to advertise, on behalf of Wedgwood & Bentley, for 'any hands who had been employ'd in painting figures or flowers upon Coaches, Fans, Waiters [trays] or China'.

In addition, the 'Vase-madness' that had broken out in 1769, had greatly increased the demand for 'encaustic'* painted vases and new methods of outlining the designs were tried so that the figures might be filled in by 'A Japaner, Fan or Waiter Painter'. All the most important decoration of black basaltes vases and Queen's ware tablewares was done at the Chelsea Decorating Studio during this period. It was closed in 1774, when the Greek Street showrooms were acquired with sufficient accommodation for the whole of Wedgwood & Bentley's London enterprise.

Chelsea Porcelain Factory
The first English porcelain factory, founded by Nicolas Sprimont and Charles Gouyn, both of Huguenot origin, in 1745 or earlier. The wares fall into three well-marked periods. The first is known as the triangle period from the mark employed, when the principal source of inspiration was French rococo* silver; the second as the raised and red anchor period (1750-56), when the primary influence was that of Meissen*; and finally the gold anchor period, from 1756 onwards, when the styles of Vincennes-Sèvres* were fashionable. Chelsea made the finest porcelain of any factory in England during its lifetime, and at its best the body approached the quality of Sèvres.

In 1769 the factory was advertised for sale with all the plaster moulds in wax, lead or brass, kilns, mills and iron presses. Wedgwood wrote to Bentley: 'The Chelsea models, moulds &c. are to be sold…There's an immense amount of fine things. Later he wrote: 'Pray inquire of Mr Thomas [Sprimont's manager] whether they are determined not to sell less than the whole of the models &c. If so, I do not think it would suit me to purchase. I should be glad if you would send me further particulars of the things at Chelsea.'

The factory was eventually purchased by William Duesbury*, who continued it until 1784, largely as a decorating studio for the Derby* factory.

It has been suggested, mainly on stylistic grounds, that Chelsea engaged painters from Meissen* during the 1750s. There are one or two painters with Germanic names recorded as working at Wedgwood's Chelsea Decorating Studio, who may have been taken on in 1769 when the porcelain factory was closed.

Chemical Wares
The name used to describe all wares, such as mortars* and pestles, retorts, crucibles*, pharmacy cups and syphons, supplied regularly to pharmacists and free of charge to Joseph Priestley*, James Watt* and others for experimental work.

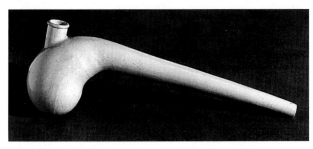

CHEMICAL WARES. Tubulated retort of white retort composition, the outer surface covered with yellow slip, glazed. Length 11½in.
Science Museum, London

Cherokee Clay
In 1745 William Cookworthy (see: Champion, Richard; Porcelain) received a visit from a fellow potter from America, now identified with some certainty as Andrew Duché, who brought with him samples of porcelain* made from kaolin* (china clay) discovered in Virginia. This was clearly the same material as that specified in the first Bow* porcelain patent as 'an Earth, the product of the Cherokee nation in America called by the natives Unaker'.

Late in 1764 specimens of porcelain made from this clay arrived in Bristol from Georgia. 'The material', according to the *Bristol Journal,* appears to be good, but the workmanship is far from being admired.' In 1765 samples of the clay arrived in Bristol, some being sent to Richard Champion and others to the Worcester* Porcelain Factory for testing; but nothing appears to have been done with them.

Wedgwood was aware of this clay at the latest by June 1766, when a Mr Vigor brought samples to Bentley* in Liverpool, which

CHELSEA DECORATING STUDIO. Queen's ware teapot decorated in the style of David Rhodes, probably painted by one of his pupils at the Chelsea studio. Height 4¾in. Unmarked. Wedgwood, c.1771.
Wedgwood Museum

he at once passed on to Wedgwood. Next year, Wedgwood sent Thomas Griffiths* to America to search for it, and, if at all practicable, to obtain a quantity of it. Wedgwood recounted the outcome of this journey in a letter written sixteen years later to W.G. Constable: 'I was so delighted with the appearance of this beautiful raw material…[that] I determined upon sending an agent to the spot to…procure me some of the clay…With much difficulty he procured about six tons, at the expense all together of about £500 but…there was no hope of any future supply upon such terms as could be complied with by any manufactory'. Later in the letter he stated that this clay was the basis of his 'new biscuit porcelain' (jasper*).

'Ayoree' (Cherokee) clay is listed as one of the ingredients of the 'encaustic' colours in Wedgwood's patent specification of 1769, and the use of clay in the pigments is confirmed by his letter written to Bentley in February of the same year. In December 1777 Wedgwood wrote to Bentley: '…it may not be a bad idea to give out that our jaspers are made of the Cherokee clay which I sent an agent into that country on purpose to procure for me, & when the present parcel is out we have no hopes of obtaining more, as it was with the utmost difficulty the natives were prevail'd upon to to part with what we now have…His Majesty [George III*] should see some of these large fine tablets*, & be told this story (which is a true one for I am not Joking) the first, as he has repeatedly enquir'd what I have done with the Cherokee clay…A portion of Cherokee clay is really used in all the jaspers so make what you please of the fact.' It is scarcely possible to believe this claim unless the quantities involved were infinitesimally small (see: Jasper).

On 12 June 1950 a marker was placed on Highway 28, five miles north of Franklin, North Carolina, to mark the position of the pit from which the Cherokee clay was dug. The discovery of Cornish china clay, and relaxations in the terms of Champion's patent, made it unnecessary to continue the search for sources of supply so far afield as North America and China.
See: Blake, John Bradby; Sydney Cove Medallion

Cherry Blossom
See: Prunus Blossom

Chert
A type of quartz which occurs in limestone. It is coarser than flint and more brittle. It is found in several colours: grey, brown, yellow, red and white. It is used as a pulverising agent in certain types of grinding mill. Wedgwood employed chert from Derbyshire for this purpose as a substitute for granite which he found was the cause of black specks in the pulverised material. Wedgwood also made trials with Derbyshire chert which he found whitened his Queen's ware* body, an effect which he put down to the presence of small quantities of limestone in this material.

CHESSMEN. Pencil and ink and wash drawing, 6⅞in. x 20⅜in., of chess pieces by John Flaxman junior. Signed, c.1785.   *Wedgwood Museum*

CHESSMEN. Set of cane and grey stoneware chessmen from the models by Flaxman. Heights 2½in. x 4in. c.1820.   *Christie's, London*

CHESSMEN. Part of the blue and white jasper set designed by Arnold Machin in 1938. Height (king) 5½in.   *Wedgwood Museum*

Chessmen

Chessmen have been a popular product in jasper* since the 18th century, and later sets have been made in other dry bodies*, Queen's ware* and Carrara*. A set was designed by Flaxman* in 1783-4 and his *trompe l'oeil* pen and wash drawing of it (invoiced in 1785 but perhaps drawn earlier) is in the Museum* at Barlaston*. Some of the original wax models have also survived, though only that of a Queen is undamaged. One of the figures of the Queen is generally thought to be a portrait of Sarah Siddons* in the role of Lady Macbeth. According to Barnard*, 130 sets in jasper of various colours were sold between 1785 and 1795. They were still being ordered in 1812.

A set of chessmen was designed by Arnold Machin* in 1940 and produced in basalt*, jasper, Queen's ware and bone china*. Chessmen made in the 18th century, and even reproductions of Flaxman's set made in the late 19th and 20th centuries, have become rare, and single pieces are collected. Machin's set was reproduced in the 1960s and 1970s.
See: Colour Plate 22
See also: Inlaid Ware; Mellor, Thomas

Chestnut Basket

Circular footed basket with domed pierced cover, surmounted by a typical rose knop*, and conforming pierced stand made by Wedgwood in Queen's ware* and illustrated as design no.32 (Plate 9) in the first (1774) Queen's ware Catalogue*. Described in the Catalogue as a Fruit bowl, this shape is known also as an 'Orange basket'. It has been been frequently reproduced in plain Queen's ware and was also made in the second half of the 19th century in coloured bodies and Queen's ware decorated with Majolica* glazes.

Chestnut Pot

A round or oval lidded pot with stand in a moulded basket-weave shape with plaited straw edge. The rose knop* to the lid is not of the early model, the centre being more open in form and the outer petals separately applied. A drawing of this piece appears as shape no.1310 in the earliest surviving Shape Drawing Book*, watermark 1802, but it was probably made at least as early as 1780.

CHESTNUT POT. Queen's ware oval 'Chestnut Pot', height 6¼in. Unmarked. Wedgwood, c.1785. This piece is illustrated as shape no. 1310 in the Shape Drawing Book with watermark for 1802.

Manchester City Art Gallery

Chetwynd, Deborah (fl.1745-80)

Third daughter of William Richard ('Black Will') Chetwynd, Master of the Mint and, from 1767, 3rd Viscount Chetwynd. 'Deb' Chetwynd held an honorary appointment at Court as Seamstress and Laundress to Queen Charlotte* and was instrumental in obtaining for Wedgwood his first royal orders: not only the Queen's teaset in 1765, but also a dinner service for the Prince of Wales four years later. As a native of Staffordshire, she was glad to promote Wedgwood's interests. In gratitude, Josiah paid her the graceful compliment of naming a fine engine-turned and gilt creamware vase (c.1766) the Chetwynd vase. He also sent her one of the first of his 'Etruscan' teapots (1768).

On the death of her father in 1770, Deborah Chetwynd decided to commission a monument in his memory to be placed in Ashley Church, Staffordshire. At her request, 'Athenian'.Stuart* designed an austere inscribed slab surmounted by a cornice and arch. Wedgwood supplied a basaltes* vase, fluted on the lower half of the body, with tall scrolled handles. From surviving correspondence it is clear that Miss Chetwynd was not satisfied with the design of the vase, but the substance of her complaint seems not to have been committed to paper. She visited the Etruria* factory with her sister in August 1771 and 'fell in love with the Faun [sic] colour & carried some of it off with them' (see: Cane Ware).

Cheverton, Benjamin (1794-1876)

English sculptor who showed his work at exhibitions held by the Royal Society of British Artists from 1835 to 1849. He is, however, remembered primarily for his mechanical inventions, most of which were connected in some way with the arts. The most important of these was a machine, patented in 1844, which would cut an accurate reduction of a figure or bust, regardless of size or material. Chiefly this was of value to the makers of Parian*, who were able to make reproductions in miniature without resort to the laborious method of casting and progressive shrinking in firing. Cheverton's original machine is preserved in the Science Museum, London.
See: Pantograph

Ch'ien Lung, Emperor (1736-96)

An Emperor of the Chi'ing dynasty during whose reign the export trade with Europe and America increased considerably in both variety and quantity. In 1793 Lord Macartney, British Ambassador at the Imperial Court, presented Ch'ien Lung with various articles of Western manufacture, including Wedgwood's Queen's ware, which much impressed the Emperor, who had some of these pieces copied in porcelain at the Imperial factory. Creamware shapes sometimes occur in export porcelain thereafter, deriving either from this source or from ware sent to China as patterns by merchants sending orders.

Children, Employment of

There is a long history of the employment of children in the Potteries, particularly in the lighter skilled jobs such as mould-running (carefully moving ware made by potters to drying rooms), wedging clay, burnishing gold or paper-cutting for transfer-printing* (traditionally employment for young girls), as well as the unskilled work of lighting fires to warm the various 'shops', and cleaning floors, work-benches and tools. Of more than 12,000 workers employed in the principal potteries in 1841, twelve per cent were under the age of thirteen and two boys interviewed stated that they had been at work since they were five years old. This position was little changed twenty years later, principally because the family pottery system, in which all members of the family played a part, had been carried into the factories. Families often continued to work together, handing down the same skills through several generations, and Wedgwood's records show many examples of this. In 1841 childrens' wages averaged about two shillings a week.

In 1831 Francis Wedgwood* instituted some reforms, insisting that no boy under ten years old be employed, and thirty years later Godfrey Wedgwood* raised the limit to eleven years of age. By 1875 no child under thirteen was permitted to work more than half-time, to allow time for education, and Clement Wedgwood* personally conducted classes for young boys on the Works during the midday meal break. Although their hours of work had been reduced, their week was still one of fifty-four hours. The proper regulation of the employment of children in the Potteries had to wait until the 20th century.

CHILDREN'S STORY SERIES. *The Sandman,* lithograph on Queen's ware. Diameter 6in. 1971.   *Wedgwood Museum*

Children's Story Series

A series of colourful Queen's ware plates decorated with lithographed* subjects of a kind likely to appeal to small children. The first, dated 1971, is *The Sandman,* after Hans Christian Andersen.

Chimaera

Fabulous monster with the front part of a lion, the middle part of a goat and the hinder part of a dragon. It breathed fire and was named after the volcano of Chimaera in Lydia. It was eventually killed by Bellerophon*. A chimaera is mentioned several times by Eliza Meteyard* *(Memorials,* pp.22 and 58), who suggests that it may have been modelled by Josiah Wedgwood, but the example she illustrates *(Life of Wedgwood,* Vol II, Fig. 42) is a hawk-faced griffin*. No example of a Wedgwood chimaera is known to exist.

Chimneypieces

The chimneypiece as a focal point of the room dates from medieval times, and those in the larger country houses during the 17th and 18th centuries were often especially ornamental and imposing. Wedgwood provided plaques* and tablets* for the decoration of chimneypieces, particularly those of wood, from about 1770. The earliest work of this kind was in either black basaltes* or terracotta*. In 1772 Wedgwood produced basaltes tablets* decorated with encaustic* paintings for a chimneypiece in Sir Watkin Williams Wynn's* house at 20 St James's Square, London, designed by Robert Adam*. The designs for the tablet and two smaller plaques were copied from drawings by Antonio Zucchi* and Sir Watkin paid Wedgwood & Bentley the sum of £26.15.0 for the three. Although it is clear from surviving records that encaustic-painted tablets for chimneypieces were produced in good quantities during the following three years, the making of such pieces was often undertaken more for reasons of prestige and the suitable acknowledgement of patronage than for profit. Wedgwood wrote at the time: I suppose it is very much in Mr Adams's [sic] power to introduce our things into use & am glad to find he seems so well dispos'd to do it'. There is some indication that Adam may have used unglazed enamelled biscuit plaques in other rooms at about this time and he certainly left a number of designs for chimneypieces incorporating Wedgwood & Bentley encaustic-painted tablets, but there is little evidence that he regarded jasper* tablets with favour.

Tablets and plaques made for decorating chimneypieces were oval or rectangular, and they had to be of definite proportions. Throughout 1776 Wedgwood experienced difficulty in making them in jasper. They were prone to a number of defects, of which the most serious were warping and the development of firecracks*

CHIMNEYPIECES. White Carrara marble chimneypiece inset with green and white jasper tablets of trophies, acanthus scrolls and Flaxman's *Apotheosis of Homer* with circular medallions of Flaxman's *Medusa* in the blocks. This fine chimneypiece was made for the Master of the Dublin Mint, c.1785.
Lady Lever Art Gallery, Port Sunlight

during cooling. The jasper tablets were of special importance to Wedgwood & Bentley because their introduction of a new collection promised to provide a different and fashionable market among the architects. It was not accidental that the colours developed in jasper so closely resembled those made popular for interiors by the brothers Adam and James Wyatt.

The outcome of Wedgwood & Bentley's efforts in this direction was disappointing. Neither Adam nor Wyatt showed much enthusiasm for jasper tablets as decoration for chimneypieces, and it was probably at Wedgwood's request that Sir William Bagot*, a loyal patron, sent three tablets to Wyatt with instructions to install them in a chimneypiece at Blithfield, Staffordshire. Wedgwood visited Bagot there in July 1779 and wrote to Bentley: 'Among other great

works of art Sr Wm particularly pointed out the chimney piece to my attention, assuring me at the same time that he esteemed it the best piece in the room'.

The attitude of Sir William Chambers* was no more helpful than Adam's, and, to Josiah's chagrin, Queen Charlotte*, probably advised by Chambers, failed to order any tablets for her palaces. 'We were', Josiah wrote in July 1779, 'really unfortunate in the introduction of our jaspers into public notice, that we could not prevail upon the architects to be godfathers to our child. Instead of taking it by the hand & giving it their benediction, they cursed the poor infant by bell book & candle, & it must have a hard struggle to support itself & rise from under their maledictions'. James Stuart* was a notable exception, ordering tablets for Mrs Montagu's house and leading Josiah to congratulate Bentley on 'the conversion of the Athenian'.

In the 1779 Catalogue* Wedgwood & Bentley advertised 'The large Cameo Pictures and Tablets for chimney-pieces in blue and white jasper [which] have been brought to their present Degree of Perfection with much Labour and Expence to the Artist' but these were for setting into entablatures only. By 1785 Wedgwood was producing complete suites of jasper for chimneypieces, with blocks and ovals for the ends of the entablature and vertical tablets for the jambs as well as horizontal friezes (long rectangular tablets) to set either side of the central tablet. Sadly few of these have survived in their original settings and many of the tablets which appear on the market or are displayed in collectors' cabinets were evidently extracted from 18th-century chimneypieces of wood or marble. Among those that have survived intact are those made for Longton Hall and for the Master of the Dublin Mint, the latter chimneypiece now in the Lady.Lever Art Gallery, Port Sunlight. Others may still lie hidden under layers of paint that have blurred the modelling and disguised the source of the work.

The almost total absence of jasper from production for nearly thirty years removed all possibility of such decoration being used for chimneypieces for much of the 19th century and there is no record of jasper being made for this purpose until 1882, when a new 'peach' colour was introduced especially for the use of Halsey Ricardo* at Buckminster Park. Ricardo designed at least twelve chimneypieces, all heavily inset with Wedgwood jasper, for bedrooms of the house, as well as a complete scheme of redecoration for the dining room, and most of the overmantels were furnished with clock faces, all in the new 'peach' jasper (later named 'Dysart'* green as a compliment to the owner of the house). The house was demolished shortly after World War II and its decorations were dispersed.

Ricardo's work was evidently considered a success and his florid designs certainly made the maximum use of jasper ornaments. Clement Wedgwood* was therefore moved to commission from Ricardo some sketches of jasper plaques 'chiefly of non-

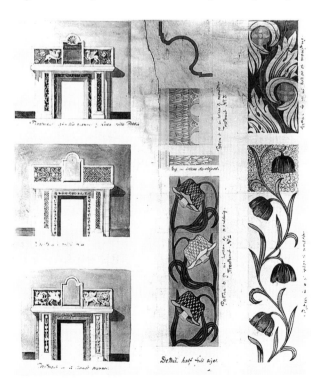

CHIMNEYPIECES. Sketches of chimneypieces attributed to Halsey Ricardo, c.1884, showing 'Classic', 'Luca della Robbia' and Art Nouveau-style Wedgwood tiles used as decoration.
Wedgwood Museum

CHINESE FLOWERS. Black basaltes pillar candlesticks and an inkstandish enamelled with flowers in the *famille-rose* style known as *Chinese Flowers.* c.1820.   *Christie's, New York*

CHINOISERIE. Queen's ware teapot with cross-over handle and rose knop decorated in polychrome enamels with an elongated 'Chinese' figure in front of buildings with 'Chinese-fret' gates. Height 5½in. c.1775.   *Norwich Castle Museum*

classic origin, worked into chimney pieces with strips and tiles'*. The sketches were duly produced and approved but nothing more seems to have come of the project.

In 1961 a quantity of small tablets in pale-blue, green and lilac jasper was produced for the use of a London company making carved pine chimneypieces, but they did not prove sufficiently popular for production to be continued.

Chinese Flowers
The name given to two different types of decoration, both in the famille rose style:
1. *Enamelled Chinese Flowers.* Sprays of flowers enamelled on black basaltes*, cane*, rosso antico* and drab*, c.1815-30. (See also: Capri Ware)
2. *Chinese Flowers.* Small sprays of flowers enamelled on bone china* of the first period. At least twelve versions have been identified, three on printed coloured grounds, and others with a bird added to the design

Chinese Pheasants (Chinese Flowers and Pheasants)
Wedgwood's name for a crowded design enamelled in *famille-rose** colours, consisting of oriental pheasants among flowers. The design appears on large pot-pourri jars* of black basaltes*, cane*, rosso antico*, and drab*, c.1820.

Chinoiserie
Fantasy Chinese scene invented by a European designer, but usually based in a general sense on a Chinese prototype. Design of this type is an expression of the European 'Vision of Cathay', based on an incomplete knowledge and little understanding of Chinese art. It is as Chinese to Europeans as it is evidently European to the Chinese. *Chinoiserie* with a strong element of fantasy was especially popular at Meissen* during the 1720s and 1730s. This later inspired much early porcelain decoration in England and the fashion spread rapidly to the decoration of pottery. The *Willow** pattern is true *chinoiserie* because it is a European invention. *Chinoiseries* in low relief occur on some of Wedgwood's early creamware* decorated with tortoiseshell* and other coloured glazes, but none is attributable to Etruria*. *Chinoiseries* as printed or enamelled decoration on Wedgwood creamware are extremely rare and it is probable that Rhodes* and his painters at the Chelsea Decorating Studio* were not encouraged to paint in this style.

Chinoiserie appeared at Etruria* with the introduction of 'bamboo'* shapes shortly before Bentley's* death in 1780. During the early years of the 19th century there was a revival, led by the

CHINESE PHEASANTS. Black basaltes pot-pourri enamelled with *Chinese Flowers and Pheasants* in the *famille-rose* palette with orange-red lines. Height 11½in. c.1820.   *Christie's, London*

CHINOISERIE. Deep (soup) plate, diameter 10¼in., printed in pale underglaze blue with *Bamboo* pattern. c.1810. *Author's collection*

CHINOISERIE. First period bone china teaware and a dessert plate decorated with pattern no. 622 'Chinese Tigers printed on the glaze in green, gold edge', c.1813. The so-called 'tigers' are fairly accurately drawn Lions of Fo (Buddhist temple guardians). *Wedgwood Museum*

Prince of Wales, of demand for *chinoiserie* decoration, and it was produced at Etruria in the form of *famille-rose*-style* painting on black basaltes*, cane*, rosso antico* and drab*, and Chinese-inspired decoration for earthenware and bone china tablewares (see: Chinese Flowers). The most original of these were the underglaze-blue printed* patterns on Pearl* ware. *Chinoiserie* has survived into the 20th century in such patterns as *Charnwood* and *Cathay*.
See: Colour Plate 23
See also: Japonaiserie; Japonisme

Chintz
Decorative style of patterns enamelled on early Queen's ware*.
See: Rhodes, David

Chisholm, Alexander (1723-1805)
Chemist, and assistant to Dr William Lewis of Kingston-upon-Thames, who was practical chemist to the Society of Arts (Royal Society of Arts*) and author of a number of scientific works. He was employed by Wedgwood in 1781 as his secretary and chemical assistant and also as tutor to his children. In Tom Wedgwood* especially, Chisholm found an apt pupil who took a close interest in chemistry. Many of the entries in Josiah's Commonplace Books* are in Chisholm's handwriting, as are also the whole of the surviving copy of Josiah's Experiment Book* and the crucial 1777 Memorandum dealing with the composition of jasper*. Wedgwood left Chisholm an annuity of £20 with the charge to Josiah II* that he should 'give him any further assistance that he may stand in need of to make the remainder of his life easy and comfortable. Chisholm was chief Works chemist until his retirement and was consulted by Josiah II as late as 1805 concerning possible improvements to the pyrometer*.

Chitqua (c.1750-96)
A Chinese artist who arrived in England from Canton in 1769, returning three years later. He exhibited at the Royal Academy in 1770, in which year he modelled a portrait of Josiah Wedgwood.

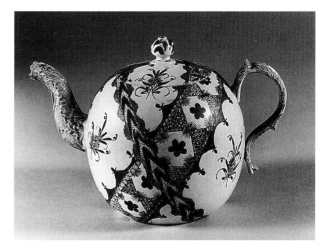

CHINTZ. Creamware teapot enamelled in purple, iron-red, black, green and yellow in a typical geometric banded and diaper pattern with sprays of flowers. Height 5½in. Unmarked. Painted at the Chelsea Decorating Studio, c.1770. *Norwich Castle Museum*

This portrait, probably a bust modelled in clay, has since been lost but Chitqua was noted for his ability to achieve a striking likeness of the sitter. He committed suicide by taking poison.

Chocolate Cup
The first London chocolate house was opened in 1657, and cups and saucers for the service of chocolate became part of the general production of the Staffordshire potter about a century later. Larger than the conventional teacup, the chocolate cup was often provided with two handles and a lid. Wedgwood made chocolate cups in his early creamware and also obtained 'Jocolates' from William Greatbatch* from 1762. A later, and more sophisticated, version of the 'chocolate' is a covered cup, the saucer having a deep well into which the foot of the cup fits. It is often described as a *trembleuse** cup and saucer, since it was convenient when held in a trembling hand. The *trembleuse* cup and saucer for the service of chocolate seems to have been made in England in porcelain from about 1755, and somewhat earlier in France. It was made as a cabinet piece* in jasper* from about 1785. Wedgwood made this type of cup and saucer for a variety of purposes in addition to the service of chocolate: for instance, it was used in the 19th century for broth cups for invalids.

Choiseul-Amboise, Etienne-François, Duc de (1719-85)
Minister of Louis XV who reorganised the army and the navy, developed trade and industry, and made himself popular by opposing the Jesuits. He enjoyed the patronage of Madame de Pompadour, but Madame du Barry succeeded in alienating him from the King. Wedgwood had written to Bentley* in September 1769 of the possibility that they might 'conquer France in Burslem', and before he went into retirement at Chanteloup in 1770, Choiseul received a letter from Josiah Wedgwood which accompanied the gift of a box containing 'an assortment of Urns, & Vases in the antique taste', which he claimed was 'the fruit of a Manufacture lately established here under the imediate protection of the Queen'. Wedgwood went on to admit that, being earthenware, it was not comparable to the wares of Sèvres and that he knew it to be 'counterband in France' (prohibited by Royal Edicts in favour of the Sèvres factory, in which the King was principal shareholder). Moreover, Josiah continued, he did not send it in the hope of opening a trade in creamware between England and France; but since all the other crowned heads of Europe enjoyed creamware, there was surely a possibility of some relaxation of the law, in this as in other matters, in favour of the nobility of France.

The response, if any, to this ingenuous and not strictly truthful attempt has not been preserved, but the French nobility of the time paid very little attention to Royal Edicts of this kind and there is little doubt that they could easily have procured what they wanted. In fact, the Pont-aux-Choux* factory had been making creamware in the English style for some five years when this letter was written, and others in France soon followed.

Cholerton, Herbert A. (1883-55)
Artist, armorial painter and gilder, employed by Wedgwood 1901-55. Cholerton worked on the bone china* service ordered by Theodore Roosevelt for the White House* in 1902. It is printed in gold with the seal of the United States of America in polychrome enamels. His son, Fred Cholerton, painted prestige patterns, especially those with raised gold patterns (e.g.*Black Astbury)* from 1927 to 1980.

Christie, James, The Elder (1730-1803). Christie's
Auctioneer in Pall Mall, London, 1766-1803, and founder of the famous firm of Christie, Manson & Woods. Wedgwood referred to him as 'Mr Christy'. In Wedgwood's day the firm was Christie & Ansell (Robert Ansell, partner 1777-84). The firm was responsible for the valuations of the properties of Sir William Chambers*, Sir Joshua Reynolds* and Johann Zoffany, among many others, and for the valuation and attribution of the Houghton pictures (Walpole collection) sold to Catherine II* of Russia in 1778.

By 1780, when Bentley* died, the firm's reputation was established and Christie & Ansell were the natural choice to sell by auction the joint stock of ornamental wares belonging to the Wedgwood & Bentley partnership. The sale was held in 1781 and the priced catalogue, preserved in Christie's archives, is one of the most valuable of existing records of Wedgwood & Bentley period production.

James Christie was described by a contemporary as 'courteous, friendly and hospitable in private life – held in great esteem by his numerous friends among whom there were many of high rank'.

Christmas Plates and Mugs
Pale-blue and white jasper* plates, 8in. in diameter, with centre relief ornament of a famous British scene or building and holly-leaf border. Each plate has the word 'CHRISTMAS' and the date moulded in blue relief. The first plate, with a centre ornament of Windsor Castle, was produced in 1969. In 1978 a limited edition of 10,000 plates in three-colour jasper (Portland blue, pale-blue and white) was issued featuring ten miniature bas-reliefs* of the scenes used for each annual plate since 1969 with a gold inscription. Pale-blue and white jasper Christmas mugs with similar ornaments have been issued since 1971. The first was ornamented with a view of Piccadilly Circus.
See: Limited Editions

Chrome Green
The first of the chromium colours to be introduced, c.1795, chrome green is derived from chromium oxide. It yields an opaque colour, variable in shade and more yellow in appearance than copper green, which inclines to blue. It has been popular with manufacturers since the beginning of the 19th century and is often used in glazes, when it yields a distinct yellowish-green. Quantities of up to five per cent mixed with clay or slip* give different shades of grey-green, such as Celadon*.

CHRISTMAS MUGS. Following the success of the Christmas plates, introduced in 1969, Wedgwood began, in 1971, a series of Christmas mugs. The first is ornamented with a view of Piccadilly Circus.
Wedgwood Museum

CHRISTMAS PLATES. Tenth anniversary three-colour jasper Christmas plate ornamented with reliefs from the previous issues. 1978.
Wedgwood Museum

Chubbard, Mr (fl.1767)
Modeller given trial employment by Bentley* in Liverpool towards the end of 1767. His attempts at modelling were ridiculed by Josiah Wedgwood in terms which are revealing of his own standards: 'The Terrine [tureen] is capitally defective in point of truth in the form of the *ends* and *sides,* which do not at all correspond with each other, there is the same fault in the ornaments & likewise in the top of the dish, & the Cover. The carv'd ornaments are not finish'd, & the whole shows such a want of the *Masterliness* necessary.' Although deemed to be 'well-dispos'd to do his best', Chubbard was reckoned by Wedgwood to require a seven-year apprenticeship and he was tactfully paid off. It is likely that he was related to the Thomas Chubbard (fl.1770-87) of Liverpool who exhibited paintings, principally landscapes, in Liverpool from 1784.

Churchill, Sir Winston Leonard Spencer K.G., O.M. (1874-1965)
A portrait medallion* of Churchill by Arnold Machin* (a companion to one of F.D. Roosevelt by the same artist) was reproduced as bas-relief decoration to an embossed Queen's ware* patriotic mug issued in 1941. The portrait was reproduced as a jasper medallion in 1945. Machin's bust of Churchill, height 10¼in., was produced in Queen's ware in 1953 and this was reduced for a black basalt* bust, height 6¾in., issued in a limited edition of 750 to commemorate the centenary of Churchill's birth. Also issued in 1974 were a jasper portrait medallion and cameo glass goblet (both in editions of 1,000) and various smaller objects ornamented with a bas-relief portrait reduced from Machin's original model.

Churchyard Works
A small pottery occupied and worked by the Wedgwood family from 1656, when Josiah Wedgwood's great-grandfather first took possession of it, and inherited by Josiah's eldest brother in 1739. Josiah served his apprenticeship there, completed in 1749. After Wedgwood's removal of his factory to Etruria*, the Churchyard Works were taken over by his cousin, Joseph, who worked them until 1795, when they were sold to Thomas Green. On his bankruptcy in 1811, they passed to John Moseley, who made basaltes in the Wedgwood style, impressed MOSELEY.

Churns
Milk churns, complete with bow or wheel construction woodwork, were made in eight sizes in Queen's ware as part of Wedgwood's Dairy ware*. A cream-coloured milk churn, transfer-printed* in brown and coloured underglaze in blue, brown, pink, orange and green, was produced c.1905.

CIGARETTE JAR AND LIGHTER SET. Basalt smoker's set, the jar and lighter base modelled to stack as a single cylinder, designed by Peter Wall for the Design '63 Exhibition, shown with engine-turned salt and pepper shakers by Robert Minkin. 1963.   *Author's collection*

Cicero, Marcus Tullius (106-43 B.C)
Roman orator and statesman, elected consul in 63 BC. As a statesman he was remarkable for his habitual errors of judgement. Some years after the murder of Julius Caesar*, he became the acknowledged leader of the republican party and attacked Mark Antony* in a series of fourteen orations known as the *Philippics.* Antony had him killed in 43 BC. Cicero's extensive letters and philosophical writings have in great part survived.
Wedgwood subjects:
Cicero, bust, 22in., supplied by Hoskins & Grant*, 1775; bust, 10-11½in., 1777
Cicero, portrait medallion 3in. x 2½in., 1777 (cameo 1773)

Cigarette Jar and Lighter Set (Smokers' Set)
Cylindrical cigarette jar and lighter sets, made in three pieces to stack as a single cylinder (the lid common to both the cigarette jar and the lighter base) and fitted with Ronson lighters were made in 1963 for the 'Design '63'* exhibition in London. The sets were produced in basalt*, ornamented with a new bas-relief designed by Peter Wall*, in gold-printed basalt, and in two silk-screen* printed patterns on bone china*

Cipriani, Giovanni Batista RA (1727?-88)
Painter, designer and engraver, born in Florence. He removed to London in 1753 and worked there for the rest of his life, becoming a member of the Royal Academy. He designed and painted ceilings for Robert Adam* and collaborated with Bartolozzi*, who produced sensitive engravings of much of his work. Sir William Hamilton* commissioned from him drawings of the Portland vase* which were engraved by Bartolozzi. Erasmus Darwin* considered using one of Bartolozzi's engravings of the vase to illustrate *The Botanic Garden* (part 2, 1791) but, on the advice of his publisher that it was 'very imperfect', commissioned a fresh drawing from William Blake*. An unidentified sacrifice* subject, taken from a Bartolozzi engraving after Cipriani and painted in encaustic* colours on a black basaltes* tablet* (probably intended as decoration for a chimneypiece*), is in the British Museum. Cipriani drew illustrations for Sir William Chambers's* *Treatise on Civil Architecture,* including the figures of 'Persians and Caryatids' later copied by Wedgwood for his 'Michelangelo' lamp* (though his immediate source was probably casts from Flaxman*).

Citharist
The Crowning of a Citharist
A Victorious Citharist
See: Apotheosis of Homer

Clam Dish
See: Oyster Dish

CLEOPATRA. Wedgwood & Bentley solid pale blue and white jasper portrait medallion of Cleopatra, modelled in 1775, probably by Hackwood, as a companion to the portrait of Mark Antony. Oval height 3¼in. c.1777.
   Dwight & Lucille Beeson Collection, Birmingham Museum, Alabama

Clarke, Esau (fl.1758-86)
Merchant, and Wedgwood's agent in Dublin from 1778, when Wedgwood closed his own Dublin showroom and warehouse. He was driven out of business by Wedgwood's opposition to the Irish Trade Treaty*. Josiah described him as 'a timerous but very safe & good man'.
See: General Chamber of Manufacturers

Classicism
Classical art is based on the principles of ancient Greek and Roman art and architecture, particularly in such aspects as mathematically-expressed rules of proportion by which the parts were related to the whole, as much in the elements of a building as in the measurements of the human body. This necessarily led to certain conventions in the representation of the subjects of classical art, and one of its principal manifestations was a well-marked symmetry in ornament, both in form and disposition. Asymmetry (deliberate departures from symmetry) marks most forms of non-classical art; for instance, the rococo*, Gothic*, and some Oriental styles, notably Japanese (see: Japonisme*). A Roman temple was always built to a fixed plan laid down before the foundations. The height, diameter and spacing of columns adhered to rules which were first enunciated by Vitruvius some time after 46 BC. He wrote a poor treatise on architecture, much of it borrowed from Greek sources, which survived when other, better books failed to do so. Gothic churches adhered to no fixed plan and were often drastically altered during the course of construction. Gothic comprehended no system of proportion, although an English rural architect, Batty Langley, attempted to impose one in the 18th century.
   Classical art is European mainstream art, although from time to time other, non-classical, styles have arisen, such as Gothic (12th to 16th centuries), which re-echoed some aspects of Islamic architecture in such features as the pointed arch and the arcade, and became widespread in northern Europe, even invading the northern towns of classical Italy.
   The decay of Gothic art was followed by the rebirth of classicism, referred to as the Renaissance. Classical principles, and the

CLOCK CASES. Green jasper dip clock case ornamented with relief figures of 'Father Time' and children from the 'Domestic Employment' series. Height 8in. c.1885. *Wedgwood Museum*

CLOCK CASES. Three-colour jasper clock case, ornamented with blue 'Sacrifice' figures and green borders on a white ground, the form based on the popular marble clocks of the period. c.1905.
Sotheby's, London

vocabulary of classical ornament, were revived with some significant differences. The model for the Renaissance artist was Rome; for the neo-classical* artist it was often Pompeii* and Herculaneum*, provincial rather than metropolitan, and for the later Empire style the model was Greek rather than Roman. Roman classicism was, of course, heavily influenced by Greek and Etruscan art, and the work of the Etruscans, including their later pottery, was much influenced by Greece.

Neo-classicism, dating from the middle of the 18th century, followed an interregnum represented by some aspects of the baroque style, the rococo and the early influence of China and Japan, as well as a brief Gothic revival shortly before mid-century. The close of the Empire period (a style marked by a return to Grecian and metropolitan models) about 1830, marked the beginning of 19th-century eclecticism. This was a view of art which assumed that one style was as good as another and that all might be mixed freely and it led to such solecisms as Minton's* classical vase on a Gothic arcaded pedestal. Classicism then tended to become one style among many, but it was a style to which Wedgwood remained largely faithful, and it accounts for the fact that although the factory produced some wares the design of which was no better than that of many of its competitors, a good deal of work, especially in Queen's ware*, was far ahead of its time in qualities of design, and its classical bias accounts to a great extent for its continued popularity in the United States, where classical styles (such as the Federal style) have always dominated the scene.
See: Gothic; Neo-classical Style; Romantic Style.

Clay
Hydrated silicate of aluminium formed from the decomposition of feldspar*. Kaolin*, or china clay, is white burning, but most other clays burn from light brown to red due to the presence of iron as an impurity. A few clays are grey after firing. Clays may be stained by the addition of metallic oxides, such as cobalt* or manganese*, commonly used as pottery colours. Clay is plastic when it contains water. It shrinks and becomes hard when dry, and can be reduced to a fine powder when in this state. Dry clay may be reconstituted by the addition of water, but, if it is fired, point-to-point attachment of the particles takes place and this state is irreversible. Although clays may be fired to this state at a comparatively low temperature, they are also refractory, and will only fuse at about 1600°C, a temperature above that of feldspar and the fusible rocks (such as barium sulphate*) used in the manufacture of fine stonewares* and porcelain*. Clay is always found with various impurities, most of which must be removed before it is fit for use in the manufacture of pottery.
See also: Cherokee Clay; Vitrification

Clay, Henry (fl.1750-1802)
Japanner, of Newhall Street, Birmingham, who took out, in 1772, a patent for the manufacture of 'panels from paper of several thicknesses dried in a hot stove for furniture etc.', a product which he called 'paper ware' to distinguish it from 'true' *papier mâché*

produced from pulped paper. Highly varnished panels of Clay's paper ware were used for trays, tables, cabinets, screens, bookcases and chairs as well as for smaller decorative objects, such as writing boxes and tea caddies which were often inset with Wedgwood cameos* or medallions*. He is first mentioned in Wedgwood's correspondence in May 1776. Clay retired from business in 1802 and his firm was taken over, in 1816, by Jennens & Bettridge.

Cleopatra
The eldest daughter of Ptolemy Auletes. Her father appointed her co-heir with her brother Ptolemy, whom she was to marry according to the custom of the Egyptian royal house. She acceded in 51 BC but was expelled by her brother's guardians. She appealed to Julius Caesar*, who replaced her on the throne. She bore him a son, Caesarion. After Caesar's death, she met Mark Antony* and accompanied him to the battle of Actium in 31 BC, but by withdrawing her fleet from the battle she sealed his fate. She opened negotiations with Augustus and caused rumours of her death to be spread abroad. Antony, hearing these, stabbed himself and, overcome by remorse, Cleopatra poisoned herself with the bite from an asp. After her death, Caesarion was executed by order of Augustus.
Wedgwood subjects:
Cleopatra, portrait medallion, 1773, remodelled, probably by Hackwood*, 1775. Companion portrait to one of Mark Antony
Cleopatra, bust 7-8in., probably supplied by Hoskins & Grant*, 1775
Cleopatra (seated on a rock), figure 9½in., produced in Carrara* 1849, also in basaltes
Cleopatra before Augustus, white terracotta* plaque painted *en grisaille* after Thomas Burke's engraving, c.1786, from the painting by Angelica.Kauffmann*

Clock Cases
The fashion, during the last quarter of the 18th century, for elaborately decorated clock cases was inspired by contemporary French styles. Many of these were made from gilt metal and marble or alabaster, often with the addition of ceramic ornament. Among the most common ornaments were Sèvres* porcelain and Wedgwood jasper* medallions and a fine clock by Benjamin Vulliamy* embellished in this manner is in the British Museum. Vulliamy also made clocks the ornamental cases of which were mounted with biscuit* porcelain figures made at Derby*, and it is now known that white jasper figures made by Wedgwood were used for the same purpose. Mounted in this manner, the difference between biscuit porcelain and white jasper figures is not immediately apparent. In the case of the latter, the mark is concealed on the sole of the foot and may be seen only when the figure is detached from its mount.

Wedgwood had seen in 1776 the profitable business being done by Boulton* in French-style ormolu* clocks and he had no doubt seen also some of the porcelain clock cases being produced by Sèvres in the form of ovoid vases with a movement inset into the body. There is evidence that Wedgwood experimented with

CLODION. Black basaltes 'Faun' and 'Bacchante' after models by Clodion. Height 15⅜in., c.1860.   *Mr & Mrs David Zeitlin Collection*

adapting his own vases for this purpose. He experimented also with watch stands*, four being sent to London in 1774. An exceptionally fine jasper clock case showing *Peace Destroying the Implements of War* (probably to celebrate the Treaty of Amiens in 1802) is in the collections of the Merseyside Museums at Liverpool.

In the 1880s clock cases with arched tops were made in jasper of various colours ornamented with the words 'TEMPUS FUGIT' and relief figures of 'Father Time', and Wedgwood Pearl* ware panels painted in enamel colours were supplied to be inset in gilt bronze clock cases. Three-colour jasper clock cases were produced about 1905, the simple rectangular shape based on that of marble cases popular at the time. Cases of a similar shape were reintroduced in 1965 and are still in production.
See: Watch-holder Vase

Clodion, Claude Michel (1738-1814)

French sculptor, born Claude Michel, in Nancy, later assuming the name Clodion. At the age of sixteen he moved to Paris, where he studied under L.S. Adam, a relation of his mother's, and Pigalle*. After nine years in Rome, executing commissions for the Empress Catherine II* and other patrons, he returned to Paris, but his work – generally small terracotta figures and bas-reliefs* of nymphs and satyrs treated with frank sensuality – did not recommend him for recognition by the Academy until 1793, when he became an Associate. Later he successfully changed his style to conform more nearly to the fashion for Greek sculpture and worked on the Calonne de la Grande Armée and the Arc de Triomphe de Carrousel. In 1798 he returned to Nancy and provided models for the Niderviller porcelain factory.
Wedgwood subjects:

Bacchante, figure 15in. } Catalogued in 1849 for Carrara* but
Faun, figure 15in. } made also in black basaltes* and
Majolica*. (Terracotta examples of these figures are at
Waddesdon Manor, Buckinghamshire *(National Trust)*

Bacchanalian Sacrifice } 'long square' tablets 9in. x 21in., nos
Bacchanalian Triumph } 71 and 70 respectively in 1773
Catalogue*

The *Wine* and *Water* ewers produced from casts supplied by Flaxman* in 1775 were after models by Clodion, but the form of the ewers suggests an earlier source, probably renaissance metalwork.

Closet Ware

Also known as Sanitary ware: including such objects as closet pans, stool pans and urinals. The Etruria* factory appears to have been among the first to manufacture ceramic closet pans, and closet ware, in a body mixed especially for it, was made there throughout the 19th century. Pans were available in a remarkable array of shapes, many of which are illustrated in the 1802 Shape Drawing Book*, and could be ordered individually to fit specified dimensions. In September 1827 Bateman* sent in an order for a ship's closet 'nearest to those dimensions given' and ten years later he obtained an order for twelve closet pans of specified dimensions 'for the Queen's Palace Buckingham House' (occupied in that year, on the accession of Queen Victoria, for the first time as a regular royal residence), adding 'as soon as these are sent the Old ones will be all taken up'. By 1818, perhaps earlier, underglaze-blue printed* patterns were being used for the decoration of closet

CLOSET WARE. Pearl ware closet pan decorated with *Camellia* pattern printed in underglaze blue. Oval length of bowl (interior) 16½in. c.1850.   *Wedgwood Museum*

pans, and later decoration included 'Marble', 'Marble gilt' and 'Mulberry marble' with 'plug basins' to match. By 1832 the closet ware body had been replaced by 'White best' and ten years later the decoration available included bands of colour – Green, Blue, Red, Celeste or Fawn – with gold lines, all with basins, closet handles and chamber ware* to match. Production of closet ware ceased in the 1930s.

Club (Vine) Jug
Jug of vase shape, with sloping shoulders, pinched lip and arching handle, made in several sizes and all Wedgwood ceramic bodies. Examples in the dry bodies* are often ornamented with vine bas-relief around the collar. Queen's ware jugs were moulded all-over with a vine in low relief, often decorated with coloured glazes.

Coach Pot
See: Bourdalou

Coade Stone
Although Coade's Artificial Stone Works in Lambeth was not the first business to manufacture artificial stone in London, it was the largest. Founded in 1769, the manufactory was managed by Mrs Eleanor Coade, from 1799 in partnership with John Sealy, her cousin. Several modellers and sculptors worked alike for her and for Wedgwood, including Voyez*, De Vaere* and Flaxman*, and the two manufacturers made copies of the work of other sculptors in common. The works closed in 1836.

Coade's success was due largely to the secret composition of the artificial stone, This was a ceramic stoneware, infinitely superior in quality to modern cement or 'reconstituted stone' compositions: fine textured, creamy-white in colour (though it could be stained to produce shades of yellow, grey or pink to tone with the stone or brick of a building) and durable. It was thus better suited to classical ornament than the later red terracotta so popular with Victorian architects.

Coade competed very successfully with Wedgwood in the sale of chimneypiece ornaments, possibly because articles of similar appearance and durability could be produced in Coade stone at lower cost than Wedgwood's jasper. Certain of Wedgwood's tablets* and plaques*, including *Bacchanalian Triumph* after Clodion, were made also by Coade but it is not certain which of the models is the earlier.

Coalport
Porcelain factory established in 1795 by John Rose, previously an apprentice at the Caughley pottery, which he acquired in 1799. From 1798 Rose was one of the pioneers of the manufacture of bone china*. At first this was marred by uneven quality and iron specks, but by 1820 Rose had achieved a fine white body with creamy translucency. In 1820 he introduced a hard transparent leadless glaze. During the 19th century the firm's china became particularly notable for flower-encrusted rococo* shapes and for reproductions or copies of large and magnificent Sèvres* and Meissen* vases of a century earlier. A small quantity of Parian* was made from about 1845. In 1967, when the name of Coalport was especially noted for the production of sentimental, but well-modelled and painted, figures as well as bone china tablewares of high quality, the firm was acquired by Wedgwood as part of the Wedgwood Group*.

Cobalt Oxide
The most commonly used colouring oxide, yielding a distinctive blue which is used underglaze, onglaze, for colouring glazes, and for staining slips and bodies. It appears to have been used first in Persia about the 10th century and it was known in China about a century later. Wedgwood used it particularly for colouring jasper*. Cobalt oxide was used in the form of smalt*. Because at this period the best quality cobalt was found in Saxony, in quantities kept small by the prohibition or rigorous control of exports, and smuggling was punishable by death, it was always both scarce and costly. In 1777 Josiah was paying three guineas a pound for it but wrote nevertheless: 'it is worth all the money'. Later, native deposits were found in Cornwall, but Josiah I always depended upon imported supplies.

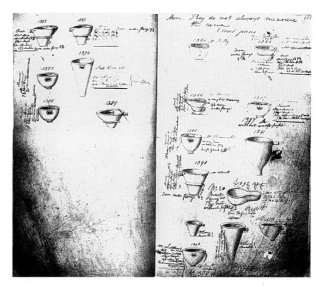

CLOSET WARE. Page from a mid-19th-century drawing book showing varied designs of Wedgwood closet pans, many of which were available with printed decoration. *Wedgwood Museum*

Codes and Formulae
The theft of manufacturing secrets was a well-established commercial practice in the 18th century. All manufacturers who employed new or significantly improved techniques were compelled to guard against industrial spies, and Wedgwood was already taking precautions against them during his partnership with Thomas Whieldon*. This partnership was undoubtedly offered to Wedgwood because, even as early as 1754, he had achieved some reputation for experiment which led to useful improvements in the ware and in methods of manufacturing. It is said that Wedgwood was able to insist that any improvements that he introduced should remain his property which he was not obliged to share, but there is no evidence for this statement. His *Experiment Book* belonging to the end of this period survives in the Wedgwood Museum* at Barlaston* and it records how he was induced 'to try for some more solid improvements, as well in the *Body*, as the *Glazes*, the *Colours*, & the *Forms*, of the articles of our manufacture.' He formulated an elaborate code to express the different degrees of heat to which trial pieces had been subjected: GO meant glost oven, and BO the biscuit oven; the letters B, M or T prefixed meant bottom, middle or top; so TBO meant top of the biscuit oven (not to be confused with T°, which is thought by some to be the mark of the modeller, Tebo*). Experiments were ranged in classes and sections, the first, second or third class being indicated by one, two or three dots respectively, and the appropriate section being indicated by a figure. Every material used by Wedgwood for experiment or production was allocated a code number, further numbers being added through the years as more materials were tried.

One of the formulae, set out numerically, is characteristic:

$$\frac{7}{} \quad \frac{3}{120} \quad \frac{17}{30} \quad \frac{33}{9}$$

This is the seventh experiment on the first page. The numbers above the line, in black ink, are materials, disguised, as usual, by their code numbers; those below the line, in red ink, are quantities. This is the formula for a copper green glaze* to be used on cream-colour* biscuit* and it is dated 23 March 1759. The date makes it doubtful that this glaze was ever used while Wedgwood was working with Whieldon, since the partnership was dissolved in April 1759 and Josiah's cousin ('Useful') Thomas Wedgwood* agreed to serve him as a journeyman from 1 May.

Little more than a year after his marriage to Sarah Wedgwood* in January 1764, Josiah was able to report to his brother: 'Sally is my chief helpmate…She hath learnt my characters, at least to write them, but can scarcely read them at present.' It is unlikely that the code was revealed to many, but Bentley* was certainly one and it would be sensible to assume that 'Useful' Thomas and, somewhat later, Tom Byerley* were among others who were required to be familiar with it. Despite Wedgwood's efforts to protect his manufacturing secrets, they were acquired by his rivals. He took out

CODES AND FORMULAE.
Trials of the rosso antico body showing Wedgwood's use of codes to designate the placing of trial pieces in the oven: MBO for Middle of Biscuit Oven; TTBO for Tip Top of Biscuit Oven, etc.
Wedgwood Museum

only one patent – for encaustic painting* – and James Neale* and Humphrey Palmer*, who infringed it, proved of how little value a patent could be in the 18th century when others were sufficiently unscrupulous to disregard it. Wedgwood eventually compromised and withdrew his action against Palmer. After this experience, he lost confidence in patents and relied more than ever upon secrecy.

This became especially marked when the trials for jasper* were nearing success. In the autumn of 1774 Wedgwood journeyed into Derbyshire in search of minerals. There he discovered cawk* or barium sulphate* (74 in Wedgwood's code and called 'radix jasperini'* in his letters to Bentley), which proved superior to the 'spaith fusible' (see: Spath) with which he was experimenting. He disclosed the formula of jasper to Bentley in February 1776. 'You desire to know a mixture', he wrote guardedly to his partner in London, always conscious of the insecurity of the mail service: 'Will you be content to have part of it now & the remainder another time – it is too precious to reveal all at once.' The figures that followed were Josiah's code numbers and the identifications were added by Bentley in French. Three days later, Josiah sent him the quantities: 'one of 17 six of 74 three of 22 & ¼ of 20.'

Before the end of the 18th century, copying Wedgwood had become a growth industry, not only in Staffordshire but throughout Europe, but by the time of Josiah's death the use of codes and elaborate precautions to maintain secrecy were becoming less vital than they had been at the outset, when Wedgwood's success depended to a large extent on keeping ahead of his rivals and exploiting his improvements and innovations undisturbed for a few years.

Such secrecy was not universally approved, probably because the need for it was never properly explained to those who considered that manufacturing processes should be public property, used for more general benefit. William Evans, a remarkable Welshman who took a leading part in forming a union (the United Branches of Operative Potters) which became a national organisation, wrote in 1846: 'Time was, when most of the Handicrafts of this country were secrets, confined in the possession of those whom Fortune, or Capital had placed in the position of EMPLOYERS. Few amongst the working, or operative class, could boast of the knowledge of the ingredients of processes, by which the most beautiful articles of British Manufacture have been brought into existence. Indeed, it has been a matter of legal prosecution for an apprentice or adult mechanic, having discovered some of the *secrets* of his profession, to divulge the same in opposition to the expressed wish or sanction of his employer. His state of mental darkness is fast passing away…Working men no longer remain the mere physical manipulators of the craftily compounded materials of hidden process and hoarded up recipes.' The existence of several notebooks kept by skilled workmen at Etruria* in the 19th century provides evidence that formulae were no longer the closely guarded secrets that they had been in the previous century, but the principal reason for this was that all but the most recent innovations were already widely known and all the largest manufacturers were, by then, using broadly the same processes.

Nevertheless, manufacturers still have their secrets, it is still illegal for an employee to disclose them, and the business of industrial espionage* is more widespread and more ruthless than ever it was in the 18th or 19th centuries. The difference, today, is that the spies are as likely to be employed by governments as by rival manufacturers.

Coffee Biggin

Forerunner of the filter-method coffeepot, and made in Queen's ware*, but more especially in the early 19th-century drab*, cane* and white 'porcelain'* (stoneware). The biggin consists of a standard teapot and a cylindrical cup (without handle), shaped and perforated at the base. The cup rests in the open top of the teapot, the teapot lid being used as a cover for the whole. Coffee, made by pouring boiling water on to the measured grounds in the cup, drips slowly into the pot below, The cup is then removed, and the lid replaced on the teapot. The biggin was invented in 1803 and Wedgwood produced versions of it in Queen's ware and the dry bodies from about 1805.
See: Tea and Coffee Infuser

Coffee Cans

Straight-sided cylindrical cups, about 2½in. high, for the service of coffee. The shape was copied from Sèvres by a number of English factories for cups of exceptional quality for display as 'cabinet'* pieces. They date from the last quarter of the 18th century. Wedgwood made them in white jasper* ornamented with various colours, in solid-colour jasper and in jasper dip. A large-size can made in porcelain at Derby* was described as a breakfast can and for these no saucers were provided. In 1773 a letter from Wedgwood to Bentley* records the preparation of coffee cans (no doubt of Queen's ware*) for the Turkish market. Although other shapes have been introduced, the can shape, generally in a size smaller than that made for display in cabinets) has remained the most popular for coffee sets in bone china*, Queen's ware, basaltes* and jasper.

Cold Painting

Painting in unfired colour, a practice quite common in some of the early porcelain factories during the first years of their existence. In England, enamelling on porcelain was not practicable until about 1750, when William Duesbury*, later proprietor of the Derby* factory, had an enamelling studio in London. Wares decorated in 'cold' colour (oil paint or coloured varnish) are now usually white after years of washing and handling, although slight traces of paint sometimes remain. There is no record that Wedgwood ever employed 'cold' colour for anything but experimental work. The background of early white biscuit* cameos* was painted with watercolour independently and, experimentally, by Wedgwood also. Other wares, mostly vases or bough pots*, painted in this manner do exist, but they are rare. They are the work of amateur painters, usually ladies. A letter to the factory dated 1 March 1796 contains a relevant request: 'The Marchioness of Blandford wishes you to send (along with the things already bespoke) a small vase for Lady's [*sic*] to paint on. What her ladyship means is made of a white composition'. Since this was written before the introduction of White ware*, the 'white composition' ordered was probably the white terracotta* biscuit.

Colonial Shape
See: Tableware Shapes

Coloured Bodies

Technically a coloured body is any ceramic body that has been stained by mixing it with ochreous earths or metal oxides so that it is of a homogeneous colour. By this definition, all the dry bodies* – black basaltes*, solid-colour jasper*, cane*, rosso antico* and drab* stoneware – and all the various coloured stonewares used for ornament are coloured bodies, as also are the stained bone china* bodies, notably *Alpine Pink*, but it is the accepted custom to use this description only for the stained and glazed (Queen's ware) earthenwares: drabware, *Celadon*, *Lavender*, *Windsor Grey* and the cane-coloured *Champagne* or *Honey Buff*.

The first of these to be introduced was drabware (not to be confused with the concurrent drab stoneware described as 'porcelain'). A beautiful saltglazed 'drabware' had been made in Staffordshire from about 1720 and this was followed by a stained drab earthenware with stamped or sprigged* ornament. Josiah made some experiments for a drab body between 1759 and 1774 but there is no evidence of its production during his lifetime. The first record of Wedgwood's drabware appears in 1811, when Bateman commented that the samples sent to him were too dark, that the interiors of hollow wares* should be glazed in white, and that the gold edge-line should be broader. His advice was taken, and from 1812 there was regular production of tea, coffee and breakfast services, sets of jugs in various shapes, candlesticks and toy* sets, with some less common objects such as incense burners* and pyrophorous vases*. White interiors were not provided by the use of an opaque white glaze as Bateman had suggested but by a wash of white slip* applied before glazing. The use of 'smalt* stain' added an attractive pale blue-green ('duck-egg') tint to the wash.

Early drabware was used also as a ground for transfer-printed* and bat-printed* sporting subjects and landscapes in black, red or purple about 1817 and for *famille-rose**-style enamelling. A few simple enamelled patterns were produced on drabware early in the 20th century. Production continued into the 1920s and, after an interval of nearly fifty years, drabware was reintroduced for Tiffany's, New York, in the 1970s.

Sage was a coloured body made in small quantities in the 1870s. Little is known about it, though its name is indicative of its colour, and it was evidently made only for a very short period. The range of pieces probably coincided nearly with drabware, but no detailed records have been found.

The *Lavender* body was certainly in production by 1858 and, although confirming evidence is lacking, it is most likely that *Celadon* was introduced at about the same time. The latter has previously been assigned to 1805, but this is an error, based on the production of a grey-green stoneware for ornaments at that date. Minton* had produced a grey-green earthenware slip* for the decoration of vases by 1845, and a grey-blue body for jugs a few years later, and these are likely to have been the inspiration for Wedgwood's similar colours. Although both of these coloured bodies were made in the 19th century, records of production are sparse, and it was not until the 20th century that they were made in large quantities on Traditional tableware shapes*. In the 1930s they were made also as slipware to produce two-colour variants (with cream-colour* rims, handles, knops* and interiors) known as

COLOURED BODIES. Covered milk jug of drabware with white slip interior, creamware crabstock handles and applied ornament touched in with green and blue. Height 4¾in. Unmarked. Staffordshire, c.1750.
Temple Newsam House, Leeds

Wintergreen and *Summer Sky*. Cane-coloured bodies, *Champagne* and *Honey Buff* (the latter for Heal's store in London's Tottenham Court Road), were added in 1930, and this colour was chosen for the Cadbury Bournvita set* in 1933. At about the same period, some distinctive *Celadon* and cane-coloured art-wares decorated with handpainted polychrome and lustre patterns were introduced (see: Hispano-Moresque Designs).

After World War II, the Traditional shapes were reintroduced and a new colour, *Windsor Grey*, was created in 1953. This was inspired by the earlier production of the *Oriental* body, primarily for export to France in 1912. This greenish-grey body lasted only a few years and was superseded by a new *Grey* body, which lasted until 1940.

The two-colour clay patterns were transferred to Barlaston shape (see: Tableware Shapes) in 1955 as *Summer Sky, Barlaston Green,* and *Harvest Moon,* and to these were shortly added *Moonlight (Windsor Grey* and cream colour) and *Havana* (a new chocolate-brown slip with cream-colour). An experimental quantity of a brick-coloured *Terracotta* was made as a two-colour clay pattern in 1958 but this was found to be unreliable in production and it was swiftly cancelled. Wedgwood's coloured bodies were withdrawn from general production in the 1970s because of a lack of sufficient continuing demand. They had never been popular in the

COLOURED BODIES. Drabware eggstand, coffeepot and oval parapet teapot with gold edge-line, typical of a breakfast service of the period 1815-30. *Christie's, London*

COLOURED BODIES.. Miniature shell-shaped drabware candlestick, height 2in. c.1820. *Wedgwood Museum*

115

COLOURED BODIES. Two-colour (Celadon and cream-colour) vase and bowl designed by Keith Murray and introduced c.1935 and reintroduced in 1953. Vase height 10¼in. *Author's collection*

United States except in the form of Embossed Queen's ware*, which sold there in great quantities.
See also: Flemish Ware; Ivory Ware; Oriental Body

Column Vase
See: Pillar Vase; Ruined Column Vase

COMMEMORATIVE WARE. Small White ware bough-pot made to celebrate the Golden Jubilee of George III in 1810. Decorated with a printed stippled ground, outline prints of the head of George III and the Garter star and badge within a border of the Garter chain, and enamelled flowers in the *famille-rose* style, this piece matches a tea and coffee service which was probably presented to the King.
Wedgwood Museum

Commemorative Ware
Throughout its history the Wedgwood firm has made wares in celebration of popular heroes and historical events. Typical examples are the 'Death of Wolfe'* teapots and jugs, c.1778, and the Wolfe bicentenary jugs and trays of 1959; the medallions commemorating George III's recovery from his illness in 1789 and the tea and breakfast service commemorating his Golden Jubilee in 1810; the 'German cameos'*; the Bastille medallions*; and in recent times the American Independence Series* of 1976. In the broadest terms, Wedgwood's early creamware teapots decorated with transfer-printed portraits, many of the 'Illustrious Moderns' portrait medallions*, and the modern Christmas plates* might be classified as commemorative, but the specific description, 'Commemorative Ware', is properly applied only to those 'named views' commissioned by Jones, McDuffee & Stratton*.
See: Colour Plate 24

COMMEMORATIVE WARE. One of sixty Queen's ware 'Charleston' jugs decorated with a tattered Confederate flag, the name of a company of South Carolina militia and a poem about war. Commissioned by Captain W.A. Courtenay of Charleston, probably for a reunion of surviving members of the company in 1891.
From the Collection of Norm Flayderman

COMMEMORATIVE WARE. Page from an earthenware pattern book showing the design for a jug commemorating Alfred, Lord Tennyson, c.1892. *Wedgwood Museum*

COMMEMORATIVE WARE. Deep blue and white jasper dip vase ornamented with De Vaere's portrait of Nelson, marking the centenary of his death at Trafalgar in 1805. Height 8in. 1905. *Wedgwood Museum*

COMMEMORATIVE WARE. Queen's ware plate decorated with a printed view of the United States Naval Academy in 1858. Issued by Jones, McDuffee & Stratton in 1935.

Wedgwood Museum

COMMEMORATIVE WARE. Queen's ware mug designed by Richard Guyatt to commemorate the American bicentennial in 1976. Edition of 5,000, described as 'limited'.

Wedgwood Museum

COMMEMORATIVE WARE. Printed and enamelled Queen's ware plate commemorating the surrender of the British army at Yorktown in 1781, commissioned by Williamsburg Restoration Inc. in 1960.

Author's collection

COMMEMORATIVE WARE. The Olympic Plate, made in blue and white jasper to celebrate the Olympic Games at Montreal in 1976.

Wedgwood Museum

Commonplace Books

Two manuscript books preserved in the Wedgwood archives at Keele University, North Staffordshire, containing an extraordinary variety of information noted by Josiah Wedgwood from his earliest days as an independent potter almost until his death. Much of it is in the hand of Alexander Chisholm*, indicating that it was copied from earlier manuscript material. The notes range from extracts from Du Halde's* account of the composition and manufacture of porcelain*, published in 1735 in his *Description...de l'empire de Chine*, through Erasmus Darwin's* prescriptions for the Wedgwood family's ailments and recipes for such delights as 'Ponche Royale' (requiring '10 gallons of Brandy or Rum'), to a list of Master Potters in Burslem in 1783. Next to Josiah's letters, the Commonplace Books are the most valuable documents relating to 18th-century Wedgwood.

Commonwealth Shape

See: Tableware Shapes

Comport

A form of dessert dish on stand (somewhat resembling a tazza*)

made by Wedgwood in Queen's ware in the 18th century. In the 19th century 'tall' and 'low' comports were essential parts of ceramic dessert services.

Compotier

A bowl or deep dish, often on stand, for serving *compôte* (cooked whole fruit). Wedgwood have also used the term to denote smaller shallow bowls in various shapes and patterns suitable for serving nuts, olives etc.

Concave Shape

The name given to flat ware (plates and serving dishes) with a slightly concave rim. An unusual feature is the lack of a footrim to the base of the plates and dishes. This shape, part of Wedgwood's Queen's ware* 'Traditional shape', appears to have been one of Wedgwood's earliest and was certainly in production by the mid-1770s. In only slightly modified form, it is still in production in the 1990s.
See: Tableware Shapes

CONCEIT. Pair of Cane ware 'Conceits', ornamented with white stoneware, simulating an iced cake. Height 5½in.

Formerly Buten Museum

Conceit

A ceramic object in the form of an iced cake used for the decoration of the dinner table when flour for real cakes was scarce. Conceits were made by Wedgwood in ornamented cane ware* early in the 19th century.

See: Game Pie Dish; Pastry Ware

Conchology

The science of the study of shells. The collecting of exotic shells was a fashionable 18th-century pursuit, and Josiah Wedgwood was an avid shell collector. In 1778 he wrote to Bentley*, then on holiday in Margate, asking him to search the beach and rummage in chalk pits for specimens. The rococo* style of the mid-18th century made much use of shells as decorative motifs, especially in the design of porcelain. Shell forms also decorated Wedgwood's early wares. The shell-edge shape was among the first of Queen's ware* tableware shapes*, and the popular green enamelled seaweed and shell pattern was introduced as late as 1776, when rococo styles had been all but discarded in favour of the more fashionable neo-classical* shell designs. Shell shapes occur as bas-reliefs for jasper, and the Triton* figure grasps a whorled shell, often erroneously described as a cornucopia*. Two different Wedgwood dessert services were made in the form of shells: the first, based on the Nautilus and Pecten shapes was made in Queen's ware with an enamelled border from c.1790; the second, the 'Wreathed shell' service based on the Argonaut shape fruit centre and stand and Anornia cream bowls and Pecten plates, was made from c.1805. The latter set was decorated, from about 1812, with variegated lustre* or coloured washes of pink, yellow, orange and pale-brown enamel,

CONCHOLOGY. Part of a White ware shell dessert service, the shapes based on the Argonaut, Anornia and Pecten shells, decorated with enamelled bands of yellow, pink and grey. Argonaut centre and stand height 8⅜in. c.1835.

Merseyside Museums

CONCHOLOGY. White bone china ornament in the form of two shells supported by branches of coral. Height 5in. c.1895.

Wedgwood Museum

and, later in the 19th century it was reproduced in Majolica* glazes. Later still, it was introduced in bone china* and it was made in Alpine Pink* c.1937. The service was still in production, in plain Queen's ware with Dysart glaze* or decorated with green glaze* in the 1960s and it was revived in bone china with a pearl lustre* glaze in the 1980s. A range of thirty-six bone china ornaments in the form of shells supported on coral stands was produced c.1895.

See: Colour Plate 25

CONCHOLOGY. Pearl ware shell-edge shape dessert service printed in dark-brown and enamelled in green with scattered compositions of shells and seaweed. c.1785-90.

Christie's, New York

Concordia

Roman goddess with several temples in Rome. She personified harmony and agreement. She is usually represented holding a cornucopia* in one hand and an olive branch in the other.

Wedgwood subject:

Sacrifice to Concordia, medallion diameter 10in. No.259 in 1787 Catalogue*. Companion piece to *Sacrifice to Hymen*.

Confederate Jug

Baluster shape Queen's ware jug, height 11in., made c.1891 to the order of Captain William A. Courtenay of Charleston, South Carolina. The jug is decorated on both sides and beneath the spout with transfer-printed* commemorative inscriptions and verse and the Confederate flag enamelled in colour. Only sixty jugs were produced, it is assumed for the sixty surviving members of the South Carolina Militia Company.

See also: Commemorative Ware

Connor (originally O'Connor), Charles Ernest Edward (1876-1960)

Painter and engraver, born in the Potteries. He studied at the Stanley School of Art, 1902-3 and 1906-8, and was Supervisor of Arts and Crafts at Newcastle-under-Lyme, 1921-2. He was headmaster of Leek School of Art from 1922 to 1939 and subsequently held the same appointment at Crewe. As an 'outside' decorator he painted a series of Wedgwood earthenware plaques, c.1910-20. He generally signed his pieces, often with a shamrock as well as his name.

Cook, Isaac

See: Wedgwood Museum

Cookworthy, William

See; Champion, Richard; Cherokee Clay; Porcelain

Cooper, Joseph (fl.1770-73)

A 'good flower painter' from Liverpool, probably in the style usually attributed to James Bakewell*, hired for three years in May 1770 at thirteen shillings a week in the country and sixteen shillings while working at the Chelsea Decorating Studio*. He worked on the *Husk** dessert service.

Cooper, Joseph (fl. 1770-80)

Printer of Drury Lane, London, who printed the 1773 and 1774 Ornamental Ware Catalogues* and the catalogue of the 'Frog'* service for Wedgwood & Bentley. He was, for a time (1772-77), and at the instigation of Josiah Wedgwood, in partnership with Du Burk* in Amsterdam. He discovered, however, 'gross mistakes' in the accounts but was overawed by Du Burk's wife. Later, Josiah wrote: 'I cannot help thinking our friend Joe [Cooper] lost a fine oppertunity of making his fortune there & all by suffering to be brow beat by that Diable of a Woman Mrs DB'. He was succeeded as Wedgwood's agent in Holland by Lambertus van Veldhuysen*.

Cooper, Nathaniel (fl.1769-74)

Painter of encaustic* vases at the Chelsea Decorating Studio*, who worked on the *Husk** service for Catherine the Great*, and painted inside borders and frog emblems on the Frog* service.

Cooper, Susie OBE RDI (b.1903)

English ceramic designer; studied at Burslem Art School from 1922; from 1925, designer for A.E. Gray & Co., Hanley; noted for abstract designs in styles influenced by Art Nouveau* and Art Deco*. In 1932 she established her own company, using a deer as her trade mark, and during the 1930s she worked principally on bone china*. In 1966 her company was taken over by Wedgwood in the formation of the Wedgwood Group* and she became one of Wedgwood's leading designers. She executed successful commissions for the Queen's Silver Jubilee in 1977. A retrospective exhibition of her work was held at Sanderson's Berners Street showrooms, London, in 1978, and a more comprehensive exhibition, 'Susie Cooper Productions', was mounted at the Victoria & Albert Museum in 1987. Susie Cooper is now widely recognised as one of the most original ceramic designers to work in 20th-century Staffordshire.

CONCORDIA. Black basaltes plaque, *Sacrifice to Concordia.* Diameter 10¼in. c.1787.   *Christie's, New York*

Copeland

See: Spode

Copper

See: Glazes, *Green Glaze;* Lustre

Coriolanus

Originally Gaius Marcellus, he was surnamed Coriolanus to celebrate his heroism during the siege and capture of the Volscian town of Corioli. His arrogance made him many enemies, however, and in 491 BC he was exiled, taking refuge among the Volscians, whose king appointed him general of the army. In 489 Coriolanus led his command to within a few miles of Rome, where he was visited by many distinguished Romans who vainly implored him to spare the city. Finally, he was persuaded by a deputation of Roman matrons, who included his mother, Veturia, and his wife, Volumnia*, accompanied by his two children. He turned away from Rome and returned to live with the Volscians.

Wedgwood subjects:

Coriolanus. With his Wife and Mother Persuading Him to Return [sic] *to Rome,* tablet 6in. x 9¾in., from a wax* model by Flaxman*, 1784. No.258 in the 1787 Catalogue*. Neither Flaxman nor Josiah Wedgwood appears to have been familiar with the history of Coriolanus

Volumnia, Wife of Coriolanus, tablet 6in. x 9⅛in. c.1790, after an engraving in d'Hancarville's *Antiquities,* 1767 (Vol.II, Plate 26). This subject is often erroneously catalogued as *Penelope and Her Maidens*

Cornish Journey

In May 1775, Josiah Wedgwood and John Turner*, accompanied by Thomas Griffiths* (who had been Wedgwood's agent in 1767 for the purchase of Cherokee Clay*), set out on a journey of exploration into Cornwall on behalf of the Staffordshire potters. Wedgwood kept a journal of his travels which was reprinted in the *Proceedings* of the Wedgwood Society*, Nos 1 and 2 (1956-7). The object of the journey was to find and assess deposits of minerals, such as china clay and feldspathic rock, likely to be of use in the pottery industry. Wedgwood paid a visit to the source of the Worcester* factory's supplies of soaprock* near Liskeard and took samples, and, not far away, he found the site from which Chaffers' Liverpool factory drew supplies. By 11 June 1775, the travellers had acquired the rights to deposits of minerals sufficient for their purpose, and Griffiths was left behind to supervise the conclusion of the arrangements. Wedgwood proposed the setting up of a joint stock company to carry out experimental work on behalf of those potters and subscribers who opposed Champion's* porcelain bill, but no agreement was possible and Wedgwood felt free to continue experiments with the Cornish materials alone.

See: Public Experimental Work

Cornish Metal Company

Company formed to exploit Cornish metal deposits. Josiah Wedgwood was a shareholder with Matthew Boulton*, James Watt* and Richard Arkwright. A letter from Wedgwood to Watt dated 17 September 1785 discusses payment for shares.

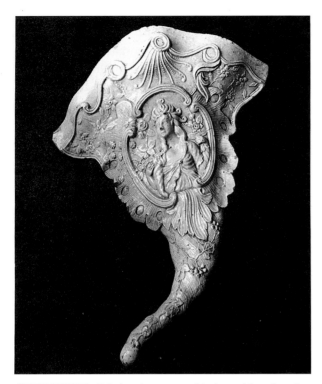

CORNUCOPIA. Saltglazed stoneware block mould attributed to William Greatbatch and probably made by Wedgwood in saltglazed stoneware and creamware (undecorated, enamelled or decorated with Green glaze) at the Ivy House. Length 10¾in. *Wedgwood Museum*

Cornish Stone
A mineral, known also as moor stone or growan stone, rich in feldspar*, used in the manufacture of porcelain*, bone china* and fine stonewares*.

Cornucopia
Horn of plenty, symbolic of happiness, concord and fortune, taking the form of a drinking horn *(cornu)* filled with corn and fruit, the two kinds of nourishment essential to man. The goddesses Abundantia*, Fortuna, Concordia* and Ceres* (Demeter) are often represented with a cornucopia spilling out fruits and corn. Wedgwood's *Triton** is sometimes erroneously described as grasping a cornucopia.

Coronation Pattern
Bone china* border pattern (no. W3369) designed by Cecily Stella ('Star') Wedgwood* in 1937 to celebrate the Coronation of George VI. Three white plumes are outlined in platinum on a ground of onglaze ruby.

CORONATION PATTERN. 'Leigh' shape teacup and saucer and can coffee cup and saucer in Star Wedgwood's *Coronation* pattern. 1937. *Wedgwood Museum*

Cost Accounting
In August 1772, in urgent response to a crisis in the business management of the Wedgwood & Bentley partnership, Josiah Wedgwood calculated detailed costings of his vases, creating what he described as a 'price book of workmanship' for 'every expence of Vase making as near as possible from the Crude materials, to your [Bentley's*] Counter in London upon each sort of Vase'. The resulting document is the first recorded exercise in cost accounting in the British pottery industry and one of the earliest surviving documents of this kind in manufacturing history.

Coupe Shape
See: Tableware Shapes

Coward, John (fl.1765-70)
Woodcarver, said to have been employed by the brothers Adam, first mentioned by Wedgwood in November 1765, when he acknowledged receipt of some carvings by Coward, sent from London. Subsequently, he carved a varied assortment of models, including the cross-ribbons to a 'neat small mahogany tea tray', some 'heavy & bad' baskets, an unidentified piece of foliage, the handle and swan's head for a vase, a triangular pedestal, spouts for lamps and a copy of a figure of Somnus*, but by the end of 1770 Wedgwood was dissatisfied with his work, which he found of little practical use. Surviving carved wood models attributed to Coward include a circular stand, a hexagonal pot-pourri* vase and a soup tureen and handle, all in the Wedgwood Museum*. Some of Coward's most valuable work was in his 'tinkering'* of black basaltes* vases. He worked also on models for the first service made for Catherine* the Great (the *Husk** service) in 1770.

COWARD, John. Carved wood block moulds for a soup tureen and circular dish stand attributed to Coward, c.1765-70. Length of tureen 15½in. *Wedgwood Museum*

Cox, William (fl. c.1763-76)
Warehouseman and book-keeper in London and Burslem. Cox was sent to London in November 1767 to take charge of the showrooms in Charles Street (now Carlos Place), off Grosvenor Square. Although apparently loyal and honest, and trusted to handle substantial sums of money – especially when, as in 1768, Wedgwood was urging him to collect large outstanding debts – Cox was both dogmatic and inexpert. His deficiencies as a book-keeper finally cost him his position in London and he returned to work in Burslem in 1769. 'I am much concerned,' Wedgwood wrote to Bentley in December, 'to find so many more blunders in Mr Cox's cash account, & as I am daily suffering in so tender a point, as that of my Character for Honesty, & all through his neglect, I cou'd not help reproving him very severely for it...It is equitable and just, that he shou'd rather lose his character as a book-keeper which he has deserved to do, than that I shou'd lose mine for honesty'. Ironically, Cox was replaced in London by the accomplished swindler Ben Mather*.

Crabstock (Crabtree)
Form of spout*, handle* and knop* moulded in relief to represent the gnarled branch of a crab apple tree. Sometimes called 'rustic'

CRABSTOCK. Creamware coffeepot with strongly modelled crab-stock spout and handle, coloured with green, yellow and brown oxides, the sides ornamented with applied Tudor roses and leaves on trailed stems. Height 7⅛in. Unmarked. Whieldon-Wedgwood, c.1756.
Temple Newsam House, Leeds

(this name was given to a 19th-century Wedgwood tableware shape which made use of a form of crabstock), the type was first introduced on saltglazed* wares c.1745 and is to be found also on early red ware* and black-glazed teapots. The crabstock spout was the first to be adopted for Staffordshire and Yorkshire creamwares* and was made by Whieldon* and by Wedgwood at Burslem.
See: Greatbach, William; Rococo

Craft, William Hopkins (c.1730-1811)
Craft's identity has proved hard to establish although his signature is on three receipts in the Wedgwood archives and also upon a number of fine miniatures, four of which are in the British Museum. It appears that he was the partner whom David Rhodes* described in a letter of June 1768 as having enamelled in Paris 'with great Elegance', and with whom he proposed to become Wedgwood's tenant for part of the Newport Street showrooms later that year. Craft, always referred to in Wedgwood's letters as 'Mr Croft' or 'Crofts', signed some of the invoices for 'D. Rhodes & Co' between 1769 and 29 March 1770, shortly before Rhodes became manager of the Chelsea Decorating Studio*, where Craft worked until about May 1771.

Craft was evidently one of the most skilled painters employed by Wedgwood in London, working chiefly on the encaustic* decoration of basaltes* vases. He was briefly entrusted with some administration and the training of painters, but he soon showed signs of artistic temperament which sorely tried Bentley's* patience. Craft demanded, and was paid, £200 a year, which Josiah considered 'too extravagant to be lasting', but the artist was still dissatisfied and threatened to move to the Derby* factory. 'Not pleas'd with our behaviour to him!', Josiah exclaimed in exasperation, 'Why if he had been a Nabob himself we could not have behaved with more respect & caution towards him'. Nevertheless, Craft's skill as a painter is not in doubt. It was he who was instructed to copy the Duke of Argyll's 'Raphael'* vases, when it was proposed that Wedgwood might attempt something in the style of the *istoriato* painting of Urbino *maiolica,* and it is most probable that it was Craft, not Rhodes as is usually assumed, who painted the First Day's Vases* in 1769. Josiah had to admit in October 1770 that 'If that coxcomb Crofts would be made any way bearable I apprehend we could find him constant employment'. Evidently the desired effect could not be achieved: Craft left about

CRAFT, William Hopkins. Self-portrait, enamel on copper. 1¼in. x 1⅛in. Signed and dated 1780.
National Gallery of Ireland

the end of April 1771 to become an independent enameller. None of his work for Wedgwood has been identified with certainty.

Crane, Walter (1845-1915)
Artist, designer, book-illustrator, writer and lecturer, born in Liverpool. An associate of William Morris, Crane was one of the leading figures in the Arts and Crafts* movement, and first President of the Arts and Crafts Society, founded in 1888. With Kate Greenaway* and Ralph Caldecott, he was one of the three 'Academicians of the Nursery': influential artists whose work as contemporary illustrators of children's books made their names household words. Strongly influenced by the Pre-Raphaelites, Crane's illustrations relied upon decorative design, for which purity of line and charm of colour were essential ingredients. He was the inventor of 'Mr Michael Mouse', a recognisable antecedent of Disney's immortal character. More formally, Crane was a member of the Royal Watercolour Society, Director of Design at the Manchester Municipal School (1893), Art Director of Reading University College (1897) and Principal of the Royal College of Art (1898). Introduced to the Wedgwoods in 1866, Crane was commissioned to design decoration for a number of Queen's ware* vases, the first two pairs of which – *The Seasons* and *The Hours, The Ages of Man* and

CRANE, Walter. Queen's ware vase decorated in enamel colours, representing 'The Ages of Man', painted in 1866-7.
Wedgwood Museum

CRANWELL VASE. Queen's ware vase finished in a speckled matt glaze over Moonstone. Height 33in. 1953. *Wedgwood Museum*

CREALOCK, Colonel H.H. Satsuma shape teapot, bowl and coffeecup and saucer printed in red by a photographic process with drawings of stags by Crealock. c.1877. *Wedgwood Museum*

The Employments – were delivered in January 1867. Later he finished two more pairs, *Knowledge* and *Imagination,* and *Science & Poetry* and *Beauty & Utility;* two single vases, *The Ten Virgins* and *Painting & Music;* and three trays, *L'Allegro, Il Penseroso* and *Gannymede* [*sic*]. He also designed 'a border for a kind of encaustic inlay they [Wedgwood] had invented applied to the decoration of a chessboard' for the 1871 Exhibition. Crane designed also for Maw & Co. and for the Pilkington Tile & Pottery Co.
See: Colour Plate 26
See also: Inlaid Ware; Mellor, Thomas

Cranwell Memorial Vase
Large Queen's ware* lidded vase on stand, height 33in., finished in a speckled matt glaze over Moonstone (see: Glazes, *Moonstone),* made for the Chapel at RAF Cranwell in 1953. The vase was designed by Victor Skellern*, with coats of arms and supporters modelled by Eric Owen*. The glaze was specially created to imitate the stone of Hopton Wood.

Crazing
A network of surface cracks on the glaze of pottery or porcelain, usually the result of an unintended disagreement between the shrinkage rates of glaze and body during the cooling stage, but sometimes caused by later reheating in a domestic oven, when the cracks are often badly discoloured. Particles of dirt or grease are inclined to collect in these glaze cracks and cannot be removed by washing, and the passage of time makes them more obvious, especially in the case of tablewares. Chinese potters were able to control crazing to a notable extent and it was employed as a form of decoration on some of the finest wares. Crazing appears on some early creamware and frequently upon Wedgwood earthenware tablewares of the mid-19th century.

Crealock, Henry Hope (1831-91)
Soldier, artist and author; served in the Crimea, in China, in India, and in the Zulu war, 1879; retired with the rank of Lieutenant-General, 1884. He sketched many scenes in the Indian Mutiny and the Chinese campaign, and during the Zulu war for the *Illustrated London News.* He also illustrated Whyte-Melville's *Katerfelto,* 1875. His *Deer-Stalking in the Highlands of Scotland,* profusely illustrated with his drawings, was published posthumously in 1892. Godfrey Wedgwood* wrote to Crealock in 1876 asking for 'a dozen good sized drawings, in pairs if possible' from which he

CREALOCK, Colonel H.H. Queen's ware plate with pierced edge, transfer-printed in brown with the head of a camel after a drawing by Crealock. c.1880. *Wedgwood Museum*

proposed to take negatives to be printed by a new photographic process. Crealock's drawings reproduced by Wedgwood included sets of 'Dogs' Heads' and stalking scenes printed on tiles* and Queen's ware plates, and stalking scenes printed by photolithography* on Satsuma* shape tea sets and on decorative plaques.

Cream-coloured Ware (Creamware)
The English name for fine lead-glazed earthenware first made in Staffordshire at some date between 1730 and 1740. The earliest documentary example is the punch bowl in the British Museum decorated in underglaze blue* and manganese* and inscribed 'E B 1743'. This is generally attributed to Enoch Booth, to whom is also credited the introduction of biscuit* firing as a process separate from glazing. Liquid glazes, replacing the traditional powdered glaze dusted on to unfired clay, were first used regularly by Aaron Wood* and William Littler. Although he is frequently credited with its invention, Josiah Wedgwood's creamware, known from 1765 as Queen's ware*, was a development of a cream-coloured earthenware body already well established in Staffordshire. But

CREAM-COLOURED WARE. Early creamware teapot with crabstock handle and spout ornamented with applied Tudor roses and leaves on trailed stems touched in with yellow, green and brown. Height 5¾in. Unmarked. Whieldon-Wedgwood, c.1756.
Temple Newsam House, Leeds

Wedgwood's refinement of the body and glaze and his use of sophisticated shapes more commonly associated with silver or porcelain, justifies the claim that he created a new form of earthenware for the table. Unlike potters who had traditionally whitened their wares by adding tin oxide to the covering lead glaze, Wedgwood produced a fine, durable ware that was white bodied, owing its colour primarily to the introduction of Cornish china clay and china stone into the body. Wedgwood's earliest creamware was buff in colour, but this shade was considerably paler by 1763, and five years later the transformation in the body and glaze, which made Wedgwood's Queen's ware the most important development in the history of British pottery, was complete. Manufacturers on the Continent started to make cream-coloured ware before 1775, but not on a large scale until the end of the century. It was known as *faience-fine, faience anglaise* or *terre de pipe* in France, as *Steingut* in Germany, *terraglia* in Italy and as *flint porslin* in Scandinavia. Before he died, in 1795, Wedgwood saw his Queen's ware copied all over Europe, where he had achieved what at one time amounted

CREAM-COLOURED WARE. Creamware coffeepot enamelled in red and black with a large rose and stylised foliage. Probably painted by David Rhodes, at Leeds, for Wedgwood, c.1764-8.
Norwich Castle Museum

almost to a monopoly of the high-quality earthenware tableware trade. By the end of the century the manufacture of the traditional European tin-glazed earthenware had virtually ceased, continuing only in small provincial potteries in France and two factories in Delft. If jasper* may be said to be Wedgwood's greatest invention, his refinement of creamware was his most influential achievement.

Decoration of early creamware was by painting with enamel colours, transfer-printing* (see: Sadler, John), moulding, engine-turning*, piercing, and covering with coloured glazes or slips*.
See also: Crystalline; Glazes, *Green Glaze*; Variegated Ware; Warburton, Anne

Cream Pan
Large, flat, oval pan or dish with a lip at one end for pouring, made in Queen's ware*, cane*, rosso antico* (perhaps only for the Anson dairy at Shugborough) and in the 19th-century coloured bodies* for use in dairies for the separation of cream.
See: Dairy Ware

Cream Vase
Ovoid Queen's ware vessel with lid and two handles designed as part of Wedgwood's dairy* ware. It was made in four parts, on the

CREAM-COLOURED WARE. Thrown and turned creamware vase of baluster shape on turned foot, the domed lid with acorn knop. Height 10½in. Unmarked. Wedgwood, c.1765. *Wedgwood Museum*

CREAM VASE. Queen's ware cream vase made in four parts on the same principle as the 'glacier' to keep cream cool. Height 11in. c.1795.
Merseyside Museums

CRUET SET. Queen's ware cruet or condiment set, height 7½in., the five containers set in a circular pierced stand with moulded scrolls and splayed feet. Shape no.781 in the 1802 Shape Drawing Book. c.1785.

Christie's, London

same principle as the 'glacier'*, to keep the cream cool. Cream vases were first made by Wedgwood some time before July 1769, when he wrote to William Cox*: 'You have lately had some Cream Vases for dairys of a new pattern which I wish you would shew & take orders from instead of the old ones'.

Creamware
See: Cream-coloured Ware

Creil (Oise)
A factory was founded at Creil in 1793 to make *faience-fine* (creamware) and other English-type wares, including agate* ware and black basaltes*. Early in the 19th century, it merged with Montereau, a factory originally founded in 1774 by English potters. A good deal of cream-coloured ware* decorated with transfer-printing*, an unusual technique on Continental wares, was made at Creil, and topographical prints of English country houses titled in French were popular, perhaps inspired by some recollection of the Frog* service. The pottery chemist, Saint-Amans, who had spent more than twenty years in England studying the industry, made soft-paste porcelain in the English manner about 1820.

Cress Dish
See: Strawberry Dish

Crest Order Books
Manuscript records, preserved in the Wedgwood Museum, Barlaston, of orders for armorial ware* executed by Wedgwood. The descriptions of crests and coats of arms are illustrated by accurate watercolour drawings, sometimes heightened with gold.

Crewe, Emma (fl.1787-1818)
Daughter of the Whig hostess, Frances Anne Crewe* and John, later Baron Crewe, of Crewe Hall, Cheshire. Emma Crewe was an amateur artist who provided sentimental designs for Wedgwood to reproduce in bas-relief* on jasper* from 1787. Her designs are similar to those of Lady Templetown*, with which they are often

confused. The following bas-reliefs were designed by her and probably modelled by William Hackwood*:
Domestic Employment, medallion 3½in. x 4¼in. and sizes down to 1½in. x 2in. No.247 in 1787 Catalogue*.
The Young Seamstress and 'companion piece' (untitled, but probably *The Reading Lesson),* two medallions 4in. x 2½in. and sizes down to 2¼in. x 1¼in. No.270 in 1787 Catalogue.
This list is probably incomplete, but no evidence has been found to support other attributions. These bas-relief subjects appear on vases, teapots and small jasper pieces as well as on medallions.

Crewe, Frances Anne (c.1740-1818)
Fashionable beauty and Whig champion, the friend of Charles James Fox*, Burke and Sheridan; married John Crewe, created Baron Crewe in 1806. Her son's portrait was modelled by Hackwood*. Wedgwood wrote to Bentley* in September 1771: 'Hackwood has been three times at Crew by Mrs Crew's particular desire to model the head of her son and heir'. This may have been the origin of Wedgwood's decision to produce contemporary portrait medallions or at least individual portraits to order, but no factory mould nor surviving example of this portrait has been identified. Her daughter, Emma*, provided designs for Wedgwood bas-reliefs.

Crisphagnia
A mysterious figure listed on Hoskins & Grant's* invoice of 5 May 1779 and unidentified until 1989. It appears on the same invoice as the figure of *Zingara*,* which, in turn, is listed as no.34 in the 1787 Catalogue*, next to a figure of the same size (17in.) described as *Ceres*.* It is a sensible deduction, therefore, that 'Crisphagnia' is nothing more than a clerk's error for 'Crispina', an alternative name for the statue now known as the 'Mattei Ceres', illustrated in Maffei's *Racolta di Statue* 1704 (Plate 108), and now in the Vatican Museum.

Crocus Pot (Crocus Basket)
Unusual crocus pots in the form of beehives and hedgehogs were made by Wedgwood from c.1815: the beehive in Queen's ware* covered with green glaze*, and the hedgehog in both black basaltes* and green-glazed Queen's ware. Both shapes, pierced at regular intervals with small round holes to allow the flowers to grow through the hedgehog or beehive cover, were provided with conforming trays. The hedgehog crocus pot has been reproduced in basaltes intermittently through the 19th and 20th centuries. A pierced crocus basket with overhead bow (bail*) handle and loose, pierced cover was produced in smear-glazed* white 'porcelain' (stoneware) c.1830. 'Bowhandle crocus pots and stands' appear in the order books as late as November 1850.

Croft or Crofts
See: Craft, William Hopkins

Croquant
Wedgwood's name for a shallow bowl, also described as a sweet-meat dish, with elaborate domed, pierced and moulded cover. It is illustrated as design no.21 (Plate 6) in the first Queen's Ware Catalogue*, 1774, and again, with the wrong caption, in the '1790' Catalogue (design no.53, Plate 11), by which time the description had been altered to 'Pierced covered bowl for fruit'. It has been reproduced in Queen's ware* in the 20th century.

Crucible
Crucible cups, made in a special 'crucible body' similar to that used for other chemical wares* were used by Wedgwood in his own experiments in chemical analysis and in conjunction with pyrometric cylinders (see: Pyrometer) to compare the performance of different clays in firing.

Cruet Set
A condiment set generally comprising a footed stand, sometimes with tall centre handle, and space for two or more containers (cruets and casters*) for oil, vinegar, salt, mustard, pepper and sugar. Plate 6 of Wedgwood's first (1774) Queen's ware Catalogue* illustrates an 'Oil and Vinegar Stand, containing from two to six Cruets' and another version of this appears in Plate 7 of the '1790' Catalogue. Far more sophisticated shapes, including

CUPID. Wedgwood & Bentley blue and white jasper medallion, *Cupid Inflaming the Mind,* height 5⅛in. c.1778.
Dwight & Lucille Beeson Collection, Birmingham Museum, Alabama

CUPID. Wedgwood & Bentley blue and white jasper plaque, *Marriage of Cupid and Psyche,* oval 11in. x 16¼in., c.1778. *Manchester Museum*

pepper and sugar casters, oil and vinegar bottles based on silver prototypes, and attractively pierced stands are illustrated in Plate 10 (drawn by William Blake*) of the '1817' Catalogue.

Crystalline

The name given by Josiah Wedgwood to the white terracotta* body used by him for his 'variegated'* vases after 1772, when it replaced creamware for this purpose. Class XV of the 1787 Ornamental Ware Catalogue* is 'Ornamental Vases of antique forms: in the Terracotta, resembling agate, jasper, porphyry, and other variegated stones of the crystalline kind.'

Crystalline glazes are those partially devitrified glazes* in which some crystallisation is apparent (e.g. Aventurine glaze – see: Glazes, *Aventurine).*

Cullet

Broken glass added to the other ingredients in the crucible before heating to promote fusion. Cullet was used also by the potter. In the 18th century it was powdered and mixed with the other substances employed to make artificial porcelain*, forming part of the fusible ingredients of the body. In 1775 Wedgwood wrote to Bentley* asking for scraps of London crown glass to be obtained for him. He also requested Bentley to ask Samuel More*, Secretary of the Society of Arts (Royal Society of Arts*), to get some poor man to work secretly on reducing it to a powder which could be 'put through a coarse hair sieve.'

The letter suggests that Wedgwood may have been experimenting with 'soft paste'* porcelain or that he was engaged in making his own enamel colours. Some Parian* bodies, first made in the 19th century, are composed of about seventy per cent of feldspar and thirty per cent of china clay to which is added a small quantity of cullet. This helps to give this type of porcelain its satin surface and glass-like body.

Cupid

Cupido, or Amor, the Roman god of love identified with the Greek Eros. Cupid was the son of Venus* by either Mars*, Jupiter* or Mercury*. He is usually represented as a boy, often winged, with arrows in a golden quiver, and torches. Sometimes he is blindfold and he frequently accompanies Venus. When depicted with Psyche* he is usually an adolescent rather than a child. There is a notable series of Cupids engaged in various crafts in the House of the Vetii in Pompeii and this has frequently been used as inspiration for decoration.

Cupids, *putti* and 'bacchanalian boys' were among the most popular and frequently used subjects of decoration and ornament in the 18th century and Wedgwood reproduced numerous designs by

Beauclerk* and Templetown*, most of them modelled by Hackwood*. Others were original models by Flaxman* or Webber*, or remodelled from casts supplied by Hoskins & Grant*. Cupids in various forms also appear in the compositions for tablets*. In the 19th century, such painters as Emile Lessore* and Henry Brownsword*, and the modeller and designer, Hugues Protât*, made frequent use of Cupids as decoration. A series of Cupids at various pursuits after Bartolozzi* was painted on bone china by Hodgkiss*, Holland* and others, c.1910. Principal Wedgwood subjects include:

Autumn and *Winter,* 'Rustic candelsticks'. Cupid figures emblematic of autumn and winter, with tree trunks in the form of candlesticks, height 10¾in. Produced in jasper, c.1785-90. Often attributed, without evidence, to Hackwood*

Cupid 'on a pedestal'. Jasper figure. Catalogued in 1787

Cupid, jasper flower vase, height 8½in. The figure of Cupid with a bird's nest against a tree trunk. Companion to a similar *Psyche* figure vase

Cupid Sitting Pensive, figure 8½in., companion to a figure of *Psyche,* after Falconet* (1757). From casts probably supplied by Flaxman senior* in 1781

Cupid and Hymen, medallion 3¼in. x 5in. No.135 in 1777 Catalogue

Cupid Inflaming the Mind, medallion 3¼in. x 5in. No.136 in 1777 Catalogue

CUPID. Green jasper dip cream jug with engine-turned dicing and ornament of yellow quatrefoils and white jasper floral scrolls and figures of *Cupid* among the scrolls. Height 3⅛in. c.1790.
Merseyside Museums

CUPID. Pair of solid grey-green and white jasper vases, the figures of *Cupid* with a bird's nest and *Psyche* with a butterfly perhaps representing *Spring* and *Summer*. Height 8½in. c.1790.
Dwight & Lucille Beeson Collection, Birmingham Museum, Alabama

Cupid on a Lion or *The Power of Love*, medallion 4⅛in x 3¼in. No.145 in 1777 Catalogue

Cupid Sharpening His Arrows, circular medallion diameter 5in. No. 267 in 1787 Catalogue

Cupid Shaving his Bow, medallion 3in. x 2¼in., down to 1½in. x 1in.'From a picture of Corregio's' (now attributed to Parmigianino). No.27 in 1773 Catalogue

Cupid Stringing His Bow, circular medallion diameter 5in. No.268 in 1787 Catalogue

Cupid Watering the Swans, tablet 4¼in. x 9in., after Lebrun*. No.246 in 1787 Catalogue

Marriage of Cupid and Psyche, tablet 11½in. x 16in. Also medallions and cameos in sizes down to 1in. x 2¾in. No. 30 in 1773 Catalogue. This subject exists in three versions: the first after the famous Marlborough sardonyx gem, possibly from a cast supplied by Mrs Landré*, 1771; the second, after the same source in 1774; and the third, after a Tassie* gem* from the same original source. Neither of the first two, however, is an accurate copy of the Marlborough sardonyx, both evidently being copied more closely from an engraving by Theodorus Netscher, which was in Wedgwood's possession in 1770

Sacrifice to Love, tablet 9½in. x 21in. or 10½in. x 25in. No. 208 in 1779 Catalogue

The Graces Erecting a Statue to Cupid, medallion 10¾in. x 9in. No.269 in 1787 Catalogue

*The Seasons**. Four bas-relief figures of Cupids representing the seasons. These were used in various sizes to ornament medallions, bough pots and pedestals, c.1785

Triumph of Love, medallion 6¼in. x 11in. No. 207 in 1779 Catalogue

Venus and Cupid, medallion 5in. x 4in. No. 168 in 1777 Catalogue.

From a model in the Newdigate* collection

Venus and Cupid, group, height 13in, after a model by Giovanni Meli*, c.1850-60

Venus in Her Car Drawn by Swans. With Attendant Cupids, tablet 4¼in. x 9in., 'From Le Brun'. No.245 in 1787 Catalogue

Winged Cupid upon a Swan, medallion 2¾in. x 2½in. No.181 in 1777 Catalogue. From a model in the Newdigate collection

Winged Cupid flying away with a Swan, medallion 2¾in. x 2½in. No.182 in 1777 Catalogue

See also: Bacchus ('Bacchanalian Boys'); Somnus

Curd Mould

A Queen's ware mould with pierced sides for making cheese. It was used with a lining of cheese cloth. Moulds of this type, in various shapes, were made by Wedgwood as part of his dairy* ware.

Custard Cups

Small covered cups of jasper* with lapidary*-polished interiors were made, usually in sets of four on an octagonal tray, c.1785. A rarer type is the covered can shape (see: Coffee Cans) or the uncovered pear or tear shape (sometimes described as a 'comma') made in solid-colour jasper with white jasper lattice-work ornament. Similar cups were made in ornamented cane ware*. Custard cups were made also in Queen's ware* (they were among the pieces included in the Frog* service) and Pearl* ware and they are

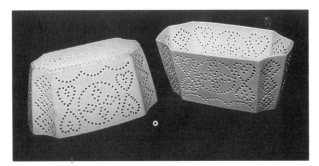

CURD MOULD. Pair of Queen's ware octagon curd moulds, 564 shape, 7½in. x 4in. c.1790. *Formerly Buten Museum*

CUSTARD CUPS. Queen's ware lidded custard cup, enamelled in blue and gilt, with bat-printed and enamelled crest and monogram. Height 3½in. c.1785. *Norwich Castle Museum*

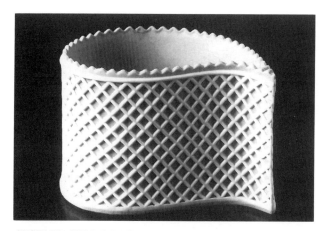

CUSTARD CUPS. Solid lilac and white jasper 'tear' or 'pear' shaped custard cup with applied lattice-work ornament. Height 2in. Unmarked. Wedgwood, c.1788-90. *Wedgwood Museum*

glazed* white 'porcelain'* (stoneware*), c.1820. Custard cups are similar in every respect to ice-cream cups*, one of which is illustrated in the 1774 Catalogue, and were interchangeable in use.

Cut-Steel Mounts
Many of Wedgwood's cameos*, seals* and medallions* were mounted in cut-steel jewellery at the Soho (Birmingham) factory of Boulton* & Fothergill and they were also sold to distributors who had them mounted elsewhere. Similar wares were sent by Adams* of Tunstall to Thomas Low of Sheffield. Steel was cut, chiselled and filed into facets which, when brightly polished, reflected the light and provided a substitute for marcasite that was both more durable and less prone to damage. Small objects of cut steel were first made in the 17th century as a cottage industry at Woodstock, and Wedgwood may have seen work of this kind when he visited Blenheim Palace. He was at Blenheim in December 1770, and on the same journey he went on to Birmingham to visit Boulton. This may have been when Wedgwood first had the idea of having his wares mounted in cut steel but it was not until some five years later that jasper was mounted in this style.
See: Colour Plate 27

Cutts, John (1772-1851)
Landscape painter at the Pinxton (Derbyshire) factory. In 1812 he began painting bone china* for Wedgwood but Josiah II's* opinion was that he would 'not suit as a flower-painter and probably not as a landscape painter'. Cutts took twelve days at five shillings a day to paint the fifty-one pieces of a tea service (pattern no.673, 'small groups of Flowers'). He seems to have left Wedgwood in 1816 to

CUSTARD CUPS. Solid pale-blue and white jasper custard set of four covered cups and a rectangular tray, 6in. square, with a large oval jasper tray, 11in. x 15¾in. c.1785. The interiors of the cups are lapidary-polished. *Wedgwood Museum*

CYBELE. Solid blue and white jasper candlestick in the form of a figure of *Cybele* holding a cornucopia which supports a moulded candleholder. Height 12½in. *Wedgwood Museum*

set up as an enameller and gilder in Hanley, taking his sons into partnership, and by 1842 the family of John Cutts & Sons was employing fifty people. He was responsible for the following patterns (and probably others not yet identified):

673	*China, small groups of Flowers,* gold edge
685	*China, small landscape* [sepia], gold edge
689	*Full Landscape* [naturalistic colour]
701	*Purple small landscapes, gold edge*
784	*New Chinese Figures on China Dessert Ware*

See: Colour Plate 28

Cybele
Roman name associated with the ancient Greek goddess Rhea, mother of Zeus (Jupiter*) and known as 'Mother of the Gods'. From the orgiastic nature of the rites accompanying the worship of Cybele her name became associated with that of Dionysus (Bacchus*). The lion was sacred to her and in art she is usually represented seated on a throne with a garlanded crown and attendant lions. Wedgwood's figure of Cybele surmounted by a candleholder was modelled in 1786 as a companion to that of Ceres* (see: Candlesticks and Candelabra). Josiah Wedgwood described this figure in March 1786 as 'Cybele representing the Earth, and being accompanied by a tame lion to shew perhaps that cultivation will subdue all things.'

Czechoslovakian (Bohemian) wares
The *faience* factory at Holic (Holitsch) made cream-coloured earthenware from about 1786 and soon afterwards factories at Byotrice and at Hranice in Moravia were imitating it. Probably the wares of Prague, founded with a privilege by Carl Hunerle and J.E. Hübel, and those of Tyne-nad-Sazavon, both founded in 1793, came closest to Wedgwood designs. Among the porcelain factories to imitate Wedgwood were Karlovy Vary (Karlsbad), Slavkov (Schlaggenwald), Klasterac (Klosterle) and Brezov (Pirkenhammer). The factory at Vranov-nad-Dyji made jasper-style wares in light blue and light brown with relief ornament (including pale blue on a brown ground), and pierced creamware decorated with excellent flower painting and transfer-printing*. Colours used for printing were blue, green, rose, brown and grey, and subjects included landscapes, architecture and hunting scenes. A fine collection of these wares is preserved at Vranov castle.

D

Da Bologna, Giovanni (1529-1608)

Sculptor; born Jean Boulogne at Douai and passed most of his working life in France. He was one of the most noted of Mannerist sculptors, and small bronzes and reductions of his large works were made in considerable quantities. In addition, his pupils and studio assistants produced work in his style. These works were drawn upon by the European porcelain factories. Six small medallions, untitled but described as by Giovanni da Bologna appear as nos 175-180 in the 1773 Catalogue*. Four measure 3in. x 4½in., and two 2⅛in. x 5in. All were obtained from models or casts in the Newdigate* collection and all but one – described in the original list of models from Arbury as 'the presenting of the cabinet' – are 'Modern Figures & modern stories'.

Daguerre, Dominique (fl.1770-95)

Marchand priviligié de la cour. Associated before 1778 with the dealer, Simon Poirier. Mainly he dealt in furniture from premises in the rue Saint-Honoré, Paris. Daguerre supplied the French Court, the Prince of Wales (later Prince Regent and King George IV) and the Duke of Northumberland. In June 1787 he was Wedgwood's agent in Paris but he retired to England in 1793 and was succeeded in Paris by Martin Eloi Lignereux. A superb *secrétaire* in the Metropolitan Museum (Kress Collection), New York, inlaid with a rare combination of Sèvres porcelain and Wedgwood jasper* medallions, may be the one catalogued by Christie & Ansell* in 1791 as 'imported from Paris by Mons. Daguerre'.

DAIRY WARE. Two matching Queen's ware cream vases enamelled in green and brown with a trailing ivy pattern, produced for the Countess Spencer's dairy at Althorp in 1786.
Photograph: Courtesy of Alison Kelly

DANCING HOURS, THE. Wedgwood & Bentley black basaltes vase, shape No.239, the body moulded with overlapping petals and ornamented with the *Dancing Hours.* Height 14¾in. c.1778.
Christie's, London

Dairy Ware

Objects, generally but not invariably of Queen's ware, for dairy use. The range includes cream vases*, ladles, milk sieves, settling pans*, skimmers*, spoons* and churns*. Some dairy wares are undecorated, others are painted with border patterns, and some have the name of the dairy or the crest of the owner added. Specimens exist from the 18th and 19th centuries, one of the most complete being at Althorp, Northamptonshire, the seat of the Spencer family. Like the dairy ware made for Queen Charlotte*, the Althorp set, made in 1786, is decorated with a painted border of ivy leaves, and Wedgwood supplied matching border tiles* for the walls of the dairy at a price of tenpence each, with complementary plain tiles at threepence. An order from the duc d'Orléans for cane-coloured ware for his dairy at Raincy is preserved in the Wedgwood archives but none seems to have survived. Dairy wares were supplied also during the last quarter of the 18th century to Warren Hastings at Daylesford House, the Duke of Marlborough at Blenheim Palace and the Duke of Bedford at Woburn Abbey. Typical shapes are illustrated in Charles Gill's* notebook. Perhaps the most curious dairy ware made by Wedgwood was ordered in 1807 by Lady Anson for the dairy at Shugborough, Staffordshire. This consisted only of octagonal and oval settling pans. As Tom Byerley, who took the order, explained: 'She has set her heart upon having some Milk pans – red outside – with Egyptian ornaments black glazed within'. At his suggestion the pans were made of rosso antico* with black Egyptian ornaments to the rims and a covering black glaze to the interiors. Four of each shape have survived at Shugborough.
See: Colour Plate 29

DANCING HOURS, THE. Black basaltes saucer dish with engine-turned centre and applied ornament of the *Dancing Hours*. Diameter 8in. c.1785.   *Lady Lever Art Gallery, Port Sunlight*

Dalmazzoni, Angelo (fl.1787-95)

Italian modeller employed by Wedgwood in Rome from 1787 to 1795, at first under the direction of Flaxman* and Webber*, but subsequently as Wedgwood's chief modeller in Italy. Several of his letters to Josiah Wedgwood have survived and the accompanying lists of models have proved valuable in identifying the work of other artists employed in Rome. None of his own work has been identified with certainty.

Dancing Hours, The

Probably the most famous of jasper* relief subjects, and one which is still reproduced today. It is believed to be the work of John Flaxman*, though positive proof is lacking, and it was probably remodelled, with some increase in the drapery, by Hackwood* in 1802. Wedgwood first mentioned the subject in 1778 as 'intended as frises to the marriage of Cupid* &c' and associated it in his letter with authenticated examples of Flaxman's work. The source from which the subject was adapted was either two engravings in Bartoli's *Admiranda Romanorum Antiquitatum,* 1693 (re-engraved for Montfaucon's *L'Antiquité expliqué,* Vol.III, Plate CLXXIII, 1719), in which figures described as 'Nuptiales Chorae' dance before an open colonnade, or a chimneypiece* of marble and lapis lazuli* installed by Sir Laurence Dundas* at Moor Park, Hertfordshire. The chimneypiece (now in the Lady Lever Gallery, Port Sunlight), from the Borghese* Collection, incorporates 'Dancing Maenads' copied from a Graeco-Roman marble relief of the first century then in the same collection and now in the Louvre as *Les Danseuses Borgheses.* Wedgwood's original tablet (no.205 in the 1779 Catalogue*) measured 6in. x 18in. or 5¼in. x 14¾in., but it has been reproduced in many sizes on many objects, including salt cellars, vases and teapots.
See: Colour Plate 30

DANCING HOURS, THE. Pale blue and white jasper drum salt cellar, ornamented with the *Dancing Hours*. Height 2⅛in. c.1790.
                                                   Wedgwood Museum

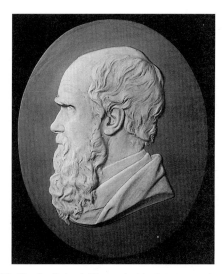

DARWIN, Charles Robert. Blue and white jasper portrait medallion, 1935.   *Wedgwood Museum*

Daniel(l), Thomas (fl.1750-65)

According to Simeon Shaw*, Daniel was the finest enameller in England, and was employed or commissioned by Wedgwood in 1762 when, in association with Daniel Steele*, he painted the flowers on a caudle set* presented by Wedgwood to Queen Charlotte*. Although there is no corroborative evidence that this presentation was ever made, it is not obviously unlikely and Shaw's account cannot be dismissed.

Daphne

Daughter of the Thessalian river god Peneus, Daphne was pursued by Apollo* and prayed for help. As he was about to seize her, she was changed into a laurel which, thereafter, was Apollo's favourite tree. A bas-relief* of *Apollo and Daphne* ('Apolow & Dafnee') was supplied to Wedgwood by Mrs Landré* in 1769 and appears as an octagonal medallion 3in. x 6in., no.9 in the 1773 Catalogue*. Webber* modelled Apollo and Daphne 'as a beaupot' (bough pot*) c.1785, but no example of this has been identified.

Darwin, Charles Robert FRS (1809-82)

English naturalist, son of Robert Waring Darwin* and Susannah Wedgwood*; educated at Shrewsbury, Edinburgh University and Christ's College, Cambridge. He married his cousin Emma Wedgwood, youngest daughter of Josiah II*. Darwin's *On the Origin of Species* was published in 1859. He was the author of numerous books and papers, including the *Descent of Man,* 1871,

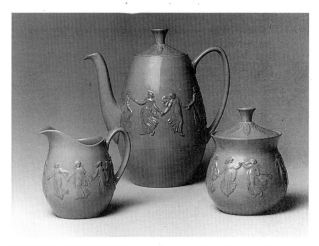

DANCING HOURS, THE. A modern use of the *Dancing Hours* on a trial coffee set designed by Norman Wilson, the chocolate-brown body covered with an opaque grey glaze. Coffeepot height 8¾in. 1956. The trials were not approved for production.   *Author's collection*

DARWIN, Erasmus. Blue jasper dip portrait medallion of Erasmus Darwin. Oval height 5in. Attributed to Hackwood, 1780.

Wedgwood Museum

DARWIN MUG. Queen's ware mug printed in underglaze blue with the Water Lily pattern for the Wedgwood Collectors' Society.

Wedgwood Museum

The Expression of the Emotions in Man and Animals, 1872, and a biography of his grandfather, Erasmus Darwin*, in 1879. A portrait medallion* of Charles Darwin was issued c.1880. The modeller has not been identified.

Darwin, Dr Erasmus (1731-1802)

Scientist, poet and physician, educated at St John's College, Cambridge, and Edinburgh University. Darwin was a doctor of medicine, who practised at Lichfield from 1756 until his removal to Derby in 1783. He declined an appointment as physician to George III*. His literary reputation rests on one long poem, *The Botanic Garden,* published in two parts in 1789 and 1791. Written in 2,192 decasyllabic rhymed couplets, the poem, a curious mixture of turgid rhetoric, original thought and self-parody, is a monument to scientific interest in nature. Erasmus Darwin was not only Wedgwood's 'favourite Aesculapius', who attended Wedgwood and his family in all their most serious ailments, but also, after Bentley*, his closest friend. His counsel and opinion were sought on the subject of canals* and turnpike* roads, Queen Charlotte's* teaset and the Portland vase*, education and the French Revolution. Wedgwood and Darwin may have been introduced by Dr Matthew Turner* as early as 1762 but there is no certain evidence of their acquaintance before 1764. Darwin was a founding member of the Lunar Circle (see: Lunar Society) and many of his closest friends were also Josiah's.

Darwin was twice married. Robert Waring Darwin*, a son by his first wife, married Josiah's eldest child, Susannah* ('Sukey') and one of their children was Charles Darwin*, who married his cousin Emma Wedgwood. By his second wife, Erasmus Darwin was grandfather to Francis Galton. Darwin's portrait by his friend Joseph Wright* of Derby, now in the National Portrait Gallery, London, was adapted (probably by Hackwood*) in 1780 for a portrait medallion*, and a portrait in a rather similar pose was painted by Stubbs* on a Wedgwood earthenware* plaque in 1783.

Darwin Mug, The

Queen's ware mug, height 6¼in., commissioned by the Wedgwood Collectors' Society*, New York, as one of several specially commissioned Queen's ware* pieces decorated with historic Wedgwood designs. The decoration is the *Water Lily* pattern, printed in underglaze blue*. The pattern was for many years believed to have been made for Erasmus Darwin* for presentation to his son, Robert, on the occasion of his marriage, but this is now known to be false. A service of *Water Lily,* printed in brown, was bought by Robert Waring Darwin* in 1808, and, for no better reason, the pattern has been connected with the Darwin name.

Darwin, Dr Robert Waring FRS (1766-1848)

Physician; third son of Erasmus Darwin* by his first wife, Mary (Howard). He married Susannah*, Josiah Wedgwood's eldest and favourite child, 1796, and Charles Darwin* was among their children. In the year of his marriage, Darwin moved to Shrewsbury, where he formed a large collection of Wedgwood, which included at least one first edition Portland* vase. Many years later, Eliza Meteyard* visited the Darwin's house and it was probably there that she first formed her abiding interest in Wedgwood.

Darwin, Susannah (1765-1817)

Eldest child of Josiah and Sarah Wedgwood*. She married, in 1796, Robert Waring Darwin*, third son of Josiah's close friend, Erasmus Darwin*, and one of her children was the great naturalist, Charles Darwin*. Susannah, known in the family as 'Sukey', was spirited, intelligent and popular, and Josiah seems to have enjoyed a closer relationship with her than with any other of his children.

Dassier (I.Dassier et cie, J. Dassier et cie)

Swiss partnerships of medallists and engravers. The partners were I. Dassier, Jean Dassier (1676-1763) and Antoine Dassier (1718-80). There seems to be no evidence to support the suggestion that the Dassiers were connected with the English Mint. Jean Dassier, who produced numerous medals of famous characters in history, worked in a style that became more or less international. Wedgwood cast many of the Dassier medals in basaltes* and also used Dassier models for his series of heads of the Popes, Kings and Queens of England, and the Roman History portraits (supplied as sulphurs* by Tassie*). The following portrait medallions of *Illustrious Moderns** were modelled from Dassier medals:

Philip Dormer Stanhope, Earl of Chesterfield
Abraham Demoivre
Cardinal Fleury
Martin Folkes
Sir Andrew Fountaine
Louis XV
Francesco Scipio di Maffei
John Churchill, Duke of Marlborough
John, 2nd Duke of Montagu

Davenport Factory

Manufactory of earthenware, black basaltes*, cane* ware, stone china*, and porcelain* founded in 1794 by John Davenport (later, with Josiah II*, member of parliament for the borough of Stoke-on-Trent). He retired in 1838, when the business was continued by his sons. They specialised in well-painted tablewares and vases, especially decorated with bold Japan patterns (see: Japonaiserie).

Painters who worked at the Davenport factory included Daniel and Edwin Steele, James Rouse and Jesse Mountford. Under John Davenport's direction, the factory produced fine creamware*, green glaze* leaf dessert plates, white stoneware, cane (including pastry ware*) and black basaltes, all in emulation, if not in direct imitation, of Wedgwood's. The creamware table services, in particular, were decorated with simple border patterns in typical Wedgwood manner.

Davies, Oscar (1894-1975)
English potter, established the Roeginga Pottery at Rainham, Kent, in association with his wife, Grace Barnsley*. He patented a combined milk and coffee pot, the *Duopour*, which was produced by Wedgwood in 1936, decorated by Grace Barnsley.

Davis, Edward (1813-78)
Sculptor, born in Carmarthen; studied at the Royal Academy Schools and exhibited at the Academy 1834-77. His bronze figure of Josiah Wedgwood was finished in 1860 and erected outside Stoke-on-Trent railway station. A copy of this figure was cast in bronze in the 1960s and now stands outside the main entrance to the Barlaston* factory.

Davison, Alexander & Co
Identified by Una des Fontaines in 1966 as the newly-formed banking house in which Josiah Wedgwood bought a partnership for his eldest son, John, in 1793. This contradicts previous statements that the firm in question was the London & Middlesex bank, which was not founded until 1862. The firm of Alexander Davison was originally registered in 1793 as Messrs Edwards, Smith, Templer, Middleton, Johnson and Wedgwood at 18 Stratford Place, London. Davison appears to have joined the partnership in 1804 when the offices moved to Pall Mall. The bank failed in 1816, when it was absorbed by Coutts. John Wedgwood, having advanced a further £10,000 in an effort to save the bank, lost the greater part of his inherited fortune.

Davy, Sir Humphry FRS (1778-1829)
English natural philosopher, educated at Penzance Grammar School. He superintended the laboratory of the Bristol Pneumatic Institution, visited London in 1799, and was appointed director of the chemical laboratory of the Royal Institution in 1801. In 1802 he was appointed Professor of Chemistry. Next year he became Fellow of the Royal Society, of which he was President in 1820. He was knighted in 1812 and created baronet in 1818.

Davy collaborated with Josiah's youngest son, Tom*, in the invention of an early photographic process by which the latter succeeded in reproducing images by the action of light on paper sensitised with nitrate. They were, however, unable to fix the images, which faded when exposed to light. The making of voltaic troughs* was first suggested to Josiah II* by Humphry Davy in 1808, when he offered to order between two and three hundred of them if Wedgwood would make them.

Day, Lewis Foreman (1845-1910)
Designer, decorative artist and critic. Day was born in London and educated at Merchant Taylor's School before studying in France and Germany. After further experience in craft workshops, he decided to specialise in the design of stained glass. A Master of the Art Workers Guild, Day exhibited at the Royal Academy and in 1870 founded a firm to design for various manufacturers of carpets, tiles, glass and wallpaper. He was commissioned by Wedgwood to produce a number of designs for tiles* during the early 1880s, shortly after the introduction of Marsden's* new process. His designs appear to have been almost exclusively of leaves and petals, strongly influenced by Art Nouveau* styles.

De Morgan, William Frend (1839-1917)
Designer and studio potter. He attended the Royal Academy Schools and worked first in stained glass before turning his attention to coloured glazes and the use of lustre* as pottery decoration. He began by decorating ware bought in white from manufacturers and small potteries. He opened his own pottery in Chelsea in 1872, which he transferred nine years later to Merton Abbey, Surrey. From 1888 he was in partnership with the architect Halsey Ricardo* at the South End Pottery, Fulham, West London. This closed in 1906. Wedgwood supplied him with 'blanks' – large dishes ('chargers') and tiles – in the white to be decorated in his own studio. De Morgan's lustre

DAVY, Sir Humphry. Queen's ware mug decorated with a lithographed portrait of Sir Humphry Davy to commemorate the bicentenary of his birth. 1978. *Wedgwood Museum*

technique and painting were unrivalled in his time and two of his best painters in lustre decoration were the brothers Charles and Fred Passenger*. De Morgan's *A Paper on Lustre Ware,* delivered to the Royal Society of Arts*, was published in 1892.
See: Colour Plate 31

De Shoning (d.1780)
Little is known of de Shoning except that he was apparently a friend, or at least an acquaintance, of Thomas Bentley's*, and that he was responsible for suggesting to Wedgwood one of the most daring experiments in marketing attempted by any manufacturer in the 18th century. The proposal was designed to broadcast Wedgwood wares throughout the smaller states of Europe, most particularly those principalities, electorates, bishoprics and duchies whose ruling families were not accessible through diplomatic introduction. The plan, simple but potentially ruinous in its cost, consisted of sending out unsolicited parcels of ware (Wedgwood called them 'Voluntaries') to large numbers of noble houses in Europe in the fond hope that these potential customers would not only pay for them but order more and advertise the excellence of the goods to others. It seemed to Josiah, 'almost the only mode in which our Goods can get into such Familys', but it was also extremely risky. The cost was likely to be enormous: Josiah was thinking in terms of 'a thousand parcels @ £20 each', and there was no guarantee that any of the goods would be either bought or returned. Nevertheless, he agreed to make the attempt 'to the utmost verge of prudence or rather beyond', and Germany was chosen for the first trial.

Just eight months later, in July 1772, Josiah was able to rejoice with Bentley on the arrival of 'some prizes from our expedition in Germany' and finally there were only three debts outstanding. This venture set the pattern for future efforts, though on a much smaller scale, to distribute Wedgwood through 'inertia selling'. By April 1772, however, de Shoning was already suspected of some dubious dealings, the details of which were not specified in Wedgwood's letters, in respect of orders from Poland, and de Shoning's name is not mentioned again.

De Vaere, John (fl.1785-1810)
Sculptor and modeller, born in France. De Vaere attended the Royal Academy Schools in 1786. He was recommended to Wedgwood by Flaxman* and succeeded Webber* as chief modeller at Etruria* in 1794, when the latter left Wedgwood's employment. Until 1790 he assisted Flaxman and Webber in Rome. Flaxman described his work as 'full of the sentiment of the fine Antique' and Josiah paid tribute to the 'spirited action & beauty of the figures' in his *Discovery of Achilles.* De Vaere's work for Wedgwood, so far identified, includes five portrait

DE VAERE, John. Solid blue and white jasper tablet, *The Discovery of Achilles,* from the wax model by De Vaere. Length 13¾in. c.1792.   *Sotheby's, London*

DE VAERE, John. Dark-blue jasper portrait medallion of Horatio, Viscount Nelson, modelled by De Vaere in 1798. Oval height 4in. c.1800-10.   *Wedgwood Museum*

medallions* – the Admirals Nelson, Duncan, Howe and St Vincent (used to ornament the jasper pedestal of the *Britannia Triumphant* group) and Alexander Allardyce, all modelled in 1798 – and the following tablets modelled in Rome between 1788 and 1790:

The Discovery of Achilles, tablet 9in. x 17in., 1789-90
Orestes and Pylades, tablet 7¾in. x 22¼in.
Judgement of Paris, tablet 7in. x 18½in.
Rape of Proserpine, tablet described as finished by De Vaere 'in a most beautiful manner' (Flaxman to Wedgwood March 1789). This is possibly the same as 'Pluto carrying off Proserpine', listed by Dalmazzoni in 1789 as the work of Angelini*

De Wilde, William (fl.1777)
Modeller, who executed commissions for Wedgwood. None of his work has been identified.

Death of a Roman Warrior
One of Wedgwood & Bentley's earliest and most impressive tablets, 11in. x 20in., which appears as no.72 in the 1773 Catalogue, in which it is described as a 'long square tablet; from an ancient sarcophagus at Rome. It was produced in black basaltes* and seems to be one of the few early subjects never to have been reproduced in jasper*. The subject is not from a single source, as the Catalogue suggests, but a composition from several sources. The central group derives from a Greek marble of the second century, formerly in the collection of Cardinal Albani and now in the Capitoline Museum, Rome. This was, for a century, called 'The Death of Meleager'*, an error which has led to the misguided renaming of the Wedgwood tablet. Other figures have been added from the monument of Hadrian (probably by way of Bartoli's* *Admiranda Romanorum)* and the Ara Pacis of Augustus. Josiah referred to this subject as 'the dead Warrior' in a letter of 6 February 1776, when it was remodelled, but it was in production at least three years earlier and may be the bas-relief of 'Antique figures' obtained from Mrs Landré in January 1769 at the relatively high price of eight shillings for the mould. *Death of a Roman Warrior* has been much reproduced, especially during the first quarter of the twentieth century, and many of the later reproductions no longer bear the distinctive 'ENGLAND' or 'MADE IN ENGLAND' impressed marks* that would identify their approximate date of production. They may be recognised by a lack of undercutting* and the flat uniformity of the back of the tablet.
See also: *Roman Procession*

DEATH OF A ROMAN WARRIOR. Black basaltes rectangular tablet, *Death of a Roman Warrior.* 10in. x 20in. c.1782.   *Wedgwood Museum*

DECANTER. Queen's ware decanter, in the form of a cloaked figure, decorated with 'satin' black glaze, made for Sandeman's port, c.1935.
Wedgwood Museum

Death of Meleager

See: Death of a Roman Warrior; Meleager

Decalomania (Decal)

See: Transfer Printing; Lithography

Decanter

Queen's ware decanters decorated with 'satin' black glaze, in the shape of a cloaked Spanish figure, height 10in., were made for Sandeman's port c.1935. These appear to be unmarked and, since the same figure with a similar glaze was made by other manufacturers, the Wedgwood decanter is not easy to identify.

Deck, Joseph-Théodore (1823-91)

Designer. One of the most important influences in French ceramics between 1850 and 1880, Deck was trained in various potteries in Europe before setting up his own studio pottery in Paris. His work was greatly influenced by Japanese art, which gained rapidly in popularity after the exhibitions in London in 1862 and in Paris in 1867. Several of his designs were reproduced by Wedgwood c.1870.

Decoration

In ceramics, there is a clear distinction, seldom scrupulously used, between decoration and ornament*. Decoration is designed to enhance the appearance of an object by the use of printed or painted pattern or colour (including gilding). It does not alter the form or outline of the object, but certain deliberate uses of decoration may deceive the eye and thus alter the object's perceived shape. Ornament, on the other hand, alters the form and outline of an object by the use of moulded or applied (sprigged) shape or pattern. Thus, an object with a moulded pattern covered in a coloured glaze is both ornamented and decorated.

Arthur Lane *(Style in Pottery,* 1948) defined the dual purpose of all decoration: to 'reaffirm the third dimension, the bulge of the shape between the profiles to right and left' and to reinforce stability by the use of 'strongly defined horizontal accent'. He recognised three principal 'rhythms' in all decoration and ornament: the single statement, which he described graphically as a 'Punctuation mark that first seizes our attention' (employed more often by the studio potter than on industrial pottery); the frieze, or border, that creates a continuous line around a three-dimensional object; and the all-over (coverall) design, often a repeating pattern, of the type favoured for the design of textiles and wallpaper. The affinity between design for textiles and the decoration of pottery and porcelain was already noticeable in the 18th century in the translation of work by such painters as Boucher* and Watteau*. The primary purpose of both decoration and ornament on pottery is to enhance its shape, either by drawing attention to its virtues or by disguising its faults. The most perfect pottery and porcelain therefore requires the least decoration, a fact inadequately appreciated in Western civilisations.

Déjeuner Set

A breakfast *(petit déjeuner)* service or cabaret*, for one person or more, consisting of tea cups and saucers, teapot, sugar box or dish, cream jug and accompanying tray. These sets were made by Wedgwood in the 18th and 19th centuries in Queen's ware*, black basaltes* and cane* ware for daily use, and also as cabinet* pieces in jasper. Towards the end of the 19th century, similar services were made in bone china*. Josiah Wedgwood had little grasp of the meaning of the word *déjeuner* (which he generally used to describe the tray for these sets) and even less of the spelling of the word, which eluded him entirely. *Déjeuner* sets were first mentioned as early as March 1773, when Wedgwood wrote 'we wil likewise make some Dejunias & furniture to them for Enameling'.
See: Trays

DEJEUNER SET. Fine solid blue and white jasper *déjeuner* set or *cabaret à deux* with an unusually large tray, ornamented with acanthus scrolls and classical figures. Tray diameter 15½in. c.1786-95.
Christie's, London

DELLA PORTA, Guglielmo. Solid blue and white jasper oval plaque ornamented with *Feast of the Gods* after Guglielmo della Porta. Oval 6¼in. x 9¼in. *Brooklyn Museum, Emily Winthrop Miles Collection*

DENMARK. Blue jasper dip plaque ornamented with a profile portrait of King Christian IX of Denmark and Norway, and the inscription 'MED GUD FOR AERE OG RET 1818 8 APRIL 1898'. Diameter 7⅛in. 1898. *Mr & Mrs David Zeitlin Collection*

Delftware

The town of Delft was not the site of the first Dutch pottery to make tin-glazed earthenware *(faience* or *maiolica)* but it became the centre for such pottery in the 17th century, becoming famous especially for its fine imitations in tin-glazed earthenware of Chinese porcelain. The name 'Delftware' was consequently adopted to describe English and Irish tin-glazed earthenware made especially at Lambeth (London), Bristol, Liverpool and Dublin. It was the potters of tin-glazed earthenwares who were most harmed by the international success of Wedgwood's Queen's ware*.

Della Porta, Guglielmo (?1510-77)

Italian sculptor celebrated especially for his tomb of Pope Paul III in the choir of St Peter's, Rome. Wedgwood reproduced five bas-relief subjects after Della Porta, probably copied from plaster casts of bronzes by Jacob Cornelisz Cobaert, in black basaltes. They are ovals, 6in. x 9in., usually with narrow basaltes frames, and they are listed as nos 2-6 in the 1773 Catalogue, described as 'fit either for inlaying, as Medallions in the Pannels of Rooms, as Tablets for Chimneypieces, or for hanging up as Ornaments in Libraries &c for which purpose some of them have rich Compartments [frames] of the same Material, modelled and burnt together with the Bas-reliefs.' The subjects are: *War of Jupiter and the Titans, Destruction of Niobe's Children, Feast of the Gods, Marriage Feast of Perseus and Andromeda* and *An Antique Boar Hunting*.

Della Robbia Ware

Tin-glazed terracotta made in Florence, Italy, by Luca Della Robbia, his nephew Andrea, and the latter's four sons, c.1438-1520. Their models were often bas-reliefs* or figures of *putti* or *amorini*, usually in white on a blue ground, but sometimes with touches of green, maroon and yellow. Hackwood* finished a number of small figures said to be after Della Robbia c.1785, but opinions are divided about the original source of them.
See: Infant Reclining Figures

Demeter

See: Ceres

Democritus

Greek philosopher, born in Thrace about 460 BC. Noted for his cheerfulness and optimism, he was known as the 'Laughing Philosopher'. A bust of 'Democrates', height 12½in., was supplied by Hoskins & Grant* in 1775. It does not appear in the Wedgwood & Bentley Catalogues* until 1779.

Demosthenes (c.384-322 BC)

Great Athenian orator. He used his eloquence to warn the Athenians against the intentions of Philip of Macedon. He poisoned himself in 322. Sixty of his orations have survived. A bust of Demosthenes, height 22in., was produced by Wedgwood in basaltes*, from a cast supplied by Hoskins & Grant* in 1775 and a portrait medallion*, 4in. x 3in., is listed in the 1777 Catalogue.

Denby, Charles (fl. 1750-80)

Painter and modeller, formerly of Derby, employed at the Chelsea Decorating Studio* from 1770. In September 1769 Wedgwood wrote that he had hired the young Hackwood* and added, 'with Denby and him I shall not want any other constant modeller at Etruria*'. In May 1770, however, Denby was dispatched to London as a painter, so great was Bentley's* need of skilled hands when demand for encaustic* painted vases coincided with the production of the *Husk** service. Wedgwood wrote of Denby: 'He applys close to business, has a delicate modesty in his manners, & I think will be an agreeable and useful assistant to us in a little time…he is really *learned* in the Anatomy & the drawing of a human figure', which suggests that Denby's work in London was the painting of vases.

Denmark

Early Danish pottery, especially the lead-glazed wares and slipwares, shows some similarity with English work of the same period. By the middle of the 18th century, the principal *faience** factories, Store Kongensgade (Copenhagen) and nearby Kastrup, were engaged in making tin-glazed wares in the rococo* style. About forty years later, the universal popularity of English creamware*, known in Denmark as Stengøds, had encouraged potters to imitate it, and some fine cream-coloured earthenware, including vases in the neo-classical* taste, were made towards the end of the century.

Prince Christian (later King Christian VIII)) of Denmark, who visited Wedgwood's York Street showrooms* in July 1822, ordered a large dinner service in drabware*, printed with his coat of arms in black and finished with a gold edge. The original order appears in the Crest Order Book* for 22 September 1822. The bulk of this service was sold, with others of the King's effects, in 1881.

A blue jasper dip* circular plaque ornamented with a profile portrait of Christian IX of Denmark and Norway within a hexagonal frame of laurel and oak was made for Goldschmidt Magazin, Copenhagen, to celebrate the King's eightieth birthday in 1898.

Dent, Catherine (fl.1769-74)

Painter at the Chelsea decorating Studio* engaged in painting the Frog* service, 1773-4.

D'Entrecolles, Père

French Jesuit missionary in China who sent descriptions of porcelain* manufacture back to Europe in 1712 and 1722, as well as samples of china clay (kaolin*) and feldspathic rock (*pai-tun tzu* or petuntse*). Unfortunately for the manufacture of porcelain in Europe, the samples could not be analysed and they were described in insufficient detail to allow them to be identified from the letters alone. D'Entrecolles was resident in the first quarter of the 18th century near Ching-tê-Chîu, a town of over one million people with at least 1,000 kilns that was a centre of porcelain manufacture. His letters, written to the Baron de Réaumur were published in 1717 and 1724 as *Lettres édifiantes et curieux,* and they circulated widely among European potters. They were undoubtedly known to Wedgwood, although no extracts from the *Lettres* appear in his Commonplace Books*.

See also: Du Halde, Jean Baptiste

Dentures

Josiah Bateman* wrote from Plymouth in 1815 enclosing an order from a Mr Edward Eardley of Exeter for 'A set of Teeth enamelled China to pattern…A quantity will be wanted for they are for a respectable dentist'. Nothing seems to have come of this request, but it was not the first of its kind to arrive at Etruria*. Porcelain* dentures had already been made by an émigré French dentist, Nicolas Dubois de Chemant, who had settled in England. He had applied unsuccessfully to Turner* for a supply of porcelain paste and turned for help to the Wedgwoods, who supplied him with substantial quantities of various pastes in 1800-1 and possibly for as much as twenty years thereafter.

In 1804, Joseph Bramah* suggested that Wedgwood should make false teeth, mentioning that 'a *French-Man* in London' (evidently de Chemant), who had a patent, nearly expired, was making a fortune out of the business 'altho managed in the most bungling manner possible and conducted with the greatest personal Importance [*sic*]'. Wedgwood's response to this attempt by one customer to steal the business of another is unlikely to have been favourable. Certainly, no false teeth were ever made by Wedgwood.

Derby

Creamware* was made at a small factory founded about 1751 and situated at Cockpit Hill, Derby, which lasted until about 1770. Specimens are fairly rare, but an example in the British Museum is transfer-printed* and inscribed 'Radford sculpsit DERBY Pot Works'. One of the proprietors, John Heath, a banker, was connected with the founding of the porcelain factory, in 1756.

Perhaps as early as 1745, but certainly by 1750, a small quantity of porcelain* was being made at Derby by Andrew Planché. The accounts of William Duesbury*, who at this time had an enamelling studio in London, refer to the enamelling of figures from Derby in 1753. This porcelain was made by Planché at Cockpit Hill. In 1756 an agreement was drafted, but never signed, between John Heath, banker, William Duesbury, enameller, and Andrew Planché, china maker, for organising a new porcelain factory at Nottingham Road, Derby. Duesbury, however, emerged as sole proprietor, and during the years 1756-8 the products of the factory were advertised as 'Derby, or the second Dresden'. The Longton Hall factory was bought in 1760 by Duesbury, who gained control of the Bow* Porcelain Factory in 1762 and of the Chelsea* Porcelain Factory in 1770. Derby specialised in figures (notably in biscuit* after about 1770) and fine quality enamel painting in the 18th century. 'Japan' patterns became a speciality towards the end of the century. Richard Holdship* went from Worcester* to Derby in 1764 and took the process of transfer-printing* with him. Rare examples of both Derby porcelain and Cockpit Hill creamware bear transfer-prints signed with an anchor, assumed to be the rebus of Holdship, the same mark occurring on earlier Worcester porcelain in conjunction with Holdship's signature. The Derby factory closed in 1848. The modern factory was founded in 1878.

No doubt Wedgwood was acquainted with Duesbury and there are numerous references to Derby painters applying to Wedgwood for work; but he rarely engaged one. Modellers who worked for both Wedgwood and Derby include Joachim Smith* and Pierre Stephan*.

Dere, John (fl.1765-80)

Landscape painter at Newport Street, London. A number of his views of Staffordshire were copied for the Frog* service.

Design

While English pottery remained a craft and its distribution and sale were confined to local markets, the design of shapes, ornament* and decoration* was dictated largely by practical considerations, such as the availability of materials and the simple requirements of neighbourhood customers. Technical developments, especially the introduction of press-moulding* and slip-casting*, gave the artist-craftsmen who designed and cut block moulds* some influence over the design of shapes and relief patterns, particularly during the period when colour decoration was limited to the random use of

metal oxides under a lead glaze (see: Tortoiseshell). The development of enamelling, and the application of transfer-printing to pottery, put the design of decoration into the hands of painters and engravers. Quality improved and, with increasing industrialisation, greater standardisation became possible. Markets expanded, and the experience of valuable export trade encouraged the owners of potteries to pay attention to the taste and changing fashions of peoples in foreign countries, particularly in Europe and America, as well as of their own countrymen in London and the major cities of Britain. Under the closer control of the owners, design became more varied and fell more evidently under the influence of fashion. 'Fashion', Josiah Wedgwood wrote in 1779, 'is infinitely superior to merit in many respects'.

Wedgwood was personally responsible for drawing and modelling both tableware and ornamental pieces, but he relied upon his modellers, not only for 'original' shapes but also for adaptations from existing silver and porcelain shapes and from engravings of sculpture and vases. Architects and sculptors also were potential sources of models and designs, and Wedgwood employed Flaxman* and Webber* and copied from Adam* and Chambers*. The design of Wedgwood's early enamelled decoration seems to have been left largely to the good taste and skill of his painters in London – Rhodes* and the painters in the Chelsea Decorating Studio* – but most services of tableware were decorated either with transfer-printed designs or simple enamelled borders. The subjects for printed decoration were carefully selected by Wedgwood, either from the engravers or from 'design books', such as Sayer's* *The Ladies Amusement.* The enamelled designs – simple running borders of leaf, flower and classical motifs – were generally adapted from nature and architecture, though some of the most striking (e.g. 'Etruscan' patterns) were copied from vases illustrated in d'Hancarville's* *Antiquités.* It was an early ambition of Wedgwood's to set up 'a regular drawing & modeling school to train up Artists', but these were to be employed in copying designs, not in creating them.

Although scarcely any of Wedgwood's work in the 18th century was original in either form or decoration, much of it was new in pottery. As a trained thrower, Josiah understood purity of form better than most pottery directors today and the elegance of the Queen's ware shapes undoubtedly helped to recommend it to Wedgwood's most discerning and influential patrons. This combination of elegance with utility has been the hallmark of the best of Wedgwood's tableware shapes throughout the firm's history, outstanding examples being the famous 146 teapot (long believed to be an 18th-century shape personally designed by Josiah I), first recorded in 1828, and the 225 shape, introduced in 1984.

The design of Wedgwood has always been strongly influenced by fashion, most notably by the neo-classical* style, but the importance of some styles – Art Nouveau* and Art Deco*, for example – has been slight, while that of Japonaiserie* and Japonisme* was, until the 1980s brought Japanese taste and the Japanese market into prominence, forgotten or ignored.

A long and distinguished history and a recognisable design style, especially in ornamental ware, such as jasper*, may be as limiting as it is valuable, and successive generations of Wedgwood directors and designers have needed to guard against the real danger that innovation may be stifled by tradition. Wedgwood has continued to follow the policy of Josiah I in the employment or commissioning of 'outside' designers. The work of Wedgwood's art directors – Thomas Allen*, John Goodwin*, Victor Skellern* and their successors – and their staff designers has deliberately been augmented, and sometimes challenged, by commissioned work from artists such as Lessore*, Alfred and Louise Powell*, Keith Murray* and Eric Ravilious*, who were able to bring a fresh vision to decoration and sometimes also to Wedgwood's shapes. In 1933, in a confidential memorandum setting out his view of the pottery industry in Britain, Josiah V noted as one of the industry's cardinal failures 'A poor standard of design' and went on to add: 'The majority of factories have no real designer. The decorating foreman or an entirely unqualified director or manager makes the designs, either according to an equally unqualified customer's or traveller's sketch, or, more usually, by using a stock lithograph*, or by imitating someone else's pattern'. These conditions have changed in the Potteries, but ignorance of design is not confined to earlier directors, and powerful but 'equally unqualified' customers continue to hamper attempts at change or innovation.

See: Decoration; Ornament; Sadler, John; Tableware Shapes

DESIGN '63. Three bone china pieces with silkscreened decoration by Peter Wall, designed especially for the Design '63 Exhibition. Cigarette jar height 4½in.   *Author's collection*

DESIGN '63. Two first trials for Queen's ware tea caddies with silk-screened decoration for the Design '63 Exhibition. Both designs were accepted for production.   *Author's collection*

Design Research Unit

The first large professional design consultancy in Britain, founded on the Morrisonian concept of a group of artists and designers working together. It first director, Henry Reed, described its principles: 'Like every aspect of modern industry, design should be a cooperative activity, and the function of DRU is to focus on every project it undertakes the combined knowledge and experience of several creative minds'. In January 1961, DRU, then under the direction of Sir Mischa Black, was commissioned to standardise the use of typefaces and colours used throughout the Wedgwood company, from invoices to delivery trucks, to present a systematic and recognisable 'image' to replace the haphazard and multiform conglomeration that had been allowed to accumulate over the centuries. This was successfully launched in January 1963.

Design '63

The name given to an exhibition held in the Wigmore Street, London, showrooms* in January 1963. It was customary to hold a reception and exhibition on two consecutive evenings in January each year to show new tableware patterns, but in 1963 they were complemented by a range of ornamental pieces by Peter Wall* and Robert Minkin* distinguished by their style, quality and originality rather than chosen for their volume-sales potential. A small number of models commissioned from Angelo Biancini* also appeared for the first time.

Deutsche Blumen

Deutsche blumen (German flowers) is the contemporary name for flowers painted in a naturalistic style introduced at Meissen* by J.G. Höroldt, c.1740. Originally the flowers were painted as specimens, but these soon gave way to a freer style of loose bouquets, sometimes accompanied by scattered sprigs. The *Deutsche blumen* style of decoration appears on enamelled Queen's ware* and Pearl* ware jugs of the last quarter of the 18th century.

Devis, Anthony (1729-1817)

Landscape painter, particularly in watercolour; received a Premium from the Royal Society of Arts in 1763; exhibited at the Royal Academy, 1772 and 1781. Devis supplied views for the Frog* service. Wedgwood wrote to Bentley* in November 1773: 'I asked [Lord Stamford's] permission to add some views of Enville to our list. He told me he had ten or a dozen color'd sketches taken by an Eminent hand...and he thought that if we were to apply to the person who took them he could furnish us with a great variety more...His name is Devis in Lamb's Conduit Street'. Wedgwood added: 'These views are exactly what we want. The inside of Pleasure Grounds taken with great taste and and perfectly picturesque'. There is no evidence to support the statement that Devis was employed at the Chelsea Decorating Studio*.

Devonshire, Georgiana Cavendish, Duchess of (1757-1806)

Famous beauty and Whig hostess; eldest daughter of the first Earl Spencer; married 1774 the fifth Duke of Devonshire. In 1778 Wedgwood named some flower pots* with green hoops and 'brown spaces' after her. Her portrait medallion*, attributed to Flaxman*, was produced in 1782.

Devoto, John (fl. c.1750-80)

Artist in watercolour who was employed, with Unwin* and Catherine Willcox*, in the encaustic* painting of tablets*.

DEUTSCHE BLUMEN. Reverse of a Pearl ware jug enamelled with a large spray of Deutsche Blumen-style flowers in naturalistic colours. Height 8⅝in. c.1780.   *Author's collection*

DEVONSHIRE, Georgiana, Duchess of. Pale-blue jasper dip portrait medallion. Oval height 4½in. c.1786. *Nottingham Castle Museum*

D'Hancarville, Baron Pierre (fl.1760-90)

Pierre Germain Hugues, a French adventurer who assumed the title of baron. As an antiquarian and art historian of some repute, he published, in 1766-7, *Antiquités Etrusques, Grécques et Romaines* (in the English edition as *Collection of Etruscan, Greek and Roman Antiques from the Cabinet of the Honble William Hamilton),* a sumptuous work in four volumes lavishly illustrating Sir William Hamilton's* collection. It is described, with Staffordshire brevity, as 'Hambleton's [*sic*] Etruscan Antiques' in the list of books belonging to Wedgwood & Bentley in 1770, and many of Wedgwood's black basaltes* vase shapes, and their 'Etruscan' decorations, were copied from it, although Wedgwood considered that the illustrations were superior to the originals. 'Mr Hambleton', he wrote to Bentley in 1770, 'has flattered the old pot-painters very much'. Many of Wedgwood's classical borders for tableware decoration also were copied or adapted from borders painted on Hamilton's vases. In 1785 the self-styled baron published *Recherches sur l'Origine, l'Esprit, et les progrès des Arts de la Grèce,* a work not celebrated for its accuracy.

Diana

Roman name for Artemis, the daughter of Zeus and Leto, and twin sister of Apollo*. She was a goddess who delighted in the chase and is usually depicted carrying a bow and quiver. She is also identified with Selene, goddess of the Moon, in love with Endymion*, and is sometimes shown with a crescent moon on her forehead. Unlike most of the inhabitants of Olympus she was noted for her chastity. She slew Orion because he attempted to violate her, and Actaeon was changed into a stag because he saw her bathing.

Wedgwood subjects:

Diana, seated figure for a candelabrum. Modelled as a companion piece to *Minerva.* Attributed to Webber*

Diana, seated figure, height 8⅞in., produced in black basaltes from c.1830 and Carrara, c.1849, described in the 1849 price lists as 'after Flaxman'

Diana and Actaeon, plaque modelled by Alec Miller*, 1906

Diana the Huntress, cameo, 1774. Commonly used also as ornament for jasper wares

Diana Visiting Endymion, tablet 8½in. x 27½in., modelled in Rome from the bas-relief of *Selene and Eros visiting Endymion* on the Sarcophagus of Gerontia in the Capitoline Museum. No.274 in the 1787 Catalogue*

Triform Goddess (Diana, Luna, Hecate), tablet 9¼in. x 7½in., modelled by Pacetti*, 1788

DIANA. Black basaltes figure described in the 1849 Carrara price list as 'after Flaxman'. Height 8⅞in. c.1860. *Formerly Buten Museum*

DIANA, Green jasper dip tablet, *Diana visiting Endymion,* 13¾in. x 30¼in. c.1875. *Wedgwood Museum*

DICED PATTERN. Small, lidded pale-blue jasper cream jug with engine-turned 'blind' dicing and an applied pattern of running oak and quatrefoils in white and green jasper. Height 4½in. c.1790. *Manchester Museum*

DICED PATTERN. Three-colour jasper teapot and lidded jug in bright blue jasper dip with engine-turned dicing ornamented with green quatrefoils. Jug height 5½in. c.1790.
Manchester Museum

Diced Pattern

A jasper pattern produced on the engine-turning lathe*, the chequered effect being obtained by cutting through a coloured dip* to a contrasting ground (usually white) at regular intervals. The diced pattern is found most frequently on vases, trophy plates*, cassolettes*, tobacco jars and coffee cans*. This type of ornament was introduced about 1785 but it was reproduced in the second half of the 19th century and small quantities of diced ware, usually for limited editions*, have been produced in recent years.
See: Colour Plate 32

Dillon, Michael (1944-76)

Studio potter, born in Bendigo, Victoria, 1944. For four years he was an art student at Bendigo Technical College before moving to England. He joined Wedgwood in 1970 and was given a free hand to create Oriental-inspired shapes with abstract clay designs and special glazes. His work demonstrated a very high quality of understanding and originality. His tragically early death robbed the world of British ceramics of a considerable artist. His work is marked with his initials 'MD' incised.

Dimcock, Thomas (fl.1760-80)

Painter employed by Wedgwood in 1770 and believed to have been responsible for dessert ware in Queen's ware enamelled with naturalistic flowers in deep pink in the style generally associated with James Bakewell*, some of which is marked with the enamelled letter 'D'.

Dimpled Jasper

See: Granulated Jasper

Diomedes

King of Argos, who sailed to Troy with eighty ships. He enjoyed the protection of Athene and fought against Hector* and Aeneas*. Diomedes and Ulysses carried off the Palladium*, which protected Troy while it remained within its walls.
Wedgwood subject:
Diomedes Carrying off the Palladium, medallion 3½in. x 2⅞in., remodelled by Hackwood* (from a mould taken by Bedson*) from a model in the Newdigate* collection in 1776. No.169 in 1777 Catalogue*

Dionysus

See: Bacchus

Dip

The process of covering solid-colour jasper* (generally white or pale-blue) with a darker jasper slip*. Some jasper pieces are dipped on one side only, some on both, with the base colour showing at the edges. Jasper dip was introduced in 1777, when the rising price of cobalt* made the cost of staining deep blue solid jasper prohibitive. The dip process is still in use, especially for 'prestige' objects and for those that rely for their decorative effect on the lines or patterns produced by engine-turning*.
See: Colour Plate 33
See also: Bas-relief Ware

Doccia Factory

Porcelain factory, near Florence, founded by the Marquis Carlo Ginori in 1735, which has remained in the hands of the Ginori family to the present day. The factory has always been renowned for porcelain of high quality, especially in regard to decoration, often in the style of Vienna or Meissen*. Blue and white portrait medallions*, usually said to be in the style of Wedgwood, in fact pre-date Wedgwood's by some twenty years, eighty-four such portraits of the Medici family being used in 1756 to ornament a single porcelain centrepiece in celebration of the *'Glorie della Toscana'*. While it is most unlikely that either Wedgwood or Bentley* ever saw this particular piece, or any illustration of it, there is good reason to suppose that they might have seen other similar Doccia medallions brought home by patrons, such as Captain Edward Hamilton or Sir Watkin Williams Wynn*, returning from the Grand Tour, or in the possession of Sir William Hamilton* or Lord Lansdowne*. The possibility that a single Doccia blue and white porcelain portrait medallion may have provided the inspiration for Wedgwood's long list of classical and modern portraits in jasper cannot be discounted.

DOCCIA. Porcelain portrait medallions of *(left)* Camilla Marteli (1547-90), wife of Cosimo, 1st Grand Duke of Tuscany, and *(right)* Vittoria della Rovere (1623-94), wife of Grand Duke Ferdinand II, the grounds enamelled in underglaze blue and inscribed with the subjects' names in relief. Ovals 3½in. x 2¾in. c.1750. Doccia portraits of this kind may have provided the inspiration for Wedgwood's jasper portrait medallions. *British Museum*

DOCUMENTARY PIECES. Queen's ware tea pot enamelled in colour with the arms of the Honourable Company of Shipwrights, a monogram and the date 1784. Height 6⅝in. (Replacement lid of earlier date).   *Sotheby's, Sussex*

Documentary Pieces

Specimens of ware which cast light upon a factory's history are described as 'documentary'. These include fragments or shards* discovered during the excavation of a factory site, examples of ware which have an impeccable provenance (such as those which are recorded as owned by successive generations of a potter's family), and pieces which bear artists' or modellers' signatures, or dates or informative inscriptions. Josiah I took active steps to prevent artists or modellers from signing their work after he discovered Hackwood's* signature on portrait medallions* and signed pieces of 18th-century Wedgwood are therefore rare. The signatures of later artists, such as Lessore*, Brownsword* and the Powells* often appear in the decoration or on the base of the piece, and Daisy Makeig-Jones* sometimes hid her initials skilfully among the complicated decoration of her Fairyland Lustre* bowls and vases.

Queen's ware* jugs and teapots sometimes bear inscriptions to individuals or to groups or associations (for example, volunteer regiments) and these are often dated. Such inscriptions on early black basaltes* or jasper* are extremely rare.

DOCUMENTARY PIECES. Queen's ware vase decorated with a carved design of leaves coloured in ochre, grey-green and blue with some gilding against a Rockingham glaze ground. Impressed 'H. Barnard TRIAL. 29.1.98'. Height 9½in. 1898.   *Wedgwood Museum*

Dod

A die through which a strip of clay is extruded in a desired form and size. After extrusion the strip is cut off and bent to the required shape. The technique is often used for the making of handles, which are then luted on.

DOCUMENTARY PIECES. Black basaltes vase and cover of shield shape, painted in encaustic orange-red and white with the figures of *Jupiter* and *Ganymede,* and *(verso)* the inscription 'W.M.MOSELEY. 1788'. Height 9¾in.   *Sotheby's, London*

Dolphin

French: *Dauphin.* Sea mammal venerated in ancient times and then, as now, protected from persecution. Representations of dolphins appear occasionally on antique coins and terracottas, in Pompeian wall paintings, and on the furniture and pottery of the Greeks and Romans. The title 'Dauphin' was taken by Guigo IV of Viennois in 1140 and surrendered to the family of Valois two hundred years later on condition that it should belong to the heir to the French throne. This explains the frequent appearance of the dolphin in French decoration, but it was popular also in Italy and England. Dolphins are used as supporters for Wedgwood tripod vases (particularly for the tripod lamps* and pastille burners*); and the well-known dolphin candlesticks*, which have been produced until the present day in basaltes* and Queen's ware*, and were also made in rosso antico* and Majolica*, are said to have been modelled by Josiah Wedgwood himself. A dolphin was chosen by Laurence Whistler* for the centre decoration for one of his few designs for Wedgwood in 1955.
See: Colour Plate 34

DOLPHIN. Pair of black basaltes Dolphin candlesticks, the shell ornament on the base applied in rosso antico. Height 10in. c.1810.
Sotheby's, London

DRAB STONEWARE. Smear-glazed Drab 'porcelain' vase moulded in the form of thistle-leaves over a reeded ground with branch handles. Height 7½in. c.1820. *Wedgwood Museum*

DRAB STONEWARE. Teapot, shape 43 ('Egyptian') ornamented with bands of fruiting vine in bright blue on a pierced stand slotted to contain a burner to keep the tea hot. Height 7½in. c.1825.
Mr & Mrs Samuel Laver Collection

Doncaster, Samuel (d. after 1841)
Engraver of Burslem; worked for Wedgwood, 1806-11.

Door Furniture
Finger plates, key escutcheons, door and drawer knobs were all made by Wedgwood, Turner* and other 18th-century potters, but in the 19th century the manufacture of these pieces tended to be concentrated among specialist factories. Early examples of Wedgwood door furniture are extremely rare.
See also: Bell Pulls

Doric Jug
Bulbous jug with tall collar and moulded mask beneath the lip, It appears in Queen's ware with lustre decoration* and in Majolica* in the second half of the 19th century.

Dossie, Robert
See: Handmaid to the Arts

Downing, William (fl.1790-11)
Engraver of Hanley; worked for Wedgwood, 1806-11.

Drab Stoneware ('Porcelain')
'Drab' is the name given to a distinctive greenish-brown ware made by Wedgwood in two different bodies: a stoneware and a stained earthenware. The latter is one of the coloured bodies* and is discussed under that heading. The stoneware was sometimes produced as a dry body*, but usually with a smear-glaze, from about 1819.

A beautiful saltglazed drabware had been made in Staffordshire from about 1720. Wedgwood's early-19th century drab body was a stained version of the white stoneware body described as 'porcelain' and the drab body was therefore called 'drab porcelain' to distinguish it from the similarly stained coloured body. The range of pieces made appears to have been almost identical with that of both the contemporary white and cane* stonewares, and included teapots, sugar boxes and cream jugs, decorative jugs ornamented in a variety of colours, small vases, flower baskets and caddy spoons*. All the earliest orders for drab porcelain were for drab with white or blue relief ornaments. 'Embossed Chinese flowers', 'New blue fruit band' and 'Lilac and white honeysuckle' ornaments were added in 1828 and the first Gothic* jugs were introduced between 1828 and 1830. Drab stoneware was made throughout the 19th century and was used in 1863 for some *Celtic* vases with raised and acid gold and white enamel decoration. One of the most unusual pieces made in this body was a five-piece inkstandish, the lid ornamented with figures of a medieval lady, her train held by two pages to form a pen tray, decorated with transparent glazes, produced in 1872. A darker brown stoneware*, made from about 1807, was known as 'Stone Brown' or 'Brown Porcelain'.

Drabware
See: Coloured Bodies

Dragon Lustre
See: Ordinary Lustres

DRAB STONEWARE. Flower basket ornamented with acanthus leaves and bell-flowers in lilac and white. Height 2in. c.1828.
Wedgwood Museum

DRAB STONEWARE. Pair of *Celtic* vases decorated with raised and acid-etched gilding and raised white enamel decoration. Height 4½in. c.1895. *Wedgwood Museum*

Drainer (Strainer)

A flat, pierced, false bottom to rest on a large platter, principally for draining boiled or steamed fish. Drainers were also made with small feet to stand in large meat dishes, the surfaces of which were sloped towards a scooped well for the collection of juices. The making of drainers in the 18th century was a skilled operation, and it is worthy of note that, when Wedgwood was finding difficulty in making flat jasper* tablets*, he brought in a maker of drainers from the Useful Works. Because they were both difficult and expensive to make (and therefore not produced in large quantities) and vulnerable, undamaged drainers from the 18th century or early 19th century are rare.

Dresser, Christopher (1834-1904)

Designer, writer and botanist, born in Glasgow. Dresser studied at the London School of Design and also at Jena University, where he obtained a Doctorate of Philosophy. In 1862 he published *The Art of Decorative Design,* the first of his studies on the subject. He differed from many of his contemporaries in his willingness to design for production by machine. While others looked backwards and tried to revive faded handicrafts, Dresser studied new manufacturing processes and adapted his design for their use. He designed domestic silver and metalwork, textiles, glass and furniture.

Dresser was never employed by Wedgwood but he created a number of designs for tableware and ornamental pieces between 1865 and 1880, the same period when he was producing designs also for Minton's*. Some of those which he created before he visited Japan in 1876-7 are clearly inspired by Egyptian motifs. Much of his best work was done after his return, and in 1883 he published *Japanese Architecture, Art and Art Manufactures,* which established his reputation as an Orientalist, but he does not appear to have designed anything based on Japanese sources for Wedgwood. Several vases decorated with designs by Dresser have been identified, some because they bear his signature in the decoration and others from drawings in surviving pattern books in the archives, but there can be little doubt that more are unrecognised.

See: Colour Plate 35

Drum

Cylindrical pedestal for a lamp, vase, figure or candelabrum. Drums for such purposes have been produced in all of Wedgwood's dry bodies*, especially jasper*, often mounted in ormolu*.

Dry Bodies

Non-porous, unglazed stonewares, usually made by adding colouring oxides to local clays. Wedgwood's dry bodies were jasper* (the only Wedgwood ceramic body which was not either an adaptation or a development of one which already existed in some recognisable form), black basaltes*, white terracotta stoneware*, rosso antico*, cane*, drab stoneware*, and white and various coloured stonewares made in the early part of the 19th century and described as 'porcelain'. Dry bodies were used for a wide variety of objects, both useful and ornamental, and were ornamented with applied reliefs (often in a contrasting colour) or by engine-turning*, or decorated with enamelling or coloured slip applied before firing. The interiors of holloware pieces intended for use (not as cabinet pieces*) were glazed to prevent staining.

Du Burk, John (fl.1760-77)

Merchant, who acted as Wedgwood's agent in Amsterdam from 1769 to 1777. He purchased £50 worth of vases in 1769 and wrote to Wedgwood in April that he had 'had a good success at the first market, which thank God I had a sale so much that I am almost out of stock'. The association soon, however, deteriorated, and Josiah was anxious about shipping large stocks to Amsterdam without prepayment. Two years later, both Wedgwood and Bentley were relieved to find a partner for Du Burk in Joseph Cooper* and an agreement was signed in April 1773, but sales did not improve and Cooper discovered 'gross mistakes' in the accounts. Nothing was done until May 1776, when (presumably on the dubious principle of poacher turned gamekeeper) Ben Mather* was sent out to count the stock. By October Wedgwood had enough evidence to condemn Du Burk as 'a bad Man, as well as a fool' and was

DRESSER, Christopher. Designs by Dresser for the decoration of ornamental pieces and tablewares, c.1866.   *Wedgwood Museum*

advised to take legal action against him. After much unpleasantness the embezzler was convicted and sent to prison, whereupon his wife demanded that Wedgwood pay Du Burk's debts. Wedgwood appropriately declared that he 'would not pay a stiver' (Dutch: *stuiver,* a small coin).

Du Halde, Jean Baptiste (1674-1743)

Jesuit missionary in China, who published *Description...de l'empire de Chine* in Paris in 1735. It contained one of the earliest descriptions of the composition and manufacture of Chinese porcelain to be published in Europe and an English translation appeared in London in 1738. Josiah Wedgwood's first Commonplace Book* contains long extracts from du Halde's work and there is no doubt that he studied it closely when he was contemplating the production of porcelain at Etruria*.

Du Roveray J.P. (fl.1760-80)

A London merchant of Swiss extraction with whom Wedgwood first established a connection in 1775. Du Roveray exported to the Continent and was noted for the unnecessary length of his letters. On his mother's side, he was related to the Dassier* family, and he offered to help Wedgwood to obtain medals.

Dublin

See: Showrooms

Duesbury, William (1725-86)

Son of a tanner; born at Cannock, Staffordshire; proprietor of a London decorating studio, 1751-3; proprietor of the Derby* porcelain factory founded in 1756. Duesbury probably controlled the Bow* porcelain factory in East London from 1762 and had a financial interest in the studio of James Giles* after 1770 in which year he bought the Chelsea* factory. The Derby factory was especially noted for the quality of its biscuit* figures and enamel painting. Wedgwood's white jasper* figures, used to ornament Vulliamy's* clocks and barometers are almost indistinguishable from Derby's biscuit figures and were evidently inspired by them.

There was talk in 1774-5 of portrait medallions* being made at Derby from models supplied by Joachim Smith* but no trace of any such portraits has been found.

Dumb Waiter
A bone china* revolving circular tray, 'Dumb Waiter' or 'Lazy Susan', 18¾in. diameter, c.1880, decorated with panels of oriental flowers in the currently fashionable *Japonisme* style, with a matching breakfast set, was sold at Christie's* in October 1973. Similar sets are recorded in both bone china and Pearl* ware c.1880-1920.

Dummy Ware
Another name for pastry ware or pie-crust* ware.
See: Game Pie Dish

Dundas, Sir Laurence (1719-81)
First baronet. Dundas began as a woollen draper in Edinburgh, being elected member of parliament for the Linlithgow burghs in 1747-8. Subsequently he moved south, representing Newcastle-under-Lyme, Staffordshire, 1762-8, and returning to Scotland to be member for Edinburgh, 1768-81. He amassed an enormous fortune (£800,000 in four years according to the unreliable evidence of Horace Walpole) in the Seven Years' War as commissary to the army and bought Moor Park, Hertfordshire, which, like his house in Arlington Street, London, he furnished lavishly. He was an early patron of Robert Adam*, Boulton* and Wedgwood and the owner of the magnificent chimneypiece of marble and lapis lazuli*, formerly in the Borghese* collection, which may have been the inspiration for Wedgwood's *Dancing Hours*. A view of Moor Park appears on one of the glaciers* made for the Frog* service.

Dunting
Cracking caused by stresses developing during the processes of firing and cooling. These may be the result of faulty design as well as incorrect or erratic firing temperatures, and may occur a month or more after manufacture. Godfrey Wedgwood* explained in a letter to Colonel Crealock* dated 26 September 1876: 'This is an accident which sometimes happens to large pieces of ware after they are finished'. Dunting is not, however, confined to large pieces of ware.

Duopour
Combined coffee- and milk-pot patented by Oscar Davies* in 1935 and made in Queen's ware* by Wedgwood about that date. The *Duopour* pot was usually sold with matching cups and saucers, all decorated by Grace Barnsley*, Davies's wife. The impressed marks are WEDGWOOD MADE IN ENGLAND and DUOPAR (*sic*).

Duquesnoy, François (1594-1643)
Born in Brussels, Duquesnoy lived in Italy from 1620 and assisted Bernini with the St Peter's, Rome, *baldacchino*. He became known by the sobriquet, *Il Fiammingo* (The Fleming). He adhered mainly to the classical tradition, and his work was notable for bronzes of *putti* – small boys in various guises and engaged in various occupations – which were a favourite form of Roman decoration, a particularly famous example being the 'Cupids as Craftsmen' painted on the walls of the Vetii at Pompeii*. The much-reproduced fountain figure, the *Manaken-pis* in Brussels, is Duquesnoy's work. Most of the 18th-century porcelain factories, including Sèvres, owed models of *putti* to his inspiration, and forty figures of Sleeping Boys* after sketches by Duquesnoy were made in Vincennes porcelain for the King of France in 1755. A dated *Somnus* figure was produced in white porcelain by the Chelsea* factory* in 1746. Duquesnoy's bas-reliefs* of boys were reproduced also in ivory, bronze and plaster. Wedgwood reproduced both figures and bas-reliefs in black basaltes* and jasper*.

The following subjects are after Duquesnoy:

Bacchanalian Boys, six bas-reliefs, casts of which were supplied by Mrs Landré* in 1769. They have not been certainly identified but are most probably those listed in the 1773 Catalogue as nos 13-14, 32, and 35-7: *Bacchanalian Boys at Play, Silenus and Boys, Boys Playing with a Goat, Bacchanalian Boys* (two plaques), and *A Bacchante and Children*

In addition, five models of *Sleeping Boys* (often erroneously called *Somnus*) were produced in basaltes by 1770 and may have been from casts supplied by Mrs Landré in 1769.

See also: Infant Reclining Figures

Dwight, John (c.1637-1703)
Studied at Christ Church, Oxford, where he received an M.A. degree. In 1671 he took out a patent for 'the mistery of transparent earthenware, commonly known by the name of porcelane in China, and of stoneware, vulgarly called Cologne ware'. From other sources we know that 'red porcelain' was a term commonly used to describe Yi-Hsing stoneware*, and some of Dwight's white (or drab-coloured) stonewares are translucent in parts where they are thin enough. Dwight established himself at Fulham, where he made some remarkable busts and figures. He also made bellarmines which are often difficult to distinguish from those made in Cologne. In 1690 Dwight started an action, alleging infringement of his patents, against the Elers* brothers and Aaron, Thomas and Richard Wedgwood, kinsmen of Josiah Wedgwood. The Wedgwoods were probably, like the Elers, making red stoneware. Dwight was the first to use calcined flint in the body of earthenware, an invention usually credited to John Astbury.

Dysart Glaze
See: Glazes

Dysart Green
In 1882, the architect Halsey Ricardo*, a leading proponent of the Arts and Crafts Movement*, remodelled the Earl of Dysart's house, Buckminster Park, in Leicestershire, installing at least twelve chimneypieces* inset with Wedgwood plaques and medallions. At Ricardo's request, Wedgwood created for this purpose a new 'Peach' jasper*, known also as 'Dysart Green'. The house was demolished shortly after World War II.

DUQUESNOY, François. Three-colour jasper figure of a *Sleeping Boy* after Fiammingo, the figure in white lying on a solid green sheet on a lilac base. c.1785-90.
Kadison Collection

Eardley, Joseph and Richard (fl.1880-1920)
Painters at Etruria, the former c.1885-1910, the latter working under the direction of John Goodwin*.

Earle, Thomas (1810-76)
Sculptor, born in Hull; son of the sculptor John Earle. Thomas Earle was employed by Sir Francis Chantrey in London before studying at the Royal Academy Schools, where he was awarded a Gold medal in 1839. He executed a number of groups which were admired and exhibited at the Royal Academy between 1843 and 1873. He was said to have died of a broken heart at hearing that his 'Alexander the Great', on which he had worked for three years, had been rejected by the Academy. His bust of the Marquis of Zetland (1846) was reproduced by Wedgwood in Carrara* in 1868.

Earthenware
An English term for all factory-made pottery which is not vitrified. It therefore excludes stoneware* and porcelain*. Since earthenware is porous, it requires a glaze. *Faïence, maiolica* and *delft* are all varieties of tin-glazed earthenware. The finest quality earthenwares are white, or near white, and since the middle of the 18th century have contained calcined flint*. Wedgwood's Queen's ware* belongs to this class. Lead-glazed cream-coloured earthenware of the type made by Wedgwood is usually called *faience-fine* in France and *Steingut* in Germany.

Eastern Flowers
Oriental-style pattern of the *famille-rose* type, designed by G. Allen in 1845. First produced with onglaze enamel and lustre* decoration on Queen's ware, it was reintroduced in 1954 as an underglaze lithograph pattern in muted shades of brown, yellow, pink and green.
See also: Lithography

Eastwood, Hanley, Staffordshire
Earthenware factory owned by William Baddeley*. He made creamware*, cane*, Egyptian black* and other wares inspired by Wedgwood during the last quarter of the 18th century and the early years of the 19th. He used the impressed mark 'EASTWOOD'.

Eberhard, Robert G.
See: Toby Jug

Ecritoire
See: Escritoire

Ecuelle
French term for a lidded shallow bowl, usually with two handles level with the rim, and a conforming stand. Shapes in English pottery and porcelain were generally based on silver or Continental porcelain shapes. *Ecuelles* were generally used for soup, but Wedgwood's jasper *écuelles*, with unglazed (sometimes lapidary polished) interiors were probably 'cabinet' pieces*. *Ecuelles* were produced until 1940 in Queen's ware* and bone china* patterns and occur, more rarely, in cane* and drab ware*.

Eden, William
See: Auckland, William Eden

Edgar, Albert (fl.1920-36)
Painter at Etruria* working under the direction of John Goodwin*.

ECUELLE. Covered broth cup (ecuelle) and stand decorated with variegated lustre. Height 4¼in. c.1815. *Formerly Buten Museum*

Edgeworth, Honora Sneyd (d.1780)
Daughter of Ralph Sneyd of Lichfield; second wife of the author R.L. Edgeworth*, a close friend of Josiah Wedgwood's. Wedgwood, who stayed with the Edgeworths in 1778, described Honora as 'a very polite, sensible, and agreeable lady...with a considerable share of beauty'. After her death in 1780, Edgeworth wrote to Wedgwood asking for her profile portrait to be made in jasper*. This was modelled, probably by Flaxman*, 'from a profile by Mrs Harrington [the well-known artist in silhouette] and an excellent picture by [John] Smart', the miniaturist. The field below the truncation is impressed 'HONORA EDGEWORTH O B 1780', and the portrait is one of the few to have been produced on a rare brown jasper ground, though it is more often seen on the black ground.

Edgeworth, Richard Lovell (1744-1817)
English author, born at Bath and educated at Trinity College, Dublin, and Corpus Christi College, Oxford, where he read both law and science. He had a lifelong fascination with vehicles and their construction and, at the age of twenty-three, designed a machine for land measurement which won him a Silver Medal from the Society of Arts (see: Royal Society of Arts), and a mechanical telegraph which predated by a quarter of a century the work of Claude Chappe. He was a founding member of the Lunar Society* and a close friend of Anna Seward, Erasmus Darwin* and Josiah Wedgwood. A man of remarkable inventive ability (his later inventions included a tracked vehicle, a hygrometer and an anemometer), his principal publications were on educational and mechanical subjects. He was four times married, and father of Maria Edgeworth, the novelist, first of his twenty-two children. Two of his books, *Practical Education,* written with Maria in 1798, and *Professional Education,* published ten years later, are among the most influential in the literature of the subject. In later years, after the death of Bentley*, Wedgwood's friendship with Edgeworth became even closer and he submitted a number of ideas for Wedgwood's approval, including one for 'oval baking dishes for meat pies in the shape of raised paste pies', a suggestion which resulted in the production of game pie dishes* and pie-crust ware*. In 1782, Edgeworth committed what was then an illegal act by marrying his deceased wife's sister and went to live on his estates in Ireland. He and Wedgwood continued to correspond on current affairs, on which they held, for the most part, divergent views.

Edme Shape
See: Tableware Shapes

Egg-and-Dart, Egg-and-Tongue
Running border patterns consisting of alternating ovoid and either dart-like or tongue forms.

EGG-BEATER. Queen's ware egg-beater, height 3⅞in. Shape no.1262 in the '1802' Shape Drawing Book. Eggs were placed in the base, the lid replaced and the whole briskly shaken.

Formerly Buten Museum

Egg Beater
A small, Queen's ware* cylindrical box with spikes arranged inside the base and lid, projecting towards the centre. Eggs were placed in the base, the lid replaced and the whole briskly shaken. A drawing of the shape appears in the '1802' Shape Drawing Book*.

Egg Cups
Footed egg cups of conventional shape have been made by Wedgwood in Queen's ware from perhaps as early as 1765 to the present day. An egg cup with ribbed cup appears as design no.26 in Plate 7 of the 1774 Catalogue*, advertised as available with or without cover, and two different shapes with covers are shown in Plate 7 of the '1790' Catalogue. Josiah mentioned having sent '6 friezed Egg Cups with plinth feet and nob on the cover' to London in January 1769. Egg cups have been made in many shapes since that date, including the open hoop or ring, pear shape and as double egg cups for the American market. They have also been made in most of Wedgwood's ceramic bodies, including 18th-century jasper with lapidary* polished interiors (probably as 'cabinet' pieces*), cane* ware and bone china* decorated to match breakfast services.

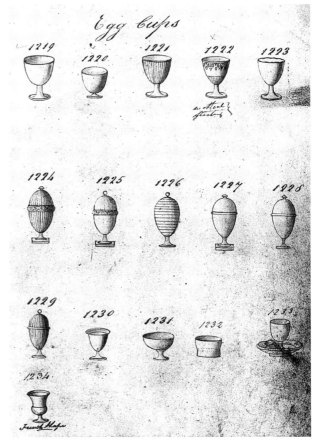

EGG CUPS. Page from the '1802' Shape Drawing Book showing sixteen shapes for Queen's ware egg cups. *Wedgwood Museum*

Egg Cup for Poached Eggs
A small circular Queen's ware tray with two lug handles, shown in Plate 7 of the '1790' Catalogue* and described in the surviving texts as an 'Egg-cup for poached eggs' or *coquetier.*

EGG CUPS. Ribbed Queen's ware covered egg cup with a moulded band of oak leaves on a waisted foot and square plinth. Unmarked. Wedgwood, c.1770. Shape no.41 in the '1790' Catalogue.
Wedgwood Museum

EGG CUPS. Set of eight solid pale-blue and white jasper egg cups with lapidary-polished interiors on a footed tray. c.1790. *City Museum & Art Gallery, Stoke-on-Trent*

EGG SEPARATOR. Queen's ware egg separator, length 3⅝in., with moulded shell handle. c.1780. *Norwich Castle Museum*

Egg Cup Stand

A circular tray on a stem foot, pierced with holes to hold egg cups, usually supplied with a tray *en suite* for spoons. Egg cup stands were made by Wedgwood in 18th-century Queen's ware* and jasper and later also in cane* ware and bone china*.

Egg Poacher

A shallow circular Queen's ware* dish with one or two handles, pierced with holes in a regular pattern but small enough to allow the egg to set without the white passing through. They were made from c.1775 and possibly earlier.

Egg Separator

A small Queen's ware pierced dish, similar in shape to the egg poacher* but with one handle only and pierced with holes of sufficient diameter to allow the egg white to pass through them, leaving the separated yolk behind in the dish. They were made by Wedgwood from the last quarter of the 18th century, perhaps earlier.

Egg Stand

A flat circular dish on a low spreading foot, pierced with a number of holes (usually six or eight) of sufficient diameter to hold a boiled egg. Such stands were made by Wedgwood in Queen's ware* in the 18th century, cane* ware, and later in bone china*.

Egyptian Black

Although pottery made from red-brown clay which burned black in firing had been known in England since the Iron Age, the use of black-stained clay in English pottery has not been confirmed before about 1750. Unglazed black ware of this type came to be known as 'Egyptian Black' and this name continued to be used until Wedgwood's black basaltes*, which was a much-refined development of it, became so well known that basaltes was adopted as a generic term for all unglazed black stonewares made from stained clay. Specimens (for example, two teapots in the City

EGYPTIAN COLLECTION. Canopic vase and bowl, ornamented in terracotta on black, and a Trophy plate with central portrait of Ankhesenamum in terracotta (red) on primrose jasper, 1978.
Wedgwood Museum

Museum, Stoke-on-Trent, and the teapot marked 'ASTBURY' in the British Museum) previously thought to date from the 1730s are now believed to belong to the middle of the century and no evidence has been found to substantiate the attribution of this type of ware to the Elers* brothers. Nor does Wedgwood mention it as part of Whieldon's* production, which it would surely have been if Shaw's* assertion about the widespread production of Egyptian Black in Staffordshire at that date were accurate. A primitive black portrait medallion has been recovered from the Whieldon site, but its date is uncertain and it seems most likely that little Egyptian Black was made before 1755 and that its quality did not promise well enough to encourage extensive production.

Egyptian Collection 1978

Limited editions* of figures, plates and plaques in terracotta* and black jasper*, terracotta and primrose jasper, and gilded basaltes*. The seated Sphinx* figures and Canopic* vases were reproduced from 18th-century models. The editions ranged from an acceptable fifty for the Canopic vases to a figure, scarcely justifiable as 'limited', of 3,000 for a miniature plaque of gilded basaltes, *Beloved of the Great Enchantress*.
See: Colour Plate 36
See also: Minkin, Robert

Egyptian Ornaments

A series of new bas-relief subjects for jasper, modelled c.1910, depicting somewhat stylised 'Egyptian' figures and motifs, some of the latter copied from earlier models after Montfaucon's* illustrations. The style does not appear to have been popular and examples are fairly scarce. The quality of the jasper (generally a purplish-blue) on which these bas-reliefs appear is poor.

Egyptian Shape

See: Tableware Shapes

EGYPTIAN BLACK. Egyptian black teapot and wasters, the bulbous bodies supported on four lions'-head-and-paw feet. Unmarked. Whieldon-Wedgwood or Wedgwood, c.1759. *Wedgwood Museum*

EGYPTIAN TASTE. Rosso antico perfume burner on tripod monopodia ornamented with black 'Egyptian' motifs, including winged discs, lotus buds, zig-zags and spirals, and hieroglyphics copied from Montfaucon's *L'Antiquité Expliquée*. This piece derives from an ormolu tripod attributed to James 'Athenian' Stuart copied by Boulton. Height 15in. c.1805. *Wedgwood Museum*

Egyptian Taste

Although most of Wedgwood's decorative products were inspired by Greek and Roman sources, interesting and surprisingly early examples of Egyptian influence also occur. Decoration in the Egyptian style first appeared in England during the second quarter of the 18th century, when it was considered a very sophisticated taste. Neither Egypt nor Greece was included in the itineraries of

EGYPTIAN TASTE. Boat-shaped black basaltes inkstandish with crocodile's and griffin's heads at the stern and prow, fitted with a canopic vase inkwell flanked by a quill holder and sander or pounce pot, ornamented in the 'Egyptian' style in rosso antico. Length 12⅛in. c.1805. *Wedgwood Museum*

the Grand Tour and few travellers ventured beyond Rome in their study of either. The most influential of the early travellers in Egypt were Frederick Norden, Charles Perry and Richard Pococke, all of whom published illustrated accounts of their journeys between 1743 and 1757, but neither Wedgwood nor Bentley* seems to have been aware of them. The principal sources used by Wedgwood & Bentley were the work of Montfaucon* and the comte de Caylus*, neither of whom had visited Egypt but whose illustrations were serious attempts at authentic detail.

The number of subjects copied from illustrations of Egyptian originals produced during the lifetime of the first Josiah Wedgwood is surprisingly large in comparison with the work of any pottery or porcelain manufacturer of his time and it is possible that he was influenced in this by Sir William Chambers*. Wedgwood & Bentley's first Ornamental Ware Catalogue*, published in 1773, advertised Egyptian sphinx* figures and candlesticks*, Egyptian lions and cameos* of subjects from Egyptian history. The 'Canopus' vases (see: Canopic Jars) in plain and encaustic*-painted black basaltes* were among the earliest of their vase shapes, and other pieces, such as a script-marked pen tray with sphinx-head ornament (Wedgwood Museum, Barlaston) provide evidence that the Wedgwood & Bentley partnership was the first firm seriously to attempt to introduce Egyptian styles into English pottery.

The early years of the 19th century saw the 'Egyptian Revival', popularly supposed to have been inspired by Napoleon's campaigns in Egypt and subsequent publications, particularly the official survey commissioned by Napoleon and the work of the Baron Denon. The

EGYPTIAN TASTE. White biscuit earthenware garden pot and stand in the 'Egyptian' style for reproduction in rosso antico and black. The moulded and applied ornaments include sphinx-head handles and branching and spiralling papyrus copied from Montfaucon. Height 11¼in. c.1805. *Wedgwood Museum*

4. EGYPTIAN TASTE. Red body 'Club' jug decorated with a sphinx in a combination of matt black and glost black and white enamels. Height 8in. Made for Woollard & Hattersley, Cambridge, 1854. *Manchester City Art Gallery*

most important influence on design remained, however, Montfaucon, with the important addition of Piranesi*, who was the first to suggest that Egyptian motifs might be used more widely in design than in their original settings. Wedgwood continued, after the death of Josiah I, to produce figures and vases first made during his lifetime and a significant number of new designs was added after about 1803. These were made in the combination of rosso antico* and basaltes* with smaller quantities in the cane* and jasper* bodies. In this period, the Egyptian style of ornament rarely appeared on 'useful'* wares, a notable exception being the remarkable dairy ware* made for Shugborough. All of these fresh designs were based on Montfaucon's illustrations, with the specific addition of hieroglyphics, copied from his second volume, which had not been used previously.

One of the few designers to produce something better than slavish imitations of the most popular 'Egyptian' motifs was Christopher Dresser*, whose rare work for Wedgwood shows true originality. Both Thomas Allen* and Frederick Rhead* also produced impressive work in the Egyptian style between 1875 and 1880 and Egyptian styles are to be found also in a series of Majolica* pieces made in 1875. Thereafter demand for this style of decoration declined, reviving only briefly in response to the Tutankhamen exhibition at the British Museum in 1972.

Elden, Matthew (fl.1860-75)
Painter and modeller who worked with Lessore* and was introduced by him to Wedgwood in 1860, working as Lessore's assistant. He later studied under Hugues Protât* at the Stoke-on-Trent School of Art and assisted with the façade of the Wedgwood Memorial Institute, Burslem. His work for Wedgwood includes unidentified modelling and some paintings on earthenware in a style very similar to Lessore's.
See also: Brownsword, Henry; Eyre, George; Wagstaffe, William

Electricity and Pottery Decoration
It is evident from a letter written to Bentley* in 1766 that Wedgwood had been invited by his friend to make his first contribution towards the costs of the experiments carried out by Dr Joseph Priestley*. It seems that Priestley thought it might be possible to adapt electricity to the decoration of pottery. Wedgwood replied in mock-rhetorical vein: 'Heavens once dreaded bolt is now called down to amuse your wives & daughters – to decorate their teaboards & baubles!' Nothing, however, seems to have come of the idea. It is difficult to imagine what the process might have been unless Priestley was anticipating Elkington* by seventy years and experimenting with the electrical deposition of metal.

Elements, The
The four Elements – *Earth, Air, Fire* and *Water* – appear in art represented either as female figures identified by their attributes or (especially in the 16th century) as classical gods and goddesses. They

ELERS, John Philip and David. Two fine examples of the red stoneware made by the Elers brothers: a tea jar with 'countersunk' reliefs of 'Chinese' designs and a mug with two bands of turned ribbing and applied prunus relief, both with contemporary silver mounts. Tea jar height 4½in. Unmarked. Elers, c.1695.   *Jonathan Horne*

ELERS, John Philip. Wax portrait modelled by Hackwood in 1777 and reproduced in jasper.
Formerly Author's collection, now Mint Museum, Charlotte, N.C.

were painted in groups or as separate figures and in the 17th and 18th centuries the names of the elements were often used as titles for pictures showing young men and women engaged in some appropriate activity. *Earth* is usually represented as a woman, often crowned, with the attributes of fertility: the cornucopia* and snake associated with Ceres*. She may be depicted gathering fruit or engaged in cultivation. *Air* was sacred to Juno* and was often represented by the goddess with her peacock; or she floats in the air, an anvil attached to each foot (Jupiter's* revenge for Juno's disobedience) surrounded by birds. *Fire* is represented by a woman with her hair in flames or wearing a head-dress in the form of a phoenix ringed by fire. She holds a thunderbolt. *Fire* may also be represented by Vulcan*, forging the armour of Achilles*, watched by Venus* and Cupid*. *Water* is personified by a river god or by Neptune*, accompanied by Triton*, dolphins*, hippocampi* and the Nereids*.

'4 Ovels of the Elements' were supplied by Hoskins & Grant* in 1774 and these were reproduced as four plaques, 13in. x 10¾in., listed as nos 88-91 in the 1774 Catalogue.

The Four Elements were used in 1930 for the ornament of Emmanuel Tjerne's* prize-winning vase commemorating the birth of Josiah Wedgwood.

Elephant
See: Animal Figures

Elers, John Philip and David (fl.1688-1710)
Brothers, originally silversmiths; believed to have been salt glaze* potters at Cologne (Rhineland). They are mentioned by Dr Martin Lister in 1699 as 'two Dutch [Deutsch] men brothers…who wrought in Staffordshire…and were not long since at Hammersmith [W. London]'. The Elers brothers made red stoneware* ('porcelaine') at Bradwell Wood. Other types of ware are more doubtfully attributed to them, and no evidence has been found to substantiate the claim that they made Egyptian black*. John and David Elers abandoned the pottery business by the end of 1700, when they were reported bankrupt. Josiah Wedgwood was in no doubt of the importance of their work, noting the information given to him by Edward Bourne*, an old bricklayer who worked at Etruria*, now remembered as the subject of one of Hackwood's* finest portrait medallions*: 'The next improvement introduc'd by Mr E[lers],' Wedgwood wrote to Bentley*, 'was the refining of our common red clay, by sifting & making it into Tea & Coffee Ware in imitation of the Chinese Red Porcelaine, by casting it in plaister moulds, & turning it on the outside upon Lathes, & ornamenting it with the tea branch in relief'. The Elers' red stoneware was evidently the forerunner of both Wedgwood's early red stoneware and also of his rosso antico*.

A portrait medallion of J.P. Elers, modelled in ivory wax by Hackwood, was reproduced in jasper in 1777. The original wax model* (then in the Reilly collection, now in the Mint Museum, Charlotte, N. Carolina) was exhibited at the National Portrait Gallery, London, in 1973.

EMAIL OMBRANT. Two green-glazed *émail ombrant* plaques moulded with intaglio subjects. Diameter 5in. and 4in. c.1875.

Wedgwood Museum

Elers Paul (1700 - after 1779)

Son of John Philip Elers*. Paul Elers corresponded at tedious length with Josiah Wedgwood in 1777 on the subject of the wares made by his father and uncle, making extravagant claims on their behalf which Wedgwood rebutted in a long letter to Bentley* in July. At Paul's request, Hackwood* modelled the original wax for the portrait medallion of John Philip, and on 19 July 1777 Wedgwood relayed a demand for 'about half a dozen more of the Portraits, for his friends are pretty numerous'. Paul Elers continued to pester Wedgwood with long letters containing exaggerated claims for his father and an array of suggestions for Wedgwood's production, urging him to rise above 'trifling trinkets' and instead to manufacture water pipes 'for London first & then for all the world'. R.L. Edgeworth's* first wife was Elers's daughter.

Elkington & Sons (Birmingham)

Silversmiths, founded in the 1830s by G.E. Elkington (1801-65) and his cousin Henry (c.1810-52). The firm developed a process of electro-plating on base metal, usually nickel-silver (EPNS), and a process of making reliefs and models in the round by the electric deposition of metal (electro-typing). They also made mounts of silver for the embellishment of pottery and porcelain. When George Elkington died in 1865 the firm employed over 1.000 workmen, occupying much the same position in the 19th century as Boulton* had done in the 18th. During the latter half of the 19th century and the first quarter of the 20th, Elkington produced EPNS mounts for Wedgwood jasper* biscuit barrels, match holders, salad bowls etc, some of which bear the name 'Elkington' impressed with the Wedgwood mark in the clay body, indicating that they were supplied to, and marketed by, Elkington.

Ellis, Ruth (fl.1920-35)

Architect and designer, in partnership with her husband, Leonard Holcombe Bucknell*; probably introduced to Wedgwood by Sir Charles Holmes*. She designed a number of patterns for Wedgwood, all for handpainted decoration of the simple stylised flower and leaf type favoured by the Powells* and Millicent Taplin* in the early 1930s.

Elysian Fields

According to Homer*, a land lying to the West, where there is neither cold, nor snow, nor rain. Favourites of the gods passed there without first dying. According to the Roman poets, Elysium is part of the Lower World to which pass the souls of the favoured dead. Angelini* modelled a large bas-relief, *Several Geniuses Representing the Pleasures of the Elysian Fields,* in 1789. This was reproduced as a jasper tablet 7⅝in. x 25in. and has been used for the ornament of vases. It is usually (and bizarrely) catalogued as *Sacrifice to Hymen,* following an incorrect identification by Meteyard*. The same relief appears on jasper made by Adams*.

Email Ombrant

French term for a form of pottery decoration, suitable only for plates, flat dishes and plaques, developed in 1842 by the Baron du Tremblay from the lithophane*, patented in Paris fifteen years earlier. The design was deeply impressed in the centre of the dish, which was then flooded with transparent coloured glaze (commonly green or brown), light and shade being defined, as in an engraving, by the varying depth of the design. Examples of *émail ombrant,* also known as 'Tremblay' ware, made at the Rubelles factory, were shown at the Great Exhibition of 1851, where they won a Gold Medal. Wedgwood conducted trials and the resulting pieces were sold exclusively at Thomas Goode, London. In 1872, about eight years after the closure of the factory, the Rubelles moulds and patent were bought by Wedgwood, Emile Lessore's* son Alfred acting as their legal representative.
See: Majolica

Embossed Queen's Ware

Tableware and ornamental ware of cream-coloured Queen's ware* or coloured bodies* ornamented by hand with relief patterns (most commonly vine) in a contrasting colour. Colour variations include CC* (cream-colour) on Lavender, Celadon or Windsor Grey; and Pink, Lavender, Celadon or CC on CC. The tablewares were produced on traditional* and shell edge* shapes. Introduced about 1850 and especially popular in the USA, the style and ornament was based on the Hackwood Vine* designed by William Hackwood* in 1812.

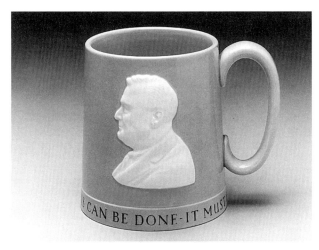

EMBOSSED QUEEN'S WARE. Cream-colour on Lavender hand-embossed mug ornamented with a relief portrait of Franklin Delano Roosevelt, modelled by Arnold Machin. Height 4¼in. Printed with special backstamp. 1941. A similar mug, ornamented with a relief portrait of Winston Churchill was issued at the same time.

Wedgwood Museum

EMBOSSED QUEEN'S WARE. Cream-colour on Cream-colour hand-embossed Queen's ware tablewares. These were available in many colour combinations and were especially popular in the USA.

Photograph: Wedgwood

EMBOSSED QUEEN'S WARE. Lavender on cream-colour hand-embossed mug and jug ornamented with portraits of Queen Elizabeth II and the Duke of Edinburgh to celebrate the Coronation in 1953. Jug height 5¼in. 1953.   *Wedgwood Museum*

Empire Shape
See: Tableware Shapes

Enamel Decoration, Enamelling
Technically the term 'enamel' applies only to colour decoration applied over the glaze (onglaze), but it is commonly used to describe all colour decoration applied by hand, whether onglaze, underglaze or on unglazed dry bodies*, such as black basaltes*. The first reference to enamelled decoration on Wedgwood cream-ware occurs in July 1763 and by November 1764 Wedgwood was supplying Rhodes* in Leeds with quantities of creamware teapots and coffeepots, presumably for enamelling, but nothing of such an early date has been identified with certainty. Several teapots in the style associated with Rhodes have been assigned to dates between 1764 and 1770 but the dates are somewhat speculative. From 1770 onwards Wedgwood's output of enamelled ware increased so fast that he had the greatest difficulty in recruiting painters to keep up with the work, and from this date the impressed mark was used with increasing regularity, making identification more sure.
See: Chelsea Decorating Studio; Decoration

Encaustic Painting
A technique of decoration developed by Josiah Wedgwood principally for the purpose of imitating Greek and Italian vases in the red figure* style. The surface of the colours is matt rather than glossy, and they are smooth and durable. They were applied in the conventional way with a brush, and the palette, although limited, consisted of several contrasting colours, including blue, green, pink, orange and white as well as red and black.

Wedgwood patented the technique in 1769, an exercise which compelled him to reveal the secret composition of the colours, which were a mixture of fine china clay slip* (the Cherokee* clay, according to the specification) and pigments, without obtaining

ENCAUSTIC PAINTING. Black basaltes chocolate-jug (also known as a coffeepot ewer) decorated with simple flower and leaf designs in encaustic colours. Height 9⅞in. c.1783.   *Wedgwood Museum*

ENCAUSTIC PAINTING. D-shaped black basaltes 'bulbous root pot' with five collared cups for bulbs on a removable grid, the body ornamented with palm trees and cupids with a wreath, painted in pink, red and white encaustic colours. Length 9½in. c.1785.
Merseyside Museums

ENCAUSTIC PAINTING. Black basaltes tablet painted in encaustic colours of flesh tones and brown with a central design of the American eagle within a wreath of bound laurel, probably produced to celebrate American victory in the War of Independence. 8in. x 13½in. c.1783.

Christie's, London

ENCAUSTIC PAINTING. Two black basaltes encaustic-painted calyx-krater vases, c.1785, and a neo-classical vase decorated in encaustic colours, c.1795. Height 9¼in. and 7¾in.   *Christie's, London*

protection against infringements by competitors, notably Palmer*. Apart from the bronzing process, Wedgwood never patented anything else.

The term 'encaustic' is properly applied to either of two methods of decoration, neither of which bears any resemblance to Wedgwood's. The first is the technique of painting with colours mixed with wax and fused by heat, usually on a wood support; the second is a method of inlaying patterns of coloured clay into lines and shapes cut out of the plain clay base, used principally for tiles. Nor, except superficially in appearance, did Wedgwood's technique of red-figure painting resemble that of the Greek or Italian vase painters.

According to the description in the 1779 Wedgwood & Bentley Catalogue*, the misleadingly named 'encaustic' colours had *'all the Advantages of Enamel,* without its *essential Defects.'* They had been invented, 'not only…completely to imitate the Paintings upon Etruscan Vases, but to *do much more;* to give to the Beauty of Design, the Advantages of Light and Shade in various Colours; and to render Paintings durable without the Defect of a varnished or glassy Surface.' This was, Wedgwood modestly observed, 'An Object earnestly desired by persons of critical Taste in all Ages, and in Modern Times, without Success.' A formidable list of patrons who possessed these 'painted Etruscans' included George III* and Queen Charlotte*, Catherine II* of Russia, and the Kings of Poland, Prussia, Sweden and Portugal, followed by Grand Dukes, Electors, Princes, Dukes and Marquesses etc., in descending order. Nevertheless, comparing his technique to that described by the Comte de Caylus*, Wedgwood was honest enough to admit: 'It is evident this kind of Painting, *in coloured Wax* has little or no Resemblance to ours but in Name'.

Included in this category of basaltes vases with encaustic painting are the First Day's vases* of 13 June 1769. The painting of these, and much else besides, was done at the Chelsea Decorating Studio* under Bentley's supervision. Among those artists who painted vases and tablets were Craft*, Rhodes*, Unwin* and Mrs Willcox*, and, from 1784, Aaron Steele*.

Manufacture of these vases began in 1768 and for a time they were in considerable demand. The principal sources of designs were Sir William Hamilton's* collection, published by D'Hancarville*, and the illustrated work of the Comte de Caylus*.

Apart from vases, tablets* and medallions, encaustic painting appears on basaltes teaware, root (bulb*) pots and, more rarely, on cane* ware. The style of red and black decoration was adapted also for the borders and centres of enamelled tableware patterns. A letter written from Paris in February 1788 testifies to the popularity of this style of tableware in France.
See: Colour Plates 37 and 38

Endymion
A youth renowned for his beauty, he was put to sleep for eternity on Mount Latmos on the command of Jupiter*, in return for the gift of perpetual youth. There Endymion was visited nightly by the moon goddess Luna, or Selene, with whom Diana* became identified. In art he is usually shown embraced by Diana or bathed in moonlight, which indicates her presence.

ENDYMION. Pink wax model of *Endymion sleeping on the Rock Latmos,* modelled by Pacetti, 1788, on a slate ground, reproduced in jasper, c.1790.   *Lady Lever Art Gallery, Port Sunlight*

Wedgwood subjects:
Endymion Sleeping on the Rock Latmos, tablet 10in. x 8in. and 9¼in. x 7½in., modelled by Pacetti, 1788
Diana Visiting Endymion, tablet 8½in. x 27½in., no.274 in 1787 Catalogue

Engine-Turning Lathe (Engine-Turned Decoration)
The engine-turning lathe is similar in general principles to the simple lathe*, but it has an eccentric motion, reciprocating in a horizontal plane while the shaft and the object being worked rotate. The cutting tool is held stationary, cutting flutes or more complex

ENGINE-TURNING LATHE. Modern engine-turning lathe at Barlaston, copied from the 18th-century lathe still in use.
Photograph: Wedgwood

ENGINE-TURNING LATHE. Vertical-striped decoration being cut on a jasper dip vase on the engine-turning lathe at Barlaston.

Photograph: Wedgwood

ENGINE-TURNED DECORATION. Wedgwood & Bentley black basaltes vase with vertical-striped engine-turned decoration. Height 10⅝in. c.1774. *Manchester Museum*

patterns as the reciprocating motion brings the object into contact with it. This enables a variety of repetitive patterns to be cut, the more elaborate of which are cut with the aid of a guide called a rosette.

Josiah Wedgwood claimed to have introduced the engine-turning process to the pottery industry in 1763 and this claim, but not the date, is confirmed by a note in the Journal of Sir Joseph Banks* written on 18 December 1767. The earliest mention of the engine-turning technique in Josiah's correspondence occurs in a letter to Bentley* dated 28 May 1764, and 'Engin'd Teapots' (evidently engine-turned redware teapots which had been in production for some time) are recorded in February 1765. On 6 July 1765 Josiah told his brother John Wedgwood* that he proposed sending 'two setts of Vases, Creamcolour engine turn'd, & printed' to the Queen. This is the first reference to engine-turned creamware and to the application of the technique to vases.

In 1767 Wedgwood made a number of important experiments with the twin aims of improving his lathe and exploiting its potential. He wrote in May of negotiating to buy a lathe fitted with rosettes from Matthew Boulton*, at whose factory in Soho he had seen it in operation. In October he was working with John Wyke*, the Liverpool watch- and tool-maker to construct his own lathes, and by the end of 1769 there were three engine-turning lathes in operation at Etruria and Wedgwood admitted to Bentley that he had 'committed a Sad Robbery upon my Burslem works to furnish it – We have not one Engine Turner left there now'.

Engine-turning is a highly skilled operation for both the turner and his assistant. Some of the patterns produced are so intricate that the lathe must be turned slowly by hand. Engine-turned patterns of the highest quality were never successfully imitated by Wedgwood's contemporaries.

The engine-turning lathe presently in use at the Barlaston* factory is little altered from the 18th-century prototype still preserved there in working condition except that it has been adapted to electrical motive power. The new machine was built in 1976 by Wedgwood's engineering staff and assembled by Arthur Ward, a fitter, and George Hughes, a pattern-maker, who had between them seventy-

four years' experience at the Etruria and Barlaston factories.
See: Colour Plate 39
See also: Processes of Manufacture, *Turning*

Englefield, John (fl.1769-74)
Painter at the Chelsea Decorating Studio* who worked on the Frog* service.

Engraving
See: Processes of Manufacture

Epergne
See: Grand Plat Ménage

Epicurus (342?-270 BC)
Greek philosopher, who taught that peace of mind arising from a cultivation of the virtues is the highest good. This precept was later misinterpreted, some of his followers suggesting that he had held the highest good to be happiness, thus opening the way for sensual enjoyment. A bust of Epicurus, supplied by Hoskins & Grant* in 1774, was worked on by Hackwood* and reproduced, about 25in. high, in basaltes*.

Eros
See: Cupid

Escritoire (Ecritoire)
French: properly a writing desk or bureau. A term appropriated in pottery and porcelain to denote a desk-set or inkstand. Wedgwood's escritoire was an inkstand, sometimes boat-shaped and combined with a pyrophorous vase*, and furnished with a candleholder. Escritoires were made in the dry bodies*.

Estimate Books
Valuable 19th- and 20th-century manuscript records of new models and their decoration, with estimates of their production costs, preserved at the Wedgwood Museum*, Barlaston.

ETRURIA FACTORY.
Photograph of the front of the Etruria Works, c.1945, showing how subsidence had sunk the level of the factory buildings as much as fifteen feet below the canal and some fifty feet below their original level.
Wedgwood Museum

Etruria (also Tuscia)

An area of central Italy, known to the Greeks as Tyrrhenia, inhabited by the Etrusci (or Tusci), who were probably of Pelasgian origin. The Pelasgians were the original inhabitants of Greece. The Etruscans were a highly civilised people from whom the Romans learned a great deal about the arts, and religious and social organisation. They became subject to Roman power in 91 BC and were completely Romanised by the time of Augustus.

Etruria Factory, Staffordshire (1769-1950)

The opening of the Etruria factory on the 350-acre Ridgehouse Estate* marks the beginning of the production of ornamental wares by the Wedgwood & Bentley partnership. The deeds of partnership were signed on 10 August 1769, but the books were opened on 14 November 1768, when the first hands started work at the new factory. Originally proposed as a 'Vase work', the Etruria factory was planned, by the end of 1767, as a complete factory, both for

ETRURIA FACTORY. Potter's throwing wheel from the Etruria factory, reputed to be one of the first used by Wedgwood. The motive power was produced by an assistant turning the large wheel.
Wedgwood Museum

wares designated as 'Useful' (tablewares) and produced in the partnership between Josiah and his cousin Thomas Wedgwood*, and for ornamental wares. It was housed in three blocks, linked by walled courts or yards, at the corners of which were eight 'hovels'* containing ovens or kilns. There were wide gateways for the delivery of clay and coal and the removal of rubbish. From the start, Etruria was equipped with a water-wheel, supplying power by water drawn from the canal. After Josiah's death the use of water and wind was abandoned in favour of steam.

When it was built, the Etruria factory was second to none in Europe for its location and the practicality of its design. There was also no doubt that conditions for work there, with new housing provided for many of the workers, and a sick club (sick benefit scheme) subsidised by Wedgwood, compared favourably with those to be found anywhere in Europe.

In 1844, the factory, Etruria Hall* and the entire estate were put up for sale by auction. The factory was described in the sale advertisement: 'An extensive and commodious set of Potworks known as the ETRURIA WORKS, consisting of Six Biscuit and Nine Glost Ovens, with Workhouses, Warehouses, powerful Steam Engine, Flint and Colour Mill, and other conveniences belonging thereto, most advantageously situated on the banks of the Trent and Mersey canal, with which two lateral Cuts from the premises communicate...'. Offered with the factory were eight houses and an option to buy 103 'well-built Dwelling Houses' with yards and gardens, 'chiefly occupied by persons employed at the Etruria Works'. Much of the estate was sold but the factory failed to reach its reserve and was withdrawn. By the 1870s there was some concern at evidence of subsidence caused by coal mining. Fifty years later, parts of the site had sunk thirty feet and the road running between the factory and the canal was fifteen feet below the towpath. By 1930 the subsidence had become too dangerous to be ignored. Long-term planning was no longer possible on the Etruria site, and the directors decided to abandon it and move the factory to a new site purchased at Barlaston*. On 13 June 1950, exactly 181 years since Josiah Wedgwood and Thomas Bentley had thrown their First Day's Vases* at Etruria, six Last Day's Vases were thrown there and the factory was closed.

ETRURIA HALL. Queen's ware oval dish (no. 1,129) from the 'Frog' service, enamelled in monochrome with a view of Etruria Hall. 1773-4. Hermitage Museum, St. Petersburg.   *Photograph: Wedgwood*

Etruria Hall

The residence of Josiah Wedgwood built by him on the Ridgehouse Estate* 1767-9. The architect was Joseph Pickford of Derby, a former plasterer who had built the Soho factory for Matthew Boulton*, and who was responsible also for the design and building of the Etruria factory*, the Bank House (intended for Bentley* but never occupied by him) and the workmen's cottages on the estate. Etruria Hall was enlarged in 1780 and sold by auction in 1844. Later it became the offices of the Shelton Iron & Steel Company. It has recently been restored and converted into a hotel.

Nothing remains of the original interior ornament of Etruria Hall and no trace has survived of the drawing-room ceiling painting, said to have been by William Blake*. The contents of the Hall were distributed among the family, and paintings by Wright* of Derby, Reynolds* and Stubbs*, once in the possession of Josiah I, are now in the Wedgwood Museum*, Barlaston.

Etruscan Patterns

Queen's ware* tableware patterns printed and enamelled in red and black in imitation of the decorative motifs found on Greek and Italian vases in the red-figure* style. These patterns were a development from the popularity of encaustic* painted vases and they were especially popular in Paris. Patterns were made with figures in black on a red ground and, more rarely, in red upon a black ground. The latter style was more difficult to make and was not introduced until about 1790. A service decorated in this manner was made in 1790 for Thomas Hope*.

Etruscan Pottery

Much ancient Etruscan pottery was inspired by the wares of contemporary Greece, and some of the finest examples of Greek wares have been found in Etruscan tombs. Later, Roman potters also copied contemporary Greek wares. Collections of vases of this kind were made in the 18th century, notably by Sir William Hamilton*, Ambassador to the Court of Naples, who subsequently sold his collection to the British Museum. Josiah Wedgwood made copies or adapted versions of some of Sir William's undecorated vases as well as those decorated in the red-figure* style. At the time the subject of ancient pottery had not been very seriously studied, and, in the absence of reliable evidence to the contrary, anything found in Italy was regarded as either Roman or Etruscan. The Etruscan *bucchero nero* ware, a black pottery with moulded or incised ornament dating from the 8th century BC, was also recovered from tombs and may have inspired some 18th-century black wares.

Etruscan School

The name given by Josiah Wedgwood to the small and private school he set up at Etruria Hall in 1778 for the education of his children, joined by the daughter and three sons of his cousin and partner 'Useful' Thomas Wedgwood*. The children were to be instructed by Tom Byerley*, Peter Swift* and the Reverend Edward Lomas, a parson from Newcastle-under-Lyme. These were joined by a young French prisoner-of-war named Potet, engaged for one year at a salary of 50 guineas. Josiah set down a detailed and rigorous daily timetable, which has survived in the Wedgwood archives.

Etruscan Ware

The description 'Etruscan' was first applied by Josiah Wedgwood to his plain black basaltes* vases before it became the term exclusively used for basaltes vases and other pieces decorated with encaustic* painting in the classical red-figure* style. He used the term for the first time in a letter of 30 August 1768, indicating that he may have shared the popular misapprehension that the ancient pottery then being excavated in Italy was Etruscan work; or he may have been influenced in his selection of a name by having seen examples of Etruscan *bucchero nero* (see: Etruscan Pottery). That the name was not reserved to vases is proved by his letter to William Cox* dated 14 September: 'Dont forget to call all the dark colour'd Etruscan Vases. I shall send my good Patroness Miss Chetwynd* her Etruscan T.pots this week end.' The description 'Etruscan bronze' was also used at this early period of the production of the black body to describe the plain basaltes and should not be confused with bronzed basaltes*, the technique for which was not invented until the following year.

After the invention of his bronzing technique in 1769, the ordinary black was known as 'Etruscan' and the bronzed basaltes as 'Bronze Etruscan'. After 1773, the plain black was referred to as 'Basaltes' and the name 'Etruscan' was reserved to pieces decorated in the red-figure style.

Eve Plaque

See: Zinkeisen, Anna

Exotic Birds

During the 1760s and 1770s the porcelain factories, especially Worcester* and Derby*, made frequent use of 'exotic birds' as painted decoration. These had first been introduced as decoration at Meissen* but the Sèvres factory developed the style and made it fashionable, taking their subjects from one or other of the popular private aviaries of the day. In London, the independent decorator, James Giles*, painted similar birds in a characteristic style for which W.B. Honey coined the apt description, 'dishevelled birds'. Some comparatively rare Wedgwood Queen's ware* and Pearl ware* is painted in this style. Less rare is creamware (cream-coloured* ware) and Queen's ware decorated with transfer-prints* of this type by Sadler* & Green. 'Birds' are first noted as being drawn for engraving in August 1763 and were in production in black or red in the following year. Renamed *Liverpool Birds,* these and similar engravings have been irregularly in production (occasionally with crude and unsuitable enamelled colouring) on Queen's ware for more than two hundred years.

See: Colour Plate 40

Experimental Work

See: Experiment Books; Public Experimental Work, 1775

Experiment Books

The manuscript records, begun during Josiah Wedgwood's partnership with Whieldon* (1754-59), in which he kept details of his experiments for the improvement of bodies and glazes. The Experiment books preserved in the Wedgwood Museum*, Barlaston, presumed to be fair copies of the originals, are in the handwriting of Alexander Chisholm* and were made after 1782. The introduction was probably written by Josiah at the same time. In this, he wrote:

> This suite of experiments was begun at Fenton Hall, in the parish of Stoke upon Trent, about the beginning of the year 1759, in my partnership with Mr Whieldon, for the improvement of our manufacture of earthen ware, which at that time stood in great need of it, the demand for our goods decreasing daily, and the trade universally complained of as being bad and in a declining condition. White stone ware (viz. with salt glaze) was the principal article of our manufacture: but this had been made a long time, and the prices were now reduced so low, that the potters could not afford to bestow much expence upon it, or to make it so good in any respect as the ware would otherwise admit of. And with regard to Elegance of form, that was an object very little attended to.

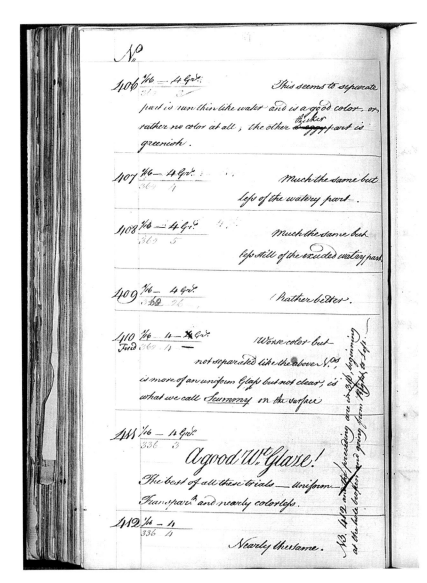

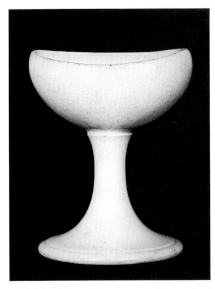

EYE BATH. Queen's ware eye bath on waisted stem and spreading foot. Height 2⅛in. c.1830.
Wellcome Institute Library, London

EXPERIMENT BOOK. Page from Josiah Wedgwood's First Experiment Book showing coded formulae on the left and the results of firing trials on the right. The figures in black above the line are quantities; those in faded red below the line are materials.
Wedgwood Museum

The article next in consequence to Stoneware was an imitation of Tortoiseshell. But as no improvement had been made in this branch for several years, the country was grown weary of it; and though the price had been lowered from time to time, in order to increase the sale, the expedient did not answer, and something new was wanted, to give a little spirit to the business.

I had already made an imitation of Agate; which was esteemed beautiful & a considerable improvement; but people were surfeited with wares of these variegated colors. These considerations induced me to try for some more solid improvement, as well in the *Body*, as the *Glazes*, the *Colours*, & the *Forms*, of the articles of our manufacture.

I saw the field was spacious, and the soil so good, as to promise an ample recompence to any one who should labour diligently in its cultivation.

Experiment no.7 in the first book is for Wedgwood's Green Glaze* (see: Glazes). Wedgwood's work with Whieldon was evidently largely experimental, and there is evidence, in the form of a page dated 28 March 1760 and headed 'at Fenton', that occasional experimental work was done at the Whieldon Works for some time after Wedgwood set up his own factory in May 1759.
See: Agate; Saltglazed Stoneware; Tortoiseshell

Extrusion
The process of forcing plastic clay through suitably shaped forms to produce rods of uniform section which may be cut off in desired lengths for the production of handles, strips for twig baskets* etc.

Eye-bath (Eye-cup)
A small ovoid cup, with concave rim to fit the eye-socket, on a stem and spreading foot. Eye-baths do not appear to have been made in ceramic bodies before the 18th century, although examples in silver are recorded in the 16th century. Porcelain eye-baths were made in England in the last quarter of the 18th century, for example at Caughley, but specimens are rare. Wedgwood, and other potters, made eye-baths in the first quarter of the 19th century, and possibly earlier, but few have survived. Wedgwood's silver lustre* eye cups, made c.1810-15, are especially rare.

Eyre, George (1816-87)
Painter at Etruria* from about 1865. He had previously worked for several other pottery and porcelain manufacturers, including both Minton* and Copeland (see: Spode*), where he had been art director. At Wedgwood's he painted earthenwares in a style which owed much to the influence of Lessore*.
See also: Brownsword, Henry; Wagstaffe, William

Faïence

Tin-glazed earthenware. The term is French and probably derives from the popularity in 16th-century France of tin-glazed wares made at Faenza (N. Italy), famous since medieval times for its *maiolica**.
See also: Delftware; Faïence Anglaise; Faïence Fine

Faïence Anglaise

One of the terms used in France to describe English creamware (cream-coloured ware*). The term is, in fact, misleading since creamware, being lead-glazed, is not a form of faïence.

Faïence Fine

French term used to describe both English creamware (cream-coloured ware*) and also French lead-glazed wares in imitation of English creamwares. Neither use is accurate since only tin-glazed* wares may properly be described as faïence.

Fairyland Lustre

The name given by Daisy Makeig-Jones* to a large range of ornamental wares decorated with commercial lustre* and produced, from her designs and under her supervision, from November 1915. These designs, combining the use of bright underglaze colours (occasionally with onglaze enamel highlights), painted-on com-

FAIRYLAND LUSTRE. Group of Fairyland Lustre patterns on bone china, designed by Daisy Makeig-Jones, c.1925: pair of *Candlemas* vases; *Daventry* bowl; and vase shape 3451 decorated with *Pillar* design. *Wedgwood Museum*

mercial lustre, and finally gold-printing*, with fantastic and often grotesque figures, scenes and landscapes, followed immediately upon the successful Ordinary Lustres*, introduced in the autumn of 1914. The production of these two new forms of decoration enabled Wedgwood, for the first time, to compete with the great English porcelain manufacturers – Worcester*, Minton*, Spode*, Derby* and Coalport* – in the production of ornamental bone china*. Enthusiastic critics wrote of the 'genuine innovation of Fairyland Ware, on which vivacious imps and fays are seen disporting themselves among fantastic trees' and the 'endless variety of colouring… the gamut reaching from light pearl tints of grey, blue, green and pink to the richest ruby, flame orange, violet, blue and deep green'. Another wrote, 'whilst many have copied, Etruria still leads.'

The Fairyland Lustres fall into three main categories: Queen's ware* plaques, 16in. x 11in. (pattern numbers with 'F' prefix); bone china plates, 10¾in. diameter ('W' prefix); and bone china ornamental pieces – vases, bowls, plaques etc. – ('Z' prefix). The method chosen for the numbering and identification of the many different shapes and patterns was unfortunately one of remarkable complexity. The six 'F' and eleven 'W' prefix numbers were often 'comprehensive', the same number covering a wide diversity of shapes, sizes and designs which had in common no more than a recognisable style of decoration or a particular combination of enamel colours. The resulting confusion has been patiently disentangled by Una des Fontaines, whose splendid *Wedgwood Fairyland Lustre* (1975) is the definitive study of this ware.

Fairyland Lustre was produced by Wedgwood from 1915 until 1931, but demand declined after 1929 and only one pattern (a new colour version of an existing design, concocted by Victor Skellern* in 1935 to meet a particular order) was added after the retirement of Daisy Makeig-Jones in 1931. The order, given by Josiah V*, for the destruction of all the copper plates was not obeyed and these were discovered by Una des Fontaines, many years later, in the engravings store at Barlaston*. Two reproductions have been made in recent times: a plaque, *The Enchanted Palace,* issued in a limited edition of 250 in 1977; and an octagonal bowl produced in 1979. Neither was made by the original techniques and the quality of the decoration is more mechanical.

Neglected for some thirty years, Wedgwood's Fairyland Lustre has enjoyed an impressive revival in popularity and esteem and is much sought after by collectors. The consequent rise in prices at auction has led to the appearance of lustre pieces, made during the 1920s by other manufacturers without any intention to deceive, but now bearing spurious Wedgwood and Portland vase* marks replacing genuine trade marks which have been removed by grinding. The surface damage done to the object by grinding, the poor quality of the printed mark, and the evidence of reglazing or varnishing, are all obvious to the eye and should deceive no one.

The pattern numbers listed below were painted on the base of Fairyland Lustre pieces by the paintresses who had decorated them,

FAIRYLAND LUSTRE. Bone china Fairyland lustre plaque decorated with *Torches* pattern. Height 10in. Signed. c.1925.
Mr & Mrs David Zeitlin Collection

155

and their appearance, with the authentic Wedgwood marks, is a valuable aid to identification. They are not, however, infallible.

QUEEN'S WARE PLAQUES
F3078)   *The Stuff that Dreams are made of* (sic)
F3080)

F3081)   *Imps on a Bridge and Tree House*
F3082)

F3083)   *Bubbles*
F3084)

BONE CHINA PLATES
W556	*Roc* centre, *Flaming Wheel* border
W557	*Firbolgs* centre, *Gnome* or *Imp* border
W558	*Roc* centre, *Twyford* border
W559	*Roc* centre, floral diaper border
W560	*Roc* centre, *Gnome* or *Imp* border
W561	*Si Wung Mu* centre, *Flame* border
W607	*Imps on a Bridge and Tree house*
W608	*Imps on a Bridge and Tree house*
W609	*White Pagodas, Gnome* or *Imp* border
W610	*White Pagodas,* triangular masks border
W1050	*Roc* centre, fruit and flower border
—	*White Pagodas, Pebble and Grass* border (unrecorded in design books)
Z5501	*Goblins on Bubbles* background

All the above plates are 10¾in. in diameter, Lincoln shape, except for Z5501 which is 9½in.

BONE CHINA ORNAMENTAL VASES, BOWLS ETC
Z4935	*Poplar Trees*
Z4968	Comprehensive pattern number (long line)
Z5125	Comprehensive pattern number for octagonal bowls: *Dana* panels
Z5157	*Candlemas*
Z5200	*Firbolgs* and *Thumbelina*
Z5217	*Angels* or *Geisha* and *Running Figures*
Z5219	*Firbolgs* and *Thumbelina*
Z5228	*Willow Fairyland*
Z5247	*Firbolgs* and *Thumbelina*
Z5252	*Woodland Elves (IV) (Big Eyes)*
Z5257	*Bubbles* (3 versions)
Z5275	*Red Firbolgs*
Z5331	*Torches*
Z5346	*Firbolgs*
Z5348	Coral and Bronze
Z5349	Coral and bronze
Z5360	Comprehensive pattern number: *Flame Fairyland* (long line)
Z5366	*Bifrost*
Z5367	*Goblins*
Z5391	*Imps on a Bridge and Tree House*
Z5392	*Imps on a Bridge and Tree House*
Z5404	Coral and bronze
Z5406	Coral and Bronze
Z5407	*Willow Fairyland*
Z5433-6	Various Fairyland patterns, borders and centres on *Daventry* shape (footed) bowls
Z5442	Comprehensive pattern number
Z5454	*Bird in a Hoop*
Z5461	*Candlemas*
Z5462	*Moonlight Fairyland* (various designs)
Z5463	*Bubbles*
Z5464	*Willow*
Z5481	*Sunset Fairyland*

BONE CHINA PLAQUES
Z5154-5 ⎫
Z5287-8 ⎬ *Elves in a Pine Tree*

Z5156 ⎫
Z5158 ⎪
Z5279 ⎬ *Picnic by a River*
Z5280 ⎭

Z5292   *Elfin Palace*
See Colour Plates 41 to 43

Fakes and Forgeries
The words 'fake' and 'forgery' are frequently used as if they were interchangeable but, correctly, their meanings are distinct. A fake is a genuine work of art, but of inferior quality, altered in such a way as to enhance its value. A forgery is a deliberate copy of a work of art, produced for the purpose of fraud (such a definition would not, of course, embrace copies made by students or for other legitimate purposes). For collectors, the best security against forgeries is connoisseurship and expertise and the proven integrity of the dealers from whom they make their purchases. The most dangerous forger is one who combines craftsmanship and expertise with a close relationship with an ostensibly reputable dealer.

Wedgwood's use of impressed marks has always made the forgery of Queen's ware* and the dry bodies* technically difficult. Cast reproductions, made by the conventional use of plaster of Paris from genuine pieces, shrink by about one-sixth in firing, their reduced size revealing the deception. The production of Wedgwood and other forgeries was openly announced in an advertisement carried by the *Staffordshire Evening Sentinel* of 20 June 1878 but none of these has been certainly identified, indicating either that the advertisement was an idle boast, or that the forgeries were of such poor quality that they never found a substantial market. It is scarcely credible that they were of such astonishing quality that they have remained undetected for more than a century.

M.H. Grant, whose *Makers of Black Basaltes* was published in 1910, was confident that Wedgwood's basaltes had rarely been faked or forged, but prophesied that increased demand and diminishing supply would encourage the forger in the future. Forged sets of 'Wedgwood and Bentley' basaltes medallions of Kings of England (Class IX, Section I of the 1773 Catalogue*) have passed through the salerooms in the past thirty years, but their reduced size and poor quality have not been deceptive. There have also been examples of other manufacturers' basaltes vases appearing with scratched or incised marks quite unlike the genuine marks impressed at Etruria.

Modern techniques have, to some extent, overcome the problem of shrinkage, and the appearance, in recent years, of a substantial number of forged jasper* and black basaltes* pieces bearing various Wedgwood & Bentley or Wedgwood marks is the cause of serious concern. Such pieces include jasper tablets (notably of *Apotheosis of Homer** and *Triumph of Bacchus**), jasper Medusa* medallions and ruined column vases*, black basaltes Stella's* ewers, basaltes and rosso antico* busts of George II* and various miniature busts.

These pieces were apparently made by Noel Thorley, a Staffordshire potter who worked at Etruria for some years before establishing his own factory in Longton about 1940. The factory, Thorley China, was closed in 1971. The precise period of these forgeries is not known but is most likely to have been between about 1955 and 1976, when Noel Thorley died. The full range of his work is still (in 1995) to be discovered, but it is not thought to have extended beyond about thirty-five models. These forgeries were sold principally, but not exclusively, to collectors in the United States of America. A valuable illustrated account was published by the Wedgwood Society of New York in 1994 (*Ars Ceramica*, No.11, April 1994).

The quality of the Thorley forgeries is variable. The jasper body is chalky, the colours are inaccurate and the bas-reliefs (in spite of being moulded from originals) are coarse and show noticeable variations from genuine examples. The basaltes body is rather more convincing, but the modelling of such reliefs as mask handles is crude to the point of caricature. The deception succeeded largely because it was too generally accepted that early impressed Wedgwood was too difficult and costly to forge. The great increase in prices of genuine Wedgwood & Bentley pieces justified greatly increased costs of forgery. Now that their existence is known, these forgeries should be more readily recognised.

In judging such pieces, it is more than ever necessary to have examined genuine specimens, or at least illustrations of them, with close attention. There is no substitute for genuine knowledge and a true understanding of quality. The first Josiah Wedgwood's insistence on the highest quality – especially in his ornamental wares

– is a guarantee that nothing crude or coarse was purposely distributed from the ornamental works at Etruria*. The Wedgwood & Bentley mark is never a guarantee of authenticity: on the contrary, it would seldom be worth the labour, cost or risk to forge a jasper or black basaltes piece without such a mark. Unmarked pieces, or those marked with the Wedgwood mark alone, because they are less desirable and less highly valued, are also less likely to be forged.

Examples of faked Wedgwood exist. Most commonly, these are 19th- and 20th-century black basaltes vases or late 18th-century variegated* vases 'improved' by the substitution of marked Wedgwood & Bentley plinths for their original Wedgwood ones. Some lustre pieces, made by other manufacturers during the 1920s in the manner of Wedgwood's Fairyland Lustre* but without any intent to deceive, appear occasionally bearing spurious Wedgwood and Portland vase* printed marks, replacing genuine manufacturers' marks which have been removed by grinding. The great prices now being realised by important Fairyland Lustre pieces suggest that it may not be long before forgeries of them reach the market.

FALCONET, Etienne-Maurice. Black basaltes figures of *Cupid Sitting Pensive* and *Psyche*, after the marbles by Falconet (1757). Height 8½in. c.1860. *Christie's, New York*

Falconet, Etienne-Maurice (1716-91)

French sculptor, whose work belongs to the early days of the neo-classical* style. A favourite of Mme de Pompadour's, he went, after her death in 1764, to Russia where he executed the colossal equestrian statue of Peter the Great at St Petersburg. His most famous work is *La Baigneuse*, a standing nude exhibited at the Salon in 1757 and later copied in porcelain by a number of factories.
Wedgwood subjects :
Cupid and *Psyche,* companion figures 8in. The sources are Falconet's marbles (1757), which were copied in Sèvres biscuit porcelain (1758 and 1761). Casts were probably supplied by Flaxman senior* in 1781 and the figures were produced intermittently in black basaltes* until the 1920s. Both figures were reproduced in Carrara* (in which they appear also on one base) and also in pink or pale blue Majolica glazes* during the 19th century.

Famille Rose

Chinese decoration distinguished by the use of an opaque enamel, ranging in shade from pink to purple-rose. The pigment, a crimson-purple discovered by Andreas Cassius of Leyden, Holland, before 1673, was introduced into China by Jesuit missionaries c.1685, appearing on Chinese porcelain before the end of the century. The finest *famille rose* porcelain was produced during the reign of Yung Chêng (1723-35). Thereafter it was exported in large quantities to Europe and the quality declined. The colour was developed at Meissen*, and at other German and French factories, particularly for porcelain decoration in the Chinese manner. The rose-purple enamel colour mixed by Rhodes* for use on early Queen's ware, including the *Husk* service, evidently owed its name, calx cassii*, to either Wedgwood's or Rhodes's knowledge of the inventor of the *famille rose* colour.

During the early years of the 19th century, there was a revival of demand for *chinoiserie* decoration and it was introduced at Etruria* in the form of *famille rose*-style painting on black basaltes*, rosso antico* and cane* *(Chinese Flowers*)*, and also on some tablewares in Queen's ware, White ware* (notably the service made to celebrate the Golden Jubilee of George III in 1810) and first period bone china*. The style reappeared in the 1860s.

FAMILLE-ROSE. Fine pair of black basaltes pastille-burners enamelled in the *famille-rose* style. Height 12½in. c.1815.
Dwight & Lucille Beeson Collection, Birmingham Museum, Alabama

157

Farrer, Katherine Euphemia, Lady (1839-1934)
Daughter of Hensleigh and Frances Wedgwood, and a great-granddaughter of Josiah Wedgwood. She married in 1873 (as his second wife) Thomas Henry Farrer, a civil servant who was created baronet in 1883 and first baron Farrer of Abinger ten years later. Between 1903 and 1906 she edited and published privately in three volumes the available letters of Josiah Wedgwood to Thomas Bentley* and a number of other letters from Wedgwood to his contemporaries. All were then in the possession of members of the family or had been bought for the firm from the Mayer* collection in 1887. The rest have since been acquired by the Wedgwood firm and now form an important part of the Wedgwood archives at Keele University. This edition of Wedgwood's letters (republished for the Trustees of the Wedgwood Museum in 1973) remains the most complete in circulation but it is unfortunately an unreliable source. In addition to omitting 'much business and technical detail' (some of it of great importance), as she claimed, Farrer also excised any material which she thought improper or too private for public view, edited punctuation and syntax, misread dates and conflated documents at will. The modern republication of this work without correction, or indeed any mention of its defects, was a sadly missed opportunity. Lady Farrer, in her own introduction to the letters, was also responsible for repeating in print an inaccurate family story upon which two later writers built the wholly erroneous theory that Josiah Wedgwood committed suicide.

In 1910 Lady Farrer generously gave 'a large sum of money' to the Wedgwood Museum* and this was spent on 'a considerable number of valuable pieces of Old Wedgwood'.

Fashion
'Fashion is infinitely superior to merit in many respects', Josiah Wedgwood told Bentley* in 1779. This judgement was, of course, a purely commercial view and, in this sense, it remains substantially accurate to this day. Although manufacturers have often denied it, and some have even sought to ignore it, fashion has always played an important part in the marketing of pottery and porcelain and has therefore been a major influence on design. Meissen* was the pre-eminent European porcelain factory during the baroque period, giving place to Sèvres as the supreme manufacturer of rococo* porcelain, which in turn yielded the lead to Wedgwood as the master potter of the neo-classical* style. The fashion for oriental design has been perhaps the strongest and most lasting of all influences on European ceramics, producing, through *chinoiserie*, *japonaiserie* and *japonisme*, a grammar that has been entirely absorbed into the western language of design for decoration and ornament.

While porcelain remained costly and its purchase represented a substantial investment that might be expected to be enjoyed by several generations of the family, fashion was slow to change. Mass-production and reduced costs made both pottery and porcelain more vulnerable to sudden changes in fashion, and manufacturers were obliged to introduce larger numbers of new patterns while retaining in production ever larger numbers of those which earlier customers expected to be able to replace. The necessary rationalisation of production was greatly aided by the restrictions of World War II, when no decorated ware was allowed to be made for home consumption and patterns for export were reduced to a small number of best-sellers. For the first time, customers were made to understand that their favoured patterns would not be manufactured for an indefinite period.

The 'heirloom' attitude to china tableware is rapidly declining: tableware has become 'disposable', almost to the extent that carpets, curtains and other household furnishings are replaced at regular intervals; and fashion has thus become more important in the design of ceramics than it has ever been.

Faun (Faunus)
Ancient Italian minor deity who protected agriculture and flocks. He later became identified with another rustic god, the Greek Pan*, and is similarly represented with goats' hooves and horns. Fauns may be defined as half-men, half-goats, with short horns, and may be identified with the Greek satyrs. Female fauns are referred to as fauna.
Wedgwood subjects:
Faun, figure 10¾in., listed in the 1774 Catalogue*
Faun, figure 15in., after Clodion*

Faun and Goat, antique figure 23½in.
Faun with Flute (Faun with Pipes: Louvre), antique figure 17in. 1849 Price List
Faun with Infant Bacchus, antique figure 18in.
Fauns Representing Four Different Stages of Life From Youth to Old Age, four medallions, 9in. x 7in., nos.38-41 in 1773 Catalogue
A Piping Faun (figure from the Borghese Vase*), medallion 4in. x 3¼ in., probably from a cast supplied by Flaxman* in 1775. No. 150 in 1777 Catalogue
Piping Faun, medallion 4in. x 3in., no.45 in 1773 Catalogue
Fauns Sacrificing, tablet 8½in. x 15in., no.140 in 1777 Catalogue
A Faun with Three Spartan Bacchantes, tablet modelled by Pacetti*, 1788
Two Fauns, Two Bacchanates & a Silenus (probably separate figures for medallions). Modelled by Angelini*, 1789

FAUN. Black basaltes figure, *Faun with Goat*, height 12¾in. c.1860-80.
Sotheby's, London

Faustina (fl. c.125-176)
Wife of the Emperor Marcus Aurelius Antoninus, noted for her licentiousness. She intrigued with Avidius Cassius to replace her husband as emperor, and died, perhaps by her own hand, during his expedition to suppress a revolt.
Wedgwood subjects:
Faustina, portrait medallion, 1774
Faustina, bust 20in., from a cast supplied by Hoskins & Grant*, 1774
Apotheosis of Faustina, modelled by Pacetti*, 1789, finished by Hackwood*

Feather Edge
See: Tableware Shapes

Feeding Bottle
Boat-shaped bottle, completely enclosed except for a spout at one end and a hole in the top through which it was filled. Made for feeding infants and invalids. Wedgwood produced feeding bottles

in Queen's ware*, including the coloured bodies*, Pearl ware* and occasionally in cane* and drab ware*.

Feeding Cup
A type of spouted cup, partly covered, for feeding infants and invalids. They were made by Wedgwood in Queen's ware* and Pearl ware*, either plain or transfer-printed*.

Feeding Jug
See: Baby Feeder

Felspar, Feldspar (Fieldspar)
Felspars are a group of minerals used as a flux* in ceramic bodies and as glazes*, or part of the composition of glazes. Felspars soften at a temperature of about 1150°C but their high alumina content prevents their becoming liquid even at 1300°C. The Chinese petuntse*, a component of many types of crystalline rock and a constituent of most true or hard-paste porcelains as well as of some glazes, is a form of felspar.

In china compositions, felspar, of which the principal constituent is silica, may be substituted for Cornish stone (which itself contains felspar) with the advantages that it is a purer material and is more stable in production. The first native deposits of felspar were found on the borders of Shropshire and Wales in 1818 by Thomas Ryan, from whom John Rose of Coalport* obtained supplies for use in his porcelain glaze. In 1821 Spode* produced 'Felspar Porcelain', using supplies bought from Ryan. The quality of bone china made with the addition of felspar was outstandingly fine, but scarcity of British deposits limited its use to a few manufacturers and a brief period. In 1865-6, and again in 1870, Wedgwood made small quantities of a porcelain body containing a proportion of felspar and some of this was used for decoration by Emile Lessore*.

Fenton Vivian
The site of Thomas Whieldon's* pottery from 1747, or possibly earlier, where he was joined in partnership by Josiah Wedgwood from 1754-9. The types of ware manufactured at Fenton Vivian are recorded in Whieldon's Account and Memorandum Book (City Museum & Art Gallery, Stoke-on-Trent) as principally white saltglazed stoneware*, tortoiseshell* and creamware (cream-coloured ware*). Excavation of the site has yielded valuable information about Whieldon's production.

Fern Leaf
Relief decoration for dry bodies* introduced c.1830.

Ferrara Pattern
Transfer-printed pattern engraved by William Brookes* in 1832 and printed in underglaze dark blue or brown. A purple version was introduced some years later. The centre pattern, within a deep floral border, depicts an Italian harbour scene with the castle of the Dukes of Este to the left, a canal which connects the harbour with the River Po, and a group of shipping taken from a set of engravings published in 1832 under the title *Lancashire Illustrated*. *Ferrara* continued to be made intermittently until 1941 and was reintroduced in the 1950s.

Festoon
A garland of flowers, fruit, leaves or drapery supported at either end and hanging in a natural curve. The motif is known also as a swag. Festoons are a common neo-classical* decorative feature and Wedgwood made much use of them as painted decoration and applied ornament. In a letter to Bentley* of December 1767, Wedgwood wrote: 'We shall want many of this branch [modellers] to work festoons and other ornaments upon Vases, free, without moulds, which Boys may be made to do at moderate expense, & they will look much richer than anything made out of moulds. Mr Pickford has a Plaisterer who can do this sort of work in miniature (the size we shall want) & he will lend him to me to instruct some Pupils.'

Fettling
The process of finishing a vessel before firing by removing cast and seam marks and other blemishes with the aid of a metal tool.

FESTOON. Solid white jasper vase, shape no.381, ornamented by Thomas Lovatt with green festoons and lilac cameos. Height 8¼in. c.1876. *Wedgwood Museum*

The presence of cast and seam marks on pottery and porcelain is evidence of poor quality control, and, if very pronounced, is due to the use of worn working moulds (see: Moulds). Such seams do not, of course, occur on ware thrown on the wheel, but other blemishes may require to be removed before firing.

Fiammingo, Il ('The Fleming')
See: Duquesnoy, François

Figures
The production of figures was never much favoured by Josiah Wedgwood, who considered that while his craftsmen had sufficient work without them figures were better left to others. Bentley*, if we may judge from Wedgwood's letters, did not favour the kind of figures made by the porcelain factories. His was probably the reaction of a fervent neo-classicist to a largely rococo* concept. Wedgwood's objections, on the other hand, seem to have been more on account of technical difficulties. He wrote in November 1769: 'If there was any such thing as getting one sober figure maker to bring up some Boys I sho[ul]d like to ingage in that branch. Suppose you inquire at Bow*; I despair of any at Derby*'.

The process of modelling figures in wax or clay was probably the least of Wedgwood's difficulties. It would not have been hard to find modellers in London capable of doing the work. The need was for craftsmen who could dissect the models, mould the various parts, cast them, reassemble them, prop them for firing and see them safely through the kiln. Repairers*, as these skilled craftsmen were called, were not numerous, and we find Wedgwood eagerly hiring one of them, a Mr Tebo*, in 1774, only to be disappointed that this repairer and modeller, who may have worked for Bow*, could not produce the quality of figures that he required. Wedgwood thought Tebo incompetent, but his principal fault was possibly that he was a rococo modeller, accustomed to porcelain, and too set in his ways to change. Had Wedgwood succeeded in tempting other figure makers from Bow or Derby, the verdict on their work might well have been the same. Wedgwood was obliged to find his own modellers and repairers and train them to work in

FIGURES. Solid white jasper figure of *Venus* with *Cupid* and a dolphin. Height 6⅝in. Unmarked. Wedgwood, c.1785.

Merseyside Museums

the neo-classical* style to his exacting standards.

In the early 1770s, when Wedgwood was beginning to take the business of figure modelling seriously, an important change was taking place in the industry as a whole. In 1752 J-J. Bachelier, art director at the factory of Vincennes (later the Royal factory of Sèvres*), introduced the use of white unglazed porcelain for figure work. These biscuit* figures were highly successful. In England the manufacture of biscuit porcelain figures was taken up at Derby, already specialising in figure making, and it was an obvious temptation to Wedgwood to enter this market with his recently developed white terracotta* body, a composition especially well suited to figures in the neo-classical style. The influence of the white marble statuary being excavated at Pompeii* and Herculaneum* that led to what André Malraux aptly described as the 'white world of neo-classicism', still prevails in the popular misconception of ancient civilisations.

There is ample evidence in the surviving factory records to prove that Derby charged more for biscuit figures than for those that were glazed and painted. Although the latter required more work, the glaze and enamelling covered many minor faults which would not have been accepted by the purchaser of a biscuit figure. Wedgwood had not developed the glazed and painted figure and his models were unsuitable for this treatment. Imperfect wares, unless he was prepared to sell them cheaply as of inferior quality ('seconds'), were wastage. Although, like all 18th-century manufacturers, Wedgwood had his share of wares which had some manufacturing defect, and must therefore be sold as 'seconds', he nevertheless appreciated the potential harm that this might do to his reputation as a manufacturer of finer quality ornamental wares and was therefore reluctant to venture into a field where 'seconds' were likely to be greater than average. He was also acutely aware of the heavy financial losses suffered by the porcelain companies, due largely to their heavy losses in production, and he was determined, as far as possible, to avoid repeating their mistakes.

The first Wedgwood & Bentley Catalogue*, published in 1773, lists a total of twenty-three figures (including sphinxes* and griffins* fitted with nozzles for candles), the largest being 24in. high *(Neptune*)* and *Triton*)*. In the following fifteen years, up to 1788 when the last Wedgwood Ornamental Ware Catalogue was issued, twenty-three more were catalogued and records exist of a further sixteen, all but four of which were produced in the 18th century but which were either omitted or produced after 1788 (see:

FIGURES. Black basaltes *Faun with Infant Bacchus,* height 18in., and *Venus* after Pigalle, height 18½in. c.1860-80.

Christie's, New York

Colour Plate 41. FAIRYLAND LUSTRE. Pair of bone china Fairyland Lustre vases decorated with *Pillar* pattern (familiarly known at Etruria as 'Fire Escape') and *(centre)* a covered vase decorated with *Demon Tree* in 'Flame Fairyland' colours, all designed by Daisy Makeig-Jones. Height 14¾in. and 12in. c.1920.   *Sotheby's, London*

Colour Plate 42. FAIRYLAND LUSTRE. Bone china Fairyland Lustre plaque decorated with *Bubbles* design by Daisy Makeig-Jones. 1916. Height 16in.
Wedgwood Museum

Colour Plate 43. FAIRYLAND LUSTRE. Fairyland Lustre vase decorated with *Candlemas* design by Daisy Makeig-Jones. Height 7in. c.1920.
Wedgwood Museum

Colour Plate 45. FLAXMAN, John. Wedgwood & Bentley solid pale-blue and white jasper tablet ornamented with the *Apotheosis of Homer,* modelled by John Flaxman junior in 1778. 7⅝in. x 14½in.
Wedgwood Museum

Colour Plate 46. FLOWER-POTS. White terracotta stoneware flower-pot and 'window vase' moulded to resemble barrel forms, decorated with green hoops and brown staves. From 1778 objects decorated in this manner were referred to as 'Devonshire' after the Duchess. Height (flower-pot) 9½in. c.1785.
Wedgwood Museum

Colour Plate 44. FIRST DAY'S VASE. Two First Day's Vases (shape no. 49) painted in encaustic orange-red, showing the front and reverse: the front painted with the figure of Hippothon, Antiochus and Clymenos from a vase in the Hamilton collection (Vol I, Plate 129 of d'Hancarville's edition). Height 10in. Unmarked. 1769.
Wedgwood Museum

Colour Plate 47. FROG SERVICE. Queen's ware Catherine shape dessert plate enamelled in polychrome with a view of 'Moor Park', Hertfordshire, a subject which appears in monochrome in the 'Frog' service. Polychrome-painted pieces were probably made at Josiah Wedgwood's particular request after the completion of the official service. Unmarked, 1774. *Wedgwood Museum*

Colour Plate 49. GUYATT, Richard. Commemorative mugs designed by Richard Guyatt to celebrate the American Bicentennial (1976), the Silver Jubilee (1977), the Silver Wedding (1974), the Coronation (1953) and the Investiture of the Prince of Wales (1969). Height 4½in. *Wedgwood Museum*

Colour Plate 48. GANYMEDE. Pale blue-grey jasper with blue jasper dip plaque ornamented with the figures of *Ganymede and the Eagle*. Height 7in. Wedgwood & Bentley, c.1778.   *Wedgwood Museum*

Colour Plate 50. HACKWOOD, William. Pale-blue jasper dip portrait medallion of Josiah Wedgwood in a rosso antico and black basaltes frame. Modelled by William Hackwood in 1782. Height 5¼in. Unmarked. c.1782.   *City Museum & Art Gallery, Stoke-on-Trent*

Colour Plate 51. HOLLOWAY, John. Pair of Queen's ware egg vases (lacking covers) on dolphin tripod supports, painted in enamel colours with continuous seascapes by John Holloway. Height 7in. c.1876.   *Author's collection*

Colour Plate 52. INLAID WARE. Glazed redware 146 shape teapot and a pair of candlesticks decorated with patterns inlaid with contrasting slip. Teapot length 8in. c.1862. *Wedgwood Museum*

Colour Plate 53. JAMES, Elwyn. Two vases by Elwyn James illustrating his fine use of decorative glazes and pierced patterns. c.1970.
Dr and Mrs Jerome Mones Collection

Colour Plate 54. JAPONAISERIE. White ware teaset and coffeeset decorated with panels of underglaze blue and oriental flowers in the 'Imari' style. Parapet teapot length 8½in. c.1812. *Wedgwood Museum*

Colour Plate 56. JASPER. Rare Wedgwood & Bentley solid grey jasper portrait medallion of Gustavus III, King of Sweden, in a polished frame of the same material. Attributed to Flaxman, 1777. Oval height 3¹⁵⁄₁₆in.
Formerly Eugene D. Buchanan Collection

Colour Plate 55. JASPER (frame of cameos). Frame of twenty-five jasper cameos illustrating a variety of colours and including a trial piece of green on black, three versions of the cameo produced by Wedgwood in 1787 from the seal of the Society for the Abolition of the Slave Trade, a small figure of Aesculapius and three of Apollo. *Wedgwood Museum*

Colour Plate 57. JASPER. A group of 18th-century jasper pieces, showing *(right),* a solid-blue jasper pedestal bulb pot with examples of blue, green and black jasper dip. c.1785-95. *Wedgwood Museum*

Colour Plate 59. JASPER. Fine blue jasper dip coffeepot or chocolate pot with engine-turned lid, white jasper handle and spout, and ornament of *Domestic Employment* after a design by Lady Templetown. c.1785-90. *Wedgwood Museum*

Colour Plate 58. JASPER. Solid pale-blue and white jasper two-handled cup with white jasper handles and ornaments of *The Young Seamstress* after designs by Emma Crewe. The interior is lapidary-polished. Height 4in. c.1790. *Nottingham Castle Museum*

Colour Plate 60. JASPER. Extremely rare solid lilac and white jasper teapot and cup and saucer, engine-turned and ornamented with figures of *Domestic Employment* after a design by Lady Templetown, and *Bacchanalian Boys* after Duquesnoy. Teapot height 5in. c.1785-95.   *City Museum & Art Gallery, Stoke-on-Trent*

Colour Plate 61. JASPER. Group of 19th- and 20th-century jasper pieces illustrating some of the colours produced between 1800 and 1930, including crimson and turquoise.   *Wedgwood Museum*

Colour Plate 62. JASPER. Crimson jasper dip bas-relief ware spill vase and teapot, the spill vase (height 8in.) ornamented by Bert Bentley. c.1930. *Wedgwood Museum*

Colour Plate 63. JASPER. Three-colour jasper goblet, ornamented with portrait medallions of George Washington and Thomas Jefferson, issued in a limited edition in 1975 to commemorate the American Bicentennial. Height 4¾in. *Wedgwood Museum*

Colour Plate 64. JASPER TEAWARE. Three tri-colour jasper can-shape coffee cups and saucers, two with engine-turned dicing. These were intended for display as 'cabinet pieces', not for use. Height 2¾in. c.1790. *Nottingham Castle Museum*

Colour Plate 65. JEWELLERY. Cut-steel comb and bracelet mounted with jasper cameos, and a small necklace of seventy-two matched blue and white jasper beads, examples of 18th-century jewellery employing Wedgwood's jasper. No marks visible. c.1785-90. *Wedgwood Museum*

Colour Plate 66. JEWELLERY. Three-colour jasper pendant and brooch, gold-mounted, from a small collection of cameos mounted in gold, gold-plated silver and rhodium-plated silver in 1979. *Wedgwood Museum*

Colour Plate 67. LESSORE, Emile. Original watercolour drawing by Emile Lessore and a Queen's ware tazza painted in enamel colours with the same subject: 'The Young Architects'. Watercolour: *Wedgwood Museum;* Tazza (length 12½in.): *L.A. Compton Collection*

Colour Plate 68. LESSORE, Emile. Fine Queen's ware plaque painted by Emile Lessore with a scene of Diana and her attendants bathing in a woodland stream. 15¾in. x 12in. Signed.
Mr & Mrs David Zeitlin Collection

Colour Plate 69. LUSTRE DECORATION. White ware combined pastille burner and bough pot, width 13½in., and a broth bowl with cover and stand decorated with variegated lustre. c.1815.
Formerly Buten Museum

Colour Plate 70. LUSTRES. Pair of 18th-century lustres: candlesticks of cut glass with drops of yellow and white glass, the black and white jasper drums mounted in ormolu bases. Height 11in. No marks visible.

Wedgwood Museum

Colour Plate 72. MAJOLICA. Majolica helmet vase decorated in opaque and transparent glazes of turquoise, red and grey with gilding. Height 8in. 1873.   *Formerly Buten Museum*

Colour Plate 71. MAJOLICA. 'Fan' garden seat decorated in transparent and opaque Majolica glazes. Height 17in. 1886.

Byron & Elaine Born Collection

Colour Plate 73. MAKEIG-JONES, 'Daisy'. Bone china Globe shape coffeeset decorated in enamel colours with *Tyrone* pattern from the Celtic Ornaments series of patterns designed by Daisy Makeig-Jones. c.1920. *Author's collection*

Colour Plate 74. MAKEIG-JONES, 'Daisy'. Bone china vases and a large plate decorated with Fairyland Lustre patterns designed by Daisy Makeig-Jones, c.1920. *Wedgwood Museum*

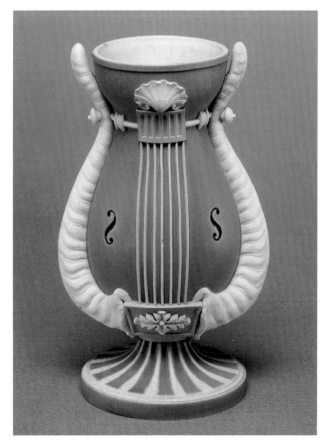

Colour Plate 75. MELLOR, Thomas. Queen's ware vase on a cylindrical plinth decorated with bands of enamel colouring and gilding and inlaid by Thomas Mellor in the *Henry Deux* manner. Height 15in. Signed. c.1885.
Wedgwood Museum

Colour Plate 76. MERCURY. Fine black basaltes bust of Mercury attributed to John Flaxman junior. Height 18½in. c.1790-5.
Wedgwood Museum

Colour Plate 77. MUSICAL INSTRUMENTS. Pale-blue jasper dip 'Viol del Gamba' [*sic*] vase, 'intended to captivate musical people'. Height 6½in. c.1801.
Wedgwood Museum

Colour Plate 78. ORDINARY LUSTRE. A group of bone china pieces decorated with Ordinary Lustre, including fish, dragon and butterfly patterns, with a Fairyland Lustre *Roc* pattern plate. *Wedgwood Museum*

Colour Plate 79. ORNAMENTING. White jasper rectangular plaque, with applied reliefs and four octagonal jasper grounds for cameos, illustrating the four stages in the making of a tricolour jasper dip cameo ornamented with *Cupid in his Car drawn by Lions.* 5½in. x 8¼in. Made by Bert Bentley, 1922. This method has remained unchanged since the 18th century. *Wedgwood Museum*

FIGURES. Basalt figures of Charles I and Oliver Cromwell. Height 6½in. c.1910.
Mr & Mrs Samuel Laver Collection

FIGURES. White bone china figure of George Washington holding the American flag surmounted by a gilded bald eagle. Height 8½in. c.1880. *Formerly Buten Museum*

Black Basaltes).

Although the principal Wedgwood body for figures has always been black basaltes, some early figures were also made by Boot* in the white terracotta* body and a small number of 18th-century figures were made also in cane* (Voltaire* and Rousseau*) and jasper* (including white jasper figures for Vulliamy*), though examples are extremely-rare. The moulds or casts of Wedgwood's early figures were bought primarily from Hoskins & Grant*, the makers of plaster casts in St Martin's Lane, London, who also supplied casts of most of the busts*, but others were obtained from Mrs Mary Landré*, Theodore Parker* and John Flaxman* senior and junior*. Hoskins charged the comparatively large sum of £5 for a 'Mould for the Morpheus* for pressing, cutting the model in pieces, and joining it together again after it was moulded'. From this it is clear that Hoskins undertook to dissect the figure and mould its components, and obvious, too, that the moulds were used to take 'squeezes' (press-moulding*) and that slip casting* was not used at that early date. Production moulding and repairing*, of course, had to be done at Etruria*, and between 1769 and 1773 the repairer was probably Boot.

There is no documentary evidence that any creamware or Pearl ware* figures were made at Etruria during the lifetime of Josiah I. The reason for this is plain: a good variety of such figures was already in production in Staffordshire, notably by Ralph Wood*. Although the best were of high quality, they could never compete for elegance or sharpness of modelling with those from the porcelain factories. Black basaltes and jasper figures were exceptional in quality and also in their markets: the first because they helped to satisfy the demand for bronze ornaments; and the second because they were part of a unique product, competing directly with biscuit porcelain. There was, nevertheless, a substantial market for earthenware figures and Josiah was obliged sometimes to supply them to his customers by buying in stocks from other manu-

facturers. He bought a large quantity of such figures from Ralph Wood in 1783. There is no evidence to show that these bore the impressed mark of either manufacturer, but similar figures exist (e.g. *Faith, Hope, Charity, Reclining Boys*) as well as a few rare busts, which bear the Wedgwood mark impressed with the distinguishing addition of a stop after the name. These were probably bought either from Ralph Wood or his cousin Enoch Wood, most probably the latter, c.1790.

In the 19th century the Parian* body was used for sixty-three figures, several of them from earlier moulds, and sixteen groups (see full list under Carrara*). Some of these were reproduced in an earthenware body with Majolica* glazes. About 1880 a small number of figures was produced in the reintroduced bone china* body decorated with enamel colours and a matt ivory glaze.

The 20th century saw several attempts by Wedgwood to compete in the market for porcelain figures. The nine well-modelled but insipid figures of her friends by Kathleen Goodwin*, the accurate but conventional 'Audubon Birds' modelled by Herbert Palliser*, a few characters from fiction (including *Long John Silver* and *Jorrocks*) by Montague Weaver-Bridgeman*, and some now forgotten figures by freelance modellers such as Joan Pyman (Celadon* figure of a Madonna), Agatha Walker (figures from *The Beggar's Opera*) and Mrs J. Lawson Peacey (figure of a lady with peacocks) made little impact on a market already dominated by Worcester* and Coalport and rapidly being captured by Doulton. Something fresh and less sentimental was needed. Alan Best's* fine Queen's ware models, produced in cream colour and matt white, might have been more successful if they had been reproduced in basalt.

Basalt was the body chosen for a series of small statuettes, c.1910, between 7½ and 8in. in height, of Charles I, Oliver Cromwell, the *Lady of the Lake, Olivia, Roderick Dhu* and the *Vicar of Wakefield*. The modeller of these remains unidentified and they seem not to have been produced in large quantities, indicating that the somewhat odd selection of subjects did not prove to be popular. No more distinguished, but commercially the best figures produced during the first quarter of the century, were the twenty-two small animals and birds modelled by Ernest W. Light* between 1913 and 1920. Produced in basalt with 'realistic' glass eyes in several of the models, they were reintroduced, the glass eyes omitted in favour of modelled sights, in 1935.

The animal figures modelled by John Skeaping* and Arnold Machin* in the 1930s were in a different, and altogether far superior, class and they were deservedly admired. Skeaping's, in particular, marked a departure from Wedgwood's traditional attitude to the modelling of figures, which had previously been entirely conventional, relying principally upon reductions of classical sculpture or naturalistic representations of birds, animals and human figures. Costs of production (largely determined by the techniques of skilled repairers) and prices were high. Skeaping modelled his figures so that they might be cast in one piece, like the cheap and colourful Staffordshire earthenware figures of the 19th century. In Machin's *Taurus* and *Ferdinand,* especially, the Staffordshire tradition of humour and simplicity in modelling was attractively combined with a new vigour and purity of line. Skeaping's figures were reproduced in the 1950s but their undecorated simplicity was not appreciated by a public too long starved of colour during the war years when decorated china was not permitted to be sold on the home market. The earlier, signed, models are now popular among collectors.

Four classical figures by Donald Brindley* – *Hercules* and *Mercury* (basalt) and *Leda and the Swan* and *Terpsichore* (jasper) – were issued in 1974-5. The last venture into figure making, in 1985-6, was a collection of seven sets of 'fine porcelain' figures variously titled *Countryside Collection – Birds, Countryside Collection – Animals, Childhood Memories, The Hyde Park Collection, The Four Seasons Collection* and *High Society Collection.* The human figures, evidently intended to be sophisticated, combine rigidity of modelling with an arch sentimentality. They bear no relationship either to anything previously produced by Wedgwood or to contemporary design and are best regarded as an ill-considered aberration.

Filter
Large cylindrical vessel with a cover and spigot, containing a porous stone filter for the purification of water. Filters were made from the 1830s in large sizes of about five-gallon capacity for kitchens and in smaller sizes for the table. They were usually of

FILTER. White stoneware and pale-blue jasper dip water purefier labelled 'SPENCER'S PATENT MAGNETIC PURIFYING FILTER'. Height 15in. c.1887.   *Formerly Buten Museum*

plain brown stoneware, often decorated with the royal coat of arms in relief, and are particularly associated with Doulton. An especially fine and decorative Wedgwood white stoneware filter with pale-blue jasper dip* and applied ornaments, 15in. high, was made in 1887. It is marked 'Spencer's Patent Purifying Magnetic Filter' in addition to the usual trade mark.

FINCH, Lady Charlotte. Wedgwood & Bentley pale-blue and white jasper portrait medallion modelled by Joachim Smith. Oval height 3in. c.1775.   *Private collection*

Finch, Lady Charlotte (1725-1813)
Second daughter of the Earl of Pomfret; governess to the daughters of George III. Horace Walpole described her as 'the cleverest girl in the world' and 'a woman of remarkable sense and philosophy'. Portraits of Lady Charlotte and her daughters Henrietta and Matilda (Mrs Fielding) were modelled by Joachim Smith* in 1774 and were among the earliest portrait medallions to be made in jasper*. Wedgwood wrote to Bentley* on 30 August 1774: 'I shall send by tomorrows Coach a number of heads of Lady CF's Daughters… Two only are pretty good.'

Finger Vase (Five-Finger Vase)
Vase with five flower holders arranged in a fan shape, sometimes called a quintal vase. Made in porcelain at Vienna and of tin-glazed* earthenware at Delft*, they were also produced in creamware by Wedgwood and Leeds*, the Don Pottery, James and Charles Whitehead and Castleford, among others. They have been reproduced intermittently by Wedgwood during the 19th and 20th centuries.

Finial
The terminal ornament of an object, but used particularly of a decorative handle* or knop* on the cover of a vase, teapot, coffee-pot, covered bowl or tureen. Finials have been made in a great variety of forms, including figures, animals, flowers and fruits (especially the pineapple, the pine cone and the acorn) and they are characteristic of their period and style. For example, flowers and certain fruits, like the lemon, are especially rococo*; acorns are neo-classical*; and sphinxes* belong to the Empire or Regency styles. Knops particularly associated with Wedgwood are the sibyl*, pierced baluster, rose, acorn, and oval and round plumes; but animals, figures, fruit, flowers and vegetables are among those which appear on pieces of 18th-century design. Rare finials of the

FINIAL. Well modelled acorn finial surmounting the lid of an engine-turned black basaltes vase of the Wedgwood & Bentley period. Height 7½in. *Wedgwood Museum*

FIRECRACKS. Jasper sphinx couchant with a candleholder between its wings. Well defined firecracks appear at the junction of the left paw with the body, just in front of the back paw separating the body from the base, in the region of the neck, and between the candleholder and the foremost supporting wing. *Merseyside Museums*

Whieldon-Wedgwood* and Ivy House* periods include a bird in flight, a conch shell and a recumbent sheep.

Fire Speckling
Minute pieces of carbon or other material embedded in the glaze either during the original firing or as a result of refiring to add enamel or onglaze transfer-printed* decoration. Fire speckling often accompanies refiring that has taken place some considerable time after manufacture, and glaze that has been enamelled at a later date to enhance the value of an undecorated piece very often displays this fault. Sadler* & Green complained to Wedgwood that they were experiencing trouble of this kind in firing transfer-printed ware and suggested that the cause might be dampness acquired during transport. The presence of fire speckling cannot be regarded as certain evidence of faking or redecoration at a much later date and should be considered in conjunction with the nature of the decoration. Much of Wedgwood's late 19th-century Queen's ware* and Pearl ware* suffered from this fault.

Fireclays
Very refractory clays able to withstand extremely high temperatures without fusing. Clays of this kind are used in the making of saggars* and kiln furniture generally.

Firecracks
Firecracks must be carefully distinguished from cracks due to damage which usually have a depressing effect upon value unless the specimen is extremely rare. Firecracks are always slightly wider at one end, and are normally due to faulty design. The thicker parts of an object take up heat in the kiln more slowly than the thinner parts, and give it off more slowly during cooling. Unless this has been taken into account in the design, tensions are created which lead to the opening of firecracks or to distortion. Firecracks are not, by themselves, a good reason for rejecting a specimen.

The term 'age crack' sometimes used is undesirable because it does not define the nature of the crack, and leaves doubt whether it is due to firing or later damage. No cracks occur simply as the result of age.

Firecracks are rare in any but 18th-century work, and then only in early specimens as a general rule. In Wedgwood wares they are most frequent in black basaltes*, and they are sometimes to be found filled with some kind of bituminous substance to make them fit for sale (see also: Tinkering). Firecracks occur occasionally in early jasper tablets and figures but are rarely seen even in the earliest creamware. In September 1776, referring to jasper tablets,

Wedgwood wrote: '…we have done with the cracking which teized [*sic*] us so much in former compositions, & only want a proper fire to make us absolute'.
See also: Dunting

First Day's Vases
The manufactory of ornamental ware was removed to Etruria* between November 1768 and the following spring, and the new factory was formally opened on 13 June 1769. The occasion was celebrated by the making of six First Day's vases in black basaltes*, thrown by Josiah Wedgwood while Bentley* cranked the wheel for him. After turning and firing, these vases were sent to London to be painted with encaustic* decoration in imitation of ancient red-figure* vases. The form of the vases was copied from one in the Hamilton* collection. The obverse painting represents Hercules in the Garden of the Hesperides, copied from Plate 129 in Hamilton's first volume, and the inscription below reads *Artes Etruriae Renascuntur* (The Arts of Etruria are Reborn). On the reverse is painted the inscription:

JUNE XIII M.DCC.LXIX

One of the First Day's Productions

at

Etruria in Staffordshire

by

Wedgwood & Bentley

Wedgwood wrote to Bentley on 19 November: 'The six Etruscan Vases, three-handled sent to you a fortnight since were those we threw & turn'd the first at Etruria, & sho'd be finished as high as you please, but not sold, they being the *first fruits* of Etruria'.

It has been customary to credit David Rhodes* with the painting of these vases, but recent research has shown that the figures are more likely to be the work of William Hopkins Craft*, while the borders and inscriptions are attributed to Rhodes or another of the painters at the Chelsea Decorating Studio*.

Fifty replicas were issued in 1930 to mark the bicentenary of Josiah Wedgwood's birth. These bear an inscription which gives the years of his birth (1730) and death (1795). The works at Etruria were finally closed on 13 June 1950, 181 years after the official opening, and the event was commemorated by the production of six Last Day's Vases.
See: Colour Plate 44

First Pattern Book
See: Pattern Books

Fish Lustre
See: Ordinary Lustres

Fish Platter
A large oval dish with moulded relief of a salmon on a bed of fern and leaves, decorated in Majolica* glazes in naturalistic colours, made c.1865.

Fish Trowel

A flat, trowel-shaped utensil, pierced for draining, with a raised handle, for serving fish. Wedgwood's fish trowels were made of Queen's ware*, with decorative piercing and a feather-moulded handle, c.1775-1850.

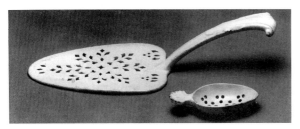

FISH TROWEL. Queen's ware pierced fish trowel with feather-moulded handle, length 11⅜in., c.1790, shown with an egg poacher of around the same date. *Formerly Buten Museum*

Fishtail Ewer

Ewer with a handle in the form of a scaled fish tail which arches from the centre of the lid to the shoulder. There is a mask below the handle and another beneath the spout, and some examples are ornamented with festoons* and a key fret*. The model, apparently in production in 1770, was adapted from an illustration in Jacques de Stella's* *Livre de Vases aux Galeries du Louvre*. Wedgwood referred to these ewers as 'Stella's ewers' in a letter of 3 September 1770 to Bentley* defining the difference between useful and ornamental wares. The ewer was made in black basaltes* and in the white terracotta* body with variegated* decoration and gilding.

FISHTAIL EWER. Wedgwood & Bentley white terracotta stoneware ewer with fishtail handle terminating in a human mask, adapted from a design by Jacques Stella. Height 12½in. c.1773. *Dwight & Lucille Beeson Collection. Birmingham Museum, Alabama*

Flags Pattern

A patriotic design, showing the flags of the Allies in World War I, produced on a Queen's ware* toy teaset, c.1914. This pattern is easily confused with the Liberty Ware* made three years later.

Flask

A flattened globular vessel with a short neck, small mouth and cover for carrying liquids. When it is provided with pierced lugs for a carrying strap, it is known as a pilgrim flask. A red body pilgrim flask with printed and enamelled *Peacock* pattern and a scene of an Edo period pageant over a printed *Mikado* ground in the *kibori gakuawase* style was made by Wedgwood, c.1875. The same shape was used for a redware pilgrim flask with slip decoration of an

Egyptian head within an *Isis* border, probably the work of Frederick Rhead*, c.1878. A Pearl ware* flask painted with sprigs of flowers in underglaze blue and ornamented with applied bows and husk wreaths, impressed with the Wedgwood mark and inscribed 'R Wedgwood' in blue (Buten Museum*) is the work of Ralph Wedgwood*, probably before his move to Ferrybridge.

Flatware

Term applied to saucers, plates, round and oval dishes, platters and trays. These are wares apt to warp in the kiln unless carefully placed.

Flaxman, John RA (1755-1826)

English sculptor, draughtsman and designer; born in York, the son of a modeller and maker of plaster casts, living from 1756 at New Street, Covent Garden, London. The family was poor and the young Flaxman suffered from ill-health and congenital curvature of the spine. He was, however, cheerful and intelligent and showed, at an early age in his father's shop, great promise in drawing and modelling. There he was befriended by a local clergyman, who lent him books and taught him Latin and Greek. In 1766, at the age of eleven, he won a premium from the Society of Arts (Royal Society of Arts*), and three years later enrolled as one of the first students of the newly founded Royal Academy Schools, where his fellow students included John Bacon* and James Tassie*. He exhibited for the first time at the Academy in 1770 and had come to the notice of Josiah Wedgwood by September 1771, when he wrote to Bentley* describing the visit to Etruria* of a Mr Freeman: 'he is a great admirer of young Flaxman & has advised his Father to send him to Rome which he has promised to do. Mr Freeman says he knows young Flaxman is a Coxcomb, but does not think him a bit the worse for it *or the less likely to be a great Artist*'.

In January 1775, when he was having some trouble with the portrait modeller Joachim Smith*, Josiah proposed to Bentley that they drop all connection with him and find 'a Modeler of our own for Portraits', and on the 14th wrote, 'I am glad you have met with a Modeler & that Flaxman is so valuable an Artist'. The earliest surviving bill for work done for Wedgwood by the Flaxmans is dated March 1775, for the modelling of a pair of vases at three guineas and a number of bas-reliefs at 10/6d each. Since the

FLAGS PATTERN. Sketches from a Wedgwood pattern book showing designs for the Queen's ware toy teaset decorated with *Flags* pattern. c.1914. *Wedgwood Museum*

FLAXMAN, John, RA. Green jasper dip portrait medallion of John Flaxman junior. A self-portrait modelled c.1787. Diameter 6in. c.1790.
Wedgwood Museum

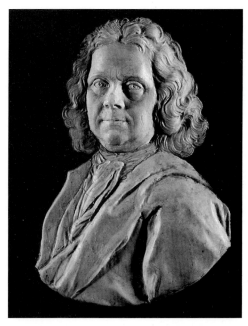

FLAXMAN, John, RA. Wax portrait of Hermann Boerhaave, the Dutch physician, modelled by Flaxman in 1782 (invoiced to Wedgwood 8 July) and reproduced in jasper later in the year. The portrait is modelled directly on to glass and illustrates Flaxman's rare ability to model the nearly full-face portrait. Maximum height of relief 3⅛in. *Formerly Author's collection*

younger Flaxman often signed invoices on behalf of his father, it is difficult to differentiate between the work of father and son.

Four months later Josiah suggested that Bentley employ Flaxman 'to model some Figures. They would do for Tablets, Vases, inlaying &c. We have nobody here who can do them'. It is clear from the context that Josiah was referring to bas-reliefs, not statuettes. The first clear evidence of the young Flaxman's original work for Wedgwood occurs in Wedgwood's letter of 8 August 1775, when he wrote: 'I wish you to see Mr Flaxman before you leave London, & if you could prevail upon him to finish Mr Banks* & Dr Solander* they would be an acquisition to us'. He went on to suggest that Flaxman should be given more work of this kind – 'some of the finest things that can be modeled, & Originals which have not been hackney'd in Wax & Plaister for a century past'. This is important evidence of Wedgwood's desire to move from the production of subjects taken from plaster casts available to other manufacturers to the reproduction of work commissioned especially for his own use.

Flaxman's work for Wedgwood was both varied and extensive but was concentrated especially on portrait medallions and classical bas-relief subjects for ornamenting vases and tablets. Most of his subjects were first modelled in wax, direct on to glass or slate grounds, using a hard greyish-white composition of his own, which contained a high proportion of white lead. The relief varied in thickness from a transparent coating of wax to about half an inch. A professional sculptor, Flaxman was one of the few modellers capable of producing convincing likenesses in the difficult three-quarter view, and some of his portraits are almost full-face. His profiles show recognisable characteristics of style: an upright figure, sharply truncated well below the shoulder; uncluttered dress; well-defined eyes (with sculpted eyeballs), mouth and nostrils; and an especially noticeable thinness of jasper at the bridge of the nose, which often shows the colour through the white relief. Josiah complained of this last feature of Flaxman's modelling as 'too flat in several parts to be made in color'd grounds, & we can sooner finish our own than raise his model'.

Flaxman's most important bas-relief design was unquestionably the *Apotheosis of Homer**, modelled in 1778 after an engraving illustrated by d'Hancarville* (Vol.III, Plate 31) of a scene from a bell krater* in the Hamilton* collection. About seven years later, Flaxman modelled a companion piece, *Apotheosis of Virgil.* Both were used for ornamenting vases and tablets.

Early in 1784 Flaxman made designs for the ceiling and cornices

of Wedgwood's drawing-room at Etruria Hall*. It is not certain that these were ever used, but it is probable that they were since the room, which is thought to have been painted by William Blake*, became a showpiece for visitors. Next year Flaxman modelled another subject from the Hamilton collection, from an engraving of the painting on a 5th-century red-figure hydria, *Hercules in the Garden of the Hesperides,* and in 1786 he was commissioned to model two important plaques to celebrate the French Commercial Treaty*. The famous and popular *Dancing Hours**, although not certainly documented, is undoubtedly Flaxman's work, as are one set of the *Muses** with Apollo*, and the superb bust of Mercury* which was probably not reproduced in black basaltes until the end of the century. Among Flaxman's documented work is also a fine set of chessmen* designed in 1783-4.

In February 1784 Flaxman wrote to recommend to Wedgwood that he journey to London especially to see Sir William Hamilton's (later Portland*) vase. This is the earliest mention of the vase in the surviving Wedgwood manuscripts and it appears likely that Flaxman was the first to draw Wedgwood's attention to it.

In 1787 Flaxman went to Rome, partly subsidised by Wedgwood, where he was supposed to do some modelling and to superintend Wedgwood's 'Roman School' of artists. In the event, Flaxman found little time for work on Wedgwood's behalf, apparently completing only one large bas-relief in wax of *The Birth of Bacchus** and a small portrait of Victor Amadeus III. He was busy on his account, making a considerable reputation for himself not only as a sculptor but also as the illustrator of the *Iliad,* the *Odyssey,* the works of Dante and the tragedies of Aeschylus, for which engravings from his drawings were made in Rome. There he made the acquaintance of Canova*, who became his friend and one of his most fervent admirers.

After seven years in Italy, Flaxman returned to London and rented a house in Buckingham Street, Fitzroy Square, where he lived for the rest of his life. He devoted himself largely to monumental sculpture, but he maintained a friendly connection with the Wedgwoods and did a small amount of work for them. He also supplied important designs for Rundell, Bridge & Rundell, silversmiths to the Prince Regent. Flaxman was elected a member of the Royal Academy in 1800 and Sir Richard Westmacott, who followed him as Professor of Sculpture at the Royal Academy, spoke of him as the greatest modern sculptor.

When Josiah Wedgwood died in January 1795, it was appropriate that Flaxman should be invited to carve a memorial portrait tablet, to be erected in the parish church of Stoke-on-Trent. He agreed to do so, basing his likeness on the portrait by Sir Joshua Reynolds*. He was paid £93.19.0 for the monument, including 'affixing & interest'.

Wedgwood's production in the 18th century would have looked very different without Flaxman's contribution. He modelled not only bas-reliefs for tablets, medallions and cameos, but important portrait medallions, a set of chessmen and probably vases and other objects that lay beyond the capabilities of modellers employed at the factory. He and his father supplied also several busts, figures and other decorative pieces, but most, if not all, of these appear to have been in the form of casts or moulds and are therefore not listed as original work. The relationship between Flaxman and Josiah Wedgwood provides an instructive illustration of the friendly working association between artist and manufacturer. Flaxman accepted Wedgwood's criticisms and suggestions, adapting his technique to reproductive processes and benefiting from the disciplines imposed by them.

Flaxman was the most complete and the most consistent artist employed by Wedgwood in the 18th century, and, with the single exception of Hackwood* (whose work was largely in adapting, re-modelling and repairing), he was also the most prolific. There has thus been a temptation to attribute to him all of Wedgwood's finest models. The list that follows is not definitive, but it includes all the major work that is documented as Flaxman's and the most important models that may be reliably attributed to him. Also included are models invoiced to Wedgwood by the Flaxmans, father and son, which are casts or moulds.

BUSTS
Mercury, the model given to Wedgwood by Flaxman in 1782, but probably not reproduced until the end of the century
Sarah Siddons, 1784 (no example of this bust has been found)
Josiah Wedgwood. Marble bust for Wedgwood's memorial
Invoices were sent to Wedgwood by the Flaxmans for moulding the following busts. The wording of the invoices and the prices charged make it clear that none was modelled by either Flaxman, although all have previously been listed as the original work of the younger Flaxman:
Dr John Fothergill*, 1781
David Garrick, 1788
Georg Friedrich Handel, 1788
*Hercules** (probably the work of Flaxman senior), 1782
Homer*, 1788
Jean-Jacques Rousseau*, 1781
Laurence Sterne* (probably invoiced in error for Voltaire), 1781. The known bust of Sterne was supplied by Hoskins & Grant* in 1779
Voltaire*, 1781

FIGURES
Apollo, height 11in., 1775
Apollo Belvedere. Cast invoiced 1789
Mercury, height 11in., 1775
Cupid Sitting Pensive and *Psyche* 'to match', height 8½in. Casts, after Falconet*, supplied in 1781

PORTRAIT MEDALLIONS
Banks*, Sir Joseph, three portraits: (1) invoiced 1775; (2) a large portrait 'classicised' from (1), 1779; (3) attributed
Banks, Dorothea, Lady, 1782
Boerhaave, Hermann, 1782
Buchan, William, 1783
Cats, Jacob, c.1782, attributed
Chatham, William Pitt, 1st Earl of, 1778
Coligny, Louise de, 1781, attributed
Cook, James, three portraits: (1) attributed; (2) enlarged from (1), 1779; (3), 1784
Cowper, George, 3rd Earl, 1786
Devonshire, Georgiana, Duchess of, c.1782, attributed
Dutens, Louis, c.1786, attributed
Edgeworth, Honora, 1781, attributed
Edward, Duke of Kent, c.1785, attributed (a second portrait is by Lochée*, 1787)
Ferdinand I of the Two Sicilies, 1781
Flaxman, Anne, c.1790
Flaxman John, two self-portraits: (1) c.1771; (2) c.1790
Fothergill, John, 1777, attributed
Fox, Charles James, c.1790, attributed
Franklin, William, c.1786, attributed

Franklin, William Temple, c.1786, attributed
George, Prince of Wales (later George IV), c.1786. A second portrait, after a drawing by E. Scott, is attributed
Goethe, Johann Wolfgang von, c.1790, attributed
Gustavus III of Sweden, 1777. Two portraits, the second attributed
Hastings, Warren, 1787
Hein, Peter, c.1782, attributed
Herschel, Sir William, c.1785, attributed (a second portrait is attributed to Lochée)
Hogerbeets, Rombout, c.1782, attributed
Johnson, Samuel, 1784
Joseph II of Austria, 1786, attributed
Kemble, John Philip, c.1784, attributed
Kortenaer, Egbert, c.1782, attributed
Lever, Sir Ashton, c.1785
Liverpool, Charles Jenkinson, 1st Earl, 1784
Maria I, Queen of Portugal, 1787 (a second portrait is attributed to Lochée)
Meerman. Anna, 1785
Meerman, Johann, 1785
Paul I of Russia, 1782
Pitt, William, c.1786
Ruyter, Michel de, c.1782
Siddons, Sarah, 178.
Solander, Daniel, two portraits: (1) 1775; (2) enlarged and classicised from (1), 1779
Victor Amadeus III of Sardinia, 1788
Witt, Cornelis de, c.1782
Witt, Jan de, c.1782
In addition, the Flaxmans supplied a set of the English Poets in 1777 and part of a set of the Kings of England (a second set being supplied complete by Thomas Astle*).

BAS-RELIEFS
Although, with few exceptions, designed for tablets and medallions, many of these subjects were adapted for use as ornament for vases and urns, and for smaller objects, such as teapots and salt cellars.
Jupiter, oval medallion 8in. x 6in.
Juno, oval medallion 8in. x 6in.
Apollo, oval medallion 8in. x 6in.
A Muse, oval medallion 8in. x 6in. (probably Euterpe)
Contemplative Muse, oval medallion 8in. x 6in. (probably Sappho)
Hercules Strangling the Lion, oval medallion 8in. x 6 in.
Hercules Binding Cerberus, oval medallion 8in. x 6 in.
Meleager, oval medallion 8in. x 6 in.
Justice, medallion 7in x 5½in.
Minerva, medallion 7in. x 5½in.
Hope, medallion 7in. x 5½in.
Melpomene, medallion 8in. x 6in.
Comedy (Thalia), medallion 8in. x 6in.
Dancing Nymph, medallion 8in. x 6in.
Head of Bacchus medallion 8in. x 6in.
Head of Ariadne, medallion 8in. x 6in.
Spring (Head), medallion 10in. x 8 in.
Summer (Head), medallion 10in. x 8 in.
Autumn (Head), medallion 10in. x 8 in.
Winter (Head), medallion 10in. x 8in.
The twenty subjects listed above were all supplied as casts to Wedgwood by Flaxman senior in 1775, the receipts being signed on his behalf by John Flaxman junior. Which of these models is original work and which, if any, may be assigned to the younger Flaxman is problematic. They are listed, in the order shown, as nos 98-117 in the 1777 Catalogue*.

Marriage of Cupid and Psyche, tablet 11½in. x 16in. No.30 in 1773 Catalogue. One of several versions of this subject, which was made in sizes down to 1in. x 2¾in., is attributed to Flaxman
*Large Head of Medusa** ('Gorgon's head'), circular, diameter 5 in. No.94 in 1777 Catalogue, Attributed
*A Piping Faun**, one of the figures from the Borghese* vase, medallion 4in. x 3¼in., 1775. No.150 in 1777 Catalogue. Attributed
Bacchanalian Triumph, figures from the Borghese vase as a tablet, 7½in. x 9¾in., 1775. No.153 in 1777 Catalogue. Attributed
*Sacrifice to Hymen**, tablet in various sizes, designed as a companion piece to Cupid and Psyche. No. 196 in 1777 Catalogue. Attributed
*Apotheosis of Homer**, tablet 7½in. x 14in. and smaller sizes, 1777.

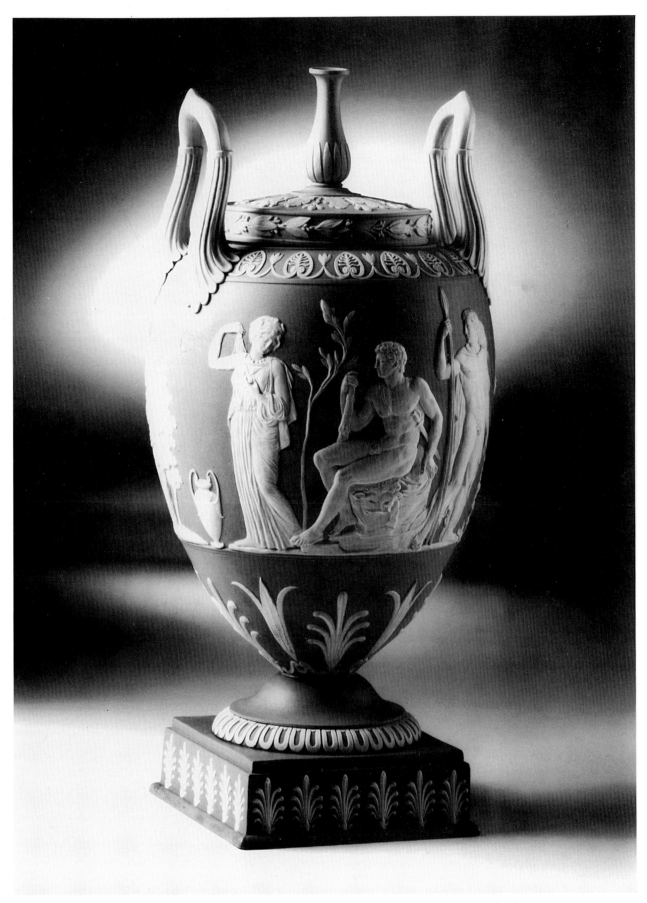

FLAXMAN, John, RA. Solid pale blue and white jasper vase, Shape no.1316, ornamented with Flaxman's figures of *Hercules in the Garden of the Hesperides.* c.1787.

City Museum & Art Gallery, Stoke-on-Trent

FLORA. Wedgwood & Bentley grey-blue and white jasper with darker-blue jasper dip tablet of *An Offering to Flora*, 8¼in. x 19in. c.1778. At that date it was the largest jasper tablet yet made by Wedgwood.

No.202 in 1779 Catalogue. Adapted to the Homeric vase, 1786
The Nine Muses*, tablet 8in. x 25in. (with festoons or garlands, 10in. x 25in.), 1778. No.203 in 1779 Catalogue. Attributed
The Muses with Apollo tablet 6in. x 18in. (or in two parts for chimneypieces*), 1778. No.204 in 177 Catalogue. Attributed
The Nine Muses and Apollo in separate pieces, 8in. x 5½in. or 3½in. x 2½in., 1778. Nos 214-223 in 1779 Catalogue. Attributed
Dancing Hours*, tablet 6in. x 18in. or 5¼in. x 14¾in., or with festoons or garlands 10in. x 25in. (also in two parts), 1778. No.205 in 1779 Catalogue. Attributed
Tragedy and Comedy with Apollo, tablet 6in. x 9½in. Melpomene and Thalia from the set of the Muses. No. 227 in the 1779 Catalogue. Attributed
Blindman's Buff, tablet 5¼in. x 13in. or 3in. x 9in., 1784
Commercial Treaty with France (Mercury joining the hands of Britain and France), tablet 11in. x 9in., 1786. No.256 in 1787 Catalogue
Commercial Treaty with France (Peace preventing Mars from bursting open the Temple of Janus), tablet 11in. x 9in., 1786. No.257 in 1787 Catalogue
Coriolanus* with his wife and Mother Persuading Him to Return [sic] *to Rome*, tablet 6in. x 9¾in., 1784. No.258 in 1787 Catalogue
Apotheosis of Homer, tablet 7½in. x 15½in., remodelled 1786. No 265 in 1787 Catalogue
Apotheosis of Virgil, tablet 7½in. x 15½in., 1786. No.266 in 1787 Catalogue
Hercules in the Garden of the Hesperides, tablet 5½in. x 17in., 1785. No.275 in 1787 Catalogue

Game of Marbles and *Triumph of Cupid* (two pieces) were designed at the same time as *Blindman's Buff* 'to decorate the sides of teapots', but only the last is listed in the Wedgwood Catalogues. See: Flaxman John, senior
See: Colour Plate 45

Flaxman, John, Senior (1726-95)
Modeller and maker of plaster casts, employed as a modeller by Louis-François Roubiliac* and Peter Scheemakers* and subsequently supplied plaster casts of busts and figures, some of which may have been from his own models, to Wedgwood. The elder Flaxman was supplying casts to Wedgwood as early as 1770, when he sent him a 'group of Hercules and Atlas', now identified as the supporting figures (*Atlantes* or *Persians)* for the so-called 'Michelangelo' lamp*. In March 1775 he supplied plaster models of 'A pair of vases one with a Satyr & the other with a Triton Handle' (the 'Wine and Water' ewers*) priced at three guineas. Because the younger John Flaxman* signed this and other invoices on his father's behalf, their work has now become inextricably confused. The elder Flaxman was probably responsible for many, if not the majority, of the moulds of busts and the twenty bas-reliefs listed above under the younger Flaxman's name

as supplied in 1775, and also for 'Moulding & making a cast from a Medall of Lennaeus' and 'Mending a Wax medall & making a Mould from it' in 1775. This was later reproduced as a portrait medallion of the Swedish botanist Carolus Linnaeus.

Flemish Ware
An earthenware body of variable colour between grey-green and bluish-sage, which, in shapes and texture, is similar to the drab* body. It was introduced c.1870 but appears to have been withdrawn after only a few years probably because of unacceptable variations in colour.

Flint
A kind of silica in the form of quartz crystals in combination with molecules of water. When it is calcined at about 400°C it can easily be crushed and powdered. It was employed by Wedgwood in both creamware and Pearl ware*, helping to confer additional strength, freedom from warping and lightness of colour.

Flint Ware
Term for saltglazed stoneware* which contains flint*.

Flora
Roman goddess of flowers and spring. The half-length figure of the goddess appears on saltglaze* wall vases in the form of cornu-

FLORA. Solid pale-blue and white jasper flower holder in the form of the figure of *Flora* resting against a sarcophagus. Companion to a similar flower holder with the figure of *Zephyr*. Height 5⅞in. c.1790.

copiae*, which are attributed to William Greatbatch* for Wedgwood or Whieldon* and also on some early tea canisters, but similar pieces were made by other factories and probably by other block-cutters. A figure of *Flora* was supplied by Theodore Parker*· in 1769 but apparently set aside. A large bas-relief head of *Flora,* 9in. x 8in., moulded by Bedson* from a marble or cast in the Newdigate* collection, is no.165 in the 1777 Catalogue, and *An Offering to Flora,* a tablet 7½in. x 17in. or 8¼in. x 19in., is no. 199 in the 1779 Catalogue. The latter is usually attributed, without evidence, to Hackwood*. The figure of *Flora* appears also on one of two jasper bough pots*, c.1795, a companion to one ornamented with the figure of *Zephyr*.*

Florentine Pattern
Wedgwood's most popular and commercially successful bone china* tableware pattern, a form of which was introduced c.1880. It was redesigned by Victor Skellern* in 1935. The border of grotesques* has its source in Urbino *maiolica.* The pattern has been made in a great variety of colours: enamelled in green, turquoise, dark blue, coral, yellow or grey over an outline print; as a black print; and as a gold print (latterly silk-screen*) on white, ivory, dark ('Arras') green, grey-green slip ('Thames Green'), ruby, and dark ('Mazarine') blue grounds.

FLORENTINE PATTERN. Bone china dinner plate and teacup and saucer printed in brown and enamelled principally in turquoise with *Turquoise Florentine* pattern no. W2714.   *Wedgwood Museum*

Flow (Flown) Blue
A technique of underglaze blue* printing which takes advantage of the tendency of cobalt oxide to bleed slightly into the glaze, lending a soft, blurred outline to the engraved design. This effect could be encouraged by adding a flow mixture (usually salt, lime and white lead) to the saggar* in which the ware was fired. This form of decoration was never fashionable in England but it found a ready market in America. Wedgwood was not among the leading manufacturers of Flow Blue (who included Samuel Alcock, Charles Meigh, Davenport* and William Adams*) but produced a varied range of patterns in this decoration from about February 1841. The number of patterns recorded is small and surviving orders are principally for *Vermicelli, Chusan, Flowers, Key Border* and *Bullfinch,* all of which appear to have been available heightened with gold. Flow Blue decoration continued to be made at Etruria* until shortly after World War I. Although the quality was good, it has never been counted among the firm's most distinguished products.

FLOW BLUE. Wall plaque printed in Flow Blue with a landscape with mill and fishermen within a rose border. The footrim is pierced for hanging. Diameter 14in. 1872.   *Author's collection*

Flower Pots
Wedgwood has made flower pots in a wide variety of shapes in Queen's ware*, white terracotta*, the dry bodies* and bone china*. See: Bough Pot; Bouquetière; Bulb Pot; Crocus Pot; Myrtle Pan; Southwell, Mrs
See: Colour Plate 46

FLOWER POTS. Solid pale-blue and white jasper flower pot and stand ornamented with 'blind' dicing and applied dots and quatrefoils below a border of enclosed anthemion. Height 3⅝in. c.1785.   *Manchester City Art Gallery*

FLOWER POTS. White stoneware flower pot (lacking stand) dipped in pale-blue jasper and ornamented with spiralling 'leaf and flower between reliefs'. Height 6¼in. c.1825.   *Merseyside Museums*

Flute and Wreath Pattern

One of Wedgwood's most distinguished Queen's ware patterns, known also as *Lag and Feather,* consisting of a fluted ribbon decorated with a continuous feathery wreath. It has been made intermittently in many colour versions, sometimes with gold, and was reproduced in red and black enamel on bone china* c.1885. The earliest version of this pattern is no.289, enamelled in dark brown and red. Similar patterns were made by other potters, including Leeds* and Spode*.

FLUTE AND WREATH PATTERN. Queen's ware rectangular covered dish, tureen and oval salad bowl enamelled with the *Flute and Wreath* pattern in brown and blue. c.1785.   *Wedgwood Museum*

Fluted Pillar Vase

See: Pillar Vase

Flux

An oxide added to glazes or ceramic bodies to lower the fusion point and thus to promote fusion during firing. Fluxes commonly used in ceramics include potash, borax and soda. When experimenting with the colouring of the grounds of white terracotta* biscuit* in 1773, Josiah recommended Bentley* to 'lay on a little flux upon the ground, fire it, & then lay on the color'. This was probably the method used to prepare the grounds of the tablets made for Stubbs* to paint in 1779.

Folgham, John (fl.1780-90)

Case and cabinet maker of 81 Fleet Street, London. Folgham made cases and cabinets for sets of Wedgwood cameos* and intaglios* and also for chessmen*. It appears also that he may have sold sets of chessmen ready boxed.

Follot, Paul (1877-1941)

French artist and interior designer, who worked largely in the Art Nouveau* and Art Deco* styles. He specialised in luxury furniture and, after World War I, became a director of the Pomona Studios of the Paris store, Le Bon Marché. During the 1930s he was co-director with Serge Chermayeff of Waring & Gillow's French furniture department. About 1911, Follot was recommended to Cecil Wedgwood* by the French retailer Georges Rouard and completed a number of designs, none of which was manufactured until 1922. Follot's designs for tableware shapes include *Sylvia, Galbia* and *Génie* and he designed also a range of twenty pieces heavily ornamented with leaves and apples, one of which is recorded as requiring twelve hours' work from a skilled ornamenter. Unsurprisingly, these pieces were made in small quantities and are now rare.

See also: Goupy, Marcel

Fonts

Wedgwood is known to have made six baptismal fonts in black basaltes* and there were perhaps others which have not survived or are not yet identified. The first may have been made as early as 1774, when Wedgwood wrote to Bentley*: 'We can make the Font very well at the price you ment[io]n & will set about it', but no further reference to production occurs before 1778. Two fonts were commissioned by members of the Whitbread family of brewers and a third was made for a church with which the Whitbreads were connected. All but one are of the same form: a large footed bowl, 22in. in diameter and 14in. high, the lip finished with a banded reed border and the body ornamented with simple swags (see: Festoons) of drapery suspended from rings. The single exception, 16½in. in diameter and 11in. high, is now in the Lady Lever Art Gallery, Port Sunlight. The difficulty in firing successfully such a large bowl without cracking or warping was considerable, but Josiah had made an even larger bowl for the Anson tripod at Shugborough (see: Black Basaltes) in 1771, so he would not have been intimidated by the challenge.

FONTS. Baptismal font ornamented with drapery festoons and a moulded rim border of bound reeds. Height 16½in. Unmarked. Wedgwood. c.1788.
Lady Lever Art Gallery, Port Sunlight

Food Carrier

A utensil consisting of several flat-bottomed bowls with handles which fit into one another, the lowest bowl for hot water, the top one with a cover. Used for keeping food warm in the kitchens and for carrying hot food from the kitchens to the dining-room (often a considerable journey through unheated passageways), the food carrier was made by Wedgwood, c.1850, in Queen's ware*. It was probably inspired by a model in Chinese porcelain.

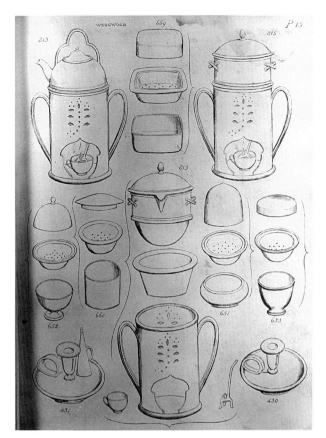

FOOD WARMER. Plate 15 engraved by William Blake for the '1817' Catalogue, showing food warmers with kettle or porringer tops.
Wedgwood Museum

FOOD WARMER. Queen's ware food warmer, *veilleuse* or night lamp. c.1785. *Wellcome Institute Library, London*

Food Warmer

A composite Queen's ware* utensil also called a *veilleuse* or, in the 18th century, a night lamp. It is usually about 12in. high and consists of a cylindrical pedestal, into the top of which is fitted a flanged bowl or teapot. The pedestal rests on a turned foot and, immediately above the base, there is an arched opening for the insertion of a small lamp *(godet)*. The pedestal is pierced with holes to allow free circulation of air and to provide a little illumination, and the bowl has a cover. When the bowl is intended to be filled with water to heat a second bowl fitted into it, the object is a *bain marie;* with a teapot it is known as a *théière*.

In the '1790' Catalogue* (Plate 11) it is described as a 'Night Lamp to provide illumination and conserve hot liquids'. Several shapes are illustrated in Plate 211 of the Shape Drawing Book*, c.1802, but the food warmer was probably in production at Etruria* some twenty years earlier.

See also: Whisky Still

Foot Pan (Bath)

A deep basin, usually oval in shape and with two lateral handles, used for washing or soaking the feet. Until about 1820 the sides were vertical, sometimes with hooped bands or moulded decoration. Later examples had curved sides and more ornate handles. Two Wedgwood foot pans with vertical sides appear as shapes 1331 and 1332 in the first Shape drawing Book*, and the '1880' Cata-

logue of Shapes shows no.2139 *Chatsworth* shape, with curved sides. From about 1820 Wedgwood made foot pans with underglaze-blue printed* decoration and these were made also by other manufacturers. Today they are much in demand as *jardinières*.

Ford, G. (fl. 1840-5)

Engraver who worked with Wedgwood, 1842-3.

Fothergill, Dr. John FRS (1712-86)

Quaker physician; MD, Edinburgh; FRS, 1763; Fellow of the Royal Society of Medicine in Paris, 1776. At Upton, Essex, Fothergill

FOOT PAN. Foot pan decorated with *Tower of London*, a *capriccio* London Thames scene, printed in underglaze blue. Length 17¾in. c.1835. *Christie's, London*

possessed one of the finest botanical gardens in Europe, a collection of shells and insects, and one of natural history drawings which was eventually bought by Catherine the Great*. His portrait by Hogarth is at the College of Physicians, and Wedgwood produced a portrait medallion* of him which was listed in the 1779 Catalogue*. Attributed to Flaxman*, it was probably based on the Medical Society medal of 1773 by Lewis Pingo (see: Pingo, Thomas). A black basaltes* bust of Fothergill, from a mould supplied by John Flaxman senior*, was made in 1781. Wedgwood and Fothergill corresponded from about 1766 and he was one of the inner circle of friends who knew of Wedgwood's experiments towards the invention of jasper* and sent him samples of earths for his experiments. In 1776 Wedgwood refers to a formula for bronzing frames and mounts which had been given to him by Fothergill, and, in September of that year, Fothergill summoned Wedgwood to meet him in Cheshire, where he gave him 'a long Lecture upon china, & Brick-making', advising him to 'relinquish the former, & take up the latter business.'

FOTHERGILL, Dr. John. Black basaltes bust of Fothergill by Flaxman. Height 13¾in. Marked with the date code for 1882, almost precisely a century after its first production. *Christie's, London*

Four Seasons
See: Seasons

Fox, Charles James (1749-1806)
English Whig statesman; born in London, the third son of Lord Holland. Member of Parliament from 1768 and one of the most skilful debaters in the House of Commons. He held office in Lord North's administration but opposed coercive policies for America, joining North's government again in 1783. The rejection of his India Bill led to their resignation and this marked the beginning of the long struggle between Fox and the Younger Pitt*. Fox supported the French Revolution and opposed war with France, but joined with Pitt in the campaign to abolish the slave trade. After Pitt's death in 1806, Fox was restored to office, but he died before the year was out.

Fox was a leading opponent of Pitt's proposals for a trade treaty with Ireland in 1785, a measure strongly resisted by Wedgwood (see: General Chamber of Manufacturers). Both men appear in an unpublished cartoon by J. Sayers, published in February 1787.

Fox was a friend of Lady Diana Beauclerk's* and he was responsible for introducing her to Wedgwood. Wedgwood's portrait medallion* of Fox, attributed to Flaxman*, was produced c.1790.

Fox's Patent Milk and Soup Pan
A pan for separating two liquids of different densities, such as milk from cream, or soup from fat. It has two pouring lips, one below the other, the lower being connected by a hole to the bottom of the pan. By tilting the pan to an angle sufficient to allow the liquid to flow only from the lower of the two pouring lips, the liquid in the lower part of the vessel may be drawn off, leaving behind the lighter liquid floating on its surface. The pan is illustrated in the '1880' Catalogue.

FRAMES. Black basaltes plaque, *Dancing Nymph*, in integral fluted frame with modern gilding. Oval height 14⅞in. Unmarked. Wedgwood & Bentley, c.1775. *Formerly Buten Collection*

Frames
Josiah Wedgwood expressed his opinion of ceramic frames in a letter to Bentley* dated 8 January 1775: 'I think it is impossible for us to make any frames of *Pottery* however fine, or color'd that will not degrade the Gem or Picture. Metal Frames Gilt, though they may Tarnish in time, are the best frames in use. I only mention this as my present opinion, despairing of ever being able to make a pitcher frame to please either our selves or our Customers'. By then he had been making frames for about four years. These were advertised as 'rich Compartments of the same material' for plaques* of both black basaltes* and white terracotta*. The earliest were simple mouldings but by March 1771 Wedgwood had begun to make wider fluted mouldings and these might be painted or gilded, though few of the latter now bear more than vestigial traces of their original gold. The same patterns were used for some portrait medallions* and they were reintroduced for jasper after 1776. The early frames in black basaltes and terracotta were cast in one piece with the plaques, but, after the invention of jasper*, the frames were made separately. A few examples exist in rosso antico* with black ornaments. Experiments were made also with

FRAMES. Blue jasper dip portrait medallion of J.P. Elers by Hackwood, 1777, in an extremely rare Wedgwood Pearl ware frame decorated with variegated lustre, c.1810. Both pieces unmarked.
Private Collection

variegated lustre* frames, c.1810, but examples are extremely rare.

In the 19th and 20th centuries frames have continued to be made for portrait medallions. The Herculaneum Pictures* were reproduced in jasper with cavetted frames in a contrasting colour in the 1870s. These are frequently mistaken for 18th-century pieces.

Fratoddi, Angelino (fl.1788-91)
Italian cameo carver who supplied Wedgwood's modellers in Rome with a quantity of 'cameos in shells' in 1788-90. None has been identified.

Frederick II (The Great), 1712-86
King of Prussia; son of Frederick William I of Prussia and Sophia Dorothea, daughter of George I of England. Frederick was an able

FREDERICK THE GREAT. Early creamware teapot, height 5in., transfer-printed in black with a portrait of Frederick the Great after the painting by Antoine Pesne. Unmarked. Wedgwood, c.1763.
E.N. Stretton Collection

and enlightened ruler who laid the foundations of Prussia's future greatness. He wrote extensively on political matters and philosophical subjects and was extremely popular in England, especially during the Seven Years' War (1756-63). The resource, courage and genius he displayed during his military adventures earned him the sobriquet of 'the Great'. During the Seven Years' War he occupied the Meissen* factory, and after the war he acquired the Berlin porcelain factory which he had previously patronised.

There are three portrait medallions* of Frederick: (1) a portrait of 1778, which exists on both oval and circular grounds, from a medal; (2) a smaller portrait reversed from (1); (3) a large portrait, so far untraced, 1779. No bust of Frederick is listed in the Wedgwood Catalogues, but a bust of Voltaire* after Houdon* was sold at Christie's on 8 July 1969 erroneously described as Frederick the Great.

A transfer-printed portrait of Frederick the Great after the portrait by Antoine Pesne, engraved by either W.W. Ryland or Jean Wille, appears on a Wedgwood creamware teapot, available in two sizes, first mentioned by Wedgwood in 1763. The portrait was also printed on half-pint mugs of the same date. The 'King of Prussia' was a popular print on Battersea enamel and Worcester* porcelain.

Freemasons
See: Masonic Ware

French Commercial Treaty
As early as 1772 Wedgwood was trying to influence English politicians to negotiate a trade treaty with France. Trade in pottery and porcelain to France was exceptionally difficult since the import of both was prohibited. The earliest French porcelain factories, and many of the *faïence* potteries, had been established with the aid of the aristocracy. Louis XV had, through Madame de Pompadour, assisted in the founding of the Sèvres* porcelain factory and after 1756 was the principal shareholder. A number of Edicts had been promulgated in favour of the factory, prohibiting the manufacture of porcelain elsewhere in France and even limiting the *faïence* factories to painting in blue only, polychrome decoration being reserved to Sèvres. Even during the lifetime of Louis XV these Edicts were, to some extent, disregarded by factories under the patronage of members of the royal family (Chantilly, for example, was owned by the Prince de Condé), and faïence factories tended to add more colour to their palettes according to their distance from Paris. It was not until the accession of Louis XVI in 1774, however, that restrictions were noticeably eased. Even so, most of the small porcelain factories which grew up in and around Paris were still under the protection of the royal family and the aristocracy, including one patronised by Marie-Antoinette. Only one factory in the Paris area, at Pont-aux-Choux*, made earthenware in the manner of Wedgwood's, although one or two small factories started by Englishmen, such as the Leigh* brothers at Douai, copied the creamware of Wedgwood and Leeds*.

An attempt to enter the closed French market is discussed in the entry relating to the Duc de Choiseul*, and since that time (1770) Wedgwood had lost no opportunity to further his stated ambition to 'Conquer France in Burslem', issuing catalogues in French and maintaining such commercial relations with French customers as were possible. Catalogues in French were not, of course, directed solely to France. French was the language of the Court in both Germany and Russia, where Wedgwood found fewer obstacles to trade.

An Edict reviving former prohibitions was promulgated in France in 1784, but by 1787 this had dwindled in force to a point where French factories were forbidden only to copy the products of Sèvres without the King's permission. That these prohibitions were well understood by Wedgwood may be seen from his letter to Choiseul in which he refers to English creamware being contraband in France, but his understanding of the market – or at least of legal and commercial French – seems to have been deficient because, in a letter of 30 June 1786 to William Eden (later Lord Auckland*), he makes it clear that he had failed to grasp the true difference between *poterie* and *fayence*. The proposed duty on *poterie* was 1 livre 8 sols, and on *fayence* 20 sols, per 100 lbs (French currency then being divided into Livres, Sols and Deniers, the origin of the English £.s.d.).

Faïence is tin-enamelled earthenware, a type of ware never made by Wedgwood; *poterie* is lead-glazed earthenware, such as creamware, also called *faïence-fine* or *faïence anglaise*. A low-fired ware covered with a transparent glaze falls into this category but true *faïence* is excluded. Stoneware is *grès*, and the term

FRENCH COMMERCIAL TREATY.
Solid blue and white jasper plaque,
Commercial Treaty with France,
modelled by John Flaxman in 1786-7.
9in. x 9⅝in. c.1787.

Christie's, London

FRENCH REVOLUTION. Circular blue jasper dip portrait medallions of leading personalities. *(Above, left to right)* comte de Mirabeau, Jacques Necker, duc d'Orléans; *(below, left to right)* Jean Sylvain Bailly, Louis XVI, marquis de Lafayette. Diameter 2⅛in.-2⅛₁₆in. 1789-90.

Dr & Mrs Alvin M. Kanter Collection

190

porcelaine admits of no mistake. Wedgwood, however, regarded the difference between *poterie* and *fayence* as residing in the decoration. The error was probably one of translation since similar errors are made by modern translators (and in modern dictionaries). The problems of language were finally resolved and a compromise agreement was reached to the satisfaction of the Staffordshire potters by the imposition of an *ad valorem* duty of twelve per cent.

Wedgwood played a useful part in the negotiations by providing technical and commercial advice to Eden. The treaty was signed at Versailles in September 1786 and Wedgwood described it later to Richard Lovell Edgeworth* as 'the most fair, & liberal treaty we have with any nation, therefore the most likely to be lasting.' It was commemorated by the production of two tablets commissioned from John Flaxman*: one showed Mercury* as the god of commerce joining the hands of Britain and France; the second was *Peace preventing Mars from bursting open the Temple of Janus.*

FRENCH REVOLUTION. Blue jasper dip medallion celebrating the French Revolution. Diameter 2½in. c.1789. The design of the medallion is only slightly amended from that of Webber's 'Sydney Cove' medallion.
Wedgwood Museum

French Revolution
In common with many Englishmen of liberal opinions and Whig persuasion, Josiah welcomed the French Revolution. He wrote to Erasmus Darwin* in July 1789: 'I know you will rejoice with me in the glorious revolution which has taken place in France. The politicians tell me that as a manufacturer I shall be ruined if France has her liberty, but I am willing to take my chance in that respect, nor do I yet see that the happiness of one nation includes in it the misery of its next neighbour.' Later, like many of his friends, as the mindless violence of the revolutionaries became apparent, he altered this opinion. Meanwhile, however, he hastily adapted the Sydney Cove* medallion to the requirements of the moment, endowing the figure of *Peace* with a staff surmounted by the Phrygian cap of revolution and hanging the French King (not too subtly symbolised by a shield bearing the royal *fleur-de-lis*) from a pillar. This thinly disguised political medallion occurs in at least two versions and was shortly joined by other medallions celebrating the fall of the Bastille* and the optimistic concept of 'France embracing Liberty'. Portrait medallions of popular revolutionary figures – Jean Sylvain Bailly, president of the National Assembly, the Marquis de Lafayette, the celebrated soldier who had distinguished himself in the American Revolution, and the Comte de Mirabeau, president of the National Assembly in 1791 – were produced on circular grounds with borders of stylised anthemion* and lily, and a similar portrait of the lamentable Duc d'Orléans (Philippe Egalité) was made with a border of laurel. Companion portraits of Louis XVI and his director-general of finance, Jacques Necker, were provided with borders of *fleur-de-lis*. Whatever his private sympathies, Wedgwood's commemorative ware was commercially suitable for any occasion.

Wedgwood's trade with France, so carefully nurtured after the French Commercial Treaty*, was ruined with the collapse of the French economy. It was many years before Wedgwood wares appeared again in any quantity in France.

French Ware
In the early months of 1765 Josiah Wedgwood wrote to his brother John that he was about to attempt 'the French ware' in earnest, but a month later he wrote again to say that he did not intend to make the French white ware at Burslem but was considering more convenient premises elsewhere for the purpose. It is not certain precisely what he meant by 'French ware', but he specified that it was white and a great deal of French porcelain, apart from that made at Sèvres, was white or very sparsely coloured. This was because the royal Edicts forbade the use of coloured decoration to any but the Sèvres factory, although these Edicts were somewhat relaxed after the death of Madame de Pompadour in 1764. The reference might have been to the porcelain* of St Cloud or Mennecy, which Wedgwood could have seen in London. It is scarcely credible that he referred to French tin-enamelled earthenware *(faïence*)* since he had already developed a lead-glazed creamware (cream-coloured ware*) which was evidently a superior product. Nor is it likely that the reference was to the whiter earthenware body that eventually appeared as Pearl* ware, for there was no French equivalent. It seems most probable that Wedgwood was writing of porcelain. From his later letters to Bentley* it is clear that he had for years studied the problems of porcelain manufacture and he was soon aware of the economic disaster that overtook many of the English soft-paste porcelain factories. Further, Richard Champion's patent stood in the way of any production of 'true' porcelain.

Fret
A decorative border pattern of continuous repetitive form made by short lines of equal length meeting at an angle of 90°, or occasionally at a slightly greater or lesser angle. Fret patterns are either painted, printed, moulded, or incised, and occur as decoration or ornament on both classical and neo-classical* pottery as well as in Chinese decorative art. They are sometimes also referred to as *meanders.*

Frit (Fritt)
Ingredients of a glaze composition melted and ground together before use in the making of the glaze. Frits have many uses, including the preparation of artificial porcelain and ceramic colour stains.

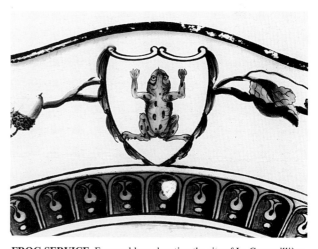

FROG SERVICE. Frog emblem, denoting the site of La Grenouillière, which appears in green enamel on all the 952 pieces of the dinner and dessert service made for the Empress Catherine II in 1773-4.
Photograph: Wedgwood

Frog Service
A Queen's ware* service made to the order of Catherine II* of Russia in 1773-4. It was intended for the palace she was building on the site known as Kekereksi or La Grenouillière (the frog marsh), near Petrodvorets, and each piece bore the emblem or crest of a green

frog. According to Bentley*, who compiled a detailed description of the service, written in French for the Empress Catherine, it comprised 952 pieces, painted in 'delicate black' (actually a mulberry-coloured enamel) with 1,244 'real views of Great Britain', all different. Two painted borders were used: a running oak-leaf and acorn for the dinner service and an ivy for the dessert, both broken on plates and dishes to accommodate the frog emblem, which appeared framed by a wreath of oak or ivy on the serving pieces.

Production of the service in plain Queen's ware represented an investment of only £51.8.4d, but the cost of decorating it (including finding or commissioning suitable views to be copied) promised to be formidable. Wedgwood must also take into account the loss of ordinary business and the disruption to everyday production caused by such a large, difficult and prestigious commission. The actual costs of materials, labour and commission paid to Alexander Baxter, the Briton appointed Russian consul in London, appears to have been about £2,290. The price finally paid for it was 16,406 roubles 43 kopeks, or approximately £2,700. It was then both the largest and the most costly earthenware service ever produced in Britain. At the outset, Wedgwood estimated that production would take between two and three years; in the event it was completed in less than twelve months.

The decoration of this service was a much more ambitious task than anything that Wedgwood had hitherto attempted. The painting was done at the Chelsea Decorating Studio* and it was accepted, from the start, that, although evidently 'Useful' ware (and therefore naturally within the Josiah and Thomas Wedgwood partnership), it should be considered as part of the Wedgwood & Bentley partnership. 'Dare you', Wedgwood asked Bentley* on 9 April 1773, 'undertake to paint the most embelish'd views, the most beautiful Landskips, with Gothique Ruins, Grecian Temples, & the most Elegant Buildings with hands who never attempted anything beyond Huts and Windmills?'

It was clear that more painters must be urgently recruited and trained, but a start was made with Catherine Willcox* and James Bakewell* painting landscapes, while borders were entrusted to Nathaniel Cooper* and Joseph Linley*. Ralph Willcox* was set to paint borders. By the beginning of August, William Mence* and Thomas Mills* were at work on inner borders and Miss Glisson* and Miss Pars* were painting landscapes. The wage sheets show the names of five other women and fourteen more men engaged on the decoration of this service. Wages ranged from thirty-one shillings and sixpence to ten shillings a week, Mrs Willcox being

FROG SERVICE. Custard or ice cup with a view 'Near Richmond', oval compotier from the dessert service with a view of part of Windsor Castle, , cover dish showing Sir William Mann's lake in Surrey, and tureen and cover with a view of Earl Gower's mansion at Trentham. Hermitage Museum, St. Petersburg.   *Photograph: Wedgwood*

the highest paid of the women with earnings of eighteen shillings. The most accessible sources of landscape views were the engravers, printers and publishers. Some of their names – John Boydell*, Thomas Major* and John Pye*, for example – have become confused with those of the small number of painters employed to paint original views for reproduction. Published sources included Sir William Chambers's* *Views of the Gardens and Buildings at Kew in Surry* (*sic*), Thomas Pennant's *Journeys to the Hebrides* and Buck's *Antiquities*. Other landscape paintings were lent by friends and patrons, such as Lord Stamford of Enville and Thomas Anson of Shugborough. Eighteen views of Enville and fifteen of Shugborough appear on the service. Least in number were the original sketches painted by artists employed for the purpose, the most regular of whom seems to have been Samuel Stringer*, who was probably a kinsman of Josiah Wedgwood's mother Mary (née Stringer). Josiah accompanied 'Young Stringer' on expeditions to sketch views at Trentham, Keele, Swinnerton and

FROG SERVICE Oval dish enamelled in monochrome with 'A View of the Duke of Montague's gardens at Richmond' (no.527 in Bentley's catalogue). Length 14in. Unmarked. Wedgwood & Bentley, 1773-4.

Dwight & Lucille Beeson Collection, Birmingham Museum, Alabama

FRUIT AND VEGETABLE SHAPES. Pear and pineapple teapots, length 4¼in. to 9¼in., decorated in coloured glazes. Unmarked. Probably Wedgwood or Whieldon, c.1763.
Christie's, New York

Enville. In August 1773 Josiah asked Bentley to buy a 'camera obscura'* for the use of artists in London. The views for the service were chosen with the intention of giving what Bentley described as 'a true and picturesque idea of the beauties of this country, both natural and artificial' and a wide variety of subjects was obtained, ranging from royal palaces to parks and gardens, from castles and cathedrals to scenes of industrial progress.

A new shape, *Catherine* shape, was modelled especially for this service, and some entirely new tableware pieces, among them some fine 'glaciers'*, were designed for it. By the end of February 1774, modelling and production of the plain Queen's ware service was almost complete. Five months later the service was ready for shipment and Josiah was able to express his relief at being free of 'this tedious business.'

A great part of the service was put on display at the Greek Street showrooms*, where it was viewed by the public (admission by ticket only) from the first week in June, and in mid-July by Queen Charlotte* and her brother, Prince Ernest of Mecklenburgh.

Much of the original service was exhibited in London in 1909 and it is now preserved in the Hermitage, St Petersburg. A few plates and dishes exist in public and private collections in Britain and America. Some of these, lacking the Frog emblem, are decorated in polychrome enamels and are thought to have been painted especially for Josiah Wedgwood, Bentley and Baxter. Others are probably either duplicates, or rejected as imperfect, or may have been from the original service but sold off, perhaps, in the state-controlled antique shop (as were pieces from the *Husk** service). Only one serving piece, a cream bowl now at Shugborough, has been located outside Russia. A dessert plate, painted in polychrome enamels with a scene named as 'Westcowes Castle, in the Isle of Wight' was sold for £7,000 at Christie's. London, in October 1983 and acquired by the British Museum after an export licence had been refused.
See: Colour Plate 47

Fruit and Vegetable Shapes
Tablewares modelled in imitation of fruit and vegetables – especially apples, pears, melons, pineapples, artichokes, cabbages and cauliflowers – were made by porcelain factories, notably Chelsea*, and potteries in Staffordshire in the 1750s and 1760s. The shapes are typically rococo* and the fashion for them declined rapidly with the rise of neo-classicism*. Apple and pear teapots are attributed to Whieldon-Wedgwood* and Wedgwood at the Ivy House*, and both cauliflower and pineapple teapots, coffeepots, jugs and sugar boxes were made at the Ivy House, making use of Wedgwood's Green glaze*. Wedgwood's melon tureens and preserve dishes, imitating the shape of a water melon lying on a leaf, were in production by 1765 and the latter have been reproduced in Queen's ware* in the 20th century.

Fruit Lustre
See: Ordinary Lustres

Frye, Thomas (1710-62)
Irish portrait painter, miniaturist and engraver in *mezzotinto*. A Quaker , born in Dublin, he took out a patent for the manufacture of porcelain* in 1748, specifying the use of Cherokee* clay. He was also the first to use calcined* bones (bone ash) in porcelain manufacture. Until 1762 he was manager of the Bow* porcelain factory. His daughter Catherine married Ralph Willcox* and was employed by Wedgwood & Bentley at the Chelsea Decorating Studio*.

Fumigating Ribbon Holder
A container in jasper-dipped stoneware for a volatile fumigating liquid which evaporated from a wick protruding through a slot in the cover. Like the earlier pot-pourri* vases, it operated on the principle of replacing an unwanted smell with one that was stronger and more tolerable. Examples, c.1892, are marked 'WEDGWOOD. PIESSE & LUBINS FUMIGATING RIBBON' impressed.

Furniture, Ornamental
The use of inset painted porcelain plaques* and medallions* for the decoration of furniture began in France in the 1760s, when Sèvres* porcelain plaques were first employed for the purpose. The use of Wedgwood ware as furniture decoration dates from about February 1774, when Josiah Wedgwood wrote to Bentley proposing that engravings be made of furniture inset with cameos and encaustic-painted* medallions, 'to shew *what might* be executed in the same stile'. There is no record that this suggestion was acted upon. Furniture dating from the 18th century decorated with encaustic-painted basaltes, white terracotta* or jasper* medallions certainly exists, most examples being in the Adam* style veneered in satinwood. English furniture predominates, but the Metropolitan Museum in New York owns a superb *secrétaire à abbatant* by the *ébéniste du roi* Adam Weisweiler*, better known as the maker of such small pieces as occasional tables, in which he has replaced the customary Sèvres plaques with Wedgwood jasper medallions surrounding a large painted porcelain plaque. This is possibly the piece catalogued by Christie* & Ansell in 1791 as 'an elegant lady's writing desk with fall-down front, ornamented with porcelain and Wedgwood medallions and a marble top…imported from Paris by Mons. Daguerre*.' One of the medallions inset dates the piece certainly to after the French Commercial Treaty* of 1786, a time when English design was briefly fashionable in Paris.

By this date Sèvres was making wares inspired by Wedgwood's jasper, using a blue body devised by Josse of the Faubourg Saint-Denis, but from surface appearance, general style and treatment of the classical subjects employed, it should not be difficult to distinguish between old Wedgwood jasper and French work.

'Adam style' is used as a generic term for neo-classical decoration and furniture. Cabinet makers who used Wedgwood as decoration for their furniture included Hepplewhite, Sheraton, Gillow, Ince & Mayhew and Seddon, and many lesser craftsmen followed their example. Sheraton used Wedgwood to decorate his cases for

FURNITURE, ORNAMENTAL. Satinwood commode mounted with three blue and white jasper medallions of boys after designs by Lady Diana Beauclerk. c.1785-90. *Lady Lever Art Gallery, Port Sunlight*

pianofortes (see: Broadwood, John). Some caution is necessary, however, in identifying Wedgwood medallions inset in 18th-century (and even 19th-century) furniture. Many of the original medallions have been removed for sale separately and replaced by modern reproductions.

When Josiah II* was in Holland in July 1790, he sought for cabinet makers and inlayers who would use jasper medallions and cameos in their furniture, and a Dutch secretaire is recorded decorated in this manner.

In the 1850s the architect Gottfried Semper* designed a cabinet which, like Weisweiler's, was decorated with a central porcelain panel surrounded by Wedgwood bas-reliefs – in Semper's design, small rectangular tablets. This was shown in the Paris Exposition of 1855. Wright & Mansfield* produced a large satinwood cabinet in the Adam style decorated with Wedgwood medallions for the 1862 Exhibition in London, and the same exhibition contained an appalling cabinet, shown by Lamb of Manchester, inlaid with various exotic woods and quantities of jasper medallions, which was nevertheless described in the *Art-Journal Catalogue* as 'very beautiful in design, of admirable proportions, and unsurpassed as an example of good workmanship'. For more popular taste in the 19th century, Wedgwood cameos were set in the various pieces comprising desk or writing sets, generally of excellent quality, either of papier mâché* or veneered in walnut or amboyna.

In addition to decorative cameos, medallions and tablets, Wedgwood also made door knobs, escutcheons and handles of jasper.

Queen's ware* printed tiles* were also occasionally used to decorate furniture, such as bamboo tables and white metal plant stands of the Arts and Crafts* style (see: Miles, Helen).

Fürstenberg (Brunswick)

A factory founded in 1747 by Duke Karl I of Brunswick. It flourished especially between 1770 and 1814 and is still in existence. From 1794 to 1814 the director was Louis-Victor Gerverot* and Wedgwood products were copied during this period. Biscuit* porcelain bas-reliefs in oval frames, sometimes with a lavender-blue ground inspired by Wedgwood's jasper*, were produced by the modeller Carl Gottlieb Schubert, the subjects (principally Greek poets, philosophers and statesmen) adapted from cameos* and gems* in the ducal collection. Gerverot added a form of black basaltes* to production in 1796 and some small busts were made. The biscuit body was improved and used for many new models in the Empire style from 1805.

FURNITURE, ORNAMENTAL. Late 18th-century satinwood box ornamented with five jasper cameos set in gold mounts. 5in. x 8½in. x 2⅜in. No mark visible. c.1795-1800. *Nottingham Castle Museum*

Gaj (Gai), Pietro (fl.1850-70)

Italian modeller and designer, and a director of Benucci e Latti of Pesaro, who experimented for some years with the use of reduced lustres (see: Lustre Decoration) on pottery. He was credited with having rediscovered, in 1848, the technique of producing the magnificent ruby-red lustre made famous at the Gubbio factory under Maestro Giorgio Andreoli c.1515-36. Gaj was awarded a medal at the Fine Art Exhibition in Florence in 1861 for tableware decorated with his own designs in liquid gold and platinum, but he failed to achieve the financial rewards to which he thought himself entitled and, in 1862, he visited England, where he approached Minton*, Copeland (see: Spode) and Wedgwood, vainly seeking employment as a senior designer. Wedgwood did, however, buy 'all his receipts together with drawings of the kiln, method of manipulation etc. for making his Maestro Giorgio & other Cinque centi lustres' for the sum of £20. Gaj agreed to 'assist Messrs. Wedgwood as far as possible in adapting these receipts to their use', an indication that some difficulty was anticipated in translating his techniques from tin-glazed wares to Queen's ware*. Gaj was to be paid a further £20 when experiments proved successful.

The trials were a failure and Gaj received no further payment. He died in 1866. Four trial pieces are in the Wedgwood Museum*, one dated 11 May 1866. All appear to have been produced in trials made by Clement Wedgwood* and Emile Lessore* several years after the association with Gaj was ended.

See also: De Morgan, William

Game Pie Dish

A deep dish, oval or circular, with cover, modelled and coloured to resemble piecrust. These dishes were made of cane* ware with ornament of leaves, vines and dead game around the bowl and on the lid, and often with a hare or vegetable handle. Production of these dishes was first suggested to Wedgwood by Richard Lovell Edgeworth* in 1786. 'I think', he wrote, 'oval baking dishes for meat pies in the shape of raised paste pies, with bunches of grapes, &c. &c, on their outsides, made of cane-coloured ware, not glazed, but nearly as possible the colour of the baked paste, would be a saleable article…They should have covers.' Wedgwood responded on 23 December: 'I mad[e] a clay pye & shewed it to my children as the best judges, but they not knowing what it was intended for, convinced me at once that it was wrong, & I have not yet made another essay'.

'Raised pies' made their first appearance in the invoices in 1795 and were produced thereafter in good quantities. Their popularity was due, no doubt, as much to recurrent shortages of flour as to their decorative qualities. Although other manufacturers, including Spode*, Davenport*, Minton* and Turner*, produced similar game pie dishes, Wedgwood's appear to have been the first. Captain Jesse's *Life of Beau Brummel* (1844) contains the following passage: 'The scarcity two years after Brummel's retirement, viz. in 1800, was so great that the consumption of flour for pastry was forbidden in the Royal Household, rice being used instead. The distillers left off malting…and Wedgwood made dishes to represent piecrust'.

Game pie dishes were made regularly throughout the 19th century, the commonest form being 'Grape & Cabbage top' oval, available in five sizes, but the same shape was made with a hare or cauliflower knop, a flower and strap handle, an ivy band with various knops or an elaborate leaf band and lid decoration sometimes called 'snipes' wings'. Similar reliefs and knops were used also on round raised pies. Flat pie shapes (see: Pastry Ware), often with basketwork moulding, were primarily for fruit. After 1850, glazed interior liners, known as 'pie middles', were used for cooking meat or game in the oven and transferred to the warmed

GAJ, Pietro. Wood-framed Queen's ware plaque decorated with a portrait, 'Cintia Bella', in underglaze blue and yellow with orange lustre. Diameter 8¾in. One of three similar trials produced in 1866, after the death of Gaj but probably based on his recipes.

Wedgwood Museum

game pie dish to be brought to the table. Early pie dishes were ornamented with applied reliefs, but from about 1850 the relief decoration was moulded in one piece with the body.

Game pie dishes in both cane ware and Majolica* appear in Wedgwood's price lists as late as 1901.

Ganymede

A youth, the most beautiful of mortals, who was carried off by Zeus in the form of an eagle. Ganymede became cup-bearer to Zeus and lived among the gods on Olympus. He is usually represented in art as a naked youth accompanied by an eagle.

Wedgwood subjects:

Ganymede, figure 'from the Florentine Museum', height 12in., from a cast supplied by Hoskins & Grant* in 1770.

Ganymede and the Eagle, medallion 5in. x 6¼in., 1777: No.225 in 1779 Catalogue*

GAME PIE DISH. Cane ware game pie dish with glazed stoneware inner dish (lining). Shape no.2006. Height 6½in., length 9½in. c.1850.

Wedgwood Museum

GARBE, Richard. Queen's ware figure of 'Syren', modelled by Garbe in 1941. *Photograph: Wedgwood*

Jupiter, Eagle and Ganymede, medallion 3½in. x 2¾in., no.262 in 1787 Catalogue
See: Colour Plate 48

Garbe, Louis Richard, RA FRBS (1876-1957)
English sculptor of figure and animal subjects. Born in London and studied at the Central School of Arts and Crafts and at the Royal Academy Schools. He exhibited subjects in marble and bronze at the Royal Academy from 1908 and was elected a member in 1936. He was Professor of Sculpture at the Royal College of Art 1929-46. Three models by Garbe, *Boy on a Shell, Syren* and *Cupid Vase* were reproduced in Queen's ware* in 1941, and the *Cupid Vase* was reintroduced, in very small quantities, in Norman Wilson's* tan and grey in 1959. Garbe was associated with Doulton between 1933 and 1939.

Garbett, Samuel (1717-1803)
Birmingham merchant and ironmaster; partner with Dr John Roebuck in a sulphuric-acid works and later the Carron Ironworks.

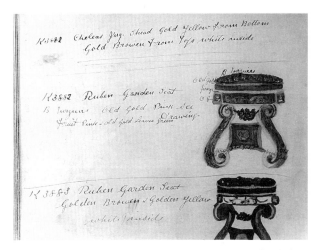

GARDEN SEAT. Page from a Majolica pattern book showing designs for the 'Rubens' garden seat. *Wedgwood Museum*

GARDEN SEAT. *St Louis,* Argenta garden seat with moulded ornament of trailing prunus between borders of simulated woven straw and sunflower heads. Height 18in. c.1885. *Christie's, London*

Garbett was closely associated with Josiah Wedgwood in the founding of the General Chamber of Manufacturers* and in representations to the government about the Irish and French Trade Treaties*. He also cooperated with Joseph Priestley* and Erasmus Darwin* in campaigning against the slave trade.

Garden Seat
Garden seats, height 17-18in., were made in Wedgwood's Majolica*, c.1875-1900. An example, the *Rubens* garden seat, is illustrated in Plate 6 of the '1878' Illustrated Catalogue of Ornamental Shapes.

Garniture de Cheminée
French for a set of vases or ornaments to decorate the shelf of a chimneypiece*. The number varied – three, five or seven – the most popular being five. The Chinese *garniture,* which became the standard at English factories in the 18th century, included a central baluster-shaped vase, a pair of smaller vases of the same shape, and two beaker-shaped vases, all decorated *en suite.* Variations on the theme included three figure groups. A *garniture de table* consisted of a set of vases or ornaments for a side-table in a reception hall or saloon; a *garniture de toilette* consisted of perfume bottles, powder boxes, rings stands, etc. for a dressing table.

Gaudy Welsh
Decoration of gaudily painted stylised flowers, distantly derived from *Imari* styles, made principally in the West of England from about 1820. The colours employed were usually cobalt blue, rust and green, often with copper lustre*. Nothing of this kind was made at Etruria*. A Pearl ware* soap dish decorated in this manner and marked 'WEDGWOOD' impressed (formerly in the Byron Born collection) is the work of John Wedg Wood*.

GARNITURE DE CHEMINEE. Three-piece cane ware garniture, comprising a set of two small flower pots 3½in. wide and a centre flower pot 6½in. wide, with moulded oval reserves and applied ornament of figures and paterae, decorated in encaustic colours of blue and white with gilded frames. The interiors are glazed. c.1790.
Christie's, London

Gaugain, Thomas (1748-c.1805)

French engraver who lived in England from his youth. He exhibited at the Royal Academy, 1778-82, and executed numerous engravings after such artists as Reynolds*, Morland, Northcote and Maria Cosway. He supplied Wedgwood with engravings, c.1790-1800.

Gems

Precious or semi-precious stones carved in cameo* or intaglio* were made from ancient times. Greek temple inventories dating from 400 BC record gold and silver rings set with seals of this kind, and by the 1st century BC gem collecting was an established enthusiasm in Rome. Julius Caesar, for instance, presented six cabinets of gems to the temple of Venus, and Pliny the Elder records the manufacture of false gems in glass paste and other materials on a large scale, so scarce had genuine examples become in the art market of the day. The carvers of false gems devoted themselves largely to well-known subjects which were already old in their day, and to this may be ascribed the numerous examples of almost identical gems.

The passion for gem collecting revived during the Renaissance and continued well into the 19th century. The practice of imitating them started once more and reached considerable proportions by the end of the 18th century. Many imitations were legitimate and were sold, without any attempt to disguise their nature, at a price related to the cost of production. In this category were Wedgwood's cameos* and intaglios* and Tassie's* glass paste gems, which were not intended to deceive anyone into thinking them antique. It is worthy of note that the earliest of all cameos, predating those carved from stone, were made from glass paste, or were impressed into terracotta and then gilded to resemble gold medallions, but it is improbable that this was known to either Wedgwood or Tassie. 18th-century forgeries were carved from precious stones using lapidary* techniques, given some signs of age, and sold at enhanced prices as Greek or Roman work.

During the 4th century BC the gem was usually a thin slice of stone with a design carved in the face (intaglio) and set in a ring or seal. Usually the stone selected was sard, varying in colour from golden to blood-red. Other fairly common stones were onyx, sardonyx, agate, chalcedony and jasper, and from the last Josiah took the name of his stoneware. His early jasper was also described by him as 'onyx', and it is clear that from the start he regarded the new jasper body as especially suitable for gems.

The introduction of cameo carving on a fairly large scale belongs to the 3rd century BC, when advantage was taken of laminated stones with variously coloured layers, such as onyx and the sardonyx, to produce carvings in relief of a different colour from the background. According to Pliny, the first Roman to possess a carved gem of sardonyx was Scipio Africanus (241-c.183). Cameo portraits appear to date from the time of Alexander the Great (356-323), who forbade the engraving of his portrait by anyone but Pyrgoteles. Portraits of those living earlier than this date (e.g. Plato*, Socrates*) were made in Graeco-Roman times and taken from sources now unknown. The Greek tendency was always to idealise the person portrayed; the Romans, in their portraiture, particularly in their bronzes, were realists.

Wedgwood made a collection of antique gems, acquired primarily for reproduction in terracotta* and black basaltes*, and in 1772 he found himself hampered by the difficulty of identifying the subjects. He wrote: 'We are continually asked...the names of gems, seals &c...imagine how foolish we look when we can scarcely tell them a single head or subject'.

Antique gems had always been collected into cabinets, and Wedgwood supposed that those who bought his gems would follow this custom. They were, he claimed with some justification, 'exactly taken from the finest Antique gems...by the favour of the Nobility &c. who are in possession of original gems, or fine impressions of those in foreign Collections. We have been able to make our list pretty numerous.' To encourage collectors, heads of the Popes – 256 cameos after medals by Dassier* – were sold at 'six-pence a piece, single, or three-pence a piece to those who take the set'.

The 1779 Wedgwood & Bentley Catalogue* lists 440 cameo and 379 intaglio subjects, a substantial collection, but modest in comparison with Tassie's. In 1782 Tassie made a cabinet for Catherine the Great* which contained 12,000 intaglios and impressions of 6,076 different subjects. Wedgwood's intaglios were intended primarily for seals, and the subjects were chiefly copies from antique gems, heraldic devices or initial letters or ciphers. Both cameos and intaglios were used for profile portraits and these might be modelled to order. In the 1779 Catalogue Wedgwood called attention to the improvements made possible by the introduction of jasper 'by polishing the bezels and giving a ground of pale blue to the flat surface of the stone, which makes them greatly resemble the black and blue onyxes, and equally ornamental for rings or seals.

Cameos have been produced by Wedgwood almost continuously since the 18th century, but the number of new subjects has been small and modern cameos generally lack the definition of 18th-century examples.

See also: Burch, Edward; Sulphurs

GENIUS. Dark-brown wax model by Giuseppe Angelini, 1789, of *Several Geniuses representing the Pleasures of the Elysian Fields.*
Lady Lever Art Gallery, Port Sunlight

General Chamber of Manufacturers

An organisation of Chambers (or Committees) of Commerce founded in 1785, at the instigation of Josiah Wedgwood, to protect the interests of British manufacturers during the negotiation of the Irish Trade Treaty*. In February Wedgwood went to Birmingham to consult Samuel Garbett* and other manufacturers about the treaty, which he opposed. He wrote to Boulton*: I mean to recommend them the measure of a Committee of Delegates from all the main factories and places in England and Scotland, to meet and sit in London…This strikes me as a measure which may be productive of many beneficial effects, principally informing and cementing a commercial band which may be great use on others as well as the present occasion.' The first delegates, who included Garbett, Boulton, James Watt* and the ironmaster John Wilkinson, met on 7 March and 1 May. On 2 May Wedgwood gave evidence on their behalf before the House of Commons select committee. In spite of strenuous opposition from the manufacturers, led by Wedgwood, the Irish Resolutions, much amended, were passed in the House of Commons, but, lacking sufficient support in the Dublin parliament, they were withdrawn.

In October 1785 Wedgwood suggested to William Nicholson, secretary to the Chamber, that joint action be taken against industrial espionage*. Later in the year, William Eden (later Lord Auckland*) was appointed to negotiate a trade treaty with France. The Chamber of Manufacturers, of which Wedgwood had been elected president, was divided in its attitude to the French Commercial Treaty*, the manufacturers of the Midlands and North in the younger, expanding, industries – potters metal workers, cotton spinners – welcoming the attempt to free trade with France from inequitable restrictions and imposts, while the older, less aggressive industries, fearful of competition, strongly opposed the negotiations. Wedgwood's expert advice played a significant part in Eden's successful negotiations and the treaty was given the formal approval of parliament on 8 March 1786. Within a month the Chamber was collapsing. While he could count on the loyal support of Watt, Boulton, Garbett and many others, Wedgwood had, by his energetic and outspoken support of the treaty, made enemies among other influential manufacturers and he was attacked in the newspapers as 'a tool of Administration'. A cartoon by J. Sayers, *The Chamber of Commerce or L'Assemblée des Not-ables* published on 14 February 1787, shows the ambitious Charles James Fox* pulling the strings of the asses of the committee, while the peg-legged Wedgwood, as a figure of Mercury* brandishing a caduceus*, dances beside a vase inscribed 'Wedgwood'.

Many 'respectable members' resigned, dissatisfied with the manner in which the business of the Chamber had been taken over by a disaffected minority. Wedgwood, 'wearied out with the nonsense of some & the pertness & abuse of others' considered whether he, too, should take the advice of his friends, resign and 'let the Chamber go to the Devil'. He was relieved of the decision: the Chamber of Manufacturers died of inanition. In June 1787 Wedgwood wrote to Eden: 'The Chamber of manufacturers sleepeth for the present, but may be waked at any time when its services are called for.'

Genius

A protecting spirit or daemon. The ancient Greeks and Romans believed that every human acquired a tutelary genius at birth, who accompanied him throughout life and guided him to the underworld at death. Genii are generally represented as winged beings, often confused with Cupids*.
Wedgwood subjects:
Genii, medallion, 3in. x 7in. 'measured diagonally', and smaller sizes down to 1¾in. x 3¾in., designed by Lady Templetown*, c.1785. No.252 in 1787 Catalogue
Several Geniuses Representing the Pleasures of the Elysian Fields, tablet, modelled by Angelini*, 1789

GENIUS. Extremely rare lilac dip jasper flower or bough pot ornamented with seven *amorini* after *Angelini's Several Geniuses.* Oval length 8¾in. c. 1790. Wedgwood's version has added drapery to hide the nudity of the figures and was frequently copied by Adams of Greengates. *Lady Lever Art Gallery, Port Sunlight*

GENTLEMAN, David. Bone china plate decorated with a silk-screened view of 'Harlech Castle'. One of a set of six 'named views' issued in a 'limited' edition of 5,000. 1977. *Wedgwood Museum*

Gentleman, David William RDI (b.1930)

English painter and graphic designer; studied at the Royal College of Art, 1950-3; Tutor, Royal College of Art, 1953-5; designer of murals and posters for the National Trust and London Transport, and of a number of important sets of postage stamps; member of the Design Council, 1974. Gentleman was awarded the Gold medal for postage stamp design, 1969, and the Design Council Poster Award 1973, 1976 and 1977. He has illustrated a number of books, including *The Shepherd's Calendar* and other limited editions.

David Gentleman designed a series of views of British Castles and Country Houses for reproduction on Wedgwood bone china* plates in a 'limited' edition of 5,000 sets. The first two views, Harlech Castle and Woburn Abbey*, were issued in 1977.

George II (1683-1760)

King of Great Britain and Ireland and Elector of Hanover; grandfather of George III*. A bust of George II, about 10in. high, is listed in the 1773 Catalogue* 'from an Ivory in the possession of Mr Ranby, carved by Mr Rysbrack*' (the ivory is now lost). This bust, for many years wrongly identified as a portrait of the first Duke of Marlborough*, is closely related to a bust by Rysbrack in the possession of H.M. The Queen at Windsor Castle and a later marble in the Victoria & Albert Museum, London. The Wedgwood bust exists in black basaltes*, jasper* and *rosso antico**. Two portrait medallions* of George II, attributed to Matthew and Isaac Gosset*, are listed in the 1779 Catalogue.

George III (1738-1820)

King of Great Britain and Ireland and Elector of Hanover; grandson of George II; married, 1761, Charlotte Sophia* of Mecklenburgh-Strelitz. The King evidently approved of Queen Charlotte's patronage of Wedgwood for, shortly after the production of the Queen's tea service, he ordered a table service for himself, on a new shape which was called 'Royal' shape. Josiah and Bentley* were granted an audience of the King and Queen in 1770 to present some bas-reliefs* ordered by the Queen, and Bentley wrote afterwards to his partner, Boardman*: 'They expressed in the most obliging and condescending manner, their attention to our manufacture...The king is well acquainted with business, and with the characters of the principal manufacturers, merchants and artists; and seems to have the success of all our manufactures much at heart, and to understand the importance of them.'

As a convinced Whig, Wedgwood can have had little personal regard for a king who had prosecuted a war against the American colonists and who was later to dismiss North and Fox* in favour of

GEORGE II. Pale-blue and white jasper portrait medallion of George II after a wax portrait attributed to Isaac Gosset. (Modern reproduction.). *Wedgwood Museum*

the younger Pitt*, but royal patronage took precedence over politics. At least ten portrait medallions* of the King were produced, of which four were modelled by Hackwood* from models by Isaac Gosset*. A rare double portrait of George III and Queen Charlotte dates from 1777. Three medallions were modelled to celebrate the King's temporary recovery from illness (he suffered from porphyria) in 1789. The King's Golden Jubilee in 1810 was celebrated by the production of a service of White ware* decorated with a printed stippled orange ground, outline prints of the head of George III and the star and badge of the Order of the Garter within a printed border of the Garter chain, and enamelled *famille-rose*-style flowers. A small bough pot* from this service is in the Wedgwood Museum* at Barlaston*.

In 1786 Wedgwood presented one of his pyrometer* sets to George III to add to the royal collection of scientific instruments at the Royal Observatory at Richmond, Surrey.

GEORGE III. Creamware teapot transfer-printed in red by Sadler with a portrait of George III, probably after James McArdell's engraving from the painting by J. Meyer. Height 5¾in. Unmarked. Wedgwood, c.1763. *Manchester City Art Gallery*

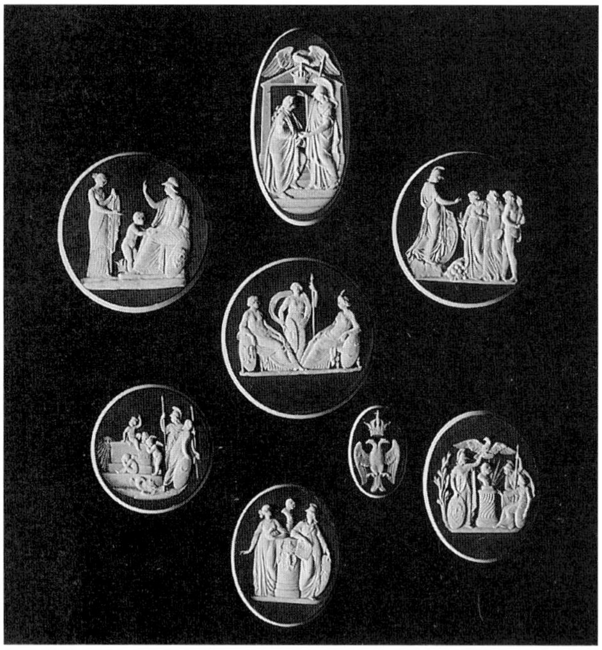

GERMAN CAMEOS. Eight blue jasper dip cameos issued to celebrate the accession and virtues of Leopold II. The cameo illustrated upper right, diameter 2⅛in., is yet another adaptation of Webber's 'Sydney Cove' design. c.1790. *Dr & Mrs Alvin M. Kanter Collection*

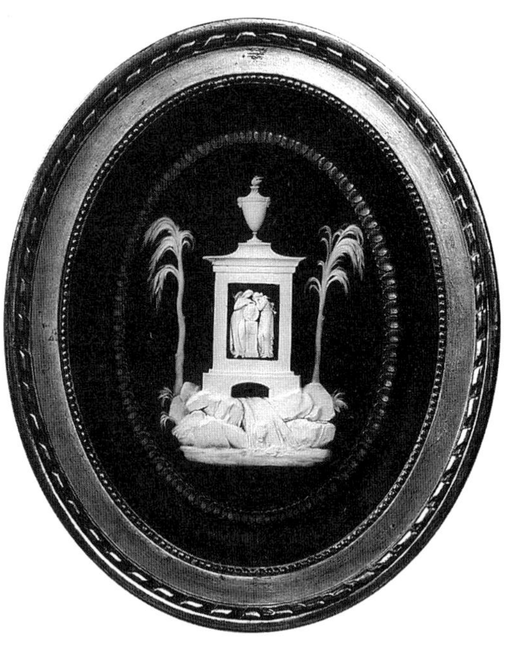

GESSNER, Solomon. Dark-blue jasper dip medallion ornamented with the Muses of painting and poetry mourning the death of the Swiss poet. Oval height 4⅝in. c.1790.
Dwight & Lucille Beeson Collection, Birmingham Museum, Alabama

Germaine, Pierre (b.1716)
Member of a family of goldsmiths of Avignon and Marseille; apprenticed to Nicolas Besnier and was received *maître* of the Guild in 1744. His book of designs, *Elements d'Orfèvrerie,* published in 1751, appears to have been in Josiah Wedgwood's library. Plate 5, with alterations in pencil, survives in the Wedgwood archives and seems to have influenced the design of some of the carved wood block moulds attributed to Coward*.
See: Rococo Style; Silver Pattern

German Cameos
Bas-reliefs designed specially to commemorate the accession and virtues of Leopold II*, who succeeded his brother Joseph II as Holy Roman Emperor in 1790. The precise number of subjects is not known but seven are listed on an invoice dated 11 September 1790:
Fame inscribing Vase to the Memory of Elizabeth (favourite niece of Joseph II, who died February 1790). Upright oval 1⅞in. or bent oval (for shoe buckles) 1⅛in.
Leopold the Lawgiver supported by Wisdom & Benevolence, 1⅞in. or 1⅜in.
The genius of Empire holding the bust of Leopold while a priestess is officiating at an altar, round, 2⅛in. diameter
Germany in the character of Minerva presents Leopold with a Civic band as a reward for his code of laws, round, 2⅛in. diameter
Mars presenting a Crown to the Genius of Germany to be placed upon the bust of Leopold which stands on an altar, round, 2⅛in. diameter
Turkey and Russia – the two belligerent powers consulting upon peace, & Germany the mediator between them, round 2⅛in. diameter
Coronation of Leopold, oval upright 2in.
Others identified are:
Germany in the character of Minerva encouraging Art and Labour with Peace to work for the prosperity of the Empire (a slightly altered version of the Sydney Cove* medallion; and see also: French Revolution)
Germany and Turkey with Amorini grieving for Elizabeth.
Two-headed eagle surmounted by the Imperial crown.

Germanicus
The son of Nero Claudius Drusus and Antonia, daughter of Mark Antony*, Germanicus was adopted by his uncle Tiberius. Germanicus was successful in subduing the German tribes but Tiberius withdrew him before his task was completed, giving him command of the eastern provinces. There Germanicus died, probably poisoned. One of his nine children became the Emperor Caligula and another the mother of the Emperor Nero. A bust of Germanicus, supplied by Hoskins & Grant* in 1774, was finished by Hackwood*.

Gerverot, Louis-Victor (1747-1829)
Painter, colour-chemist, potter and arcanist. Gerverot was a porcelain* painter at Sèvres* (1764-5), Niderviller, Fulda, Ludwigsburg, Höchst, Frankenthal, Offenbach, Weesp (c.1771), Schrezheim (1773-5) and Oude Loosdrecht (1777-8). Gerverot visited England in 1786 to barter his knowledge of the secrets of porcelain for knowledge of English creamware and stonewares. Wedgwood offered him employment, which he declined, but he evidently visited Etruria*, of which he was later able to give a detailed description to the directors of the Fürstenberg factory. He reached agreement with John Turner* to build a porcelain factory on the latter's land at Lane End, but this was still uncompleted when Turner died. In 1797 he became manager of Fürstenberg, where he supervised the production of busts and medallions in imitation of Wedgwood's and Turner's.

A porcelain beaker, made by the Turner-Gerverot factory in 1787, was decorated in reddish-brown enamel with two scenes (one signed by Fidèle Duvivier) showing the interior of a pottery. These designs were reproduced on a jug, and perhaps other pieces, by Wedgwood in 1887.
See: Industrial Espionage

Gessner, Solomon (1720-88)
Swiss poet, who was born and died in Zürich, where he was a bookseller. His poetry, written in German, was exceedingly popular. He painted landscapes in a romantic* neo-classical* style and did excellent engraving. He was one of the founders of the Zürich porcelain factory and supplied subjects for the decoration of the ware. He also painted occasional landscapes on the porcelain of this factory.

His portrait medallion* was issued by Wedgwood in 1790, but the source is not known. Wedgwood also produced a medallion of about the same date which shows a classical tomb or monument surmounted by an urn with the Muses* of Poetry and Painting weeping over Gessner's profile. Flanking the monument, which stands above a rushing stream and rockwork, are two palm trees. This bas-relief* was designed by Brandoin*. A second, simplified, version of this memorial medallion uses only the figures of the two Muses weeping over the profile of Gessner.

Gilbert and Sullivan Mug

Half-pint mug issued in 1961 to commemorate the fiftieth anniversary of the death of W.S. Gilbert. It bears portraits of Gilbert and Arthur Sullivan, with that of Richard D'Oyly Carte under the handle. The backstamp lists eleven Gilbert and Sullivan operas with the dates of their first performances and the body of the mug is decorated with transfer prints* of characters from these operas between bands of pink and blue enamel. The mug was designed by Victor Skellern*.

Gilding

The application of gold to pottery and porcelain. It has been extensively used for the decoration of European porcelain since about 1710 but appeared first on faïence of the mid-16th century. It was not in regular use, however, for another hundred years or so. Before about 1755, gilding was applied in the form of gold leaf over a sticky size (usually a boiled mixture of linseed oil and litharge), which was then allowed to dry. 'Size gilding' was excessively vulnerable to wear and has now mostly worn off. Another method, by which ground gold leaf was mixed with a thick varnish and applied with a brush, was as impermanent. These early forms of gilding were succeeded by honey-gilding, which substituted honey for varnish and was made more durable by a low-temperature firing. This was the method used throughout the 18th century for fine gilding on porcelain and some high quality pottery, including Wedgwood's. Gilding of this type was usually laid on thickly and was attractively soft in tone. Mercury-gilding was invented about 1785. An amalgam of gold and mercury, applied with a brush, was lightly fired, the mercury being vaporised in the kiln. The gilding produced by this method was thin and burnished to a rather garish brilliance.

The use of gilding was characteristic of baroque* and rococo* porcelain, greatly restrained during the period of neo-classical* taste, and wholly unrestrained during the Empire or Regency period, when it was applied to larger surfaces, such as handles and plinths, and as grounds for painted panels, simulating solid gold.

Raised gilding, or raised gold – relief decoration worked up as a paste, fired and gilded – was introduced about 1802 in imitation of earlier decoration, especially at Sèvres, in which gold applied very thickly was tooled to the desired design.

A liquid gold, introduced about 1855, produced a brassy-bright finish without burnishing, but its cheap appearance confined it to use on goods of lower quality. Bright burnished gold was used from 1860.

A technique for transfer-printing* in gold was patented by Peter Warburton (1773-1813) in 1810, and gold-printing dates from this time.

Gilding was seldom used in the Staffordshire Potteries during the 18th century and in 1765, when Wedgwood accepted Queen Charlotte's* commission for a teaset 'with a gold ground', he appears to have been the only potter prepared to accept the challenge of producing it. The gilding was certainly his principal anxiety. He asked his brother John to obtain 'some gold powder such as is burnt in upon China', made solely by a Mr Shenton at the enormous price of seven guineas an ounce, and referred John to the enameller James Giles*, who could supply Shenton's address and might also provide instructions about the best method of using the gold. Wedgwood did not know how to burnish it, and asked John to consult Jenks, a gilder recently transferred from the Chelsea* porcelain factory to Bow*. By the end of August he had completed his first trial in making his own powder gold. This all suggests that Wedgwood had little or no experience of applying gold to earthenware prior to making the Queen's teaset, but he was evidently successful at his first attempt. A year or so later, some of his green glazed ware* was gilded, but it does not appear to have been popular in England. Specimens exist of Queen's ware* tableware, c.1772, transfer-printed in black, with the feather-edge honey-gilded, and the set is unlikely to have been unique. A shell-edge Pearl* ware glacier*, enamelled in turquoise and gilded, c.1780-5, was in the Buten* collection.

Gold was used also in the decoration of Wedgwood & Bentley vases, both variegated* and plain Queen's ware. From the end of 1769 most variegated vases were gilded, on handles, finials and all applied ornament including figures and cameos. In 1772, however, Bentley* passed on to Wedgwood Sir William Hamilton's* severe criticism of this form of embellishment and Wedgwood agreed to

GILDING. Auro basalt vase illustrating the use of raised gold paste in a leafage design. Height 15¾in.   *Christie's, London*

'make a good use of his hints…by greatly reduceing, if not totally banishing this *offensive Gilding*'. He was anxious lest his customers should equate gilding with value, but later in the year he reported: 'They cannot bear anything Gilt beyond a picture frame…Gold, the most precious of all metals, is absolutely kicked out of doors.' The reaction against gold was temporary, but it was always more popular as a finish for porcelain than for earthenware. It was used extensively on Wedgwood's bone china* of the first period and from its reintroduction in 1878. In the 18th century gilding was rarely used on black basaltes*, although traces may be found on frames and vases. An exceptional white terracotta* plaque (Holburne of Menstrie Museum, Bath) is gilded all over the upper surface. Gilding appeared again on bronzed and gilt basaltes* and the bronze and gold* body in the late-19th century. Gilding and transfer-printed or silk-screen* gold patterns have been an essential part of Wedgwood's 20th-century bone china production and gilding has been used also, but less regularly, on modern Queen's ware, basalt and jasper*.

See also: Acid Gold; Auro Basalt; Golconda Decoration; Lustre

Giles, James (1718-80)

Independent decorator, described by Mortimer's *Directory* of 1763 as a 'china and enamel painter'.' His style has been identified on porcelain imported from China, and also that of Chelsea*, Worcester* and Bow*. In 1763 he claimed to copy 'patterns of any china with the utmost exactness, both with respect to the design and the colours, either in European or Chinese taste'. Among the best known of his decorations are the so-called 'dishevelled birds' (see: Exotic Birds) inspired by earlier bird painting at Sèvres*, and some excellent painting of sliced fruit. In 1765 Wedgwood sought his advice about gilding* for Queen Charlotte's* teaset. Five years later, when Wedgwood was contemplating an action against Palmer* and Neale* for the infringement of his patent for encaustic* colours, he wrote to Bentley* speculating that the offending wares might have been painted by James Giles. This was not improbable since Giles was experiencing difficulties at the time in obtaining supplies of white porcelain to paint and was soon in financial straits in consequence. Although there is no evidence that Giles ever painted Wedgwood Queen's ware*, it is not unlikely that he did so.

GLADSTONE, William Ewart. Black and white jasper portrait medallion, modelled by Charles Toft, in solid white jasper frame with green oak-leaf ornament. Oval height 8in. c.1877. *Christie's, New York*

GLACIER. Glacier from the "Frog' service, enamelled in monochrome with views of Lord Paget's Staffordshire mansion, Beau Desert, and Sir Laurence Dundas's estate, Moor Park, in Hertfordshire. The elaborate finial of three sibyls appears to have been designed especially for this piece. Hermitage Museum, St Petersburg.
Photograph: Wedgwood

Gill, Charles (fl.1805-26)

Traveller, who shared the British territory with Josiah Bateman* during the greater part of the first quarter of the 19th century. Little is known of him personally but his traveller's pattern book – a small volume containing details of patterns and shapes of tableware and ornamental wares, meticulously drawn in watercolour – is preserved in the Wedgwood archives. It is an invaluable reference for details of Wedgwood's production during this period.

Glacier

The term 'glacier' appears to be Josiah Wedgwood's own for a covered ice-cream bowl or refrigerator. These pieces were commonly made for French porcelain services and were known in France as *rafraîchissoirs*. A *glacier* in France is either a maker of mirrors or an ice-cream vendor, while a *glacière* is an ice-house or ice-box. Wedgwood wrote to Bentley* in February 1774: 'I am preparing the Glauciers [*sic*], the only things now wanting from hence...to complete it [the Frog* service]'. This is the earliest reference to Wedgwood glaciers. They were modelled especially for the Frog service and it is said that the three sibyl* finials were modelled by Josiah himself. A glacier in four parts appears as design no.5 in Plate 2 of the 1774 Catalogue* with a detailed description of its use as a refrigerator for ice-cream but the drawing is not repeated in the '1790' Catalogue. From 1774 until about 1850 these pieces were made in Queen's ware* in many patterns and several shapes, including shell-edge, some decorated with crests, coats of arms and gilding.

Gladstone, William Ewart, Rt. Hon. (1809-98)

English Liberal politician and Prime Minister; collector of English and Continental pottery and porcelain, especially Wedgwood wares. His eulogy of Josiah Wedgwood, delivered in 1863, is often quoted. His collection was dispersed in London in June 1875. A bust of Gladstone by Joseph Edgar Boehm*, 1879, was reproduced in Celadon jasper* and black basaltes* in 1880. His portrait medallion, modelled by Charles Toft*, was produced in jasper, c.1877.

Glass Ware

Wedgwood first added the manufacture of glass ware to their range of production in 1969, when they acquired King's Lynn Glass Ltd (later Wedgwood Glass). The first chief designer was Ronald Stenett-Willson and the product range included drinking glasses, decanters, candlesticks and ornamental objects, some incorporating jasper* cameos as decoration. The purchase of the Galway Crystal Company of Galway, Eire, followed in 1974, but this second, and more ambitious, acquisition was not a success and the company was sold again six years later.

Glazes

Glaze is a form of glass applied to the surface of biscuit* and other porous ware to render it impermeable (in the case of earthenware) and to prevent surface staining (vitrified wares). Wedgwood's earliest glaze for creamware was a distinctive yellow-green and, contrary to the pronouncements of his eulogists, was sometimes disfigured by crazing*. This fault was almost eliminated by about 1763, when a refined creamware body was accompanied by a finer glaze which shows a paler green tinge and was applied more evenly. The green tint is especially noticeable on the inside of foot rims and the interior of teapots and coffeepots. By the end of the 18th century the glaze had become almost colourless, except on Pearl* ware, the 'blue-bag' tint of which is, unlike that of Leeds*, also greenish. Glaze may be coloured (usually by the addition of metallic oxides) or almost colourless, transparent or opaque. It is now usually applied by spraying or dipping (see: Processes of Manufacture) but may be dusted on, brushed or sponged.

The earliest-known specimens of glazed pottery are blue and green beads made in Egypt perhaps 14,000 years ago. Alkaline copper glazes were in use by 3000 BC. Glazes were used to add a waterproof and hygienic covering to porous earthenware from about 1500 BC. Lead glazes were used by Chinese potters early in the 3rd century and in ancient Rome and continued in common use in Europe through the Middle Ages until the end of the 19th century.

GLAZES. Green glaze dessert plates and dessert dish with moulded fruit, leaf, sunflower and basketwork patterns. Dish, c.1843; plates, c.1850-60.
Wedgwood Museum

GLAZES. Matt Glazes. Moonstone vase, height 10in., from a series of ribbed vases and two-handled bowls, designed by Victor Skellern in 1954-5 for Moonstone and Ravenstone glazes, especially for sale in the Wedgwood Rooms but available also for general sale. c.1955.
Wedgwood Museum

The first yellow or brown coloured glazes were stained by the accidental presence of iron in the clay or galena (the natural sulphide of lead), and the deliberate colouring of glazes was developed quickly. T'ang dynasty (619-906) pottery shows a variety of colours derived from metallic oxides – blue, green, yellow, orange and brown – often sponged on to produce a splashed or dappled effect.

Dry glazes produced by a mixture of powdered galena and ground flint were gradually superseded in England by the invention, credited to Enoch Booth about 1740, of a fluid lead glaze. During the 18th century the poisonous effect on workers in the pottery industry was widely recognised. For his later Queen's ware* Wedgwood developed a glaze made from white clay and flint, using smaller quantities of lead, but he failed in his attempts to make a satisfactory leadless glaze. In 1898 the Home Office ordered an official inquiry into the incidence of lead poisoning in the pottery industry, and a year later manufacturers were instructed to discontinue the use of raw lead.

The following are the principal Wedgwood glazes:

Aventurine Glaze
A glaze so called from its resemblance to the natural stone. The glaze usually has copper particles suspended in it which imitate gold. The Venetians, among others, made glass of this kind. Wedgwood's Aventurine glaze was developed by Norman Wilson* in the 1950s for the decoration of ornamental pieces produced in small quantities under the general description of Unique* ware. The glaze is of a distinctive deep reddish-brown with flecks of metal which reflect light as dull gold. The glaze was used principally for the interior of Queen's ware bowls, the exterior usually being glazed black. Examples are scarce.

Champagne Glaze
Pale yellow glaze used on tablewares and a few Skeaping* animals in the 1930s.

Dysart Glaze
A deep creamy-yellow glaze introduced, c.1885, at the request of the Earl of Dysart, who wanted a colour closer to ivory than the pale 19th-century cream-colour glaze. It has been continuously in use ever since that time.

Green Glaze
Probably Wedgwood's most famous and distinctive glaze, Green glaze was developed by Wedgwood during his partnership with Whieldon* and used from 1759. The copper scales from which it was made were bought from Robinson & Rhodes* of Leeds.

Wedgwood's formula for 'A Green Glaze to be laid on Common white biscuit ware' is the seventh recorded in his Experiment Book* and shows the composition to be a mixture of white lead, calcined flint and calcined copper. Green glaze is often described as Wedgwood's invention but, although he devised his own formula, shades of green had been achieved in glazes made by the Romans, and primitive examples are to be found on specimens of Norman and medieval pottery made in England. The colour enjoyed widespread popularity in 16th-century Europe. Nothing made earlier, however, surpassed the brilliance of Wedgwood's clear green lead glaze, especially when it was applied to his creamware.

Wedgwood's Green glaze was used on its own, especially on simple leaf shapes and teapots, occasionally enriched with gilding*, and combined with other colours for the apple, pear, cauliflower and pineapple shapes. The glaze was copied and used extensively by other potters and by mid-1766 Wedgwood was 'heartily sick of the commodity' and stopped making it. By 1779 it had been reintroduced for the decoration of flower pots and during the 19th century it enjoyed a substantial revival as decoration for leaf dessert services. It was important again as one of the early Majolica* glazes and has been intermittently in use for dessert ware during the 20th century.

Lead Glaze
Transparent glaze containing lead, often called Galena glaze during the 18th century, and employed to cover creamware, Queen's ware* and Pearl* ware (see: Pearl Glaze).

Majolica Glazes
Transparent and opaque glazes, stained with metal oxides, introduced at Etruria* in 1860 for the decoration of dessert services, a few small figures and a wide range of ornamental wares known as Majolica*.

Matt Glazes
Glazes with an 'egg-shell' or 'satin' sheen, somewhat resembling marble in surface finish. Introduced in 1933, the Wedgwood matt glazes include moonstone*, matt green, matt straw, turquoise, silver grey and black (later called 'ravenstone'). All were extensively used for the shapes modelled by Keith Murray* and moonstone has been in production continuously to the present day. Except for occasional use, none but the moonstone and ravenstone glazes has been in production since 1941. The original matt white was a mixture of leadless frit*, china clay and whiting and the different colours were obtained by the addition of metal oxides (for example, uranium oxide for green) but the composition has since been altered, by the use of 'matting agents', to improve appearance and durability.

GLAZES. Veronese Glaze. Simple thrown and turned Queen's ware vase decorated with transparent green 'Veronese' glaze and outlines of leaves and flowers in platinum, probably after designs by Louise Powell. Height 10½in. c.1935.　　　*Author's collection*

Moonstone
See: Matt Glazes
Peacock
A deep blue glaze, mottled to resemble the markings of peacocks' feathers, devised by Norman Wilson* especially for the decoration of his 'Unique'* wares. The effect, being impossible to control, varied from piece to piece.
Pearl Glaze
Glaze containing a small quantity of cobalt oxide, giving it a blueish tint. It was used at first on Queen's ware* to whiten it, and from 1779 on the new Pearl* body.
Ravenstone
See: Matt Glazes
Rockingham Glaze
Purplish-brown transparent glaze introduced at Etruria* no later than 1823, when it superseded the London Brown glaze used for a short period in the early years of the 19th century. The name was taken from the manganese-stained glaze developed at the Rockingham factory, Swinton, Yorkshire at the end of the 18th century, extensively copied by Staffordshire and Yorkshire potters and as far away as the Bennington Pottery in Vermont, USA. The glaze was at first used almost exclusively for teapots and coffee biggins* but the range was later extended to tea and coffee services and, in conjunction with underglaze painting in slip, for vases (see: Magnolia Ware). Perhaps its most important use was with acid-etched decoration (see: Vigornian Ware).
See also: Rockingham Ware
Smear Glaze
A deposit of glaze by volatilisation on the surface of pottery produced by smearing the inside of the saggar* with a lead glaze preparation. It is sometimes erroneously described as a form of saltglaze* and is often mistaken for it. It was introduced on the white stoneware* ('porcelain'*) body in 1815 and its use on basaltes* was suggested by Bateman* in 1817. It was applied extensively also to the cane* and drab* bodies, both for interior and exterior glazing. It was considered suitable for ornamented or moulded stonewares because it did not blunt the relief to the same degree as lead glaze applied by dipping.
Veronese Glazes
Translucent coloured glazes in rich hues of red, purple, blue, turquoise, green, yellow and black developed by Norman Wilson*

about 1933, devised specifically for use with ornamental shapes and lustre decoration* in platinum or gold. Wilson was responsible also for some of the shapes while others were drawn from existing Wedgwood models. The range was introduced to supply a comparatively cheap range of ornamental ware and to provide work for skilled throwers and paintresses. Ware decorated with Veronese glazes continued in production until 1941.
Yellow Glaze
Wedgwood's first yellow glaze was produced in 1760 for the decoration of fruit and vegetable* shapes, especially cauliflower teapots and coffeepots. These were seldom made after 1766 and no evidence has been found to show that yellow glaze was used again during the 18th century. A bright yellow glaze was made by a number of potters, including Leeds*, Spode*, Davenport*, Samuel Alcock and Shorthose, during the first half of the 19th century. Wedgwood's yellow glaze dates from about 1820 and no reference to it occurs after 1833. Production was evidently small and examples are rare.
See also: Jackfield Ware; Salt Glaze

Glisson (Glesson), Miss (fl.1769-74)
Painter at the Chelsea Decorating Studio who worked on the Frog* service, painting topographical views for a weekly wage of 12/6d.

Globe Shape
See: Tableware Shapes

Glost Oven
Glazing oven.
See: Kilns; Processes of Manufacture – *Firing*

Glover, Thomas (fl.1769-74)
Painter at the Chelsea Decorating Studio* who worked on the Frog* service.

Godet
Small cup, in which a wick was suspended or floated in oil, used in the lower part of a food warmer* or *veilleuse**.

Golconda Decoration
Decoration in raised gold paste and enamel on bone china* ornamental wares, introduced at Etruria* c.1885 by George Marsden*. The style of decoration, principally floriate, was similar to that used for Auro Basalt* and belongs to the same period.

GOLCONDA. Bone china vase with *Golconda* decoration in raised gold paste. Height 8in. c.1885.　　　*Wedgwood Museum*

GOLD-PRINTING. Fine Queen's ware punch-pot decorated with gold-printed patterns and gilding with 'The Punch Party' and 'The Smoking Party' transfer-printed in black in oval reserves. Length 12½in. c.1820.

Mr & Mrs Herbert Jacobs Collection

GOODWIN, John. Queen's ware coffeepot and coffee cup and saucer from the *Edme* shape designed by Goodwin in 1908. *Edme* has been, for more than eighty years, Wedgwood's most popular earthenware shape in the North American market.

Wedgwood Museum

Gold

See: Gilding

Gold-printing

The technique for transfer-printing in gold was patented by Peter Warburton (1773-1813) in 1810. The modern printing technique is by silk-screen. (See: Gilding.)

Goodden, Robert York (b.1909)

Architect, designer and silversmith; Professor of Silversmithing and Jewellery at the Royal College of Art, 1948. Goodden collaborated with R.D. Russell in the design of the Lion and Unicorn Pavilion at the Festival of Britain in 1951 and, with Russell, redesigned Wedgwood's London Showrooms* in Wigmore Street. In 1959 he was commissioned to design the decoration for one of the mugs produced to celebrate the bicentenary of the Wedgwood firm and, about a year later, he designed Wedgwood tableware for the P & O liner *Oriana*. His brother, Wyndham Goodden, was introduced to Wedgwood in the 1930s by Sir Charles Holmes* and worked in the art department at Etruria* for two years, producing a number of tableware designs, including the Leipzig pattern.

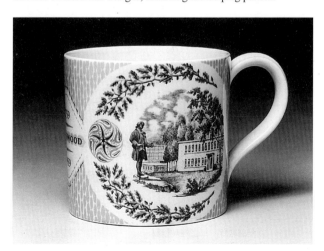

GOODDEN, Robert York. Queen's ware mug with lithographed decoration in blue and dark rose-pink designed by Robert Goodden to commemorate the bicentenary of the founding of the Wedgwood factory in 1759. Height 4in. 1959. *Wedgwood Museum*

Goode, William James (1831-92)

Son of Thomas Goode, founder of the noted firm of china and glass retailers of South Audley Street, London, of which he became a partner in 1857. William Goode was also a talented artist and designer who painted on earthenware and porcelain for Minton* and devised a method of etching on porcelain which was praised at the Paris Exposition of 1878. He supplied some designs to Wedgwood in the 1860s. His private collection of Sèvres porcelain was exhibited at Thomas Goode's premises until his death in 1892, when it was sold. A small Queen's ware dish, painted with caricature figures and subtitled '1742', is in the Wedgwood Museum. It is inscribed on the underside: 'Oh! What a charming Cup & Saucer', with Goode's monogram, signature and the date 1864. The figures are copied from Hogarth's *Taste in High Life; or dress in 1742.*

GOODE, William James. Small Queen's ware lobed dessert dish painted by William Goode and dated 1864. *Wedgwood Museum*

Goodwin, John Edward (1867-1949)

English ceramic designer; art director at Etruria 1904-34 in succession to Thomas Allen*. Goodwin designed a number of Queen's ware* tableware shapes*, some adapted from 18th-century originals, the most successful of which, *Edme*, is still in production. He drew his inspiration particularly from bas-relief* ornament previously used for jasper* and other dry bodies*. Goodwin also designed some distinguished tableware patterns, including the White House* service for Theodore Roosevelt in 1903. Under

Goodwin's influence Wedgwood design was reinvigorated and during the period of his directorship the powder blue* ground on bone china* and the Ordinary Lustre* and Fairyland Lustre* ornamental wares were introduced. Among the artists who worked under his direction were Alfred and Louise Powell*, James Hodgkiss*, Daisy Makeig-Jones* and Arthur Dale Holland*. Goodwin retired in 1934. Although his own designs were commercially successful, and several have proved to be persistant, Goodwin was not a designer of impressive originality. His gifts lay in understanding the needs of the markets, especially the crucial North American market, and in management. He laid sound foundations on which his successor, Victor Skellern*, was able to build with confidence.

Goodwin's designs for Wedgwood include the following:
Queen's ware Tableware Shapes
Annular shape, with Tom Wedgwood* and Keith Murray* (produced with matt glazes – see: Glazes)
Colonial shape, 'in typical style of the…American Colonial period'
Edme shape, 1908
Osier shape, a basketware shape 'after the style of old Meissen', 1906
Patrician shape, 1926
Wellesley shape, 1932
Tableware Patterns
Montreal pattern on Queen's ware, 1930
Ruby Tonquin pattern on Audley shape bone china, 1930
Ulander pattern on bone china, 1912
White House service, 1903 (reissued, without coat of arms, as *Colonnade* pattern, 1960)
Ornamental Wares
Hispano-Moresque* designs on cane coloured body* art wares
Apollo vase 1930

Goodwin, Kathleen H.M. (1902-76)

Artist and modeller, born and studied in the Potteries. Her bronze figure *Will o'Wisp* won a bronze medal from the Royal Society of Arts in 1923* and was one of nine models that were reproduced in bone china by Wedgwood. All were enamelled by Arthur Dale Holland*. Although well modelled, the figures, which are of Kathleen Goodwin's young friends, are insipid and bear no relation to anything in Wedgwood's modelling tradition. The figures are: *Will o' Wisp, Brenda, Bojey, Jacky, Molly, Nancy, Ninette, Pas de Deux* and *Undine*.

GOSSET, Isaac. Blue jasper dip portrait medallion of George III from a wax model by Isaac Gosset. Oval height 3½in. c.1785. *Wedgwood Museum*

Gosset, Isaac (1713-99)

Member of a family of Huguenots who invented his own wax composition for modelling relief portraits. He exhibited at the Society of Arts (Royal Society of Arts*) and the Free Society 1740-78. Gosset modelled many portraits of the famous, including several members of the royal family. Wedgwood portrait medallions* adapted from his models include, Augusta, Princess of Wales, Frederick Louis, Prince of Wales, William, Duke of Cumberland, George III*, Queen Charlotte* and the naturalist, George Edwards.

Gosset, Matthew (1683-1744)

Modeller in wax; uncle of Isaac Gosset*. Several of his wax portraits*, including those of George I, George II* and Lord North, were copied by Wedgwood for portrait medallions* in the 'Illustrious Moderns' series.

Gothic

The Gothic style, of which the pointed arch is a particular feature, prevailed in England from the end of the 12th to the end of the 16th century. It was revived briefly in the middle of the 18th century, when Horace Walpole converted his villa at Strawberry Hill, but it did not attract the potter at the time, and in consequence of the rising

GOTHIC. Gothic-style jugs in white and drab stonewares with coloured ornaments and *(extreme left)* in tinted glazed Parian. The moulded architectural pillars, arches, statuesque figures and rosettes are typical of this 'Revival'. All c.1830.   *Wedgwood Museum*

GOODWIN, Kathleen. Bone china figure, *Undine,* modelled by Kathleen Goodwin and decorated in enamel colours by Arthur Dale Holland*. Height 7½in. c.1923.   *Photograph: Wedgwood*

tide of neo-classicism* it almost disappeared until the early years of the 19th century, surviving most popularly in the 'Gothick' novel. Examples of 18th-century Gothic are rare in ceramics, among the most interesting being John Flaxman's* chessmen* modelled for Wedgwood in 1783-4. Gothic began to return to favour in architecture in the opening decade of the 19th century, when William Beckford commissioned Fonthill Abbey (a country house based on the design of Salisbury Cathedral) from James Wyatt, and a limited use of Gothic motifs appeared on pottery soon afterwards.

About 1825, Wedgwood introduced the underglaze blue* printed pattern now known as *Gothic Ruins* (possibly that called *Abbey* in Bateman's* orders of the period). Wedgwood's Gothic jugs, coffee biggins*, bowls and wine coolers* are illustrated as additional plates to the '1817' Catalogue*, probably issued c.1835. Introduced about 1825, they appear to have been the first of their type to be produced in Staffordshire and they were widely imitated. They are most often found in white stoneware* with coloured reliefs, cane* or drab* stoneware, usually finished with smear glaze*. The design of Wedgwood's Gothic jugs ornamented with applied classical figures beneath moulded arcades was probably derived from a Rhineland stoneware source of the end of the 16th century when this form of ornament – the moulded arcade, each niche containing a figure (usually one of the Apostles) – was favoured. Early German stoneware became popular among collectors early in the 19th century and German influence gained strength with the arrival of Albert of Saxe-Coburg-Gotha, the Prince Consort.

Wedgwood was little influenced by Gothic taste, which is more noticeable in occasional products of Minton*, for whom A.W.N. Pugin worked, and in the series of jugs produced by Charles Meigh & Son, T.J. & J. Mayer, T.R. Boote and W. Ridgway, Son & Co between 1840 and 1860.

Gould & Associates
American international design studio, led by Jerome Gould, responsible for the design of Wedgwood's 225 Shape (see: Tableware Shapes), produced, in 1984, in bone china* and basalt, to celebrate the 225th anniversary of the founding of the firm.

Goupy, Mme Apolline (fl.1880-1915)
French sculptor; sociétaire des Artistes Français from 1898. Wedgwood portrait medallions* of Albert I, King of the Belgians, Marshall Joseph Joffre, Field-Marshal Horatio Herbert, 1st Earl Kitchener and Victor Emmanuel III, King of Italy, were produced in 1915-16 from models by Mme Goupy.

Goupy, Marcel (fl.1909-54)
French designer, closely associated from 1909 with the leading French retailers, Georges Rouard, with whom he was for many years artistic director. Goupy produced a number of tableware designs for Wedgwood but production of them was interrupted by World War I. His Goupy pattern for Queen's ware* dinnerware and toilet sets was designed c.1912 but not produced until 1923.

Goutard, Leonce
See: Mallet, Pierre

Gower, Granville Leveson Gower, 2nd Earl
See: Stafford, 1st Marquis

Graces, The Three
The three Charities: Aglaea (Brilliance, Radiance); Euphrosyne (Mirth, Joy); and Thalia (Bloom, Flowering). Daughters of Zeus and goddesses of beauty and grace, they attended Aphrodite*, and presided over physical exercise and dancing and were the patrons of poetry and art. The Graces were closely associated with the Muses* and are usually represented naked, holding hands. Wedgwood produced two cameos of this subject: the first, which appears also on black basaltes* vases, shows the central figure nude and appears to have been copied from an engraving of a vase in the Hamilton* collection; the second, showing all three figures draped, is probably after a Tassie* gem. Other Wedgwood subjects are:
The Graces erecting the Statue of Cupid, plaque 10¾in. x 9in., no 269 in the 1787 Catalogue
The Three Graces, medallion 3in. x 2¼in. and sizes down to 2in. x 1½in. No.29 in the 1773 Catalogue. Reproduced in jasper, 1777

GRACES, THE THREE. Black basaltes plaque, height 9in. c.1880.
Christie's, New York

Granby. John Manners, 1st Marquis of (1721-70)
Lieutenant-General; eldest son of the 3rd Duke of Rutland; commanded the Royal Horse Guards ('the Blues') at the battle of Minden, 1759 and further distinguished himself during the Seven Years' War. He became a public hero after Minden and has been immortalised in pottery and porcelain and upon the signs of numerous public houses throughout Britain. A transfer-printed* portrait occurs on Wedgwood creamware, the print by Sadler* probably taken from Richard Houston's engraving of 1760 after the painting by Sir Joshua Reynolds*. The portrait is first mentioned by Sadler in a letter to Wedgwood dated 27 March 1763.

Grand Plat Ménage
Term applied to a large centrepiece in the Leeds* catalogue of creamware. Wedgwood described such pieces as *plats de ménage* or *épergnes,* although the latter term was more often applied at the time to glass centrepieces. The *plat de ménage* stood in the centre of the dining table. A very elaborate example is illustrated as Plate 10 of the '1790' Catalogue* and surviving Queen's ware* examples are about 19in. high, terminating in a large pineapple*. The 'Large Epergne for the centre of the table' has two tiers of hanging pierced sweetmeat baskets and sugar containers, all of recognisable silver patterns.

GRAND PLAT MENAGE. Queen's ware pineapple *grand plat ménage,* table centre or *épergne* of the same design as no.52 in the '1790' Catalogue with three contemporary sweetmeat dishes of the style used with the centre. Height 19in. Unmarked. Wedgwood, c.1770-5.
Wedgwood Museum

GRANITE. Unusually large Wedgwood & Bentley white terracotta stoneware vase with sibyl finial and applied drapery swags decorated with evenly applied sponged blue-grey glazes ('Granite'). Height 18½in. c.1776.
Christie's, London

GRANULATED JASPER. Solid blue and white jasper 'Vase teapot', the body ornamented with Lady Templetown's *Domestic Employment* figures on a granulated or 'dimpled' ground. Height 8in. c.1787-95.
Wedgwood Museum

Granite
Variegated* ware mottled in imitation of greyish granite.

Grant, Duncan (1885-1978)
Scottish artist and theatre designer; studied at Westminster School of Art 1902-5, La Palette, Paris 1906-7, and for one term at the Slade School of Art. Grant showed six canvases at the Second Post-Impressionist Exhibition and was co-director of the Omega Workshops 1913-19. In 1916 he settled at Charleston, Sussex, with Vanessa Bell*, and remained there for the rest of his life. Duncan Grant painted his own designs on Wedgwood blanks and was commissioned to decorate a Queen's ware* dinner service for Kenneth (later Lord) Clark in 1932.

Granulated Jasper
A surface finish consisting of small 'dimples', providing a textured ground in contrast to the smooth finish of bas-relief* ornament. It is found on fine examples of jasper* produced during the lifetime of Josiah I and also, but rarely, on solid blue jasper made after 1860.

Gravy Cup, Gravy Warmer
See: Argyll

Great Newport Street, St Martin's Lane
See: Showrooms

Greatbatch, Daniel (fl.1768-85)
Principal vase modeller at Etruria, c.1768-85. Possibly the same Daniel Greatbatch whose baptism is recorded at Little Fenton in 1738. His relationship, if any, to William Greatbatch* is not known.

Greatbatch, Thomas (fl.1830-64)
Modeller at Etruria*. He modelled the tercentenary bust of Shakespeare* produced from the original bust by F.M. Miller* in 1864.

Greatbatch, William (1735?-1813)
Potter, modeller and block-cutter. Greatbatch was apprenticed to Whieldon* during the period of Wedgwood's partnership with him. In 1762 Greatbatch started his own pottery from which, for a period of a little more than two years, he supplied Wedgwood with large quantities of biscuit* ware. This business declined rapidly as Wedgwood's own production increased and probably ceased altogether c.1771, when Wedgwood began regularly to use his own impressed mark*. Greatbatch seems to have suffered heavy losses which finally ruined him. He was declared bankrupt in 1782. Thereafter he may have worked for other potters, including

GREATBATCH, William. Pair of creamware candlesticks, covered with green glaze of the Wedgwood type, moulded with leaves and owls' heads. The design of the candlesticks, shards of which have been recovered from the Greatbatch factory site, was copied from silver prototypes. Height 11in. Unmarked. Greatbatch, c.1765-70.
City Museum & Art Gallery, Stoke-on-Trent

Turner*, but by the end of August 1786 he was employed at Etruria*, making enamel colours and, later, apparently as general manager following the termination of Wedgwood's partnership with his cousin 'Useful' Thomas Wedgwood*, and the latter's removal to the Hill Works, Burslem. Greatbatch appears to have retired in 1807-8. His three sons, Hugh, William junior and Richard were all employed at the Etruria factory. The excavation and study of shards from the Greatbatch factory site conducted

GREATBATCH, William. Creamware teapots printed and enamelled with 'The Prodigal Son feasted on his Return' and 'The Prodigal Son in Misery' by Greatbatch. Unmarked. c.1780. *Norwich Castle Museum*

over a period of about twelve years by David Barker, Keeper of Archaeology at the City Museum & Art Gallery, Stoke-on-Trent, have revealed Greatbatch to be a potter of extraordinary virtuosity.

Greek Fret
Border pattern in which the lines, vertical and horizontal, are at right angles to each other. A meander* border.

Greek Street, Soho, London
See: Showrooms

Green Glaze
See: Glazes – *Green Glaze*

Green, Guy (fl.1750-99)
Partner with John Sadler* in Liverpool and possibly co-inventor of the transfer-printing* process applied to earthenware. His signature, 'Green, Liverpool', appears on some subjects. He continued to operate the firm of Sadler & Green for ten years after Sadler's death, finally retiring in 1799. Wedgwood's business connection with Guy Green was maintained at least until 1791.

GREEN, Guy. Queen's ware punch-pot decorated with a popular example of Guy Green's transfer-printing, 'The Smoking Party' *(verso* 'The Pipe and Punch Party'). Height 7½in. c.1775.
Norwich Castle Museum

Green, Thomas (fl.1760-80)
Painter employed by Wedgwood in 1770 and believed to be responsible, with Thomas Dimcock*, for the decoration of parts of dessert services painted with naturalistic flowers in purple monochrome, in the style generally attributed to James Bakewell*, some of which are marked with the enamelled letter 'G'.

Green Ware
Ware that is fully formed but not sufficiently dried to be ready for firing.

Greenaway. Kate (1846-1901)
English illustrator and writer of children's books erroneously credited, on the basis of style, with designs for Wedgwood plates and tiles* which are now identified as the work of Helen Miles*.

GREEN, Guy. Portrait, reputed to be of Guy Green, who continued to provide transfer-printed decoration to Wedgwood's Queen's ware for at least twenty years after Sadler's retirement. Attributed to William Dixon, c.1801. *Merseyside Museums*

GREENAWAY, Kate. Drawing from an Etruria shape book, of the 'Greenaway' umbrella stand for production in Majolica glazes. The design was registered in 1881. No evidence has been found to suggest that Kate Greenaway was responsible for designing it.
Wedgwood Museum

GRIFFIN. Black basaltes griffin candlestick with (later) gilded brass candleholder. Wedgwood experienced considerable difficulty in making the tips of the wings stick to the head of the figure in firing and was obliged, in 1771, to alter the design to fix them instead to the candleholder. Height 12¾in. c.1785.

Lady Lever Art Gallery, Port Sunlight

Griffin (Gryphon)

Fabulous animal having the head of an eagle and the body and hindquarters of a lion. It was believed by the Greeks to inhabit the region of Scythia and to guard its gold. The figure of a griffin, 13¼in. high, was produced as a candlestick* in black basaltes* in 1770. It was later reproduced in jasper* and has been reproduced in basaltes in the 19th and 20th centuries. The modelling is of extremely fine quality and, although often attributed to Josiah Wedgwood, is recorded as Hackwood's* work. Wedgwood is known to have modelled a chimaera* and it is likely that the two creatures were confused at the factory as well as in Meteyard's *Life of Wedgwood* (Vol.II, Plate 42). Boulton's* almost identical model in ormolu* was apparently copied from a model lent to him by Sir William Chambers* and it seems likely that Wedgwood's original model came from the same source.

Griffiths, John (fl.1776-79)
See: Lapidary

Griffiths, Ralph (1720-1803)

Ralph Griffiths, founder, proprietor and publisher of the *Monthly Review* and a member of the Wednesday Club*, spent many years of his life in America, principally in South Carolina and Philadelphia, where he was awarded his LL.D. degree. As Wedgwood's surviving letters testify, Griffiths's friendship with both Wedgwood and Bentley* was close and it may have been his residence in Turnham Green that persuaded Bentley to settle there.

GRIFFITHS, Ralph. Blue jasper dip portrait medallion. Oval height 3in. c.1790. *Wedgwood Museum*

It was Ralph Griffiths who broke to Wedgwood the distressing news of Bentley's final illness. Wedgwood produced a portrait medallion* of Samuel Griffiths, c.1790.

Griffiths, Thomas (fl. 1750-75)

Thomas Griffiths, like his elder brother Ralph*, had spent much of his youth in South Carolina and was commissioned by Wedgwood in 1767 to search for Cherokee* clay. Griffiths's journey was both arduous and hazardous and it was only with extreme difficulty that he was able to obtain some six tons of the clay at the enormous cost of about £500. His journal of the journey is in the Wedgwood archives.

Grignion (Grignon), Charles, the Elder (1717-1810)

Engraver; studied under Gravelot and Le Bas. Grignion worked with Hogarth on the engraving of some of his paintings, produced illustrations for Walpole's *Anecdotes of Painting* and engraved Cipriani's* illustrations to Sir William Chambers's* *Treatise on Civil Architecture* (see: Michelangelo Lamp). His engravings, after Michel-Vincent Brandoin*, of the *Pretty Mantua Maker* and *An Opera Girl of Paris* were reproduced on a Wedgwood Queen's ware* jug, c.1775. Versions of both engravings appear also on the creamwares of other potters. Grignion also engraved E.F. Burney's drawing of 'an artistic representation' of the objects in the Portland Museum (see: Portland Vase). Charles Grignion was the uncle of the painter of the same name.

Grotesques

French term for a form of ornament or decoration characterised by fantastic shapes based on a combination of human, plant (acanthus*) and animal forms. Grotesques are Roman in origin and first came to light when the frescoes in the Golden House of Nero were discovered during excavations at the end of the 15th century. The name reflects the fact that grotesques were first discovered below ground in what appeared to be a cave (*grotta*). Raphael used grotesques in his frescoes for the *loggie* of the Vatican in 1509 and they were especially popular with the *maiolica* potters, notably in Urbino. The fashion for grotesques continued in 17th-century Europe and they appear occasionally in designs of the 18th and 19th centuries during Renaissance revivals. Wedgwood's popular *Florentine** pattern is based on 16th-century grotesques.

Groundlaying
See: Processes of Manufacture; Powder Colours

GUYATT, Richard. Bone china plate from a dinner service designed by Guyatt for King's College Cambridge, 1952. The design, printed in black enriched with gold, incorporates ciphers of the royal founder and patrons of the college – Henry VI, Henry VII and Henry VIII – with representations of the Tudor Rose, True Lover's Knot and the dragon which appears in the stained glass of the Chapel. *Wedgwood Museum*

GUYATT, Richard. Queen's ware mug designed by Guyatt to commemorate the Coronation of HM Queen Elizabeth II, 1953. The design is printed in brown and heightened with pink (gold) lustre and gold. It was repeated in a black print with gold and also printed in gold on glazed basalt. Height 4in. 1953. *Author's collection*

Growan Stone
See: Cornish Stone

Gubbio Lustre
A brilliant iridescent lustre* developed by Maestro Giorgio Andreoli and applied from c.1498 to *maiolica* made at Deruta, Faenza, Castel Durante and (later) Gubbio. Best known is a ruby colour, but lighter colours also were employed, all probably derived from gold. Wedgwood attempted to reproduce this lustre in 1862-4 with the aid of Pietro Gaj*, and a further attempt was made in 1866, but without much success.
See also: De Morgan, William

Guyatt, Richard Talbot, CBE (b.1914)
Artist and designer; co-designer of the Lion and Unicorn Pavilion at the Festival of Britain, 1951; consultant designer to Wedgwood 1952-55 and 1967-70; Principal of the School of Graphic Design, Royal College of Art. For Wedgwood, Guyatt designed the prize-winning commemorative mug for the Coronation of Queen Elizabeth II, 1953, the Prince of Wales Investiture mug, 1969, the Royal Silver Wedding mug, 1973, the American Bicentennial mug, 1976, the Silver Jubilee mug, 1977 and the *Oranges and Lemons* lemonade set (for Liberty's, London), all on Queen's ware. A sporting mug in black and white jasper* was designed in 1966. The latter, issued in a limited edition of 500, features bas-relief* views of British sporting centres: St Andrews, Cowes, Brands Hatch, Twickenham, Wimbledon, Lord's, Epsom, Wembley and Henley. Guyatt also designed the decoration for a bone china* dinner service commissioned for King's College, Cambridge in 1952. Guyatt's commemorative work, with its strong heraldic inspiration, has been justly praised for its elegance in a souvenir market which has been widely condemned for its poor quality and vulgarity of design.

See: Colour Plate 49

H

Hackwood, Louis (Lewis) (fl.1775-1800)
Engraver at Etruria* around 1799, working on engraved borders for tablewares.

Hackwood Vine
An embossed vine leaf pattern produced in three versions on Wedgwood's first period bone china*, said to have been designed by William Hackwood*.

Hackwood, William (c.1757-1839)
Modeller for Wedgwood, 1769-1832; chief resident modeller of ornamental work at Etruria*. Hackwood was the 'ingenious boy' hired by Wedgwood in September 1769 and doubtfully permitted two years later to attempt a portrait medallion* of Master Crewe (brother of Emma Crewe*). Later he was to become indispensable, particularly in the work of adapting, remodelling and finishing busts*, bas-reliefs* and designs bought in London, and he was especially skilled in work of intricate detail. Many of Wedgwood's cameos*, although unattributed, are undoubtedly his work. Wedgwood wrote in 1774: 'Hackwood is of the greatest value & consequence in finishing fine small work, & of this kind we shall have enough to employ him constantly'. Many portrait medallions* are by his hand, including those of Josiah Wedgwood, George III* and Queen Charlotte*. His portraits of Garrick and Shakespeare were signed on the truncation but Wedgwood disapproved and Hackwood was instructed not to repeat this practice.

By 1776 Hackwood was working on important tablets and Wedgwood told Bentley* that he could do with 'half a dozn more Hackwoods'. Hackwood seems, indeed, to have been capable of fine modelling on almost any scale. Besides his work in re-modelling and finishing large busts obtained from Hoskins & Grant*, he did much restoration and remodelling to gems*, the foundation of jasper cameo work, and modelled many, perhaps all, of the designs supplied by Lady Templetown*, Lady Diana Beauclerk* and Emma Crewe.

HACKWOOD, William. Engraving from a portrait in oils, probably by a local Staffordshire artist, c.1820, in the City Museum & Art Gallery, Stoke-on-Trent.   *Photograph: Wedgwood*

HACKWOOD, William. Wedgwood & Bentley blue and white jasper portrait medallion of David Garrick modelled by Hackwood in 1777. Oval height 3½in. Examples of this portrait are signed on the truncation.   *Christie's, London*

It was perhaps inevitable that Hackwood should have acquired a high opinion of himself. In March 1777 when Hackwood was just twenty, Wedgwood complained that he was 'growing very extravagant in his prices' and that he did not 'find it possible to keep him reasonable upon the subject'. Evidently this difficulty was overcome and Hackwood settled down to be one of Wedgwood's most loyal and highly valued servants. In November 1778 he wrote to Bentley: 'Some of the tablets lately sent are finish'd very high by Hackwood at a considerable expence...you will easily percieve the difference in the hair, faces, fingers &c, & more palpably by all the parts capable of it being undercut* which gives them the appearance, & nearly the reality of models.'

In 1802, seven years after Josiah I's death, Byerley* wrote to Josiah II* expressing his fears that Josiah Spode II might be trying to entice Hackwood to work for him. Hackwood was not to be tempted: he remained with Wedgwood for an astonishing sixty-three years of service. His work for Wedgwood displays both vigour and fine detail. He was not in the true sense a creative artist, for very little of his work was original, but the best of his modelling – especially evident in his portraits of Edward Bourne* and Willet* – is unsurpassed by any of the artists regularly employed by Wedgwood.

An exhaustive catalogue of Hackwood's work is not possible. The list below includes all the authenticated work and much that is reliably attributed:

BUSTS (supplied by Hoskins and believed to have been re-modelled or finished by Hackwood).
Agrippina, 18in., 1774
Antinous, 22in., 1774
Antoninus Pius 22in., 1774
Augustus Caesar, 22in., 1774
Brutus, Lucius Junius, 25in., 1774
Brutus, Marcus Junius, 25in., 1774
Cato, 20in., 1774
Epicurus, 25in., 1774
Faustina, 20in., 1774
Germanicus, 16½in., 1774
Homer (2), 25in. and 15in. 1774
Horace, 20in., 1775
Jones, Inigo, 22in., 1774
Marcus Aurelius, 16½in., 1774
Minerva, 22in., 1774
Palladio*, 22in., 1774
Pindar, 25in., 1774
Plato, 25in., 1774
Seneca, 20in., 1774
Venus de Medici, 18in., 1774
Zeno, 25in., 1774

HACKWOOD, William. Wedgwood & Bentley blue jasper dip tablet, *Triumph of Bacchus,* modelled by Hackwood in 1776. 6⅜in. x 12⅛in.
Wedgwood Museum

BUSTS from models supplied by Veldhuysen*, 1779
Boerhaave, Hermann, 15in., c.1780
De Ruyter, Michel, 15in., c.1780
De Witt, Cornelis, 25in., c.1780
De Witt, Jan, 25in., c.1780
Grotius, Hugo, 20in., c.1780

PORTRAIT MEDALLIONS
D'Alembert, Jean le Rond. Attributed, after Pesez*, 1776
Anglesey, Henry Paget, 1st Marquis, c.1821
Bentley*, Thomas, three portraits 'al antique', attributed 1778-82
Bourne*, Edward, 1778
Queen Charlotte*, two portraits, both after I. Gosset*, c.1776
Darwin*, Erasmus, attributed, after Wright* of Derby, c.1780
Elers*, John Philip, 1777
Franklin, Benjamin, two portraits, one attributed, c.1779
Garrick, David, two portraits, one signed, 1777-9
George III*, at least four portraits after I. Gosset, 1774-7
Keppel, Augustus, 1st Viscount. Attributed, 1779
Louis XVI, c.1779
Mead, Richard, attributed, after Silvanus Bevan*, 1778
Penn, William, attributed, after Silvanus Bevan, 1779
Priestley*, Joseph, two portraits, both attributed, after Ceracchi*
Shakespeare*, William, signed, 1777
Temple, George, attributed, after G. Leader*, 1794
Voltaire*, signed, 1776
Wedgwood*, Josiah, signed, 1782
Willet*, William, 1776
Woodward, John, attributed, after Silvanus Bevan, 1778

BAS-RELIEFS
Birth of Bacchus, medallion, 5¾in. x 7½in., 'from the antique', 1776. No.118 in 1777 Catalogue
Birth of Bacchus, tablet 11in. x 23in. 'From Michelangelo's seal', 1779. No.206 in 1779 Catalogue
Dancing Hours. Flaxman's* models redraped, 1808
Slave Medallion, 1786
Triumph of Bacchus, tablet 6½in. x 14in. and 7½in. x 10in., no.201 in 1779 Catalogue
See also lists for Lady Diana Beauclerk and Lady Templetown.
Hackwood modelled a bulb pot* with arched top, and the Rustic candlesticks* (figures of *Autumn* and *Winter*) are attributed to him. He also worked with Josiah I, Josiah II, Webber* and William Wood* on the Portland vase*.
See: Colour Plate 50

Hades
God of the Underworld
See: Pluto

Hales, William, (fl.1790-1815)
Engraver. He executed engravings for the 12in. and 14in. oval dishes for the *Water Lily** pattern in 1807-8, part of the *Bamboo* (1808), *Hibiscus* (1806-8) and *Peony* (1808) patterns and the engravings for underglaze red *Water Lily* (c.1807-8).

Half Figures
Figures modelled at the front and flat at the back to enable them to be fixed to a wall or flat surface. Made in white terracotta* stoneware* and white jasper*, they were intended for the use of architects as an inexpensive substitute for carved marble ornament (Wedgwood to Bentley, 27 October 1778). Specimens are very rare and are notable for sharply detailed modelling.

HALF FIGURES. Pair of white terracotta biscuit half-figures of 'Herculaneum Dancers'. Probably trials. Height 10in. c.1769.
Wedgwood Museum

HALF TEAPOTS AND JUGS. A selection of white and drab smearglazed stoneware ('porcelain') half teapots and a Gothic jug made as travellers' samples. All c.1819-35. *Wedgwood Museum*

HAMILTON, Sir William. Blue and white jasper portrait medallion modelled by Joachim Smith and first produced in 1772. Oval height 7in. c.1772.
Formerly Eugene D. Buchanan Collection

Half Teapots and Jugs
Half teapots and jugs with fixed lids, cut vertically through the vessel just behind the handle, were made in smear-glazed* stoneware 'porcelain', and possibly in other bodies, c.1819-35, for the use of travelling salesmen. Bateman* wrote to the factory on 20 February 1819: 'please to prepare for JB jugs in halves 36s size new wt porcelain…all the patterns…' and on 20 August 1831 he ordered 'halves made of porcelain teapots with borders, selling patterns'.

Hall, Douglas (fl.1900-15)
Painter at Etruria* under the direction of John Goodwin*.

Hambleton
Wedgwood's frequent mis-spelling of 'Hamilton'*, which has led

a number of scholars to believe in the existence of another patron, 'Sir William Hambleton'. A close study of Wedgwood's references to 'Sir William Hambleton' makes it certain beyond doubt that such references are to Sir William Hamilton.

Hamilton, Sir William (1730-1803)
Grandson of the 3rd Duke of Hamilton; Knight of the Bath, 1772; Ambassador to the Court of Naples, 1764-1800; husband of Emma, Lady Hamilton, Nelson's mistress. Sir William took a close interest in the excavations at Herculaneum* and Pompeii* and made a notable collection of Greek and Italian vases which he sold in 1772 to the British Museum. The publication of his collection in 1766-76, in a four-volume work compiled by d'Hancarville* entitled *Antiquités étrusques, grecques, et romaines*, greatly

HAMILTON, Sir William. Plate 129, Vol. I, from d'Hancarville's *Collection of Etruscan, Greek and Roman Antiquities from the Cabinet of the Honble William Hamilton*, 1776, showing the composition copied for the decoration of Wedgwood & Bentley's First Day's Vases.
Photograph: Wedgwood

influenced a number of manufacturers. Wedgwood was lent prints from the volumes by Lord Cathcart* in 1768 before they were available in England and was later presented with a set by Sir Watkin Williams Wynn*.

These illustrations, and examination of the original vases in the British Museum, were the foundation of Wedgwood's success with his encaustic-painted* vases in the red-figure* style. Hamilton was free with valuable advice: 'Continue to be very attentive to the simplicity and elegance of the forms, which is the chief article', he told Wedgwood, 'You cannot consult the originals in the museum too often'. It was Hamilton, also, who urged Bentley* to rid the variegated* vases of 'offensive Gilding'*.

Wedgwood referred to Hamilton (frequently mis-spelled as 'Hambleton'*) as 'Our good, & very polite friend' and freely acknowledged his 'repeated favours'. In return, Wedgwood reproduced in black basaltes* and white terracotta* stoneware Joachim Smith's* fine portrait medallion* of Hamilton, c.1772 (later produced in jasper*). A superb and probably unique example of this portrait, in black basaltes with encaustic-painted ground is in the Beeson* collection, Birmingham Museum of Art, Alabama. A second, truncated, version of Hamilton's portrait was modelled c.1778, and a third portrait, remodelled and 'classicised' from the first, was included in the series of large (10in.) portraits of celebrities in 1779. Hamilton was also the recipient of one of the first jasper tablets* ornamented with Flaxman's *Apotheosis of Homer*ic bas-relief, the source of which was a calyx krater* previously in the Hamilton collection. Sir William wrote in July 1779: 'I have the pleasure of receiving safe your Delightfull Bas-relief of the Apotheose of Homer…it is far superior to my most sanguine expectation'.

A few years later, Hamilton bought the Barberini vase (see: Portland Vase*) from James Byres*, but sold it on to the Duchess of Portland in 1784. When, two years later, Wedgwood borrowed the vase in order to copy it, he naturally turned to Hamilton for advice about the propriety of restoring surfaces 'partially decayed by time', of making copies of single figures from the bas-relief ornament, and of making simple copies, cast in a single colour, for the use of students. In 1790, Hamilton was among the first to congratulate Wedgwood on his achievement in copying the vase, writing on 23 July. 'I am wonderfully pleased with it'.

Wedgwood's debt to Hamilton as a source of designs – for vase shapes and decoration, for tableware patterns (many of which were copied or adapted from borders on Hamilton's vases) and for bas-reliefs – is scarcely calculable.

Hammersley, Godfrey (fl.1906-49)
Painter at Etruria* and Barlaston*, at first under the direction of John Goodwin* and later of Victor Skellern*.

Hammersley, James Astbury (1815-69)
Painter, born in Burslem, who studied under James Baker Pyne (1800-1870). In 1844-5 Hammersley was either briefly employed at Etruria or supplying Wedgwood with models. He modelled the portrait medallions* of Queen Victoria and Albert, the Prince Consort, produced in 1844. Hammersley was later head of the Manchester School of Design, becoming first President of the Manchester School of Fine Arts 1857-61.

Hampton, Herbert (1862-1929)
Sculptor and painter; studied at Lambeth, Westminster and Slade Schools of Art and also in Paris. Hampton exhibited at the Royal Academy from 1886. Several of his models were reproduced as portrait medallions* in 1910-11, including those of Edward VII (two portraits), George V (two ·portraits) and Queen Mary (Consort of George V).

Hancock, John (1757-1847)
Ceramic decorator, born at Nottingham. He claimed to have invented the gold (pink) and platinum (silver, steel) lustres which were used at Spode's* factory in Stoke-on-Trent. He worked for Wedgwood from 1816 and died at Etruria in 1847.
See: Lustre Decoration

Hancock, Robert (1730-1817)
Engraver, probably a pupil of John Brookes at Battersea. Hancock, who worked at Battersea, Bow*, Worcester* and Caughley,

pioneered transfer-printing* on porcelain*. His two most widely known prints are probably a portrait of Frederick the Great* and *The Tea Party*, several versions of which appear, printed by Sadler & Green*, on Wedgwood Queen's ware*.
See: Ladies' Amusement, The; Sadler, John

Hand-basin
Also known as a washing bowl; an essential component of chamber* ware (toilet ware) made in a great variety of bodies and decoration during the 19th century. Basins were generally about 14-15in. in diameter. Their production was not discontinued until 1941.

Hand-embossed Queen's ware
See: Embossed Queen's ware

Handleing
The process of fixing handles on to cups, jugs, teapots, coffeepots and the like. The handles are made separately and are attached to the unglazed vessel by luting them into position, using slip* as an adhesive. In 1744 the fourteen-year-old Josiah Wedgwood was apprenticed to his eldest brother to be taught the 'Art of Throwing and Handling'.

Handles
The attribution of early, unmarked Wedgwood cream-colour wares* depends largely upon the detailed comparison of their shapes with those of later, marked objects. A few shapes of handles are characteristic of Wedgwood alone; others were used extensively by Wedgwood but are found also on the wares of other contemporary creamware potters. Identified as exclusive to Wedgwood are: first, a strap handle with overlapping leaves or scales and a neat foliate terminal; and second, a reeded strap handle of almost identical form but lacking the leaf or scale moulding. Handles similar to these shapes are known, notably from Leeds*, but they vary in detail. The scroll handle with the split terminal is common on early Wedgwood ware, and shards of this shape were recovered from the Whieldon-Wedgwood site at Fenton Vivian, but it appears to have been used in precisely the same form by other factories. The same applies to the cross-over strap handle with foliate upper terminals and curled lower terminals. Both of these handles, however, are useful indications of origin if combined with recognisable Wedgwood spouts* and knops*.
See also: Bail Handle

Handmaid to the Arts, The
A treatise, published by Robert Dossie in 1758 (reprinted 1764), containing many valuable instructions and recipes for the making and decoration of a variety of objects, including soft-paste* porcelain and papier mâché. A 110-page section dealt with enamel painting and the preparation of colours. In August 1765, while he was trying to perfect the gilding* of Queen Charlotte's* teaset, Josiah wrote to his brother John* instructing him to buy a copy of 'Vol 1st of the Handmaid of [*sic*] the Arts' and to send it to Burslem at once by coach.

Hangers
See: Sword Hilts

Hardening-on
The process of firing underglaze decoration on biscuit* ware prior to glazing. This firing, which is usually at a fairly low temperature (700°-800°C), burns out the oils in the pigment and fuses it sufficiently to adhere to the biscuit body.

Hard-paste porcelain
Correctly, true porcelain*, made from china clay and natural fusible rock. The ingredients of Chinese porcelain were kaolin, a local white china clay, and petuntse* *(pai-tun-tzu)*, feldspathic rock, a closely guarded secret discovered in Europe by Johann Friedrich Böttger at Meissen* in 1708-9.
See also: Soft-Paste Porcelain

Hardstones
See: Cameos; Variegated Wares

HANDLES.
1. Scroll handle with characteristic divided end, the commonest of early Wedgwood handles, shards of which have been excavated from the Whieldon-Wedgwood site at Fenton Vivian. Shown on a transfer-printed mug, c.1763-4.
E.N. Stretton Collection

2. Cross-over strap handle with foliate upper terminals and curled ends shown on a Wedgwood creamware teapot, c.1770. *Wedgwood Museum*

3. Strap handle, moulded with overlapping leaves or scales, with a neat foliate terminal, shown on a painted teapot, c.1768. The most easily identified of all Wedgwood handles, commonly used on teapots and mugs and not apparently copied by any contemporary manufacturer. *Author's collection*

Harrache, Thomas (fl.1750-75)
Jeweller, china seller and art dealer of Pall Mall, London. Wedgwood wrote from London to Bentley* in Staffordshire, 21 November 1768: '…at Harraches this afternoon, where we have amongst us spent near twenty pounds…Harrach has just return'd from Paris & has bro[ugh]t a great many fine things with him. I bid £30 for 3 pr of Vases, they asked £32 and wo[ul]d not abate a penny. There's spirit for you! – must we not act in the same way?'
See also: Raphael Ware

Harrison, John (1716-98)
Tradesman of Newcastle-under-Lyme and partner with Thomas Alders* and Josiah Wedgwood in a potworks at Cliff Bank, Stoke-on-Trent, making agate* and marbled knife-handles, tortoiseshell* and black wares, 'scratch blue' and saltglazed* ware, 1752-54.

Heath, John (fl.1830-77)
Engraver of Hanley who worked for Wedgwood, 1840-77.

Hebe
The goddess of youth, daughter of Zeus and Hera. She filled the cups of the gods before the arrival on Olympus of Ganymede*. Hebe married Hercules* when he became immortal. She was reputed to be able to renew the youth of the aged.
Wedgwood subjects:
Hebe 'on a pedestal'. Small statuette, no.37 in the 1787 Catalogue, modelled for production in jasper*
Hebe and the Eagle, medallion 7in. x 4½in., 1776. Moulded by Bedson* from a model in the Newdigate* collection. No.155 in 1777 Catalogue*.

Heberden, Dr William FRS FRCP (1710-1801)
Fashionable physician in London, who numbered among his patients Samuel Johnson and the poet William Cowper. Heberden was the first to describe *angina pectoris*. Josiah Wedgwood consulted him in April 1788 about recurrent headaches, when Heberden prescribed a 'blister' and a holiday. His son, also William, was physician in ordinary to George III* and Queen Charlotte*.

Hector
Eldest son of Priam* and Hecuba, husband of Andromache*, and hero of the Trojans. During the siege of Troy, Hector fought with the bravest of the Greeks and slew Patroclus, the friend of

Achilles*. Hector fled from Achilles but was killed and his body, tied to the chariot of Achilles, was dragged three times round the city walls. At the command of Zeus*, Achilles surrendered Hector's body to Priam.
Wedgwood subjects:
Three versions of the subject *Achilles dragging the body of Hector round the walls of Troy:*
1. Tablet, 6¼in. x 18¼in., modelled by Pacetti*, 1788
2. Medallion 3in. x 4⅝in., c.1790-5
3. Similar medallion, but reversed to face in the opposite direction and with notable alterations to the figures and composition (the heroic figure of Achilles dwarfs his horses). Probably copied from a cast from Tassie* after a gem by Pichler*
Priam kneeling before Achilles begging the Body of his Son Hector, also modelled by Pacetti in 1788, was produced as a tablet 6in. x 15½in. and in a larger size, length 22½in.

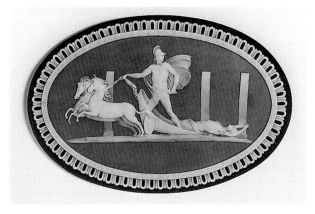

HECTOR. Green, lilac and white jasper dip medallion, *Achilles dragging the body of Hector round the walls of Troy.* Oval 3in. x 4⅝in. c.1792. *Manchester City Art Gallery*

Hedgehog Crocus Pot
A hollow receptacle realistically modelled in the form of a hedgehog, its bristly body pierced with holes large enough to admit a crocus bulb. It was accompanied by a shaped shallow tray to hold water.

Moss or soil was placed inside the hedgehog, which was then placed on the tray and planted with bulbs. Hedgehog crocus pots were made by Wedgwood in black basaltes* and green-glazed* Queen's ware* from c.1815 and are still reproduced in modern basalt.

Heels
Heels for women's shoes were first made in blue and white jasper* in 1959 at the request of Edward Rayne, Chairman of the luxury shoemakers H. & M. Rayne. The heels, which were made in both the low and high styles, were soon afterwards produced in other jasper colours and marketed successfully, although briefly, in both Britain and America. In frequent use they proved to be more decorative than practical.

Henning, John (1771-1851)
Modeller of portraits in wax and plaster, born at Paisley, Scotland. He moved to Glasgow in 1800 and made his reputation by modelling the portraits of many of the most celebrated inhabitants of the city. From 1811 he lived in London, where he completed models of the Parthenon and Phigaleian friezes from the Elgin marbles and a series of small copies in plaster of the Raphael cartoons, as well as portraits and larger friezes for architectural ornament. Many of his portraits were modelled from pencil drawings of his sitters and a number were reproduced in Tassie's* glass paste. It was probably through the Tassies that Henning first made contact with Wedgwood. Letters from Henning to Josiah II*, starting in 1811, are in the Wedgwood archives and he sent Wedgwood a list of his 'medallion portraits done from life'. The following were reproduced in jasper: James Grahame, 1813; Sir Samuel Romilly, 1813; Sir Walter Scott, 1813; Dugald Stewart, 1811; and the Duke of Wellington, 1813.

Henri Deux Ware
Properly, Saint-Porchaire ware. A very rare type of pottery made in France during the 16th century, principally during the reign of Henri II, decorated with grotesques*, arabesques* and strapwork* by inlaying with coloured clays. Fewer than one hundred specimens are known to have survived, and these were much sought by wealthy collectors during the 19th century and were copied or imitated at that time by a number of factories. Some of the best copies were made by Charles Toft* for Minton*. Toft was also chief modeller at Etruria*, 1877-88, and there is in the Wedgwood archives the description of a chess board decorated in the Henri Deux manner as an exhibition piece. This is generally attributed to Charles Toft. The border was designed by Walter Crane*, and the chessmen* (after Flaxman's* original models) were by Thomas Mellor*, who was evidently responsible for the inlaying of the bases of the figures.
See: Inlaid Ware

Henshaw (also Henshall), William (fl.1769-74)
Painter at the Chelsea Decorating Studio* who worked on the Frog* service. He is possibly the painter and engraver of that name, a pupil of Bartolozzi*, listed as an exhibitor at the Royal Academy from 1775.

Hepworth, Dame Barbara DBE (1903-92)
Sculptor; born in Yorkshire; studied at Leeds College of Art and the Royal College of Art, London; married first (1924), John Skeaping*, and second, Ben Nicholson. Both Hepworth and Skeaping submitted designs in the international competition for a contemporary vase* to celebrate the bicentenary of Wedgwood's birth in 1930.

Herculaneum
An ancient city of Campania in the shadow of Vesuvius, situated between Neapolis (Naples) and Pompeii*. It was captured by the Romans in 88 BC and partly destroyed by the earthquake of AD63. With Stabiae and Pompeii, it was buried by ashes and lava in AD79. Much of the site was afterwards built over and the old city is now some seventy feet below ground level. It was accidentally discovered in 1738 as the result of the sinking of a well. Many buildings have now been excavated and important works of art have been discovered. Sir William Hamilton* collected vases and other works recovered from this site. A Liverpool* creamware factory was named after it at the end of the 18th century. The design of Wedgwood's ornamental wares was strongly influenced by Herculaneum. Early in the 1770s Lord Lansdowne* granted

HEDGEHOG CROCUS POT. Black basaltes Hedgehog crocus pot on quatrefoil stand. Height 7in., length 11¼in. c.1820.
Christie's, New York

Wedgwood permission to copy some bas-reliefs* which had been made to his order after wall-paintings in the Villa dei Papyri (see: Herculaneum Pictures).

Herculaneum Pictures
A series of fourteen circular or oval plaques, thirteen of which were inspired by Roman wall-paintings at Herculaneum* (illustrated in *Le Antichita di Ercolano Esposte*, Vol.I, Naples, 1757) but moulded directly from a set of casts in the possession of the Marquis of Lansdowne* in 1770. They are listed as nos. 51-65 (omitting no.63) in all of Wedgwood's Catalogues of ornamental wares from 1773 and were made in white terracotta* or black basaltes*, sometimes with painted grounds and usually with moulded frames* of the same composition, which might be painted or gilded. From 1778 they were available also in jasper*. These plaques were intended 'for the decoration of large Halls and Staircases', and the frames were described as 'rich compartments of the same material, modelled and burnt together with the Bas-reliefs'.

Herculaneum Pictures were reproduced in solid blue and white and solid green and white jasper throughout the 1870s and examples are frequently mistaken for 18th-century pieces.

HEPWORTH, Dame Barbara. Original drawing by Barbara Hepworth for her entry in the international competition for a vase to commemorate the bicentenary of Josiah I's birth. *Wedgwood Museum*

HERCULANEUM PICTURES. White terracotta stoneware biscuit plaque, *A Female Centaur and Bacchante* in integral moulded fluted frame. Diameter 16in. Unmarked. Wedgwood & Bentley, c.1772.

Victoria & Albert Museum, London

The list of Herculaneum pictures is as follows (measurements include frames):

Dancing Nymph (holding tambourine)
Dancing Nymph (holding cymbals)
Dancing Nymph (with tray of figs)
Dancing Nymph (with branch and sceptre)
Dancing Nymph (holding veil)
Dancing Nymph (with tray)
} Nos. 51-6

All Ovals
10in. x 7¾in.

Centaur (with Bacchante* on his back)
Centaur (female, with child on her back)
Centaur (teaching Achilles*)
} Nos. 57-9
diameter 11½in.

Polyphemus, no.60, diameter 11½in.
Marsyas and Young Olympus, no.61, diameter 11½in.
Papyrius and His Mother, no.62, diameter 11½in.
Bacchanalian Figure (male dancer), no.64, diameter 11½in.
Bacchanalian Figure (male dancer), no.65, diameter 11½in.

Hercules

Greek Herakles. Hercules was the son of Zeus* by Alcmena, the wife of Amphitryon. Hera (see: Juno), always jealous of her husband's amours with mortal women, sent serpents to destroy Hercules in his cradle, but he slew them by crushing them in his hands. In his youth he was instructed in the martial arts, and became renowned for his great physical strength. He killed a huge lion which had wrought havoc among the flocks and herds of Mount Cithaeron, and from this time wore its skin, and sometimes a helmet in the form of its head and upper jaw. Driven mad by Hera, he slew his own children by Magara, as well as the children of his half-brother. In his grief he consulted the oracle of Delphi who told him to serve Eurystheus for twelve years, after which he was to become immortal.

The twelve Labours of Hercules, undertaken at the behest of Eurystheus, have often been depicted in art. The most frequently represented is his fight with the Nemean lion, which he killed by tearing its jaws apart. He exhausted the Erymanthean boar, which he had to capture alive, by chasing it through the snow and then carrying it off in a net. A popular subject has been his seizure of the Golden Apples of the Hesperides, which had been given to Hera at her wedding and entrusted to the care of the Hesperides (the daughters of Atlas* and Hesperis) and the dragon, Ladon, on Mount Atlas. It was during his journey to find the Golden Apples that Hercules, to persuade Atlas* to fetch them for him, shouldered the heavens in his place. Another labour often depicted is his binding of

HERCULES. Wedgwood & Bentley solid blue and white jasper medallion of *Hercules Farnese.* Oval height 7¼in. *Wedgwood Museum*

the great dog Cerberus, the fearsome triple-headed guardian of the portals of Hades, to transport him to the upper world.

When these labours were completed, Hercules became ill and again consulted the Delphic oracle, which prophesied that he would be restored to health if he would serve for three further years. He became the servant of Omphale*, Queen of Lydia, and legend tells of a period of intimacy with her, during the course of which he became effeminate, and Omphale wore his lion-skin and carried his club. When Hercules died a cloud carried him to Mount Olympus amid peals of thunder, where he became reconciled to Hera and married to her daughter Hebe*.

In works of art Hercules is usually represented with a lion's skin and a large club. In Rome he was sometimes connected with the Muses*, and hence, like Apollo*, was called Musagetes (leader of the Muses).

Wedgwood subjects:
Hercules, bust invoiced by Flaxman* (senior?), 1782

HERCULES. Wedgwood & Bentley grey-blue and white jasper oval plaque, *Judgement of Hercules.* 9⅞in. x 13in. c.1778. The ormolu frame may be from Matthew Boulton's Soho workshop.

Wedgwood Museum

HERCULES. Solid blue and white jasper medallion, *Hercules and Cerberus.* Oval 9in. x 6¼in. c.1870 (first catalogued 1777).

Christie's, New York

HERCULES. Basalt figure of *Hercules* modelled by Donald Brindley in 1974. Height 8in.   *Wedgwood Museum*

Hercules, figure invoiced by Theodore Parker*, 1769

Hercules, figure modelled by Donald Brindley*, 1974

Hercules, medallion 4in. x 3¼in. No.149 in 1777 Catalogue

Hercules Farnese, medallion height 7¼in., from a model in the Newdigate* collection. No.157 in 1777 Catalogue

Farnesian Hercules, medallion 4in. x 3in. No.42 in 1773 Catalogue*

Hercules and Antaeus, encaustic-painted* framed circular plaque, diameter 13⅝in., c.1774

Hercules and Theseus Supporting the World, or The Power of Union, medallion 3½in. x 2¾in. No.75 in 1773 Catalogue

Hercules Binding Cerberus, oval medallion 8in. x 6in. From a model supplied by Flaxman, 1775. No.104 in 1777 Catalogue

Hercules in the Garden of the Hesperides, tablet 5½in. x 17in., 'From a beautiful Etruscan vase in the collection of Sir William Hamilton, now in the British Museum'. Modelled by John Flaxman*, 1785. No.275 in 1787 Catalogue. A bas-relief subject used also on fine vases

Hercules in the Garden of the Hesperides, encaustic-painted subject on obverse of First Day's* vases, 1769, copied from Hamilton's Antiquities, Vol.I, Plate 129

Hercules Strangling the Lion, oval medallion 8in. x 6in. From a model supplied by Flaxman, 1775. No.103 in 1777 Catalogue

Infant Hercules with the Serpent, figure 20in. x 23in. Model obtained from Hoskins & Grant*, 1770

Judgement of Hercules, tablet 11in. x 15in. No.69 in 1773 Catalogue

Young Hercules, medallion 2in. x 2¼in. No.26 in 1773 Catalogue

Young Hercules, medallion 4in. x 6¼in. No.224 in 1779 Catalogue

Among the medallions supplied to Catherine II* is one listed as *Hercules and Thetis,* presumably an error for *Hercules and Theseus* (above) or possibly *The Birth of Achilles** (Achilles and Thetis).

See also: Meleager

Hermes

See: Mercury

Hero and Leander

Hero was a priestess of Aphrodite in Seatus, Leander a youth of Abydos who was in love with her. Every night Leander swam across the Hellespont to visit his beloved until he was over-whelmed by a sudden storm and drowned. Next day his body was washed ashore and found by Hero, who took her own life by throwing herself into the sea. A Wedgwood tablet in two sizes, 17in. x 8in. or 20in. x 9in., is listed as no.210 in the 1779 Catalogue.

HERRING DISH. Pearl ware herring dish decorated with the *Mared* pattern in underglaze blue, shown with a shell-edge strawberry dish in the same pattern. Herring dish 6½in. x 11¾in. c.1785-90.

Byron & Elaine Born Collection

Herring Dish

A Queen's ware* or Pearl* ware dish of rectangular form with a moulded centre design of one or two herrings and usually a simple hand-painted or printed border. Length about 11in. First made in the last quarter of the 18th century.

Hesiod

One of the earliest of the Greek poets, whose name is frequently associated with that of Homer*, although he lived about a century later. His *Theogony* gives an account of the origin of the world and the birth of the gods. The mention in Wedgwood's letters of 'Homer and Hesiod', a name he gave originally to the bas-relief* now known as *The Apotheosis of Homer*,* has given rise to the misapprehension that a separate bas-relief depicting 'The Crowning of Hesiod' exists.

Hindshaw, M. (fl.1900-20)

Designer and paintress, associated with Alfred and Louise Powell* in the handcraft department at Etruria*. Some of her work was included in the Arts and Crafts Exhibition held in London in 1916.

Hinks, J. & Son

Birmingham metal manufacturers associated with Wedgwood in the late 1870s in the making of oil lamps for domestic lighting. Wedgwood made the oil reservoir in Queen's ware* or jasper* on a pedestal foot, the Queen's ware usually printed and enamelled with designs of figures and flowers in the aesthetic* style of the period. Hinks made the metal parts, the wick holder, shade and chimney carrier.

HIPPOCAMPI. Rectangular Queen's ware plaque painted by Emile Lessore with a scene of *Venus* in her car drawn by dolphins and hippo-campi. Signed. c.1863.   *Photograph: Wedgwood*

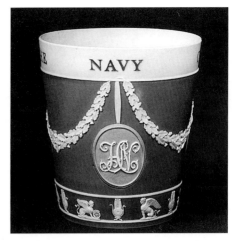

HIPPOCAMPI. Black basaltes volute-krater vase painted in encaustic colours with the figure of *Venus* riding on the backs of two hippocampi. Height 11¾in. c.1785-95. *Mr & Mrs Samuel Laver Collection*

Hippocampi
Sea horses, usually depicted in conjunction with Poseidon (Neptune*), Nereids* and Tritons*. Under the influence of the Renaissance grotesque* the hippocampus was sometimes given a dolphin's* tail to replace its hindquarters and fish-like fins instead of fore hoofs. Hippocampi exist as figures in Chelsea* porcelain and appear on encaustic-painted* Wedgwood vases, on the *Nereids* tablet* variously attributed to Webber* or Pacetti*, c.1790, and on other painted pieces of the 19th century.

Hippocrates (c.460 - c.357 BC)
The most celebrated physician of antiquity, born on the island of Cos. His best known work is the *Aphorisms,* which was widely disseminated in both ancient and medieval times. He died at the age of 104. A bust, supplied by Hoskins & Grant* in 1775, was reproduced in black basaltes.

HN MONOGRAM. Dark-blue jasper dip beaker, or 'drinking can', ornamented with two lilac and white jasper cameos showing *Neptune* and the monogram 'HN'. c.1798-1801. *Manchester City Art Gallery*

Hispano-Moresque Designs
Lustre* designs by John Goodwin*, c.1925, painted principally in copper or pink lustre on the cane coloured body*. This style of decoration was intended to imitate the lustre-painted tin-glazed earthenwares produced in Spain, especially between the 15th and 18th centuries.

HN Monogram
The monogram 'HN' is found on one of two applied medallions ornamenting a three-colour jasper dip* cylindrical beaker. The second medallion bears the figure of Neptune*. The beaker is ornamented with acorn and oak-leaf swags (representing the oak timbers of the navy) and a band of 'Egyptian' reliefs around the foot. The inscription around the rim, 'THE NAVY OF BRITAIN', is inlaid in blue. The ornament suggests a celebration of Nelson's victory at the battle of the Nile in August 1798 but no record of the manufacture of this beaker has been found for a date earlier than 1801.

Hoadley, Thomas (1793-1888)
Engraver of 40 Charles Street, Hanley (1834) who worked for Wedgwood, 1824-47. He supplied engravings also to Ridgway's.

Hodgkiss, James (1867-1937)
Artist and designer at Etruria*, c.1900-23, under the direction of John Goodwin*, with whom he was closely associated. With Goodwin,

HISPANO-MORESQUE DESIGNS. Cane coloured body dish hand-painted in purple (gold) lustre with a design by John Goodwin in the Hispano-Moresque style introduced in 1925. Diameter 12⅜in. *Author's collection*

HODGKISS, James. Bone china vase, shape 2034, decorated with figures of mice, printed and enamelled on a powder-blue ground and covered with mother-of-pearl glaze. Designed by James Hodgkiss, c.1916. Height 8in. *Wedgwood Museum*

HOLLAND, Arthur Dale. Bone china plate from a dessert service painted by Holland with fish in naturalistic colours within a powder-colour border and beaded gilt rim. Diameter 8in. c.1930
Wedgwood Museum

and George Adams (successor to William Burton* as resident chemist), Hodgkiss was responsible for the development of powder colours*. He also designed patterns, notably of birds and landscapes, for the decoration of bone china* tablewares and ornamental pieces. The latter included a long line of bowls and vases decorated with gold-printed Oriental designs over a powder blue ground and also patterns of flowers, animals and birds in white reserves against powder blue. Hodgkiss painted a series of bone china dessert sets decorated with birds in natural landscapes. His work is often signed.
See also: Fairyland Lustre; Ordinary Lustres

Holdship, Richard and Josiah (fl.1740-70)
Engravers; brothers and part-owners of the Worcester* porcelain factory from 1751-59. In 1764 Richard Holdship moved to Derby*, where he revealed the recipe for soaprock* porcelain and others of Worcester's secrets. Josiah Wedgwood's Commonplace Books* contain evidence that he consulted the brothers about the manufacture of porcelain and it is likely that Wedgwood's cousin and partner in the 'Useful' Works, Thomas Wedgwood*, worked for the Holdships at Worcester before joining Josiah in 1759 at Burslem.

Holland, Arthur Dale (1896-1979)
Painter in the decorating department at Etruria*, 1910-35 and 1941-44, under the direction of John Goodwin* and Victor Skellern*. Holland was a painter of considerable versatility, producing fine (sometimes signed) decoration, notably of fish, fruit or flowers, on bone china* dessert ware, sporting subjects on Queen's ware*, *Cupids* after Bartolozzi*, and animals reserved against powder colour* grounds. He was also responsible for enamelling Palliser's* 'Audubon Birds' and the figures modelled by Kathleen Goodwin*.

Holloway, John (fl.1870-90)
Painter at Etruria*, working under the direction of Thomas Allen* in the late 1870s. Little of his work has been identified with certainty, but it includes paintings of animals and birds and some fine, freely-painted continuous seascapes on Queen's ware* vases.
See: Colour Plate 51

Hollow Ware
The collective name in the Potteries for cups, bowls, teapots, coffeepots, vegetable dishes, soup tureens and all similar objects designed for holding liquids.

Holmes, Sir Charles (1868-1936)
Landscape painter, etcher, designer and art-historian and critic; born in Preston, Lancashire; educated at Eton and Brasenose College, Oxford; editor of *The Burlington Magazine*, 1903-09; Slade Pro-

HOLLOWAY, John. Pair of Pearl ware snake-handle vases painted with continuous seascapes by Holloway. Height 14¼in. c.1876.
Mr & Mrs David Zeitlin Collection

fessor at Oxford, 1904-10; Director of the National Portrait Gallery, 1909-16, and of the National Gallery, 1916-28. Holmes was knighted in 1921 and made KCVO, 1928. He was Vice-President of the Royal Watercolour Society and the author of a large number of books on art subjects. This highly distinguished public figure was the choice of Josiah V* to be art consultant to Wedgwood in 1930. The appointment lasted only two years but it was one of considerable importance for its influence on Wedgwood's design policy in the 1930s. Holmes was interested in contemporary design and had useful connections with young artists and designers. Among those

WEDGWOOD "SUN-BIRDS" (AK 8723)

This design by Sir Charles J. Holmes is modernist in the best sense. Painted under the glaze, on Wedgwood "Queensware," the design is as durable as the ware itself.

HOLMES, Sir Charles. Advertising leaflet for *Sun-Birds* pattern, printed in black and painted underglaze in dark-red on Pearl ware, designed by Sir Charles Holmes. 1931. *Wedgwood Museum*

HOMER. Black basaltes bust of Homer. Height 13⅞in. c.1790.
Formerly Buten Museum

whom he introduced to Wedgwood were Wyndham Goodden and Harry Trethowan*. Holmes also designed some tableware patterns but only two have so far been identified: *Sunbirds* and *Aegean.*

Holmes-Wedgwood Lampshade
Pendant lampshades were made in the Lavender coloured body* in 1937 to fit a patent fixture. They are marked: 'The Holmes-Wedgwood shade Patent No.326610 WEDGWOOD MADE IN ENGLAND.

Holy-Door Marble
One of the crystalline* or variegated* bodies of mixed coloured clay or slip* in imitation of natural stones. It is first mentioned in a letter from Wedgwood to Bentley* dated June 1768, but its precise colour is not known. The name has been frequently misused to describe a variegated lustre* introduced about 1809.

Homer
Greek epic poet, whose dates and birthplace are both disputed. He is generally regarded as the author of the *Iliad,* which recounts the exploits of Greek warriors during the Trojan war, and the *Odyssey,* concerned with the adventures of Odysseus (Ulysses*) during the course of his erratic journey homewards to Ithaca after the fall of Troy. Nothing is certainly known about Homer's life and antecedents, but tradition places him about 950 BC and regards him as both blind and poor in old age. Most representations of Homer seem to be based on the bust in the Naples Museum, but this, itself, is conjectural.

Wedgwood obtained a cast of this bust from Hoskins & Grant* in 1774 and it was produced in black basaltes* in two sizes (height 25in. and 15in.). A miniature bust (about 4½in. high) was modelled by 1779 and produced in basaltes, jasper* and glazed white terracotta*, all on basaltes plinths. Flaxman's *Apotheosis of Homer*,* first produced as a bas-relief for a tablet* in 1778 and subsequently adapted as ornament for the Homeric* vase, was inspired by an illustration in Hamilton's* *Antiquities* (Vol.III, Plate 31). A portrait medallion* of Homer was among Wedgwood's earliest and was made both framed* and unframed in black basaltes before 1773.

Homeric Vase
See: Apotheosis of Homer

Honey-Buff
Cane-coloured Queen's ware* body made especially for Heal's store in Tottenham Court Road, London, in 1930, probably at the instigation of Harry Trethowan*. A series of handpainted patterns was commissioned for the decoration of the body, all supplied exclusively to Heal's. A slightly paler body, named Champagne* was introduced for other customers and these two colours continued in production until 1941. Both were superseded by the cane coloured body* produced in 1956.

Honey Pot
Honey pots in the beehive* shape were first produced by Wedgwood c.1800, and a remarkable model of a beehive honey pot

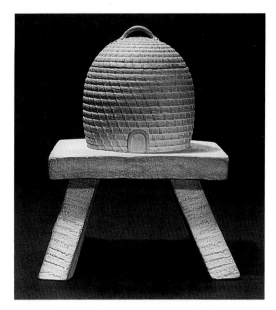

HONEY POT. Cane beehive bench honey pot. Height 7in. A sketch of this piece appears in the Oven Book for 8-15 January 1802. It was evidently in production for at least fifty years, but few examples have survived
Judge J. Trabue Collection

on a bench is sketched in an Oven Book* for 1802. This 'Beehive Bench' was continued in production for at least fifty years but – probably because of its excessively vulnerable shape – surviving examples are rare, The beehive honey pot (without bench) has continued to be produced in the 20th century and examples of various periods, some with fixed stands, are known in Cane* ware, Lavender coloured body*, and Queen's ware* with Green glaze, Yellow glaze or Dysart glaze (see: Glazes).

Honeysuckle Border
See: Anthemion

Honourable Society of Bucks
Society whose mottoes were 'Industry Produces Wealth' and 'Freedom with Innocence'. The members of the Society were apparently dedicated to 'Nimrodism', the principles of which, although hard to define, were generally 'to promote all good Fellowship, Freedom of

HONOURABLE SOCIETY OF BUCKS. Creamware mug transfer-printed in black with the arms of the Society of Bucks. Sadler's signature appears below the arms. Height 4¾in. *E.N. Stretton Collection*

HOOKAHS. Bell hookahs: *(left)* cane ware ornamented with figures of the *Muses* after Flaxman, height 7½in.; *(right)* blue jasper dip ornamented with 'Acanthus and Bell' and floral scroll reliefs, height 10¼in. Both c.1800.   *Wedgwood Museum*

Conversation, Innocent Mirth and every social Virtue'. The pursuit of these admirable objectives was evidently accompanied by the consumption of great quantities of wine. The Society of Bucks flourished in Liverpool, where Bentley* was a member, and a Wedgwood creamware mug transfer-printed* in black with the arms of the Society was produced in 1764.

Hookahs
Wedgwood & Bentley made their first attempt on the Turkish market in 1773 when Josiah reported 'setting our people at the ornmental works of making a few each of the Turkish articles' and it is likely that Sir Robert Ainslie* supplied Wedgwood with models of hookahs in 1777. Tobacco bowls were in production by March 1781 but no specific reference to the production of hookahs before 1800 has been found. Hookahs were known also as chillums.

Hooker, Sir Joseph Dalton (1817-1911)
English botanist: son of Sir William Jackson Hooker; director of the Royal Botanic Gardens at Kew in succession to his father; intimate of Charles Darwin*. Sir Joseph made many journeys of exploration and his published works are numerous. He was an enthusiastic collector of Wedgwood and chose a combination of jasper* and marble for the memorial to his father on the north wall of Kew parish church. Designed by Sir Reginald Palgrave* in 1911, the memorial included a large blue and white jasper portrait medallion* by Frank Bowcher surrounded by four shaped plaques of green and white jasper ornamented with ferns. The latter were designed by Matilda Smith, an illustrator for the *Botanical Magazine*.

Hope, Thomas (1769-1831)
Collector, author and designer of furniture in the 'Greek' and 'Egyptian' styles; born in Amsterdam of a Scottish family of bankers who had settled in Holland towards the end of the 17th

century. Hope embarked in 1787 on a Grand Tour lasting eight years, studying architecture, design and costume, collecting antiquities and sketching buildings in France, Italy, Spain, Germany, Greece, Egypt, Syria and Turkey. In 1799 he bought a house in Duchess Street, London, which he filled with his collections, especially of marbles, sculpture and costly furniture. He commissioned chimneypieces* for the house from John Flaxman* and was a patron also of Canova* and Thorwaldsen. In 1807 Hope published (anonymously) *Household Furniture and Interior Decoration*. He was one of the original subscribers to Wedgwood's Portland vase* and his copy is now in the Wedgwood Museum*, Barlaston.

Horace (65-8 B.C)
Quintus Horatius Flaccus, Roman poet; celebrated for his *Odes, Satires, Epodes* and *Epistles*, the last being considered the most perfect of Horatian poetry. Wedgwood produced two busts of Horace: the first, about 22in. high, appears in the 1773 Catalogue*; the second, 15in. high, was supplied by Hoskins & Grant* in 1775 and finished by Hackwood*.

Horae
Spirits in Greek and Roman mythology personifying the Seasons, later identified with the Hours. The daughters of Luna (Selene – see: Diana), they are generally represented in art carrying fruit and flowers and are sometimes depicted with butterfly's wings. A set of four jasper* medallions of the *Horae* was issued by Wedgwood c.1785. They are usually catalogued as the *Four Seasons* or even the *Four Winds*, but in art the latter are usually depicted as male. See also: Dancing Hours

Horne, Matthew (fl.1750-76)
Josiah Wedgwood I frequently received applications for employment from workmen who had been at other factories, but these were rarely in writing. The precise date of the application from Matthew Horne of Lambeth, South London, is uncertain but it may reasonably be placed towards the end of December 1775, when Wedgwood was at last successfully completing his long series of experiments to perfect jasper* and had abandoned his Public Experimental Work*. Nothing more is known of Horne, nor is much information available about porcelain manufacture in Lambeth, although there is evidence of porcelain production at nearby Vauxhall. There is little doubt that Horne's claims were exaggerated, but they were probably not entirely unfounded.

'Sir', he wrote, 'I hear they are all going to make China in Staffordshire, which I am afraid will be of hurt to some. I at last by long practice, have found out the best body in this kingdom it will make figures or ornaments four or five feet high without supports or props. It will make dishes any [size] it workes allmost as well as your cream color clay it burns quite Transparent [*sic*] and will be maid very cheap. I have three Glazes that sute it very well. But have no where to [burn] them but in a house fire – I saw your man Gorge he promised to come to Lambeth – I tould him I had something to send to you as he Did not come I could not tell how to send them to you – This again I whall [will] to you and no One Else if you will avail me with a little Monney. – So you may understand that when my Brother John and Taylor Broke I was bound for some Monney for him which I must pay soon. I am certain that if you would see the Troyals [trials] you would approve

HORAE. Set of four blue jasper dip on solid blue-grey jasper oval medallions ornamented with figures of the four *Horae: (left to right)* 'Summer', 'Winter', 'Autumn' and 'Spring'. c.1785-90.
Dr & Mrs Alvin M. Kanter Collection

HOSKINS & GRANT. Four black-painted plaster busts on waisted rectangular socles: *(left to right)* Ben Jonson, Matthew Prior, John Fletcher and William Congreve. These are possibly the original plasters supplied by Hoskins & Grant in 1775.
Wedgwood Museum

of it. I Don't want to make any Troyals but make a whole Kiln which I can as easy and certain as a Kiln of Staffordshire ware if you please I will take some things and show them to Mr Bentley* and you will have [h]is opinion of it. If you have a mind to Do Anything in it I will come down as soon as possible and worke for you half a year without wages and then if you find it to answer I shall leave it to you what I deserve yearly, and hope I shall be with you for Life. Your answer to this by return...will greatly oblige, Sir, Your humble servant to command, Matthew Horne'.

On 30 December Wedgwood sent a reply to Bentley: 'Please tell Mr Horne that our experimental work is over...it does not suit with my business to begin upon Porcelain at present.'

Hoskins & Grant
Hoskins & Oliver

Not much is known of the early life or antecedents of James Hoskins, but he held the position of moulder and caster in plaster to the Royal Academy from its foundation in 1768 until his death in 1791. He was, until 1774, in partnership with Samuel Euclid Oliver at premises in St Martin's Lane, London. Oliver was evidently a modeller since he exhibited a wax portrait* of a nobleman at the Royal Academy in 1769. He may have died in 1774, for in that year Hoskins took Benjamin Grant into partnership. Grant (fl.1760-1809) was a plaster figure-maker for the Royal Academy. Towards the end of his life Grant was in financial difficulties and applied three times to the Academy for relief. On each occasion he was granted the sum of ten guineas.

As Hoskins & Oliver the firm supplied Wedgwood & Bentley with both moulds and casts of figures from 1770 and as Hoskins & Grant supplied busts from 1774 until 1779. Most of their models were undoubtedly cast 'from the antique', or from more recent work in marble, bronze or, occasionally, ivory, but some were probably modelled especially for their use. Hoskins and his partners charged high prices for their moulds and casts. Oliver's method, according to Josiah, was 'to take a mould, then prepare that mould & cast a plaster one out of it, from which he makes what sho[ul]d be a working mould for us, & this long process makes them come dear.' He suggested that Bentley try to buy the original moulds of any busts cast for Wedgwood & Bentley for about half a guinea to one guinea each, giving Oliver a decent profit and yet allowing Wedgwood to make his own block mould* and working moulds as he required them. Eventually it was agreed that Wedgwood & Bentley should buy 'Plaster Casts Prepar'd to Mould from': that is, full plaster copies of busts – roughly the equivalent of block moulds – from which Wedgwood could take his own (intaglio*) working moulds. These casts from Hoskins were at first finished with some form of varnish, presumably to lend them added strength, but this practice was discontinued when

it was found that it greatly complicated the business of taking clay moulds from them. Wedgwood's baked fireclay moulds lasted far longer than any in plaster of Paris.

It was an important aspect of all of Wedgwood's transactions with suppliers of plaster casts that his business was, in some respects, directly in competition with theirs. From the moulds he obtained from them, Wedgwood proposed to make reproductions in a far more attractive and durable form than anything reproduced in plaster. Not only was Wedgwood's business certain to interfere with the sale of plaster busts and figures, but it might in the near future make them unsaleable and reduce the work of the plaster cast makers to mould-making. Although Hoskins must undoubtedly have valued his business with Wedgwood, he was not blind to the dangers of supplying him and he kept his prices, as Wedgwood complained, 'horrid dear'. From about 1775 Wedgwood began to make his own casts and moulds.

Plaster casts or moulds of the following were supplied to Wedgwood & Bentley by Hoskins and his partners between 1770 and 1779:

FIGURES
Bacchus*, height 11in., 1770. After Sansovino
Ceres*, height 17in., 1779. Almost certainly the figure invoiced as 'Chrispagnia'
Ganymede*, height 12in., 1770
Infant Hercules* with the Serpent, 20in. x 23in., 1770
Mercury* (seated, tying his sandal), height 20in., 1779. After Pigalle*
Morpheus*, length 25in., 1770
Polyphemus*, 19in. x 16in., 1770
Venus* (seated) height 20in., 1779. After Pigalle
Zingara*, height 17in., 1779

BUSTS
Joseph Addison, 15in., 1775
Agrippina, 16½in. , 1774
Alexander, 1779
Antinous, 22in. 1774
Augustus 22in., 1774
Antoninus Pius, 22in., 1774
Ariadne, 10-11½in., 1779 (attributed)
Bacchus, 10-11½in., 1779 (attributed)
Francis Bacon, 18in., 1774
Francis Beaumont, 15in., 1775
Robert Boyle, 18in., 1774
Cato, 20in., 1774
Geoffrey Chaucer, 15in., 1775
Cicero, 20in. and 15in., 1774

HOT-WATER PLATE. Queen's ware hot-water plate enamelled in brown with *Oak* pattern no. 343. The base has a double wall and the dish is moulded with channels and two pockets for gravy.

Formerly Buten Museum

Cleopatra, 10-11½in., 1775, (attributed)
William Congreve, 15in., 1775
Democritus, 15in., 1775
Demosthenes, 22in., 1775
John Dryden, 15in., 1775
Epicurus 25in., 1774
Faustina. 20in., 1774
John Fletcher, 15in., 1775
Galen, 15in., 1775
David Garrick, 1779
Germanicus, Young, 16½in., 1774
William Harvey, 1775
Hippocrates, 15in., 1775
Homer, 25in., 1774
Horace, 15in., 1775
Ben Jonson, 18in. and 15in., 1774
Inigo Jones, 22in. 1774
Julia, 15in., 1775
John Locke, 15in., 1775
Madonna, 15in., 1775
Marcus Aurelius, Young, 16½in., 1774
Marcus Aurelius Antoninus, 25in., 1774
Marcus Brutus, 25in., 1774
Marcus (Junius) Brutus, 25in., 1774.
Mark Antony, 10-11½in., 1775 (attributed)
Mercury*, 1779
John Milton, 15in., 1775
Minerva*, 22in., 1774
Sir Isaac Newton, 18in. and 15in., 1774
'Palladio'* (an unidentified male, certainly not Palladio), 22in., 1774
Pindar, 25in., 1774
Plato, 25in. 1774
Alexander Pope, 15in., 1775
Matthew Prior, 15in., 1775
Sir Walter Raleigh, 18in., 1774
Sappho, 15in., 1775
Seneca, 20in. and 15in., 1775
Socrates, 20in., 1775
Edmund Spenser, 15in., 1775
Jonathan Swift, 20in. and 15in., 1775
Venus de Medici, 18in., 1774
Vestal, 15in., 1774
Virgil, 15in., 1775. Finished by Josiah Wedgwood
Zeno, 25in., 1774
TABLETS. PLAQUES AND MEDALLIONS
'4 Ovels of the Elements', 13in. x 10¾in., 1774: *Fire, Air, Earth, Water*
Lyre and Two Sphinxes, 10in. x 22in., 1774
PORTRAIT MEDALLIONS
Lord Orford (Sir Robert Walpole). Sulphur cast, 1774

Hot Lane, Burslem

Site of the first enamelling kiln in Staffordshire, established about 1750. The art of enamelling is traditionally supposed to have been introduced by two Dutchmen. According to Simeon Shaw*, Ann ('The Widow') Warburton*, who lived at Hot Lane, enamelled creamware teawares for Josiah in the early 1760s.

Hot-Water Plate

Hot-water plates were made with double walls in one piece, with a hole for filling the intervening space with hot water; or an ordinary plate was set into a hot-water container of pewter. In the 18th century they were generally made of porcelain in China, but Wedgwood was making both plates and dishes of the first type by about 1790, the meat dishes being moulded with gravy channels and pockets.

Houdon, Jean-Antoine (1741-1828)

French sculptor, born at Versailles. He studied under Slodtz, winning the Premier Prix in 1761. From 1764 to 1774 he was in Rome and he became an Academician in 1777. He spent five years in America between 1787 and 1792. Houdon made busts in marble, bronze and terracotta of many celebrated people of his time and his seated figure of Voltaire*, dated 1781, is especially well known. Wedgwood's busts of Voltaire and Washington are after models by Houdon.

Hovel

Also hovel kiln. A Potteries term for the common bottle kiln in which the chimney is an extension of the outer wall. In December 1767 Josiah Wedgwood sent Bentley* a sketch of the ground-plan of Etruria*, showing eight hovels, which might be, as Wedgwood reminded his partner, a variety of shapes, ranging from beehive to pepper-pot, from milk churn to castellated castle keep. Not all were intended to be taken seriously and he was alarmed when Bentley expressed a preference for 'Gothic Battlements'. The Etruria hovels were eventually built of conventional bottle shape.

Howell & James

Retail store established in 1820 in Regent Street, London, to sell millinery, silks and all kinds of 'art' products, especially pottery and porcelain. Beginning in 1876, Howell & James organised exhibitions to encourage amateur porcelain painting and they had their own backstamp added to wares ordered from industrial and 'art' potteries of the day. The Wedgwood Tercentenary bust of Shakespeare (see: Shakespeare Subjects) bore the unusual impressed mark 'Wedgwood & Son' and the inscription 'The Shakespeare Memorial Bust Published under the special sanction of the National Shakespeare and Stratford on Avon Tercentenary Committees by Howell James & Co London April 23 1864.' The firm made a donation of £50 to the Committee.

Howorth, John (fl.1800-30)

Salesman and Manager of Wedgwood's York Street, London, showrooms* from 1814 to 1829. Howorth had been recommended by Tom Byerley* for the job of 'housekeeper' at York Street in 1802, when he described him as 'a man decidedly honest from principle'. Howorth succeeded Josiah Byerley* as manager in 1814 and retired after the sale of stock and abandonment of the showrooms in 1829. His son, also John, was employed briefly at the new rented offices in Charles Street but was described by Bateman* as a rake, a drinker and a poor worker. When later the younger Howorth applied to Josiah II* for financial assistance, Bateman advised strongly against it, advising Josiah II that Howorth senior owned three or four houses: 'I think', he wrote, 'Mr Howorth has a comfortable income – there is every appearance of it, he looks well and Mrs H is very dressy – they keep a good house – and a servant maid.'

Hubertusburg, Saxony

Faïence factory founded in 1770 by J.S. Tännich. It came under the directorship of Count Marcolini of Meissen*, who made *Steingut* (creamware) in the Wedgwood manner at Hubertusburg. Styles were copied from Queen's ware* and some pieces were even marked WEDGWOOD impressed (1815-35). Pierced borders of the type generally associated with Leeds* also were favoured. The factory closed in 1848.

Hulme & Walmsley

Merchants of Manchester and Cadiz (Spain) who exported Wedgwood wares. Copies of Wedgwood's Catalogue* in French were sent to Mr Walmsley in Cadiz in 1774. In November of that year, Wedgwood referred to the demand there for crucifixes and portraits of saints, the latter to be inserted into bracelets, lockets, snuff boxes etc. The small medallion portraits of the Popes, listed

HUSK SERVICE. Queen's ware plate, Queen's shape, enamelled in rose-pink with the *Husk* pattern . Diameter 9¾in. c.1770.
Wedgwood Museum

in the first (1773) Ornamental ware Catalogue, were eminently suitable for export to Catholic countries, but sales were disappointingly small.

Hulme, Jesse (1789-1852)
Engraver, designer, portrait artist; worked for Wedgwood at Etruria*, 1842-44.

Hulme, Paul (fl.1900-51)
Engraver at Etruria* and Barlaston*, 1913-51; worked on the Barlaston mug of 1940.

Hunt Pattern
Wedgwood have used two moulded relief Hunt patterns for jugs and mugs. The first, produced also by other potteries, including Spode*, New Hall*, Davenport* and Turner*, is well known. It appears on 19th-century stoneware jugs with glazed blue, black or brown (very rarely, yellow) slip* backgrounds and white reliefs or with the collars of the jugs in one of those slip colours. The Wedgwood version, produced c.1830-60, usually has an unglazed brown or blue slip collar and was made in five sizes. Small white stoneware ('porcelain'*) Hunt mugs with a blue slip band at the lip were made during the same period. The relief pattern appears to be identical among the leading factories, showing two dismounted huntsmen with their horses close to a gate on the obverse, and hounds in at the kill on the reverse.

The second version, which appears to be exclusively Wedgwood's, shows two huntsmen, one mounted and the other on foot, in conversation, with hounds at their side. First produced c.1820 on the Club* jug, the relief design was later (c.1850) adapted to a specially modelled collared shape with hound handle which was produced in large quantities until the 1960s in green glaze*, Dysart glaze*, and in cream colour with enamelled figures or with a ground of silver lustre* to the relief. A similar pattern was produced c.1900 with a portrait of John Peel (1776-1824), the Cumberland huntsman, surrounded by the inscription, 'D'ye ken John Peel, 1829'.

Huquier, Gabriel (1695-1772)
See: Bouchardon, Edmé

Husk Service
A Queen's ware* dinner and dessert service made for the Empress Catherine II* of Russia in 1770 and decorated with the *Husk* pattern. The dinner service was produced on Queen's shape (see: Tableware Shapes) and enamelled in rose-purple with a border of husk festoons* and botanical flowers* in the well of the plates. The dessert service, on shell edge shape with the addition of decorative pierced stands for some serving pieces, was decorated with sprays of flowers. The decoration was executed at the Chelsea Decorating Studio* under the supervision of Bentley* and Rhodes*. Wedgwood, fully aware of the prestige of this order and its potential value in enhancing his reputation in Russia, was extremely anxious about the quality of the painting on the service and the lack of time allowed for its completion. He 'trembled for the Russian service' and told Bentley in May: 'Mr Rhodes has hands who can do husks, which is the pattern of the Table service, & I think I shall not wait yr reply to send you two or three for flowers'. For the painting of the dessert service, therefore, Ralph Unwin*, Joseph Cooper* and James Bakewell* were sent at once to Chelsea. Some Queen's ware shapes were modelled by Coward* especially for this order.

Much of the *Husk* service has survived and is displayed in the palace of Petrodvorets (Peterhof). Some was sold in the state-controlled antique shop in 1931. Copies of certain pieces, presumably replacements for breakages, were produced by the Poskotchin* factory about 1810. The *Husk* pattern was not reserved to this service and shards from another 18th-century set have been excavated at Williamsburg, Virginia.

HUSK SERVICE. Queen's ware oval cream bowl and pierced stand painted in rose-purple with scattered sprays of flowers in the manner of James Bakewell. The bowl matches those supplied for the dessert service of the *Husk* service in 1770. *Christie's, London*

HYDRIA. Black basaltes hydria painted in encaustic colours with classical figures and a palmette border. Shape no.943. Height 11in. Unmarked. Wedgwood, c.1790. *Wedgwood Museum*

HYGEIA. Solid grey-blue and white jasper medallion, *Hygeia,* height 3¼in. Unmarked. Wedgwood & Bentley, c.1778.
Dwight & Lucille Beeson Collection, Birmingham Museum, Alabama

Hutchins, Thomas (fl.1769-77)
Painter and printer for Wedgwood in London; formerly at Boulton's* Soho, Birmingham, Works. Hutchins was hired in 1770 to print outlines on black basaltes* vases for encaustic* painting. When that experiment failed, no attempt was made to use his skills for the printing of outlines for enamelled tableware patterns and he was employed as a painter. He worked on the Frog* service in 1773-4 and three years later was put by Bentley* to 'stopping the Jaspers': repairing and colouring imperfections caused in firing (see: Tinkering). 'I daresay', Josiah wrote to Bentley, 'he will do them neatly and we shall always have occasion for such a hand'.

Hydria
Greek term for a vase used for storing and carrying water. It is large, urn*-shaped, and has two or three loop handles for lifting. The shape was made by Wedgwood in black basaltes*, sometimes with encaustic* decoration.

Hygeia
Goddess of health; wife (or daughter) of Aesculapius*. She is usually represented as a virgin in a long robe feeding a serpent from a cup.
Wedgwood subjects:
Aesculapius and Hygeia, rectangular plaque 8¼in. x 6⅞in. and 9½in. x 8¼in. Modelled by Pacetti*, 1788.
Hygeia, medallion 4in. x 3¼in., no.142 in 1777 Catalogue.

Hymen
God of marriage, personified by a handsome youth, taller than Eros (Cupid*) and carrying a torch. He was thought to be the son of Apollo* and one of the Muses*.
Wedgwood subjects:
Cupid and Hymen, medallion 3¼in. x 5in., no.135 in 1777 Catalogue*
Hymen, medallion 5in. x 3¾in., no.264 in 1787 Catalogue
Sacrifice to Hymen, tablet 11½in. x 16in. and various sizes to match *Marriage of Cupid* and Psyche*. Attributed to Flaxman*, 1777. No.196 in 1777 Catalogue
Sacrifice to Hymen, circular medallion, diameter 10in., no.259 in 1787 Catalogue. Companion piece to Sacrifice to Concordia

HYMEN. Blue and white jasper plaque, *Sacrifice to Hymen,* the companion piece to *Marriage of Cupid and Psyche,* attributed to Flaxman, c.1777. *Wedgwood Museum*

228

I

Ice Cream Bowl
See: Glacier

Illustrious Moderns
A series of portrait medallions* of 'modern' subjects, produced in black basaltes*, white terracotta*, jasper* and, more rarely, cane ware* and rosso antico*, the first 122 of which were listed in the first (1773) Wedgwood & Bentley Catalogue*. By 1788 the number had risen to 233 and the subjects included royalty, statesmen, military heroes, artists, poets, actors, scientists and judges. The choice was carefully made to embrace not only the eminent, but also those whose popularity or notoriety would assist sales both at home and abroad, and there was a liberal sprinkling of American and European portraits.

Ilmenau, Thuringia
Porcelain factory founded in 1777 and taken over in 1782 by the Duke of Weimar. From 1786 to 1792 it was leased to Gotthelf Greiner and in 1808 it was bought by Christian Nonne, who had leased it since 1792. Under Nonne's management the factory produced biscuit* porcelain medallions in the style of Wedgwood's blue and white jasper*, the subjects including 'modern' portraits and classical and mythological groups and figures. The medallions are often in glazed porcelain frames* and occasionally bear the modeller's mark 'Senff' or Senft'.

ILMENAU. White biscuit porcelain medallion with a pale blue slip ground in the Wedgwood style, ornamented with a 'Sacrifice' group, perhaps after Clodion. Unmarked. Made at the Ilmenau factory, c.1800.
Kestner-Museum, Hanover

Imari Style
Imari is the common name in Europe for the Japanese porcelains of Arita (province of Hizen) exported to Europe from the early part of the 18th century. The name is taken from that of the port from which they were shipped. The Imari style of decoration is based largely on two colours – a dark underglaze blue and dark red – and is crowded. The designs, in which stylised floral shapes predominate, derived from native textiles. Imari styles became popular in England during the early years of the 19th century and appear in patterns on Wedgwood's Queen's ware*, White ware* and bone

IMPERIAL QUEEN'S WARE. Covered box, height 4½in., and fruit bowl of pierced cream colour similar in style to Belleek. c.1875.
Wedgwood Museum

china* of the first period. In Wedgwood's catalogues, orders and invoices such patterns on tableware are usually described as 'Japan' patterns, and some were reproduced on bone china in the 1880s.

The earlier, more sparsely decorated porcelain of Arita is called Kakiemon, after the great Japanese potter believed to have been the first to apply enamelling to Japanese porcelain, c.1660. Kakiemon painting was much imitated at Meissen*, Chelsea*, Bow* and Worcester*, but not in the Potteries.
See: Japonaiserie; Japonisme

Imperial Queen's Ware
Delicately pierced Queen's ware* ornamental pieces – vases, bowls and covered boxes – produced c.1865-85, closely resembling in style the popular pierced basketwork of Belleek. Some of the scroll and festoon ornaments are borrowed from 18th-century models used on early Queen's ware and jasper. These pieces are fragile and undamaged examples are now scarce.

Impressed
Indented, as distinct from incised* or cut in. Impressed marks were made with a stamp while the clay was still soft, before firing, and are thus difficult to forge.
See: Marks

Incense Vase (Incense Burner)
See: Pastille Burner; Pot-pourri Jar

Incised
Scratched into the body of a piece of pottery or porcelain with a sharp tool, such as a metal or diamond point. Decoration may be incised, or the technique may be used to add a name, inscription or date. Individual potters' marks are often incised, but manufacturers marks are generally either impressed*, printed or painted onglaze.
See: Sgraffito

India Rubber
See: Inkstone

Industrial Design
As early as 1888 the architect John D. Sedding advocated the closer involvement of the designer in the process of production: 'The designer should be part of the working staff of the factory, see his design take shape, and be consulted as required.' The founding of the Design and Industries Association in 1915 gave new impetus to this concept. Its philosophy of 'decent design for ordinary people' and the precepts it sought to define and propagate – fitness for purpose, the proper use of materials, suitability of ornament, the beauty of nature and of commonplace objects – were not new: they were the guiding principles of the Arts and Crafts Movement*. Nor was the DIA the first organisation to emphasise the importance of a national effort to improve standards of design in British industry, but it was the first to receive government support.

The principles of modern industrial design were first enunciated before the end of the 19th century but it was not until the 1920s that the influence of the DIA began to be seen. A new partnership was formed between professional designers and artist-craftsmen and a new name, Industrial Design, was found for its product. The relationship between the Wedgwoods and Alfred Powell*, a professional architect and artist and a disciple of Sedding's, was a striking example of that of manufacturer and industrial designer: the manufacturer supplying organisation and the essential technical and practical knowledge to a designer of undoubted quality but limited experience or understanding of factory methods. The experience of Alfred and Louise Powell in working for the Wedgwoods was common to other disciples of the Arts and Crafts Movement who chose to work in industry: they were awakened to the realities of production, costing, and the relationship between profit and security of employment.

Among the consequences of the burgeoning interest in industrial design in the 1930s were the formation of the Council for Art and Industry (1933), of which Josiah Wedgwood V* was a founder member, the establishment by the Royal Society of Arts* of the Faculty of Royal Designers for Industry (1936), which brought together the elite of designers from different disciplines with varied industrial experience, the development of education for designers, especially the opening of the Central School of Arts and Crafts in London, and the commissioning by Staffordshire potters of original designs by established artists. After World War II the drive to improve design standards was given new momentum by the establishment of the Council of Industrial Design (now the Design Council) in 1947. One of the Council's first members was Josiah V.

The profession of industrial design is a 20th-century invention but its basic principles have been practised since man first began to shape objects for use, and their application to machinery has been understood at least since the 18th century. Josiah Wedgwood I's insistence on the close relationship between formal beauty and functional efficiency, and his employment of professional artists, especially of the sculptors Flaxman*, Webber* and Pacetti*, are evidence of his recognition of the elements of industrial design, of which he may be considered one of the true founders.

Industrial Espionage
Britain in the 18th century was a honey-pot to the industrial spy, who came from almost every country in Europe and Scandinavia, and most especially from France, to learn the secrets of British manufacturing. His particular interests included machinery of all kinds, iron and steel, textiles, watches, glass and pottery. Where the secrets could not be stolen on their own, or where their use depended upon training and skills that could be demonstrated but not easily described, the enticement of key workers was a practical alternative. Legislation to prevent the loss of skilled workers to foreign competitors was introduced as early as 1719. Josiah Wedgwood took his own course, first by caring for his workers – by the provision of health care, housing and fair wages – and second by issuing in 1783 An Address to the Workmen in the Pottery on the Subject of Entering into the Service of Foreign Manufacturers. This pamphlet contained a stirring appeal to patriotic loyalty, warnings against the easy acceptance of exaggerated promises of fortune, and a number of deliberately shocking stories relating the fate of those who had been seduced to defect. Since these stories concerned local people known to many of Wedgwood's workers at Etruria*, they were doubly effective.

Wedgwood's care for his workers was central to his policy of demanding their loyalty, which was often tested. They were sometimes privy to secrets of considerable value to competitors and, although Wedgwood told Bentley* that the copying of his work by others held few anxieties for him, he was constantly afraid that his inventions, innovations or developments might be stolen before he could fully exploit them. From the time of the Whieldon-Wedgwood* partnership Josiah had recorded his experiments in code and, as the years passed and his inventions were more and more widely copied or imitated, he became more and more secretive. His letters to Bentley contain frequent allusions to the lack of security in the mail coaches. 'Our Postmasters open just what letters they please', he complained, '& seem to have a particular curiosity to be peeping at mine'.

The increasing stream of visitors to Etruria, from home and abroad, posed additional problems of security which were not easy to solve without giving offence to potential customers. Josiah told Bentley in 1779 of 'several foreigners here lately & most of them extremely anxious after the composition of the black [basaltes*] of which we make our vases & busts, & quite hurt & disappointed when they are told we do not shew that part of the manufactory. Boulton* at Soho had a sign written in gold above his door which read: 'Entry to these works forbidden to all persons whatsoever, because of the problems which have already arisen from it'.

Wedgwood's security was tightened by the organisation of his factory. The separation of the 'Useful' Works from the 'Ornamental' and the detailed separation of processes resulted in few of his workers, apart from managers, having access to more than a small part of the production processes. An enterprising French spy of the period wrote: 'There is no country where labour is so divided as here...No worker can explain to you the chain of operations, being perpetually occupied only with a small part...it is this little understood division which results in the cheapness of labour, the perfection of the work and the greater security of the property of the manufacturer.'

Nevertheless, Wedgwood complained in 1785 to the secretary of the General Chamber of Manufacturers* about 'three different sets of spies upon our machines & manufactures...from different nations...some of them exhibited the greatest share of impudence ever known upon like occasions. For having been refused admittance by one clerk, they have come again when he has been absent, and almost forced their way to the machines they wanted to see...Sometimes they pretend to be possessed of improvements to the machines they want to take drawings or models of, at other times they procure recomendations from gentlemen who are not aware of their intentions...no time should be lost, nor any diligence on our part to prevent them.'

One of the most professional spies of the period was Louis-Victor Gerverot*, who evidently visited the Wedgwood factory several times, to judge by the detailed descriptions of it that he was able to send to the directors of the Fürstenberg factory. In 1789, two years after Gerverot's return to the Continent, Josiah wrote to Sir John Dalrymple: 'Our pottery here is at this time in a considerable ferment, occasioned by a person having lately been detected in seducing & bribing our workmen to give him drawings of our kilns, samples of our clays & raw materials, & specimens of our goods in different stages of mfre [manufacture]. The person has made his escape, but we are endeavouring to take & prosecute him. The foreign agent, for such he proves to be, has been 16 years in England employed upon the same plan respecting the different mfres of G.B & has taken drawings of our machinery for mining & mfres from Cornwall to Yorkshire.'

Dangerous as these foreign spies might be, the greatest potential threat to Wedgwood's secrets came always from the defection or dismissal of skilled hands who had come with high qualifications or remained long enough to be trained to Wedgwood's exacting standards. One such craftsman was John Voyez*, who was to give Wedgwood greater cause for concern than all the foreign visitors.

Infant Academy
The Infant Academy, the subject of one child painting the portrait of another, was painted by Sir Joshua Reynolds in 1782. This work, depicting children playing at the serious activities of adults, is closely related to Van Loo's Allegory of Painting and comments humorously on the art of the fashionable portrait painter (an art in which Reynolds had no contemporary peer). Wedgwood was evidently permitted by Reynolds to copy the painting in bas-relief* and the subject was modelled, with a companion piece, Music, by William Hackwood*, c.1785. Both bas-reliefs were produced as medallions and as ornament for large saucer dishes in jasper of various colours. The Infant Academy was used again in 1973 to ornament fluted plates in Portland Blue jasper* and black basalt. The latter version was produced in a limited edition of 2,500 with a gold inscription.

Infant Reclining Figures
Figures of naked babies, lying down and holding apples or other articles. These small figures do not appear in any of Wedgwood's catalogues* of ornamental ware but they were first produced in black basaltes* and in white jasper* with coloured jasper bases, c.1785-90 and have been reproduced intermittently in the 19th and 20th centuries. They were reproduced also in Majolica* glazes

INFANT RECLINING FIGURES. Four black basaltes or jasper figures of *Sleeping Boys,* c.1790-1810, after Duquesnoy, with *(extreme left and right)* two black basaltes *Infant Reclining Figures,* c.1850. Lengths 4¼in. to 5⅛in.
Byron and Elaine Born Collection

c.1870. A wax model* of one of the figures is preserved in the Wedgwood Museum*. The origin of these figures is uncertain. They have been attributed, on grounds of style, to Della Robbia*, but their resemblance to the five similar figures by Duquesnoy* suggests that they may be copies of others of the fifty figures made at Vincennes (see: Sèvres) for Louis XV.

Infuser
See: Coffee Biggin

Ink Pot, Ink Standish
No potter ever paid so much attention to the improvement of the design of the inkpot and inkstand as Wedgwood. The Wedgwood & Bentley Catalogue* of 1775 contained drawings and details of a

new shape, available in black basaltes*, which prevented the ink from soiling the pen or the fingers, avoided the blunting of the nib against the bottom of the well, and helped to inhibit evaporation. Next year Wedgwood wrote to Bentley*: 'Our Ink Pots being the best in the World, & every Body wishing to have one of them – Why do not we sell an immense number?' Sales improved and Wedgwood himself modelled eight or ten new sizes 'to fit all sizes & sorts of the wood stands in the shops, & private houses.' The inkstandish included a pen tray, ink pots, a pounce pot or sander, a taper stick and sometimes a spill vase. Wedgwood referred to his inkstandishes as 'ecritoires' (see: Escritoire). He modelled vase shapes, boat shapes with swans' heads at prow and stern, canopic* shapes and 'ruined columns'*. Ornament, in renaissance, neo-classical* and 'Egyptian'* styles, was moulded or applied. A few

[88]

CLASS XXI.
INK-STANDS, and EYE-CUPS.

INK POT. Engraving from the Wedgwood & Bentley 1777 Catalogue showing a new shape of ink pot designed to avoid the ink soiling the fingers or pen of the user and to prevent the nib being blunted by striking the bottom of the well.
Photograph: Wedgwood

THE Proprietors of this Manufactory have made a confiderable Variety of Ink-Veffels, and Ink

INKSTANDISH. Wedgwood & Bentley black basaltes inkstandish with ink pot and sander, the centre handles formed around a vase shape for a 'wett Spunge', decorated in encaustic colours. Length 6¾in. c.1778
Wedgwood Museum

231

INKSTANDISH. Important Wedgwood & Bentley black basaltes inkstandish with inkwell, pierced sander, candleholder and box for seals and wax, the body moulded with oak scrolls on a 'dimpled' ground. Length 7⅛in. *Dr & Mrs Alvin M. Kanter Collection*

rare examples were painted in encaustic* colours. Bentley was soon complaining that too great a variety complicated customers' choice. Wedgwood's inkpots and inkstandishes were usually made in basaltes but they exist also in jasper*, cane*, rosso antico*, smear-glazed* white stoneware* and decorated Queen's ware*. In the 19th century, they were made also in both first and second period bone china*.

INK POT, INKSTANDISH. Watercolour sketches of fourteen inkpots and inkstandishes drawn by Josiah Bateman, Wedgwood's senior traveller, in September 1823. *Wedgwood Museum*

Inkstone

Inkstones or 'India rubbers' were designed by James Watt* and made by Wedgwood in response to Watt's request, dated 10 February 1782, for 'some vessels for rubbing down India inks of various colours, all the present contrivances being defective'. The form of Wedgwood's inkstone, which was made of Queen's ware*, is a flat cylinder, about 3in. in diameter, with a closed biscuit* top in the centre of which is a small glazed depression. The ink was prepared by putting a few drops of previously boiled water into the

INKSTONE. Queen's ware inkstone or 'India rubber' designed by James Watt and made by Wedgwood in 1782. From Watt's workshop. *Science Museum, London*

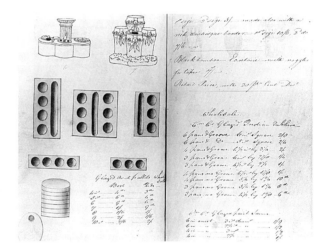

INKSTONE. Page from the 1832 Price Book showing several types of Queen's Ware inkstone ('India rubbers') for the making of ink. Prices ranged from 6d to 2/8d a dozen (wholesale). *Wedgwood Museum*

glazed depression, dipping the ink stick in the water, and then rubbing the stick round the rough biscuit disc. The particles of ink abraded from the stick dissolved in the water to form ink of the density required. Wedgwood sold large quantities of these pieces in the early part of the 19th century, when they were confusingly described on orders and invoices as 'India rubbers'.

Watt's own Wedgwood inkstone is preserved in the Science Museum, South Kensington, London.

Inlaid Ware

1. Ware decorated by impressing the unfired clay body with an intaglio* design which is then filled with slip* of a contrasting colour in the manner of Henri Deux* ware. Inlaid wares were made by a number of English factories during the 19th century, notably at Minton* by Charles Toft*. The Wedgwood Inlaid Pattern Book for 1859 lists eight separate bodies and glazes for inlaid decoration: lavender, sage, and red bodies; brown glaze; black; white stone; 'orange porous'; and 'white porous'. The inlaid patterns, often two-colour, were floral, chequered or key designs, sometimes with simple lines inlaid in contrasting colour. The range of pieces made in this style included candlesticks*, ale jugs*, spill vases*, tobacco jars, vases*, porous water bottles* with stoppers and matching saucers, teapots and inkpots*. In the 1870s Thomas Mellor* produced inlaid chessmen*, after the Flaxman* models, and other ornamental Queen's ware decorated in this manner,

2. Two-colour coloured bodies*, introduced with *Wintergreen* (Celadon body with cream-colour rims, handles and knops) in 1954. The success of this pattern was quickly followed by the production of other colours with cream-colour: Summer Sky

INLAID WARE. Glazed red body teapot, 146 shape, inlaid with lines and meander and bead borders. c.1862.   *Wedgwood Museum*

INLAID WARE. Miniature Queen's ware tazza with inlaid decoration of scrolls and stylised flowers by Thomas Mellor. Signed. Height 2½in. c.1885.   *Wedgwood Museum*

(Lavender), Barlaston Green (Celadon) and Havana (Chocolate), all on Barlaston shape (see: Tableware Shapes). A similar technique was used with bone china*. Almost every piece was cast, jiggered* or jollied* twice, one colour upon the other: a *Wintergreen* plate, for example, would be jiggered first in thin Celadon without a rim, and a second plate of cream colour would then be placed on top of the first on the jigger, providing a cream-colour base and rim. Inlaid patterns of this type were discontinued early in the 1970s.
See: Colour Plate 52

Intaglio

An Italian term, from the verb *intagliare* (to carve or incise), for a design created by incising and carving below the surface, which is flat and even; the opposite of cameo*, where the design is in relief. Wedgwood made intaglios in black basaltes* and variously coloured dry bodies* for use as seals, either mounted in holders or as signet rings. Those intended for mounting in holders were made available with shanks for the purpose. Early intaglios were

INTAGLIO. Twenty-one black basaltes intaglios varying in size from ⅝in. to 1⅛in. Three (unmarked) are double-sided, and eleven are impressed 'Wedgwood & Bentley'. The subjects include *Venus and Cupid*, *Hercules and the Nemean Lion* and a portrait of George II.

Christie's, London

lapidary* polished. Production of seals started in 1769 and from 1771 they were impressed with the catalogue number as well as the initials 'W&B', or (after Bentley's death) 'Wedgwood'. Some 1,700 different subjects were available, most of them also to be had in cameo form, and they could be obtained mounted back to back or mounted similarly with a cameo of the same size. The principal mounters were Boden & Smith of Birmingham, but from the end of 1773 Boulton* also was supplied direct. In 1774 Wedgwood obtained evidence that Voyez* was selling his seals with a forged 'W&B' mark. The seals made by Voyez were described by Wedgwood as 'sad trash' and it was therefore not the copying of them so much as the forgery of the Wedgwood & Bentley mark which concerned him. Later he admitted to Bentley: 'Mr Tassie* and Voyez have made terrible depredations upon our Seal Trade.' With the development of jasper* colours and of the techniques of laminating*, dipping and polishing, Wedgwood could compete with Tassie but he was never able to overshadow him in the quality of imitation seals or gems*.

Intaglio China
See: Lithophanes

Iphigenia
By common tradition the daughter of Agamemnon and Clytemnestra, but, according to some, daughter of Theseus and Helena. Agamemnon, having killed a hart in the grove of Artemis (see: Diana), was punished by a calm which prevented the fleet from sailing against Troy. To appease the goddess, he sacrificed Iphigenia, who was rescued by Artemis and taken to Tauris, where she became the priestess of the goddess. There she later saved her brother Orestes* and fled with him to Greece. She appears twice in the tablet *Orestes and Pylades,* modelled by De Vaere*, c.1790. The bas-relief frequently but erroneously described as *Sacrifice of Iphigenia* is the version of *Achilles in Scyros* attributed to Pacetti*.

Iris Kenlock Ware
See: Kenlock Ware

Irish Trade Treaty
Trade treaty proposed and vigorously pursued by the Younger Pitt as prime minister in 1784-5 in an attempt to remove the artificial restrictions that impoverished the Irish and consequently to provide an increasingly valuable outlet for English goods. The freeing of trade was intended to be the first step in a logical progression that would eventually achieve the reform of the Dublin parliament and the emancipation of the Catholic population of Ireland. Pitt proposed that in return for the mutual reduction of duties on all manufactures and produce, the Irish should make an agreed contribution, varied according to the rise and fall of Irish revenue, to the cost of their defence. Josiah Wedgwood was among those called to give evidence to the Board of Trade and he advocated the removal of all duties on earthenware imported into both countries, but otherwise voiced no objection to the proposals. Less than three weeks later he took the chair at the first executive committee of the newly formed General Chamber of Manufacturers of Great Britain*, pledged to oppose the Irish Resolutions.

Allowing for the fact that Wedgwood was honestly representing the views of most members of the Chamber (the 'gentlemen of the iron trade', for example, were convinced that they would be ruined by Pitt's proposals), it is nevertheless clear that his sudden change of mind was influenced by his regular contacts with the most formidable Whig opponents of the treaty, Lord Sheffield and William Eden (see Auckland). There is equally no doubt that Wedgwood and his friends were deliberately misled into believing that Pitt's intention was to increase duties on British goods. The Resolutions, much amended, passed the British parliament but, lacking sufficient support in Dublin, were withdrawn. Wedgwood's opposition made him few political friends, the most useful of whom, William Eden, was soon working for Pitt's administration, but many important enemies and the cost to his trade in Ireland was great. His agent there, Esau Clarke, was compelled to give up his business. Wedgwood wrote to Edgeworth*: 'I have offended the Irish & they will buy no more of Wedgwood's double-damned ware.'

Ironstone China
An opaque stone china patented by Charles James Mason in 1813

and imitated by many English potters, including Wedgwood, H. & R. Daniel, Davenport* and Hicks & Meigh. Although porcellaneous, Stone china is not technically porcelain*, but some of it satisfies both the European and the Chinese definitions: that it should be translucent and ring when struck. The first stone china was made by William and John Turner* of Lane End, who patented a new ceramic body using 'Tabberner's Mine Rock' in 1800. The body was often slightly translucent. Spode's* Stone China, introduced about 1813, was advertised as 'newly invented', but may have been based on Turner's composition. Josiah Byerley* wrote to Josiah II* in March 1814: 'Every one enquires for the stone china, made by Spode and Mason and it has a very great run...it is a thick coarse china body, not transparent'. Three months later, after Queen Charlotte* had bought a set of Spode's Stone China, Bateman* wrote to Josiah II: 'Since the Queen went to Mr Spode the Stone China is much inquired for and is got more into repute – indeed a dealer cannot be without it'. It appears that trials of a stone china body were made at Etruria* in 1817, but in April 1819 John Howorth* wrote from London that stone china was repeatedly asked for but that 'the great quantity of this ware made and making by several manufacturers' must make the competition for prices unprofitable.

No record has been found of Wedgwood's production of stone china before 1821 and Bateman's first order for it is dated December of that year. Although trials continued for a further twenty-four years there is evidence of production for only a fraction of this period. It appears almost certain that it was produced regularly for only about eight years, probably ending in 1830, and that quantities were never large. This supposition is reinforced by the scarcity of surviving examples.

Wedgwood's stone china is generally opaque and was decorated with patterns of two types: printed and enamelled chinoiserie* or Japan patterns, most of them already popular on Pearl* or White ware*; and underglaze blue* printed patterns previously applied to the Pearl body. Some of these were edge-lined with a brown iron lustre* first developed for use with blue printed wares. Most of Wedgwood's stone china is marked 'WEDGWOOD'S STONE CHINA', printed in blue or red, but unmarked pieces are not unknown and other specimens bear the single word 'WEDGWOOD' in the manner of bone china* of the first period.

Isaacs, Miss (fl.1769-74)
Painter at the Chelsea Decorating Studio* said to have worked on the Frog* service in 1773-4.

Isis
Egyptian deity; the wife of Osiris and mother of Horus. Isis was worshipped as the goddess of the earth and later as goddess of the moon. She was identified by the Greeks with Demeter (see: Ceres). Wedgwood subjects:
Isis (Head), medallion 3in. x 2½in., no.119 in 1777 Catalogue
Isis border decoration designed by Christopher Dresser*, c.1875
Procession to Isis, encaustic*-painted tablet* after a Hadrianic relief in the collection of Alessandro Maffei and now in the Vatican Museum
Meteyard* (*Life of Wedgwood,* Vol.II, p.363) mentions a medallion of *Iris,* evidently a misprint for *Isis.*

Ivory Wares
An ivory-coloured stained Queen's ware* body was introduced at Etruria* towards the end of 1882, evidently in an attempt to compete with Worcester's* popular Ivory porcelain, but it proved difficult in production and was withdrawn after only a few years. It was replaced by an ivory glaze, used for Queen's ware ornamental wares (especially some fine bronzed busts and *japonisme* vases) and the Ivory 'Vellum'* bone china*.

Ivy House Works, Burslem
'House and Work Houses' rented by Josiah Wedgwood I from 1 May 1759 from his kinsman John Wedgwood of the Big House, Burslem, for £15 per annum. They were occupied by Wedgwood as his first factory until the end of 1762 or the beginning of 1763, when he moved his business to the larger Brick House* Works nearby. The Ivy House Works came complete with 'Wheele' and 'Flagg Stone' for an additional rent of £2.6.0. According to the recollections of one who saw the Works, the Ivy House had two

IVY HOUSE. The Ivy House Works, Josiah Wedgwood's first pottery. Reproduced from the line engraving published in Meteyard's *The Life of Josiah Wedgwood,* 1865. After a drawing from memory by Aaron Wedgwood of Burslem.   *Photograph: Wedgwood*

ovens in 1759, one of which might have been used for lead-glazed earthenware while the other was reserved for redware*. Simeon Shaw* records that Wedgwood rented 'a second small manufactory only across the high road', where he made white saltglazed* stoneware. No evidence has been found to support this statement, but it is likely that Wedgwood would have needed to make saltglazed wares and their manufacture would have required a separate oven.

Rent for the first year was paid in five instalments and almost a quarter of the total was settled in goods. No dated records of manufacture, and few of orders placed with Wedgwood, during this period have survived, so there is little firm evidence to show what sort of ware Wedgwood made at the Ivy House. According to Shaw, Wedgwood continued there 'the manufacture of Knife Hafts, Green Tiles, Tortoiseshell and Marble Plates, glazed with lead ore, for his previously formed connections', while saltglazed

wares, 'then increasing in demand', were produced at the smaller rented factory. In essentials, this account is likely to be accurate, although it is remarkable for containing no mention of either redware or Wedgwood's green glazed* wares.

The *Ivy House* pattern, a lithographed ivy pattern on bone china*, was designed by Peter Wall* in 1957.

Ivy Leaf
A border pattern of ivy leaves, sometimes of double ivy leaves. Originally Greek, it was employed by Wedgwood in the 18th century and has been revived, in various forms, in the 19th and 20th centuries. Wedgwood's London Ledger for 1793-1806 contains an entry for 'green ivy plates' supplied to Queen Charlotte* in 1795.
See: Napoleon Ivy

J

Jackfield Ware

Red earthenware covered with a lustrous black glaze made at Jackfield (Shropshire), c.1750, by Maurice Thursfield. Similar ware was made by a number of Staffordshire potters, including Whieldon* and it was almost certainly included among Wedgwood's early productions (Robinson & Rhodes* ordered 'Black Decanters' and 'Black cream juggs' from Wedgwood in 1763, some years before his introduction of black basaltes*). The name of Jackfield has become associated with any brilliant black glaze on early earthenware, although only a small percentage of surviving examples were made in Shropshire. A black glaze of the Jackfield type was used by Wedgwood c.1860, in conjunction with enamelled flowers in the *famille-rose* style, to decorate teapots and probably other tewares, and a similar glaze was used with platinum lustre* decoration by Louise Powell*, c.1923

James, Elwyn (1942-78)

Designer; born in North Wales; studied at Wrexham College of Art, gaining a National Diploma in Design, before going on to study at Liverpool College of Art. James joined Wedgwood at Barlaston* and worked primarily as a studio potter, being allowed a fairly free hand to develop his own shapes and glazes for bone china* and stoneware. Before his tragically early death, he had already begun to fulfil his early promise as a potter-designer of exceptional gifts.
See: Colour Plate 53

Janus

Ancient Italian deity with two faces, one looking forward and the other back. The month of January was sacred to him. The doors of his temple in the Roman Forum were shut during periods of peace and open in time of war. The symbolism of the jasper* tablet* modelled by John Flaxman* in 1787 to celebrate the signing of the French Commercial Treaty*, *Peace preventing Mars* from bursting open the Gates of the Temple of Janus*, is thus explained.

JACKFIELD WARE. Creamware teapot with crabstock handle and spout decorated with 'Jackfield' black glaze and gilding. The body is ornamented with applied fruiting vine and trailed stems in the manner associated with Whieldon. Possibly Whieldon or Whieldon-Wedgwood, c.1757-63. *Wedgwood Museum*

JACKFIELD WARE. Red body 'Rockingham' shape teapot decorated with black 'Jackfield'-type glaze and enamelled flowers in the *famille-rose* style. c.1860. *Author's collection*

JANUS. Solid blue and white jasper plaque, *Commercial Treaty with France*, depicting Peace preventing Mars from breaking open the gates of the Temple of Janus, modelled by John Flaxman junior in 1786-7. c.1787. *Christie's, London*

Japanese Influence

Apart from the bamboo* wares and the occasional *chinoiseries* on early creamware teapots, there is little sign of oriental influence on Wedgwood's wares of the 18th century. The influence of Japanese design appears in two distinct periods: the early 19th century, when the designs are properly known as *japonaiseries;* and the thirty years or so immediately following the London Exhibition of 1862, when the styles became known as *japonisme.*

The earlier of the two, the *japonaiseries,* were derived from designs in the Imari* style then being produced by the English porcelain companies, notably at Derby* and Worcester*. Wedgwood's patterns in this style were produced primarily on Queen's ware*, Pearl* or White ware*, but at least eight of the *Japan* patterns designed for earthenware were transferred to bone china* of the first period. The second, and far more popular, fashion for Japanese design arose from the international exhibitions held in London in 1862 and in Paris in 1867, 1878 and 1889. The vocabulary of Japanese decoration was provided by pictorial dictionaries printed for the use of European designers and these provided the foundation of *japonisme:* a style which made use of accurately copied Japanese motifs and images in conjunction with traditional European materials and techniques.

The British porcelain manufacturers were quick to produce ornamental wares for the newly created market. Worcester made vases and other ornaments decorated with Japanese motifs and painted in oriental styles as early as 1862, and Minton's* vases in similar styles were not far behind. Wedgwood, having no porcelain or bone china until the reintroduction of the latter in 1878, was at first limited to earthenware and the 'dry bodies'*. The popularity of Japanese partly gilt bronzes* inspired the gilded and bronze and gilt basaltes of this period, a curious use of neo-classical shapes and ornament which seems not to have been successful. *Auro basalt** vases were a more genuine attempt to imitate Japanese bronze styles, but the bizarre mixture of Japanese motifs with classical reliefs which appears on some mercifully rare jasper* pieces is more obscurely motivated. Natural forms regarded as typically Japanese – the iris, the chrysanthemum and certain leaf-and-berry designs, as well as the generally oriental prunus branch and blossom – were used for the decoration of vases and a large number of tableware patterns was created from authentic Japanese sources. The *Satsuma* shape (see: Tableware Shapes) was modelled especially for decoration in the Japanese style but was nevertheless frequently used with entirely western designs. Japanese designs were adapted also for Majolica* and Argenta* wares and the decoration of several sets of tiles* was derived from woodblock *(ukiyo-e)* prints.

Japanese art remained the dominant influence on European fashion for the rest of the 19th century, though its grammar and idiom have been so completely absorbed into the language of western art and design that their presence may pass almost unnoticed. *Chinoiserie* patterns are still noticeable in Wedgwood's 20th-century wares, especially the bone china tablewares (popular patterns such as *Charnwood, Cathay* and *Kutani Crane,* for example), but neither the early *Imari* styles nor the *japonismes* of the late 19th century have been revived.

JAPANESE INFLUENCE. Japanese woodblock print of about 1870 depicting Josiah Wedgwood (recognisable by his stump and stick and identified in the inscription) at Etruria. Apparently one of a set of 'foreign worthies', this print reflects the intense Japanese interest in foreigners and western cities. This interest was strongly reciprocated in Europe after the second Great Exhibition of 1862
Photograph: Wedgwood

Japonaiserie

Like *chinoiserie,* the term *japonaiserie* is used for art or design that is imaginatively based on incomplete or inaccurate understanding of the style it is intended to imitate. The Imari*-style patterns produced by the English porcelain companies and by Wedgwood in the first quarter of the 19th century are examples of *japonaiserie.* The term is not properly applied to design produced after 1862 in response to the fashion for Japanese goods and styles.
See: Colour Plate 54
See also: Japanese Influence; Japonisme

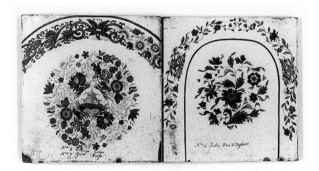

JAPONAISERIE. Two earthenware reference tiles printed and enamelled with Japan patterns: *(left)* no.7 with gold edge and no.8 with orange enamel edge; *(right)* no.4. In common with many 'Japan' patterns of this period, both are more Chinese than Japanese in style. Unmarked. Wedgwood, c.1820. *Wedgwood Museum*

JAPONAISERIE. *Chrysanthemum* pattern printed in brown and enamelled on *(left)* a rectangular White ware dessert dish, 7½in. x 9¼in., c.1815, and *(right)* a Queen's ware sugar box (lacking lid), height 4¼in., c.1885. The latter provides an interesting example of early 19th-century *japonaiserie* repeated in the period of *japonisme.*
Author's collection

Japonisme

Term invented by the French art critic Philippe Bury in 1872 to describe the new styles inspired by Japanese design. By *japonisme* is meant European design, after 1862, grounded in Japanese art or securely based on authentic Japanese motifs and styles.

See: Japanese Influence; Japonaiserie

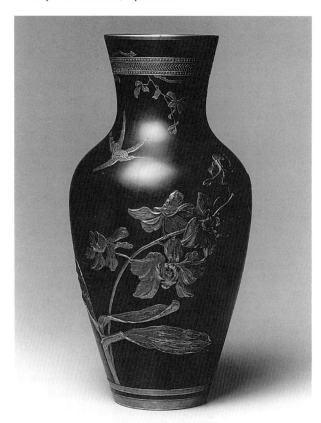

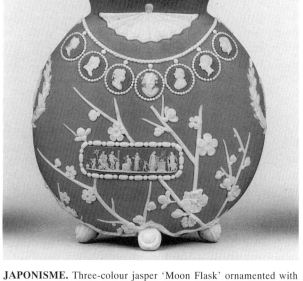

JAPONISME. Three-colour jasper 'Moon Flask' ornamented with white fans and prunus branches, framed portrait medallions and octagonal cameos. Height 5¾in. c.1875. This bizarre piece, evidently intended to appeal to the fashionable desire for Japanese styles, bears little resemblance to anything Japanese.   *Christie's, New York*

JAPONISME. Auro basalt vase decorated with a gilded raised paste design of a swallow and a single spray of orchids. Although scarcely recognisable to the Japanese, this style clearly shows the influence of Japanese design and the popular gilded bronzes imported from Japan in the last quarter of the 19th century. c.1885. Height 17in.
Wedgwood Museum

JAPONISME. Queen's ware *Satsuma* shape teapot and teacup and saucer decorated with the *Peacock* pattern and a Shinto shrine in a landscape, in reserves on a deep-blue ground. c.1887-9.
Wedgwood Museum

JAPONISME. Bone china teaset of octagonal form decorated in the *Imari* style with iron-red flowering shrubs on alternating gilt and ivory panels within mazarine blue panels. c.1885.
Christie's, New York

JAPONISME. Queen's ware plate decorated with a central scene of an Edo village pageant copied from a woodblock engraving and border motifs of bamboo trellis, leafy bamboo, palm and a fire tower. c.1887.
Wedgwood Museum

Jardinière

French term for an ornamental bowl, generally large and raised on feet, used to hold flowering or otherwise decorative plants. *Jardinières* became popular in England during the 19th century and Wedgwood produced some imposing examples in Majolica*. In the 1920s, Paul Follot* designed a *jardinière* in his *Pomona* shape.

Jasper

Wedgwood's most important contribution to ceramic art and the most significant innovation in ceramic history since the Chinese invention of porcelain* nearly a thousand years earlier. Jasper is a dense white stoneware* which, when thinly potted and fired at a slightly higher temperature than usual (above 1,250°C) may be translucent like porcelain. The body may be stained by metal oxides to a wide variety of colours, and – like other dry bodies* – moulded, ornamented, engine-turned*, laminated*, and lapidary-polished*. Less happily, it may also be glazed (although this is strictly unnecessary for any reason but decoration), painted in enamel colours and gilded. It is commercially the most successful and enduring range of ornamental ware and gift ware ever manufactured, and, except for a short interval in the 19th century and periods of wartime government restrictions, it has remained continuously in production at Etruria* or Barlaston* for more than two hundred years.

The composition of jasper was Wedgwood's most closely guarded secret and it was revealed to Bentley* in February 1776 in code and in two separate letters to protect it against spies (see: Industrial Espionage). The formula was: calcined flint 1, Purbeck clay 3, alabaster (fired and washed) ¼, and sulphate of barium* 6.

JASPER. Numbered and coded jasper trials, showing differing compositions and colours, fired in various positions in the ovens.
Wedgwood Museum

JASPER. Solid pale blue and white jasper vase, ornamented with a framed figure of *Apollo* and laurel swags. Height 13⅜in. c.1787.
Nottingham Castle Museum

JASPER. Three early solid pale-blue and white jasper trial medallions with moulded frames: *(left to right) A Vestal, Orestes at Delphi* and *Hercules and the Nemean Lion.* Oval 4½in. x 3½in. Unmarked. c.1775. These trials illustrate the problems of blistering and cracking in firing.
Wedgwood Museum

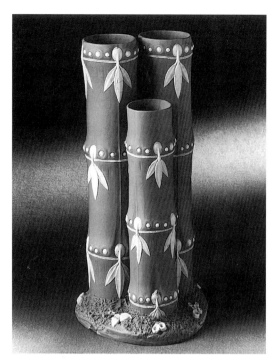

JASPER. Solid blue and white jasper bamboo flower-holder. Height 10½in. c.1790. *Wedgwood Museum*

A knowledge of this formula is necessary to a full understanding of Wedgwood's difficulties in perfecting the body and of the problems that faced his successors in reproducing it in the 19th century. It is significant that the general principle of its manufacture – a high proportion of fusible material (barium sulphate) held in shape during firing at a temperature of about 1200°-1250°C by refractory clay while fusion takes place – was that of porcelain*, and it is no great surprise that, when thinly potted and high-fired, some jasper is translucent and rings like a bell when struck, thus satisfying both the European and the Chinese definitions of porcelain. Josiah Wedgwood himself described the body as 'my porcelain'.

JASPER. Small five-colour jasper 'Altar flowerpot with basketwork cup', the solid blue jasper body on a base of white jasper ornamented in chocolate-brown, the lilac jasper top ornamented in a basketwork pattern with green binding to the rim. Height 6⅞in. c.1792. *Wedgwood Museum*

While there is no doubt that Wedgwood was for some years interested in the manufacture of 'true' porcelain, it is clear from his rejection of Matthew Horne's* offer at the end of 1775 that he had, by that date, abandoned any intention to make it. His search, from the end of 1772, was clearly for a new composition, an original ceramic body, and this occupied much of his time and energy for more than two years. By February 1773 he had made 'some very promising experimts', but for the next fourteen months he had little time to spend on them. In March 1774 he wrote: 'I have…such *Roots,* such *Seeds* as would open & branch out wonderfully if I

JASPER. Solid blue and white jasper footed bowl with cover ornamented with *Bacchanalian Boys* after Duquesnoy, the interior lapidary polished, set on a pedestal ornamented with bas-reliefs of the Seasons in rectangular panels. Height 13in. c.1790.
Manchester City Art Gallery

JASPER. Tricolour dark-blue jasper *pot-pourri* vase, the body with engine-turned spiral dicing ornamented with green quatrefoils and bands of laurel, with solid white jasper internal lid (to seal the *pot-pourri* mixture when not in use), the lid surmounted by two doves. Height 8¾in. c.1795-1810. *Lady Lever Art Gallery, Port Sunlight*

JASPER. White stoneware *pot-pourri* vase dipped in bright blue jasper and ornamented with solid white jasper handles, finial and large applied flowers and leaves. Height 15½in. c.1850. *Merseyside Museums*

JASPER. Bright-blue jasper dip vase ornamented with ferns, flowers and butterflies. Height 10in. c.1876-86. Possibly ornamented by Charles Toft. *Sotheby's, London*

JASPER. One of a pair of electroplated nickel silver girandoles mounted with solid pale-blue and white jasper plaques and candleholders. Height 13⅜in. For many years catalogued as 18th-century pieces, these are now known to have been made for the 1871 International Exhibition. *Wedgwood Museum*

JASPER. Black jasper dip vase ornamented with bands of engine-turned dicing and yellow quatrefoils. Height 14½in. c.1875. *Christie's, New York*

JASPER. Three yellow-buff jasper dip vases ornamented in black. Height 7in. and 10¼in. 1919-32.

could nail myself down to the cultivation of them for a year or two'. By July he was deep in experiments but experiencing difficulties with his materials: 'At one time the body is white & fine as it should be, the next we make…is a Cinamon color. One time it is melted to a Glass, another time dry as a Tob: Pipe'. Next month he sent the first trial portrait medallions* in the new body to London to have the grounds enamelled, but he was far from satisfied with them. 'I cannot work miracles in altering the properties of these subtle & complicated (though native) materials', he told Bentley: 'If I had more *time,* more *hands,* & more *heads* I could do something – but as it is I must be content to do as well as I can. A Man who is in the midst of a course of experimts *shod not be at home* to anything or anybody else but that cannot be my case. Farewell – I am almost crazy.'

Early in November he made his first bas-relief* figures, but encountered fresh difficulties with blistering during firing. He sent Bentley a sample of a new composition, a 'seed of consequence'. Bentley, meanwhile, was experimenting with various methods of colouring the grounds of medallions in the new body, none of which had proved wholly successful. A month later an important development had taken place: Josiah told Bentley not to enamel any more samples, and on 18 December he sent him '4 black & Blue onyx intaglios*'. Much remained to be done before it was perfected, but these four intaglios were the first examples of the new (stained) coloured jasper. By Boxing Day 1774 Wedgwood had made his first laminated* seals* in blue and white. He warned Bentley of the future importance of lapidary polishing in their business and suggested that he 'hire a proper person' to work in London.

Secrecy was now of paramount importance and Wedgwood arranged to have his materials sent to him via London to disguise their origin. As he explained: 'If our Antagonists should overtake us at this stage, we cannot again take a step before them, to leave them behind'. When he had established a satisfactory lead he would meet any competition: 'taking it for granted they will in time come at our compositions &c, we shall still have *variety of subjects – Execution – Character,* & *connections* in our favour

sufficient to continue us at the head of this business'.

At the beginning of 1775 Josiah declared himself 'absolute' in the white jasper, blue, 'likewise a beautifull Sea Green, & several other colors *for grounds* to Cameo's, Intaglio's &c', and was confident of being able to make bas-reliefs from the largest size then in production in black basaltes* or terracotta* to the smallest gem*, but this claim proved to be over-optimistic. He had still not fully understood the crucial difference between barium sulphate* (cauk) and barium carbonate ('Wheat stone') and he had not yet solved the problem of staining or 'bleeding'*. He was experimenting with making the heads and figures separately, undercutting* them at the edges and fixing them before firing to avoid staining. Throughout 1775 he continued to struggle with intractable materials which produced unpredictable results under conditions that were as nearly constant as he could make them. In August he wrote to Bentley: 'I have so many of these raw materials, & different compositions under my immediate care, & in which nobody can assist me that I am almost crazed with them'. Although the New Year brought new hope and the successful firing of several large plaques and 'a Medusa* large & very fine…too fine to sell', Wedgwood's troubles were not over and in June 1776 he wrote in frustration: 'This Jasper is certainly the most whimsical of any substance I ever engag'd with.' He was especially anxious about the huge losses in production: seventy-five per cent of jasper tablets in May. The first 'deep' blue jasper was made in April 1777 and, to reduce the costs of staining this with cobalt* at thirty-six shillings a pound, he had introduced jasper 'dip', a new technique of applying a thin wash (slip*) of one colour over a ground of another (usually blue over white, but other colours were used). The 'dip' technique superseded lamination and opened the way to engine-turned decoration, cut through the dip to the base colour.

At last, on 3 November 1777, Wedgwood was able to assure his partner that his principal difficulties were at an end: 'I have tried my new mixing of Jasper, & find it very good. Indeed I had not much fear of it, but it is a satisfaction to be certain, & I am now ABSOLUTE in this precious article & can make it with as much facility, & certainty as black [basaltes*] ware. Sell what quantity you please'. It was a bold claim after so many years of false hopes, but it was one that he was able to justify. The colours he offered were pale blue, a 'middle' or 'deeper' blue and a still deeper 'mazarine', green, lilac, yellow, pale grey, black and chocolate-brown, and there were accidental variations of shade or tone which have given rise to such distinguishing names as 'pink', 'peach', 'olive-green' and 'mauve', but these were not used by Wedgwood.

In November 1777 Wedgwood set down in a memorandum a technique to enable him to make vases and other large objects which would not otherwise hold their shape in firing. This involved the use of a coarsely ground jasper body, to lend strength to the object, disguised by a thin covering of fine-ground jasper. This memorandum, which appears to have been lost for some years and neglected for many more, is of the greatest importance to the understanding of Wedgwood's production of jasper vases, and especially of his copies of the Portland vase*. In December Josiah wrote to Bentley proposing that they publish the information that jasper was 'made of the Cherokee* clay', but this suggestion, the truth of which is extremely doubtful, was dropped, probably on Bentley's advice.

The precise date of the introduction of 'diced' patterns created on the engine-turning* lathe is not known, but this type of decoration appears to date from about 1785. Extremely beautiful effects were obtained by using jasper ornament of various colours in simple trellis and strapwork patterns which required great delicacy and skill in application.

The range of objects made in jasper was enormous: cameos*, intaglios*, buttons*, beads, medallions*, plaques*, tablets*, portrait medallions*, candlesticks*, figures*, miniature busts*, cabinet pieces*, chessmen*, bough pots* and vases* were all made during Josiah I's lifetime. Medallions and cameos were mounted in cut-steel by Boulton* and others. The first vases were not shown until after the auction* sale of Wedgwood & Bentley stock in December 1781. Wedgwood's greatest achievement in jasper was undoubtedly the Portland vase*, produced, after four years of trials, in 1790, but he personally considered the Homeric vase (see: Apotheosis of Homer) to be his finest.

After the death of Josiah I, although the popularity of jasper had begun to wane, it continued to be made in wide variety and good quantities. Cameos were supplied to Vulliamy*, the clock maker, three- and four-colour jasper and the difficult deep blue jasper were regularly produced, and a deliberate attempt was made to give jasper a fresh appearance by exploiting unfamiliar colours and introducing new shapes. Undoubtedly the most important piece of jasper made in this period was the large group, *Britannia Triumphant*, now in the Birmingham Museum of Art, Alabama (see: Beeson Collection).

Throughout this period there is no indication that any difficulty was being experienced in the manufacture of jasper at Etruria*. From about 1811, however, there was a steep decline in the making of larger pieces until, in the early 1820s, in spite of frequent experiments with the body, the manufacture of jasper was confined to such small and nondescript pieces as spill vases*, taper candlesticks and caddy shells* and spoons. Apart from caddy shells, no solid jasper of any description was made between 1829 and 1844. No record of the production of jasper vases has been found for the years 1817 to 1845. Jasper was confined to dip and ornaments on a new white stoneware* body, known as 'white porcelain', Frank Wedgwood* noted in 1836: 'We formerly used to make large pieces of ware of jasper body, therefore am much surprised to find almost every piece that I attempt of any size dunt* as soon as it comes out of BO [Biscuit Oven].' The explanation for this failure is not certainly known but it appears to lie in the loss of the important 1777 Memorandum and the retirement and death of many of Josiah Wedgwood's most skilled managers and potters.

After many years of experiment, jasper was reintroduced in 1844, but as jasper dip only. Solid jasper was not produced again until 1860, when pale blue, green and lilac made their appearance. The body was different from Josiah I's original composition, and Frank wrote of it: 'it is not so good as the old has not such a waxy surface & is not so sharp & yet dryer so that it soils & when the soiling is well rubbed in a nailbrush & soap will not get it out – it seems that the surface is full of little broken bubbles which hold the dirt.' Laurence Wedgwood* wrote that the dark blue, made only as a dip, was inferior to the 18th-century colour. The jasper

JASPER. Solid black and white jasper mug with a wide glazed band, ornamented with the words 'A SOUVENIR' in leafage designs, each letter enclosing a cameo view of a British sporting centre: St Andrews, Cowes, Brands Hatch, Twickenham, Wimbledon, Lord's, Epsom, Wembley and Henley. Designed in 1966 by Richard Guyatt and issued in a limited edition of 500. Height 4in. *Wedgwood Museum*

dip, however, produced fewer problems and could be made in all colours, including yellow. Some interesting attempts were made to introduce floral and foliate relief ornament, but it was difficult to persuade a public accustomed to neo-classical* reliefs on jasper that any other form of ornament was suitable. In the 1870s and 1880s many of the finest 18th-century models were reproduced, including some large solid tablets and 'Herculaneum Pictures'*, and much diced jasper was made on the engine-turning lathe. New colours appeared – 'Quaker Grey' and 'Celadon' (especially for Boehm's* bust of Gladstone*) and Dysart Green* (see: Ricardo, Halsey) – and modellers Frederick Schenck* and Charles Toft* were employed to create new bas-relief subjects and models.

The principal developments in jasper during the 20th century have been in colour and, after World War II, in the 'reinvention' of the body. Crimson and dark olive green were introduced as dips in 1910 but both bled so badly into the white that they were withdrawn after a few years. An attempt was made to reintroduce the crimson dip between 1929 and 1935, also as a dip on white stoneware, but the costs in faulty wares were too great. Yellow dip on stoneware was made also in 1932 and a yellow-buff jasper with black ornaments appeared in small quantities from 1929 to 1932.

The production of jasper was halted in 1941 and it was not made again until 1948, when Norman Wilson* developed the new composition, more reliable and economical than the old, which is still

JASPER. Primrose jasper teapot, cream jug and sugar box of bamboo form with terracotta jasper ornaments. 1976. *Wedgwood Museum*

JASPER TEAWARE. Solid pale-blue and white jasper *déjeuner set, cabaret* or *solitaire,* ornamented with reliefs of *Poor Maria, amorini* and groups from the *Domestic Employment* series, typical of teaware designed as 'cabinet pieces'. c.1786-95.   *Wedgwood Museum*

in use. Pale blue, green and black jasper were made for the first few years and lilac was added from 1960 to 1962. A new jasper colour, a solid orange-red called terracotta (not to be confused with Josiah Wedgwood I's white terracotta stoneware* or the various red bodies of the 18th and 19th centuries), appeared between 1957 and 1959 with either white or black reliefs. Trials of solid white and solid grey were made in 1960 but neither was accepted for regular production. 'Royal' blue jasper was created to celebrate the coronation of Queen Elizabeth II in 1953, and 'Portland' blue (a dark slate-blue) in 1980 to commemorate the 250th anniversary of Josiah Wedgwood's birth. 'Primrose' jasper, some pieces in old bamboo* shapes, with terracotta (red) or white reliefs, was produced from 1976. A regrettable pink (predictably known to some as 'dentures') was introduced in 1982, and two inappropriate 'Fashion' colours, 'taupe' and 'teal', enjoyed a brief appearance in 1984. Least appropriate of all was certainly the mutation of Beatrix Potter's* 'Peter Rabbit' characters from lithographed nurseryware to bas-relief on jasper. By these basic errors of taste, Wedgwood's jasper, the pride of Josiah I's ornamental wares, was debased into 'giftware'.

In 1960-1 a laudable, but unfortunately unsuccessful, attempt to introduce new design into Wedgwood's jasper was made by inviting Lucie Rie* to make prototypes of teaware pieces. It is one of the great virtues of jasper, but also one of the perennial problems of marketing it, that it is associated so closely with neo-classical ornament. The jasper dip technique and engine-turned decoration add substantially to costs, and any reduction in ornament results in an approximately equal reduction in the employment of ornamenters whose skills are acquired only after years of training. The problem, which is both complex and recurrent, is, however, not solved by cheapening the product or by multiplying the colours available.

The immediate and widespread popularity of Wedgwood's jasper in the 18th century inspired imitations throughout Europe. The best was the jasper made by Adams* of Greengates, which closely resembled Wedgwood's in all but colour. Turner's* jasper, a slightly greyer-blue and closer in composition to porcelain, is of excellent quality. Palmer*, Neale*, Wilson and Samuel Hollins all made stonewares which more or less resembled jasper. Sèvres* copied jasper in a porcellaneous body devised by Josse of the Faubourg Saint-Denis; other factories used biscuit porcelain. The

blue and white bas-relief porcelain portrait medallions of Doccia* are hardly to be described as imitations of Wedgwood's jasper, since they predate it, and it may even be argued that the reverse is true. In Germany, Meissen's* *Wedgwoodarbeit* was a porcelain with a blue ground and integrally cast white reliefs; and the Ilmenau (Thuringia) factory made biscuit medallions with a blue ground and white reliefs, c.1792-1808. The Vienna state factory attempted to produce imitations of jasper at the turn of the 18th century. The Poskotchin* factory at Morje (St Petersburg), where much of Wedgwood's production was imitated, produced a blue stone ware with white reliefs in the jasper style, c.1835. None of these European imitations is deceptively close to Wedgwood's jasper in appearance and the technical difficulties inherent in manufacture appear to have discouraged forgeries.

JASPER COLOURS AND VARIATIONS

Black. Solid for frames*, small objects (e.g. Machin's* chessmen) and ornament, 1778-c.1826, c.1866-1941, 1948-86; dip, 1778-c.1826, 1844-1941, 1948-86 (principally for 'prestige items and special orders)

Barberini Black. Mixture of blue and black, solid, dipped in black, created especially for the Portland vase, 1789-90

Blue.   1. Pale blue. Solid, 1775-c.1820, 1860-1941, 1948-6; dip, 1777-1826, 1843-1941, 1948-86 (infrequently)
       2. Dark/Deep Blue. Dip, 1777-c.1820, 1866-1941
       3. Mazarine. Dip, 1777-c.1820
       4. Portland. Solid only, 1980
       5. Royal. Solid only. Introduced 1953

Brown. Solid, for ornament only, c.1778-1820; dip, trials c.1778, small quantities medallions, 1779-1820. See also: Taupe

Cane. Dip only, recorded only once, 1805

Celadon (very faint green). Solid only. Introduced 1879 for Boehm's bust of Gladstone; not known in any other form

Crimson. Dip only, 1910 and 1929-35

Dysart Green (peach green). Solid only. Introduced 1882 for Buckminster Park (see: Ricardo, Halsey)

Green. Solid 1775-c.1820, 1860-1941, 1950-86; dip 1777-1826, 1843-1941; reintroduced after 1948 for trials and special orders only. See also: Teal; Dysart Green

Grey. Solid, 1777-c.1820 (rare), 1960 trials only; dip, 'Quaker' Grey 1879

JASPER TEAWARE. Solid blue and green dip engine-turned teaware made in 1955, illustrating the quality still attainable with modern materials and compositions, and by modern, but costly, methods of manufacture. *Wedgwood Museum*

Lilac. Solid 1777-c.1790 (very rare, probably trials only), 1960-62; dip, 1777-c.1820, 1869-c.1885
Peach Green. See: *Dysart Green*
Pink. Solid, 1982
Primrose. Solid, with white or terracotta (red) reliefs, 1976-82.
Taupe. 1984
Teal. 1984
Terracotta. Solid only, with white or black reliefs, 1957-59
Turquoise. Dip only 1875-c.1885
White. 1774-c.1826, 1844-1941, 1948-86
Yellow. Solid and dip 1777-c.1820; dip, 1869-90
Yellow-Buff. Dip with black ornaments, 1929-33
See: Bas-relief Ware; Cabinet Pieces; Granulated Jasper; Jasper Teaware; Porcelain; Stoneware; Waxen Jasper
See: Colour Plates 55 to 63

Jasper Teaware

Although teapots, tea cups, chocolate cups, coffeepots and coffee cans were made from jasper, no complete services of the kind available in Queen's ware* or Pearl* ware were produced in the 18th century. The cabaret*, popular with the Continental porcelain factories, was probably the commonest set. Cups and saucers were made in great variety, sometimes in three or more colours. They were often engine-turned* and lapidary* polishing of the rims was not uncommon. Cups and saucers, and other jasper teaware pieces of high quality, were not intended for use but for display in cabinets. The interior of such 'cabinet pieces*' was not glazed, but was occasionally lapidary polished, a finish that may be mistaken for glaze. In the 19th century, and until the reintroduction of jasper after World War II, teawares in this style were generally of white stoneware with a coloured jasper dip* (see: Bas-relief Ware), although true jasper teawares were made from 1800 to about 1820 and occasionally after 1860. Since 1948 solid-colour jasper teawares, intended for use and with interiors glazed, have been made regularly in a variety of colours, especially pale-blue and green. A small quantity of solid blue and white and green and white dip* jasper teawares with engine-turned* decoration was made in 1955 but the high production costs of these pieces and their limited market made production uncommercial.
See: Colour Plate 64

Jelly Mould

A vessel for making gelatinous desserts. Wedgwood's Queen's ware* and Pearl* ware jelly moulds were made in two parts: a hollow mould to be filled with jelly or coloured gelatine, and a decorated inner core (also hollow), which was inserted into the outer mould until the jelly was set. The outer mould was then removed, leaving the painting on the inner core visible through the jelly. Such pieces were purely for table decoration, and Parson Woodforde, dining with the local squire on 28 March 1782, noticed 'a very pretty pyramid of Jelly in the Centre [of the table], a Landscape appearing thro' the Jelly, a new device and brought from London'. Tom Byerley* mentioned a 'jelly pyramid' 8½in. high in a letter to Etruria* dated March 1788 and orders for them were accepted at least as late as 1802. Shapes included a wedge, a tall cone and a pyramid, and decoration was usually floral,

JELLY MOULD. Queen's ware jelly mould, the central core enamelled in polychrome, the outer mould fluted and undecorated. The rectangular base of the core is provided with two holes through which the liquid jelly was poured. Height 9in. c.1785. *Wedgwood Museum*

JONES, McDUFFEE & STRATTON CO. Queen's ware plate, transfer-printed in red, commemorating the bicentennial of the founding of the State of Georgia by James Edward Oglethorpe in 1733. Available in red, blue or mulberry prints and issued in a limited edition of 250 sets of twelve plates, each with a different portrait or view. Diameter 10½in.   *Author's collection*

although rare landscape painting is known on these pieces. Drawings of several shapes with enamelled decoration appear in the '1802' Shape Drawing Book* preserved in the Wedgwood archives.
See: Blancmange Moulds

Jewellery
Large quantities of Wedgwood's 18th-century and early 19th-century terracotta*, black basaltes* and jasper* cameos and beads were mounted in gold, ormolu, pinchbeck, silver or cut steel* by Boulton*, Boden & Smith and Green & Vale, all of Birmingham, Thomas Copestake of Uttoxeter, and Hasselwood & Vernon of Wolverhampton. Such jewellery included jasper bead necklaces, brooches, bracelets, buckles, rings, ear-rings, hat pins, pendants, and tiaras. Much of it is either unmarked or mounted in such a manner that the mark is not visible. Jasper by Adams*, Turner* and others was similarly mounted and the identification of Wedgwood pieces may often depend on close familiarity with other distinguishing features such as colour, bas-relief subject and quality. Wedgwood jasper and black basaltes cameos were mounted in metal, notably in silver and gold-plated silver, in the second half of the 19th century.

Original jasper and basalt jewellery was designed for Wedgwood in 1982 by Wendy Ramshaw*, some made in limited editions by the artist herself and other pieces produced in larger quantities from her prototypes. Unlike the jewellery of the 18th century, Ramshaw's work concentrated on innovative use of the ceramic materials, the metal mounts being minimal and incidental to the design. Since the acquisition of Merseyside Jewellers in 1969, Wedgwood has done much of its own metal mounting and a wide range of brooches, pendants, rings, cufflinks and ear-rings has been made in jasper of various colours and in basalt*.
See: Colour Plates 65 and 66

Jewitt, Llewellyn Frederick William (1816-86)
Illustrator and engraver who became successively Chief Librarian of Plymouth Public Library and Curator of the Museum, Curator of the Derby Museum, and founder of the *Daily Telegraph,* which he edited until 1869. He also founded an illustrated magazine, *The Reliquary,* principally devoted to historical and biographical subjects. His best known work, *The Ceramic Art of Great Britain,* was published in two volumes in 1878. That part of the work which concerned the 19th century was revised and expanded by Geoffrey Godden in an edition of 1972. Jewitt's *Life of Josiah Wedgwood,* written without benefit of access to the Mayer* manuscripts, was published in 1865, shortly before Meteyard's* two-volume biography.
See: Wedgwood's Biographers

Jigger
A revolving mould which shapes the front of a plate from a bat of clay placed on it. It is used in conjunction with a stationary tool called a profile, which is brought into contact with the back of the revolving plate, removing excess clay and forming the back and footring. The method is a very old one and the jigger was certainly in use in the 18th century.
See: Jolley; Spreader

Jolley
A revolving mould used in the quantity production of cups. The mould forms the outside, the profile being pressed into the mould to form the inside.
See: Jigger

Jones, McDuffee & Stratton Company
Wholesalers and importers of pottery, porcelain and glassware who trace their history back to 1810, when Otis Norcross founded a crockery business on Fish Street, Boston, Massachusetts. The present company dates from 1871 and by the turn of the century was established as one of the largest importers of pottery and glass in the USA. In 1881 Wedgwood produced the first calendar tile* for Jones McDuffee & Stratton and others were designed annually until 1929. In 1899 thirty-five 'Wedgwood Old Blue Historical Plates' were copyrighted and this quantity was rapidly increased until, when the association was ended in the 1950s, more than 1,000 different views had been produced, transfer-printed* in various colours. The quality of engraving was almost uniformly fine and the many sets comprise a remarkable series of 'named views' which are not without historical value.

Jorrocks, Mr
A fictional Cockney grocer, one of three famous sporting characters (the others are Mr Soapey Sponge and Mr Facey Romford) created by the author R.S. Surtees. Jorrocks first appeared in sketches published in the *New Sporting Magazine,* later collected as *Jorrock's Jaunts and Jollities* (1838). His later adventures in the hunting field were recorded in *Handley Cross* (1843) and *Hillingdon Hall.* Wedgwood produced a series of bone china* plates with powder green borders, the centres decorated with scenes from these classic stories after illustrations by James E. Callahan, c.1912, and a bone china figure of Jorrocks, modelled by Montague Weaver-Bridgeman*, c.1925.

Joseph, Felix (1840-92)
Son of a Bond Street, London, antique dealer and collector; joined his father's firm, inheriting, in 1870, a large fortune. Felix Joseph amassed a formidable collection of ceramics, enamels and drawings, and his collection of Wedgwood was one of the finest among the great hoards accumulated towards the end of the 19th century. On the opening of the Castle Museum, Nottingham, in 1878, Joseph offered the whole of the Wedgwood collection on indefinite loan and it was bequeathed to the Museum on his death fourteen years later. The collection contains many important pieces, including a rare greenish-buff dip *Apotheosis of Homer** vase and an extraordinary George, Prince of Wales vase* or centrepiece which appears to be unique. An exhibition entitled 'Mr Wedgwood' was held at Nottingham Castle in 1975 when the Felix Joseph collection was shown, probably for the first time, to its full advantage.

Judgement of Paris
See: Paris

Julia (39 BC-AD14)
Daughter of Augustus* by Scribonia. She was thrice-married: to M. Marcellus, to Marcus Agrippa and to the future Emperor Tiberius. In consequence of her profligate life, Augustus banished her to the island of Pandataria. A bust of Julia, 15in. high, was supplied by Hoskins & Grant* in 1775 and is listed in the 1777 Catalogue*.

Juno
Roman name for Hera, wife of Zeus (Jupiter*). To the Romans, Juno was the queen of heaven and the female counterpart of Jupiter. She was regarded as the Genius* of womanhood. As Hera, she occupies the same position in Greek mythology and is the only

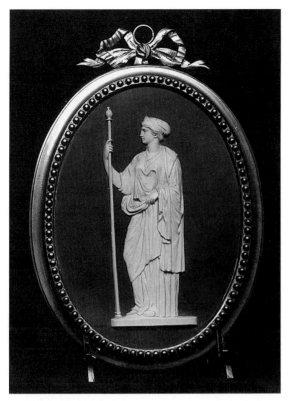

JUNO. Wedgwood & Bentley solid pale-blue and white jasper medallion. Oval height 7½in. 1776-80.
Dwight & Lucille Beeson Collection, Birmingham Museum, Alabama

married goddess (the *mésalliance* between Hephaestus and Aphrodite excepted). She was notable for the way in which she pursued and harried her husband's illegitimate offspring by mortal women. She resented the judgement of Paris* and became hostile to the Trojans in consequence. Juno usually wears a crown, a veil hangs down the back of her head, she may carry a spear and she is often accompanied by a peacock.

Wedgwood subjects:

Juno, Oval medallion 8in. x 6in. No.99 in 1777 Catalogue. From a cast supplied by Flaxman*, 1775, the invoice receipted by the younger Flaxman

Jupiter

Roman name for Zeus, son of Cronos and Rhea, who married his sister Hera (Juno*). When Zeus and his brothers shared the world between them, Poseidon (Neptune*) obtained the sea, Hades (Pluto*) the underworld and Zeus the heavens, the earth being common to all. Zeus, called the father of gods and men, was the supreme ruler, dwelling on Mount Olympus. He is often described as the 'cloud-gatherer' or the 'thunderer' and frequently carries a conventionally represented bolt of lightning as a symbol of his power. He had many amours with mortal women as well as with other goddesses, of whom Hera was extremely jealous. By his wife he had two sons, Ares (Mars*) and Hephaestos (Vulcan*), and one daughter Hebe*. The eagle and the oak were sacred to Zeus, and in art he carries a sceptre, a lightning bolt, or a statuette of Victory in his hand.

Wedgwood subjects:

Jupiter, oval medallion 8in. x 6in. No.98 in 1777 Catalogue. From a cast supplied by Flaxman*, 1775, the invoice receipted by the younger Flaxman

Jupiter and Semele,* medallion 3in. x 2in. No.83 in 1774 Catalogue*

Jupiter, Eagle and Ganymede,* medallion 3½in. x 2¾in. No.262 in 1787 Catalogue

See also: Procession of Deities

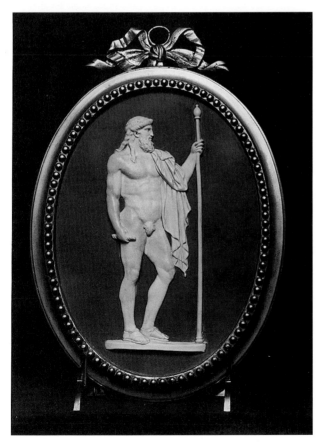

JUPITER. Wedgwood & Bentley solid pale-blue and white jasper medallion. Oval height 7½in. 1776-80.
Dwight & Lucille Beeson Collection, Birmingham Museum, Alabama

JUPITER. Solid white jasper figure of *Jupiter* on a pale-blue and white jasper drum pedestal. Height 10¾in. c.1785.
City Museum & Art Gallery, Stoke-on-Trent

K

Kantharos
Greek drinking cup, commonly associated with Bacchus*, having a tall footed stem and two loop handles extending from the bottom of the bowl to the rim, or with long looped handles. Variants of this classical shape were made by Wedgwood in the 18th and early 19th centuries, particularly in black basaltes* with encaustic* painting.

Kaolin
A china clay, owing its whiteness to a lack of iron impurities. It has little plasticity but is refractory*, with a melting point of over 1770°C. In Britain, kaolin, or china clay, is found in Cornwall; in the USA it is mined in Georgia, Florida and Carolina. Kaolin is one of the two essential ingredients of 'true' porcelain*.
See: Champion, Richard; Cherokee Clay

Kauffmann, Angelica (1741-1807)
Swiss painter; the daughter of a painter; married, 1781, Antonio Zucchi*. During the course of a visit to Italy she painted Winckelmann's portrait and became an enthusiast for the neo-classical* style. A founder member of the Royal Academy, where she exhibited from 1768 to 1797, she numbered Sir Joshua Reynolds* among her friends. Her popular classical and allegorical subjects were sentimental, and through the medium of

KENLOCK WARE. *Iris Kenlock* decoration printed and enamelled on a red-body vase, shape 1501. Height 8½in. c.1898.
City Museum & Art Gallery, Stoke-on-Trent

Bartolozzi's* stipple engravings her works were widely disseminated. They were popular as decoration for interiors in the form of wall and ceiling panels and painted furniture, and were the inspiration of a number of Derby* porcelain figures and groups. A painting *en grisaille, Cleopatra before Augustus* after Thomas Burke's engraving from Kauffmann's painting, appears on a Wedgwood white terracotta* stoneware circular plaque, c.1786-90, acquired by the British Museum in 1909.

Keeling Isaac (1789-1869)
Designer and Engraver at Etruria*. A Wesleyan minister, he was the author of pamphlets, verses and sermons.

Keeling William (fl.1763-90)
Modeller and repairer* of large busts from 1769, he is thought by some to be the modeller of objects bearing a large letter 'K' scratched on the base. A bust of Jan de Witt and a figure of Voltaire* are among those noted with this mark. He is credited with having worked on busts of Francis Bacon, Democritus, Ben Jonson, Spenser and Shakespeare. Many other models, including the Ruined Column* vase and *Triton* figure have been attributed to him but without reliable evidence.

Keir, James FRS (1735-1820)
Scottish chemist. Keir studied medicine at Edinburgh, where he became acquainted with Erasmus Darwin*, but left without graduating and joined the army. He served in the Seven Years' War and in Ireland for eleven years before resigning his commission and returning to the study of chemistry. He visited the Wedgwood factory in 1767, introduced by Darwin, and was an early member of the Lunar Society*. Keir translated and published Pierre Joseph Macquer's huge *Dictionary of Chemistry* and became a partner in a Stourbridge firm of glass manufacturers. He was among those friends, notably Wedgwood and James Watt*, who helped to support Joseph Priestley* after the destruction of his house and laboratory in the Birmingham riots of 1791.

Keith, Sir Robert Murray (1730-95)
Soldier and diplomat, who served with distinction in the Seven Years' War. He was appointed British Minister in Saxony, 1769-71, and, a year later, as envoy in Copenhagen, was appointed KB for rescuing George III's sister, Sophia Matilda, from an angry mob. In the same year he was appointed ambassador at Vienna, where he remained for twenty years. During this period he successfully promoted Wedgwood's tablewares and ornamental wares at the Courts of the Empress Maria Theresa and the Emperors Joseph II and Leopold II. Keith was promoted lieutenant-general in 1781.
See also: German Cameos

Kenlock Ware
Designs, notably *Iris* and *Dragon*, produced as enamelled decoration on red-body vases and jugs, c.1895-1900. Some of Christopher Dresser's* designs were adapted as part of the range and there were also some lighthearted designs for jugs, of which *Golf Girl* is an example. Specimens of Kenlock ware, which was given a special backstamp printed in black or red, are now rare enough to indicate that quantities were small.

Kettle
See: Rum Kettle; Tea Kettle

Key Fret
Repetitive border pattern of short lines meeting at right angles (occasionally at an oblique angle) in a continuous design reminiscent of the wards of a key. Sometimes called a Greek fret* or Chinese fret.
See: Meander Border

Keys, Edward (1798-c.1860)
Modeller of figures and flowers; trained at Derby*, where he was foreman of the figure department, 1821-26; worked for H. & R. Daniel, 1826-31; modeller with Minton*, 1831-42. In 1842 Keys attempted to set up his own porcelain factory but this failed and in 1845 he joined Wedgwood, where he remained until 1853. At Etruria* he modelled Carrara* figures of *Poor Maria* and *Water Nymph* and two groups, *May Day* and *The Surprise*.

KILNS. 'Placing' ware (protected by saggars) inside a 'bottle' ('bee-hive') oven at Etruria, c.1910.   *Photograph: Wedgwood*

KILNS. Firing a bottle oven at Etruria, c.1910.

Photograph: Wedgwood

Kiev-Mezhegorsky

The State factory of Kiev-Mezhegorsky was set up in 1798 and quickly became the largest Russian ceramics factory, producing *faïence* that was later advertised as the best in the country. The wares manufactured there included marbled*, red and chocolate coloured bodies*, and cream-coloured earthenware, often decorated with coloured glazes. The quality was high and an unusually wide variety of goods was made, including barrel-shaped garden seats, picture and mirror frames, icons and Easter eggs. The cream-coloured tablewares, with simple border patterns, and the later green-glazed* moulded leaf-pattern plates and dishes, were in obvious imitation of Wedgwood styles. The factory closed in 1875.

Kilns

A ceramic body is the product not only of the degree of heat to which it is subjected but also of the length of time over which that heat is applied in the kiln or oven.

In Josiah Wedgwood's day all firing was done in intermittent kilns, usually bottle shaped and made of brick. The kiln was packed when cold with the ware to be fired. The fire was then started and, when it had reached maximum temperature, was maintained at that heat for several hours, after which it was cooled slowly to a point where it was cold enough for the ware to be removed. Although some kilns of this type were converted from coal to oil firing early in the 1960s, even small manufacturers, who might have continued to use them, were forced by the Clean Air Act to abandon them. What may be the last firing of a bottle kiln took place as a museum demonstration in 1978 in the Potteries, and this particular kiln is being preserved as an industrial archaeological specimen.

The modern kiln is fired by gas, oil or electricity. The first gas-fired tunnel oven, 100ft. long, was introduced at Etruria* for the firing of bone china* in 1927 by Norman Wilson*. This was followed three years later by the installation of the first earthenware glost tunnel oven, 150ft. long and fired by oil. All Wedgwood's firing is now electrical. The first Brown Boveri contra-flow oven was built in 1940 and fired continuously for the next seven years.

Under the contra-flow system, twin tunnels fire biscuit* in one direction and glost* in the other. The ware is closely stacked on shelves mounted on wheeled trucks which are fireproof, and these move extremely slowly, in a continuous line, through a tunnel 272ft. long, the truck taking seventy hours to traverse its length. The first 90ft. is a pre-heating zone; the next 70ft. the firing zone; and the last 112ft. the cooling zone. Wares which do not distort (those which are refractory*) may be packed on the truck without supports, and many may be placed one upon the other. Those wares which soften at high temperatures, like stonewares and porcelain compounded of clay and fusible materials which are liable to distortion, are supported with props made of highly refractory material.

In the old bottle kilns, wares likely to be damaged by contact with the flames were packed in fireclay boxes known as saggars*, the lids of which were sometimes sealed with plastic clay to prevent the entry of unwanted gases which, in the case of enamelled wares or coloured glazes, could spoil the decoration by reacting with the colouring oxide.

The glost oven is fired at a lower temperature than that of the biscuit oven, the heat required being sufficient only to melt the glaze particles and spread them over the surface. Care must be taken that none of the objects touch one another in the glost firing: they would otherwise be irretrievably stuck together.

A muffle kiln is a low temperature kiln used for firing enamel painting and other forms of onglaze decoration. The heat is sufficient slightly to soften the surface of the glaze and to convert the enamel into a kind of glass akin to glaze in its composition, but firing at a lower temperature. Some colours need a higher temperature to develop them than others, and these are fired first, the others being fired-on subsequently at a lower temperature. Enamels fired in the old muffle kilns were invariably enclosed in saggars to protect them. Muffle kilns vary greatly in size and some may be little larger than a domestic oven. Writing to Bentley*, Wedgwood recommended using the bread oven at Greek Street for the purpose on one occasion, and gave directions for doing so, adding that the normal temperature for baking bread would suffice. It is not un-

common for enamel colours to be referred to as 'muffle' colours, as distinct from the high-temperature colours like cobalt* and manganese*, which are capable of bearing the full heat of the kiln used to fire the ware itself.
See also: Pyrometer

Knife Hafts (Handles)

Marbled* and variegated* hafts for knives and forks have been excavated from the Whieldon* site and early examples of this type of ware are confidently attributed to Wedgwood. Simeon Shaw* states that Wedgwood, while still in partnership with Harrison*, 'supplied the tradesmen of Birmingham and Sheffield with Earthenware hafts for Table knives &c in imitation of Agate, Tortoiseshell, Marble and other kinds'. By about 1800 Wedgwood was making jasper knife handles with bas-relief* ornament and small quantities of jasper handles were made in the 19th and early 20th centuries. These were reintroduced in 1959 in solid pale blue and white and green and white jasper. Queen's ware* knife hafts painted to match 18th-century tableware patterns are also known, but they are usually unmarked and are extremely rare. In the 19th century decorative Queen's ware handles were made but the quantities were always small and comparatively few have survived.

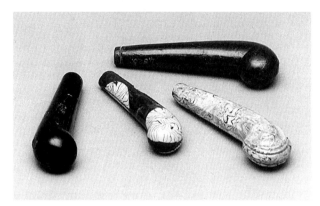

KNIFE HAFTS. Four knife hafts or handles, two with decoration imitating agate, of the type believed to have been made by Wedgwood both before and shortly after his partnership with Whieldon. Length about 4in. c.1752-60. *Wedgwood Museum*

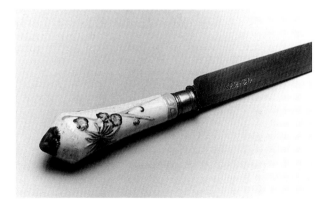

KNIFE HAFTS. Argenta knife handle with moulded relief of flowers decorated in coloured glazes over an opaque white glaze. Unmarked. Wedgwood, c.1880. *Wedgwood Museum*

Knight, Dame Laura (née Johnson) D.B.E., R.A. (1877-1970)

Painter and etcher; studied at Nottingham School of Art and at the Royal College of Art; exhibited at the Royal Academy from 1903; married the painter Harold Knight, 1903. Laura Knight was noted especially for scenes from the theatre, ballet, circus and music hall, and also of gipsies and their encampments. She was created D.B.E. in 1929. Her autobiography *Oil Paint and Grease Paint* was published in 1936. In the same year she was commissioned by Wedgwood to design a loving cup in bone china* to celebrate the

KNIGHT, Dame Laura. Bone china mug designed by Laura Knight to commemorate the Coronation of King George VI and Queen Elizabeth in 1937. The design is printed in blue and enriched with enamel colours and gold. Height 8¾in. *Wedgwood Museum*

Coronation of Edward VIII due to take place in the following year. This design was hurriedly adapted for the Coronation of George VI. The result is not pleasing. The ornate two-handled mug, with lid surmounted by a lion standing on a crown, is lavishly gilded and overdecorated. Ravilious*, also commissioned to design a mug for the same occasion, described Knight's as 'bloody beyond description' and it is difficult to dissent from this opinion.

Knops

Knobs used as handles on the lids of such objects as teapots, coffeepots, covered jugs, vegetable dishes, sauce tureens, soup tureens, mustard pots etc. Certain shapes were used exclusively by Wedgwood in the 18th century and others are especially associated with wares produced at Etruria*. These may often be of considerable assistance in the identification of unmarked pieces, especially if they are found with characteristic Wedgwood spouts* and handles*.

The typical early Wedgwood rose knop is raised above the surface of the lid and rests on a pad of clay. The clay support for the flower head was not used by any other manufacturer. The second shape typical of the period c.1763-90 is the pierced baluster. The third is the pierced ball. Neither of these, however, was exclusive to Wedgwood. Other knops in regular use by Wedgwood in the 18th and early 19th centuries include the acorn*, artichoke, flattened flower, 'plume', oval ring, sibyl* and spaniel (found almost exclusively on dry bodies*). Since about 1810, the most popular knops for Traditional shape (see: Tableware Shapes) Queen's ware* covered dishes and tureens have been the round and oval plume.
See also: Stephan, Pierre

Krater

Greek pottery vase for mixing wine and water. It has a wide mouth and body, a small circular foot and two handles. One of the most common of South Italian vase shapes, it is well known in four forms: bell, calyx, columnar and volute*. Wedgwood favoured particularly the bell krater and volute krater, both of which were produced in plain black basaltes* and basaltes decorated with encaustic* painting.

KNOPS.

1. Typical early Wedgwood rose knop, the flower head raised above the lid and supported on a pad of clay, on a creamware shell-edge shape teapot, c.1770. This form is exclusively Wedgwood's. *Wedgwood Museum*

2. Leeds creamware rose knop, the flower head typically resting its petals on the lid. c.1785. This form was not used by Wedgwood. *Temple Newsam House, Leeds*

3. Flower or 'plume' knop from the lid of a sauce tureen, enamelled with *Flute and Wreath* pattern, c.1785. *Author's collection*

4. Acorn knop from the cover of a Pearl ware root dish, decorated in underglaze blue, c.1790. *Author's collection*

5. Grape-bunch knop from a Pearl ware rum kettle, c.1790-1800. This form of knop is found also on black basaltes kettles. *Wedgwood Museum*

6. Lion knop from a Wedgwood & Bentley black basaltes engine-turned teapot, c.1776. The lion is possibly the model invoiced by Pierre Stephan in September 1774. *Wedgwood Museum*

KRATER. Vase of volute-krater shape with mask handles, painted in encaustic colours with the figure of a young warrior and a horse within a funerary *naiskos* or *heroön*. The decoration is copied from a volute krater in the Hamilton collection. Height 14in. *Mr & Mrs Samuel Laver Collection*

Kuntze, Edward J. (1826-70)

Pomeranian sculptor and modeller, who spent most of his working life in New York. He exhibited portraits in marble at the Royal Academy in the 1860s. Parian* figures after original work by Kuntze were produced by Worcester*, and in 1863 Wedgwood reproduced Kuntze's *Hiawatha* in Carrara*, paying the artist a commission of ten per cent on sales.

Kylix

A Greek pottery shallow cup on a tall footed stem, similar in shape to the tazza. Wedgwood produced this shape in black basaltes* decorated with encaustic* painting.

KYLIX. Black basaltes kylix, shape no.662, painted in encaustic colours. Width 8in. c.1810. *Merseyside Museums*

L

La Charité-sur-Loire (Nièvre)

Factory founded by Francis Warburton (grandson of Anne Warburton*) in 1802 where he made white earthenware (faïence-fine), black basaltes* and other English-style wares. It was taken over in 1803 by Le Boult. The manager was an Englishman, Michael Willis.

Ladies' Amusement, The

Subtitled *The Whole Art of Japanning Made Easy,* this design book, compiled by Robert Sayer*, was published in London in 1762. The designs, including those after Pillement* and many by Robert Hancock*, were reversed so that they could be copied directly on to a copper plate. They include genre subjects, flowers, insects and *chinoiseries.* Copies of them occur on transfer-printed* pottery, porcelain and enamels and some were adapted for use on Wedgwood Queen's ware*.

Ladles

Large ladles for use with soup tureens and a smaller size for sauces and gravy were made by Wedgwood to match many of the early Queen's ware* patterns. The smaller ladle was sometimes pierced. Such ladles continued to be made in the 19th century, especially to match underglaze blue printed* patterns, but ladles are among the most vulnerable of all tablewares and few have survived.

LADLES. Queen's ware sauce tureen and fixed stand, decorated with *Flute and Wreath* pattern in brown and red, with a pair of matching ladles, one pierced. Ladle length 6½in. c.1790-5. *Author's collection*

Lag and Feather Pattern

See: Flute and Wreath Pattern

Laminated Jasper

Jasper of two contrasting colours bonded together so that a two-colour intaglio* gem* or seal* may be made from the layered blank before firing. Laminated gems and seals were made by Wedgwood in the 18th century, and these were usually lapidary* polished, but the technique was costly and it was abandoned by about 1810. Laminated jasper was occasionally used for the grounds of cameos* and small portrait medallions* but examples are extremely rare.

LAMP BASES. Embossed Queen's ware *Edme* fluted lamp base, finished in Dysart glaze. Height 10¾in. 1956. *Author's collection*

Lamp Bases

Wedgwood jasper*, basaltes* and Queen's ware* components were used in the 19th century for the manufacture of oil lamps and brackets, as jasper and basaltes were used in the 18th century for the components of candelabra and girandoles, but shapes made specifically for use as lamp bases were not made until after 1878, following the invention of the electric filament lamp. Earlier bases were adapted from vases, pedestals and bough pots. Wedgwood bases exist in jasper and basaltes (though the majority are vases converted after production), and in bone china*, but only Queen's ware lamp bases were ever made in large quantities. These have been produced in various shapes in plain cream colour, coloured bodies*, embossed Queen's ware*, and Queen's ware decorated with enamel or lithographed* patterns such as *Napoleon Ivy*, Peter Rabbit*, Circus, Charnwood* and *Liverpool Birds.*
See: Lamps

Lamps

Wedgwood made pottery lamps similar to those commonly used in the classical world, excavated specimens of which were fairly numerous in 18th-century collections of antiquities. These were of

LAMPS. Two Wedgwood & Bentley variegated oil lamps of Queen's ware or white terracotta decorated with sprinkled 'pebble' in blue-green and black: *(left)* dolphin tripod lamp with candleholder, height 7½in.; *(right)* lamp with three handles and burners on applied masks, height 9½in. c.1774. *Private Collection. Photograph: Courtesy of David Buten*

LAMPS. Wedgwood & Bentley black basaltes lamp with two burners. Height 9½in. c.1775. *Kadison Collection*

flattened oval shape, covered, and contained colza oil. The wick protruded through a small spout at one end, and a small handle was placed at the other. Eighteen brown earthenware lamps in this Roman style were invoiced by Wedgwood in July 1774 at one shilling and sixpence each. In January 1771 Wedgwood wrote to Bentley*: 'We are making Lamps of various sorts some of which will be fired in our next Oven' and in July he mentioned lamps with three handles and 'masque' faces to the spouts as available from stock. These were certainly of black basaltes* or variegated* ware, and they are described in the 1779 Catalogue* as: 'Lamps…both of the variegated Pebble and black [basaltes] composition. They bear the flame perfectly well, and are fit for Chambers, Halls, Stair-cases, &c. The Tripod Lamps with several Lights are highly en-riched, and will be suitable Ornaments for the finest Apartments'.

Elaborate lamps of black basaltes or, after 1776, of jasper, were priced between one-and-a-half and two guineas. Probably the most elaborate of these was the so-called Michelangelo* lamp, and among the most popular were certainly the 'Vestal'* and 'Reading'* lamps – boat-shaped, turned or ornamented, on stems and plinths, the handles formed by finely modelled figures of seated women – and the rather similar oval footed lamps with lights at both ends. The Michelangelo, Vestal and Reading lamps were originally made in black basaltes in the Wedgwood & Bentley period, but all were reproduced in jasper towards the end of the 18th century and in Majolica* and bone china* in the 19th century. All have been frequently reproduced in black basaltes and were readily available in the 1920s. An extremely rare jasper hanging lamp, c.1795, is in the Lady Lever Art Gallery, Port Sunlight. An unusual Queen's ware 'toy lamp' – a small pierced bowl of inverted bell shape on three short splayed feet, with two loop handles – is illustrated in the '1802' Shape Drawing Book and an example was in the Buten* Museum.

See also: Argand Lamp; Food Warmers (Night Lamps); J.Hinks & Son; Lamp Bases; Oil Lamp

Lampshades
See: Light Shades

Landré, Mrs Mary (fl.1768-74)
Mrs Landré supplied Wedgwood and Bentley with casts between 1768 and 1774 and invoices from her are preserved in the Wedgwood archives. From the prices charged, it is clear that the models obtained from her were not original work. Wedgwood's letter to Bentley* dated 31 October 1768 makes it plain that he was already, at that date, making copies from her casts. It was John Voyez* who warned him that she was 'the D---l at finding out Pirates' and Wedgwood told Bentley: 'If once she finds me out, I shall never be able to get a Cast from her.' Evidently, at this time, Wedgwood was making and marketing black basaltes bas-relief subjects from Landré's casts without her knowledge, and he

arranged for future orders to be placed by Bentley in London.
Subjects listed on Landré's invoices which are identifiable in Wedgwood & Bentley catalogues are as follows:

Apollo and Marsyas ⎫ A set of three bas-reliefs, 1769
Apollo and Daphne ⎬ Nos 8-10 in 1773 Catalogue*
Apollo and Python ⎭

Bacchanalian Boys at Play, 1769. No.13 in 1773 Catalogue
Bacchanalian Triumph. Probably the 'Antique Bacchanalians' sup-plied in 1769 for 7/6d. No.12 in 1773 Catalogue
Five Bacchanalian Figures (probably figures from the Borghese* vase), 1769. Nos 126-30 in 1777 Catalogue

Head of Apollo ⎫ Probably the 'heads from Mrs.
Head of Venus ⎬ Laundre' mentioned in January 1771.
⎭ Nos. 17-18 in 1773 Catalogue

Set of twelve Caesars with six Empresses, 1769
Silenus and Boys, 1769. No.14 in 1773 Catalogue
Other subjects (all bas-reliefs unless otherwise described) invoiced are:
Battle piece (possibly *War of Jupiter and the Titans*)
Female Virtues (Faith, Hope and *Charity*)
Four Quarters of the Earth
Six Friars
Horse
Jesus dead, with Virgin and Boys
Joseph
The Last Supper
Magdalen
Moses and the Serpent (probably Aesculapius*)
Naiad*, figure for a pair of candelabra
Neptune*, large figure, 1769
Six Passions (Vices)
The English Poets, set of portrait heads
Scripture Pieces, set of four
Shepherd
*Signs of the Zodiac**
Vintage (set of three)
It is probable that Mrs Landré supplied more of the early bas-relief subjects and also the five figures of Sleeping Boys* after Duquesnoy*.

Landskip Pattern
A moulded pattern, made c.1762-3 in saltglazed* stoneware, enamelled creamware and green glaze*, by Wedgwood, the design attributed, without certain evidence, to William Greatbatch*. Block moulds for this pattern are in the Wedgwood Museum* and ver-sions of it were made by Whieldon* and other Staffordshire potters.

LANDSKIP PATTERN. Saltglazed stoneware teapot moulded with the 'Landskip' pattern, the reliefs painted in green, pink, yellow and brown enamel colours. Height 4in. Unmarked. Probably Whieldon or Wedgwood, c.1760. *Mrs R.D. Chellis Collection*

Lansdowne, Sir William Petty, 1st Marquis and 2nd Earl of Shelburne (1737-1805)
Statesman. President of the Board of Trade, 1763; Secretary of State, 1766-8; Home Secretary, 1782; First Lord of the Treasury, 1782-3. As Lord Shelburne, he consistently advocated conciliation of the American colonies, although he opposed the recognition of

American independence. His rejection of political parties and faction laid him open to charges of insincerity and he was one of the least popular of 18th-century statesmen. A generous patron of the arts, he allowed Wedgwood to take moulds from fourteen plaster bas-reliefs inspired by Roman wall-paintings at Herculaneum*. Black basaltes* and white terracotta* copies, usually described by Wedgwood as 'Herculaneum Pictures'*, were first catalogued in 1773.

Lapidary

A carver of hardstones, semi-precious stones and gemstones, who makes use of the principle that a substance will always be cut by one which is harder and will cut one which is softer. The chief decorative hardstones are agate, amethyst, lapis lazuli*, turquoise, rock crystal, sardonyx, chalcedony and cornelian, but other stones, such as granite, also reveal a decorative surface when cut and polished. All these stones exhibit a hardness of between 5.5 and 7 on Moh's scale. A substance which is hard enough to cut these stones easily is emery (carborundum), well known to the Egyptians, which is 9 on Moh's scale. Industrial diamonds, hardest of all, have a factor of 10. Steel, unless of a specially hardened variety, falls into a position of 5 on Moh's scale, so it will not cut any of the hardstones mentioned. Wedgwood's jasper* and basaltes* vary in hardness between 6 and 7 (i.e. between turquoise and agate), and he employed lapidary techniques for a variety of processes, including the polishing of seals* and cameos*, the edges of the finest medallions* and tablets*, and the rims and interiors of cups. The usual method of working is to remove the unwanted material rapidly with a coarse abrasive, and then polish with a fine abrasive. Emery cloth, used in the engineering trades, cuts basaltes and jasper without trouble and polish may be added by using the finest grade obtainable.

By 1774, lapidary polishing of gems and seals had become 'a capital branch of our Manufacture', as Wedgwood told Bentley, and it was soon decided that this work should be done on their own premises in London. The first lapidary employed by Wedgwood & Bentley was John Griffiths*, engaged in 1777 at the comparatively high wage of twenty shillings a week. Just one hundred years later, the lapidary and glassworker, John Northwood* was employed to finish an edition of the Portland vase*.

Lapis Lazuli

Natural lapis lazuli is an azure-coloured stone. Highly prized since ancient times, it was originally the source, in powdered form, of the artist's pigment ultramarine. The name, lapis lazuli, was used by Wedgwood to describe an especially fine and rare form of variegated* ware which was a deep variegated blue with gold veining.

Last Day's Vases

See: First Day's Vases

Lathe

A machine tool in which the ware is held between rotating centres on a horizontal axis, and various stationary cutting tools are brought into contact with it as it turns for the purpose of uniformly paring down the surface or incising simple ornament such as stepped rings. There are two types of lathe in use in the pottery industry: the simple lathe, described above; and the engine-turning* lathe.

The lathe has been employed for wood-turning since the Bronze Age, when the pole lathe was in use, and for metal turning for many centuries. It was reputedly introduced into Staffordshire by the Elers* brothers shortly after 1700. Writing to Bentley* in July 1777 about the improvements brought to Staffordshire by John Philip and David Elers, Wedgwood stated: The next improvement introduc'd by Mr E. was the refining of our common red clay...& turning it on the outside upon Lathes'.

Lathes for the pottery industry were made in the early part of the century by Randle of Congleton. Improvements were devised by William Baddeley* in 1764, and by Wedgwood himself a little later. Wedgwood attempted to prevent the improved lathe from becoming generally available by offering Baddeley a high price, but with little success. He used the lathe extensively in the manufacture of early creamware*, red ware*, black basaltes* and white terracotta* and it has continued in use for the production of many types of ware ever since. The use of the more highly skilled

LATTICE WORK. Solid yellow and white jasper custard cup and cover ornamented with trellis or latticework, the cover intricately pierced. Height 2½in. c.1785-90.   *Wedgwood Museum*

engine-turning* technique was largely confined to the dry bodies*, although some of the earliest creamware vases were given engine-turned decoration. Wedgwood made good use of an illustrated guide to turning, Plumier's *L'Art de Tourner,* published in Paris in 1701.

Lattice Work

Applied lattice or trellis work was used as jasper* ornament in the last quarter of the 18th century. Such intricate and delicate ornament, usually in white jasper over a ground of contrasting colour, required exceptional skill and examples are scarce.

Lauraguais, Louis-Léon-Félicité, Comte de (1733-1824)

Duc de Brancas. Owner of a laboratory at the Château de Lassay, where he produced, c.1765, the first French 'true' (hard paste*) porcelain. His porcelain was of poor colour and was never made in quantity. He later came to England and found kaolin* in Cornwall. He attempted to take out a patent for the manufacture of porcelain in England in 1766 and to sell the secret of its manufacture for £2,000. Wedgwood was well informed about this work by October 1767 and took a copy of the patent application for his Commonplace Book*.

Laurel Border

A border pattern consisting of a series of laurel leaves placed horizontally and separated by flowers and berries. It was used commonly on Queen's ware* and jasper* during the period of the neoclassical* style and has appeared at irregular intervals in the 19th and 20th centuries, mostly as reproductions of earlier patterns.

Lavender

A grey-blue stained body introduced in 1858.
See: Coloured Bodies

Lawson Peacey, Mrs J (fl.1920-38)

Sculptress. She modelled a figure of a lady with peacocks which was moulded at Etruria* to her order in 1930. It is not certain that this was ever produced commercially by Wedgwood.

Lazy Susan

See: Revolving Tray

Lead

See: Glazes

LE BRUN, Charles. Black jasper dip vase with Etruscan scroll handles and bas-relief ornament of *Cupid watering the Swans* after a design by Charles Le Brun. Height 10½in. c.1790. *Wedgwood Museum*

Le Brun, Charles (1629-90)

French painter and principal decorative artist of the reign of Louis XIV; founder member of the Académie. Lebrun's output was prodigious and included decorative work of all kinds. The following, sometimes erroneously attributed to Mme Vigée Le Brun, are derived from designs by Charles Le Brun:

Cupid Watering Swans, no.246 in 1787 Catalogue*
Venus in her Car drawn by Swans, no.245 in 1787 Catalogue

Both bas-reliefs* were made as tablets* 4¼in. x 9in., but they are more commonly found as ornament for jasper snake-handled vases and an example of this vase was chosen as the subject of a full-page illustration in Wedgwood's 1787 Catalogue. The design of the snake-handled vase, often attributed to Le Brun, is more likely to have been based on late 16th-century Italian *maiolica* from Urbino (the type known as Raphaelesque), in which Wedgwood is recorded as showing a close interest.

See: Raphael Ware

Le Marchand, David (1674-1726)

Ivory carver of Dieppe, who produced, according to George Vertue, 'a vast number of heads from ye life in basso relief'. The earliest dated portrait in ivory by Le Marchand appears to be that of Sir Isaac Newton, 1718, but there is reason to believe that he was in England some years sooner. Wedgwood portrait medallions* copied

LE MARCHAND, David. Carved ivory portrait medallion of Sir Christopher Wren by David Le Marchand, c.1723. Oval height 5in. This portrait was copied by Wedgwood in black basaltes as early as 1773, and later in jasper.
National Portrait Gallery, London

LEAFAGE. White ware jug enamelled in bright green and purple. Height 5⅝in. c.1820. *Formerly Buten Museum*

from his work include those of Boileau-Despreaux (the French critic), Anne Dacier, Sir Isaac Newton, Sir Christopher Wren, Matthew Raper II (Huguenot banker) and his wife, and Charles Chester Eyre. All but the last three, which were probably private commissions, appear in the 1773 Catalogue. Wedgwood busts of Newton and John Locke are also after ivories by Le Marchand.

Leader, G. (fl.1792-1804)

Wax modeller who exhibited a number of relief portraits, including those of George Stubbs*, Paul Sandby and Admiral William Bligh, at the Royal Academy between 1792 and 1801. In 1794 he modelled the portrait of the banker, George Temple, from which Wedgwood's jasper portrait medallion was copied, probably by Hackwood*. This appears to have been a private commission.

Leaf Dish

A dish naturalistically moulded in the form of a leaf, or of overlapping leaves, usually with veins in slight relief. This was a popular Wedgwood rococo* style in the 18th and 19th centuries, being made in large quantities with green glaze* and for a shorter period in Majolica*.

Leafage Ware

Dessert ware and jugs moulded with patterns of large leaves in low relief made c.1804-20 in White ware* with enamelled decoration. The plates were available with green, brown, red, blue or gilt fibres, or with green and red fibres and green or brown rays in the centre. The same shape of plate was available decorated with green glaze. Leafage ware was made also in the Cane* body and is illustrated in the 1804 Price Book.

Leather Hard

Also, cheese hard. The state of an unfired piece of pottery after the evaporation of some of the moisture content. It is not unlike leather in firmness and pliability, and in this condition it can be turned on a lathe* or ornament may be incised by engine-turning*. Slip* is applied to the surface of ware in this state in the making of marbled* ware.

Leda

Wife of Tyndareus, King of Sparta. She was visited by Zeus (Jupiter*) in the guise of a swan and subsequently laid two eggs. From one of these eggs came the twins, Castor and Pollux, and from the other, Helen of Troy. Leda also became the mother of Clytemnestra, but in a more conventional manner. The story of Leda and the swan has long been a favourite among painters and

LEDA. Solid pale blue and white jasper vase with swan handles, the finial in the form of figures of *Leda and the Swan*. Height 16⅞in. c.1795.

Dwight & Lucille Beeson Collection, Birmingham Museum, Alabama

sculptors, the Wedgwood version, modelled in the round as an elaborate finial* to a vase (shape no.274) being less explicit than most. It was, perhaps surprisingly, Bentley* who thought the subject of Jupiter and Leda 'too warm' for Wedgwood & Bentley's customers. A figure of *Leda* was modelled by Donald Brindley* and reproduced in jasper in 1975.

Ledward, Richard Arthur (1857-90)
Sculptor and modeller; studied at the Wedgwood Institute, Burslem, before working briefly at Etruria*. He later became modelling master at the South Kensington College of Art. His son, Gilbert Ledward R.A. (1888-1960) was one of the most distinguished British sculptors of his time.

LEECH JAR. Queen's ware leech jar, shape no.1111, with perforated lid, decorated in dark-red enamel. Height 11½in. c.1810.

York Castle Museum, Long Collection

LEEDS POTTERY. Creamware vase-candlestick, shape no.116 in the Leeds Pattern Book. Height 12⅜in. c.1785. The winged figure handles are similar to those on contemporary and earlier Wedgwood black basaltes and variegated vases. *Temple Newsam House, Leeds*

Leech Jar
A jar, usually on a pedestal stem and circular foot, with pierced lid, used in apothecaries' shops. Leech jars, which are often inscribed with the word 'Leeches' in blue or black, were part of the Pharmacy ware* made by manufacturers of tin-glazed earthenwares in the 17th and 18th centuries and by some creamware potters between c.1770 and 1850. Wedgwood examples are rare.

Leech John (1817-64)
Humorous artist, who subscribed more than 3,000 drawings, including some 600 cartoons, for *Punch* magazine between 1841 and 1864. He illustrated several books and his sporting sketches, in particular, were often reproduced. A series of his drawings, 'The Fisherman', was copied as the decoration for a set of Wedgwood Queen's ware* plates, c.1905, and others, which had appeared in Punch, were copied by William Wagstaffe* on dessert plates c.1868.

Leeds Pottery
The Old Pottery was founded in the 1750s (the precise date is uncertain). In 1774 its style was Humble, Green & Co., and in 1781 it became Hartley Greens & Co. The factory flourished until 1820 and subsequently changed hands several times before closing in 1878. The Hunslett Old Pottery, founded before 1792, made similar wares, and Slee's Modern Pottery (founded 1888) has used old moulds and patterns for wares with the old mark. Old Leeds is rarely marked, except for those pieces illustrated in the Pattern Books, but after 1790 a fair proportion of Pearl ware, blue-printed wares and figures was impressed* 'LEEDS POTTERY'. The greater part of the Leeds output was of creamware of excellent quality. Much use was made of pierced* work in imitation of contemporary silver, and elaborate centrepieces were a speciality. Like Wedgwood, Leeds issued a number of catalogues, the earliest in 1783 being printed in French, German and Spanish language editions. Transfer-printing* was largely done at the factory. Some painted wares are decorated in a style which appears also on Wedgwood's creamware and early Queen's ware* and these are the work of Jasper Robinson* and David Rhodes*, or of enamellers employed by Robinson & Rhodes at Briggate, Leeds.

Some gilded creamware of outstanding quality was probably decorated by James Giles's* studio, but much of the gilding* at Leeds (attributed to Robinson & Rhodes) was applied gold leaf and has now worn away. Early Leeds creamware was, like Wedgwood's, a deep cream or buff colour, but after 1775, when Champion's* patent was withdrawn, it became paler, closely resembling Queen's ware. Among other wares made by Leeds may be included an agate* body, variegated* ware, red stoneware*, black basaltes*, saltglazed*

LEIGHTON, Clare. Queen's ware plate printed in black with 'Ice Cutting' from Clare Leighton's set of twelve wood engravings of 'New England Industries'. Diameter 10in. 1950.   *Wedgwood Museum*

LEMONADE CUP. White ware biscuit *trembleuse* lemonade cup with cover and stand, the interior lead-glazed. Height 4½in. c.1830.
Author's collection

stoneware, green-glazed* creamware, Pearl ware*, lustre* and slip-decorated creamware with engine-turned* and dice-pattern* decoration. The quality is seldom inferior to Wedgwood's and some of the pierced ware is unsurpassed in creamware.

Leg Pan
See: Foot Pan

Leigh, Charles and James (fl.1775-1820)
Proprietors of a factory making *faïence-fine* in imitation of English creamware, opened at Douai (Nord) in 1781, with the assistance of a French merchant, George Bris. Their commonest products imitated Leeds rather than Wedgwood, and they specialised in pierced wares. They also made variegated* ware, biscuit* wares ornamented with bas-reliefs* and unglazed black and red stone-wares. Workmen were engaged from England to instruct craftsmen who later moved to other factories in France, where they made similar wares. The Douai factory closed about 1820. A letter addressed to Bris by Samuel Jones, a painter at Etruria, was inter-cepted in 1784 and returned to Wedgwood. Jones offered his own services and also those of four others, 'a turner, a presser and handler a modeller and a man that cann make as good a China glaze and Enamel coulers as any man in the country'. The risk taken by Jones is emphasised by his offer to negotiate on behalf of the others, all of whom were married – 'to run the hazard of anything happening from the masters in this country' – and by his providing only an accommodation return address in Derbyshire although his letter is clearly headed 'Staffordshire Pottery'.
See also: Industrial Espionage

Leigh Shape
See Tableware Shapes

Leighton, Clare Veronica Hope (1898-1989)
Painter, wood-engraver and author; born in London and studied at the Brighton School of Art, the Slade and the Central School of Arts & Crafts, where she specialised in wood engraving under the tuition of Noel Rooke. Clare Leighton illustrated a number of books, including her own pioneering book about the process of wood-engraving, published in 1932. From 1939 she lived and worked in America. In 1951 she designed the decoration for a series of twelve Queen's ware* plates illustrating New England Industries. The twelve subjects, transfer-printed* in black, are: Whaling, Marble Quarrying, Cranberrying, Ice Cutting, Logging, Farming, Grist-milling, Shipbuilding, Sugaring, Codfishing and Tobacco Growing.

Leith Hill Place, Surrey
A 16th-century mansion with substantial 18th-century additions and façade bought by Josiah Wedgwood III* and his wife Caroline (Darwin) in 1847, who made further alterations to the building. From 1875 it was the home of their widowed daughter Margaret, and thus also of her son Ralph Vaughan Williams, one of England's greatest

20th-century composers, who became the owner of the house in 1944. He presented the property to the National Trust and in 1947 it was let to his cousin, Sir Ralph Wedgwood Bt, brother of Josiah IV* (Lord Wedgwood of Barlaston) and of Francis Hamilton Wedgwood*, who had been Chairman and Managing Director of the firm until his death in 1930. In 1956 the tenancy passed to Sir John Wedgwood*, Sir Ralph's son, who surrendered it to the National Trust in 1965.

Lemonade Cup
Footed cup with two handles, lid and saucer with a deep (*trembleuse*) well; often erroneously called an ice-cream cup. Lemonade cups were made by Wedgwood in biscuit White ware* with glazed interiors, 1824-32, and were sometimes supplied to amateur artists to decorate (as was the white terracotta stoneware* before White ware was introduced). Lemonade cups with a single handle were made also in smear-glazed* stoneware with coloured reliefs, c.1815-35.

Lemonade Set
A set comprising a tall jug and six beakers for the service of fresh lemonade. Wedgwood has produced two Lemonade sets of par-ticular distinction: the set decorated with *Garden Implements* pattern, designed by Eric Ravilious* in 1939, printed in black with 'pink' lustre* or yellow enamel; and that decorated with *Oranges and Lemons,* designed by Richard Guyatt* in 1955, printed in black with enamel wash bands.

LEMONADE SET. Queen's ware *Oranges and Lemons* lemonade set, printed in black with views of London churches and decorated with enamelled wash bands, designed by Richard Guyatt, 1955. Jug height 7¹/₁₆in.   *Wedgwood Museum*

LESSORE, (Elaine) Thérèse. Queen's ware dish decorated in purple (gold) lustre, c.1920. 7¼in. square. *Wedgwood Museum*

Leopold II, Holy Roman Emperor (1747-92)
See: German Cameos

Leslie, Sir John (1766-1832)
Scottish mathematician and physicist; private tutor to Wedgwood's family 1790-2; elected professor of Mathematics, Edinburgh, 1805; member of the Institute of France, 1820; knighted 1832. Tom Wedgwood* (Josiah's youngest son) first met Leslie, who was five years his senior, at Edinburgh University and invited him to Etruria. He proposed to set up house with him in order to pursue his scientific studies, but Josiah refused permission for this arrangement and, instead, took Leslie into his family for two years 'bringing his sons to a more intimate acquaintance with some branches of philosophy than the time they were at Edinburgh would allow them to acquire.' It was during this short period that Tom made his first experiments with the chemical action of light. After Josiah's death in January 1795, Tom set off on a five-month walking tour in Germany with Leslie, to whom, in 1797, he gave an annuity for life of £150.

Lessore. Elaine Thérèse (1884-1945)
Painter of landscapes, interiors and scenes and characters from the circus. Daughter of Jules Lessore*, grand-daughter of Emile Lessore.

LESSORE, Emile. Lessore's 'reversed' monogram (shown on the base of a creamware plate) which appears on early plaques and some later small pieces. *Photograph: Wedgwood*

She studied at the Slade School and married, as his third wife, the painter Walter Sickert. She painted occasional pieces for Wedgwood, some of them in lustre*, probably using 'blanks' obtained for her by her sister Louise (Powell*). Her style is free and distinctively French, not infrequently reminiscent of the work of Lautrec.

Lessore, Emile (1805-76)
Painter on pottery and porcelain at Bourg-la-Reine and at Sèvres, 1852-58. Lessore painted Queen's ware* tablewares, plaques* and tablets* for Wedgwood, 1858-63, and worked as a freelance decorator for Wedgwood, 1863-75.
Lessore studied in the studio of Ingres and exhibited regularly at the Paris Salon for thirty-eight years, winning his first medal in 1831. His style, which, in his treatment of landscape and his favourite rustic

LESSORE, Emile. Engraved portrait after the drawing by his son, signed 'E. Lessore fils' and dated 1878. *Photograph: Wedgwood*

LESSORE, Emile. Footed dish painted by Emile Lessore with a group representing *Charity* on a deep-blue ground, within a boldly decorative border of naked figures. Diameter 15in. Signed with reversed monogram. c.1860. *Author's collection*

LESSORE, Emile. Five examples of Emile Lessore's painting on Queen's ware, including a *jardinière* modelled by Hugues Protât and decorated in the Watteau style and Wedgwood's vase no.1 shape painted with a scene of children playing with a pet rabbit. c.1865.   *Wedgwood Museum*

scenes owes something to the Barbizon school, is easily recognised. His drawing is free and attractive, in a manner much praised at the time, especially because it was new to ceramic decoration, and his colouring, at first experimental, is muted. Lessore was driven to leave Sèvres because of the jealousy of other painters – proof, if any were needed, that the cult of mediocrity is no modern phenomenon. After a brief period at Minton* he moved in 1860 to Wedgwood, where he gained a great reputation and was paid the handsome salary of £400 a year. His work, often signed, was exhibited by the firm in the London International Exhibition of 1862, the Paris Exposition Universelle of 1867 and the Vienna Exposition of 1873.

Lessore's relations with Wedgwood were extremely amicable but he could not stand the English climate: 'I shut myself up at Etruria as in a tomb' he wrote later, 'without seeing the sun more than six times a year.' He returned to France, settling at Marlotte in 1862, and negotiated a new agreement with Wedgwood which allowed him to live and work in France on condition that he spent ten days of each month in the summer at Etruria. During the next five years, Lessore acted as design consultant to the firm, advising on matters of taste and fashion, recommending modellers and engravers, creating designs for tablewares and assisting Clement Wedgwood* in his early experiments with ruby lustre* in 1865. Stocks of his work grew too large and in 1867 a new agreement was forged under which Lessore and Wedgwood shared costs and profits. This was unsatisfactory to both parties but continued until Lessore's death in 1876.

Claims that Lessore 'accomplished quite a revolution in the decoration of pottery' or created a school of ceramic painting are exaggerated. Although his style was imitated by a number of contemporary artists working at Etruria – Wagstaffe*, Eyre*, Rochfort*, Brownsword* and Rischgitz*, for example – there is little evidence that Lessore's work exerted any lasting influence.

Appreciation of his work was not widespread during his lifetime and its significance lies primarily in the originality of his technique. Like Stubbs, but on a more domestic scale, he used Wedgwood ware as his canvas; and, like Stubbs's, his work produced no discernible effect on the development of ceramic decoration. Lessore was extremely productive and his work is consequently not rare; but the large and vulnerable tablets and plaques are often of exceptional quality and are sought by collectors.

A price book of Lessore's work after February 1866, preserved in the Wedgwood archives, gives descriptions of many of his subjects.
See: Colour Plates 67 and 68

Lessore. Jules (1847-92)
Painter. Son of Emile Lessore* and father of Louise and Elaine Thérèse. He exhibited regularly at the Paris Salon and also nine landscapes at the Royal Academy between 1879 and 1892. He painted small quantities of Wedgwood Queen's ware* pieces in a style closely resembling his father's.

Lessore, Louise
See: Powell, Ada Louise

Lessore, Thérèse (1849-1909)
Daughter of Emile Lessore*. She painted occasional pieces for Wedgwood which were sent to Etruria* with her father's work. After Emile's death, Godfrey Wedgwood wrote to her: 'Should you find in work the distraction from thoughts of your loss, which I have found from experience to be one of the greatest benefits of work, we shall be glad if you will continue your work on buff coloured Creil plain.' From this it appears likely that much of Thérèse Lessore's work may have been on *faïence fine* from this French factory.

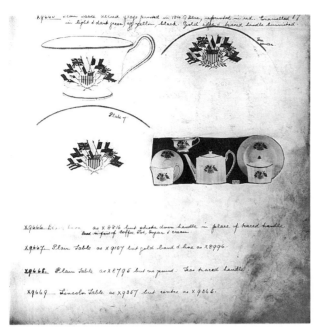

LIBERTY WARE. Sketches from a Wedgwood pattern book showing designs for Liberty ware sold in aid of the War Relief Fund, 1917-18.

Wedgwood Museum

Liberty Bell
See: Paperweights

Liberty Ware
Bone china* and Queen's ware* 'patriotic' tablewares decorated in enamel colours with the shield of the United States of America and the flags of the Allies in World War I. The idea was conceived by Mrs Robert Coleman Taylor of New York and translated into a design by Mrs H. Snowden Marshall. The ware was sold by subscription and more than $14,000 was raised by this means in aid of the War Relief Fund. This ware is easily confused with *Flags** pattern.

Light, Ernest William (d.1932)
Sculptor and modeller; studied at South Kensington School of Art; Headmaster of Hanley School of Art; Master-in-Charge of Stoke-

LIGHT SHADES. Rare bone china Fairyland Lustre light shade decorated with *Garden of Paradise*, designed by Daisy Makeig-Jones and introduced in 1916. Diameter 12in. c.1925.   *Sotheby's, Chester*

on-Trent School of Art, 1920-32. Light was commissioned to model at least twenty-six small bird, insect and animal figures, which were reproduced in basalt from 1913. Several of the models, which were competent and attractive rather than original, were not improved by the addition of 'realistic' glass eyes. When the series was reintroduced in 1935, the glass eyes were omitted in favour of modelled sights. Light's models included *Alighting Bird, Cockatoo, Crane, Egret, Flamingo*, four versions of *Flying Bird, Kingfisher Hornbills, Pelican, Raven, Toy Jap Bird, Woodpecker, Bear, Bulldog, Cat, Elephant, Poodle, Rabbit, Squirrel, Dragonfly* and four models of a *Butterfly*.

Light Shades
Bone china* lithophane* light shades were made by Wedgwood for conventional light fixtures, candelabra and girandoles c.1920. Lavender coloured body* lampshades were produced for a light fixture patented by Holmes in 1937 (see: Holmes-Wedgwood Lampshade). Wedgwood's most important production in this form, however, was in Fairyland Lustre*. At least three of Daisy Makeig-Jones's designs – *Willow Fairyland, Dogs and Deer* and *Garden of Paradise* – were applied to light shades. Examples are rare.

Lily Border
A border pattern of stylised lilies, with four petals and side leaves, the flowers set in adjacent pointed arches. The pattern appears on 18th-century and later plinths to vases in Wedgwood's dry bodies*.

LIGHT, Ernest W. Basalt figures of an egret, a cat, a bulldog and a raven, modelled c.1913. All have the glass eyes of the original edition. Bulldog, height 5in.

Christie's, New York

LINDSAY WARE. Queen's ware 'Lindsay Ware' vase decorated with enamelled butterflies and leaves on a darker ground. Height 5in., c.1901. *Wedgwood Museum*

Limited Editions

Once a respectable method of marketing small numbers of objects of special quality, often at a high price that was justified by rarity and the high costs of production, and sometimes sold by subscription, the production of limited editions was essentially confined to book publishing. The general concept gradually spread to the marketing of other goods, especially commemorative wares of various kinds. The advertisement and sale of an edition of 15,000 as 'limited' may be strictly accurate but debases the term, which is now widely regarded as disreputable and designed to appeal to the ignorance and greed of customers buying entirely (and unwisely) for investment. But, with few notable exceptions (as experts at the leading auction houses have often made plain), objects of this kind produced in this quantity have no genuine investment value and in many cases their quality is no better than that of any others in unlimited production. These illusory 'limited' editions are often 'hyped' by advertising so misleading as to border on the fraudulent. Such descriptions as 'strictly limited to only 15,000' and 'limited to the quantity fired before (date)' should be taken as warnings, not invitations. It is a matter of fact that, if even 5,000 were taken as the number of a limited edition, the majority of books published in Britain each year would qualify for the description. It can only be regretted that Wedgwood has been encouraged, since the 1960s, to lend its name – in association with professional marketing companies – to such dubious marketing practices.
See: American Heritage Series; Christmas Plates; Egyptian Collection

Lindner, Doris (1896-1979)

Welsh sculptor and modeller; studied sculpture at St Martin's School of Art, the British Academy at Rome and Calderson's Animal School, London. Lindner worked as a freelance modeller and was especially noted for her fine animal figures modelled for the Royal Worcester* Porcelain Co. She also created figures for Minton*. In 1934 she designed a pair of Reclining Girl book-ends* for Wedgwood in the form of a seated, naked figure. These were reproduced in a matt white glaze and Dysart* glaze on Queen's ware*.

Lindsay Ware

Vases in the Art Nouveau style designed by the freelance designer Courtney Lindsay in 1901. These vases, of Queen's ware* with covering enamel decoration of typical Art Nouveau* motifs, such as stylised butterflies and peacocks and patterns of leaves, were marked with a 'Lindsay Ware' printed backstamp, created especially for them. Lindsay was responsible also for designing the shapes of some of the vases, and he created designs for Wedgwood tiles* at about the same time. Lindsay ware has in the past been erroneously attributed to the artist and designer Lindsay Philip Butterfield, but a letter dated 2 November 1900 from Kennard

Wedgwood* to Courtney Lindsay leaves no room for doubt as to the correct authorship of these designs. It appears that quantities were never large, and examples are consequently uncommon.

Linley, Joseph (fl.1769-74)

Painter at the Chelsea Decorating Studio*, who worked on tableware borders and later on the pierced fruit baskets of the Frog* service.

Lions

'Egyptian Lions from the Capitol', 5in. x 8½in., appear in the Wedgwood & Bentley Catalogue* for 1773. They are copies in miniature of the pair of massive basaltic rock sculptures of lions *couchants* in the Egyptian style originally placed at either side of the staircase leading from the Piazza Araceli to the Capitol in Rome. Wedgwood's source of these figures, which were produced in black basaltes*, was probably Sir William Chambers*. Examples are uncommon, possibly indicating that they were not reproduced in the 19th century.

Liqueur Bottles

See: Apricot Brandy Bottle

Liston, Sir Robert (1742-1836)

Diplomatist; minister plenipotentiary at Madrid, 1783-8; envoy extraordinary, Stockholm, 1788-93; ambassador to Constantinople, 1793-6 and 1811-21; ambassador to Washington, 1796-1802. Liston bought Wedgwood tableware for use in his embassies in Lisbon and Stockholm and, like Cathcart* in St Petersburg and Murray Keith* in Vienna, helped to promote Wedgwood's manufactures abroad.

Lithography

A method of decorating pottery and porcelain first used experimentally in Staffordshire in 1840 in conjunction with engraving. The process was patented by Pierre Auguste Ducoté in 1839 and given first trials at the firm of Ridgway, Morley Wear & Co. of Shelton. Frank Wedgwood* made detailed notes of the method, of which he saw a demonstration in 1842, but no further action was taken, and, when lithographic transfers were submitted to Wedgwood by printers in 1863, they were rejected. Apart from a very limited use of photolithographic* techniques in the late 1870s, lithography was not used for decoration at Etruria* until 1940.

The term 'lithograph' implies drawing on stone, and the stone employed was absorbent limestone. Ceramic colour is attracted by grease and repelled by water in the same way as printer's ink, so the picture to be reproduced is drawn in greasy crayon on the surface of the stone. The stone is then moistened with water and inked. The oily ink adheres to the greasy crayon, but is rejected by the moisture, and impressions are then taken on paper from the stone. Later developments included the substitution of metal plates for

LITHOGRAPHY. *Charnwood* pattern, Wedgwood's first bone china tableware to be decorated by lithography, introduced in 1944.
Photograph: Wedgwood

LITHOPHANE. Two glazed bone china lithophane light shades in plain white with intaglio decoration. Height 6¼in. c.1920.
Wedgwood Museum

stones since these can be made in cylindrical form to act as rollers, and more recently the use of rubber has led to vastly improved methods of colour printing. In the case of photolithography, zinc and aluminium surfaces can be given a light-sensitised coating.

Lithographs for ceramic printing are made with a backing of special paper, using pigments that can be fired in the enamelling kiln*. The glaze is coated with varnish, and when this is tacky the picture is pressed on to it, causing it to adhere to the glazed surface. The backing paper is then peeled off and the ware is fired again.

The earliest lithographs were monochrome, but multi-coloured designs applied in one operation were developed as a cheaper method of producing polychrome-decorated wares than outline printing and hand enamelling.

An experiment with the use of lithograph decoration on Queen's ware* was made by Wedgwood with the Barlaston mug*, designed by Eric Ravilious* and produced in 1940. The first bone china pattern to be decorated by this method was *Charnwood,* introduced in 1944. Lithograph decoration on Wedgwood bone china was pioneered by Victor Skellern* and from 1947 until the 1960s, when it was largely superseded by silk-screen* printing, it was the most popular form of decoration.

Modern patterns decorated by lithography are often described, especially in the USA, as 'Decals' (from Decalcomania).

Lithophane (Berlin Transparency)
A translucent panel of unglazed porcelain with moulded intaglio* decoration which becomes visible only by transmitted light. The process was patented in Paris in 1827 and the manufacturing rights

LITHOPHANE. Pair of lithophanes in the form of lampshades in use on a jasper-mounted wall sconce and lit to show the intaglio decoration. c.1920. *Formerly Buten Museum*

LOCHEE, John Charles. Dark coral-pink wax portrait of Prince Charles von Ligne modelled by Lochée and supplied to Wedgwood in 1787, when it was reproduced in jasper. Height of wax relief 3⅛in.
Formerly author's collection

were bought by Meissen*. After the expiry of the French patent, lithophanes were made by several factories in Germany, at Sèvres, at the Royal Copenhagen Porcelain Company, and in England by Minton*, Copeland (Spode*) and W.H. Goss. Wedgwood made some so-called lithophanes, c.1920, from bone china, some of them in the form of glazed light shades*. Although the decoration was intaglio, they were not true lithophanes since they were cast from relief models and not from carved wax intaglios.
See also: Email Ombrant

Liverpool
See: Bentley & Boardman; Sadler, John

Liverpool Birds
See: Exotic Birds

Lochée, John Charles (1751-after 1791)
Sculptor and modeller; enrolled at the Royal Academy Schools in 1772 and first exhibited at the Academy in 1776. Between 1784 and 1788 he supplied Wedgwood with a number of moulds from portraits in wax from which Wedgwood made portrait medallions* in jasper*, but Josiah did not find his work entirely satisfactory. Lochée's wax portraits* were intended for commercial reproduction in wax and he therefore generally supplied Wedgwood with moulds, not with the original models (which were, like John Flaxman's*, modelled directly on to grounds of slate or glass). According to Josiah II*, Lochée's moulds were 'in general very bad', appeared already to have had waxes taken from them and were always 'very full of pin holes'. Lochée's style is individual and easily recognisable: the truncation below the shoulder is concealed by an opulently folded cloak, sometimes fur-lined; ribbons and sashes are ornately creased or folded; the hair is naturalistically modelled; and the lace is reproduced in fine detail. In 1791 he was declared bankrupt. The following portrait medallions are from wax originals by Lochée:
Prince Adolphus Frederick, 1787
Prince Augustus Frederick, 1787

LOCHEE, John Charles. Pale blue jasper with blue jasper-dip portrait medallion of George, Prince of Wales (later George IV), modelled by Lochée c.1787.
Wedgwood Museum

LOVATT, Thomas. Lovatt finishing the bas-relief ornament on a jasper Portland vase at Etruria, c.1905.
Photograph: Wedgwood

Prince Edward Augustus, Duke of Kent, 1787
Charles Ferdinand, Duke of Brunswick, 1787 (attributed)
Princess Charlotte Augusta, Princess Royal, 1788
George Grenville, 1st Marquis of Buckingham, 1788
Mary, Marchioness of Buckingham, 1788
Prince Ernest Augustus, 1787
Prince Frederick Augustus, Duke of York, 1787 (two portraits)
George IV as Prince of Wales, 1787
Samuel, 1st Viscount Hood, 1787
Princess de Lamballe, 1787
Charles Joseph, Prince de Ligne, 1787
Charles Macklin, 1784
Prince Charles of Mecklenburgh-Strelitz, 1787
Anne, Lady de la Pole (attributed)
Prince William Henry, 1787

London Jug
A black-printed Queen's ware* jug, designed by Victor Skellern* and made for Liberty & Co. of Regent Street, London, in 1959. On one side is printed Wordsworth's poem, *On Westminster Bridge,* and on the other the words of Dr Samuel Johnson: 'When a Man is tired of London, he is tired of Life'. The base originally bore the Wedgwood bicentenary symbol in addition to the usual backstamp, but it has since been reproduced without the symbol.

London Shape
See: Tableware Shapes

London Showrooms
See: Showrooms

Longmore, Thomas (fl.1795-1810)
Engraver who supplied Wedgwood with engravings for onglaze red-printed *Botanical Flowers** and *Chrysanthemum* patterns, 1809.

Lovatt, Thomas (1850-1915)
Skilled ornamenter at Etruria* during the latter part of the 19th century and the early years of the 20th. Lovatt was one of the few employees ever to be permitted to sign his work. He used his initials 'TL' or initial and surname 'T.Lovatt' incised*. This break with tradition is all the more surprising in view of the critical comments about his work made by Laurence Wedgwood*, who complained in 1870 of 'Or[namen]ts bad in Lovatts work', and again in 1875 of Lovatt's vases 'not nicely ornamented'. Lovatt ornamented a number of jasper Portland vases*, which he signed, c.1875-80, and in 1912 he was responsible for ornamenting a three-colour jasper plaque* commemorating the 250th anniversary of John Wesley's birth.

Lucretia
Wife of Tarquinius Collatinus. The outrage of her rape by Sextus Tarquinius led to the deposition of his father, Tarquinius Superbus, and the establishment of the Roman republic. A bust of Lucretia was modelled by Arnold Machin* in 1944 and reproduced, 22in. high, in a reddish-brown terracotta body. The bust is also known, somewhat unkindly, as *The Harlot*.

Luna
See: Diana

LUSTRE DECORATION. 'Steel' lustre finger bowl, candlestick-bough-pot (height 10½in.) and footed cup. c.1812.
Wedgwood Museum

Lunar Society
The Lunar Society (originally Lunar Circle) of Birmingham was founded in 1765 as an informal association of friends with interests in common. They met in members' houses, or occasionally in a Birmingham hotel, once a month, at or near the full moon to ensure sufficient light for members returning home after their discussions. Meetings, of which no minutes were kept, took the loose form of unsystematic exposition, demonstration and discussion, to which suitable visitors might be invited. It was a select group, never more than fourteen members strong in the twenty-five years or so of its existence. The Society grew from the friendship of Matthew Boulton* and Erasmus Darwin*, and they were soon joined by John Whitehurst*, Dr William Small and Richard Lovell Edgeworth*. Later members of particular importance to Wedgwood were James Watt* and Dr Joseph Priestley*.

Josiah Wedgwood's membership of the Lunar Society is un-proved and it appears that he was not formally a member, although he was a welcome guest at meetings. The Society has fairly been described as 'an intellectual galaxy' and it attracted guests who were among the brightest stars of other galaxies – Benjamin Franklin, Sir William Herschel, Sir Joseph Banks* and Dr Daniel Solander* among them. The rationalism and the search for scientific explanations that motivated the members of the Lunar Society and informed their proceedings were characteristic of the Enlightenment. The British Enlightenment principles of humanitarianism and utilitarianism, of self-improvement and progress through scientific experiment and discovery, were articles of faith among the 'Lunatics', as they called themselves, and they applied those principles to the progress of industry.

Lustre Decoration
The term applied to the deposition of a thin film of metal on the surface of a glaze, using an oxide or sulphide of the metal fired in a reducing kiln* (a kiln from which the oxygen is removed at a certain point in firing, thus 'reducing' the metal oxide to free metal). The application of the technique to pottery is at least 1,100 years old (probably 500 years earlier applied to glass) and some of the most beautiful surviving examples come from 13th-century Persia. In Europe, the tradition of lustre decoration on tin-glazed earthenware *(faïence*)* was established at Malaga in the first half of the 13th century and reached a peak of perfection as an art in 16th-century Italy, notably in the Umbrian potteries of Deruta and Gubbio (the latter presided over by Maestro Giorgio Andreoli).

Interest in this type of decoration declined for 300 years but was revived in the middle of the 19th century by the Castan family of Manises in Spain, by Ginori's Doccia* factory in Florence, and by Carocchi, Fabri* Co.* of Gubbio. Important developments in the form of in-glaze lustres were the work of the brothers Clément and Jérôme Massier of Vallauris, and the French ceramist, Louis Franchet.

LUSTRE DECORATION. Ovoid pastille burner with pierced cover decorated with copper (gold) lustre. The deep bronze colour of the lustre suggests that the underlying body is black basaltes. Rosso antico produces a paler golden colour. *Mrs Robert E. Chellis Collection*

Three principal types of lustre have been used to decorate English pottery and porcelain, and all have been applied to Wedgwood earthenwares: the ancient 'reduction-fired' lustre described above, which shows a metallic or prismatic sheen; early 19th-century 'metallised' lustre, imitating solid metal and always fired in an oxidising atmosphere; and modern liquid or 'commercial' lustres, which purists do not consider to be true lustre.

Two inventions, both in Germany, were fundamental to the early development of lustre decoration in England. The first was the discovery by Johann Friedrich Böttger at the Meissen* factory about 1716 that a lavender or purple lustre with copper reflections could be made with gold. The second was an experiment by the chemist Martin Klaproth which showed that a solution of platinum in *aqua regia* could be made to adhere to porcelain, giving it a polished metallic appearance. The latter experiment was published

in England in 1803 and was almost immediately followed by the invention, generally credited to John Hancock, of metallised lustre using platinum. Metallised lustre was produced by suspending an acid solution of gold or platinum in an oily resin and applying it over the fired glaze. The medium was burnt away in the oxidising atmosphere of the fire, reducing the metal compounds to a thin film of free metal which was drawn ready-polished from the kiln. Hancock's invention of 'steel' lustre, probably in 1804, was developed to produce 'silver' and 'gold' lustre by the end of that year.

Steel lustre was the product of a single application of platinum; the brighter silver lustre was obtained by a second application over the first; and gold lustre (also known as 'copper') was produced in varying shades from a compound of gold and tin. The gold lustre was generally applied over a dark-red or brown body to conceal the purple cast which gold gives to the underlying glaze. 'Pink' lustre with copper metallic reflections was made by the application of gold lustre over creamware or a white body, such as White ware*.

The first record of Wedgwood's interest in lustre of any form occurs in 1776, when Bentley* made several experiments which he recorded in the London Experiment Book. The first, 'Gold coloured glazing on Earthen ware by fumigation', based on German work published by the Royal Society in 1734, produced 'true *copper glaze,* looking like that metal, or betwixt that and Gold.' Two others, 'to produce prismatic Colours on the surface of glazed vessels – by a partial reduction of metals in the glaze' also succeeded, producing 'an agreeable variety of changeable colours with perfect smoothness' and 'some beautiful prismatic colours', but no use appears to have been made of any of these experiments and no reduction-fired lustre was attempted by Wedgwood for nearly a century.

Wedgwood's production of metallised lustre dates, though probably experimentally, from February 1805, when a number of pieces, which are precisely (although in varying forms) dated 2 February 1805 (see: Appendix II), were decorated with gold lustre. This early date has been challenged on the grounds that the generally accepted date for the invention of gold lustre has been 1806, but the suggestion that Wedgwood's pieces were deliberately antedated or kept in stock for several years before being decorated does not accord with the evidence yielded by the latest research and must now be rejected.

During the next ten years steel, silver and gold metallised lustre was made at Etruria* in good quantities as decoration for such objects as jugs, teapots, candlesticks* and eye cups*, and both silver and gold lustre were used for some extremely grand chamberpots and shaving basins in 1815. Copper lustre appeared as decoration for escritoires* with swan handles and for leafage pen trays in 1812. A 'bronze' lustre – a darker version of gold lustre applied over black basaltes* or a brown glaze – was used for some handsome teapots with white or purple lustred interiors, and purple

LUSTRE DECORATION. 'Wreathed shell' dessert service with rare pierced ladle decorated with variegated lustre. c.1810. *Christie's, London*

LUSTRE DECORATION. Cane coloured body vase handpainted in pink (gold) lustre. Height 7in. c.1925-30. *Manchester City Art Gallery*

lustre appears also inside gold lustre tea cups. Steel lustre jugs with bas-relief* ornament were made with 'flowered' decoration or with white ornament. The 'flowered' decoration was a form of 'resist' lustre, a technique by which a pattern was painted over the glaze with a water-resistant or viscous material (wax, gum and honey were all used for this purpose) before dipping the article in lustre. The 'resist' was then washed off before firing or burnt off in the kiln, leaving the pattern, of the same colour as the body, contrasted against lustre of a different colour (usually silver or gold).

About 1809 Wedgwood introduced 'variegated' lustre, described as 'a solution of gold with a little tin mixed with sweet wort & laid on with a feather.' This produced an attractive pink or purple 'splashed' effect with a gold reflection. An exceptionally wide range of articles, including full tableware sets, decorative jugs, drinking horns, Nautilus* flower vases, hand basins, pastille burners* and pyrophorous vases*, was produced in this decoration. The colours were principally a rose-purple (varying from pale pink to a deep plum), orange and shades of grey-blue that sometimes approached violet, obtained by the use of gold and brown lustres, the latter containing both iron and platinum. Metallic reflections are red-gold and some pieces show slight iridescence. The name 'marbled lustre' is occasionally given to this combination of colours. Gold lustre alone produced variations of pink and rose-purple shades with a copper-gold sheen and, incomprehensibly, this decoration has become known as 'moonlight lustre', although this description was never used at Etruria during the 19th century. Wedgwood made no distinction between these two types, both of which were described simply as 'variegated'. Much of this variegated lustre was produced on the recently-introduced White ware*. It was not produced much after 1825.

One more type of lustre was developed especially for the edging of plates, particularly underglaze blue* printed and stone china* patterns. This was a thin yellowish-brown lustre, later strengthened to an orange-brown with gold reflections. This does not appear to have lasted in production beyond about 1860.

In 1862, Wedgwood made another attempt to make reduction-fired lustre when Frank Wedgwood* bought the recipes and techniques for its production from Pietro Gaj*. However, the experiments, carried out during the next two years, failed and the only trial pieces still surviving in the Wedgwood Museum* were made by Emile Lessore* and Clement Wedgwood* in experiments made after Gaj's death in 1866. Reduced lustre decoration appeared again on Queen's ware blanks supplied to William De Morgan* and Charles Passenger*, c.1878-85, and the technique was used at Etruria by Alfred and Louise Powell*, although for most of their work in lustre they made use of liquid lustres and gold resinates.

Liquid lustres, also known as 'lustre solutions' or 'commercial lustres', are a modern development from the work of the German, Heinrich Kühn, about 1837, and that of the French chemist, Jules

LUSTRE DECORATION. Two bone china plates, 'Audley' shape, painted in enamel colours and platinum lustre with designs by Millicent Taplin. Diameter 10⅞in. c.1950. *Wedgwood Museum*

Brianchon, a few years later. They are described here under Ordinary Lustres* and were used also for the decoration of all Fairyland Lustre*.
See: Colour Plate 69

Lustres
Candleholders with pendant drops of prismatically-cut glass similar to those employed for making chandeliers. Jasper* of various colours and black basaltes* were sometimes used for the drum bases, mounted in ormolu*, in the 18th and 19th centuries, and a few examples exist from a later date. Some specimens from the 18th century were mounted by Boulton*, and some of the glass is identified as Waterford.
See: Colour Plate 70

Lysimachus (361-281 BC)
One of Alexander's generals who became King of Macedonia and died in battle at the age of eighty. A portrait medallion* of Lysimachus, 4in. x 3in., described as 'a fine head', is listed in the 1774 Catalogue* but appears to be a copy of Tassie's* portrait of Alexander the Great.

LUSTRES. Pair of lustres in the 18th-century style with cut-glass and brass fittings on yellow and black jasper drums. No mark visible. Wedgwood, c.1929-32. *Sotheby's, London*

McFall, David (1918-88)

Sculptor of a bronze bust, height 33in., of Josiah Wedgwood V in 1975. This bust is now in the Wedgwood Museum*, Barlaston.

Machin, Arnold OBE, RA (b.1911)

Sculptor, modeller and designer, born in Stoke-on-Trent; studied at the Stoke and Derby Schools of Art and worked as a figure painter at Minton*, where Eric Owen* taught him the art of throwing. Later Machin resumed his studies at the Royal College of Art, 1937-40. He first exhibited at the Royal Academy in 1940, while still a student, and was elected Member of the Academy in 1956. He designed the new coin effigies in 1964 and 1967 (decimal coinage), the definitive postage stamp in 1967, and the commemorative crown pieces for the Silver Wedding, 1972, and the Silver Jubilee, 1977. In 1968 he modelled a set of four hard-paste porcelain figures allegorical of the *Four Seasons* for the Worcester* Porcelain Co., which were mounted in ormolu* and issued in a limited edition* of 1,500 sets.

Machin was employed by Wedgwood in 1940, when Josiah V wrote: 'His modelling is much the most interesting that I have seen from either students or Professors at the College and…I think he would do a series of animal figures very well.' Machin was allocated a studio on the Barlaston* estate, where he modelled a number of figures, using a brownish-red (terracotta) clay. Among his earliest models for Wedgwood were his chessmen*, reproduced in jasper*, basalt and Queen's ware*, and *Bridal Group,* one of several in the Staffordshire tradition of 'flatbacks' for the cottage chimneypiece. Machin continued to model for Wedgwood during the 1940s and 1950s, creating figures, busts, portrait medallions* and bas-reliefs*. His most celebrated model is probably *Taurus,* the figure of a bull which combines strength, vigour and purity of

MACHIN, Arnold. Queen's ware model of Machin's 'Bridal Group', 1941. Height 11in. *Wedgwood Museum*

line with traditional Staffordshire humour.

Machin's work has occasionally been criticised for its conventionality, but it must be judged in the proper context, which is a distinctively English pottery tradition which stretches from John Dwight* to Staffordshire flatbacks. Machin has added creatively to that tradition and the best of his figures must rank among the most satisfying and authentic in 20th-century pottery.

Machin's work for Wedgwood includes:

Alcock and Brown, bas-relief, 1941

Aphrodite, Queen's ware figure, 12½in. high 1941

Beatrice, terracotta figure, 30in. high, 1944

Bridal Group, Queen's ware flatback group, enamelled, 10½in. high (also Windsor Grey coloured body*), 1941

Cherub, terracotta head with salt glaze*, 5in. high, 1944

Chessmen, set produced in black basalt, white jasper*, blue jasper, black jasper, and Queen's ware (cream colour and Lavender coloured body*), 1940-1

Winston Churchill, bust, Queen's ware or basalt, 8in. high

McFALL, David. The Hon. Josiah Wedgwood (Josiah V). Bronze bust by David McFall, 1975. Height 33in. *Wedgwood Museum*

MACHIN, Arnold. Enamelled Queen's ware figures of a 'Thrower', a 'Saggar Man' (height 11in.) and a 'Paintress', modelled by Machin c.1941. (Replicas made in 1975). *Wedgwood Museum*

Cupid with Violin, Queen's ware figure, 7in. high, 1941

Country Lovers, Queen's ware flatback group, enamelled, 12¼in. high, 1941

Elizabeth II, portrait medallion (two versions), 1971 and 1977

Ferdinand, figure of a bull, Queen's ware, enamelled, 12½in. long, 1941

Helen, terracotta figure, 11½in. high, 1941

Lucretia,* terracotta bust, 22in. high, 1944

Paintress, Queen's ware figure, enamelled, 10½in. high, 1941

Penelope, Queen's ware figure (also Windsor Grey coloured body), 11in. high, 1941

Philip, Duke of Edinburgh, portrait medallion (two versions),1971 and 1977

Potter's Oven Placer, Queen's ware figure, enamelled, 11½in. high, 1941

Franklin D. Roosevelt, bust, Queen's ware or basalt, 7¼in. high, and portrait medallion

Saggar-maker, Queen's ware figure, enamelled

Sea Nymph, terracotta figure, 9½ in. 1941

Sylvia, Queen's ware figure, 13½in. high, 1941

Taurus, Queen's ware figure, 14¾in. long, 1945. Decorated with print and enamel *Zodiac* design or *Avon* pattern. Other versions were made in plain basalt, glazed and gold-printed basalt, and gold-printed porphyry

Thrower, Queen's ware figure, enamelled

Magnolia Ware

A range of large ornamental pieces made in the 1890s as part of the Art Pottery* of the period developed by Thomas Allen*. The red body* was painted with flowers in pale-coloured slip* and dipped in Rockingham* glaze (see: Glazes) which thinned sufficiently over the raised painting to allow the design to show through it.

MAGNOLIA WARE. Three red body vases decorated with floral designs in thick pale-coloured slip and finished with purple-brown Rockingham glaze. Tallest vase height 18in. c.1895.

Wedgwood Museum

MAJOLICA. A selection of Majolica, decorated primarily in brown, green and yellow glazes, including a three-handled mug (height 6½in.) with opaque turquoise-glazed interior and silver mounts in the 'Egyptian' style. c.1860-73.   *Author's collection*

MAJOLICA. Water ewer, after the model supplied by Flaxman, decorated with coloured glazes. Height 17in. c.1867.   *Christie's, London*

Majolica

The trade name for a type of ware made in the second half of the 19th century by a number of factories, beginning with Minton*. It was made in Germany under the name of 'Majolika'. The word is derived from the Italian *maiolica,* which is a kind of reddish earthenware covered with a glaze made white and opaque by the addition of tin oxide and usually noted for the quality of its painted decoration. But English Majolica is nothing like this. It is what was termed an 'Art pottery'*, decorated with coloured glazes, usually transparent but sometimes opaque. It was introduced at Minton by Léon Arnoux in 1850 and seems to have been inspired by the 16th-century pottery of Bernard Palissy, who spent many years searching for the secret of Italian *maiolica* and developed a coloured glaze ware instead. This was similar in some respects to ware made by the Whieldon-Wedgwood* partnership and later by

Wedgwood himself. Whieldon tortoiseshell* ware resembles the mottled coloured glazes which Palissy used on the reverse side of his dishes. When Arnoux first introduced this type of decoration the pottery of Palissy was much in demand among collectors.

Wedgwood Majolica was the product of covering with coloured glazes a white earthenware body moulded with high quality relief ornament. The range of objects made in this decoration was large

MAJOLICA. Fish platter with moulded relief of a salmon on a bed of fern and leaves. Length 25¼in. c.1865.   *Christie's, London*

MAJOLICA. Floor vase, decorated with coloured glazes and enamel colours and oval painted medallions of a Greek warrior and a classical maiden. Height 31½in. c.1871.
           Christie's, London

MAKEIG-JONES, Daisy. Photograph, c.1915.
Photograph: Courtesy of Una des Fontaines

and included umbrella stands, wall brackets, plaques, figures and groups, as well as quantities of dessert ware.

By strict definition, Wedgwood's Green glaze of this period could be included under this heading and the earliest Majolica made at Etruria* about 1860 was dessert ware decorated with mixtures of green, brown and yellow or blue, yellow and brown transparent glazes. The meagre selection of shapes was rapidly expanded to include figures by Carrier de Belleuse* and impressive decorative pieces specially commissioned from Hugues Protât*, some of which were painted by Emile Lessore*. The palette of colours also was greatly extended.

Wedgwood's Illustrated Catalogue of Ornamental Shapes, published in 1878, contains drawings of some of the most popular of the Majolica shapes but these were only a small proportion of the whole range, which was remarkable both for its diversity and for its mixture of styles. A large number of the shapes, such as the shell and leaf dessert wares, the Wine and Water* ewers and the dolphin* candlesticks were revivals of those produced up to ninety years earlier for production in black basaltes*, jasper* or the original Green glaze, and game pie* dishes took their place beside shapes that were recognisably from the renaissance or the neo-classical period. The largest piece of Wedgwood Majolica so far recorded is the 'Swan' vase, displayed by Harrods, London, in 1973, which (including its 16in. plinth) stood 54in. high, though this is scarcely significant in relation to Minton's 36ft. high fountain built for the 1862 Exhibition.

About 1878 Wedgwood introduced a different style of Majolica, with decoration in opaque or transparent coloured glazes on pale-coloured grounds. This was named Argenta* and it provided a medium for the production of new shapes, the greater number of which were moulded with decoration in the 'Japanese' style made fashionable largely by the Paris Exposition of 1867. In both forms, Majolica continued to be made, in decreasing quantities, until 1940.
See: Colour Plates 71 and 72
See also: Email Ombrant; Japonisme

Major, Thomas (fl.1770-80)

Well-known engraver, from whom Wedgwood obtained six views of the river Thames for the Frog* service. It has frequently been stated that Major was employed at the Chelsea Decorating Studio* as a painter but no evidence has been found to substantiate this.

Makeig-Jones, Susannah Margaretta ('Daisy') (1881-1945)

Artist and designer, employed at Etruria*, 1909-31; daughter of Dr William Makeig-Jones; studied at Torquay (now Torbay) School of Art. In 1909, as the result of her own characteristically direct application to Cecil Wedgwood*, she joined Wedgwood as an appren-

tice hand-paintress. Two years later she was accepted on to the staff, and in January 1912 she was recognised as a designer in the Art Department directed by John Goodwin*. Her first designs were insignificant: toy tea sets and nursery ware* decorated with rather woodenly drawn animals, aeroplanes, toy soldiers etc, which gave little hint of any particular talent or invention. Later in the year she produced some dessert plates and bowls decorated with designs from Hans Andersen's story of *Thumbelina,* and in the following year the first of her designs using Oriental dragons appeared.

In 1909 Messrs Ashworth of Hanley had exhibited in London the first of their 'Lustrosa Ware', an impressive range of lustred pottery developed by their director, J.V. Goddard. Commercial painted-on lustres were commonly in use in Staffordshire, but Goddard relied for his effects upon reduction lustres, described by the *Connoisseur* four years later as 'jewel-like in their brilliance and lustre'. Powder blue, the first of the powder colours*, had been produced successfully at Etruria in 1912, and it was these two techniques which inspired the use by Daisy Makeig-Jones of powder colours in combination with commercial lustres in the autumn of 1914. Her earliest ten 'Ordinary Lustres'* – pieces decorated with dragons, birds, butterflies, fish, fruit and small animals – were followed less than two years later by the first of the Fairyland Lustre* designs. For the next thirteen years. designs for Fairyland Lustre, Ordinary Lustre and tableware decoration flowed from Daisy's studio. Their success, in a country tired of wartime austerity, was considerable, and by 1920 these commercial lustre decorations had lifted Wedgwood for the first time into the forefront of manufacturers of ornamental bone china*. After the Wall Street crash of 1929 the popularity of lustre declined, and by the time the demand for it had revived in the mid-1930s, Daisy Makeig-Jones had left the firm.

In 1930, following the death of Major Frank Wedgwood*, Josiah V* became Managing Director. Adverse economic conditions dictated radical changes in production and organisation. Under such conditions it was probably inevitable that Daisy Makeig-Jones should have been invited to retire; but there were other reasons why Josiah wished her to leave. Her behaviour, never conventional, had become increasingly – and often embarrassingly – eccentric; she had become dictatorial and over-demanding, treating the production departments as tiresome but necessary extensions of her studio; and she created designs for which the new generation of directors had little regard. In April 1931 she was asked to retire. Predictably, she refused. After an acrimonious interview with Josiah she left, having ordered the destruction of every piece of lustre in her studio. She retired to a life of stormy domesticity with her mother and two sisters, and died on 21 July 1945.

Daisy Makeig-Jones does not merit serious consideration as an artist. Her draughtsmanship was scarcely competent and, although not lacking in imagination, she seems to have been entirely without artistic invention. Her designs were thinly disguised adaptations of the work of others. She was not legitimately influenced by better artists: she deliberately plundered their work, hiding the thefts

MAKEIG-JONES, Daisy. Bone china covered vase (Malfrey pot) and Lily tray covered in a matt blue glaze and decorated in black and gold with *Celtic Ornaments.* Vase height 9½in. c.1919. *Private collection*

MAKEIG-JONES, Daisy. Oueen's ware 'Emily' sugar caster designed by Daisy Makeig-Jones. Height 8⅜in. c.1923.
Byron & Elaine Born Collection

MAKEIG-JONES, Daisy. Bone china vase decorated with black Fairyland lustre *Butterfly Women,* and a Celadon-coloured bone china dish decorated with *Papillon* pattern in underglaze colours and mother-of-pearl lustre, diameter 13½in. c.1925.   *Christie's, London*

beneath brilliant colours and glazes. Her principal sources for Fairyland Lustre were the work of H.J. Ford, Edmund Dulac and Kaj Nielsen. For her 'Celtic Ornaments' she turned to the sixth-century Book of Kells. Her 'Graeco-Roman' animals and *Istria* designs were taken from D'Hancarville*. There were embarrassing errors: her *Lahore* design includes African and North American animals entirely foreign to India; and her *Persian Cup* is a tasteless and illiterate travesty of a superb 13th-century Syrian glass cup (now in the Metropolitan Museum, New York), with one of its Arabic inscriptions applied upside down. The colours and lustres employed were rich and individually beautiful, but they were too often combined to produce a garish and ostentatious appearance. The drawing of the Fairyland Lustre figures is poor and the attempt to temper sentimentality with humour results in an unfortunate archness. The Ordinary Lustres benefit by relying less on Daisy's draughtsmanship than the beauty of in-glaze lustre decoration, and some of the Celtic Ornaments* designs, in which her draughts-manship is not tested, are both sophisticated and satisfying.

While it is true that Daisy Makeig-Jones's work has little appeal for professional designers or design critics, it is undeniable that it provided, in its time, precisely the commercial success that Wedgwood needed. Nor can it be denied that her Fairyland Lustre pieces currently command greater prices from collectors than any other Wedgwood ware produced since the 18th century. Her place in Wedgwood's design history is assured.

In addition to the Celtic Ornaments, Ordinary Lustre and Fairy-land Lustre designs described separately under those headings, Daisy Makeig-Jones was responsible for the following:

QUEEN'S WARE TABLEWARE PATTERNS
Blue Willow, plate 10in. (Wedgwood's *Willow* with *Coq du Bois* figures superimposed, enamelled in colour)
Cobble Bead and Zoo, nursery ware
Coq du Bois, nursery ware
Cretan, teaware
Moa, nursery ware
Yellowstone Zoo, nursery ware
ORNAMENTAL QUEEN'S WARE
Istria, bowls and plates
Leaping Chamois, bowls (*Imperial* shape)
Silenus, bowl
Sphinx, bowls, mugs, jugs
Chick, pepper and salt
Emily, sugar caster
Dawg salt
BONE CHINA TABLEWARE
Hawk, teaware and coffeeware
Magpie, teaware and coffeeware
Nizami, coffeeware
The Street that ran away, teaware
BONE CHINA ORNAMENTAL WARES (Lustre Decoration)
Amherst Pheasant, bowls, melba cups and lily trays

Argus Pheasant, vases, bowls, *Lincoln* plates 10¾in.
Crane and Rock, bowls
Daventry, vases, bowls, cups
Dogs and Deer, vase, lampshade (see: Light Shades)
Endymion, bowls
Flame Daventry, vases, bowls, cups
Hares, Dogs and Birds, bowl
Hindu-Persian, Persian Cup
Lahore, bowls and vases.
Nizami, bowls, *Lincoln* plates 10¾in., melba cups
Rhages bowls
Silenus, dessert sets, bowls
See: Colour Plates 73 and 74
See also: Lustre Decoration

Makinson, Norman (b.1923)
Artist and designer. Makinson joined Wedgwood at Etruria* as an apprentice in 1937, but joined the Royal Marines in 1940, with whom he served throughout the rest of World War II. He returned to Wedgwood's art department after the war and his designs included the much-praised mug commemorating the Festival of Britain in 1951. Sponsored by Wedgwood, he studied at the Royal College of Art, returning to Barlaston* in 1952. He left in 1955 to take up a new career in teaching design. His best known tableware design is *Partridge in a Pear Tree* (1953), for Coupe-Savoy shape (see: Tableware Shapes).

MAKINSON, Norman. Celadon coloured body 'coupe' shape plate decorated with the figure of a kangaroo enamelled in white and black over a black print. Unmarked trial. Wedgwood, c.1946.
Wedgwood Museum

MALFREY POT. Queen's ware 'Malfrey Pot' decorated with *Celtic ornaments* designed by Daisy Makeig-Jones in black over a matt yellow ground. Height 7in. c.1920. *Dr & Mrs Jerome Mones Collection*

Malachite

A decorative stone which, when polished, is a fine dark copper green with darker veins. It is one of the ores of copper, and was among the natural stones which Wedgwood attempted to copy in his variegated* or crystalline* wares.

Malfrey Pot

A bulbous jar, similar in style to the Chinese ginger jar but with a wider cover, produced in Queen's ware* in the 1920s decorated with *Persian* patterns, *Celtic Ornaments* by Daisy Makeig-Jones* and other contemporary designs. It was made in several sizes and also in a taller shape, height 9½in.

Mallet, Pierre (fl.1870s)

French painter and designer. With Léonce Goutard he designed for the London retailers A. Borgen & Co the decoration for several Pearl* ware services decorated with naturalistically drawn birds, fish or vegetables, printed in black or brown and enamelled in colour. These were printed with a special backstamp in addition to the Wedgwood impressed mark.

MALLET, Pierre. Soup plate from a service printed and enamelled with figures of birds. Diameter 9⅝in. c.1875. *Author's collection*

Manganese Oxide

A metal oxide used to colour bodies, glazes and ceramic pigments. It yields variable colour, from purple-brown to rich brown, similar in shade to that obtained by adding permanganate of potash to water. With iron and cobalt* oxide, manganese produced the dense black of black basaltes* ware.
See: Coloured Bodies; Rockingham Ware

Mangiarotti, Michelangelo (fl. 1787-90)

Modeller in Rome under the direction of Webber*, c.1787-90.

Manzolini

A name generally quoted as that of a modeller who worked under Webber's* supervision in Rome, c.1787-90. He is, however, mentioned in the correspondence from Dalmazzoni* only as the supplier of '140 pieces of Marbles', for which he was paid fourteen zequins (about thirty shillings).

Marbled Lustre

See: Lustre Decoration

Marbling (Marbled Ware)

The mingling of coloured slips* on the surface of an object or the wedging of variously coloured clays in imitation of the marbled end-papers of books or the surface marking of some decorative stones. Ware decorated by this technique is known also as 'combed' ware and it was developed, but not invented, by Josiah Wedgwood in the early 1760s. The same technique was used by Norman Wilson* in the 1950s for some of the bowls and plates in his range of 'Unique' ware.
See: Variegated Ware

MARBLING. Two trial 'marbled' plates of mixed cream-colour and black and stained green and black clays by Norman Wilson. Diameter 10in. Unmarked. Wedgwood, 1955. These were never put into production. *Author's collection*

Marchant, Nathaniel, RA (1739-1816)

Gem* engraver and medallist who studied under Edward Burch* and at Rome; exhibited at the Royal Academy; elected RA, 1809; assistant engraver at the Mint, 1797. He was especially noted for fine intaglios*, several of which – including *Garrick looking into the face of Shakespeare* and *Priam and Achilles* – were copied by Wedgwood.

Marcus Aurelius Antoninus

Roman Emperor, adopted by the Emperor Antoninus Pius*, whose daughter, Faustina*, he married. Marcus Aurelius is remembered especially for his devotion to the Stoic Philosophy and his *Meditations* on the subject have survived. Wedgwood produced two busts of Marcus Aurelius: *Marcus Aurelius Antoninus,* height 25in. and *Young Marcus Aurelius,* height 16½in., both from plaster casts invoiced by Hoskins & Grant* in March 1774.

Mared Pattern

Underglaze blue-painted pattern which appears principally on shell edge shape (see: Tableware Shapes) Pearl* ware, although examples (with painting that has turned a blackish-blue) are known on Queen's ware* and Queen's ware with a Pearl* glaze. The

MARBLING. Two Wedgwood & Bentley terracotta stoneware vases and a gilded ewer (height 11⅛in.) decorated with marbled slip in shades of green, brown and cream, grey, brown and black, and blue, green, brown and black respectively. The vases are on white biscuit terracotta plinths, which do not appear to have been used before 1772.   *Dwight and Lucille Beeson Collection, Birmingham Museum, Alabama*

MARED PATTERN. Fine Pearl ware sauce tureen and fixed stand, shell-edge shape, decorated in underglaze blue. c.1782.

City Museum & Art Gallery, Stoke-on-Trent

pattern, which consists of borders of a shape somewhat similar to the Meissen* *Zwiebelmuster* (Onion) pattern and scattered small sprigs of flowers, which were used both together or separately, appears to have been especially popular during the period c.1778-

90. The origin of the name is unknown but a clue to it may be found in Wedgwood's letter to Bentley* of April 1778 with which he sent a sample of a new 'marine pattern table ware' decorated with blue at low cost at the suggestion of the Duke of Northumberland.

MARS. Solid white jasper figure of *Mars*. Height 7in. c.1785.
Merseyside Museums

Maria Feodorowna, Empress of Russia (1759-1826)

Daughter of Duke Eugen of Württemberg; married, 1776, Paul, son and heir of Catherine II*, who succeeded her as Tsar in 1796. Maria Feodorowna modelled a number of portraits of the Russian royal family, including one of Catherine as Minerva*, and a double portrait of her own sons, Alexander and Constantine, which were reproduced in Wedgwood's jasper* in 1791. These, and other portraits of her sons, and of the Empress Elizabeth, were reproduced also by James Tassie* in his glass paste, and it is possible that Wedgwood obtained his models from him. Maria Feodorowna's drawing of her six children, three of whom became Tsar, was engraved by J. Walker in 1790.

Marks

A mark on a piece of pottery or porcelain, if genuine, is a statement about its origin. In the 18th century regular marks were few. They were used by a select number of exceptionally powerful and influential manufacturers, whose products were bought because they came from that particular source. The first 18th-century manufacturers of porcelain* in Europe, the Meissen* factory, employed a mark consistently from a very early stage, while many of their competitors, especially the smaller enterprises, either used no mark at all or one calculated to be mistaken for the Meissen crossed swords mark (e.g. the crossed hayforks of Rudolstadt, or the crossed Ls of Limbach). Even the powerful royal factory of Sèvres, in its first year or two at Vincennes, imitated Meissen, and a bowl of this period marked with the crossed swords is recorded.

In England the first porcelain factory at Chelsea* was, for a good many years, the only factory to mark its wares. The Bow* porcelain factory, started a few years afterwards, never marked its wares. The few marked specimens known were painted by a decorator such as James Giles*, and it is noteworthy that even this mark contains the Chelsea anchor as well as the dagger which came from the arms of the City of London. Worcester* marked its early wares with pseudo-Chinese ideograms because Chinese porcelain was the ware they were copying. No Derby* porcelain was marked until after its proprietor had bought the Chelsea factory in 1770, although, when it was founded, it called itself 'the second Dresden' (i.e. Meissen). About the same time Champion's Bristol factory, as well as Worcester, was putting the Meissen mark on the base of English vases.

Apart from a mere handful of very exceptional pieces, no mark appeared on Staffordshire pottery before Wedgwood started to stamp his name on his products. With a few rare exceptions, no one in Europe put his name, or that of the factory on his wares, only some kind of device, and Wedgwood's action was a new departure which marks the beginning of modern marketing methods. It is significant that Wedgwood's mark was impressed into the unfired

clay, instead of being painted, which made it less vulnerable to forgery. It is noteworthy too that he did not adopt this policy until he began to break away from improvements on the standard wares of the Potteries, such as those he had made while in partnership with Whieldon*.

The earliest Wedgwood wares were unmarked. Certain pseudo-Chinese seal marks incorporating the letter 'W' have been attributed to Wedgwood but no solid evidence has so far been found to sustain these attributions. There are also some exceptionally rare incised script marks, which are evidently of an early date preceding regular marking. The first manuscript reference to the use of marks occurs in a letter to Bentley* dated 9 July 1771 in which Wedgwood writes: 'If we alter the large characters it must be by having new moulds. The letters are stamped with printers letters & we want a middle size betwixt those large ones & the least.' In November next year he writes of his plan to start marking all his wares. It is clear that marking was not new to Wedgwood in July 1771, but neither was it the rule before the end of 1772 to mark all ware made at Etruria. It is clear also that by 1771 (probably from 1769) the mark was being made by a single impression from a mould. Impressed marks which are clearly made by the impressing of single letters individually, sometimes in a curve, belong to an earlier date. After 1772, unmarked ware was the exception (the most notable being the first-edition copies of the Portland vase*). Even the smallest seals* were impressed, if not with 'Wedgwood & Bentley' in full then at least with 'W & B', and Wedgwood was reluctant to see his cameos* and intaglios* set by Boulton* 'with a Pebble at the back' because, as he told Bentley in 1773, 'This is bad for us…as it hides *our name.*'

In 1877 Isaac Falcke, whose large and distinguished collection may be said to have formed the foundation of the British Museum collection of Wedgwood, wrote to Eliza Meteyard* deploring 'the forgery by [the] Wedgwood present firm of the Wedgwood & Bentley mark.' There is no evidence to support this extraordinary accusation, which would certainly have been challenged in the Courts had it ever been published before 1989.
See: Appendix II

Marlborough, John Churchill, 1st Duke of (1650-1722)
See: George II

Marryat, Joseph (1790-1870)

Member of parliament for Sandwich; brother to Captain Frederick Marryat RN, author of *Mr Midshipman Easy*. Joseph Marryat retired to Swansea in 1850 and published his *History of Pottery and Porcelain,* which was followed by revised editions in 1857 and 1868. This was the first book of its kind and it contains information, much of it inaccurate, about 18th-century Wedgwood wares. According to Marryat, Josiah Wedgwood II*, while travelling in Germany in 1790, offered to rent the Meissen* factory, but no evidence has been found to support this statement. Marryat's own collection, which was extensive and contained good examples of Wedgwood production, was sold by Christie's in a ten-day sale from 9-19 February 1867.

Mars

Roman name for Ares, the god of war. The son of Zeus and Hera, Ares carried on an adulterous liaison with Aphrodite* (Venus*). He delighted in battle, slaughter and the destruction of cities, but was conquered by Hercules* and forced to retire to Mount Olympus. *Mars* is the subject of one of Wedgwood's rare small statuettes, which appear for the first time in the 1787 Catalogue*. Made in white jasper* with a coloured jasper base, as a companion to one of Venus, this is thought to have been reduced from a figure by Bacon* supplied in 1769. The tablet *Peace preventing Mars from bursting open the Temple of Janus* (see: French Commercial Treaty), 11in. x 9in., no.257 in the 1787 Catalogue, was modelled by Flaxman* in 1786. *Vulcan with Mars and Venus in the Net,* a medallion 5½in. x 6in., no.184 in the 1777 Catalogue, is from one of the casts obtained from the Newdigate* collection in 1776.

Marsden, George Anthony (fl. 1860-1900)

Decorator and inventor. In 1880 Wedgwood bought from Marsden the patent for an 'Improvement in the Manufacture of Coloured or Ornamental Tiles, Bricks and other like Articles'. Marsden's technique produced textured patterns in low relief with a

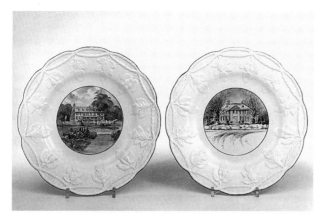

MARSHALL, Isabel. Two dessert plates with moulded borders and 'named views' painted in puce. Diameter 9in. Signed and dated 1927.
Christie's, London

MASKS. Basalt wall masks. Height 7⅛in. c.1932. *Wedgwood Museum*

hand-decorated appearance. Patterns were obtained from independent designers and production was begun at the end of 1881. The agreement was cancelled in 1888 after a severe drop in the tile* business and Marsden was briefly employed at Etruria* to decorate Art Pottery* with moulded and raised slip patterns. He was responsible for the introduction of Golconda* decoration.

Marshall, Isabel (fl. 1920s)
Painter of a dessert set, decorated in puce monochrome with 'named views' of American scenes. The plates are signed and dated 1927.

Marsyas
A satyr of Phrygia, who found a flute discarded by Athene (Minerva*) which played beautiful melodies of its own accord. He challenged Apollo* to a musical contest, the victor to do as he pleased with the vanquished. The Muses* decided the contest in favour of Apollo, who tied Marsyas to a tree and flayed him alive.
Wedgwood subjects:
Apollo and Marsyas, octagonal medallion, 3in. x 6in., from a cast obtained from Mary Landré*, 1769. No. 8 in 1773 Catalogue
Marsyas and the Young Olympus, circular plaque, diameter 11½in.
  One of the Herculaneum Pictures'*, in production by June 1769.
  No.61 in the 1773 Catalogue

Masks
Painted wall masks were produced by a number of Staffordshire potteries, including Susie Cooper*, in the 1930s. Wedgwood produced pairs of female masks, height 7⅛in., in plain basalt, c.1932.

Mason, Charles and James
See: Ironstone China

Masonic Ware
Pottery or porcelain decorated with Masonic insignia. On Wedgwood Queen's ware* and other English earthenware the decoration is usually transfer-printed* and consists of the arms of the Freemasons supported by two Masons and pyramids surmounted by celestial and terrestrial globes. An early Queen's ware mug, c.1763, formerly in the Buten Museum*, is transfer-printed by Sadler* with the Arms of the Free and Accepted Masons, and a later mug, c.1791, from the same collection is similarly decorated with the 'Arms of the Antients', Athol Grand Lodge. Williams-Wood *(English Transfer-Printed Pottery and Porcelain, 1981)* illustrates an unmarked creamware mug, which he assigns to Wedgwood, decorated with a Masonic print after an engraving by James Ross, which appears also on Worcester* porcelain. Neither the body nor the shape of the mug

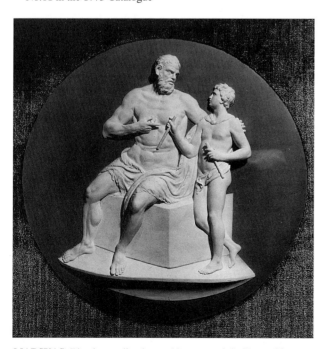

MARSYAS. Blue jasper dip plaque, *Marsyas and the Young Olympus.* Diameter 11¼in., c.1790-95.
Dwight & Lucille Beeson Collection, Birmingham Museum, Alabama

MASONIC WARE. Queen's ware tankard transfer-printed with the 'Mason's Arms' in black with enamel inscription and contemporary Danish silver mounts. Height 6¼in. c.1785. *Christie's, London*

MASONIC WARE. Interior of a large footed bowl, decorated with red groundlay and gold-printed borders, the centre transfer-printed in black with three figures and emblems of the Freemasons. Diameter 11¼in. c.1810-20.   *Merseyside Museums*

MAYER, Elijah. Cane ware engine-turned bowl with applied ornament, including *Poor Maria, Bourbonnais Shepherd* and *Domestic Employment,* all copied from Lady Templetown's designs for Wedgwood, lined with bright blue enamel. c.1800. *Author's collection*

closely resemble Wedgwood's; nor does the print look like the work of Sadler, so this attribution must be dismissed. A similar engraving after Ross, however, appears as the interior decoration of a superb Wedgwood Pearl* ware footed bowl, c.1810-20, in the Merseyside Museums collection, Liverpool. This is inscribed 'Etruscan Lodge 327, Bridge Inn, Etruria'. The same inscription appears with the printed interior decoration of another such bowl, formerly in the collection of the late Byron and Elaine Born. The Wedgwoods were not, themselves, Masons, but they evidently permitted the establishment of a Lodge on, or nearby, the Etruria factory estate.

Match Block
A rectangular container on a flat stand intended as a decorative holder for a box of safety matches. It appears in the '1878' Illustrated Catalogue of Ornamental Shapes (Plate 14) and was made in Majolica* and Argenta*.

Match Holders, Match Pots
Containers for loose matches made in Majolica* and Argenta*. Two shapes of match holders – mask (slotted for hanging) and double mask (mask heads back-to-back for the table) – are illustrated in the '1878' Catalogue of ornamental shapes (Plate 14). Three match pots – fish barrel, Berlin (a truncated cone, with ribbed exterior as striker, on circular foot) and fish basket – appear in the same illustration.

Mather, Ben (fl.1769-80)
Head clerk in Wedgwood's London showrooms from September 1769, in succession to William Cox*, who returned to Burslem. In 1772 it was discovered that he was guilty of embezzlement and had indulged in 'a course of extravagance & dissipation'. Wedgwood's informant told him that he and others of the London staff had been too frightened of Mather to report him sooner. Further, it appeared that Mather's recent illness, for which he had received much sympathy, was 'the foul disease'. It might have been expected that Wedgwood would have dismissed him instantly. That he did not do so was due to two considerations: first, he was anxious lest Mather collect thousands of pounds owing from creditors before they could be informed of his dismissal; and second, as he told Bentley, 'He should have *some hope left him* that upon a change of conduct he may still be restor'd to the favor & confidence of his friends.' This surprising lenience was not repaid by Mather. He was finally dismissed in 1780, 'an abandoned worthless wretch.' The discovery of Mather's dishonesty and of his bad influence on other employees in London, led to reforms in showroom and warehouse administration and also to the payment of commission on sales made by the staff at Newport Street.

Mayer, Elijah (1750-1813)
Potter of Hanley, who made creamware*, black basaltes* and cane* ware of fine quality from c.1780. He used engine-turned* decoration, and some of his applied reliefs, especially of 'baccha-

nalian boys' are identical to Wedgwood's. The mark 'E. Mayer' appears impressed either on the extreme edge of the base or on the projecting rim around it, and is often not immediately visible.

Mayer, Joseph (1802-86)
19th-century antiquary and collector of coins, antiquities, manuscripts, Liverpool pottery and porcelain and Wedgwood wares. Mayer was born in Newcastle-under-Lyme and moved to Liverpool where he studied to be a goldsmith and silversmith. He later opened a shop in Liverpool, making a considerable fortune, much of which he spent on his collections. A man of little formal education, he believed passionately in the provision of education for the people and opened his own museum and library in Liverpool for this purpose. In 1848 Mayer discovered by chance in Birmingham a huge quantity of Wedgwood manuscript material, disposed of as scrap by Francis Wedgwood* and then being sold to shopkeepers as wrapping paper. This hoard included the greater part of Wedgwood's letters to Bentley* and large quantities of invoices and factory records. These were generously made available to Eliza Meteyard* for her *Life of Josiah Wedgwood,* published in 1865-6, and, since their purchase by the Wedgwood firm in 1887, have remained the principal primary source for all original research into Josiah Wedgwood's life and work. The greater part of Mayer's great collections was donated to the City of Liverpool. Sadly, the Liverpool Museum received a direct hit from a bomb during an air raid in 1941 and much of its contents, including most of the Wedgwood collection, was destroyed.

Mazarine Blue
The English name for an exceptionally rich underglaze blue groundlay colour produced by the use of ground cobalt. The original name for this colour at Vincennes (later Sèvres*) was *Gros bleu.* The connection with Cardinal Mazarin is untraced. Mazarine blue grounds appear on Wedgwood bone china services of the 19th and 20th centuries.

MEDALS. Solid pale-blue and white jasper portrait medal of John Paul Jones. Diameter 2in. Cast from a medal by Augustin Dupré, struck in 1779, and first produced in jasper in 1906.
Dwight & Lucille Beeson Collection, Birmingham Museum, Alabama

MEDUSA. Wedgwood & Bentley solid blue and white jasper medallion head of *Medusa,* attributed to Flaxman. Diameter 5in. c.1776.
Christie's, London

Meander Border
A type of Greek fret in which one or two continuous lines turning at right angles at equidistant intervals make a repetitive labyrinthine pattern.
See: Fret

Medals
Flat circular medallions, some double-sided, of historical scenes or portraits and inscriptions moulded from bronze medals. Wedgwood & Bentley medals include sixty Roman History medals after Dassier*, Heads of the Popes, Kings of England supplied by Thomas Astle*, and Kings of France. A rare late production is the jasper medal of John Paul Jones, made to the order of Frederick Rathbone in 1906.

Medallions
Medallions were originally large medals issued by the Roman Emperors to mark special occasions, and when of gold or silver their weight was usually a multiple of the standard coin. Wedgwood medallions, thin and flat, of white terracotta*, black basaltes*, jasper*, or less frequently of other dry bodies*, bear a portrait or other design in relief. They are intermediate in size between the cameo* and the plaque* or tablet*. Some of the very large portrait medallions* (about 10½in. across the long axis) might more accurately be described as portrait plaques, but they fall under the general heading of medallions. Medallions were used principally for cabinet display. Plaques were made to ornament furniture and such architectural features as chimneypieces*, but medallions were often used as ancillary ornament. Portrait medallions, usually in basaltes or jasper, were produced with frames* of the same material or might be framed in metal or turned wood.

Medea
Daughter of the King of Colchis, the city to which Jason came to steal the Golden Fleece. In this undertaking he was abetted by Medea, who fled with him to Greece as his wife. There Jason deserted her. In revenge she murdered their two children and destroyed Jason's new wife with a poisoned garment. Ovid *(Metamorphoses)* dwells on her powers of sorcery, which she used to rejuvenate Jason's father (Aeson) by replacing his blood with a powerful brew of herbs.
Wedgwood subject:
Medea Rejuvenating Jason's Father, medallion 4in. x 3¼in., no.152 in 1777 Catalogue*

Medical spoon
A spoon with a loop handle, the terminal of which curves under the bowl to serve as a foot on which it will stand. Spoons of this kind were made in creamware throughout the 19th century by

MEDUSA. Wedgwood & Bentley solid pale blue and white jasper medallion head of *Medusa* or Gorgon's head. Diameter 4in. c.1778.
Manchester City Art Gallery

Wedgwood, Leeds and other potteries. Some examples, subsequent to 1875, have graduated markings in the interior of the bowl.

Medusa
The hair of the young and beautiful Medusa was changed into hissing serpents by Athene (Minerva*) who objected to Medusa's copulation with Poseidon in one of her temples. Medusa's appearance became so terrible that anyone who saw her was turned to stone. Perseus* slew her by using his polished shield as a mirror against her, an event depicted in Guglielmo della Porta's* *Marriage Feast of Perseus and Andromeda* reproduced in black basaltes*, c.1768. Athene placed the image of the head of Medusa in the centre of her shield and breastplate. A superb bas-relief head of Medusa 'from an exquisite marble in the possession of Sir W. Hamilton'* (no.94 in 1777 Catalogue), described also by Josiah as 'Gorgons head', is attributed to Flaxman*, 1776. Three more Medusa heads were made, all catalogued for the first time in 1777:
Medusa, circular medallion, 3in. diameter, no.95.
Medusa, medallion 1½in. x 2in., profile 'with wings', no.96
Medusa, medallion 1½in. x 2in., another profile, no.97

Meissen (Saxony)
The oldest European porcelain factory, established as the Royal Saxon Porcelain factory at Meissen, about twelve miles from the city of Dresden, in 1710. A true porcelain* body on the same principle as

MEISSEN. Green dip biscuit porcelain plaque, *Apotheosis of Homer* after the model by Flaxman. Diameter 12¾in. Meissen, c.1810.
British Museum

that of the Chinese was made there from the first. The formula was discovered, after many years of research and experiment, by E.W. von Tschirnhaus and J.F. Böttger, the latter an alchemist originally employed by Augustus the Strong, Elector of Saxony and King of Poland, to make gold. Augustus was a notable patron of the arts, and of the factory artists: J.F. Höroldt, the *Obermaler* (chief painter), was also Court Painter, and J-J. Kändler, the *Modellmeister* (chief modeller), was Court Sculptor. Augustus was a voracious collector of porcelain, who bought a palace (the *Japanische Palais)* especially to house his collection of Oriental porcelain and a representative selection of the products of his new factory.

The early factory style was predominantly Oriental, which rapidly gave way to a well-marked baroque. The artists enjoyed access to all kinds of sources of inspiration, from the designs of the Court Goldsmith, Dinglinger, to the exotic birds of the Moritzburg aviaries. Especially admired products of those early years are the figures of Kändler and his assistants, and the series of superb table services, of which the Swan service, made for the factory's Director, the Count von Brühl, is probably the most famous.

In the first half of the 18th century Meissen had little competition, but factories were gradually established elsewhere, usually under royal or aristocratic patronage, and they took their styles from Meissen which, until the start of the Seven Years' War (1756), dominated the European scene. The Chelsea* factory, founded in England in 1745 by Huguenot silversmith, Nicolas Sprimont, started by copying or adapting French silver shapes but soon went on to copy Meissen with a series of distinguished figures and some of its service ware, turning to Sèvres* instead as that factory's reputation grew and Meissen was occupied by the troops of Frederick the Great*.

After the end of the war in 1763, Meissen recovered with great difficulty, and the next sixty years or so was a period of mounting troubles which culminated in the Napoleonic Wars and the bombardment of Dresden. The factory adopted a neo-classical* style and employed a French modeller, Michel-Victor Acier, who brought with him the current Sèvres styles. Meissen introduced a number of novelties in an attempt to revive flagging trade, including *Wedgwoodarbeit* (Wedgwood work) which was an imitation of blue and white jasper* in a porcelain body. After Waterloo, the factory's fortunes began gradually to recover, and during the 19th century it became increasingly prosperous. It survived both World Wars and is now generally known by the name of Dresden.

According to the Meissen Jubilee Catalogue published in 1910, the Direktor Oppel obtained in 1814 'cases of ornaments in the classical style from Etruria'* to help with new designs. Few in Germany could then afford the high quality hand-painted porcelain which had been a speciality of Meissen, and most of the wares selling at the time were either stonewares *(Steinzeug)* (some being of the black basaltes* or jasper types) or creamware *(Steingut).* These styles were not necessarily imported from Staffordshire directly, since many of the former German *faïence** and stoneware factories had changed to making wares in the Wedgwood manner in order to stay in business. Later, when the German States had recovered from the devastation of the Napoleonic Wars, these factories reverted for the most part to porcelain, and created a thriving export trade in wares based on their early styles, although these did not become so fashionable in the luxury trade as the reproductions of early Sèvres porcelain produced by Minton*, Coalport* and many others.

Wedgwood's own period of prosperity came when Meissen had passed its 18th-century zenith, and it had little effect on the style of his later wares; but some of his early wares, such as the cauliflower and pineapple tureens, certainly came originally from Meissen, probably at secondhand by way of English factories (Chelsea, for instance) who copied the German factory's rococo* wares. It is possible that Wedgwood's cauliflower ware* may have been inspired by the local porcelain of Longton Hall, which must have been known to him. In 1765, he acknowledged the gift of a Meissen dessert service, sent to him by Sir William Meredith* 'to pattern from'.

There are few references to Meissen in Wedgwood's correspondence and memoranda, where he refers to the factory as either 'Dresden' or 'Saxon', but there is enough material to make it clear that he well understood the nature of the product, classifying it with Chinese porcelain. In the notes of his experiments with his newly-invented pyrometer*, Josiah noted that his Queen's ware*

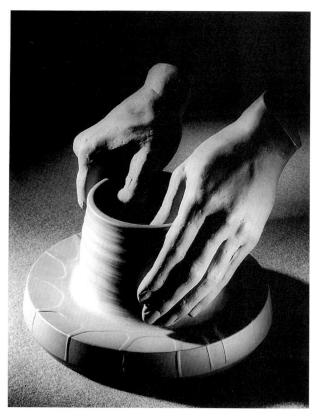

MELBOURNE, Colin. 'The Hands of the Potter', a sculpture in terracotta (orange-red) jasper, issued in a limited edition in 1978. Height 7in. *Wedgwood Museum*

bore 'the same heat as the Dresden'.

According to Marryat*, writing soon after 1850, Josiah II, while travelling in Germany in 1790, offered a rental of £3,000 per annum to take over the Meissen factory, an offer that was apparently refused. If the offer was ever made, it was a fortunate escape for Wedgwood that it was not accepted, since the area was to be overrun by Napoleon's armies within fifteen years and the Continent, in general, was already heading for a severe trade recession.

Melbourne, Colin (fl.1978-94)
Modeller; head of the Faculty of Art and Design at the North Staffordshire Polytechnic College. Melbourne modelled *Hands of the Potter,* a terracotta jasper* sculpture, height 7in., issued by Wedgwood in 1978 in a limited edition of 500.

Meleager
Son of Oeneus, King of Calydon and leader of the Argonauts. With a band of hunters, including Atalanta, Meleager slew the boar which ravaged the woods, an animal 'Scotticised' by Wedgwood as the 'Caledonian boar'.
Wedgwood subjects:
Meleager and Atalanta Killing the Calydonian Boar, medallion 6in. x 7in., no.81 in 1773 Catalogue*
Meleager, oval medallion 8in. x 6in., from a model or cast supplied by Flaxman* in 1775 (the subject invoiced as 'Hercules and the Boar'). No.105 in 1777 Catalogue

Meli, Giovanni (c.1815-85)
Sicilian sculptor and modeller, who came to England c.1839 and worked first for S. Alcock and later for Adams* of Tunstall and Copeland (Spode*). He set up on his own account as a manufacturer of Parian*, c.1858, and sold his business to Robinson & Leadbeater in 1865, when he returned to Italy. Some years later he emigrated to the USA, becoming a manufacturer of terracotta at a factory in Chicago. Meli modelled a group, *Venus and Cupid* ('Cupid Disarmed'), c.1850-60, which was reproduced in black basaltes* and Carrara*.

MELI, Giovanni. Black basaltes group, *Venus and Cupid* or *Cupid Disarmed* after a model by Meli. Height 13in. c.1850-60.
Christie's, London

Mellor, Thomas (fl.1870-95)

Pâte-sur-pâte* artist at Minton's*, where he was, with Charles Toft* and Frederick Rhead*, trained by M.L. Solon. In the 1870s he moved to the Etruria* factory, where he made inlaid* ware. A chess board made as an exhibition piece in the manner of Henri Deux* ware in 1871, was furnished with inlaid Queen's ware chessmen* after the original models by Flaxman*, and one of the surviving examples is signed by Mellor. Mellor's signature appears also on a fine inlaid Queen's ware* vase and an inlaid miniature tazza (height 2½in.) in the Wedgwood Museum*. Towards the end of the century Mellor worked for Wedgwood as an ornamenter. His wife, Lucy Shaw, was a paintress at Etruria*.

See: Colour Plate 75

MELON. Melon-shaped creamware teapot with rouletted body, decorated with green and yellow glazes in vertical bands. Height 5in. Unmarked. Attributed to Wedgwood, c.1765. *City Museum & Art Gallery, Stoke-on-Trent*

MELON. Pair of melon-shaped tureens on fixed stands coloured with green and yellow glazes. Length 9½in. Unmarked. Attributed to Whieldon, c.1763.
Christie's, New York

Melon

Tureens, teapots and covered preserve dishes moulded in the form of a melon, often on a leaf stand, were popular during the second half of the 18th century, and were made by Wedgwood, Leeds*, Castleford*, James and Charles Whitehead*, the Don Pottery and others. A porcelain version was made at Chelsea*. 'Mehons' [*sic*] were among the pieces ordered for Queen Charlotte's* tea service in 1765. The 'Melon Preserve', produced in Queen's ware*, and also decorated with Green glaze (see: Glazes) from about 1763, was still in production in plain Dysart glaze* two hundred years later.

Menai Suspension Bridge

The bridge, one of Thomas Telford's most important works, with a span of 580ft., was opened in 1826, forming the only road link between Anglesey and the Welsh mainland. To mark the 150th anniversary, Wedgwood produced 2,000 Queen's ware* plates printed in green with a view of the bridge designed by Islwyn Williams, a graphic art student at Liverpool polytechnic. The commemorative backstamp is unusually in both Welsh and English.

Mence, William (fl.1769-74)

Painter at the Chelsea Decorating Studio* who worked on border designs of the Frog* service in 1773-4.

Menu Holder

Menu holders supported by enamelled figures of clowns were produced in bone china*, c.1880. Jasper* medallions* were mounted in Chester silver menu holders in 1907-8.

Mercury

The Greek Hermes; god of commerce, gain and good fortune; the messenger of the gods, who usually carries the caduceus* and wears wings on his helmet and sandals. The helmet is perhaps better described as a travelling hat. As Hermes, Mercury was the son of Zeus and Maia. He invented the lyre. As the messenger of Jupiter*, he was charged with leading Venus*, Juno* and Minerva* to be judged by Paris* and is often seen in art handing the apple of Discord to him. In allegory Mercury represents Reason and Eloquence.

MERCURY. Basalt bust of *Mercury*. Height 10½in. Probably the model supplied by Hoskins & Grant in 1779. 20th-century reproduction, c.1910.
Wedgwood Museum

279

MERCURY. Black basaltes figure of *Mercury* from the model supplied by Flaxman in 1775. Height 12¾in. c.1860-80.

Sotheby's, London

Wedgwood subjects:

Mercury, bust 10½in., invoiced by Hoskins & Grant*, May 1779

Mercury, bust 18½in., attributed to Flaxman*, 1781, but probably not reproduced in black basaltes until 1790-5

Mercury, figure, height 11in., from a cast supplied by Flaxman, 1775

Mercury, figure by Donald Brindley*, 1974, produced in basalt with gold inscription

Mercury (seated), figure, height 20in., after Pigalle's* figure of Mercury tying his sandal, 1779

Mercury joining the Hands of Britain and France (Commercial Treaty), tablet 11in. x 9in., modelled by Flaxman, 1786

The figure of Mercury appears also in several tablets, including *Birth of Bacchus*, Judgement of Paris* and *Procession of Deities**.

See: Colour Plate 76

Meredith, Sir William (d.1790)

3rd baronet, of Henbury, Cheshire; M.P. for Wigan, 1754-61, and Liverpool, 1761-80; Privy Councillor and Comptroller of the Royal Household, 1774. Meredith was one of Wedgwood's earliest and most influential patrons. As M.P. for Liverpool he was certainly acquainted with Bentley*, to whom Wedgwood may have owed the introduction. In 1765 Wedgwood completed a large Queen's ware* dinner service for Sir William, who exerted his considerable influence to obtain for him the loan or gifts of antique gems*, prints, pottery and porcelain (see: Meissen). Prior to 1770, he was one of those who urged Wedgwood to introduce a whiter earthenware body (a proposal which Wedgwood resisted) leading to the production of Pearl* ware in 1779. Josiah's father-in-law, Richard Wedgwood*, lent Sir William the sum of £1,900, a substantial debt which led to an acrimonious dispute between them and nearly to a duel. Josiah made an unsuccessful attempt to resolve this quarrel at a meeting with both parties at the studio of Joseph Wright* of Derby in 1773.

Metallic Oxides

The oxides of certain metals are used as pigments in pottery and porcelain decoration, either underglaze (applied to the surface of the ware before glazing) or onglaze (applied to the glazed and fired ware in the form of enamels). These oxides are suspended in an oily medium to make them suitable for application with a brush, the medium burning away in the kiln, the final colour being developed by subsequent firing. In modern times ceramic colours usually have a vegetable dye added as a guide to the developed shade, but in the 18th century a system of numbered palettes was often used, together with a similarly numbered guide to the appearance of the colours after firing. The oxides most widely used were cobalt* (blue), copper (green), iron (yellow-brown, black, and rust-red at high temperatures), manganese* (brown, purple), and antimony (yellow). Variations of colour could be obtained by simple mixing. The colours obtainable were variable, depending on firing temperature, kiln atmosphere and the composition of the glaze on which they were used. Copper, for instance, yielded a bluish-green in the presence of a plentiful supply of oxygen, but a reddish-purple in the presence of carbon monoxide (reducing atmosphere). In the 19th century, new colouring oxides, such as chromium (normally grey-green, orange in soft lead glazes), uranium (red and orange) and vanadium (yellow with tin oxide) came into use. White glazes and enamels are usually the result of opacifying a transparent glaze with tin oxide.

Colouring oxides are also added to glazes to stain them (e,g. Green glaze – see: Glazes) and mixed with clay bodies to make solid colours (coloured bodies*, solid-colour jasper*). Mixed with slip*, colouring oxides will produce coloured dip* or slip ground-lays (see: Processes of Manufacture: Groundlaying).

Meteyard, Eliza (1816-79)

Author, born in Liverpool, the daughter of a doctor, who was appointed in 1818 surgeon to the Shropshire militia, whose headquarters were in Shrewsbury. There she later visited the home of Dr Robert Waring Darwin*, who had formed an important collection of Wedgwood ware including a first edition copy of the Portland vase*. Her father died in 1842 and, at the age of twenty-six, Eliza went to live in London to try to support herself by her writing. She was both a feminist and a reformer, holding what she later described as 'communistic' opinions and campaigning for social equality, women's rights, the industrial co-partnership of owners and workers and popular education. Between 1845, when she published her first book, *Struggles for Fame,* and 1865, she wrote eight novels (several under the pseudonym of 'Silverpen') and collections of short stories and a guide to *The Hallowed Spots of Ancient London.*

She had 'formed the idea of writing a life of Wedgwood as early as 1850', but, according to her own account, 'found materials so scanty and so little seemed be known of our great ceramic artist as to lead me to the resolution to write as exhaustive a memoir as possible as soon as time permitted.' In 1862 she applied to Godfrey Wedgwood* for information. He replied: 'I am fully satisfied that there are not materials for a really satisfactory life of my great-grandfather. I am sorry that such a man should have left so little to chronicle behind him.' This must have come as something of a surprise to Eliza Meteyard, who had already, in 1856, met Joseph Mayer* and been promised free use of the huge hoard of Wedgwood manuscript material that he had discovered in Birmingham, open access to his great collection, and introductions to the other collectors of Wedgwood among his extensive acquaintance. He was also generous with financial help to her, and the publishers Hurst & Blackett offered her £1,000, a huge sum by the standards of the day, for a biography of Josiah Wedgwood.

Eliza Meteyard's *Life of Josiah Wedgwood* was published in two large volumes in 1865-6. Nearly half of the first volume is devoted to a general history of pottery, which is open to criticism for being inappropriate to a biography, but much of the material was not easily accessible at the time and it provided a useful, if unnecessarily detailed, background to the remarkable story that followed. A more serious defect is her uncritical admiration for her subject, which led her to ignore his faults and failings and to draw false conclusions from the evidence. She was neither a professional historian nor a ceramist and her knowledge of business was too limited to allow her fully to understand the manufacturing and commercial problems faced by Wedgwood. Nor did she appreciate the extent of the contributions to Wedgwood's success made by Bentley* and Thomas Wedgwood*. Her biography is none the less an extraordinary achievement by any standards, a monumental work of pioneer inquiry which compels admiration. It remained the standard work on Josiah Wedgwood and the products of his factory for more than a century.

Eliza Meteyard wrote several more novels, but the greater part of her energies after 1765 continued to be given to the study of Wedgwood. In 1871 she published *A Group of Englishmen,* a useful and original study of Wedgwood's sons and their circle of literary friends, who included Coleridge and Wordsworth. She admittted, however, that she had 'suppressed everything which might have been considered of a private nature' and credited Tom Wedgwood* with the invention of photography, reproducing what she described (quite erroneously) as 'almost certainly the first photograph'. This was followed by *The Wedgwood Handbook,*

MICHELANGELO. Black basaltes bust of Jesus Christ after Michelangelo. Height 8in. c.1810.   *Wedgwood Museum*

1875, a reference work for collectors, which contained practical notes on marks and other methods of identification, part of the Christie* & Ansell 1781 Auction Sale* Catalogue, a valuable collation of the Wedgwood & Bentley and Wedgwood Catalogues of Ornamental wares (1773-1788), and lists and prices of ware from four important collections (Marryat*, De la Rue, Barlow and Carruthers) sold by auction between 1867 and 1870. Three books of (autotype) illustrations – *Wedgwood and His Works, Memorials of Wedgwood* and *Choice Examples of Wedgwood Art,* were published in 1873, 1874 and 1879 respectively.

Michelangelo Buonarotti (1474-1564)

Possibly the foremost sculptor of the Renaissance (at least to modern taste) although he himself awarded the honour to Cellini. Nothing by Michelangelo in bronze survives but a number of marbles exist, including the *tondo* belonging to the Royal Academy, which was reproduced in Parian* by Wedgwood in 1981. The following of Wedgwood's earlier models are described in his catalogues as after work by Michelangelo:

Bacchus*, figure 11in., 1773

Jesus Christ, bust 8in., c.1810

Triton*, figure 11in. Wedgwood's pair of tritons appears to have been modelled from the cast of a single figure, described by Bentley* on 28 December 1769 as after a model by Michelangelo. The original carnelian gem from which Hackwood* drew inspiration for his tablet, *Birth of Bacchus,* modelled in 1779, reputedly once belonged to Michelangelo.

See also: Michelangelo Lamp

Michelangelo Lamp

Sometimes described as the 'Michelangelo vase', this lamp is in the form of a large covered bowl with three burners, either fluted or ornamented with acanthus* scrolls upon a triangular pedestal and column support. The cover is surmounted either by a palm-tree candle-holder and stopper or three sibyls* seated beneath a palm. Around the column and supporting the bowl are three stooping male figures. It was made in black basaltes*, its low shape number (180) indicating that it was in production by about 1772, and later in jasper*. The three supporting figures, described as 'Persians' (an architectural term for the male equivalent of caryatids*) were copied from figures on a silver-gilt crucifix by Antonio Gentile da Faenza, c.1582, two of which were illustrated by Sir William Chambers* in *Treatise on Civil Architecture,* 1759. Three figures, obtained as casts from John Flaxman* senior in 1770, were used by Boulton* for a magnificent 'Geographical clock' and it is almost certain that Wedgwood obtained his models from the same source. Chambers

MICHELANGELO LAMP. Black basaltes 'Michelangelo' lamp. Height 13½in. Unmarked. Wedgwood & Bentley, c.1772.
                                        Courtesy of Country Life

described the figures as 'copied from candelabres, in St Peter's of the Vatican…cast from models of Michael Angelo Buonaroti and repaired either by himself, or under his direction'. The Michelangelo Lamp was reproduced in the 19th century in basaltes and jasper, and, with somewhat bizarre effect, in Majolica*. It was reproduced also in enamelled and gilded bone china*, c.1885.

Miles, Helen Jane Arundel (fl.1860-93)

Painter (especially in watercolour), illustrator and designer; studied at the South Kensington School of Art and was a regular exhibitor between 1860 and 1883, also illustrating a number of books. She designed several series of tiles* for Wedgwood, including *Midsummer Night's Dream* and *Months,* the latter frequently attributed to Kate Greenaway*.

MILES, Helen. Speltre plant-pot, the four sides inset with tiles from the set of the 'Months' by Helen Miles printed in underglaze blue. Height 8in. c.1878.   *Author's collection*

281

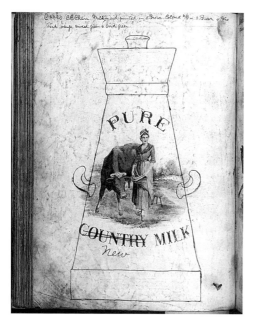

MILK CHURN. Design for a Queen's ware milk churn printed in brown and painted in underglaze colours. c.1905. *Wedgwood Museum*

Milk Churn

Queen's ware* milk churns were made, for advertising purposes and for display in shops selling dairy produce, c.1905. They were decorated with suitable printed and enamelled designs and supplied to such companies as Wiltshire United Dairies and the Dairy Supply Co.
See also: Dairy Ware

Milk Cooler

Tall cover with low stand made of a porous Orange body*, introduced c.1811, to contain a milk bottle. When kept damp, the container cooled the contents by the process of evaporation. Similar containers, with liners, were made for butter.

Miller Alec (b.1879)

Sculptor; born in Glasgow. Miller studied at the Glasgow School of Art and in Florence. He taught at the Cambridge School of Arts and Crafts, 1902-14, and Oxford City School of Art, 1919-23. Miller lived for some years in Monterey, California. His Wedgwood plaque, *Diana and Actaeon,* 1906, was in the Buten* Museum.

MINERVA. Bronzed basaltes bust of *Minerva,* probably a reduced version of the model supplied by Hoskins & Grant in 1774. Height 14in. c.1870. *Christie's, London*

MINERVA. Wedgwood & Bentley solid blue and white jasper medallion, *Minerva.* Height 6½in. 1776-80.
Dwight & Lucille Beeson Collection, Birmingham Museum, Alabama

Miller, Felix Martin (1820-after 1880)

Sculptor; brought up in an Orphan School; joined the Royal Academy Schools in 1842; exhibited at the Academy, 1842-80. He specialised in bas-relief* and his work was favourably discussed on several occasions in the *Art Journal.* Several of his models were reproduced in Parian* by Minton* and Copeland (Spode*) and of these *Emily and the White Doe of Rylston* (Copeland, c.1862) is probably the most widely known. For Wedgwood, Miller sculpted a bust of Shakespeare, 11½in. in height, which was reproduced in Carrara* to mark the tercentenary of the latter's birth in 1564.
See: Howell & James; Shakespeare Subjects

Mills, Anne (fl.1769-74)

Painter at the Chelsea Decorating Studio* who worked on borders of the Frog* service.

Mills, Thomas (fl.1773-74)

Painter at the Chelsea Decorating Studio* for the inside borders of the Frog* service.

Minerva

Roman goddess of wisdom, patroness of the arts, professions and trades and agriculture. She was identified by the Romans with Pallas Athene, the daughter of Zeus (Jupiter*), in whom power and wisdom were harmoniously blended. Minerva represents prudence, courage and perseverance and is usually clad in armour, with helmet and shield. The traditional figure of Britannia was no doubt based on representations of Minerva. The Palladium* was an image of the goddess preserved at Troy, on which the safety of the city depended. It was stolen by Ulysses* and Diomedes* and taken by the latter to Greece.
Wedgwood subjects:
Minerva, bust 22in., from a cast supplied by Hoskins & Grant*, 1774. Reproduced in the 19th century in bronzed basaltes*, bronze and gold*, and ivory-glazed Queen's ware* enamelled and gilt
Minerva, oval medallion 6in. x 5in., no.19 in 1773 Catalogue*
Minerva, medallion 2½in. x 2in., no.23 in 1773 Catalogue
Minerva, medallion 7in. x 5½in., from a model or cast supplied by Flaxman*, 1775. No.107 in 1777 Catalogue
Minerva, seated figure candelabrum (companion to Diana), height 13¾in. Variously attributed to John Flaxman* and Webber*. In production by the end of 1782
Diomede Carrying off the Palladium, medallion 3½in. x 2⅞in., from a model in the Newgate* collection. No.169 in 1777 Catalogue
See also: Cassandra

Minkin, Walter Robert, Des.RCA, FSIAD (b.1928)

Designer at Barlaston* 1955-86; Chief Designer; Group Design Manager; and from July 1979 to 1986, Design Director. Bob Minkin was responsible for a large number of tableware designs, including the outstandingly successful *Ice Rose* on Coupe shape

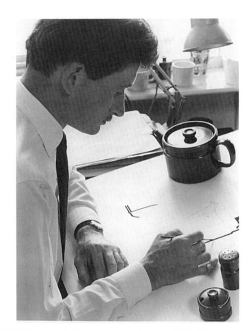

MINKIN, Walter Robert. Design Director, 1979-86, at work on his designs for *Sterling* oven-to-table ware. *Photograph: Wedgwood*

(see: Tableware Shapes) bone china* (1959) and *Mayfield* in two versions on Barlaston shape Queen's ware*. The design for which he received the greatest critical acclaim was his cylindrical coffee set, produced originally in black basalt and later in Ravenstone glaze (see: Glazes) on Queen's ware. Others of his designs include: *Sterling* (oven-to-table ware*), *Faversham, Seander, Sun Flower* and *Moonlight* (Barlaston shape); *India Rose* (Galaxie shape); *Summer Rose* and *Yellow Diamond.* In 1978 he was responsible for the adaptation of the Egyptian Collection* gilded plaques from originals in the Tutankhamun treasure.

MINKIN, Walter Robert. Basalt cylindrical coffeeset, designed by Robert Minkin in 1963. Coffeepot height 9in. *Wedgwood Museum*

Minton, Stoke-on-Trent

The firm was founded by Thomas Minton in 1793 (operating from 1796) with the aid of William Pownall, who financed the enterprise, Joseph Poulson (master potter) and Samuel Poulson (modeller and mould maker). Thomas Minton's brother acted as London agent. When Minton died in 1836, his place was taken by his son, Herbert Minton. At first the principal products were blue-printed earthenware and bone china*, but plain and enamelled creamware was made and there is a record of Minton's purchasing '50 tons of Mr.Wedgwood's blue clay at 10/6' in August 1817 for the manufacture of a coloured body*. Wedgwood bought considerable quantities of blue-printed ware from Minton between 1801 and 1806, including *Tulip, Willow, Pine* and *Nankeen Temple* patterns. The firm became more adventurous after it employed J.-L.-F. Arnoux from France as art director. He introduced, among other wares, one which he called Majolica*, which became one of the successes of the Great Exhibition of 1851, where the Medieval Court contained objects designed by Pugin and made by Minton. Artists of importance came from France in 1848 (July Revolution) and 1870 (Franco-Prussian War). Marc-Louis Solon, who arrived from Sèvres in 1870, brought with him the *pâte-sur-pâte* technique. Parian* was successfully adopted by Minton in the 1840s, and models by John Bell* and Hiram Powers (notably *The Greek Slave*) enjoyed great popularity. Carrier de Belleuse* also was among those who supplied models. Some fine figure work was done by Minton, both free-standing figures and as part of ornamental dessert services. Emile Lessore*, Thomas Allen*, Hugues Protât, Charles Toft* and Eric Owen* all came to Wedgwood from Minton's, as did John Boyle*, Herbert Minton's partner 1836-41 and equal partner with Francis Wedgwood* at Etruria 1843-5. Since the 19th century Minton has enjoyed a high reputation for richly decorated bone china table services, many in the style of Sèvres*. In the 1960s, like all the other great names in the Fine China Group except Wedgwood, Minton was put up for sale and, with Doulton, was acquired by the Pearson Group.

MINKIN, Walter Robert. *Ice Rose* pattern on Coupe shape, designed by Robert Minkin in 1959. *Wedgwood Museum*

MISS PIT. Creamware teapot enamelled in iron-red and black with the figure known as 'Miss Pit'. Probably decorated by Robinson & Rhodes, Leeds. Height 5½in. Unmarked. Wedgwood, c.1765.
Mr & Mrs David Zeitlin Collection

Miss Pit

A half-length portrait of a young woman, over a scroll inscribed 'Miss Pit', occurs on a Leeds* salt-glaze* teapot, and the same young woman is depicted seated in a garden on both saltglaze and creamware teapots from the same factory, the reverse being decorated with a design of stylised buildings. A similar figure, painted in iron-red, with almost identical buildings painted on the reverse, is recorded on a Wedgwood creamware teapot, c.1765. The painting is attributed to David Rhodes*.

Mollart, J (fl.1806-11)

Engraver who supplied Wedgwood with engravings of 'Minton's* Willow' (see: Willow Pattern) in 1806, though it does not seem to have been produced until 1818. He was also partly responsible (with Hales* and Brookes*) for the *Blue Bamboo* pattern.

Mongenot, Joseph (1769-1814)

Swiss modeller and designer who came to England in 1788 and designed bas-reliefs* for Adams* of Greengates, including *Sacrifice to Apollo, Sacrifice of Diana, Sacrifice to Pomona* and *Sacrifice to Aphrodite,* all in the Wedgwood style. He worked also as an engraver.

MONOCULAR. Single-lens telescopic opera glass (monocular) with ormolu and ivory mounts and a decorative sleeve of blue jasper dip ornamented with the *Marriage of Cupid and Psyche.* Length 3in. No mark visible. Wedgwood, c.1790.
Wedgwood Museum

Monocular

An opera glass with a single eye-piece. Made about 1785-90, the ornamental jasper* outer case was used with brass tubes and lens carriers and an ivory eye-piece. Similarly ornamented opera glasses in the form of binoculars with twin eye-pieces were also made.

MONOPODIA. Three-colour jasper vase ornamented with four lions'-head simulated monopodia, borders of ribbon and ivy, floral swags and paterae. Height 7½in. c.1875-85.   *Wedgwood Museum*

Monopodia

Masks, usually of lions, goats or satyrs, surmounting a single leg or foot, used as supports for a vase or entablature. Wedgwood's early vases and candlesticks* in variegated* wares and the dry bodies* were often supported in this manner, and sphinx-head monopodia appear supporting objects in the revived Egyptian* taste of 1800-10.

Monteith

An oval bowl with an elaborately scalloped rim which is turned slightly inwards. Its purpose was to cool the bowls of wine glasses, which were suspended from the rim by the foot, the bowl resting in very cold water. The name is derived from a Scotsman named Monteith who, at Oxford during the reign of Charles II, wore a cloak with a scalloped hem.

Monteiths are comparatively rare, but they exist in silver, pewter, glass and porcelain* and they were made also by Wedgwood in Queen's ware* and jasper*. A monteith is illustrated in Plate 5 (design 16) of Wedgwood's first (1774) Queen's ware Catalogue*, and an early enamelled example is among the pieces of the Frog* service preserved in the Hermitage Museum, St. Petersburg. The type has also been made in recent times as a decorative piece in transfer-printed* Queen's ware and glazed black basalt.

MONTEITH. Queen's ware monteith from the Frog service, painted in monochrome with a view of Cliveden House, Buckinghamshire.
Hermitage Museum, St.Petersburg. Photograph: Wedgwood

Montfaucon, Bernard de (1655-1741)

Montfaucon served in Germany in the army of Marshal Turenne before entering the Congregation of Saint-Maur in 1675 and devoting the rest of his life to scholarship. His most celebrated work is the somewhat inaccurate *L'antiquité expliquée et representée en figures,* published in five volumes in 1719. A five-volume *Supplément* followed in 1724. An English version by D.

MOORE, Arthur. Moore in his studio preparing detailed art work for commemorative ware. c.1965. *Photograph: Wedgwood*

Humphreys, London, appeared between 1721 and 1725. This important, lavishly-illustrated reference work was in Wedgwood's library and it is evident that he made frequent use of it. It was probably from this source that some of his models of sphinxes* were derived, and both relief ornament and encaustic-painted* decoration in the Egyptian* taste as well as the Canopic* jars can be traced to it. Wedgwood quoted Montfaucon in his letter of 2 November 1786 to Flaxman* about designs for the French *Commercial Treaty* tablets, and Flaxman appears to have used Montfaucon as a source for his Medusa*-head terminals to the handles of the Homeric vase (see: Apotheosis of Homer). In his early attempts to copy the Portland vase*, Wedgwood worked from Montfaucon's four illustrations of it.

Monti, Raffaelle (1818-81)
Italian sculptor who visited England in 1846 and lived in London from 1848 until his death. He executed some architectural sculpture, including the *relievo* over the proscenium arch of the Covent Garden Opera House in 1858, and was responsible for the interior decoration of Mentmore, Buckinghamshire, but he is best known for a form of sculpture, probably originated by Antonio Corradini, which gave solid marble statues and busts the appearance of being covered by a diaphanous veil. An example of this work is *A Veiled Woman* in the Wallace Collection, London. He also sculpted more conventional marble busts and statues, and his bust of Thomas Henry Huxley (1825-95) was reproduced in Wedgwood's Carrara* and in basaltes* in 1865. Several of his figures were reproduced in Copeland's (see: Spode) Parian*.

Moonlight Lustre
See: Lustre Decoration

Moonstone Glaze
See: Glazes – *Matt*

Moore, Arthur (b.1916)
Artist; born and raised in Etruria* village; joined Wedgwood as an apprentice gilder, 1930. In 1932 Moore became a junior assistant in the art department under the direction of John Goodwin* and was promoted in 1937 to be senior assistant to art director Victor Skellern*. In 1968 he was appointed Design Studio Manager. Arthur Moore was a skilled draughtsman who made more than 2,000 drawings for the 1940-50 Shapes Catalogue and detailed drawings for all commemorative ware* for the USA after 1934. He was largely responsible for initiating the use of silk-screen* printing in 1953.

MORE, Samuel. Dark-blue jasper dip portrait medallion of Samuel More. Oval height 3¼in. c.1785. *Wedgwood Museum*

Moorstone
A feldspathic rock or 'china stone' similar in properties to the Chinese petuntse (see: Porcelain) and Cornish growan stone. Wedgwood made extensive tests with moorstone in his experiments to produce jasper* but wrote of it in 1776: 'As Moor stone varies so much, being a compound mixed at random perhaps by the waves & Tides of the Ocean, I despair of making it a Principal ingredient in a Porcelain Manufactory'.

More, Samuel (fl.1769-99)
Secretary to the Society of Arts* and a friend of both Wedgwood and Bentley*. As early as 1772, Wedgwood wrote to Bentley: 'I have a very friendly letter from our good friend Mr. More with advice of the China Earth being sent. I beg you will make my thanks & affectionate regards known to him.' In the late summer of 1774 More and his wife visited Etruria* and More encouraged Wedgwood to begin a collection of Wedgwood & Bentley's products for posterity. In 1774 the Society of Arts moved to the Adelphi*, where it maintained a laboratory for the purpose of assaying specimens of ore. It was to More that Wedgwood applied in 1775 when he needed supplies of ground glass for his porcelain experiments, and it was More who sent Wedgwood quantities of zaffre* when, in 1777, the price of cobalt* doubled in less than six months, threatening the production of blue jasper*. More also gave Wedgwood practical advice on the design of mortars* and pestles and he supplied a 'very poor head' of William Penn from which Wedgwood reproduced a surprisingly satisfactory portrait medallion*. More's own portrait medallion was produced in black basaltes* by 1773 and later reproduced in jasper*. In 1787, More, on behalf of the Society of Arts, sent enamels to Etruria to be tested.

Morgan, J. (fl.1760-70)
China dealer who occupied premises at the corner of Arlington Street and Piccadilly, London. In 1769 Wedgwood wrote to Bentley* asking whether Craft* had taken a drawing of the 'Seve [Sèvres*] vases' at Morgan's, which he thought 'composed in a very masterly stile'. This is evidence not only that the porcelain of the Manufacture Royale was being exported to England but also that, at that date, Wedgwood was still taking an active interest in rococo* styles.

Morpheus
The son of Sleep and the god of Dreams, who was responsible for the shape and content of dreams.
See: Somnus

Morris, Rowland James (1847-1909)
Ceramic sculptor and modeller; studied at Hanley School of Art under Hugues Protât* and, from 1863, at South Kensington School of Art. He was the sculptor of the 'Processes of the Pottery Industry'

MORTAR WARE. Three Wedgwood & Bentley mortars and pestles, mortars varying in height from 3½in.-1¼in., pestles 12¾in.-5in. length. c.1779.
Kadison Collection

MORTLOCK, John. Printed backstamp of John Mortlock, the Oxford Street, London, retailers who commissioned a number of commemorative pieces from Wedgwood, taken from a 'Carlyle' jug, 1881.
Private collection

and 'Labour of the Months' panels for the façade of the Wedgwood Institute, Burslem, 1865-73, and also worked at this time at Etruria* as a modeller, especially of Majolica*. Later he modelled for a number of Staffordshire potters, including Bernard Moore.

Mortar Ware

A very hard vitreous (see: Vitrification) stoneware* body introduced by Wedgwood in 1779 for the manufacture of mortars, pestles and other chemical ware. The body is non-absorbent and acid-resistant, a fact which Veldhuysen* of Amsterdam reported as 'incredible history to several physicians', and mortars made from this body are still probably the best available. Wedgwood had first considered the possibility of making mortars as early as 1762, when he consulted Dr Matthew Turner* on the subject, but nothing further was done until about 1777, when, after reading Priestley's* *Experiments and Observations on different kinds of Air,* Wedgwood noted in his Commonplace Book*: 'The Dr seems much at a loss for a mortar, not metal, for pounding in. Make him one or two.' Until then, mortars had commonly been made of metal (usually bronze) or marble, imported from Holland or Italy. Metal was liable to flake, causing poisoning, and marble was not impervious to oil or attack from acids.

Wedgwood & Bentley mortars (they were made in the Ornamental ware partnership and marked as such) were of two kinds: a brown body, which Wedgwood described as 'of an excellent porcelain texture'; and a white, 'so much more beautiful…and quite equal in point of texture'. Samuel More* offered practical advice about the design of mortars and pestles, and they were 'proved with the severest necessary tests' at Apothecary's Hall. In 1780 Wedgwood was able to tell Bentley: 'mortars…go everywhere'.

Two years later James Watt* supplied Wedgwood with a design for triturating mortars, intended for mechanical operation, and these were produced in three sizes. It was Wedgwood's policy not to charge for chemical wares used for experimental work and he declined all payment from both Watt and Priestley for chemical wares supplied to them and to other scientists. Wedgwood's mortar ware is described in his 1787 Catalogue* as 'A porcelain *bisqué* of extreme HARDNESS, little inferior to that of agate. This property, together with its resistance to the strongest acids and corrosives, and its impenetrability by every known species of liquids, adapts it happily for mortars, and different kinds of chemical vessels…This compact hard porcelain is excellently adapted also for evaporating pans, digesting vessels, basons, filtering funnels, syphons, tubes, such as Dr Priestley uses in some of his experiments.'

Wedgwood's mortars and pestles continued to be made throughout the 19th century and production was continued at Etruria* and later at Barlaston* in the 20th century.

Mortlock, John, London

China dealer and merchant who ordered wares from various factories marked with his own backstamp. His transfer-printed* mark added to the jug commemorating Thomas Carlyle is in the form of a globe with radiating lines on which is inscribed 'John Mortlock, Oxford Street, London W.' A flagstaff and flag with the figures '1748' suggest that the firm may have been founded in that year. Shortly after Lessore's* death in 1876, Mortlock took over much of the remaining stock of his work and most of it was sold in a successful exhibition in 1877.

Morye, St Petersburg

See: Poskotchin

Moscow

The Gardner factory at Verbilki was the foremost porcelain factory in the neighbourhood of Moscow. It was founded about 1765 by an Englishman, Francis Gardner, and no earthenware was made there until 1833. Some of the early tableware border designs used to decorate the 'Opaque ware' closely resembled Wedgwood's 18th-century Queen's ware* patterns, but later designs were more florid.

Mother-of-Pearl Lustre

A liquid lustre, based on bismuth or titanium, which produces a mother-of-pearl iridescence.
See: Ordinary Lustres

Mould

A matrix, usually of plaster of Paris or fireclay, used for the casting of figures and other ceramic wares which cannot be made on the potter's wheel. Moulds can be taken from a variety of sources: from an original model in clay, wax or carved wood; from another piece of ceramic ware; or even from a natural object. There are three stages in the making of a pottery mould:
1. A hollow case mould is formed over the original model, made in as many parts as may be necessary (see: Casting)
2. The case mould is used to make a block mould (patrix), which is a replica of the original object
3. The block mould is used to make a working mould, and it is from the latter that the work is cast. New working moulds can be made from the block mould as they are required

Intaglio moulds have sometimes been made by carving or modelling, and block moulds of wood or alabaster were often employed in the 18th century, made by craftsmen known as block-cutters. Two of the most celebrated Staffordshire block-cutters were Aaron Wood* and William Greatbatch*. Coward* carved wooden block moulds for Wedgwood, several of which are in the Wedgwood Museum*. The plaster of Paris mould was introduced into

MOULD. Saltglazed stoneware block moulds of leaf and shell spouts and a 'Landskip' teapot and sauceboat. Teapot mould height 4½in. c.1760. *Wedgwood Museum*

Staffordshire about 1745, reputedly by Ralph Daniels of Cobridge. Wedgwood's 18th-century block moulds were made of fired clay for durability and many of them have lasted in good condition until the present day.

Moulds from Silver

Apart from wares which are plainly copies of silver patterns*, some Wedgwood creamware objects give the impression of having been made from moulds taken from actual pieces of silver. In a letter of February 1769, Wedgwood refers to the gift of an inkstand from Ralph Griffiths* which he had been asked to transmit to Bentley*, and concludes '…but I have a notion of moulding from it first'. This suggests that the practice was not uncommon.

Moulds, Queen's Ware

Decorative Queen's ware* moulds were made in the 18th and 19th centuries in many shapes and sizes for jellies, butter and meat and fish pastes.
See: Blancmange Mould; Jelly Mould

MOULDS, QUEEN'S WARE. Two Queen's ware 'double-star pettys' – two-tier, star-shaped moulds for jellies. Width 3⅜in. c.1770-85. Similar objects were made in saltglazed ware by John and Thomas Wedgwood as early as c.1745 and later supplied to Josiah Wedgwood.
Mr & Mrs Samuel Laver Collection

Mounts, Metal

The mounting of porcelain in gilt-bronze or ormolu* was fashionable during much of the 18th century and vase mounts were made by Boulton* at Soho, Birmingham. Wedgwood reported to Bentley* in November 1768: 'Mr Boulton is picking up Vases, & going to make them in Bronze. You know how old China bowles, Jarrs &c are mounted in Metal, he proposes an alliance betwixt the Pottery & Metal branches, Viz, that we shall make such things as will be suitable for mounting, & not have a *Pott* look, & he will finish them with the mounts.' Bentley was not enthusiastic about any regular arrangement of this kind, but a few vases of various

MOUNTS, METAL. Cane ware mug with moulded 'bamboo' foot and handle and applied figures, *Bringing Home the Game*, the canted rim and interior covered with opaque white glaze enamelled with an egg-and-tongue pattern in blue. The rim is mounted in Sheffield plate. c.1786. *Wedgwood Museum*

types, including variegated*, were mounted at Soho. Large quantities of cameos* and seals* were mounted in metal in Birmingham, and jasper* was widely used in metal mounts.
See: Boden & Smith; Drum; Lustres; Monocular

MOUNTS, METAL. Blue jasper dip miniature engine-turned cream jug, ornamented with yellow strapwork and white beads and leaves, mounted in Sheffield plate. Height 4½in. c.1795. The body of the jug is formed from an oval bell-pull, a shape used also for scent bottles.
Wedgwood Museum

MOUNTSTEPHEN, Eley George. Solid blue and white jasper portrait medallion of General Sir Eyre Coote, modelled by Mountstephen in 1788. Oval height 5in. c.1790.

Formerly Eugene D. Buchanan Collection

Mountstephen, Eley George (fl.1776-91)

Modeller in wax, born in County Meath, Ireland. Mountstephen moved to London in 1781 and exhibited wax portraits* at the Royal Academy between 1782 and 1791. His style varied, probably because his portraits, many of which were not 'taken from life', reflected more closely the style of the portrait used as a source than his own. The following Wedgwood portrait medallions* are from original wax models by Mountstephen:

Lord and Lady Auckland*, two portraits, 1790

Sir Eyre Coote, 1788, from a 1779 marble bust by Nollekens. This portrait was for many years catalogued as Ferdinand of the Two Sicilies

Duc d'Orléans ('Philippe Egalité'), 1788

Christopher Wyvill, modelled 1776, first appearance in the Oven Books*, 1780

Moustache Cup

A tea or breakfast cup with a pierced ledge immediately below the rim for the purpose of protecting the fashionable bushy moustaches of the late 19th century from contact with the liquid in the cup. This type of cup, introduced as a novelty c.1880, was made by most porcelain manufacturers of the day, including Wedgwood.

Muffin Dish (Muffineer)

Round dish with a domed cover for the service of warm muffins. Muffin dishes were made by Wedgwood in Queen's ware* and in bone china* of both the first and second periods.

Muffle

See: Kilns

Murray, Keith Day Pierce, MC, RDI, FRIBA (1892-1981)

Architect and designer of pottery, glass and furniture; born in New Zealand and educated at King's College, Auckland, and Mill Hill School, London. During World War I, Keith Murray served with distinction in the Royal Flying Corps, being five times mentioned in dispatches and awarded the Military Cross and the Croix de Guerre Belge. After the war he studied architecture, and during the depression of the early 1930s he produced many successful designs for glass manufactured by Stevens & Williams of Brierley Hill. Through Arthur Powell (a cousin of Alfred Powell's*) he was introduced to the Wedgwoods and in 1932 visited Etruria*, where he was invited to design for the firm on a freelance basis. His first commission was the design of vegetable dishes for the *Annular* shape then being created by John Goodwin* and Tom Wedgwood*. In 1933 Murray was formally engaged to work for Wedgwood for three months a year.

MURRAY, Keith. The architect and designer at work on his drawings for the 'Commonwealth' shape in 1947. *Photograph: Wedgwood*

Murray's employment coincided with the development by Norman Wilson* of white and coloured matt glazes (see: Glazes), soon followed by two-colour Queen's ware* ('CC and Celadon Slipware') which proved to be exceptionally well suited to Murray's uncluttered, rational shapes, which relied upon purity of form with a minimum of decoration in lines, bands and fluting added on the lathe*. His work is characterised by strong shapes, securely based, with well-defined outlines, and his bowls and vases are as functional as they are aesthetically satisfying. Murray's designs were well received at their first exhibition in London later in the year and he won a gold medal at the 5th Triennale in Milan. An exhibition at John Lewis's store in London in November 1933 showed no less than 124 shapes designed for Wedgwood by Keith Murray, a startling example of his industry. He was later described as 'used to working from 10 in the morning till 11 at night every day of the week including Sundays'. Most of his designs were made in Queen's ware decorated with matt glazes in various colours, but there were also small quantities made in a modern version of rosso antico* and a new copper basalt body, examples of which are now extremely scarce.

During the following five years Murray designed more vases, bowls, beakers, mugs, jugs, inkstands, cigarette boxes and ash trays, tobacco jars and powder bowls, and also some tableware patterns, which included *Lotus, Radio, Iris, Pink Flower, Red Pimpernel* and *Weeping Willow* (also known as 'Green Tree'). His designs for tablewares were slight: economical drawings, handpainted in one or two colours, often enhanced with platinum, with simple matching

MURRAY, Keith. Moonstone glazed Queen's ware coffeeset with platinum handles and knops designed by Keith Murray, c.1935. Coffeepot height 8in. *Wedgwood Museum*

MURRAY, Keith. Three Queen's ware vases in versions of the two-colour clay technique, using cream-colour with stained grey and Celadon coloured bodies. c.1935 *(centre)* and c.1953.

Author's collection

border lines. These would now be considered fairly representative examples of Art Deco* design, but they did not last beyond 1940 (unlike Ravilious's* more original designs of the same period). Many of Murray's shapes for bowls, vases and mugs, on the other hand, were reintroduced in the 1950s and some are now regarded as among the best ceramic shapes of the century. Most of his pieces made before 1940 are printed with his signature in facsimile in addition to the Wedgwood backstamp and impressed mark.

In 1936 Murray formed his own architectural firm in partnership with Charles S. White, and this firm was chosen by the Wedgwoods to design the new factory at Barlaston*. Intended to provide for '40 to 50 years life', Murray's buildings are still central to the Barlaston factory. The close friendship he formed with Josiah V* lasted until the latter's death in 1968.

Muses

The nine female divinities presiding over the arts and sciences; daughters of Zeus and Mnemosyne. They are: Clio, the Muse of history, represented with a roll of parchment or a chest of books; Euterpe, the Muse of lyric poetry, with a flute; Thalia, the Muse of comedy, with a mask or an ivy wreath, or as the Muse of idyllic poetry with a shepherd's staff; Melpomene, the Muse of tragedy, with the tragic mask and cothurnus (a kind of high shoe to increase the height of the tragic actor); Terpsichore, the Muse of dance and song, with a lyre and plectrum; Erato, the Muse of erotic poetry and mimicry, sometimes with a lyre; Polyhymnia (Polymnia), the Muse of the sublime hymn, usually seated in a pensive attitude; Urania, the Muse of astronomy, standing pointing with a staff at a globe; and Calliope, the Muse of eloquence and epic poetry, with a tablet and stylus. Mount Parnassus was sacred to the Muses, who are often found with Apollo* Musagetes. Figures of the Muses were made in sets at several of the porcelain factories and they are found also as painted decoration or relief ornament.

The attribution of Wedgwood bas-relief* ornaments depicting the Muses is complicated. Before 1778 Wedgwood owned casts of a set of the Muses by Edmé Bouchardon* but he was doubtful

MUSES. Pair of Wedgwood & Bentley blue and white jasper dip tablets, each 6⅛in. x 15¾in., ornamented with figures of *Apollo* and the nine *Muses,* attributed to Flaxman, 1778-80.

Kadison Collection

MUSES. Pair of pale-blue jasper dip vases, 1316 shape, with pale-green ('Celadon') jasper handles and ornaments of *Apollo* and the nine *Muses* with garlands of flowers. Height 11½in. c.1880. *Wedgwood Museum*

about using them because they were 'not sufficiently finish'd for an unlearned modeler to copy'. Wedgwood had also an incomplete set in plaster – comprising Melpomene, Thalia, Terpsichore and Euterpe, with the companion figure of Apollo – obtained from Flaxman senior* in March 1775. It is not clear whether these bas-relief figures were casts from the antique (in which case their origin is unknown) or original work by the younger Flaxman. In October 1777 Wedgwood told Bentley*: 'You may permit Mr Flaxman to proceed with the Muses of the size he had begun…we have Apollo, Melpomena, Thalia & Terpsichore, so that we want only 6 more to complete our suite.' It appears that the figure of Euterpe previously supplied was either forgotten, mislaid or not identified, for Wedgwood almost immediately countermanded the order and wrote: 'Having laid all our bass-relief Goddesses & ladies upon their backs…I instantly perciev'd that the Six Muses we want might be produc'd from this lovely group at half the trouble & expence they will be procur'd from Flaxman…I hope you may not have order'd them to be model'd as I desir'd you would'.

It is thus not clear whether all or only part of the set is Flaxman's. Giuseppe Angelini* modelled a set of the Muses for Wedgwood in 1789, probably copied direct from the Sarcophagus of the Muses, then in the Capitoline Museum, Rome, and now in the Louvre. The set attributed to Flaxman is to be found as a single

large tablet or as two tablets, with the figure of Apollo Musagetes balancing the number of figures to ten (nos 203-4 in 1779 Catalogue). Many of the figures from both the 'Flaxman' and the Angelini sets exist singly as oval medallions.
See also: Brindley, Donald *(Terpsichore);* Gessner, Solomon

Musical Instruments
Musical instruments appear both as painted decoration on Wedgwood's Queen's ware* and as relief ornament on jasper* and other dry bodies* (e.g. Hackwood's* *Music,* modelled in 1785 as a companion piece to *The Infant Academy* after Reynolds*). The most notable Queen's ware example is a tableware service of about 1780 painted in onglaze green and depicting a number of early instruments from antique sources. This service was first researched by J.C. Holdaway (Wedgwood Society *Proceedings* 13, 1990). In February 1801 Tom Byerley* wrote to London of the production of 'four new [jasper] ornaments in the form of Viol del [*sic*] Gamba or Violoncello for Musical Amateurs – to be used either as flowerpot, bulbous-root, or candlestick. they belong to a set intended to captivate musical people. 'A rare specimen of the Viol da Gamba vase in blue and white jasper dip* is in the Wedgwood Museum. 'Lyre Candelabras' were ordered through London in 1802 and 1803.
See: Colour Plate 77

MUSICAL INSTRUMENTS. Dark-blue jasper dip plaque, *Music,* modelled by Hackwood in 1785. Oval length 5¾in. c.1785-90.
Wedgwood Museum

MUSICAL INSTRUMENTS. Queen's ware Royal shape plate transfer-printed with the music and words of *Non Nobis Domine* and border decoration of musical instruments. Diameter 9in. c.1780.
Merseyside Museums

Mussill, William (fl.1871-1906)
Painter, mostly of flowers and birds, at Minton's* factory from 1872 until his death in 1906. His work, often signed, has been identified on both Davenport* and Wedgwood wares, although he does not appear to have been formally employed by either factory.

Myrtle Pan
Name given to a long rectangular flower pot* or bough pot* with rounded corners made in white terracotta* stoneware decorated with coloured slip* c.1770-1820. Large quantities of these pieces were sold in the Christie & Ansell Auction Sale* in 1781 but few appear to have survived.

MYRTLE PAN. White terracotta stoneware Myrtle pan with moulded *guilloche* rim and fluted body, decorated with brown slip under a clear glaze. Length 19½in. c.1785.
Wedgwood Museum

Naiads (Naiades)'

Inferior deities, or nymphs, who presided over rivers, springs, wells and fountains. Naiads lived in the countryside, in woods and meadows close to the water which they had made their own. In art they are generally represented as young and beautiful maidens, sometimes leaning on an urn from which water flows. *The Crouching Venus** reproduced in black basaltes* was probably intended to be one of these nymphs. A 'Naiad Centre' – an oval basket supported at each end by two female figures on a base moulded to represent waves – was produced by Wedgwood in plain Queen's ware* and Majolica*. This dessert bowl or table centre is illustrated in the '1878' Catalogue of Ornamental Shapes.

NAIADS. Queen's ware 'Naiad Centre' fruit bowl or table centre. Length 20in. c.1878.   *Wedgwood Museum*

Named Views

See: Topographical Painting

NAPOLEON IVY. Dessert plate decorated with the so-called 'Napoleon Ivy' pattern printed in brown and enamelled in green and brown. Diameter 8in. c.1815.   *Wedgwood Museum*

NAUTILUS. Pair of 'Nautilus flower vases' or wall pockets decorated with variegated lustre. Height 6in. c.1812.   *Formerly Buten Museum*

Napoleon Ivy

Persistent pattern* of large ivy leaves, arranged as a running border, printed in brown and enamelled in dark green. This pattern is often described as having been supplied to Napoleon in exile on the island of St Helena. 'Green Ivy' patterns are recorded from about 1812, but no factory record has been found of any such pattern ordered for Napoleon's use.

Nautilus

Shell shape used for the footed fruit bowl (fruit centre) of Queen's ware* dessert services, usually decorated with handpainted border patterns, from c.1790.
See: Conchology

Neale, James (1740-1814)

Humphrey Palmer's London agent who took over Palmer's* business in 1778 when Palmer failed. Robert Wilson became a partner in 1786 and eventually succeeded Neale. Other partners were admitted, and the style changed from Neale & Wilson to Neale & Co. The factory was noted for many close imitations of Wedgwood's productions, not infrequently precise copies. Neale's creamware, variegated* and black basaltes* vases and jasper wares are all of excellent quality.

Neo-classical Style

The style of most of Wedgwood's production after 1769.

The term was not in use before the 1880s. In the 18th century the style was known as the 'true' or 'correct' style or the 'revival of the arts'. It was looked upon as a new, or revived, Renaissance classicism*, supplanting the rococo*, which had developed from the baroque. The discoveries at Herculaneum* and Pompeii* were part of the foundations on which was built not only what was tantamount to a revolution in the arts but also great intellectual, social and political changes, of which the French Revolution eventually became a part. Neo-classicism, in its early stages, was as much an expression of opposition to Louis XV and his Court as it was a new fashion in the arts. In the 1750s the beginning of the new style in France was almost an underground movement. Influenced by the King, the Court remained faithful to rococo and antagonistic to the new classicism and to those who promoted it, almost until Louis's death in 1774. It is fair to say that at first neo-classicism was a contrived style which was one of the overt signs of political opposition. It appealed to intellectuals, financiers, tax-farmers and the affluent *bourgeoisie,* whose capital was in cash, and it was directed against the ruling aristocracy, whose capital was in land, and whose efforts were directed towards keeping the *bourgeoisie* from positions of influence at Court. To attack rococo was a relatively safe way of attacking those who favoured it.

Neo-classicism therefore came to comprehend a variety of ideas, not all of them classical in origin, held by the loosely knit group opposed to the *régime* which they hoped to see become *ancien*. In particular, it had to find room for the emerging Romantics. At first sight this seems hardly possible, but, as the century wore on, Romantic Classicism became well marked in almost every department of art: in painting, in literature and in pottery and porcelain.

Rococo never gained a notably firm hold in England, but its principal manifestations – Chippendale's furniture, silver (mainly by silversmiths of Huguenot descent who used French design books) and the early work of the porcelain factories, largely copied from the designs of Meissen* and Sèvres* – were among the finest of the 18th century. Architecturally, the principal English style was Palladian, and Josiah Wedgwood made a black basaltes* bust and two portrait medallions* to honour its first great English exponent, Inigo Jones. Perhaps surprisingly, he produced no such tributes to William Kent or Colen Campbell.

Neo-classicism, sometimes termed the 'Adam style', was regarded as little more than a passing fashion by those who took architecture seriously. Sir William Chambers* thought it trivial, as did his knowledgeable King, George III* ('The Adams have introduced too much of neatness and prettiness'). Horace Walpole, who spent much of his long life Gothicising his villa at Strawberry Hill, Twickenham, thought Palladian the only conceivable style for important buildings and complained that 'from Kent's mahogany wc are dwindled to Adam's filigree' and of 'Mr Adam's gingerbread and sippets of embroidery'. Elizabeth Montagu, on the other hand, told Lord Kames in 1766 that Robert Adam* had created a ceiling, chimneypiece and doors for her house in Hill Street, London, 'pretty enough to make me a thousand enemies'.

In England, as in France, the period from about 1760 was one of reaction against rococo, which hardly survived the decade. But the English did not adopt the luxurious French Louis Seize style in its stead. In the forefront of the new movement were the Adam brothers, and James 'Athenian' Stuart*, both of whom published books which were employed by contemporary architects, designers and manufacturers, who also used the catalogue of Sir William Hamilton's* collection and the works of the Comte de Caylus*, among others. The illustrations to these works were sometimes directly copied, but more often they were adapted or employed for the purpose of making pastiches, new objects combining parts of old ones. Wedgwood's 'Etruscan'* vases, for example, are usually copies of antique vases in form and decoration, although the decoration of one may appear on the shape of another and the finial may be taken from a third.

One of the features of the neo-classical style was the employment of fresh sources of inspiration, mainly from Herculaneum and Pompeii. These were small towns, affluent but provincial. One of the discoveries made during excavations was a type of wall painting, not hitherto known, which aroused a good deal of controversy because it did not wholly accord with the notion, derived from literary sources, of ancient painting. Wedgwood used the wall paintings of Herculaneum as subjects for bas-relief (see: Herculaneum Pictures) and Webber's* Sidney Cove* medallion made use of a figure from a wall painting at Pompeii.

These discoveries brought in their train a revised, and not always accurate, outlook on ancient history. As André Malraux pointed out, the excavations at Herculaneum and Pompeii uncovered large quantities of white marble statues, and it was assumed that this was how they had appeared in antiquity. This false notion led directly to the the introduction of white biscuit* porcelain figures at Sèvres and Meissen*, and in England especially at Derby*, and accounted later for the popularity of Parian* and Carrara*. In the north, white marble is relatively uncommon and expensive. It occurred to no one that it was not in the least uncommon in Italy, and that the Romans might have painted both structural marble and statues. This fact had not been lost sight of during the Renaissance, but by the 18th century it was forgotten and later the Victorian sculptor, John Gibson, caused a sensation at the London International Exhibition of 1862, when he showed his *Tinted Venus,* a carefully coloured, realistically carved marble nude. The 'white world' of the neo-classicist was an 18th-century invention. So, too, were the pastel colours used for much of 18th-century decoration, which strongly influenced Wedgwood's choice of jasper* colours. The Romans generally preferred strong colour.

There is much to be said for the proposition that the Rome of the 18th-century neo-classicist was his own invention. Certainly Piranesi* provided a new view of Rome which was entirely his own and had little to do with verisimilitude. In 1761 he published a work which stated that the Etruscans had elevated the arts, especially architecture, sculpture and painting, to a perfection which

NEALE, James. One of a pair of solid agate vases by Neale, the bodies of wedged blue, green, orange, black, brown and cream-coloured clay, ornamented and gilded. Height 9½in. c.1776-8. Mark: I.NEALE HANLY [*sic*]. *Mr & Mrs David Zeitlin Collection*

the Romans maintained but the Greeks debased. It is possible that this is one source of the confusion which assigned to Italian potters the Greek vases recovered from Etruscan tombs and ultimately to the naming of Wedgwood's factory.

Throughout the 18th century classical learning was a large and essential part of education. The Latin and Greek languages were either fed into one end of the schoolboy or beaten into the other. Most of the literate population were at least as familiar with ancient literature, art and history as they were with the literature and arts of their own times. Most of the subjects of Wedgwood's bas-reliefs were recognisable (although his first catalogue of cameos* and intaglios* was undoubtedly intended to assist salesmen in the showrooms and warehouses) and the stories attached to them well known to his customers.

NEALE, James. Creamware plate, similar in shape to Wedgwood's Royal shape, transfer-printed in black and enamelled in colours. Diameter 9½in. Mark: NEALE & CO. c.1785.
Temple Newsam House, Leeds

NEREIDS. Solid pale-blue and white jasper tablet, *The Nereids*, 6⅜in. x 21½in. c.1870.   *Mr & Mrs David Zeitlin Collection*

Leaving aside such obviously contemporary subjects as portraits of the *Illustrious Moderns** series, more than three-quarters of all 18th-century Wedgwood bas-reliefs and figure subjects were classical in derivation. Most of the forms of basaltes and jasper pieces were classically based and can be traced to marble, pottery or metalwork prototypes. The commonest Greek shape to inspire Wedgwood's painted basaltes vases was the krater*. Other shapes include the amphora, the hydria*, the kylix* (rare), the kantharos* and the oenochoe*. But many such shapes were adapted and given applied relief ornament and decoration in techniques which were never employed by potters of antiquity. For example, relief ornament was never applied, and the reliefs on the finer Samian wares were moulded integrally. Both black basaltes and rosso antico* may be said to resemble ancient pottery, but jasper bears no resemblance to any kind of pottery from classical sources and is more closely related in appearance, if not in technique, to cased glass (e.g. Portland vase*) or carved gem stones.

Many Queen's ware shapes were classically based, but Queen's ware never lost all traces of its rococo origins. The shell shapes, so often attributed to Josiah I's interest in conchology*, were common rococo themes, going back at least to the silver shapes of Meissonnier and the porcelain crayfish salts of Chelsea*, and Wedgwood's Shell-edge shape tablewares continued to be made throughout the last quarter of the 18th century. Although an obviously rococo pattern of printed shell and seaweed enamelled in bright green was introduced as late as 1777-8, most Queen's ware patterns, especially border designs, were derived from classical sources. The acanthus*, in various forms, was the most widely used of ancient foliate ornaments, and it was extensively used on black basaltes and jasper. The fashion for striped grounds, painted in enamel colours, popular with such porcelain factories as Derby*, was followed by Wedgwood, both in the form of stripes cut on the engine-turning lathe* and by the use of contrasting slip* decoration.

The neo-classical style employed the classical vocabulary for ornament which had persisted for millennia. The difference was largely in the type of ornament selected. It is relatively easy to distinguish designs which are purely 18th-century from those (like the Wine and Water* ewers and the so-called Michelangelo lamp*) which were derived from Renaissance metalwork. Designs created in the 18th century were relatively plain and simple, confining ornament to such details as swags (see: Festoons) and garlands, repetitive acanthus leaf borders, and the goat's head, which is an old Roman motif with its origin in metalwork, often found at the base of handles. Human masks, employed for the same purpose, are based on the ancient theatrical mask, descended from Roman painting and metalwork by way of the grotesques* popularised by Raphael*.

At the end of the 18th century the neo-classical style began to veer in the direction of Greece rather than Rome and the Romantic movement grew in strength. In France, under Bonaparte, neo-classicism gave place to the Empire style, which in England became the Regency style. The Empire style was an extension of the neo-classical, but florid and elaborate, with the emphasis, at the

larger porcelain factories, on meticulously detailed topographical painting and large areas of solid gilding. By this time Josiah I was dead and his place had been taken by Josiah II*. The production of jasper dwindled and was eventually suspended, lustre* was introduced, and the first Wedgwood bone china* was made. Wedgwood's principal concession to the Empire style was the greater use of Egyptian ornament (see: Egyptian Taste).

The Empire style survived until about 1830, its end being marked in France by the accession of Louis-Philippe, the Bourgeois King. By this time a notion had become widespread that one style was as good as another, that all were equally valid, and thus that they might be mixed without offence to artistic sensibilities. Such eclecticism would not have dismayed Josiah I, who had never distinguished too nicely between ornament that was Renaissance, Egyptian, Greek or Roman in his choice of figures or of ornament for his vases; but his design solecisms were accidental. About 1830 revived rococo and neo-Gothic made their appearance, and wares partly in one design and partly in another became common. Throughout this period Wedgwood remained generally faithful to its classical traditions. The suspension of jasper production had less to do with changing fashion than a technical inability to make large pieces, such as tablets* and vases, and the introduction of a new white stoneware* body. The ornaments continued to be classical, with the addition of floral and foliate reliefs. Although Wedgwood has not been unaffected by the changing demands of fashion and the market, and has been among the leaders in ceramic design in modern times, that classical tradition has survived.

Neptune

Roman name for Poseidon, god of the Mediterranean. He was the brother of Zeus and Hades and was given dominion over the sea. With Apollo* he built the walls of Troy but the Trojans cheated him of his promised reward, thus incurring his enmity. After the blinding of his son, Polyphemus*, he was also hostile to Ulysses*. Neptune was the creator of the horse and the patron of racing. He was married to Amphitrite, and Triton* was one of his sons. Neptune's symbol of power was the trident; and the dolphin*, the pine tree and the horse were sacred to him. In art he is usually depicted with Amphitrite, Tritons, Nereids*, dolphins or hippocampi*.

A figure of *Neptune*, 2ft. high, was listed in the 1773 Catalogue* as as a companion to one of Triton.

Nereids

The fifty daughters of Nereus and Doris, of whom Thetis, mother of Achilles* was among the most celebrated. *The Nereids*, a tablet 6in. x 21⅞in., probably modelled in Rome in 1790, is variously attributed to Webber* or Pacetti*. It is a faithful copy of the relief on a Pentelic marble sarcophagus then in the Capitoline Museum, Rome, and now in the Louvre. A plaque, 7⅞in. x 13½in., of Nereids and a triton* with fantastic sea creatures, probably after Clodion*, was produced in Majolica* in the 1880s and it is likely that this existed earlier in black basaltes* and jasper*.

NEWDIGATE, Sir Roger. Wedgwood & Bentley solid pale blue and white jasper medallion, Fame, moulded in 1776 from a model at Arbury Hall. Oval height 4½in. c.1777. This model was adapted for several commemorative occasions. *Mr & Mrs David Zeitlin Collection*

Neunberg, G.V. (fl. 1780s)
An 18th-century china dealer at 75 Cornhill, London, who, to judge from the extent of his purchases (he spent about £4,000 with Wedgwood in the first half of 1784) was a principal stockist of Wedgwood in London. A Wedgwood bill head of 1787 directs inquiries to the Wedgwood showrooms* in Greek Street or to Mr Neunberg's premises as the only places in London where Wedgwood wares could be obtained. Neunberg is possibly identifiable as the buyer, noted only as 'N', of many lots of Wedgwood & Bentley ware in the 1781 auction sale* of the partnership stock.

New Hall Factory
In 1781 Wedgwood was approached by Richard Champion* for help in disposing of his patent for the manufacture of porcelain, for which he had exclusive rights to the use of Cornish clay and china stone. By 1781, Wedgwood, who in 1775 had led the opposition to Champion's application to parliament for an extension of the patent, was no longer interested in it, but he appears to have helped him to the extent of introducing him to a number of master potters who together founded the New Hall Company, at Shelton, Staffordshire. The company made domestic wares, for the most part sparsely decorated, and abandoned the 'true' (hard-paste*) porcelain body in favour of bone china* in 1835.

Newdigate, Sir Roger Bt (1719-1806)
Antiquary; M.P. for Middlesex, 1741-7 and for Oxford University, 1750-80; founded the Newdigate prize for English verse. Newdigate owned Arbury Hall, a great house in Warwickshire which he gothicised to rival Walpole's Strawberry Hill at Twickenham and filled with casts and marbles brought home from the Grand Tour. In 1776 Wedgwood obtained his permission to take casts from this collection, and in June William Bedson* visited Arbury and made thirty-four casts of bas-reliefs* which were reproduced as nos.154-87 in the 1777 Catalogue. These included two casts from which *Offering to Flora** and part of Hackwood's* *Sacrifice to Bacchus** were composed, and other single figures which appear both as individual medallions and as additions to groups that were required to be enlarged to make them suitable as tablets*. Newdigate was among those who ordered Wedgwood's tiles* for his dairy. These were supplied, undecorated, in 1784.

Night Lamp
See: Food Warmer

NORTHWOOD, John. Solid black and white jasper copy of the Portland vase finished by John Northwood. Height 10in. Signed with monogram in the fork at the base of the tree-trunk behind the figure of Nereus and dated 1877. *Wedgwood Museum*

Northwood, John (1837-1902)
Glass worker who revived the art of carving glass in the manner of the Roman cameo carvers and *diatretarii,* and made the first cased glass copy of the Portland vase*, using a blank of dark blue glass cased with white opal glass provided by Philip Pargeter and the methods of Roman craftsmen. The task took him three years and was finished in 1876. In 1877 Northwood was engaged by Wedgwood to finish the reliefs of a jasper* edition of the vase, using lapidary* methods. Northwood's monogram 'JN' and the date 1877 are incised in the forked root of the tree almost immediately below one of the handles and above the impressed Wedgwood mark. Thirteen copies of this edition of the vase were sold by W.P.

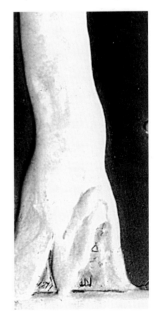

NORTHWOOD, John. Detail of Northwood's monogram found in the same position on all Portland vases finished by him. The date 1877 is incised to the left of the monogram.
Wedgwood Museum

NUNN. Walter J. Pair of Queen's ware vases decorated with framed portraits of Oliver Cromwell and Sir Walter Raleigh on a ground of leaves and scrolls. Height 11in. c.1895.
Wedgwood Museum

& G. Philips of Oxford Street, London. In 1877 Northwood's glass-engraving firm, Perkes & Co. of Stoke-on-Trent, also engraved a small number of Wedgwood's Vigornian* ware pieces.

Nunn, Walter J. (fl.1890-1910)

Painter who worked for Wedgwood, c.1900, probably as a freelance decorator. His subjects were historical portraits with back-

NURSERY WARE. Queen's ware plate printed and enamelled with a design from Yellowstone Zoo nursery ware designed by Daisy Makeig-Jones in 1923. Diameter 8⅛in. 1924. *Wedgwood Museum*

grounds painted in subfusc colours. Nunn later produced work in a similar palette for Doulton.

Nursery Ware

Tableware, usually of Queen's ware* and including small mugs, porringers, plates and teacups and saucers, for the use of children. Wedgwood's most celebrated Nursery ware is the Peter Rabbit* set, reproduced from Beatrix Potter's* original paintings and introduced in 1949. Earlier Nursery ware patterns by Daisy Makeig-Jones* were *Cobble Bead and Zoo, Coq du Bois* and *Moa*. Ravilious* created some distinguished Nursery ware, *Alphabet*, first produced, transfer-printed and decorated with pink or blue enamel wash bands, in 1937 and reproduced in the 1950s. After an interval, it was reintroduced, silk-screened in black or rust in 1982.

Nymphs

Minor female deities who peopled all parts of nature. The nymphs of the ocean (daughters of Oceanus) were Oceanids; those of the Mediterranean were Nereids*; the Naiads* were the nymphs of fresh water; and the Dryads and Hamadryads were nymphs of the trees and forests. The Oreads were associated with the mountains. Nymphs were believed to have the gift of prophecy and to be able to inspire men.

Wedgwood subjects:

Bathing Nymphs, medallion 5½in. x 6in., from a cast or marble in the Newdigate* collection. No.187 in 1777 Catalogue

Dancing Nymphs, six oval plaques 10in. x 7¾in., 'Herculaneum Pictures'* from models in the collection of the Marquis of Lansdowne*, 1769. Nos.51-6 in 1773 Catalogue

Nymph at the Fount, figure 10½ in. x 11½in. produced in Carrara* and black basaltes*, c.1865.

Observatory, The Royal

A bone china* plate in a limited edition* of 1,000 was issued in 1975 to mark the tercentenary of the founding of the Greenwich Observatory by Charles II. The centre of the plate shows a 17th-century star map of the Northern Hemisphere, on which are superimposed portraits of the first eleven Astronomers Royal, beginning with John Flamsteed (1675-1719). The border illustrates the old Royal Observatory at Greenwich and the later establishment at Hurstmonceux, with astronomical instruments and star motifs between.

OBSERVATORY. THE ROYAL. Bone china plate, silkscreen-printed in black and gold, commemorating the tercentenary of the Royal Observatory, 1975. *Wedgwood Museum*

Octagon Shape

See: Tableware Shapes

Odysseus

See: Ulysses

Oenochoe

Greek term for a wine jug with a vertical loop handle and trefoil (pinched) lip. The shape was used by Wedgwood in the 18th century for variegated* wares and black basaltes. It reappeared in the 19th century, notably in the decorative Art Pottery* of the 1870s and 1880s.

Oil and Vinegar Set

See: Cruet Set

Oil Lamp

An exceptionally rare solid green jasper* hanging oil lamp with rounded gadrooned cover surmounted by three Sibyls* is in the Lady Lever Art Gallery at Port Sunlight. The form of the lamp is the same as that of the upper part of the Michelangelo lamp* and it is furnished with three white jasper taper holders. Meteyard*

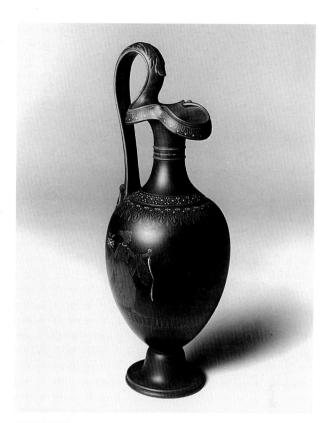

OENOCHOE. Black basaltes *Oenochoe,* shape no.489, painted in encaustic colours. Height 10½in. c.1815. *Merseyside Museums*

described the lamp in 1874 as 'comparatively modern', but it was illustrated in Marryat's* *History* in 1850 and the latest research makes it certain that it was not made between 1810 and 1850. It may therefore be dated to c.1795 and it is unlikely to be a unique example.

See: Lamps

Old Wedgwood

The term is strictly used only for Wedgwood ware of any kind made at the Ivy House*, the Brick House*, or at Etruria* during the lifetime of the first Josiah Wedgwood (e.g. between 1759 and 1795).

OIL LAMP. Extremely rare solid green jasper hanging oil lamp, the cover surmounted by three sibyls. No visible mark. Wedgwood, c.1795. *Lady Lever Art Gallery, Port Sunlight*

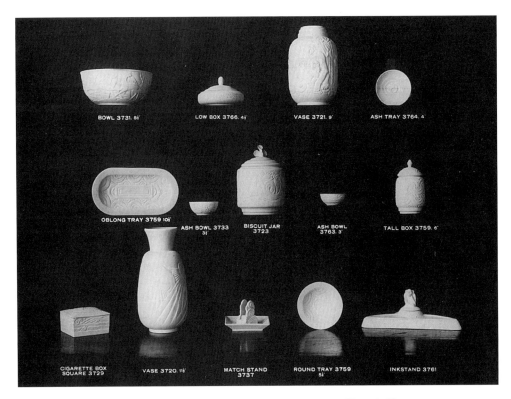

Olsen, Erling B. ('Eric') (b.1903)

Norwegian designer and modeller; studied at Oslo School of Art, at Sèvres* and at St Martin's School of Art, London. In 1931 he designed for Wedgwood a range of Art Deco* ornamental pieces which included lamps, book ends and vases, first shown in an exhibition in Copenhagen. The wares were decorated with white or coloured matt glazes* or Veronese* glazes. Olsen continued to model for Wedgwood on a freelance basis until 1935, when he joined Spode*. After service with the Norwegian army in World War II, Olsen went to live in America, where he became design director of Haeger Potteries, Dundee, Illinois.

OMPHALE. Wedgwood & Bentley dark-blue jasper dip medallion, *Omphale.* Oval height 3⅜in. c.1776-80.
Dwight & Lucille Beeson Collection, Birmingham Museum, Alabama

Olympic Shape

See: Tableware Shapes

Omphale

Queen of Lydia to whom Hercules* was in bondage for three years.
Wedgwood subject:
Omphale, medallion 4in. x 3in., no.43 in 1773 Catalogue (companion to no.42, *Farnesian Hercules*)

O'Neale, Jeffryes Hamett (1734-1801)

Irish miniaturist who was also a porcelain painter at the Chelsea* factory about 1752. He later painted an impressive series of plates and vases for Worcester*, working as an independent decorator. He was especially noted for his amusing depiction of animals. In 1771 he did some unidentified work for Bentley* at the Chelsea Decorating Studio*, and it is most likely that he was painting encaustic* decoration on black basaltes vases. His employment there does not appear to have been for more than a few months at most.

Onyx

Wedgwood's first name for his white jasper* body. In November 1774 he sent Bentley* a sample of a new white body, a 'seed of consequence', which he described as containing 'neither Zaffer, smalt nor anything but white materials' and 'a beautiful Onyx color'. Two months later he was confident of making the body in 'any tint of a fine blue from the Lapis Lazuli, to the lightest Onyx', and for the next few years, until the name 'jasper' became established, he continued to refer to 'our Onyxes'.

Orange Body

A porous composition of Cambria slip* and red clay, introduced about 1811 for functional domestic objects such as 'evaporating butter & wine coolers', porous water bottles and for decorative garden pots, some of which continued to be made until about 1940. The porous body for the production of containers which, when kept damp, cooled their contents by the process of evaporation was largely made obsolete by the widespread use of refrigerators, but a similar orange body is still made for this purpose by a few Staffordshire potters.

Ordinary Lustres

Lustre decorations consisting of underglaze stainings (powder colours*, stippled or mottled) covered by modern commercial lustre and finally printed in gold with designs of dragons, butter-

ORDINARY LUSTRES. 'Butterfly Lustre' trumpet vase, the interior decorated with an apricot lustre, the exterior printed and enamelled in blue and yellow with gilding on a mottled pale-blue lustre ground. Pattern no.Z4832. Height 11¼in. c.1925. *Christie's, London*

flies, birds, fish, fruit, Oriental motifs or diaper patterns. The first ten of the lustre patterns were produced in October 1914, and twenty-seven were designed between 1914 and 1928, some continuing in production until 1931. These designs, now known more specifically as 'Dragon Lustre', 'Butterfly Lustre' etc., are often wrongly described as part of the Fairyland Lustre* range of ornamental bone china*. They were the work of the same designer, Daisy Makeig-Jones*, and many of the same shapes were used, but the style of decoration is quite distinct from that of Fairyland Lustre and should not be confused with it. Both, however, relied for their effect largely on the artistic use of liquid lustres.

Commercial (liquid) lustres were developed from the invention, in 1837, by Dr Heinrich Gottlob Kühn (Director of Meissen*, 1849-70) of a technique for producing iridescent ground colours, based on the use of different metals, including uranium, lead and bismuth, as well as gold, silver and copper. A few years later, the French chemist Jules Joseph Henri Brianchon patented his formula for 'imparting to ceramic substances the colour of gold, white and coloured mother-of-pearl, the variegated and changing reflections of shells, of all kinds of minerals, and of the optical prism.' The lustre colours used by Wedgwood included mother-of-pearl, orange, purple, dark green, yellow, bronze, drab, ruby, pink and black; and on bowls, vases and mugs they were often used in pairs, the interior lustre contrasting with the lustre colour of the exterior.

ORDINARY LUSTRES. 'Dragon Lustre' vase, in imitation of the Chinese mei ping shape, with mottled blue ground and gold-printed dragon and mother-of-pearl lustre decoration. Height 16in. c.1916. *Wedgwood Museum*

A wide range of vases and bowls was made, and there were also mugs, buttons, brooches, and a miniature (and somewhat incongruous) Portland vase*. Technically accomplished, the so-called 'Ordinary Lustres' lack the startling juxtaposition of colour, the crowding of decoration and the bizarre designs of Fairyland Lustre. For this reason they are, perhaps, less representative of their period. They are certainly less highly valued by collectors.
See: Colour Plate 78

Orestes

The son of Agamemnon and Clytemnestra, and brother of Iphigenia*. After the murder of his father by Clytemnestra and Aegisthus, Orestes was saved by his sister and taken in secret to King Strophius of Phocis, who was married to Agamemnon's sister. There Orestes formed a close friendship with his cousin, Pylades, with whom he journeyed to Agos, where he slew Clytemnestra and Aegisthus. His murder of his mother turned his brain and he wandered from land to land pursued by the Eumenides (Furies), finally taking refuge in the temple of Athena, where he was acquitted by the court appointed by the goddess to try him.

ORESTES. Black jasper dip tablet, *Orestes and Pylades*, 9½in. x 22½in. c.1795. *Dwight & Lucille Beeson Collection, Birmingham Museum. Alabama*

ORMOLU. Pale-blue jasper dip vases ornamented with lilac medallions, the finials, rims to lids, handles, stems and feet of ormolu. Height 11in. c.1870-80.

Christie's, London

Wedgwood's tablet, *Orestes and Pylades,* modelled in Rome by De Vaere,* c.1790, was adapted from bas-reliefs on a sarcophagus then in the Palazzo Accoramboni and now in Munich.

Oriental Body
A greenish-grey coloured body* created in 1907 especially for the production of patterns on Catherine shape. These were made at the request of Georges Rouard, the influential Paris retailer for whom Wedgwood designed the Osier and Annular shapes (see: Tableware Shapes). Early in 1907, Rouard lent Wedgwood an old Rouen tin-glazed plate, from which both the *Vieux Rouen* pattern and the Oriental body were copied.

Oriental Patterns
See: Chinoiserie; Japonaiserie; Japonisme; Underglaze Blue Printing

Ormolu
A term derived from the French *or moulu* ('ground gold') used to denote gilded metal – usually brass, but sometimes bronze or copper – which has been gilded either by fire-gilding or mercurial gilding. Matthew Boulton* appears to have been one of the first to use the term in this sense in England. In France, the gilding of bronze by the mercuric process was referred to as *dorure d'or moulu* (gilding with ground gold or gold paste). That the term was current in England by 1776 is proved by a letter from Wedgwood to Bentley* in which he refers to the enormous quantity of 'D'Or Moulu' being made by Boulton, whose ormolu-mounted vases were considered by Lady Cathcart (see: Cathcart, Charles, 9th Baron) to be 'superior in every respect to the French.' In

November 1768 Wedgwood reported to Bentley that Boulton had suggested buying their variegated* and black basaltes* vases for mounting, 'you know how old China bowles, Jarrs &c are mounted in Metal, he proposes an alliance betwixt the Pottery & Metal branches, Viz, that we shall make such things as will be suitable for mounting, & not have a *Pott* look, & he will finish them with mounts...We can make things for mounting with great facility, & dispatch, & mountg will enhance their value greatly.' Bentley was less enthusiastic about this proposal but, although no regular arrangement was made to supply Boulton, a few vases of various types were mounted. Boulton also mounted quantities of jasper cameos* in ormolu settings. It would be a serious mistake, however, to assume that all ormolu-mounted ware belongs to this period. Much jasper was mounted in metal during the 19th century.

Ornamental Ware
Wedgwood's partnership with Bentley* was specifically for the production of 'ornamental Earthenware or Porcelain Viz Vases, Figures, Flowerpots, Toylet Furniture, & such other Articles as they shall from Time to Time agree upon.' 'Useful' wares were produced by Wedgwood's partnership with his cousin Thomas. The division between the two categories was not always clear and it led to the only serious disagreement recorded between Wedgwood and Bentley (see: Useful Ware). One of the complications arose from Bentley's supervision of the Chelsea Decorating Studio*, where much of his time was spent in the organisation and management of tableware decoration which, by the terms of Wedgwood's agreements with both of his partners, should properly be classified as 'useful'. As a result of Bentley's

ORNAMENTING. Ornamenters at work at the Etruria factory, c.1900.
Photograph: Wedgwood

dissatisfaction with this arrangement, not only was he allowed a share of the 'Frog'* service in 1773-4, but also he was given the benefit of all black basaltes*, cane*, jasper* and rosso antico*, whether decorated or undecorated, regardless of its use or ornamental qualities. Thus all dry body* wares of the Wedgwood & Bentley period, including tea and coffee services, should bear the appropriate impressed mark.

In his last catalogue, Wedgwood divided his ornamental wares into twenty different categories, or classes, as follows:
1. Small cameos and intaglios
2. Large Bas-reliefs, medallions, tablets etc.
3. Medallions of Kings and Queens and illustrious persons of Asia, Egypt and Greece
4. Ancient Roman History subjects. 60 medals
5. Portrait medallions of Illustrious Romans
6. The Twelve Caesars and their Empresses (portrait medallions)
7. Portrait medallions of the Caesars from Nerva to Constantine
8. Portrait medallions of the Popes
9. Portrait medallions of the Kings and Queens of England and France
10. Portrait medallions of Illustrious Moderns
11. Busts and Statues
12. Lamps and candelabra
13. Tea and coffee services
14. Flower pots and root pots
15. White terracotta and variegated vases
16. Black basaltes vases
17. Encaustic-painted vases, tablets etc.
18. Jasper vases and other ornaments
19. Inkstands, escritoires, paint chests, eye cups, mortars, chemical wares
20. Thermometers (see: Pyrometer)

Ornamenting
The process known also as sprigging (see: Sprigged Ware): the process of applying small figures and other kinds of relief ornament made in 'pitcher' moulds* to a background, such as the surface of a vase or plaque*. The ornaments are applied to a slightly moistened surface and affixed with gentle pressure from the fingers, a task requiring considerable skill. Wedgwood's 18th-century jasper is noted for the fine quality and detail of its white relief ornament which is pressed in fired earthenware moulds, smoothed on the back, lifted from the mould and fixed to the coloured ground.

The finely detailed relief ornament is the result of using hard-fired earthenware moulds instead of moulds of plaster of Paris. They were once made from a model of comparatively large size which shrank by about one-sixth during firing. Another mould was made from this reduced model and this was fired, again shrinking by one-sixth. This process was repeated until the desired size was attained. The clay employed for the moulds was extremely refractory (it had no tendency to fuse at the temperatures necessary to fire it) and therefore the model in its reduced size retained its sharpness and clarity of detail, a point to be borne in mind when making assessments of quality. This lengthy process is now seldom used.
See: Colour Plate 79
See also: Pantograph; Processes of Manufacture

Osier Shape
See: Basket Work; Tableware Shapes

Otto Factory
Founded by Karl Otto in 1801, at Perovo, near Moscow, the Otto factory was one of the earliest to produce Russian *faïence*. The factory was sold to Ivan Krause in 1812 and shortly afterwards ceased production. The wares were finely potted and glazed and a good cream-coloured ware was made. During the short existence of the factory, some faithful reproductions of the Wedgwood *Husk** service were made, presumably as replacements for breakages.
See also: Poskotchin

Oven Books
Day-to-day manuscript records, preserved at the Wedgwood Museum*, of ware fired at the Wedgwood factory at Etruria*. Apart from an important break in the early 19th century records, the books are almost complete. The descriptions of ware often require both deciphering and translating, but their value is frequently enhanced by thumbnail sketches which have permitted the identification of many otherwise unrecognised objects (e.g. Myrtle Pan*).

Oven-to-Table Ware
Wedgwood's first oven-to-table ware was produced in 1850 as a complement to the popular Game Pie* dishes. A dish or 'liner' of glazed vitrified stoneware, impervious to normal domestic oven heat, was used for cooking meat or game in the oven. When the contents were cooked, the liner was placed inside an ornamental pie dish to be brought to the table. Surprisingly, no further development of such ware appears to have taken place until the introduction of the *Pennine* range of oven-to-table ware in 1965. Designed and modelled by Eric Owen*, this ware was immediately popular and has been followed by many patterns, notably Robert Minkin's *Sterling* and *Wild Strawberry,* which were available either in a full range of tableware or to match existing patterns in Queen's ware* or bone china*.

OVEN-TO-TABLE WARE. Sterling oven-to-table ware designed by Robert Minkin in 1967. The functional shapes are covered with a hard-wearing metallic brown glaze. *Wedgwood Museum*

Overton-Jones, Edward (d.1963)
Born in Stone, Staffordshire, into a family of potters. Designer at Etruria* and later employed at Josiah Wedgwood & Sons, Inc., New York, as a sales representative, becoming a vice-president of the Company in 1947. He retired in 1957. His designs included *Prairie Flowers,* an enamelled border pattern on bone china*; *Laurentia,* decoration for a bone china dinner plate based on a brocade once worn by Martha Washington; and *Richborough,* a printed and enamelled design on the *Celadon* coloured body*.

OWEN, Eric. Basalt bust of Dwight D. Eisenhower modelled by Eric Owen. Height 8in. 1961. *Wedgwood Museum*

OWEN, Eric. Pennine oven-to-table ware designed and modelled by Eric Owen in 1962, covered in metallic brown glaze. 1963.
Wedgwood Museum

Ovolo

Classical (Roman) decorative motif in the form of a convex quarter-round profile; also known as an echinus. Continuous ovolo moulding appears on the plinths of some early Wedgwood vases and also as enamelled border patterns on Queen's ware*.

Owen, Eric (1903-74)

Chief modeller and sculptor for Wedgwood, 1946-67, and freelance modeller with facilities at Barlaston* from 1967 until his death. Born in the Potteries, Owen was apprenticed to a tile factory before joining Minton*, where he was chief modeller for twenty-five years. During his time with Wedgwood, Owen was responsible for modelling many tableware shapes, including the *Barlaston* shape, and he both designed and modelled the first modern oven-to-table* ware, *Pennine,* introduced in 1963. He also modelled a number of portrait medallions*, some of unusually large size. He travelled and lectured widely, teaching for a short period at the Royal College of Art, and was elected a member of the Society of Industrial Artists in 1957. In 1967, the year of his retirement, he was awarded a Gold Medal at the International Exhibition of Artistic Ceramics, Faenza, for a series of figurines.
Eric Owen's work for Wedgwood includes the following:
PORTRAIT MEDALLIONS
H.M.Queen Elizabeth II, 1953
H.R.H. Prince Philip, Duke of Edinburgh, 1953
H.R.H. Princess Margaret, Countess of Snowdon
Ludwig van Beethoven
Winston Churchill
Thomas Jefferson
John F .Kennedy, 1962
Jacqueline Kennedy, 1962
Richard Nixon
Hon. Josiah Wedgwood (Josiah V*)
Tom Wedgwood* (large bas-relief set in the wall facing Etruria Park, inscribed 'To commemorate the work of THOMAS WEDGWOOD of Etruria Hall, Pioneer of Photography'. Unveiled 11 June 1953 by the President of the Royal Photographic Society).

OWEN, Eric. Enamelled Queen's ware pastiche of a Staffordshire 'Pew Group' of the first half of the 18th century by Eric Owen. Although modelled, decorated and fired at Barlaston, using Wedgwood materials, this was never part of Wedgwood production. Height 4⅜in. Mark: ERIC OWEN, inscribed. c.1953. *Author's collection*

TABLEWARE, BAS-RELIEFS AND FIGURES
Bull in Chains, bas-relief for mug presented by Queen Elizabeth II and Prince Philip to the Cider Makers' Association
Barlaston shape tableware designed by Norman Wilson*
Pennine, Oven-to-table ware, designed and modelled by Owen
William Shakespeare, bust, 1964
Josiah Wedgwood, full-length figurine after the statue by Edward Davis*
Two 'Queen's Beasts' for the Queen's vase*
See also: Cranwell Memorial Vase

P

Pacetti, Camillo (1758-1826)

Son of a Roman gem engraver, and younger brother of the sculptor Vincenzo Pacetti (1746-1820), to whom he acted as assistant. One of the group of artists employed by Wedgwood in Rome from 1787, Camillo Pacetti modelled copies of antique reliefs under the supervision of Webber* and Angelo Dalmazzoni*, who described him as 'a proud imperious fellow'. Josiah Wedgwood, however, was particularly impressed by his work. Records are incomplete, but the following bas-reliefs (not all of which have been identified in jasper*) were listed as his models in correspondence between Wedgwood and Angelo Dalmazzoni, 1788-90:

Aesculapius and Hygeia, tablet 8¼in. x 6⅞in. (also 9½in. x 8¼in.), 1788.

The Whole Life of Achilles in five pieces, 1788:
1. *The Birth and Dipping of Achilles*
2. *Thetis Delivering Achilles to Centaur* and *Achilles on the back of Centaur Hunting the Lion*
3. *Achilles in Scyros among the Daughters of Lycomedes*
4. *Achilles and Hector in combat Before the Walls of Troy*
5. *Achilles Dragging Hector around the Walls of Troy*

(These five subjects were copied or adapted by Pacetti from the Luna marble disc or puteal given to the Capitoline Museum, Rome, by Pope Benedict XIV. See also: *Priam Kneeling before Achilles* below)

A Faun, with Three Spartan Bacchantes, 1788

Apotheosis of Faustina, Wife of Marcus Aurelius, 1789 (finished by Hackwood*)

Endymion Sleeping on Mount Latmos, tablet 10in. x 8in. (also 9¼in. x 7½in.)

Fable of Prometheus, 1788

Marcus Aurelius Making His Son Commodus Caesar, 1789

Priam Kneeling before Achilles Begging the Body of his Son Hector, tablet 6in. x 15½in. (also larger size, length 22½in.), 1788. This sixth scene for the *Life of Achilles* (see above) was taken from the so-called sarcophagus of Alexander Severus in the Capitoline Museum

The Simulacrum of Hygeia, to Whom a Woman is Making an Oblation, 1788

Triform Goddess (Diana, Luna, Hecate), tablet 9¼in. x 7½in., 1788

The following are reliably attributed to Pacetti:

Achilles in Scyros Among the Daughters of Lycomedes (usually, and erroneously, described as *Sacrifice of Iphigenia*). A second version of this subject adapted from the same source as *Priam Kneeling before Achilles,* to which it may have been intended as a companion piece.

Three Warriors and a Horse) Copied from the 'Alexander
Two Warriors and a Horse) Severus' sarcophagus

Some of Pacetti's bas-reliefs, first produced as tablets and medallions, were used also as ornament for vases.

PAINT CHEST. White terracotta biscuit paint box with dolphin finial, furnished with palette and twelve small pots for colours in a tray, the exterior decorated with matt black slip, the interior glazed. Length 6¼in. c.1781. *Wedgwood Museum*

Paint Chest

A paint box for the amateur artist, made by Wedgwood in white terracotta* stoneware with slip* decoration, in black basaltes* and in jasper*. It is described in the 1779 Catalogue*: 'The paint-chest contains a set of large and small vessels and neat palats [*sic*] for the use of those who paint in water colour.' Paint chests were reproduced in solid blue and white jasper in a special edition for collectors in the 1970s.

Painted Etruscan

Black basaltes*, and more rarely Cane* ware painted in Wedgwood's encaustic* colours in imitation of the red-figure* style of antique Greek and Roman pottery. During the period 1769-80, all such ware, whether apparently useful or ornamental, was included in the Wedgwood & Bentley partnership stock.

PAINTED ETRUSCAN. Wedgwood & Bentley black basaltes cream jug painted in encaustic orange-brown and white with a band of running anthemion. Height 3½in. c.1778. *Wedgwood Museum*

PACETTI, Camillo. Olive-green jasper tablet, *Thetis delivering Achilles to Centaur* and *Achilles on the back of Centaur hunting the Lion.* Modelled by Pacetti, 1788. 6⅛in. x 18in. c.1910-28. *Dwight & Lucille Beeson Collection, Birmingham Museum, Alabama*

PALLADIO. Wedgwood & Bentley period black basaltes bust, height 22¾in., from a cast supplied by Hoskins & Grant. Unmarked, c.1775. An 'invented' bust taken from a fake portrait. *Wedgwood Museum*

Palgrave, Sir Reginald Francis Douce (1829-1904)

Clerk of the House of Commons, 1886-1902; edited *Rules of the Procedure of the House of Commons,* 1886-96. A proficient water-colourist, Palgrave designed the memorial to Sir William Hooker in Kew Parish Church for Sir Joseph Hooker* and modelled the floral ornament. A Wedgwood portrait medallion* of his father, the historian Sir Francis Palgrave, was modelled by Woolner* in 1899.

Palin, William Mainwaring (1862-1947)

Portrait and landscape painter, born in Hanley, Staffordshire. He was apprenticed for five years to Wedgwood before being awarded a scholarship to the South Kensington School of Art. Later he studied in Rome and in Paris, under Boulanger and Lefebvre. He exhibited at the Royal Academy from 1889 and at the Paris Salon, and he was elected Vice-President of the Royal Society of British Artists in 1914. At Etruria* he painted tableware decoration of birds, figures, fruit and flowers under the direction of Thomas Allen* from 1876. He also cooperated with Allen in painting a series of Shakespeare subjects* on Queen's ware plaques*.

Palissy Ware

Ware decorated with coloured lead glazes, made in France in the 16th century by Bernard Palissy, who attempted to imitate Italian *maiolica* but did not succeed in discovering the tin-enamel glaze. The undersides of Palissy's dishes are mottled in blue, brown and manganese* and are similar in appearance to Whieldon's* tortoise-shell and mottled glazes, also made by Wedgwood in his early years at the Ivy House*. In the 19th century the popularity of Palissy's pottery among collectors was responsible for the intro-duction by Minton*, Wedgwood and others of Majolica*. This was probably inspired by the vogue for exact copies of Palissy's rustic ware at Continental factories, for which they had gained a number of awards at exhibitions.

Palladio, Andrea (1508-80)

Architect, born Andrea di Pietro della Gondoa, whose work re-verted to the principles of Vitruvius and of ancient Rome. His own designs were published in several works, of which *I Quattro Libri dell' Architettura* and *L'Antichità di Roma,* translated in many languages, were the most influential in disseminating his theories throughout Europe. His most important surviving buildings are in Vicenza (Palazzo Chiericati and the Villa Capra) and Venice (the churches of S. Giorgio Maggiore, 1565, and Il Redentore, 1577-92). The Palladian school of architecture in England was named after him, although it derived equally from the work of Inigo Jones. Under the patronage of Lord Burlington and in the architecture of William Kent and Colen Campbell, it developed into a style that was particularly English. Lancelot ('Capability') Brown* owed much of his fame to his ability to create suitable settings for Palladian country mansions.

Wedgwood's black basaltes* bust of Palladio, 22in. high, was produced from a cast supplied by Hoskins* & Grant in 1774, probably copied from a marble by J.M. Rysbrack*. This, in turn was taken from an engraving by B. Picart after a painting said to be by Paolo Veronese. In 1970, R. Wittkower showed that this was a fake by Giacomo Leoni and Sebastiano Ricci, concocted especially for reproduction in Leoni's *Palladio,* published in 1716. Wedgwood's bust is therefore an 'invented' likeness.

Palladium, The

Properly, any image of the goddess Pallas Athene (see: Minerva), but the term is used specifically to refer to one of the sacred images of Troy stolen by Ulysses* and Diomedes*. According to another story, only an imitation was stolen from Troy, and Aeneas bore the genuine image to Italy, where it was lodged in the Temple of Vesta, in Rome. Wedgwood subjects:

Cassandra medallion 7¼in. x 4½in., 'A fine figure in high relief', often attributed to John Bacon* senior. No.33 in 1773 Catalogue*

Diomedes Carrying Away the Palladium, medallion 3in. x 3in., also attributed to John Bacon senior. No.34 in 1773 Catalogue

Diomede Carrying off the Palladium, medallion 3½ins x 2⅞in., cast from a model in the Newdigate* collection. No.169 in 1777 Catalogue

Palliser, Herbert W. (1883-1963)

Sculptor, born in Northallerton, Yorkshire; studied at the Central School of Arts and Crafts and at the Slade School of Art. He taught sculpture at the Royal College of Art and exhibited at the Royal Academy from 1922. In 1940 Palliser was commissioned to model a series of figures of birds after Audubon's engravings in *Birds of America.* These were reproduced in bone china* and enamelled in naturalistic colours by Arthur Dale Holland*.
See: Colour Plate 80

PALLISER, Herbert W. Two bone china figures of ducks, modelled by Palliser after Audubon's *Birds of America* and painted by Arthur Holland. Height 8in. and 6in. c.1940. *Byron and Elaine Born Collection*

Colour Plate 80. PALLISER, Herbert W. Pair of bone china figures of owls modelled by Herbert W. Palliser and enamelled by Arthur Holland. Height 7½in. and 7¼in. c.1940. *Byron & Elaine Born Collection*

Colour Plate 81. PAOLOZZI, SIR Eduardo. Two from a set of six bone china Coupe shape plates decorated with silk-screen designs entitled 'Variations on a Geometric Theme' by Sir Eduardo Paolozzi. 1971. *Wedgwood Museum*

Colour Plate 82. PATE-SUR-PATE. A pair of important *pâte-sur-pâte* vases, the obverse of each decorated with a design of a bird and irises on a dark chocolate-brown ground, the sides with buds and leaves in green and red enamel, and the reverse with butterflies and reeds, finished with fine gilding. Height 7¾in. c.1878. *Wedgwood Museum*

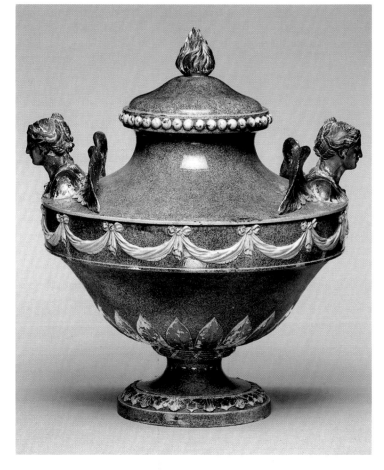

Colour Plate 84. PORPHYRY. White terracotta stoneware funerary urn with gilded handles and finial, the body decorated with sponged blue-green in imitation of porphyry. Height 20in. c.1785. *Wedgwood Museum*

Colour Plate 83. PIERCED DECORATION. Queen's ware oval basket stand with pierced border enamelled in rose-purple in the manner of James Bakewell. 9in. x 10in. c.1772. *Author's collection*

Colour Plate 85. PORTLAND VASE. An exceptionally fine 'first edition' example of Wedgwood's jasper copy of the Portland vase, supplied to Thomas Hope, one of the original subscribers, in June 1793. Height 10⅛in. Unmarked.
Wedgwood Museum

Colour Plate 86. PORTRAIT MEDALLIONS. Rare Wedgwood & Bentley solid yellow and white jasper portrait medallion of George Washington, copied from a medal by Voltaire struck in Paris in 1777. Height 3¼in. 1777-80. *Formerly Eugene D. Buchanan Collection*

Colour Plate 87. PORTRAIT MEDALLIONS. Rare Wedgwood & Bentley chocolate-brown jasper dip portrait medallion of Admiral Keppel, attributed to William Hackwood.1779-80. *Private collection*

Colour Plate 88. PORTRAIT MEDALLIONS. Deep-blue jasper dip portrait medallion of William Pitt the Younger, modelled by John Flaxman junior. Height 3⅝in. c.1786. *Wedgwood Museum*

Colour Plate 89. POT-POURRI JAR. Large rosso antico combined pot-pourri jar, pastille burner and bough pot decorated with *Chinese Flowers*. In addition to the pierced cover, the jar is supplied with two interior lids, one pierced for flowers, the second solid 'for the pastilles to lie on'. Height 13½in. c.1820. *Wedgwood Museum*

Colour Plate 91. PROTAT, Hugues. Large Majolica jardinière modelled in the Sèvres style by Hugues Protât and decorated with opaque and transparent glazes and oval panels of figures by Emile Lessore, 17in. x 10¼in. 1871. *Wedgwood Museum*

Colour Plate 90. POWELL, Alfred. One of a pair of Queen's ware chargers painted by Alfred Powell with a peacock (the companion charger has an owl at the centre) surrounded by an intricate pattern of animals, flowers and foliage. Diameter 18½in. c.1920.
Mr & Mrs David Zeitlin Collection

Colour Plate 92. QUEEN'S WARE. Group of 18th-century Queen's ware, including (centre) an enamelled jelly mould and undecorated cover. c.1785.
Wedgwood Museum

Colour Plate 93. RAVILIOUS, Eric. Queen's ware lemonade set decorated with the *Garden Implements* pattern designed by Eric Ravilious, printed in black and enriched with 'pink' (gold) lustre. Jug height 7½in. c.1930.   *Wedgwood Museum*

Colour Plate 94. RHODES, David. Queen's ware teapot with typical overlapping leaf or scale handle, pierced ball knop and cabbage spout, enamelled in naturalistic colours with a bouquet of flowers centred on two large roses in the style associated with David Rhodes. Unmarked. c.1770.   *Author's collection*

Colour Plate 95. ROCOCO. Pair of Queen's ware plates with feather-edge and moulded rose-centre, the feather-edges gilded, transfer-printed in black with 'exotic' birds by Sadler & Green, with a similarly decorated tureen stand of rococo shape. The plates have retained most of their original gilding, perhaps indicating that they were never used. Plate diameter 8in. All unmarked. c.1768.   *Author's collection*

Colour Plate 96. ROMANTIC STYLE. Pale-green jasper dip Brewster shape teapot and bowl, engine-turned and ornamented with scenes of 'Domestic Employment' after designs by Lady Templetown. Teapot height 4½in. c.1785-90. *Nottingham Castle Museum*

Colour Plate 97. ROSSO ANTICO. Parapet teapot of rosso antico ornamented with *White Chinese Flowers*. Height 4½in. c.1810-15. *Wedgwood Museum*

Colour Plate 98. SADLER, John. Early transfer-printed creamware cream jug and small lidded jug, transfer-printed for Wedgwood by Sadler & Green with, respectively, 'The Tea Party' in black and 'exotic' birds in orange-red. Lidded jug height 6in. Both unmarked. c.1763-4. *E.N. Stretton Collection*

Colour Plate 99. SCENT BOTTLE. Four scent bottles, one of cut-glass with a gold screw-top, the body inset with a black and white jasper cameo of a girl with doves (attributed to Emma Crewe) and three of pale-blue and white jasper variously ornamented with the figure of 'Winter' from the set of *Horae*, a warrior with his armour, and portraits of George III and Queen Charlotte. No marks visible. c.1785-90. *Wedgwood Museum*

Colour Plate 100. SIDDONS, Sarah. Deep-blue jasper dip portrait medallion of Sarah Siddons, modelled by John Flaxman junior. Height 4½in. c.1784.
Wedgwood Museum

Colour Plate 101. SKEAPING, John. Queen's ware 'Standing Duiker', modelled by John Skeaping and decorated with Champagne glaze. Height 7½in. c.1930.
Wedgwood Museum

Colour Plate 102. SORROWS OF THE YOUNG WERTHER. Grey-blue and white jasper teapot with engine-turned foot and lid ornamented with 'Charlotte at the Tomb of Werther' *(verso 'Sportive Love')* modelled by William Hackwood after designs by Lady Templetown. Height 6in. c.1785-90. This teapot and its ornaments were copied precisely by Turner.
Wedgwood Museum

Colour Plate 103. STEELE, Aaron. Pair of bone china violet baskets with pierced covers, painted with birds in naturalistic colours by Aaron Steele. Height 2½in. c.1816.   *L.A. Compton Collection*

Colour Plate 104. STUBBS, George. The Wedgwood family in the grounds of Etruria Hall. Oil on panel, 47¾in. x 72½in., by George Stubbs, 1780. *(Right to left:* Josiah Wedgwood, his wife Sarah, and their children John, Josiah II, Susannah, Catherine, Thomas, Sarah and Mary Anne.)
Wedgwood Museum

Colour Plate 105. STUBBS, George. Portrait of Josiah Wedgwood by George Stubbs. The portrait is painted in ceramic colours on an oval Wedgwood earthenware support, 20in. x 16in. Signed and dated 1780. *Wedgwood Museum*

Colour Plate 106. TAURUS. Queen's ware figure of 'Taurus the Bull' modelled by Arnold Machin, c.1946, and decorated with lithographed Signs of the Zodiac finished in brown enamel. Length 15in. c.1950. *Wedgwood Museum*

Colour Plate 107. TEA CANISTER. Octagonal tea canister of ribbed ivory and tortoiseshell, each side inset with a gold-mounted blue and white jasper cameo. The subjects include figures of Minerva, Juno, Neptune and Hope. Height 5¾in. c.1790-1800.
Nottingham Castle Museum

Colour Plate 108. TERRACOTTA. Fine Wedgwood & Bentley white terracotta stoneware portrait medallion of Henri IV, King of France and Navarre, the ground and reverse enamelled in encaustic reddish-brown over a thin glaze of 'flux'. Height 4⅝in. Unmarked. c.1773.
Dr David Williams Collection

Colour Plate 109. TERRACOTTA. Two white terracotta stoneware bulbous-root pots, one decorated with surface agate and the other with sponged colour, both under a Pearl glaze. Height 7in. and 7¼in. c.1790. *(Left)* Wedgwood Museum; *(right)* Author's collection

Colour Plate 110. THORLEY, John Palin. Queen's ware charger painted by John Palin Thorley with a parrot among foliage in underglaze blue within a wide onglaze enamelled border. Diameter 22¼in. c.1910. *Author's collection*

Colour Plate 111. UNDERGLAZE BLUE PRINTING. Pearl ware soup tureen, cover and stand printed underglaze in blue with *Peony* pattern. Height 10½in. c.1815. *Author's collection*

Colour Plate 112. VARIEGATED WARE. Wedgwood & Bentley white terracotta stoneware vase and plinth, the body and cover of the vase decorated with surface agate. Height 12in. c.1773. *Wedgwood Museum*

Colour Plate 113. VARIEGATED WARE. Wedgwood & Bentley white terracotta stoneware ewer, decorated with sprinkled grey 'granite' veined with black and brown, on a black basaltes plinth. Height 13½in. c.1774. *Wedgwood Museum*

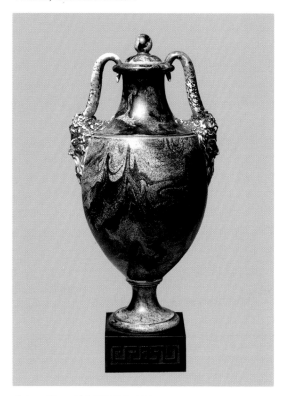

Colour Plate 114. VASES, ORNAMENTAL. Wedgwood & Bentley white terracotta stoneware vase (shape no. 1), decorated with sprinkled grey 'granite' veined with black and touches of brown, on a black basaltes plinth. The handles retain traces of their original gilding. Height 9⅞in. c.1775.
Merseyside Museums

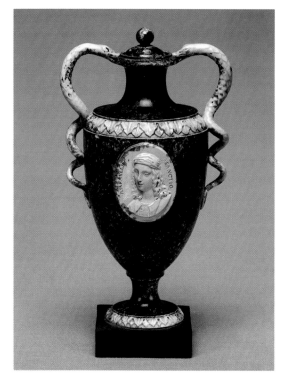

Colour Plate 115. VASES, ORNAMENTAL. Wedgwood & Bentley Queen's ware or white terracotta stoneware vase with snake handles and an applied medallion of Raphael inscribed 'RAFFAELLE SANCTIO', the body sponged with blue and manganese, on a black basaltes plinth. Height 8½in. c.1771-4.
Wedgwood Museum

Colour Plate 116. VASES, ORNAMENTAL. Wedgwood & Bentley black basaltes documentary vase (shape no. 93) painted principally in encaustic white with green foliage and sepia shading. Dated (in the memorial inscription) 1774. Height 14¾in.
Wedgwood Museum

Colour Plate 117. VASES, ORNAMENTAL. Pair of miniature blue and white jasper vases. Height 6¾in. c.1785.
Wedgwood Museum

Colour Plate 118. VENUS. Carrara bust of Venus after the model by Antonio Canova. Height 25in. c.1849-60. *Wedgwood Museum*

Colour Plate 119. VICTORIA WARE. Glazed and gilt Victoria ware vase with Cupid finial, heavily ornamented with swags and medallions within frames of Signs of the Zodiac. Height 12½in. c.1876-85.
Wedgwood Museum

Colour Plate 121. WATER LILY PATTERN. Pearl ware plate decorated with brown-printed *Water Lily* pattern with 'Botanical' border, introduced in 1808. Diameter 9¾in. c.1808. *Wedgwood Museum*

Colour Plate 120. VOLTAIRE. Wedgwood & Bentley cane figure of Voltaire after the small marble by Jean-Claude Rosset dated 1773. Height 12¼in. Unmarked. 1779. This appears to be the only example of this figure in the cane body to have survived. *British Museum*

Colour Plate 122. WEDGWOOD IN THE 19TH CENTURY. A group of teawares from five first period bone china patterns, illustrating Wedgwood's use of groundlays and gilding, c.1815.
Formerly Buten Museum

Colour Plate 123. WEDGWOOD IN THE 19TH CENTURY. Three stoneware ('porcelain') smear-glazed teapots: a white stoneware arabesque moulded teapot with spaniel knop, height 5in; a similar cane teapot, height 3in; and a cane basketweave teapot with wheatsheaf knop, height 2½in., c.1830.
Author's collection

Colour Plate 124. WEDGWOOD IN THE 19TH CENTURY. Victoria ware vase decorated with coloured slips and gilding, ornamented with Signs of the Zodiac. Height 11in. c.1876-80.
Wedgwood Museum

Colour Plate 125. WEDGWOOD IN THE 19TH CENTURY. Queen's ware 'Pegasus' vase painted with large bouquets of flowers and leaves, the finial and snake-and-mask handles bronzed to match the borders to the lid, neck and foot. Height 19½in. c.1876.   *Byron & Elaine Born Collection*

Colour Plate 126. WEDGWOOD IN THE 20TH CENTURY. Bone china trumpet vase decorated with *Manilla* pattern, printed and enamelled over a canary-yellow groundlay. Height 11⅛in. c.1913.   *Author's collection*

Colour Plate 127. WEDGWOOD IN THE 20TH CENTURY. Bone china lidded vase no. 2410, height 9¾in., decorated with Flame Fairyland *Willow* pattern designed by Daisy Makeig-Jones. c.1920.   *Wedgwood Museum*

Colour Plate 128. WEDGWOOD IN THE 20TH CENTURY. Queen's ware coffeepot, 129 shape, handpainted with a simple border design of flowers and leaves in the style promoted by the Powells and interpreted by such designers as Millicent Taplin, Star Wedgwood, Ruth Ellis and L.H. Bucknell. Height 8in. c.1932.   *Author's collection*

Colour Plate 129. WEDGWOOD IN THE 20TH CENTURY. Pale-blue and white jasper portrait medallions of Queen Elizabeth II, Charles, Prince of Wales, Anne, Princess Royal and Prince Philip, Duke of Edinburgh. Height 4½in. 1972-4.   *Wedgwood Museum*

Colour Plate 130. WEDGWOOD, Josiah. Portrait of Josiah Wedgwood by Sir Joshua Reynolds, 1782. Oil on canvas, 29½in. x 24¾in. *Wedgwood Museum*

Colour Plate 131. WEDGWOOD, Sarah. Portrait of Sarah Wedgwood by Sir Joshua Reynolds, 1782. Oil on canvas, 29½in. x 24¾in. *Wedgwood Museum*

Colour Plate 132. WHITE HOUSE SERVICE. Bone china plate and sauce tureen and stand decorated with the *Colonnade* border in gold and enamelled representation of the Great Seal of the United States of America, made for the White House in 1903.

Wedgwood Museum

PALMER, Humphrey. Two variegated vases by Palmer with sponged decoration and ornaments of medallions and swags. The medallion suspended from a loop and hook is typical of vases by Palmer and Neale. Height 10⅛in. and 12¼in. Mark: H PALMER HANLEY. c.1776.

Christie's, London

Palmer, Humphrey (fl.1760-78)

Potter, from 1760, at the Church Works, Hanley, who became bankrupt in 1778, when the business was continued by the London agent, James Neale* (of Neale & Bailey, Staffordshire [pottery] and Glass warehousemen), first as Neale & Palmer and then as Neale & Co. Robert Wilson, Neale's manager, became a partner in 1786. In the 19th century the firm was absorbed by Ridgway. Enoch Wood* served his apprenticeship with Palmer and later claimed that he used calcined bone in earthenware during this

period, being the first to do so.

Palmer imitated Wedgwood's production and as early as 1768 he was making basaltes vases with moulded relief ornament. In August 1768 Wedgwood wrote to William Cox* in London: 'the Bronze Vases sent you last will be down here [Staffordshire] in a fortnight for coppying…Caravalla supplies Mr P with all my patterns as they arrive at my rooms in London.' About a year later he admitted: 'P[almer]s black Vases – I saw one…The body is very good – the shape & composition very well…We must proceed or they will tread upon our heels.' The danger of serious competition was increased by Palmer's acquisition of John Voyez*, until recently employed as a modeller by Wedgwood.

By the autumn of 1770 Wedgwood had evidence that Neale was selling vases decorated with encaustic* painting, which infringed Wedgwood's 1769 patent, but Josiah was undecided whether action should be taken against Palmer or Neale. As he explained to Bentley*: 'the *selling* you can prove easily & clearly, the *Making* I cannot prove at all…neither could we prove that Palmer has really enameld these things, Neale may have got them done by Giles*, or some of the Enámelers in Town.' An injunction was granted to prevent Neale from continuing to sell the offending vases and, after many months of negotiation, a compromise was reached in 1771 which allowed Palmer a share in the patent in return for the payment of an undisclosed sum to Wedgwood & Bentley.

After 1778 Neale continued to manufacture ware in the Wedgwood style, including creamwares of excellent quality, black basaltes vases and some large portrait medallions*. He also made green-glazed* ware with gilding, and some good jasper*. Of all the Staffordshire potters who attempted to compete with Wedgwood in the 18th century, none came so close to succeeding as Palmer.

Palmette

Decorative ornament in the form of a stylised palm resembling a spread fan. In appearance it is not unlike the Greek anthemion*. When divided in half it is termed a half-palmette. A palmette border is a pattern consisting of a series of palmettes. This motif occurs frequently on copies of old red-figure* vases and it is used also on the plinths of jasper*, basaltes and other dry body* vases.

PALMETTE. Black basaltes volute krater vase painted in encaustic colours with a formalised palmette and scroll design. Height 14in. c.1781-95.

Mr & Mrs Samuel Laver Collection

PAN. Wedgwood & Bentley grey-blue jasper medallion with pale-blue jasper dip, *Pan and Syrinx*. Oval length 5⅛in. c.1778.

Dr & Mrs Alvin M. Kanter Collection

Pan

Son of Hermes (see: Mercury). The god of flocks and shepherds, who wandered among the mountains and valleys of Arcadia. Pan is usually depicted with goat's horns and feet, in the act of playing the syrinx* which he is supposed to have invented. His sudden appearance before mortals induced feelings of terror, described as Panic fear. The Romans identified him with the god Faunus (see: Faun).
Wedgwood subjects:
Pan (head), medallion 3in. x 2⅜in., no.122 in 1777 Catalogue
Pan Reposing with Young Satyrs, medallion 6in. x 8in., no.139 in 1777 Catalogue

Pantograph

An instrument for making precise copies of an object, usually a plan or drawing, on a larger or smaller scale. A more sophisticated version of the instrument used to reproduce drawings known as a pointing machine may be employed to copy statuettes or relief ornament and this is used to enlarge or reduce bas-reliefs*. In the past, reduction of bas-reliefs was achieved by progressive shrinking in firing.
See: Cameo; Cheverton, Benjamin; Ornamenting

Paolozzi, Sir Eduardo Luigi, CBE, RA (b.1924)

British sculptor, born in Edinburgh; studied at Edinburgh College of Art and at the Slade School of Fine Art, Oxford and London;

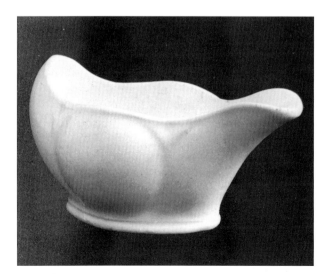

PAP BOAT. Queen's ware pap boat with scalloped rim and lobed sides. Length 4⅛in. c.1790. *Wellcome Institute Library, London*

Lecturer in Sculpture at the St Martin's School of Art 1955-8; Visiting Professor at Hochschule für Bildende Künste, Hamburg, 1960-2; Visiting Lecturer, University of California, Berkeley, 1968; Lecturer in Ceramics at the Royal College of Art from 1968. Paolozzi's many awards include First Prize for Sculpture at the Carnegie International Exhibition, 1967. He was elected Member of the Royal Academy in 1979 and knighted in 1989.

In 1970 Eduardo Paolozzi created for Wedgwood *Variations on a Geometric Theme,* a set of six silk-screen* designs reproduced, in a limited edition* of 200 sets, on bone china*. Each set was issued with a numbered certificate.
See: Colour Plate 81

Pap Boat

Small vessel, much the same in shape as a sauce or gravy boat without the handle, used for feeding soft or semi-liquid food (pap), such as bread and milk, to infants or invalids. The lip is extended to be placed in the mouth of the feeder. Later 19th century examples were covered above the lip to form a spout. Wedgwood's early Queen's ware* pap boats appear to have been adapted from a sauceboat, shape no.10 in the 1774 Queen's ware Catalogue*.

Papera, Benjamin (fl. late 18th-early 19th century)

Figure maker. Little is known of Papera, who appears in the Soane archives as the supplier of busts to Lord Bridport in 1802. In the Wedgwood archives he is recorded as supplying busts of Mrs Siddons*, Lord Nelson and Mrs Deamour (probably Mrs Anne Damer, the modeller and sculptor) and 'one vase with lamp', all in 1802.

PAPERWEIGHTS. Blue jasper *Liberty Bell* paperweight with the inscription 'Proclaim Liberty throughout all the Land' in gold, made for the Wedgwood Collectors' Society in 1978. The Liberty Bell was cast at Whitechapel, London, in 1751, damaged in transit, and recast in Philadelphia and hung in 1753. It has been rung on many historic occasions, including the invasion of Normandy in 1944.

Wedgwood Museum

Paperweights

The 18th-century house was a draughty place in winter and summer, as its numerous draught screens testify, and the odours arising from inadequate sanitary arrangements led to windows being opened whenever possible. The effect of this was to make it difficult to leave papers safely on a desk or table, and paperweights were devised to hold them down. Popular in France as *presse-papiers,* they were made in bronze and in porcelain from Sèvres*. Wedgwood made basaltes* sphinxes* for this purpose, and the small figures of *Sleeping Boys** on flat bases were probably intended as paperweights (similar Sèvres models were certainly intended for such use). Since the 19th century the tendency has been for the paperweight to be primarily a decorative object.

PAPYRIUS. White terracotta biscuit plaque, *Papyrius and his Mother,* one of the 'Herculaneum Pictures'. Diameter 12¼in. Unmarked. Wedgwood & Bentley, c.1772.   *Wedgwood Museum*

Papier Mâché
One of the commonest methods of preparation for making decorative objects was to paste sheets of coarse paper together, one upon another, with a paste of flour, water and size. The pressed paper could then be packed into moulds, or sawn or cut to shape and joined when dry. The completed object, which was both light and strong, was then sized and japanned. Henry Clay* of Birmingham, Japanner in Ordinary to the King and the Prince of Wales, patented a new process of this type in 1772, the finished product being stoved, japanned black, crimson or green, and finally varnished. Soon after Clay began to market his new product he was making tea canisters*, small writing desks, dressing cases and other objects inset with Wedgwood cameos*. Wedgwood wrote to Bentley* on 14 July 1776: 'Mr Clay has made three sets of Dressing-boxes very fully set with our cameos, and wants his assortment made up complete again.

Papyrius (Papirius)
Son of a Roman Senator, who took him, when a youth, to hear a debate. Reluctant to betray the secrets of the Senate to his importunate mother, Papirius invented a subject of debate to amuse her: whether it would be preferable to give two wives to one husband or two husbands to one wife. His mother spread this to other Roman matrons who petitioned the senate in favour of two husbands for one wife. Until the time of Augustus, no child except Papirius was thenceforth allowed to attend senate debates.
Wedgwood subject:
Papyrius and His Mother, circular plaque ('Herculaneum Picture'*) from a cast in the collection of the Marquis of Lansdowne*, 1771. No.62 in 1773 Catalogue*

Parapet Teapot
Teapot, usually oval in section, with the lid deeply recessed inside a parapet, the rim of which curves slightly outwards towards the spout. It was popular in the early decades of the 19th century but was introduced in the 1770s and occurs in Wedgwood's dry bodies*, Queen's ware*, White ware* and bone china*.

Pargeter, Philip (1826-1906)
Stourbridge glassmaker. His uncle was Benjamin Richardson, who offered a reward of £1,000 to anyone making an accurate replica of the Portland vase*. Pargeter persuaded his cousin, John Northwood*, to work with him on the production of a copy, Pargeter providing the cased glass blanks for Northwood to carve. Subsequently he made three *tazze,* signed by Northwood, emblematic of Science, Art and Literature. These were decorated with

portraits of Newton, Flaxman* and Shakespeare (see: Shakespeare Subjects) respectively, which were copied from Wedgwood portrait medallions*.

Parian
A creamy-white, smooth, unglazed porcellaneous body with a natural sheen, produced in conscious imitation of marble and named after the Greek island of Paros, famous for the quality of the marble quarried there. Known also as 'statuary porcelain', Parian was introduced about 1845 (the date is debated) and its invention is claimed variously by Copeland & Garrett (see: Spode), Minton* and T. & R. Boote. The body is slightly translucent and is a composition of china clay, felspar* and a frit* (in this case a mixture of white sand, Cornish stone and potash). The body was suitable for slip casting*, and Parian figures were invariably made by this method.

The reproduction in miniature of sculpture from all periods had been made easier by Benjamin Cheverton's* invention in 1828 of a machine (belatedly patented in 1844) to reduce figures and busts to the size of table ornaments without resort to the traditional and laborious method of progressive casting and shrinking in firing (see: Ornamenting).

Parian was popularised among the middle classes by the Art Unions, which held annual lotteries in which the top prizes were contemporary works of art. Lesser prizes were cheaper objects, including commissioned ceramic pieces, and in 1846 Parian was added to their lists with the favourable comment: 'We attach very great importance to this material as offering a valuable medium for the multiplication of works of a high order of art, at a price that will render them generally available.' Another enthusiastic patron of Parian was Sir Henry Cole, Chairman of the Society of Arts, who founded, under the pseudonym of Felix Summerly in 1847, Summerly's Art Manufactures*. He commissioned work in the new Parian body, which included two small pieces designed by John Bell* and one by Richard Redgrave*, all made by Wedgwood.

No precise date is recorded for the introduction of Wedgwood's Parian, which was named 'Carrara' after the white statuary marble from the quarries at Carrara in northern Italy, but it was probably not before 1848.

Some manufacturers, notably Minton, made figures and other objects in the Parian body tinted with pink, yellow, green and blue. See: Carrara; Pâte-sur-Pâte; Victoria Ware

Paris
Second son of Priam and Hecuba; married to Oenone. Commanded by Zeus, through the agency of Hermes (Mercury*), to adjudicate between Hera, who promised him the sovereignty of Asia, Athena, who promised him renown in war, and Aphrodite*, who promised him the fairest of women for his wife, he awarded the golden apple for beauty to Aphrodite. Under her protection he sailed for Sparta, whence he abducted Helen, the wife of Menelaus and the most beautiful woman in the world. This gave rise to the Trojan war in

PARAPET TEAPOT. Pearl ware parapet-shape teapot enamelled in polychrome with a sentimental subject typical of one aspect of Romantic art. Height 5in. c.1790-5.
Dr & Mrs Alvin M. Kanter Collection

PARIS. Solid black and white jasper tablet, Judgement of Paris, 7in. x 18½in. c.1790. *Photograph: Wedgwood*

PARIS. Black basaltes bust of Paris. Height 19½in. c.1840. *Author's collection*

which Paris is said to have killed Achilles*. Wounded, Paris returned to Oenone, who refused to heal his wound. Paris died, and Oenone, overcome with remorse, killed herself. Paris is represented as a beautiful beardless youth, usually wearing a Phrygian cap.

Wedgwood subjects:

Paris, bust, height 19½in. Probably not produced before 1790-1800. Reproduced in Carrara* in the 19th century.

Judgement of Paris, medallion 2½in. x 3in, no.31 in 1773 Catalogue*

Judgement of Paris, medallion 5½in. x 6in., moulded by Bedson* from a model in the Newdigate* collection, June 1776. No.183 in 1777 Catalogue

The Judgement of Paris, tablet 7in. x 18½in., modelled in Rome, c.1790. Attributed to De Vaere*

Rape of Helen, a long oval plaque 5½in. x 6in., moulded from a model in the Newdigate collection in June 1776. No.185 in the 1777 Catalogue

See also: Portland Vase

Paris Shape
See: Tableware Shapes

Parker, Richard (fl.1769-74)
Modeller and plaster cast maker; perhaps the son or brother of Theodore Parker*. Richard Parker had a studio in the Strand, London and had acquired sole rights to the making of plaster casts from the work of the sculptor Joseph Wilton RA, 'statuary to His Majesty'. Parker is recorded as supplying Wedgwood in 1774 with busts of Zingara* and a Vestal*, and the model of a 'Pug Dog'. The last was William Hogarth's dog 'Trump'*, after a model by Roubiliac*. Parker is known for his sets of plaster library busts* after Roubiliac and Rysbrack* but none of them is recorded as being reproduced by Wedgwood. In view of Parker's monopoly of casts from Wilton's work, however, it is likely that Wedgwood's bust of Lord Chatham (the elder William Pitt), after Wilton, was obtained from Parker.

Parker, Theodore (fl.1769-74)
Very little is known of this modeller, who may have been the father or brother of Richard Parker*. According to an invoice for September-October 1769, Parker supplied Wedgwood with models (probably casts) of 'statues' of *Flora*, Ceres*, Prudence, Juno*, Hercules*, Spenser, Shakespeare, Milton,* and 'A Boy on a Couch'. The last is identifiable as the figure catalogued in 1773 as *Morpheus* (see: Somnus), and the figure of *Ceres* is probably 'A young female figure in the character of Ceres, sitting', catalogued next in order to Morpheus in 1773. The 'Shakespeare statue' is the figure after Scheemakers*, and Milton the companion figure (both commonly found in Derby* porcelain). The rest are not to be found in the Wedgwood catalogues and appear to have been set aside, unused.

Pars, Miss (fl.1773-74)
Artist employed at the Chelsea Decorating Studio* to paint ruins and landscapes for the Frog* service. She is thought to have been the sister of William Pars (1742-82), one of the leading artists in watercolour of his day, whose Greek drawings were used to illustrate the second and third volumes of Stuart* and Revett's *Antiquities of Athens* (1789 and 1795). Another brother, Henry, also an artist, conducted an art school, founded by William Shipley, in the Strand.

Partnerships
See: Alders, Thomas; Harrison, John; Proprietors of Wedgwood; Whieldon, Thomas

Passenger, Charles (fl.1875-1907)
Artist, engaged, with his brother Fred, by William De Morgan* in 1875 to decorate lustre* wares. The Passenger brothers became partners in the business in 1898, when Halsey Ricardo* withdrew, and continued until 1907, when De Morgan withdrew and the Sands End factory was closed. Charles and Fred Passenger continued to produce pottery until 1911. Charles Passenger's monogram 'CP' appears on some fine examples of Wedgwood Queen's ware* decorated at the De Morgan factory.

Pastille Burner
A vase, or more rarely a dish or *tazza,* popular during the 18th and 19th centuries for burning cassolette* perfumes (powdered willow wood charcoal mixed with fragrant oils and gum arabic in the form of cone-shaped pastilles) to counteract the smells of stuffy rooms and inadequate drains. Pastille burners served the same purpose as cassolettes and pot-pourri* jars, but the contents of pastille burners

PASSENGER, Charles. Underside of a Queen's ware footed dish decorated in crimson lustre by Passenger for William De Morgan at Fulham, showing Passenger's monogram. Diameter 9½in. c.1902. *Mr & Mrs David Zeitlin Collection*

PASTILLE BURNER. Large 'Dolphin' tripod pastille burner, shape 496, as supplied to the special order of the Bishop of Winchester in 1807. Height 12½in. 1807. *Wedgwood Museum*

were dry and easily replaced throughout the year. Wedgwood's small dolphin* tripod shape was first produced as an oil lamp in the 1770s and this was adapted for use as a pastille burner about 1804. In 1807 Wedgwood received a request from Tom Byerley*, who wrote: 'I have just been attending the B[isho]p of Winchester who has laid out some Guineas in ornaments – and wanting a Vase for perfuming large Halls of the form 290 Dolphin Tripod – about 5 times as large as what we now make that 3 or 4 pastils may be burnt at once…it is to be in black ornamented as the small ones are.' A fine example of this type of burner is in the Wedgwood

PASTILLE BURNER. Deep-blue jasper dip combined bough-pot and pastille burner. Overall height 6⅜in. c.1820.
Dwight & Lucille Beeson Collection, Birmingham Museum, Alabama

Museum. A second large pastille burner in black basaltes* was in the shape of a plain classical vase with two loop handles and a pierced lid with acorn* knop. This was supplied with an internal lower plate 'for the pastilles to lie on'.

Pastry Ware
Shallow pie dishes of buff stoneware were made during the period of the Flour Tax after 1800. Wedgwood had already made some Game Pie dishes* in the Cane* body and by about 1795 had added dishes consisting of an ornamented lid, separate 'crust' edge and shallow base for fruit pies. These were made also by Turner* and Spode*.

PASTRY WARE. Cane ware pie dish made in three pieces – base dish, 'crust' edge and 'crust' lid – the dish only being glazed. Width 13½in. c.1795. *Dr & Mrs Alvin M. Kanter Collection*

Patera
Latin. A shallow vessel, similar in form to a deep saucer, with or without handle, originally intended for wine to be drunk in a libation. *Paterae* were made in gold, silver, bronze or earthenware, the interior often ornamented with a type of rosette. Wedgwood made *paterae* in various bodies, especially black basaltes*, but he used the term primarily to describe circular or oval rosettes or palmettes* which resembled the interior ornament of Roman *paterae*.

Pâte-sur-Pâte
Pâte-sur-pâte is the French name given to the technique of painting on porcelain in white slip*, using successive layers to build up a semi-transparent relief on a coloured or tinted ground, The details are then carved or undercut* before firing. This costly style of decoration was used in China during the 18th century and introduced at Sèvres* about 1851. The technique was perfected at Meissen* in 1880 and was brought to England by Marc-Louis Solon, who moved to Minton* from Sèvres during the Franco-Prussian war of 1870. Among Solon's pupils at Minton were Charles Toft*, Thomas Mellor* and Frederick Rhead*, all of whom later worked for Wedgwood.

Rhead's work has been identified from Wedgwood pieces bearing his signature, but, although the differing styles of decoration suggest that more than one artist was employed in this work, no marked Wedgwood piece of pâte-sur-pâte bearing the signature of any other artist has yet been found. When Toft was first employed, Godfrey Wedgwood* asked him specifically, 'Have you turned your attention to the pâte sur pâte modelling?', and it would be surprising if Toft's expertise in this technique was not used. A fourth artist who may have used pâte-sur-pâte at Etruria* was Frederick Schenck*, who later made a spurious form of this decoration (applying layers of slip to moulded figures) for George Jones & Sons.

Wedgwood's pâte-sur-pâte, like Minton's, was made from the Parian* (Carrara*) body, or a variation of it known as White Vitreous Body or 'WVB', and the first record of its production occurs in October 1875. There is some confusion in the Wedgwood records between genuine pâte-sur-pâte pieces, which were made in very small quantities, and Victoria ware*, which was made by a cheaper and more conventional technique and in larger quantities. Production of pâte-sur-pâte ended in 1879, probably the date at which Rhead left the firm, but Victoria ware continued until at least 1893.
See: Colour Plate 82

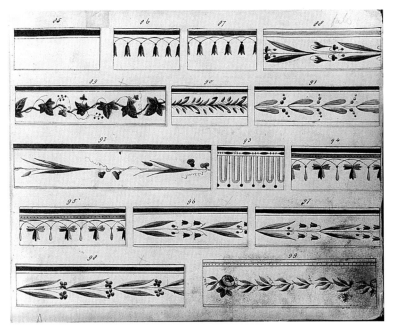

Patrician Shape
See: Tableware Shapes

Pattern Books
The Wedgwood pattern books – hand-painted factory records which have never been published, although extracts from some of them have been used as illustrations in several books dealing with Wedgwood wares – are of particular value in the identification of Wedgwood tableware decoration. The first pattern book, preserved in the Wedgwood Museum*, was probably started in 1769 (the precise date is uncertain) and records patterns, principally border decoration, used for Queen's ware*. It was continued until c.1814 and includes also some White ware* and bone china* patterns. The book, which is a copy made c.1810 of an earlier one, contains 55 unnumbered pages showing sketches of 663 numbered patterns with their descriptions. Since some of the earliest patterns are not included, it is evident that the record is not complete. There are eight tableware pattern books covering the period 1770-1870. It is difficult to date them with certainty, but J.K. des Fontaines *(The Wedgwood Catalogue of Shapes)* has estimated the dates from the watermarks on the paper. Details are given below:

Book No.	Pattern Nos	Watermark
1.	1-663	1810
2	672-1284	1811-14
Duplicate	709-104	1823
3	1298-1950	1831
4	1403-1930 (apparently duplicate)	1831
5	1939-3285	1844
6.	3289-4329	1851
7	4330-7074	1855
8.	7055-9998	1864

It is interesting to note that approximately 2,000 different patterns had been recorded by 1844, and another 8,000 were added to this total in the following twenty years – testimony to the enormous increase in demand for wares thus decorated.

Uncatalogued pattern books are also preserved at Barlaston* for later bone china and Queen's ware patterns, for Majolica* and for tiles*.

Peace Destroying the Implements of War
The figure of *Peace*, holding a burning torch in her right hand setting fire to the accoutrements of war, was a subject considered by Wedgwood and Flaxman* in 1786 to celebrate the French Commercial Treaty*. Wedgwood wrote to him: 'The burning of the implements of war, and the figure of Peace must then form another group for Medallion No.2.' This subject seems to have been abandoned in favour of *Peace preventing Mars from bursting open the Temple of Janus* but it appears again about 1802 as the ornament for a Louis Seize style jasper clock case celebrating the Peace of Amiens.

Peace Plaques
A set of three plaques made by Wedgwood for Soane & Smith of Oxford Street, London, in a limited edition* of 250 sets and issued in 1919. The larger plaque (17in. diameter) is painted with the head of Bellona, goddess of war, with the inscription '1919 Peace'. One of the two smaller plaques (14in. diameter) shows a bust of Britannia and the other a bust of France, each in front of her national flag, the borders with the inscriptions *'Honi Soit Qui Mal Y Pense'* and *'Liberté, Egalité, Fraternité'* respectively. The marks are both printed and impressed.

Pear Shape
Pear-shaped teapots and covered sugar dishes were made of creamware decorated with coloured glazes during Wedgwood's period at the Ivy House factory. The Pear teacup (approximately in the form of an inverted pear with the base sliced off) with turned foot has been one of the most popular forms in Queen's ware* of the Traditional shape for about 150 years and has been made also in bone china* since 1878.
See also: Tableware Shapes

PEACE DESTROYING THE IMPLEMENTS OF WAR. Deep-blue jasper dip clock case with the solid white jasper figure of *Peace* holding a firebrand to the implements of war. Height 16¾in. c.1802.
Merseyside Museums

PEACE PLAQUES. Queen's ware printed and enamelled plaque commemorating the peace of Versailles. Diameter 14½in. 1919.
Sotheby's, London

PEARL WARE. Jug printed in black and enamelled in colour with 'The Farmer's Arms', a popular subject on pottery of the period. Height 8in. c.1790-5.
City Museum & Art Gallery, Stoke-on-Trent

Pearl Glaze

About five years before his formal introduction of Pearl* ware and soon after telling Bentley* of his need to produce a new glaze to make 'Tea-ware a *little* whiter' in February 1774, Wedgwood began to whiten the appearance of his Queen's ware* by the use of a small quantity of cobalt* in his glaze. This is noticeable where the glaze 'pools' in the foot ring of such pieces as jugs, and these are usually mistaken for Pearl ware.

Pearl Ware

A white earthenware body containing a greater proportion of white clay and flint than the creamware body. The glaze had a small quantity of cobalt oxide added further to whiten the appearance of the body. A cream-coloured earthenware with a bluish glaze was produced in Staffordshire in the 1740s, and Wedgwood used cobalt* in his Pearl glaze* from about 1774, but the name 'Pearl White' (later 'Pearl ware' or simply 'Pearl') was Wedgwood's and the body and glaze he produced in 1779 were also his own, the result of experiments over a period of at least five years.

Josiah Wedgwood was reluctant to make Pearl ware, finally produced it in response to continuous pressure from influential

PEARL GLAZE. Two Wedgwood & Bentley Queen's ware *pot-pourri* vases (one lacking lid), both covered with a Pearl glaze, the smaller *(left)* with replacement lid and relief ornament decorated with blue enamel. Height 9¼in. and 11½in. c.1779.
Byron & Elaine Born Collection (left); Jacobs Collection (right).

PEARL WARE. Pearl ware plate decorated with *Convolvulus* border and a botanical flower centre, printed in underglaze blue. c.1825.
Author's collection

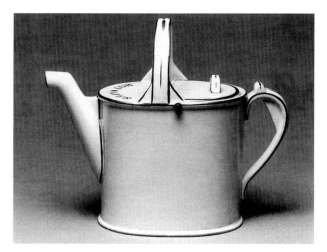

PEARL WARE. Hot-water jug with enamel lines and the inscription 'HOT WATER' on the lid. Height 8in. 1911.
Byron and Elaine Born Collection

patrons (especially Sir William Meredith*) and customers to do so, and appears to have been little satisfied with the result. He rightly regarded his Queen's ware*, in its final pale-cream colour, as near to perfection and unrivalled among earthenwares, and he was constantly aware of the necessity to maintain the evident difference between Queen's ware (and the patterns used to decorate it) and English blue-and-white painted and printed porcelain or earthenwares. Some fine blue-painted patterns (including the Mared* pattern) were produced, and the Pearl body was used also for some exceptionally well painted decorative jugs and teapots, but no blue-printed patterns were produced until ten years after Josiah's death.

The name 'Pearl' became generic for English white lead-glazed earthenware and its production lasted at Etruria* almost without a break into the 20th century. 'Pearl' was, confusingly, used also as the name for a white 'dry body'* stoneware made by Chetham & Woolley of Lane End for ornamental wares from about 1795.
See: Underglaze Blue Printing

Peart, Charles (1759-98)
Sculptor and modeller. Peart entered the Royal Academy Schools in 1781 and in the following year he was awarded a Gold Medal for a group, *Hercules and Omphale*. He later worked as assistant to John Charles Lochée*, and modelled portraits in wax for Wedgwood between 1788 and 1794, including those of Lord Hillsborough (1786), the style of which shows signs of Lochée's influence, Sir William Chambers* (1787), and probably that of Princess Charlotte Augusta. Peart has been credited with Wedgwood's portrait of Warren Hastings, but Flaxman's* invoice of January 1784 contradicts this attribution.

Pebble Vases
Vases of white terracotta* stoneware (the 'crystalline' body) decorated with mottled coloured glazes to resemble the cut and

PEART, Charles. Pale-blue jasper dip portrait medallion of Lord Hillsborough modelled by Peart in 1787. Oval height 4¾in. c.1790.
Private collection

polished surface of natural stones. Introduced in 1768. Marbled and agate* wares were produced at least ten years earlier but the decoration was not extended to vases until about 1765.

Pecten Shell
The scallop shell; a rococo* decoration popular in the 18th century and much used by Wedgwood as enamelled decoration for tablewares and relief ornament for dry bodies*. The pecten shell shape is among those used for the 'Wreathed Shell' dessert service of which drawings appear in the '1802' (watermark) Shape Drawing Book.

Pegasus
The winged horse which sprang from the blood of Medusa* when Perseus cut off her head. Pegasus was caught by Bellerophon*, and with his aid Bellerophon conquered the Chimaera*. Riding Pegasus towards the heavens, Bellerophon fell to earth. Pegasus continued upwards to dwell among the stars and is associated with the Muses*. Two bas-reliefs for cameos* – *Muses watering Pegasus on Helicon (Pegasus cared for by Nymphs)* and *Muses watering Pegasus* are attributed to Flaxman* and Hackwood* respectively. The Pegasus finial* for the Homeric vase*, used also for the Pegasus vase*, was modelled by Flaxman.

Pegasus Vase
The name loosely given to a number of different vases with the Pegasus* figure as finial. A glass vase of this name was made also by John Northwood*, who worked on the 1877 edition of Wedgwood's Portland vase*. The Northwood Pegasus vase, ornamented with *Venus and Adonis,* is surmounted by a Pegasus finial which is obviously derived from Flaxman's* model.

Pemberton & Son, Samuel (fl. c.1770-1800)
Silversmiths of Soho, Birmingham, who bought seals for mounting from Wedgwood, and also from Palmer* and Voyez*.

Pen Tray
Shaped rectangular tray, often separated into two compartments and with a shallow raised ledge to protect pen nibs from damage. Ornamental pen trays were made in black basaltes* as early as 1769 and appear in various bodies, including Queen's ware* and the dry bodies*. Toothbrush trays, which are of similar shape but were originally supplied with lids, are often mistaken for pen trays.

Penelope
Wife of Ulysses*, King of Ithaca, by whom she had one son, Telemachus. During the long absence of Ulysses she was beset by suitors, who assumed that Ulysses was dead. She deceived them by declaring that she would not yield to them until she had finished the piece of cloth she was weaving. Every night, however, she unravelled her day's work. At length the suitors perceived the stratagem and began to press for an answer, but Ulysses returned in disguise and slew them all with arrows from the bow which only

he could string. Another tradition makes Penelope the mother of Pan*, either by Hermes (Mercury*) or by all the suitors, and records that Ulysses repudiated her when he returned.

Wedgwood subjects:

Penelope, bust modelled by Arnold Machin*, 1941

Penelope and Her Maidens, the name given erroneously to the tablet, *Volumnia, Wife of Coriolanus**

The painting, *Penelope unravelling Her Web,* by Joseph Wright* of Derby was purchased by Josiah Wedgwood in 1784-5.

Pennant, Thomas (1726-98)
Naturalist and traveller, notable especially for his *British Zoology* (1766) and *History of Quadrupeds* (1781). Drawings for illustrations to his *Journeys to the Hebrides* were copied, before publication, for several landscapes of the Frog* service, 1773-4.

Pennine
The name given to Wedgwood's first modern oven-to-table ware* designed by Eric Owen* in 1965. The name was adopted also for the rich chestnut-brown semi-matt glaze used for this shape.

Pennington, Joseph
Painter, apprenticed at Etruria*, who left to work for Worcester* towards the end of the 18th century. He may have been related to John and James Pennington and Seth Pennington, potters of Liverpool.

Pepin
A name which appears, almost invariably within quotation marks, as a signature on some handpainted vases made in the 1870s. It is possibly an invented or assumed name since no painter of this name has been found in the records of Wedgwood or of any of the porcelain companies of the period.

Pepper, Elisha (fl.1839-after 1865)
Engraver of Slack Lane, Hanley, 1851-65, who carried out work for Wedgwood between 1839 and 1865. He was a partner in the firms of Green, Sergeant & Pepper, Green & Pepper and E. Pepper & Son.

Percival, Dr Thomas (1740-1804)
Manchester physician and one of the pioneers of public health administration, who wrote a pamphlet on lead poisoning which referred to Queen's ware*. This was a cause of considerable concern to Josiah Wedgwood. Percival later wrote a second article, published in 1774, in which he stated that there was 'no objection to the common use of this beautiful pottery, but...vessels of it are improper for the preserving of acid fruits and pickles.' All reference to Queen's ware was deleted in later reprints. In 1773 a Dr Goulson followed Percival's first pamphlet with one on the same subject. Wedgwood remarked that 'quieting one of these Gentlemen was only lopping off one of the Hydra's heads.' He began experimenting with a leadless glaze but he was not successful in perfecting it. In 1793 the Society of Arts* offered a premium for a leadless glaze which was claimed by Coalport* in 1820. What both Percival and Goulson had failed fully to understand was that lead glazes posed no danger to the user of the finished product but they were deadly to workmen handling the raw glaze before firing.

Perfume Bottle
See: Scent Bottle

Perfume Burner
An ormolu tripod perfume burner in the form of an ornamental lidded bowl on three tall monopodia* was made by Boulton* after a design attributed to James Stuart* in 1771, and four more such tripods were produced for the Earl Gower (see: Stafford) in 1777. Wedgwood copied one of these burners in rosso antico* ornamented in black with fashionable 'Egyptian'* motifs replacing the original acanthus* and scroll ornament, c.1805.

Perissoire Stand
The *perissoire* is a single-seat river canoe, the shape of which, with the figure of a male or female canoeist, was used for a Majolica* piece, c.1875-80. The precise purpose of this piece is not clear but it was probably a trinket tray for the dressing-table.

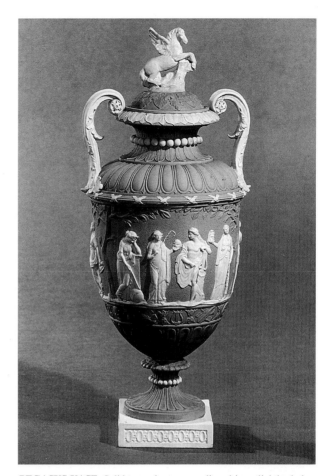

PEGASUS VASE. Solid green jasper vase dipped in a slightly darker shade of green and ornamented with figures of *Apollo and the Nine Muses,* the lid surmounted by the *Pegasus* finial. Height 15in. c.1795-1820. *Lady Lever Art Gallery, Port Sunlight*

Perrier, François (1590-1650)
French artist who published two books of engravings, *Segmenta nobilium signorum et statuarum que temporis que dentem invidium evase* (Paris and Rome, 1938) and *Icones et segmenta illustrium e marmore tabularum que Romae adhuc exstant* (Paris and Rome, 1645). The former, containing etchings of one hundred of the finest antique statues (and one then considered modern: Michelangelo's *Moses)* was the first illustrated volume of its kind to be published

PENELOPE. Handpainted biscuit and glazed Queen's ware busts of Penelope modelled by Arnold Machin, c.1941. Height 11in. *Wedgwood Museum*

PERSEPHONE. Queen's ware 'Round Plume' vegetable dish and plate decorated with *Persephone* pattern, designed by Eric Ravilious in 1936. *Wedgwood Museum*

and was a major influence on sculptors and students for about two hundred years. 'Perrico's Statues' (undoubtedly Perrier's *Segmenta nobilium...*) was listed among the books belonging to the Wedgwood & Bentley partnership and was evidently used for reference by Wedgwood and probably by his modellers at Etruria. It is likely also that Wedgwood owned a copy of *Icones et segmenta....*

Persephone
The Greek name for Proserpine*, daughter of Jupiter* and Ceres*. The name was chosen for a transfer-printed* pattern in black, with linear scroll border and centre motif representing fruit and fish,

PERSIAN STYLE. A handpaintress at work on a large 'Persian' vase, c.1920. The vase is rotated on a turntable and the natural light source is to the right and rear of the paintress. *Photograph: Wedgwood*

designed by Eric Ravilious* in 1936. It was decorated with blue, yellow or pink enamel wash. The pattern was known also as *Harvest Festival*. In 1937-40, when it was first produced, *Persephone* was a commercial failure, but it was reintroduced in 1952 and stocked in the Wedgwood Rooms* from 1953, rapidly becoming one of Wedgwood's most popular Queen's ware* patterns. It provides a satisfactory modern example of Wedgwood's traditional policy of employing, and putting faith in, young contemporary designers. This pattern, printed in gold on bone china*, and with the Royal Arms substituted for the central motif, was chosen for the dinner service to be used at the Foreign Secretary's banquet celebrating the Coronation of Queen Elizabeth II in June 1953.

Perseus
Son of Zeus (Jupiter*) and Danaë, the daughter of Acrisius, King of Argos. Polydectes, King of Seriphos, who was in love with Danaë, sent Perseus on a quest for the head of Medusa*, one of the Gorgons, the sight of whom turned men to stone. Perseus cut off the head of Medusa, looking at the reflection of her head in a mirror, and, on his way home, married Andromeda*, whom he had rescued from a sea monster. Attacked by Andromeda's uncle, Phineus, at his wedding feast, he used the head of Medusa to turn him to stone. He later gave the head to Athene (Minerva*), who placed it in the middle of her shield or breastplate. At the games at Larissa, he accidentally slew his grandfather, Acrisius, with the discus, thus fulfilling a prophecy made before his birth.
Three Wedgwood bas-reliefs* illustrate parts of the story:
Marriage Feast of Perseus and Andromeda, plaque 6in. x 9in., copied or adapted from bas-reliefs by Guglielmo della Porta*, probably by way of plaster casts from bronze reliefs by J.C. Cobaert (d.1615). No.5 in 1773 Catalogue*
Perseus, medallion 4¾in. x 4in., no.22 in 1773 Catalogue (the companion medallion, *Andromeda,* is no. 23)
Perseus and Andromeda, medallion 6in. x 5in., no.124 in 1777 Catalogue

Persian Figures
See: Michelangelo Lamp

Persian Style
So-called 'Persian' styles became fashionable towards the end of the 19th century and Wedgwood produced a range of decorative vases decorated in this manner on Queen's ware*. Large chargers and vases decorated in Islamic styles using enamel colours and lustre*, some of which may have been designed by Alfred and Louise Powell*, were also produced by Wedgwood in the early 1920s. These ornamental pieces, which required a high standard of craftsmanship, were never made in large quantities and examples of them are now fairly scarce.
See also: Rhodian Ware

Group of "Wedgwood" Vases. Turquoise, Roses, and gold decoration Prices range from 12/0 to £6 6 0

PERSIAN STYLE. Old photograph showing a range of elaborately modelled and decorated ornamental pieces in the 'Persian' style fashionable in the 1890s. *Photograph: Wedgwood*

Persistent Patterns

Name given to patterns and shapes which have persisted more or less unmodified from the 18th and early 19th centuries to the present day (e.g. *Napoleon Ivy**).

Pesez

Medallist of Amsterdam, whose medals depicting portrait heads were 'picked up' by Bentley* during a visit to Paris, in 1776. Wedgwood wrote of these portraits: 'I observe *Pesez* is a strong mannerist, & has given a Family likeness to them all in the thickness of their Lips, & a peculiar, bold opening of the Nostril. However, he has a free bold touch, – Slight & Masterly, & superior to the common run of Head makers.' Nothing otherwise appears to be known of this medallist.

The following Wedgwood portrait medallions* are after medals by Pesez, the majority of them probably remodelled by Hackwood*:

Comtesse du Barry, c.1780
Anne Marie Fiquet de Boccage, c.1776
Dr Herman Boerhaave. Modelled by Flaxman* after Pesez, 1782
Nicolas Boileau-Despreaux, c.1776
Jean Jacques Burlamaqui (attributed), c.1776
Gabrielle Emilie, Marquise du Châtelet-Lomont, c.1776
Josepha Hippolyte Léris Clairon de la Tudi, c.1776
Pierre Corneille, c.1776
Prosper Jolyot de Crébillon (attributed), c.1776
Anne Dacier (attributed), c.1776
René Descartes, c.1776
Antoinette Deshoulières, c.1776
Gabrielle D'Estrées, Duchesse de Beaufort, c.1776
Françoise Marguerite, Comtesse de Grignan, c.1776
Pieter Hein, modelled by Flaxman, 1782, probably after Pesez
Jean de La Fontaine, c.1776
Anne L'Enclos (Ninon de L'Enclos), c.1776
Eustache Le Sueur, c.1776
Molière, c.1776
Michel Eyquem, Seigneur de Montaigne, c.1776
Blaise Pascal, c.1776
Jean-Baptiste Racine, c.1776
Michel Adriaanszoon de Ruyter, modelled by Flaxman after Pesez, 1782
Madeleine de Scudéry, c.1776
Marquise de Sévigné, c.1776
Agnes Sorel, c.1776
Henriette de Coligny, Comtesse de la Suze, c.1776

Peter Rabbit Nurseryware

From 1949 Wedgwood had exclusive rights to the production of Peter Rabbit nursery ware*, the patterns reproduced from Beatrix Potter's* original paintings, the copyright of which was owned by Frederick Warne & Co. In 1980 these designs were translated into bas-relief* ornament for jasper*, a scarcely credible lapse of taste and degradation of Wedgwood's most valuable ornamental ware for short-term commercial gain.

PETER RABBIT. Porringer, plate, oatmeal bowl, teacup and saucer, mug and eggcup with lithographed decoration after Beatrix Potter's watercolour drawings. *Photograph: Wedgwood*

Petuntse

A corruption of the Chinese name (*pai-tun-tzu*) for the local equivalent of Cornish stone. It is a feldspathic mineral which is one of the two essential ingredients of 'true' porcelain*, the other being kaolin* (white china clay). Fired at a sufficiently high temperature, petuntse becomes a natural glass. In porcelain, it fuses the white clay and lends hardness and translucency to the fired body.

Phaeton

Son of Helios, the sun god, who importuned his father for permission to drive the chariot of the Sun. Helios yielded reluctantly, but Phaeton was not strong enough to hold the horses in their course, and, coming too close to the earth, the heat from the chariot began to consume it. Zeus saved the earth from destruction by killing Phaeton with a thunderbolt, hurling him into the river Eridanus.
Wedgwood subject:
The Fall of Phaeton, tablet 10½in. x 19⅜in. Modelled by George Stubbs*, 1780. No.236 in 1787 Catalogue*

PHAETON. Solid blue and white jasper tablet, *The Fall of Phaeton,* designed and modelled by George Stubbs in 1780. c.1785.
Lady Lever Art Gallery, Port Sunlight

PHARMACY JARS. Queen's ware pharmacy jar with printed label inscribed 'S.E.SPIN.C.'. Height 7¾in. c.1820.
Wellcome Institute Library, London

Pharmacy Jars
Sets of lidded storage jars, the shapes and decoration designed by Robert Minkin*, were included in the new pieces shown in the Design '63* Exhibition in London in January 1963. Pharmacy jars of more conventional shapes were among the Chemical Wares* produced at Etruria* in the late 18th and 19th centuries.

Pharmacy Wares
See: Chemical Wares

Phidias (c.490-417 BC)
One of the greatest of Greek sculptors, born at Athens. He directed the erection of the Parthenon, and the sculptures from this source now in the British Museum were carved under his supervision. The

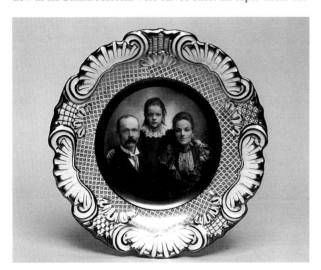

PHOTOLITHOGRAPHY. Bone china shell-moulded and gilt plate decorated with a photographic print of a family portrait. Diameter 8¼in. c.1892. *City Museum & Art Gallery, Stoke-on-Trent*

cast of a 'Fragment by Phidias' was invoiced to Wedgwood by Flaxman* in September 1782, but it is not known whether any use was made of it. The bas-relief* known as *Two Warriors and a Horse*, attributed to Pacetti*, c.1790, has been erroneously identified with this cast.

Philadelphia Bowl
Large Queen's ware* bowl, diameter 12½in., transfer-printed* in black with reproductions of engravings commemorating the signing of the Articles of Federation at Philadelphia on 9 July 1778. Designed by Alan Price*, 1959.

Photographic Printing
See: Photolithography; Tableware Shapes – *Satsuma*

Photolithography
It is not inappropriate that the Wedgwood firm should have been among the earliest users of photographic decorative techniques since Josiah I's youngest son, Tom Wedgwood*, had been one of the pioneers of photography at the end of the 18th century. The first photographic process to be used in the decoration of porcelain* and enamels was the invention of a Paris manufacturer, Lafon de Canarsac*, in 1854. He exhibited a cup and saucer decorated with a photographic portrait at the London Exhibition of 1862, where he was awarded a Gold Medal. In the 1860s a technique for transferring photographs on prepared backing paper to the surface of pottery and porcelain glazes was devised, and several methods of applying photographs to enamel and wooden surfaces were patented during the 1870s. Wedgwood made limited use of the new technique from 1875-6 but it never achieved great popularity. Some of Henry Hope Crealock's* drawings were reproduced in this manner as decoration but Godfrey Wedgwood* wrote to him in March 1876: 'I am rather at a loss to know what to say about the subject of photography. As far as we have got with it, it does not show signs of being a quick process, so that we have not been able to sell our productions in quantities.' W.E. Henry and H.S. Wood published a book entitled *Photoceramics* in 1896.

Physic Cup
Queen's ware* spouted feeding cup with two side handles and a third (opposite the spout) moulded in the shape of a dog's head. Made by Wedgwood in the 19th century. Otherwise known as a pap boat*.

Pianofortes
See: Broadwood, John

Pichler, Johann or Giovanni (1734-91)
Gem* engraver, born in Rome into an Austrian family of engravers. His gems* were highly esteemed and it is even said that his own copies of ancient gems were brought to him for copying by collectors who had bought them believing them to be antique. Pichler lived in England, c.1764-76, and engraved gems, many of which were reproduced in James Tassie's* glass pastes. After the purchase of the Portland vase* by James Byres*, and before it was sold to Sir William Hamilton*, Pichler was commissioned to take a

PHYSIC CUP. Queen's ware physic cup, shape no.1244, the spoon dish at the side for pills or small quantities of medicine. Overall length 7¼in. c.1820. *Formerly Buten Museum*

PIERCED DECORATION. Fine pierced Queen's ware basket and stand, transfer-printed in purple with a view usually described as 'Corinthian Ruins'. Oval length (stand) 10¼in. c.1775-85.
Mr & Mrs Samuel Laver Collection

mould from it. This was subsequently used by Tassie for sixty copies cast in plaster. Many of Wedgwood's seals* were probably copied from gems by Pichler, either supplied directly or in the form of copies by Tassie, but these have not yet been identified.

Piece Mould
A plaster mould made of several interlocking parts so arranged that each will draw from the surface of a cast without damaging it, leaving the mould to be reassembled and used again.

Piecrust Ware
See: Pastry Ware

Pierced Decoration
Type of decoration found principally on cream-coloured ware and on creamware decorated with coloured glazes from Wedgwood and Leeds* during the last quarter of the 18th century, which consists of piercings similar to those used for the decoration of contemporary silver. The clay was pierced when in a state of leather-hardness* with punches in a variety of shapes. Plates and dishes, baskets*, cruet stands, punch glass stands*, fish trowels*, food warmers* and other wares capable of being pierced may all be recognised as having silver prototypes.
See: Colour Plate 83

Pigalle, Jean-Baptiste (1714-85)
French sculptor. A pupil of Lemoyne and Robert Le Lorrain, he worked at the Academy in Rome, returning to Paris in 1744, exhibiting two plaster statues in the Salon in the same year. He was a regular exhibitor until 1753, and executed several commissions for Louis XV, including the statues of Mercury* and Venus*, and the figure of Mercury tying his sandals copied by Wedgwood. He was among the 'outside' sculptors (who included Caffiéri and Houdon*) employed by the Sèvres factory after 1766 to model reduced versions of their most celebrated work for reproduction in biscuit* porcelain. Pigalle became an Academician in 1744 and was elected Chancellor of the Academy in 1785.
See: Carrara; Figures

PIGALLE, Jean-Baptiste. Unpolished black basaltes figure of *Mercury* after the model by Pigalle, first produced by Wedgwood in 1779. Height 20in. c.1840.   *Merseyside Museums*

PIGALLE, Jean-Baptiste. Unpolished black basaltes figure of *Venus* after the model by Pigalle, first produced by Wedgwood in 1779. Height 20¾in. c.1840.   *Merseyside Museums*

PILL JAR. Queen's ware lidded pill jar. Height 4in. Unmarked. Wedgwood, c.1782-6. From James Watt's garret workshop at Heathfield, near Birmingham. *Science Museum, London*

Piggin

A small pail-like receptacle with a single handle, used as a dipper for milk or cream. Made in engine-turned red ware, c.1765, and also in creamware. The type was made in porcelain at Bow* and Worcester*.

Pill Jar

Cylindrical lidded pill jars, height 4in., were made by Wedgwood in Queen's ware* for the use of apothecaries and druggists in the last quarter of the 18th century and in the first half of the 19th century.

Pill Slab

A flat rectangular slab for rolling pills, a feature of apothecary ware in one form or another in England from the 17th century. Wedgwood made pill slabs but few have survived. A specimen formerly in the Buten* Museum is of Queen's ware*, marked with a painted scale for cutting a long cylinder of the mixture into equal parts before rolling them into spheres.

Pillar Vase

Vase in the form of a fluted pillar without capital. The 'fluted pillar' or 'column' vase was produced by Wedgwood as early as 1770, when Wedgwood wrote to Bentley*: 'I cannot fix any price to the fluted Pillars, the principal expence being the modelling and

PILLAR VASE. White terracotta stoneware fluted pillar vase decorated with fawn-coloured slip, on a black basaltes plinth. Height 12¼in.
Mr & Mrs David Zeitlin Collection

PINEAPPLE WARE. Pineapple teapot decorated with green and orange-yellow glazes. Height 4¾in. Unmarked. Probably Wedgwood or Whieldon, c.1764. *City Museum & Art Gallery, Stoke-on-Trent*

moulding in London, they are otherwise no worse making than Vases of the same size.' This was an extraordinarily early use of a shape that became popular in England some twenty years later. These vases were first made in Queen's ware* and soon afterwards in white terracotta*, often decorated with contrasting slip* in a striped pattern. See also: Ruined Column Vase

Pillement, Jean (1728-1808)

French landscape painter and designer, born in Lyons, the son of an *ornemeniste*. His own work consisted principally of fantastic rococo* *chinoiseries*** and *singeries*, many of which were published in Paris and London. Designs after Pillement are illustrated in *The Ladies Amusement**, a design book compiled by Robert Sayer*, where they were engraved by Robert Hancock*. Designs after Pillement are to be found on English silver and porcelain, especially on transfer-printed* Worcester*. Some Wedgwood transfer-prints for 18th-century Queen's ware* decoration were derived from this source and the first period bone china* pattern no.724 *Pillement Flowers* acknowledges the debt.

Pinchbeck

An alloy of copper and zinc simulating gold introduced by Christopher Pinchbeck (1670-1732) and employed for the manufacture of jewellery and small objects of vertu. The best were mercurically gilded to increase their deceptive appearance. Wedgwood black basaltes* and jasper* cameos are to be found mounted in pinchbeck settings made in Birmingham.

Pindar (518-438 BC)

Greek lyric poet, born near Thebes. The only poems of his which have survived are in commemoration of victories in the games. A bust, 25in. high, was supplied by Hoskins & Grant* in 1774 and refinished by Hackwood*. A miniature bust, 4½in. high, was produced in 1778.

Pineapple

The pineapple, a tropical fruit, was grown under glass in a hot bed during the 18th century. It was introduced into England early in the 1660s, and the first pineapple was grown by the King's gardener. A painting of the gardener presenting the first fruit to King Charles II is in Ham House, South-West London.

In addition to Wedgwood's early pineapple* ware, which is regarded as rococo*, the shape survived as a knop* to the cover of teapots, tureens and similar vessels by Wedgwood and others during the currency of the neo-classical* style, and it formed part of the design of a large Queen's ware* centrepiece or epergne (see: Grand Plat Ménage) which appears as design no.52 in the '1790' Catalogue.

Pineapple Ware

Creamware naturally modelled and decorated with coloured glazes to represent the pineapple*, usually in the form of a teapot, coffee-pot or covered sugar dish, made by Wedgwood for several years from c.1760.
See: Fruit and Vegetable Shapes

Pingo, Thomas (1692-1776)
Medallist, born in Italy, who came to England c.1743 and became assistant engraver at the Mint. The Wedgwood portrait medallions* of David Garrick and Lord Camden were modelled from Pingo's medals, the former by Hackwood*. Pingo was also responsible for the copper plaques of the battles of Pondicherry and Plassey and the *Birth of a Prince* invoiced in 1769 by John Ireland on behalf of 'Mr Pingo'. In 1800 Mrs Theodosia Pingo wrote to Wedgwood to inform him of her husband's illness and inability to attend to business. This probably refers to one of Thomas Pingo's sons, Thomas or Lewis, although no evidence has yet been found of their employment by Wedgwood.

Pink Lustre
Metallic pink reflection produced by the use of gold lustre on a glazed body of white, cream or buff. The earliest known Wedgwood example is dated 2 February 1805 (see: Appendix II). Variegated lustre, in shades of pink to purple, was produced by Wedgwood from 1809.
See: Lustre Decoration

Pipe Clay
A fine white clay used to make tobacco pipes* and sometimes for earthenwares of high quality, but lack of plasticity generally limited its use to applied or 'trailed' ornament or to slip* washes over bodies of a darker colour.

Pipes, Tobacco
Heads for tobacco pipes were made by Wedgwood in several different shapes and bodies, notably, during the Wedgwood & Bentley period, in ornamented black basaltes* and jasper*. The Christie* & Ansell auction sale* catalogue of 1781 lists a number of them and examples were in the Mayer* collection in Liverpool before it was largely destroyed by bombing in World War II. Quantities of red body pipe heads, some with black relief ornament, were produced in 1849 marked 'STAITE'S PATENT'. The same mark appears on a practical but highly ornamental jasper-dip* white stoneware pipe and stand of about the same date.

Pipkin
A small pot, usually circular, with a straight, horizontally disposed handle, principally used for warming brandy. The term was employed also for small earthenware cooking vessels. Wedgwood refers to 'pots and pipkins' in a letter to Bentley* of February 1780.

Piranesi, Giovanni Battista (1720-78)
Italian engraver who specialised in recording the architectural aspects of the city. His engravings were popular and were often reprinted and imitated. Piranesi is noted for fantastic interiors and dramatic effects of shadow and perspective. Much of his work exhibits a Romantic distortion which leads to highly imaginative views of Rome, to many of which the term *capriccio* could properly be applied. He also published some original and inaccurate interpretations of history, alleging that the Greeks debased classical art, and attacking Vitruvius. Piranesi's *Diverse Maniere d'adornare i Cammini*, published in 1769, launched the concept that Egyptian motifs might be divorced from their original setting and formed into compositions to suit contemporary taste, and it is likely that Wedgwood's interest in Egyptian ornament (see: Egyptian Taste) was influenced by this work.

Piranesi's engravings were used by Wedgwood in 1958 for a set of views of Rome, printed in black on Edme shape (see: Tableware Shapes).
See: Neo-classical Style

Pitcher Mould
Small mould of fireclay* into which clay is pressed in the making of such ornaments as leaves, scrolls, swags, figures and other kinds of relief ornament for application to a variety of wares, most notably jasper*.

Placing
The packing of ware into saggars*.

PIPES, TOBACCO. Turned and cast rosso antico pipe heads. Length 2¼in.-3⅞in. (Right and bottom) marked 'WEDGWOOD STAITE'S PATENT'; others unmarked. c.1849. *Wedgwood Museum*

Plant, John Hugh (fl.1885-1917)
Painter employed at Etruria*, c.1890-1902. He painted landscapes and topographical subjects, later painting in the same style at the Coalport* and Doulton factories.

Plant Labels
Plant labels in matt mortar* ware were made specially for Kew Gardens, c.1830. These were produced in a pointed 'T' shape, in several sizes, and stamped 'KEW'. They were made also for general sale in a variety of shapes, including one with a moulded snowdrop pattern, priced at 2d.-3½d. per dozen.

Plaque
Flat, thin tablet* of ceramic ware (creamware*, terracotta*, black basaltes*, jasper*, rosso antico*, bone china*, Carrara* etc.) ornamented in relief or decorated in enamels. Plaques or tablets were used principally as wall decoration, for insertion into chimney-pieces* and furniture, and for the ornamenting of such objects as clock cases. Some plaques were made with a raised surround (usually cast in one piece with the ground) simulating a picture frame*; others were decoratively framed in metal, often by Boulton* & Fothergill. Although it would be desirable to confine the term to oval or circular examples, using 'tablets' to denote those that are square, rectangular, hexagonal or octagonal, the word actually refers to any of these shapes. The size is not defined, but is usually not less than 6in. on the long axis. 'Cameo'* is generally used for bas-reliefs* which are small enough to be mounted as jewellery or inset in such objects as patch-boxes, toothpick cases or chatelaines*, and 'medallion'* refers to an intermediate size, such as that of the portrait medallion*, seldom greater than 5in. on the long axis.

Platinum Lustre
See: Lustre Decoration

Plato (c.428-347 BC)
Greek philosopher, born in Athens; perhaps a descendant, on his mother's side, from Solon*. Plato was a pupil of Socrates*, and after travels in Egypt and Italy returned to teach in the Academy. Many of his philosophical writings have survived, and to him we owe the account of the death of Socrates and the story of Atlantis.

Two busts were produced by Wedgwood: the first, 25in. high, from a cast supplied by Hoskins & Grant* in 1774; the second, 15in. high, after a bust by John Cheere*, supplied by Hoskins & Grant in 1775. A portrait medallion was catalogued in 1774 and a larger version, 4in. x 3in., appeared in 1777.

Platter
A large shallow dish, usually oval (but also octagonal), for serving food; known in Scotland as an 'ashet'. Large platters of the 18th and 19th centuries were often made with feet, so arranged as to tilt the dish towards one end, where the juices collected in a shallow well. Platters were sometimes provided with drainers*.

Platter Tilter

A rectangular wedge-shaped slab placed under one end of a platter* so that the juices or gravy flow to the opposite end. Wedgwood made Queen's ware* platter tilters in 18th and 19th centuries, often decorated to match tableware services and sometimes crested. They are frequently described erroneously as knife rests.

Playing Cards

A set of twelve playing card designs for plates was produced in 1909 after drawings by the American artist Augustus L. Jansson. These designs, which featured the Court cards in the four suits, were issued with various borders and reproduced as a toy set c.1921.

Plume Knops

Round and oval handles or knops for covered serving dishes in the form of curled plumes of feathers. Knops of this shape do not appear in the illustrations to the '1790' Catalogue* but are to be seen on tureens from c.1815. From about that date they became the standard knops for Traditional shape (see:Tableware Shapes) Queen's ware*, Pearl* ware and White ware*, and they were taken into regular use for bone china* at about the same time, appearing on bone china teaware of the first period.

Pluto (Hades)

Hades was god of the Underworld, brother of Zeus (Jupiter*) and Poseidon (Neptune*) and husband of Persephone*. As king of the Underworld he was supposed to provide men with metals, which came from under the earth, and hence with riches. The name of Hades was hated and feared, and Pluto was commonly used instead. Wedgwood subject:

Pluto Carrying Off Proserpine (also described as *The Rape of Proserpine* or *The Procession of Persephone into the Underworld),* tablet 9in. x 26¼in., modelled by Angelini*, 1789, (possibly 'finished' by De Vaere*).

Pollard, Robert (1755-1838)

Painter and engraver employed by Wedgwood to polish seals* and gems* in the 1770s. His friend, Thomas Bewick*, may have been responsible for introducing him to Wedgwood. Pollard painted landscapes and seascapes, exhibiting his work at the Free Society in 1783 and becoming a member of the Society of Artists. Later he concentrated on engraving, mostly from his own work.

Polyphemus

A son of Poseidon (Neptune*); one of the Cyclopes. Polyphemus was a giant with one eye in the centre of his forehead, who lived in a cave near Mount Aetna. When Odysseus (Ulysses*) was shipwrecked on the coast of Sicily and seized by Polyphemus, he escaped by putting out the monster's single eye. A large figure of Polyphemus, 19in. x 16in., was reproduced from a cast supplied by Hoskins & Oliver* in 1770, and is one of the earliest figures listed in the 1773 Catalogue*,

but no specimen of it appears to have survived. *Polyphemus* is also the subject of one of the 'Herculaneum Pictures'*, after models in the collection of Lord Lansdowne*, and is listed as a circular plaque, diameter 11½in., no.60 in the 1773 Catalogue.

Pomona

Roman divinity of fruit trees. The name was adopted by Paul Follot* for the fruit-encrusted shapes he designed for Wedgwood's Queen's ware* and basalt c.1921.

Pompeii

A city of Campania in the shadow of Mount Vesuvius. It was once on the coast but is now two miles from the sea. It was overwhelmed by an eruption of the volcano in AD79, at the same time as the neighbouring towns of Herculaneum* and Stabiae. Pompeii was buried in a fall of ashes and cinders, but the lava flow did not reach it and it is consequently in an excellent state of preservation. Much of the city has been excavated since the discovery of the site shortly before the middle of the 18th century. The best contemporary account of the destruction of Pompeii is to be found in the letters of Pliny the Younger, whose uncle, the elder Pliny, was killed while attempting to evacuate some of the inhabitants. The discoveries made during the excavations at Pompeii and Herculaneum were fundamental to the development of the neo-classical* style and thus to Wedgwood's stylistic development, and a number of his bas-reliefs* were adapted from wall paintings still to be seen at both sites.

In 1976 Wedgwood issued a limited edition* of 1,000 pale-blue and white jasper compotiers* to be sold by the Royal Academy of Arts to mark the exhibition *Pompeii AD79* held at Burlington House, London. The bas-relief* ornament was a much-reduced version of one of the Herculaneum Pictures*.

Pont-aux-Choux, Paris

A factory founded in 1740 which began by making tin-glazed earthenware *(faïence*),* but from 1765 it produced cream-coloured* ware of excellent quality for which it became widely known. In 1772 the factory was advertised as the 'Manufacture royale de terres de France à l'imitation de celles d'Angleterre'. The wares are moulded in relief with flowers, foliage etc., inspired by contemporary (rococo*) silver; the colour is pale cream; and the glaze is soft and easily abraded. Precise imitations of Staffordshire saltglaze* ware shapes are known.

PORCELAIN. White biscuit 'porcelain' (stoneware) mug ornamented with 'Borghese' figures, and basketwork-moulded bail-handled basket and flower pot and stand. c.1811.   *Wedgwood Museum*

Porcelain

Porcelain manufacture was a matter of serious interest to most 18th-century potters, including Josiah Wedgwood. Properly defined, porcelain is a compound of refractory refined clay and a fusible rock, with the addition of a small quantity of flux* to assist fusion. This is fired to the point of vitrification, when it becomes translucent if it is about 5mm or less in thickness. The type of porcelain usually termed 'true' ('hard-paste') porcelain was first made in China during the Yüan dynasty (1280-1366), although translucent wares had been made for several centuries before that. Because of the difficulty of finding a suitable clay and a fusible

PORCELAIN. Extremely rare example of Wedgwood hard-paste porcelain, a ginger jar decorated in underglaze blue. Possibly a trial. Height 8in. c.1890.   *Wedgwood Museum*

rock possessing the necessary properties, Chinese porcelain was known in Europe for several centuries before the secret of its manufacture was discovered.

The first European true porcelain was produced as the result of the experiments of Ehrenfried Walther von Tschirnhaus and Johann Friedrich Böttger at Meissen* about 1709. The most admired property of Chinese porcelain, specimens of which had been seen in Europe in the 12th century, was translucency, and it was imitated in the 16th century in Italy (at Florence) and late in the 17th century in France (by Louis Poterat at Saint-Sever and at Saint-Cloud) in a body prepared from white-burning clay and what was, in principle, ground glass, the latter taking the place of fusible rock. This 'artificial' porcelain, made also at Chantilly and Mennecy, was brought to its highest point of development in France at Vincennes shortly before 1752, at a factory purchased by Louis XV and removed to Sèvres* in 1756.

In England, a patent for the manufacture of 'transparent earthen-ware, commonly known by the name of Porcelain or China' was granted to John Dwight* in 1671 but it is now considered unlikely that he ever succeeded in making it. The first factory making artificial ('soft-paste') porcelain was located at Chelsea*, where a body ('paste') was produced which was admired by the Vincennes directors. Chelsea was founded in 1745, to be followed by Bow*, Derby*, and the Pomona factory and Longton Hall (both in Staffordshire) all producing soft-paste porcelain before 1750. At Bow calcined cattle bones (bone ash) were added to the body, which reduced kiln wastage at the expense of quality, and this substance was later employed in the manufacture of bone china*. The Worcester* factory, founded in 1751, made a type of porcelain from 1752 which employed soaprock as a fusible rock, thus using the same principle as the Chinese, although the soaprock fused at a lower temperature.

In 1768, William Cookworthy, Quaker apothecary and chemist of Plymouth, who had been experimenting with Cornish material similar to those of China, took out a patent for the use of china clay and feldspathic rock (Cornish stone* or growan stone) in the manufacture of true porcelain. The Plymouth factory was transferred to Bristol, where the manager was Richard Champion*, who bought the factory and patent in 1775. Almost throughout the 18th century porcelain was the most fashionable ceramic material among the wealthier classes (although Wedgwood's Queen's ware* had a wider following) and most manufacturers on a reasonably large scale were interested in making it.

It would be an error to assume that Wedgwood was never interested in adding porcelain to his range of products. As early as 1769 he noted details of the Worcester china body and glaze in his Commonplace Book* and in April 1773 he recorded Cookworthy's patent in full. The same manuscript volume contains extracts from a translation of Du Halde's* *Description Géographique*, de Lauraguais'* patent of 1766, and information obtained from John Bradby Blake* and others. An undated experiment carried out by Wedgwood at Etruria* between 1769 and 1774 is recorded as yielding 'True porcelain, and a good color, extremely firm, and a fine close texture, superior to most India [sic] China. NB Confirmed by repeated trials, but fear it will be apt to warp in dishes and large ware.' Such experiments were continued until January 1776. Thereafter the success of jasper* probably persuaded him not to add yet another body to the large range of them already in regular production.

It is clear, however, that Josiah was never enthusiastic about the production of artificial or soft-paste porcelain. There was little reason for him to expose his successful business to the great risk of producing artificial porcelain, an undertaking which had already ruined the Chelsea, Bow, Pomona and Longton Hall factories, and which would put him directly in competition with Worcester and Derby, when he could perhaps, at no greater risk, produce true porcelain. It is clear, too, that by January 1776 he was perfectly able to produce true porcelain, but chose not to do so.

It is unlikely that Wedgwood was apprehensive of the consequences of infringing Champion's patent, which was extended in 1775. He had already seen how easily his own patent on encaustic* colours had been evaded by Palmer* and Neale*, and Champion was not in any position to pursue expensive lawsuits. Nevertheless, Bentley* did, on several occasions, urge him to avoid firing jasper to the point of translucency (to be noticed in some early examples) to avoid infringements of Champion's patent. By 1778, when

PORPHYRY. Queen's ware vase, shape no.14, decorated with deep purple-red and white surface slip colouring in imitation of 'true porphyry', ornamented with applied swags suspended from goats' heads, on a marble plinth. Height 16½in. Unmarked. Wedgwood & Bentley, c.1770. *Wedgwood Museum*

Champion decided to abandon his factory and to try to sell his patent, Wedgwood was 'absolute' in jasper and leading the market, not following it. He had no commercial need of porcelain, nor of the financial risk involved in making it.

Porcelain, in the form of bone china* was introduced by Josiah II* in 1812, but it was not a commercial success and, after about eight years when production dwindled to 'matchings', was finally abandoned in 1831. It was reintroduced in 1878 and has been a staple product of the firm ever since. About 1890 a small quantity of true, hard-paste, porcelain was made, and a ginger jar in this body, decorated in underglaze blue and marked WEDGWOOD ETRURIA ENGLAND in green, is in the Wedgwood Museum*.

During the early 19th century, white and stained stonewares (including cane* and drab*) were misleadingly described as 'porcelain'.

See: Carrara; Pâte-sur-Pâte; Stoneware

Porphyry

A decorative stone of purplish or reddish-brown or mottled green colour imitated on terracotta* (crystalline) body vases by the use of coloured glazes.

See: Colour Plate 84

See also: Variegated Ware

PORTLAND VASE. Original wax model on slate, probably by Henry Webber, for the figure identified as *Hermes*. *Wedgwood Museum*

Porta, Guglielmo della (d.1577)

Italian Renaissance artist, sculptor and designer whose work was copied or adapted by Wedgwood. Five oval bas-reliefs, 6in. x 9in., after della Porta were listed in the 1773 Catalogue* (nos.2-6) and all were probably in production at least three years earlier. It is most likely that they were copied by way of plaster casts of bronze reliefs by Jakob Cornelisz Cobaert (d.1615). The Wedgwood subjects are:

War of Jupiter and the Titans
Destruction of Niobe's Children
Feast of the Gods
Marriage of Perseus and Andromeda
An Antique Boar Hunting

Some of Della Porta's reliefs were copied also by the Doccia* factory for reproduction in porcelain.

Portland, William Henry Cavendish Bentinck, 3rd Duke of (1738-1809)

Whig statesman; educated at Eton and Christ Church, Oxford. He succeeded to the dukedom in 1762 and married Lady Dorothy Cavendish, daughter of the Duke of Devonshire, in 1766. He was prime minister in 1786 and again in 1807. At the auction after the death of his mother, the Dowager Duchess, he bought the Portland vase* and lent it to Josiah Wedgwood to copy in jasper*. Wedgwood's London showrooms* at Portland House*, Greek Street, rented from James Cullen, were owned by the Duke, who was then the freeholder of much of the property in the vicinity.

Portland House

A late 17th-century mansion at 12 Greek Street, Soho, London, chosen for the Wedgwood & Bentley showrooms from 1774 to 1795. Part of the estate of the 3rd Duke of Portland*, the house was leased to James Cullen, a cabinet-maker, who sub-leased it to Wedgwood & Bentley, for a term of twenty-one years, at a rental of £200 (later revised to £300) per annum. Although a comprehensive plan of alterations was far from completed, the new showrooms were opened on 1 June 1774 and a special exhibition of the Empress Catherine's Frog* service was mounted throughout the month.

The property was considerable: a four-storey brick house finished with pilasters on the north and south sides and with a frontage of nearly 55ft. Behind the façade, more buildings and two spacious yards opened into Manette Street. A second lease of No.11 Greek Street provided accommodation for Bentley*. In 1778 many of the staff employed at Greek Street were struck by a series of mysterious illnesses and it has been conjectured that the cause might have been an old and unfumigated dissecting-room, built by a previous medical lessee at the rear of the building, or the proximity of the Manette Street workhouse. However, the illnesses seem to have cleared up as mysteriously as they appeared, so a more commonplace explanation may be found for them.

In the 1980s, after considerable expansion and redecoration, Wedgwood's London showrooms at 34 Wigmore Street were renamed Portland House, but, in spite of further costly alterations after the Waterford take-over in 1986, the premises were vacated in 1990. See: Showrooms

Portland Vase, The

The name used since about 1784 for the Barberini vase, a superb example of cameo glass-cutting and probably the most famous of all surviving Roman works of art, now in the British Museum. Its early history is uncertain, but it is believed to have been made at Rome, c.27 BC-AD 14 (during the reign of Augustus), probably by Alexandrians or craftsmen trained in Alexandria, the centre of glass-making in the ancient world. The vase is of cased glass: a foundation of dark blue (almost black) glass covered with a layer of white glass. The bas-relief* design was carved out of the white by gem* engravers, or *diatretarii,* and its meaning is still debated. Most modern authorities are agreed that it represents the myth of Peleus and Thetis* (mother of Achilles*) but the precise identification of episodes in the myth with the two sides of the vase is unsure. The shape of the vase was originally an amphora, similar to the large terracotta amphorae used for the storage of oil or wine, but the base has been broken off or removed, and the present flat disc base on which the vase stands is a slightly later piece of cameo glass of a paler colour, cut from another composition and attached to the body of the vase at some date before 1600 (when the vase is first recorded in its present shape). The bas-relief decoration of the disc is thought to represent the head of Paris*.

At one time it was widely believed that the vase was a cinerary urn, that the decoration portrayed the Emperor Alexander Severus and his mother, Mamae, and that it had been found in 1582 in a marble sarcophagus. None of these beliefs is accurate. The vase was first recorded in the winter of 1600-1 by Nicolas de Peiresc, a Provençal scholar and antiquarian, when it was in the collection of Cardinal Francesco Maria del Monte (1549-1627). On his death, the vase was bought by Cardinal Barberini, nephew of Pope Urban VIII, and it remained in the possession of his family until 1780, when it was sold to settle the gambling debts of Donna Cornelia

PORTLAND VASE.
Badly blistered and firecracked trial of the jasper Portland vase, illustrating two of the problems encountered by Wedgwood in making his first copies. Height 9⅞in. Unmarked. Wedgwood, c.1787.
Wedgwood Museum

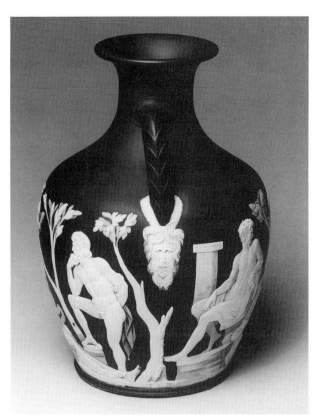

PORTLAND VASE. The first edition jasper Portland vase traditionally believed to be Josiah Wedgwood's own copy. Some of the reliefs have broken away from the body of the vase, probably some considerable time after firing. Height 10⅛in. Unmarked. Wedgwood, 1790.   *Wedgwood Museum*

PORTLAND VASE. Side view of the 'Hope' copy of the Portland vase, perhaps the most perfect first-edition example surviving. The undercutting and shading are especially fine. The handles slope noticeably from upper left to lower right (on the original vase the slope is from right to left).   *Wedgwood Museum*

Barberini-Colonna, Princess of Palestrina, the last of the Barberini family. The purchaser was James Byres*, the Scottish antiquarian and dealer, who commissioned sixty plaster casts of the vase by James Tassie* from a mould by Giovanni Pichler*. Byres sold the vase to Sir William Hamilton* in 1783 for £1,000, and in the following year Hamilton brought it to England, where he resold it to the eccentric Dowager Duchess of Portland, 'a simple woman', according to Horace Walpole, 'and intoxicated only by *empty* vases'. After her death in 1785, the vase was bought at auction by a Mr Tomlinson acting for the 3rd Duke of Portland*, who lent it to Josiah Wedgwood to copy, in return (it is said) for Josiah's agreement not to bid for the vase at the sale.

Broken at least twice before it reached the hands of Josiah Wedgwood, the Portland vase was deposited on loan to the British Museum by the 4th Duke of Portland in 1810. There, in February 1845, it was comprehensively smashed by a young Irishman, who gave his name as William Lloyd and admitted that he had been 'indulging in intemperance for a week before' and was suffering from 'nervous excitement.' Three years later, more than 200 fragments were patiently pieced together. In 1945 the vase was purchased for the Museum from the Portland family, and, just one hundred years after the first reconstruction, the vase was restored again, adding some missing chips of glass and employing modern colourless adhesives to replace discoloured glue. Between 1988 and 1990, after some years of research, the entire vase was dismantled and reassembled, using slow-drying epoxy resin as the principal adhesive, and incorporating all the slivers of glass that had previously been omitted. The entire operation, which was undertaken by Nigel Williams and Sandra Smith of the British Museum's Conservation Department, was filmed by the BBC Archaeology and History Film Unit. The vase is now again on exhibition in the Museum galleries, with the base disc, displayed separately, beside it.

WEDGWOOD'S COPIES

It was probably Flaxman* who first drew Wedgwood's attention to

the Portland vase. 'I wish', Flaxman wrote in February 1785, 'you may soon come to town to see Wm Hamilton's Vase, it is the finest production of Art that has been brought to England and seems to be the very apex of perfection to which you are endeavouring to bring your bisque & jasper; it is…made of dark glass with white enamel [*sic*] figures. The Vase is about a foot high & the figures between 5 & 6 inches, engraved in the same manner as a Cameo & of the grandest & most perfect Greek Sculpture.' It is not certain when Wedgwood first saw the vase for himself, but within eighteen months he had both decided to try to copy it in jasper* and obtained permission to do so.

Wedgwood put several modellers, including Webber*, Hackwood* and William Wood* to work on the vase, supervising the modelling himself and involving his second son, Josiah II*, in the project from the first. The technical difficulties were greater than he had anticipated and he was also uneasy about the shape of the vase, which he rightly considered to be 'not so elegant as it might be'. He consulted Hamilton about these problems and also about the propriety of making copies of different quality 'to suit the tastes, the wants, & the purses of different purchasers.' When the figures were satisfactorily modelled, there remained the difficulty of making a jasper colour that would satisfactorily imitate the blue-black of the original. It was a happy coincidence that Wedgwood had already perfected his pyrometer* for without such an accurate method of assessing firing temperatures his problems would have been much greater.

In July 1789 Wedgwood told Lord Auckland* that 'after having made several defective copies' he saw his way clear to the completion of the vase. Two months later he sent the first perfect vase to Erasmus Darwin*, who later included a description of it in his long poem, *The Botanic Garden*, with an illustration of it engraved by William Blake*. Wedgwood decided to sell the vase by subscription and by 9 May 1790 he had received subscriptions for twenty vases. Queen Charlotte* had already viewed a copy of the vase in London a week earlier, and it was displayed to a distinguished gathering at

'a correct and faithful imitation both in regard to general effect, and the most minute detail of the parts.' By the end of the month, Josiah II and Tom Byerley* were on their way to Holland at the start of a promotional tour of Europe that lasted until December.

Production of the vase continued to be slow, difficult and costly. Some fine blue Portland vases were produced in 1791 when supplies of 'Barberini black clay' temporarily ran out, and specimens of this colour are in the British Museum (presented by Josiah II in 1802) and the Beeson* Collection in the Birmingham Museum, Alabama.

The number of 'first edition' vases (potted, if not finished, during the lifetime of Josiah Wedgwood I) is not known. The best estimate puts the figure at forty-five, of which as many as thirty-one may have been considered of first quality. Josiah II wrote in 1839 that he believed his father had never sold more than ten copies. Josiah Byerley noted ten vases, '4 of them tolerably perfect' in stock in London in 1814. Some, possibly all, of the black jasper first edition vases were marked inside the lip of the vase with a number inscribed in manganese pencil, but blue copies were not so marked. All vases appear to be of solid colour jasper, but all were made by the jasper dip* method, using a coarse body washed with a finer slip, the technique specifically invented for jasper vases in November 1777 (see: Jasper).

The finest of Wedgwood's first-edition Portland vases are indisputably among the greatest technical achievements of European pottery and their production provided a triumphant finale to Wedgwood's career. They are, however, works of craftsmanship, not of art. Whatever their undoubted technical excellence, they are copies in the wrong material, reproduced by entirely different techniques, of a vase which had already been deprived of much of its original grace. The beauty of the original is now in the colour and nature of material – glass – and the exquisite artistry of the cameo-cutter. Neither of these qualities could satisfactorily be reproduced in jasper.

There is no reliable record of any jasper Portland vases being made in the 19th century before 1845. This omission was due to the difficulties being experienced in making the jasper body, and especially in the production of the larger pieces, such as vases. From 1836, however, the white stoneware ('porcelain') body was used to produce vases in several sizes with a jasper dip, in blue, green and lilac. Black was still giving trouble in 1845, even used with the 'porcelain' body. In 1846 six sizes were in production (4in. to 10in. in height), some cast in one piece with the relief ornament, some without the base disc relief, and some 'draped' (the male figures, originally nude, modestly covered to spare Victorian sensibilities). Colours included mazarine blue* and an enamelled black ground on white stoneware. Carrara* copies of the

PORTLAND VASE. List of subscribers to the first edition of Wedgwood's Portland vase. From Thomas Bentley's notebook, 1789.
Wedgwood Museum

Sir Joseph Banks's* house in Soho Square on 5 May. Two weeks later Sir Joshua Reynolds*, president of the Royal Academy, signed a certificate declaring Wedgwood's copy of the Portland vase to be

PORTLAND VASE. Late 19th-century jasper copy of the Portland vase. Height 10½in.   *City Museum & Art Gallery, Stoke-on-Trent*

PORTLAND VASE. Base disc of the vase made in a limited edition for Charles Bellows in 1914. The surface of these vases has a disagreeable sheen.   *Wedgwood Museum*

PORTRAIT MEDALLIONS. Three relief portraits of Dr Richard Mead illustrating stages of production of a Wedgwood portrait medallion: (a) original ivory carving by Silvanus Bevan, sent to Etruria in 1778; (b) wax portrait, probably by Hackwood, after Bevan's model; (c) Wedgwood & Bentley solid grey-blue and white jasper portrait medallion, height 3⅜in. c.1779.

British Museum

vase were produced c.1843. On these vases, the figures were moulded in one piece with the body, the ground sometimes being painted in mazarine blue or black and glazed.

Continuing problems with the jasper body required almost continuous trials until 1860, when the solid jasper body was reintroduced. In April of that year Portland vases are listed in three sizes in solid colours but it was not until 1871 that the solid black and white jasper vases could be produced with confidence.

In 1876 John Northwood* completed the first cased glass copy of the Portland vase and next year Wedgwood engaged him to finish the reliefs of a special edition of the jasper Portland vase. The figures on Godfrey Wedgwood's* copy were shaded, as they had been on vases of the first edition. Thirteen copies of the Northwood edition were sold by Phillips, the London retailer, all marked with Northwood's monogram. Another special edition was made for Phillips in 1878, using a blacker jasper body and a higher quality of ornamenting, but of the thirteen copies fired, none was thought fit to be finished. The 'ordinary' Portland vase, without undercutting* or shading of the figures, however, continued to be made in fair quantities. Some were ornamented by Thomas Lovatt*, who signed his work with his initials. A limited edition was produced in 1914 for Charles Bellows and some of these vases were finished by Bert Bentley*, but the quality of the jasper body was poor and has an extremely unattractive gloss.

There appears to have been a gap in the production of black and white jasper vases between about 1885 and 1919, when Harry Barnard* was instructed to produce a new edition. It took him four years to make his first perfect vase, but in 1923-4 he produced seven good out of thirteen and thereafter he made them with ever greater ease until, by the bicentenary of Josiah I's birth in 1930, he had made 195, of which only thirteen had been unfit for sale.

Throughout the whole period from about 1840, small Portland vases, between 4in. and 8in. in height, were made in a variety of colours. Most of these were bas-relief ware* – white stoneware washed and ornamented with jasper – and their production continued until 1941.

Small editions of the full-size (10in. high) Portland vase have been made since World War II. The first was produced in solid green jasper for use in the stage and film production of Wolf Mankowitz's *Make Me an Offer*. A limited edition in the new Portland Blue jasper was made in 1973, and another limited edition in solid Royal Blue jasper was issued in 1977 to celebrate the Silver Jubilee of Queen Elizabeth II.

Since much misleading information has been published about Wedgwood's Portland vases, it may be useful to summarise some of the evidence regarding solid black-and-white jasper vases of the full 10in. size – the only type that could be mistaken for a first-

edition vase. Apart from trial pieces, the first reliably recorded 19th-century Portland vases of this description were made in the period 1870-85, when they were made in good quantities and in two qualities: the lower quality being without undercutting or shading of the figures. The second period when vases of this type were made in quantity was between 1923 and 1930, when Barnard's well-finished edition was in production. Most surviving vases belong to one of these two periods. Of the rest of the 19th-century black-and-white vases, the majority are of jasper-dipped white stoneware.

See: Colour Plate 85

Portland Vase Mark

A trade mark depicting the outline of the Portland vase*, printed in various colours on Wedgwood bone china* since its reintroduction in 1878. The mark appears occasionally on Queen's ware, especially vases, of the period 1878-95.

See: Appendix II: Trade Marks

Portrait Medallions

Medallions, usually oval in shape and between 2in. and 5in. in height (the long axis), ornamented with a portrait in relief. Such portraits are commonly in profile but appear more rarely in either half-face, three-quarter-face or full face.

The last quarter of the 18th century was a period in which the British passion for portraiture amounted almost to frenzy. A number of disparate influences – which included the excavations at Herculaneum* and Pompeii*, the improvement in communications and consequent recognition of public heroes, and the desire of a prosperous middle class to equip their houses in the manner of the aristocracy – combined to create a feeling for the importance of the individual, a celebration of the family and a reverence for history. Likenesses of the great, of family and friends were demanded and provided in a bewildering variety of media. Portraits in oils; miniatures in watercolour on ivory; figures and busts in marble and bronze or cast in plaster; small busts in relief, modelled or cast, in ivory, wax, glass paste, jasper* and black basaltes*; profiles cut out or painted in silhouette; bronze medallions; even needlework portraits worked in the sitters' own hair: all illustrate a fashion never equalled in any country.

Josiah Wedgwood was not slow to take advantage of this fashion. In 1771 he wrote to Bentley* of his proposal to produce portrait medallions of George III* and Queen Charlotte*, 'fully perswaded a good deal may be done in that way with many of Their Majesty's subjects.' Two years later he published the first of his Catalogues* of Ornamental Ware. This listed 609 portrait medals* and medallions which included 254 Popes and the first

PORTRAIT MEDALLIONS. Wedgwood & Bentley solid pale-blue jasper portrait medallion of Dr Daniel Solander from the Wedgwood & Bentley edition of large-size portraits issued in 1779. Oval height 13in. 1779.   *Lawrence Pucci Collection*

122 of the important medallions known as 'Heads of Illustrious Moderns'*. In the introduction to this Catalogue, Wedgwood advertised his ability to supply portraits, in cameo* or intaglio*, in sizes from those 'proper for a ring, seal or bracelet', to 6in. in diameter. The original wax portrait* (from which most of Wedgwood's portraits in black basaltes*, terracotta*, jasper* or other dry bodies* were replicated) cost from three to six guineas; copies in black basaltes or 'polished biscuit [terracotta*] with cameo grounds' were 10/6d each for not less than ten. Portrait medallions from the 'Illustrious Moderns' series might be bought, according to size and body, for between 2s and 7/6d each.

The idea was not new. In the 1750s the Doccia* manufactory, near Florence, had produced quantities of portrait medallions, the heads in white relief against a blue ground. The invention of stained jasper in 1775-6 gave Wedgwood the variety of colours he

sought for grounds. By 1788 he had catalogued 857 portrait medals and medallions, of which 233 were 'Illustrious Moderns', and this list did not include a substantial number of portraits of family and friends, or those private commissions which were thought to lack public appeal. Many of the subjects were undoubtedly chosen to flatter patrons (e.g. Lord and Lady Auckland*, Sir Joseph and Lady Banks*) or to assist the passage of Wedgwood wares into other countries (e.g. the Queen of Portugal, Charles III of Spain, Gustavus III of Sweden) rather than in the expectation of large sales of the portraits themselves. The majority of Wedgwood's portrait medallions were not original. They were copied or adapted from existing medals, reliefs cast in glass paste, carvings in ivory, wax portraits or horn medallions. The rest were either modelled in wax *ad vivum* or from engravings, drawings, portraits in oils or sculpture, by artists employed or commissioned by Wedgwood. The largest source was the medallists, and many of the classical and French portraits were copied from medals by the Dassier* family and Pesez*. Glass paste portraits were obtained from James Tassie*. Among the principal modellers whose work was reproduced by Wedgwood were John Flaxman* (the younger), William Hackwood*, John Charles Lochée*, Eley George Mountstephen*, Joachim Smith* and John De Vaere*. A series of large-size portrait medallions, about 10in. high, was produced in 1779, the subjects including, Sir Isaac Newton, Benjamin Franklin, Priestley*, Captain Cook, Sir William Hamilton*, Sir Joseph Banks and Daniel Solander*.

Portrait medallions have continued to be produced by Wedgwood to the present day, though the number of additional subjects has been small in comparison with the late-18th century, when the fashion for them was at its height. Many of the most popular portraits from that period have been reproduced at irregular intervals and as commemorative portraits to celebrate centennials of events, and some, such as the portraits of admirals on the 'Britannia Triumphant'* group, have been used to ornament vases and other decorative objects. Recent additions have included portraits of H.M. Queen Elizabeth II, the Duke of Edinburgh, the Queen Mother, the Prince of Wales and Earl Mountbatten of Burma.
See: Colour Plates 86 to 88

Poseidon
See: Neptune

Poskotchin
Sergei Poskotchin's factory in Morye (Schlisselburg district of the province of St. Petersburg) manufactured high quality *faïence* and heat-resistant wares for the kitchen and for technical use. The factory was founded early in the 19th century by E. Friedrichs, but its reputation rests on the ware produced after it passed into the hands of Poskotchin (1817-42). These included various coloured bodies*, black ware and cream-coloured* ware. Many of Poskotchin's products were in conscious imitation of Wedgwood's, and an attempt was made to manufacture a blue stoneware body with white ornaments in the jasper* style. In about 1810 Poskotchin made some well potted and decorated replacements for the *Husk* service.

PORTRAIT MEDALLIONS. Pair of 20th-century solid black and white jasper portrait medallions of Edward VII and Queen Alexandra. Oval height 8½in. 1902. The modeller, recorded only as 'Watkin', has not been identified.   *Christie's, New York*

POSKOTCHIN. Creamware dessert dish painted in rose-purple in imitation of the *Husk* pattern at the Poskotchin factory, c.1810. Length 13½in. Mark: CII impressed.   *Wedgwood Museum*

POT-POURRI VASE. Hexagonal Queen's ware pot-pourri vase, the model attributed to John Coward. Height 11in. Unmarked. Wedgwood, c.1768. *Wedgwood Museum*

Pot Bank

A term which has come to mean any pottery factory, though it is generally used to describe smaller factories. The word 'bank' was, however, used by Josiah Wedgwood to denote his stock of ware, made by other potters, which he could not (or did not find it convenient to) supply from his own manufacture. Josiah expressed extreme irritation when Tom Byerley* was unable, on one occasion, to distinguish between Wedgwood creamware and that of the 'bank'.

Pot-Pourri Jar (Vase)

A jar or vase, sometimes mounted in ormolu*, which is characterised by piercing on the shoulders and in the cover. It was used for holding pot-pourri, a liquid deriving its odour from decomposing flower petals and herbs, as the word *pourri* (rotten) suggests. In England, dry mixtures of flowers and herbs were placed in open bowls as well as vases, and received the same name of pot-pourri, although it is strictly incorrect. Wedgwood made pot-pourri jars and vases in Queen's ware* and the dry bodies*, especially in the first half of the 19th century.
See: Colour Plate 89
See also: Cassolette; Pastille Burner; Scent Box

Potter, Beatrix (1866-1943)

Writer and illustrator of childrens' books, born in South Kensington, London. Her first books, *The Story of Peter Rabbit* and *The Tailor of Gloucester,* failed to attract a publisher and were privately printed in 1900 and 1902. Soon afterwards she began a personal and professional association with Frederick Warne & Co., who published twenty-four of her books during the following thirty years. In

POT-POURRI VASE. Black jasper dip pot-pourri vase with lattice-work lid, the body ornamented with 'Torches'. Height 8⅜in. c.1790-1800.
Lady Lever Art Gallery, Port Sunlight

POWELL, Alfred. Alfred Powell painting one of his bowls, c.1925.
Photograph: Wedgwood

1902 she became engaged to Norman Warne, but he died a few months later. She married a solicitor, William Heelis, in 1913. Her portrait by Delmar Banner is in the National Portrait Gallery, London. Wedgwood's Peter Rabbit* nursery ware*, decorated with accurate reproductions of Beatrix Potter's illustrations, was produced under licence from Frederick Warne & Co.

Pottery

Properly, the generic term for all ceramic wares, whether of earthenware, porcelain or stoneware, but generally limited in use to those wares which are not porcelain. Thus Wedgwood's Queen's ware* and all the dry bodies* are designated as forms of pottery, but bone china* and Carrara* are not.

Pottery Memos

Manuscript Memorandum Books kept by Francis Wedgwood* between 1816 and 1860 and later by his sons, containing notes of ceramic bodies, compositions, blendings, techniques, prices and experiments, and occasionally also of business arrangements and factory organisation. These books, which are preserved with the rest of the Wedgwood archives at Keele University, are a mine of information about Wedgwood in the 19th century.

Pounce Pot

A small box with a pierced top for containing pounce (powdered gum sandarac) used to prepare the surface of parchment for writing or to restore it after erasures. The pounce pot usually formed part of the early inkstandish and was sometimes included as part of Wedgwood's 18th-century black basaltes* 'escritoires'*.

Powder Colours

Colours imitating in appearance the powder-blue ground of the Chinese, made at several porcelain factories during the 18th century and revived by Wedgwood in 1910. The Chinese applied the colour in powder form by blowing it through a silk screen at the bottom of a bamboo tube on to a surface prepared by a light application of oil, hence the French term for this ground, *bleu soufflé*. It was imitated in England by first laying a ground of solid colour and then stippling it with a fine-grained sponge. This technique has been used by Wedgwood to produce powder colour grounds for bone china* tableware border patterns (e.g. *Whitehall, Ulander, Columbia*) in a variety of colours, including blue, turquoise, shagreen, ruby, pink, lilac and grey; and the ruby and blue have been used also for 20th-century bone china vases designed by James Hodgkiss* and Daisy Makeig-Jones*.
See: Ordinary Lustres; James Powell & Sons

Powell, Alfred Hoare (1865-1960) and Ada Louise (1882-1956)

English potters and ceramic designers. Alfred Powell was a gifted painter who trained as an architect at the Slade School of Art and

POWELL, Alfred. Queen's ware charger handpainted by Alfred Powell with his 'White Hart' design. Diameter 16¼in. Signed with the artist's monogram. c.1920.   *Wedgwood Museum*

joined the firm of J.D. Sedding, whose pupils included Ernest and Sidney Barnsley (father of Grace Barnsley*) and Ernest Gimson. In 1901 Powell joined Gimson and the Barnsleys in setting up craft workshops in Gloucestershire and two years later, on the strength of some designs submitted to Wedgwood, he was invited to Etruria*. The association with Wedgwood lasted for more than forty years. The first exhibition of Powell's work for Wedgwood was held in London in 1905 and next year agreement was reached that Wedgwood should pay him a salary and contribute to the rental of a studio in London. Later in the year he married Louise Lessore, a grand-daughter of Emile Lessore*, and they worked together on designs for Wedgwood in a studio in Red Lion Square. They also made prolonged visits to Etruria, where, under their tuition and with the aid of the old pattern books*, the old techniques of handpainting were revived. Many of the patterns painted at this time were made exclusively for sale by James Powell & Sons*.

The paintresses trained by the Powells worked also on tableware patterns designed by them, and they developed a collective style, generally based on stylised interpretations of fruit, flowers and leaves, so homogeneous that it is difficult to distinguish between the work of Alfred and Louise. Their designs for ornamental wares were more individual, but, although they painted many of the pieces themselves in London, many were also designed to be copied by paintresses at the factory.

Louise, the elder daughter of Jules Lessore*, had been trained at the Central School of Art, specialising in calligraphy and illumi-

POWELL, Louise. Queen's ware charger decorated by Louise Powell in platinum lustre over a black groundlay. Diameter 16¼in. c.1928.
                              Christie's, London

nation. Later she assisted in the completion of William Morris's unfinished illuminated manuscript of Virgil's *The Aeneid*. The influence of this disciplined training is often discernible in her work on pottery, whereas Alfred, who had exhibited nine landscape paintings at the Royal Academy (the first when he was only fourteen years old) was more often concerned with architecture and landscape and his border decoration was less heraldic than his wife's.

After World War I the Powells created many designs using lustre or a combination of enamel and lustre decoration*. The designs employed on the Veronese wares (see: Glazes) introduced about 1930 closely resemble Louise Powell's in style and were probably by her or adapted from her work. Although the Powells produced designs for bone china* teawares (e.g. simple 'gold spot' edge patterns), both preferred to work with Queen's ware. Much of their own painted work was signed with their personal monograms (see: Appendix II).

Alfred Powell designed and painted some large and important plaques, bowls and vases, some of which were private commissions, including a fine circular plaque decorated with a view of Barlaston Hall* in purple lustre.

POWELL, Louise. Bone china bowl and covered broth cup and saucer decorated with black glaze of the 'Jackfield' type and various designs in platinum lustre with a similarly decorated earthenware jug made by the same artist at Millwall. c.1923.   *Author's collection*

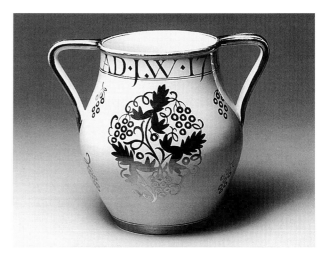

POWELL, Louise. Queen's ware vase, decorated with white matt glaze and platinum lustre, designed by Louise Powell to commemorate the bicentenary of the birth of Josiah Wedgwood. Issued in a limited edition of fifty. Height 9½in. 1930.   *Wedgwood Museum*

POWELL, James & Sons. Queen's ware dessert ware handpainted over Dysart glaze. Except for the matching pierced fruit centre (1951) all the pieces were made between 1908 and 1912.

Wedgwood Museum (fruit centre);
Author's collection (dessert service).

The reintroduction by the Powells of handpainted decoration at Etruria was largely responsible for a revival of interest in Wedgwood's Queen's ware among a section of the public which had grown unaccustomed to fine earthenware, and a number of their pupils, notably Millicent Taplin* and 'Star' (Cecily Stella) Wedgwood*, went on to become successful designers of Wedgwood tableware patterns.

Alfred and Louise Powell ceased to be formally employed by Wedgwood in 1930, but they continued to execute commissions and made frequent visits to Etruria to collect Queen's ware 'blanks' which they decorated in London or at Tarlton, in Gloucestershire, and returned to the factory for firing. Louise died in 1956 and Alfred four years later. Their achievement for Wedgwood was threefold: first, in their own work, which was of the highest quality and helped to reinvigorate Wedgwood's reputation for traditional artistry and craftsmanship; second, in their training of a large number of paintresses, whose skills, under the discerning eye of Millicent Taplin, were still evident at Barlaston into the 1960s; and third, in their introduction to Wedgwood of other artists, including Louise's sister Thérèse Lessore* and Grace Barnsley.

See: Colour Plate 90

POWELL, James & Sons. Bone china vase, height 11in., decorated with birds in reserves on a powder-blue ground. Made for James Powell & Sons, c.1916.

Christie's, London

James Powell & Sons

Manufacturers of Whitefriars glass and retailers of china and glass of Conduit Street, London. Early in the 20th century, Powell's commissioned from Wedgwood a number of reproductions of 18th-century tableware designs chosen from the old Queen's ware* pattern books and decorated, as they had been formerly, by hand-painting. These were produced for sale exclusively by Powell's, and most of the pieces bear a special printed backstamp. Some of these patterns, withdrawn from production during World War II, were reintroduced in 1950 and made for several years without the Powell backstamp. Arthur M. Powell, a director of the firm and a family connection of Alfred Powell's*, visited Etruria in 1910 in search of decoration in the Japanese style. Later, after a visit with James Hodgkiss* to the Victoria & Albert Museum, he suggested that Hodgkiss might try to reproduce the Chinese *bleu soufflé*. The important consequence of this was the introduction of Wedgwood's powder colours*.

Press Moulding

A process in which a body is pressed by hand into a mould of plaster of Paris or fired clay, used in the making of small ornaments, such as the reliefs to ornament jasper. The absorbent mould removes some of the moisture from the body, which shrinks slightly in consequence, facilitating removal from the mould. In former years, quite large objects, such as busts, were made by pressing, but the process has now been replaced to a great extent by slip casting*.

Pretty Mantua Maker, The

See: Brandoin, Michel-Vincent

Priam

King of Troy during the Trojan war. According to Homer* he had fifty sons, nineteen of whom were by his second wife, Hecuba. His eldest son, Hector, was slain by Achilles*. When Troy was captured, Priam was killed by Pyrrhus, son of Achilles. Wedgwood's tablet, *Priam kneeling Before Achilles Begging the Body of His Son Hector*, 6in. x 15½in. (also length 22in.), was modelled by Pacetti* in 1788. The subject appears also as a small bas-relief* used to ornament cameos* and small tableware objects, such as cream jugs.

Price, Alan, Des.RCA (b.1926)

Artist and designer; studied at Leamington School of Art, Leeds College of Art and the Royal College of Art, London; joined Wedgwood at Barlaston* in 1953, shortly afterwards becoming Wedgwood's first resident designer in the USA. He designed many commemorative pieces for Wedgwood, including the *Philadelphia Bowl*, the *Boston Bowl*, the *Washington Presidential Bowl* and the *St Lawrence Seaway* plate, and his best known tableware designs are *Potpourri* for Queen's ware*, and *Honesty* for bone china*, for which he was awarded the Gold Medal for pottery design at the

PRICE, Alan. Large bowl transfer-printed in black with reproductions of engravings commemorating the signing of the Articles of Federation of Philadelphia on 9 July 1778, designed by Alan Price in 1959. Diameter 12½in. *Author's collection*

Californian State Fair. A successful painter, who has had five one-man exhibitions at the prestigious Kennedy Galleries in New York, Price has been designing tableware patterns for Lenox, the American porcelain manufacturer since 1990.

Priestley, Dr Joseph FRS (1733-1808)

Born a cloth dresser's son at Fieldhead, near Leeds, Joseph Priestley was educated at a dissenting academy and became a dissenting minister at Needham Market, Suffolk, in 1755. Three years later he was appointed Minister at Nantwich, and later tutor of

PRIESTLEY, Dr Joseph. Wedgwood & Bentley blue and white jasper portrait medallion adapted from a model by Giuseppe Ceracchi (1751-1802). One of the large-size portrait medallions issued in 1779. Oval height 11in. *Brooklyn Museum, Emily Winthrop Miles Collection*

languages and *belles-lettres* at Warrington Academy, soon to become one of the most celebrated dissenting academies in Britain. He was elected Fellow of the Royal Society in 1766 and published *The History and Present State of Electricity* in the following year. His history of optics, the first in the English language, was published in 1771 and the subscribers included Wedgwood, Bentley* and Benjamin Franklin. In 1774 Priestley isolated oxygen but without realising the significance of his discovery. He was elected to the French Académie des Sciences in 1772 and to the St Petersburg Academy in 1789. In 1777 he went to live in Birmingham, where his reply to Burke's *Reflections on the French Revolution* incited a mob to plunder and destroy his home, and in 1794 he emigrated to America, settling in Pennsylvania. His numerous scientific works have never been published in a collected edition, but his *Theological Works,* in twenty-six volumes, were published in London between 1817 and 1832.

Josiah Wedgwood's friendship with Priestley was of long standing and they corresponded over many years. When he heard of Priestley's move to Birmingham, Wedgwood immediately offered to subscribe to a fund for his support, so that he might give all his time to scientific research, and, when Priestley's house and library were destroyed in 1791, Wedgwood at once offered him financial assistance and sanctuary at Etruria Hall*. From about 1779 onwards, Wedgwood supplied Priestley, and other scientists, with free chemical wares* for their experimental work. Priestley was a member of the Lunar Society* from 1777.

Two portrait medallions* of Priestley were produced. The first, modelled by Giuseppe Ceracchi*, was remodelled, probably by Hackwood*, for the series of large-size portraits issued in 1779. Wedgwood wrote to Bentley*: 'Dr Priestley is arriv'd & we are with great reverence taking off his presbyterian parson's wig.'
See also: Electricity and Pottery Decoration; Mortar Ware

Prime Movers

Until the 18th century prime movers were limited to the human being, horses and oxen, the water mill, and the windmill. Human beings provided motive power by working a treadle or turning a wheel. The horse or ox trudged in a circle, harnessed to a bar turning a central mechanism which could be geared either up or down. The longer the bar (within reason), and the nearer to the end of it the point of attachment to the animal, the greater the power which could be exerted. Windmills and water mills were more sophisticated, and Staffordshire, which was provided with numerous rivers with strong currents, made great use of water power for grinding materials for the pottery industry.

The project for a windmill at Etruria* was first discussed in 1768 when Erasmus Darwin* sent Wedgwood a drawing for a mill with horizontal sails. Wedgwood doubted the efficiency of the design, and eleven years later he went to Lichfield to consult Darwin, R.L. Edgeworth* and James Watt* about it. There is no evidence that this mill was ever built and in 1782 Wedgwood ordered his first rotary steam engine from James Watt, thus becoming a pioneer of the use of steam power in the industry. A watercolour by Stebbing Shaw dated 1794 shows the top of a windmill just visible over the roof of the building fronting the water. This seems to have been in existence since 1774, and before that time Wedgwood used the mill owned by his wife's kinsmen, John and Thomas Wedgwood* of the Big House. The Etruria mill appears to have been used principally for grinding glaze material and enamel colours, but Wedgwood probably utilised subsidiary belt drives off the main shaft for other purposes. The mill was demolished about 1796, when Boulton* & Watt supplied a new 10h.p. rotary steam engine. Watermills have continued in use in Staffordshire for grinding pottery colours and similar materials until modern times.

Prince of Wales Vase

An important centrepiece of three-colour jasper* (white, blue and olive-green) in a restrained rococo* style. The form is unusual for a piece made at so late a date (c.1790-5) and it may reflect some deference to the taste of the recipient. The base is octagonal, with figures of a lion and a unicorn flanking the central vase. On the front of the vase, an oval medallion of George, Prince of Wales (later George IV) is flanked by a wreath and surmounted by the Prince of Wales's feathers; on the reverse is a bas-relief* of Flora* holding a cornucopia*. Surmounting the domed cover is the figure of Britannia, which, like other such figures, is modified from one

PRINCE OF WALES VASE. Solid pale blue and white jasper vase ornamented with a portrait of George, Prince of Wales, surmounted by the Prince of Wales's feathers. The finial is in the form of the figure of Britannia. The vase stands on a solid white jasper plinth ornamented with green festoons, the upper surface covered with greenish-brown jasper on which lie the solid white figures of a lion and unicorn. Height 14¾in. Unmarked. Wedgwood, c.1783-95. *Nottingham Castle Museum*

of Minerva*. This bizarre, but apparently unique, piece (in the Nottingham Castle Museum) is reputed to have been presented to the Prince on the occasion of his 21st birthday in 1783 but the bas-relief* portrait suggests an older man and a later date and the vase is more likely to have been presented at the time of the Prince's marriage in 1795. The design is doubtfully attributed to Webber*.

Print and Enamel Decoration
Decoration that is first transfer-printed* in outline and then filled-in with enamel colours. This form of decoration was first employed by Wedgwood in 1776, although he had suggested the use of the technique to Bentley* at least six years earlier. Bentley was reluctant to accept it, and, in spite of Wedgwood's urging, did not do so until the first shell and seaweed patterns were received from Guy Green*. The introduction of this type of decoration created some unrest among the painters employed at the Chelsea Decorating Studio* and at Etruria*, who thought that it threatened their jobs, and, as late as 1789, Josiah II* (in his father's absence in London) had to deal with a dispute at Etruria which lasted for several days. Although patterns of this kind were produced for Wedgwood from 1776, printed and enamelled wares were never a significant part of production at Etruria during Josiah I's lifetime. Nevertheless, as he told Bentley: 'I make no doubt but Painting, & Printing may exist together, I hope we shall do both in quantities…Many patterns cannot be printed, & those will employ the pencils.' After about 1810, print-and-enamel became an essential decorating technique for Queen's ware* and, after 1878, for bone china*. It has now been largely superseded by lithography* and silk-screen* printing.

Printing
See: Transfer-printing

Processes of Manufacture
The principal processes of manufacture are summarised below. The more important are discussed at greater length under the appropriate headings in the main text. These are marked with an asterisk.

BURNISHING. Gold-printed *Florentine* pattern plates being burnished, after firing, on a rotating turntable.

Burnishing. 1. Polishing clay objects, while in the leather-hard* state, with a hard object, such as a smooth pebble. Coatings of fine slip over a coarser body (such as Wedgwood used in his production of larger jasper* pieces after 1777) may also be polished in this manner. 2. Polishing gold, which has a dull surface when applied to pottery or porcelain, with a metal tool (French: *brunissage au clou*) or an agate or dog's-tooth burnisher.

CASTING (1). Slip being poured into plaster of Paris moulds.

CASTING (2). A slip cast coffeepot being separated from its plaster mould.

Casting. The process of formation by pouring slip* into plaster of Paris moulds*. When the cast is dry enough it is removed for further processing, and the parts of the mould reassembled for further use. Casts made in plaster of Paris instead of slip are used for a variety of purposes, including the making of fresh working moulds to replace those that have become worn.

DIPPING. Queen's shape plates decorated with an underglaze lithograph pattern being dipped in liquid glaze.

Dipping. The process of glazing by submerging an article in liquid glaze* material (see also: Dip).

ENAMELLING. Adding blue enamel colour to a printed, glazed and fired plate of the Florentine pattern.

Enamelling. Adding colours over the glaze (onglaze colours). They are fixed by a low-temperature firing in the enamelling or muffle* kiln. Several firings may be required for elaborately decorated articles. Enamel colours may be applied freehand or to fill in printed outlines (print and enamel decoration*). See: Enamel Decoration.

ENGRAVING. Using a scorper to incise the lines of *Florentine* pattern in a copper plate.

Engraving. The cutting of designs on a copper plate with the aid of a tool known as a scorper. It leaves a line of variable depth and width according to the pressure exerted on it, which governs the amount of ink the line will hold. Prints from the engraved plate inked with ceramic colour are used for transfer-printed* decoration.

FETTLING. Removing seams and mould marks from a *Sterling* coffeepot before glazing.

Fettling. Finishing an article after removal from the mould by trimming off seams, mould marks, etc., and touching up blemishes.

FIRING. Ware being wheeled into an electrically fired continuous tunnel oven at the Barlaston factory, c.1960.

Firing. The process of subjecting an object to heat of varying intensity according to the purpose and body. Earthenware bodies are fired at a lower temperature than vitreous bodies; glazes are fired at a lower temperature than the body; and enamel colours receive the lightest firing of all. Stonewares and porcelain are referred to as 'hard' fired wares; earthenware receives a 'soft' firing.

GLAZING. Modern semi-automatic glazing machine at the Adams factory (one of the Wedgwood Group).

Glazing. The application of glaze (a kind of glass) to the surface of the ware. Modern ware is usually given a preliminary firing to biscuit*, and it is then covered with glaze and fired in the glost or glazing kiln. See: Glazes.

GROUNDLAYING. Powder colour being applied to the oiled surface of a glazed bone china plate.

Groundlaying. The process of giving the ware a coloured ground. A coating of oil is applied to the surface of glazed ware in places where the ground colour is required. Powdered colour is then dusted on to the oil until it will absorb no more. Firing burns off the oil, leaving the colour fixed to the glaze. See: Aerograph.

JIGGERING. Forming a plate on a rotating mould, the upper surface of which shapes the upper surface of the plate, while the metal profile forms the base and removes surplus clay.

Jiggering. The process of making plates by placing a bat of clay on a revolving disc in the form of a plaster mould, which forms the front of the plate. A profile having the shape of the back is then brought into contact with the clay as it revolves, and this, by removing surplus clay, shapes the back. The process dates back at least to the 18th century.

JOLLEYING. Forming a cup inside a rotating white plaster mould by lowering a metal form into it.

Jolleying. A process for forming cups which is on the same principle as jiggering for plates (see above). The mould forms the exterior of the cup, the profile the interior.

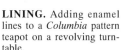
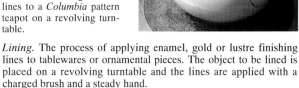

LINING. Adding enamel lines to a *Columbia* pattern teapot on a revolving turntable.

Lining. The process of applying enamel, gold or lustre finishing lines to tablewares or ornamental pieces. The object to be lined is placed on a revolving turntable and the lines are applied with a charged brush and a steady hand.

MODELLING. Preparing a clay model of the Houses of Parliament for a Christmas plate.

Modelling. The making, in a plastic material such as clay or wax, of the pattern or design from which the master mould is taken. The original model is usually taken from a design which has been drawn or sketched, and it is important that the model be made larger than the size required for the finished object, since clay shrinks by about one-sixth during firing.

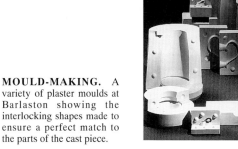

MOULD-MAKING. A variety of plaster moulds at Barlaston showing the interlocking shapes made to ensure a perfect match to the parts of the cast piece.

Mould-making. The replication of objects in the course of manufacture requires the making of moulds from an original model. The

349

making of a working mould from the wax or clay model is usually done in three stages. The first mould to be made is a hollow mould (matrix), which is used to reproduce the object (patrix) in plaster. The patrix is used to make a series of working moulds (matrices), which can be replaced when worn out by casting fresh moulds as required. In this way the standard of reproduction is maintained. Instead of wax or clay, the original model from which the matrix was taken was sometimes of carved wood. The Wedgwood Museum* at Barlaston* has examples of carved wood models by John Coward* which were used for this purpose. Aaron Wood* was a notable 18th-century block cutter, who supplied almost everyone of note in the Potteries, including Wedgwood.

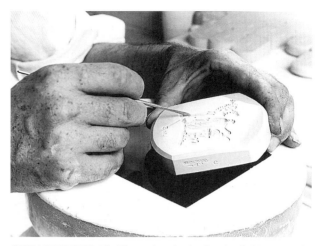

ORNAMENTING (4). Sharpening the details of a finished intaglio mould ready for use.

ORNAMENTING (1). A pug of clay being placed on top of a relief block to receive an intaglio impression.

ORNAMENTING (5). Clay being pressed into a fired clay intaglio mould.

ORNAMENTING (2). The clay being hammered on to the relief block mould.

ORNAMENTING (6). The clay relief being lifted from the mould.

ORNAMENTING (3). The block mould and the intaglio clay mould taken from it.

Ornamenting. The process of applying relief ornament to the ware. The reliefs are made in pitcher* moulds and applied to the moistened surface of the background by skilful pressure of the craftsman's fingers. Although the commonest example of Wedgwood ornamenting is blue jasper*, many other colours and bodies were used, including black basaltes*, rosso antico* with black ornaments and cane* ware with various colours.

ORNAMENTING (7). Applying an acanthus relief ornament to a modern basalt bowl. The surface is dampened to allow the relief to adhere. Firing completes the process of adhesion.

ORNAMENTING (8). Sharpening the detail of the relief ('undercutting') before firing.

Overglaze (Onglaze) decoration. Painting, groundlaying or transfer-printing* on the surface of the glaze which has been fixed by a light firing in the muffle* or enamelling kiln. See below: Underglaze decoration.

Painting. The application of ceramic colours with brushes either on biscuit* ware subsequently glazed (underglaze painting) or on the surface of the glaze (overglaze, onglaze or enamel painting). The finest brushes are known as 'pencils' (as watercolourists' brushes were known in the 18th and early 19th centuries) – hence the occasional use of the term 'pencilled ware' for hand-drawn linear decoration.

Photographic decoration. Decoration based on photographic processes, first used by Wedgwood in 1875. See: Photolithography.

PRINTING (1). Taking a print from between the twin rollers of a modern printing machine. The upper roller is the engraved and inked cylinder which transfers the print to the paper.

PRINTING (2). Applying a coloured lithograph transfer sheet to a 'Globe' shape coffeepot. When the transfer has adhered to the glaze, which has been coated with varnish, the backing paper will be peeled away and the transferred design will be ready to be fired on.

Printing. The technique of transferring engraved patterns to the ware by means of tissue paper and ceramic colour instead of printer's ink. Ceramic printing was invented by John Brooks and developed independently by Sadler* & Green of Liverpool about 1757. Wedgwood bought the right to do his own printing in 1763 but continued for many years to send creamware to Sadler & Green for printing. See also: Lithography; Silk Screen Printing.

THROWING. Forming a vase on a rotating potter's wheel. All thrown pots are by definition circular in section.

Throwing. The art of making ware on the potter's wheel. A ball of soft clay is thrown on to the revolving wheel, centred, and worked into shape with the hands. All wares thus made are circular in section; wares of oval or square section are slip cast*. The jigger*, the jolley* and the lathe* are all developments of the potter's wheel.

TURNING. Shaving excess clay from a vase, in the 'leather' hard state, refining its shape by the use of a horizontally rotating lathe.

Turning. The art of shaping (or turning) on a horizontal lathe*. The ware, in a leather-hard* state, is placed on the 'chum', a hollow drum which holds it in place, and the surface is then shaved with rotary tools as it turns. See: Engine-turning Lathe; Rose Engine-turning.

Underglaze decoration. Decoration which is painted or printed on biscuit* ware (before the glaze is applied). The most common colours are cobalt* blue and the less popular manganese* purple, but many new underglaze colours were added during the 19th century.

Procession of Deities

A large bas-relief* which does not appear in any of Wedgwood's Catalogues up to 1788 but is to be seen on black basaltes*, jasper* and rosso antico* vases of the period c.1800-10. It was probably modelled in Rome, before 1790, by one of the artists working under the supervision of Flaxman* and Webber*, after the *Puteal of the Twelve Gods,* formerly in the collection of Cardinal Albani and now in the Capitoline Museum.

Prodigal Son, The

A series of six scenes illustrating the New Testament parable, possibly engraved by Thomas Radford and certainly printed and enamelled by William Greatbatch* at his pottery, c.1770-80. These prints, which usually appear in pairs on teapots, have not so far been identified on Wedgwood Queen's ware*, but the existence of a Queen's ware teapot enamelled with another subject – *Aurora* – in the same group of decorations by Greatbatch, suggests that they may have been produced. A full set of *Prodigal Son* prints is to be seen on teapots in the Castle Museum, Norwich (Bulwer Collection).

Prometheus

Son of Iapetus and Clymene, and brother of Atlas*. He is the great benefactor of men, stealing fire from heaven to give to them. He also taught them the useful arts. In retribution Zeus chained him to a rock on Mount Caucasus where, every day, an eagle came to feed on his liver, which regenerated itself during the night. Hercules* killed the eagle and released Prometheus.
Wedgwood subject:
The Fable of Prometheus, modelled by Pacetti*, 1788. The description and price paid for this bas-relief suggests that it was a very large composition but no example of it has been found. Individual figures or groups from it may have been reproduced as ornament for vases or medallions.

Proportion

Classical architecture was founded on a fairly rigid system of proportion which has survived in the works of Vitruvius, a Roman military engineer (1st century BC) who wrote the *Ten Books of*

Architecture (now lost) based on Greek authorities. The same system was employed by Renaissance classical architects, and especially by the Palladians, who regarded the works of Vitruvius as a kind of Holy Writ. The system was still employed, with minor modifications, by such neo-classical* architects as the Adam* brothers, with the result that chimneypieces*, for instance, followed more or less the same proportional rules, whatever their size. For this reason, Wedgwood's chimneypiece tablets* were of standard proportions.

During the Renaissance, representation of the human figure was subject to these mathematically-based rules until the development of the Mannerist school after the middle of the 16th century, and a good deal of classical sculpture, including Wedgwood's derivations from classical sources, still followed the proportional tradition. Vitruvius laid down that a man standing with his legs apart and his arms raised and extended to form an X, should be contained within a circle of which the navel was the centre. The unit of measurement was the head, and the body was divided in halves at the pubic bone and subdivided into 'heads'. For example, two 'heads' were allowed from the pubic bone to the knee, and two from the knee to the sole of the foot. Certain special cases, like the muscular Hercules*, were permissible exceptions to some of these rules.

Proprietors of Wedgwood

1759	Josiah Wedgwood I
1766-88	Josiah I and Thomas Wedgwood* (one-eighth share for useful* wares only). Style: Wedgwood
1768-80	Josiah I and Thomas Bentley* (equal shares for ornamental* wares only). Style: Wedgwood & Bentley
1780-88	Josiah Wedgwood I (ornamental wares only). Style: Wedgwood
1788-90	Josiah Wedgwood I (all wares). Style: Wedgwood
1790	Josiah I, his sons John*, Josiah II* and Thomas Wedgwood*, and Thomas Byerley* (one-quarter to each son, one-eighth each to Josiah I and Byerley) Style: Wedgwood, Sons & Byerley
1793	Josiah I, Josiah II and Thomas Byerley (one-half Josiah II, three-eighths Josiah I, one-eighth Thomas Byerley). Style: Josiah Wedgwood, Son & Byerley
1795	Josiah II and Thomas Byerley (Josiah II three-quarters, Byerley one-quarter). Style: Wedgwood & Byerley
1800	Josiah II, John Wedgwood and Thomas Byerley (one-half Josiah II, one quarter each John Wedgwood and Thomas Byerley. Style: Wedgwood & Byerley

1811	Josiah II. Style: Josiah Wedgwood
1823	Josiah II and his son Josiah III* (three-quarters Josiah II, one-quarter Josiah III). Style: Josiah Wedgwood & Son
1827	Josiah II and his sons, Josiah III and Francis* (one half Josiah II, one-quarter each Josiah III and Francis. Style: Josiah Wedgwood & Sons
1841	Josiah III and Francis (equal shares). Style: unchanged until 1895
1842	Francis
1843	Francis Wedgwood and John Boyle* (equal shares; Boyle's half-share to be paid in instalments, profits to be shared equally)
1845	Francis Wedgwood and Robert Brown (Francis three-fifths, Brown two-fifths for four years; thereafter equal shares)
1859	Francis and his son, Godfrey* (Francis four-fifths, Godfrey one-fifth, later altered to three-quarters and one-quarter respectively)
1863	Francis and his sons, Godfrey and Clement Francis* (one-half Francis, one-quarter each Godfrey and Clement)
1868	Francis and his sons, Godfrey, Clement and Laurence* (equal shares)
1870	Godfrey with his brothers, Clement and Laurence (equal shares)
1891	Laurence with his nephews, Cecil* and Francis Hamilton* (equal shares)
1895	Incorporation as Josiah Wedgwood & Sons Ltd
1919-55	Overseas companies formed in America (Josiah Wedgwood & Sons Inc.), 1919; in Canada (Josiah Wedgwood & Sons, Canada Ltd) 1948; and in Australia (Josiah Wedgwood & Sons, Australia, Pty) 1955
1959	Registration of Wedgwood Rooms Ltd
1967	Registration as a Public Limited Company and the shares admitted to the London Stock Exchange. Formation of the Wedgwood Group
1986	Take-over by Waterford Glass. Registration of Waterford Wedgwood PLC

Proserpine

Roman name for Persephone*, the daughter of Zeus (Jupiter*) and Demeter*. She was the wife of Hades (Pluto*) and Queen of the Underworld. With her husband she ruled over the souls of the dead. Wedgwood subject:

Pluto Carrying off Proserpine (also described as *The Rape of Proserpine* or *The Procession of Persephone into the Underworld*), tablet 9in. x 26¼in., modelled by Angelini*, 1789 (possibly 'finished' by De Vaere*).

Protât, Hugues (fl.1825-71)

French sculptor, modeller and designer, who exhibited at the Paris Salon between 1843 and 1850. He came to London where he executed some of the stone carvings adjoining the India Office and worked for a time for Jackson & Graham, makers of elaborately decorated furniture which was said to be in the style of 'all the Louis'. From about 1852 to 1864 he acted as Modelling Instructor

PRUNUS BLOSSOM. Primrose jasper ornamented with white prunus blossom, introduced in 1976.   *Wedgwood Museum*

at the Hanley and Stoke Schools of Design and in 1855 he became chief modeller at Minton's*. Protât settled in London in 1864-5 and about 1871 returned to live in Paris.

The date of Protât's first work for Wedgwood is uncertain. Although there is no documentary evidence of his association with the firm before 1870, it is possible that a few of his models date from a few years earlier. Some of his models are described briefly in the Estimates Book for 1869-80, and surviving examples confirm that the decoration of his larger pieces combined the use of transparent and opaque Majolica* glazes. Some were also decorated with paintings by Lessore*.
See: Colour Plate 91

Prunus Blossom

Raised flowering sprigs of prunus and the tea plant were first used in England about 1690 by the Elers* brothers to ornament their red stoneware teawares and then, in the 1750s, at the porcelain factories, especially Bow* and Chelsea*. They were copied from similar ornament on *blanc de Chine* imported from Tê Hua (Fukien Province, China) and from the red teapots of Yi Hsing. Wedgwood refers to the Elers' use of the tea branch 'in imitation of the Chinese method of ornamenting their ware' in a letter to Bentley* of July 1777. By the 1760s this kind of ornament was already becoming unfashionable, but some rare early creamware pieces are thus ornamented. Josiah Wedgwood made little use of this pattern, but it was used at Etruria*, especially on the dry bodies* during the period of revived popularity of Oriental patterns during the early 19th century, although there are distinct divergences from the Tê Hua types.

Raised prunus blossom was again employed for the ornament of some Majolica* pieces and on Auro basalt* (in both cases with the intention of creating *japonisme** ornament), and it was revived for the ornament of primrose jasper* in 1977.

PROSERPINE. Red wax model *Pluto carrying off Proserpine,* modelled by Giuseppe Angelini in 1789 and reproduced in Wedgwood's jasper shortly thereafter.   *Lady Lever Art Gallery, Port Sunlight*

The prunus blossom appears also on enamelled Queen's ware and bone china* patterns of the second half of the 19th century, again intended as *japonisme*.

Psyche
Psyche is the personification of the human soul. She excited the jealousy of Aphrodite (Venus*) by her beauty. In revenge, Cupid* was ordered to inspire her with love for the meanest of men but fell in love with her himself. Unseen, and unknown, he visited her every night, but one of her sisters. curious about the mysterious lover, brought a light to see him asleep. A drop of hot oil fell on Cupid's shoulder and, waking, he fled. After many wanderings in search of him, Psyche was made immortal and united with her lover.
Wedgwood subjects:
Psyche, figure, height 8in., after the marble (1757) by Falconet*, supplied, probably in the form of a cast, as a companion to that of *Cupid* by Flaxman senior* in 1781. Both figures were produced in black basaltes* (frequently reproduced in the 19th and early 20th centuries), in Carrara* and in Majolica* glazes, and they exist both as single figures and together on a common oval base. This pair of figures was reproduced by Sèvres* in biscuit* porcelain in 1758
Psyche, jasper flower vase, height 8½in. The figure of Psyche with a butterfly kneels beside a tree trunk. Companion to a similar *Cupid* vase
For details of *Cupid and Psyche* tablet*, medallions* and cameos*, see: Cupid.
See also: Flora

Public Experimental Work, 1775
As a consequence of the opposition, led by Wedgwood, to Champion's* application to extend Cookworthy's patent, other potters were free to make what use they wished of Cornish clay and local china stone so long as it did not infringe the patented specification for porcelain. In 1775, Wedgwood, accompanied by John Turner* and Thomas Griffiths*, made an expedition into Cornwall to search for clay on behalf of the Staffordshire potters. As a result of this journey, they decided not to grant exclusive rights, 'which would soon degenerate into a pernicious monopoly', to any factory or company, but to create a 'Public experimental work' controlled by a joint stock company composed of 'potters and subscribers to the opposition to Champions porcelain bill, and the journey into Cornwall'. The primary purpose of this company would be to conduct trials with Cornish materials for the benefit of all members. A committee was elected and agreement was reached to make trials of Cornish and other materials in order to 'improve

our present manufacture, and make an USEFUL WHITE PORCELAIN BODY, with a colourless glaze for the same and a blue paint under the glaze'. As this specification makes clear, the intention was not, as has been suggested, to produce underglaze blue* patterns on Queen's ware* (which Wedgwood had excellent reasons for wishing to avoid) but to create a porcelain body with decoration to compete directly with the underglaze blue-painted porcelains of Worcester* and Liverpool. The project foundered on the rock of disagreement over subscriptions and Wedgwood was left to pursue his own course, which shortly culminated in the invention of jasper. Thereafter, he was no longer greatly interested either in the production of porcelain or in cooperative manufacturing or experimental ventures with other potters.

Public Relations
Wedgwood's Public Relations department was set up in 1955, with Alan Eden-Green, a past-President of the Institute of Public Relations, as its first director. The department was represented on the firm's board of directors by John Hamilton Wedgwood*.

Pug Dog
See: Trump

Pug Mill
A cylindrical mill fitted with knives which ensures the homogeneity of plastic clay by slicing and compressing it, forcing it through a tapered outlet.

Punch and Judy
Teasets with 'Punch and Judy' moulded handles and spouts, and salad bowls with similar handles, decorated with transparent and semi-opaque Majolica* glazes (pattern no.M2730), were made at Etruria* c.1878. *Punch* designs were also registered in 1878 for the decoration of a variety of objects, including teaware and a beer set, of Queen's ware* with an ivory glaze.

Punch Bowl
A large circular bowl, without cover, for the service of punch. Wedgwood made Queen's ware* punch bowls, about 10½in. in diameter, from c.1764, usually decorated by Sadler* & Green with transfer-printed* scenes, such as *The Pipe and Punch Party, The Sailor's Farewell* and *The Sailor's Return*. Some were decorated with as many a eleven prints and Sadler complained in 1764 that they were 'so tedious in firing and attended with so great Loss'. Later punch bowls, made in the 19th and 29th centuries, were larger, measuring up to 32in. in diameter and being raised on a

PUNCH BOWL. Queen's ware punch bowl, the interior enamelled with a coat of arms and a band of fruiting vine, the exterior with a band of *Strawberry* pattern no.84. Diameter 12½in. c.1790.
Manchester City Art Gallery

waisted circular foot. Bowls of this type were in production, in such patterns as *Napoleon Ivy*, as late as 1955.

Punch Glass Stand
A circular stand, with pierced and moulded gallery, standing on three paw feet with a central baluster stem supporting a pierced basket or cup, used for punch glasses or cups, the central cup being used for sliced fruit and spices.

PUNCH GLASS STAND. Queen's ware punch glass stand with pierced and moulded gallery. Height 8¼in. c.1785.
Temple Newsam House, Leeds

Punch Pot (Punch Kettle)
A large vessel resembling in shape an outsize teapot, but usually lacking the interior strainer at the base of the spout. Punch pots were used for brewing and serving hot punch (a blend of spirits and milk or water, flavoured with oranges, lemons, sugar and spices).

PUNCH POT (KETTLE). Queen's ware punch pot transfer-printed with hunting scenes after James Seymour. Height 7in. c.1775.
Formerly Buten Museum

Some examples have bail handles* of the type associated with rum kettles*, but the latter are smaller in size and usually have beak-shaped pouring lips instead of curved spouts. Whieldon-Wedgwood* and Wedgwood punch pots were made in creamware decorated with coloured glazes, in Queen's ware* (often decorated with Sadler* & Green transfer-prints* or enamelled flowers), black basaltes* and other dry bodies*.

Purple of Cassius
A ceramic pigment, varying in shade from purple to pink, but generally a reddish-purple colour, precipitated from chloride of gold mixed with chloride of tin by a process invented by Andreas Cassius of Leyden, c.1673. Taken to China by Jesuit missionaries, it became the principal pigment of the *famille-rose** palette. It has been much used for the decoration of porcelain, especially at Meissen* and at Strasbourg, where it was used also for *faïence*. Rhodes mixed a pigment of this kind for use on Wedgwood's Queen's ware*.
See: Calx Cassii; Rhodes, David

Puxley, David (b.1943)
Studio potter at Barlaston*, 1964-7; studied at Oxford School of Art and taught at St Edward's School. His work is marked 'DP' impressed.

Pye, John (1745- after 1775)
Engraver who worked for Sadler* & Green, Liverpool. A pupil of Thomas Major*, he engraved the nine plates for the first Wedgwood Queen's ware* Catalogue of 1774, which he both prepared and printed. Pye engraved landscapes for the print seller, John Boydell*, and supplied views for the Frog* service.

Pylades
See: Orestes

Pyrometer
The word 'thermoscope' is often used as an alternative term for an instrument for measuring those extremely high temperatures which are beyond the range of the ordinary mercury thermometer. Modern conditions demand an ability to measure temperatures in excess of 3000°C, but when Josiah Wedgwood began his career as an independent potter the only way in which a kiln master could judge the temperature of a kiln was by observing the colour of the interior fire, which he did by withdrawing a small plug set in the kiln wall. Success or failure depended to a great extent on this man's skill and experience.

No one with Josiah Wedgwood's logical mind and desire for experiment could remain content with a state of affairs which left so much to chance, and he began by placing trial pieces in different parts of the kiln to observe the effect of variations in temperature arising from position in the oven. These wares were marked 'GO', 'BO, and 'WO', meaning Glost (or Gloss) Oven, Biscuit Oven and White Oven respectively. The glost oven was used to fuse the glaze,

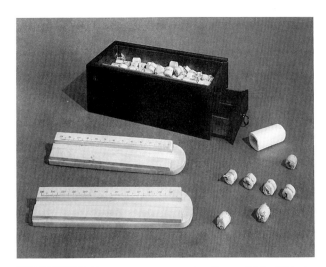

PYROMETER. Pyrometer set presented to George III in 1786, the mahogany box containing stock of pyrometric clay cylinders.

Science Museum, London

the biscuit oven to fire ware to the biscuit* or unglazed state, and the white oven for hard-fired stonewares* or porcelain*. Of these, the glost oven had the lowest temperature and the white oven the highest. The letters 'B', 'M' or 'T' prefaced to the letters denoted the bottom, middle or top of the oven, the letters 'TT' referring to the highest point of all. The letters 'TBO' which have in the past been

mistaken for the sign manual of Mr Tebo*, actually meant 'Top of the biscuit oven'. These letters are normally seen only on trial pieces.

In 1780, Wedgwood experimented with a red-burning clay by withdrawing trial pieces from the kiln at two-hourly intervals while the temperature was still rising, and the colour changes in these trials suggested to him the possibility of constructing a thermoscope which would enable clay cylinders of a standard composition to be matched against a set of cylinders fired at known temperatures and ranging in colour from buff (low temperature) to red (high temperature). This instrument has recently been re-constructed at Barlaston* when the temperature range was found to be from 950° to 1250°C. In 1781 Sir Joseph Banks*, then President of the Royal Society*, advanced the objection that few people could reliably match colours. Wedgwood then turned to the possibility of using the shrinkage of clay during firing as a method of temperature measurement. No doubt he had noticed that the cylinders of his thermoscope became uniformly smaller as the firing temperature increased.

His first sketch for his pyrometer (which he always referred to as a thermometer) was dated 1 January 1782. This consisted of two straight-edged wooden rulers mounted on a baseboard. They were half-an-inch apart at the top and one-third of an inch apart at the bottom. One of the rulers was marked with a graduated scale. He then prepared small clay cylinders two-fifths of an inch high and a half-inch in diameter. The clay cylinder was fired and allowed to cool, shrinking as it did so by an amount proportinate to the temperature to which it had been subjected. It was then placed between the rulers and pushed along until it would go no further, and the temperature at this point was read off the scale, graduated in degrees Wedgwood, which ran from 0 to 240. This pyrometer soon

PYROPHOROUS SET. Six biscuit models for pyrophorous sets, some combined with inkstands, for reproduction in Wedgwood's 'dry' bodies. c.1815-20.

Wedgwood Museum

became widely known, and since it was the first instrument to provide anything like an accurate estimate of temperature it was in great demand for many scientific purposes, apart from potters' kilns.

Wedgwood began by having the pyrometers made in brass, but this was an expensive metal in the 18th century, and by the autumn of 1783 he was experimenting with pyrometers of stoneware and porcelain. From 1786 pyrometer sets were being made in buff stoneware and boxed. Two gauges were supplied, one reading from 0 to 120, the other from 120 to 240, 60° Wedgwood on the pyrometer scale being equivalent to 1100°C. A set presented to George III for his collection of scientific instruments is now in the Science Museum, South Kensington. Additional clay cylinders were obtainable ready packed from the Etruria* factory, and an instruction booklet, probably included with the boxed sets, was available from 1784. One thousand copies of a French translation were printed in 1785, and 500 copies in German in the following year.

Wedgwood noted in his Commonplace Book* the temperatures on his own scale at which a number of different bodies were fired: Delftware 'by a heat of 40 or 41 degrees' (Wedgwood); Queen's ware by 86; and 'Stoneware, called by the French *pots de grès'*, by 102. He was able also to determine at what temperatures examples of finished pottery and porcelain of any age had been fired, and discovered that his own samples of Roman and Etruscan pottery had been fired at between 20 and 32 degrees on the pyrometer scale. In another experiment, he found to his gratification that Queen's ware 'bears the same heat as the Dresden [Meissen* porcelain], and the body is as little affected by this intense fire.'

On 9 May 1782 Wedgwood's paper entitled *An Attempt to make a Thermometer measuring the higher Degrees of Heat, from a red Heat up to the strongest that the Vessels made of Clay can support* was read to the Royal Society*, and eight months later, proposed by James Stuart*, Josiah Wedgwood was elected Fellow of the Royal Society. He presented further papers to the Society in 1783, 1784 and 1786, the last two concerned with improvements to the pyrometer. Wedgwood's invention of the pyrometer greatly assisted him in the long series of trials which resulted in the successful production of jasper copies of the Portland vase* in 1790.

In his experiments to develop the pyrometer, Wedgwood was ably assisted by Alexander Chisholm*, and he was consulted again in 1805, when Josiah II sought to make further improvements to the instrument. The experiments made at that time have special relevance to the mysterious '2 February 1805' mark (See: Appendix II, Marks).

Buller's rings are a development of Wedgwood's pyrometer,

still in use today. After firing, the ring is put into a brass gauge engraved with a temperature scale and fitted with a pointer. Temperature is judged by the amount of shrinkage.

Until recent times temperatures were commonly measured by cones invented by Seger at the Berlin porcelain factory. In Europe they are usually known as Seger cones, and a similar device in America is called the Orton cone. Seger cones are in the form of a small three-sided pyramid, and there are about sixty different compositions, ranging from low-temperature glaze material to pure alumina, with a temperature range of 5000° to 2000°C. The attainment of the temperature for which a particular cone is designed is indicated by the tip of the pyramid, which softens and curves over. In the modern tunnel kiln temperatures are maintained at the correct level by thermo-couples which adjust the gas or electricity supply as necessary.
See: Kilns

Pyrophorous Vase
A sophisticated form of the 'Instant Light Box', a contrivance introduced in 1810 to provide ignition more conveniently than by use of the flint-and-steel tinder box and before the invention of the sulphur-tipped match. It consisted of a sliver of wood, the head tipped with sulphur (later coated with a mixture of chlorate of potash, sugar and gum), which ignited on touching concentrated sulphuric acid. It was marketed in the form of a metal box of 'matches' and a small glass bottle containing the acid. Wedgwood appears to have been the first pottery manufacturer to make these objects as decorative ceramic pieces, and they were produced at Etruria* in good quantities and in every type of dry body* and in bone china* between 1812 and 1817. Production of dwindling quantities continued until about 1827 when the first friction matches, known as 'Lucifers' or 'Congreves', were invented by John Walker of Stockton-on-Tees. Until the publication of an important article by John des Fontaines and Lynn Miller (*Ceramics,* III, May-June 1986), Wedgwood's pyrophorous vases were invariably catalogued as inkwells, several shapes of which were adapted for this use, with additional apertures for the acid bottle and the 'matches'. Other shapes included the 'beehive' and the popular dolphin* tripod which had been used for both pastille burners* and oil lamps*. Wedgwood's pyrophorous vases were probably made at the instigation of Accum & Garden, a firm of chemists in Compton Street, Soho, to whom they were supplied. They were made also by Spode*, and Josiah Byerley* remarked with some irritation in 1812: 'I do not know how it is he [Spode] gets up every new thing we have almost directly…I almost think he must get patterns from Etruria.'

QUEEN'S WARE. Queen's ware turned jug enamelled in polychrome with a mounted cavalryman within a *Green Oat* cartouche. Height 8in. c.1786.
Wedgwood Museum

QUEEN'S WARE. Part of a *garniture* of early Queen's ware vases with covers, the bodies and lids engine-turned, with moulded and applied ornament. Height 11in., 12in. and 13in. Unmarked. Wedgwood, c.1765. *From the Saltram House Collection, National Trust. Photograph: Courtesy of* Country Life

Queen's Shape
See: Tableware Shapes

Queen's Vase, The
Bone china* vase with heraldic figures of the 'Queen's Beasts' co-operatively made to commemorate the Coronation of Queen Elizabeth II in 1953 and presented to Her Majesty by the British Pottery Manufacturers' Federation. The decoration and moulding of the vase were shared by the Wedgwood, Worcester*, Minton*, Derby* and Copeland (Spode*) factories. A replica of the vase was sent to each country of the Commonwealth.

Queen's Ware
Wedgwood's cream-coloured ware*, or creamware was renamed Queen's ware in 1766, after the official announcement of Josiah Wedgwood's appointment as 'Potter to Her Majesty [Queen Charlotte*]'. This was some months after the delivery of the Queen's tea service, late in 1765, the date usually given for the change of name. Wedgwood's creamware and also coloured bodies* are still known as Queen's ware and the name has come to be used, erroneously, as a generic term for the creamware of other factories.
See: Colour Plate 92

QUEEN'S WARE. Large teapot transfer-printed by Guy Green with a portrait of Admiral Keppel within a floral and scroll cartouche. Height 7½in. 1779-82. *Dr & Mrs Alvin M. Kanter Collection*

QUEEN'S WARE. Egg stand with five footed egg cups and two matching custard cups decorated with a vine border and agricultural and other devices in brown enamel. Tray diameter 9¼in. c.1802.
Merseyside Museums

QUEEN'S WARE. Early 19th-century Queen's ware, including a water or milk ewer, food warmer or nursery lamp with kettle top, porringer, soup tureen and stand with ladle and parapet-shape coffeepot, all illustrated in the '1817' Catalogue. *Wedgwood Museum*

QUEEN'S WARE. Charger painted by Alfred Powell in shades of brown and gold. Diameter 18in. c.1923. *Formerly Buten Museum*

QUIVER VASE. Pair of solid blue and white jasper 'Quiver' vases, the domed lids ornamented with pairs of doves. Height 8⅝in. c.1795.

Dwight & Lucille Beeson Collection, Birmingham Museum, Alabama

Quintal Vase
See: Finger Vase

Quirk, William (fl. 1769-74)
Painter at the Chelsea Decorating Studio* who worked on the Frog* service.

Quiver Vase
Jasper* vase in the shape of four quivers mounted back to back on a circular base, the feathered arrow shafts forming a gallery to the top. The domed cover (usually missing) has a finial in the form of two doves. The fronts and sides of the quivers are moulded with panels of horizontal fluting. A fine pair of these vases, complete with covers, is in the Beeson* collection. Quiver vases, which first appeared in solid jasper towards the end of the 18th century, were reproduced, also in solid jasper, after 1860. A similar, though not identical shape was made in Queen's ware* and decorated in panels with figures of children by Emile Lessore*.

QUIVER VASE. Pair of Queen's ware 'Quiver' vases painted with figures of children by Henry Brownsword in the style of Emile Lessore. Signed with monogram. Height 6¼in. c.1870.

Sotheby's, London

Radish Dish
An oval, lobed dish, about 8½in. x 11½in., made in Queen's ware* (shape no.1318), c.1770 onwards. An example, painted in rose-purple with a single flower centre and *Husk* border, is in the Wedgwood Museum*.

Radix Amethyst
See: Blue John

Radix Jasperini
Wedgwood's name for cawk* or barium sulphate*, (no.74 in Wedgwood's code), the principal ingredient of jasper*. 'Radix jasperini' was an invented term, used by Wedgwood as an alternative to the numerical code in his letters to Bentley*.
See: Codes and Formulae; Industrial Espionage

Raised Gold
See: Gilding

Ramshaw, Wendy FSIAD (b.1939)
Jewellery designer; Freeman of the Worshipful Company of Goldsmiths; winner of a Council of Industrial Design Award, 1972 and the De Beer Diamond International Award, 1975. In 1982 an exhibition of Wendy Ramshaw's jewellery produced from or incorporating Wedgwood jasper and basalt was held at the Victoria & Albert Museum, London. The jewellery was deliberately designed in three categories: individual pieces made up by the artist from jasper or basalt supplied by Wedgwood to her specifications; limited editions* of pieces also made by the artist; and pieces produced in larger quantities by others from her prototypes. Wedgwood's cooperation in this new venture was described by Ramshaw as 'a generous form of patronage', which enabled her to take advantage of materials and the special skills of the turners (see: Processes of Manufacture – *Turning*) at Barlaston*, neither of which would otherwise have been available to her.

Raphael (Raffaelle) Ware
Raffaello Sanzio da Urbino (1483-1520), the great Renaissance painter, employed motifs decorating the then newly-discovered Golden House of Nero to ornament the walls of the *loggie* of the Vatican. These motifs, now known as grotesques*, became popular with the painters of *maiolica**, especially those of Urbino, where Raphael's paintings were also copied with the aid of engravings by Marcantonio Raimondi. For this reason Urbino *maiolica* became widely and inaccurately known as Raffaelle ware, and it was believed that he had painted some of it himself. In England, certain types of Italian *maiolica,* notably that decorated with grotesques and *istoriato* painting, became known as 'Raphael ware' and this term lingered well into the 19th century.

In November 1768 Wedgwood wrote to Bentley* from London: 'Do you remember what Harrach [Thomas Harrache*] asked for the Raphael bottles? I think it was 10 Guineas. They now want twenty-five!'. Next year Craft* was deputed to copy the Duke of Argyll's 'Raphael' vases when it was proposed that Wedgwood should attempt something in that style on Queen's ware*, but the idea was abandoned, probably because of the shortage of sufficiently skilled painters. All the painters that Wedgwood, and Bentley in London, were able to train to their high standards were needed for encaustic* painting on black basaltes* vases and, in 1773-4, to decorate the Frog* service.

In the 1860s 'Raphaelesque porcelain', an ivory-toned body sometimes decorated with coloured reliefs in the style of 18th-century Doccia*, was made by Worcester*.

Rattlesnake Seal
Black basaltes seal* made by Wedgwood & Bentley showing a coiled rattlesnake (with thirteen rattles) and bearing the motto

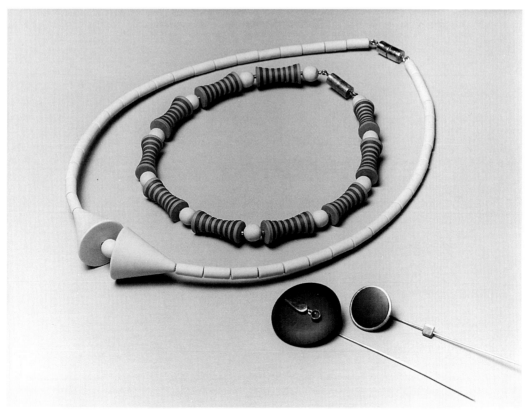

RAMSHAW, Wendy. A selection of jasper jewellery designed for Wedgwood by Wendy Ramshaw in 1982. *Wedgwood Museum*

RAVILIOUS, Eric. Four Queen's ware mugs decorated with designs by Ravilious: *(left to right)* 'Alphabet' printed in black with enamel wash bands; 'Barlaston' mug, decorated by lithography, to commemorate the removal of the Wedgwood factory from Etruria to Barlaston, 1940; Coronation mug, 1937, printed in black and enamelled in Marina green; Coronation mug, 1953, printed in black and enamelled in pink and yellow.

Wedgwood Museum

'DON'T TREAD ON ME', adapted from the design chosen for the Union flag. The original conception has been attributed to Benjamin Franklin, and a description of a Union flag bearing the design appeared in the *London Chronicle* of 1 January 1776. The design was, however, copied from the flag of Christopher Gadsden, a distinguished South Carolinian. The Wedgwood & Bentley seal was intended for distribution to sympathisers with the American cause but, for good commercial reasons, Wedgwood was not anxious to broadcast his own sympathy with the revolutionaries too widely and he therefore warned his partner that it would be prudent to 'keep such unchristian articles for Private Trade.' For this reason the rattlesnake seal, unlike the rest of the Wedgwood & Bentley seals, was usually unmarked.

Ravenstone Glaze
See: Glazes – *Matt*

Ravilious, Eric William (1903-42)
Artist, designer and book-illustrator, born in West London; studied at Eastbourne (Sussex) School of Art and the Royal College of Art, where his tutor was Paul Nash and his fellow students included Henry Moore and Edward Bawden*. In 1935 Cecilia, Lady Sempill introduced Ravilious to the Wedgwoods, who invited him to submit trial designs for tableware patterns and a mug to commemorate the Coronation of Edward VIII. The latter design Ravilious himself described as a 'submerged royal arms with the heads of the royal beasts sticking out of the fireworks above'. It was approved and produced, with enamelled bands of blue and yellow over the design transfer-printed* in black, but withdrawn at the time of the King's abdication. It was reproduced, with minor changes and altered colours, for the coronations of both George VI in 1937 and Elizabeth II in 1953.

RAVILIOUS, Eric. Part of a *Travel* pattern tea service printed in black with underglaze colouring in pale blue on *Windsor Grey* coloured body. Designed 1938, introduced 1953. *Wedgwood Museum*

RAVILIOUS, Eric. Bone china plate printed in gold with *Golden Persephone* border and the Royal Coat of Arms, the pattern, adapted from Ravilious's *Persephone* design, chosen for the Foreign Secretary's Coronation banquet service in June 1953.

Author's collection

362

READING LAMP. Black basaltes oil lamp, the companion model to the 'Vestal' lamp, introduced in the 1770s, reproduced in the 1870s with bronze and gilt ornaments and additional gilding. Height 8½in. c.1875. *Formerly Buten Museum*

Ravilious's first attempts at tableware design, however, were considered too sophisticated for the market and he was asked for something less demanding. He described the firm's 18th-century patterns, which he had examined in the old Pattern Books*, as 'the most perfect pottery designs' he had ever seen, and thought the Wedgwoods 'too timid', and he was irritated by their rejection of his most adventurous drawings. Josiah V*, on the other hand, was ready to produce adventurous and innovative design, and did so, but not at the price of jeopardising the market for Queen's ware*. Like many designers, Ravilious had little understanding of the commercial realities of manufacture or the marketplace.

Josiah V nevertheless had faith in Ravilious and a number of his designs were produced in the full expectation that they were unlikely to prove commercially successful. *Harvest Festival* (later *Persephone)* was introduced at the end of 1936 with wash bands of blue or yellow enamel; and two further versions, banded in green or pink, were added next year. *Garden,* a far more complicated design, was produced in three versions – yellow, blue or green – in 1938, and was made available also, in the same colours, without the centre decoration to the plates. *Alphabet* nurseryware*, *Afternoon Tea,* the *Boat Race* bowl and vase, and *Garden Implements* lemonade sets* were all in production by 1939, and samples of *Noel* (one of the most commercially promising of all Ravilious's designs) were made in 1939 but shelved at the outbreak of World War II. Incomprehensibly, *Noel* has never been revived. Designs for the remarkable *Travel* pattern were also completed and engraved by 1938 but laid aside until 1953. Ravilious's last design for Wedgwood was the mug commemorating the firm's removal to Barlaston* in 1940.

Ravilious's contract with Wedgwood was for only six weeks of the year. On the outbreak of war he resigned and was appointed an official war artist, commissioned as a captain in the Royal Marines. In 1942 the Air Sea Rescue aircraft in which he was travelling failed to return from an operational search off the coast of Iceland.

As an artist, and notably as a war artist, Ravilious's work displays his sure draughtsmanship in a distinctive linear style and a dry use of colour that gives full value to the texture and light provided by the paper. His illustrations for the Golden Cockerel Press, the Cresset Press and the Golden Hours Press show an imaginative use of texture and an unassuming humour, and these qualities are evident, too, in his designs for Wedgwood. In 1953, *Persephone, Garden* and *Travel* patterns were reintroduced (the last on the new Windsor Grey coloured body*) and brought to public notice in the Wedgwood Rooms* (thus circumventing the prejudices of store buyers). They were almost instantly a success. Wedgwood also revived the *Boat Race, Garden Implements* and *Alphabet* pieces to similar effect, and these three designs were reproduced by the silk-screen printing* process in the 1980s. In 1953, the *Persephone* border, printed in gold on bone china* with the Royal Arms as the centre decoration, was chosen for the Foreign Secretary's Coronation banquet service, and the *Persephone* pattern in gold was introduced as a regular bone china service for public sale.

Ravilious is now recognised as one of the most original of the ceramic designers of the 1930s, whose sadly small body of work was of inestimable value to the modern reputation of Wedgwood. His premature death on active service robbed the industry of an artist who would surely have enlivened the appearance of British pottery in the third quarter of the 20th century.
See: Colour Plate 93

Reading Lamp

Boat-shaped lamp on a raised foot and shaped triangular or hexagonal plinth, the handle formed by the finely modelled figure of a seated woman reading a book. A companion to the Vestal* lamp, this model was produced in black basaltes* from c.1775 and reproduced intermittently during the 19th and early 20th centuries. In the latter half of the 19th century it appeared in black basaltes with bronze and gilt ornaments, in bronze and gold basaltes* and enamelled bone china*.

RED CHINA. Teapot with crabstock handle and spout and applied stamped ornament. Height 5⅜in. Unmarked. Staffordshire, c.1755.
Temple Newsam House, Leeds

Red Body
See: Redware; Rosso Antico

Red China (Red Porcelain)
Fine red stoneware usually imitating that of Yi-Hsing which, in the 17th century, was especially popular for teapots. It was made in Germany at Meissen* by J.F. Böttger, in Holland by Arij de Milde, and in Staffordshire by the Elers* brothers, who had originally come from the Cologne region, home of German stoneware. The Elers made red stoneware into the early years of the 18th century, and it continued to be produced as a more or less standard ware by various manufacturers, and especially by Wedgwood, who refined it further and called it rosso antico*. It was never very popular with him (he referred, in a letter to Bentley in 1776, to 'the extreme vulgarity of red wares'). The firm, however, expanded production of it after his death and production of a red body continued into the early 20th century.

Red china, as it is frequently referred to in 18th-century manuscripts, was not a revival of the so-called 'Samian' ware, made in Roman Britain, which was made from a red-burning clay unsuitable for firing above 1100°C and requiring to be dipped in a refined slip to make it impermeable. However, some of the techniques of decoration employed for red china were closely related to those used in Roman times.

Red Figure Style
The decorative style of Greek pottery, c.530-400 BC, the distinctive feature of which is red figures and ornaments reserved on a black ground. A red-burning clay was used for the body of the vase, reserving the figures by covering the remainder of the red surface with a black slip* mixed with wine lees or urine to promote an even flow over the surface. The type was imitated more or less contemporarily in Southern Italy, although the style of decoration differs to a sufficiently marked degree to make it fairly easy to separate Italian from Greek work. The style also inspired Wedgwood's black basaltes* ware painted with encaustic* enamels. The secret of the black slip was supposed, by the 18th century, to have been lost, and there seems to be no evidence that Wedgwood ever experimented with the production of red-figure vases using the ancient slip technique. The Buten* Museum, however, contained a very rare example of a rosso antico* krater* on which the red figures were achieved by painting the remainder of the surface with a black enamel in place of slip, a far more laborious process than the one adopted by Wedgwood of painting red figures on an existing black ground. No Wedgwood example has been found of black-figure painting, the earlier type of Greek vase decoration in which the figures were painted in black slip on a red ground, but copies of Greek pottery thus decorated were made elsewhere in the 19th century.

Red Stoneware
See: Rosso Antico

Red Workhouses
A small pottery for the production of redware rented by Josiah Wedgwood from John Wedgwood of the Big House, Burslem, in 1766 for £10 per annum. Josiah vacated these premises in March 1772, more than three years after production was started at Etruria* and several months after the 'Useful' Works were removed there from the Brick House*.

Reda von Redern, Sigismund Ehrenreich, Baron (1719-89)
Born in Brandenburg, director of the Berlin Academy of Sciences, and a Curator of Berlin University. He retired to France, receiving letters of naturalisation from Louis XV in 1769. He studied physics and chemistry and visited England in 1782, when he accompanied Josiah Wedgwood to Cornwall in search of china clay and pottery materials generally. A jasper portrait medallion* is listed in the 1788 Catalogue.

REDA VON REDERN, Baron Sigismund Ehrenreich. Blue jasper portrait medallion of Baron Reda von Redern, chemist and physicist, who accompanied Josiah Wedgwood on his Cornish journey in 1782. Oval height 3⅜in. c.1787. *Mrs Stanley Rose Collection*

Redgrave, Richard RA (1804-88)
Painter and designer; studied at the Royal Academy Schools; elected member of the Royal Academy 1851; appointed inspector-general for art in the government school of design, 1857; surveyor of the crown pictures. A remarkable shaving-pot entitled 'Heroes Bearded and Beardless' was commissioned from him by Summerly's Art Manufactures and produced in Wedgwood's Pearl* ware with a Parian* lid about 1849.

Reducing Kiln
A kiln the atmosphere of which is heavily charged with carbon monoxide instead of oxygen. It is employed for firing wares coloured with metallic oxides* which yield different colours according to the prevailing kiln atmosphere. For instance, copper oxide used as a glaze colouring will, in the presence of oxygen, yield a variable colour from bluish-green to turquoise, according to the constituents of the glaze itself, but in the presence of carbon monoxide it will give crimson-purple or bluish-red.
See: Lustre Decoration

Redware
Earthenware bodies made from red-burning clays were familiar in Britain from Roman times, when the so-called 'Samian' ware was imported from Gaul and made at Colchester. Later this type of ware was made in much of the country from Hampshire to Carlisle. The body was hard and brittle, unsuitable for firing at temperatures above 1100°C, and required a covering of refined slip to make it impermeable for use with liquids. The slip usually employed contained illite, a mineral which vitrifies at comparatively low temperatures and accounted for the lustrous surface, somewhat similar in appearance to a thin glaze.

Staffordshire redware (known also as red china* or red por-

celain), after the arrival of the Elers* brothers in the final years of the 17th century, was closer in composition to the Chinese red stoneware of Yi-Hsing and the European red china made in imitation of it, notably Böttger's fine red stoneware made at Meissen* from about 1708. Wedgwood made redwares at least as early as 1764, when he is recorded as supplying them to Rhodes* in Leeds, and probably from 1759. Later to avoid any possible association of his refined red stoneware with common Staffordshire redwares, Josiah Wedgwood, who never cared for it, gave it the name 'rosso antico'. After his death, when the body was made in a wider variety of objects and larger quantities, the name was discarded in favour of the older and less pretentious 'redware' or 'red body'.
See: Rosso Antico

Reeding
Also called ribbing. Moulded or turned relief ornament in the form of parallel convex reeds. The reverse of fluting. Reeded moulding appears on certain shapes of all the dry bodies* and on Queen's ware* vases and tablewares.

Refractory
Resistant to the action of heat. Refractory materials which will withstand high temperatures are used by potters for building kilns and for kiln furniture, such as shelves and saggars*. Refractory powder, such as alumina, is used to prevent objects sticking together in the kiln (see: Repairers).
See also: Fireclays

Refrigerator
See: Glacier

Regency Style
The English version of the French Empire style. It is a continuation of the neo-classical* style and is generally accepted as extending from 1805 to 1837, although the Regency itself lasted only from 1810 to 1820. The vocabulary of neo-classical ornament continued to be used, with the addition of Egyptian motifs (see: Egyptian Taste) resulting largely from Napoleon's Egyptian campaign and renewed interest in Egyptian archaeology. Marine motifs, anchors, twisted rope etc., were inspired by Nelson's naval victories. Egyptian motifs, such as the canopic jar* and the sphinx*, employed during the lifetime of Josiah I, were derived principally from illustrations to Montfaucon's *L'Antiquité expliquée* and Caylus's* *Recueil D'Antiquités,* both of which were in Wedgwood's library.

Registry Mark
A Patent Office mark on British manufactured goods using registered designs. The scheme was started in 1842 and was discontinued in 1883, when its place was taken by a system of registered numbers. The mark shows the day, month and year of manufacture and places the object in one of several categories.
See Appendix II, Marks

Rendel, Emily Frances (1840-1921)
Amateur artist; married, in 1866, Clement Francis Wedgwood*; decorated some Wedgwood Queen's* ware during the 1870s but little of it has been identified.

Repairers (Repairing)
Those skilled in the art of making figures, and certain vases, candlesticks etc., from moulded components. The original model was made of clay or wax, and this was dissected by the moulder into convenient parts. Each part was moulded and cast separately and luted together with slip* by a craftsman known as a repairer, who rebuilt the original model from the moulded parts. Those features of the model which might sag under their own weight during firing, such as arms unsupported at the elbow or hand, were propped with clay strips dusted with a refractory* powder (in modern times, alumina) to prevent adhesion to the model.

The design of a figure is very important if it is to be produced in quantity. The designer has to bear in mind the necessity for adapting the figure so that it can be moulded in the fewest number of pieces, and to see that, wherever possible, supports are incorporated into the design so that temporary props are not required during firing. For this reason many figures either have drapery from the waist downwards or are leaning against a tree trunk or a

REDWARE. Engine-turned lidded jug and separate lid. Jug height 4¾in. The separate lid is said to have been found on the Brick House site. Marked with pseudo-Chinese ideogram incorporating the letter 'W', sometimes attributed to Wedgwood. c.1765. *British Museum*

pillar. Parts which are unduly thick and might for this reason lead to firecracks* also have to be avoided. If Wedgwood's figures of Voltaire* and Rousseau* are examined, it will be seen that if they had been posed on their legs alone, there would have been considerable danger of the legs bending or collapsing during firing. Voltaire was therefore given a long cloak and Rousseau a short tree trunk as supports. The jasper* figure of Jupiter* has one hand attached to his head and the other to his body, thus supporting both arms, and his legs are supported to the ankles. In the case of candlesticks*, we find the figures closely clasping the shaft on which the candleholder rests. Good design makes repairing easier and ensures the minimum of kiln wastage.

Slight variations in the poses of figures may arise during the repairing process, but in recent times they have been kept to a minimum by a rigid adherence to a standard, to which the repairer works, and systematic inspection of the finished product. Variations due to this cause are more likely to occur in 18th-century wares.

Wedgwood demanded very high quality in figure work (as in all his wares), not only because it was his policy but also because his figures were unglazed. Jasper and (apart from its colour) black basaltes* are strictly analogous to the biscuit* porcelain body of Derby* (which specialised in biscuit porcelain figures) whose price list has survived. There, only perfect figures were sold in biscuit form. Those with minor imperfections were glazed and painted to disguise the faults and sold more cheaply than the biscuit versions. This is sufficient proof of the market requirements which were being supplied by Wedgwood and Derby.

Resist Lustre
An onglaze process of lustre decoration* ordinarily used in conjunction with 'silver' (platinum) lustre. Designs are painted or printed on ware by using 'resist' material, such as china clay mixed with honey or treacle, wax, varnish or even paper stencils. The lustre, a metallic oxide suspended in an oily medium, is brushed over the surface of the ware, which is then fired. The lustre, of course, does not adhere to the parts treated with the 'resist' material, which burns away in the kiln, leaving behind its simulacrum in the underlying colour of the body or glaze – usually white, but sometimes yellow – the remainder of the glaze being covered with lustre.

Retailing
See: Showrooms; Wedgwood Rooms

Retorts
See: Chemical Wares

Revere, Paul (1735-1818)
American silversmith of Huguenot descent who worked at Boston, and took part in the notorious Boston Tea Party in 1773. Two years later he rode from Charleston to Lexington, rousing the Minute Men on the Way, and in so doing became the hero of Longfellow's poem, *The Midnight Ride of Paul Revere.* Two Wedgwood bowls are based on engravings of his silverwork: the *Boston Bowl,* designed by Alan Price*, and the *Harvard Old Buildings* bowl.
See also: American Independence Series

REVOLVING TRAY. Bone china *déjeuner* set decorated with panels of oriental flowers in typical 'Imari' colours on a revolving circular tray. Diameter 14in. c.1880.

Christie's, London

Revolving Tray

Bone china*, and more rarely Queen's ware* or Pearl* ware, revolving trays (popularly known as 'Lazy Susans') were made at Etruria* during the last quarter of the 19th century and the first quarter of the 20th. They were decorated with handpainted or print and enamel* patterns to match the patterns of tea, coffee and breakfast services.

Reynolds, Sir Joshua PRA (1723-92)

Artist, widely regarded as one of the greatest of British portrait painters. A founder member of the Royal Academy (1768) and its first President, Reynolds was also one of the earliest members of the Incorporated Society of Artists. He was born in Plymouth, came to London to study in 1740, and was in Rome, where he studied the work of Raphael and Michelangelo*, from 1749 to 1752. Returning to London, he rapidly achieved a high reputation as a portrait painter. He was knighted in 1769 and was appointed painter to the King in 1784. He ceased to paint in 1789, when his eyesight failed, and died two years later. His portraits of Josiah Wedgwood and Sarah Wedgwood* (now in the Wedgwood Museum*) were painted in 1782, the former being engraved in mezzotint by John Taylor Wedgwood* and Samuel W. Reynolds. Reynolds introduced the modeller Henry Webber* to Wedgwood and gave a testimonial to the quality of Wedgwood's copy of the Portland vase*. His portrait medallion*, sometimes attributed (without evidence) to Flaxman*, was modelled c.1787.

Wedgwood bas-relief subjects inspired by paintings by Reynolds include *Infant Academy,* 1787; and *Music* (modelled by Hackwood* as a companion to the last).

REYNOLDS, Sir Joshua. Lilac jasper dip engine-turned saucer dish ornamented with a group, *Infant Academy,* probably modelled by Hackwood after Reynolds. Diameter 8in. c.1785-90.

Holburne of Menstrie Museum, Bath

Rhead, Frederick Alfred (1856-1933)

Painter and designer; younger brother of G.W. Rhead*; trained at Minton's* under Marc Solon as a pâte-sur-pâte* artist from 1872 but left, with his younger brother Louis, to work for Wedgwood in 1878. Frederick Rhead specialised in the use of slip* decoration and sgraffito* on art pottery* and examples of his work were exhibited in the Paris Exposition of 1878. He later worked for a number of other Staffordshire potteries, becoming art director of Brownfield's in the 1890s. He was co-author, with his brother George, of *Staffordshire Pots & Potters,* published in 1906.

Rhead, George Woolliscroft (1855-1920)

Artist and designer; apprenticed (like his brothers Frederick* and Louis*) to Minton's, where he instructed the artist W.S. Coleman in the use of ceramic colours. Although no evidence has been found that he worked at Etruria*, he is noted in Godfrey Wedgwood's* Letter Books as the designer of commemorative jugs decorated with portraits of Longfellow, Disraeli and Carlyle, c.1880. With his brother Frederick, he was author of *Staffordshire Pots and Potters,* 1906, a work by no means uncritical of Wedgwood.

REYNOLDS, Sir Joshua. Pale-blue jasper dip portrait medallion. Oval height 3¼in. c.1790.

Nottingham Castle Museum

RHEAD, Frederick Alfred. Redware plaque or charger painted with slip and decorated in the sgraffito technique by Frederick Rhead. Diameter 14½in. Signed and dated. 1878. *Christie's, London*

Rhead, Louis (1858-1927)

Painter, poster designer and illustrator; youngest brother of Frederick Rhead* and G.W. Rhead*; trained at Minton's*. With his brother Frederick, he moved from Minton to Wedgwood in 1878, continuing his studies at the Newcastle-under-Lyme School of Art. He moved to London but returned in 1882 to work at Etruria*. In 1883, however, he went to live in the USA and did not return to England until 1896.

Rhodes, David (fl.1763-77)

Independent enameller and partner with Jasper Robinson in the firm of Robinson & Rhodes, 'Chinamen' of Leeds, trading in 'a good Assortment of Foreign China, and a great Variety of useful English China…and all Sorts of Fine Earthenware.' They also undertook ceramic repairs 'without rivetting'. From 1763 they bought various types of ware from Wedgwood, especially colour-glazed teapots in moulded fruit and vegetable shapes, while in return they supplied him with copper dust for the production of his green glaze*. In March 1763 Rhodes took over the business and by the end of the next year Wedgwood was supplying him with creamware teapots and coffeepots (probably for enamelling) as well as colour-glazed wares and redwares*. Rhodes continued to supply Wedgwood with copper, in the form of scales, invoicing 60lb at 7½d a pound in December. In 1768 Rhodes moved to London. Robinson resumed control of the Leeds firm and maintained contact with Wedgwood until 1778-9.

In March 1768 Wedgwood informed Bentley* that he had acquired the lease of premises for showrooms* and offices in Newport Street, London, and had 'already agreed with one very useful Tennant, a Master Enameler, & China piecer [restorer]', whom he described as 'sober & steady….He paints flowers, & Landskips very prettily, prepares a pretty good powder gold, & has a tolerable notion of colours.' This tenant was David Rhodes, and this agreement was the start of a most useful association. Rhodes brought with him a partner, William Craft*.

Rhodes's style of enamelling has now been identified with some confidence, due largely to the pioneer work of Donald Towner (*English Cream-coloured Earthenware,* 1957, and *Creamware,* 1978). The designs, which are known principally on teapots and, more rarely, coffeepots, include varied subjects painted in iron-red and black; simple figures in landscapes, painted in a palette of distinctive rose-pink, red, blue, green, black and yellow; landscapes, in a similar palette, usually on the reverse of teapots painted with figure subjects; naturalistic bunches of flowers, always centred on one or more large roses; bold banded and diaper patterns, sometimes described as 'Chintz'; scale* patterns, usually combined with

RHEAD, George Woolliscroft. Commemorative jug printed with a portrait of Thomas Carlyle within a printed and enamelled thistle frame, designed by George Rhead, 1880-81. Height 8in. 1881. *Private Collection*

flower, landscape or diaper patterns; and rare *chinoiseries* – simple paintings of 'Oriental' figures in landscape or interior settings. Until the end of March 1770 Rhodes remained independent, but soon after that date he became Wedgwood's manager at the Chelsea Decorating Studio and he remained there until his death in 1777. During that period he developed into one of Wedgwood's most valued employees, trusted with closely guarded secrets and with confidential negotiations and purchases of porcelain. Some of his own work is recorded: he is known to have painted some table-wares, candlesticks, 'hooped' flower pots and encaustic-decorated black basaltes* vases and to have worked on the Frog* service; and he is reputed to have been partly responsible for the painting of the First Day's vases*, although Wedgwood's opinion of his skill as a red-figure painter was not high. It was Rhodes who mixed Wedgwood's 'calx cassii'*, and it was he who was given the task of discovering whether Wedgwood's newly-invented white jasper* would take an enamelled finish to provide coloured grounds for bas-relief* ornament. His death in 1777 was undoubtedly a serious loss to Wedgwood and marked the end of the London premises as the centre of high-quality Queen's ware decorating. It was

RHODES, David. Queen's ware teapot enamelled in polychrome with the figure of a man in a typical Rhodes setting, the reverse inscribed 'Success to Sir Charles Holte'. Unmarked. Wedgwood, 1774. *Norwich Castle Museum*

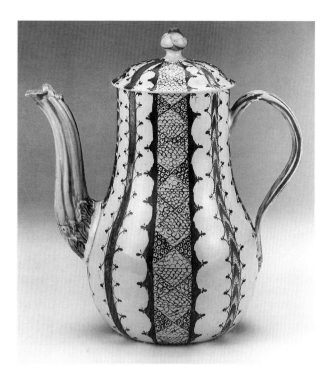

RHODES, David. Creamware coffeepot enamelled with a banded and diaper pattern, the knop, handle and spout enamelled in rose-purple. Height 8⅝in.   *Harrogate Museum*

probably an even greater loss to Bentley* who, after Rhodes's death, bore the whole weight of management in London.
See: Colour Plate 94

Rhodes, James (fl.1880-1923)
Designer and art pottery* decorator who worked at Etruria* between 1885 and 1923.

Rhodian Ware
A series of large Queen's ware* vases and plaques* or chargers handpainted in a mixture of lustre* and enamel colours with decoration in Islamic styles. Some of these designs were probably the work of Alfred and Louise Powell* but the painting was executed by paintresses trained by them and much of it was by Millicent Taplin*. Like the *Persian*-style wares, *Rhodian* designs were produced in the early 1920s.

Rhyton
See: Stirrup Cup

Ribbon and Leaf Border
Neo-classical* border pattern consisting of a continuous twisting ribbon with a leaf in each curve.

Ricardo, Halsey (1854-1928)
Architect and designer, and a leading proponent of the Arts & Crafts Movement*; teacher at the Central School of Art; in partnership with William De Morgan*, 1888-98. In 1881-2 Ricardo was responsible for the redecoration of Lord Dysart's house, Buckminster Park, in Leicestershire, for which he designed at least twelve chimneypieces*. In the colour scheme of the house, he used a particular peach green of his own mixing which was copied by Wedgwood to create a new jasper* colour, generally known as 'Dysart green'. This was used for large rectangular plaques*, tablets* and medallions* to ornament some of the Buckminster chimneypieces. Clement Wedgwood* sent a sample of the new 'peach green colour' jasper to his cousin George Darwin in October. 'This', he wrote, 'is the colour that Mr Ricardo has been using so largely lately in decorating Lord Dysart's house at Buckminster & suits present style of furniture very well.' Evidently Ricardo's work was deemed a success, for Wedgwood commissioned him to produce sketches of jasper plaques 'chiefly of non-classic origin worked into chimneypieces with strips

and tiles' for travellers to use to promote the sales of jasper for this purpose. Although the sketches were produced, nothing seems to have been made of them.

Ridgehouse Estate
A property of about 350 acres, close to Burslem, Staffordshire, overlooking the valley towards Newcastle-under-Lyme. The estate was bought by Josiah Wedgwood in 1767 for £3,000 from the executors of a Mrs Ashenhurst, with whom Wedgwood had been negotiating for more than a year before her death. Although it was not the only property he considered for the site of his new factory, which he later named Etruria, Wedgwood was particularly anxious to buy the Ridgehouse Estate because he knew that it lay directly in the path of the proposed Trent & Mersey Canal*. By the simple addition of a short access canal, this would give him the ability to load goods for conveyance by barge to the ports of Liverpool in the west and Hull in the east.
See: Etruria Factory

Riding, Jessie M. (fl.1919)
Modeller, who executed portrait medallions* of the French World War I leaders, Georges Clemenceau and Ferdinand Foch, in 1919. They were reproduced in jasper* and both are signed on the truncation. The mould of the Clemenceau portrait at Barlaston* is inscribed and dated.

RHODIAN. Design for *Rhodian* pattern no. C5470 handpainted in black and shades of blue, green and purple under a mother-of-pearl glaze with orange lustre edge and band. c.1926.   *Wedgwood Museum*

Rie, Dame Lucie DBE (1902-1995)
Artist-potter, born in Vienna, the daughter of Professor Gomperz, a prosperous medical specialist; married, in 1926, Hans Rie (divorced 1940). DBE, 1990. Lucie Rie studied art at the Kunstgewerbeschule, specialising in ceramics, and by 1925 her work was being exhibited in Paris. Twelve years later she won a prize at the Paris International Exposition. In 1938 Hans and Lucie Rie moved to England, where her growing international reputation as a potter was ignored, although William Staite-Murray at the Royal College of Art helped her to obtain a work permit and W.B. Honey of the Victoria & Albert Museum used his influence to save her from internment during World War II. Although he did not greatly admire her work, Bernard Leach became her friend and strongly influenced her approach to the art of pottery. A second, and – from the point of view of her own development as a potter – more significant influence, was her close friendship with Hans Coper. The market for her work, produced from her studio in Albion Mews, London, grew with her reputation, until, by the 1960s, she was widely recognised as one of the most important artist-potters in Britain.

RICARDO, Halsey. Chimneypiece designed by Ricardo for Buckminster Park, inset with plaques, tablets and a clock face in peach ('Dysart') green jasper. *Photograph: Courtesy Alison Kelly*

In 1960-1 Wedgwood made an attempt to introduce a new style of jasper* by inviting Lucie Rie to make prototypes of teawares. A small quantity of blue and white jasper clay was delivered to her and from this material she created some teacups and coffee cups of solid blue decorated with simple inlaid lines of white. The shapes were original. These were sent to Barlaston*. Sadly for all concerned, Lucie Rie's technique of inlaying was not considered suitable for modern methods of controlled quality production and it was not thought possible to reproduce her designs commercially. The transition from studio pottery to industrial pottery is seldom possible to achieve and the influence on industrial pottery design of the great studio potters of 20th-century Britain – for example, Bernard Leach, Michael Cardew, Hans Coper and Lucie Rie – has been regrettably slight. The criticism of Wedgwood's failure to use Lucie Rie's work has not been well informed (see: Robin Reilly, *Wedgwood,* Vol.II, pp.533 and 776-7).

Rischgitz, Edouard (1828-1909)
Porcelain painter of French origin employed by Minton*, c.1864-70. His figure subjects, landscapes and birds appear principally on Queen's ware* vases and his style and palette are sometimes mistaken for Emile Lessore's*.

Roberts, Ann, Grace and John (fl.1769-74)
Painters at the Chelsea Decorating Studio* who worked on the decoration of the Frog* service. Anne and Grace are recorded as painting borders.

Robinson & Rhodes
See: Rhodes, David

Robinson, Jasper (fl.1761-78)
Partner, with David Rhodes* in Leeds, trading in English and imported china and earthenare, enamelling creamwares and repairing broken china 'without rivetting'. He left the partnership in 1763, at about the time when Wedgwood began supplying various types of ware to Robinson & Rhodes and obtaining copper dust from them.

RISCHGITZ, Edouard. Pair of Queen's ware vases painted with figures. Height 7in. c.1871. *Sotheby's, London*

Robinson again became head of the firm in 1768, when Rhodes moved to London, and maintained some connection with Wedgwood until 1778 or 1779, when he retired and was succeeded by Leonard Hobson.

RISCHGITZ, Edouard. Large Queen's ware vase with snake handles painted with bird subjects. Signed on the foot. Height 20¾in. 1865.
Photograph; Courtesy Earl Buckman

ROCHFORT, J.D. Queen's ware scalloped oval dish painted by Rochfort with a framed self-portrait supported by the skeletal figure of *Death* and an angel holding a cross. Inscribed and dated. 9in. x 11½in. 1863. *Author's collection*

Robinson, John (fl.1793-1819)

Engraver, printer and print-seller of London, who supplied Wedgwood with engravings of the onglaze red-printed *Water Lily* pattern in 1807, the underglaze blue-printed *Water Lily* with cut reed border in 1809, and a large part of the *Corinth* pattern in 1811. See: Underglaze Blue Printing

Rochfort, John D. (fl.1860s)

Independent designer and enameller who either painted on Queen's ware at Etruria* or was supplied with 'blanks', His style often resembles Emile Lessore's so closely as to be indistinguishable from it without an identifying signature and some designs are near-copies of Lessore's work. Others are strange compositions which suggest an oppressive concern with his own mortality. His work is almost invariably signed on the reverse, and sometimes also on the painting.

Rockingham Ware

Ware made in England and America (Bennington Pottery, Vermont), distinguished by a thick, lustrous, often treacly brown glaze, the colour of which was due principally to manganese* and varied from purple through a brownish-red to dark-brown. It was originally developed at the Rockingham factory, Swinton, Yorkshire, c.1796. At Etruria* it was introduced no later than 1823, when it replaced the London Brown glaze and it was used at first for teapots and coffee biggins*, the range later being extended to full tea and coffee services. It was also employed for Magnolia* ware and Vigornian* ware. Wedgwood used the name 'Rockingham' both for the glaze and for the shape on which it usually appeared. Teapots and coffeepots in this shape (which was made in 19th-century black basaltes* and redware*, sometimes enamelled or covered with a contrasting glaze) were given a sibyl* finial. Rockingham ware made at Etruria was frequently impressed 'ROCKINGHAM' as well as 'WEDGWOOD' (although both marks tended to be obscured by the thick glaze) causing some Wedgwood pieces to be attributed to the Swinton factory.

Rococo Style

Term, from the French *rocaille* (shell-work), used originally to describe the ornamenting of grottoes, which became a popular feature of gardens from the end of the 16th century.

The mainstream of European art is classical*, which is also to say that for the most part it adheres strictly to a system of symmetry and proportion* that altered remarkably little in 2,000 years. There was, however, an interregnum provided by the Gothic style, beginning at the end of the 12th century, which had its roots in the architecture of Islam, and another to be found in the short-lived rococo style which begins to be apparent at the end of the 17th century, and for most practical purposes may be regarded as over before the accession of Louis XVI in 1774. This, too, owed much of its original inspiration to the Orient, but in this instance to China and Japan. The Gothic style manifested itself mainly in architecture, the rococo style in the decorative arts, and especially in porcelain and silver. Both Gothic and rococo abandoned the

ROCHFORT, J.D. Two painted Queen's ware chargers illustrating the similarity between the styles of Lessore and Rochfort. *(Left)* Diameter 12¼in., signed by Lessore, 1862; *(right)* diameter 12½in., signed and dated by Rochfort, 1865. *Mr & Mrs David Zeitlin Collection*

strict principle of symmetry and it is not entirely coincidental that a revival of the Gothic style took place around 1750, when rococo was at its most fashionable. The rococo style was followed by the neo-classical*, sometimes known in England as the Adam* style and in France as the Louis Seize style.

The impact of rococo in England was not so great as it was on the Continent. It is chiefly to be seen in the furniture of Chippendale and his followers, the silver of those of Huguenot descent, or the work of more recent arrivals such as Paul de Lamerie or Nicolas Sprimont (the latter one of the founders of the Chelsea* porcelain factory) and of the early porcelain factories.

It has been said that Wedgwood did not work in the rococo style, and more frequently asserted that he produced no rococo shapes or designs after the start of his partnership with Bentley*, under whose influence he became a convinced neo-classicist. Neither statement is accurate. Wedgwood's early wares, especially the colour-glazed wares in fruit and vegetable shapes, are evidently rococo; and for many years after the start of his partnership with Bentley, who was certainly a confirmed classicist, Wedgwood continued to copy the shapes of rococo Sèvres* and to produce shell-edge tablewares and shell-shaped dessert wares. Although it cannot be said that Wedgwood ever entirely abandoned the rococo style, he nevertheless became, with the help of Bentley, Sir William Hamilton* and John Flaxman*, in particular, the leading manufacturer in the neo-classical style.

Wedgwood's rococo products include those early wares with crabstock* handles and spouts or rococo silver-pattern handles; probably some moulded *chinoiseries** patterns on teapots and tea canisters, though none of these is proved to be Wedgwood's; fruit and vegetable (notably pineapple and cauliflower) shapes; moulded fruit, flowers or landscape patterns; cornucopiae* (the tips twisted to one side in typical rococo asymmetry); scale patterns (see: Rhodes, David); twisted double strap handles terminating in moulded leaf-shapes; floral knops; all shell shapes, and especially the shell-edge tableware shape*; shell and seaweed patterns (introduced as print and enamel patterns by Guy Green* in 1776); and shell terminals to handles of jasper pieces. Wedgwood's transfer-printed patterns include a number which are obviously rococo, such as the 'exotic' birds* (later called 'Liverpool' birds), which are not too distantly derived from Sèvres bird painting in the rococo style by Evans and Aloncle.

During the 19th century, in spite of the eclecticism of the time, the revival of rococo in the 1830s and the application of revived Gothic to pottery design by A.W. Pugin and others, Wedgwood remained remarkably faithful to the neo-classical style. The style of some of the more ornate wares of the 1860s might be termed neo-baroque, but hardly rococo, a particular example being the ewer designed by Protât* and painted by Lessore*, which is remarkable for scrolling acanthus, a female figure perched precariously on the shoulder, and an infant clutching the entwined foliate handles. This is obviously based on 17th-century metalwork, and Protât probably took it from a design book of the period, of which there were many in existence. In

ROCKINGHAM WARE. Queen's ware coffeepot with sibyl knop decorated with Rockingham glaze. Height 11¼in. c.1870. *Kadison Collection*

ROCOCO. Queen's ware coffeepot, printed in brown and enamelled in bright green with sprays of flowers. Height 9½in. c.1778. *Sotheby's, London*

the 20th century the factory has continued to develop its own style which is soundly based on tradition inherited from the 18th century, and it is instructive to see, in the 1990s, tableware designs from the first Pattern Book* being successfully revived.
See: Colour Plate 95

Roman Procession
Tablet, 9½in. x 21in., no.237 in the 1787 Catalogue*, sometimes described as *Procession of Senators*. The subject is a composition based on the relief on the north side of the Ara Pacis, celebrating

ROMAN PROCESSION. Black basaltes tablet, *A Roman Procession*. 9¾in. x 20½in. c.1790. *Kadison Collection*

ROMANTIC STYLE. Green jasper dip medallion, *Study,* modelled by Hackwood from a design by Lady Templetown. Oval length 4½in. c.1790.   *Mr & Mrs David Zeitlin Collection*

the victories of Augustus. The original now shows much late restoration which differs noticeably from the Wedgwood version. In addition, the latter includes the figure of a youth (also appearing on the extreme left of the *Death of a Roman Warrior** tablet), from a relief on the second-century monument of Hadrian. Its appearance in the 1787 Catalogue suggests that the *Roman Procession* composition was not, as has previously been supposed, modelled at Wedgwood's Rome atelier but rather supplied as a cast or mould from Mrs Landré* or Hoskins & Oliver* and set aside until the 1780s.

Romantic Style
The Romantic Movement in the arts in Europe was a widespread reaction, which took place during the late 18th and early 19th centuries, against the accepted principles (see: Proportion) of classical art developed by the Greeks. The distinction between the aims of classical and romantic art was made by Heinrich Heine: 'Classical art had to express only the finite, and the forms could be identical with the artist's idea; romantic art had to represent, or rather to typify, the indefinite and the spiritual, and had therefore to be expressed symbolically.' While classical art aimed at symmetry and perfection of form, romantic art sought to express individuality and emotional intensity. But it is precisely this search for individuality which – because of the diversity of the work that it inspired – makes the movement so hard to define. The Romantics claimed to possess heightened sensibilities, which were deemed necessary to the creation of art, and may be discerned in the work of such supreme artists as Schubert, Brahms, Delacroix, Turner, Goethe, or Wordsworth, but which were also responsible for an outburst of sentimentality. The most important influence on Romantic art in the 18th century was undoubtedly Goethe's autobiographical novel, *The Sorrows of the Young Werther,* 1774.

The Romantic style of ornament may be seen on Wedgwood's jasper from about 1785, most notably in the work of Lady Templetown* and Emma Crewe*, the bas-reliefs of *Maria* and *The Bourbonnais Shepherd* (no.251 in 1787 Catalogue*) taken from Sterne's *Sentimental Journey,* 1768, and *Charlotte at the Tomb of Werther* (no.272 in 1787 Catalogue) being the most obvious examples.
See: Colour Plate 96
See also: Classicism; Neo-classical Style

Rome
Rome in the 18th century was not only the most important staging post on the Grand Tour but also a place of pilgrimage for artists, and especially for sculptors. Despite the attention paid to Pompeii* and Herculaneum*, the importance of Rome to the neo-classical* artist and designer was undiminished. It is not surprising, therefore, that Wedgwood should decide to employ a number of artists in Rome under the direction of John Flaxman* and Henry Webber*. The work of those artists was either adapted on the spot to the

needs of the factory by Flaxman, Webber or De Vaere*, or sent on to Etruria* to be worked on by Hackwood* and the factory modellers. In addition to De Vaere, several Italian modellers were employed, notably Dalmazzoni* (whose letters to Josiah Wedgwood and accounts supply most of the surviving evidence about the atelier and the modellers employed there), Angelini*, Pacetti* and Mangiarotti*. The names of Manzolini*, Fratoddi* and Cades* also are recorded, but as suppliers of 'pieces of marbles', shell cameos* and gems* respectively, and it is not certain that any of them produced models or casts.

The modellers were principally engaged in making copies, adaptations and reductions of the work of classical and Renaissance sculptors, much of it from the Capitoline Museum and much of it 'improved' to supply missing heads and limbs or to complete compositions. Such models cannot properly be described as 'copies' from the antique although their classical source is often both evident and traceable.

In 1790 Wedgwood complained to Flaxman about the 'nakedness of the figures' on a number of compositions, especially De Vaere's, after the antique. This was an objection which he described as 'insurmountable.' As he explained: 'To clothe them would not only be a great increase of labour, but would require the hand of an experienced master in the art, & besides the piece would not then be a copy of the antique. I know the nudities could be covered with leaves but that is not enough…none either male or female of the present generation will take them as furniture if the figures are naked.' Evidently Wedgwood was persuaded, probably by Flaxman, that a certain amount of classical nudity (distinct from offensive nakedness) was respectable, for several of the bas-reliefs modelled in Rome, as well as a number taken from earlier casts, include male and female nudes in their compositions. Many of the original models were of wax and a number of them are preserved in the Lady Lever Art Gallery, Port Sunlight.
See: Wax Portraits, Wax Models

Root Dish
An early term, used by Wedgwood in 18th and early 19th-century catalogues, for a covered vegetable dish.

ROOT DISH. Pearl ware root dish printed underglaze in blue with *Botanical Flowers* pattern. 7¼in. x 13in. x 6½in. c.1815.
                    Author's collection

Root Pot
See: Bulb Pot

Rose Engine-Turning
Curved, symmetrically-disposed, repetitive ornament of a geometric kind incised into the body of some stonewares (and, more rarely, Queen's ware*) with the aid of the engine-turning lathe by using a guide tool known as a rose or rosette*.

Rosette
1. A stylised rose with the petals equally disposed on a circular plan, sometimes with leaves in addition. The 'Tudor rose' characteristic of some Whieldon* and Whieldon-Wedgwood* relief ornament on creamware and redware is a rosette of this type.
2. A special tool which, when fitted to the engine-turning lathe*, enables curved patterns to be cut.

ROSSO ANTICO. Inkstandish in the form of a boat with griffin's and crocodile's heads at the prow and stern, a lotus-shaped candleholder, canopic vase inkwell, and pounce pot and sander, ornamented in black with 'Egyptian' motifs, including hieroglyphics. Length 11¾in. c.1810.
Merseyside Museums

ROSSO ANTICO. Rosso antico vase, the body dipped in black slip and engine-turned, the interior glazed. Height 6¾in. c.1785.
Wedgwood Museum

Rosset, Jean Claude, 'Du Pont' (1703?-86)
See: Voltaire

Rosso Antico

Wedgwood's name for a refined red dry body*, similar in properties to black basaltes* and cane* ware, developed from Staffordshire redware*. It is the single example of a type of ware suggested by Bentley* and made against Josiah Wedgwood's inclination. Conscious of the inevitable comparison between any red stoneware he might make, however fine, and what he called a 'red-Pot-Teapot', Wedgwood was reluctant to develop it, unsatisfied with it when he had succeeded, made little use of it, and never listed it in his catalogues.

To judge by unmarked examples which are attributed to them, the redwares made by both Whieldon* and Wedgwood* were of excellent quality, and the use of the engine-turning lathe, after 1763, greatly increased the styles of decoration which could be achieved.

In 1770 Wedgwood had a plan for lightening the colour of the body and using it for red-figure* vases by painting the black ground around the figures. This was the reverse of his patented method and technically more difficult and the proposal was soon abandoned. Two years later, he made his first fluted teapots and bough pots*, the hollows of the fluting decorated with black slip to produce a handsome striped effect. Other projects, notably the production of the Frog* service and experiments for the production of jasper*, hindered any further progress until 1776, when Bentley* asked for cheap cabinet medals to be made in the red body, and in March Josiah mentioned the body for the first time by the new name he favoured, telling Bentley: 'we shall never be able to make a *Rosso Antico* otherwise than to put you in mind of a red-Pot-Teapot.'

Nevertheless, he went ahead with production of the body, even producing some tablets*, evidently intended for sale to architects and builders, but these were not a success and production of them was stopped at the end of 1776, although Wedgwood expressed his willingness to make them again if they were required. An un-

ROSSO ANTICO. D-shaped bulbpot, the rosso antico body dipped in black basaltes slip and engine-turned in a diced pattern, with applied paterae. The loose grid is furnished with two cups for large bulbs, such as hyacinths, and pierced holes for smaller bulbs. Width 7¼in. c.1790.
Christie's, London

ROSSO ANTICO. Pastille burner vase, shape no.43, ornamented with figures from the Borghese vase. Height 15½in. c.1830-50.
Christie's, New York

marked medallion of *Venus and Cupid* in rosso antico on a black basaltes ground (City Museum & Art Gallery, Stoke-on-Trent) may be a trial from this period, but portrait medallions* of Shakespeare and Milton, in the collection of Dr Alvin Kanter (illustrated in Eleventh Wedgwood International Seminar *Proceedings,* 1963, p.26) are probably c.1785-90. Rosso antico busts of George II* and John Locke are recorded and others from this period may exist, but such pieces are rare. After Bentley's death in 1780, there was little incentive for Josiah Wedgwood to continue to produce wares in a body which he considered 'vulgar' and production of it between 1780 and 1795 seems to have been extremely small. The colour of rosso antico varied considerably in the 18th century, but it is clear from the correspondence that both Wedgwood and Bentley aimed for a rich, deep red, nothing like the bright orange-red of later wares.

Josiah II* evidently did not share his father's misgivings about the rosso antico body, although the name was soon discarded in favour of the older and simpler 'red body'. Black basaltes was no longer used to ornament it, being discarded in favour of a new black body, 'red-black', created specially for the purpose, and during the first half of the 19th century good quantities of redware were made with 'Egyptian' reliefs in either black or white. Border ornaments in these colours included 'husk', 'leafage', 'leafage with flower between', 'grape' and 'ivy'; and decorative groups of *Domestic Employment* were also used. Vases of this period were ornamented with either 'Egyptian' or classical reliefs. Among the most unusual pieces were the oval and octagonal settling pans made for the Shugborough Dairy (see: Dairy Ware).

Enamelled *Chinese Flowers* and *Chinese Pheasants*∗ in the

famille-rose∗ style, appeared on the red body (as on black basaltes and cane* ware) c.1815, and plain red teawares were produced both unglazed and with the purple-brown Rockingham* glaze. The British Museum owns pieces from a teaset said to have belonged to Queen Adelaide (consort to William IV) which is made of the red body decoratively mounted in silver hallmarked 1839-40. About 1860, the red body was given a glossy black glaze of the Jackfield* type and decoration in the *famille-rose* style, and inlaid* wares are of about the same date. Some extraordinary so-called 'Egyptian' pieces were decorated with a combination of matt and gloss enamels for Woollard & Hattersley, Cambridge, in 1854, and the same firm commissioned the Cambridge Ale Jugs* which were supplied from about 1850. The same red body was used for Magnolia* and Kenlock* wares near the end of the century. The body was revived briefly for small quantities of some Keith Murray* shapes in the 1930s but has not been made since 1940. Rosso antico, or red body, should not be confused with the softer, porous orange* body made during the 19th century or the orange-red terracotta jasper*, introduced with white or black ornaments in 1957.

See: Colour Plate 97
See also: Orange Body; Redware

Roubiliac, Louis-François (1695-1762)

French sculptor, born at Lyon, who became a pupil of Balthasar Permoser's at Dresden. He was later employed as assistant to Nicolas Coustou, and came to England in 1732, where he was introduced to Sir Henry Cheere, a well-known sculptor and brother to John Cheere*. He became godfather to the daughter of Nicolas Sprimont, proprietor of the Chelsea* porcelain factory, to whom he is said to have supplied models. One of his minor works, a model of Hogarth's pug dog Trump*, was certainly reproduced in porcelain around 1750 and Wedgwood's black basaltes* model is from the same source.
See: Parker, Richard

Roulette (wheel)

A small wheel, the circumference of which is cut or moulded with patterns. When the wheel is held against a rotating (unfired) pot, these patterns, are transferred to the clay. The wheel is attached to a handle or spindle which, in use, is held between finger and thumb. Rouletted patterns are simple to apply and rouletting was a popular and effective method of decoration in the 18th century. Josiah Wedgwood made use of this technique for impressing lines, beads and other decorative border patterns into the clay bodies of his early creamware vases and several examples of 18th-century roulettes, with metal or *lignum vitae* handles, are preserved in the Wedgwood Museum*.

Round Plume

See: Plume Knops

Rousseau, Jean-Jacques (1712-78)

French philosopher and author, born in Geneva of a Huguenot family. After many vicissitudes he arrived in Paris in 1741, where he became acquainted with Diderot and wrote articles on music and political economy for the *Encyclopédie* while he scratched a

ROUSSEAU, Jean-Jacques. Wedgwood & Bentley pale-blue and white jasper portrait medallion. Oval height 2⅛in. c.1778.
Private Collection

living copying music and writing. His *Paradoxical Oration on the Arts and Sciences,* 1750, earned him fame with its paradox of the superiority of the savage state, and in the *Discourse on the Origin of Inequality,* 1753, he advocated the return to a primitive life, holding that wealth is criminal, government tyrannical and social legislation unjust. His reputation was confirmed by *The New Heloïse,* 1760, and *The Social Contract,* 1762. In the same year he published *Emile,* which expounded his views on education and was to have a widespread influence on educational theory in Europe. Josiah Wedgwood sought Bentley's* advice on *Emile,* which he proposed to buy 'notwithstanding His Holiness has forbid its entrance into his domains', in 1762. Rousseau fled to Switzerland to avoid arrest and came to England at the invitation of David Hume in 1766, but suspecting the intentions of the British government, he returned to France, finally settling at the Château d'Ermenonville, where he died.

Rousseau was a popular figure in England and small busts were produced in both porcelain and earthenware by various factories well into the 19th century. Two Wedgwood busts of Rousseau are listed in Wedgwood's 1777 Catalogue: the first about 20in. high, sometimes erroneously attributed to Flaxman*; the second, a miniature, about 4½in. high. Flaxman charged for moulding a bust of Rousseau in 1788 but, if this was produced, it was too late for Wedgwood's catalogues. A portrait medallion* of Rousseau was listed in 1773 but was probably issued earlier. It was copied in glass paste by Tassie*.

Rousseau was also the subject of one of Wedgwood's rare 18th-century figures of contemporary personages. Intended as a companion piece to the figure of Voltaire*, the statuette of Rousseau, about 11¾in. high, was modelled after a full-length drawing sent to Wedgwood by Sir Brooke Boothby, who had been Rousseau's host in Derbyshire. It portrays the philosopher going botanising at Ermenonville, a walking stick in his left hand and a small bunch of flowers in his right. Wedgwood was doubtful whether it was appropriate: 'our statue, if it gives him any character at all, should bestow that upon him for which he is most the famous, & that I

ROUSSEAU, Jean-Jacques. Wedgwood & Bentley black basaltes bust of Rousseau. Height 18in. c.1777.   *Christie's, London*

apprehend is not the botanist.' However, the figure was made in black basaltes in 1777-8 and has been reproduced intermittently since then, as late as the 1920s. At least one copy was made also in the cane* body, but no example has been found.

Royal, Bella (b.1898)
Painter of Rhodian* and Persian* wares at Etruria* from 1919.

Royal Shape
See: Tableware Shapes

Royal Society of Arts
Learned society, founded in 1754 as the Society for the Encouragement of Arts, Manufactures and Commerce, in the words of its founder, William Shipley, 'To embolden enterprise, to enlarge science, to refine art, to improve our manufactures and to extend our commerce.' The Society was responsible for the first exhibition of contemporary art in England, the success of which led to the founding of the Royal Academy; the first industrial exhibition, 1761; and the first international exhibition, 1851. The Royal Charter of Incorporation was granted in 1847 and the title of Royal in 1908. In the present century, the Society, whose title is now informally abbreviated to the Royal Society of Arts, has been concerned particularly with industrial design. Her Majesty the Queen is Patron of the Society, HRH Prince Philip, Duke of Edinburgh is President, and Fellows of the Society in 1993 numbered more than 15,000 world wide. Josiah Wedgwood, who received considerable assistance from Peter Templeman and Samuel More*, successively Secretaries of the Society, was elected a Fellow in 1786.
See: Adelphi; More, Samuel

Royal Society of London for Improving Natural Knowledge
Generally known briefly as the Royal Society, it is one of the oldest European societies devoted to scientific inquiry, being granted its first charter by Charles II in 1662. The King was one of the founding members. They met regularly to read scientific papers which were subsequently published in the *Philosophical Transactions.* Josiah Wedgwood was proposed for election as a Fellow in May 1782 and his candidature was supported by no less than fourteen Fellows, headed by James ('Athenian') Stuart*. The Royal Society Club held meetings in less formal surroundings than those of the official meetings, usually at an inn. Non-members, especially those likely to be candidates for Fellowship, were invited as guests. Wedgwood was Stuart's guest in 1780 and 1781.

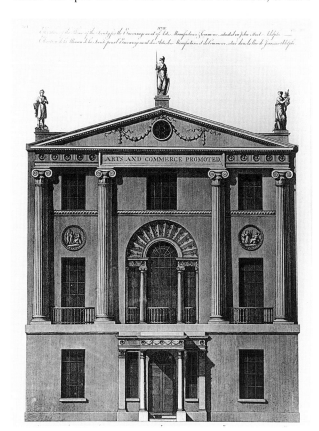

ROYAL SOCIETY OF ARTS. Engraving of the front of the Society of Arts in John Street, the Adelphi, London, erected by Robert Adam for the Society and leased from him from June 1774.
Photograph: Wedgwood

RUINED COLUMN VASE. Rare solid blue and white jasper triple ruined column vase, the base moulded with a central panel derived from 'A Roman Procession'. Height 9in. c.1786-95.
Dwight & Lucille Beeson Collection, Birmingham Museum, Alabama

Wedgwood's paper relating to the invention of his thermometer was read to the Society on 9 May 1782, and he presented further papers to the Society in 1783, 1784 and 1786.
See: Banks, Sir Joseph; Pyrometer

RUINS. Queen's ware teapot transfer-printed in black with a scene of classical ruins with two figures sketching in the foreground. Height 5⅜in. Unmarked. Wedgwood, c.1771. *Merseyside Museums*

Ruined Column Vases
Classical ruins* were fashionable subjects of decoration during the second half of the 18th century and both natural and artificial ruins appear in transfer-printed* decoration on Wedgwood's Queen's ware* and Worcester* porcelain. Wedgwood's 'ruined column' vases are composed of one, two or three columns, broken about a third of the way up, mounted on a time-worn base, moulded with lichen, inscriptions and panels of figures. These vases were made in cane* ware and two-colour jasper* of various colours from about 1786, when they were priced from one guinea to three guineas according to the number of columns.

Ruins
Classical ruins and obelisks were fashionable subjects in painting and many forms of decoration from about 1750. Artificial ruins were built as garden ornament, and artists such as Piranesi* and Hubert Robert found in them a source of inspiration – the latter to an extent where he became known as 'Robert les Ruines'. The vogue was undoubtedly inspired by the excavations at Herculaneum* and Pompeii* and contemporary interest in these and other classical sites. Thomas Chippendale designed a 'ruined' chimneypiece; Chelsea* porcelain was painted with ruins before 1760, probably by Jeffryes Hamett O'Neale*; Robert Hancock's* transfer-prints* of this subject occur on Worcester* porcelain; and Sadler* & Green transfer-printed several landscape subjects with ruins on Wedgwood's Queen's ware*. In addition to his 'broken column' vases*, Wedgwood produced a jasper 'ruined vase' modelled in imitation of an excavated classical vase with simulated damage, c.1785-90. An example of this extremely rare model is in the Beeson* collection.

RUINS. Blue jasper dip 'ruined vase' ornamented with figures, trees and a floral scroll. Height 6¾in. c.1786.

Dwight & Lucille Beeson Collection, Birmingham Museum, Alabama

Rum Kettle

An 18th-century vessel, somewhat smaller than a tea kettle, with a short beak-shaped pouring lip or spout and bail handle*. Kettles 5in. and 10in.-11in. in height were made in black basaltes* during the Wedgwood & Bentley period, and the smaller version was reproduced in bone china* of the second period, c.1880. Jasper* kettles of about 1785, the interiors left unglazed, were intended as cabinet pieces*.

Russel, Frederick Bret (fl.1860s)

Designer of several decorative pieces, including the *Caterers* Jug and *Flowering Rush* Jug illustrated in the '1878' Illustrated Catalogue of Ornamental Shapes and reproduced in Majolica* glazes. Russel marked some of his work with his monogram impressed.

Rustic Handle

See: Crabstock

Ryles, Robert Daniel (fl.1816-65)

Engraver of Lane End, who worked for Wedgwood at Etruria*, 1816-54. He engraved the *Old Vine* pattern, 1854, which was still in production on Shell Edge Queen's ware* a hundred years later.

Rysbrack (Rijsbrack), John Michael (1694-1770)

Sculptor; the son of a landscape painter of Antwerp. Rysbrack arrived in England about 1720 and rapidly gained a reputation for his portrait busts. He was responsible for an enormous amount of statuary and carving of all kinds, from chimneypieces to monuments. There is no suggestion that Rysbrack worked directly for Wedgwood but busts of George II* and Robert Boyle were taken (probably by way of casts from Hoskins & Grant*) from his originals.

RUM KETTLE. Pearl ware rum kettle with bail handle and grape-bunch knop. Height 9in. c.1795. *Wedgwood Museum*

Sacrifice

An offering to a deity; usually a prayer or an act of thanksgiving, penitence or propitiation. Wedgwood's sacrifice groups are not always easy to identify with certainty because some of the figures composing them were apparently considered interchangeable and might be increased or reduced in number to suit the size and shape of the ground (tablet*, medallion* or vase). The titles also have become confused and duplicated in various later publications. The sacrifice subjects recorded in Wedgwood's catalogues and price lists are as follows:

GROUP

The Sacrifice, Carrara* group 24in. x 14in., modelled by William Beattie*

BAS-RELIEFS

A Sacrifice, plaque 10in. x 14in., moulded from a model in the Newdigate* collection. No.173 in 1777 Catalogue*

Bacchanalian Sacrifice, 'long square tablet' 9in. x 21in., after Clodion*. No.71 in 1773 Catalogue

Fauns Sacrificing, tablet 8½in. x 15in., no.140 in 1777 Catalogue

Offering to Love, circular medallion diameter 4in., or oval 4½in. x 5½in., no.260 in 1787 Catalogue as companion piece to *Conjugal Fidelity*

Offering to Peace, tablet 6½in. x 11½in., 'from a design of lady Templetoun's [sic]' (finished by Hackwood*). No.238 in 1787 Catalogue

Sacrifice to Aesculapius, medallion 4in. x 3⅜in., no.28 in 1773 Catalogue

Sacrifice to Bacchus,* tablet 6½in. x 14in. and 7½in. x 10in. No.200 in 1779 Catalogue

Sacrifice to Concordia, circular plaque, diameter 10in., no 259 in 1787 Catalogue as companion piece to *Sacrifice to Hymen*

Sacrifice to Flora, tablet 7½in. x 17in. and 8¼in. x 19in. Sometimes catalogued, and bought by Sir Laurence Dundas*, by this name, but catalogued by Wedgwood as *An Offering to Flora* (no.199 in 1779 Catalogue)

Sacrifice to Hymen, medallion, various sizes to match those of *Marriage of Cupid** and *Psyche**, attributed to Flaxman*. No.196 in 1777 Catalogue

Sacrifice to Hymen, circular plaque, diameter 10in., no.259 in 1787 Catalogue as companion piece to *Sacrifice to Concordia*

Sacrifice to Love, tablet 9½in x 21in. or 10½in. x 25in., no.208 in 1779 Catalogue

Sacrifice to Peace, medallion 3¾in. x 2¾in., moulded from a model in the Newdigate collection. No.171 in 1777 Catalogue

Sacrificing Figure, plaque, height 7in., moulded from a model in the Newdigate collection. No.158 in 1777 Catalogue

Sadler, John (1720-89)

Transfer-printer; partner in the firm of Sadler & Green of Liverpool, who may also have been manufacturers of earthenware, although no specimens have been identified. Sadler is said to have invented transfer-printing of earthenware about 1750. The technique was invented also independently by John Brooks in London before 1753 and used at the Bow* porcelain factory and the Battersea enamel works. By 1756 it was also in use at the Worcester* factory. From 1761 Sadler & Green decorated increasingly large quantities of Wedgwood cream-coloured ware*, which was sent to Liverpool for that purpose, and some of their accounts survive in the Wedgwood archives. They also decorated tiles* with a great variety of subjects, including scenes from Aesop's* Fables, and figures from the contemporary theatre which are much prized by collectors.

John Sadler withdrew from the partnership in 1770 and the business was continued by Guy Green, who continued to decorate Wedgwood Queen's ware* at least until Josiah Wedgwood's death in 1795 and possibly as late as 1799. The subjects, some of which were suggested by Sadler and most of which were engraved in London, were varied, but mainly fall into five categories: contemporary portraits; landscape, pastoral and sporting subjects; 'exotic' birds*; armorial* wares (including Masonic* pieces and wares decorated with the arms of clubs and societies); and subjects taken from Sadler's repertoire of engravings for tiles*. All were transfer-printed in monochrome, principally in black but also in iron-red or purple. Some experimental prints were produced in green and onglaze blue. Transfer-printed wares have been of great importance to Wedgwood, especially in the decoration of 18th-century Queen's ware, and for more than 200 years the technique has also provided the outlines for print and enamel* patterns.
See: Colour Plate 98

Sadler & Green
See: Sadler, John

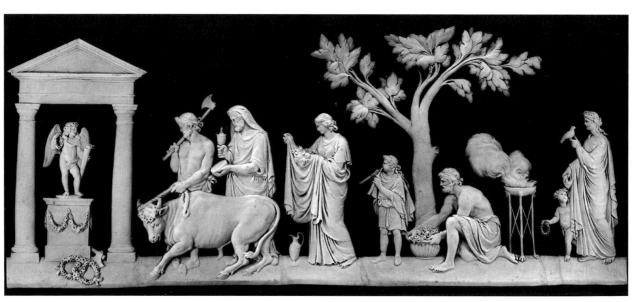

SACRIFICE. Green jasper dip tablet, *Sacrifice to Love.* 9¼in. x 24⅞in. c.1790.

Sotheby's, London

SADLER, John. Tin-glazed earthenware tile transfer-printed in black by Sadler & Green with 'The Sailor's Farewell'. 5in. x 5in. c.1759.
Author's collection

Sage Stoneware

A brownish-green stoneware recorded between 1843 and 1857 for the production of Stilton cheese dishes*, jugs and pot-pourri jars* and vases. It is likely that the range of objects was much more varied than these records suggest, but examples are extremely rare and quantities were probably small.

Saggar

A protective box of highly refractory* fireclay used to enclose objects during firing to prevent contact with the flame or gases. Some are pierced at irregular intervals with triangular holes through which the saggar pins are inserted to support ware during firing.

St Lawrence Seaway Plates

Two designs were commissioned in 1959 to commemorate the opening of the St Lawrence Seaway: one, a sepia print by Peter Wall* for Manchester Lines Ltd., whose ships use the seaways, and the other by Alan Price* for the *Toronto Evening Telegram*.

Salpion (fl. AD 100)

Greek sculptor. Hackwood's* tablet, *Birth of Bacchus*, was modelled from Montfaucon's* engraving of Salpion's original bas-relief* now in the Naples Museum.

Saltglazed Stoneware

Stoneware covered with a thin, hard glaze having a minutely pitted surface reminiscent of the appearance of orange peel. It is produced by throwing a shovelful of salt (sodium chloride) into the kiln when the fire is at its hottest. The salt splits into its components – sodium and chlorine. The sodium combines with the silica on the surface of the ware to form the characteristic glaze; the chlorine passes out of the kiln chimney. Saltglazed stoneware was manufactured in Germany at least as early as the 15th century and vitrified stoneware (fired to about 1200°-1400°C) was produced in Fulham, London, long before it was common in Staffordshire. The finely potted white stoneware, thinly coated with saltglaze and made into lightweight tablewares, however, was in a different class from the coarser greyish-bodied saltglazed stonewares of Cologne (often coloured blue, black, purple or brown by the use of stained slip*, manganese* or cobalt* oxide) and the body was a significant improvement on that produced at Fulham, though the magnificent busts produced by Dwight* show its suitability for work on a larger scale. From the end of the 17th century until about 1765 saltglazed stoneware was by far the most important product of the Staffordshire potteries. The body was

SADLER, John. Queen's ware feather-edge plate transfer-printed in black by Sadler & Green with a rustic scene and six flower sprays. Unmarked. Wedgwood, c.1770. *Temple Newsam House, Leeds*

white and strong and it was beautifully potted, and the introduction of the techniques of mould-making and slip casting* made it possible to reproduce intricate shapes. Decoration was by incising* patterns ('scratch blue'), by enamelling and, after 1754, by transfer-printing. By the third quarter of the 18th century Staffordshire saltglazed ware had been superseded by creamware but production of a coarser saltglazed stoneware for jugs, flasks and tankards was continued elsewhere.

SALTGLAZED STONEWARE. Two sauceboats, moulded in relief: *(left)* similar to a Longton Hall model attributed to Aaron Wood; *(right)* a pattern that relates to a block mould in the Wedgwood Museum. c.1755. *Formerly Buten Museum*

SALTGLAZED STONEWARE. White saltglazed stoneware teapot moulded with the 'Landskip' pattern. Height 5¼in. Unmarked. Whieldon or Wedgwood, c.1760. *Mrs R.D. Chellis Collection*

SALTGLAZED STONEWARE. Block mould of a sauceboat moulded with the 'Foxglove' pattern. Height 3⅝in. c.1760.
Wedgwood Museum

Wedgwood probably produced saltglazed stoneware during his partnership with John Harrison* and Thomas Alders* and, according to Wedgwood's own account, it was 'the principal article of our manufacture' during his years with Whieldon* although it was already becoming unfashionable and 'reduced so low [in price], that potters could not afford to bestow much expence upon it.' There can be little doubt that Wedgwood continued to produce saltglazed stoneware in his years at the Ivy House*, between June 1759 and Christmas 1762. Its continued production after 1762, when he moved to the Brick House*, is far less likely. By that date he had made considerable progress in the improvement of the creamware (cream-coloured*) body (his first delivery to Sadler* & Green for transfer-printing* was made in September 1761) and the move probably marked the end of Wedgwood's production of saltglazed stonewares.

Saltram
Saltram, a mansion near Plympton, Devon, was purchased by George Parker, ancestor of the Earls of Morley, in 1712, and his son John began to enlarge the house after 1743. The grandson, also John, inherited the property in 1766 and employed Robert Adam* to make extensive alterations to the east wing. John Parker was created Baron Boringdon in 1784 and was succeeded by his son in 1788. Sir Joshua Reynolds* visited Saltram, painted the family portraits and advised the owner on the acquisition of pictures. The house, which now belongs to the National Trust, still contains many of the original furnishings, including some early creamware*, black basaltes* and variegated* Wedgwood vases, which are made the more interesting by the preservation of documents and invoices relating to them. Four creamware vases with engine-turned* decoration, part of a larger *garniture*, are among the finest of their type and date (c.1765) surviving.

Sand Box
A box with a pierced top for sprinkling fine sand or pumice powder on to paper for the purpose of drying the ink. Sand boxes were used until c.1820, when they were replaced by blotting paper. They should not be confused with pounce pots*. Wedgwood produced sand boxes in black basaltes from about 1775.

Sandby, Paul (1730-1809)
Painter. A founding member of the Royal Academy, Sandby was one of the most celebrated and influential artists in watercolour of the 18th century. His work included landscape, architecture, portraits and even caricature. Prints from several of Sandby's views of Windsor Park and his *Gate of Coverham Abbey* (British Museum), were copied by Wedgwood for the Frog* service.

Sandeman's Port Decanter
See: Decanter

Sanitary Ware
See Closet Ware

Sappho (fl. c.600 BC)
One of the leaders of the Aeolian school of lyric poetry. She was born on the island of Lesbos, where she was the centre of a female literary coterie, most of the members of which were her pupils. Only fragments of her works survive.
Wedgwood subjects:
Sappho, bust, height 15in., from a cast or mould supplied by Hoskins & Grant*, 1775
Sappho, bas-relief supplied by Flaxman* senior in 1775. Probably the oval medallion 8in. x 6in. listed as *Contemplative Muse,* no.102 in 1777 Catalogue

Sarreguemines
See: Utzschneider, Paul François

Satsuma Shape
See: Tableware Shapes

Satyr
See: Faun; Pan; Silenus; Wine and Water Ewers

Sauce Boat
Boat-shaped vessel, usually with a loop handle and spout, resting on a flat or footed base or four short legs, for the service of sauces or gravy. Some models have lips at both ends and two handles at the sides. The former style, in three versions, appears in the first (1774) Queen's Ware* Catalogue* (Plate 4) and both shapes are illustrated in Wedgwood's '1790' Queen's Ware Catalogue (Plate 5). The simpler shape with single handle has survived, in various forms, to the present day in both Queen's ware and bone china*. The sauce boat with fixed stand, now made primarily for the American market, exists in 18th-century Queen's ware.

Sauce Tureen
Small tureens ('terrines') with stands for the service of sauces and gravy, generally in shapes conforming to those of covered vegetable dishes or soup tureens in the same service, were made in Wedgwood's Queen's ware* from the late 1760s. One of the earliest shapes is illustrated in the 1774 Queen's Ware Catalogue* (Plate 4). Three more shapes, round and oval, appear in Plates 4 and 5 of the '1790' Catalogue. The oval shape was usually supplied with a fixed stand, and all were provided with matching ladles.

Saucer Dish
A round shallow dish in the shape of a large saucer (without indented well). The shape was originally Chinese but was adopted for European tableware services in both earthenware and porcelain. Wedgwood produced saucer dishes in Queen's ware* and bone china* during the 18th and 19th centuries.

Savoy Shape
See: Tableware Shapes

Sayer, Robert (1725-94)
One of the principal print and map sellers in Britain, trading from the Golden Buck, 53 Fleet Street, London. In business on his own account for twenty-four years, Sayer was in partnership with J. Bennett, 1775-84. Thereafter he again traded alone until his death. His publications include *The Complete Drawing Book*, 1758; *The Dramatic Characters or Different Portraits of the English Stage,* 1770; *The Artist's Vade Mecum;* and *The Draughtsman's Assistant,* 1777. *The Ladies Amusement*, issued in at least two editions between 1758 and 1762, is described on the title page as 'extremely useful to the PORCELAINE and other Manufacturers depending on Design.' The illustrations by Pillement*, Robert Hancock* and others were certainly used by Wedgwood, Sadler* & Green and the Bow*, Chelsea* and Worcester* porcelain factories.

Scale Patterns
Patterns of overlapping scales handpainted on teapots and coffee-pots by David Rhodes* or his assistants at the Chelsea Decorating Studio*. The scale pattern was often accompanied by small landscapes or bunches of flowers in reserves.

SCALE PATTERNS. Queen's ware teapot painted in black and red with a scale pattern and a landscape in a circular reserve, the spout, knop and handle enamelled in bright green. Height 5½in. Unmarked. D. Rhodes & Co for Wedgwood, c.1768.　　*Manchester City Art Gallery*

SCENT BOX. Documentary smear-glazed white stoneware ('porcelain') scent box with pierced lid and thumb-scoop handle, ornamented with blue quatrefoils and floral borders. 3⅝in. x 4¾in. x 1⅞in. Printed inscription. 1824.　　*Formerly Buten Museum*

Scent Bottle

In former times scent bottles were usually notable for qualities of design and workmanship and were made in a variety of precious metals. In the 1750s and the early 1760s the Chelsea* porcelain factory made a series of small porcelain scent bottles which are now keenly sought. Wedgwood's jasper* scent bottles are less elaborate because they are generally neo-classical* in design and they had to be in shapes suitable for bas-relief* ornament. The mounted stoppers were often attached to the neck by a thin metal chain, and the screw tops were usually of gold, silver-gilt, silver or pinchbeck*. Most 18th-century scent bottles have by now lost their original mounts. In addition to flat octagonal 'smelling bottles' with classical ornaments and circular ones, often ornamented on both sides with pairs of small portrait medallions (e.g. George III* and Queen Charlotte*, George Prince of Wales and Frederick, Duke of York), Wedgwood also used the shape and styles of ornament created for bell pulls* to make less conventional scent bottles. Wedgwood cameos also appear as ornament for metal stoppers to glass smelling bottles of the period.

Most of these styles were reproduced during the 19th century, especially after the reintroduction of the solid jasper body in 1860, and original larger shapes for the dressing table were produced in Queen's ware*, some with decoration by Lessore* from 1862. Several of the small shapes designed for jasper were reproduced also in bone china* between about 1880 and 1920. In the 1950s a quantity of small, flat bottles in solid blue jasper with simple ornament and metal screw tops was produced for a special commission and the substantial residue was sold to the Buten* Museum at low prices. These bottles were resold without mounts or stoppers and have frequently appeared on the market falsely described as 18th-century pieces.

See: Colour Plate 99

Scent Box

In May 1824 Josiah Bateman* took an order from the 4th Duke of Portland for a set of four 'long square scent boxes, pierced cover, the holes to be a little larger than *pattern* and a small notch as thumb part cut in the cover to take it up by'. These objects were to be made in white smear-glazed (see: Glazes) stoneware ('porcelain'), ornamented with 'blue cymbals [*sic*] or group of flowers.' A surviving example (Buten* Museum) is 3⅝in. x 4¾in. x 1⅞in. (deep), with a pierced removable lid, and was evidently designed to hold liquid pot pourri*.

Scheemakers, Peter (1691-1781)

Sculptor, born in Antwerp, who spent some years in Rome before settling in London c.1741 in which year he had a studio in Vine Street. Scheemakers became even better known and more successful than Rysbrack*, and the Shakespeare monument in Westminster Abbey is among his many works. Lord Radnor bought

SCENT BOTTLE. Queen's ware scent bottle with stopper painted with three agricultural scenes by Emile Lessore. 1862-3.
Wain Antiques

SCHEEMAKERS, Peter. Black basaltes figure of Shakespeare after the figure by Scheemakers, 1740. Invoiced by Theodore Parker, 1769. Height 16in. c.1870. The companion figure of Milton is possibly from the same source.　　*Christie's, New York*

SEASONS, THE. Rare green jasper dip head of *Ceres,* representing *Summer,* one of four heads of the Seasons invoiced by Flaxman in 1777. Diameter 7¾in.   *Manchester Museum*

a head of Zingara* from him and a statue of the same subject by Scheemakers was among the lots in the sale of Dr Richard Mead in 1755. Wedgwood's figure of Shakespeare, possibly supplied by John Cheere*, was copied from Scheemakers, and the companion figure of Milton may be from the same source. Both figures are commonly found in Derby* porcelain. Scheemakers left England and returned to Antwerp in 1771.

Schenck, Frederick (fl.1870-90)
Modeller at Etruria* in 1872-3. He was engaged at a daily wage of five shillings from 3 August 1872 but no record of his work before January 1873 has survived. In the following three months he repaired or remodelled two bas-reliefs*, 'Satyr & two Bacchantes' and its companion piece by Clodion*, and another of Diana*. He also modelled a companion plaque to 'Flying Figures with Torch', a pair of plaques entitled 'Vanity' and 'War', '4 Seasons…out of a frieze for a Vase', a figure of Minerva* and figures or groups representing 'Utility', 'Beauty', 'Hector and Andromache', 'Poetry', 'Homer Muse' and Science'. Presumably this exhausted his invention for he left shortly afterwards to join George Jones & Sons as a modeller of a spurious form of pâte-sur-pâte* produced by applying layers of slip to moulded figures.

Schliemann, Heinrich (1822-90)
German archaeologist and traveller; lived in California and amassed a great fortune in the 1850s, being granted American citizenship. From 1863 he devoted himself to the study of Homeric archaeological sites, conducting excavations in Asia Minor, especially in what he believed to be the site of ancient Troy. He undertook other excavations elsewhere and was the author of several books on the subject. In the late 1870s Wedgwood produced at least one vase shape copied from one discovered by Schliemann at the 'Trojan' site, though the various decorations applied to it have little obvious relevance to its origin and belong to the Art Pottery* of the period. 'Trojan Revival' pottery was produced by several European potteries, notably in Germany.

Scott, Sir Peter Markham (b.1909)
Painter, notably of birds in flight or their natural habitat, and naturalist; founder of the Wild Fowl Trust at Slimbridge, Gloucestershire. Son of Captain Robert Falcon Scott, the Antarctic explorer. Peter Scott studied at the Munich State Academy and Royal Academy Schools, and exhibited at the Academy from 1933. His illustrations appear in several books on natural history subjects. Early in the 1930s Scott visited Etruria*, where he painted a few bird subjects on bone china* plates. Examples of these are scarce and it is unlikely that many were produced.

Scum
Whitish marks, caused by the surface crystallisation of soluble salts in the clay, appearing on biscuit* ware and also on fired dry bodies*. Wedgwood experienced much difficulty with this problem on the 19th-century red body* and orange body*.

Seals
Intaglio seals were made at the Chelsea* porcelain factory from about 1755, and Wedgwood's black basaltes* seals, or intaglios*, were marketed from the autumn of 1771. They were principally of three categories: classical subjects and heads; modern' subjects and heads; and ciphers and initial letters. Factory prices in 1773 were 10/6d a dozen for 'heads unset' and 16s for 'Figures & devizes'. The first catalogue was issued in 1773 and six years later the catalogue listed 379 numbered intaglios of subjects from mythology and ancient history and classical and modern portraits. In his introduction to the 1779 Catalogue, Wedgwood wrote: 'The Improvements made in the Intaglios, since the publication of the First Edition of our Catalogue require some Notice. We have found that many of them take a good Polish, and when polished have exactly the effect of fine black Jasper, but this operation must be performed with great Care, or the Work will essentialy suffer by it…We have also found out another Method of adding very considerably to the the Beauty of these Intaglios, by polishing the Bezels, and giving a Ground of pale blue to the Surface of the Stone, which makes them greatly resemble the black and blue Onyxes, and equally ornamental for Rings or Seals…They are also now made in fine blue Jasper*, that takes as good a Polish as Turquois Stone or Lapis Lazuli.' He added that portraits suitable for seals might be obtained at 'moderate Expence', a model for a portrait costing about three guineas and any number of copies ('not fewer than ten') in black and blue onyxes for seals and rings at 5s each.

Many of the original gems copied by Wedgwood were lent to him by such friends and patrons as Sir Watkin Williams Wynn* and Sir Roger Newdigate*, but the greatest number were supplied to him by James Tassie*.

Seasons, The
The Four Seasons were popular subjects in art from Roman times until the 18th century and their attributes have been remarkably constant. In Renaissance art, as in antiquity, they are often represented by pagan divinities. Spring is portrayed as a young woman with flowers (Flora* or Venus*); Summer as a female

SEASONS, THE. Basalt figures of *Summer* and *Winter* from a set of the Seasons by an unidentified modeller. Height 10in. and 9½in. c.1849.   *Mr & Mrs David Zeitlin Collection*

SENECA. Black basaltes bust on a plain waisted socle. Height 14in. c.1790.   *Formerly Buten Museum*

figure with a sickle and a sheaf or ears of corn (Ceres*); Autumn as a male figure with grapes and vine leaves (Bacchus* or Silenus*); and Winter as a male figure, usually an old man, wrapped against the cold or tending a fire (Boreas or Vulcan*). From the 18th century, the Seasons were more often represented allegorically.

Wedgwood subjects:

Four Seasons: *Spring, Summer, Autumn* and *Winter,* plaques 10in. x 8in. 'Heads' invoiced by Flaxman* at 2 guineas the set, 1775. 1777 Catalogue

Four Seasons, 'in separate pieces', medallions of putti 3¾in. x 4in. or 1½in. x 2in., often erroneously attributed to Flaxman. Nos.231-4 in 1779 Catalogue. These bas-relief figures appear also on bulb pots*, square pedestals etc.

Four Seasons, 'out of a frieze for a Vase', bas-relief(s) modelled by Schenck*, 1873, but not yet identified

Four Seasons, separate figures listed in 1849 for Carrara and black basaltes, modeller unidentified

Autumn) Companion figures attributed to Hackwood*, modelled
Winter) for jasper*candlesticks* and later used also with Majolica* glazes

The pair of jasper flower holders supported by figures of Cupid* with a bird's nest and Psyche* with a butterfly, c.1785, possibly represent *Spring* and *Summer.*

See: Horae

Seder Set

Gold-printed bone china* set, made in 1959 for Blancol Ltd., consisting of a tray, 15½in. in diameter, illustrating the order of the Passover ceremony, with six footed cups to hold the ceremonial foods.

Seigmund, George (fl.1769-74)

Painter at the Chelsea Decorating Studio* who worked on the Frog* service.

Semele

The daughter of Cadmus, founder of the city of Thebes. Carrying Jupiter's child, she was advised by Juno*, who schemed to destroy her, to receive Jupiter in all his divine splendour. The power of his lightning consumed Semele but Mercury* rescued her unborn child who became Dionysus (see: Bacchus). *Jupiter and Semele* was the subject of a small medallion, 3in. x 2in., no.83 in the 1774 Catalogue.

Semper, Gottfried (1803-79)

German architect and designer; member of the Prince Consort's circle in Britain. He designed an ebony cabinet on stand with gilt metal mounts, the door of which was inset with a painted porcelain panel surrounded by Wedgwood medallions. The panel was painted by George Gray with a copy of William Mulready's *Crossing the Ford* (exhibited RA 1842), and the cabinet was made by Holland & Sons and shown in the Paris Exposition of 1855. It is now in the Victoria & Albert Museum.

Seneca, L.Annaeus (?5 BC - AD 65)

Roman Stoic philosopher, who wrote largely on moral philosophical subjects, but was also the author of ten tragedies. In his early years he gained a reputation as a pleader of causes. His most important surviving work is *De Beneficiis* in seven volumes. He killed himself on the orders of Nero, to whom he had been tutor and chief counsellor.

Wedgwood subjects:

Seneca, bust, height 20in., from a cast supplied by Hoskins & Grant*, 1774.

Seneca carried dead from his bath. A tablet with this title is mentioned in Wedgwood's letter to Bentley* of 15 January 1771 but it is not listed in any of the Catalogues* and it seems probable that the title is wrong.

Settling Pan

A large oval pan, usually of Queen's ware* but made also in dry bodies*, about 17in. long with a pouring lip at one end. Milk was poured into it and allowed to stand until the cream or butter had risen to the surface and this was taken off with a skimmer.

See: Dairy Ware

Sèvres, Manufacture Royale de

This porcelain factory, originally housed in the fortress of Vincennes to the south-east of Paris, was removed to Sèvres, to the south-west, in 1756. By this time Louis XV, persuaded by Mme de Pompadour, had become the principal shareholder as well as being the factory's principal customer for its finest quality wares. The King was a powerful patron and protector, who issued edicts preventing the manufacture of porcelain elsewhere in France, and limiting the colours which might be employed to decorate *faïence.* Despite these royal prohibitions, a few small porcelain factories managed to operate clandestinely under the protection of the King's relations, a fact known to Wedgwood and mentioned obliquely in his letter to the Duc de Choiseul* when he was attempting to promote the sale of Queen's ware* in France. After the death of Mme de Pompadour in 1764 these edicts were progressively relaxed, although there were periods of more stringent application, and by the time the factory was inherited by Louis XVI they were hardly enforced at all.

It is pertinent to note that the date of Wedgwood's first Queen's ware Catalogue in French is 1774, the year in which Louis XV died. The situation was finally regularised by the Anglo-French Trade Treaty of 1786, in the negotiation for which Wedgwood advised William Eden (later Lord Auckland*) on aspects affecting tariffs and the export of English wares. The treaty was more or less terminated by the Revolution of 1789. During the Revolution the

SEVRES. Blue and white biscuit porcelain portrait medallion of Henri IV in imitation of Wedgwood's jasper. Diameter 3½in. Sèvres, c.1820.   *Formerly Author's collection*

SGRAFFITO. Deep-blue jasper dip vase with sgraffito and modelled slip decoration by Harry Barnard. Height 11¾in. Script signature incised. 1898-1902. *Wedgwood Museum*

SHAKESPEARE SUBJECTS. Modern basalt bust of William Shakespeare, remodelled from the cast supplied by John Cheere, 1774. Height 11½in. *Wedgwood Museum*

Sèvres factory became the Manufacture Nationale, and under Napoleon I the Manufacture Imperiale, reverting to the title of Manufacture Royale at the time of the restoration of Louis XVIII.

From about 1750, and for some thirty years thereafter, Sèvres was the supreme arbiter of ceramic taste in Europe, taking the lead from Meissen* before the start of the Seven Years' War. Sèvres yielded this place to Wedgwood in the 1780s, at about the time when a potter named Josse invented a biscuit* porcelain in which Wedgwood's jasper could be imitated. During this period Sèvres enjoyed the assistance of several distinguished painters and sculptors, who acted as designers and supplied models. Usually they were recruited by Mme de Pompadour, who exercised much influence in artistic circles, and they included such artists as Boucher*, Falconet* and Pigalle*, whose occasional influence may be traced in Wedgwood's products.

From the first, the Vincennes-Sèvres factory worked in the rococo* style and departed from it only slightly before the death of Louis XV, who remained faithful to rococo until the last. Sèvres specialised in fine quality ground colours and miniature painting in reserves and many of the more important pieces made at this time are considerable works of art. Exotic birds*, painted by such artists as Evans and Aloncle, shipping scenes by Morin, and cupids after Boucher were favourite subjects copied elsewhere. In 1752 the art director J-J. Bachelier introduced the use of biscuit* porcelain for figure work. This became extremely fashionable and many high quality figures were issued. They influenced both Derby* and Wedgwood contemporarily in England, and the Parian* body was a 19th-century descendant.

Wedgwood certainly regarded his jasper* as a form of biscuit porcelain and his dry bodies* followed the same general principles of manufacture. Several of his vases were closely based on Sèvres porcelain models and there can be no doubt of his interest in the products of the royal factory. These he was able to examine at some of the great houses he visited, notably the Duke of Bedford's Woburn Abbey*. He wrote to Bentley in October 1765 that he had been 'three days hard & close at work taking patterns from a set of French China at the Duke of Bedford's, worth at least £1500, the most elegant things I ever saw'; in August 1770 Craft* was sent to 'take a drawing of the Seve Vases in Morgans*', which Josiah thought 'composed in a very Masterly stile'; and two months later he expressed a wish to have drawings of the Sèvres vases in the collection of Lord March. As late as the 1880 Shape Book* there are several forms which owe their inspiration to 18th-century Sèvres. This is hardly surprising considering the wide popularity of

the numerous porcelain copies and reproductions of early soft-paste Sèvres (referred to as *vieux Sèvres)* by Minton*, Copeland (Spode*) and others.

When, in 1770, suitable materials for the manufacture of true porcelain, similar to that made by Champion* in England, were found at Saint-Yrieix, near Limoges, the Sèvres factory started to abandon the soft-paste body and, at the same time, to adopt the neo-classical style. One result of the change was that the wares lost a great deal of their former artistry and, in consequence, Wedgwood began to assume the leadership of European fashion, factories all over the Continent imitating Queen's ware, jasper and black basaltes*. With the onset of the Revolution, and the period of maladministration and reduced trade which followed for the royal factory, Wedgwood became supreme, but the general disruption of trade in Europe prevented him from fully exploiting his advantage.

The Sèvres factory, and the artists and designers trained there, dominated Staffordshire quality production during the second half of the 19th century, some of them coming to England during the political upheavals of 1848 and the Franco-Prussian War of 1870. Wedgwood, with its strong tradition of neo-classical styles, was less affected than the porcelain factories, but Wedgwood's 19th-century production would have been much the poorer without the work of Emile Lessore*.

The Manufacture Nationale de Sèvres is still the leading French porcelain factory.

Seward, Anna (1747-1809)
Author and poet, apostrophised as 'The Swan of Lichfield'; acquainted with Samuel Johnson and James Boswell; the friend of Erasmus Darwin*, who introduced her to R.L. Edgeworth* and probably also to Josiah Wedgwood. Wedgwood wrote at length to her, discussing the opposing arguments for abolition or regulation of the slave trade. Anna Seward was an anti-abolitionist, whom he was especially anxious to enrol in his campaign, and he wrote to her of 'the absolute despair of the West Indian slave, wearing out by immoderate & incessant labour'.
See: Society for the Abolition of the Slave Trade

Sgraffito
Decoration resulting from incising a design through slip of a contrasting colour to the body beneath. This operation is carried out before glazing. It is a very ancient technique and is almost universal. Wedgwood examples of the technique exist in some Art Pottery* and notably in the work of Harry Barnard* and Norman Wilson*.

SHAKESPEARE SUBJECTS. Carrara tercentennial bust by Felix Martin Miller. Height 16in. Inscribed and printed with lengthy commemorative backstamp. 1864. *Author's collection*

Shakespeare Subjects

Bardolatry is a British national pursuit and Wedgwood has been making objects of interest to lovers of Shakespeare for more than two hundred years, beginning in 1774 with the first 15in. black basaltes* bust after a mould or cast supplied by John Cheere*. A second bust, 14in. high, described as 'after John Flaxman junior' was evidently produced too late for inclusion in the 1788 Catalogue* but appears in an 1859 price list for Carrara*. It seems not

SHAKESPEARE SUBJECTS. Mug designed by Victor Skellern to commemorate the 400th anniversary of Shakespeare's birth, decorated with engravings of great Shakespearian actors of the past in their most celebrated roles. Height 4¾in., 1964. *Wedgwood Museum*

to be an original model by Flaxman but rather a remodelled version of Cheere's. A third bust, by Felix Miller*, was issued in two sizes (11½in. and 16in. high) in 1864 to commemorate the tercentenary of the poet's birth. These last busts bear a special backstamp which reads: 'Published under the Special Sanction of the National Shakespeare and Stratford-on-Avon Tercentenary Committees by Howell & James & Co. London April 23 1864'. They were reissued in Carrara and black basaltes in 1867.

A standing figure of Shakespeare, height 16in., copied from the statuette by Peter Scheemakers* (a companion figure to one of Milton) appears to have been produced too late for inclusion in the 18th-century catalogues. It was probably supplied by Cheere* and was reproduced in the 19th century in both black basaltes and Carrara.

At least three portrait medallions of Shakespeare were produced in the 18th century. One, facing to left, was modelled by Hackwood in 1777 from a print, and examples were signed by him

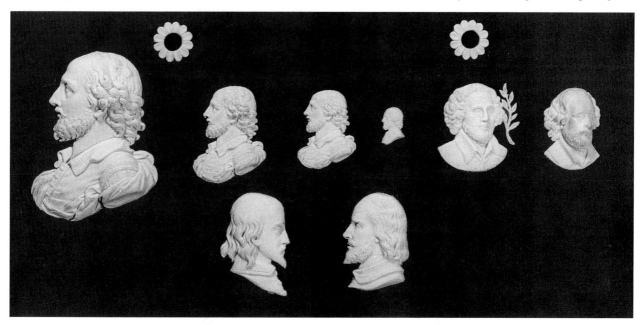

SHAKESPEARE SUBJECTS. 20th-century jasper reference tablet ornamented with the various portrait medallions of Shakespeare of which moulds were available. The largest portrait on the left was modelled by Hackwood in 1777. Those on the lower line are attributed to Charles Toft, c.1878.

Wedgwood Museum

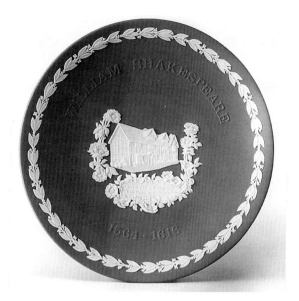

SHAKESPEARE SUBJECTS. Blue and white jasper plate ornamented with a view of Shakespeare's birthplace, Stratford upon Avon, issued to commemorate the 400th anniversary of his birth. 1964.
Wedgwood Museum

on the truncation. This portrait has been issued at various times in at least five sizes. A three-quarter face portrait, sometimes with a sprig of laurel, was in production by the end of 1775. Two later profile portraits are assigned to the 19th century but the modeller (perhaps Charles Toft*) has not been certainly identified.

A series of Queen's ware* circular plaques was painted in 1881-2 by Thomas Allen* and W.M. Palin* with portraits of characters from Shakespeare's plays on richly-patterned raised gold (see: Gilding) grounds.

To celebrate the four hundredth anniversary of Shakespeare's birth, Wedgwood issued a mug, designed by Victor Skellern*, decorated with prints of 18th-century actors in characters from twelve of the plays. These are listed in the special backstamp. This mug was the first of a series of six historical mugs by Skellern which received a Council of Industrial Design award in 1966. The design of the Shakespeare mug was adapted for the decoration of a Queen's ware plate, the characters arranged round a central view of the Globe Theatre, Southwark.

Shape Books
A name often confusingly used, without discrimination, for the printed Queen's ware* Catalogues*, the Shape Drawing Books* and the Vase Shape Drawing Book.

Shape Drawing Books
Unpublished drawings of tableware shapes preserved in the Wedgwood archives. The earliest surviving book of these drawings has 236 pages watermarked for 1802 and contains drawings of many shapes copied from records of an earlier date which no longer exist.
See also: Catalogues

Shapes
See: Tableware Shapes; Vases, Ornamental

Shard (Sherd)
A pottery or porcelain fragment, or ceramic 'waster', such as may be found in the excavation of abandoned kiln sites or potters' waste tips. Excavated shards may often provide reliable evidence of the existence of a pottery and of the type of ware made there, but the industrial archaeologist has to distinguish with care between wasters found on kiln sites, which are probably (but not certainly) from the pottery concerned, and those from tips, which may be from potteries far afield. Fairly accurate dating of shards is often possible from the levels at which they are found. Among the most significant excavations of recent times have been those of the Whieldon* and Greatbatch* factories.
See: Shraft

Sharp, William (1749-1824)
Engraver. Early in life he specialised in heraldic engraving but later became well known for his reproductions of the work of such classical painters as Guido Reni and Carracci as well as portraits by Reynolds*, Benjamin West, J.S. Copley and others. He supplied Wedgwood with engravings, c.1795-1805.

Shaving Pot
See: Redgrave, Richard

Shaw, Simeon (1784?-1859)
Author; born in Manchester; principal, 1818-51, of a private educational establishment described as an 'Academy for Young Gentlemen' in Hanley and later in Tunstall. Shaw's *History of the Staffordshire Potteries,* 1829, despite its inaccuracies, is still an important source of information about the Potteries in the 18th century. For many years dismissed as too unreliable to be of serious interest, his work is now understood, in the light of modern research and excavation, to be of considerable value to historians. Shaw is the only near-contemporary source for the story of Wedgwood's presentation of a caudle* set (misprinted in his *History* as 'Candle Sett') to Queen Charlotte*. He died in the County Lunatic Asylum, in Stafford.

Shelburne
See: Lansdowne

Shell Edge Shape
See: Tableware Shapes

Shell Shapes
See: Conchology

Shenton, Miss E (fl.1850-9)
Sculptor who exhibited at the Royal Academy, 1850-9. Her figures *Wanderer, Strawberry Girl* and *Broken Heart* were reproduced in Carrara*, 1858-9.

Shepherd, (Richard) David OBE (b.1931)
Painter of wildlife. A series of six Queen's ware* dinner plates and six side plates decorated with scenes after his paintings were produced for the World Wildlife Fund in 1970. These were available also in bone china* in a limited edition of 100 sets.

Sherwin, Henry (fl.1839-64)
Engraver and decorator; worked for Wedgwood 1860-4; engraved *Cornflower* pattern, 1860. Sherwin exhibited a series of designs for plates at the International Exhibition, 1862, based on the parsley leaf and other botanical subjects. He engraved a number of local topographical views in 1839.

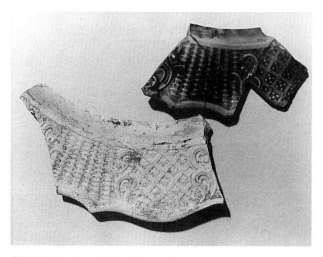

SHARD. Biscuit and glazed shards of two moulded patterns recovered from the Whieldon factory site at Fenton Vivian. Whieldon or Whieldon-Wedgwood, c1760.
City Museum & Art Gallery, Stoke-on-Trent

SHOUT, Robert.
Black basaltes bust of Admiral Sir Horatio Nelson by Robert Shout, inscribed and dated 1798. Height 11in.

Sotheby's, London

Sherwin, John (fl. early 19th century)
China painter, believed to have been employed at the Spode* factory in 1806 and the painter of Spode's pattern 3449, 'Sherwin's fruit and flowers in centre.' He was probably the painter (and possibly also the designer) of Wedgwood's bone china patterns 725 and 768 listed respectively as 'Shirwin's Flowers' and 'Shirwin's rich border of flowers'.

Shout, Robert (fl.1778-1819)
Sculptor and maker of plaster casts, in partnership at Holborn, London, with his father, Benjamin Shout, with whom he was responsible for a large number of monuments. Their work included casts of Canova's* figures of Hebe*, Venus*, Paris* and Perseus*. Wedgwood reproduced Robert Shout's bust of Nelson in black basaltes* in 1798, and a bust of Venus, height 9½in., after Canova was probably supplied by Robert Shout from a plaster copy made by him in 1819. This was reproduced in black basaltes and also in Carrara*.

QUEEN's WARE and ORNAMENTAL VASES, manufactured by Josiah Wedgwood, Potter to her Majesty, are sold at his Warehouse, the Queen's Arms, the Corner of Great Newport Street, Long Acre, where, and at his Works at Burslem in Staffordshire, Orders are executed on the shortest Notice.

As he now sells for ready Money only, he delivers the Goods safe, and Carriage free to London.

☞ His Manufacture stands the Lamp for Stewing, &c. without any Danger of breaking, and is sold at no other Place in Town.

SHOWROOMS. Advertisement for Wedgwood's 'Pattern Warehouse' at 1 Great Newport Street, London, opened in 1768.

Wedgwood Museum

Showrooms
Unlike some of his successors, Josiah Wedgwood always recognised the importance of a London address, and for some years his affairs were looked after by his brother John*, of Wedgwood & Bliss, London general warehousemen, with premises at Cateaton Street (now Gresham Street), near the Guildhall. He is listed in the Directories for 1763 and 1765 but not for 1766. In October of that year John Wedgwood went to live in Liverpool. While his brother was handling his affairs in London, Josiah Wedgwood had two rooms for display purposes at the Sign of the Artichoke, Cateaton Street.

After his brother's move in the autumn of 1766, and until Thomas Bentley's* arrival in London in August 1769, Wedgwood's business in London was handled by his Burslem book keeper, William Cox*, who was despatched to London for that purpose, from two rooms at the Queen's Arms, Charles Street (now Carlos Place), off Grosvenor Square. These were modest premises which Wedgwood regarded as temporary. By April 1768 he had settled on a house on the corner of Great Newport Street and St Martin's Lane, '60 feet long, the streets wide which lye to it, & carriages may come to it from Westminster or the City without being incommoded with drays full of timber, Coals &c which are allways pouring in from the various Wharfs, & making stops in the Strand

SHOWROOMS. The Wedgwood & Byerley, York Street, London, showrooms, reproduced from Ackermann's *Repository of Arts*, 1809.

Photograph: Wedgwood

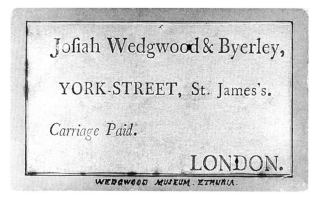

SHOWROOMS. Trade card for Wedgwood & Byerley's London showrooms, c.1809. *Wedgwood Museum*

very disagreeable & sometimes dangerous'. The rent was 100 guineas a year, but Josiah's friends assured him that it was the 'best situation in all London' for his rooms. Joseph Pickford, architect of the Etruria* factory, was sent to London to oversee the necessary alterations, including the regilding and resiting of the Royal Arms, which proclaimed Wedgwood potter to Her Majesty, and by August the rooms were open for business. The building consisted of two shops with fronts on to the street, one of which was sub-let to a linen draper. The showrooms occupied the whole of the first floor, where dinner and dessert services were laid out, as Josiah had planned, on tables. The ornamental wares were arranged on shelves around the walls, which were lined with paper in colours chosen to enhance shape and decoration (yellow for black basaltes*, blue or green for Queen's ware*).

At the close of 1769, Wedgwood & Bentley acquired a house in Cheyne Row, Chelsea, which became their Chelsea Decorating Studio*, and in 1770 Bentley, who had been living at Newport Street, moved to the Chelsea premises. Wedgwood feared that this might make the supervision of cash transactions more difficult and his apprehensions were proved to be well founded when the chief clerk, Ben Mather*, was discovered misappropriating funds. At Newport Street both James Tassie* and Hoskins & Grant* were neighbours.

By the end of 1770 Wedgwood was again on the hunt for new premises, and both he and Boulton* considered establishing show-rooms at the Adelphi*. Wedgwood had detailed plans prepared, but in spite of the temptation to be so permanently and so 'nobly situated', the plan was finally abandoned in November 1772. By this time the Wedgwood & Bentley showrooms had become a place of fashionable resort, where people foregathered to view the newest displays and to gossip. Circumstances also made it extremely desirable to house Bentley and his new wife with the showrooms, the painting studios and the warehouse under one roof. New premises were at length found at 12 Greek Street, near Soho Square, in 1774. Portland House*, as the mansion was known, was leased for twenty-one years at an annual rental of £200, later revised to £300, and the new showrooms were opened there on 1 June 1774 with a special exhibition of the Frog* service. The main galleries were on the first floor, and the ground floor included a spacious entrance hall, a large room for display purposes and a counting house. The outbuildings in the large courtyard at the rear afforded room for a painting shop, a laboratory, a 'retort room' (no doubt where the muffle kiln was situated for firing-on decoration), printing and pattern room, and a packing house. Mr and Mrs Bentley moved into No.11, next door.

SHOWROOMS. The Ornamental wares showroom at Etruria, c.1908, illustrating a large number of reproductions of 18th-century wares.

Photograph Wedgwood

Entry to the opening exhibition of the Frog service was by ticket only, an arrangement which says much for the strength of Wedgwood's position in fashionable London. According to a breathlessly inaccurate account in Mrs Mary Delaney's diary, the service occupied three rooms below and two above, and many of those who came to view it owned houses depicted on the plates and dishes.

Bentley's health was apparently affected by living in Soho and in 1777 he decided, despite the real risk of highwaymen, to move to the more rural surroundings of Turnham Green. The last exhibition at Portland House was staged in April 1790, admission again by ticket only, when the Portland vase* was displayed. The lease of the Greek Street premises terminated in 1795, within a month of Josiah's death, and renewal was complicated by the wish of the Duke of Portland, who owned the freehold, to sell the whole estate.

New Showrooms were found in St James's Square, at the corner of Duke Street, and the house was bought for £8,500, a further £7,500 being spent on alterations and furnishings. The building has now been demolished to make way for government offices but a view of the interior of the principal showroom is provided by Plate 7 of Ackermann's *Repository of the Arts* of February 1809. The neighbourhood at this time was exclusively residential, but it was not isolated, being just a minute or two's walk from Jermyn Street and Piccadilly, and no great distance from Buckingham House (now Palace), which George III* had bought for Queen Charlotte*. Tom Byerley was in charge until his death in 1810, when he was succeeded in the job by his son, Josiah. From 1814 to 1829, when the house was sold, the manager was John Howorth*. By 1828 the need for retrenchment had become so pressing that a clearance sale was held, and during that winter and the following spring many irreplaceable models, moulds and trial pieces were disposed of. Some of these may now be identified in public and private collections.

In 1875 Wedgwood returned to London with the acquisition of premises at 4-6 St Andrew's Buildings, Holborn Circus, thus moving back towards the City. Fifteen years later the showrooms were moved to 108 Hatton Garden, on the other side of the Circus. In 1902 Harry Barnard* became manager, remaining until 1918, when he returned to Etruria*. In 1911 the showrooms were moved again to 24-7 Hatton Garden, where they were maintained until 1941, when they were closed. In 1948, some three years after the end of World War II, new showrooms were opened at 34 Wigmore Street, where they remained until the 1980s, when they were considerably enlarged and redecorated, reopening again under the old name of Portland House. In spite of further considerable expense in redecoration after the Waterford take-over in 1986, the showrooms were vacated in 1990.

Josiah Wedgwood established showrooms and warehouses in Bath and Dublin during his lifetime. The former was opened in 1772 and managed by William Ward and his wife Ann (Stamford), the sister of Bentley's second wife. The Dublin warehouse, opened in 1773 and run by William Brock, was given up in 1778 and the business delegated to an agent. In the 20th century, showrooms have been opened in New York, Toronto, Sydney, Melbourne and Tokyo, providing also headquarters offices for Wedgwood's companies in the United States, Canada, Australia and Japan. The Wedgwood Rooms* retail organisation provides smaller but more widespread displays of tableware and ornamental wares based on the ideas originally formulated by Josiah I for his London showrooms.

The management of the London showrooms was, from the first, of exceptional importance to the Wedgwood firm and the appointment of London Manager (later Director) – responsible for all wholesale business in the southern counties, the management of all Wedgwood Rooms in Britain (from 1955 to 1963), and with final responsibility for European sales – became one of increasing authority and prestige in the pottery industry. The list of Wedgwood's London Directors is as follows:

John Wedgwood*	1765-6
William Cox*	1766-9
Thomas Bentley*	1769-80
William Brock	1780
James Jennings	1781
Thomas Byerley*	1781-1810
Thomas Howship	1810
Josiah Byerley*	1810-14

SIBYL FINIAL. The sibyl finial most commonly found on Wedgwood vases and teapots (from a Wedgwood & Bentley 'Sugar Dish' vase, height 7in., c.1775). *Kadison Collection*

John Howorth*	1814-29
– 1829-75 Showrooms closed –	
Charles Bacchoffner	1875-85
James Buttle	1885-97
S.H. Dyer	1897-1902
Harry Barnard*	1902-18
Felton Wreford	1918-41 and 1948-53
Arthur Bryan	1953-60
Robin Reilly	1960-64
Charles Dean	1964-66
Fred de Costobadie	1966-74
Roy Wadland	1974-81
Paul Hutchinson	1981-87

Shraft
An accumulation of shards*. A 'shraft tip' is a dump of broken ware from one or more potteries, often used also for general pottery factory waste.

Shuter, William (fl.1770-91)
Painter at the Chelsea Decorating Studio* who was responsible for the view of Fortescue House and other landscapes for the Frog* service. Principally a painter of portraits and flowers, he exhibited six landscapes in the exhibitions of the Incorporated Society of Artists and the Free Society of Artists.

Sibyl Finial
A finial in the form of a woman seated on the ground with a shawl drawn over her head. Often erroneously described as a 'widow' finial, it was properly noted by Josiah Wedgwood as a sibyl (in ancient times a mouthpiece of the gods, endowed with prophetic or oracular powers). Sibyl finials appear on Wedgwood Queen's ware* vases, in triple form (said to have been modelled by Josiah I) on the glaciers* of the Frog* service and some versions of the Michelangelo lamp*, and singly upon black basaltes* teapots and kettles from the 18th century until the 1930s. They appear more rarely on teapots of cane* ware and the other dry bodies* They are also found on teapots of the Rockingham* shape, both those of enamelled Queen's ware and those decorated with Rockingham or Jackfield-type glazes.
Wedgwood's sibyls are of three types:
1. (Perhaps the earliest). A seated draped figure, right leg crossed over left, left hand resting on right knee.
2. A similar figure but with legs uncrossed, the right foot extended forward, the left knee bent, arms folded.
3. A similar figure but left foot crossed over right, the left hand holding a book or scroll, the right arm held to the breast.
Sibyl finials of slightly different forms were used by Turner*, Davenport*, Spode* and Warburton*. Widow* finials, used by several other factories, but not by Wedgwood, are all provided with a barrel of meal and a cruse of oil and hold a cake in one hand.

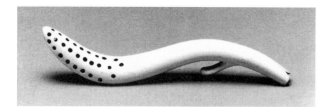

SICK SYPHON. Queen's ware sick syphon. Length 6½in. c.1790.
Byron and Elaine Born Collection

Sick Pot
Term used in the 18th century for an invalid's feeding cup*.

Sick Syphon
A combined strainer and feeding tube, open at one end and pierced at the other with holes large enough to allow the passage of fairly thick liquid. Wedgwood's version of this feeder is of Queen's ware* in the form of an elongated 'S', curved to rest on the edge of a broth bowl and provided with a small hook on the underside to prevent it from slipping. It was adapted from a silver prototype and appears as shape no.1246 in the '1802' Shape Drawing Book*.

Sickert, Walter Richard RA (1860-1942)
Painter and etcher, born in Munich; studied at the Slade School of Art and under J.A.McN. Whistler before living and working in France, 1883-1905. Returning to London, Sickert became one of the founders of the Camden Town Group in 1911. In 1926 he married, as his third wife, Elaine Thérèse Lessore*. In the late 1920s he was supplied with Wedgwood 'blanks' to decorate.

Siddons, Sarah (1755-1831)
English tragic actress; daughter of Roger Kemble and sister of John Philip Kemble; married William Siddons, 1773. In 1775 she was engaged by David Garrick for Drury Lane. She achieved fame in many roles, both in London and in the provinces, one of her most notable being Lady Macbeth, in which she made her farewell appearance in 1812. Her portrait as the *Tragic Muse* by Reynolds*

SICKERT, Walter R. Sickert with his third wife, (Elaine) Thérèse Lessore. *Photograph: Wedgwood*

SILENUS. Wedgwood & Bentley white terracotta biscuit plaque, *Silenus and Boys,* after Duquesnoy, the obverse oil-gilded all over. Oval length 6½in. c.1774. *Holburne of Menstrie Museum, Bath*

hangs in the Dulwich Gallery, London.

Wedgwood is believed to have owned models or moulds for two busts of Mrs Siddons but it is not certain that either was produced. The first, by John Flaxman*, was the subject of a letter from Josiah Wedgwood to the sculptor in February 1784; the second was supplied by Benjamin Papera* in 1802. Two portrait medallions were issued: the first, produced in 1782, is by Flaxman; the second, the identity of which is less sure, may be based on an engraving of 1795 by T. Burke after J. Bateman. Flaxman's chessmen* include the figure of Siddons in the role of Lady Macbeth as the Queen, and the king is said to represent Kemble as Macbeth.
See: Colour Plate 100

Silenus
The satyr who accompanied Bacchus* on his travels, and by whom he is said to have been brought up and instructed. Silenus was a son either of Mercury* or of Pan*. He is usually represented as a fat, jovial old man with a bald head, carrying a wine skin. Since he was drunk for most of the time, he is depicted asleep or supported by other satyrs, or riding on an ass.
Wedgwood subjects:
Silenus and Boys, medallion 6in. x 8in., probably after Duquesnoy* and obtained from Mrs Landré* in 1769. No.13 in 1773 Catalogue*
Triumph of Silenus, medallion 4½in. x 7½in., 'from a gem', no. 189 in 1777 Catalogue
A miniature bust of Silenus was made in the form of a term with a small circular base as a pipe stopper for tamping the tobacco in the bowl of a pipe, c.1780. An example in cane* ware is in the Wedgwood Museum* and it is likely that others were made in all the dry bodies*.

Silk-screen Printing
A modern process employed by Wedgwood for fine quality multi-colour printing in which colour is sifted through the interstices of an appropriately woven silk screen. The early colour range was somewhat limited, but in the 1960s-70s wide ranges of colour and subtle gradations of tone were achieved, making the process a preferable substitute for printing by lithography*. Printing in gold by this method was introduced in 1960, producing a perfection and clarity of line that was seldom achieved by earlier methods.

Silver Deposit
A decorative technique for glass, developed by the Stevens & Williams Glassworks, Brierley Hill, in the 1870s, which produced the effect of silver-cased glass. It was employed at Etruria* for the decoration of black basaltes*, c.1895, but examples are extremely scarce.

Silver Lustre
See: Lustre Decoration

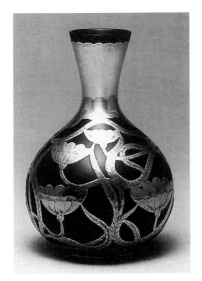

SILVER DEPOSIT.
Small black basaltes vase decorated by the 'Silver Deposit' technique. Height 6in. c.1895.
Formerly Buten Museum

Silver Pattern

Pottery the design of which has been copied or adapted from silver prototypes, or is decorated with ornament first used on silver ware. 'Silver shape' means pottery which is more or less directly copied from a silver prototype. Many of Wedgwood's early creamware* and black basaltes* shapes are closely related to contemporary silver but it is not always possible to determine whether the prototype was silver or ceramic.

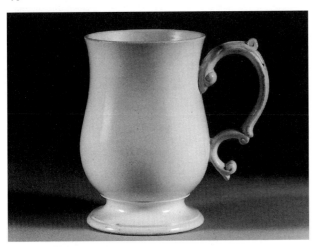

SILVER PATTERN. Queen's ware mug of bellied silver shape with ornate scroll handle. Height 4in. c.1775. *Norwich Castle Museum*

SILVER PATTERN. Silver shape teapot. Height 4⅛in. c.1800.
Formerly Buten Museum

SILVER PLATING. White stoneware cream jug, 146 shape, the exterior covered with 'silver-plating'. c.1890. *Formerly Buten Museum*

Silver Plating

A method of of decorating tableware and small ornaments with a layer of platinum giving the effect of silver plated ware. The technique was described by William Burton*, chemist at Etruria* from 1887 to 1892, in an undated memorandum of c.1890: 'A solution of platinum in aqua regia was slowly poured with careful stirring, in about three times its bulk of an oily menstruum, such as balsam of sulphur or spirits of tar. This forms an oily pigment which can be applied to a piece of glazed pottery…When the oily coating has become tacky by drying, a film of finely divided platinum, obtained by charring ammonium-platina-chloride, is dusted upon it, and when the ware is fired again at a low heat, say 700-800°C., a brilliant metallic deposit of platinum is found fixed to the glaze.' Examples of this fairly costly technique, which was applied principally to relief-ornamented white stoneware, are scarce enough to indicate that quantities were small.

Silvered Basaltes

An early attempt to use silver as decoration for black basaltes* was made by Tom Wedgwood* in 1790. He wrote to his brother Jos (Josiah II*) in April, 'I think a good deal might be done with silver & gold embossed work. These polished medallions may be set with metal melting at 220 or thereabouts.' Nothing came of the proposal for embossed ware but a method of inlaying silver decoration was found which resulted in 'silvered ware' being sent to London in February 1791, and 'Black silverd ware' appears in the London list of 'enameled' stock in 1793. A clue to the appearance of this ware exists in an order of 14 August 1814 from London for teapots, sugar boxes and cream jugs in 'Black with Silver Etruscan [pattern]'. Several examples of this pattern have survived.

SILVERED BASALTES. Black basaltes teaware pieces decorated with meander and laurel borders and an Etruscan border inlaid with silver. c.1793-1814.
Manchester Museum

Simpcock, Thomas (fl.1768-74)

A 'new made flower painter who promises to be a very dispatchfull hand', according to Josiah Wedgwood, who sent him to London with Bakewell* in 1768, to work at the Chelsea Decorating Studio*. In 1772 Simpcock was asked to send Josiah an account of a new method of printing which was being considered for the outlines of both vase and tableware decoration, and in 1773-4 he is recorded as one of the painters employed on the decoration of the Frog* service. Owing to a misreading of the initial of his first name, he has been recorded also as 'J' Simpcock.

Simon, Joseph (fl.1767-74)

Enameller employed by Wedgwood from 1767 and later on at the Chelsea Decorating Studio*, who worked on the decoration of the Frog* service.

Simons, George (fl.1769-74)

Painter at the Chelsea Decorating Studio*, employed on the Frog* service

Skeaping, John Rattenbury RA (1901-80)

Sculptor, draughtsman and engraver; born at South Woodford, Essex, the son of a painter, Kenneth Mathieson Skeaping; studied at Goldsmiths' College, at Central School of Arts and Crafts, 1917-19, and at the Royal Academy Schools, 1919-20. In 1924 he was awarded the Prix de Rome and in the same year he married Barbara Hepworth*. The marriage was dissolved in 1933. Skeaping first exhibited at the Royal Academy in 1922. Four years later he produced the first of many animal figures for Wedgwood and these were reproduced in Queen's ware*, finished with matt glazes or champagne glaze (see: Glazes), in coloured bodies* and in basalt*.

SKEAPING, John. Leaflet describing the ten animal figures by Skeaping, produced from 1927. In addition to Moonstone, cream-colour and basalt, small quantities of these figures were made in the Champagne and Celadon coloured bodies and with various 'satin' glazes. In the 1950s they were reproduced in Moonstone and Norman Wilson's tan glaze on Windsor Grey body. *Wedgwood Museum*

SKEAPING, John. Sea Lion, modelled by John Skeaping in 1927 and available in Moonstone glaze (illustrated), cream-colour or black basaltes. Height 8in. *Wedgwood Museum*

During World War II he served in Intelligence and with the SAS. In 1953 he became Professor of Sculpture at the Royal College of Art and seven years later was elected a member of the Royal Academy.

John Skeaping was a prize winner in the international competition of 1930 to design a vase to commemorate the birth of Josiah Wedgwood, and his original drawing is preserved in the Wedgwood Museum*. Skeaping's figures, cast in one piece, combined economy of line with ease of production and his emphasis on a 'rhythm of total volume and design' rather than precise representation was in the idiom of the period. His figures were reproduced in the 1950s, some in the Windsor grey coloured body with a rust glaze devised by Norman Wilson*, but they were too plain for a public starved of decoration since 1941. The figures produced before 1939 bore his signature in facsimile in addition to their Wedgwood trade marks; those reproduced after 1950 do not.

See: Colour Plate 101

Skellern, Victor George, ARCA, FSIA, NRD (1909-66)

Artist and designer. Born at Fenton, in the Potteries, Victor Skellern began work in the Design Department at Etruria* in 1923, studying part-time at the Burslem and Hanley Schools of Art, where he won several prizes for design. He was released in 1930 to take up a scholarship at the Royal College of Art, where he studied under Edward Bawden* and specialised in the design of stained glass. In 1934 he returned to Etruria to become Wedgwood's first professionally trained and educated art director. He brought to his new job an unusual combination of qualities – of management ability, perception, humour and lack of pretension – which, added to his outstanding ability as a ceramic designer and his insistence on work of the highest quality, made him the ideal choice to guide Wedgwood's design through the crucial period of transition over which Josiah V* presided. He succeeded, as few designers have ever done, in combining a proper respect for the traditions of Wedgwood design with an understanding of commercial necessity. This balance was reflected in own tableware patterns, which attracted admiration among his design contemporaries as well as success in the various markets for which he was called upon to create designs. His own contacts with artists and freelance designers enabled him to introduce to Wedgwood a number of artists whose work became important to the firm, including Rex and Laurence Whistler*, Clare Leighton*, Edward Bawden, Eric Ravilious* and Richard Guyatt*, and his continuing association with the Royal College of Art enabled him to choose qualified and especially suitable designers for his department, among them, Peter Wall* and Robert Minkin*.

Skellern's influence over Wedgwood design was paramount for more than thirty years and he was largely responsible for the decision to introduce lithograph* decoration at Barlaston. Ill-health

SKELLERN, Victor. Victor Skellern at work in his studio, handpainting prototype pieces of *Husk* pattern for the Williamsburg Restoration scheme.

Photograph: Wedgwood

obliged him to retire in 1965 and he died the following year. His loss to Wedgwood is well documented by the fact that he was not found to be replaceable: Wedgwood appointed five art directors in the following fourteen years.

The long list of Skellern's important contributions to Wedgwood tableware design includes the following:

Ashford, 1951, bone china, lithograph
Asia, 1956, bone china, silk screen
Avocado, 1959, Queen's ware, *Catherine* shape
Corinthian shape, 1935, in collaboration with Kennard Wedgwood*
Evenlode, 1947, Queen's ware, *Corinthian* shape
Fairford, 1941, bone china
Green Leaf, 1949, Queen's ware, *Queen's* shape, lithograph
Greyfriars, 1937, bone china
Hampton Court, 1937, Queen's ware, *Corinthian* shape
Lichfield, 1953, bone china, lithograph
Mandarin, 1949, Queen's ware, *Queen's* shape, lithograph
Meadow, 1940, Queen's ware, *Edme* shape
Morning Glory, 1936, Queen's ware, *Patrician* shape
Moselle, 1957, bone china, silk screen

Persian Pony, 1936, bone china
Pimpernel, 1947, bone china
Runnymede, 1940, bone china
St James, 1936, bone china
Sandringham, 1947, bone china
Santa Clara, 1951, bone china, lithograph
Seasons, 1935. Queen's ware, *Catherine* shape
Strawberry Hill, (with Millicent Taplin*) 1956, bone china, lithograph. Council of Industrial Design 'Design of the Year' award, 1956

SKELLERN, Victor. Queen's ware plate printed in underglaze blue with the 'Squirrel' from Skellern's *Forest Folk* pattern, 1934.

Wedgwood Museum

SKELLERN, Victor. *Wild Oats* pattern designed by Skellern in shades of grey enriched with platinum on Coupe shape, 1954.

Wedgwood Museum

SKELLERN, Victor. *Strawberry Hill* pattern, lithograph on bone china, designed by Skellern and Millicent Taplin in 1957, when it won the Council of Industrial Design award for Design of the Year.
Wedgwood Museum

Wild Oats, 1954, bone china, *Coupe* shape
Wildflower, 1945, bone china
Winchester, 1947, Queen's ware, Patrician shape
Woodstock, 1939, bone china
Skellern also designed engine-turned jasper vases for presentation to H.M. Queen Mary in 1936 and 1939, and the mug commemorating the Wedgwood bicentenary in 1959.

SKELLERN, Victor. Oval dessert dish, Catherine shape, printed in blue with Skellern's *Avocado,* designed in 1959. 9½in. x 14½in. x 2¼in. 1959.　　　　　　　　　　*Author's collection*

Skimmer

Shallow perforated bowl with a pouring lip for separating and straining cream from the surface of milk. Wedgwood made skimmers of Queen's ware as part of the range of dairy ware*.

Sleeping Boys

Five figures of *Sleeping Boys,* naked infants lying in characteristic poses, were produced by Wedgwood by 1773 in basaltes* and subsequently they were made in jasper*. These were reproduced from

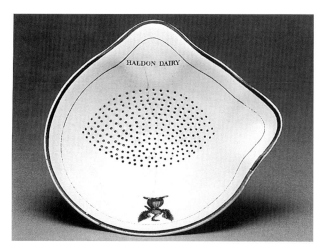

SKIMMER. Queen's ware skimmer enamelled in brown with the crest of the Palk family of Haldon House, Devonshire, and the name 'HALDON DAIRY'. c.1790.　　　　　*Formerly Buten Museum*

casts (probably supplied by Mrs Landré*) after the originals by Duquesnoy*. They are almost identical to the five *Enfants du Roi* produced by Sèvres* from the same source. Considerable confusion has arisen from the practice of calling these figures *Somnus*, a name which properly applies only to the similar but much larger figure after Algardi. The *Sleeping Boys* were reproduced in the 19th century in basaltes, jasper and Majolica*. The same figures occur also in Pearl ware* but are considered to be the work of Ralph or Enoch Wood* (see: Figures).
See: Infant Reclining Figures; Morpheus

Slip

Clay, or a ceramic body, diluted with water to the consistency of thin cream. As decoration it is washed over the entire body in a contrasting colour, often with a design incised through it (*sgraffito*) or applied as a trailing pattern of lines and dots. Slips of various colours are sometimes applied and combed together to give an effect of marbling*. Slip-cast ware is produced by pouring slip into plaster of Paris moulds. This process was introduced into Staffordshire about 1745, reputedly by Ralph Daniels of Cobridge. Wedgwood thought that plaster of Paris was first used by J.P. Elers*. The process of decorating ware with two different and contrasting coloured slips – two-colour slip – is a modern development (1936) of an old technique.
See: Slip Casting; Slip Decoration

Slip Casting

Casting with slip* in plaster of Paris moulds. The plaster absorbs water from the slip, leaving a layer of firm clay adhering to the walls of the mould. Surplus slip is poured off when the layer is thick enough, and the cast allowed to become leather hard*. In doing so it shrinks away from the walls of the mould, which facilitates extraction. Slip casting is now employed to make a good deal of hollow ware, and it is generally used for anything that does not have a circular section.

SLEEPING BOYS. Black basaltes figure of a Sleeping Boy, one of five such figures after Duquesnoy. Length 5in. c.1785.
Christie's, London

SMITH, Joachim. Blue jasper dip portrait medallion of the Prussian naturalist and philosopher, Johann Reinhold Forster, modelled by Joachim Smith, c.1776. Oval height 3½in. c.1785.
Nottingham Castle Museum

Slip Decoration

The product of applying slip* to the surface of a ceramic object by a technique similar to that employed in decorating a cake with icing, by trailing it in lines and dots (trailed slip), or by applying differently coloured slips which are combed to produced marbled* or variegated* wares. Speckled ware is produced by spraying slip on to the surface of the ware.

Slipper

A term used by Wedgwood for a bourdalou*, also known as a crinoline slipper or, more formally, as a coach pot. Correctly, the term 'slipper' refers to the normal wedge-shaped bed pan which was part of the sanitary or closet ware* made by most potters in the 18th and 19th centuries.

Smalt

A deep blue pigment made by fusing together zaffre*, potassium carbonate and a form of silica (e.g. sand) to produce a coloured glass. This was ground to a fine powder and could be used as the pigment for cobalt blue painting (either as an enamel or underglaze), transfer-printing* and groundlaying. It was employed also to make coloured bodies* including jasper*. Smalt in the 18th century was imported from Saxony until native deposits of cobalt were found in Cornwall.
See: Cornish Journey

Smear Glaze
See: Glazes

Smiles, Samuel (1812-1904)

Author; born in Haddington, East Lothian; qualified as a doctor at Edinburgh University but gave up medical practice in 1838 to become editor of the *Leeds Times*. Seven years later he was employed as an executive of the new Leeds and Thirsk Railway, which led to his interest in George Stephenson, whose biography he published in 1857. This was followed by *Self Help,* his best known work, which became a best seller in Victorian England and was translated into several European languages. The book is a series of homilies illustrated by anecdotes from the lives of famous men, mainly on the improving theme of failure conquered by perseverance and hard work. It was addressed principally to young men, and some of the biographical material, which included a number of references to Josiah Wedgwood, is inaccurate. The lives of several of the more illustrious potters were glanced at, including those of Böttger and Palissy, as well as Wedgwood's, and various worthy lessons were drawn.

Smiles's *Life of Josiah Wedgwood* came much later, in 1894, and was his last work. It was commissioned by Godfrey Wedgwood*, whose first choice for the task had been Charles Tindall Gatty (1851-1921), Curator of the Liverpool Museum, but he was unable to undertake it. Smiles's biography failed to add anything of importance to the earlier work of Eliza Meteyard* and Jewitt*.

Smith, Joachim (fl.1758-1803)

Portrait modeller. In 1758 he received a premium of ten guineas from the Society of Arts (Royal Society of Arts*) for a wax portrait. He had apparently devised a method of colouring wax so as to make it suitable for modelling portrait miniatures, but he was certainly not the first to do so, and it was common for modellers in wax to create their own wax compositions for modelling (cf. John Flaxman* junior and Isaac Gosset*). Smith appears to have been the first 'outside' modeller to supply Wedgwood with wax portraits* for reproduction. This was a reversal of Wedgwood's normal practice, which was to buy, commission or borrow models which he reproduced in black basaltes*, white terracotta* or jasper* for sale. Smith's portraits, reproduced in terracotta, were supplied to him for distribution as well as being available to Wedgwood. His portraits of Lady Charlotte Finch* and her daughters (1774), and of John Bradby Blake* (1776) are undistinguished and give little hint of the mastery displayed in that of Sir William Hamilton* (1772), a portrait as dignified and finely modelled as any in the entire series of 'Illustrous Moderns'* portraits. Nearly as fine are his companion portraits of Josiah Wedgwood and Thomas Bentley* in Court dress (c.1776), and those of Captain Edward Hamilton (c.1774) and the Prussian philosopher and naturalist Johann Reinhold Forster (1776).

In 1775 Wedgwood learnt from 'a Man from the Derby China Works', who sought employment at Etruria*, that Derby* had been 'making h[ea]ds for Smith & have many more to make.' Josiah was then making good progress with the experiments which resulted in the invention of jasper and was therefore anxious to drop all connection with Smith. This he did not do until he had acquired the services of another portrait modeller, the younger Flaxman. No record of Derby biscuit* porcelain portrait medallions has been found so it is possible that the story of Smith's connection with Derby was false.

Smith, John (fl.1773-4)

Painter at the Chelsea Decorating Studio* who worked on the Frog* service. He is sometimes listed as John 'Warwick' Smith (1749-1831) the noted painter of landscapes in watercolour, who appears to have been in London studying with Sawrey Gilpin at the time when the Frog service was being painted. It is possible that he worked for a short time at the Chelsea Decorating Studio.

Smith & Co, William

Earthenware manufacturers of Stockton-on-Tees, founded in 1824. They were principally imitators of Wedgwood, employing the impressed 'WEDGEWOOD' mark. Presumably they hoped that the misspelling would protect them from the consequences of plagiarism, but in 1848 Wedgwood applied for an injunction restraining Smith's from continuing to copy the products of Etruria* and this was granted. William Smith & Co made a considerable variety of wares, among them creamcolour and white ware. Their marks included: 'W.S. & Co's WEDGEWOOD' and 'W.S. & Co's QUEEN'S WARE'.

Sneyd Family

Lords of the Manor of Tunstall, Staffordshire, since the 14th century and owners of Keele Hall, now Keele University. The Sneyds were well known to the Wedgwoods in the 18th century, and

SNEYD FAMILY. Bone china plate decorated with the arms of the Sneyd family in red, black and gold. This plate is from the only first period bone china dinner service so far recorded. *Wedgwood Museum*

SOAP BOX. Three-piece soap box printed in dark underglaze blue with the *Peony* pattern. 5in. x 3¾in. x 3in. c.1840. *Author's collection*

William Sneyd of Belmont was a close friend of Josiah II's*. An armorial* plate of first period bone china* in the Wedgwood Museum* bears the arms of the Sneyd family.

Sneyd, T., Hanley
Name found on crude imitations of the Portland vase* dating probably from the early years of the 19th century.

Snuff Bottles
Snuff bottles, about 2½in. high, the form inspired by Chinese snuff bottles made during the reign of Chia Ch'ing (1796-1820), were produced by Wedgwood in Pearl* ware and bone china*, c.1900. Examples are scarce.

Snuffers and Stands
Wedgwood made jasper* chambersticks with snuffers and stands as early as c.1785-90. Snuffers and stands were made in jasper-dipped stoneware early in the 19th century and decorative snuffer stands were produced in Majolica* from about 1869.

Soap Box (Dish)
The three-piece soap box – rectangular, circular or oval – with lid and loose, pierced liner, was an essential part of chamber ware* (toilet ware) sets throughout the 19th century and until 1940. They were produced in a wide variety of patterns, notably underglaze blue prints* and in coloured bodies*, but also decorated with gold, platinum and variegated lustre*.

Soap Cup
A more elaborate version of the soap box, a footed cup with lid, height about 4in., made in Queen's ware* during the latter part of the 18th century and, from c.1820, in ornamented white stoneware ('porcelain').

SOAP CUP. Queen's ware Globe soap cup, shape no.652. Height 4½in. c.1820. *Wedgwood Museum*

SOCIETY FOR THE ABOLITION OF THE SLAVE TRADE. Medallion of a Slave in Chains issued in support of the Society of which Josiah Wedgwood was a committee member. Black on yellow jasper (probably a trial). Diameter 1⅜in. 1787. *Wedgwood Museum*

Soaprock
Hydrated silicate of magnesium, possibly discovered by Cookworthy (see: Champion, Richard; Cherokee Clay; Porcelain); first recorded in use at Lund's Bristol porcelain factory. Its special quality is resistance to thermal shock. It was used by the Worcester* porcelain factory (in place of the feldspathic rock of 'true' porcelain) from about 1752, the year in which the Bristol factory was united with Worcester. 'Useful' Thomas Wedgwood*, while at Worcester, would certainly have acquired some knowledge of the manufacture of steatitic or soaprock porcelain and this would have been valuable to Josiah Wedgwood in his early experiments to make porcelain and jasper*.

Society of Antiquaries, The
London society, founded c.1572, and incorporated in 1751, whose members were devoted to the study of antiquities. Wedgwood was elected a Fellow in May 1786, proposed by seven members, all Fellows of the Royal Society*, one of whom was Sir Joseph Banks*.

Society for the Abolition of the Slave Trade
Society founded originally as the 'Committee for the Abolition of the Slave Trade' in 1787. Its first Chairman was Granville Sharp and other members of the Committee included Thomas Clarkson, William Wilberforce and Josiah Wedgwood. The title of the Committee was carefully chosen, recognising a clear, and politically critical, distinction between slavery and the slave trade. The poem, *The Dying Negro,* written by Thomas Day, a member of the Lunar Society*, in 1773, may have been partly responsible for enlisting Wedgwood's practical opposition to the slave trade, of which, as a frequent visitor to Liverpool, he was better informed than many of his contemporaries.

In 1787, Hackwood* modelled a cameo*, after the seal of the Society, depicting a kneeling slave in chains, the outer edge moulded with the words 'AM I NOT A MAN AND A BROTHER?'. This was produced principally in black and white jasper (though examples exist in other colours) and distributed by Wedgwood free to all those closely concerned with the movement for abolition. Clarkson wrote: 'Some had them inlaid in gold on the lid of their snuff-boxes. Of the ladies, several wore them in bracelets, and others had them fitted up in an ornamental manner as pins for their hair. At length the taste for wearing them became general, and thus a fashion…was seen for once in the honourable office of promoting the cause of justice, humanity and freedom.' In 1788 Wedgwood sent a quantity of these cameos to Benjamin Franklin, President of the Pennsylvanian Society for the Abolition of Slavery. This cameo was reproduced in 1959 and modern examples are not rare.

Wedgwood's efforts were not confined to the production of a few hundred cameos. He promoted meetings, publications and petitions and actively canvassed the support of anyone whose voice might command respect, such as Anna Seward*. In spite of the best efforts of both William Pitt and Charles James Fox, the motion for abolition was lost in the House of Commons in April 1792 and it was not until 1807 that the bill was passed. Of the Lunar Society members who had most actively supported the campaign – Wedgwood, Darwin*, Boulton*, Day and Priestley* – Boulton alone lived to see it succeed.

Society of Arts
See: Royal Society of Arts

Society of Bucks
See: Honourable Society of Bucks

Sock Boot
A hollow utensil approximately in the shape of a short riding boot, made in Queen's ware c.1890. Filled with hot water it was used for drying or warming a sock or stocking drawn over it.

Socle
A low plinth used as a pedestal for a statue or bust. Wedgwood's 18th-century socles for black basaltes* busts were usually circular in shape with a simple turned foot, often ornamented with a meander or key pattern. Some, however, were a more elaborate, waisted rectangular shape. Early in the 19th-century the circular shape was changed to one with a much flatter foot and this shape was retained for most busts throughout the century and up to 1940.

Socrates (469-349 BC)
Celebrated Greek philosopher, the son of a sculptor. His method of teaching was to bring his hearers to an understanding of what he wanted to impart by posing a series of carefully framed questions. His influence became so great that he was eventually charged with corrupting the youth of Athens and of trying to replace the divinities of the State with his own. He died by drinking hemlock. Hoskins & Grant* supplied a cast for a bust in 1775.

Soft-paste Porcelain
Artificial porcelain made from white-burning clays and what was, in principle, ground glass. It takes its name from its relatively soft firing temperature (about 1200°C), as opposed to 1450°C for hard-paste* or 'true' porcelain. Soft-paste porcelain was first made in Europe in the 16th century and reached its peak of perfection at Vincennes. In England, it was made first at Chelsea* and Bow*, where bone ash was added to the body. At Worcester*, from about 1752, the body contained soaprock*. There is no evidence that Wedgwood ever made soft-paste porcelain and he was probably deterred principally by the many failures in the industry, including Chelsea* and Bow*, and the potential damage to sales of Queen's ware*.

Soho Factory, Birmingham
See: Boulton, Matthew

Solander, Dr Daniel (1736-82)
Swedish naturalist, a pupil of Linnaeus. He travelled to London in 1760 to obtain employment at the British Museum. Eight years later he accompanied Sir Joseph Banks* and Captain Cook to Otaheite to observe the transit of Venus. Solander was a guest at Lunar Society* meetings in Birmingham, where Wedgwood probably met him, and his London house in Soho Square was close to Wedgwood's Greek Street showrooms. A portrait medallion* was modelled by Flaxman* in 1775 and adapted for a large portrait in 1779.

Solid Agate
Coloured clays (usually white, blue and brown) wedged (mingled by slicing and kneading) either at random or in a predetermined sequence to imitate agate and other natural stones. Wedgwood used the technique for his early teapots and knife handles and later, in a more sophisticated form, for vases. Solid agate was made also at Apt (Vaucluse), and at Kassel and Königsberg in Germany.
See: Variegated Ware

Solitaire Service
Another term for a *déjeuner* set for one.

SOLID AGATE. Wedgwood & Bentley egg-shaped vase of wedged red, brown and cream-coloured clay, with gilded *putto* finial. Height 8¼in. c.1774.   *Wedgwood Museum*

Solon (c.639- ?559 BC)
Athenian legislator, chosen archon (head of State) in 594, introducing many reforms, a new system of weights and measures and a revised calendar. He is known also for philosophical and moral wisdom expressed in verse form. Hoskins & Grant* supplied casts of busts described as Solon and Demosthenes in March 1774, but Wedgwood wrote to Bentley* in May 1777: 'We are at a loss about the Solon Bust order'd, having no other Solon than what we have called Demosthenes…Mr Cox* says it was called Demosthenes when it first came here in Plaister & continues under that name in our Catalogue'. Confusion (of which there has been plenty) in the naming of Wedgwood subjects is not confined to the 19th and 20th centuries

Somnus
God of Sleep, the son of Night and the brother of Death. Wedgwood produced a large figure, 25in. long, of a sleeping boy after a black marble (or basalt) by Alessandro Algardi (1602-54) now in the Galleria Borghese, Rome. The original figure was illustrated in an engraving published in 1704 (Maffei and Rossi, *Raccolta di Statue Antiche e Moderne,* Pl.151). The Wedgwood copy in black basaltes* is illustrated by Meteyard* *(Life of Wedgwood,* Vol.II, facing p.230) with the correct title. Wedgwood, however called this figure *Morpheus* and it is listed under this name in the 1773 Catalogue. It may be the figure described as 'Boy on a Couch' invoiced by Theodore Parker* in 1769. Hoskins & Grant* also charged for a 'Mould for a Morpheus for Pressing, cutting the model in pieces and joining it together again', suggesting that Parker's figure may have been sent to Hoskins for moulding and repairing* by a figure maker.
See also: Coward, John

Sophonisba
Daughter of the Carthaginian general, Hasdrubal; married the King of Numidia. She died from drinking a poisoned draught sent by her husband after Scipio Africanus insisted that she become a Roman captive.
Wedgwood subject:
Sophonisba, medallion 4in. x 3¼in., no 148 in 1777 Catalogue*

Sorrows of Young Werther, The
Goethe's *Die Leiden des Jungen Werthers,* 1774, was one of two works of contemporary fiction employed as inspiration for ornament in the Romantic* style on Wedgwood's jasper*. The other was Sterne's* *Sentimental Journey.* Goethe's sentimental best-selling romance was suggested by the suicide of a fellow student at Leipzig University, who shot himself while possessed of a hopeless passion

SPHINX. One of a pair of 'modern' sphinxes, the heads popularly supposed to be portraits of the actresses Peg Woffington and Kitty Clive. Height 7¼in.

Mr & Mrs David Zeitlin Collection

for the wife of another man. The work was an instantaneous success and was soon translated into several languages. Young men and women gave way to imaginary sorrows to emulate Werther, and men even committed suicide holding a copy of the book. Werther and Charlotte were widely used as porcelain decoration, Meissen* producing tea services decorated with different scenes from the book about 1780. A favourite subject of a number of factories was Charlotte weeping at the tomb of Werther, the Wedgwood jasper version of which was designed by Lady Templetown* about 1785.
See: Colour Plate 102

Southwell, Mrs (fl.1750-75)
A visitor, with her husband, to Etruria* in July 1772. Wedgwood wrote to Bentley: 'They like our new flower & bow [bough] pots very much. They are both adepts in these matters & I did not miss the opportunity of profiting from their knowledge...We fixed some general principles, & then examin'd every flowerpot we had by these principles, & we found all those we have hitherto made & *which have not sold,* to be very deficient in some of these *first principles.*' He added 'Mrs Southwell is a Charming Woman I am more & more in love with her every time I see her.' The popularity of Wedgwood's terracotta* bough pots, which sold in great quantities, was undoubtedly due in large measure to their practical design.

Sparks, Thomas (1773-1848)
Engraver of Hanley, who supplied engravings for tableware patterns to Ridgway, Spode*, Stevenson's of Cobridge and Wedgwood, among others. He was responsible, in 1810, for a number of engravings for the *Peony, Bamboo* and *Hibiscus* patterns. In 1818 he wrote from London to Josiah II* soliciting work and suggesting 'designs after the manner of the antique, printed, coloured and gilt in imitation of Bronze' for Wedgwood's Stone China*.
See: Underglaze Blue Printing

Spath (Spaith)
An 18th-century term, equivalent to the modern 'spar', for kinds of crystalline or non-lustrous minerals which can easily be cleaved, such as fluorspar, calcite, etc. The term 'spathic' is used today of a mineral resembling a spar, particularly in the property of breaking along lines of cleavage, as in 'feldspathic'. The word spath is of German origin and is still used in France to mean spar. Wedgwood used the term 'spath [or spaith] fusible' to denote the fusible part of his fine stonewares, as distinct from the refractory clay.

Speckled Agate (Speckled Ware)
The effect of coloured slips* sprayed on to the surface of the ware to produce a speckled pattern. The technique was employed by Wedgwood, the Woods* of Burslem and others.

Spence, Benjamin Edward (1822-66)
Sculptor who studied under R.J. Wyatt and John Gibson; exhibited at the Royal Academy on five occasions between 1849 and 1866. His *Joseph Interpreting Pharoah's Dream* was modelled by William Beattie* for Wedgwood in 1867 and reproduced in Carrara* under the title *The Interpretation.*

Sphinxes
The sphinx is a combination of the human form with that of the lion. There are two types: the Greek and the Egyptian. The Greek sphinx derived originally from Egypt but was said to be the daughter of Hades (Pluto*) and the Chimaera*. She is represented as seated upright in a typically feline position, and has the head and breasts of a woman, the body of a lion and a pair of wings. The Egyptian sphinx, originally male, is represented as reclining, the upper part human, the remainder of the body that of a lion. In 18th-century England the Greek sphinx was known, in particular, from black-figure vases, the Egyptian from illustrations in work by such antiquarians as Montfaucon* and Caylus*. Wedgwood produced versions of both varieties of sphinx from about 1769 in black basaltes* and later in jasper* and rosso antico*. Some good reproductions were included in the Egyptian Collection* produced

SPHINX. Black basaltes seated Greek sphinx, a form derived from Egypt. Height 8in. c.1785.
Wedgwood Museum

SPITTOON. Black basaltes engine-turned spittoon with wide everted rim. Height 3½in. c.1785. *Wedgwood Museum*

in 1978. The modelling of the original figures is of excellent quality and has been assigned to various artists. Probably they were obtained, like other figures, as casts from one of the London plaster cast makers such as Hoskins & Oliver*, Mrs Landré* or Richard Parker*, and repaired* by Ralph Boot*, the young Hackwood* or Josiah Wedgwood himself.
See: Candlesticks and Candelabra; Canopic Jars; Egyptian Taste; Figures

Spies
See: Industrial Espionage

Spilsbury, Jonathan (fl.1770-1800)
Engraver and modeller, briefly employed by Wedgwood in 1770-1. Excessive prudishness impelled him to write to Bentley* complaining of being asked to model nude figures. 'I cannot', he wrote, be reconcil'd to those Figures which are quite naked. Whether there be any immodesty in making such Representations I can't say, but to Me such an employment wou'd be at least exceedingly disagreeable.' Transfer-prints* by Sadler* & Green after Spilsbury, which have been identified on Queen's ware*, suggest that he supplied engravings to the firm for nearly thirty years.

Spill Vase
A small cylindrical vase to contain folded slips of paper or thin strips of wood known as spills. They were used, lit from the grate, for lighting candles and tobacco pipes. Spill vases of various sizes were made by Wedgwood in Queen's ware* and all the dry bodies* from c.1775 and later in bone china*, Carrara* and Majolica*. Spill vases are still in production in basalt and jasper*.

SPODE. Creamware *pâté* dish on fixed stand enamelled with *Flute and Wreath* pattern in rose-purple and dark brown. Height 3¾in. Mark: Spode. c.1795. *Author's collection*

Spirit Barrel
Large containers for spirits were made by several pottery manufacturers, the earliest being of saltglazed* stoneware. They were made for bulk storage in public houses and bars. Wedgwood made spirit barrels of Pearl* ware with printed and handpainted decoration with the name of the spirit – brandy, rum, whisky – lettered prominently and fitted with a pewter spigot for drawing off the contents. These were produced at Etruria* c.1890-1915.

Spittoon
A cuspidor, or receptacle for spittle; usually a flat cylinder with a concave hole in the centre or globular in shape with a wide rim and a funnel-shaped mouth, sometimes containing sawdust. Some models have a spout for emptying. Wedgwood made spittoons of the latter shape in both Queen's ware and black basaltes* (including some handsome engine-turned* pieces of small size, evidently not intended for use in a public place) from c.1775.

SPODE. White stoneware teapot, dipped in blue, ornamented with *Charlotte at the Tomb of Werther.* Height 4⅜in. Mark: SPODE. c.1820. *Norwich Castle Museum*

Spode
Josiah Spode I was apprenticed to Whieldon* in 1749 and by the time of Wedgwood's partnership with Whieldon (1754) he appears to have graduated to journeyman. Shortly thereafter he joined William Banks and John Turner* at Stoke. Between 1764 and 1779 he was a partner at factories at Shelton and Stoke. From 1779 he was in business on his own account at Stoke. At first his production was probably confined to Egyptian Black*, creamware and a form of Pearl* ware painted in blue and it was left to Josiah Spode II (1754-1827), who assumed the direction of the firm after his father's death in 1797, to convert a successful pottery into a major force in the pottery industry. When he died thirty years later, Spode had taken the lead from Wedgwood.

He was succeeded by his son Josiah Spode III, who survived him by only three years. The firm was then bought by William Taylor Copeland, who was already a partner, and it became successively 'Copeland late Spode' and 'W.T. Copeland & Sons.' Josiah Spode II is credited with having introduced the manufacture of bone china* into Staffordshire about 1805, and he made many improvements in the art of transfer-printing*. Outline transfers as an aid to the painters were used on bone china.

Spode captured a large share of the porcelain market and made a speciality of 'Japan' patterns. In the 1840s Copeland introduced Parian* ware, later manufactured by Wedgwood under the name of Carrara*. Under the Copelands the firm produced elaborately gilded wares with rich coloured grounds, drawing heavily on Sèvres for inspiration.

The range of wares produced by Spode during the 18th and early 19th centuries was wide and conformed closely to Wedgwood's. It included creamware, black basaltes*, a white stoneware body with coloured slip ornamented in imitation of jasper* (but not a true jasper body), a red body similar to rosso antico*, cane* ware, a drab* body, Pearl* ware, lustre* (including variegated lustre*) and bone china. Many of the shapes and ornaments are indistinguishable from Wedgwood's and it is plain (or certainly appeared so to the Wedgwoods) that Spode deliberately copied some of Wedgwood's styles and patterns. In 1802 Tom Byerley warned Josiah II: 'He [Spode] is very anxiously endeavouring I believe to get into the

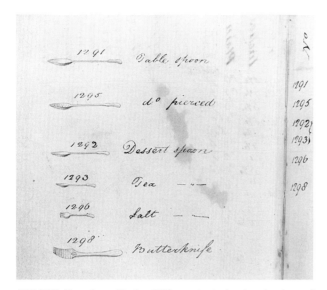

SPOONS. Page from Charles Gill's notebook showing drawings of shapes of Queen's ware spoons and a butterknife with curved ridged surface. c.1815. *Wedgwood Museum*

same tracks as we are in – and to improve his articles by our models – and I dont think he will be too scrupulous in the means.'

Eight years later Josiah II wrote to Bateman: 'I believe Mr Spode has copied our Chrysanthemum [pattern] and I should be glad to know his price & how it is executed.' Bateman's reply makes it clear that the Spode version, although not a precise copy, was so near to one as to be immediately recognisable. He had already reported in April: 'the Japan [patterns] 9 and 10 and the Rock…Mr Spode has made a similar pattern, it is a combination of the Japan No 9 and the Rock…Mr Spode has copied most of our flower pots, Green, Buff, and different coloured glazes with black spots &c.' Spode tried also to entice some of Wedgwood's workmen into his employ, and it was rumoured that he had approached William Hackwood* for this purpose. Hackwood, however, was not to be bought.

In the 20th century the relationship between the two firms was distinctly friendly, but, while Wedgwood prospered and regained the lead in the industry, Spode's business failed to develop. In the 1960s the firm was put up for sale and serious talks were held in the hope of coming to an agreement for its purchase by Wedgwood. These failed and the firm was bought by London International Group, a company specialising in the manufacture of contraceptive and other rubber goods, which also acquired the Royal Worcester* Porcelain Co and subsequently bid unsuccessfully for Wedgwood itself (see: Wedgwood in the Twentieth Century).

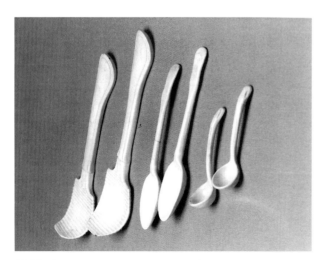

SPOONS. Queen's ware salt and dessert spoons and two butter knives. Salt spoons c.1840, the rest c.1790. *Byron and Elaine Born Collection*

Sponged Ground
A ground colour applied underglaze by dabbing with a sponge. Examples are the early mottled and tortoiseshell* grounds, in which several colours were applied in much the same way, and the so-called powder-blue ground introduced in 1910-12.
See: Powder Colours

Spoons
Wedgwood made Queen's ware* spoons of all sizes, from table spoons to salt spoons, from c.1770 until the second half of the 19th century. These were generally plain but were supplied also to match handpainted or printed patterns, and long-handled spoons were part of the dairy ware* available. Ladles, in sizes suitable for cream, gravy and soup were made, some being pierced for straining. Salt spoons and caddy spoons* were produced in jasper* and the dry bodies* from c.1785. Ceramic spoons are exceptionally vulnerable to breakage and examples from the 18th century are extremely scarce.

Spoon Warmer
Spoon warmers in the form of finely modelled shells raised on feet moulded and decorated to simulate waves were made in Argenta* (Majolica*) in the 1880s.

Spouts
The shapes of handles*, knops* and spouts often provide the only indication of the source of a piece of unmarked pottery. Three shapes of spouts are characteristic of Wedgwood's early creamware teapots and coffeepots, although they should not be taken as conclusive evidence of Wedgwood manufacture without confirming factors, such as similarly characteristic handles* and knops*. The crabstock* spout, with conforming handle and knop,

SPOUTS. The commonest of early Wedgwood teapot spout shapes, the so-called 'cabbage' or 'overlapping leaf' spout, shown on a Rhodes-painted teapot of about 1768. *Author's collection*

SPOUTS. Moulded rococo shell spout shown on a Wedgwood Queen's ware teapot, c.1770. *Wedgwood Museum*

SPROSON, Kenneth. Barlaston-shape teaware decorated with *Covent Garden* pattern, designed by Sproson in 1959.
Wedgwood Museum

was used by Wedgwood in the early 1760s but was employed also by so many other Staffordshire potters as to be of little aid in identification. The commonest Wedgwood spout shape, in use between 1760 and 1768 was a well defined, elongated 'S' shape moulded with overlapping cabbage or cauliflower leaves. This shape was used by other potters but on Wedgwood pieces it was normally (not invariably) accompanied by the scroll handle and either the rose or pierced ball or baluster knop. A rococo* shell-moulded spout is also found at the same period but lasted well into the late 1780s. Shapes used after about 1772 pose fewer problems since the ware is almost invariably impressed or printed with Wedgwood's mark.

Spreader
A tool, nowadays operated automatically, used for flattening a ball of clay into a circular bat for use with a jigger*.

Sprigged Ware (Sprigging)
Pottery ornamented in low relief with motifs stamped or moulded separately and applied to the ware using water or slip* as an adhesive. The process of sprigging was extensively used by Wedgwood, for instance for the ornamenting of jasper*, but it was in use before his time, notably at some of the porcelain factories, where sprays of prunus or tea blossom were applied in this way.

Sproson, Kenneth (b.1932)
Designer; studied at the Royal College of Art; joined Wedgwood's design staff at Barlaston, 1955. Next year he transferred to the New York office, where he became staff designer, concentrating on commemorative wares and patterns for the American market. In 1959 he designed *Covent Garden,* one of the most outstandingly successful patterns produced for Barlaston shape, and in 1963 he created *Galaxie* shape for bone china* (see: Tableware Shapes).

Spurs (Stilts)
Small pieces of fired refractory* clay used to separate ware stacked in the glost oven*. Three spur or stilt* marks are usually visible on the underside of earthenware plate rims.

Stafford, Granville Leveson-Gower, 1st Marquis of (1721-1803)
Eldest son of the 1st Earl Gower, whom he succeeded in 1754; member of parliament for Westminster; Lord of the Admiralty, 1794; Lord Privy Seal, 1755 and 1784; Lord President of the Council, 1767-1769 and 1783. Friend and patron of Josiah Wedgwood's, a frequent visitor at Etruria*, and host to Josiah at Trentham Hall, Lord Gower is frequently mentioned in Wedgwood's letters to Bentley*. He exercised his considerable influence on behalf of the Staffordshire potters in general and Josiah Wedgwood in particular, and was one of Wedgwood's most constant admirers

and most liberal customers. He was created Marquis of Stafford in 1786. His portrait medallion*, attributed to Hackwood*, was issued c.1782.

Stafford Pottery
An earthenware pottery at Stockton-on-Tees which, from 1826 to 1853, traded as William Smith & Co*. They used the name 'WEDGEWOOD' or 'WEDGEWOOD & CO' until Wedgwood obtained an injunction to stop this infringement of their trade mark in 1848.

Staite's Patent Pipe
A patent pipe bowl made by Wedgwood in jasper-dipped white stoneware* ('porcelain') with jasper* ornaments, c.1849. It was produced also in an elaborate version with a circular stand. The '1843' Price Book contains details of prices for pipes of several patterns, including Staite's patent, on 28 December 1849, and an entry for 'Stand No 1 and large pipe to it 5/4d'.

STAITES PATENT PIPE. Pipe and stand of white stoneware dipped in blue jasper and ornamented with various classical cameos. Height 6⅛in. c.1849.
Author's collection

STAMPED. Teapot of deep ochre-coloured clay with creamware handle and spout and stamped applied ornament touched in with green and brown. Height 5⅜in. Unmarked. Probably Whieldon-Wedgwood, c.1755. *Manchester City Art Gallery*

Stamped, Stamping
1. Impressed with a stamp, as in the case of the mark impressed by Wedgwood from about 1770 onwards.
2. The process of making small ornaments from intaglio moulds for attachment by sprigging.
3. The technique of decoration in which unfired clay is impressed with ornament with the aid of metal stamps.

Statuary Porcelain
A mid-19th century term for Parian* or Carrara* porcelain. It was originally intended that this body be employed for the reproduction of statuary in miniature.

Steam Engines
See: Prime Movers; Watt, James

Steel Lustre
See: Lustre Decoration

Steele, Aaron (fl.1780-1845)
Painter at the Greek Street decorating studios (see: Showrooms) from April 1784. He appears to have specialised in the decoration of Etruscan* vases and as late as 1807 Tom Byerley* was suggesting that he should be put to work on these again. 'He is,' Byerley wrote in April of that year, 'the only man in the country with much knowledge of that work, & as such very valuable.' Steele was responsible also for some fine bird painting, principally on dessert ware but seen also on some small violet baskets of first period bone china*, c.1816. The name of the bird is inscribed on the base of each piece.
See: Colour Plate103

STEELE, Aaron. Bone china scalloped dessert plate painted by Steele with a central portrait of a bird and rim decoration of groups of feathers, shown with two bone china dessert plates of the same period. c.1816. *Formerly Buten Museum*

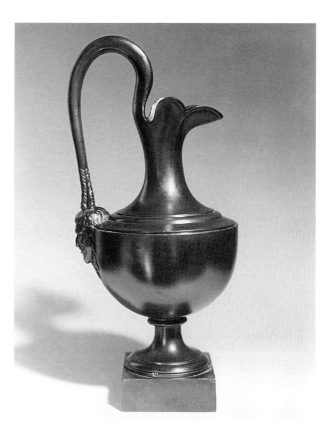

STELLA, Jacques de. Wedgwood & Bentley black basaltes ewer with tall looped handle terminating in a male head, the shape adapted from a design by Stella. Height 12in. c.1774. *Schaefer Collection*

Steele, Daniel (fl.1762)
Painter with Thomas Daniel(l), credited with the decoration of the caudle set* said by Simeon Shaw* to have been presented by Wedgwood to Queen Charlotte* about 1763.

Stella, Jacques de (1596-1657)
French painter and etcher, born in Lyon, who belonged to a family of painters and engravers of Flemish origin. Jacques de Stella spent a number of years in Rome, where he met Poussin, who became his friend and later greatly influenced his work. In Paris, Stella received royal patronage and was responsible for some important decoration in churches. He is particularly noted today for his decorative work. The *Livre de Vases aux Galeries de Louvre* (Paris, 1667) contained illustrations of vases by Stella, engraved by his niece, Françoise Bouzonnet. Wedgwood's fish-tail* ewer was copied from the title-page to this book (although the handle had previously appeared on French *faïence*). A copy of *Livre de Vases* was in Wedgwood's library in 1770 and Josiah wrote of the book as 'an admirable one indeed' and referred to his copies of the vase as 'Stella's ewers'. These varied from the original design only in the addition of scales to the tail handle and a simplification of the terminal. On some copies, which were made in black basaltes* and white terracotta* with variegated* decoration, the applied ornament was altered or omitted.

Stephan, Pierre (fl.1770-95)
A French modeller, who worked for Derby*, Coalport* and Wirksworth. He was at Derby from 1770 to 1773, probably as resident modeller, but worked thereafter as a freelance. In May 1774 he applied to Wedgwood from Wirksworth, seeking employment, describing himself as capable of working in 'Figures, Vasses, or any sort of Useful as Business may require' and requested that he might be employed partly in London in order to improve his modelling. No evidence has been found that he was employed at Etruria* but he supplied moulds to Wedgwood later in 1774. Josiah wrote of them in August: 'I have rec'd Mr Steven's [*sic*] moulds of Hope & the conquer'd Province & am glad to find the drawing & proportions so well serv'd, but in everything else they are infinitely short of the

STEPHAN. Pierre. Derby biscuit porcelain figure of Admiral Rodney modelled by Stephan, c.1781-2. Height 10¾in., Unmarked, but inscribed 'STEPHAN'. This figure exists unmarked in black basaltes and is assigned to Wedgwood. *Merseyside Museums*

STERNE, Laurence. Black basaltes figure of *Poor Maria*, modelled by Edward Keys, c.1850. It was reproduced also in Carrara. Height 11½in. *Formerly Buten Museum*

exquisite originals. The Drapery is hard & unfinish'd, the characters of the faces are those of common Mortals *of the lower Class*.' Next month Stephan supplied models of a lion, a greyhound and a 'Lap Dog' as knops for teapots. No further mention of his name appears in the Wedgwood archives. Stephan's name (possibly his signature) appears on a figure of Admiral Rodney which is known both in Derby biscuit* porcelain and in black basaltes*. The latter is assigned to Wedgwood, but no evidence has been found to confirm this attribution. (A full discussion of this figure appears in Robin Reilly's *Wedgwood,* Vol.I, pp.469-71).

Sterne, Laurence (1713-68)
English novelist, born in Ireland and educated at Halifax and Cambridge University. He entered the Church and procured a living at Sutton, Yorkshire. The first two volumes of his most famous work, *Tristram Shandy,* were published in 1760 and were an instant success. The remaining volumes appeared over the next seven years. *A Sentimental Journey through France and Italy* was published in 1767. Wedgwood's bas-reliefs* of *Poor Maria* (adapted from a painting by Joseph Wright* of Derby) and the *Bourbonnais Shepherd,* both characters from this work, were modelled by Hackwood* in 1783 after designs by Lady Templetown*. A figure of *Poor Maria* by Edward Keys* was reproduced in black basaltes and Carrara*. c.1850.

Still
See: Whisky Still

Stilt (Spur) Marks
Small defects in the surface, or the glaze (where this is present) on the underside of flatware* which is not supported on a footing during firing. These mark the places where the object stood on small pointed stilts or 'cockspurs' in the kiln. They occur on Wedgwood earthenware (but not on bone china*, which is supported on a footrim), but they are, on modern Queen's ware*, ground out before being passed for distribution. They are so invariable on Chelsea* and Japanese (Arita) porcelain as to be a reason for instant rejection when they are absent. They are very widely found on other wares, especially earthenware.

Stirrup Cup
An English drinking vessel adapted from the ancient Greek rhyton. Usually it is in the form of the head of a fox or hound, but less often it is shaped like the head of a hare or some other animal, or even a fish head. The cups have no handle or foot and were made

to be drained at one draught. Principally they were for huntsmen to drink a toast to the day's sport, or for the rider who wanted a drink without dismounting.

Wedgwood made a hare's head stirrup cup in black basaltes*, possibly modelled by Tebo*, foxes' heads (often mounted in silver), and a classical head in the form of a handled and footed ewer copied from an antique bronze now in the Louvre.

Stone China
Dense, hard, porcellaneous ware generally composed of china clay, china stone, flint, blue clay and a bluish stain, first developed by Turner* of Lane End in 1800 and made in quantity by Spode* under the name of 'Stone China', and by others – including Wedgwood, H. & R. Daniel, Davenport* and Hicks & Meigh – using such names as 'Opaque china' and 'Semi porcelain'. Charles and James Mason patented a similar body under the name of 'Ironstone china' in 1813.

Josiah Byerley* wrote to Josiah Wedgwood II* in March 1814: 'Every one enquires for the stone china, made by Spode and Mason and it has a very great run – I presume you know what it is – it is a thick coarse china body, not transparent, with china patterns, but in texture similar to old stoneware*.' He rightly considered Mason's body inferior to Spode's. Bateman* added, two years later: 'The stone china is mostly inquired for amongst the better sort, they say the blue printed is so common – Spode, Davenport & Mason are

STIRRUP CUP. Two black basaltes stirrup cups: *(left)* hare's head, height 5¾in., c.1785in.; *(right)* fox's head with Sheffield plate mount, length 5¼in., unmarked, Wedgwood, c.1775.
Byron and Elaine Born Collection

STONE CHINA. Stone china dessert centre and saucer dish printed underglaze in blue and enamelled in a *chinoiserie* pattern. Dessert centre 8in. x 11in. c.1825. *Author's collection*

the best makers.' The first evidence of Wedgwood's Stone china is an undated entry in Josiah III's* Pottery Memos* of about 1819, which shows that the body was already in production. It is described as 'not vitrified enough to ring like china' and too costly because of the high proportion of china clay used. Other evidence indicates that trials of Stone china were made at Etruria* at least as early as 1817 and that the composition was altered, replacing the greater part of the china clay with china stone, to produce a body close to Spode's New Stone china body introduced in 1822.

It has been stated that production of Wedgwood's Stone china was limited to the years 1822-5 but there is sufficient evidence to show that these dates should be extended at least to c.1817-29 and probably later. Trials were continued as late as 1853. The scarcity of surviving examples suggests that quantities were never large. Wedgwood's Stone china patterns were of three types: printed and enamelled *chinoiseries** or 'Japan' designs, most of them already popular on Pearl* or White ware*; and underglaze-blue printed* patterns also previously applied to Pearl ware. A number of these were edge-lined with a brown lustre* first developed for use with blue printed wares.

Stone china is technically not porcelain, although it is certainly porcellaneous, much of it being slightly translucent and also ringing when struck. Wedgwood's Stone china is generally opaque, although specimens have been noted that show some degree of translucency in the thinnest parts. The Wedgwood impressed mark does not usually appear on Stone china, which is printed with the words 'WEDGWOOD'S STONE CHINA' or 'WEDGWOOD' alone in underglaze blue or onglaze black On gilded patterns the pattern number is added in gold (See: Appendix II, Marks).

Stoneware
A type of pottery, composed of clay and fusible rock, midway between earthenware and porcelain. It is fired to a point where vitrification of the fusible part renders it impervious to liquids, but not sufficiently to make it translucent, except in the case of the thinnest and most refined of these hard-fired wares. Vitrification makes a glaze unnecessary, but a glaze of some kind is usually added to those wares intended for domestic utility, usually a salt glaze, since this can be added at the same time as the ware is fired. Lead glazes have been employed occasionally, as they are on most porcelain, but this was most often for decorative purposes. Vessels for domestic use were always glazed *inside* for aesthetic reasons and to avoid staining. Some of Wedgwood's finer stonewares, such as jasper*, were lapidary* polished rather than glazed in the 18th century. Wedgwood's stonewares include early saltglazed wares, white terracotta*, all the dry bodies*, and also the so-called 'porcelain' introduced early in the 19th century.

A white body, known as 'porcelain' but in fact a stoneware body, made in biscuit* but in greater quantities covered with a smear glaze (see: Glazes), was in production by 1810, when the name was also in use. It appears to have been closely related to the white terracotta stoneware body, which it superseded, the principal difference being that, in its final form and thinly potted, the new 'porcelain' was slightly translucent. By 1817 successful trials had been made with a wash of jasper slip* and jasper reliefs to give the new body the appearance of jasper dip*. By the end of 1821, the blue ornaments were being made of a composition that was made almost entirely of jasper shavings.

The range of objects made in this body was at first limited, consisting mostly of decorative jugs and garden pots moulded with basketwork patterns sometimes edged with blue slip*. Hunt* pattern jugs and mugs, of the type made also by Turner*, Spode*

STONE CHINA. Part of a Stone china dinner service printed in brown and enamelled with *Japan* no.4 pattern. c.1830. *Christie's, London*

and Davenport* were especially popular, the necks often decorated with blue or brown slip, and these were made in five sizes until the 1850s. Smear glaze was in use by 1818, and many other forms of moulding and ornament – beehive*, arabesque*, wreathed laurel, fern, border sunflower, embossed Chinese flowers, and rose, thistle and shamrock – were introduced with different colours of ornament, which included a bright blue, grey, green and brown. Gothic* jugs were produced from 1828 and 'artichoke' teapots were available as late as 1845.

The principal function of the white stoneware ('porcelain') body was as a replacement for jasper during the years when the jasper body could not be made. As well as being ornamented in colour, it was dipped in jasper or stained to colours associated with jasper and its versatility is illustrated by its employment for such diverse objects as Flaxman's* chessmen*, figures of *Psyche** and *Ariadne**, *Triton** candlesticks, Portland vases* and tubes of various sizes for pharmaceutical use. It was still in production with a jasper dip and reliefs (Bas-relief ware*) in 1941, when it was finally discontinued.
See: Saltglazed Stoneware

Stothard, Thomas RA (1755-1834)
Painter and book illustrator; studied at the Royal Academy Schools, 1777; exhibited at the Society of Artists 1777 and at the Royal Academy, 1778; elected RA 1794. Stothard, a friend of Flaxman* designed the Wellington Shield (now at Apsley House, London), His three sons were all sculptors. Several Wedgwood bas-reliefs* are said to have been designed by Stothard, including *Blind Man's Buff* (certainly Flaxman's) and the four *Horae** (also, erroneously described as 'Aerial Figures' or 'Zephyrs'), which appear to have been adapted from illustrations by Bartoli* (*Pitture Antiche*, 1750).

Strainer
See: Drainer

Strapwork, Applied
Ornament in the form of vertical strips interwoven with horizontal strips applied to the surface of, for instance, a jasper* bowl. The vertical and horizontal strips might be of different colours, such as yellow and white. This type of ornament occurs most often on wares which, because of their shape, could not easily be worked on the engine-turning lathe* or were not suitable for more conventional applied ornament. Its application required exceptional skill on the part of the ornamenter and examples are scarce.

Strawberry Dish
Pierced dish, standing on four pointed feet, and usually provided with a conforming, slightly dished, plate to be used for draining strawberries. Four shapes – round, diamond, octagonal and oval – appear in the '1817' Queen's ware* Catalogue* (Blake's* Plate 12), and they were certainly in production at least thirty years earlier. They are usually decorated with handpainted patterns to match table services and they exist also in the shell edge shape (see: Tableware Shapes), decorated in underglaze blue. These pieces are often described as cress or salad dishes and were no doubt used as such.

STRAPWORK. Solid pale-blue jasper centrepiece ornamented with strapwork of white and yellow jasper and applied flowers inside the bowl. Height 9in. c.1785-95. *Wedgwood Museum*

Stringer, Samuel (1750?-82)
Josiah Wedgwood's mother was a Stringer, and it is probable (but not certain) that the Knutsford family of artists of that name – who included Samuel (exhibited, Society of Artists, 1774), James (architect) and Daniel – were her kinsmen. Young Samuel, or 'Young Stringer' as Josiah Wedgwood generally referred to him, was a competent landscape painter. Although a 'sad, untutor'd raw young fellow', he was engaged by Wedgwood to paint more than thirty views for the Frog* service, and a view of Etruria Hall* enamelled on a Wedgwood plaque* is attributed to him. This appears to be the original from which the Frog service view of Etruria Hall was copied and is of particular interest since it pre-dates by at least three years the work of George Stubbs* on Wedgwood supports. For about twenty years 'Young Stringer' was identified with Edward Stringer, a painter from Lichfield, an error corrected by Michael Raeburn, whose extensive researches into the sources of the Frog service landscapes are to be published in 1995.

Strobl, Kisfaludy Sigismund de (1884-1975)
Hungarian portrait sculptor; studied at Budapest Royal Academy (Professor from 1924) and in Vienna, Paris and Italy; awarded the Hungarian Order of Merit 1954. Strobl worked extensively in London between the wars, exhibiting at the Royal Academy and sculpting portraits of British notables, including Field Marshal Lord Allenby and George Bernard Shaw. Strobl's bust of Princess Elizabeth Alexandra Mary (later Queen Elizabeth II), height 16½in., was reproduced in basalt and Carrara* in 1937.

STRAWBERRY DISH. Queen's ware pierced strawberry dish and stand enamelled with a border of flowers and foliage. Dish 11in. x 9¼in. c.1790.
Byron & Elaine Born Collection

STROBL, Sigismund Kisfalud de. Matt white glazed Queen's ware bust of HRH The Princess Elizabeth Alexandra Mary (Queen Elizabeth II) at the age of eleven. Height 16½in. Signed and dated 1937.
Wedgwood Museum

Stuart, James 'Athenian' (1713-88)

Painter and architect, authority on classical art, and member of the Dilettanti Society. Stuart began his professional career as a fan painter. He visited Rome in 1741 and ten years later went to Greece in company with Nicholas Revett. The product of this journey was the publication of the first volume of *The Antiquities of Athens,* written with Revett and completed in four volumes between 1762 and 1816. Wedgwood acquired the first volume for his library and immediately subscribed for the second, which finally appeared in 1787, the year before Stuart's death. Stuart was both friendly to Wedgwood and, through his many connections with the aristocracy for whom he designed houses, influential. He lent Wedgwood original works of art to copy, discussed with him the proposal to open showrooms in the Adelphi*, and travelled with him to visit Oxford, Blenheim and Boulton's* works at Soho, Birmingham, in 1770. Two portrait medallions* of Stuart were produced, the first being listed in the 1773 Catalogue*, somewhat flatteringly under the heading of 'Princes and Statesmen' (evidently an error for Prince James Francis Edward Stuart, the 'Old Pretender'). Stuart was one of the few distinguished architects to make use of Wedgwood's jasper tablets* (Wedgwood wrote to Bentley* in November 1778 to congratulate him on 'the conversion of the Athenian') and he was among those who composed epitaphs for Thomas Bentley after his death in 1780.

Stubbs, George (1724-1806)

Painter, especially of animals, and now considered to be the greatest of British painters of horses. His *Anatomy of the Horse,* for which he engraved his own detailed anatomical drawings, was published in 1766. Through his friend, the miniature painter Richard Cosway, he became interested in miniature painting in enamel colours on copper, but soon found that limits of size and weight made copper plates unsuitable for his purpose and turned instead to ceramic plaques. He made enquiries with Coade* and by 1775 his search for a ceramic support for his painting had come to the attention of Thomas Bentley*. Wedgwood was enthusiastic about the proposal that he should make them and wrote in his Commonplace Book*: 'Tablets for Mr Stubbs – The proportions he likes are 3 feet by 2 and 3 by 2ft 4 – or in general 4 by 3 and 3 by 2.' These proved to be more difficult to produce than he supposed and two years passed before he was able to write, 'He shall be gratified, but large tablets are not the work of a day.' The body he chose is generally described either as Queen's ware* or biscuit*, but neither is technically accurate. It was a porous earthenware, probably a lower-fired version of the terracotta* body whose strength and suitability for firing in large sizes, such as the grounds for the Herculaneum Pictures*, was already proved. A thin, light glaze (a form of flux* such as Wedgwood had recommended previously for the preparation of terracotta grounds) was applied to the surface to seal it.

At the end of November 1777 Wedgwood fired two tablets but they were only about 22in. x 17in. and both were cracked or warped. Two more were fired next month, one of them successful, and the latter may have been used for *Lion attacking a Stag,* the only Stubbs plaque known to be signed and dated 1778. After eleven months more of experiments, Wedgwood wrote to Bentley: 'When you see Mr Stubs pray tell him how hard I have been labouring to furnish him with the means of adding immortality to his excellent pencil.' At the end of May 1779 he was at last able to to make tablets of the type required without undue loss, but only of sizes up to 30 inches, 'perhaps ultimately up to 36 inches by 24', but the costs had been heavy: special kilns had been built and later altered, a new body had been developed, and the correct firing temperature had been found only after many trials and costly losses. Josiah suggested that Stubbs should contribute towards these costs and told Bentley: 'we will take the payment in paintings.' Tablets continued to be supplied to Stubbs at least as late as 1786, and his last paintings on them, *Haycarting* and *Reapers,* were completed in 1790. The tablet for *Reapers,* at 30½in. x 41½in., was the largest delivered, though probably not the largest attempted.

Commercially the experiment was a failure: the paintings were received with almost universal disapproval when they were exhibited at the Royal Academy in 1781-2 and most of them remained unsold when Stubbs died. *The Gentleman's Magazine* of 1791 hoped that Stubbs would never again 'experience the disgrace... attendant on mounting his *hobby horse* of enamel portrait

STUART, James ('Athenian'). Solid blue and white jasper portrait medallion. Oval height 3¼in. c.1785. *Mrs Edward J. Warren Collection*

painting.' History has reversed this judgement: the plaques are now among the most highly prized of all examples of English pottery. Three portraits by Stubbs on oval ceramic grounds are of particular Wedgwood interest: those of Josiah and Sarah Wedgwood*, painted in 1780 when the artist paid a prolonged visit to Etruria*; and that of Erasmus Darwin*, painted in 1783.

In July 1780 Stubbs visited Etruria as Wedgwood's guest and stayed for several months, teaching the Wedgwood boys the elements of drawing, making sketches for a large painting on panel of the Wedgwood family, painting portraits on ceramic grounds of Josiah I and Sarah, and on panel of her father Richard Wedgwood*, and modelling two large bas-reliefs*, *The Frightened Horse* and *The Fall of Phaeton. The Frightened Horse* was modelled, at Stubbs's suggestion from his own engraving of *The Lion and the Horse.* Josiah was not pleased with the choice of subject but he was surprised at the artist's quick mastery of modelling tools and delighted with the excellence of the final model, a copy of which he immediately sent to Bentley*. It was produced in both jasper* and black basaltes* and has been reproduced at least twice in the 20th century in modern basalt. The second bas-relief was adapted from Stubbs's painting on copper, *The Fall of Phaeton,* and this, too, met with objections from Josiah, who wrote to Bentley that the *Frightened Horse* was 'a piece of natural history', while *Phaeton* was 'a piece of un-natural fiction' and would therefore, make an unsatisfactory companion for the first. As the finished tablet shows, this criticism was just, and the composition is quite unlike any other produced by Wedgwood in the 18th century; but the strength and vigour of the modelling amply justify Stubbs's steadfast defence of his subject. It was reproduced in jasper and examples are extremely rare.

Stubbs's large painting on panel of the Wedgwood family was also the subject of dissatisfaction and disagreement. He worked on the picture for nearly two months but Josiah thought the likenesses 'strong, but not very delicate' and some parts 'a little caricatur'd'. He was particularly disappointed with his own portrait and those of his wife and their daughters, Susannah* (Darwin) and Mary Anne. Although he was never entirely satisfied with it, he finally agreed that there was in the picture 'much to praise, & a little to blame.'

The following work by Stubbs is associated with Wedgwood:

OIL PAINTINGS

The Wedgwood Family in the park of Etruria Hall*, 1780, on panel, 47½in. x 59½in.

Richard Wedgwood*, 1780, on panel, 28in. x 23in.

ENAMEL (Ceramic colours) ON WHITE TERRACOTTA BODY PLAQUES

Lion attacking a Stag, oval 17in. by 23½in., 1778

Lion and dead Tiger, 17¼in. x 24in., 1779

Panther, 7½in. x 11in. c.1779

Josiah Wedgwood, oval portrait 20in. x 16in., 1780

Sarah Wedgwood, oval portrait 20in. x 16in., 1780

George Stubbs, oval self-portrait 27in. x 20in, 1781

STUBBS, George. White terracotta tablet painted with an equestrian self-portrait by George Stubbs. Oval 36½in. x 27½in. Unmarked, but inscribed 'Geo. Stubbs pinxit 1782'. Wedgwood, 1782.

Lady Lever Art Gallery, Port Sunlight

STUBBS, George. Black basaltes oval plaque, *The Frightened Horse,* modelled by Stubbs in 1780. 8¾in. x 14¼in. *Wedgwood Museum*

Labourers, oval 27½in. x 36in., 1781
Stallions Fighting, oval 22in. x 3 in., 1781
Young Gentleman loading a gun, oval 18in. x 24½in., 1781
Isabella Saltonstall as Una in Spenser's *Faerie Queene,* oval
 18⅞in. x 25⅛in., 1782
The Farmer's Wife and the Raven, oval 27½in. x 37in., 1782
George Stubbs on a white hunter, oval self-portrait 36½in. x 27½in.,
 1782. Sometimes erroneously catalogued as a portrait of Josiah
 Wedgwood
Erasmus Darwin, oval portrait 26in. x 20½in., 1783
Warren Hastings on horseback, oval portrait 43in. x 25½in., 1791
Haymakers, oval 28½in. x 39½in, 1794
Reapers, oval 30½in. x 41½in., 1795
Haycarting, oval 28½in. x 39½in., 1795
(Eleven enamel paintings, some of which may have been on
ceramic supports, listed in the sale of Stubbs's effects in 1807, are
still untraced.)

BAS-RELIEFS
The Frightened Horse, oval 11¼in. x 17½in, 1780
The Fall of Phaeton, 10½in. x 19⅜in., 1780
Nineteen small bas-reliefs of horses were modelled by Edward
Burch* in 1788-90. Several of these have been identified as after
drawings by Stubbs.
See: Colour Plates 104 and 105

Sugar Caster
See Caster

Sugar Dish Vase
Small lidded vases of squat baluster shape on a waisted, turned foot
and square socle, produced in black basaltes* and terracotta* with
variegated* decoration, c.1770-85.

STUBBS, George. Queen's ware teapot transfer-printed in black with a
sporting scene adapted from Stubbs's 'Two Gentleman going a
shooting with a view of Creswell Crags', engraved by W. Woollett,
1767. Height 6½in. c.1775-80. *Norwich Castle Museum*

SUGAR DISH VASE. Wedgwood & Bentley black basaltes Sugar
dish vase. Height 8in. c.1775. *Mr & Mrs Samuel Laver Collection*

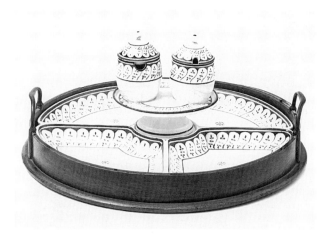

SUPPER SET. Queen's ware supper set enamelled in red and brown in contemporary mahogany tray. Diameter 13in. c.1795.
Wedgwood Museum

Sulphurs

Casts or impressions of gems* made in wax and sulphur composition were very popular during the 18th century. The mixture made sharp and accurate casts from ancient gems and originals of all kinds, and sulphurs were collected into cabinets in the same way as antique* gems and Wedgwood's cameos* and intaglios*. James Tassie* and others supplied Wedgwood with sulphurs from which cameos and intaglios in black basaltes* were reproduced.

Summerlys' Art Manufactures

An organisation founded in 1847 by Sir Henry Cole (founder of the South Kensington Museum, London, of which he became Director in 1860) using the pseudonym of Felix Summerly, intended to encourage the cooperation of artists and industry. In pursuit of this aim he commissioned designs from a number of artists, including John Bell* and Richard Redgrave*, both of whom designed objects for Summerly's which were produced by Wedgwood.

Sunflower, The

A favourite decorative motif of the Aesthetic Movement* in the 1880s. The sunflower appears as decoration on objects of all kinds, and dessert ware moulded with this form with a pierced border is illustrated in the 1880 Catalogue* of Shapes. It was made with decoration in enamel colours, green glaze (see: Glazes) or Majolica* glazes. Sunflower heads form part of the relief ornament of the *St Louis* Argenta* garden seat* of c.1885.

Supper Set

A service for use on a sideboard or supper table, consisting of several fan-shaped dishes which, placed side by side, form a circle, often within a wooden tray specially made for the purpose. In the centre is a space for a circular dish or tureen. These dishes were often provided with covers (now usually missing) and in this case the rims are concave to accommodate them. Supper sets were first made in China, from European models, towards the end of the 17th century and were made of Queen's ware* from the last quarter of the 18th century.

Surface Agate

Coloured clay slips trailed on to the surface of the ware to be decorated and combed to mingle them with an effect similar to the marbled end-papers of books. Surface agate vases were decorated after they were formed, and applied ornament, handles and finials were usually left uncoloured for later gilding. All such pieces are easily distinguished by their interiors, which are often left undecorated. Where the interior has been finished with slip, it will be seen that the pattern differs from that of the exterior.

Surtees, R.S. (1803-64)

See: Jorrocks, Mr

Swag

See: Festoon

SURFACE AGATE. Wedgwood & Bentley pear-shaped vase with gilded handles and band of laurel, the white terracotta body decorated with coloured slip to imitate agate, on a square terracotta plinth. Height 11in. c.1773. *City Museum & Art Gallery, Stoke-on-Trent*

Sweetmeat Set

A set of dishes in the form of segments of a circle which surround a central dish or stand, similar to a supper set*. A sweetmeat dish is one with several compartments similar to an *hors d'oeuvre* dish. Both were made by Wedgwood in late 18th- and 19th-century Queen's ware*.

Swift, Peter (fl.1766-90)

Peter Swift, described by Wedgwood as 'Cashier, Paymaster General and Accountant General', was one of his most valuable and trusted employees. He was engaged, on the recommendation of Thomas Bentley*, in November 1772 at a salary of £25 per annum for two years and £30 for the third. In that year he was sent to London to investigate Ben Mather's embezzlement. Early in 1777 he bought the Leopard Inn, Burslem, and entered into partnership with one Cobb, formerly Wedgwood's warehouseman, to manufacture a brown saltglazed* ware known locally as 'critch' ware (a similar ware was made also in Derbyshire under the name of 'Crouch' or 'Critch'). After about a year Swift tired of his new responsibilities and offered to return. Wedgwood accepted and, sensing that Swift would now settle down, wrote: 'I am not sorry he has made the trial'. With practical but not disinterested generosity he offered to lend him money to pay his debts. In 1779 Peter Swift acted as tutor to the Wedgwood children.

SYDNEY COVE MEDALLION. Pale fawn biscuit Sydney Cove medallion, designed by Henry Webber, 1789. Diameter 2⅜in. 1789.
Wedgwood Museum

Sword Hilts

Wedgwood jasper cameos* and beads were used to ornament the cut-steel hilts and guards of Court swords c.1790. Such a sword is in the Nottingham Castle Museum, the case bearing the name of 'I.Dawson, small steel worker, Goldsmith and Jeweller, 21, Hyde Street, Bloomsbury, London'. A second, similar, sword was in the Buten* Museum. Wedgwood made also some trial short sword or dagger ('hanger') handles in 1777, writing to Bentley* in October: 'The Griffins head makes an excellent handle for an Hanger but I wish you had given me some dimensions for the length & thickness. The Tritons head will make another for a Sea Captain, & a Tygers head we have wod make a third.' He adds that he will send the griffin first for Bentley's inspection. Since none of these pieces appears to have survived it is not known whether they were made in jasper* or black basaltes*. There is no evidence that they were ever put into production.

Sydney Cove Medallion

Circular commemorative medallion designed by Henry Webber* and issued in 1789-90. The 'First Fleet' – eleven ships, carrying some 850 convicts and 200 naval officers and men commanded by Captain Arthur Phillip, first governor of New South Wales – arrived in Sydney Cove on 26 January 1788. In November Phillip wrote to Sir Joseph Banks*, President of the Royal Society*, about local deposits of a white clay, used by the natives to paint themselves, which he had been informed might be suitable for porcelain manufacture. Samples sent to Banks were passed on to Josiah Wedgwood for trials. He replied to Sir Joseph on 12 March 1790: 'I have the pleasure of acquainting you, that the clay from Sydney Cove…is an excellent material for pottery, and may certainly be the basis of a valuable manufacture for our infant colony there. Of the species of ware which may be produced from it, you will have some idea from the medallions I have sent for your inspection.' In his Commonplace Book*, he noted that the clay was likely to be 'very useful where fine impressions are wanted' but that it did not 'agree with cobalt', producing an ugly grey colour which made it unsuitable for jasper*.

Webber's design represents Hope encouraging Art and Labour under the influence of Peace and was modelled by William Hackwood*. One of the first medallions made was sent to Erasmus Darwin* towards the end of November 1789, and a consignment of medallions (the quantity is not recorded) was sent out to Botany Bay with the 'Second Fleet', sailing on 19 January 1790. An engraving of the medallion, accompanied by some suitably prophetic verses by Darwin, appeared on the title page of John Stockdale's *The Voyage of Governor Philip* [sic] *to Botany Bay,* published in November 1789.

Medallions of the original issue, made of Sydney Cove clay, exist in two colours: a pale fawn and a dark brown that is almost black. They are impressed on the reverse with a special commemorative backstamp which has not been repeated on any later edition. They were moulded in one piece, to include the inscription. Later two-colour jasper editions were taken from a mould using a technique developed for the Bastille medallions*.

The design of the Sydney Cove medallion was adapted twice: first for a medallion commemorating the French Revolution* (the figure of Hope given a staff surmounted by the Phrygian cap of Liberty), and second for another celebrating the accession of the Emperor Leopold II (see: German Cameos).

Sykes, Mr

A merchant of Paris and Bordeaux supplied by Wedgwood under an agreement, initially for one year, concluded after the signing of the French Commercial Treaty* of 1786.
See also: Daguerre, Dominique

Synovec, Anita (b.1938)

Studio potter; studied at Cranbrook Academy of Arts, Detroit; worked at Barlaston* 1967-8, producing experimental pieces which are incised 'Anita'.

Syp Teapot

The Simple Yet Perfect teapot was designed by Lord Dundonald and produced at Etruria* from c.1905 in Queen's ware decorated with printed patterns (e.g. *Oaklands* and *Peony*) and Majolica* glazes. Some teapots bear the inscription 'THE CEYLON TEAPOT' on the front section of the lid.

A horizontal, perforated ledge separates the dry tea from the hot water. When the teapot is tilted backwards it rests on two short legs at the back and on the curved handle, allowing the hot water to pass through the perforations on to the tea leaves. When the tea is brewed, the pot is set down on its base and the tea is ready to be poured through the conventional spout. The separation of the used tea leaves from the prepared tea prevents it from becoming 'stewed'.

Syrinx

A nymph of Arcady who, pursued by Pan*, fled into the river and prayed to be changed into a reed. Of this reed Pan made his pipes, which became known as a syrinx.
Wedgwood subject:
Syrinx, medallion head, 3in. x 2in., no.123 in 1777 Catalogue. A companion piece to the medallion of Pan. The two heads sometimes appear on a single medallion. Both were probably copied from Montfaucon's* *L'Antiquité expliquée,* Plate 49.

SYP TEAPOT. 'Simple Yet Perfect' teapot decorated with *Oatlands* pattern printed in underglaze blue. Height 7½in. c.1910.
Wedgwood Museum

T

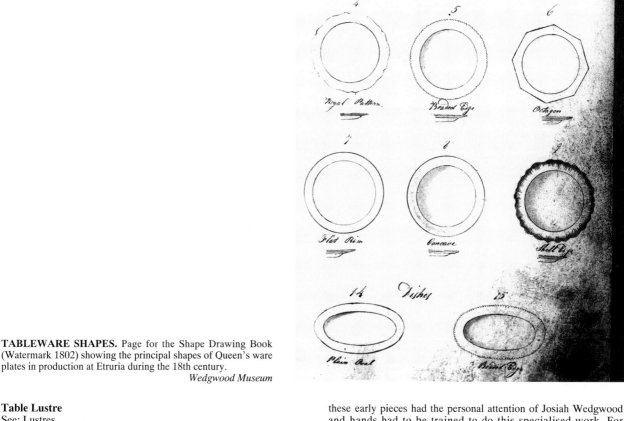

TABLEWARE SHAPES. Page for the Shape Drawing Book (Watermark 1802) showing the principal shapes of Queen's ware plates in production at Etruria during the 18th century.
Wedgwood Museum

Table Lustre
See: Lustres

Tablets
It would be desirable to define the term 'tablet' to mean a flat, tile-like object, rectangular in shape and either painted or ornamented in bas-relief*, reserving the term 'plaque'* for those objects which are oval or circular, and larger than (and of a different character from) those ordinarily defined as medallions*. Tablets, like plaques, were made principally for the decoration of furniture, walls and chimneypieces*. Unfortunately, this admirably logical arrangement is not always practicable, since Wedgwood himself used the word 'tablets' with less discrimination. Wherever possible, however, this distinction is made in this book.

The first tablets were made in 1768-9, soon after the black basaltes* body had been perfected. In November of that year Wedgwood wrote to Bentley*: I have lately had a vision by Night of some new Vases, Tablets &c. with which we shall certainly serve the *whole World.'* These earliest pieces, which from 1770 were made in the white terracotta* body as well as black basaltes, were all moulded in one piece. Tablets with figures applied by sprigging* were introduced in 1772, and that technique of ornamenting, described as being 'in a new vein', soon became the principal method used to ornament the dry bodies*.

Technical troubles were frequent. In November 1772 Wedgwood complained to Bentley* of the difficulty of making long narrow tablets: 'we cannot keep them straight.' Some difficulty was experienced also in making exact sizes to customers' requirements ('we shall make the black tablets for Lady Wynne as near to size as we can and the Glass grinders must do the rest'). All

these early pieces had the personal attention of Josiah Wedgwood and hands had to be trained to do this specialised work. For instance, in November 1774, Wedgwood wrote to Bentley: 'our fish-drain[er] maker at the Usefull works has been trying his hand at long square [rectangular] tablets for two months past & has made some tolerable good ones.'

Plain black basaltes tablets were sent to London from 1771 to have figure subjects painted on them in encaustic* colours. This type of encaustic painting was in a more extensive palette than that employed for copies of red-figure* vases. One of the first of such tablets, and perhaps the only one to survive in its original setting, was made in 1772 for Sir Watkin Williams Wynn's* house at 20 St James's Square, London, a house designed by Robert Adam*, whose original drawing for the chimneypiece is in the Soane Museum. The designs for the tablet and for two smaller plaques were copied from drawings by Zucchi*, and Sir Watkin paid Wedgwood £26.15.0 for the three. The making of these few encaustic-painted tablets for chimneypieces – objects requiring exceptional skill in painting and vulnerable to losses in firing – was undertaken more for reasons of prestige and the acknowledgement of patronage than for profit. All tablets, whether of basaltes or terracotta, were difficult and costly to make. In May 1776 Wedgwood reported that kiln wastage was currently as high as seventy-five per cent. Hackwood's *Birth of Bacchus** and *Triumph of Bacchus* were made in five separate pieces to reduce such losses.

Further problems were encountered with jasper* tablets, and it was not until the end of 1777, after the development of the technique of covering a coarse-ground base with a fine-ground slip (for a note about the November 1777 memorandum, see: Jasper) that Wedgwood was able to make them with any confidence.

Jasper tablets were of special importance to Wedgwood & Bentley because they hoped, through the production of this new collection, to acquire a market among the architects. They were to be disappointed. Adam made a number of designs for chimney-pieces incorporating encaustic-painted tablets, but there is little evidence that he favoured the use of jasper. James Wyatt and Sir William Chambers* were no more helpful, and it was more the good will of patrons, such as Sir William Bagot*, than the good offices of architects that kept Wedgwood's hopes for his tablets alive. He wrote to Bentley in July 1779: 'We were really unfortunate in the introduction of our jaspers into public notice, that we could not prevail upon the architects to be godfathers to our child. Instead of taking it by the hand & giving it their benediction, they cursed the poor infant by bell, book & candle, & it must have a hard struggle to support itself, & rise from under their maledictions.' Only his old friend 'Athenian' Stuart* made any serious attempt to use jasper tablets.

This setback was temporary, but it lasted until after Bentley's death. Records of 115 suites of tablets and plaques for chimney-pieces have been found (see: Alison Kelly, *Decorative Wedgwood,* p.12) and the list is unlikely to be complete. Most of the subjects used for ornamenting tablets were classical, and many of them had been seen earlier on basaltes or terracotta tablets. Between 1776 and 1791, however, new ornamental subjects were commissioned from or supplied by Flaxman*, Stubbs*, Lady Diana Beauclerk* and the artists employed in Rome*. The largest jasper tablet was *The Nine Muses** (10in. x 25in.) attributed to Flaxman, the longest *Diana Visiting Endymion** (8½in. x 27½in.). The most celebrated among them are probably *The Dancing Hours*, Apotheosis of Homer** and the two tablets of *The Muses with Apollo**. Jasper tablets were never produced in large quantities and fine specimens from the 18th century are among the rarest of surviving examples of early Wedgwood.

Tablets continued to be made during the 19th century but generally on a smaller scale. A green jasper dip* example of *Diana visiting Endymion* in the Wedgwood Museum*, however, is the largest known in a single piece, 13¾in. x 30¼in., proving that such sizes were still possible; but none was made between 1817 and 1870. In 1882 a number of tablets and large rectangular plaques was made in peach jasper to the order of Halsey Ricardo* for Lord Dysart's Buckminster Park. Small jasper tablets have been made at intervals throughout much of the 20th century and these are occasionally to be found with the 'MADE IN ENGLAND' mark ground out in the hope that they may be mistaken for earlier examples.

Tableware Shapes
The following are the principal tableware shapes made by Wedgwood:

129
Bulbous shape with a flat base used for coffeepots and jugs in Queen's ware* and jugs in bone china*. Although often described as an 18th-century shape, it was not produced until about 1820. The 129 coffeepot, which became the standard for all patterns produced on Traditional* shapes, was originally designed as a tall teapot.

146
Probably the most celebrated of all Wedgwood's teapot shapes and made with *en suite* cream jugs and sugar boxes in Queen's ware, dry bodies* and (from about 1920) bone china. The teapot has frequently been described and illustrated as an outstanding example of Wedgwood's 18th-century design, but modern research has proved that it was not introduced until about 1828, and belongs therefore to the Regency period. For more than 160 years it has been the standard shape for patterns on Queen's ware Traditional* shapes, and it has been the most popular bone china shape since about 1920.

225 Shape
Tableware shape designed for bone china and basalt* and modelled by Tom Kellogg of Gould & Associates* to celebrate the 225th anniversary of the founding of the Wedgwood firm. From the initial presentation to the production of a range of nineteen items and four patterns the introduction of this shape took a full three years.

146 SHAPE. Modern basalt teapot. *Wedgwood Museum*

225 SHAPE. Bone china dinnerware, decorated with *Tranquillity* pattern in gold, and basalt teaware, partly glazed. *Wedgwood Museum*

ANNULAR SHAPE. Queen's ware teaware covered with Matt Green glaze. 1935. *Wedgwood Museum*

Annular
Queen's ware* shape designed by Tom Wedgwood* and John Goodwin* in 1932. The vegetable dishes were added by Keith Murray* as his first commission from Wedgwood. Annular shape was designed especially for decoration with matt glazes* of various colours and was occasionally also decorated with hand-painted patterns over matt glazes.

Audley
Bone china* scalloped-edge shape introduced about 1920. It was used for a series of platinum lustre* handpainted patterns (some designed by the Powells* and Millicent Taplin*) during the 1930s and notably also for *Ruby Tonquin* pattern.

BARLASTON SHAPE. Tablewares decorated with *Ruby Mayfield* (Robert Minkin), *Covent Garden* (Kenneth Sproson), *Box Hill* (Robert Minkin) and *Hereford* (Peter Wall). *Wedgwood Museum*

Barlaston
Queen's ware shape, the flatware having a narrow concave rim, designed by Norman Wilson* and modelled by Eric Owen* in 1955. It proved to be extremely popular for both two-colour coloured bodies* and lithographed* designs, and it replaced Traditional shapes for about twenty years.

BEADED EDGE. Queen's ware deep plate transfer-printed with a ship flying the American flag. c.1790. *Formerly Buten Museum*

Beaded Edge
One of Wedgwood's early Queen's ware shapes illustrated in the '1802' Shape Drawing Book*. It appears to have been in production by about 1785, but examples are scarce and no dates of production have been authoritatively ascribed to it.

Boston
A name given to small cylindrical coffeecups and also to small bowls and squat bulbous jugs in both Queen's ware and bone china.

Bute
A squat circular shape for teacups and breakfast cups, without feet, made of both Queen's ware and bone china.

Catherine
Queen's ware shape created in 1773 especially for the Frog* service. A variant of the Royal* shape.

Colonial
Queen's ware shape, moulded with a laurel border 'in typical style …of the American Colonial period', designed by John Goodwin*.

Commonwealth
Queen's ware shape designed by Keith Murray* with Wedgwood's

CATHERINE SHAPE. Queen's ware tableware decorated with Victor Skellern's *Avocado* pattern, printed in brown and enamelled in yellow and dark green. 1959. *Wedgwood Museum*

COLONIAL SHAPE. Queen's ware tableware designed by John Goodwin. *Photograph: Wedgwood*

production staff in 1947 intended for production on a large scale to meet the requirements of export markets for decorated wares and those of the home market which was still restricted to undecorated tableware. The shape was designed for economy in production as well as utility and suitability for the markets.

Concave
One of the earliest of all Wedgwood Queen's ware flatware shapes, having a curved base without footrim and a practical concave rim. It is illustrated in the '1802' Shape Drawing Book but was in production by about 1770. It has lasted, with only occasional breaks in production, ever since.

CONCAVE SHAPE. Documentary 'Champagne' body plate transfer-printed in red with an inscription commemorating the election of Josiah Clement Wedgwood (Josiah IV) to Parliament in 1922. *Formerly Buten Museum*

CORINTHIAN SHAPE. Queen's ware shape designed by Victor Skellern and Kennard Wedgwood in 1935   *Photograph: Wedgwood*

Corinthian
Moulded Queen's ware border shape designed by Victor Skellern* in collaboration with Kennard Wedgwood* in 1935.

COUPE/SAVOY SHAPE. Bone china decorated with *Royal Barge* pattern, enamelled in turquoise and scarlet with gold, designed by Lady Robertson for the Savoy Hotel, London.   *Wedgwood Museum*

Coupe/Savoy
Rimless 'Coupe' plates and dishes teamed with flattened pear-shaped teacups and oval teapots, cream jug and sugar box in bone china, designed for the Savoy Hotel, London, in 1939 but not produced until 1954.

Edme
Ribbed Queen's ware shape designed by John Goodwin for Pannier Frères, 1908. One of the most popular tableware shapes ever made by Wedgwood, and sold in enormous quantities in the USA. It has been continuously in production (including the war years) since its introduction.

Egyptian
A banded shape for teapots, cream jugs and sugar boxes originally introduced with sphinx* or crocodile knops for dry bodies and later continued in Queen's ware, Pearl* ware and White ware* with flattened rose or ball knops. The shape was used also for tea and coffee biggins*.

EDME SHAPE. Queen's ware designed by John Goodwin in 1908.
Photograph: Wedgwood

EGYPTIAN SHAPE. Two rosso antico teapots and a sugar box in Egyptian shape with crocodile knops, moulded with zig-zag pattern and ornamented in black with bands of mixed hieroglyphs and other motifs in the 'Egyptian' taste. Larger teapot width 8¼in. c.1810-20.
Christie's, New York

FEATHER EDGE SHAPE. Creamware plate, feather-edge and rose-moulded centre, transfer-printed in black with 'exotic' birds. Unmarked. Wedgwood, c.1770.   *Author's collection*

Feather Edge
One of Wedgwood's earliest Queen's ware tableware shapes and almost certainly copied from the Chelsea* porcelain feather-edge shape. Like Chelsea's, the Wedgwood shape has twenty-four feathers, each of seven barbs, divided four and three with a clear gap between the fourth and fifth. Certainly in production by 1770 and probably from about five years earlier. 'New Feather Edge', with the border moulding divided into twelve groups of twelve feathers (four sets of three) is first mentioned in a letter from Wedgwood to Bentley dated 19 August 1772.

GLOBE SHAPE. Bone china coffeeset designed by Norman Wilson, c.1935. *Wedgwood Museum*

Galaxie
Semi-fluted shape designed by Kenneth Sproson* for bone china in 1963.

Globe
Coffeeware shape originally designed for bone china in the 1880s and re-designed by Norman Wilson* c.1935.

Leigh
The shape of a bone china teacup raised on a turned foot, introduced c.1910 and reintroduced in the late 1950s. The name was then extended to a teapot, cream jug and sugar box, and a vegetable dish of similar shape with flattened lid and disc knop, all designed by Norman Wilson*.

Lincoln
Bone china flatware shape with a broad, almost flat, rim. Lincoln has been the standard flatware shape for bone china patterns for most of the 20th century.

London
Popular teacup and coffeecup shape used, with little variation apart from the shape of the handle, by many manufacturers. Wedgwood used it for first period bone china from 1812 and it was reintroduced in 1878.

OLYMPIC SHAPE. Queen's ware teapot from the Olympic shape designed by Peter Wall, decorated with *Mosaic* pattern by Robert Minkin. *Wedgwood Museum*

New Feather Edge
Queen's ware shape introduced c.1772.

Octagon
Octagonal Queen's ware flatware was illustrated in the '1802' Shape Drawing Book and was probably in production by 1775.

Olympic
Queen's ware shape designed by Peter Wall* in 1964, some of the shapes being multi-purpose and designed for stacking.

Osier
Queen's ware moulded basketware border shape designed by John Goodwin 'after the style of old Meissen*', 1906.

Paris
Queen's ware flatware shape with a flattened rim, wider than that of the concave* shape.

NEW FEATHER EDGE. Queen's ware plate decorated in monochrome green enamel. Unmarked. Wedgwood, c.1772. *Wedgwood Museum*

OSIER SHAPE. Queen's ware basketwork-shape designed by John Goodwin in 1906. *Photograph: Wedgwood*

PATRICIAN SHAPE. Queen's ware shape designed by John Goodwin in 1926. *Photograph: Wedgwood*

QUEEN'S SHAPE. Plain Queen's ware vegetable dish with plate and coffeepot decorated with *Pot-pourri* and *Chinese Teal* patterns.
Wedgwood Museum

Patrician
Queen's ware moulded arabesque* border shape designed by John Goodwin, 1926, adapted from an 18th-century wax model found in the Museum*.

PEAR SHAPE. Queen's ware teacup with enamelled ribbon scroll decoration. *Wedgwood Museum*

ROYAL SHAPE. Queen's ware dish painted with an inscription signed and dated by Enoch Wood testifying that it was modelled by his brother William in 1770. *Wedgwood Museum*

Pear
Teacup and coffeecup shape resembling the form of an inverted pear (cut square at the base) on a turned foot. It was popular in both Queen's ware and bone china from the latter part of the 19th century.

Peony
Low teacup of open shape with turned foot, extensively made in bone china from the late 19th century, especially for the American market.

Queen's
A simplified form of an older saltglazed* stoneware shape with hexafoil lobed rim. Wedgwood's Queen's ware version is generally believed to have been modelled especially for Queen Charlotte* but there is some evidence that it was already in production by February 1765 and merely named after her. With hollowware of a much later date, it has been in production ever since.

Royal
Lobed Queen's ware shape, similar in appearance to Queen's* shape but without the border divisions. Said to have been created especially for George III* in 1770 and at least partly modelled by William Wood*.

Satsuma
A shape introduced c.1865 and inspired by Japanese lacquer or metalwork (not ceramic) shapes. The teapot is flat-sided, the mouth of the vessel being rectangular with a stepped cover. The flat sides were easily decorated and lent themselves particularly to designs in Japanese styles and to photolithographic* prints. The Wedgwood Museum* contains examples decorated with typical Highland scenes by Crealock*.
See: Japonisme

Savoy
See: Coupe/Savoy

Shell Edge
Rococo moulded Queen's ware shape, also seen on Chelsea porcelain, and possibly the earliest of Wedgwood tableware shapes. It was extensively used with gilding, with transfer-printed patterns and with underglaze-blue and onglaze enamelled edging. It remained in production during the late 1770s and 1780s, during the height of the fashion for neo-classical* design, and has seldom been withdrawn in more than 230 years.

SATSUMA SHAPE. Queen's ware 'Satsuma' shape teapot painted with a rustic scene in France by Emile Lessore. Height 5¼in. c.1874.
Wedgwood Museum

SHELL-EDGE SHAPE. Queen's ware plate transfer-printed in black with a landscape and a border of sprigs of flowers. c.1785.
Mr & Mrs Samuel Laver Collection

WELLESLEY SHAPE. Moulded Queen's ware shape designed by John Goodwin in 1932. *Photograph: Wedgwood*

Traditional Shapes
Blanket name given to the Queen's ware combination of Concave* shape flatware*, round or oval plume* vegetable dishes, Pear* or Bute* teacups and breakfast cups and 129/146* shape jugs, coffee-pot and teapot.

Wellesley
Queen's ware shape designed by John Goodwin, 1932, primarily for the American market. The border is moulded with a pattern of fruit and flowers adapted from old factory moulds.

Tabor, Samuel (fl.1763-91)
Merchant in Rotterdam who wrote to Wedgwood on 22 April 1763, more than two years before the latter's name became famous through royal appointment, asking for supplies. Tabor's correspondence with Wedgwood during 1763-4 has been preserved and provides useful information about Wedgwood's production during those two years. Tabor, who was one of the earliest recorded of Wedgwood's agents abroad, appears to have been a good customer for many years, perhaps up to the date of his retirement in 1791.

Tankard
A mug with a hinged lid, originally made with a capacity of about one quart. Smaller lidded mugs are generally described as tankards to distinguish them from similar objects without lids. Wedgwood Queen's ware* mugs were occasionally mounted with metal lids, usually of pewter and more rarely of silver or Sheffield plate, during the 18th century.

Taplin, Millicent MSIA NRD (1902-80)
Paintress and designer, who became manager of Wedgwood's hand-painting department at Etruria* and Barlaston*. 'Milly' Taplin joined Wedgwood in 1917, after working briefly as a trainee paintress at Minton's* and while completing a scholarship course at the Hanley School of Art. She became closely associated with the Powells* and founded, in 1928, a 'hand crafts' department at Etruria which was merged after about twelve months with the hand-painting department. In the 1930s she designed a number of simple floral patterns – reminiscent of early New Hall painting and the work of Louise Powell – and some more original patterns in the then fashionable Art Deco* style (with which Wedgwood is seldom associated). Several incorporated the use of platinum lustre (see: Lustre Decoration). After World War II, while managing the hand-painting department, she continued to design for Wedgwood, producing two best-selling lithograph* designs for bone china* tableware, *Kingcup* and *Strawberry Hill* (with Victor Skellern*).
Her designs for bone china include the following:
Autumn, 1938
Buds and Bells, 1938
Cynthia, 1942
Falling Leaves, 1930
Kingcup (lithograph), 1948
Papyrus, 1934

TAPLIN, Millicent. Part of a bone china Globe shape coffee set hand-painted in grey and green, lined in platinum, with Millicent Taplin's *Falling Leaves* pattern. c.1953. *Wedgwood Museum*

TAPLIN, Millicent. Two Norman Wilson 'Unique Ware' bowls decorated by Millicent Taplin in platinum over a crackled, transparent turquoise glaze. The exterior is covered in a stone-coloured glaze over 'Moonstone'. Diameter 8in. 1953. *Author's collection*

Silver Buttercup
Strawberrry Hill (lithograph), 1957, with Victor Skellern
Westover
Windrush
In addition, Milly Taplin decorated a number of vases and some platinum-painted Norman Wilson* unique ware. She occasionally signed individual pieces with her monogram, but this is easily confused with that of a senior paintress, Mabel Tatton*.

Tartlett Stand

An arrangement of small round tartlett dishes, disposed on several levels at varying heights, on a circular stand. This piece, no.605 in the Shapes Book* appears in an Oven Book* entry for January-February 1800 and was made in jasper*, cane* ware and terracotta* biscuit. It was evidently intended as a centrepiece to display small tarts or pies containing sweetmeats or fruit. A biscuit* example, coloured with black slip*, discovered among the Wedgwood archives and researched by Mrs Lynn Miller (Wedgwood Society *Proceedings,* No.11, 1982) appears to be the only one surviving, although it is possible that individual dishes remain unrecognised.

TASSIE, James. Portrait by David Allan. Oil on canvas 30in. x 25in. *Scottish National Portrait Gallery*

Tassie, James (1735-99)

Born at Pollokshaws, near Glasgow, Tassie started life as a stonemason and went to Dublin in 1761 in the hope of becoming a sculptor. There he met Dr Henry Quin, who was engaged in reproducing gems* and precious stones, and in copying antique cameos*. Working with Quin, Tassie produced a white material resembling porcelain but made from finely powdered glass which could be moulded in plaster of Paris moulds taken from original wax models* or sulphurs*.

Tassie came to London about 1769 and obtained financial help from the Society of Arts (Royal Society of Arts*). He took premises not far from Wedgwood's showrooms in Great Newport Street. From about that date he supplied Wedgwood with moulds of cameos and intaglios* for reproduction, especially in black basaltes*, and, in return, Wedgwood supplied him with similar moulds from his own stock. Tassie was commissioned to take plaster moulds of the Portland vase*, several of which have survived. He produced nearly 900 small portraits and 114 larger portrait medallions*, many of them modelled *ad vivum,* in his glass pastes, some of which were supplied to Wedgwood (in the form of sulphurs or as glass paste models) to reproduce in jasper*. After his death, Tassie's business was carried on by his nephew William (d.1860).

Wedgwood's connection with Tassie was mainly through Bentley* and dates from 1769. In a letter of 1776, Wedgwood admitted: 'Mr Tassie & Voyez*, between them, have made terrible depredations on our Seal Trade. The former by making them more beautifull, & the latter by selling them cheaper…It will be a credit to emulate the one, & the other we may fight in his own way as far as we think prudent.' The relationship between the rivals was, however, always friendly, Wedgwood reproduced Tassie's portraits complete with his signature or initial on the truncation and recent research has revealed that Tassie reproduced portraits obtained from Wedgwood. An important catalogue of Tassie's gems and cameos was compiled by R.E. Raspe and published in two volumes in 1791. It lists 15,800 reproductions from the antique.

Tatton, Mabel (1885-1973)

Designer and paintress at Etruria*, succeeding her sister Ethel as head of the enamelling department. She worked with James Hodgkiss* and was awarded a medal at the 1925 Paris Exposition. She sometimes signed her work with her monogram, giving rise to confusion between her painting and that of Millicent Taplin*.

Taurus
See Colour Plate 106
See also: Machin, Arnold

Taylor, Christopher (fl.1769-75)
Painter at the Chelsea Decorating Studio* who worked on the Frog* service.

TAZZA. Majolica tazza ('Boucher fruit centre') decorated in transparent coloured glazes. Height 9¼in. c.1875.   *Sotheby's, London*

TEA CANISTER. Documentary Queen's ware tea canister transfer-printed with the 'Tea Party' in black and dated 1782 on the reverse. Height 5¼in.
Byron and Elaine Born Collection

Tazza

The Italian for a cup, mug or basin; a term commonly used for an ornamental shallow dish or flat bowl, raised on a long or short stem and circular base. It is generally, but not invariably, without handles. Wedgwood's *tazze* are usually described as 'fruit centres' ('tall' or 'low').

Tea Caddy

The term 'caddy' is probably a corruption of the Malayan word *kati,* which is a quantity of about a twenty-two ounces. Sheraton's *Catalogue* of 1803 mentions the word 'caddy' as being applied to a variety of tea chests of square, octagonal or circular section. Decorative caddies occur in ivory and tortoiseshell ornamented with jasper* cameos*, most of them made towards the end of the 18th century. Earlier tea jars, of Queen's ware* (plain, transfer-printed* or decorated with coloured glazes) or black basaltes* are properly described as tea canisters*.

Tea Canister

The correct term for small ceramic containers for tea. Wedgwood's early Queen's ware* canisters were produced from about 1765. They were most commonly octagonal in shape, with curved sloping shoulders and domed round lids, some decorated with Green glaze (see Glazes – *Green Glaze)* or marbling* or transfer-printed* decoration by Sadler & Green*, and others with moulded ornament. They were made also in fruit and vegetable shapes* (especially cauliflower and pineapple). Later they were produced in the dry bodies*, generally in shapes that were round or oval in section. The height varied between about 4in. and 6in.
See: Colour Plate 107

TEA CANISTER. Pale-blue jasper dip tea canister with flattened disc stopper, *Domestic Employment* ornament and engine-turned fluting. Height 5½in. c.1785-90.
Temple Newsam House, Leeds

Tea and Coffee Infuser

Another name for the Coffee Biggin*, the forerunner of the filter-method coffeepot, invented in 1803. Two shapes appear in the '1802' Shape Drawing Book*, showing alternative uses either for tea or coffee. These practical objects were made in Queen's ware*, the dry bodies* and smear-glazed* stonewares. A Gothic-shape coffee biggin is illustrated in one of the unnumbered plates added c.1835 to the '1817' Catalogue*.

TEA AND COFFEE INFUSER. Component parts of a Queen's ware infuser. Height (assembled) 6in. 1867.   *Victoria & Albert Museum*

TEA KETTLE. Wedgwood & Bentley black basaltes kettle with sibyl knop and short S-shaped spout, the interior without strainer confirming its use as a kettle. Height 7¼in. c.1776.

Dwight & Lucille Beeson Collection, Birmingham Museum, Alabama

Tea Kettle

On 14 April 1774 Wedgwood wrote to Bentley*: 'We shall send some T. kettles on Saturday to have wicker handles.' An example of a black basaltes* kettle, c.1774, in the Wedgwood Museum has a low curved spout and wicker (over metal) bail* handle attached to holes in the shaped rim. The lid has a sibyl* knop. Other kettles with conventional handles survive in black basaltes, Queen's ware* and jasper*. Tea kettles are distinguishable from large-size teapots by their lack of internal perforated strainers.
See: Rum Kettle

Tea Party (Tea Drinkers)

One of the most popular transfer-printed* designs of the 18th century, and to be found on Caughley*, Worcester* and Liverpool porcelains and the creamares produced at the Liverpool Herculaneum* pottery, at Cockpit Hill, Derby, and by Wedgwood. The print appears in several versions, most often on teapots, tea canisters* and jugs, but also, more rarely, on plates. It shows a man and woman seated at a tripod tea table, typical of the period, in the garden. The man gestures with his right hand towards a black page boy on the left of the composition. That this subject was in use by Wedgwood by 1763 is clear from Sadler's* letter of 8 July 1763 apologising for the quality of an engraving of 'The Tea Drinkers' applied to a large creamware teapot: 'thee Engraver sent it down not half finished…but we shall mend that Matter very soon I hope.'

Tebo, Mr (fl.1750-80)

'Tebo' is probably an anglicisation of the Huguenot name Thibaud or Thibault. For many years it has been believed, largely on the evidence of the mark 'T°', which appears on products of a number of factories, that he acted as a repairer* and modeller at the Bow*, Chelsea*, Plymouth, Bristol and Worcester* porcelain factories, but this mark is no longer regarded as associated with Tebo, and what little is known about him is based almost entirely on Wedgwood archive material. The 'T°' mark does not appear on Wedgwood wares. Signatures were not permitted at Etruria* and an occasional 'TBO' found on Wedgwood experimental ware indicated 'Top of Biscuit Oven' and has nothing to do with Tebo the modeller.

Tebo began to work for Wedgwood, who had a poor opinion of his abilities, in 1774. His models of heads of hares were described witheringly by Wedgwood as 'like the head of a drown'd Puppy' and 'full as like Pigs as Hares.' Wedgwood's standards had been set by his early purchases of moulds from such suppliers as Hoskins & Grant* and John Flaxman senior*, who were working from classical sculpture, and the carvings of such sculptors as Rysbrack*. By the middle of 1775 Tebo was regarded as a useful hand for repairing figures, but he was not capable of original work to Josiah's exacting standards. None of his models is certainly recorded as having been produced, although he is known to have worked, generally unsuccessfully, on a hare's head for a stirrup

TEA PARTY. Queen's ware teapot transfer-printed in black with the 'Tea Party'. Height 5¾in. c.1777. *Sotheby's, London*

cup*, a tablet for a chimneypiece* (which he made 'ten times worse'), a 'Shocking Ugly thing' of a lamp, and three figures forming the tripod support for vase no.232, no illustration of which appears to have survived. He left in the autumn of 1775 and travelled to Dublin, where he started to model portraits which he asked Wedgwood to fire for him. In a letter of July 1776 to his Dublin agent, Wedgwood agreed to do this but stated that Tebo was not to be regarded as his modeller.

Teeth, Porcelain
See: Bramah, Joseph; Dentures

Temminck, Egbert de Vrij (fl.1778-81)

Burgomaster of Amsterdam, who ordered in November 1778, through Van Veldhuysen*, ten large black basaltes* busts*. A further order for seventy such busts followed in the spring of 1779. Subjects included Admiral de Ruyter, Jan and Cornelis de Witt, Herman Boerhaave and Johan Oldenbarneveldt.

Temple

Tom Byerley* wrote from Etruria* in January 1798: 'We have got our Temple put together, and the effect answers my expectations. The dome, the entablature, the columns, and the base are all to be thrown and turned.' Both Hackwood* and Theed* appear to have worked on this piece and it has, for many years, remained unidentified. The description and date, however, corresponds well with the temple shown as a centrepiece to the engraving of the York Street showrooms*, published in 1809, and also with the estimated date of the large group, *Britannia Triumphant**, which may be identified with the figure shown under the dome of the temple in the same illustration. Temples in the classical style as part of table decoration originated at Meissen* in the 1740s, and several examples have survived, wholly or in part. They were made in several parts and erected on the table.

Templetown, Elizabeth, Lady (1747-1823)

The daughter of Shuckburgh Boughton of Poston, Hereford, Elizabeth married, in 1769, Clotworthy Upton, who was raised to the peerage as Lord Templetown in 1776. An amateur artist, Lady Templetown supplied Wedgwood with 'cut Indian paper' designs between 1783 and 1789. These were in the sentimental manner popular in the last quarter of the 18th century and they were translated to bas-relief* models by William Hackwood*. Josiah Wedgwood wrote to her in June 1783 to express his pleasure at hearing that his first bas-relief copies of her work had met with her approval, and, somewhat obsequiously, soliciting more. Two years later he sent bas-reliefs to Charles James Fox* to demonstrate the method he proposed to follow in copying Lady Diana Beauclerk's* drawings.

The identification of Lady Templetown's work presents some problems. No bills survive (nor, probably, were any presented), her style closely resembles that of Emma Crewe*, and to a lesser extent that of Lady Diana Beauclerk*, and Hackwood's modelling of the work of all three has tended to obscure stylistic differences.

The following fifteen subjects may, however, be assigned to Lady Templetown on the evidence of Josiah's own notes to the 1787 Catalogue* (from which all catalogue numbers shown are taken):

An Offering to Peace, tablet 6½in. x 11½in. No.238

Bourbonnais Shepherd, medallion 3¾in. x 3in., and sizes down to 2¼in. x 1¾in. (Companion piece to *Maria.* See: Laurence Sterne)

Charlotte at the Tomb of Werther, medallion 5in. x 4in. and sizes down to 2¾in. x 2¼in. No.272. (See: *Sorrows of the Young Werther*)

Contemplation, and 'Companion piece' (untitled), medallions 4in. x 3¼in. No.273

Domestic Employment, medallion 4½in. x 5¾in., and sizes down to 2½in. x 3in. No.248

Family School and 'Companion Piece' (untitled), medallions 4½in. x 5¾in. and sizes down to 2in. x 3¼in. No.249

Friendship Consoling Affliction, medallion 7in. x 8¾in. and sizes down to 3in. x 4in. No.240

Genii, medallion 3in. x 7in., 'measured diagonally', and sizes down to 1¾in. x 3¾in.. No.252. Companion piece (untitled), 1¾in. by 3¾in. No.253

Maria (Poor Maria), medallion 3¾in. x 3in. and sizes down to 2¼in. by 1¾in. No.251. (Companion piece to *Bourbonnais Shepherd.* See: Laurence Sterne)

Sportive Love, medallion 4in. x 3¼in., and sizes down to 2¾in. x 2¼in. No.271

Study and 'Companion piece' (untitled), medallions 3in. x 3¾in. and sizes down to 1¾in. x 2¼in. No.250

The following subjects, unlisted in the Catalogue but named in the Oven Books* and Price Books, may be identified with the untitled 'companion pieces' catalogued at nos.249, 250, 253 and 273:

Juvenile Conversation
Juvenile Feast
Love Consoled by Friendship
Rural Employment

Terminal

Sprigged ornament employed to finish the lower end of a handle where it meets the main body of the vessel. It is usually moulded in the form of a flower, leaf, shell or human mask. Wedgwood's earliest terminals, notable especially with scroll handles, curved away from the body of the vessel, ending in a split knop. Such a shape is known as a 'kick terminal'.

Terracotta

Literally, 'baked earth' (Latin: *terra cocta*). Before the publication of Reilly's two-volume study in 1989 *(Wedgwood,* Vol.I, pp.347 and 365-82), Wedgwood's terracotta body had been wrongly described in every book on the subject for more than a century. Contrary to almost all general perception, terracotta is not necessarily an orange-red colour but may, as the name suggests, be of any colour natural to fired clay, from white, through cream or grey,

TEMPLETOWN, Elizabeth, Lady. Engine-turned blue jasper dip jug ornamented with figures of *Domestic Employment,* modelled by Hackwood from designs by Lady Templetown. Height 5⅞in. c.1785-90. *Temple Newsam House, Leeds*

to a strong red. Wedgwood's early terracotta biscuit was a vitrified*, or porcellaneous, unglazed white stoneware body especially developed for use in the production of cameos* and further used for medallions*, plaques* and tablets* and to replace Queen's ware* in the production of variegated* vases.

In its earliest form, when it was described as 'polished biscuit', it was a pale buff colour, which was disguised by coloured glazes (variegated vases) or brown or grey slip grounds (cameos, medallions, plaques and tablets, especially the framed Herculaneum pictures*). Since the body, although high-fired, was not entirely impermeable, it was covered (in London) before being coloured, with a light flux*. Later the body was refined to a clean white, which required no disguise and which, when covered with a lead glaze (as on ungilded handles, finials or ornaments of variegated vases) is almost indistinguishable from creamware. With moulded ornament, the white terracotta was often used for the plinths of vases and lamps*.

In its various stages of development, the terracotta body was

TERRACOTTA. Three white terracotta stoneware vases, engine-turned with rouletted borders, decorated with various coloured slips and ornamented with drapery swags, c.1785, with a Wedgwood & Bentley terracotta biscuit vase of similar form, c.1775. Heights 5in. to 6⅝in. *Author's collection*

TERRACOTTA. White terracotta biscuit vase covered with black slip cut on the lathe to produce white bands at the lip, upper edge and base and a pattern of graduated white spots. Height 7in. c.1810.

Christie's, London

described in the 1773, 1779 and 1787 Catalogues*; and in the Christie* & Ansell auction sale* catalogue of 1781 it is mentioned specifically as 'resembling *Porphyry*, *Granite*, *Egyptian Pebble** and other beautiful Stones of the *Chrystalline Clays*', a clear reference to variegated wares which leaves no doubt as to their composition. A last, and almost equally important use of the terracotta body was in the production of flower pots*, of which there were 108 lots in the sale, arranged in sets of three, five or seven, with as many as twenty-eight to a single lot. Like the dry bodies*, all terracotta made between before 1781 was within the Wedgwood & Bentley partnership.

The only orange-red body made by Wedgwood which is properly called 'terracotta' is the terracotta jasper*, made with black or white ornaments in the 1950s.
See: Colour Plates 108 and 109
See also: Orange Body; Red China; Rosso Antico

Theatrical Awards
The Executive Committee of the Society of West End Theatre Awards chose a Wedgwood vase in Portland blue and white jasper* for twelve awards to be made annually. The vases of 1977 were ornamented with reliefs of the Muses* and Apollo* Musagetes, god of music and poetry. For 1978 they bore medallion portraits of David Garrick and Sarah Siddons*. There is an inscription in gold of the base of each vase.

Theed, William, RA (1764-1817)
Painter, sculptor and designer. Theed studied at the Royal Academy Schools in 1786 and exhibited portraits and paintings in the neo-classical* style from 1788-1805. He visited Rome in 1791, remaining there for three years, and it was during this period that he met Flaxman*. He began to work for Wedgwood in 1799 but left in 1804 to work for Rundell, Bridge and Rundell, the London silversmiths. About 1810 he accepted a commission from Wedgwood to model a portrait of Tom Byerley* and this was reproduced in jasper*. He is recorded also as the modeller of the capital for a column for a temple*. No other work of his has been certainly identified.

Thermoscope, Colorimetric
An instrument, invented by Josiah Wedgwood in 1780-1 to measure heat in pottery kilns by observing changes of colour in fired clay. First experiments, recorded in his Experiment Book*, were made with a red-burning clay. Trial pieces were withdrawn at two-hourly intervals while the temperature was rising and the gradual change of colour was noted. These colour changes suggested to him the possibility of constructing a thermoscope which matched clay of a standard composition against a set of cylinders fired at known temperatures, ranging in colour from low-temperature buff to high-temperature red. A practical difficulty lay, however, in the consistent matching of colours by different users of the thermoscope, and Sir Joseph Banks* cast doubt on the method of calculation. Josiah therefore abandoned the project and turned, instead, to experiments in shrinkage during firing, which led to his invention of the pyrometer*.

THORLEY, Joseph Palin. Bone china dessert plate painted by Thorley with a cupid riding a goat after Bartolozzi, and a border of fruiting vine with acid-gold edge. Diameter 8in. Signed. c.1910.

Sotheby's, London

Theseus
Greek hero, King of Athens and a famous slayer of monsters. In antique art he is usually represented as naked except for cloak and sandals and sometimes a helmet. Often, confusingly, he holds the sort of club generally associated with Hercules*.
Wedgwood subject:
Hercules and Theseus Supporting the World, or The Power of Union, medallion 3½in. x 2¾in. No.75 in 1773 Catalogue*

Thetis
A sea nymph, daughter of Nereis and Doris. Although both Zeus (Jupiter*)and Poseidon (Neptune*) sued for her hand, a prophetic divinity, Themis, told Thetis that her son would be greater than his father so she married Peleus and became the mother of Achilles*. It is accepted by most modern scholars that the principal ornament of the Portland vase* represents the myth of Peleus and Thetis, although the precise identification of episodes in the myth with the two sides of the vase is still a matter for argument. The figure of Thetis appears also on the second of the tablets representing *The Whole Life of Achilles,* modelled by Pacetti* in 1788. *Thetis delivering Achilles to Centaur* was usually produced with *Achilles on the back of Centaur hunting the Lion* as a single tablet, 6½in. x 18½in., but both subjects are known as separate medallions.

Thorley, Joseph Palin (fl.1906-25)
Painter who joined Wedgwood at Etruria* in 1906 and worked with James Hodgkiss* and Arthur Dale Holland* under John Goodwin's direction. Palin painted bone china* dessert wares with figures of *putti* after Bartolozzi* prints and two large chargers (one signed) finely painted in underglaze blue with a parrot among foliage show the quality of his work.
See: Colour Plate 110

Thorwaldsen, Bertel (1770-1843)
Danish sculptor, living in Rome between 1797 and 1838, where he carved many busts and figures for English patrons. He was an ardent admirer of the work of Flaxman*. Much of the best of Thorwaldsen's work is collected in the museum which bears his name in Copenhagen. His allegorical bas-relief* of 'Night' (in profile) was reproduced in biscuit porcelain by the Royal Copenhagen factory and also in Wedgwood jasper*, c.1875, and the same subject was adapted by Emile Lessore*, as a composition viewed from the front, painted on a Queen's ware* dish, diameter 15in., c.1863.

Throwing
See: Processes of Production

Thyrsus
A wand, tipped with a pine cone, the symbol of fertility. It is the attribute of *Bacchus* and his attendant satyrs*.

TILES. View of the Countess Spencer's dairy at Althorp, furnished by Wedgwood in 1786, showing Wedgwood creamware tiles used as a frame to a window. *Photograph: Courtesy of Alison Kelly*

Tiles

Before Wedgwood's time, tiles were of tin-enamelled ware (delft*), made primarily in London, the West Country (Bristol, Wincanton, Brislington) or Liverpool, or in Holland, whence they were exported in large quantities. The production of tiles in cream-coloured ware was considered by Wedgwood at least as early as August 1767, when he asked Bentley* to 'look out for a sober Tyle maker' in Liverpool, but he appears to have reconsidered this request and it was not until September 1769 that he again 'sent to Liverpool to enquire after a Tile maker that article being very much called for for dairys baths Temples &c.' He added: 'Lady Gower [see: Stafford] will build a dairy on purpose to furnish it with Cream Couler if I will engage to make Tiles for the Walls, & many others I make no doubt will follow her example.'

Sadler* supported this proposal, writing in September: 'We think the Cream Colour for Tiles wou'd have a great Run. If you send us a few we'll print open Landskips on them which will look very pretty.' He was, however, unable to find a tile maker willing to go to Burslem, and, perhaps because he was fully occupied with the production of Queen's ware tablewares, Wedgwood was prepared to leave creamware tiles to others, telling Bentley in 1772: 'They wod not be a good article for our work at present.' Later in the year he wrote: '*Ornamental* Cream Colour tiles will never be paid for – Plain ones perhaps, but our hands are too expensive & do not know how to make them. They wod charge more for workmanship, than we could sell them for.'

By the autumn of 1776, however, tiles were in production and Josiah wrote to Bentley of the 'rising fashion of furnishing Baths, Dairys &c with Tiles. I cannot help thinking you may do something considerable in them in Greek St. They are a fine wholesale Article, as a Bath will take 4 or 500 doz to furnish it, & Mr Green* allows us a good profit upon them.' This is clear evidence that by this time Wedgwood was making tiles for transfer-printed, and probably also for printed and enamelled, decoration (the Duchess of Argyll was supplied with both in 1783). A letter of 1 June 1779 gives further details: 'The tiles made at Etruria are 7 inches square...those made at Liverpool are only 5 inches...so that one dozn of the former covers nearly as much surface as two dozn of the latter, & have greatly the advantage over them in several respects from being so much larger.'

Plain tiles were supplied in 1783-4 to two regular patrons, Sir Roger Newdigate* and Sir Watkin Williams Wynn*, and in 1786 to Lavinia, Countess Spencer for the dairy at Althorp, Northamptonshire. The latter ordered also some tiles with a painted trailing ivy design as decoration for walls and windows, and the pattern was matched on Queen's ware dairy ware*. Lady Spencer was charged threepence each for the plain and tenpence for the painted tiles. During the last quarter of the 18th century, tiles and dairy ware were supplied also to Warren Hastings at Daylesford, the Duke of Marlborough at Blenheim Palace, the Duke of Bedford at Woburn Abbey* and the duc d'Orléans at the Château de Raincy.

There is some evidence that Josiah Wedgwood seriously considered the production of tiles in black basaltes* and jasper*. He wrote to Bentley in June 1776 about 'Patterns of Bricks for a Jasper floor 9 squares long by 6 broad, with a border of Porphyry & Black ones sufficient for one side & one end'. The jasper tiles were to be in a 'combed' or marbled pattern. made as thin as practicable, and the 'porphyry' ones were to be of a red body splashed with black and white. This floor may have been laid experimentally at the Greek Street showrooms*, but no evidence has been found that such tiles were made for general sale.

Wedgwood continued to make tiles in creamware and in various other bodies until the closure of the tile section at Etruria in 1902. In the first half of the 19th century tile business declined (the largest order obtained by Bateman* between 1813 and 1834 was for 1,000 plain 6-inch tiles) but there is evidence of interesting decoration, including underglaze-blue prints*, variegated lustre* and marbling*, unmarked examples of which have still to be identified. Small quantities of Majolica* and *émail ombrant*￼ tiles were produced and among patterns introduced during the last quarter of the century were printed and enamelled designs to satisfy the

ETRURIA, STOKE=ON=TRENT.

TILES. 'Tile House' created to advertise varieties of tiles manufactured at Etruria. From a catalogue, c.1885. *Wedgwood Museum*

TILES. Tile with incised decoration of a kingfisher, enamelled and enriched with gold on a bright blue ground. 8in. square. c.1882.
Wedgwood Museum

demand for *japonisme**. After the appointment of Thomas Allen* as art director, the number and variety of designs increased, several of the most popular being adapted from his own tableware patterns, such as *Banquet, Ivanhoe* and *Greek Musicians*. Others were the work of Helen Miles* or adapted from drawings by Crealock*.

The most significant development in the design of Wedgwood's tiles in the 19th century came with the acquisition in 1880 of a new process, patented by G.A. Marsden*, for textured tiles resembling the Barbotine process of painting in raised slip. Production began in 1881 and contemporary tile catalogues show a very large number of designs and types of tile available. The separate tile section, set up in 1881, did not, however, produce the encaustic tiles that Wedgwood offered for sale: those were commissioned from G. Wooliscroft & Son, Hanley, and it is possible that other specialised types may have been supplied to order by local manufacturers. Nevertheless, Clement Wedgwood* noted in October 1882: 'the tile business is not going right. We dont get the Contracts.' Some valuable government contracts – for the Admiralty, the India Office and the Colonial Office – were obtained, but business continued to decline until, in October 1902, the building and contents of the tile section, including the pattern books, were offered for sale and the department was finally closed.
See: Calendar Tiles; De Morgan, William

Till, Henry (fl. 1875-83)
Artist and modeller at Etruria* under the direction of Thomas Allen*.

Tin Glaze
An opaque white glaze, owing its colour and opacity to the addition of tin oxide. A small quantity of cobalt* was sometimes added to counteract yellowing and other metallic oxides might be added to colour the glaze. Tin glaze has been in use for about 3,000 years and reached Europe from Persia by way of the Moors in the 11th century. It was first used in England about 1550. Tin-glazed wares are usually known as *maiolica*, faïence** or *delft* ware*, according to their country of origin. The manufacture of tin-glazed earthenwares for tableware in Europe was virtually destroyed by the perfecting of English creamwares* in the 18th century, and especially by the popularity of Wedgwood's Queen's ware*.

Tinkering
Josiah Wedgwood's term for the repairing of vases, especially those of black basaltes* but also, later, of jasper*, which had suffered damage or were otherwise imperfect after firing. In February

1769 he wrote to Bentley: 'I have settled a plan & method…to Tinker all the black Vases that are crooked, we knock off the feet & fix wood ones, black'd to them, those with tops, or snakes wantg, are to be supply'd in the same way.' Much of this repair work was carried out in wood by John Coward*. Such vases were sold at greatly reduced prices. Some of these restored 'invalids' have survived with their original wood replacements, but many repairs are more modern. Similar techniques were used for the repair of both early creamware and gilt vases and, after 1781, jasper vases.
See: Hutchins, Thomas

Titans
The sons and daughters of Uranus (Heaven) and Gaea (Earth), and creators of the world, who were subdued by Jupiter* (Zeus) and shut up in the underworld. Among the descendants of the Titans were Prometheus*, Hecate, Latona, Helios (the Sun), Selene (the Moon – see: Diana)) and Circe, all of whom were divine or semi-divine.
Wedgwood subject:
War of Jupiter and the Titans, oval plaque, 6in. x 9in. One of four subjects copied or adapted from bas-reliefs by Guglielmo della Porta*, probably by way of plaster casts from bronze reliefs by Jakob Cornelisz Cobaert (d.1615). No.2 in 1773 Catalogue.

Tjerne, Emmanuel (fl.1930)
Danish designer. Winner of Wedgwood's international competition for a vase to mark the bicentenary of the birth of Josiah Wedgwood. Tjerne's original drawing is in the Wedgwood Museum*. The ovoid vase, height 17¾in., was reproduced in Queen's ware*, covered with a turquoise matt glaze* and ornamented with white matt-glazed figures emblematic of the Four Elements*. The name 'WEDGWOOD' and the dates '1730' and '1930' are raised in gold bands on the neck and foot, and the base is striped in vertical lines cut through the coloured glaze with some gilding. It was made in a very small edition (about sixteen), copies being presented to the artist and the competition judges.

TJERNE, Emmanuel. Queen's ware vase covered with turquoise matt glaze and ornamented with white matt-glazed figures emblematic of the *Four Elements,* designed by Tjerne and winning entry in the international bicentenary competition in 1930. Height 17¾in. 1930.
Wedgwood Museum

TOBY JUG. Queen's ware Toby Jug representing Elihu Yale, modelled by Robert Eberhard, decorated in amber-coloured glaze. Height 6⅜in. c.1933.

Mr & Mrs David Zeitlin Collection

Toby Jug

A pottery jug, in the form of a seated man holding a mug and usually also a pipe. He wears a tricorn hat, the brim of which provides a pouring lip. The removable crown was sometimes a small cup. Probably named after 'Toby Philpot', the nickname of Harry Elwes, whose fondness for alcohol was celebrated in the song, *The Brown Jug* published in 1761. The earliest Toby jugs are thought to have been made by Ralph Wood I. They were later made by his son, Ralph

TOFT, Charles. Important solid black and white jasper vase, *Peace and War,* designed and modelled by Toft for the 1878 Exhibition. Height 24½in. *Manchester Museum*

TOFT, Charles. Basalt plaque, *Winter* from Toft's set of 'Four Ages', finished by Bert Bentley, c.1921. Oval height 10¼in.

Christie's, New York

Wood II* and copied by many of the English potteries. Innumerable reproductions and forgeries exist, and the general form has been adapted, notably by Doulton, to commemorate modern statesmen and military commanders. Wedgwood have produced only one model of this type, a jug 6⅜in. high, covered in a transparent amber, dark brown or blue glaze, representing Elihu Yale, benefactor of Yale University. It was modelled by Robert G. Eberhard after a portrait by Enoch Zeeman, 1717, and produced in 1933.

Toft, Albert (1862-1949)

Sculptor and modeller of portraits and figures, son of Charles Toft*; studied at Hanley and Newcastle-under-Lyme Schools of Art; exhibited at the Royal Academy from 1885. He worked for Wedgwood at Etruria*, 1877-81 and again in 1882-3.

Toft, Charles (1831-1909)

Modeller; the father of Albert* and Joseph Alfonso Toft*. Charles Toft was employed by Minton*, especially in the production of Henri Deux* inlaid ware, and also by Kerr & Binns and Elkington. He joined Wedgwood at Etruria* in 1876 at a salary of £350 a year rising to £370 over five years. 'We think', Godfrey Wedgwood* wrote to him, 'there is an opening for fresh figure (bas-relief*) models and shapes of vases in our jasper ware.' One of Toft's first commissions was a portrait medallion* of Gladstone.

Toft was employed as principal modeller for twelve years, working in pâte-sur-pâte* and inlaid wares as well as jasper. His principal models included:

Four Ages – Youth, Adolescence, Autumn and Winter, oval medallions, about 10½-12in. long axis

Peace and War, jasper vase, height 24½in., made for the 1878 Exhibition

Seven Ages of Man, after designs painted on a vase by Walter Crane*

Portrait medallions of Geoffrey Chaucer and W.E. Gladstone.

Toft, Joseph Alfonso (1866-1964)

Landscape painter, son of Charles Toft* and younger brother of Albert Toft*; studied at the Birmingham and Hanley Schools of Art; employed by Wedgwood at Etruria* as an apprentice painter, 1882-7; studied at the Royal College of Art; exhibited at the Royal Academy from 1892.

Toilet Wares

See: Chamber Ware

TORTOISESHELL WARE. Tortoiseshell lead-glazed plate with moulded border of stars and dots within a diaper, a shape found also in white saltglazed stoneware. Diameter 7½in. Unmarked. Attributed to Whieldon, c.1750-55. *Wedgwood Museum*

Tool Marks

Marks scratched, incised or stamped in the unfired clay by the potter who made the piece. Also known as potters' marks. The accurate identification of such marks with a particular period may be a useful guide to dating but should always be considered with other evidence of date.

Toothbrush Box

Long rectangular box with lid, usually provided with shaped ledges, close to either end, to keep the bristles of the toothbrush from resting on the floor of the box. Such boxes are often found without their lids, when they are erroneously described as pen trays. They were part of the standard set of Wedgwood chamber ware*.

Topographical Painting

Detailed representations of existing scenes, usually landscapes with buildings but occasionally street scenes. This type of painting became extremely popular as ceramic decoration during the last quarter of the 18th century and the early decades of the 19th and, where the scene was named on the reverse, it was referred to as a 'Named View'. An outstanding example of topographical painting is the Frog* service made for the Empress Catherine II*, which played an important part in popularising in England a type of decoration which had hardly then become fashionable on the Continent.

Tortoiseshell Ware

Earthenware covered with a lead glaze which is mottled with blue, brown, and green, by the use of the oxides of cobalt*, manganese* and copper. The tortoiseshell glaze, popular in mid-18th century Staffordshire, and notable among Whieldon* and Whieldon-Wedgwood wares, was in many ways similar to that employed by Bernard Palissy in the 16th century for the reverse of his rustic dishes. Wedgwood made tortoiseshell ware during the first years of production at the Ivy House*.

Tower of London

A pale-blue and white jasper* plate, 6½in. in diameter, was produced in 1978 to commemorate the 900th anniversary of the Tower of London (1078-1978). It is ornamented with a bas-relief* of the Tower within an oak-leaf border. A dark-blue backstamp gives a brief description of the Tower.

Toys

1. Miniature pieces of pottery, generally of tableware shapes. Examples exist of unmarked toys of this type, usually decorated with green or tortoiseshell* glaze and sometimes in fruit or vegetable shapes, which are attributed to Whieldon-Wedgwood* or Wedgwood, but all 18th-century specimens are rare. After about 1800 Queen's ware* toy services became popular and were produced in good quantities, either plain, enamelled with current designs or decorated with underglaze blue prints*. They were made also in Drab* earthenware. Miniature teapots have survived also in engine-turned black basaltes* and cane* ware. In the 20th century several toy sets were designed by Daisy Makeig-Jones*.
2. In the 18th century the word 'toys' was understood to refer to the enormous variety of metal trinkets, such as snuff boxes, scent bottles, seals and buckles, of which Birmingham was the centre of production in England. Many such objects of silver, Sheffield plate or cut steel were ornamented with Wedgwood's terracotta* or jasper* cameos*.

Traditional Shapes

See: Tableware Shapes

TOYS. Child's tea and coffee service painted with Etruscan pattern in orange-red and black. Coffeepot height 5½in. c.1810. *Sotheby's, London*

TRANSFER PRINTING. Queen's ware punch pot of fine quality, transfer-printed in black by Guy Green with the figure of Diana and her hounds in a landscape setting. The enamelled name 'JACOB DE CLERK' was evidently added (and ill-placed) later. Height 7¾in. c.1780. *Sotheby's, London*

Transfer Printing

A process of decorating pottery and porcelain by transferring a print from an engraved plate to a glazed or unglazed surface so that, after firing (and where necessary glazing), the impression remains as permanent decoration. The making of a transfer print requires considerable skill, its quality depending partly on the excellence of the engraved plate and partly on the dexterity of the operative taking the print from it. A heated mixture of oil and colouring oxide is applied to the plate and wiped off, leaving the engraved lines charged with colour. A sheet of wet tissue paper is then laid on the plate and a thick pad of flannel placed on top of it. The sandwich is then put in a press, usually in modern times a pair of spring-loaded rollers, after which the tissue paper can be peeled off. It bears the engraved design in reverse. The paper is applied to the surface of the ware and the back rubbed with a flannel pad to transfer the design to the object to be decorated. The paper can then be gently washed off with water and the design fired in the muffle* or enamelling kiln*. The commonest colour employed in the 18th century was black, but red was popular and brown, purple and green occur occasionally. Since the 18th century a number of mechanical improvements have been made to this method but the principle remains the same.

The art of transfer-printing was invented by an Irishman, John Brooks, in 1752, and was subsequently used at the Battersea Enamel Works, the Bow* porcelain factory, and, from 1757, at the Worcester* porcelain factory. The process appears to have been discovered independently by John Sadler* of Liverpool, who was in partnership (c.1756-70) with Guy Green*. Sadler & Green decorated Liverpool delft* tiles* made by Zachariah Barnes by printing them at their works in Harrington Street, Liverpool. These tiles, 5in. square, were decorated with portraits of actors and actresses, scenes from Aesop's* Fables after Francis Barlow* or from Samuel Croxall's edition, and a variety of other popular subjects. They were often signed 'J.Sadler, Liverpool' and could be supplied at an extremely low price in comparison with the painted Dutch tiles then being imported.

The earliest record of a business transaction between Wedgwood and Sadler occurs on 23 September 1761 when Sadler bought a small quantity of creamware, probably for trials. In December he sent Wedgwood samples of his printing, including the Tythe Pig*, on porcelain, and three months later he returned a full crate of printed creamware to Burslem. Within twelve months the two firms were doing regular business, which averaged about £30 a month by the end of 1763. The arrangement was that Wedgwood sold glazed creamware to Sadler & Green, who decorated it and sold it back to him, or (from their Liverpool warehouse) to other customers. Notwithstanding statements to the contrary, this remained the method of business throughout their association.

In return for Sadler's agreeing to give him a monopoly on his transfer-printing of creamware, Wedgwood undertook to supply him with all the ware he wanted for resale (after Wedgwood's own requirements had been satisfied). 'You may rest assured,' Sadler wrote to Wedgwood in October 1761, 'that we never printed a Piece for any Person but yourself.' The existence of what appear to be authentic Sadler prints on ware which is unquestionably not Wedgwood's is most credibly explained by Sadler's buying in a few plain creamware pieces and printing them to make up an order which could not otherwise be completed in time (for shipping, for instance). It is possible also that plain creamware from other manufacturers, bought for sale, undecorated, from his Liverpool warehouse, was occasionally transfer-printed in error. The dependence of Sadler & Green on Wedgwood's business was such that any deliberate contravention of their agreement was extremely unlikely. After ten years of trading, this was averaging about £650 a month, representing the decorating and resale to Wedgwood of

TRANSFER PRINTING. Queen's ware oval dish, feather-edge shape, transfer-printed by Guy Green with a landscape and distant ruins, the border decorated with six printed sprays of flowers. Oval length 14½in. c.1780. *Wedgwood Museum*

TRANSFER PRINTING. A craftswoman transferring a print of one of Clare Leighton's *New England Industries* designs to a plate. 1952.
Photograph:Wedgwood

some 18,000-24,000 dozens of ware a year (in addition to Wedgwood ware decorated and sold to other customers). Wedgwood, on the other hand, may have been tempted to install his own printers at Etruria* after the new factory was built. That he did not do so was due probably to two sound commercial reasons: first, Guy Green, after Sadler's retirement in 1770, continued to provide an outlet from Liverpool for large quantities of decorated and undecorated Queen's ware; and second, while the monopoly agreement was continued, Green could not print for anyone else, thus reducing competition from other manufacturers of creamware.

There were rivals to Sadler & Green in the business of transfer printing, most of them their pupils. They included Jeremiah Green, formerly a London engraver; Richard Abbey, apprenticed in 1767, who left in 1773 to set up his own business as an engraver and printer; Thomas Rothwell, probably employed in the 1760s; and Thomas Bilinge. Neither Sadler nor Green was an engraver, and most of their engravings were obtained from London. As early as 1763 they were employing three engravers in London and another in Liverpool. The subjects were principally of five types: prints already familiar to the public in other forms (e.g. *The Tythe Pig*, The Fortune Teller, The Sailor's Farewell, Pipe and Punch Party*);

TRANSLUCENCY. Demonstrating the translucency of a modern bone china plate of the dark-blue *Florentine* pattern.
Photograph: Wedgwood

contemporary and commemorative portraits (e.g. George III*, Queen Charlotte*, Frederick the Great*, Lord Rodney, John Wesley*); landscapes and pastoral scenes; 'Exotic' birds*; and armorial* wares, including Masonic* wares, although these were produced in comparatively small quantities. Prints were chiefly in black, or one of two shades of iron-red, the second of which, described as 'orange-red', was introduced in 1764. Purple was made, from 1764, but was, according to Sadler, 'very difficult', and both blue and green were attempted experimentally without much success. No underglaze blue printing* on Wedgwood Queen's ware was done until the early 19th century.

Transfer printing continued to be used throughout the 19th century and into the 20th, but only in underglaze blue did the style of decoration ever again reach the heights of popularity and the quantity of production and sales achieved during the 1770s. It enjoyed a considerable revival with the production of commemorative ware commissioned by Jones, McDuffee & Stratton* during the first half of the 20th century, and has continued to be used regularly for individual commemorative pieces. The technique has remained the foundation for all print and enamel* decoration, the first examples of which were produced for Wedgwood by Guy Green in 1776.
See also: Bat Printing; Burdett, Peter Pever; Gold-printing; Lithography; Silk-screen Printing

Translucency
If, when a ceramic body is held up to a source of light, it is seen that light is transmitted, then it is said to be translucent. Only sufficiently thin vitreous* bodies of good quality which have been fired at a high temperature will be translucent, and porcelain is the most translucent of all ware. Nevertheless a thickness of 5mm will usually prevent light from passing. At one time translucency was regarded as an essential property of porcelain in Europe and all translucent ware was so described. Wedgwood sometimes described his jasper* as 'biscuit porcelain' because thinly potted examples are sometimes translucent. It is for this reason that Bentley* urged Wedgwood not to fire jasper at too high a temperature so that it became translucent. By this time jasper contained Cornish materials in the form of china clay and Bentley was anxious lest Wedgwood infringe Champion's* patent which gave him a monopoly on the use of Cornish materials in the manufacture of porcelain. Bone china* of the first period was the first body produced by Wedgwood which is normally translucent.

Travellers (Travelling Salesmen)
The use of travellers or 'riders' as they were often called, was uncommon in the pottery industry before the end of the 18th century. Thomas and John Wedgwood of the Big House, Burslem, are said to have employed travellers, but the evidence is thin. Josiah Wedgwood was certainly among the first to consider the idea, when he wrote to Bentley* in September 1771 to suggest that William Brock might be employed 'continually among the Merch[an]ts *shewing them Patterns, bringing them to the Rooms, taking their orders, & receiving their money'.* Seven years later he proposed that Joseph Brownbill be equipped with a 'travelling machine' to take round 'patterns of flower pots, & little bouquet pots, Tablets – Figures – Patterns – Ink pots & stands – Seals &c, & some pieces of usefull ware'. Brownbill set out in the spring of 1778 but, through a series of misadventures which Josiah later described as 'like a dream, or one of Don Quixots adventures', succeeded only in making himself ridiculous. Shortly afterwards, Tom Byerley* made a successful first attempt and, in 1779 he was sent out 'into the tremendous North', carrying samples and a small stock of easily portable pieces such as portrait medallions*, seals and ink pots*. He was on the road for thirty-six days, covering 590 miles, taking orders, selling from his small stock and, as important, collecting debts.

From that time on, salesmen travelled fairly regularly for Wedgwood and it was one of their most important duties to collect outstanding debts. This involved their being entrusted with large sums in cash. Byerley and Josiah II* travelled in Holland and Germany together in 1790-1, selling jasper and seeking orders for the Portland vase*.

In the early years of the 19th century the job of traveller assumed a new significance. The depletion of European trade by war and blockade increased the importance of provincial sales in Britain. Between 1810 and 1842 Wedgwood's most senior and most trusted traveller was Josiah Bateman*, whose orders have

TRAVELLERS. Page from Charles Gill's notebook showing various shapes of teapot then in production in Queen's ware and bone china. c.1815. *Wedgwood Museum*

TRAVELLERS. White stoneware ('porcelain') half-jug, moulded with the *Hunt* pattern, the neck ornamented with fruiting vine over a blue slip wash. Height 6½in. c.1820. *Wedgwood Museum*

Trays

Trays, which were made by Wedgwood in the 18th century in black basaltes*, jasper* and cane* ware, were, according to Josiah Wedgwood, always 'very hazardous' and, because they could not be potted thinly without cracking or warping, tended to be unpractically heavy. Consequently few were made and even fewer have survived. John Coward* may have carved the original model for a rare, late rococo* example, c.1785, in the Manchester Museum (Haworth Collection). Usually the trays were of simpler design, plain round or oval shapes with dished rims, made for use with 'furniture' as *déjeuner* sets*. No doubt for this reason, Josiah used the term *déjeuner* (spelt variously 'dejunia' or 'dejunier') to denote the tray rather than the set. In the 19th and 20th centuries, trays have been made also in Queen's ware* and bone china*, generally as part of *déjeuner* sets but also as tops for tea tables and in the form of revolving trays* or 'Lazy Susans'. All examples are scarce.

Tremblay Ware
See: Email Ombrant

survived almost intact in the Wedgwood archives, providing a remarkably detailed record of the bodies, shapes and designs in production as well as a reliable picture of a traveller's business and his relationship with his employer. In addition to taking orders from samples and collecting debts (as much as £2,000 cash in a month), he organised the journeys of junior travellers, commented on quality and prices, advised on the introduction of new wares, reported on the wares of competitors and passed on the complaints of his customers, as well as providing valuable information about their creditworthiness. Complaints were frequent: 'It certainly must be painful to me to be always complaining', Bateman wrote in 1817, 'yet it would be injurious to withhold incessant accusations of neglect and misconduct – I never notice trifles.'

Travelling was never an easy job, even when trade conditions were favourable, and extra hazards were offered by the state of the roads and the weather, especially in the north country and Scotland. In April 1820 Bateman's carriage was overturned in the Exe river in Devonshire and he was fortunate to escape alive.

Since the latter half of the 19th century, Wedgwood's travellers have been allotted territories for which they have assumed managerial responsibility, the most significant of these being Europe, where regular visits have been made to agents and established retail outlets. During his period as Sales Director in the 1950s, Sir John (Hamilton) Wedgwood* made many sales journeys abroad, sometimes accompanying the traveller for the territory, and as Chairman and chief executive Sir Arthur Bryan* never allowed Wedgwood's travellers or customers to forget that he was first a salesman. This insistence on the importance of selling at all levels has been crucial to the firm's success since World War II.
See also: Gill, Charles

TRAYS. Black basaltes tray with shell-edge rim and foliate handles, probably copied from a carved wood model attributable to John Coward. Overall length 16½in. c.1785. *Manchester Museum*

TREMBLEUSE. Covered broth bowl, decorated with *Gold wreath* pattern and red enamel lines, and a tea bowl decorated in blue and gold, both with deep *trembleuse* saucers. c.1800-10.   *Author's collection*

Trembleuse
Term used to describe a saucer with an unusually deep well to accommodate the foot of a cup so that it might be held by a trembling hand with less danger of upsetting or spilling the contents. Such cups and saucers were made by Wedgwood in the last quarter of the 18th century and during the first half of the 19th century in several versions and many bodies, notably Queen's ware*, jasper*, White ware* and bone china*. The shapes include lidded chocolate cups and saucers and lemonade cups and saucers.

Trent & Mersey Canal
See: Canal, Trent and Mersey

Trethowan, Harry (1884-1960)
Designer, who was closely associated with, and for many years a director of, Heal's, Tottenham Court Road, London. As buyer of the china and glass department, a member of the Council for Art and Industry (the Pick Council) of which Josiah Wedgwood V* was a founder member, and spokesman on ceramics for the Design and Industries Association (DIA), Trethowan occupied a position of considerable influence in the pottery industry. He was instrumental in obtaining *Honey Buff* coloured body* for Heal's in 1920 and was probably responsible for commissioning patterns used on it. He designed some tableware patterns himself in the early 1930s but they have not been identified.

Triform Goddess
A reference to Diana*, who was identified with Selene (Luna – see: Diana) and Hecate She was thus a threefold goddess and for this reason was called Triformis.
Wedgwood subject:
Triform Goddess, rectangular plaque 9¼in. x 7½in., modelled by Pacetti*, 1788

Trinket Set
A set, generally comprising a tray with ring stand, pin box, powder box, and pair of small candlesticks, for a woman's dressing-table. Some eccentric and oddly jokey sets were produced in Majolica* and Argenta* in the last quarter of the 19th century and more conventional sets in silver shapes* appeared in bone china* and jasper*, c.1895-1920.

Triptolemus
Son of Celeus, King of Eleusis. A protégé of Ceres*, he invented the plough and became the hero of the Eleusinian mysteries. Wedgwood's early plaques entitled *Night* (nos.77 and 79 in 1773 Catalogue*), copied from an antique gem, are known also as *Ceres and Triptolemus* (1779 Catalogue).

Tritons
Triton, half-man, half-fish, was the son of Poseidon (Neptune*) and Amphitrite. Tritons and Nereids* accompany Neptune, playing in the waves and blowing trumpets in the shape of the conch shell.

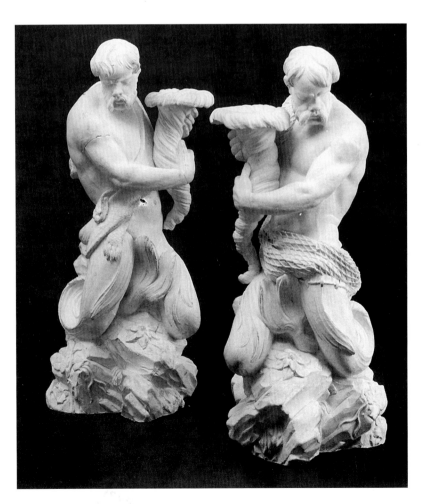

TRITONS. Biscuit models of candlesticks in the form of Tritons carrying whorled shells. Height 11in.   *Wedgwood Museum*

TROPHIES. Pair of black basaltes vases, the necks ornamented with garlands and trophies. the bodies with figures of *Apollo and the Muses*. Height 19¾in. c.1790.

Christie's, London

Wedgwood's Triton candlesticks*, height 11in., are in the form of bearded, naked Tritons with seaweed or fishing net clinging to their thighs. Each holds a conch shell. Tritons of this size 'after Michael Angelo' are listed in the 1773 Catalogue*. They have been attributed to Flaxman* but it appears from Josiah's letter of 19 November 1769 that one of the pair was first obtained as a carved model, probably in wood. It is possible that the companion figure was modelled by Flaxman. A single figure of Triton, height 24in., is also listed in the 1773 Catalogue but no example of this large figure has been found.

Triton candlesticks, first produced in black basaltes*, were reproduced in jasper* and rosso antico* with black basaltes before the end of the 18th century. In the 19th century they were reintroduced in Majolica*. They have been reproduced in modern basalt intermittently during the 20th century. Tritons appear also on the Wine and Water Ewers*.

Triumph

Originally a grand military procession in which the victorious general entered the city at the termination of a campaign. Roman processions were led by the Senate, the members of which went out to meet the army, and they terminated in the Temple of Jupiter on the Capitoline Hill. Other processions commemorating success or victory came to be known as triumphs, and Wedgwood made a number of bas-relief* subjects representing such processions. See: Ariadne; Bacchus; Cupid; Silenus; Venus

Trophies

Although trophies were a fashionable sort of decoration during the 18th century, they were not often employed by Wedgwood. Originally, trophies were the arms of a beaten enemy, which were hung up in a tree to celebrate a victory. Later, weapons were grouped together as a form of modelled or painted ornament. The notion was extended to a variety of objects: musical instruments were emblematic of music, and a palette and brushes of the visual arts. Trophy-like ornaments occur on vertical tablets made by Wedgwood for the jambs of chimneypieces* and also occasionally as the ornament for jasper* and black basaltes* vases.

TRIUMPH. Wedgwood & Bentley solid pale-blue and white jasper plaque, *Triumph of Bacchus,* modelled by Hackwood in 1776. 7⅛in. x 9⅝in. c.1778.

Dwight & Lucille Beeson Collection, Birmingham Museum, Alabama

TROPHY PLATE. Pair of sold pale blue and white jasper Trophy plates heavily ornamented with borders of flowers, fruit and ribbons, the centres with *Venus Bound* and *Venus and Cupid,* mounted in carved and gilt wood frames. Height 16½in. (plates diameter 8¾in.).
Christie's, New

Trophy Plate

A jasper* plate, often of several colours, diameter about 8¾in., the surface of which is almost entirely covered by jasper ornament surrounding a central bas-relief*. The number of reliefs varies between 150 and 180, and the production of this piece, which has continued intermittently since about 1870, requires great technical expertise. The total effect is generally ostentatious and more nearly resembles the work of an over-enthusiastic confectioner than an example of the potter's art.

Trump

William Hogarth's pug dog which appears in his self-portrait. In a reclining pose Trump was portrayed by Chelsea* in porcelain c.1749-50. The Chelsea model was adapted from a terracotta by L-F. Roubiliac*. Richard Parker* supplied Wedgwood with the model of a 'Pug Dog' for 10/6d in 1774 and it is likely that Parker either bought a mould at the sale of the contents of Roubiliac's studio in 1762 or that he obtained a model from Joseph Wilton, who had studied with Roubiliac in Rome. This was reproduced in black basaltes*, 'One Pug Dog' being catalogued in 1774, and 'Two Pug Dogs', evidently a pair, in 1777, indicating that Wedgwood had caused a second, mirror-image, to be modelled during the interval. The 1781 Christie's* Auction Sale* catalogue lists 'two pug dogs from Hogarth' and 'a pair of pug-dogs from a favourite dog of Hogarth's', all in black basaltes. The known Wedgwood models are all unmarked and examples are extremely rare. In recent years a much smaller and inferior model, also unmarked, has appeared, attributed to Wedgwood. It bears no resemblance to Roubiliac's original and neither the quality of the modelling nor that of the black body inspire confidence in the attribution.

TRUMP. Black basaltes figure of Hogarth's 'Trump'. Length 11¼in. Unmarked. Wedgwood, c.1774.
Christie's, London

TULIP VASE. Earthenware biscuit Tulip vase with three tiers of spouts or cups, each to hold a single tulip, shown with a biscuit tartlett stand. Vase height 18½in. Unmarked. Wedgwood, c.1786.
Wedgwood Museum

Tudor Rose Ornament

Forms of the 'Tudor rose' appear as sprigged* ornament on ware excavated from the Whieldon* site at Fenton Vivian, both on redware* and on early creamwares decorated with colouring oxides of the Whieldon-Wedgwood* partnership period. It is likely that Wedgwood continued to use this style of ornament at the Ivy House* and the Brick House* Works.

Tulip Vase

A vase in the general form of a pyramid on a tall rectangular pedestal, the pyramidal centre ornamented with tiers of spouts or tubes, each to hold a single tulip. Vases of this type with up to eleven such tiers were made in tin-glazed* earthenware in much of Europe, especially in Holland, and porcelain vases of this shape were made in Vienna and also in China for export to Europe. An earthenware biscuit tulip vase is preserved in the Wedgwood Museum and has been researched by Lynn Miller (Wedgwood Society *Proceedings* No.11, 1982). An Oven Book entry for January 1786 indicates that such a vase ('Blue and white promide [*sic*] for flower things') was fired in jasper*. A drawing of the piece appears as Shape No.291 in a factory Shape Drawing Book*. It is unlikely that many of these remarkable objects were ever made, and none is known to have survived in jasper.

Tureen

A serving bowl, usually circular or oval, for soup or vegetables, or in a much smaller size for sauces. Wedgwood's later 18th-century Queen's ware* tureens were generally of simple, elegant shapes copied, or slightly adapted, from contemporary silver. In his catalogues they were invariably described as 'terrines'.

Turner, H. Thackeray (1853-1937)

Architect and designer; a pupil of Sir George Gilbert Scott. Turner painted a few ornamental pieces of Wedgwood's bone china, in a style resembling that of Alfred Powell*, c.1917-27.

TUREEN. Pearl-glazed Queen's ware soup tureen and stand, shape no.3 in the '1790' Catalogue, with matching ladle. Height 19¾in. c.1790-1800. *Wedgwood Museum*

Turner, John (1738-87)

Potter at Lane End, 1762-87. The factory was continued after his death by his two sons, John and William, until 1803, when it was enlarged and became Turner & Co. Turner manufactured creamware*, stoneware*, jasper*, black basaltes* and dry bodies* generally. The quality was excellent and his wares were similar in style to those of Wedgwood, with whom he was on excellent terms. In 1775 he was involved with Wedgwood in an attempt by the Staffordshire potters to prevent an extension of Champion's* patent and together they leased clay mines at Redruth and St Austell. John Turner later became a member of the New Hall* porcelain company. Although Turner's sons continued to make high quality wares in the manner of their father, and produced and patented the first Stone china* in 1800, the firm came to an abrupt end in 1806 with the bankruptcy of the younger Turners, due to the wartime blockade and the loss of their very considerable Continental trade. Like the Wedgwoods they had a flourishing business with Holland, and like Leeds* they shipped creamware there for decoration. John Hancock*, who was employed by Turner's sons, introduced a technique for burnishing gold.

Turner's jasper body closely resembles that of Wedgwood but the blue differs in shade and is closer to slate blue. Its surface also shows a slight but perceptible sheen. Although he often copied Wedgwood's bas-relief subjects, Turner's style is less severely classical. His cane* ware, a vitreous body containing china clay and china stone, is light buff in colour and of fine quality.
See: Cornish Journey

TURNER, John. Black basaltes jug with moulded and applied ornament, horizontal turning and vertical engine-turning, the principal ornament of Cupids with a wreath probably copied from Wedgwood's and applied over a textured ground. Height 6⅜in. c.1785. Mark: TURNER. *Author's collection*

Turner, Dr. Matthew (d.1788?)

Surgeon, anatomist, chemist and scholar of Liverpool; a founder of the Liverpool Academy of Art, 1769. Turner was called to attend Josiah Wedgwood when the latter injured his leg in 1762, on a visit to Sadler & Green*. On one of his routine visits to his patient, Turner brought with him his friend, Thomas Bentley* and was thus responsible for introducing the two men who were to form one of

TURNER, John. Creamware sauce tureen and stand with pierced ladle, enamelled with a continuous ivy pattern. Height 5¾in. Mark: TURNER. c.1780-5. *Merseyside Museums*

TURNER, John. Solid blue-grey and white jasper teapot apparently identical in shape to a Wedgwood teapot of the same period and ornamented with *Sportive Love,* designed for Wedgwood by Lady Templetown and modelled by Hackwood. Height 5¾in. c.1785-90. *Temple Newsam House, Leeds*

TWIG BASKET. The modern Queen's ware 'Twig' basket is made by the same method as those of the 18th century. *Photograph: Wedgwood*

the most important partnerships in industrial history. It is probable that he was responsible also for introducing Wedgwood to Erasmus Darwin*, another of his close friends.

Turner prepared varnishes and colours for Wedgwood, and it was his brown varnish that was first used as a ground for the bronze powder in the production of bronzed basaltes* vases. Wedgwood consulted him on the subject of making crucibles* in 1762 but appears to have taken no further action until about 1777, when his interest in chemical apparatus was reawakened by his reading of Dr Joseph Priestley's* *Experiments and Observations on different kinds of Air.* Through a series of lectures he gave at the Warrington Academy in 1765, Turner was responsible for introducing Priestley to the subject of chemistry.

Turner's Jaspe Ware
A reddish terracotta body covered with slips* of various colours (blue, green, chocolate, buff, black) ornamented with bas-reliefs*. These wares, made by Gildea & Walker of Duke Hall, near Burslem, in the third quarter of the 19th century were said to be ornamented from moulds originally in the possession of John Turner*.

Turning
See: Processes of Production

Turnpike Roads
A turnpike is a barrier placed across a road to prevent passage until a toll has been paid. Turnpike roads were those highways main-

TWIG BASKET. Queen's ware 'Twig' fruit basket and stand. Length (basket) 9⅝in. c.1778. *Temple Newsam House, Leeds*

TYTHE PIG, THE. Creamware mug transfer-printed in black by Sadler & Green, signed 'Sadler' and 'Liverpool' in the corners. Height 5in. Unmarked. Wedgwood, c.1763-4. *E.N. Stretton Collection*

tained by tolls levied on all vehicles and cattle using them. Tollbars in England originated in 1267 and the first English turnpikes were set up in 1663. One of the principal obstacles to the development of the pottery industry in Staffordshire was the appalling state of the roads serving the Potteries. The construction of turnpike roads to improve communications was strongly supported by the potters and by influential coal owners, but often strenuously opposed by local merchants (who thought their interests would be injured by roads which passed by their towns instead of through them). Whieldon* was among those who subscribed in 1759 to the first turnpike road in the neighbourhood, and Josiah Wedgwood became a leading figure in the fight for turnpikes. He enlisted the help of Lord Gower (see: Stafford), whose vast coal resources gave him a particular interest in the transport of freight. He used his influence to have a petition presented to Parliament in February 1763 for a turnpike to connect the existing Liverpool-London road to the north of the Potteries with the Derby-Uttoxeter-Newcastle-under-Lyme road to the south. Strong opposition resulted in a compromise route being agreed, and two years later Josiah again took the lead in having the Burslem and Uttoxeter turnpikes joined, subscribing £500 on behalf of himself and his brother, John, at interest of five per cent 'and good security'.
See also: Canal, Trent and Mersey

Twig Basket
A circular or oval fruit dish made up of strips of clay woven together by hand to form an open basket shape. An example, with matching stand, appears in the 1774 Catalogue* (Plate 8) and twig baskets have been made intermittently ever since.
See: Baskets

Two-colour Clay Bodies
See: Coloured Bodies

Tythe Pig, The
A popular 18th-century transfer-print* which exists in several versions. It depicts a parson, a farmer and his wife. The farmer holds a pig, the wife a child. The couple are refusing to part with the tenth (or tithe) pig to the parson unless he agrees also to take the tenth child. There are some lines of verse below the print. The origin of the design is an engraving after Boitard dated 1751. A version signed by Sadler* is found occasionally on Wedgwood creamware and it is the earliest design mentioned in correspondence between Sadler and Wedgwood in 1763. The print appears on the creamware of other factories and Derby* made a porcelain group and a set of three figures of the subject.

U

Ulfsunda, Sweden

A minor *faïence* factory which began to make black basaltes* and red and white stoneware in the Wedgwood style at the end of the 18th century. In 1819 the factory was called the *Wedgwood-Fabriket.*

Ulysses

Roman name for the Greek hero of the Trojan war, Odysseus. Homer's *Odyssey* recounts the adventures of Ulysses after the war, when he set out for home. For some reason he was not popular with Wedgwood and only one bas-relief* illustrating any of his exploits is recorded. This is a cameo* attributed to Hackwood*, *Ulysses staying the Chariot of Victory.* Penelope* the wife of Ulysses, is the subject of a painting by Joseph Wright* of Derby, *Penelope unravelling Her Web,* bought from the artist by Josiah Wedgwood in 1785.

Umbrella Stand

Umbrella stands of various shapes were made by Wedgwood in Majolica* glazes from c.1875. One such stand in Argenta*, bearing the date mark for 1882, is of the fan shape associated with both the Aesthetic* Movement and the fashion for 'Japanese' design.

Unaker

See: Cherokee Clay

Undercutting

The method of hand-finishing a bas-relief*, after it is removed from the mould* and while it is in the leather-hard* state, to sharpen the modelling and to accentuate the contrast between the

UNDERCUTTING. Detail of the head of a Triton from a solid blue and white jasper Triton candlestick, c.1785, showing fine undercutting, especially noticeable in the mouth, eyelids and ears.
Brooklyn Museum, Emily Winthrop Miles Collection

relief and the ground. It is especially noticeable where the cutting is on a plane horizontal (parallel) to that of the ground (e.g. in nostrils and ears of portraits) and provides an extra dimension which cannot be obtained from the mould. Undercutting is a feature of the finest 18th-century jasper* and is seen also on the small number of portrait medallions* finished by A.H. ('Bert') Bentley* in 1922. Josiah I wrote to Thomas Bentley* in November 1778: 'Some of the tablets lately sent are finish'd very high by Hackwood* at a considerable expence…you will easily perceive the difference in the hair, faces, fingers &c, & more palpably by all the parts capable of it being undercut which gives them the appearance, & nearly the reality of models.'

UNDERCUTTING. Solid blue and white jasper plaque, *Bacchanalian Figure,* diameter 12in., c.1790, the shadows behind the right foot and arm showing the depth of relief and the use of undercutting.
Dwight & Lucille Beeson Collection, Birmingham Museum, Alabama

UNDERGLAZE BLUE PRINTING.
Oval fruit centre decorated with *Peony* pattern printed in dark underglaze blue 'richly gilt'. Height 6½in. c.1820.   *Sotheby's, Chester*

Underglaze Blue Printing

Underglaze blue printing was the most significant addition to Wedgwood production during the first half of the 19th century. The technique appears to have been introduced to the Potteries about 1780, although some authorities credit William Adams* with having brought it to Staffordshire some five years earlier. Josiah I had always declined to produce underglaze blue decorated ware, even after the creation of the Pearl* body and glaze which did not discolour the blue, because he wished to distinguish his wares from the style most typical of the Continental tin-glazed earthenware manufacturers and also from the most popular style of decoration on English porcelain. He was determined to avoid any unflattering comparison between his Queen's ware* and the blue-painted or blue-printed porcelains of Bow*, Caughley*, Worcester*, Lowestoft or the Liverpool factories, and for the same reason he was generally unwilling to produce *chinoiserie** designs.

The original proposal to introduce blue-printing at Etruria* is usually credited to John Wedgwood*, but the earliest surviving reference occurs in a letter from Tom Byerley* to Josiah II* dated 31 March 1805. By then it was clear that Wedgwood could no longer afford to ignore the rising demand for this type of decoration, which was already obliging Byerley to buy in goods from other factories. Within a few years blue-printed earthenware was being produced in larger quantities than any other type of ware in the pottery industry and probably accounted for more than half of English earthenware production in the first quarter of the 19th century.

The Wedgwoods put their cousin Abner*, the fifth son of 'Useful' Thomas Wedgwood*, in charge of the blue-printing department, and he sought advice from his brother, Ralph Wedgwood* of the Hill Top and Ferrybridge factories, who had evidently inherited their father's notebooks. The 'body used for blue-printing used Decr. 30th 1805' at Etruria – the 'Printing body' – was not identical to the Pearl body, but it deviated so slightly from it that the two are generally considered as the same. Josiah II's own description of the process is definitive:

> Blue printed is quite different [from other colour printing] the colour being given under the glaze. The intended impression is first taken from the copper-plate by a rolling press upon a sheet of thin paper washed with soap which is immediately transferred by being rubbed hard upon the Biscuit*. The paper is then washed off & the impression remains on the ware which is then placed in the gloss-ovens to drive off the oil with which the colour is laid on...The ware is then glazed and hardened on in a stove to drive off the moisture otherwise the colour is dull: it is then put in a Glost oven & upon this third firing is finished. Blue printed is fired with a stronger fire...than the Cream Coloured ware which prevents crazing* & improves the blue...A particular glaze is used for Blue printed with which it strikes a better colour... Zaffre* produces an inferior blue...The best cobalt* comes from Sweden.

The choice of design was important and the first produced at Etruria, *Blue Bamboo* and *Blue Basket,* were *chinoiseries** engraved by William Brookes*. The next five patterns, produced between 1806 and 1811, reflected John Wedgwood's* interest in botany: *Hibiscus* and *Peony,* engraved by William Hales* and Thomas Sparks*; *Water Lily,* first engraved by Semei Bourne* in 1896 and re-engraved in various versions by Hales and John Robinson* between 1807 and 1809; *Chrysanthemum,* engraved by Thomas Longmore*; and *Blue Botanical Flowers* engraved by Robinson and Longmore. Several of these patterns were re-engraved also for printing in brown, red and what Josiah II noted as a 'dingy green'. The *Chrysanthemum* pattern was closely imitated by Spode*, although there was little apparent need for such copying since Spode's patterns of this period achieved standards of quality reached only occasionally by other factories. Of Wedgwood's patterns the most distinguished and the most original were unquestionably the botanical prints, in particular *Water Lily* and *Botanical Flowers.*

Largely in response to almost continuous calls from Bateman*, Josiah II introduced a landscape pattern, *Corinth,* which was well received, but then incomprehensibly reverted to *chinoiseries,* producing no further European or classical landscapes for eleven

UNDERGLAZE BLUE PRINTING.
Serving dish decorated with *Claude* pattern, introduced in 1825, printed in underglaze blue. Length 16in. c.1825.
Wedgwood Museum

UNDERGLAZE BLUE PRINTING.
Soup tureen decorated with *New Chinese Temples* pattern printed in underglaze blue. Height 10in. c.1830.   *Sotheby's, Chester*

years. During this period (1811-21) the patterns were exclusively 'Chinese' and included *Chinese Economy of Time* (later *Blue Bridge on a Scroll*), *Blue Pagoda, Chinese Lions, Blue Palisade, Blue Broseley* and *Blue Group [of Flowers]*. The *Willow* pattern was engraved in 1806 from Minton's but, probably by agreement, was not marketed for about twelve years. For the next ten years, 1822-32, there was a revival of interest in floral patterns and landscapes and *Blue Convolvulus* border produced also with a flower centre), *Blue Melon, Blue Rose, Blue Poppy, Blue Pavilion, Blue Claude, Abbey, Blue Landscapes* and *New Chinese Temples* were among the patterns added to the range. Towards the end of this period patterns became heavier, with more ornate borders (including a moulded anthemion* called 'honeysuckle embossed') often with printed or embossed gadroon or beaded edges. One of the most long-lived of these patterns, *Ferrara* was introduced in 1832.

Abner Wedgwood, who had been responsible for the excellence of Wedgwood's underglaze printing, the quality which, more than any other, distinguished the underglaze blue printed wares of Etruria from those of lesser factories, died in 1835. The importance of this loss to Wedgwood is signalled by the absence of any new patterns of this type during the next seven years.

Underglaze blue printed patterns continued to be made through-out the rest of the 19th century and some of the early designs – notably *Landscape, Ferrara* and *Willow* – survived into the 1970s. Among the most distinguished of the new designs during this period were those engraved for Jones McDuffee & Stratton* (1899-1957) and the blue version of Victor Skellern's* *Avocado* pattern (1959).
See: Colour Plate 111

Underglaze Colour
Decoration, either painted or printed, applied to the biscuit* surface of the ware, before the application of glaze and therefore lying under it. Until the 19th century was fairly well advanced the only two pigments which could be employed in this way were blue from cobalt* oxide and purple, or a brownish-purple, from manganese* oxide. Josiah I employed coloured glazes, but underglaze printed decoration is known only after 1805. The underglaze palette is still limited, and no satisfactory method has yet been devised for the application of gold underglaze.
See: Underglaze Blue Printing

Unique Ware
A range of ornamental vases, bowls and small trays designed and produced under the direction of Norman Wilson*, 1932-9 and

UNIQUE WARE. Four examples of Norman Wilson 'Unique Ware' decorated in a variety of glazes, usually superimposed one upon another. The tall vase (height 10¼in.), for example, is decorated with brown and blue glazes over Moonstone glaze, the interior with a dark-green glaze.   *Author's collection*

1954-63. Many decorating techniques were employed, including *sgraffito** and painted lustre*, but the majority of these wares rely for their effect on the sensitive use of brilliant glazes – sometimes as many as seven of different colours superimposed and separately fired. Shapes of Chinese or Korean origin predominated, but vases and bowls with turned horizontal or vertical fluting were also popular. Since the patterns of glazes could not be precisely controlled in firing, each finished piece was unique. Production of Norman Wilson Unique Ware was limited by cost, and the finest pieces, which are both beautiful and technically accomplished, are already attracting the attention of discerning collectors.

Unique wares are marked with the initials 'NW', printed or impressed, in addition to the appropriate Wedgwood marks.

Uniques
Josiah Wedgwood's name for single commissions, often requiring special modelling and decoration, usually undertaken for valued patrons. The acceptance of individual commissions was common practice in small potteries where they could be made with little disruption to regular production, but in factories organised for long production runs of the same article such orders were (and are still) costly to make and, because they could seldom be priced to take full account of true costs without defeating the object by offending the customer, were almost invariably sold at a loss. Josiah I warned Bentley in November 1769 against *'time loseing with Uniques* which keep ingenious Artists who are connected with Great Men of taste, poor & would make us so too if we did much in that way', and less than two months later added: 'Defend me from particular orders.' He was, however, obliged to change his mind about these orders, telling Bentley: 'We must please these great Friends who are warm Patrons of this little Manufacture.'

Unwin, Ralph, (fl.1770-1812)
Miniaturist and enameller, from Liverpool, who occasionally painted landscapes. He exhibited thirty-three works, mostly miniatures, at the Royal Academy. He was hired by Wedgwood in May 1770 as a flower painter at the Chelsea Decorating Studio* where he painted part of the *Husk** service and landscapes for the Frog* service (1773-4). Unwin also painted the grounds for Herculaneum Pictures* and copied a painting of 'Dead Game' by P.P. Burdett*. A miniature portrait of Josiah I by him has been lost.

Urn
The word 'urn' has many meanings, although it is often stated that the Roman *urna* were used only for cinerary purposes. The name was primarily given by the Romans to a narrow-necked, full-bodied pitcher, on a circular base of relatively small diameter, used for carrying water from a fountain. The cinerary urn *(sepulcrum)* was less full-bodied, with a wide mouth, two upstanding handles on the shoulder, and a cover. The First Day's Vase* is a sepulcrum (or *Lebes gamikos)* in shape. The name, *urna*, was applied also to a receptacle of slender form used for collecting votes or drawing lots. The term need not therefore be strictly confined to vessels used for cinerary purposes. It is, however, applied loosely. Most garden urns, for instance, are far closer in form to the krater*, and most tea urns, such as those of Adam design in Sheffield plate, are based on the sepulcrum. A sepulchral shape in black basaltes* was employed on a number of occasions as part of a monument. One such urn was ordered by Deborah Chetwynd* when her father, Lord Chetwynd, died in 1773, and another of the same period, painted in encaustic* colours to commemorate Henry Earle, is in the Wedgwood Museum*. Urns were made also of Queen's ware*, terracotta* with variegated* decoration, and later in jasper* and rosso antico*.

Wedgwood, unsure of the difference between an urn and a vase, attempted to consult William Chambers* on the subject in Decem-

ber 1768. The architect assured him that there was 'a real difference between *Urns & Vases',* but could not spare the time to explain it as he was on his way 'to wait upon the Queen.' Josiah decided that the principal character of urns was simplicity: 'to have covers but no handles, nor spouts…ornamental…either high or low, but sho'd not seem to be Vessels for culinary or sacred uses.' It is plain from his own orders, however, that he quickly abandoned such fine discrimination in favour of a simple all-embracing description – vases.

About 1778 Wedgwood experimented with the production of sideboard urns in the style popularised by Robert Adam*, used either for holding water for washing glasses or for storing knives, but it proved difficult to arrive at an efficient design which would not topple over when the lid was opened and allowed to fall back. The project was therefore abandoned.
See: Vases, Ornamental

Useful Ware
The difference between 'useful' and 'ornamental' wares was of considerable importance since Wedgwood's partnership with his cousin Thomas Wedgwood was limited to the former, and that with Bentley* to the latter. Josiah defined these terms to Bentley, in a letter of 3 September 1770: 'May not usefull ware be comprehended under this simple definition, of such vessels as are *made use of at meals.* This appears to me the most simple & natural line, & though it does not take in Wash-hand basons & bottles or Ewers, Chamberpots & a few such articles, they are of little consequence & speak plain enough for themselves: nor would this exclude any superb vessels for sideboard, or vases for deserts [*sic*]…as these articles would be rather for shew than use.' In spite of this admirably simple definition, the whole of the Frog*, service was credited to the ornamental partnership, as were, on Bentley's insistence, all wares, whether useful or ornamental, of black basaltes*, terracotta*, cane*, rosso antico* and jasper*. Thomas Wedgwood's reaction to this scarcely equitable arrangement is not recorded.

Utility Ware
During World War II the sale of decorated ware to the home market was prohibited and similar prohibitions were extended to the production of articles listed officially as 'non-essential' (e.g. ashtrays, jam pots, figures, vases). Wedgwood production was rationalised to maximise profit while making room for government contracts, principally for the armed forces. From 1942 limited-price 'Utility Ware' – a short range of essential pieces in undecorated white earthenware in strong, simple shapes – was an important part of production for the home market, but the controlled price was too low for it to register as a high percentage of sale or to yield much profit. Although it was made in great quantities, very little of this ware appears to have survived.

Utzschneider, François Paul (1771-1844)
Partner, with Joseph Fabry, in the firm of Utzschneider & Cie, the largest manufacturers of fine earthenware in France during the 19th century. Founded at Sarreguemines (Moselle) in 1778 by Nicolas-Henri and Paul Augustin Jacobi and Joseph Fabry, the factory produced *faïence* until 1799, when the Jacobi interests were transferred to Utzschneider in a new partnership for the manufacture of 'English' earthenware and stoneware. Price lists of 1810 advertised products 'in the English taste', including Queen's ware*, black basaltes*, agate* and marbled* wares, and various stained dry bodies*. Known as 'the French Wedgwood', Utzschneider specialised in wares of this type, winning Gold Medals at Expositions in Paris in 1806, 1819, 1823, 1827 and 1834. In 1836 Utzschneider handed over direction of the factory to, his son-in-law, Alexandre de Geiger (1808-91), in partnership with Fabry's heirs.

Variegated Lustre
See: Lustre Decoration

Variegated Ware

Term applied to all ware of coloured clay, or decorated with coloured slip* or glazes, whose colours have been mixed to imitate marble, agate*, granite, porphyry* or similar decorative natural stones. 'Crystalline'* is the name given by Josiah Wedgwood to the ceramic body (a white vitrified stoneware* which he called 'terracotta'*) which replaced creamware as the body used for all variegated vases after 1772.

There are four principal methods of producing variegated effects: by mixing or 'wedging'* clays of contrasting colours; by trailing or painting coloured slips on the surface of the ware; by the application of metallic oxides; and by decorating the ware with opaque white glaze veined or marbled with colouring oxides. Wedgwood made use of the first three. The fourth is seen only on the 18th-century *faïence* of the Marieberg factory in Sweden.

The technique of wedging stained clays of two or more colours was employed by the Romans, and specimens are known from the T'ang period in China. Dwight* made grey and black stoneware in this manner in the 17th century, and Böttger used the technique effectively at Meissen* during the first quarter of the 18th century. A teapot of 'agate ware' in the Victoria & Albert Museum is believed to have been made in Staffordshire about 1745, nearly ten years before Wedgwood joined Whieldon*. In the introductory remarks to his Experiment Book*, Wedgwood states that prior to 1759 he 'had already made an imitation of Agate; which was esteemed beautiful & a considerable improvement; but people were surfeited with wares of these variegated colours.' Variegated wares produced by wedging are described as 'agate' or 'solid agate' to distinguish them from those whose decoration is on the surface only, which are known as 'surface agate' or by the name of the natural stone (such as pebble or porphyry) which the decoration is intended to imitate. Solid agate pieces exhibit identical patterns inside and out, and, if the object has been press-moulded*, there are breaks in the pattern (usually below the handles) where parts of the mould have been joined.

The second method of decorating variegated ware was by dabbing or trailing stained slips on the surface of the ware and 'combing' them into patterns in imitation of agate or marble. It dates from the Middle Ages, when pilgrim bottles were often decorated in this manner, and an early Staffordshire earthenware cup of this type, dated 1701, is in the Victoria & Albert Museum. Ware decorated by this technique is known as 'surface agate', 'marbled' or 'veined'. All surface agate ware is decorated after it has been thrown or moulded and the interior is often left uncoloured. Where the interior has been finished in coloured slip, the pattern differs from that of the exterior. The external pattern is carried round the piece without any break at the mould seams.

The third and most versatile technique was developed by Wedgwood from his work with tortoiseshell and coloured glazes. It was a type of decoration known to the Chinese at least 1,000 years earlier and the most successful of Whieldon's decorative techniques, requiring the application with a brush or sponge, of powdered metallic oxides to the surface of the ware before glazing. In firing, the colour melted into the glaze, forming patterns which could be controlled sufficiently to produce some consistency of effect, although uniformity of pattern was never possible and the perfect matching of pairs of vases, for example, could not be achieved. The colours most often used were manganese* (violet, purple, brown), cobalt* (blue), iron (rust-red, brown, yellow), anti-

VARIEGATED WARE. Wedgwood & Bentley white terracotta stoneware ewer with snake handle, decorated with sprinkled colour, on a black basaltes plinth. Height 11in. c.1775.
Christie's, London

mony (yellow) and copper (green), which produced a great variety of shades and colours, the tone and pattern being changed by varying the density of application. Ware decorated by this method is distinctive in appearance, the patterns being mottled rather than linear (as in combed or wedged agate) and the colours being mingled rather than deliberately contrasted. The interiors of such pieces are seldom decorated.

All three techniques were first developed for 'useful' wares, and even Whieldon seems not to have attempted to use them for the decoration of vases. Wedgwood's principal use of the three techniques was in the production of vases, but he was persuaded in 1769 reluctantly to make pebble tea ware for a special order, and two years later he was producing quantities of pebble tea ware and coffee ware, although he complained that it was 'too like the Agat pottery which has been made before.' The same stricture did not apply to vases, as he told Bentley*: 'it is *forms* more than the *colours* of many of the Vases which has raised & unvulgarised them. Make exactly the same pebbles into Tea ware & they are let down to the class of common Pott again, many degrees below *Queens ware.*' An extremely rare Wedgwood & Bentley teapot decorated in imitation of Lapis Lazuli ('Vein'd Granite – with Gold') is in the British Museum.

Wedgwood used a great many names for the varied patterns produced by the use of colouring oxides – pebble, blue pebble, variegated pebble, grey pebble, dark pebble, Egyptian pebble, granite, blue granite, porphyry, true porphyry, green porphyry, porphyry with white spots – and some more grandiose names, such as 'Jaune Antique' and 'Holy Door Marble' for combed decoration. Although he made a brief attempt to define some of these decorations to Bentley, their identification with surviving vases remains largely a matter of educated guesswork. Wedgwood's variegated vases and lamps achieved enormous popularity and the technique was given a new lease of life by the introduction of flower pots* and bough pots* with surface agate or sponged colour decoration, sometimes enriched with gilding. As late as 1778 Josiah was introducing new styles. Grandest of the vases were those mounted in ormolu by Boulton* at his Soho (Birmingham) Works.

Production of Wedgwood's variegated vases, lamps and flower pots continued into the late 1780s, when finally Josiah wrote to Josiah II*: 'the granite is now vulgar'. There was a brief revival in the popularity of this style of decoration shortly after Josiah's death, but it was then neglected for many years and little appreciated by collectors. Some solid agate and marbled vases and candlesticks were made in the 19th century, between about 1830 and 1880, the coarseness of their patterns betraying their period. In

VARIEGATED WARE. Wedgwood & Bentley white terracotta stoneware vase, shape no.1, with satyr's mask handles, the horns piercing the rim of the vase, the body decorated with mottled 'pebble' colours. Height 10in.
Mr & Mrs Samuel Laver Collection

1961 Norman Wilson* made some experimental marbled plates in black and white and green and black, which were not approved for production, and some small combed clay bowls in black and white with beaded edges were marketed among the varied range of his Unique Ware*.

Wedgwood's solid agate vases were imitated by a number of Continental factories, notably Apt, in the Vaucluse, and Kassel and Königsberg in Germany. In England, Neale* made variegated vases of excellent quality and somewhat similar decoration was produced by Ralph Wedgwood* at Ferrybridge.
See: Colour Plates 112 and 113

Vase Candlestick

A vase with a reversible cover, one side of which is surmounted by a conventional finial*, the other being provided with a candle nozzle. When the shoulders and cover are pierced it becomes a cassolette*. Vase candlesticks were made by Wedgwood in Queen's ware*, white terracotta* with variegated* decoration, black basaltes* and, after 1781, in jasper*.

Vases, Ornamental

In Europe, the ornamental, or purely decorative, vase was largely a product of the 18th century and became one of the hallmarks of the period. The sophisticated forms and decoration of Greek vases made between 2,000 and 4,000 years ago tend to obscure the fact they they were made for use, and it was not until the 18th century that they came to be prized and collected as decorative objects.

The ornamental ceramic vase, generally adapted from earlier designs for stone or bronze, was developed at Meissen* from about 1710. Böttger made a number of vases, some of them marbled* and faceted, in stoneware, and his porcelain was used at Meissen for vases in recognisable Chinese shapes, decorated with well-painted *chinoiseries** in 1730. The fashion, as it became, was further developed at Sèvres*, where superb vases in the rococo* style were made after the removal of the factory from Vincennes. Tin-glazed* earthenware vases were made at Berlin from about 1730 and other factories which produced vases enamelled with *chinoiseries* in the 1740s and 1750s included Fulda and Höchst. By the middle of the 18th century the fashion for ornamental porcelain and tin-glazed earthenware vases was established on the Continent and it is surprising to find so little evidence of it among English potters. Although vases were made at some of the English porcelain factories – Chelsea*, Bow*, and even Longton Hall, in Staffordshire (although examples are extremely rare) – there appears to be nothing in English pottery which may accurately be described as a decorative vase before 1763-4, when Josiah Wedgwood began to make them in creamware. In July 1765, after he had obtained the order from Queen Charlotte* for a 'A complete

VASE CANDLESTICK. Tricolour green jasper dip vase candlestick with lotus finial, the lid reversing to a candleholder, the upper part of the body diced and ornamented with yellow quatrefoils. Height 9¾in. c.1790.   *Lady Lever Art Gallery, Port Sunlight*

sett of tea things' he told his brother John* to enclose, with a selection of patterns that he proposed sending to the Queen, 'two setts of Vases, Creamcolour engine turn'd, & printed.'

This is the earliest documentary evidence of Wedgwood's vases and it appears that he was the first English potter to introduce vases as a material part of his manufacture. 'Vases & ornaments of various sizes' appear among the first objects in the list of 'The articles to begin the work with', sent to Bentley* in November 1766, when Wedgwood was trying to persuade the latter to enter into partnership with him; and 'ornamental Earthenware or Porcelain Viz Vazes' are first among the articles mentioned in their partnership agreement a year later. It is extremely unlikely that the transfer-printed* vases sent to the Queen were the first to be made, and it is reasonable to conclude that the first Wedgwood creamware vases, probably turned and with some rouletted decoration, were produced at the Brick House* by 1763-4, and by May 1764 they were probably being decorated on the engine-turning lathe. A documentary source for early Wedgwood vases is Saltram*, Devon, where the unmarked, rococo*, engine-turned* creamware vases date to 1764-5.

Creamware vases, both plain (with turned or rouletted decoration) and decorated with transfer prints (though an example of this type of early vase decoration has yet to be found) and in the variegated* form using creamware, wedged or mingled with stained bodies or slips, continued to be made until the end of 1772, when the creamware body was superseded by the more durable terracotta* ('crystalline') body in the production of vases and flower

VASES, ORNAMENTAL. Three early creamware vases with moulded and rouletted patterns, one with applied floral swags and lions' heads, two on conforming pedestals. Height (with pedestals) 14in. Unmarked. Wedgwood, c.1765.

Wedgwood Museum

VASES, ORNAMENTAL. Wedgwood & Bentley black basaltes vase shape no.1 ornamented with a medallion of *The Three Graces* and drapery swags. Height 14¼in.   *Manchester Museum*

VASES, ORNAMENTAL. Wedgwood & Bentley Queen's ware or white terracotta stoneware vase with entwined serpent handles, shape no.8, the body sprinkled with blue, brown and black to imitate porphyry and ornamented with a bas-relief of *Venus and Cupid*. Height 15in. c.1772.

Dwight & Lucille Beeson Collection, Birmingham Museum, Alabama

pots. Black basaltes* vases date from August 1768 and bronzed basaltes* and encaustic* painting on black basaltes vases from 1769. By 1773 Wedgwood had five principal types of vases concurrently in production: creamware, variegated, undecorated basaltes, bronzed basaltes and encaustic-painted basaltes; and there were further subdivisions of ornament and decoration within these broad categories.

At first, all bas-relief* ornament was moulded with the vase, but by the autumn of 1769 Josiah was producing enlarged cameos* for sprigged* ornament and these were soon combined with applied wreaths and swags. It was not until 1776, however, that the technique had been perfected for the application of groups of figures, which date from the summer of that year but were not marketed until the winter lest they be imitated by rival manufacturers before the season was out. Once these various forms of ornament could be applied with confidence and without uneconomic losses in firing, the variety of vases became almost infinite. Handles, finials, ornaments – even the shapes of lids – might be interchangeable.

Designs for vases were mainly copied or adapted from engraved illustrations, notably from the work of de Caylus*, Joseph Marie Vien*, Jacques de Stella*, Edmé Bouchardon*, Fischer von Erlach, Friedrich Kirschner, Bernard de Montfaucon* (especially for Egyptian-style shapes) and, most particularly, Hamilton* and d'Hancarville*. Wedgwood also had drawings made of vases in the collections of friends and patrons – the Duke of Bedford, the Marquis of Rockingham, the Earl of Orford – and named some of the shapes accordingly. Sèvres vases at Morgan's, the London dealer, and in the collection of Lord March, were sketched for copying. Sarah Wedgwood* wrote to Bentley in August 1772: 'my good man is on the ramble continually and I am almost affraid he

wil lay out the price of his estate in Vases he thinks nothing of giving 5 or 6 guineas for.' In 1777 Wedgwood was able to boast that he had 'upwards of 100 Good Forms of Vases for all of which we have the moulds, handles & ornaments.'

Wedgwood saw himself as 'Vase maker General to the Universe' and it is no exaggeration to say that Wedgwood & Bentley's vases caused a sensation in London. There was nothing like them, and only Boulton* and Palmer* ever offered any serious competition. Wedgwood's sister, Margaret Byerley, returned from a visit to London in May 1769 with a 'strange acc[oun]t of their goings on' at the Newport Street showrooms*: 'No getting to the door for Coaches nor into the rooms for Ladies & Gentn & Vases…Vases was all the cry'. A year later, 'a violent *Vase madness'* was reported in Dublin.

Wedgwood visited London himself and sent back to the factory enormous orders for vases – more than 1,200 of three shapes – confident that he could sell [£]1000 worth of such Vases if I had them before I am come home', but by the end of the year he was experiencing 'cash flow' problems, the classic symptom of over-expansion with insufficient capital resources or management expertise. He owed a 'tide of money' to his suppliers and was owed a tide at least as large by his customers. There were rumours of his bankruptcy and he urged Bentley to 'Collect – Collect'. By February 1771 he had identified other serious problems: 'a vast increase in stock', the result of a total lack of production planning, which accounted for all, and more, of the annual profits; and a failure properly to cost production. He immediately put in hand

VASES, ORNAMENTAL. Documentary black basaltes vase and cover of shield shape painted in encaustic orange-red and white with the figures of Jupiter and Ganymede, the reverse inscribed for 'W.M.MOSELEY' and dated 1788. Height 9¾in. *Sotheby's, London*

VASES, ORNAMENTAL. Solid green and white jasper snake-handle vase ornamented with *Sacrifice to Cupid* on a solid white jasper plinth and green jasper dip pedestal. Height 22½in. c.1790. *Christie's, New York*

effective planning of the production of vases, so that manufacture was not dictated by demand or invention (resulting in uneconomic, short production runs) and personally calculated a detailed 'price book of workmanship' for every vase, one of the first examples of cost accounting* in British manufacturing, from which prices were to be calculated. The crisis passed, but it is instructive that Wedgwood & Bentley's greatest production and marketing success should so nearly have caused their downfall.

From the middle of 1771 the bodies of vases were affixed to their feet and plinths by the use of brass screws and nuts, with the interior of the vase protected and made watertight by the use of a thin leather washer. The earliest vases, like all other ware before 1769-70, were unmarked. Thereafter various forms of the Wedgwood & Bentley mark were used (see: Marks) on the base of the plinth only, and it is well to bear in mind that missing plinths may be replaced and older plinths added to newer vases. Both black basaltes and white terracotta plinths were used with variegated vases after 1772.

No jasper* vases were made until 1781 and none was sold to the public before the beginning of 1782. The delay in making them was due to Wedgwood's inability to make the jasper body, in larger forms, stand up in the fire, and this problem was not solved until the end of 1777. It was a further three years before Josiah hinted to Bentley that he was 'contriving some vases for bodies and bodies for vases', and two weeks later Bentley was dead. No new ornamental wares could be introduced until after the auction sale* of the Wedgwood & Bentley partnership stocks in December 1781, and Byerley* later wrote: 'it was determined to open the [show]rooms after the public sale of W&B with works of original merit...at this period Jasper Vases were first introduced.' They

were an immediate success. Many of the shapes were variations of those already popular in other bodies but in the following ten years Josiah added fresh shapes and styles of ornament and decoration, experimenting with new colours, and the effects of dip* and engine-turning to produce striped, fluted and diced patterns. Bas-relief ornament was adapted largely from existing models for tablets. The *Apotheosis of Homer** vase was described by Wedgwood in a letter to Sir William Hamilton as 'the finest & most perfect I have ever made', and he presented a copy of it to the British Museum, but the pinnacle of his achievement in jasper was undoubtedly his copies of the Portland vase*.

During the lifetime of Josiah I, more than 250 vases shapes were made and this number was greatly increased during the 19th century, when some excellent painting on Queen's ware vases was carried out by Emile Lessore*, Thomas Allen* and others. The decorative vase form has been used also, with considerable success, for decoration with coloured and matt glazes* (see: Majolica; Murray, Keith; Unique Ware) and with Fairyland Lustre*. Small black basaltes and jasper vases have continued to be made to the present day, but it is unlikely that anything will ever again equal the pebble vase, 5ft. in height and ornamented with bas-reliefs, listed in the Auction Sale of 1781. Josiah Wedgwood I was unquestionably the most versatile and innovative manufacturer of decorative vases in the history of the pottery industry, and neither his descendants, nor his competitors have matched his success in this field.

See: Colour Plates 114 to 117

Veilleuse
See: Food Warmer

Veined Ware

1. Ware decorated by dabbing or trailing stained slips on to the surface of ware and 'combing' them into patterns in imitation of agate* or marble. Known also as 'surface agate' or 'marbled'.

2. Ware decorated by skilled painters with enamel colours or gold. Some rare variegated* decoration in imitation of lapis lazuli was decorated in this manner. In November 1769 Wedgwood wrote to Bentley: 'I have reserv'd my house at Burslem for Mr Rhodes & his men…& when he comes you shall have Mr Bakewell, but we must have somebody here to vein & finish the Vases, & if Bakewell goes, before Mr Rhodes comes we have nobody.' The veining technique required considerable skill if both David Rhodes* and James Bakewell* were employed on it.

Veldhuysen, Lambertus van (fl.1760-90)

Amsterdam merchant, who was appointed Wedgwood's sole agent in the Netherlands in July 1777, in succession to Du Burk* (imprisoned for peculation) and Joseph Cooper*, who had returned to England. None of Wedgwood's agents in Europe has been so well trusted and few have been as successful as Van Veldhuysen, whose business was carried on by his son and grandson, Lambertus II and Lambertus III. Lambertus II was responsible for translating the 1774 Wedgwood & Bentley Catalogue* for publication in Amsterdam in 1778. Van Veldhuysen warned Wedgwood from the start that he would be unable, because of price, to sell his ware to 'the middle sort of People' and that every article must be of the best quality and clearly marked with Wedgwood's name. In 1778-9 Van Veldhuysen sent in special orders for eighty black basaltes* busts*, principally of eminent Dutchmen, including Admiral de Ruyter and the brothers De Witt, and portrait medallions* were commissioned at about the same time. 'I am told', Wedgwood wrote to Bentley* in November 1778, 'this warehouse is fitted up very elegantly & believe he [Van Veldhuysen] is likely to do very well both for himself & us.' He was not to be disappointed. Lambertus I, his descendants and successors, continued to do business with Wedgwood for more than two hundred years.

Vellum Ware

Ivory-glazed ornamental wares with a slightly textured surface, introduced at Etruria c.1880. The Vellum ground, often with enamelled and raised gold decoration, was used primarily for decorative vases, some in styles reflecting the fashion for *Japonisme*.

Venus

Formerly the Roman goddess of Spring, she became identified with the Greek Aphrodite*, goddess of love and fertility, in the 3rd century B.C. The worship of Venus was fostered by Julius Caesar*, who traced his ancestry back to Aeneas, son of Mars* and Venus. The goddess is often depicted with Cupid*, her son, or with the most famous of her human lovers, Adonis*. The Three Graces are her attendants. Her attributes include a pair of doves or swans, which may draw her chariot, dolphins*, a flaming torch and a scallop shell.

The principal Wedgwood subjects include the following:

BUSTS

Venus, height 14in., after Canova*, probably from a cast supplied in 1819 by Benjamin and Robert Shout*. Reproduced in black basaltes* and later in Carrara*

Venus de' Medici, height 20in., from a cast supplied by Hoskins & Grant*, 1774

FIGURES

Crouching Venus, height 13in. A 19th century figure, reproduced in black basaltes and Carrara after the 'Venus de Vienne'. See also: Naiads

Venus (seated), height 20in., after the figure by Pigalle*, from a cast supplied by Hoskins & Grant in 1779. Later reproduced in Carrara

Venus and Cupid, height 27in. A 19th-century figure produced in Carrara

Venus and Cupid (also 'Cupid Disarmed'), height 15in,, after Giovanni Meli*, c.1855. Reproduced in black basaltes and Carrara

Venus de' Medici, height 10½in. No.24 in 1774 Catalogue

Venus on a pedestal. One of the six small jasper* figures described in the 1787 Catalogue

Venus Reclining, length 10in. No 30 in 1787 Catalogue

VELLUM WARE. Queen's ware *oenochoe* decorated in the Worcester manner over an ivory glaze. The form is Greek, but the decoration, in iron-red and gold, is Japanese in intention. Height 11½in. c.1880.   *Formerly Buten Museum*

Venus Rising from the Sea 'upon a pedestal richly ornamented with figures representing the seasons', height 6½in. No.29 in 1779 Catalogue

Venus Victrix, height 9½in. A 19th-century figure reproduced in Carrara and also in enamelled bone china* c.1880. This figure is actually a miniature version of the Venus de Milo, excavated in 1820 and now in the Louvre. The true 'Venus Victrix' is the 'Belvedere Venus' in the Uffizi, Florence.

BAS-RELIEFS

A Head of Venus, circular medallion, diameter 2in, no. 17 in 1773 Catalogue. Probably one of two 'heads from Mrs Laundre [Landré]' mentioned in 1771

Sleeping Venus ('Clothed'), tablet 4in. x 11in., from a cast of a model in the Newdigate* collection. No.166 in 1777 Catalogue

Triumph of Venus, tablet 8in. x 17in. or 9in. x 20in., no.210 in 1779 Catalogue

Venus, medallion 4in. x 3in., no.46 in 1773 Catalogue

Venus and Cupid, medallion 5in. x 4in, from a cast of a model in the Newdigate collection. No.168 in 1777 Catalogue

Venus and Cupid, medallion 7in. x 5½in. after an antique gem, catalogued as *Night*, no.77 in 1773 Catalogue

Venus Belfesses (Callipygous), medallion 4in. x 3in., no.49 in 1773 Catalogue

Venus Belfesses (Callipygous), plaque 10½in. x 7¾in., no.66 in 1773 Catalogue

Venus Belfesses (Callipygous), medallion height 7in., from a cast of a model in the Newdigate* collection. No.156 in 1777 Catalogue

Venus in Her Car Drawn by Swans, With Attendant Cupids, medallion 4½in. x 9in., after Le Brun*. No.245 in 1787 Catalogue. A companion piece to *Cupid Watering the Swans,* with which it is often paired on vases

Vulcan with Mars and Venus in the Net, medallion 5½in. x 6in., from a cast of a model in the Newdigate collection. No.184 in 1777 Catalogue

See: Colour Plate 118

VENUS. Black basaltes figure of *Crouching Venus* (the 'Venus de Vienne'). Height 15in. c.1900.   *Christie's, London*

VENUS. Black basaltes figure of *Venus* seated on a rock, after Pigalle. Height 19in. c.1785.   *Mr & Mrs David Zeitlin Collection*

VENUS. Black basaltes framed plaque, *Venus Belfesses* ('Callipygous'). Height 14¾in. Unmarked. Wedgwood & Bentley, c.1775.   *Christie's, London*

VENUS. Wedgwood & Bentley solid blue and white jasper medallion *Venus and Cupid*, (catalogued from 1773 as *Night*). Oval height 6½in. c.1777.   *Wedgwood Museum*

VENUS. Solid blue and white jasper vase ornamented with *Venus in her Chariot drawn by Swans,* after Lebrun, on a solid white jasper plinth. Height 15½in. c.1786.

Lady Lever Art Gallery, Port Sunlight

VESTAL LAMP. Black basaltes oil lamp, the companion to the 'Reading Lamp', introduced in the 1770s and made intermittently, with various ornaments and moulded decoration and on different shapes of plinth, into the 1920s. Height 8½in. *Christie's, London*

Verde Antique

Name given to a kind of green marble very much prized in France for the tops of *commodes* and *console* tables, and for pedestals. Josiah Wedgwood used the name to describe one of his variegated* bodies in colours of dark-green, grey and black.

Veronese Ware

See: Glazes – *Veronese Glazes*

Vestal

A virgin priestess who helped to keep the eternal fire burning on the goddess Vesta's hearth or altar. Vesta was one of the great Roman divinities, goddess of the Hearth and therefore connected with the Penates (household gods). The temple of Vesta was situated in the Forum, between the Capitoline and Palatine hills. Wedgwood made a medallion, *A Vestal,* 5in. x 4in., no.143 in the 1777 Catalogue*, and a bust, height 15in., from a cast supplied by Hoskins & Grant* in 1775.
See: Vestal Lamp

Vestal Lamp

Boat shaped lamp on a raised foot and shaped triangular or hexagonal plinth, the handle formed by a finely modelled figure of a seated woman pouring oil from a jug. A companion to the Reading Lamp*, produced in black basaltes* from c.1775 and in jasper* from c.1780, and reproduced intermittently during the 19th and early 20th centuries. In the latter half of the 19th century it appeared also in black basaltes with bronze and gilt ornaments, bronze and gold basaltes* and enamelled bone china*.

Victoria Ware

A range of ornamental pieces made in the Carrara* body and decorated with enamelled or coloured slip grounds, ornamented in the same manner as jasper*. These pieces were glazed and usually gilded, and the ornaments, generally overcrowded, were taken from moulds previously used for jasper and black basaltes. From Laurence Wedgwood's* memoranda of 22 October and 9 December 1875 it is clear that there was some confusion between this ware and pâte-sur-pâte*, which was made by an entirely different technique. The Victoria ware vases, plaques and medallions are not pâte-sur-pâte but the misunderstanding evident in Laurence's notes has persisted.
See: Colour Plate 119

VIEN, Joseph Marie. Design for a vase, from *Suite de vases composée dans le goût de l'antique* (1760), engraved by his wife, Thérèse Reboul Vien. *Photograph: Wedgwood*

Vien, Joseph Marie (1716-1809)

French painter, who studied in Italy, 1743-50; elected a member of the Academy, 1754; Director of the French Academy at Rome. David was his pupil. He created a number of designs for vases, thirteen of which were etched by his wife under the title, *Suite de Vases Composée dans le Goût de l'Antique,* published in Paris in 1760. Wedgwood's Vase No.1 shape was adapted from Plate 13.

VIEN, Joseph Marie. Pair of Wedgwood & Bentley variegated ('porphyry') vases, no.1 shape, the general form and the handles adapted from Plate 13 of Vien's *Suite de vases.* *Christie's, London*

Vigornian Ware

The name given to a variant of Rockingham ware*, decorated with the purple-brown Rockingham glaze (see: Glazes) and acid-etched patterns. Vigornian ware 'which will no doubt have its admirers', was first shown at the Paris Exposition Universelle in 1878. The technique, employed also by Doulton and Minton*, involved the use of the Rockingham glaze, and also a much rarer deep blue glaze, as grounds through which patterns of flowers, plants, butterflies and birds were acid-etched to the white beneath the stained glaze. The patterns were etched by John Northwood's* glass-engraving firm, Perkes & Co. of Stoke-on-Trent. Vigornian ware is sometimes marked with the name 'ROCKINGHAM' impressed in addition to the Wedgwood trade mark, a practice that has led to confusion where the Wedgwood mark is indistinct.

Viol da Gamba

See: Musical Instruments

Violet Basket

Small circular or oval baskets, generally about 4in. wide and 2½in. high, with pierced and slightly domed loose covers intended for dried pot-pourri or the arrangement of small flowers. They were made in bone china* of the first period, handpainted and gilded, and also in white and stained stoneware* (porcelain) with coloured applied relief ornament, c.1820.

Virgil, P. Vergilius Maro (70-19 BC)

The greatest of the Roman epic poets, and author of the *Aeneid,* the *Georgics, Eclogues, Bucolics* and possibly of other, lesser works. Virgil died at Brundisium and was buried near the road from Puteoli to Naples, where a monument supposed to be his tomb still exists. A painting of it by Joseph Wright* of Derby is dated 1779. On 2 August 1779, dissatisfied with the attempts of others to remodel the cast of a head supplied by Hoskins & Grant*, Josiah Wedgwood sat down at the modelling bench. He wrote to Bentley*: 'I this morning resumed my old employment, took the modelling tools into my hands, and made one side of the head pretty near like the gem…I have opened his mouth, & shall send him to you saying some of his own divine poems'.

VIRGIL. Black basaltes bust of Virgil on waisted and moulded socle. Height 15in. Unmarked. Wedgwood & Bentley, c.1777.
Wedgwood Museum

VIGORNIAN WARE. Teapot, 159 shape, with sibyl knop, the design of birds, butterflies and flowers acid-etched through Rockingham glaze. Height 4½in. c.1878. *Wedgwood Museum*

Wedgwood subjects:

Apotheosis of Virgil, tablet 7½in. x 15½in., modelled by Flaxman*, c.1786. Companion piece to the *Apotheosis of Homer*, modelled by Flaxman in 1779. No.266 in 1787 Catalogue*. Both bas-relief compositions were used as ornament for vases

Virgil, bust, height 15in., from a cast supplied by Hoskins & Grant, remodelled by Josiah Wedgwood with the aid of an antique gem (intaglio*) portrait

Vitalba

Painter at the Chelsea Decorating Studio*, who executed landscapes for the Frog* service. He is listed also as 'Nitalba'.

Vitreous Bodies

A term which embraces black basaltes*, jasper*, the dry bodies* and stonewares* of all kinds, and also porcelain*, although it is rarely employed to include the last, which is regarded as a separate category. Ordinary earthenware is fired at a comparatively low temperature which results in point-to-point attachment of the particles. For this reason it remains porous. Vitreous bodies have almost no porosity because they are fired at a temperature (about 1200°-1400°C) high enough to convert all but the clay in their composition into an amorphous mass which, in effect, is a kind of glass. Chips and fractures have much the same appearance as those in ordinary thick glass. The principle is the same, whether the material be common stoneware or the finest porcelain, the differences in quality being largely due to differences in the materials used and the refinement of the processes. The basic composition is refractory* clay and fusible rock, with the addition of a flux*. Clay is so refractory that most reasonably pure clays will only fuse or melt at temperatures in the region of 1600°C. The rock employed will fuse into an amorphous mass (i.e. natural glass) at a much lower temperature, between 1100° and 1400°C, according to its nature. The flux is added to promote fusion, which it induces at a lower temperature than would otherwise be possible.

Clay is plastic, and when blended with the rock in powdered form, the flux and a certain quantity of water, it yields a substance capable of being shaped in any of the ways commonly used by the potter. When firing is taking place, the clay holds the object in shape during the vital period when the rock is at fusion point. Porcelain, jasper and black basaltes are all fired at higher temperatures than the commoner stonewares or stone china*, and one result of this is that thinly potted examples of jasper and certain other fine stonewares, fired at a temperature above 1250°C, are sometimes translucent. Porcelain of less than 5mm in thickness is invariably so. Stonewares, because the body is impervious, do not ordinarily need a glaze, although they are sometimes given one for aesthetic reasons. Jasper and black basaltes teaware intended for domestic use is glazed on the inside because the surface might otherwise be stained. Porcelain also is glazed for these reasons.

Vitrification

The last stage of a ceramic body in firing before it collapses. A vitrified body is generally considered to be non-porous, although an absolutely non-porous body would fracture too easily to be practical in use.

Vitruvian Scroll

Classical ornament, a favourite of the brothers Adam*, consisting of convoluted scrolls resembling stylised waves. It is known also as the Greek wave pattern. Wedgwood delivered '2 oblong tablets* Vitruvian Scroll to pattern, 10 guineas' to the architect, James Wyatt, in March 1786, and two Vitruvian scroll friezes to the order of the same customer in 1788. The tablet illustrated as a Vitruvian scroll by both Meteyard* (*Memorials of Wedgwood* Plate XXIII) and Frederick Rathbone *Old Wedgwood*, Plate VI), however, is not in any sense Vitruvian.

Voltaic Troughs

See: Davy, Sir Humphry; Batteries, Electric

Voltaire, Jean-François-Marie Arouet de (1694-1778)

Educated by Jesuits, Voltaire was banished in 1716 for a satire on the profligate Régent, the duc d'Orléans, and an even more scurrilous effort in 1717 earned him a spell in the Bastille. He arrived in England in 1726, where he became acquainted with many influential people, and later he was appointed Chamberlain to Frederick the Great* of Prussia. Voltaire settled in Switzerland in 1755 and published the first of his anti-Christian writings in 1762. He enjoyed considerable success as a dramatist and his philosophical writings were widely esteemed.

There are two Wedgwood portrait medallions* of Voltaire: the first, catalogued in 1773 and modelled as a companion to one of St Evremond; the second, modelled by Hackwood* in 1777 and signed with his initials on the truncation. A bust, height 10-11½in., was produced in time for the 1779 Catalogue* and a miniature bust, about 4-4½in., appeared in 1777. This was produced in both black basaltes* and jasper*. Voltaire was also the subject of one of Wedgwood & Bentley's rare models of contemporary figures. The source of this figure was a small marble dated 1773 by Jean Claude Rosset ('Du Pont'), a cast of which was received from Bentley* in July 1777. Early in November it was reproduced in black basaltes, priced at one and a half guineas. A companion figure of Rousseau* was made a year later, and both figures were reproduced in 1779 in the cane* body. Wedgwood wrote to Bentley on 26 September: 'We have made Voltaire & Rousseau in cane color ready for firing.

VOLTAIRE, Jean-François-Marie Arouet de. Wedgwood & Bentley solid white on yellow jasper experimental portrait medallion, modelled by Hackwood, 1778. Oval height 3¼in. *Wedgwood Museum*

VOLTAIRE, Jean-François-Marie Arouet de. Wedgwood & Bentley black basaltes figure of Voltaire after the marble by J-C. Rosset dated 1773. Height 11¾in. c.1778. *Sotheby's, London*

They will have the appearance of models, & to strengthen that idea in the very offset I would not shew more than one pair in the rooms at a time.' Five days later he sent one example of each figure, but he was disappointed that they were 'so much discolor'd in burning as to stand in need of a wash of paint.' Only one cane ware figure of Voltaire is known (now in the British Museum) and none of Rousseau appears to have survived. Black basaltes figures were, however, reproduced intermittently until the 1920s and are not especially rare.

See: Colour Plate 120

Volumnia

Wife of Coriolanus*. There seems to have been some confusion at Etruria* about the history of Coriolanus and his relationships, and this has been further confused by the erroneous re-titling of bas-reliefs by later authors. The figure of Volumnia appears in two Wedgwood subjects;

Coriolanus, With his Wife and Mother Persuading him to Return (in fact persuading him to turn away from Rome), tablet 6in. x 9¾in., from a model by Flaxman*, 1784, No.258 in 1787 Catalogue*

Volumnia, Wife of Coriolanus, tablet 6in. x 9⅛in., c.1790, after an engraving in d'Hancarville's* *Antiquities,* 1767 (Vol.II, Plate 26)

See: Penelope

Voluntaries

See: De Shoning

Volute

A spiral curve; a helix. An architectural term for the spiral scroll flanking an Ionic capital. A volute handle, to be found on some kraters*, terminates above the vessel in a helical scroll.

VOLUTE. Black basaltes vase of volute-krater shape with mask handles, the body encaustic-painted in red, buff, cream and white with the figure of a young warrior and a horse copied from a vase in the Hamilton collection. Height 14in. c.1781-95

Mr & Mrs Samuel Laver Collection

450

VOYEZ, John. Solid blue and white jasper portrait medallion reputed to be a self-portrait of Voyez. Replica from an old mould inscribed and dated 1768. Oval height 5in. c.1922.   *Wedgwood Museum*

Voyez, John or Jean (1735-1800)

Sculptor and modeller engaged by Wedgwood in 1768 to serve for three years. Voyez had spent several years with Robert Adam* and was reputed to be 'a perfect Master of the Antique stile in ornaments, Vases &c.' He arrived at Etruria* in July and on 28 January 1769 was sentenced to transportation for seven years for stealing '11 Models of Clay val[ue] 5£.15 Moulds of Clay val. 50s and 15 moulds of Plaister val. 50s Goods of Josiah Wedgwood.' It appears that he may have suffered a whipping and five months' imprisonment instead for he was released and employed by Humphrey Palmer* before the year was out. Although Voyez' work at Etruria had been far from satisfactory, Wedgwood was appalled at the prospect of his working for Palmer, his only serious rival (apart from Boulton*) in the vase trade. What his competitors needed, he told Bentley, was 'Some person to instruct them to compose good form, & to ornamt them with tolerable propriety. V[oyez] can do this much more effectually than all the potters in the Country put together'. He even proposed paying Voyez a retainer of thirty-six shillings a week to prevent his working for another pottery, for

'The selling a single V[ase]: say a Medallion, less per w[ee]k through such competition wod be a greater loss to us than paying him his wages for nothing!' Voyez's connection with Palmer appears, however, to have been short lived. He is thought to have been in partnership with John Hales soon afterwards, and in 1772 was in business on his own account in Cobridge.

In 1773 Wedgwood found seals* by Voyez being sold cheaply in Birmingham, and although he described them as 'sad trash', he was uncomfortably aware that they were being bought and mounted as jewellery by some of the mounters whom he supplied with black basaltes and terracotta* gems*. When he discovered that Voyez was impressing his seals with the 'W & B' mark used by Wedgwood and Bentley on their smallest gems, he contemplated legal action against him but was advised that this would be unlikely to succeed as a country jury would not understand the nature or consequences of the offence. Josiah admitted privately to Bentley that 'Mr Tassie* & Voyez, between them, have made terrible depredations upon our Seal Trade.'

By the summer of 1780, Voyez had, in Josiah's words, 'done our country the favour of turning his back upon it.' He left a quantity of models and moulds behind in pawn and they were offered to Wedgwood, who rejected them. It appears from the 'Fair Hebe' jugs in the Ralph Wood style signed 'I.VOYEZ 1788' that he returned to England, but he did not trouble Wedgwood again.

Apart from the 'Fair Hebe' jugs, Voyez is known especially for a signed vase in black basaltes manufactured by Palmer and moulded with a scene of the torture of Prometheus, a fine example of which is in the Birmingham Museum, Alabama (Beeson Collection*). The Wedgwood Museum* owns a signed plaster model of a candlestick, possibly the one described by Josiah as 'that Solomangundy'. The mould of a portrait* medallion inscribed 'Mr John Voyez's likeness, Sept 20th 1768' is in the Wedgwood archives and may be a self-portrait, though it precedes by about four years the earliest 'modern' Wedgwood portrait medallion recorded. Some examples of spurious 'W & B' seals and cameos which appear occasionally in the auction rooms are probably the work of Voyez.

Vulcan

Roman god of fire and furnaces, identified by the poets with Hephaestos. He was represented in art as vigorous but lame, bearded and carrying a hammer or some other instrument of the smith. He wears an oval cap and the chiton, leaving the right shoulder bare.

Wedgwood subjects:

Vulcan forging the Armour of Achilles (known also as 'Venus at the Forge of Vulcan'), rectangular plaque, 6½in. x 10⅛in. A cameo of *Vulcan forging the Armour of Achilles at the request of Venus* is listed in the 1787 Catalogue but no tablet or plaque of this subject is catalogued. It was probably made c.1790

Vulcan with Mars and Venus in the Net, medallion 5½in. x 6in., cast from a model in the Newdigate collection*, 1776. No.184 in 1777 Catalogue

VOYEZ, John. Plaster model of a candlestick signed by Voyez, c.1769. Possibly the model described by Josiah I as 'that Solomangundy'.
Wedgwood Museum

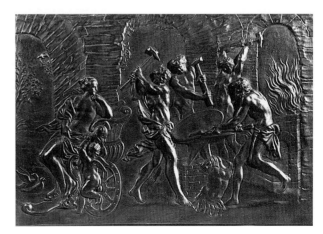

VULCAN. Black basaltes plaque, *Vulcan forging the Armour for Achilles at the Request of Venus.* Length 10½in. c.1790.
Christie's, London

451

VULLIAMY, Benjamin. Ormolu, onyx and Derby biscuit porcelain clock by Benjamin Vulliamy, the pedestal mounted with blue and white jasper medallions of Apollo. Height 17in. Signed and dated 1800.
Lady Lever Art Gallery, Port Sunlight

Vulliamy, Benjamin (1747-1812)
English clockmaker to George III*; the son of Justin Vulliamy, a Swiss who came to England in 1730, and Mary, daughter of Benjamin Gray, clockmaker to George II*. During the last quarter of the 18th century Benjamin Vulliamy produced mantel clocks in the Louis Seize style ornamented with figures from the Derby* factory which were modelled by John Rossi and the Swiss, Jean-Jacques Spängler. At least one Vulliamy clock is known with supporting figures in white jasper* instead of Derby biscuit* porcelain, the name 'WEDGWOOD' being impressed on the soles of the feet. It is

probable that more such clocks remain to be discovered.

The Vulliamy Clock Book, preserved in the British Horological Institute Library (Ilbert Bequest), shows that twenty-six clocks made between 1797 and 1806 were ornamented with Wedgwood medallions or cameos inset, and it is certain that Vulliamy clocks (probably the work of Justin, who died in 1797) were inset with Wedgwood ornaments at least ten years earlier. The Wedgwood Ornamental Ware Order Book for 7 November 1801 records cameos in black and white and lilac and white jasper 'for Mr Vulliamy'.

W

Wafer Mark
Also 'pad' mark. A circular wafer of black basaltes* with the words WEDGWOOD & BENTLEY or WEDGWOOD & BENTLEY ETRURIA impressed or in raised letters around the circumference. This mark appears on the inside corner of the black basaltes plinths of early vases and sometimes on the pedestals of busts and large figures.
See: Appendix II

Wagstaffe, William (fl.1855-80)
Painter at Etruria*, whose style is occasionally mistaken for that of Emile Lessore*, He painted a series of decorative earthenware plates with scenes after John Leech's* sketches for *Punch*, c.1868.

Wakral, H.
Doubtfully identified signature of an unrecorded modeller incised into the foot of a late 19th-century or early 20th-century basalt figure of a maiden seated on a high conical rockwork base with scrolling foliage (Christie's, London, December 1976). No other example of this artist's work has come to light.

Wale, Samuel (d.1786)
London painter, illustrator and engraver of 'landskips'. After an apprenticeship as a silver engraver, he became a pupil of Francis Hayman. He was a founder member of the Royal Academy, where he exhibited fourteen paintings between 1760 and 1778. His work occurs on early Wedgwood creamware printed by Sadler* & Green, and in July 1765 Wedgwood wrote to his brother John* in London asking him to procure a copper plate from Wale suitable for decorating creamware vases.

WAGSTAFFE, William. Shell-shaped dish painted in blue by Wagstaffe in a style similar to Emile Lessore's. Height 8¼in. 1868.
Mr & Mrs David Zeitlin Collection

WAKRAL, H. Black basaltes figure of a female nude seated upon a rock, bronzed in verdigris green. Signature illegible but identified as possibly 'H.Wakral'. Height 11in. c.1880.   *Christie's, London*

Wall, Peter, ARCA, Des.RCA, MSIA (b.1926)
Designer at Barlaston* from 1951; studied at Woolwich Polytechnic, Wimbledon School of Art, Burslem School of Art and the Royal College of Art under Professor Robert Baker*; Deputy Art Director, Barlaston, 1954-66; Design Manager, 1966-8. Peter Wall designed tableware patterns for bone china* and Queen's ware*, nurseryware and ornamental wares. He also designed Olympic shape (see: Tableware Shapes) in 1964. In 1970 he became head of the School of Ceramics at Birmingham (Warwickshire) College of Art (later Birmingham Polytechnic). He retired in 1988.
The following are among his principal designs:
Argosy, silkscreen* on Olympic shape
Big Top, nurseryware*, 1958
Beaconsfield, lithograph* on bone china, 1956
Greenwood, lithograph* centre and *Thames Green* slip border (two-colour clay technique) on bone china, 1955
Hathaway Rose, lithograph on bone china, 1959. One of the most commercially successful of all Wedgwood's bone china lithograph patterns
Ivy House, lithograph on bone china, 1957
Louisiana, lithograph on bone china *Galaxie* shape
Marguerite, gold silkscreen* on bone china *Galaxie* shape. Used also for the decoration of smokers' sets, 1963 (see: Cigarette Lighter)
Penshurst, lithograph on Barlaston shape, 1956
Spring Morning, lithograph on bone china, 1959
Starflower, lithograph on bone china (teaware and coffeeware only), 1953
Woodbury, lithograph on Barlaston shape, 1955
See over for illustrations

Wall Brackets

Pairs of wall brackets were made in Majolica*, c.1875. A pair in the Buten Museum* was moulded and glazed in colours to simulate wooden brackets with braided curtains parted by figures of garlanded *putti*. Examples are rare.

Wall Pocket

A flower vase, often in the form of a cornucopia* (see: Flora), a shell or a mask, flat on one side, made to be hung on a wall, and pierced at the top for suspension. Made by Wedgwood, wall pockets occur in creamware and decorated with coloured glazes in the early period. In the early 19th century a wall pocket was made in the form of the nautilus* shell, with variegated lustre* decoration, and this was reproduced in Queen's ware* with a Moonstone glaze (see: Glazes) in the 1950s. Elaborate wall pockets were made also in Majolica*.

Wallace, Nathaniel (fl.1769-74)

A painter at the Chelsea Decorating Studio* who worked on the Frog* service.

War Relief Fund

See: Liberty Ware

Warburton, Mrs Anne (1713-98)

Anne Daniel (probably related to Ralph Daniel of Cobridge, often credited with having introduced the use of plaster of Paris moulds from France, c.1745) married John Warburton, a potter of Cobridge, who died in 1761. 'The Widow Warburton' was herself a master potter, in partnership with her son, Thomas, as Anne Warburton & Son of Hot Lane, Burslem. She decorated wares manufactured elsewhere but her cream-coloured wares were also bought by other potters. Bills of sale exist showing that Josiah Wedgwood bought creamware from her during his early years at the Ivy House* and Brick House* Works. According to Simeon Shaw*, Wedgwood sent creamware to be enamelled by the Warburtons, but no documentary evidence has been found to substantiate this. It is likely, on the other hand, that early cream-coloured ware attributed to Wedgwood is actually the work of the Warburtons. Her son, Jacob, became a founding partner in the New Hall* factory, and her grandson Peter Warburton, a manufacturer

WARWICK VASE. Black basaltes copy of the Warwick vase. Height 14in. c.1820.
Mr & Mrs David Zeitlin Collection

WALL, Peter. *Hathaway Rose*, a delicate lithograph pattern, designed by Peter Wall for bone china in 1959. *Wedgwood Museum*

of creamware and also a partner in the New Hall company, took out a patent for transfer-printing* in gold (see: Gold-printing) in 1810. Another grandson, Francis, founded the French firm of La Charité-sur-Loire.

Wareham (Warham), William (fl.1860-74)

Engraver, of Newcastle-under-Lyme, who worked for Wedgwood between 1860 and 1874, engraving plates for tiles* and tableware patterns.

Warwick Vase

One of the most famous Roman antiquities in Britain. The colossal carved marble vase, 9ft. high and weighing seven tons, was discovered at Hadrian's Villa in 1771 by the Scottish artist and antiquary, Gavin Hamilton, who sold it to his kinsman, Sir William Hamilton*. Sir William had it restored and sold it to the Earl of Warwick and it remained at Warwick Castle until, along with other treasures from the castle, it was sold in 1985 to a foreign buyer. The National Art Collections Fund opposed the application for an export licence and the vase was acquired by Glasgow Museums and Art Galleries at a cost of £253,808. Piranesi*, who may have overseen the restoration of the vase in the 1770s, published engravings of it in 1778 and it was probably from these that Wedgwood made his copy in black basaltes*.

Watch Cases

Jasper cameos*, convex and about 1½in. in diameter, were made to be fitted into the cases of verge watches, being mounted by the bezel in the same manner as a glass. They are thinner than the normal cameo and ornamented with classical subjects in low relief. Because of their fragility few have survived.

Watch-holder Vase

Shape no.59 in the vase Shape Drawing Book* is a goblet-shaped vase with satyr handles, applied husk swags and a laurel wreath round the circular hole cut in the centre of the body. An angled shelf, fixed behind the hole, supported a pocket watch so that the face was visible through the aperture. The shape was copied closely from a design by Friedrich Kirschner. Josiah wrote to Bentley* on 16 December 1769 of '2 Vases for Watch Stands & three Egg vases, all finishing with figures at top, & shall be glad to have your opinion of them.'

WALL BRACKETS. Pair of Majolica wall brackets, glazed in colours to simulate wooden brackets with turquoise curtains parted by single figures of garlanded *putti*. Height 9½in. c.1875.
Formerly Buten Museum

WATCH HOLDER VASE. Wedgwood & Bentley black basaltes watch holder vase. Height 8¾in. c.1774.
Brooklyn Museum, Emily Winthrop Miles Collection

WATER LILY PATTERN. Three pieces of the *Brown Water Lily* pattern, c.1820.
Wedgwood Museum

Water Bottle

Porous water bottles, employing the method of cooling the contents by the natural process of evaporation, were made in the orange body* from about 1850 until 1940. The bottles were bulbous with tall necks, and flat saucers of the same composition were provided to catch the droplets of water running down the exterior of the bottles.

Water Lily Pattern

Unquestionably the most distinguished of Wedgwood's early 19th-century underglaze-blue printed* patterns, and one of the few to have any claim to originality. The pattern, almost certainly suggested (and possibly designed) by John Wedgwood*, was engraved originally by Semei Bourne* in 1806 and re-engraved in various versions by John Robinson* and William Hales* between 1807 and 1809. The *Water Lily* design is a composition adapted from four separate engravings in the *Botanist's Repository* (October 1803 and September 1804) and the *Botanical Magazine* (December 1804 and February 1806). It was engraved originally for printing in brown with enamelled decoration, and a dinner service for twenty-four in 'Brown printed Water Lily, shaded in red and cut up with gold, and gold outside edge' was bought from his brother-in-law (Josiah II*) by Dr Robert Waring Darwin* in 1808. The pattern was, however, expensive and difficult to make and Josiah II sent instructions to London in May 1811 that it should be removed from

WATER LILY PATTERN. Foot pan decorated with *Water Lily* pattern, printed in underglaze blue. Width 17¾in. c.1820.
Carolyn Stoddart-Scott

display, adding 'we will print some in Blue'. The resulting pattern was one of the finest of the period. It was made in large quantities between 1811 and 1845, supplied as an onglaze red print from 1809 and in underglaze red after about 1828, was revived as 'Old Water Lily' at the end of the century and was re-engraved in 1907 for 12in. plaques enamelled in a remarkably tasteless combination of blue, yellow, green and mauve. A red-enamelled and printed version appeared on White ware* in 1837. In 1978 a tall 'Darwin mug'*, printed in underglaze blue, was produced in a limited edition for the Wedgwood Collectors' Society*.
See: Colour Plate 121

Water Purifier
See: Filter

Watercress Dish
See: Strawberry Dish

Waterford Wedgwood

A new company, formed in 1986, after the takeover of the Wedgwood Group* of companies by Waterford, an Irish glass company originally founded in 1785 by a Stourbridge (Worcestershire) manufacturer. Although the Waterford firm's history of production was not continuous, the modern company's reputation was founded on the manufacture of fine quality cut glass in the tradition of the late 18th and early 19th century, using many of the old patterns.

In 1985-6 Wedgwood was the target of hostile bids and the appearance of Waterford in the guise of a 'white knight', coupled with the somewhat surprising offer of £253 million, was greeted with relief by most people concerned with Wedgwood's future. The reality has proved rather different from the expectation. By the spring of 1989 it was plain that without the purchase of Wedgwood, which provided regular and rising annual profits, a positive cash flow, and the bulk of Ir£100 million in sales of assets, Waterford would have faced disaster. In spite of Wedgwood's contributions, the amalgamated company contrived, in less than three years, to increase net debt from Ir£25 million to Ir£109 million. Sir Arthur Bryan, who had masterminded the takeover in 1986, publicly declared his support for another takeover that would produce a change of management, and many powerful shareholders agreed with him. At Waterford, continuing and almost insupportable losses and the admission of accounting errors (the magnitude of which could not be quantified, according to the Chairman, Paddy Hayes), the deterioration of labour relations leading to a fourteen-week strike in 1990, and the resignation of both Hayes and his successor Paddy Byrne, did nothing to build confidence in the Company. The injection of Ir£96.2 million

(£87.14 million), put together by Dr Tony O'Reilly and Morgan Stanley in return for a 29.9 per cent stake in 1990, has helped to revive the fortunes of the Company. By 1994, with O'Reilly as Chairman and a stronger team of senior executives in control, there were encouraging signs, notably in vigorous design of high quality, that a revival of Wedgwood's fortunes was well on the way.
See: Wedgwood in the Twentieth Century

Watt, James LL.D, FRS (1739-1819)

Engineer; partner with Matthew Boulton* in the firm of Boulton & Watt, 1775-1800. Watt began life as a scientific instrument maker and in 1764, while repairing a model of Newcomen's steam engine, he discovered the reason for its waste of power. He patented his own steam engine in 1769 and renewed the patent ten years later. He began to experiment to convert the reciprocating engine to rotary motion about 1789 and supplied a rotary engine to Wedgwood about two years later, subsequently making many improvements to this type of engine, which was of course, essential for driving factory machinery. In 1789 he invented copying ink, which enabled documents to be duplicated, and four years later he designed a screw propeller for ships. His son, also James, became a partner in Boulton & Watt in 1794. He specialised in marine engines.

The elder James Watt was a member of the Lunar Society* and became a loyal friend of Josiah Wedgwood's, supplying him with samples of clay and stone, discussing with him a proposal to unite the manufacturers of England into a single society, which became the General Chamber of Manufacturers*, giving him support and encouragement when members of the Chamber turned against Wedgwood after the successful negotiation of the French Commercial Treaty*, and designing a triturating mortar* to be added to Wedgwood's range of chemical wares*.

E.W. Wyon* modelled a bust of James Watt, height 15in., for Wedgwood which was reproduced in black basaltes in the 1850s. The omission of any portrait medallion* of either Watt or Boulton among the long list of 'Illustrious Moderns' or the shorter number of Wedgwood's friends for whom he made portraits is unexplained.
See also: Cornish Metal Company

Watteau Subjects

Scenes of 18th-century figures in a landscape in the manner of painting by Antoine Watteau (1684-1721). 'Watteau scenes' as they were called in the 18th century, appear on Sèvres* and Meissen* porcelain, and on the wares of other factories in imitation. These subjects were copied or adapted from engravings of the work of Watteau (or occasionally Lancret). Watteau scenes appear on Wedgwood Queen's ware* of about 1775, and again, in a slightly altered style, c.1800-10. Emile Lessore* reintroduced this type of painting at Etruria*, c.1865.

WAX PORTRAITS, WAX MODELS. Relief portrait of Paul I of Russia, modelled in greyish-white wax by John Flaxman junior, on painted glass, illustrating important aspects of Flaxman's technique: modelling direct on to a ground (some of the relief being too thin to mould from); a nearly full-face view; sculpted eyes and fine detail. Modelled relief 3⅜in. x 2¼in. Wedgwood reproduced this portrait in jasper in 1782. *Formerly Author's collection*

Wax Portraits, Wax Models

Wax is one of the earliest known media for portraiture, dating at least from 300 BC, and wax portraits were extremely popular from 1760 until well into the 19th century. Wedgwood bought wax models for cameos* and portrait medallions* and supplied black basaltes* tablets* and medallions* to the modellers to serve as grounds for their wax reliefs. Many of the subjects modelled for Wedgwood in Rome, notably by Pacetti*, were modelled in wax, and several examples have survived.

The method used by professional modellers of wax portraits has remained unchanged since early times except for the introduction in the 18th century of plaster of Paris for moulding. The original subject was modelled and carved from wax and an intaglio mould taken from it. Into the recesses of this mould the modeller pressed a thin sheet of wax, pushing it into all the crevices of the mould. The mould was then filled with molten wax which was left to harden. The cast was extracted from the mould and finished by

WATTEAU SUBJECTS. Queen's ware dessert service, painted by Emile Lessore with scenes in the style of Watteau. Signed. c.1870.
Christie's, London

457

WAX PORTRAITS, WAX MODELS. Pink wax model on slate, *Triform Goddess* modelled by Camillo Pacetti in 1788. Height (wax figure) 9in. This model was copied in jasper in 1788-9.

Wedgwood Museum

WEAVER-BRIDGEMAN, Montague. Bone china figure of *Long John Silver* decorated in enamel colours. Height 9in. c.1924.

Dr & Mrs Jerome Mones Collection

hand, a process that would include undercutting* features such as nostrils, ears and hair (a technique adopted by Wedgwood for his jasper*). The portrait was then ready for mounting on a suitable background, which might be painted glass, a sheet of wax, a tablet of plaster of Paris covered by a thin layer of dark wax, or a basaltes medallion. Portraits were made also in coloured waxes and were often painted in addition. Finally they were framed and glazed, a flat glass being used before 1700 and often a convex glass thereafter.

Such portraits were generally intended for reproduction in small quantities, copies being made for distribution to the sitter's family and friends. Larger quantities were made of subjects such as popular heroes, which might have a wider appeal, and these were usually finished, with rather less expert attention to detail, by the modeller's assistants. Original portraits were expensive: around 1820 the prices charged for a model from life were seven guineas for the portrait of a gentleman (two guineas for copies) and ten guineas for a lady (three guineas for copies), the difference being accounted for by the additional complication of ladies' hair styles and dresses and their more critical attitude to the modeller's finished work. Clergymen were charged at the same rate as the ladies.

The most celebrated modellers of wax portraits exhibited their work at the Royal Academy. Most portraits were profiles, of no more than bust length, but full-length portraits in the round are known and Samuel Percy, in particular, almost abandoned the profile in favour of three-quarter or full-face portraits modelled in high relief. Portraits of this kind required great skill and they are consequently much less common than profiles. Wedgwood's jasper portrait medallions include several full and three-quarter face portraits, examples being those of J.P. Elers* by Hackwood*, Paul I of Russia and Admiral De Ruyter by the younger Flaxman*, and the exceptionally fine portrait of Eyre Coote by E.G. Mountstephen* after the bust by Nollekens.

Some of the best modellers in wax were also accomplished sculptors, and many modellers – notably the Gossets*, Mountstephen and Flaxman – created their own wax compositions. Both Matthew and Isaac Gosset worked in low relief, using a distinctive wax which has the appearance of old ivory. Mountstephen favoured a pale pink wax. Flaxman, on the other hand, used a greyish-white composition which contained a high proportion of white lead. Flaxman's evident indifference to the appearance of his composition underlines the important distinction to be drawn

between the wax portraits delivered to Wedgwood by professional modellers in wax and those commissioned from sculptors. The former were intended for reproduction and sale *in wax,* and the models supplied were frequently from moulds. Wedgwood complained that the models obtained from Lochée* were 'full of pin holes', indicating that they were moulded copies of an original wax. Flaxman's waxes, on the contrary, were originals, intended for reproduction only in black basaltes or jasper and neither for public sale nor for duplication in wax. They were modelled, by the sculptor's technique, direct on to glass in his own especially hard wax composition, particularly suited to Wedgwood's purpose of taking an intaglio mould in plaster of Paris. Flaxman's technique of modelling directly on to glass, however, caused Wedgwood to complain that the relief was too thin for moulding.

The essential distinction between work by modellers who intended to reproduce and market their own models in wax (the Gossets, Lochée, Mounstephen, Joachim Smith*) and those whose original bas-reliefs in wax were modelled for reproduction in jasper (Flaxman, Hackwood, Pacetti) is that several more or less identical copies of portraits by the former are likely to exist, whereas the wax models of the latter are unique. All models are larger than their stoneware reproductions by about one-eighth. No wax portrait that is the same size or smaller than Wedgwood's version of the same subject is likely to be an original model. It could only be so it had been remodelled in an enlarged version for production. The vast majority of waxes purporting to be original models are spurious, but some original works have survived, notably a small collection of Flaxman's work discovered in damaged condition in London in 1972 and the fine tablets by Pacetti now in the Lady Lever Art Gallery, Port Sunlight.

Waxen Body, Waxen Jasper

'Waxen jasper' is a name given by collectors to jasper* of especially fine composition which exhibits a slight gloss, the result of fine grinding of the body, or to jasper which Wedgwood described as of a 'glossy composition' which he attributed to the mixture having been 'ground upon the Wind[mill] instead of the water mill' at Etruria*. Josiah I was always careful to differentiate between the 'waxen body', which was, as he made clear in his letter of 24 September 1776, not jasper but a planned development of the terracotta* or 'granite' body, and the glossy jasper composition which was an unintentional product.

Weaver-Bridgeman, Montague A. (fl.1924-50)

Canadian modeller, introduced to Wedgwood in 1924 by Tom Wedgwood*. Weaver-Bridgeman worked at Etruria* for about two years, modelling a number of figures, including those of *Jorrocks*, Long John Silver, Sitting Squaw, Harlequin* and *Columbine,* all of which were produced in bone china* with enamelled colouring. The figures were reproduced in 1941 but the production runs on both occasions appear to have been short and examples are not common.

Webber, Henry (1754-1826)

Sculptor; modeller for Wedgwood and head of the ornamental department at Etruria*, 1785-1806. The son of a Swiss sculptor and a pupil of John Bacon* the Elder, Henry Webber attended the Royal Academy Schools, where he won a Silver Medal in 1774 and the Gold medal two years later. He was recommended to Josiah Wedgwood by both Sir Joshua Reynolds* and Sir William Chambers* in 1782, arriving at Etruria in June. He signed a seven-year contract with Wedgwood on 17 January 1785. In 1787 he was sent to Rome 'for the purpose of making Models, Drawings and other improvements in the Arts of Modelling and Designing for the benefit of...Josiah Wedgwood'. He travelled home by way of Switzerland and Paris with John Wedgwood*, who also had been in Rome. Upon his return, Webber was not only engaged in translating his Italian drawings and models into jasper and basaltes but also played an important part in the modelling of figures for Wedgwood's jasper copies of the Portland vase*.

In 1795 Webber received the commission for David Garrick's monument in Westminster Abbey and it is probable that after the expiry of his contract in 1792, he worked for Wedgwood on a part-time basis. Little of his work for Wedgwood has been recorded, although many important figures, groups and bas-relief subjects have been attributed to him on the evidence of style. His involvement with the modelling of the figures on the Portland vase was noted by Josiah and there is documentary evidence of his having designed the Sydney Cove* medallion. This was adapted, probably by Webber himself, for a medallion celebrating the French Revolution* and for one of the 'German cameos'*. It is extremely likely that he was responsible for others in both the French Revolution and the German cameos series but no certain evidence has been found for them. The attribution to Webber of the portrait medallion of Sarah Wedgwood* is now shown to be flawed, and nothing has been found to connect him with *Britannia Triumphant*, the Prince of Wales vase* or the candlestick* figures of Diana* and Minerva*, all of which have been credited to him by various writers. None of these figures would, however, have been beyond his capabilities, and, apart from Flaxman (the more likely modeller of *Britannia* and the candlesticks), it is not easy to suggest who else might have modelled them. He is recorded as the modeller of 'Apollo and Daphne as a beaupot [*sic*]' but this has not been identified. Until further evidence comes to light, the extent of Webber's contribution to Wedgwood's jasper production during the last quarter of the 18th century must remain largely conjectural. Until his death in 1826, Webber remained on friendly terms with Josiah II* whom he appointed executor of his will.

Webber's elder brother, John, an accomplished artist, accompanied Captain Cook on his third voyage in 1776-9.

Wedg Wood, John

See: Wood, John Wedg

Wedging

The technique of mixing clays of contrasting colours to imitate natural stones, such as agate, and one of the principal methods of making variegated* wares. Wedgwood's method of mixing clays for agate* ware involved beating out 'bats' (flat sheets) of clay in contrasting colours and arranging them in layers which could be folded or rolled, and then cut into sections for moulding. Josiah I wrote of the difficulties of this technique in a letter to Bentley* of January 1776: 'the mixtures and colours too...are liable to so many accidents and alterations from the workmen's *unhandiness* and want of ideas...For instance, when the clays are perfectly mixt, to produce a *wildness* and *extravaganza* in the pebble, if the workman gives the batts a twist *edgeways,* instead of keeping them flat when he puts them into the mould, a line of stringiness is produced which shows the pott instead of being finely variegated.'

WEDGWOOD & CO. Creamware mug transfer-printed with 'The Virtuous Woman' engraved by R. Abbey. Height 6in. c.1796. Mark: R.WEDGWOOD & CO. *Byron & Elaine Born Collection*

Wedgwood & Co

There were two pottery manufacturers of this name. For the Burslem firm, see: Ralph Wedgwood. An earthenware factory was established about 1840 by Enoch Wedgwood (1813-79) and Jabez Charles Wedgwood. The style was E. Wedgwood & Co., and it became a limited company in 1900. After a dispute regarding the use of the Wedgwood trade mark in the USA, the firm of Enoch Wedgwood was bought by Wedgwood in 1978. It was shortly afterwards closed down. The threat to Wedgwood's trade was doubtful and the wisdom of legal action against Enoch Wedgwood questionable. The subsequent purchase and closure of the firm was not widely regarded as being in the interests of either company.

Wedgwood, Abner (d.1835)

Fifth son of Thomas Wedgwood*, Josiah I's partner in the production of useful* wares, and brother to Ralph Wedgwood* of the Hill Top and Ferrybridge factories and John Taylor Wedgwood*, the line engraver. Abner was put in charge of the underglaze-blue printing* department at Etruria* in 1805 and continued to direct it until his death thirty years later. He made trials of cobalt* which resulted in the production of colours of exceptional quality, the

WEDGWOOD & CO. Pale-blue jasper dip small portrait medallion of Lord Thurlow. Oval height 1⅝in. Mark: Wedgwood & Co. c.1796-1800. *Holburne of Menstrie Museum, Bath*

WEDGWOOD, CECIL. Partner in the firm, 1884-1916.
Photograph: Courtesy of Hensleigh Wedgwood

strength and depth of the blue being varied deliberately between patterns. One of his recipe books has survived and was reprinted in the *Journal* of the Northern Ceramic Society (Vol.I, 1972-3), and another of his notebooks is in the Wedgwood archives. There is no doubt that what most clearly distinguished Wedgwood's early blue-printed patterns from the work of lesser potters was the quality of the printing. This was Abner's achievement, and Wedgwood's reputation in the first half of the 19th century owed much to him.

Wedgwood's Biographers

It is remarkable that although more has been written about Wedgwood ware than about the products of any other pottery or porcelain manufactory in the world, Josiah Wedgwood I has been the subject of only five biographies of any significance, four of them published between 1865 and 1915.

Llewellyn Jewitt's *The Wedgwoods, being a Life of Josiah Wedgwood...* (London 1865), was, by a few months, the first to be published. Jewitt was a professional engraver and the author of a number of books on such diverse subjects as the *History of Plymouth,* and *Rifles and Volunteer Rifle Corps.* In 1878 he was to produce *The Ceramic Art of Great Britain* (revised and enlarged, 1883), the first serious study of the subject and one which is still consulted (especially in Geoffrey Godden's edited, revised and expanded version, published in 1972) for its contemporary accounts of 19th-century potteries. Jewitt's biography of Wedgwood was, however, crippled by his inability to consult the crucially important Mayer* collection of papers, access to which had been given exclusively to Eliza Meteyard*. Under such circumstances, it must be wondered at that Jewitt attempted the task at all. The resulting biography, which was never adequate, has been eclipsed by Meteyard's.

The second biography of Josiah Wedgwood, and for more than 100 years the most authoritative, was Eliza Meteyard's* two-volume study of the man and the production of his factories, *The Life of Josiah Wedgwood* (London 1865-6). This enormous labour, completed in spite of Godfrey Wedgwood's* assertion that there were 'not materials for a really satisfactory life' of his great-grandfather, laid the foundations for all later studies of Wedgwood. The work may be criticised for attempting too much: for the inclusion of a lengthy account of pottery in England before Wedgwood's time; and for the decision to combine a detailed study of Wedgwood products with a biographical account of the man responsible for them. It suffers most seriously, however, from the author's undisguised devotion, amounting to veneration, for her subject and her consequent reluctance to make use of any material that showed him as less than perfect by the exacting standards of Victorian morality. She was certainly guilty, also, of creating imaginative accounts of Wedgwood's personal life (especially in

descriptions of his early years) which she recorded as fact, and of drawing false conclusions. Nevertheless, Meteyard's research was thorough and her unrestricted access to the Mayer manuscript collection made it possible for her to marshal huge quantities of essential material not available to others. Her understanding of Wedgwood's early wares was certainly unrivalled in her time and her book remains a monument to her enthusiasm and industry.

Meteyard's biography was not admired by the Wedgwood family, who thought it inadequate, and their objections were expressed more clearly in 1871, when she published *A Group of Englishmen,* which, it was felt, suggested that the behaviour of Tom Wedgwood*, Josiah's youngest son, was due to insanity, and dealt harshly with friends of the family who had borrowed money from Josiah II*. Godfrey Wedgwood therefore approached Samuel Smiles* to write a new biography, which was published in 1894, when the author was eighty-two. With Meteyard's great work so recently published, Smiles's biography was unlikely to add much to the subject, but the opinion of Godfrey's wife, Hope, that it was 'wretched twaddle' and not worth six shillings (one which appears to have been generally shared by the family) is ungenerous. It is an uninspired work, admiring, uncritical and lacking in originality or insight, but it is readable and, but for Meteyard, might have been more highly regarded.

For many years the most original and dispassionate biography of Josiah I was that written by his great-granddaughter Frances Julia ('Snow') Wedgwood*. Julia Wedgwood was an experienced writer and *The Personal Life of Josiah Wedgwood,* published in 1915, was the first to put the subject into his historical context and to contemplate him with less than veneration. The biography does, however, owe much to the sensitive work of Charles Harold Herford, Professor of English Literature at Manchester University, who not only finished but substantially rewrote the book after Julia Wedgwood's death.

For nearly fifty years nothing more was attempted, until, in the late 1950s, the distinguished Cambridge 18th-century historian J.H. (now Sir John) Plumb was invited by the Wedgwood directors to write a new biography. Plumb was too busy to undertake the task, which he passed on to Dr Neil McKendrick. In order to facilitate his research, the Wedgwoods permitted very large quantities of original manuscript material from the archives to be transported to Cambridge, where many of them remained, effectively inaccessible to other scholars, for several years. McKendrick, meanwhile, published several articles examining Wedgwood's abilities as a sales-man and entrepreneur, his partnership with Bentley* and his factory management, which – allowing for some errors of interpretation usually resulting from an inadequate understanding of pottery production – gave promise of a forthcoming biography of exceptional depth and interest, the first by a professional historian. This 'major life' was announced by McKendrick as 'virtually complete' in 1978 and was scheduled for publication in 1980 with a shorter biography of Thomas Bentley by the same author (in time for the 250th anniversary of Josiah Wedgwood's birth and the bicentenary of Bentley's death and the ending of the Wedgwood & Bentley partnership). It was formally announced again under the title *Josiah Wedgwood and the Industrial Revolution* in 1982. It has not yet (1995) been published.

The repeated announcements of McKendrick's biography effectively deterred other historians from attempting the task, but in 1992 Robin Reilly's *Josiah Wedgwood,* the first truly objective and fully documented assessment of Josiah Wedgwood, received widespread critical approval.

Wedgwood, Cecil, DSO (1863-1916)

Only son of Godfrey Wedgwood*; educated at Clifton College; partner at Etruria* from 1884, at first with his uncle Laurence* and later with his cousin Francis Hamilton Wedgwood*. After the incorporation of the firm as Josiah Wedgwood & Sons Ltd in 1895, it was controlled by representatives of three branches of the fifth generation: Cecil, Frank (Francis Hamilton) and Kennard Wedgwood*. The newly-formed company suffered severe reverses. The Spanish-American War had a depressing effect on American sales, and the Boer War took both Cecil and Frank away from their business. Cecil was awarded the DSO in 1902. After their return strenuous attempts were made to reinvigorate the company and business improved. Kennard resigned in 1903 and was not replaced. By the end of 1913 the demand for revived neo-

WEDGWOOD, CECILY STELLA ('STAR'). Cane coloured body plate decorated with Star Wedgwood's *Turkey Oak* pattern and a circular box of the same body handpainted by her in brown and orange over a Champagne glaze. 1932. *Wedgwood Museum*

classical* design had so raised the company's performance and profits that the auditors produced, in March 1914, the most optimistic forecast of its future for seventy years. Five months later the First World War broke out and Cecil immediately rejoined the army. He was killed leading the regiment he had raised, the 8th North Staffordshire Regiment ('The Potters'), at La Boiselle in July 1916.

Wedgwood, Cecily Stella, 'Star' (1904-1995)

The daughter of Francis Hamilton ('Major Frank') Wedgwood* and sister to Clement Tom Wedgwood*, Star was a pupil of Alfred and Louise Powell*, quickly graduating from a place on the bench of trained paintresses at Etruria* to a position as a successful designer of tableware patterns. She created a number of patterns for Queen's ware* and coloured bodies*, all showing the influence of the Powells and a preference for simple border designs in keeping with the Wedgwood tradition. Her bone china* designs tended to be bolder, making use of ground colours and platinum. They included *Lady Jane Grey* and *Coronation,* the latter produced to celebrate the Coronation of George VI in 1937. In the same year she married

Frederick Maitland Wright MBE, a director of Twyford's, who in 1945 joined the Wedgwood board of directors as Company Secretary. He was joint Managing Director, with Norman Wilson*, from 1961 to 1963. Some of Star Wedgwood's work was marked with a painted five-pointed star and the initials CW.

Wedgwood, Dame Cicely Veronica OM, DBE, FBA (b.1910)

Celebrated historian; daughter of Sir Ralph Wedgwood Bt, and sister to Sir John Hamilton Wedgwood* Bt. Dame Veronica has been awarded numerous honorary degrees by both British and American universities and is the author of many distinguished works of history and biography, including *Strafford* (1935), *The Thirty Years' War* (1938), *William the Silent* (1944), *The King's Peace* (1955), *The King's War* (1958), *Truth and Opinion* (1960) and *The Political Career of Rubens* (1975). Her biography of her uncle, Josiah Clement, 1st Baron Wedgwood of Barlaston*, *The Last of the Radicals* was published in 1951. She was a Trustee of the National Gallery, 1962-76.

Wedgwood, Clement Francis (1840-89)

Second son of Francis (Frank) Wedgwood*; educated privately and at Mannheim and Paris; partner at Etruria* from 1863, at first with his father and later with his brothers, Godfrey* and Laurence*. During the period of his partnership, cut short by his premature death at the age of forty-nine, the manufacture of bone china* and tiles* was reintroduced, and Victoria ware*, Worcester-style* wares and commemorative ware* were added to the factory's range of production. Clement was much concerned with the development of jasper* during this period, and, with Lessore*, conducted experiments with ruby lustre* in 1865. Clement also took a close interest in the employment and education of young people and personally conducted classes for boys on the Works during their midday meal break.

Wedgwood, Clement Tom (1907-60)

Son of Francis Hamilton ('Major Frank') Wedgwood* and brother to Cecily Stella ('Star')*; joined the firm in 1930 becoming director in charge of plant and building, a position he retained until ill-health obliged him to retire to Rhodesia in 1950. During the period of the move from Etruria* and the building of the new factory at Barlaston*, Tom bore the heaviest burden of planning and reorganisation, working closely with Norman Wilson*. During the war years he accepted the additional responsibility for production and he was long remembered with affection for his charm, energy and inventiveness. Never one to stand on his dignity as a director, he was often to be found, his overalls caked with clay, wrestling with recalcitrant machinery on the factory. With John Goodwin* and Keith Murray* he designed the *Annular* shape in 1932. His son, Dr F. Alan Wedgwood* became a non-executive director of the company in 1966.

WEDGWOOD, Clement Francis. Partner in the firm, 1863-89.
Photograph: Wedgwood

WEDGWOOD, Clement Tom. Director in charge of factory plant and building until his premature retirement in 1950.
Photograph: Courtesy of Dr John Wedgwood CBE

461

WEDGWOOD COLLECTORS' SOCIETY. Modern Queen's ware tea canister transfer-printed in black with *The Tea Party,* adapted to portray Josiah I and his wife Sarah in the garden of Etruria Hall. Produced in a special edition for the Wedgwood Collectors' Society of America, 1977. *Photograph: Wedgwood*

Wedgwood Collectors' Society

A society, administered from the New York offices of Josiah Wedgwood & Sons Inc., whose members have exclusive rights to purchase special editions of Wedgwood pieces made in limited quantities for them. Some of the objects are reproductions of earlier work, or colour variations on well-established jasper* pieces, but many have been specially designed. The first exclusive edition was the Zodiac* plate, 9in. in diameter, in pale-blue and white jasper. Since that date many unusual designs have been created for jasper, basalt, Queen's ware* and bone china* in editions as small as 250, and some of these have already become rarities.
See: Darwin Mug

Wedgwood, Doris Audrey (1894-1969)

Second daughter of Cecil Wedgwood*. During his absence at the war, and after his death in action in 1916, his widow Lucie represented their branch of the family on the board of directors. Audrey joined the company at the same time, her appointment as Company Secretary being officially confirmed in 1918. In 1928 she married Geoffrey, youngest brother of her close friend, Daisy Makeig-Jones* and she retired from business in the same year. Her portrait medallion* was modelled in 1928 to celebrate her marriage and produced in blue and white jasper* for limited distribution to friends and relations.

WEDGWOOD, Doris Audrey. Solid pale-blue and white jasper portrait medallion of Doris Audrey Wedgwood, produced to celebrate her marriage to Geoffrey Makeig-Jones in 1928.
Mr & Mrs David Zeitlin Collection

Wedgwood, Frances Julia, 'Snow' (1833-1913)

Eldest child of Hensleigh Wedgwood (grandson of Josiah I). Handicapped in conversation by her deafness, Julia Wedgwood applied herself to supplementing her formal education, which had been meagre, and a wide and energetic correspondence. At the age of twenty-five she published two novels, *An Old Debt,* in two volumes, and *Framleigh Hall,* in three. Neither was especially distinguished or successful, but she was sufficiently encouraged to continue to write, publishing a study of John Wesley* in 1870 and 'a systematic study of ethical history in the civilisation of the world', published in 1888, after nearly twenty years of labour, as *The Moral Ideal.* She was a close friend of Robert Browning's and corresponded with many literary figures of her day, including Harriet Martineau and George Eliot. *The Personal Life of Josiah Wedgwood* was unfinished at the time of her death and was completed for her by Professor Charles Herford, who later claimed, probably with truth, that he had written or re-written about two-thirds of the text. Whoever may justly claim the greater credit for it, the biography was far superior to the efforts of either Jewitt* or Smiles* and offered a more realistic portrait of Josiah I than Meteyard's*.
See: Wedgwood's Biographers

Wedgwood, Francis (1800-80)

Third son of Josiah II*; educated at Rugby School and Cambridge, and joined his eldest brother Josiah III* as a partner in the family firm in 1827. After the withdrawal of Josiah II and Josiah III, Frank Wedgwood was in sole charge of the Etruria* factory, but in 1843 he entered into a partnership with John Boyle*, which lasted for two years, and from 1846 to 1859 he was in partnership with Robert Brown*. In the interim the factory, Etruria Hall* and the entire estate were put up for auction. The factory failed to reach its reserve and was withdrawn from sale. In the latter years Frank was joined by his eldest son Godfrey* and later by his younger sons Clement Francis* (1863) and Laurence* (1868).

Frank was a staunch Unitarian, a reluctant potter and somewhat ascetic in his way of life. He was by turns jovial and irascible. His grandson (Josiah Clement Wedgwood*) later recalled that he never saw him lose his temper, nor ever saw him smile. Frank was one of the first pottery employers to concern himself with reforming the working conditions of children and he established an enviable reputation for fair dealing with both customers and employees. He retired in 1876.

Frank Wedgwood presided over some important changes and developments at Etruria, including the introduction of Carrara*, inlaid ware* and Majolica*, and it was during this period that the employment of Emile Lessore* created a new style of decoration that gained prestige for the firm at international exhibitions. He was, nevertheless, reactionary by nature and did much to slow or prevent change. His will, dated 9 May 1874, in which he left the

WEDGWOOD, Francis. Partner in the firm, 1827-76. From a painting by an unidentified artist. *Wedgwood Museum*

WEDGWOOD, Francis Hamilton. 'Major Frank' Wedgwood, partner in the firm from 1889 and chairman and managing director, 1916-1930. *Photograph: Wedgwood*

WEDGWOOD, Godfrey. Partner in the firm, 1859-1891.
Photograph: Wedgwood

Stubbs* painting of the Wedgwood family to his son Godfrey, contains the remarkable bequest to his youngest daughter of 'my ass and the ivory screen which belonged to Lady Mackintosh'.

Wedgwood, Francis Alan (b.1937)
Scientist; son of Clement Tom Wedgwood*. A department manager at Harwell Laboratory, Alan was appointed a non-executive director of Wedgwood in 1966 and of Waterford-Wedgwood in 1991.

Wedgwood, Francis Hamilton (1867-1930)
Eldest son of Clement Francis Wedgwood*, educated at Clifton College, at Mannheim and at Trinity College, Cambridge; partner at Etruria* from 1889, following the early death of his father. After the incorporation of the firm as Josiah Wedgwood & Sons Ltd in 1895, and the retirement of Laurence Wedgwood*, three first cousins, Cecil*, Frank and Kennard*, represented the fifth generation of the family at Etruria. The adverse effects of the Spanish-American War, which depressed American sales, and the Boer War, in which Frank served as a Captain in the North Staffordshire Regiment, brought the company's fortunes to a low ebb. Kennard resigned and went to Rhodesia and the successful efforts of Frank and Cecil to restore the company to profit were brought to a halt by the outbreak of World War I in which Cecil was killed. Frank, who was gazetted major on the special list, was fortunately employed on recruiting duties, working from his headquarters at Lichfield, from where he was able to maintain almost daily contact with the factory. He succeeded Cecil as Chairman and Managing Director in 1916. He died suddenly in October 1930 at the age of sixty-three.

Major Frank' as he was known at Etruria and more widely in the Potteries, was greatly respected for his integrity in personal and business matters. His quiet and unassuming manner disguised real ability. His wise guidance of the company through the difficult years of revival after the war laid sound foundations for his successors. With the help of John Goodwin*, the Powells* and Daisy Makeig-Jones*, something like a transformation of Wedgwood's designs had been achieved, and the first of many technical improvements which were to put Wedgwood on the road to expansion – the installation of the first gas-fired tunnel oven – had been put in hand. Wedgwood's later prosperity owed much to his prudence and foresight.

Wedgwood, Godfrey (1833-1903)
Eldest son of Francis (Frank) Wedgwood*; partner at Etruria* from 1859 to 1891, first with his father, and later with his younger brothers Clement* and Laurence*. Godfrey concerned himself with the overall direction of the firm, with particular attention to design. With his brothers he was responsible for the reintroduction of bone china* in 1878 and the manufacture of tiles*, and also for the intro-

duction of Victoria ware*, pâte-sur-pâte*, Worcester-style* wares and commemorative ware*.

Godfrey Wedgwood was sensitive, reticent and earnest, conscientious rather than clever, and suffered from the deadening lack of energy which had become sadly characteristic of the eldest sons of the family. He was, however, largely responsible for the employment of both Emile Lessore* and Thomas Allen*, and for the expansion and improvement of the range of Majolica*. In 1898 he had suffered the amputation of his right leg, a loss which he cheerfully told the Etruria workmen, who had sent him an illuminated address, 'entitles me to the same nickname my great-grandfather was known by on the works, viz, Owd Woodenleg'. He stumped around the factory for more than two years while his son and nephew were serving in the Boer war.

In 1887 Godfrey arranged to buy the Mayer* collection of manuscript material when it was offered for sale at Sotheby, Wilkinson & Hodge. He paid the derisory sum of £20 for the entire hoard, which now forms the nucleus of the Wedgwood archives. Of all Godfrey's work for his firm, none has proved to be more valuable.

Wedgwood Group
Formed in 1966, the Wedgwood Group has been comprised of the following companies (shown with their dates of acquisition):
Josiah Wedgwood & Sons Ltd
William Adams*, 1966
Royal Tuscan, 1966 (Hotelware from 1976)
Susie Cooper*, 1966
Coalport, 1967
Johnson Brothers, 1968
King's Lynn Glass (Wedgwood Glass), 1969
Merseyside Jewellers, 1969
J. & G. Meakin, 1970
Midwinter, 1970
Crown Staffordshire, 1973
Mason's Ironstone, 1973
Precision Studios, 1973
Galway Crystal, 1974 (sold 1980)
Enoch Wedgwood, 1979 (closed 1980)
Franciscan, California, 1979 (sold 1986)

Wedgwood, Hensleigh Cecil (1908-91)
Great-grandson of Hensleigh, youngest brother of Josiah II*; joined Wedgwood at Etruria* in 1927, moving to America in 1931; served through the war with the Royal Canadian Navy, returning to become President of Josiah Wedgwood & Sons Inc. of America, in succession to Kennard Wedgwood*, in 1947; retired, 1960; co-author, with John Meredith Graham II of *Wedgwood – A Living Tradition*, a short illustrated history of Wedgwood wares to

WEDGWOOD IN THE NINETEENTH CENTURY. White ware meat dish printed in brown and enamelled in orange-red and deep blue with *Japan* pattern no.4. The Arabic inscription and the enamelled note on the reverse show that this was part of a service made for the King of Persia in 1810.   *Wedgwood Museum*

accompany an important exhibition held in the Brooklyn Museum in 1948, and, with his second wife Barbara, of *The Wedgwood Circle 1730-1897* (1980). Hensleigh was trained in all departments of factory production, before joining the sales department. He was responsible for reviving the manufacture of crimson jasper*, but it failed, as it had previously, owing to the 'bleeding'* of the colour. For thirteen years, between 1971 and 1984, he was a management consultant in London before retiring to live in Texas.

Wedgwood in the Nineteenth Century
This entry provides an outline of production during the 19th century with references to key entries elsewhere in the *Dictionary*.

After Josiah I's death in January 1795, Tom Byerley*, who held a quarter interest, continued in partnership with Josiah II*, the style of the firm being Wedgwood & Byerley. Josiah's eldest and youngest sons, John* and Tom*, had both withdrawn from the firm in 1793 and none of the three brothers showed much inclination to give up their lives as country gentlemen to return to the Potteries. The French Revolution and the Napoleonic wars had seriously damaged Continental trade, relations with the United States of America were deteriorating (prior to the War of 1812) and the general prospect was worse than at any time since the firm had been established. Josiah II, who had inherited the factory, thought the business not worth continuing. Most of the large European pottery and porcelain manufactories were in an equally precarious condition, and for some years Meissen* was on the verge of closing down.

It has been generally accepted that under Byerley's sole direction the business declined, that this was due at least as much to Byerley's

WEDGWOOD IN THE NINETEENTH CENTURY. Three plates decorated with *Blue Chinese Temples* pattern printed in underglaze blue. c.1828. This pattern is an early example of providing different designs for each size of plate.   *Author's collection*

incompetence as to adverse trade conditions and that the loss of profits contributed to John's financial straits. The most recent research, however, shows this to be far from the truth. The surviving accounts for the five years after Josiah's death show profits at a high level, and providing a better return on capital employed than during the best years of the 19th century. In 1802, moreover, orders exceeded production capacity. John's financial difficulties, like

WEDGWOOD IN THE NINETEENTH CENTURY. Black basaltes pillar candlestick and bough pot-pastille burner enamelled with flowers in the *famille-rose* style and a posy pot enamelled with flowers in the conventional European style. Candlestick height 7in. c.1815-20.   *Author's collection*

those of both Josiah II and Byerley, were due entirely to extravagance funded by irresponsible overdrawing of his share of profits.

The decline was not in sales and profits but in standards of pro-

WEDGWOOD IN THE NINETEENTH CENTURY. White ware 'Wreathed Shell' dessert ware decorated with variegated pink and purple (gold) lustre. 'Argonaut' shell centre height 8⅜in. c.1812.   *Christie's, London*

WEDGWOOD IN THE NINETEENTH CENTURY. Teaware in white stoneware ('porcelain') dipped in pale-lilac jasper and ornamented in blue. c.1820.   *Christie's, New York*

WEDGWOOD IN THE NINETEENTH CENTURY. Pair of white stoneware ('porcelain') candlesticks, height 6¾in., ornamented in blue with 'wreathed laurel' and a similar vase dipped in yellow jasper and ornamented in light blue. Candlesticks, c.1835; vase, c.1850.

Christie's, New York

WEDGWOOD IN THE NINETEENTH CENTURY. White stoneware and dark-blue jasper dip 'Portland' jug clumsily ornamented with prudishly draped figures. Height 6¼in. c.1846.

Wedgwood Museum

duction and discipline at the factory. Byerley had found himself unable satisfactorily to control both the factory and the London showrooms* and moved in 1796, at great expense, to York Street. This was scarcely surprising since it was a double task which even Josiah I had found overtaxed his strength. The decline in manufacturing standards was matched by a failure in design, especially in ornamental goods. The popularity of jasper* and black basaltes* was waning. The neo-classical* forms of ornament which had played a crucial part in the success of the Wedgwood & Bentley partnership were no longer so much admired. By March 1805 the Ornamental Works was running at a loss.

In October 1800, at John's request, a new partnership was drawn up, allocating one-quarter to him and a half to Josiah II, while Byerley retained his one-quarter share. John spent a few months of each year at Etruria and there is some evidence that this intermittent presence at the factory, by lessening Byerley's authority and control, contributed to the spread of indiscipline and falling standards. In 1802 Josiah II made plans to return to Staffordshire and by 1806 he and John had taken over active management of the factory. Byerley and his family were installed in London. Important developments in production had by then been put in hand. Proper discipline and higher production standards were restored. White Ware*, lustre decoration* and the first underglaze blue printed* patterns were introduced in 1805. In 1810 Tom Byerley died and was succeeded in London by his son, Josiah. Proper accounts of the partners' shares were drawn up, revealing a huge deficit attributable to John, and Josiah II seized the opportunity provided by the dissolution of their partnership with Byerley to persuade John to withdraw for the second time. For the next twelve years, until joined by his eldest son, Josiah II was in sole charge of the firm.

Bone china* was introduced in 1812 and Stone china* about 1821, but neither was a commercial success. In 1824, the firm

made a small profit, the first in eight years. The inability to make ornamental jasper* between 1826 and 1844 was a serious loss, which was not compensated by the production of white and stained stoneware (described as 'porcelain') with similar ornaments and a covering of smear glaze* (see: Glazes).

In 1823 Josiah II took his eldest son, Josiah III, into partnership, and four years later he extended the partnership to include his third son, Francis (Frank). In 1828 the York Street showrooms* were sold and a sale was held of stocks of tablewares and ornamental wares and also of irreplaceable models, moulds and trial pieces. The younger Byerley had been succeeded in 1814 by John Howorth*, who retired in 1829. Josiah II represented the borough of Stoke-on-Trent in parliament between 1832 and 1835, delegating the management of the factory to his sons. In 1841 he retired from the partnership, and in the following year, Josiah III also retired, leaving Frank in sole control. Between 1834 and 1841, the firm made satisfactory profits of £5,000-£6,000.

In 1842 Frank took John Boyle* into partnership and less than a year later the factory, Etruria Hall* and the entire estate were put

WEDGWOOD IN THE NINETEENTH CENTURY. Carrara bust of George Stephenson by E.W. Wyon. Height 15in. c.1858.

Sotheby's. London

WEDGWOOD IN THE NINETEENTH CENTURY. Smear-glazed white stoneware ornamented variously in brown and bright blue. Combined bough pot and pastille burner height 7in. c.1820-40.

Author's collection

WEDGWOOD IN THE NINETEENTH CENTURY. Solid blue and white jasper flower pot ornamented with mixed leaves and bulrushes. Height 6in. c.1860-5.

Wedgwood Museum

WEDGWOOD IN THE NINETEENTH CENTURY. A page from the *Art-Journal Catalogue* of the 1862 Exhibition, showing pieces decorated by Lessore, a figure after Clodion and replicas of 18th-century jasper pieces.

Photograph: Wedgwood

WEDGWOOD IN THE NINETEENTH CENTURY. Lilac jasper dip vase ornamented with bouquets and garlands modelled directly on to the surface, perhaps by Charles Toft. Height 7¾in. c.1876-86.

Christie's, London

up for sale. Although the Hall and much of the land was sold, the factory failed to reach its reserve and was withdrawn. Five months later Boyle died and Frank became responsible to the executors of Boyle's estate for the latter's share – £15,280. One of them, Robert Brown*, gave his personal security for the whole debt and in return accepted a partnership with a two-fifths share of the business. He retained this until his death in 1859. During this period, Carrara* was introduced and jasper was produced again (although not in the solid colour until 1860). Although Wedgwood's was not one of the displays chosen for viewing by Queen Victoria when she visited the Great Exhibition in 1851, its 'quota of beautiful works' received favourable comment in the *Art Journal.*

WEDGWOOD IN THE NINETEENTH CENTURY. Ivory vellum vase decorated in the Japanese *cloisonné* style. Height 10in. c.1885.

Wedgwood Museum

WEDGWOOD IN THE NINETEENTH CENTURY. Two gilded bone china vases painted by Thomas Allen, and a Majolica ewer, the design attributed to Hugues Protât, painted by Lessore. Ewer, c.1865; vases, c.1894.   *Christie's, London*

The profits of the factory, and Frank's personal finances, had recovered sufficiently to enable him to buy Brown's share, and, towards the end of 1859, he took his eldest son, Godfrey into partnership, allotting him a one-fifth share. While both Josiah II and Frank had been reluctant caretakers of the family business, the fourth generation of Wedgwoods at Etruria – Godfrey, Clement* and Laurence*, all partners by 1868 – was more dedicated and also more adventurous. In 1870, when Frank handed over the firm in equal shares to his sons, it was valued at £56,000, excluding land, buildings and fixtures still rented from the estate of Josiah II, which were bought by the three brothers for £17,000 in 1876. In 1864 the firm employed 445 people: 232 adult men, seventy-nine adult women, sixty-six youths and twenty young women between the ages of thirteen and eighteen, and forty-five boys and three girls under thirteen years old. A system of fines for indiscipline or breaches of factory regulations was balanced by generous incentive payments to workers who made practical suggestions for improvements or economies in production.

Godfrey Wedgwood was responsible for the overall direction of the firm and concerned himself especially with design; Clement worked on the improvement of manufacturing processes; and Laurence was particularly interested in the production of jasper and the other dry bodies*, and Carrara. In 1870, when they took over the direction of the firm, it recorded a small loss. Twelve years later this had been converted into a profit of nearly £14,000. This remarkable improvement was due particularly to four factors: the return to full production of jasper in all colours and including solid-colour jasper vases; the reintroduction of bone china* in 1878; the employment of Emile Lessore* (1860) and Thomas Allen* (1875) and their influence on design; and the more strenuous efforts, made in the 1870s, to penetrate the American market. The first Majolica* was marketed in 1860. The second Great Exhibition in London in 1862 started the fashion for *japonisme* which, in turn, resulted in Wedgwood's gilded black basaltes*, bronze and gold (see: Gilding), Auro Basalt* and Japanese-inspired shapes and patterns on Queen's ware, Majolica and (after 1878) bone china. The manufacture of tiles was reintroduced in 1879, and the first calendar tile* was produced for Jones, McDuffee & Stratton* in 1881. Wedgwood's jasper was again used for the decoration of furniture (see Furniture, Ornamental) and Halsey Ricardo* designed chimneypieces* inset with jasper tablets in a specially created shade of Dysart* green.

The Portland vase* printed mark for bone china was introduced in 1878, and has remained, in various increasingly sophisticated versions, the hallmark of Wedgwood's bone china ever since. In 1891 the word 'ENGLAND' was added to the Wedgwood mark to comply with the McKinley Tariff Act for exports to the United States. The mark MADE IN ENGLAND was substituted in 1898 but was not in general use until about ten years later (see: Appendix II).

The three Wedgwood brothers became shareholders of the North Staffordshire Railway Company (of which Godfrey was a director) and in July 1875 the firm was permitted to buy access to railway sidings at Etruria. From that date the canal barge was gradually superseded by the railway truck as the principal method of transport.

Under the terms of an agreement signed in 1885, each of the three brothers had been given the right to introduce one of his own sons into the firm to succeed his father in the partnership. Clement died in 1889 and two years later Godfrey decided to retire. A new partnership was drawn up between Laurence as senior partner and his two nephews, Cecil* (Godfrey's son) and Francis Hamilton (Frank)*. Four years later Laurence handed over his share to his son, Kennard*, and the firm was incorporated as a private company under the limited Liability Act of 1855 as Josiah Wedgwood & Sons Ltd.

See: Colour Plates 122 to 125

Wedgwood in the Twentieth Century

This entry provides an outline of the firm's development from 1900 to 1986, with reference to key entries elsewhere in the *Dictionary*.

The turn of the century found the company, incorporated in 1895, once more in difficulties. The Spanish-American War had depressed trade in America, and the Boer War had taken Cecil* (who won the DSO in 1902) and Frank* from Etruria*, leaving Kennard* in sole charge of the factory. In 1903 Kennard resigned and in 1906 he went to America, where he opened a branch sales office (incorporated as a subsidiary company in 1919). The parent company made record losses in 1901 and 1902 and Cecil considered the closure of the factory, but he and Frank were persuaded to carry on, and some encouragement was found in the order for a large formal china service for the White House*, Washington. Ornamental ware sales gradually revived but the improvement in tableware business was fluctuating and slow. Useful publicity was obtained by the exhibition, in Conduit Street in 1909, of the Frog* service, on loan from the Tsar Nicholas II. The profit for 1910 – more than £2,200 – was a startling change for the better, and this trend was confirmed by an increased profit for 1911. In April of that year new London showrooms* were opened in Hatton Garden. Increased manufacturing costs and a coal strike reduced profits in 1912, but next year, when King George V and Queen Mary visited the factory, profits rose to nearly £4,500. The principal obstacle to the company's assured prosperity was the increase in wages in comparison with prices: in 1913 wages were 54% of sales.

The improvement in Wedgwood's fortunes at this period was due partly to good management and partly to changes in taste and fashion. There was a revulsion against over-decoration and ostentation and a return to a desire for elegance, which was translated into a demand for furniture of modified Sheraton and Adam* styles. This revival of demand for classical and neo-classical* forms and decoration was one which Wedgwood was uniquely qualified to satisfy. The report of the auditors in March 1914 presented the

WEDGWOOD IN THE TWENTIETH CENTURY. Bone china dinner plate and tureen from a service decorated in deep blue and gold in a revived neo-classical style, printed in gold with a coat of arms. Tureen length 11½in. c.1900. *Wedgwood Museum*

most optimistic picture of the company for seventy years. Five months later saw the outbreak of World War I and in September both Cecil and Frank left on active service. The factory was closed for two days a week and all managers and salaried staff accepted cuts in pay in order to keep the Works going for as long as possible.

In spite of conscription, which took all able-bodied men from the industry, and the loss of all European business, the factory was kept working. Orders continued to arrive from America and the home market was surprisingly solid. The business was no longer

WEDGWOOD
BLACK BASALT.

WEDGWOOD IN THE TWENTIETH CENTURY. Advertising leaflet showing some of the basalt pieces in production, c.1913, including figures by Ernest Light and a 'Dancing Hours' bowl. *Photograph: Wedgwood*

WEDGWOOD IN THE TWENTIETH CENTURY. Queen's ware ewer and basin from a *Sussex* toilet set, handpainted in shades of green, blue and purple, probably after a design by Alfred or Louise Powell. Ewer height 10½in. 1921. *Author's collection*

WEDGWOOD IN THE TWENTIETH CENTURY. Two Queen's ware vases with designs handpainted by (left) John Goodwin and (right) Millicent Taplin. Height 8¼in. and 8in. c.1930.
Dr & Mrs Jerome Mones Collection

profitable, but dividends, passed throughout the war, were resumed in 1918, showing that wartime losses had not been large.

A more damaging loss was the death of Cecil, killed in action in 1916. Frank was fortunately employed on recruiting duties, working from headquarters in Lichfield, which allowed him to make frequent visits to the factory. He succeeded Cecil as Chairman and Managing Director and was temporarily joined on the board of directors by Cecil's widow, Lucie. Cecil's daughter (Doris) Audrey* assumed the duties of company secretary, an appointment confirmed immediately after the war.

In the design department, Thomas Allen* had been succeeded in 1904 by John Goodwin*. He was not an artist of the quality of Allen or Emile Lessore*, but he was an excellent ceramic designer, especially of tableware shapes, many of which were commissioned by Kennard in New York or by important French retailers. Two French designers, Paul Follot* and Marcel Goupy* also designed tablewares, though production of them was interrupted by the war. At about this time, Wedgwood made a series of reproductions of 18th-century patterns on Queen's ware to the order of James Powell &

Sons*, and it was during a visit of A.M. Powell to Etruria in 1910 that the idea of trying to produce powder blue (see: Powder Colours) was first discussed with James Hodgkiss*. Experiments led to the production of a valuable range of bone china* ornamental pieces decorated by Hodgkiss, Arthur Dale Holland* and others, using the new powder blue ground. It was during the early years of the century, also, that Alfred and Louise Powell* began to design patterns for Wedgwood and, from 1907, regular exhibitions of their work were held in London. Their training of the paintresses at Etruria (some of whom, like Millicent Taplin* and Star Wedgwood*, became designers in their own right) was another notable contribution to Wedgwood's success during this period and after the war.

An entirely different influence was exercised by Harry Barnard*, whose 'appliqué' slip* and stencilled and modelled clay designs were used to decorate bone china, Queen's ware and jasper*. His large number of reproductions of the Portland vase*, made between 1923 and 1930, included vases of better quality than any others produced in the 20th century, and the portrait medallions* which he made with Bert Bentley* have often been mistaken for 18th-century specimens.

Probably the most important development of this period was the introduction of Wedgwood's first commercial lustre decoration*. Ten Ordinary lustre* patterns, combining powder colour with lustre, were produced in 1914. The first *Fairyland Lustre* patterns, the work of Daisy Makeig-Jones*, followed a year later. These

WEDGWOOD IN THE TWENTIETH CENTURY. Two bone china Fairyland Lustre vases, designed by Daisy Makeig-Jones, decorated with *Imps on a Bridge and Tree House* and *Willow Fairyland*. Height 10¼in. and 8¼in. c.1925. *Sotheby's, London*

WEDGWOOD IN THE TWENTIETH CENTURY. Bone china part early morning teaset painted in bright green and platinum in the Art Deco manner. c.1933-5. *Author's collection*

WEDGWOOD IN THE TWENTIETH CENTURY. Queen's ware plate decorated with *Weeping Willow* pattern in bright green enamel and platinum over Moonstone glaze, designed by Keith Murray in 1934.
Wedgwood Museum

WEDGWOOD IN THE TWENTIETH CENTURY. Annular shape dinner service decorated with a leaf pattern printed in red over Moonstone glaze. 1936.
Wedgwood Museum

designs, complemented by Dragon, Fish, Fruit, Dragonfly and Butterfly lustre patterns, lifted Wedgwood, for the first time, into the first rank of ornamental bone china manufacturers and they are widely regarded as among the most original of Wedgwood's contributions to modern ceramic art. They enjoyed an immense vogue during the war and their popularity lasted through the 1920s.

Once more the Company was enjoying prosperity. The home market was strong, trade to Europe had recovered, orders from America reached record levels and record dividends were declared in 1928 and 1929. Once more the golden prospect was shattered by unfavourable circumstances beyond the control of the directors. The decline of the national economy was exacerbated by rising unemployment and labour disputes, culminating in a general strike in 1926. The damage was completed by the collapse of the Wall Street boom in 1929. At Etruria, the gloom of economic collapse was further darkened by the death of 'Major Frank' Wedgwood in 1930, coinciding nearly with bicentenary celebrations of Josiah I's birth. To mark the anniversary, an international competition was held for the design of a vase in contemporary style, and entries were received from both John Skeaping* and his wife Barbara Hepworth*. The prize was won by Emmanuel Tjerne*. Louise Powell also designed a vase to mark the occasion and this was produced in a limited edition* of fifty.

Frank Wedgwood was succeeded as Chairman by his cousin,

Kennard, but four members of the younger generation – all great-great-great-grandsons of the founder – had already joined the Company. Josiah V* (second son of Frank's brother Josiah Clement*) had been appointed company secretary in 1927 and he was followed by Hensleigh Cecil*, John Hamilton* (son of Frank's brother Ralph), and Frank's own son Clement Tom*. Josiah, the eldest of the cousins, was thirty-one years old, and the youngest, Hensleigh, was twenty-two. Josiah succeeded Frank as managing director, a position he held for thirty-one years; Tom assumed responsibility for factory plant and buildings; John entered the sales department and, in 1931, Hensleigh joined Kennard in New York.

One of the first decisions of the new management was to require the retirement of Harry Barnard, then on the eve of his seventieth birthday, who left sadly but with good grace, and Daisy Makeig-Jones, who stormed out in a fury of resentment. Josiah V conducted a detailed review of the pottery industry and of the management of Wedgwood, setting down his conclusions in a confidential memorandum to his fellow directors. A plan of rationalisation was put into operation, reducing both the number of

WEDGWOOD IN THE TWENTIETH CENTURY. Celadon and cream-colour slipware vase and turned bowl designed by Keith Murray and introduced c.1935. Vase height 10¼in. *Author's collection*

WEDGWOOD IN THE TWENTIETH CENTURY. Pair of Queen's ware preserve jars decorated with *Afternoon Tea* pattern designed by Eric Ravilious, c.1937. Height 5½in. *Wedgwood Museum*

WEDGWOOD IN THE TWENTIETH CENTURY. 'Honey Buff' coloured body breakfast set handpainted with sprigs of roses in underglaze red. c.1939. *Author's collection*

WEDGWOOD IN THE TWENTIETH CENTURY. Queen's ware mug designed by Eric Ravilious for the Coronation of Edward VIII in 1937 (cancelled because of his abdication) and subsequently adapted for the Coronations of George VI (1937) and Queen Elizabeth II (1953). Height 4in. 1937. *Wedgwood Museum*

patterns in production and also the different shapes available in each pattern. Subsidence of the Etruria factory site, already a cause of serious concern sixty years earlier, now threatened the continuing existence of the factory and made the modernisation of plant and machinery a doubtful investment, but such investment was nevertheless essential. The first straight tunnel oven for the firing of enamelled bone china had been installed at Etruria in 1927 and this was followed, under Norman Wilson's* direction, by the first gas-fired tunnel oven and the first oil-fired glost tunnel oven. Wilson also introduced a flow-line belt system, first employed for the mass-production of the Cadbury-Bournvita* beaker in 1933.

Josiah V was particularly critical of design standards in the Potteries, which he identified as one of the principal reasons for the depression of the industry. In 1930, design was still under the direction of John Goodwin, who had proved his value both as a designer of commercially successful tableware shapes and as a manager, but he was now sixty-three years old and a successor must be found. Meanwhile, he introduced to Wedgwood three artists who were strongly to influence the Company's style and reputation in the next decade: Sir Charles Holmes*, John Skeaping* and Keith Murray*. Holmes acted as consultant for only two years, but his connections with the world of art and design proved to be invaluable; Skeaping and Murray were to be rated among the most distinguished and original pottery designers of the period and both made admirable use of the matt glazes* newly developed by Norman Wilson.

In 1934 Goodwin retired and was succeeded as art director by Victor Skellern*, whose talents, both as designer and manager, were second to none in the industry. For more than thirty years he guided Wedgwood design with wisdom, clarity of vision and an unerring understanding of excellence. Among those artists he introduced to the Company were Rex and Laurence Whistler*, Clare Leighton*, Laura Knight*, Edward Bawden* and, most notably, Eric Ravilious*.

Josiah V's review of the industry had emphasised the need for rationalisation, modernisation and the improvement of design and

WEDGWOOD IN THE TWENTIETH CENTURY. Josiah Wedgwood V, architect of Wedgwood's revival in the 20th century, outside the factory at Barlaston. *Photograph: Wedgwood*

WEDGWOOD IN THE TWENTIETH CENTURY. Queen's ware group, 'Country Lovers' with light enamel decoration, designed by Arnold Machin R.A., c.1941. *Wedgwood Museum*

WEDGWOOD IN THE TWENTIETH CENTURY. *Mandarin* pattern, an early lithograph on Queen's shape, designed by Victor Skellern in 1949. *Photograph: Wedgwood*

he took immediate action on all three fronts at Etruria. The problem of subsidence, however, could not be solved by good management and could not be ignored. Parts of the factory were between ten and fifteen feet below the level of the canal and some forty to fifty feet below their original levels. Longterm planning for the factory was no longer possible, and in 1935 the decision was taken to buy the 380-acre Barlaston Hall* estate for £30,000 and there to build a new factory. Keith Murray and his partner Charles White were commissioned to design the factory, the responsibility for internal layout and equipping of the buildings being assigned to Tom Wedgwood and Norman Wilson. It was to be the most modern pottery manufactory in Europe, using electricity for all firing. The foundation stone of the Barlaston* factory was laid on 10 September 1938. Less than twelve months later, Britain was again at war with Germany. John and Hensleigh Wedgwood and Norman Wilson were among the first to enlist and took no further active part in the business until the war was over. Wedgwood's work-force was depleted by the voluntary enlistment of many of

the men and women, and later by the introduction of conscription.

The earthenware Works were due to be finished before the end of 1939 and work was permitted to continue until they were completed in April 1940 and production was transferred to Barlaston in the summer. Construction of the fine china factory was postponed until 1945. The sale of decorated ware to the home market was prohibited and similar prohibitions extended to 'non-essential' articles, such as ash trays and jam pots. Production was rationalised to maximise profit while making room for government contracts. Almost all ornamental ware, including all jasper, was withdrawn from production and tableware patterns were reduced to twenty-one in Queen's ware (including four versions of embossed* Queen's ware) and twelve in bone china. The work-force was reduced from 909 to 678. Government contract work, which in 1942 amounted to 87% of home sales, included heavily potted earthenware crockery for the armed forces. From 1942, limited-price 'Utility ware' was an important part of production for home consumption. There was a compensating boom in sales to the United States of America, and in 1942 the Company's sales were 50% higher than they had been in 1939. Throughout the war, the factory was managed by Josiah V and Tom, who had been invalided out of the army in 1940.

Wedgwood's reputation in America was enhanced by the war and, when Hensleigh succeeded Kennard as President of the New

WEDGWOOD IN THE TWENTIETH CENTURY. Embossed Queen's ware *Edme* fluted vases, produced in four sizes from 6in. to 12in. high, especially popular in North America. 1956.
Wedgwood Museum

WEDGWOOD IN THE TWENTIETH CENTURY. *Asia* pattern, one of the first of Wedgwood's silk-screen printed patterns, designed by Victor Skellern in 1956. *Wedgwood Museum*

WEDGWOOD IN THE TWENTIETH CENTURY. A group of 'Fancies' (giftware pieces) decorated in Robert Minkin's *Ice Rose* pattern, with gift boxes making use of the standardised typeface and colours designed for the company by Design Research Unit in 1963.

Photograph: Wedgwood

WEDGWOOD IN THE TWENTIETH CENTURY. 'Plateau', a bone china model by Glenys Barton, issued in a limited edition of ten in 1977. *Wedgwood Museum*

York company in 1946, Wedgwood's products, especially bone china, had the lead in exports of quality pottery and porcelain from England. In England, Josiah V succeeded Kennard as Chairman of the parent Company, retaining the position of Managing Director. After the end of the war in Europe, building was permitted to resume at Barlaston. The earthenware factory was extended and the new china section established there in 1949. On 13 June 1950, six 'Last Day's Vases' were thrown on the wheel at Etruria and the old factory was closed. Tom Wedgwood, who had borne the burdens of planning and production since 1940, retired as soon as the new factory was completed. Norman Wilson became production director and was joined on the board of directors by Frederick Maitland Wright, husband of Star Wedgwood*, as company secretary.

The 1950s was a period of great opportunity. The new factory was efficient and it was matched by the quality of production and the high standard of design. Wedgwood now recruited a sales force capable of winning business. In July 1952 the home market was opened to decorated goods. The Barlaston factory was planned for a work-force of 800. Within ten years of its completion the floor space had been almost doubled and the work-force totalled 2,000. The London showrooms* were reopened at 34 Wigmore Street in 1948, and in 1953 the first three Wedgwood Rooms*, the Company's own shops in retail stores, were opened in London and Birmingham. The home market was stronger than it had ever been. The Canadian company, formed in 1949 and under the direction of Charles Cooper, made good progress, and in 1955 an Australian

company had been formed successfully under the direction of Ian Taylor. Only in the United States of America was it evident that greater impetus was required. In 1961 Hensleigh retired and was succeeded as president by Arthur Bryan*, joined as vice-president of the New York company by Frederick de Costobadie, who had previously served with Bryan in London and for three years in Canada. Sales in that market improved dramatically.

These developments were all signs of a change in Wedgwood's structure: both at home and overseas the Company was growing, subsidiary companies gradually coming under the control of young, forceful managers who were not members of the Wedgwood family. In 1961 Josiah V relinquished the post of managing director and was succeeded jointly by Maitland Wright and Norman Wilson. Josiah remained Chairman, with Sir John (who had inherited his father's baronetcy in 1956) as his deputy. John's son Martin joined the company in 1962, the first member of the seventh generation to do so. Wedgwood's success during this period owed much to vigorous and intelligent management, high quality of design and production and increased demand, and it was achieved against strong competition, not only from British manufacturers but also from wares imported from Europe, Scandinavia and the Far East. Bone china sold particularly well in America, and there was a strong revival in demand for jasper. Expansion was carefully controlled, partly as a deliberate policy and partly by the limitations imposed by the original design of the factory.

A department of public relations and advertising* was set up in 1953, under the direction of Alan Eden-Green, a past president of the Institute of Public Relations, and ten years later the Design Research Unit* was commissioned to modernise the company's 'image' by standardising the use of typefaces and colours, from invoice headings to delivery trucks.

Skellern's contribution to the company's success was of the utmost importance. His judgement was trusted and his advice respected, and it was he who was most responsible for persuading

WEDGWOOD IN THE TWENTIETH CENTURY. Ornamenting a jasper plate commemorating the first landing on the moon in 1963.

Photograph: Wedgwood

WEDGWOOD IN THE TWENTIETH CENTURY. Partly glazed basalt teapot in the '225' shape, introduced in 1981 to celebrated the company's 225th anniversary. *Wedgwood Museum*

the directors to use lithograph* decoration for both earthenware and bone china tableware. An early experiment was made with the Barlaston mug, designed by Eric Ravilious in 1940 and the first bone china tableware pattern, *Charnwood* was introduced in 1944. Many of the most successful designs of the 1950s and 1960s were lithograph patterns created by Skellern or by his two most important staff designers, Peter Wall* and Robert Minkin*. Among others whose work was of special significance in this period were the sculptor and modeller Arnold Machin*, and Richard Guyatt*, whose designs for commemorative mugs were of exceptional distinction in a field generally dominated by tawdry rubbish. Wedgwood's Design '63* exhibition in London was evidence of a lively commitment to innovation as well as a healthy respect for tradition.

In January 1963 Maitland Wright and Wilson retired and Arthur Bryan returned from America to succeed them as Managing Director. He was the first chief executive of Wedgwood to be appointed from outside the family. Further important changes took place during the following two years, including the appointment of Peter Williams (formerly company secretary) as financial director and Frank Morrall as production director, and the resignation of Alan Eden-Green. In 1965 Sir John Wedgwood left the company after thirty-five years in which he had been principally in charge of sales and later of public relations. His son Martin resigned shortly afterwards, leaving Josiah V as the sole representative of the family still on the board of directors. In 1966 F. Alan Wedgwood* was appointed a non-executive director. In 1967 Wedgwood became a public company, and shortly afterwards, with the introduction of the company's shares to the London Stock Exchange, Josiah V retired. He was elected first honorary life president. He died a year later. Arthur Bryan became Chairman and Managing Director.

Less than twelve months before he took up his duties as Chairman, Arthur Bryan orchestrated the acquisition of three pottery and porcelain companies – William Adams*, Royal Tuscan and Susie Cooper* – laying the foundations of the Wedgwood Group*. This was merely an indication of a radical change in the company's policy. Six more companies were added during the next four years, including Johnson Bros, one of the largest earthenware manufacturers in Britain, a small glass factory and a firm specialising in jewellery mountings. Bryan and Peter Williams (promoted to joint Managing Director) set out on a programme of expansion by acquisition to create the largest pottery and porcelain tableware manufacturing group in the western world. The new policy was an almost unqualified success. By 1986 the number of companies in the Group, had risen to eleven and a fourth overseas company, Wedgwood Japan Ltd, had been established in Tokyo; a hotel division was gaining important business; and in less than twenty years sales had been increased from £3.25 million to £152 million (profits in the same period rose from £516,000 to £19.5 million). Such figures are undeniably impressive, even when a high proportion of the increases is attributable to acquisitions and accelerating inflation. Bryan was knighted in 1976 for services to export.

There were also mistakes and failures: Galway Crystal was sold after only six years; the Franciscan Pottery in Glendale, California, bought for $13 million to provide a manufacturing base in the United States, was closed after only five years; Wedgwood & Co* (Enoch Wedgwood), bought for reasons which many suspected as insufficient and lacking in judgement, was almost immediately obliterated. Rising interest rates penalised manufacturers whose expansion was financed by heavy borrowings, and Wedgwood was now vulnerable to such increases in costs.

More serious was the over-expansion of factory production. This was especially damaging in departments (such as ornamenting) where extended and costly training produced skilled craftsmen who were put on short time or dismissed in times of adverse trading conditions. Such conditions in 1981-2 halted an ambitious £9.5 million programme for further expansion and resulted in nearly twenty per cent of the work-force being laid off.

Design policy during this period was an awkward mix of attempted innovation (some of it – the experimental employment of such individual potters as Elwyn James* and the creation of '225' shape, for example – wholly admirable), timid and uninspired repetition (such as the reintroduction of past best-sellers and the production of jasper and Florentine* pattern in a seemingly endless succession of so-called 'fashion colours'), and expressions of debased taste (e.g. Peter Rabbit jasper and some truly dreadful figures). Commissioned designers included Guyatt, Eduardo

Paolozzi*, Glenys Barton*, Wendy Ramshaw* and David Gentleman*, all artists and designers of distinction in their different fields, whose work for Wedgwood was usually satisfying, sometimes adventurous and seldom commercially successful. The patronage of such artists was part of an honourable tradition which was properly maintained. The general impression is, however, of a company that has mislaid its character. The full extent of the loss of Victor Skellern was not felt until the final retirement of Josiah V. The degradation of jasper to common giftware during this last period of Wedgwood's independence was the sad consequence of over-distribution to a market that became saturated. The price for this fundamental error of marketing is still being paid.

In 1985-6, at the end of a period when every other firm in the Fine China Group – Minton*, Doulton, Spode*, Worcester* and Derby* – had been absorbed into a larger group whose principal business was not the manufacture of pottery and porcelain, Wedgwood became the target of take-over bids. The first of these, from London International Group (specialising in the manufacture of rubber goods), valued Wedgwood at £150 million and was rejected by Sir Arthur as 'unwelcome, hostile and unattractive in every sense'. London International Group already owned both Spode and Worcester, and the bid was therefore referred to the Monopolies Commission. Some twenty-five counter-proposals were studied before an offer of £253 million was agreed from Waterford Glass. In October the two companies were consolidated as Waterford Wedgwood. Sir Arthur Bryan was appointed first president with Waterford's chief executive, Patrick Hayes, as chairman. A Wedgwood family presence was preserved by the election of F. Alan Wedgwood* as a non-executive director. For the next seven years the consequences of this take-over were seen to be unfavourable to Wedgwood, while the parent company was lamed by the dead weight of Waterford's losses and the high interest rates payable on massive loans. It was not until the arrival of a second 'white knight' in the person of Dr Tony O'Reilly, who took over as Chairman in 1994, that faith in the company was restored and welcome signs appeared of a revival of vigour and prosperity.
See: Colour Plates 126 to 129
See also: Waterford Wedgwood; Wedgwood Museum

Wedgwood, John (1721-67)
Josiah Wedgwood's elder brother, who, from 1751, had been in business in the partnership of Wedgwood & Bliss, general warehousemen, at 3 Cateaton Street (now Gresham Street), London, not far from the Guildhall and the present Bank of England. Apparently he retired from business at the end of 1764 but remained in London until 1766, executing commissions for Josiah: paying bills, buying gold leaf for gilding*, obtaining books of designs and recipes, supervising shipments through the port of London and arranging for the engraving of copper plates for use by Sadler* in Liverpool. He was, in effect, Wedgwood's London agent and first London Manager. In June 1767 he was tragically and mysteriously killed, drowned in the Thames after spending the evening at Ranelagh Gardens and later dining at an inn near Westminster Bridge. While it was presumed that he had died accidentally, the possibility that he had been murdered was evidently considered.

Wedgwood, John (1766-1844)
Josiah's eldest son; studied at the Warrington Academy and at Edinburgh University; partner at Etruria*, 1790-3 and 1800-12; married, 1794, Louisa Jane ('Jenny') Allen, younger sister of his brother Josiah's wife, Bessie.

John had worked intermittently in the factory and at the London showrooms* as early as 1781 and by 1786 was considered capable of taking charge of the Works in his father's absence. Towards the end of that year he went to Paris, accompanied by Tom Byerley*, and in the following year he set off, with Henry Webber*, on an extended visit to Germany, Switzerland and Italy. He returned home in 1789, having plainly decided that he had no wish to make the pottery business his life's work. In spite of this, Josiah made him a partner in 1790, reminding him that he must take his share 'in the business as well as the profits.' In April 1793 John resigned his partnership and obtained, through Josiah's influence and generosity, a partnership in the newly-founded banking house of Alexander Davison & Co. He continued to be paid a share of the profits of the Wedgwood firm, and his younger brother, Josiah II* (by then also a partner) generously refused John's offer to forego part of his share. After his father's death in 1795, John sold his house in London and moved to Wiltshire, acquiring a large house and estate where he pursued his interest in botany and horticulture, building extensive greenhouses and cultivating exotic plants and tropical fruit. He was responsible (by proposing it to William Forsyth, the King's gardener at St James's and Kensington) for founding the Society for the Improvement of Horticulture, later the Royal Horticultural Society, taking the chair at its first meeting in March 1804 and acting as its first treasurer.

Davison's bank was soon in financial difficulties, which cost John much of his inherited fortune and he consistently overspent his share of the Wedgwood profits. A new partnership agreement, signed in October 1800, allocated a one-quarter share to John, who, from 1804, took a more active part in supervising the factory. During this period he did much to reform factory production, which had become dangerously slack, and he was primarily responsible for the introduction of underglaze blue printing* at Etruria. It is considered possible that he designed the *Water Lily* * pattern. Byerley described him as 'extremely active and intelligent'. In December 1811, after some correspondence with Josiah II which revealed the full extent of John's profligacy and indebtedness, he once more resigned his partnership. Neither he nor any of his descendants was ever again actively concerned in the business. John and his children became dependent upon family trusts set up for them by other members of the family in recognition of his incompetence to manage his own affairs.

Wedgwood, Sir John Hamilton, Bt (1907-89)

Son of Sir Ralph Lewis Wedgwood, CB, CMG, 1st Baronet, fourth son of Clement Francis Wedgwood*; educated at Winchester College and Trinity College, Cambridge; married, 1933, Diana Mildred Hawkshaw, a great-granddaughter of Francis Wedgwood*, who died in 1976; succeeded to the baronetcy on the death of his father in 1956; married, 1982, the art historian Pamela Tudor-Craig.

John Wedgwood joined the firm at Etruria* in 1931, becoming a director in 1935, and was one of the four young directors most closely concerned in the decision to abandon the old Etruria factory and build anew at Barlaston*. As a territorial officer he was called to the colours in 1939 and was part of the abortive expeditionary force intended to aid the Finnish army in its resistance against the Russian invasion. He served with the 5th North Staffordshire Regiment in Italy and later as an instructor with SOE, being demobilised in 1946 with the rank of major. After the war he became Wedgwood's Sales Director, travelling extensively, especially in the USA and Europe, on the company's business, and in 1955 he was appointed Deputy Chairman with special responsibility for Public Relations. He was largely responsible for the deposit of the Wedgwood archives (formerly housed in a Nissen hut at Barlaston) on loan to Keele

WEDGWOOD, Sir John Hamilton Bt. Sales director and Deputy Chairman (1955-65).   Photograph: *Courtesy of Sir H. Martin Wedgwood Bt*

WEDGWOOD, John. Eldest son of Josiah I. After a portrait miniature by an unidentified artist, c.1805.   *Wedgwood Museum*

University. 'John Ham', as he was known in the family, retired from the company in 1966 but continued to indulge his passion for travel and mountaineering (his conquests included the Matterhorn and Mont Blanc) and to excel as a lecturer on Wedgwood.

Wedgwood, John Taylor (1783-1856)

Line engraver; the youngest son of 'Useful' Thomas Wedgwood* (Josiah's cousin and first partner) and brother of Abner Wedgwood*, manager of the printing department at Etruria in 1805. Their eldest brother was Ralph Wedgwood* of the Hill Top Works and Ferrybridge. John Taylor Wedgwood was well known for his portrait engravings, and also engraved Plates 19 and 20 for the '1817' Catalogue*. He was official engraver to the Royal College of Surgeons and was responsible for an engraved portrait of Josiah Wedgwood after the painting by Sir Joshua Reynolds*.

Wedgwood, Josiah I, FRS, FRSA, FSA (1730-95)

Youngest child of Thomas Wedgwood*, potter of the Churchyard Works*, Burslem, Josiah belonged to the fourth generation of a family of potters whose traditional occupation continued through another five generations. No other instance of a family business surviving in this way has been recorded.

From about the age of six, Josiah walked to school in Newcastle-under-Lyme (a round journey of seven miles), where he learnt the rudiments of reading writing and arithmetic. His father died in 1739 and on 11 November 1744 Josiah was apprenticed for five years to his eldest brother, Thomas*, who had inherited the Churchyard Works, to learn the 'Art of Throwing and Handleing', a significant contract since the difficult art of throwing (see: Processes of Production) was the most highly rated of all the potter's skills and only those expected to become master potters served such an apprenticeship. At some stage of this indenture, probably around 1745-6, Josiah suffered a severe attack of smallpox, which left his right knee permanently weakened. He continued to work for his brother for three years after the end of his apprenticeship until, in 1752, he formed a partnership with John Harrison* and Thomas Alders* of Cliff Bank, Stoke. Two years later he was taken into partnership by Thomas Whieldon*, already one of the most respected potters in the Potteries, at his factory at Fenton Vivian.

According to Wedgwood's account in his Experiment Book*, his work with Whieldon was largely experimental and concerned with the improvement of bodies, glazes, colours and shapes, and it is clear that his principal efforts were directed to the development of creamware* and the improvement and creation of coloured glazes.

In 1759 Wedgwood left Whieldon to become an independent potter, renting the Ivy House* Works from his kinsmen, Thomas* and John* Wedgwood of the Big House, Burslem, for £15 a year. Josiah's cousin, Thomas*, agreed to serve him as a journeyman (a skilled artisan working for wages) for six years at an annual salary of £22. By 1765 Thomas was Wedgwood's principal assistant and in 1766 he was taken into partnership with a one-eighth share of the profits. The partnership was limited to the manufacture of 'useful'* wares and it lasted until 1788, the year in which Thomas died. Little evidence exists of Wedgwood's production at the Ivy House, but it was probably of well tried types of ware, such as he had made with Whieldon, for which there was an established market: saltglazed* stoneware, agate*, marbled* and tortoiseshell* wares and redware*. To these he would have been anxious to add wares decorated with his new green and yellow glazes perfected in March 1759 and March 1760, and his first moulded cauliflower and pineapple wares (see: Fruit and Vegetable Shapes) probably date from this period. His success with these early wares enabled him, after three and a half years, to move to the larger Brick House* Works. By this time he had made considerable progress in the improvement of the creamware body and a compatible pale-coloured lead glaze and in September 1761 a small quantity of this ware was bought from him by Sadler*, probably for experiments in transfer-printing*. The first delivery of Sadler's printing on Wedgwood's creamware was made in March 1762. Wedgwood's move to the Brick House coincided also with the start of regular production at William Greatbatch's* factory, which provided supplies of moulded shapes, large quantities of biscuit* hollow ware*, and a source of supply for saltglazed ware, which by May 1763 Wedgwood had ceased to produce in his own factory.

From the first Wedgwood demonstrated an initiative unique among potters of his time, and he was usually the first to adopt or adapt technical aids and techniques. For example, he brought the engine-turning lathe*, primarily a metal-working tool, to Staffordshire in 1763, and it was so efficient for its purpose that when, in the 20th century, the demand for engine-turning became too great for the 18th-century machine to satisfy, another was created by copying the old one. To the purist, pottery decorated by engine-turning perhaps resembles metalwork too closely, but the bronzing of black basaltes* was also an attempt to imitate metalwork, and these were the effects at which Wedgwood was aiming.

In the spring of 1762, while on a visit to Liverpool (probably to Sadler & Green), Josiah damaged his vulnerable right knee in a fall. Confined to bed, he was attended by Dr Matthew Turner*, who introduced his patient to Thomas Bentley*, a cultivated man, already experienced in commerce, who had acquired both classical learning and a knowledge of languages. This meeting was to have a profound influence on both Wedgwood and his business. Bentley was a convinced neo-classicist and was largely responsible for directing Wedgwood's production towards this style. More than a thousand of Wedgwood's letters to Bentley (now preserved at Keele University), the first of which was written on 15 May 1762, form the basis of all studies of the firm. Bentley's letters to Wedgwood, which must have been almost as numerous and were described by Josiah as 'my Magazines, Reviews, Chronicles, & I had allmost said my Bible', have sadly not been found, although Josiah had them bound and referred to them constantly. A few which escaped 'stitching' have survived to give us a flavour of Bentley's style.

In 1764 Wedgwood married his distant cousin, Sarah* (Sally), the daughter of Richard Wedgwood*, a prosperous cheese merchant of Spen Green, Cheshire, who was the elder brother of Thomas and John Wedgwood of the Big House, Burslem. Sally Wedgwood was a substantial heiress (her only brother, John, died in 1774) and brought with her a considerable (though unrecorded) dowry and it is clear that part of this was used to finance Wedgwood's expansion during the next ten years. In the early years of their marriage, Sally helped Josiah with his work, even learning his codes and formulae*, and giving practical advice on shapes and decoration. She bore him seven children who survived infancy, the eldest of whom, Susannah (Sukey) married Erasmus Darwin's* son Robert and became the mother of Charles Darwin*.

By 1765 the name of Wedgwood was becoming increasingly well known in London and in November 1766 he opened his first showrooms* in London in Charles Street, Grosvenor Square. In June, he received, through the medium of Deborah Chetwynd*, a commission to make a tea service for Queen Charlotte*, to be decorated with raised flowers in green on a gold ground (see: Gilding), and in the following year he was officially appointed 'Potter to Her Majesty' and his creamware was renamed Queen's ware*.

In 1766 Wedgwood bought the Ridgehouse Estate* of some 350 acres, situated between Burslem, Hanley and Newcastle, and there he built a factory which he named Etruria*. A crucial advantage of the estate as the location of a new factory was its position in the path of the projected Trent & Mersey Canal*. Bentley, meanwhile, had

WEDGWOOD, Josiah I.
Black jasper dip portrait medallion modelled by Joachim Smith, 1773-4. Oval height 5in.
E.N. Stretton Collection

formed a partnership in Liverpool with Samuel Boardman*, and, from 1764, had built up a solid and expanding trade in Wedgwood wares, much of which he shipped to America and the West Indies.

In the following year Bentley agreed to become Wedgwood's partner in the production of ornamental* ware. Wedgwood had planned this partnership for several years and his purchase of the Ridgehouse Estate and the building of the Etruria factory were evidence of his investment in it. The entire project was threatened when, in April 1768, Josiah 'over walk'd & over work'd' his weakened right knee. Four weeks later, his leg was amputated, without anaesthetic, in his own house by a local surgeon. Bentley stayed in Burslem until the immediate danger was past and, by the first week in July Josiah was sufficiently recovered to visit his factories and go 'rambleing into Cheshire'. Shortly afterwards he was fitted with the first of the wooden legs which he wore for the rest of his life.

The Wedgwood & Bentley partnership books were opened in November 1768 and the factory was inaugurated on 13 June 1769, commemorated by the production of six First Day's Vases*, thrown by Wedgwood on a wheel turned by Bentley.

The Wedgwood & Bentley partnership is rightly regarded as one of the most important in British industrial history and, by the happy accident of the survival of so many of Wedgwood's letters and other records, it is one of the best documented. The abilities of the two partners were complementary: Wedgwood's vision, inventive genius, technical expertise, urgent ambition and tireless industry combined perfectly with Bentley's commercial experience, entrepreneurial skill, educated taste and restraining good sense. Thomas Wedgwood, meanwhile, secured the essential groundwork of Wedgwood's business – the production of 'useful' Queen's ware – without which the 'ornamental' work could not have been contemplated.

The most important early products of the Wedgwood & Bentley partnership were ornamental vases*, an innovation in English pottery. By the end of August 1768 Wedgwood had vases of three different types in production – creamware (in declining quantities), variegated* and black basaltes* – and before the end of the year the variegated vases were of such quality that Boulton* proposed to mount them in ormolu*. Less than a year later the first 'encaustic'* red-figure* vases were painted in London and in November 1769 Wedgwood patented the process (see: Humphrey Palmer). In 1769 the partners acquired a house in Chelsea to be used as an enamelling studio, managed by David Rhodes* and supervised by Bentley, and new showrooms, opened in Great Newport Street in August 1768, rapidly became a fashionable meeting place.

From 1772 virtually everything made at Etruria was marked. Wedgwood was the first earthenware potter consistently to mark his wares and a notable innovation, which set him apart from such porcelain manufacturers as Meissen*, Sèvres*, Chelsea* or Derby*, was his use of his own name, impressed in the clay, instead of a painted device. Other British potters, such as Spode*, Turner* and Adams* soon followed his lead. This form of marking was part of Wedgwood's sales policy. He and Bentley undertook market research, cultivating influential patrons and customers (several of whom lent him, or permitted him to copy, gems*, sculpture, plaster casts, vases and tablewares in their private collections), enlisting the assistance of ambassadors (see: Sir Robert Ainslie; Lord Auckland; Earl Cathcart; Sir William Hamilton; Sir Robert Liston) and taking pains to produce wares suitable for specific markets. In this aspect of their business they were many years in advance of their time. Their ambitious plan to spread the fame of Wedgwood through the German states in 1771-2 (see: De Shoning) was not typical of their methods but it was characteristic of their bold, innovative approach to commerce.

In 1770 Wedgwood received an important order for a dinner and dessert service, painted with the *Husk** pattern, for the Empress Catherine II* of Russia. Three years later, the Empress commissioned another Queen's ware dinner and dessert service, of nearly 1,000 pieces, for the Chesmenski Palace, familiarly known as La Grenouillière (the frog marsh). This service, then the largest ever ordered from a British potter, was decorated with handpainted landscapes and a frog emblem at the Chelsea Decorating Studio*. Its completion in 1774 marked the removal of the showrooms from Great Newport Street to Greek Street, Soho, and the new premises were opened to the public on 1 June with an exhibition of the Frog* service before its despatch to Russia.

By this time Wedgwood was well advanced with his experiments towards the jasper* body but it was not until November 1777 that he was finally able to assure his partner that he could make it 'with as much facility & certainty as black [basaltes] ware'. Jasper was the most significant innovation in ceramic history since the Chinese discovery of porcelain nearly a thousand years earlier and it proved to be singularly well suited to the neoclassical* style of ornament. John Flaxman junior* was the first artist of note to design for this important medium and he was one of a number of artists, later to distinguish themselves as sculptors or painters, who provided designs for Wedgwood. They included George Stubbs*, Joseph Wright* of Derby, Sir Joseph Reynolds* and Henry Webber*. Many of the bas-relief designs, originally modelled for black basaltes, were used for Wedgwood's other dry bodies* – jasper, cane* and rosso antico* – but in jasper they were transformed by the two-colour cameo appearance. It was no coincidence that Wedgwood's jasper colours so nearly matched those used by Robert Adam*, and jasper tablets*, plaques* and medallions*, notably those intended for chimneypieces*, were intended to complement the colours then most fashionable in interior decoration. No jasper vases were made until 1781 and they were not offered to the public until the beginning of 1782.

Wedgwood led the potters when, in 1775, they contested the renewal of Richard Champion's* patent for the exclusive use of Cornish clay and china stone, and the patent was amended to refer only to the manufacture of porcelain*, thus freeing the materials for use in the manufacture of creamware. Since the Trent & Mersey Canal*, in the promotion of which Wedgwood had played a very active part, was nearing completion, the carriage of raw materials from Cornwall no longer presented any great obstacle. Wedgwood knew quite well how to make porcelain from a variety of materials and a long letter written to Bentley in January 1776 gives his considered views on the technicalities and difficulties of its manufacture. He was, however, aware of the crippling losses associated with the manufacture of porcelain (especially of softpaste* porcelain) and the consequent failure of many of the English factories which had made it. An attempt to establish a Public Experimental Work*, in cooperation with other leading Staffordshire potters, for the manufacture of 'an useful white Porcelain body', foundered and, by then, Wedgwood's experiments with the jasper body were yielding such results that porcelain was no longer a desirable product for either the Wedgwood & Bentley partnership or the 'Useful' Works at Etruria.

Bentley died in 1780, at the age of fifty, and no one ever replaced him either as an intimate friend or as a business partner. Thereafter, Wedgwood's closest friends were Erasmus Darwin and Richard Lovell Edgeworth*, both of whom were members of the Lunar Society*, at whose meetings Wedgwood (although apparently not a member) was a welcome guest. In business he made increasing use of his nephew, Tom Byerley*, and his sons were reaching an age when they could be trained to help him. Alexander Chisholm* was engaged to assist with experiments and correspondence, and many of Wedgwood's most valuable surviving memoranda are in his hand.

In January 1783 Wedgwood was elected a Fellow of the Royal Society*. He contributed five papers to the *Philosophical Transactions* of the Society, three (dated 1782, 1784 and 1786) on the measurements of high temperatures and his invention of the pyrometer*. In March 1786 he became a Fellow of the Society of Antiquaries* and in October of the same year a Fellow of the Society

WEDGWOOD, Josiah I. PORTRAITS AND STATUES. Marble copy of Flaxman's memorial head of Wedgwood for the tablet erected in the parish church of Stoke-on-Trent, 1802. *Wedgwood Museum*

for the Encouragement of Arts, Manufactures and Commerce*. He was on friendly terms with Joseph Priestley*, whom he assisted in his researches by providing chemical wares* free of charge.

By this time Wedgwood's reputation had spread widely through the western world and his skilled workmen received tempting offers from abroad, especially from France and America. Wedgwood published in 1783 a pamphlet entitled *An Address to the Workmen in the Pottery on the Subject of Entering into the Service of Foreign Manufacturers,* containing a stirring appeal to patriotic loyalty and dire warnings against exaggerated expectations of fortune and improved conditions. This was part of his continuous campaign to prevent competitors from acquiring his formulae and techniques and to guard against industrial espionage*. In spite of his efforts, all his wares were copied, in Staffordshire as well as on the Continent, and both Meissen and Sèvres made wares in the jasper style.

Wedgwood was the initiator of the General Chamber of Manufacturers of Great Britain* and was closely concerned in opposition to the Irish Trade Treaty* of 1785. He was consulted by William Eden (see: Lord Auckland) about the drafting of the French Commercial Treaty* of 1786 and was also active in support of the Society for the Abolition of the Slave Trade*.

In 1790 Wedgwood took his three sons, John*, Josiah II* and Tom*, and his nephew Tom Byerley* into partnership. John and Tom resigned their partnerships in 1793. In 1790 also Wedgwood finally completed his first copies of the Portland vase* and from that year he began progressively to retire from business. In December 1792 Josiah II married Elizabeth ('Bessie') Allen. Sarah Elizabeth Wedgwood, their eldest child and Josiah and Sally Wedgwood's first grandchild, was born next year. In 1794 John married Louisa Jane Allen, Bessie's sister. Josiah died on 3 January 1795, after an illness of about three weeks.

In 1863 William Ewart Gladstone*, the Liberal statesman who was also a collector of Wedgwood ware, said of Wedgwood that he was the greatest man who ever, in any age or country, applied himself to the important work of uniting art with industry. The tribute is generally considered to be extravagant, but it would be difficult to find any suitable rival to Wedgwood in this field. He was certainly far ahead of his time and his contemporaries in factory organisation, production management, cost accounting, marketing, public relations, industrial design and labour relations and welfare. Nevertheless, Josiah himself might have preferred the less fulsome tribute which appears on his monument: 'He converted a rude and inconsiderable Manufactory into an elegant Art and An important part of the National Commerce.'
See: Colour Plate 130

Wedgwood, Josiah I, Portraits and Statues of
There are two contemporary portraits of Josiah Wedgwood, both

WEDGWOOD, Josiah I. PORTRAITS AND STATUES. Bronze statue by Edward Davis commanding the entrance to the administration building at Barlaston. *Photograph: Wedgwood*

WEDGWOOD, Josiah II. Partner in the firm, 1790-1841. From the portrait by William Owen RA, c.1805. *Wedgwood Museum*

preserved at the Wedgwood Museum*, Barlaston. The first, by George Stubbs, was painted in ceramic colours on a Wedgwood white earthenware oval tablet, 20in. x 16in., and is signed and dated 1780. The second portrait, in oils on canvas, 29½in. x 24¾in., was painted by Sir Joshua Reynolds* in 1782. Both portraits have been engraved, the latter by both S.W. Reynolds and John Taylor Wedgwood*. A miniature portrait by Ralph Unwin* has been lost. An equestrian portrait by Stubbs (Lady Lever Art Gallery), thought for many years to be of Wedgwood, is now known to be a self-portrait of the artist.

A bust portrait of Wedgwood was modelled, probably in clay, by the Chinese artist Chitqua*; this does not appear to have survived. A shortened bust of Wedgwood was carved in marble by John Flaxman junior* for the memorial tablet erected in the parish church of Stoke-on-Trent, the likeness based on the Reynolds portrait. A fine marble roundel copy of this is in the Wedgwood Museum*. Flaxman was paid £93.19.0 for the monument in September 1803. Wedgwood's bust was modelled for reproduction in black basalt by Arnold Austin*, c.1940, the likeness being copied from Flaxman's tablet.

Three portrait medallions* are recorded: the first, by Joachim Smith, c.1773, shows Wedgwood in court dress with his wig tied in a queue; the second, attributed to Hackwood*, c.1778, is a classical bust, truncated at the neck; and the third, also attributed to Hackwood, c.1782, shows Wedgwood in day dress, his customary powdered toupée parted in the centre and curled over the ears.

The suggestion that a statue should be erected to Josiah Wedgwood is thought to have originated with Joseph Mayer*. Public subscriptions were invited and Edward Davis* commissioned to carry out the work. When completed, the bronze was sent to the International Exhibition of 1862 before being erected in front of the railway station at Stoke-on-Trent. It was ceremoniously unveiled on 24 February 1763 and, at the banquet which followed, the great potter's name was toasted in champagne of a vintage felicitously named Crème de Bouzy. A plaster of this statue, discovered in a storeroom at Barlaston in 1955, was repaired by Eric Owen* and cast by the Corinthian Bronze Company of

Peckham. This bronze was placed in its present position, outside the executive offices at the Barlaston factory, in 1957. The statue of Wedgwood on the facade of the Victoria & Albert Museum, London, is by Albert H. Hodge (1875-1918).

Wedgwood, Josiah II (1769-1843)

Second son of Josiah Wedgwood I and partner at Etruria* from 1790 to 1841. 'Jos' was educated principally at home, tutored by Tom Byerley*, Peter Swift* and a young French prisoner of war, M. Potet, and later at Edinburgh University. Josiah always intended that his second and third sons should be potters, and, like his brothers, Jos was given a thorough grounding in the techniques of pottery manufacture and the management of the factory. But in common with his brothers he acquired a prejudice against manufacturing industry and commerce. Privately he despised the business and was disappointed that he had never been offered the sort of extended tour of Europe that was given to John*. He regarded his journeys with Byerley in Holland and Germany in 1790, showing the Portland vase* and other samples of ornamental wares, as the job of a traveller*. Josiah I nevertheless took him into partnership, with his brothers, in 1790. In the following April, when Byerley was temporarily unable to manage the London showrooms*, Jos offered to take his place, but he made it clear that he would confine himself to management and correspondence and would not serve in the shop. His interest in the firm was not entirely feigned, but he regarded the work as a duty and, although (unlike his brothers) he never resigned his partnership, he distanced himself from it as soon as his father had died, leaving him the factory.

In 1795 Jos moved to Surrey, leaving Tom Byerley in sole charge of both the factory and the London showrooms. Not until after his brother Tom's death in 1805, did Jos take his responsibilities seriously enough to return to Staffordshire to take over the active management of the firm he had inherited. With John he succeeded in restoring proper standards of production and discipline at Etruria, and he presided over the introduction and development of White ware*, lustre decoration* and underglaze blue printed* patterns. After Byerley's death in 1810, Jos lost little time in ridding the firm of John, whose extravagance and indebtedness were a real threat to its future. In spite of his opinion that 'The business is now not worth carrying on, and if I could withdraw my capital from it I would tomorrow', Jos determined to continue it and, for the next thirty years he did his worthy best to save the firm for his family. Bone china* was introduced in 1812 but, although the quality was fine and the shapes satisfactory, the style of decoration was not rich enough and it was progressively withdrawn from 1828, the last 'matchings' order being taken by Bateman* in

WEDGWOOD, Josiah III. Partner in the firm, 1823-41. From a photograph, c.1855. *Wedgwood Museum*

1831. The technique of making large objects of jasper* was incomprehensibly lost and, after a brief period when only the smaller pieces were made, it was withdrawn from general production and replaced by white and stained stonewares* (known misleadingly as 'porcelain'*), usually ornamented with jasper reliefs and given a thin covering of smear glaze*.

Jos was responsible for the decision to sell off stocks of tableware at York Street prior to disposing of the showrooms, which were sold in October 1828. Tragically for later generations, these sales included also irreplaceable models, moulds and trial pieces, some of which have subsequently come to light in public and private collections.

In 1823 Jos took his eldest son, Josiah III*, into partnership, and four years later his younger brother Francis* joined the firm. Jos became Member of Parliament for Stoke-on-Trent in 1832 but did

WEDGWOOD, Josiah V. Chairman and Managing Director (1930-61) and Chairman (1946-67), photographed in the London showrooms, 1961. *Photograph: Courtesy of Tom Hustler*

not stand for re-election after the dissolution of 1835. In 1841 he retired from the firm and he died two years later. He was by nature earnest, taciturn and high-principled and, from a keen sense of duty and responsibility, he gave the better part of his life to a business which he disliked. Having allowed it to drift close to liquidation, he left a firm which was making respectable profits. His nephew, Charles Darwin*, described him as 'silent and reserved, so as to be rather an awful [awe-inspiring] man', and added: 'He was the very type of an upright man, with the clearest judgment. I do not believe that any power on earth could have made him swerve an inch from what he considered the right course.'

Wedgwood, Josiah III (1795-1880)
Eldest son of Josiah II*; educated at Eton, Edinburgh University, where he studied chemistry and natural history, and privately in Germany. 'Joe' was even more serious and unsociable than his father: unimaginative, solemn, introspective and dull. Although there is little evidence that he showed any keen interest in the business, Joe was given a thorough training in the materials, processes and techniques of pottery manufacture, and in 1823 Jos took him into partnership. Four years later they were joined by Francis*. In 1837, at the age of forty-two, Joe married his cousin Caroline Darwin (daughter of R.W. Darwin* and Josiah I's daughter Susannah*) and bought a four-hundred-acre estate, Leith Hill Place, in Surrey. Four years later, he resigned his partnership and settled there. Caroline bore him three daughters, the second of whom was to become the mother of Dr Ralph Vaughan Williams, OM, the distinguished composer.

Wedgwood, Hon Josiah V (1899-1968)
Chairman, Managing Director, and from 1967 first honorary Life President of Wedgwood. The second son of Josiah Clement, 1st Baron Wedgwood*, Josiah V was the great-great-great-grandson of the founder of the firm. He was educated at Bedales School (from which, with his elder brother, Charles, he ran away) and University College, London, where he took a second-class honours degree in economic history. He was awarded a PhD for his thesis, later published as *The Economics of Inheritance,* in which he attacked the principle of inherited wealth. He joined Wedgwood as Company Secretary in the winter of 1927, becoming business manager and, in 1930, Managing Director in succession to Kennard Wedgwood, who had become Chairman on the death of Frank*.

Trading conditions, immediately after the Wall Street crash, were exceptionally difficult, and Josiah V was faced with harsh decisions, which included the retirement of Harry Barnard* and Daisy Makeig-Jones*. In 1933 he wrote a private memorandum setting out his view of the pottery industry. This document, unpublished until 1989 (when substantial extracts appeared in Robin Reilly's *Wedgwood,* Vol.II) is of exceptional importance to historians of the industry, identifying the problems of the industry and proposing practical but innovative solutions to them. Josiah was especially concerned to solve the problems of Wedgwood, not all of which had been caused by the world depression. Immediate action was required in four principal areas: rationalisation of the product; modernisation of plant and machinery; investment in technical research; and improvement of design. He was uncomfortably aware that the entire Etruria* factory needed modernising, but that long-term planning was made almost impossible by the progressive and dangerous subsidence of the factory site. Nevertheless, some investment was crucial and this was concentrated on improvements to firing methods (which Josiah V described as 'the most important field for the potter'). Modernisation of equipment was directed by Tom Wedgwood* and Norman Wilson*. Modernisation of design was personally directed by Josiah V, who consulted Sir Charles Holmes*. John Goodwin*, who had been in charge of design since 1904, was succeeded in 1934 by Victor Skellern*, and a number of young artists and designers of outstanding ability – notably Keith Murray* and John Skeaping*, and a few years later Eric Ravilious* and Edward Bawden* – were commissioned to produce Wedgwood design more in tune with the period.

No improvements, however, could disguise the sad fact that the famous Etruria factory was no longer suitable for the manufacture of fine pottery and porcelain. With his cousins and fellow directors, John* and Tom, Josiah V made the decision to abandon the old factory and to rebuild elsewhere. After consulting his father (Josiah

IV*), he arranged to buy the Barlaston* estate and employed Murray and his partner Charles White as architects for the new factory. The foundation stone was laid on 10 September 1938. In spite of the restrictions imposed after the outbreak of World War II, building at Barlaston was allowed to continue and the earthenware factory was completed in April 1940. The bone china* factory was postponed until 1945. During the war, in the absence of John and Norman Wilson, the factories at Etruria and Barlaston were run by Josiah V and Tom, and survived well on government contract work and substantial orders from the USA. The first earthenware lithograph* decoration was produced in 1940. In October 1946 Kennard Wedgwood* was persuaded to retire and was succeeded in America by Hensleigh*. Josiah V became Chairman of the company, retaining his position as Managing Director.

In 1948 the London showrooms were reopened at 34 Wigmore Street. Five years later Josiah V, who had always been dissatisfied with the operation of retail distribution, decided to open the first of the company's 'shops-within-shops', to be known as Wedgwood Rooms*. Lithograph decoration was extended to bone china tablewares, and one such pattern, *Strawberry Hill,* designed by Skellern in collaboration with Millicent Taplin* won the Council of Industrial Design award for the Design of the Year in 1957. Skellern's design team was strengthened by the employment of Peter Wall* and Robert Minkin* and the policy of commissioning 'outside' designers and artists from other fields was continued. The distinguished sculptor, Arnold Machin*, was personally chosen by Josiah V, while still a student at the Royal College of Art, and he was allocated his own studio on the Barlaston estate. Others who designed for Wedgwood in this period were Richard Guyatt*, Robert York Goodden*, Laurence Whistler* and Clare Leighton*. A subsidiary company was founded in Canada in 1949 under the direction of Charles Cooper, and another in Australia, directed by Ian Taylor, in 1955. In New York, Hensleigh was replaced as President of the American company by Arthur Bryan* in 1960. A year later Josiah V relinquished the post of managing director which he had held for thirty years and was succeeded jointly by Maitland Wright and Norman Wilson. Josiah retained the chairmanship with his cousin Sir John Wedgwood (appointed in 1955) as his deputy. Sir John left the company in 1965. Two years later Wedgwood became a public company and Josiah retired.

Josiah V died on 5 May 1968, just two years after the company, under the executive direction of Arthur Bryan, had embarked on a policy of acquisition which was to make the Wedgwood Group* the world's largest pottery and porcelain manufacturer.

Josiah V's achievements for Wedgwood were second only to those of the founder. In 1930, when he became managing director, the company's sales were less than £200,000; when he handed executive control to Arthur Bryan, sales had been increased to

WEDGWOOD, Laurence. Partner in the firm, 1868-95.
Photograph: Wedgwood

WEDGWOOD, Kennard. Founder of Wedgwood's North American subsidiary company with headquarters in New York.
Photograph: Wedgwood

£3.25 million and profits were £516,000. He had inherited an outdated and inefficient factory, time-honoured but antiquated, and threatened by progressive subsidence. Its most valuable assets were its reputation and the skilled and loyal work-force of craftsmen who looked to him to save their livelihood during the worst slump in the history of the pottery industry. He bequeathed to his successors a factory that was still, twenty years after its completion, one of the most modern in Europe, with a work-force doubled in numbers but accustomed to the personal, often paternalist, style of management that had been traditional in the potteries. He succeeded, where many others failed, in holding the essential balance between commercial prosperity and the active encouragement of innovation and he achieved, as his successors have not always achieved, wider distribution without any cost in loss of quality or reputation. He shrewdly resisted all temptation to over-expand departments (such as the ornamenting department) that were particularly vulnerable to rapid swings in the market. His creation of the Wedgwood Rooms organisation provided the company with a direct connection, then unique in the industry, with the public which bought its goods.

Josiah V possessed exceptional qualities of leadership, courage and foresight, combined with business acumen and a deep devotion to his family firm. His gifts were widely recognised: he was a director of the Bank of England and of the District Bank; a part-time member of the Monopolies Commission; chairman of the Advisory Council of the Royal College of Art (of which he was one of the six senior Fellows); a founder member of the Council of Industrial Design; and a honorary Fellow of the London School of Economics. A modest and retiring man, he sought no personal honours and received none. He was the last member of the family to hold executive control of the company.

Wedgwood, Josiah Clement, PC DSO. 1st Baron Wedgwood of Barlaston; Josiah IV (1872-1943)
Politician. Born at Barlaston, the second surviving son of Clement Francis Wedgwood*; naval architect; served in the South African War; Liberal MP for Newcastle-under-Lyme, 1906-19; served in World War I, being awarded the DSO at Gallipoli. He joined the Labour party in 1919, continuing to represent the constituency of Newcastle-under-Lyme until the year before his death. Vice-Chairman of the Labour party, 1921-24 and Chancellor of the Duchy of Lancaster in the first Labour Cabinet, he was created a baron in 1942. His publications include *Staffordshire Pottery and its History* (1913) and *Memoirs of a Fighting Life* (1942), to which Winston Churchill wrote the Foreword. A radical idealist, Josiah IV was known for his vigorous, outspoken opinions, his sincerity, and his generosity, especially to refugees from Nazi Germany.

Dame C.V. Wedgwood's* biography of her uncle Josiah Clement Wedgwood, *The Last of the Radicals,* was published in 1951. His second son, Josiah V*, became Chairman and Managing Director of the Wedgwood company.

Wedgwood, Kennard Lawrence (1873-1950)

Eldest son of Laurence Wedgwood*; educated at Uppingham; director, with his cousins Cecil* and Francis Hamilton* at Etruria*; and, from 1906, in America, where he represented the firm and then founded the subsidiary company in New York. Chairman of Wedgwood, 1930-46.

Wedgwood, Laurence (1944-1913)

Third son of Francis Wedgwood*; partner at Etruria* with his father and elder brothers, Godfrey* and Clement Francis*, 1868-70, with his brothers, 1870-91, and with his nephews, Cecil* and Francis Hamilton Wedgwood*, 1891-95, when the firm was incorporated as Josiah Wedgwood & Sons Ltd. During the period of his partnership the firm introduced the first of the distinguishing prefix letters for pattern numbers (see: Appendix II), reintroduced the manufacture of bone china* and tiles* and employed Thomas Allen* as art director. Laurence's son, Kennard Wedgwood*, founded the subsidiary company in the USA.

Wedgwood Museum

The first museum at Etruria* was housed in a small single storey building. It was opened in 1906 and Isaac Cook was appointed first curator. The opening of the Museum was commemorated by the production of a miniature blue and white jasper* spill vase ornamented with a profile portrait of Josiah I and the coat of arms of the Wedgwoods of Staffordshire. The base is impressed 'WEDGWOOD ETRURIA ENGLAND MUSEUM 1906'. Frederick Rathbone, the well-known dealer and author of *Old Wedgwood* (1893), was commissioned to compile an illustrated catalogue of the 448 pieces exhibited, which was published in 1909. A year later the Museum received the gift of a 'large sum' of money from Lady Farrer*, which was spent on 'a considerable number of valuable pieces of Old Wedgwood'.

After the move to Barlaston, part of the collection was displayed in the Long Gallery, a semi-subterranean passageway connecting the factory offices to the farther end of the production area. The rest of the collection and and the highly important accumulation of

WEDGWOOD MUSEUM. Miniature jasper dip spill vase issued in 1906 to commemorate the opening of the Museum, ornamented with a portrait of Josiah I after the original model by Hackwood.

Wedgwood Museum

manuscript material was inadequately housed in Nissen huts at the back of the factory. In 1965, following a suggestion made by Robin Reilly three years earlier, Sir John Wedgwood* organised the removal of the manuscript material to Keele University Library, where it is conserved and the long task of cataloguing it has been undertaken.

In 1969 the Wedgwood Museum Trust was established and three years later the first professionally qualified curator, Bruce Tattersall, was employed. In 1974 a new museum was built at Barlaston, with an adjoining picture gallery to show the family portraits by Stubbs*, Reynolds*, George Romney and John Singer Sargent, and other original work by artists connected with Wedgwood. It was officially opened by Lord Clark, former Director of the National Gallery.

In 1979 Tattersall was succeeded by Gaye Blake Roberts, from

WEDGWOOD MUSEUM. Isaac Cook, first curator, photographed in the Wedgwood Museum on opening day, 7 May 1906.

Photograph: Wedgwood

WEDGWOOD MUSEUM. Part of the Wedgwood Museum picture gallery, opened in 1974, showing portraits by Reynolds, Romney and attributed to Wright of Derby.
Photograph: Wedgwood

the ceramics department of the Victoria & Albert Museum, who was elected Fellow of the Museums Association in 1987. The Museum was entirely rebuilt in 1985-6 to the concept of a 'living museum', showing the exhibits in chronologically ordered period settings. It was opened by Sir David Wilson, Director of the British Museum, and won the Unilever Award for Best Industrial and Social History Museum. The Museum and Visitors' Centre now

(1994) attract more than 200,000 visitors every year.

Curators of the Wedgwood Museum since its inception have been:
Isaac Cook, 1906-19
Harry Barnard*, 1919-31
John Cook, 1931-45
Tom Lyth, 1945-60
William Billington, 1960-72
Bruce Tattersall, MA, 1972-8
Gaye Blake-Roberts FMA, 1979-

Wedgwood, Ralph (1766-1837)

The eldest son of Thomas Wedgwood*, Josiah I's cousin, and partner in the manufacture of 'useful' wares*. After the death of his father in 1788, Ralph and his elder brother Samuel took over the Hill or Hill Top Works. Samuel died in 1790 and Ralph continued there alone, making creamware and stonewares* in imitation of Josiah Wedgwood's. Josiah warned Tom Byerley* in December 1790 that Ralph was sending for pieces from Etruria* with the

WEDGWOOD MUSEUM. A view of the Wedgwood Museum, opened in 1986, showing Josiah Wedgwood's original throwing and engine-turning wheels. *Photograph: Wedgwood*

WEDGWOOD, Ralph. Potter at the Hill Top and Ferrybridge factories. From a drawing. *Photograph: Wedgwood*

WEDGWOOD, Ralph. Pearl ware flask painted with sprigs of flowers in underglaze blue, impressed 'R.WEDGWOOD'.

Mrs R.D. Chellis Collection

WEDGWOOD, Richard. Portrait of Josiah I's father-in-law, oil on panel by George Stubbs. 28in. x 23in. Signed and dated 1780.

Wedgwood Museum

intention of taking moulds from them in order to supply copies to his customers, and Ralph wrote some thirty-six years later: 'I aimed at the identical objects of our Father, some of which (the Jasper* branch) were very injurious.' The Hill Works were sold in 1798 and Ralph moved his business to Ferrybridge, Yorkshire, where he continued to make wares, including creamware, Pearl* ware and jasper in the Wedgwood style, in partnership with Tomlinson & Foster. Their wares of this period were marked 'Wedgwood & Co.' The partnership was dissolved in 1800 and Ralph's subsequent career was an extraordinary mixture of experiment, incurable optimism and poverty. Josiah had always looked on him with affection, calling him 'Wedgwoodikin' and encouraging him with the dictum: 'Everything gives way to experiment'. In his later years, Ralph was frequently sent presents of money by Josiah II*.

Wedgwood, Richard (1701-82)

Cheese factor and merchant of of Spen Green, Cheshire; eldest brother of Thomas* and John Wedgwood* of the Big House, Burslem, and father of Sarah (Sally) Wedgwood*, who married Josiah I. Richard Wedgwood was evidently highly successful in his business for his books of accounts show a turnover of £1,200-£1,800 a month in the 1760s as well as regular receipts of interest on loans. He was understandably reluctant to see his only daughter married to a young kinsman who, whatever his prospects, had no fortune to match her dowry. A marriage settlement was, however, finally agreed and this would certainly have involved some financial commitment by Josiah. There is ample evidence to show that Richard came thoroughly to approve of his son-in-law, whom he accompanied on some of his travels in search of materials for his experiments with jasper*, and on at least one occasion Richard took charge of the factory in Josiah's absence. For his part, Josiah cared for the older man, and spent two weeks with him in 1770 until he recovered from a fever, although this required him to make daily journeys to Burslem. Shortly after the death of his only son John, in 1774, Richard went to live with Josiah and Sally, and he remained with them until his death. Although documentary evidence is lacking, there is strong reason to believe that Richard's wealth was used, either directly or through Sally's dowry and inheritance, to help finance the purchase of the Ridgehouse Estate*, the building of the Etruria factory and subsequent expansion.

Wedgwood Rooms

An organisation of specialist 'shops-within-shops' (shops in department or multiple stores, stocked, staffed and administered by Wedgwood), started in the autumn of 1953.

Since the 1930s Josiah V had privately disapproved of the retail distribution of Wedgwood, deploring the ignorance or timidity of many retailers and most particularly of the china buyers of depart-

WEDGWOOD ROOMS. A view of the thirtieth Wedgwood Room, designed by Alick Smithers and opened in Brown's store at Chester in 1963

Photograph:Wedgwood

WEDGWOOD ROOMS. Moonstone glaze shell-handled vase designed by Victor Skellern and modelled by Eric Owen in response to a request from Wedgwood Rooms in 1954.

Author's collection

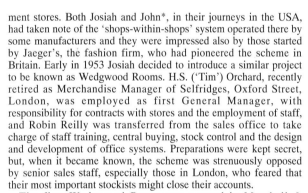

WEDGWOOD, Sarah. Wife of Josiah I. Enamel portrait on Wedgwood earthenware of Sarah Wedgwood at the age of forty-six by George Stubbs. Oval 28in. x 23in. Signed and dated 1780.

Wedgwood Museum

ment stores. Both Josiah and John*, in their journeys in the USA, had taken note of the 'shops-within-shops' system operated there by some manufacturers and they were impressed also by those started by Jaeger's, the fashion firm, who had pioneered the scheme in Britain. Early in 1953 Josiah decided to introduce a similar project to be known as Wedgwood Rooms. H.S. ('Tim') Orchard, recently retired as Merchandise Manager of Selfridges, Oxford Street, London, was employed as first General Manager, with responsibility for contracts with stores and the employment of staff, and Robin Reilly was transferred from the sales office to take charge of staff training, central buying, stock control and the design and development of office systems. Preparations were kept secret, but, when it became known, the scheme was strenuously opposed by senior sales staff, especially those in London, who feared that their most important stockists might close their accounts.

The first Wedgwood Room was opened in Marshall & Snelgrove, Oxford Street, London, in September 1953 and was followed, before the end of the year, by two others, in Marshall & Snelgrove, Birmingham and Robinson & Cleaver, Regent Street, London. Within ten years more than thirty Rooms had been installed and they are now established in every city in the British Isles. No major retailer threatened to close his account and Wedgwood's sales increased substantially throughout the country. In 1955 Orchard retired and was succeeded as General Manager by Arthur Bryan, who retained his position as London Manager (see: Showrooms). On his appointment, in 1960, to be President of the New York company, he was succeeded in both jobs by Robin Reilly. On his retirement four years later, Colin Wright became the fourth General Manager and subsequently Managing Director of the subsidiary company, Wedgwood Rooms Ltd.

The Wedgwood Rooms took the company, for the first time, into the heart of retailing and provided a unique opportunity to offer to the public advanced shapes and designs (such as patterns by Ravilious*) which would otherwise have received little public exposure. The success of this organisation and the unique experience it provided significantly influenced Wedgwood design, sales and production, and transformed standards of display and stock policy.

Wedgwood, Sarah (1734-1815)

Wife and distant cousin of Josiah Wedgwood*; daughter of Richard Wedgwood* of Spen Green, elder brother of Thomas and John Wedgwood* of the Big House, Burslem. Josiah and 'Sally' were married in January 1764 at Astbury, Cheshire, after prolonged delays while Josiah and Sally's father negotiated a suitable marriage settlement. A year later, when Josiah was engaged in experiments for the improvement of creamware, he wrote 'Sally is my chief helpmate…She hath learnt my characters [code] at least to write them but can scarcely read them at present.' Later, when Josiah had trouble with his eyesight, she wrote his letters for him and she was free with practical advice on shapes, decoration and even property values. Josiah told Bentley*: 'I speak from experience in Female taste, without which I should have made but a poor figure among my Potts, not one of which, of any consequence, is finished without the approbation of my Sally.' A shrewd, devoted and considerate woman, she bore eight children, one of whom died in infancy. Sally suffered from rheumatism but her constitution was strong and she outlived Josiah by twenty years. In 1802 she moved to Parkfields, a substantial cottage at Tittensor, where she died in April 1815.

Sally was a considerable heiress, who inherited the whole of her father's estate, and there is little doubt that her fortune helped to finance the building of the Etruria* factory and Etruria Hall*.

Her portrait was painted by George Stubbs* and Sir Joshua Reynolds*, and her portrait medallion*, probably by Hackwood*, was reproduced in jasper* in 1782.

See: Colour Plate 131

Wedgwood Society, London

A society formed in 1954 by a group of enthusiasts to encourage the study and appreciation of the wares and history of the Wedgwood factory, to publish research and to promote friendly social activity among members. Meetings are held about six times a year in London and membership is open to all genuine students and collectors of ceramics. The first chairman was Sir George Barnes. Publications: *Proceedings of the Wedgwood Society*

WEDGWOOD SOCIETY, London. Queen's ware plate, transfer-printed in sepia with a view of Etruria Hall, issued in a limited edition of 300 to commemorate the twenty-fifth anniversary of the founding of the society, 1954-79.   *Author's collection*

WEDGWOOD, Thomas. Youngest son of Josiah I. From a chalk drawing by an unidentified artist, c.1805.   *Wedgwood Museum*

(periodically); *The Wedgwood 1880 Illustrated Catalogue of Shapes.*

Wedgwood, Susannah (Sukey)
See: Darwin, Susannah

Wedgwood, Thomas (1685-1739)
Potter of the Churchyard Works*, which he had inherited from his father. Having failed to prosper in his craft and sired thirteen children, he died, leaving the potwork to his eldest son, also Thomas*, with instructions to care for the younger children and to pay to each (excepting only Anne, who was already married) the sum of £20. The youngest, then nine years old, was Josiah Wedgwood.

Wedgwood, Thomas (c.1717-73)
Eldest son and heir of Thomas Wedgwood* (1685-1739) of the Churchyard Works, Burslem, and eldest brother of Josiah I. Five years after their father's death, Josiah was apprenticed to Thomas, but left him in 1752 to take up his first partnership, with Harrison* and Alders*. Besides the Churchyard Works, Thomas inherited also the greater part of the estate of his cousin Catherine Egerton, which included the Overhouse Works. After Thomas's death, Josiah had the disagreeable task, as his brother's executor, of dealing with his second wife, who disliked her step-children.

Wedgwood, Thomas (1734-88)
Josiah Wedgwood's first cousin and his partner in the manufacture of 'useful' wares. On 30 December 1758 Thomas and Josiah signed an agreement which bound Thomas to serve his cousin for some six years from 1 May 1759 as a journeyman at an annual wage of £22. In this agreement, Thomas is described as a potter in the city of Worcester, which suggests that he was probably employed at the Worcester* porcelain factory. In 1766 Wedgwood took Thomas into partnership, allocating him a one-eighth share in the profits on useful wares. The partnership lasted until 1788.

Although Bentley*, Wedgwood's partner in the production of ornamental wares, was included in the profits of the Frog* service and, after some heated discussion, was permitted to include in his partnership account all production of black basaltes*, terracotta*, cane*, rosso antico* and jasper* (whether useful* or ornamental*), Thomas appears to have made no complaint. He served his cousin faithfully and patiently until 1788, when he decided to set up his own pottery at the Hill or Hill Top Works, Burslem. It appears, however, that he never began potting there, for his partnership with Josiah was officially ended on 11 November and Thomas was

drowned on 10 October. His contribution to Wedgwood's success has been consistently underrated. Without it, the quality of Wedgwood's Queen's ware*, the essential core of his business, might have been less reliable, and the time available to Josiah for experiment and the development of his ornamental ware would have been severely depleted.

Wedgwood, Thomas (1771-1805)
Third surviving son of Josiah and Sally Wedgwood* and always regarded as the cleverest of the brothers. Tom was educated principally at home, but spent a few terms at Edinburgh University, where he formed a close friendship with John Leslie*, a scientist and mathematician five years his senior, whom he invited to Etruria*. Josiah intended Tom to be 'the traveler & negociator' for the firm and brought him into the partnership with his brothers in 1790, but it was soon apparent that he had little interest in the business and he resigned his partnership in 1793. Tom suffered from chronic ill-health and, after the death of his father (from whom he inherited about £30,000), he spent his last years travelling and moving from one country house to another. He became addicted to opium, prescribed by Erasmus Darwin*, and contemplated suicide. When he died, at the age of thirty-four, Josiah II* wrote: 'I had long ceased to look on him with any hope and may be said to have seen him die for two years.'

Tom's inventive ability is well recorded. In 1790 he proposed the introduction of silvered basaltes* and he appears to have been instrumental in its production in 1791. He conducted experiments which were published by Humphry Davy* in the *Journal* of the Royal Institution under the title 'An Account of a Method of Copying Paintings upon Glass and of Making Profiles by the Agency of Light upon Nitrate of Silver, invented by T. Wedgwood Esq'. This has sometimes been described as the earliest record of photography in England, but he was unable to discover any method of fixing the images he obtained. He deserves the credit for being the first to understand and publish the concept that the chemical action of light might be utilised for the purpose of copying images, but the images he produced were photograms, not photographs, and his experiments were abandoned before they were fully exploited. He was generous and had many friends, including the poets Samuel Taylor Coleridge, William Wordsworth, Robert Southey and Thomas Campbell. Wordsworth wrote of him: 'His calm and dignified manner, united with his tall person and beautiful face, produced in me an impression of sublimity beyond what I had ever experienced from the appearance of any other human being.'

WEDGWOODARBEIT. Blue and white biscuit porcelain teaware in imitation of Wedgwood's jasper made at Gotthelf Greiner's factory at Groszbreitenbach, Thuringia, c.1790.   *Kestner-Museum, Hanover*

Wedgwood, Thomas (1703-76) and John (1705-80)
Younger brothers of Richard Wedgwood* of Spen Green and distant cousins of Josiah I, their common ancestor being Gilbert Wedgwood (1588-1678). Master potters of the Big House, Burslem, Thomas and John were fourth generation potters, whose father, Aaron, was said to have been an associate of the Elers* brothers. The Wedgwoods of the Big House were notable makers of saltglaze*, and the Big House, which they built, was the first considerable brick residence in Burslem. From May 1759 until the end of 1762, Josiah rented from them his first independent potwork, 'The House & Workhouses' known as the Ivy House*.

Wedgwood, Tom
See: Wedgwood, Clement Tom

Wedgwood Ware
A term properly applied to all wares manufactured by the Wedgwood factories but sometimes applied specifically to Wedgwood's jasper* ware.

Wedgwoodarbeit
Literally, Wedgwood-work. The name used to describe wares in imitation of jasper* made at Meissen* during the directorship of Count Marcolini, 1774-1814. The material used was porcelain ornamented in low relief with an enamel blue ground.

Wednesday Club
A London Club whose members met at the Globe Tavern, Fleet Street, for convivial evenings. Josiah Wedgwood was an occasional visitor. Sir Joseph Banks* wrote to Wedgwood on 6 April 1784: 'We attend the [Wednesday] Club with tolerable regularity. Hodgson makes punch and talks of politics; [Ralph] Griffiths* drinks it and makes jokes, but we all look for your assistance.'

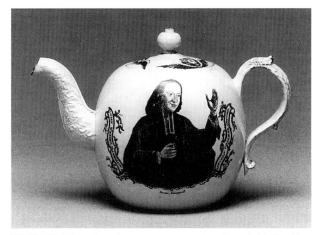

WESLEY, John. Queen's ware teapot transfer-printed in black with a portrait of Wesley within an inscribed scroll. The print is signed 'Green, Liverpool' below the truncation, Height 4¾in. 1770-1.
    Byron & Elaine Born Collection

Weisweiler, Adam (fl.1770-1810)
Ebéniste of German origin who assisted David Roentgen and arrived in Paris in 1777, becoming a *maître-ébéniste* in the following year. Weisweiler was noted for small pieces of furniture made for royal palaces, especially the Château of Saint-Cloud. He used Sèvres* porcelain plaques in the decoration of his furniture and several pieces by or attributed to him are inset with Wedgwood plaques or medallions (e.g. a *secrétaire à abattant* in the Metropolitan Museum, New York, and a console table in the Walker Art Gallery, Baltimore).

Wellesley Shape
See: Tableware Shapes

Wesley, John (1703-91)
Evangelical preacher and founder, with his brother Charles, of English Methodism; scholar of Christ Church, Oxford, and Fellow of Lincoln College. Wesley preached in Virginia among the Indians and later visited Germany. The first regular society of Methodists was formed near Bristol in 1739. During Wesley's working life of about fifty years, he is said to have travelled an average of 4,500 miles a year, delivering up to four sermons a day. He broke with tradition by employing laymen to preach, and his power in the society was absolute. The Deed of Declaration, 1784, marks the effective foundation of Methodism as a separate sect. Wesley's portrait, transfer-printed in black by Guy Green* and accompanied by the inscription, 'JOHN WESLEY M.A. FELLOW OF LINCOLN COLLEGE, OXFORD' appears on Wedgwood's Queen's ware* teapots from about 1770. A portrait medallion*, after a medal, was issued in the last quarter of the 18th century but is not listed in Wedgwood's catalogues of the period.

Whieldon, Thomas (1719-95)
Master potter and, from about 1740, one of the pioneers of English pottery manufacture at Fenton, Staffordshire. Records have survived of his letting his potbank, leased by him since about 1747 and owned by him from 1750 to 1761, but it is not certain whether he ever manufactured pottery there himself. His principal pottery was at the nearby Fenton Vivian site and in 1749 he bought Fenton Hall and its flint mill. Five years later he took Josiah Wedgwood into partnership with him, and Wedgwood's Experiment Book* begins: 'This suite of Experiments was begun at Fenton Hall, in the parish of Stoke-on-Trent...in my partnership with Mr Whieldon.' The suggestion that Whieldon's business was failing through lack of enterprise before his recruitment of Wedgwood is plainly false, and the frequently repeated statement that their agreement allowed Wedgwood to keep secret the details of his own experiments is unlikely to be true. Nevertheless, it is apparent that Wedgwood was the more inventive of the partners and that Whieldon benefited from his work. In return, Wedgwood gained experience of the organisation of a successful and substantial pottery and the opportunity for experiment unhampered by

WHIELDON, Thomas. Glazed and coloured creamware shards of teapot lids from the Fenton Vivian site showing typical leaf-shaped reliefs associated with 'Tudor Rose' ornament on Whieldon ware. c.1760. *City Museum & Art Gallery, Stoke-on-Trent*

administrative duties. Whieldon was probably the first employer in the Potteries to provide rented accommodation for his work-people, an incentive which Wedgwood was later to provide for his own employees at Etruria*.

Whieldon's reputation attracted to his employment some of the most important figures in the early history of Staffordshire pottery, among them Aaron Wood*, reputedly the best ceramic block-cutter in the country, Josiah Spode*, founder of the great factory that came to rank second only to Wedgwood's, and William Greatbatch*, the creative potter, block-maker and ceramic decorator.

Whieldon was a principal subscriber to the Trent & Mersey* canal and a keen supporter of the campaign for turnpike roads to improve communications with the Potteries. He retired from potting about 1780, when his factory was demolished. He was said to have accumulated a fortune of £10,000 and was appointed High Sheriff of Staffordshire in 1786. He died nine years later at the age of seventy-five.

See: Whieldon-Wedgwood Ware

Whieldon-Wedgwood Ware

Earthenware and saltglazed* stoneware made during the partnership of Thomas Whieldon* and Josiah Wedgwood at Fenton Vivian, 1754-9. According to Wedgwood's Experiment Book* the greater part of their production was 'White [saltglazed] Stone Ware' and this is borne out by the excavations carried out on the site in 1768-72 under the direction of Arnold Mountford, Director of the City Museum & Art Gallery, Stoke-on-Trent. Other shards* recovered from the site indicated the production of tortoiseshell* and solid agate* wares, creamware and red ware*. Shards of green

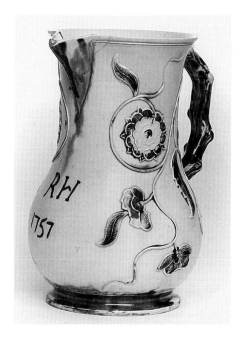

WHIELDON-WEDGWOOD. Cream-colour jug ornamented with applied Tudor roses, leaves and trailed stems touched in with colour and inscribed 'RH 1757', traditionally supposed to have been made by Whieldon for his milkman in payment. Height 7¼in. Unmarked. Whieldon-Wedgwood 1757.

City Museum and Art Gallery, Stoke-on-Trent

glazed* wares and cauliflower shapes probably belong to a later period. The applied ornament of Tudor roses with trailing stems is particularly associated with Whieldon-Wedgwood.

Whisky Still

Queen's ware* still, the cylindrical upper part with a condenser with pyramid-shaped lining, lid, and protruding outlet for the cooler, resting on a two-handled stand similar in form to the lower half of a food warmer* or *veilleuse*. The still is illustrated as lamp shape no.814 in the '1802' Shape Drawing Book* but was probably in production some twenty or more years earlier. An example of this rare object is in the Colonial Williamsburg collection and may be dated c.1775-80. It may originally have been intended for laboratory use.

WHISKY STILL. Queen's ware whisky still and burner. Height 17½in. c.1785. *Sotheby's, London*

WHIELDON, Thomas. Redware teapot ornamented with fruiting vine on trailing stems. Height 6⅛in. Unmarked. Whieldon or Whieldon-Wedgwood, c.1755. *City Museum & Art Gallery, Stoke-on-Trent*

WHISTLER, Laurence. 'New Delhi' and 'Clifton Suspension Bridge', from Whistler's set of six *Outlines of Grandeur* transfer-printed in black on a Lincoln-shape bone china plate, diameter 10¾in., with gold-printed border, and on a small coupe-shape bone china plate, diameter 5in. 1955. *Wedgwood Museum*

Whistler, Laurence, CBE (b.1912)

Artist, engraver on glass, poet and author; educated at Stowe and Balliol College, Oxford (Hon. Fellow, 1974); winner of the first King's Gold medal for Poetry, 1935; first President of the Guild of Glass Engravers, 1975; younger brother of Rex Whistler*. Indisputably the greatest British glass engraver of the 20th century, and possibly of all time, Whistler has engraved windows or panels for many buildings, including Stowe School, Buckinghamshire, St Hugh's College, Oxford, Sherborne Abbey, Dorset, and the Guards Chapel, London. His varied publications include: *Sir John Vanbrugh* (1938); *Rex Whistler, His Life and Drawings* (1948); *The World's Room* (collected poems, 1949); *Engraved Glass* (1952-8); *Pictures on Glass* (1972); and *The Image of Glass* (1975). In 1955-6 Whistler designed for Wedgwood a series of six *Outlines of Grandeur,* representing famous architecture characteristic of six periods of British history, for reproduction on Lincoln shape china dinner plates and on small coupe-shaped plates (see: Tableware Shapes). Three other designs, *Dolphin, Swan Song* and *Rose Window,* were not produced beyond the trials stage.

Whistler, Rex John (1903-44)

Painter, especially of murals and portraits, stage designer and book illustrator; studied at the Slade School of Art, 1922-6, and in

WHITE WARE. Two dessert plates painted with boldly drawn flowers over coloured grounds, a style of decoration especially associated with White ware, c.1815. *Author's collection*

Rome; painted murals for the restaurant of the Tate Gallery, London, 1926-7, and for many private houses. Introduced to Wedgwood by Victor Skellern*, he designed the *Clovelly* pattern in the *toile de Jouy* style in 1932, reproduced on both bone china* and Queen's ware*, transfer-printed* in black, blue, green, brown or crimson. He also designed 'OHO' portraits (heads which may be viewed either way up to produce contrasting characters) of 'Cinderella' and 'The Fairy Godmother' for the decoration of mugs. Examples of these are now uncommon.

White House Service

A dinner service of bone china* made for the White House, Washington, in 1903 during the Presidency of Theodore Roosevelt. It is decorated with the *Colonnade* border printed in gold and a polychrome enamel representation of the great Seal of the United States. The service was the work of John Goodwin* and Herbert A. Cholerton*.
See: Colour Plate 132

White Ware

A white earthenware body introduced, at the suggestion of Tom Byerley*, in 1805. It was a blending of flint, china clay, blue clay and china stone, fired at a higher temperature than either Queen's ware* or Pearl* ware. Both the body and the glaze are whiter than any others produced by Wedgwood at that period and the body has a thin, brittle feeling to the hand, unlike that of any contemporary body made at Etruria but similar to that of the earliest creamware.

WHISTLER, Rex. Group of *Clovelly* ware designed in 1932 by Rex Whistler for transfer-printed decoration in various colours on Queen's ware. *Wedgwood Museum*

WHITE WARE. Jug with moulded fluting, the collar painted in gold with a meander design, the body painted in colour with a view of monastic ruins and *(verso)* a huntsman and hound. An unusually rich piece of decoration intended to compete with the styles of porcelain manufacturers, notably Derby. Height 6¼in. c.1812. *Christie's London*

White ware was intended primarily for the production of tea-wares, to compete with the porcelain and bone china* of other manufacturers, but dinnerware is known, not infrequently in the same patterns as Wedgwood's bone china teaware services produced from 1812. Large quantities of dessert ware, especially the popular 'leafage'* and 'wreathed' shell* shapes, were produced and the body was used also for a variety of mugs and jugs, often with bands of coloured slip* at the neck and moulded ornament below. Vases up to 10in. in height of shapes previously used for black basaltes* or variegated* decoration on terracotta*, and lemonade cups* and stands (usually identified as white jasper, biscuit creamware, white stoneware or white terracotta) were made in the period 1824-32. Among the more unusual pieces recorded in this period are '4 Vases shape & size of the *Portland Vase** for good customers' in Birmingham in 1822, paint saucers and incense vases. The strength of the body made it suitable also for chamber ware*, which was produced in several simple patterns on White ware in the 1830s. Other useful objects made in White ware around the middle of the century included small candlesticks, funnels and the linings for butter coolers. The date when the White ware body was finally discontinued is not certain, but it was not listed among the bodies in production in 1896.

Whitehall Pattern
A bone china* tableware design consisting of a narrow vine border printed in gold. It was designed in 1942 and has since been produced in conjunction with a variety of coloured grounds, including ivory, Mazarine (underglaze) blue, Arras (underglaze) green, crimson and powder colours* (blue, turquoise, green, ruby, pink and grey).

Whitehead, James and Charles (fl.1793-c.1810)
Two sons of Christopher Whitehead, a saltglazed* stoneware potter near Bucknall and later of Shelton New Hall (taken over by the New Hall* company, c.1777). James and Charles Whitehead took over the factory of their uncle Ephraim Chatterley, in Hanley, about 1793 and they are listed in the directories as earthenware manufacturers from 1796. They were declared bankrupt in 1813. In 1798 the Whitehead brothers issued an illustrated catalogue of creamware tablewares (possibly not their first) advertising a large number of shapes which closely resemble, or are identical to, shapes produced earlier by Wedgwood and Leeds*. The catalogue is of particular importance in the attribution of unmarked creamware pieces.
See also: Castleford

Whitehurst, John FRS (1713-88)
Horologer, maker of chronometers and scientific instruments; Fellow of the Royal Society*, 1779. He lived at Derby, 1736-75, removing to London in 1778. Whitehurst constructed a time recorder for use at the Etruria* factory and he was among those consulted by Wedgwood when he was planning his factory, where a kiln was built to Whitehurst's design. In 1778 Whitehurst published *A Inquiry into the Original State and Formation of the Earth* to which Wedgwood subscribed. Wedgwood was critical of this work but decided to 'forbear' because, as he told Bentley*, 'I love the man, though I have some objections to his manufacturing of the world.' Whitehurst was a friend of Erasmus Darwin's* and Matthew Boulton's*, and, like them, one of the founding members of the Lunar Society*. 'Philosopher John', as Wedgwood dubbed him, supplied Josiah with samples of clays and rocks and he was on several occasions Josiah's guest at Etruria.

Widow Finial
A finial*, representing the Widow of Zaraphath, in the form of a woman seated on the ground with a shawl drawn over her head. At her side is a barrel of meal and a cruse of oil, and she holds a cake in her hand. Although this finial appears commonly on English pottery (notably the black basaltes* of Leeds*, Elijah Mayer*, Birch and Turner's 'Salopian' factory), it was never used by Wedgwood, who preferred the sibyl* finial to which the 'widow' finial bears some superficial resemblance.

Wilbraham, Jesse (1891-1963)
Modeller and master-craftsman. Jesse Wilbraham joined Wedgwood at Etruria* at the age of thirteen and served the firm for

WHITEHALL PATTERN. 'Round Plume' vegetable dish of *Ruby Whitehall* pattern, the wide powder-ruby band finished with a narrow border of gold-printed vine. c.1955. *Wedgwood Museum*

fifty-four years. One of his first jobs was to assist in setting up the Wedgwood Museum*, when he was responsible for finding some of Josiah I's trial pieces. In 1906 he became an apprentice figure-maker and won a scholarship to Newcastle Art School. He was wounded in the right hand in World War I and returned to Etruria to start a training school for modellers which earned him the nickname of 'The Schoolmaster'. After World War II he became head of the ornamental department at Barlaston*. His own models included portrait medallions* of Josiah V*, Hensleigh Wedgwood*, Norman Wilson* and of his close friend Tom Lyth (Curator of the Wedgwood Museum). Of the latter he said: 'I have made him a great deal nicer looking than he really is just to please his wife.' His self-portrait, inscribed in gold, was presented to him to commemorate his fifty years' service in 1953.

Willcox, Mrs Catherine (fl.1769-76)
The daughter of Thomas Frye, the engraver, and one of the founders of the Bow* porcelain factory; married Ralph Willcox*, a painter of porcelain employed at Worcester*. Catherine was a skilled painter ('an excellent copyer of figures, & other subjects, & much better than himself', according to her husband), who came with him to Etruria* from Worcester. She worked at the Chelsea Decorating Studio* from December 1769, painting encaustic* vases and landscapes for the Frog* service, for which she was paid eighteen shillings a week, the highest wage paid to a woman painter. Josiah was highly impressed with her painting of figures, and it is possible that she had a part in the decoration of the First Day's Vases* in 1769.

Willcox, Ralph (fl.1769-76)
Porcelain painter at Shaw's Brow, Liverpool and at Worcester*; husband of Catherine Willcox*, with whom he joined Wedgwood at Etruria* in 1769. With her he worked at the Chelsea Decorating Studio* from December 1769. He was known to be a heavy drinker and indiscreet, two faults which did not endear him to Josiah Wedgwood, who probably kept him on because he greatly valued the work of Ralph's wife.

Willet, William (c.1698-1778)
Unitarian minister at Newcastle-under-Lyme, Staffordshire; married, 1754, Josiah Wedgwood's sister Catherine (b.1726). Willet knew Joseph Priestley* at Warrington Academy, and may have been responsible for introducing him to Josiah. Willet and Wedgwood were on terms of warm friendship. Hackwood* modelled Willet's portrait medallion* in 1776 and Wedgwood wrote of it to Bentley*: 'I send you this head of Mr Willet as a specimen of Hackwood's modelling. A stronger likeness can scarcely be conceiv'd. You may keep it as the shadow of a good Man who is marching with hasty strides towards the Land of Forgetfulness.' Produced for private circulation, early examples of this rare portrait, considered one of Hackwood's finest, are usually unmarked.

WILLOW PATTERN. Modern Queen's ware 'Concave' shape plate and 'Bute' teacup and saucer decorated with Wedgwood's version of *Willow* pattern, transfer-printed in underglaze blue. *Wedgwood Museum*

Williamsburg Husk Service

A service, similar in form and decoration to the *Husk** service produced for Catherine the Great* in 1770. Shards have been excavated on the site of Colonial Williamsburg, Virginia, which was the political, social and cultural centre of the colony. The State government was transferred to Richmond in 1780 and Williamsburg subsequently declined, but since 1926 it has been restored to its 18th-century appearance under the sponsorship of John D. Rockefeller Jr.

Willow Pattern

The classic example of English *chinoiserie**. A transfer-printed* decorative subject originally engraved by Thomas Minton for Thomas Turner and introduced at Caughley, c.l780. The more familiar versions of this well-known pattern were not engraved until the 19th century and the 'Chinese' scene represented is a purely English invention. Wedgwood's *Willow* pattern, based on Minton's*, was engraved by J. Mollart in 1806 but (probably by agreement with Minton) was not produced until 1818. It has been manufactured intermittently ever since.

Wilson, Norman (1902-88)

Master potter, ceramic designer and inventor; Works Manager at Etruria*, 1927; Production Director, 1946; Joint Managing

WILSON, Norman. Production director at Barlaston, 1946-61 and joint managing director, 1961-3.   *Photograph: Wedgwood*

WILSON, Norman. Three pieces of Norman Wilson 'Unique Ware', of the style first produced in the 1930s, decorated with coloured slips and glazes, some of which were of his own invention. Vase height 10½in.   *Wedgwood Museum*

Director (with F. Maitland Wright) 1961-3.

The son and grandson of china and Parian* manufacturers, Norman Wilson was educated at Ellesmere College and graduated, as Silver Medallist, from the North Staffordshire Technical College, where he was later to serve for many years as examiner and Governor. After two years working for his father, he spent several months breaking in polo ponies in Canada. He was recalled from this diversion by 'Major Frank' Wedgwood*, who appointed him Works Manager at Etruria in 1927. After Frank's death in 1930 and the unprecedented slump which followed the Wall Street crash, the firm's success in its struggle for survival was largely due to the single-minded determination and economic brilliance of Josiah Wedgwood V* and the technical inventiveness and managerial skills of Norman Wilson.

In 1928 Wilson had introduced the first gas-fired china glost tunnel oven (and three years later he installed the first oil-fired earthenware glost tunnel oven in Britain). He also introduced ceramic bodies – *Alpine Pink** bone china* (an improved version of the stained bone china body produced in the 1880s) and two-colour earthenware – and designed the new Globe shape coffee pot, sugar box and cream jug, and lamp bases for decoration with Veronese* glazes. His matt glazes* – Moonstone, Matt Straw, April Green, Dark Green and Turquoise – sometimes decorated with platinum, were triumphantly successful and provided a purity of finish for the designs of Keith Murray* and John Skeaping* that was perfectly in accord with the Art Deco* styles of the period.

With Tom Wedgwood*, Wilson was intimately concerned in the detailed planning of the new factory at Barlaston*. During World War II Wilson served with the Royal Artillery, reaching the rank of lieutenant-colonel. On his return in 1946, he was appointed Production Director and applied himself to the formidable task of reviving manufacture, expanding and training the work-force, and reintroducing the production of jasper* (with a reinvented jasper body which he developed himself) in a newly-built factory. These objectives achieved, he found time during the following fifteen years to design Leigh shape hollow ware for bone china, the Barlaston shape and the range of vases, lamps and bowls decorated with brilliant original glazes known as Norman Wilson Unique ware*. From 1961 until his retirement in 1963 he was joint Managing Director with F. Maitland Wright.

WINE AND WATER EWERS. Pair of Wedgwood & Bentley black basaltes ewers, height 16in. c.1778. *Wedgwood Museum*

Norman Wilson's achievement was threefold: he exercised a strong and beneficial influence on the design of Wedgwood tableware shapes; as an inventor and technician he raised Wedgwood to a pre-eminence in production standards and efficiency unknown since the 18th century; and as Production Director he selected and trained a team of young and talented managers who would build upon the secure foundations he had laid. It would be difficult to overestimate his contribution to the success of Wedgwood's struggle for modernisation during the crucial years of depression or to the company's growing prosperity after the war. He must be considered among the most versatile, inventive and effective manufacturing potters of his generation.
See also: Tableware Shapes

Winckelmann, Johann Joachim (1717-68)
German art historian and, with the Comte de Caylus* and Sir William Hamilton*, one of the most important influences on the

WINE COOLERS. Two white biscuit stoneware wine coolers ornamented with bands of green arabesque and red stylised leaf reliefs. Height 9½in. c.1820. *City Museum & Art Gallery, Stoke-on-Trent*

WINE COOLERS. One of a pair of solid pale-blue and white jasper wine coolers ornamented with 'blind' dicing, the interiors lapidary-polished. Height 6⅜in. c.1785.
Dwight & Lucille Beeson Collection, Birmingham Museum, Alabama

neo-classical* style. As librarian to Cardinal Albani in Rome, he took a close interest in the excavations at Herculaneum*, Pompeii* and Paestum. He was made Superintendent of Antiquities in Rome in 1763 and was murdered at an inn five years later. His *Monumenti antichi inediti* (Rome, 1767) and *Description des pierres gravées du feu Baron de Stosch* (Florence, 1760) were probably known to Wedgwood although they do not appear in the list of his library.

Windsor Grey
See: Coloured Bodies

Windmills
See: Prime Movers

Wine and Water Ewers
A pair of ewers, height 16in., occasionally described as 'Sacred to Neptune and Bacchus' (T. Byerley* to P. Swift* 2 January 1782), one of which (Water) has a triton* seated on the shoulder, clasping the neck, and the other (Wine) a satyr* in the same position. The Water ewer is ornamented with a festoon* of aquatic leaves and the head of a marine monster below the lip; the Wine ewer with a vine festoon and a goat's head. Models of these ewers were supplied by John Flaxman* senior in 1775 but the designs were copied or cast from models by Clodion*. The form of the ewers suggests an earlier source, perhaps renaissance metalwork. These ewers continued in production in black basaltes* into the 20th century, and they were reproduced in jasper* and cane* ware. In the 19th century, they were reproduced in Majolica* and in enamelled and gilded bone china*. Basalt examples, especially from the late 19th century or the first quarter of the 20th century, are not uncommon, but all others, especially 18th-century jasper specimens, are rare.

Wine Coolers
Ornamented jasper* wine coolers, height about 7in., were made about 1785-90. Larger wine coolers of almost ovoid shape, about 9½in. high, of white stoneware often ornamented with wide

WINE COOLERS. One of a pair of blue jasper dip wine coolers ornamented with water lilies in modelled slip. Height 11½in. c.1880.
Formerly Buten Museum

borders of coloured reliefs, were produced c.1810-30. A pair of rare jasper dip* wine coolers in the form of a bell krater* ornamented with large flowers and trailing stems, c.1850, were in the Buten* Museum.

Wine Funnel

Queen's ware* wine funnels (for the transference of wine from bottles to decanters), copied from metal shapes, were produced from about 1785.

Wine Label

A small Queen's ware* or Pearl* ware plaque drilled with a hole for a suspensory chain, made to be hung around the neck of a bottle and lettered with the name of the bottle's contents. Wine labels of this type were made by Wedgwood from the last quarter of the 19th century. In the 1920s bone china labels in leaf and other decorative shapes with enamelled decoration were made for the retailer Thomas Goode, North Audley Street, London.
See: Bin Labels

WINE FUNNEL. Queen's ware wine funnel with interior pierced strainer. Length 7in. c.1790.
Formerly Buten Museum

WOLFE, James. Queen's ware jug transfer-printed in black with an adaptation of Woollett's engraving after Benjamin West's painting of 'The Death of Wolfe'. Height 9½in. c.1778.   *E.N. Stretton Collection*

Woburn Abbey

A classically designed house in Bedfordshire, built in 1744, the seat of the Dukes of Bedford. John Russell, the fourth Duke, and his duchess, were valued patrons of Josiah Wedgwood's. As early as 1765 he was at Woburn taking patterns from the Duke's French (probably Sèvres*) and Oriental china and the first mention of the Bedford vase* occurs four years later. Francis Russell, the fifth Duke, began to buy Wedgwood in 1786, and many of the invoices for his goods have survived in the Wedgwood archives. A Queen's ware* service ordered in 1789 was handpainted in brown with the fruiting vine pattern now known as *Bedford Grape*. Six years later eighty dozen tiles* were ordered for the Chinese Dairy designed by Henry Holland. Woburn Abbey is now open to the public.

Wolfe, James (1727-59)

English soldier; as major-general in command, killed at the siege of Quebec, 1759. Wolfe's death in the hour of one of the three great British victories of 'the year of victories' made him a national hero. Benjamin West's painting *The Death of Wolfe* was exhibited in 1771 and the engraving by William Woollett (1776) achieved greater sales than any of the period. Wedgwood reproduced this engraving on Queen's ware* teapots and tall jugs, c.1778. There was evidently an earlier representation of Wolfe (probably the same dubious 'portrait', signed 'Sadler', which appears on a Liverpool delft* bowl), for Sadler* mentions this as 'in hand' in October 1763. In 1959 Wedgwood commemorated the bicentenary of the Battle of Quebec by issuing a Queen's ware jug printed in black with a reproduction of Houston's full-length mezzotint portrait of Wolfe superimposed over an engraving of the Anse au Foulon (the British landing place before the battle). The reverse shows a view of Quebec from the south-east. The three engravings, were used also on rectangular Queen's ware trays.

Wood, Aaron (1717-85)

Modeller and block-cutter; the brother of Ralph Wood, the elder, and father of Enoch* and William Wood*. Aaron was apprenticed to Thomas and John Wedgwood* of the Big House, Burslem, in 1731, and served them as a journeyman for a further five years after his indenture was completed. He was later employed as chief modeller and block-cutter by Whieldon* between 1746 and 1750 and for seven years by Thomas Mitchell of Burslem. His son, Enoch Wood*, described him as 'modeller to all the potters in Staffordshire' towards the end of the period when saltglazed stoneware was at the height of its popularity and he was reputed to be the best ceramic block-cutter in the country. Although it has not proved possible to identify his work, it is extremely likely that he

WOLFE, James. Queen's ware commemorative jug, transfer-printed in black, designed by Victor Skellern in 1959 to celebrate the bi-centenary of Wolfe's victory at Quebec.   *Author's collection*

WOOD, Enoch. Cane ware plaque ornamented with a figure of Jupiter, apparently identical with that supplied to Wedgwood by John Flaxman senior in 1775 and reproduced in jasper. Height 8⅛in. c.1820.
City Museum & Art Gallery, Stoke-on-Trent

supplied block moulds to Wedgwood, as he did to many other leading Staffordshire potters of the period. His sons William and Enoch both worked for Wedgwood.

Wood, Enoch (1759-1840)

The youngest of the eight children of Aaron Wood* and brother of William Wood*. At the age of nine Enoch was employed by Wedgwood at the Brick House* and five years later he was apprenticed to Humphrey Palmer*. By 1783 he was in partnership with his cousin Ralph Wood II* making 'all kinds of useful and ornamental Earthenwares, Egyptian black*, Cane* and various other colours also Black figures, Seals* and Cyphers' *(Bailey's Western Directory* 1784). In 1789 Wood dissolved this partnership and formed another with James Caldwell, whose share he bought twenty-eight years later when he took his sons into partnership. Enoch Wood & Sons gained a high reputation for their underglaze blue printed* wares which were sold in large quantities in the United States of America. Many of Enoch Wood's earlier wares were, however, in direct imitation of Wedgwood's. Bronzed basaltes Triton* candlesticks* are recorded which appear to be identical to Wedgwood's apart from the turned brass nozzles, and when the Wood & Caldwell factory at Fountain Place was closed after the expiry of Hope & Carter's lease in 1880, block moulds for bas-reliefs* were found, the subjects of which were indistinguishable from Wedgwood's.

An accomplished modeller and highly successful potter, Enoch Wood was also a major benefactor to his home town of Burslem, a keen antiquarian and local historian and the first significant collector of Staffordshire pottery, of which he formed an extensive and important historical collection. The collection was broken up in 1835, when a substantial (perhaps the best) part of it was exchanged, at the request of the Elector of Saxony, for examples of Meissen* porcelain. Other pieces were given to the Mechanics Institution in Hanley, and a third part of the collection was purchased by the South Kensington (now Victoria & Albert) Museum, London. A fourth section, acquired in 1846 by the Museum of Practical Geology, Jermyn Street, London, is now also in the Victoria & Albert Museum.

A large circular Queen's ware* dish of Royal shape (see: Tableware Shapes), preserved in the Wedgwood Museum*, bears an inscription, painted and signed by Enoch Wood and dated 'September 26 1826'. Part of this inscription reads: 'This dish was made at Etruria by Messrs Wedgwood & Bentley [sic] removed from Burslem to Etruria…it is my brother William's modeling.'

In 1827 Enoch Wood & Sons issued a small booklet, *A Representation of the Manufacturing of Earthenware, with twenty-one*

quaint copper-plate engravings and a short explanation of each showing the whole process of Pottery. This little book, published in London, consists entirely of illustrations of processes of manufacture and is an invaluable social and historical record.

There is no evidence that Josiah Wedgwood ever made enamelled earthenware figures, but in 1783, during the Enoch Wood-Ralph Wood partnership, Wedgwood bought a large quantity of such figures from them. There is no indication that these figures were marked, but similar figures exist, all apparently from moulds used by Ralph and Enoch Wood, and later by Wood & Caldwell, which bear the WEDGWOOD mark impressed and these are believed to have been bought from Enoch Wood about 1790. Wedgwood's London bank account records an unusually large payment of £260 to Enoch Wood at the end of that year.

Wood, John Wedg (1813-57)

Master potter of Brownhills and Hadderidge (Burslem) and Woodlands (Tunstall); great-grandson of Ralph Wood I and (through his great-grandmother Mary Wedgwood, Josiah's first cousin) a distant kinsman of the Wedgwoods of Etruria*. Wedg (however improbably, that was the second name given to him at baptism) manufactured earthenware tablewares which were exported in

WOOD, John Wedg. Pearl ware soap dish decorated in underglaze blue, with orange and green enamel and 'pink' (gold) lustre edges in the 'Gaudy Welsh' style. Mark: WEDGWOOD impressed (the first W and last D in slightly larger capitals than the rest). c.1850.
Byron and Elaine Born Collection

WOOLNER, Thomas. Black basaltes group, *Eros and Euphrosyne* after the sculpture by Woolner, 1848. Height 12¾in. c.1860-80.

Sotheby's, London

quantity to the United States of America. The patterns were mostly printed, a few being handpainted and others decorated in the style known as 'Gaudy Welsh'*. None of his wares bears any strong resemblance to Wedgwood's, but some confusion has been caused by his use of the WEDGWOOD mark impressed, sometimes (but not invariably) with a space or a full stop between the WEDG and the WOOD. It has been vigorously argued by Una des Fontaines (Northern Ceramic Society *Journal,* Vol.6, 1987) that the use of these marks implies no deliberate deception, but suspiciously little care was taken to distinguish them from those of the Etruria factory.

Wood, Ralph II (1748-95)
Son of the potter Ralph Wood I who was noted especially for his Toby jugs* and well-modelled earthenware figures decorated with coloured glazes. The younger Ralph Wood also made figures, generally decorated with enamel colours. He was in partnership with his cousin Enoch Wood* from 1783 to 1789, making a wide variety of wares, many of them in imitation of Wedgwood's.

Wood, William (1746-1808)
Eldest son of Aaron Wood* and brother to Enoch Wood*; apprenticed to Wedgwood in 1762 and trained five years later as a modeller. At the end of December 1767 Wedgwood wrote of him to Bentley*: 'I have just taken a Boy apprentice for seven years to Model, & am beginning to teach him to draw, he has serv'd three years to handleing &c, has good fingers, & is a pretty active well-behav'd Lad. We shall want many of this branch to work festoons* & other ornaments upon Vases, free, without moulds, which Boys may be taught to do at moderate expence.' William Wood was soon put to modelling tablewares and he was later to become chief modeller of 'useful' wares at Etruria*.

Scarcely any record of his work has survived. Wedgwood wrote as early as 1767 of setting him to work on upon 'Lady Torrington's cover'd dishes' which he expected to be a 'tedious business', and some five years later of starting him on the modelling of knife handles. One positive and probably reliable identification of William Wood's modelling survives in the shape of a large round Queen's ware* dish of Royal shape, inscribed and signed by his brother Enoch. This shape is said to have been made especially for King George III* in 1770, a date which conforms with the inscription, which states that the dish was modelled by William Wood 'the first year after Messrs Wedgwood & Bentley removed from Burslem to Etruria.' It is at least probable that William Wood modelled other pieces for this service and also that he played a part in the modelling of the Catherine shape three years later. The quality of his work as a modeller is confirmed by the decision that he should join Josiah, William Hackwood* and Henry Webber* in the modelling of Wedgwood's copy of the Portland vase*.
See: Tableware Shapes

Woolner, Thomas RA (1825-92)
Poet, painter, modeller and sculptor of portrait busts. Woolner was one of the original Pre-Raphaelite brotherhood. He modelled the portrait medallion* of Sir William Hooker*, 10in. in diameter, which forms part of the memorial to him in Kew Parish church, and the portrait medallions of Robert Browning (1856), Thomas Carlyle (1855), Sir Francis Palgrave (1899) and Alfred, Lord Tennyson (1866). His model of *Eros and Euphrosyne,* exhibited at the Royal Academy in 1848, was reproduced by Wedgwood in both black basaltes* and Carrara*.

Worcester Porcelain Factory
This factory, established in 1751 by absorbing Lund's Bristol factory, was the largest and most productive maker of porcelain* in England during the 18th century, using a body which contained soaprock instead of the Cornish stone employed in Champion's* porcelain. Dr John Wall was among the founders of the factory. In 1783 the factory was bought by its London agent, Thomas Flight, for his sons Joseph and John. In 1862 it was incorporated as the Worcester Royal Porcelain Company, and it is the oldest manufactory in England with unbroken continuity. Throughout the whole of this period it has manufactured porcelain of various compositions and has produced relatively little earthenware.

There are few references to the factory in Wedgwood's correspondence, but it is evident that he knew about the part played by soaprock in their porcelain. This information could have been given to him either by his cousin and partner, Thomas*, who was almost certainly employed at the Worcester factory before he joined Josiah in May 1759, or by Robert and Catherine Willcox*, both of whom had been painters at Worcester.

Some of the transfer-printed* subjects used on Worcester porcelain, including the *Tythe Pig* and the *Tea Party* are found, in altered versions, on Wedgwood's creamware printed by Sadler* and several of Wedgwood's early tableware shapes are evidently related to Worcester porcelain. In the 19th century Wedgwood followed the lead of Worcester and Derby* in the production of designs in the Imari* style and later imitated Worcester's Ivory* porcelain.
See: Worcester Style

Worcester Style
Bone china* ornamental pieces, the exterior covered with an ivory ground and decorated in enamel and gilding in imitation of Worcester's* popular ivory porcelain. Designs were varied and included birds, leaves and traditional flower and swag patterns, sometimes with heavy raised gilding and often in 'Japanese' styles.
See: Ivory Wares; Japonisme

World's Columbian Exposition
Exhibition held in Chicago, 1893. Wedgwood produced a set of six commemorative Queen's ware* plates decorated with printed views of the temporary exhibition buildings and marked with the Portland vase* outline and the number '23' printed in brown.

Wright & Mansfield (fl.1860-80)
London cabinet-makers. They were represented in the London International Exhibition of 1862, where they exhibited a satinwood cabinet ornamented with marquetry, ormolu* mounts and Wedgwood medallions*. This was acquired by the Victoria & Albert Museum. Wright & Mansfield's copies of Adam satinwood furniture in particular have often been mistaken for 18th-century work, but they also made fairly close copies of other 18th-century types, including Chippendale.

Wright, Joseph of Derby (1734-97)
Known as the 'Candlelight painter' from his frequent choice of subjects lit by candlelight. Wright spent most of his life in his native Derby, but paid a visit to Italy in 1773-5. He was not a member of the Lunar Society* but some of his paintings, such as the well-known 'Experiment with an Air-pump' (Tate Gallery, London) of 1768, relate to the varied interests of its members and he painted portraits of several of them, including Erasmus Darwin* and Thomas Day. Wright, often described as the first painter to express the spirit of the Industrial Revolution, was specially interested in problems of painting light. He was elected to the Royal Academy in 1782, but later resigned.

WRIGHT & MANSFIELD. Important cabinet in the Adam style with ormolu mounts, ornamented with framed Wedgwood medallions, made by Wright & Mansfield for the 1862 Exhibition.

Victoria & Albert Museum, London

Perhaps recommended by Darwin, whose portrait he had painted in 1770, Wright was Wedgwood's first choice to paint the family group later commissioned (in an entirely different composition) from Stubbs*. In 1773 Wedgwood met Wright at his studio and five years later Josiah asked Bentley* to speak to the artist about a commission. This enquiry later led to Wright's visit to Etruria* and the purchase by Wedgwood in 1785 of three of his paintings – *The Corinthian Maid, Penelope Unravelling Her Web* and *The Lady in Milton's 'Comus'* – but not before some controversy about the first of these. In April 1784 Wedgwood wrote to Wright about the *Corinthian Maid* in terms of excessive delicacy: 'I could not speak to you when I was with the ladies at your house about the particular part of the drapery of the Corinthian Maid which I liked the least…My objections were the divisions of the posteriors appearing too plain thro' the drapery, & its sticking so close, the truly Grecian, as you justly observe gave that part a heavy hanging like (if I may use a new term) appearance, as if it wanted a little shove up.' The problem was resolved by Wright's agreeing to 'cast a fuller drapery' upon the offending figure. The two men became friends and Josiah bought Wright's self-portrait for the then huge price of £300 (double the price charged by Reynolds for a full-length portrait in 1782). Wright acknowledged Wedgwood's generous patronage by presenting him with a painting of Dovedale, Derbyshire (now in the Wedgwood Museum*), which he inscribed on the reverse: 'The gift of Joseph Wright of Derby to his friend Josiah Wedgwood Esq., the patron and encourager of living artists, 1787.' Josiah responded in 1789 with the gift of a 'table service green shell edge…about 10 guineas value to be looked out very good.'

Wright has occasionally been confused with Patience Lovell Wright's* son, Joseph, of whom he was no connection.

Wright, Mrs Patience Lovell (1725-86)
Painter and modeller in wax, born in Bordentown, New Jersey. She came to London in 1772 and was described effusively in the

London Magazine of December 1773 as having been 'reserved by the hand of nature to produce a new style of picturing superior to statuary and peculiar to herself and the honour of America, for her compositions, in likeness to the originals, surpass paint or any other method of delineation; they live with such a perfect animation, that we are more surprised than charmed, for we see art perfect as nature.' Her wax portrait* of Benjamin Franklin was reproduced by Wedgwood in jasper* and black basaltes* and an engraving of George Washington by her son, Joseph (not to be confused with the painter Joseph Wright of Derby*) was copied for a portrait medallion* in 1789.

Wyke, John (fl.1766-81)
Longcase clock, watch and instrument maker of Wykes Court, Liverpool, who carried out modifications to Wedgwood's engine-turning* lathe and supplied him with punches. In 1767 Wedgwood wrote to Bentley*, who was acquainted with Wyke: '[Sally] hath sent you a watch, by way of a love token I suppose, she says it is a little out of order, but one Docter Wyke of your Town perfectly understands its constitution & Complaints, & would set it to rights again if you will be kind enough to send it to him.'

Wynn, Sir Watkin Williams (1748-89)
Fourth baronet; member of parliament for Salop, 1772-4. The rich and youthful head of a respected Welsh family, Sir Watkin was an enthusiastic and generous patron of Wedgwood's. No less than 240 of the first 414 intaglios* or seals* catalogued by Wedgwood & Bentley were copied from gems* lent to them by Sir Watkin and he presented Wedgwood with the first volume of Sir William Hamilton's* *Antiquités*. The Wedgwood archives bear witness to the quantity and variety of Sir Watkin's purchases, which included tiles* for his dairy in 1783, but from the connoisseur's point of view the most important is the encaustic* painted tablet* made for the chimneypiece* at 20 St James's Square. This tablet, of black basaltes*, is painted and shaded in natural colours after a design by Antonio Zucchi* and appears to be the only surviving example of such a full palette of encaustic colours applied to a tablet.

WYNN, Sir Watkin Williams. Adam chimneypiece at 20 St James's Square, showing the black basaltes encaustic-painted tablet, made for Sir Watkin by Wedgwood in 1772.

Photograph: Courtesy of Alison Kelly

WYON, Edward William. Carrara bust of General Sir Colin Campbell (later Lord Clyde) by E.W. Wyon. Height 16in. 1858.

Author's collection

Wyon, Edward William (1811-85)
Sculptor and modeller; student at the Royal Academy Schools, 1829; exhibited at the Royal Academy, 1831-76, showing nearly one hundred busts, medallions* and wax portraits*. At the Great Exhibition of 1851 he exhibited a 'Tazza modeled from a Greek Design for the Art Union of London', and in the following year he sculpted a bust of the Duke of Wellington for reproduction by Wedgwood. This began an association with the firm which lasted at least until 1859. The following models by Wyon were reproduced in black basaltes* and Carrara*:

BUSTS
John Bunyan
Robert Burns
Lord Byron
Sir Colin Campbell
Sir Henry Havelock
John Milton
George Moore
Lord Palmerston (two sizes)
Sir Walter Scott
George Stephenson
Robert Stephenson
James Watt*
Duke of Wellington

FIGURES and GROUPS
Hope
Nubian Water Carrier
Oberon
Titania

PORTRAIT MEDALLIONS
C.F. Huth (first produced 1892)
Reginald Huth

Yellow Glazed Ware
See: Glazes

Yi-Hsing Stoneware
Chinese red stoneware which first arrived in Europe in the 17th century in the form of small spouted wine pots used for making the new drink of tea. These pots were extremely popular and much sought. They were imitated by Böttger at Meissen*, by Arij de Milde in Holland, by John Dwight* at Fulham and by the Elers* brothers in Staffordshire. The Elers brothers made the red ware* from which Josiah Wedgwood developed his rosso antico* body.

Zaffre
A word of Arabic origin, in use during the 18th century for the composition made by the fusion of cobalt* with sand. It was the colouring agent used in the manufacture of smalt*.

Zeno (335-263 BC)
Founder of the Stoic philosophy, born in Cyprus. Shipwrecked in the neighbourhood of the Piraeus, he studied philosophy under the Cynic, Crates and at the Academy. After many years of study he formed his own school and his followers were called Stoics after the Stoa Poicile where it was founded.

Wedgwood subjects:
Zeno, bust 25in., from a cast supplied by Hoskins & Grant*, 1774
Zeno, full-length bas-relief* figure as a framed oval plaque*, 10½in. x 7¾in., produced in terracotta* and in black basaltes*, sometimes with encaustic* painted ground. No.67 in 1773 Catalogue*

Zephyr
The god of the west wind, usually represented as a winged youth. He was married to Chloris (whom the Romans called Flora*). Jealous of Apollo's* love for Hyacinthus, one of his companions, Zephyr killed him by directing a discus to strike him down. A pair of jasper* flower holders, c.1790, is supported by figures which are usually identified as Cupid* and Psyche*. This identification has recently been corrected by Dr Nicholas Penny, Keeper of Western Art at the Ashmolean Museum, Oxford, and the figures are now recognised as Zephyr and Flora*.

Zeus
See: Jupiter

ZEPHYR. Pair of solid pale-blue and white jasper flower holders or bough pots in the form of figures of *Zephyr* and *Flora* (usually described as figures of Cupid and Psyche) resting against sarcophagi. Height 5½in. c.1790.
Sotheby's, London

ZINGARA. Rare black basaltes figure of Zingara. Height 17¾in. c.1785.

Mr & Mrs Samuel Laver Collection

Zingara

Zingara is the Italian word for a gypsy woman. A Zingara figure was illustrated in 'Perrier's Statues' (F. Perrier, *Segmenta nobilium signorum et statuarum*…Paris, 1638) which was in Wedgwood's library and it was well known in the 18th century. The statue, now in the Louvre collection at Versailles, is a composition of a fine Greek marble trunk (c.300 BC), perhaps originally a statue of Diana*, and a bronze head, hands and feet attributed to Nicolas Cordier (1567-1612) or a contemporary working in his style. The head of this figure was reproduced in Derby* porcelain and by Ralph and Enoch Wood* in enamelled earthenware. Wedgwood's black basaltes* reproduction was taken from a cast supplied by Richard Parker* in 1774. A full-length figure, much reduced from the original, was reproduced also in black basaltes from a cast obtained from Hoskins & Grant* in May 1779. Both the bust and the figure are rare.

Zinkeisen, Anna Katrina (1901-78)

Painter and sculptor; studied at the Royal Academy Schools, where she won Bronze and Silver Medals for sculpture; exhibited at the Royal Academy. Anna Zinkeisen later became well known as a war artist and for her murals for the passenger liners *Queen Mary* and *Queen Elizabeth.* In 1924 she modelled for Wedgwood three bas-relief* subjects for reproduction in jasper: *Adam* and *Eve,* which won a silver medal at the Paris Exposition of 1925, and *Sun and Wind.* All three plaques have been reissued in more recent times.

ZINKEISEN, Anna. Solid pale-blue and white jasper plaque, 'Adam', modelled by Anna Zinkeisen in 1924. Diameter 6¾in. Replica made in 1959. *Wedgwood Museum*

ZINKEISEN, Anna. Solid pale-blue and white jasper plaque, 'Sun and Wind', modelled by Anna Zinkeisen in 1924. Diameter 4¾in. Replica made in 1972. *Wedgwood Museum*

Zodiac, Signs of the

The word 'zodiac' is derived from the Greek *zodion,* meaning the sculptured figure of an animal, and seven of the twelve divisions of the heavens are represented by animals. Wedgwood was supplied with a set of Signs of the Zodiac by Mrs Mary Landré* in 1776. They were remodelled by Hackwood* and used as a frieze on some fine black basaltes* vases of the Wedgwood & Bentley period. They were also reduced in size for use as cameo borders and for the ornamenting of jasper* vases and smaller objects. In recent times they have been reproduced as separate figures for setting in cuff links, brooches and pendants. Other examples of the use of these motifs include the decoration of Arnold Machin's* figure of *Taurus.*

Zucchi, Antonio (1726-95)

Painter and engraver; son of the painter Francesco Zucchi and a pupil of his uncle, the theatrical designer, Carlo Zucchi. He travelled in Italy with the Adam brothers, designing classical monuments and ruins*. Later he came to live in London, where he exhibited for fourteen years, being elected an Associate of the Royal Academy in 1770. He designed and painted the decorations of a number of great houses, notably the ceiling at Osterley Park. He was regularly employed by Robert Adam* and was responsible for the original gouache designs for the encaustic* painted tablets* produced by Wedgwood for Sir Watkin Williams Wynn's* house at 20 St James's Square, London. In 1781 Zucchi married Angelica Kauffmann* and returned to Rome where he spent the last years of his life.

ZODIAC, SIGNS OF THE. Three-colour jasper dip cameo in lilac, blue and white, ornamented with a central sacrifice subject and a border of Signs of the Zodiac. Diameter 1½in. c.1790. *Wedgwood Museum*

Appendix I

Wedgwood Chronology

1719	Birth of Thomas Whieldon
1719-24	Publication of Montfaucon's *L'Antiquité expliquée*
1730	Birth of Josiah Wedgwood
	Birth of Thomas Bentley
1734	Birth of Sarah Wedgwood
	Birth of ('Useful') Thomas Wedgwood (Josiah's cousin)
1738	Discovery of Herculaneum
1739-44	Josiah apprenticed to his eldest brother, Thomas Wedgwood
1747	Birth of Thomas Byerley
1748	Discovery of Pompeii
1752-4	Josiah in partnership with John Harrison and Thomas Alders
1754	Society for the Encouragement of Arts, Manufactures and Science (later Royal Society of Arts) founded
1754-9	Whieldon-Wedgwood partnership
1756-70	Publication of Comte de Caylus's *Receuil d'Antiquités*
1759-64	Ivy House Works: Wedgwood production including saltglazed stoneware, creamware, redware, variegated wares, green glaze, fruit and vegetable shapes
1759-95	Period of wares traditionally described as 'Old Wedgwood'
1761-99	Creamwares transfer-printed by Sadler (until 1770) & Green in Liverpool
1762	Josiah's first meeting with Bentley
1762-71	Greatbatch supplying wares to Wedgwood
1762-1808	William Wood employed
1763-72	Brick House ('Bell Works')
1763	Wedgwood's introduction of engine-turning lathe to the Potteries
1763-81	Boulton & Fothergill partnership
1764	Marriage of Josiah and Sarah Wedgwood
1765	Tea service supplied to Queen Charlotte
1766	Queen's ware named
1766-76	Publication of Hamilton and d'Hancarville's *Antiquités Etrusques, Grecques et Romaines*
1766-88	Thomas Wedgwood (cousin) in partnership with Josiah in the production of 'useful' wares
1768	Black basaltes introduced. Josiah's leg amputated
1768-9	Voyez employed
1768-74	Newport Street, London Showrooms
1768-77	David Rhodes employed in London
1768-80	Wedgwood & Bentley partnership for the production of Ornamental wares
1769	Etruria Works opened. First Day's Vases produced. Encaustic painting introduced on black basaltes
1769-74	Mrs Landré supplying casts
1769-74/5	Chelsea Decorating Studio
1769-1832	William Hackwood employed
1770	First black basaltes busts produced. *Husk* service produced for Catherine II of Russia. 'Herculaneum Pictures' moulded
1770-9	Hoskins & Grant supplying casts and models
1771	Terracotta biscuit ('crystalline') body introduced. First trials of 'Fawn' ware (later developed to Cane ware). First portrait medallions produced
1772	Joachim Smith supplying portrait medallions
1773	First Ornamental Ware Catalogue
1774	First Queen's ware ('Useful ware') Catalogue. 'Frog' service completed for Catherine II of Russia. Goethe's *Sorrows of the Young Werther* published
1774-95	Greek Street, London Showrooms
1775	Jasper perfected and introduced
1775-86	Wedgwood attempting to make, and from 1777 supplying, tablets to George Stubbs for painting
1776	Rosso antico introduced. First tiles produced
1776-83	American War of Independence
1777	Jasper dip introduced. Important 'Jasper Memorandum' recording the use of coarse and fine jasper bodies
1778	*Apotheosis of Homer* relief modelled by Flaxman
1779	Mortar ware introduced
1780	Death of Bentley: end of Wedgwood & Bentley partnership
1781	Auction sale of Wedgwood & Bentley partnership stock
1782	First jasper vases offered for sale
1783-9	Designs for bas-reliefs supplied by Lady Templetown
1784-c.1815	Aaron Steele employed
1785-9	Designs for bas-reliefs supplied by Lady Diana Beauclerk
1785-1806	Henry Webber employed
1786	French Commercial Treaty medallions modelled by Flaxman
1787	Slave medallion modelled by Hackwood. Lochée's wax portraits of the royal princes reproduced in jasper. Designs for bas-reliefs supplied by Emma Crewe
1787-92	Wedgwood's studio of modellers in Rome
1788	Death of cousin Thomas Wedgwood. End of Useful ware partnership. Josiah assumes sole control of the firm
1789	Fall of the Bastille
1789-90	French Revolution medallions produced
1790	Josiah's sons – John, Josiah II and Tom – and Tom Byerley taken into partnership. Portland Vase produced. German cameos produced
1793-1802	War with France
1793	John and Tom Wedgwood withdraw from partnership
1795	Death of Josiah I
1795-1829	York Street, London Showrooms
1798	De Vaere's portrait medallions of British admirals produced
1800-10	John Wedgwood returns to partnership
1803-15	War with France
1805	Underglaze blue printing introduced at Etruria. First lustre decoration produced

c.1809	Variegated lustre introduced	1904-34	John Goodwin, Art Director
c.1810	White stoneware ('porcelain') introduced. From c.1815 decorated with smear glaze, 1817 with jasper dip and 1821 with jasper ornaments	1905-30	Alfred and Louise Powell working for Wedgwood (freelance work continued until 1942)
1810	Gold-printing technique patented by Warburton	1906	Wedgwood Museum opened
1811	Drabware introduced	1909	'Frog' service, on loan from the Tsar Nicholas II, exhibited in London
1811-23	Josiah II sole proprietor	1909-31	Daisy Makeig-Jones designing at Etruria
1812-31	Bone china, first period	1912	Powder blue decoration on bone china introduced
1815	Smear glaze introduced	1914	First 'Ordinary Lustre' decoration
c.1817-29	Stone china produced	1914-18	World War I
1817-45	Production of jasper vases discontinued	1915	Fairyland Lustre decoration introduced
1823	Josiah III taken into partnership	1919	Josiah Wedgwood & Sons Inc., New York, founded
c.1823	Rockingham glaze introduced	1923-30	Barnard edition of Portland vase
1827	Francis Wedgwood taken into partnership	1926	John Skeaping animal figures introduced
1828	Clearance sale of models, trials and moulds in London	1927	First straight tunnel oven installed for firing bone china
1829	York Street Showrooms sold	1927-41	24-27 Hatton Gardens, London Showrooms
1829-60	Solid jasper discontinued	1927-63	Norman Wilson working for Wedgwood (Works Manager, Production Director, Managing Director)
1842-3	Francis Wedgwood sole proprietor		
1842-83	Registry marks (Appendix III) used (not on all wares)	1928	First gas-fired china glost tunnel oven installed
1843-5	John Boyle in partnership with Francis	1929-40	Wedgwood sans serif mark (not invariably used)
1845	Francis sole proprietor	1930-64	Josiah V, Managing Director (Chairman, 1947-67)
1846-59	Robert Brown in partnership with Francis		
c.1848	Carrara (Parian) introduced	1931	First oil-fired earthenware glost tunnel oven in Britain installed at Etruria
1851	Great Exhibition, Crystal Palace		
c.1858	Lavender coloured body introduced	1933-40	Keith Murray designing for Wedgwood
1858-75	Emile Lessore decorating ware for Wedgwood	1934-65	Victor Skellern, Art Director
1859	Godfrey Wedgwood in partnership with Francis	1935-9	Eric Ravilious designing for Wedgwood
1860	Solid jasper reintroduced. Majolica ware introduced. Three-letter impressed dating code introduced for earthenwares and (occasionally) for stonewares	1938	Foundation stone of Barlaston factory laid 10 September
		1939-45	World War II
		1940	Barlaston factory opened. First lithograph decoration on earthenware
1862	Second Great Exhibition, London	1941-8	Production of jasper discontinued
1863	Clement Wedgwood in partnership with Francis and Godfrey	1944	First lithograph decoration on bone china
		1948	New jasper body introduced by Norman Wilson
1866-71	Walter Crane designing for Wedgwood	1948-90	Wigmore Street, London Showrooms
1868	Laurence Wedgwood in partnership with Francis, Godfrey and Clement	1949	Bone china factory completed at Barlaston
		1950	Etruria factory closed. Last Day's vases produced.
1871	Letter prefixes introduced for the designation of pattern numbers by type of body and decoration	1952-5	Richard Guyatt as Consultant Designer (also 1967-70)
1875/6-1904	Thomas Allen employed by Wedgwood. Art Director from 1880	1953	First Wedgwood Rooms opened
		1955-6	Laurence Whistler designs produced
1875-90	Holborn Circus, London Showrooms	1960	Wedgwood Group formed
c.1875-90	Period of *japonisme* designs, including Satsuma shape, bronzed and gilt basaltes and Auro basalt	1961	Josiah V succeeded as Managing Director jointly by Norman Wilson and F. Maitland Wright
1877	Northwood copies of Portland vase	1963	Arthur Bryan appointed Managing Director (Chairman 1967-86)
1878	Bone china reintroduced. Portland vase mark introduced for bone china	1967	Wedgwood registered as a public company: shares quoted on the London Stock Exchange
1879-1929	Calendar tiles produced	1968	Death of Josiah V
1879-1953	Commemorative ware produced for Jones, McDuffee & Stratton	1969	New Museum and Visitors' Centre opened. Wedgwood Museum Trust established
1890-1927	108 Hatton Gardens, London Showrooms	1979	Acquisition of Wedgwood's first American factory by purchase of Franciscan, USA (sold 1984)
1891	'ENGLAND' mark introduced		
1891-5	Laurence Wedgwood in partnership with nephews Cecil and Francis Hamilton		
1895	Incorporation of firm as Josiah Wedgwood & Sons Ltd	1979-86	Robert Minkin, Design Director
		1985-6	Wedgwood Museum redesigned and rebuilt.
1898	'MADE IN ENGLAND' mark introduced (not in general use until c.1908)	1986	Wedgwood Group acquired by Waterford Glass. Waterford Wedgwood company formed
1902	Tile department finally closed		
1903	White House service supplied		

Appendix II

Wedgwood Trade Marks

| 1 | Impressed: the letters being stamped individually and sometimes in a curve.
The first marks, irregularly used c.1759-69. Much of the Wedgwood of this period was unmarked. |

| 2 | Impressed, in varying sizes, on useful wares from 1769-80, and on all wares from 1781 onwards unless otherwise stated below. |

| 3 | Impressed. The earliest form of the Wedgwood & Bentley mark. Ornamental wares only, c.1769. |

| 4 | Impressed or raised, sometimes lacking the word ETRURIA, this mark appears on the inside corner of plinths of early basaltes vases, and sometimes on the pedestals of busts and large figures, 1769-80. |

| 5 | Circular stamp, with an inner and outer line, placed round the screw of basaltes, variegated and Etruscan vases, 1769-80. Never on jasper vases, but sometimes found on white jasper plinths of variegated vases. |

| 6 | Extremely rare script mark, 1769-80, ornamental wares only. |

| 7 | Wedgwood & Bentley 356 — Impressed on very small cameos and intaglios, 1769-80, with the Catalogue number. |

| 8 | W. & B. — Impressed. Used on very small cameos and intaglios with the Catalogue number. Sometimes the Catalogue number only was used. |

| 9 | Rare oval impressed mark found on some chocolate and white seal intaglios, usually portraits made of two layers of jasper with polished edges. |

| 10 | WEDGWOOD & BENTLEY / WEDGWOOD & BENTLEY / ETRURIA — Impressed mark on plaques, tablets, medallions and other ornamental wares. The addition of ETRURIA is uncommon. |

| 11 | Wedgwood. / wedgwood. — Impressed marks, varying in size, used for all types of ware from 1780 until c.1795. Known as the 'upper and lower case' mark and 'lower case' mark. |

503

| 12 | WEDGWOOD & SONS | Impressed mark, c.1790. Very rare. |

| 13 | JOSIAH WEDGWOOD
Feb. 2nd 1805 | Rare mark found on some lustre wares, and basaltes, *rosso antico* and jasper pieces, usually tripods. |

| 14 | WEDGWOOD | Printed on bone china c.1812-22, in red, blue or gold. |

| 15 | WEDGWOOD'S STONE CHINA | Printed on stone china, 1820-61. |

| 16 | WEDGWOOD ETRURIA | Impressed mark in various sizes, c.1840-45. |

| 17 | PEARL
P | Impressed 'PEARL' on pearl body c.1840-68; initial 'P' only thereafter. |

| 18 | JBS | Impressed three-letter marks were used to date earthenwares from 1860-1906. The first letter indicated the month, the second the potter, and the third the year. As may be seen from the table below, the third letter may indicate two possible dates for the years 1860-64 and 1886-90. After 1891 the word ENGLAND was added. The words MADE IN ENGLAND appear from c.1898 but were not in general use until about 1908 (see trade marks 21 and 24). The example shown, JBS, indicates a date of January 1864 or 1890. |

Code (first) letters for months:

January	J		July	V (1860-63)
February	F			L (1864-1907)
March	M (1860-63)		August	W
	R (1864-1907)		September	S
April	A		October	O
May	Y (1860-63)		November	N
	M (1864-1907)		December	D
June	T			

Code (third) letters for years:

A		1872	1898
B		1873	1899
C		1874	1900
D		1875	1901
E		1876	1902
F		1877	1903
G		1878	1904
H		1879	1905
I		1880	1906
J		1881	
K		1882	
L		1883	
M		1884	
N		1885	
O	1860	1886	
P	1861	1887	
Q	1862	1888	
R	1863	1889	
S	1864	1890	
T	1865	1891	
U	1866	1892	
V	1867	1893	
W	1868	1894	
X	1869	1895	
Y	1870	1896	
Z	1871	1897	

19	3BS		From 1907 the figure 3 was substituted for the first (month) letter. From 1924 the figure 4 was
	4BD		used. The last letter continued to indicate the year as shown below:

J (3)	1907
K	1908
L	1909
M	1910
N	1911
O	1912
P	1913
Q	1914
R	1915
S	1916
T	1917
U	1918
V	1919
W	1920
X	1921
Y	1922
Z	1923
A (4)	1924
B	1925
C	1926
D	1927
E	1928
F	1929

From 1930 the actual date was impressed, at first as the last two figures of a mark including the month numbered in sequence and a potter's mark (e.g. 3B35 = March 1935) and later simply as two figures (e.g. 57 = 1957).

Workmen's errors occur in the numbers and letters of marks 18 and 19, and the letters are not always legible.

20   *E Lessore*   Signature of Emile Lessore c.1858-76.

21   ENGLAND   Impressed or printed from 1891 to conform with Mckinley Tariff Act. 'Made in England' added from c.1898, but not invariably used until c.1908.

22   WEDGWOOD   Printed on bone china (and occasionally, on Queen's ware ornamental wares) from 1878. 'England' added below from 1891. Some bone china bears the standard Wedgwood's impressed mark.

23   WEDGWOOD ETRURIA. ENGLAND   Rarely found impressed on Queen's ware ornamental wares c.1891-1900.

24   MADE IN ENGLAND   Impressed or printed with standard WEDGWOOD mark from c.1898, but not in general use until c.1908.

25   WEDGWOOD   Printed on bone china from c.1900 with ENGLAND or MADE IN ENGLAND added below.

26   WEDGWOOD BONE CHINA MADE IN ENGLAND   Printed on bone china from c.1902 (BONE CHINA added).

27   a. Painted monogram of Alfred Powell.

b. Painted monogram of Louise Powell.

28   **WEDGWOOD**   Sans serif type impressed from 1929. The old type continued to be used for a short time after this date, but no sans serif marks were used before 1929.

29   WEDGWOOD BONE CHINA MADE IN ENGLAND   Rejafix machine-printed mark used on bone china from c.1950-62.

30   WEDGWOOD Bone China MADE IN ENGLAND   Improved bone china mark introduced in 1962.

31   OF ETRURIA WEDGWOOD MADE IN ENGLAND BARLASTON   Queen's ware printed mark from c.1940.

32   **BARLASTON**   Address of the firm added to standard marks from 1940.

33   N W or NORMAN WILSON   Impressed or painted on Norman Wilson Unique Ware, added to standard mark for the period.

34   **ENGRAVED BY WEDGWOOD STUDIO**   Printed on engraved patterns from 1952.

35   WEDGWOOD ETRURIA BARLASTON   Extremely rare mark impressed on basaltes vases, replicas of those laid in the foundations of the factory at Barlaston in September 1938.

Appendix III

Registry Marks

Introduced in 1842 to protect designs from being pirated by other manufacturers, registry marks were widely used throughout England, but seldom on Wedgwood wares. The marks were printed or impressed.

1842-67

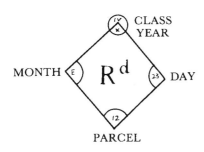

1842	X	1855	E
1843	H	1856	L
1844	C	1857	K
1845	A	1858	B
1846	I	1859	M
1847	F	1860	Z
1848	U	1861	R
1849	S	1862	O
1850	V	1863	G
1851	P	1864	N
1852	D	1865	W
1853	Y	1866	Q
1854	J	1867	T

1868-83

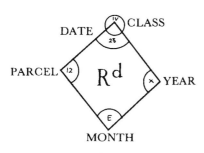

1868	X	1876	V
1869	H	1877	P
1870	C	1878	D
1871	A	1879	Y
1872	I	1880	J
1873	F	1881	E
1874	U	1882	L
1875	S	1883	K

Appendix IV

Pattern Number Prefixes

Pattern numbers prefixed by a code letter were introduced by Wedgwood in 1871. The prefixes were as follows:

A   Queen's ware, 1871-1932.
B   Queen's ware toilet-ware from 1872.
C   Queen's ware 'fancies' (ornamental pieces) from 1872.
F   Hand-painted designs from 1875-1927.
G   Queen's ware tableware gilt from 1875.
Z   Bone china 'fancies' (ornamental pieces) gilt from 1879.
W   Bone china tableware from 1879.
X   Bone china tableware from 1879-1915.
Y   Bone china tableware and coffeeware 1879-1921.
Q   Tiles from 1884-1902.
R   Marsden pattern tiles, 1888.
K   Majolica patterns, 1888.
O   Ornamental Majolica, 1888.
H   Hand-painted designs from 1928.
K   Underglaze decoration from 1928.
L   Underglaze print and onglaze enamel decoration from 1928.
M   Onglaze decoration from 1928.
P   Powder-blue patterns from 1929.
S   Bone china teaware patterns from 1931.
T   Queen's ware tableware patterns from 1932.
D   Bone china and Queen's ware lithograph decoration 1945-58.
N   Queen's ware lithograph decoration from 1958.
R   Bone china lithograph or silkscreen decoration.

(Example: TKD = Queen's ware underglaze lithograph)

Appendix V

The Wedgwoods of Etruria

I The Family of Josiah Wedgwood

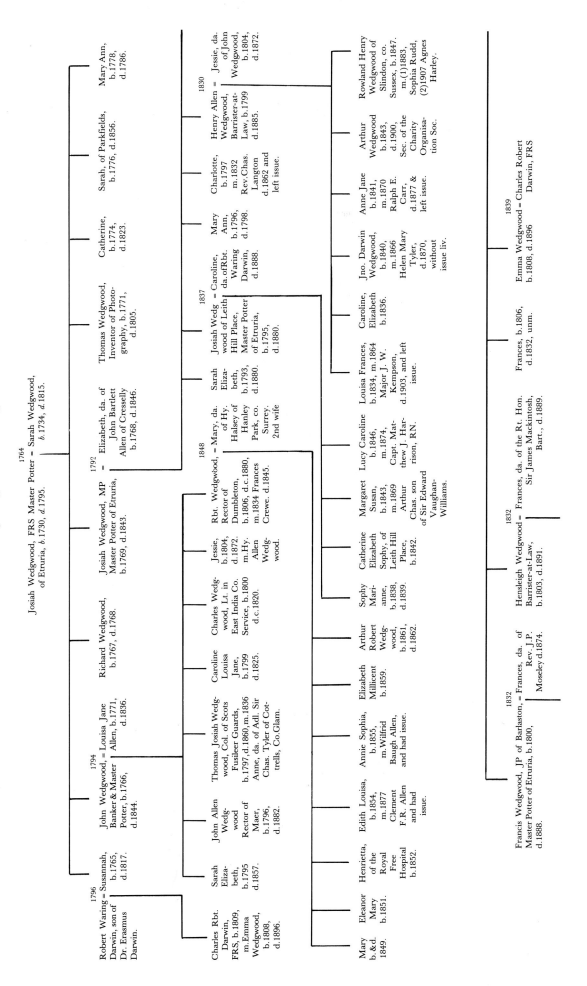

II The Families of Francis and Hensleigh Wedgwood

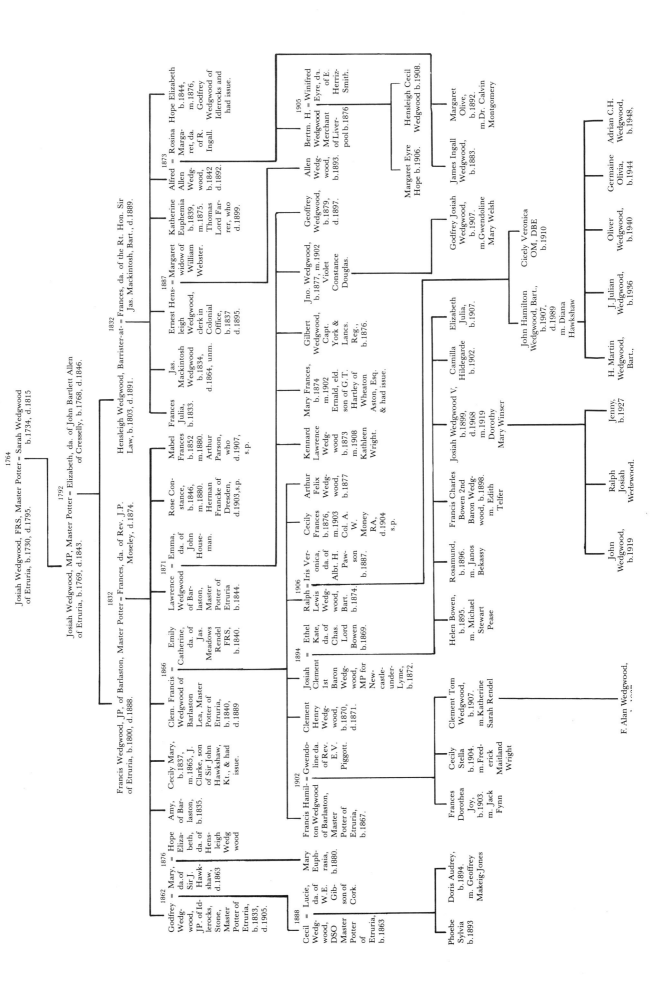

Bibliography

The following list includes those published works which have been consulted by the author in the preparation of this work and all those to which reference has been made in the text. Such consultation may not be assumed to imply agreement.

1. MANUSCRIPT MATERIAL

The Wedgwood collection of manuscripts deposited at Keele University and held temporarily at the Wedgwood Museum, Barlaston, has provided most of the primary source material for this book. The principal subdivisions of the collection are: Etruria Collection (E prefix), which includes the greater part of the surviving letters from Josiah Wedgwood to Thomas Bentley; Liverpool Collection (L prefix); Leith Hill Place Collection (LHP prefix); and Mosley Collection (W/M prefix). The E and L prefixes have been discarded here for all but the Wedgwood-Bentley letters unless the box and manuscript reference numbers are insufficient for identification.

2. PUBLISHED BOOKS

Adams, Elizabeth, and Redstone, David, *Bow Porcelain,* London, 1981

Amaya, Mario, *Art Nouveau,* London, 1966

Anscombe, Isabelle, and Gere, Charlotte, *Arts & Crafts in Britain and America,* London, 1978

Antichità die Ercolano Esposte, edited by the Accademia Ercolanense, 8 volumes, Naples, 1755-92

Aslin, Elizabeth, *The Aesthetic Movement: Prelude to Art Nouveau,* London, 1981

Atterbury, Paul (ed.), *The Parian Phenomenon,* London, 1989

Auckland, R.J., third Baron, Bishop of Bath and Wells (ed.), *The Journal and Correspondence of William, Lord Auckland,* 4 volumes, London, 1862

Austwick, J. and B., *The Decorated Tile,* London, 1980

Barker, David, *William Greatbach, A Staffordshire Potter,* London, 1990

Barnard, Harry, *Artes Etruriae Renascuntur,* London, 1924
Chats on Wedgwood Ware, London, 1924

Barrett, F.A., *Worcester Porcelain & Lund's Bristol,* London, 1966

Bartoli, Pietro Santi, *Admiranda Romanarum Antiquitatum ac Veteris Sculpturae Vestigia...,* 2nd edn, Rome, 1693

Bartoli, Pietro Santi, Bartoli, F., Bartoli, G.P., and de la Chausse, M., *Picturae Antiquae, Cryptarum Romanarum, et Sepulcri Nasonum,* 3 parts, Rome, 1750

Batkin, Maureen, *Wedgwood Ceramics 1846-1959,* London, 1982

Batkin, Maureen, and Dalrymple, Robert, *Ravilious and Wedgwood: The Complete Designs of Eric Ravilious,* London, 1986

Beard, Geoffrey, *The Work of Robert Adam,* Edinburgh, 1978

Bénézit, E., *Dictionnaire des Peintres, Sculpteurs, Dessinateurs et Graveurs,* 8 volumes, Paris, 1960

Bentley, G.E., *Blake Records,* Oxford, 1969

Bentley, Richard, *Thomas Bentley,* London, 1927

Bindman, David, *John Flaxman R.A.,* London 1979

Binyon, Helen, *Eric Ravilious: Memoir of an Artist,* London, 1983

Birks, Tony, *Lucie Rie,* London, 1987

Boardman, James, *Bentleyana,* Liverpool, 1851

Boardman, John, *Athenian Red Figure Vases: The Archaic period,* London, 1975

Bourgeois, Emile, *Le Biscuit de Sèvres: Recueil des modèles de la manufacture de Sèvres au XVIIIe siècle,* Paris, 1909

Bradley, H.G. (ed.), *Ceramics of Derbyshire,* London, 1978

Branyan, Lawrence, French, Neal, and Sandon, John, *Worcester Blue & White Porcelain 1751-1790,* London, 1981

Bubnova, E., *Old Russian Faience,* Moscow, 1973

Burton, William, *Josiah Wedgwood and His Pottery,* London, 1906

Buten, David, *18th-Century Wedgwood,* New York, 1980

Buten, David, and Pelehach, Patricia, *Wedgwood and America; Wedgwood Bas-Relief Ware,* Monographs in Wedgwood Studies, Nos 1 & 2, Merion, Pennsylvania, 1977
Emile Lessore 1805-1876: His Life and Work, Monographs in Wedgwood Studies, No. 3, Merion, Pennsylvania, 1979

Buten, Harry M., *Wedgwood ABC but not Middle E,* Merion, Pennsylvania, 1964
Wedgwood and Artists, Merion, Pennsylvania, 1960
Wedgwood Counterpoint, Merion, Pennsylvania, 1962
Wedgwood Rarities, Merion, Pennsylvania, 1968

Byng, Hon. John, *The Torrington Diaries,* ed. C. Bruyn Andrews, 4 volumes, London, 1936

Caiger-Smith, Alan, *Lustre Pottery,* London, 1985

Caylus, Anne-Claude-Philippe de Thubières, comte de, *Recueil d'Antiquités Egyptiennes, Etrusques, Grecques et Romaines,* 7 volumes, Paris, 1752-67

Church, Sir Arthur H., *Josiah Wedgwood, Master Potter,* London, 1984

Clifford, Anne, *Cut-Steel and Berlin Iron Jewellery,* Bath, 1971

Coke, Gerald, *In Search of James Giles,* Wingham, 1983

Constable, Freda, *The England of Ravilious,* London, 1982

Constable, W.G., *John Flaxman,* London, 1927

Crane, Walter, *An Artist's Reminiscences,* London, 1907

Crelin, J.J., *Medical Ceramics: A Catalogue of the English and Dutch Collections in the Museum of the Wellcome Institute of the History of Medicine,* London, 1969

Cunningham, Alan, *Lives of the Most Eminent British Painters, Sculptors and Architects,* 2nd edn, 6 volumes, London, 1830

Curl, James Stevens, *The Egyptian Revival,* London, 1982

Darwin, Charles, *Life of Erasmus Darwin,* London, 1879

Dawson, Aileen, *Masterpieces of Wedgwood in the British Museum,* London, 1984

Delieb, Eric, and Roberts, M., *The Great Silver Manufactory. Matthew Boulton and the Birmingham Silversmiths, 1760-90,* London, 1971

Des Fontaines, Una, *Wedgwood Fairyland Lustre,* London and New York, 1975

Edgeworth, R.L. and Maria, *Memoirs of Richard Lovell Edgeworth,* 2 volumes, 1820 (reprinted Shannon, 1969)

Emmerson, Robin, *British Teapots and Tea Drinking,* London, 1992

Erskine, Mrs Steuart, *Lady Diana Beauclerk, Her Life and Work,* London, 1903

Evans, William, *Art and History of the Potting Business,* Shelton, 1846

Falkner, Frank, *The Wood Family of Burslem,* London, 1912

Farrer, K.E. (Lady Farrer) (ed.), *Letters of Josiah Wedgwood,* 3 volumes, Manchester, 1903-6

Finer, Ann and Savage, George (eds.), *The Selected Letters of Josiah Wedgwood,* London, 1965

Forty, Adrian, *Objects of Desire: Design and Society 1750-1980,* London, 1986

Fothergill, Brian, *Sir William Hamilton, Envoy Extraordinary,* London, 1969

Gaunt, William, and Clayton-Stamm, M.D.E., *William De Morgan,* London, 1971

Gilhespy, F. Brayshaw, *Derby Porcelain,* London, 1965

Godden, Geoffrey A., *British pottery and porcelain 1780-1850,* London 1963
Caughley and Worcester Porcelains 1775-1800, London, 1969
English China, London, 1985
Mason's China and the Ironstone Wares, revised edn., Woodbridge, 1980
Minton Pottery and Porcelain of the First Period 1793-1850, London, 1968
(ed.) *Staffordshire Porcelain,* St Albans, 1983

Goodison, Nicholas, *Ormolu: The Work of Matthew Boulton,* London, 1974

Gorely, Jean, *Wedgwood,* New York, 1950

Gorely, Jean and Schwartz, Marvin D., *The Emily Winthrop Miles Collection: The Work of Wedgwood and Tassie,* Brooklyn, 1965

Grant, M.H., *The Makers of Black Basaltes,* London, 1910

Granville, Mary (Mrs Delany), *Autobiography and Correspondence,* London, 1862

Gray, J.M., *James and William Tassie,* Edinburgh, 1894

Greenslade, M.W., and Jenkins, J.G. (eds), *The Victoria History of the County of Stafford,* Vol. II, London, 1967

Gunnis, Rupert, *Dictionary of British Sculptors, 1650-1851,* revised edn, London 1968

Hamer, Frank, *The Potter's Dictionary of Materials and Techniques,* London and New York, 1975

Hamilton, Sir William, and d'Hancarville, P.H., *Antiquités Etrusques, Grecques et Romaines,* 4 volumes, Naples, 1766-76

Hannah, Frances, *Ceramics,* London, 1986

Hardie, Martin, *Watercolour Painting in Britain,* 3 volumes, London, 1966-9

Harris, John, *Sir William Chambers,* London, 1970

Haskell, Francis, and Penny, Nicholas, *Taste and the Antique: The Lure of Classical Sculpture 1500-1900,* New Haven and London, 1982

Haynes, D.E.L., *The Portland Vase,* 2nd revised edn, London, 1975

Hillier, Bevis, *Master Potters of the Industrial Revolution: the Turners of Lane End,* London, 1965
Pottery and Porcelain 1700-1914, London, 1968

Honey, W.B., *English Pottery and Porcelain,* London, 1933
European Ceramic Art, 2 volumes, London, 1949-2
The Art of the Potter, London, 1946
Wedgwood Ware, London, 1948

Honour, Hugh, *Chinoiserie: The Vision of Cathay,* London, 1961
Neo-Classicism, London, 1968
Romanticism, London, 1978

Hower, Ralph M., *The Wedgwoods: Ten Generations of Potters,* privately reprinted from the *Journal of Business and Economic and Business History,* Vol. IV, Nos 2 and 4, 1932, New York, 1975

Impey, Oliver, *Chinoiserie: The Impact of Oriental Styles of Western Art and Decoration,* London, 1977

Irwin, David, *John Flaxman, 1755-1826,* London, 1977

Jarry, Madeleine, *Chinoiserie: Chinese Influence on European Decorative Art, 17th and 18th Centuries,* London, 1981

Jewitt, Llewellyn, *The Ceramic Art of Great Britain,* 2 volumes, London, 1878 (2nd revised edn, London, 1883)
Life of Josiah Wedgwood, London, 1865

John, W.D., and Simcox, Jacqueline, *Early Wedgwood Lustre Wares,* Newport, Monmouth, 1963

Jonas, Maurice, *Notes of an Art Collector,* 2nd (enlarged) edn, London, 1907

Jones, H. Stuart, *A Catalogue of the Ancient Sculptures preserved in the Municipal Collections of Rome: The Sculptures of the Museo Capitolino,* Oxford, 1912

Jones, Owen, *The Grammar of Ornament,* London, 1856

Jouveaux, Emile, *Histoire de trois potiers célèbres: B. Palissy, J. Wedgwood, F. Böttger,* Paris, 1874

Kelly, Alison, *Decorative Wedgwood,* London, 1965
Wedgwood Ware, London, 1970

Keynes, Geoffrey, *Blake Studies,* London, 1949
The Letters of William Blake with Related Documents, Oxford, 1980

King-Hele, Desmond, *Erasmus Darwin,* London, 1963
Doctor of Revolution: The Life and Genius of Erasmus Darwin, London, 1977

Klingender, Francis D., *Art and the Industrial Revolution,* London, 1972

Lane, Arthur, *Style in Pottery,* 2nd edn, London, 1973

Lessore, Emile, *Five years in the Potteries,* London, 1863

Lewis, John and Griselda, *Pratt Ware,* Woodbridge, 1979

Litchfield, H.E. (ed.), *Emma Darwin: A Century of Family Letters,* 2 volumes, Cambridge, 1904

Litchfield, R.B., *Thomas Wedgwood,* London, 1903

Lockett, T.A., *Collecting Victorian Tiles,* Woodbridge, 1979
Davenport Pottery and Porcelain, Newton Abbot, 1972

Loewy, Raymond, *Industrial Design,* London, 1979

Lucie-Smith, Edward, *A History of Industrial Design,* Oxford, 1983

Lyte, Charles, *Sir Joseph Banks,* Newton Abbot, 1980

Macarthy, Fiona, *British Design since 1880: A Visual History,* London, 1982

Macht, Carol, *Classical Wedgwood Designs,* New York, 1957

McKendrick, Neil, Brewer, John, and Plumb, J.H., *The Birth of a Consumer Society: The Commercialization of Eighteenth-century England,* London, 1982.

Maffei, Paolo Alessandro, *Raccolta di statue antiche e moderne...,* Rome, 1704

Malet, Hugh, *The Canal Duke: A Biography of Francis 3rd Duke of Bridgewater,* Newton Abbot, 1961

Mankowitz, Wolf, *The Portland Vase and the Wedgwood Copies,* London, 1952
Wedgwood, London, 1953

Mankowitz, Wolf, and Haggar, Reginald G., *The Concise Encyclopedia of English Pottery and Porcelain,* London, 1957

Manners, Lady Victoria, and Williamson, G.C., *Angelica Kauffmann,* London, n.d.

Mantoux, P., *The Industrial Revolution in the Eighteenth Century,* London, 1947

Marryat, Joseph, *A History of Pottery and Porcelain,* 3rd revised edn, London 1868

Matthias, Peter, *The First Industrial Nation: An Economic History of Britain 1700-1914,* 2nd edn, London and New York, 1983.
The Transformation of England, London, 1979

Meteyard, Eliza, *A Group of Englishmen 1795-1815,* London, 1871
Choice Examples of Wedgwood's Art, London, 1879
Memorials of Wedgwood, London, 1874
The Life of Josiah Wedgwood, 2 volumes, London, 1865-6
The Wedgwood Handbook, London, 1875
Wedgwood and his Works

Miller, J. Jefferson II, *English Yellow-Glazed Earthenware,* London, 1974

Molfino, Alessandra Mottola, *L'Arte della porcellana in Italia,* 2 volumes, Busto Arsizio, 1976-7

Montfaucon, Bernard de, *L'Antiquité expliquée,* 5 volumes and Supplement 5 volumes, Paris, 1719

Moore, T. Hudson, *The Old China Book,* London, 1903

Mountford, Arnold, *The Illustrated Guide to Staffordshire Salt-Glazed Stoneware,* London, 1971

Nicolson, Benedict, *Joseph Wright of Derby,* 2 volumes, London, 1968

Pargeter, P., *Red House Glass Works,* Stourbridge, 1877

Pearson, Hesketh, *Doctor Darwin,* London, 1930

Penderell-Church, J.J., *William Cookworthy 1705-80,* Truro, 1972

Price, E.Stanley, *John Sadler,* privately printed, 1948

Prideaux, J., *Relics of William Cookworthy,* privately printed, 1948

Rackham, Bernard, *English Pottery,* London, 1924

Rado, Paul, *An Introduction to the Technology of Pottery,* London, 1969

Raspe, R.E., *Catalogue raisonné d'une Collection Générale de Pierres Gravées Antiques et Modernes,* London, 1791

Rathbone, Frederick, *Old Wedgwood,* London, 1898

Ray, Anthony, *English Delftware Pottery in the Robert Hall Warren Collection,* Ashmolean Museum Oxford, London, 1968

Read, Herbert, *Art and Industry,* 3rd edn, London, 1953

Reilly, Robin, *Josiah Wedgwood,* London, 1991
  The Collector's Wedgwood, New York, 1980
  Wedgwood, 2 vols, London, 1989
  Wedgwood Jasper, London (Letts), 1972
  Wedgwood Jasper, London (Thames & Hudson), 1994

Reilly, Robin and Savage, George, *The Dictionary of Wedgwood,* Woodbridge, 1980
  Wedgwood: The Portrait Medallions, London, 1973

Reinach, Salomon, *Repertoire de la statuaire grecque et romaine,* 6 volumes, Paris, 1897-1930

Rhead, G.W. and F.A., *Staffordshire Pots and Potters,* London, 1906

Roussel, Diana Edwards, *The Castleford Pottery 1790-1821,* Wakefield, 1982

St Fond, B.Faujas de, *Voyage en Angleterre, en Ecosse et aux Iles Hébrides,* 2 volumes, Paris, 1797

Sandon, Henry, *An Illustrated Guide to Worcester Porcelain,* 2nd edn, London, 1974

Savage, George, *Dictionary of 19th Century Antiques,* London, 1978
  Eighteenth-Century English Porcelain, London, 1952
  Seventeenth and Eighteenth Century French Porcelain, London, 1960

Savage, George, and Newman, Harold, *An Illustrated Dictionary of Ceramics,* London, 1974

Sayer, Robert, *The Ladies' Amusement: or, Whole Art of Japanning Made Easy...,* London, 1762

Schofield, R.E., *The Lunar Society of Birmingham,* Oxford, 1963

Sedding, J.D., *Art and Handcraft,* London, 1893

Shaw, Simeon, *History of the Staffordshire Potteries,* Hanley, 1829

Shinn, Charles and Dorrie, *The Illustrated Guide to Victorian Parian China,* London, 1971

Skeaping. John, *Animal Drawing,* 2nd edn, London, 1940

Smiles, Samuel, *Josiah Wedgwood,* London, 1894
  Self-Help, London, 1887

Smith, Alan, *The Illustrated Guide to Liverpool Herculaneum Pottery,* London, 1970

Smith, L. Richard, Captain James Cook: *The Wedgwood Portrait Medallions,* Sydney, 1979, and *The Sydney Cove Medallion,* Wedgwood Society of Australia, New South Wales Chapter, Sydney, 1978, reprinted in *Monographs in Wedgwood Studies,* No.4, Merion, Pennsylvania, 1979

Solon, M.L.E., *The Art of the Old English Potter,* London, 1883

Spencer, Isobel, *Walter Crane,* New York, 1975

Stanton, Sir G., *Embassy of Lord Macartney to the Emperor of China 1792-3,* London, 1797

Stringer, G.E., *New Hall Porcelain,* London, 1949

Stuart, James, and Revett, Nicholas, *The Antiquities of Athens,* 4 volumes, London, 1762-1816

Tassie, James, *Catalogue of Impressions in Sulphur of Antique and Modern Gems,* London, 1775.

Taylor, Basil, *Stubbs,* London, 1971

Thomas, John, *The Rise of the Staffordshire Potteries,* Bath, 1971

Towner, Donald C., *Creamware,* London, 1978
  English Cream-Coloured Earthenware, London, 1974
  The Leeds Pottery, London, 1963

Turner, William (ed.), *William Adams, An Old English Potter,* London, 1904

Wakefield, Hugh, *Victorian Pottery,* London, 1962

Walcha, Otto, *Meissen Porcelain,* London, 1981

Walton, Peter, *Creamware and Other English Pottery at Temple Newsam House, Leeds,* Bradford and London, 1976

Ward, John, *The Borough of Stoke-upon-Trent,* London, 1843

Waring, J.B., *Masterpieces of Industrial Art and Sculpture at the International Exhibition, 1862,* London, 1863

Warrilow, Ernest J.D., *History of Etruria, Staffordshire 1760-1951,* Hanley, 1962

Watkin, David, *Athenian Stuart: Pioneer of the Greek Revival,* London, 1982

Watney, Bernard, *English Blue and White Porcelain of the Eighteenth Century,* 2nd edn, London, 1979
  Longton Hall Porcelain, London, 1957

Weatherill, Lorna, *The Pottery Trade and North Staffordshire 1660-1760,* Manchester, 1971

Wedgwood, Barbara and Hensleigh, *The Wedgwood Circle 1730-1897,* London, 1980

Wedgwood, Dame C.V., *The Last of the Radicals,* London, 1951

Wedgwood, John, *A Personal Life of the Fifth Josiah Wedgwood 1899-1968,* Barlaston, 1979

Wedgwood, Josiah, *Account of the Barberini, now Portland Vase...,* London, 1788 (?)

Wedgwood, Josiah (V), *The Economics of Inheritance,* revised edn, London, 1939

Wedgwood, Josiah Clement, *A History of the Wedgwood Family,* London, 1908
  Staffordshire Pottery and Its History, London, 1913

Wedgwood, Josiah Clement, and Ormsbee, T.H., *Staffordshire Pottery,* New York, 1947

Wedgwood, Josiah Clement, and Wedgwood, Joshua G.E., *Wedgwood Pedigrees,* Kendal, 1925

Wedgwood, Julia, *The Personal Life of Josiah Wedgwood,* London, 1915

Whiter, Leonard, *Spode,* London, 1970

Wichmann, Siegfried, *Japonisme: The Japanese Influence on Western Art Since 1858,* London, 1981

Wiener, Martin J., *English Culture and the Decline of the Industrial Spirit 1850-1980,* New York, 1981

Williamson, G.C., *The Imperial Russian Dinner Service,* London, 1909

Williams-Wood, Cyril, *English Transfer-Printed Pottery & Porcelain,* London, 1981

Wills, Geoffrey, *Wedgwood,* London, 1980

Wilson, C., *England's Apprenticeship,* London, 1965

Wilson, Norman, and others, *Lectures on Wedgwood,* Barlaston, 1959

Wornum. Ralph, *Analysis of Ornament,* 6th edn, London, 1879

Yamada, Chisaburoh (ed.), *Dialogue in Art: Japan and the West,* London, 1976

3. UNPUBLISHED MATERIAL

Barnard, Harry, 'Record', c.1931

Gater, Sharon, 'A House of Long-Standing: A Study of Josiah Wedgwood & Sons in the Second Half of the Nineteenth Century', MA dissertation, Keele University, 1986

4. PUBLISHED CATALOGUES

A. Wedgwood's Catalogues of Queen's ware and Ornamental Wares

A Catalogue of cameos, intaglios, medals and bas-reliefs; with a general account of vases and other ornaments, after the antique, made by Wedgwood & Bentley (60 pp.), London, 1773

Catalogue of cameos, intaglios, medals, busts, small statues, and bas-reliefs; with a general account of vases and other ornaments after the antique, made by Wedgwood & Bentley (73 pp.), London, 1774

2nd edn, French translation (82 pp.), 1774

3rd edn, 1775 (reissue of 2nd edn with 6 additional pages and woodcut illustration of inkstand)

4th edn, (93 pp.), London, 1777 (Dutch translation, Amsterdam, 1778)

5th edn, London, 1779 (French and German translations, 1779)

Catalogue of cameos, intaglios, medals, bas-reliefs, busts and small statues; with a general account of tablets, vases, escritoires, and other ornamental and useful articles..., 6th edn (107 pp.), Etruria, 1787 (French translation, 1787)

A catalogue of different articles of Queen's ware, which may be either plain, gilt, or embellished with enamel paintings, manufactured by Josiah Wedgwood, potter to her Majesty (9 engraved plates, 35 numbered shapes), 1774

The '1790' Queen's ware Catalogue, with texts in English or French (13 engraved plates, 80 numbered shapes), c.1793. It is doubtful whether this catalogue was ever published.

The '1817' Queen's ware Catalogue, issued in three editions between c.1817 and 1849 (39-46 engraved plates; the 3rd edn illustrates 386 numbered shapes)

Illustrated Catalogue of Shapes March 1873 (55 engraved plates, 369 numbered shapes), Hanley, 1873

Illustrated Catalogue of Shapes (44 engraved plates, 319 numbered shapes), Hanley, n.d. (1878-80)

Illustrated Catalogue of Ornamental Shapes (24 engraved plates, 107 shapes of which 24 only are numbered), n.d. (1878-80)

Catalogue of Bodies, Glazes and Shapes, current for 1940-50 (218 pp.), Hanley, 1940

B. Select List of Catalogues of Collections and Exhibitions

Adams, Elizabeth Bryding, *The Dwight and Lucille Beeson Wedgwood Collection at the Birmingham Museum of Art, Birmingham, Alabama,* Alabama, 1992

Art Journal, Special Issue, *The Crystal Palace Exhibition, Illustrated Catalogue,* London, 1851

Arts Council of Great Britain, *The Age of Neo-Classicism,* London, 1972

Barnard, Harry, *Exhibition of replicas of eighteenth-century sculptured miniatures: Wedgwood's portrait medallions of illustrious moderns made and finished by Bert Bentley,* London, n.d. (1922)

Birmingham Museum & Art Gallery, *An Exhibition to Commemorate the Bicentenary of the Lunar Society of Birmingham,* Birmingham, 1966

Chaffers, William, *Catalogue of an Exhibition of Old Wedgwood at Phillips' Galleries, London,* London, 1877

Collins, Michael, *Christopher Dresser 1834-1904,* London, 1979

Conner, Patrick (ed.), *The Inspiration of Egypt: Its Influence on British Artists, Travellers and Designers, 1700-1900,* Brighton, 1983

Crafts Council, *The Omega Workshops 1913-19: Decorative Arts of Bloomsbury,* London, 1984

Delholm Gallery Guide, English Pottery, Charlotte, North Carolina, 1982

Des Fontaines, J.K., with Chaldecott, John, and Tindall, John, *Josiah Wedgwood: 'The Arts and Sciences United',* London, 1978

Early Wedgwood Pottery (Catalogue of the Eustace Calland Collection), London, 1951

Fairyland Wedgwood Ware. Some Glimpses of Fairyland, Etruria, 1921

Fine Art Society Ltd, *The Arts & Crafts Movement: Artists, Craftsmen & Designers 1890-1930,* London, 1973

Friedman, Terry, and Clifford, Timothy, *The Man at Hyde Park Corner: Sculpture by John Cheere, 1709-1787,* London, 1974

Gatty, T., *Catalogue of a loan exhibition of the works of Josiah Wedgwood, exhibited at the Liverpool Art Club,* Liverpool, 1879

Gorely, Jean, and Wadsworth, Mary, *Old Wedgwood from the bequest of Grenville Lindall Winthrop,* Fogg Museum of Art, Harvard University, 1944

Graham, John Meredith II, and Wedgwood, Hensleigh C., *Wedgwood: A Living Tradition,* Brooklyn, 1948

Gunsaulus, Frank W., *Old Wedgwood 1760-95: a collection acquired by...W. Gunsaulus, loaned to the Museum of the Art Institute of Chicago,* Chicago, 1912

Hayden, Arthur, *Catalogue of the Wedgwood Exhibition held in Conduit Street,* London, December 1909

Henry E. Huntington Library and Art Gallery, *Wedgwood & Bentley Pottery from the Kadison Collection,* San Marino, California, 1983

Hobson, R.L., *Catalogue of English Pottery and Porcelain in the Department of British Mediaeval Antiquities and Ethnography, British Museum,* London, 1903

Record of the Collection in the Lady Lever Art Gallery, Port Sunlight, 3 volumes, Vol.II: *Chinese Porcelain and Wedgwood Pottery,* London, 1928.

Kenwood House, *Exhibition of Wedgwood at Kenwood House, Iveagh Bequest,* London County Council, 1954

Lane, Arthur, *Guide to the Collection of Tiles* (Victoria & Albert Museum, London), 1939

Lessore, Emile, *A Catalogue of the works on Queen's ware painted for Messrs Wedgwood by the late Emile Lessore. On exhibition at Messrs Mortlock's Galleries,* London, 1876

mededelingenblad nederlandse vereniging van vrienden van de ceramiek, Dordrecht, 1982

Niblett, Kathy (ed.), *Wedgwood of Etruria & Barlaston,* Hanley, 1980

Northern Ceramic Society, *Creamware & Pearlware,* Stoke-on-Trent, 1986

Staffordshire Porcelain 1740-1851, Stoke-on-Trent, 1979

Stonewares & Stone Chinas of Northern England to 1851, Stoke-on-Trent, 1982

Nottingham Castle Museum, *Catalogue of the Wedgwood in the Felix Joseph Bequest,* Nottingham, 1930

Mr Wedgwood, Nottingham, 1975

Rackham, Bernard, *Catalogue of English Porcelain Earthenware Enamels and Glass collected by Charles Schreiber Esq. M.P. and Lady Charlotte Schreiber...,* 3 volumes, Volume II, London, 1924-30

Rathbone, Frederick, *A Catalogue of the Wedgwood Museum,* Etruria, 1909

A catalogue of a collection of plaques, medallions, vases &c in coloured jasper and basaltes: produced by Josiah Wedgwood, 1760-1795...formed by Lord Tweedmouth, London, 1905

Old Wedgwood and old Wedgwood Ware: Handbook to the collection formed by Richard and George Tangye (Birmingham Museum & Art Gallery), London, 1885

Reilly, Robin, *Wedgwood Portrait Medallions: An Introduction* (National Portrait Gallery exhibition), London, 1973

Sanderson, Arthur, *Catalogue of a collection of plaques, medallions, vases, figures etc., in coloured jasper and basalte, produced by Josiah Wedgwood F.R.S., at Etruria, in the county of Stafford: 1760-1795, the property of Arthur Sanderson,* London, 1901

Scheidemantel, Vivian J., *Josiah Wedgwood's Heads of Illustrious Moderns* (loan exhibition at the Chicago Art Institute), Chicago, 1958

Stoke-on-Trent, *Commemorative exhibition of ceramics, paintings, drawings, documents and maps, held at the City Museum and Art Gallery, Stoke-on-Trent,* Stoke-on-Trent, 1930

Taggart, Ross E., *The Frank P. and Harriet C .Burnap Collection of English Pottery in the William Rockhill Nelson Gallery,* revised and enlarged edn, Kansas City, Missouri, 1967

Tate Gallery, *George Stubbs 1724-1806,* London, 1984

Tattersall, Bruce, *Stubbs & Wedgwood,* catalogue of an exhibition held at the Tate Gallery, London, 1974

Wedgwood Portraits and the American Revolution, National Portrait Gallery, Washington, 1976

Victoria & Albert Museum, *Rococo: Art and Design in Hogarth's England,* London, 1984
Wedgwood Bicentenary Exhibition 1759-1959, London, 1959
Wedgwood In London: 225th Anniversary Exhibition 1759-1984, Barlaston, 1984
Wedgwood Institute, *Catalogue of the Wedgwood Institute,* Burslem, 1869
Weisberg, Gabriel P., Cate, Phillip Dennis, Needham, Gerald, Eidelberg, Martin, and Johnston, William R., *Japonisme: Japanese Influence on French Art 1854-1910,* Cleveland, Ohio, 1975
Wolverhampton Art Gallery, *Lustre Ceramics from British Art Potteries,* Wolverhampton, 1980

C. Related Catalogues of Shapes

Designs of Sundry Articles of Queen's or Cream-colour'd Earthen-Ware, manufactured by Hartley, Greens, and Co. at Leeds pottery..., reprinted by Donald Towner, *The Leeds Pottery,* London, 1963
Don Pottery Pattern Book, Doncaster, 1983 (reprinted from the catalogue published in Doncaster, 1807)
James & Chas Whitehead, Manufacturers, Hanley, Staffordshire, Designs of Sundry Articles of Earthenware, Milton Keynes, n.d. (reprinted from the catalogue published in Birmingham, 1798)
The Castleford Pottery Pattern Book, Wakefield, 1973 (reprinted from the catalogue published by D. Dunderdale & Co., Castleford, 1796)

5. SELECT LIST OF SALE CATALOGUES

Agnew, Thomas, *The Collection of Wedgwood Ware of Messrs Thomas Agnew & Sons, Manchester,* n.d.
Barlow, Thomas Oldham, *Catalogue of the very choice collection of Wedgwood ware,* Christie's, London, 1887
Braxton-Hicks, J., *Catalogue of the collection of J.Braxton-Hicks,* Christie's, London, 1887
De la Rue, Thomas, *Catalogue of Old Wedgwood Ware,* Christie's, London, 1866

Jacobs, Herbert and Sylvia, *The Herbert and Sylvia Jacobs Collection of 18th and Early 19th Century English Pottery,* Christie's, New York, 1994
Milestone, Milton, *The Milton Milestone Collection of Early Wedgwood Pottery,* 2 parts, Sotheby Parke Bernet, New York, 1975-6
Oster, Catherine G. and Samuel B., *Catalogue of the Well-known Collection of Wedgwood Pottery,* 2 parts, Sotheby's, London, 1971-2
Rathbone, Frederick, *Catalogue of Wedgwood ware and Old English Pottery, the property of J.F. Rathbone,* Christie's, London, 1919
Sibson, Francis, *Catalogue of the collection of old Wedgwood...the property of Francis Sibson,* Christie's, London, 1877
Towner, Donald, *Catalogue of the Well-known Collection of English Creamware, The Property of Donald C. Towner Esq.,* Sotheby's, London, 1968
British Pottery, Porcelain and Enamels [including] *The collection of the late Donald C. Towner,* Sotheby's, London, 1986
Victor, Mr and Mrs Samuel, *Important English Pottery: The Collection of Mr and Mrs Samuel Victor, Highland Park, Illinois,* Sotheby Parke Bernet, New York, 1978
Walker, T. Shadford, *Catalogue of the collection of Old Wedgwood...the property of T.Shadford Walker,* Christie's, London, 1885
Wedgwood & Bentley, *A Catalogue of cameos, intaglios, bas-reliefs, medallions, busts, vases, statues...now in joint property of Mr Wedgwood & Mrs Bentley,* Christie & Ansell, London, 1781

6. JOURNALS, PROCEEDINGS AND TRANSACTIONS

English Ceramic Circle *Transactions*
Northern Ceramic Society *Journal*
Royal Historical Society *Transactions*
Royal Society of Arts *Journal*
Wedgwood Society *Proceedings*
Wedgwood International Seminar *Proceedings*